6730 enter

Firmly

UNIVERSITY CASEBOOK SERIES

CASES AND MATERIALS

PROPERTY LAW: OWNERSHIP, USE, AND CONSERVATION

by

PAUL GOLDSTEIN
Stella W. & Ira S. Lillick Professor of Law
Stanford University

BARTON H. THOMPSON, JR.
Robert E. Paradise Professor of Natural Resources Law
Director, Woods Institute for the Environment
Stanford University

FOUNDATION PRESS

2006

THOMSON
WEST

395 Hudson Street
New York, NY 10014
Phone Toll Free 1–877–888–1330
Fax (212) 367–6799
foundation-press.com
Printed in the United States of America

ISBN–13: 978–1–59941–141–5
ISBN–10: 1–59941–141–5

To Jan and Elizabeth
P.G.

To Holly, Hobie, Maggie, and Eliza
B.H.T.

*

PREFACE

This casebook takes a new approach to property law by not only covering the traditional elements of a basic law school course in property but also incorporating emerging environmental issues associated with the use of land and other resources. The expanded coverage reflects the reality that issues such as wetland protection, conservation easements, and water scarcity are today as important, if not in some cases more important, to many property lawyers as more traditional concerns such as nonconforming structures, adjacent land support, and the rule against perpetuities.

In deciding on this casebook's coverage, we have consciously chosen evolution over revolution. The casebook examines all of the major property law doctrines found in a more traditional casebook. Indeed, this casebook is to a large degree a new edition of Professor Goldstein's *Real Property* (Foundation Press 1984). Like that classic casebook, this book aims to expose students to the theoretical and historical foundations of America's legal property system, while also introducing them to the more worldly, day-to-day practice of lawyers engaged in handling property matters for their clients. Our experience in academe convinces us that theory and principle must play a substantial role in guiding the application and future of property law. Our experience in practice convinces us that both lawyers and policymakers must understand the practicalities of property arrangements in advising clients and proposing changes in property law.

The coverage of this book differs from *Real Property*, however, in two significant respects. First, the book covers not only real property (i.e., land) but also other significant forms of property ranging from water and petroleum to intellectual property and cyberspace. Second, the casebook provides an introduction to the growing number of environmental questions arising from land use. In some instances, the environmental coverage represents merely an expansion of the traditional coverage. The section of this casebook dealing with private and public nuisances, for example, discusses the various regulatory approaches to pollution that have effectively replaced nuisance lawsuits as the principal means of reducing pollution. The material on property in wildlife examines current legislative approaches to protecting wildlife from extinction. The discussion of servitudes includes a lengthy examination of modern conservation easements. In other instances, the book introduces legal issues and doctrines that, while highly relevant to modern property practice, are not found in other property law casebooks. While other property casebooks cover only local regulation of land use, for example, this book also considers the federal government's expanding regulation of land use through statutes such as the Endangered Species Act and section 404 of the Clean Water Act.

Looking at property law through an environmental lens provides new insights and new ways of conceptualizing property doctrines. For example, a number of legal authors have observed that property law has historically favored the use versus preservation of land. In the words of Professor John Sprankling, many property doctrines have displayed an "antiwilderness bias."[1] This book considers the reasons for that bias and asks whether the reasons remain valid today. The casebook also considers the implications for property law of the recognition by ecologists that land in its natural condition can provide a variety of valuable services ("ecosystem services" or "natural services") ranging from water purification to carbon sequestration.

We hope that, as with all evolution, this casebook represents only the first step toward a rethinking and reconfiguration of the basic property law course. We invite all faculty and students who use this book to send us thoughts on other environmental laws, doctrines, concepts, and critiques that should be incorporated into future editions of this casebook. Please send ideas and thoughts to property@law.stanford.edu.

Many, many people have helped to bring this casebook to its present form. Several generations of Stanford law students have provided inestimable help in preparing research memoranda, using and commenting on drafts of the manuscripts, and attending to countless other important details. We are deeply indebted to Donna Fung for attending to all the administrative tasks that have been essential in bringing this book to print. Thank you to all.

A Note on Style. Most of the cases and other materials appearing in these pages have been edited. Most footnotes have been excised. Although ellipses indicate the deletion of sentences and paragraphs, we have not indicated the deletion of citations. On occasion, we also have expanded or added citations for greater clarity. Author's footnotes are lettered.

P.G.
B.H.T.

Stanford, California
July 2006

[1] John G. Sprankling, The Antiwilderness Bias in American Property Law, 63 U. Chi. L. Rev. 519 (1996).

ACKNOWLEDGMENTS

We are indebted to the following authors and publishers for their generosity in giving us permission to reprint excerpts or illustrations from the materials listed below.

Acheson, James M., The Lobster Gangs of Maine (1988). Copyright © 1988 University Press of New England. Reprinted by permission.

American Law Institute, Restatement (Second) of Property, Landlord & Tenant (1977). Copyright © 1977 American Law Institute. All rights reserved. Reprinted by permission.

American Law Institute, Restatement (Second) of Torts (1979). Copyright © 1979 American Law Institute. All rights reserved. Reprinted by permission.

American Law of Property (A.J. Casner ed., 1952). Copyright © 1954 Little Brown. Reprinted by permission.

Arnold, Craig Anthony, Introduction: Integrating Water Controls and Land Use Controls: New Ideas and Old Obstacles, in Wet Growth: Should Water Law Control Land Use? (2005). Copyright © 2005 Environmental Law Institute. Reprinted by permission.

Bade, Edward S., Cases and Materials on Real Property and Conveyancing (1954). Copyright © 1954 Foundation Press. Reprinted by permission.

Brown, Curtis M., Boundary Control and Legal Principles (2d ed. 1969). Copyright © 1957, 1969 John Wiley & Sons, Inc. Reprinted by permission of John Wiley & Sons, Inc.

Burke, D. Barlow, Jr., Law of Title Insurance (2d ed. 1993). Copyright © 2000 Aspen Law & Business. Reprinted by permission.

Cronon, William, Changes in the Land: Indians, Colonists and the Ecology of New England (1983). Copyright © 1983 Farrar, Straus, and Giroux. Reprinted by permission.

Cunnyngham, Wilkie, Making Land Surveys and Preparing Descriptions to Meet Legal Requirements, 19 Missouri Law Review 234 (1954). Reprinted by permission.

Dukeminier, Jesse & James E. Krier, The Rise of the Perpetual Trust, 50 University of California at Los Angeles Law Review 1303 (2003). Copyright © 2003 The Regents of the University of California. All Rights Reserved. Reprinted by permission.

Robert C. Ellickson, Of Coase and Cattle: Dispute Resolution Among Neighbors in Shasta County, 38 Stanford Law Review 623 (1986). Reprinted by permission.

Robert C. Ellickson, Property in Land, 102 Yale Law Journal 1315 (1993). Reprinted by permission of The Yale Law Journal Company and Fred B. Rothman & Company from *The Yale Law Journal*, Vol. 102, pages 1315-1400.

Flick, Clinton P., Abstract and Title Practice (2d ed. 1958). Copyright © 1958 West Publishing Company. Reprinted by permission.

Randy G. Gerchick, No Easy Way Out: Making the Summary Eviction Process a Fairer and More Efficient Alternative to Landlord Self-Help, 41 University of California at Los Angeles Law Review 759 (1994). Copyright © 1994 The Regents of the University of California. All Rights Reserved. Reprinted by permission.

Greater Boston Real Estate Board, Standard Form Purchase and Sale Agreement. Copyright © 2005 Greater Boston Real Estate Board. This form has been made available through the courtesy of the Greater Boston Real Estate Board and is protected by the copyright laws.

Guzman, Katheleen R., Give or Take an Acre: Property Norms and the Indian Land Consolidation Act, 85 Iowa Law Review 595 (2000). Reprinted by permission.

Johnson, Corwin W., Purpose and Scope of Recording Statutes, 47 Iowa Law Review 231 (1988). Reprinted by permission.

Johnstone, Quintin, Land Transfers: Process and Processors, 22 Valparaiso University Law Review 493 (1988). Reprinted by permission.

Kennedy, Duncan, The Effect of the Warranty of Habitability on Low Income Housing: "Milking" and Class Violence, 15 Florida State University Law Review 485 (1987). Copyright © 1987 Florida State University Law Review. Reprinted by permission.

Llewellyn, Karl N. & E. Adamson Hoebel, The Cheyenne Way (1941). Copyright © 1941 University of Oklahoma Press. Reprinted by permission.

Mahoney, Julia D., The Illusion of Perpetuity and the Preservation of Privately Owned Lands, 44 Natural Resources Journal 573 (2004). Reprinted by permission.

Mattis, Taylor, Recording Acts: Anachronistic Reliance, 23 Real Property, Probate, and Trust Journal 17 (1990). Reprinted by permission.

McLaughlin, Nancy A., Rethinking the Perpetual Nature of Conservation Easements, 29 Harvard Environmental Law Review 421 (2005). Reprinted by permission.

National Conference of Commissioners on Uniform State Laws, Uniform Land Transactions Act (1975). Reprinted by permission.

Note, The Tract and Grantor-Grantee Indices, 47 Iowa Law Review 481 (1962). Reprinted by permission.

Photograph of Susette Kelo. Photo by Isaac Reese. Copyright © 2004 Institute for Justice. Reprinted by permission.

Pompe, Jeffrey, The Nature of Sand: South Carolina's Shifting Shoreline, South Carolina Policy Forum Magazine, Summer 1999. Reprinted by permission.

Porter, Douglas R., The Lucas Case, Urban Land, Sept. 1992. Copyright © 1992 Urban Land Institute. Reprinted by permission from publisher, ULI - The Urban Land Institute, 1025 Thomas Jefferson Street, N.W., Suite 500W, Washington, D.C. 20007-5201.

Radin, Margaret Jane, Residential Rent Control, 15 Philosophy and Public Affairs 350 (1986). Copyright © 1986 Princeton University Press. Reprinted by permission of Princeton University Press.

Reitze, Arnold W., Jr., & Sheryl-Lynn Carof, The Legal Control of Indoor Air Pollution, 25 Boston College Environmental Affairs Law Review 247 (1998). Reprinted by permission of Arnold W. Reitze, Jr., J.B. and Maurice C. Shapiro Professor of Environmental Law, The George Washington University Law School.

Ruden, Bernard & Hywel Moseley, An Outline of the Law of Mortgages (1967). Copyright © Estates Gazette. Reprinted by permission.

Ruhl, J.B. & R. Juge Gregg, Integrating Ecosystem Services into Environmental Law: A Case Study of Wetlands Mitigation Banking, 20 Stanford Environmental Law Journal 365 (2001). Reprinted by permission.

Salzman, James & Barton H. Thompson, Jr., Environmental Law and Policy (2003). Copyright © 2003 Foundation Press. Reprinted by permission.

Sax, Joseph L., Property Rights and the Economy of Nature: Understanding *Lucas v. South Carolina Coastal Council*, 45 Stanford Law Review 1433 (1993). Reprinted by permission.

Simes, Lewis M. & Clarence B. Taylor, Improvement of Conveyancing by Legislation (1960). Copyright © 1960 University of Michigan Law School. Reprinted by permission.

Sunstein, Cass R., On Property and Constitutionalism, 14 Cardoza Law Review 907 (1993). Reprinted by permission.

Thompson, Barton H., Jr., The Trouble with Time: Influencing the Conservation Choices of Future Generations, 44 Natural Resources Journal 601 (2004). Reprinted by permission.

*

A NOTE ON NAMES AND HYPOTHETICALS

Hypotheticals in legal casebooks typically use stock names like John and Mary or just letters like X, Y, and Z. To make the hypotheticals in this book a bit more interesting, we often use the names of historical figures. In some hypotheticals, we still use letters because we have found that real names can sometimes complicate and confuse complex hypotheticals. Wherever possible, however, the book uses real names. Keeping with the themes of much of the book, moreover, the historical figures who populate this book's hypotheticals either were important to the development of environmental perspectives and policy in the United States or helped shape the settlement of the western United States.

Try to see how many of the historical figures named in this book you know.

If you find that you don't recognize a name, we've provided below very brief biographies of many of the people whom you will find in the hypotheticals. We encourage you to read more about the figures appearing in this book – all of whom were fascinating characters in varied ways.

Mary Austin (1868–1934): Author of books about the Southwest United States, with a keen eye for issues of water and the environment. Famous books include Land of Little Rain, The Basket Woman, The Ford – and her autobiography, Earth Horizon.

Black Kettle (??–1868): Cheyenne leader who had a unique vision for potential coexistence between white settlers and Native Americans.

Jim Bridger (1804–1881): One of the foremost "mountain men," Bridger was one of the first European explorers to see Yellowstone and its natural wonders. Instrumental in spreading word about the wonders and beauty of the West.

John Burroughs (1837–1921): American writer known as the Hudson River naturalist. Wrote over twenty volumes of essays extolling nature. Married to Ursula North.

Rachel Carson (1907–1964): Zoologist and marine biologist who helped create the modern environmental movement when she published Silent Spring, which examined the environmental risks of DDT and other modern pesticides.

George Washington Carver (1864–1943): African-American botanist. Advocated crop rotation and other important agricultural conservation practices among poor southern farmers. Also helped increase demand for peanuts and other plant crops through invention of hundreds of uses of these plants.

Caroline Nichols Churchill (1830–1926): Colorado suffragist and journalist.

William Clark (1770–1838): Scottish-American explorer who helped lead the Lewis & Clark expedition.

Rosalie Edge (1877–1962): One of the first female leaders in the American conservation movement. Campaigned for creation of Olympic and Kings Canyon National Parks. Also created an important wildlife refuge at Hawk Mountain, Pennsylvania.

Eliza Farnham (1815–1864): Early western feminist and author. Most famous book was Life in Prairie Land about frontier life on the Illinois Prairie.

John Charles Fremont (1813–1890): American explorer and first Republican candidate for President of the United States in 1856 (when he lost to Buchanan). Through his journeys, Fremont contributed significantly to Americans' understanding of the plants and natural amenities of the western United States.

Jessie Ann Benton Fremont (1824–1902): A gifted writer and wife of John Charles Fremont. Helped write important accounts of his explorations and accompanied him on later journeys.

Ferdinand Vandeveer Hayden (1829–1887): American geologist noted for his pioneering survey of the Rocky Mountains. Instrumental in convincing Congress to make Yellowstone the nation's first national park.

Josephine Hensley (1846–1899): Early Montana business woman. Nicknamed "Chicago Joe," Hensley was the first woman in Montana to own her own dancehall (or hurdy-gurdy).

Aldo Leopold (1887-1948): Ecologist, forester, and environmentalist. Perhaps the most instrumental person in the formation of the modern ecology movement. Author of Sand County Almanac.

Meriwether Lewis (1774–1809): American explorer who helped lead the Lewis & Clark expedition. Later became governor of Missouri.

John Muir (1838–1914): Founder of the modern conservation movement and the Sierra Club. Wrote numerous essays and books on the Sierra Nevada.

John Wesley Powell (1834–1902): Geologist and explorer. In 1869, led a 3-month river trip down the Green and Colorado River, including through the Grand Canyon. Later became the second director of the U.S. Geological Survey.

Parley P. Pratt (1807–1857): Leader in early Mormon Church. Was one of the original Quorum of the Twelve Apostles under Joseph Smith.

Red Cloud (1822–1909): Sioux leader who helped lead successful battles against the United States army over control of Powder River county in northwestern Wyoming and southern Montana.

Sitting Bull (1831–1890): Leader of Hunkpapa Sioux, who led warriors against Custer in the Battle of Little Bighorn.

Jedediah Smith (1799–1831): Hunter, trapper, fur trader, and explorer in Rocky Mountains and Southwest.

*

SUMMARY OF CONTENTS

CHAPTER 12 Federal Environmental Land Use Regulation 1070

CHAPTER 13 Regulatory Takings ---- 1111

*

TABLE OF CONTENTS

*

TABLE OF CASES

Principal cases are in bold type. Non-principal cases are in roman type. References are to Pages.

*

CASES AND MATERIALS

PROPERTY LAW: OWNERSHIP, USE, AND CONSERVATION

*

PART I

PERSPECTIVES ON PROPERTY

Property has long been a subject of immense interest and debate. William Blackstone claimed that nothing "strikes the imagination, and engages the affections of mankind, as the right of property; or that sole and despotic dominion which one man claims and exercises over the external things of the world, in total exclusion of the right of any other individual in the universe." 2 Commentaries on the Laws of England *2 (1766). Yet Blackstone's concept of property, and the precepts underlying it, have been the subject of continual controversy. Until recently, the debates over property have focused on competing human demands for the use of land and other natural resources. Why should one person have exclusive and "despotic" dominion over the "external things of the world"? What should be the limits, if any, to that dominion?

In the past several decades, a second, environmental front has opened in the controversies over property. Blackstone, like most traditional writers about property, assumed that property law should promote human interests, which courts traditionally assumed meant the development of property—its transformation into a valuable economic good. Yet as ecologists have emphasized, nature itself provides people with valuable services (often called "ecosystem services") which can be lost through development. Wetlands along the banks of a river, for example, can protect water quality and reduce downstream flood risks. Forested areas can provided habitat for pollinating insects that benefit neighboring farmers. Majestic lands such as

Yellowstone National Park provide recreational and aesthetic value. Some writers have argued that nature itself enjoys rights that should limit the manner in which we utilize nature's bounty. Such environmental concerns are forcing courts and legislatures to rethink many traditional property concepts.

Part I of this book looks at the concept of property. What purposes are served by awarding people exclusive control over land and other resources? What justifications have been given for exclusive property rights? What competing approaches have been suggested for arranging the relationship between people and the Earth's resources? Answers to these and related questions provide a framework that will help in examining the more specific contours of American property law with which the rest of the book is concerned.

This book focuses on the rights that society recognizes in land—or what is known more technically as "real property."[1] Chapter 1 provides a history of real property in the United States. Blackstone lamented how few people ask where existing property rights originated. "Pleased as we are with the possession [of our property], we seem afraid to look back to the means by which it was acquired, as if fearful of some defect in our title; or at best we rest satisfied with the decision of the laws in our favor, without examining the reason or authority upon which those laws have been built." Id. Pushing aside any fears, Chapter 1 wades into the origin of land rights in the United States. The history of these land rights provides insights into the possible justifications for private property and the purposes that property serves. The history also permits us to consider alternatives to our current system of property rights.

Chapter 2 examines some of the basic rights that the common law gives an owner of real property in the United States. True to Blackstone's image of property, the most basic and defining right remains a landowner's right to exclude other people and things from his or her land. Yet there have always been limits, and the exceptions to a property owner's right to exclude are growing in response to humanitarian, equitable, and political concerns over the "despotic" character of exclusive rights. The common law also constrains how property owners use their lands. One landowner's right to use his land as he sees fit can clash with the right of a neighbor to do the same, as when one landowner's desire to build a factory impinges on a neighbor's air quality. Land uses can also impact society's interests in the

1. The law divides property into two broad categories: "real property" (i.e., land) and "personal property" (tangible and intangible items that are not part of the land—e.g., cars, furniture, and jewelry). The reference to land as "real" property does not reflect a belief that land is more palpable or important than personal property but instead reflects the historic fact that someone suing for the theft of real property brought a "real action" in the king's courts. In a "real action" (deriving from the Latin term for thing, or *res*), one could recover the property itself. By contrast, in a "personal action" (which was the only action one could bring for the theft of personal property), one could recover the value of the property, but not the property itself. As you will see, property law is filled with such obscure distinctions.

environment and other amenities and values. For these reasons, the law limits how each property owner uses her land.

Although this book focuses on the law of real property, Chapter 3 concludes by surveying property rights in a number of other tangible and intangible assets, including fish and wildlife, petroleum, water, "intellectual property," cyberspace, and human organs. The assignment and characteristics of such rights provides a final chance to consider the purposes of property rights and how society resolves the conflicting interests inherent in giving one person control over a resource to the exclusion of others. Chapter 3 also considers again whether there should be limits to the things over which society awards private property rights. Should society recognize private property in wildlife? in ideas? in human organs?

CHAPTER 1

A BRIEF HISTORY OF REAL PROPERTY IN THE UNITED STATES

Courses in property law often plunge into existing property rights without stopping to ask how the United States got to today's property allocations. Yet the history of U.S. property rights provides a window onto many of the central issues of property theory and many of today's major property controversies. The history also forces us to consider whether existing property allocations are the result of past injustices, and if so, how we should deal with those injustices today.

A. NATIVE AMERICAN PROPERTY CLAIMS

When the first English colonists settled on the eastern seaboard of North America, much of the area was already occupied by Native American tribes. Could colonists settle on these lands without the approval of the Native Americans? If not, how could rights be acquired from Native Americans?

Many colonists concluded that they could assert ownership over such lands without obtaining the tribes' approval. Colonists distinguished between property rights that might exist in a "state of nature" and property rights that civil society should recognize. Native Americans might have had a "natural" right to occupy the land, but if they had not built permanent structures on or cultivated the land, they did not have a right that needed to be recognized by civil society. According to John Winthrop, the orthodox leader of the Massachusetts Bay colony, there are two types of property rights, both God-given:

> [T]he first right was naturall when men held the earth in common every man soweing, and feeding where he pleased; and then as men and the cattle increased they appropriated certaine cells of ground by enclosing, and peculier manurance, and this in tyme gave them a Civil right.... And for the Natives in New England they inclose noe land neither have any setled habitation nor any tame cattle to improve the land by, & soe have noe other but a naturall right to those countries.

Winthrop concluded that most tribal land was *vacuum domicilium* and that Massachusetts Bay could gain a right to it "by building an house there."

For support, Winthrop and other early settlers often pointed to Biblical edicts. In Genesis, God had instructed his people to replenish the Earth and subdue it. "Double morall & naturall that man might enjoy the fruites of the earth & god might have his due glory from the creature." Putting land to economically productive use was central to carrying out God's will and, as a result, "that which lies comon & hath never been replenished or subdued is free to any that will possesse and improve it."

Not all European settlers agreed with Winthrop. Roger Williams, a Puritan who rebelled against many of his community's precepts, wrote a pamphlet in 1632 attacking his colony's claim to Native American lands. To Williams, the colonists' arguments boiled down to the belief that being white and Christian was sufficient to justify taking over "Heathen lands"—that "Christian Kings (so calld) are invested with Right by virtue of their Christianitie, to take and give away the Lands and Countries of other men."

Williams also challenged the assertion that Native American lands were merely *vacuum domicilium*. According to Williams, Native Americans recognized the concept of property ("I have knowne them make bargaine and sale amongst themselves") and rightly believed the land belonged to them. As to the argument that Native Americans had never put the land to valuable use, Williams noted that the Native Americans "hunted all the Countrey over, and for the expedition of their hunting voyages, they burnt up all the underwoods in the Countrey, once or twice a yeare." Perhaps Native Americans did not engage in permanent agriculture, but their hunting and burning activities provided them with as much entitlement as the King of England could claim for his royal game parks. If the Native Americans did not have a civil right to their property, neither did the King of England.

The rebuttal to Williams took several forms. First, defenders of the colonists' rights challenged Williams' factual claims. English game parks were used not just for hunting, but for timber harvesting and grazing cattle. It was these economic uses that justified the King's claim. Second, it was absurd to argue that Native Americans could claim a large continent of land based on mere hunting and burning. "We did not conceive that it is a just Title to so vast a Continent, to make no other improvement of millions of Acres in it, but onely to burn it up for pastime." Finally, the colonists' divinely inspired success was proof of their right to occupy the land. "[If] God were not pleased with our inheritinge these partes, why did he drive out the natives before us?. . . . [W]hy dothe he still make roome for us, by dimishinge them as we increase?. . . . If we had no right to this lande, yet our God hathe right to it, & if he be pleased to give it us . . . who shall controll him or his terms?"

Complicating the debate over the colonists' right to the land was a fundamental disagreement between the colonists and Native Americans over what is "property." We have largely inherited the English concept of property: individuals own land to the exclusion of all other individuals. Most Native American tribes in New England had a very different conception of property. Tribal villages, through their "sachem" or leader, held collective rights over land. As Professor William Cronon, one of today's leading environmental historians, has explained, the sachem

> "owned" territory in a manner somewhat analogous to the way a European monarch "owned" an entire European nation: less as personal real estate than as the symbolic possession of a whole people. A sachem's land was coterminous with the area within which a village's economic subsistence and political sanctions were most immediately expressed....
>
> The distinction becomes important in the context of how such territorial rights could be alienated. Williams said that he had "knowne them make bargaine and sale amongst themselves for a small piece, or quantity of Ground," suggesting that Indians were little different from Europeans in their sense of how land could be bought or sold. When two sachems made an agreement to transfer land, however, they did so on behalf of their two political or kinship communities, as a way of determining the customary rights each village would be allowed in a given area....
>
> That this was so can best be seen by examining how a village's inhabitants conceived of property *within* its territory. Beginning with personal goods, ownership rights were clear: people owned what they made with their own hands. Given the division of labor, the two sexes probably tended to possess the good that were most closely associated with their respective tasks: women owned baskets, mats, kettles, hoes, and so on, while men owned bows, arrows, hatchets, fishing nets, canoes, and other hunting tools. But even in the cases of personal goods, there was little sense either of accumulation or of exclusive use. Goods were owned because they were useful, and if they ceased to be so, or were needed by someone else, they could easily be given away. "Although every proprietor knowes his own," said Thomas Morton, "yet all things, (so long as they will last), are used in common amongst them." Not surprisingly, theft was uncommon in such a world....
>
> When it came to land, however, there was less reason for gift giving or exchange. Southern New England Indian families enjoyed exclusive use of their planting fields and of the land on which their wigwams stood, and so might be said to have "owned" them. But neither of these were permanent possessions. Wigwams were moved every few months, and planting fields were abandoned after a number of years. Once abandoned, a field returned to brush until it was recleared by someone else, and no effort was made to set permanent boundaries around it that would hold it indefinitely for a single person. What families possessed in their fields was the *use* of them, the crops that were produced by a woman's labor upon them. When lands were traded or sold in the way Williams described, what were exchanged were usufruct rights, acknowledgments by one group that another might use an area for planting or

hunting or gathering. Such rights were limited to the period of use, and they did not include many of the privileges Europeans commonly associated with ownership: a user could not (and saw no need to) prevent other village members from trespassing or gathering nonagricultural food on such land, and had no conception of deriving rent from them. Planting fields were "possessed" by an Indian family only to the extent that it would return to them the following year. In this, they were not radically different in kind from other village lands; it was *European* rather than Indian definitions of land tenure that led the English to recognize agricultural land as the only legitimate Indian property. The Massachusetts Court made its ownership theories quite clear when it declared "what landes any of the Indians, within this jurisdiction, have by possession or improvement, by subdueing of the same, they have just right thereunto, accordinge to that Gen: i:28, chap: 9:1, Psa: 115, 16."

The implication was that Indians did *not* own any other kind of land: clam banks, fishing ponds, berry-picking areas, hunting lands, the great bulk of a village's territory. (Since the nonagricultural Indians of the north had *only* these kinds of land, English theories assigned them no property rights at all.) Confusion was easy on this point, not only because of English ideologies, but because the Indians themselves had very flexible definitions of land tenure for such areas. Here again, the concept of usufruct right was crucial, since different groups of people could have different claims on the same tract of land depending on how they used it. Any village member, for instance, had the right to collect edible wild plants, cut birchbark or chestnut for canoes, or gather sedges for mats, wherever these things could be found. No special private right inhered in them. Since village lands were usually organized along a single watershed, the same was true of rivers and the coast: fish and shellfish could generally be taken anywhere, although the nets, harpoons, weirs, and tackle used to catch them—and hence sometimes the right to use the sites where these things were installed—might be owned by an individual or a kin group. Indeed, in the case of extraordinary plentiful fishing sites—especially major inland waterfalls during the spawning runs—several villages might gather at a single spot to share the wealth. All of them acknowledged a mutual right to use the site for that specific purpose, even though it might otherwise lie within a single village's territory. Property rights, in other words, shifted with ecological use.

William Cronon, Changes in the Land: Indians, Colonists and the Ecology of New England 57–63 (1983).

Despite early efforts to justify expropriating Native American lands, most English settlements tacitly conceded Native American rights of occupancy. The Crown left to the colonial governments the task of acquiring land from the natives. Occupancy rights were sometimes seized outright but more commonly purchased, either by colonial governments or by individual settlers. Because most tribes did not think of land as a commodity, such purchases were typically not arms-length bargains between willing sellers and buyers. Confusion abounded over who had authority to sell land on behalf of a tribe. Bribes were commonplace.

Over time, land trades between individual settlers and tribes began to lead to violence and warfare. Tribes and settlers disagreed over the validity and terms of trades. Native Americans complained to colonial governments that white settlers were "squatting" on their land. Exchanges of liquor for land further aggravated disputes. The various colonies, beginning with Massachusetts in 1635, responded by forbidding private parties from acquiring native lands without permission from the colonial government. These efforts, however, did little to discourage settlers from land trading and squatting.

In the Proclamation of 1763, the British Crown acted to prevent such practices from spreading to the frontier area acquired in the French and Indian War. The British government closed the "Indian country" west of the crest of the Appalachian Mountains to all settlement, required the removal of squatters from the area, forbade trade with the natives without a license, and stipulated that Indian lands were to be negotiated for and purchased only by representatives of the Crown. The proclamation was never effectively enforced (and mainly served to worsen relations between colonies and the British government). But it provided a model for the settlement policy later adopted by the United States.

After United States independence, the question of Native American land rights made its way to the Supreme Court in the case of Johnson v. M'Intosh, 21 U.S. (8 Wheat.) 543 (1823). The case involved a land dispute between two groups of United States citizens, one group who claimed title based on an earlier purchase of the land directly from Native Americans, the other who had purchased the land from the United States government. For an excellent history of *Johnson v. M'Intosh*, see Eric Kades, History and Interpretation of the Great Case of *Johnson v. M'Intosh*, 19 Law & Hist. Rev. 67 (2001)

Johnson v. M'Intosh concerned the ownership of approximately 11,000 acres of land (or 20 square miles) in Southern Illinois. The Piankeshaw and Illinois Indian tribes had long inhabited the region. In the late 18th century, a number of speculative land syndicates purchased property from Native Americans in the hope that, despite the British prohibition on such purchases, the government would ultimately approve their acquisitions. Among the most renowned of the syndicates were the Illinois & Wabash Land Companies, financed by many prominent politicians and merchants, including Benjamin Franklin.[1] In July 1773, Illinois Indians sold two large

1. The land syndicates used any technique, legal or not, in acquiring property. According to one historian, "In this manner they paid a delicate and undeserved compliment to the economic conscience of the American people." Thomas P. Abernethy,

tracts of land along the Mississippi River to an Illinois & Wabash syndicate for $24,000 (a large sum at the time). In 1775, Piankeshaw Indians sold two additional tracts of land in the vicinity of the Ohio, Wabash, White, and Cat Rivers to another Illinois & Wabash syndicate for $31,000.

The syndicates found it difficult to get governmental approval of their purchases. Four years after the second purchase, the Colony of Virginia (in whose territory the land lay) followed Britain's lead by enacting a statute that rejected all private land claims based on purchases from Native Americans. In the statute, Virginia asserted an exclusive right to acquire Native American lands. Virginia later ceded ownership of its lands within the northwest territories, including the land at issue in *Johnson*, to the United States. For years, the Illinois & Wabash syndicates petitioned Congress to recognize their purchases, without success—probably because Congress saw the lands as a potential source of revenue for paying off Revolutionary War debts. In 1818, according to the Supreme Court, the United States sold 11,560 acres, much of which overlapped the earlier purchases, to William M'Intosh, an attorney and British major during the Revolutionary War.

One of the many prominent members of the Illinois & Wabash syndicates was Thomas Johnson, who served many roles in the early United States, including Governor of Maryland and Associate Justice on the U.S. Supreme Court. In 1819, Johnson died and left his share of the syndicate's land by will to his son, Joshua Johnson, and his grandson, Thomas Graham. Johnson and Graham subsequently filed suit against M'Intosh, seeking to establish that they and not M'Intosh owned the land. Following the legal formality of the day, Johnson and Graham claimed that they had leased the land to one "Simeon Peaceable" whom M'Intosh had prevented from using the land. The title of the case thus became *Johnson & Graham's Lessee v. M'Intosh.*

Johnson & Graham's Lessee v. M'Intosh

Supreme Court of the United States, 1823.
21 U.S. (8 Wheat.) 543.

MR. CHIEF JUSTICE MARSHALL delivered the opinion of the Court.

The plaintiffs in this cause claim the land, in their declaration mentioned, under two grants, purporting to be made, the first in 1773, and the

Western Lands and the American Revolution 116 (1959). "But 'for ways that were dark and for tricks that were vain,' the Illinois and Wabash Companies were peculiar." Id.

To convince local British officials to let them negotiate land acquisitions with native tribes in the face of British prohibitions, agents for the Illinois and Wabash Companies tampered with a 1757 legal opinion of the English Attorney General. The opinion originally read that "In respect to such places, as have been or shall be acquired by treaty or grant from the Grand Mogul or any of the Indian princes or governments, your Majesties letters patents are not necessary, the property of the soil vesting in the grantees by the Indian grants." British agents of the syndicates made a copy of the opinion, leaving out reference to "the Grand Mogul," and passed it off as a letter referring to Native American tribes.

last in 1775, by the chiefs of certain Indian tribes, constituting the Illinois and the Piankeshaw nations; and the question is, whether this title can be recognized in the Courts of the United States?

The facts, as stated in the case agreed, show the authority of the chiefs who executed this conveyance, so far as it could be given by their own people; and likewise show, that the particular tribes for whom these chiefs acted were in rightful possession of the land they sold. The inquiry, therefore, is, in a great measure, confined to the power of Indians to give, and of private individuals to receive, a title which can be sustained in the Courts of this country.

As the right of society, to prescribe those rules by which property may be acquired and preserved is not, and cannot be drawn into question; as the title to lands, especially, is and must be admitted to depend entirely on the law of the nation in which they lie; it will be necessary, in pursuing this inquiry, to examine, not singly those principles of abstract justice, which the Creator of all things has impressed on the mind of his creature man, and which are admitted to regulate, in a great degree, the rights of civilized nations, whose perfect independence is acknowledged; but those principles also which our own government has adopted in the particular case, and given us as the rule for our decision.

On the discovery of this immense continent, the great nations of Europe were eager to appropriate to themselves so much of it as they could respectively acquire. Its vast extent offered an ample field to the ambition and enterprise of all; and the character and religion of its inhabitants afforded an apology for considering them as a people over whom the superior genius of Europe might claim an ascendency. The potentates of the old world found no difficulty in convincing themselves that they made ample compensation to the inhabitants of the new, by bestowing on them civilization and Christianity, in exchange for unlimited independence. But, as they were all in pursuit of nearly the same object, it was necessary, in order to avoid conflicting settlements, and consequent war with each other, to establish a principle, which all should acknowledge as the law by which the right of acquisition, which they all asserted, should be regulated as between themselves. This principle was, that discovery gave title to the government by whose subjects, or by whose authority, it was made, against all other European governments, which title might be consummated by possession.

The exclusion of all other Europeans, necessarily gave to the nation making the discovery the sole right of acquiring the soil from the natives, and establishing settlements upon it. It was a right with which no Europeans could interfere. It was a right which all asserted for themselves, and to the assertion of which, by others, all assented.

Those relations which were to exist between the discoverer and the natives, were to be regulated by themselves. The rights thus acquired being exclusive, no other power could interpose between them.

In the establishment of these relations, the rights of the original inhabitants were, in no instance, entirely disregarded; but were necessarily, to a considerable extent, impaired. They were admitted to be the rightful occupants of the soil, with a legal as well as just claim to retain possession of it, and to use it according to their own discretion; but their rights to complete sovereignty, as independent nations, were necessarily diminished, and their power to dispose of the soil at their own will, to whomsoever they pleased, was denied by the original fundamental principle, that discovery gave exclusive title to those who made it.

While the different nations of Europe respected the right of the natives, as occupants, they asserted the ultimate dominion to be in themselves; and claimed and exercised, as a consequence of this ultimate dominion, a power to grant the soil, while yet in possession of the natives. These grants have been understood by all, to convey a title to the grantees, subject only to the Indian right of occupancy.

The history of America, from its discovery to the present day, proves, we think, the universal recognition of these principles.

Spain did not rest her title solely on the grant of the Pope. Her discussions respecting boundary, with France, with Great Britain, and with the United States, all show that she placed it on the rights given by discovery. Portugal sustained her claim to the Brazils by the same title. France, also, founded her title to the vast territories she claimed in America on discovery.... The States of Holland also made acquisitions in America, and sustained their right on the common principle adopted by all Europe....

No one of the powers of Europe gave its full assent to this principle, more unequivocally than England. The documents upon this subject are ample and complete. So early as the year 1496, her monarch granted a commission to the Cabots, to discover countries then unknown to Christian people, and to take possession of them in the name of the king of England. Two years afterwards, Cabot proceeded on this voyage, and discovered the continent of North America, along which he sailed as far south as Virginia. To this discovery the English trace their title.

In this first effort made by the English government to acquire territory on this continent, we perceive a complete recognition of the principle which has been mentioned. The right of discovery given by this commission, is confined to countries "then unknown to all Christian people"; and of these countries Cabot was empowered to take possession in the name of the king of England. Thus asserting a right to take possession, notwithstanding the occupancy of the natives, who were heathens, and, at the same time, admitting the prior title of any Christian people who may have made a previous discovery.

The same principle continued to be recognized. [An omitted section of Justice Marshall's decision discusses the numerous charters from the English crown that granted lands in America.]

Thus has our whole country been granted by the crown while in the occupation of the Indians. These grants purport to convey the soil as well as the right of dominion to the grantees. In those governments which were denominated royal, where the right to the soil was not vested in individuals, but remained in the crown, or was vested in the colonial government, the king claimed and exercised the right of granting lands, and of dismembering the government at his will. The grants made out of the two original colonies, after the resumption of their charters by the crown, are examples of this. The governments of New–England, New–York, New–Jersey, Pennsylvania, Maryland, and a part of Carolina, were thus created. In all of them, the soil, at the time the grants were made, was occupied by the Indians. Yet almost every title within those governments is dependent on these grants. In some instances, the soil was conveyed by the crown unaccompanied by the powers of government, as in the case of the northern neck of Virginia. It has never been objected to this, or to any other similar grant, that the title as well as possession was in the Indians when it was made, and that it passed nothing on that account.

These various patents cannot be considered as nullities; nor can they be limited to a mere grant of the powers of government. A charter intended to convey political power only, would never contain words expressly granting the land, the soil, and the waters. Some of them purport to convey the soil alone; and in those cases in which the powers of government, as well as the soil, are conveyed to individuals, the crown has always acknowledged itself to be bound by the grant. Though the power to dismember regal governments was asserted and exercised, the power to dismember proprietary governments was not claimed; and, in some instances, even after the powers of government were revested in the crown, the title of the proprietors to the soil was respected....

Further proofs of the extent to which this principle has been recognized, will be found in the history of the wars, negotiations, and treaties, which the different nations, claiming territory in America, have carried on, and held with each other....

Thus, all the nations of Europe, who have acquired territory on this continent, have asserted in themselves, and have recognized in others, the exclusive right of the discoverer to appropriate the lands occupied by the Indians. Have the American States rejected or adopted this principle?

By the treaty which concluded the war of our revolution, Great Britain relinquished all claim, not only to the government, but to the "propriety and territorial rights of the United States," whose boundaries were fixed in the second article. By this treaty, the powers of government, and the right to soil, which had previously been in Great Britain, passed definitively to these States. We had before taken possession of them, by declaring independence; but neither the declaration of independence, nor the treaty confirming it, could give us more than that which we before possessed, or to which Great Britain was before entitled. It has never been doubted, that either the United States, or the several States, had a clear title to all the lands within the boundary lines described in the treaty, subject only to the

Indian right of occupancy, and that the exclusive power to extinguish that right, was vested in that government which might constitutionally exercise it.

Virginia, particularly, within whose chartered limits the land in controversy lay, passed an act, in the year 1779, declaring her

> exclusive right of pre-emption from the Indians, of all the lands within the limits of her own chartered territory, and that no person or persons whatsoever, have, or ever had, a right to purchase any lands within the same, from any Indian nation, except only persons duly authorized to make such purchase; formerly for the use and benefit of the colony, and lately for the Commonwealth.

The act then proceeds to annul all deeds made by Indians to individuals, for the private use of the purchasers.

Without ascribing to this act the power of annulling vested rights, or admitting it to countervail the testimony furnished by the marginal note opposite to the title of the law, forbidding purchases from the Indians, in the revisals of the Virginia statutes, stating that law to be repealed, it may safely be considered as an unequivocal affirmance, on the part of Virginia, of the broad principle which had always been maintained, that the exclusive right to purchase from the Indians resided in the government.

In pursuance of the same idea, Virginia proceeded, at the same session, to open her land office, for the sale of that country which now constitutes Kentucky, a country, every acre of which was then claimed and possessed by Indians, who maintained their title with as much persevering courage as was ever manifested by any people.

The States, having within their chartered limits different portions of territory covered by Indians, ceded that territory, generally, to the United States, on conditions expressed in their deeds of cession, which demonstrate the opinion, that they ceded the soil as well as jurisdiction, and that in doing so, they granted a productive fund to the government of the Union. The lands in controversy lay within the chartered limits of Virginia, and were ceded with the whole country northwest of the river Ohio. This grant contained reservations and stipulations, which could only be made by the owners of the soil; and concluded with a stipulation, that "all the lands in the ceded territory, not reserved, should be considered as a common fund, for the use and benefit of such of the United States as have become, or shall become, members of the confederation," & c. "according to their usual respective proportions in the general charge and expenditure, and shall be faithfully and bona fide disposed of for that purpose, and for no other use or purpose whatsoever."

The ceded territory was occupied by numerous and warlike tribes of Indians; but the exclusive right of the United States to extinguish their title, and to grant the soil, has never, we believe, been doubted....

The United States ... have unequivocally acceded to that great and broad rule by which its civilized inhabitants now hold this country. They hold, and assert in themselves, the title by which it was acquired. They maintain, as all others have maintained, that discovery gave an exclusive right to extinguish the Indian title of occupancy, either by purchase or by conquest; and gave also a right to such a degree of sovereignty, as the circumstances of the people would allow them to exercise.

The power now possessed by the government of the United States to grant lands, resided, while we were colonies, in the crown, or its grantees. The validity of the titles given by either has never been questioned in our Courts. It has been exercised uniformly over territory in possession of the Indians. The existence of this power must negative the existence of any right which may conflict with, and control it. An absolute title to lands cannot exist, at the same time, in different persons, or in different governments. An absolute, must be an exclusive title, or at least a title which excludes all others not compatible with it. All our institutions recognise the absolute title of the crown, subject only to the Indian right of occupancy, and recognise the absolute title of the crown to extinguish that right. This is incompatible with an absolute and complete title in the Indians.

We will not enter into the controversy, whether agriculturists, merchants, and manufacturers, have a right, on abstract principles, to expel hunters from the territory they possess, or to contract their limits. Conquest gives a title which the Courts of the conqueror cannot deny, whatever the private and speculative opinions of individuals may be, respecting the original justice of the claim which has been successfully asserted. The British government, which was then our government, and whose rights have passed to the United States, asserted a title to all the lands occupied by Indians, within the chartered limits of the British colonies. It asserted also a limited sovereignty over them, and the exclusive right of extinguishing the title which occupancy gave to them. These claims have been maintained and established as far west as the river Mississippi, by the sword. The title to a vast portion of the lands we now hold, originates in them. It is not for the Courts of this country to question the validity of this title, or to sustain one which is incompatible with it.

Although we do not mean to engage in the defence of those principles which Europeans have applied to Indian title, they may, we think, find some excuse, if not justification, in the character and habits of the people whose rights have been wrested from them.

The title by conquest is acquired and maintained by force. The conqueror prescribes its limits. Humanity, however, acting on public opinion, has established, as a general rule, that the conquered shall not be wantonly oppressed, and that their condition shall remain as eligible as is compatible with the objects of the conquest. Most usually, they are incorporated with the victorious nation, and become subjects or citizens of the government with which they are connected. The new and old members of the society mingle with each other; the distinction between them is gradually lost, and they make one people. Where this incorporation is practicable, humanity demands, and a wise policy requires, that the rights of the conquered to property should remain unimpaired; that the new subjects should be governed as equitably as the old, and that confidence in their security should gradually banish the painful sense of being separated from their ancient connexions, and united by force to strangers.

When the conquest is complete, and the conquered inhabitants can be blended with the conquerors, or safely governed as a distinct people, public opinion, which not even the conqueror can disregard, imposes these restraints upon him; and he cannot neglect them without injury to his fame, and hazard to his power.

But the tribes of Indians inhabiting this country were fierce savages, whose occupation was war, and whose subsistence was drawn chiefly from the forest. To leave them in possession of their country, was to leave the country a wilderness; to govern them as a distinct people, was impossible, because they were as brave and as high spirited as they were fierce, and were ready to repel by arms every attempt on their independence.

What was the inevitable consequence of this state of things? The Europeans were under the necessity either of abandoning the country, and relinquishing their pompous claims to it, or of enforcing those claims by the sword, and by the adoption of principles adapted to the condition of a people with whom it was impossible to mix, and who could not be governed as a distinct society, or of remaining in their neighbourhood, and exposing themselves and their families to the perpetual hazard of being massacred.

Frequent and bloody wars, in which the whites were not always the aggressors, unavoidably ensued. European policy, numbers, and skill, prevailed. As the white population advanced, that of the Indians necessarily receded. The country in the immediate neighbourhood of agriculturists became unfit for them. The game fled into thicker and more unbroken forests, and the Indians followed. The soil, to which the crown originally claimed title, being no longer occupied by its ancient inhabitants, was parcelled out according to the will of the sovereign power, and taken possession of by persons who claimed immediately from the crown, or mediately, through its grantees or deputies.

That law which regulates, and ought to regulate in general, the relations between the conqueror and conquered, was incapable of application to a people under such circumstances. The resort to some new and different rule, better adapted to the actual state of things, was unavoidable. Every rule which can be suggested will be found to be attended with great difficulty.

However extravagant the pretension of converting the discovery of an inhabited country into conquest may appear; if the principle has been asserted in the first instance, and afterwards sustained; if a country has been acquired and held under it; if the property of the great mass of the community originates in it, it becomes the law of the land, and cannot be questioned. So, too, with respect to the concomitant principle, that the Indian inhabitants are to be considered merely as occupants, to be protected, indeed, while in peace, in the possession of their lands, but to be deemed incapable of transferring the absolute title to others. However this restriction may be opposed to natural right, and to the usages of civilized nations, yet, if it be indispensable to that system under which the country has been settled, and be adapted to the actual condition of the two people, it may, perhaps, be supported by reason, and certainly cannot be rejected by Courts of justice....

It has never been contended, that the Indian title amounted to nothing. Their right of possession has never been questioned. The claim of government extends to the complete ultimate title, charged with this right of possession, and to the exclusive power of acquiring that right....

After bestowing on this subject a degree of attention which was more required by the magnitude of the interest in litigation, and the able and elaborate arguments of the bar, than by its intrinsic difficulty, the Court is decidedly of opinion, that the plaintiffs do not exhibit a title which can be sustained in the Courts of the United States; and that there is no error in the judgment which was rendered against them in the District Court of Illinois....

Notes & Questions

Johnson v. M'Intosh & Native American Land Rights

1. Why did the Supreme Court rule for M'Intosh? In concluding that the United States, and Virginia before it, enjoyed the exclusive right to acquire land from Native Americans, Marshall refers to implicit understandings among European governments, to colonial charters and grants, to Virginia laws, and to Virginia's northwest grant to the United States. Native Americans, of course, played no role in these various agreements and laws. Could the agreements bind Native Americans? Does it matter to Marshall's analysis?

At several points, Marshall emphasizes that "almost every title" within the original colonies "is dependent" on grants from the English crown. Marshall also says that it is "not for the Court of this country to question the validity of this title, or to sustain one which is incompatible with it." Is Marshall suggesting that the Supreme Court had to rule for M'Intosh as a matter of political or practical necessity? See Philip P. Frickey, Marshalling Past and Present: Colonialism, Constitutionalism, and Interpretation in Federal Indian Law, 107 Harv. L. Rev. 381, 389 (1993) ("*Johnson* seemed to establish a rigid dichotomy between power and law. Colonialism, *Johnson* seemed to say, raises almost exclusively nonjusticiable, normative questions beyond judicial authority and competence").

Although Marshall says that the Court does "not mean to engage in the defence of those principles which Europeans have applied to Indian title," he proceeds to do so at length. Why? How convincing do you find his defense?

2. Under *Johnson v. M'Intosh*, what rights do Native American tribes enjoy in the lands that they historically occupied? Chief Justice Marshall says that "discovery" of North America gave "exclusive title to those who

made it," but that Native Americans nonetheless retain a "right of occupancy." Later he says that Native Americans retain "Indian title" and "title of occupancy." As you will see in Chapter 2, private property is frequently described as a "bundle of rights"—which can include the right to occupy the property, exclude others from the property, profit from the property's use, sell the property, determine who the property should go to upon the landowner's death, and demand compensation if the government takes the property. The individual sticks in the "bundle of rights" can be divided up among individuals, with some going to one person and other rights going to another. Under *Johnson*, what rights does the discoverer get? What rights do the Native Americans retain? Under what circumstances can the Native American rights be terminated?

3. ***Worcester v. Georgia***. In 1832, Chief Justice Marshall had an opportunity to revisit the property rights of Native American tribes. In ruling that Georgia could not regulate who resided on Cherokee lands, Marshall wrote that the "doctrine of discovery" elaborated in *Johnson v. M'Intosh*

> regulated the right given by discovery among the European discoverers; but could not affect the rights of those already in possession, either as aboriginal occupants, or as occupants by virtue of a discovery made before the memory of man. It gave the exclusive right to purchase, but did not found that right on a denial of the right of the possessor to sell. . . .
>
> Soon after Great Britain determined on planting colonies in America, the king granted charters to companies of his subjects, who associated for the purpose of carrying the view of the crown into effect, and of enriching themselves. The first of these charters was made, before possession was taken of any part of the country. They purport, generally, to convey the soil, from the Atlantic to the South Sea. This soil was occupied by numerous and warlike nations, equally willing and able to defend their possessions. The extravagant and absurd idea, that the feeble settlements made on the sea-coast, or the companies under whom they were made, acquired legitimate power by them to govern the people, or occupy the lands from sea to sea, did not enter the mind of any man. They were well understood to convey the title which, according to the common law of European sovereigns respecting America, they might rightfully convey, and no more. This was the exclusive right of purchasing such lands as the natives were willing to sell. The crown could not be understood to grant what the crown did not affect to claim; nor was it so understood.

Worcester v. Georgia, 31 U.S. (6 Pet.) 515, 544–45 (1832).

4. Disputes over Native American property rights have continued to this day. Over the first 150 years of the nation's history, the United States acquired approximately two million square miles of land by conquest or purchase from Native American tribes. See Felix S. Cohen, Original Indian Title, 32 Minn. L. Rev. 28, 36 (1947). Until 1871, the United States usually

acquired tribal territory by entering into treaties that provided the tribes with financial compensation and guaranteed them "reservations" to maintain as homelands. Over $800 million changed hands in the course of signing almost 400 treaties. Id. at 34. After 1871, the United States continued to acquire Native American lands and to create reservations through Congressional legislation, "executive orders" signed by the President, and various forms of agreements. See Felix S. Cohen, Handbook of Federal Indian Law 48–49 (1982 ed.).

5. ***Tee–Hit–Ton Indians.*** In some cases, however, the United States simply stripped tribes of aboriginal land or other resources without providing any compensation—raising the question of whether such uncompensated takings were legal under *Johnson* and *Worcester*. In *Tee–Hit–Ton Indians v. United States*, 348 U.S. 272 (1955), a small Native Alaskan clan sued the United States for taking timber from their lands. The Supreme Court, with three justices dissenting, held that the clan was not entitled to any compensation for the timber:

> The nature of aboriginal Indian interest in land and the various rights as between the Indians and the United States dependent on such interest are far from novel as concerns our Indian inhabitants. It is well settled that in all the States of the Union the tribes who inhabited the lands of the States held claim to such lands after the coming of the white man, under what is sometimes termed original Indian title or permission from the whites to occupy. That description means mere possession not specifically recognized as ownership by Congress. After conquest they were permitted to occupy portions of territory over which they had previously exercised "sovereignty," as we use that term. This is not a property right but amounts to a right of occupancy which the sovereign grants and protects against intrusion by third parties but which right of occupancy may be terminated and such lands fully disposed of by the sovereign itself without any legally enforceable obligation to compensate the Indians....
>
> In 1941 a unanimous Court wrote, concerning Indian title, the following:
>
> > "Extinguishment of Indian title based on aboriginal possession is of course a different matter. The power of Congress in that regard is supreme. The manner, method and time of such extinguishment raise political, not justiciable, issues." United States v. Santa Fe Pacific R. Co., 314 U.S. 339, 347.
>
> No case in this Court has ever held that taking of Indian title or use by Congress required compensation....

348 U.S. at 279–281. Is *Tee–Hit–Ton* consistent with the Supreme Court's decision in *Johnson v. M'Intosh*? in *Worcester*? After *Tee–Hit–Ton*, what rights do Native Americans have in the lands that they historically inhabited? For an argument that *Tee–Hit–Ton* purposefully abandoned *Johnson v.*

M'Intosh, see Nell Jessup Newton, At the Whim of the Sovereign: Aboriginal Title Reconsidered, 31 Hastings L.J. 1215 (1980).

6. Under *Johnson v. M'Intosh*, do the property rights of a Native American tribe depend on its form of government, how it has used its lands, or its concept of property? Should these factors matter? In *Tee–Hit–Ton*, the Native Alaskan plaintiffs urged that "their stage of civilization and their concept of ownership of property takes them out of the rule applicable to the Indians of the States." The Court, however, concluded that the Tee–Hit–Tons' historic approach to property was "wholly tribal":

> It was more a claim of sovereignty than of ownership.... From all that was presented, the Court of Claims concluded and we agree, that the Tee–Hit–Tons were in a hunting and fishing stage of civilization, with shelters fitted to their environment, and claims to rights to use identified territory for these activities as well as the gathering of wild products of the earth. We think this evidence introduced by both sides confirms the Court of Claims' conclusion that the petitioner's use of its lands was like the use of the nomadic tribes of the States Indians.

348 U.S. at 287. In a footnote, the Court suggested that "even ... the Pueblo Indians of the Mexican Land Sessions, despite their centuries-old sedentary agricultural and pastoral life," would not be entitled to compensation for a taking of their land by the United States. Id. at 288 n.20.

7. Congress occasionally has provided voluntary compensation for the taking of aboriginal lands of Native American tribes. The best example is the Alaska Native Claims Settlement Act of 1971, 43 U.S.C. §§ 1601 et seq., which awarded native Alaskans $962.5 million plus approximately 40 million acres of federal public lands.

8. Where the United States has created reservations or otherwise recognized Native American property rights in treaties, legislation, or executive orders, the United States Supreme Court has held that the United States cannot unilaterally deprive Native American tribes of that land without compensation. See Confederated Bands of Ute Indians v. United States, 330 U.S. 169 (1947); United States v. Shoshone Tribe, 304 U.S. 111 (1938). Courts, however, will not second guess whether Congress has provided "full value" for Native American property where Congress has made a "good faith effort" to do so. United States v. Sioux Nation of Indians, 448 U.S. 371 (1980).

In the 19th century, moreover, treaties were often renegotiated, with the size of a tribe's reservation dwindling with each new treaty. And between 1887 and 1934, Congress effectively reduced tribal land from 138 million acres to 34 million acres through the General Allotment Act of 1887, 24 Stat. 388. 2 Francis Paul Prucha, The Great Father: The United States Government and the American Indian 896 (1984). Claiming that Native Americans would be better off under a system of private property than under communal reservations, Congress in the General Allotment Act provided for the "allotment" of 160–acre parcels of land to each tribal member and the sale of "surplus" common lands. Non–Indians purchased not only surplus lands, but also thousands of the allotments. By 1934, the allotment policy was deemed a failure, and Congress passed the Indian Reorganization Act, 48 Stat. 984, returning any remaining Native American lands to the tribes. Today, Native American tribes and tribal members own approximately 100 million acres of land (44 million of which resulted from the Alaskan Native Claims Settlement Act)—or approximately 4.2 percent of the nation. David H. Getches, Charles F. Wilkinson, & Robert A. Williams, Jr., Cases and Materials on Federal Indian Law 20 (5th ed. 2004).

9. Throughout the various stages of United States policy toward Native American lands, the United States has adhered to the position that only the United States can authorize the acquisition of Native American lands. States, for example, cannot divest tribes of unused property. See Worcester v. Georgia, 31 U.S. (6 Pet.) 515 (1832). Under a variety of Nonintercourse Acts dating from the end of the 18th century, Native American tribes cannot convey their land without Congressional approval. The current version of the Nonintercourse Act is codified at 25 U.S.C. § 415. Conveyances not approved by Congress are invalid, and tribes can generally bring lawsuits to recover lands purportedly "sold" in such conveyances without worrying about statutes of limitations. See, e.g., Oneida v. Oneida Indian Nation, 470 U.S. 226 (1985) (finding that a 1795 transfer of approximately 100,000 acres from the Oneida Nation to the State of New York was void for lack of federal approval).

10. According to Professor Robert Williams, the decision in *Johnson v. M'Intosh* preserved a

> legacy of 1,000 years of European racism and colonialism directed against non-Western peoples. White society's exercise of power over Indian tribes received the sanction of the Rule of Law in *Johnson v. McIntosh*. The Doctrine of Discovery's underlying medievally derived ideology—that normatively divergent "savage" people could be denied rights and status equal to those accorded to the civilized nations of Europe—had become an integral part of the fabric of the United States federal Indian law.... While the tasks of conquest and colonization had not yet been fully actualized on the entire American continent, the original rules and principles of federal Indian law set down by Marshall in *Johnson v. McIntosh* and its discourse of conquest ensured that future acts of genocide would proceed on a rationalized, legal basis.

Robert A. Williams, Jr., The American Indian in Western Legal Thought: The Discourses of Conquest 317 (1990). If you had been on the Supreme Court in 1825, how would you have resolved *Johnson v. M'Intosh*?

11. For other valuable recent discussions of *Johnson v. M'Intosh* and Native American land issues, see Eric Kades, History and Interpretation of the Great Case of *Johnson v. M'Intosh*, 19 Law & Hist. Rev. 67 (2001); Eric Kades, The Dark Side of Efficiency: *Johnson v. M'Intosh* and the Expropriation of American Indian Lands, 148 U. Pa. L. Rev. 1065 (2000); Raymond Cross, Sovereign Bargains, Indian Takings, and the Preservation of Indian

Country in the Twenty–First Century, 40 Ariz. L. Rev. 425 (1998); Christine A. Klein, Treaties of Conquest: Property Rights, Indian Treaties, and the Treaty of Guadalupe Hidalgo, 26 N.M.L. Rev. 201 (1996).

Justifications of Property

1. *Johnson v. M'Intosh* and the early conflicts over Native American lands provide a useful window onto the underlying assumptions, justifications, and purposes of private property. For example, both Chief Justice Marshall and early colonial leaders like John Winthrop suggested that Native Americans were not entitled to full property rights because they had not "improved" their land by building fences, planting crops, and constructing buildings. The argument reflects a view that land should be developed rather than left as wilderness. See John G. Sprankling, The Antiwilderness Bias in American Property Law, 63 U. Chi. L. Rev. 519 (1996). As Professor Joseph Sax has noted, there is an alternative "ecological" view of how land should be perceived:

> The conventional perspective of private property, the transformative economy, builds on the image of property as a discrete entity that can be made one's own by working it and transforming it into a human artifact. A piece of iron becomes an anvil, a tree becomes lumber, and a forest becomes a farm. Traditional property law treats undeveloped land as essentially inert. The land is there, it may have things on or in it (e.g., timber or coal), but it is in a passive state, waiting to be put to use. Insofar as land is "doing" something—for example, harboring wild animals—property law considers such functions expendable. Indeed, getting rid of the natural, or at least domesticating it, was a primary task of the European settlers of North America.
>
> An ecological view of property, the economy of nature, is fundamentally different.... Land is already at work, performing important services in its unaltered state. For example, forests regulate the global climate, marshes sustain marine fisheries, and prairie grass holds the soil in place. Transformation diminishes the functioning of the economy and, in fact, is at odds with it.

Joseph L. Sax, Property Rights and the Economy of Nature: Understanding *Lucas v. South Carolina Coastal Council*, 45 Stan. L. Rev. 1433, 1442–43 (1993). For more information on the types and importance of services provided by land in its unaltered state, see Nature's Services: Societal Dependence on Natural Ecosystems (Getchen C. Daily ed., 1997).

2. **First Possession.** The very fact that Chief Justice Marshall and early colonial leaders labored fiercely to justify European encroachments on lands historically occupied by Native Americans also suggests that they believed that whoever first possessed a piece of land normally should own it. As you will see throughout Part I of this book, the principle that the first person in possession of a resource should have a right to that resource has long carried tremendous force in both the law and in the informal norms that govern our society. (For example, how would you feel if, having found

a parking spot in a crowded area, another car zipped in ahead of you and took the parking space? Many people would complain that the other car had "stolen *their* parking space.") That people have long been attracted to the principle of "first possession," however, does not necessarily justify the principle. Why should first possession matter to ownership?

3. **Labor Theory of Property.** John Locke's answer to the question was that someone who mixes his or her labor with a piece of land gains an equitable claim to the land itself. An individual has "a property in his own person" and thus his labor. If the person modifies a parcel of land (e.g., by planting corn on the land), the person "thereby makes it his property"; the land now has "something annexed to it that excludes the common right of other men. For this labour being the unquestionable property of the labourer, no man but he can have a right to what that is once joyned to, at least where there is enough, and as good left in common for others." John Locke, Second Treatise on Government ¶ 27 (1698).

Locke's justification for awarding property to the first user raises a variety of questions. Why do you have a property right in your labor? Why should you gain a right to something to which you have annexed your labor? Absent others' permission, why shouldn't you just lose the fruits of your labor? In Arnold v. Mundy, 6 N.J. Law 1 (1821), the New Jersey Supreme Court held that the owner of land along a public, navigable river did not gain exclusive rights to oysters growing on the adjacent river bed by planting oysters there. The closest analogy, according to that court, was "the case of a stranger voluntarily throwing his grain or money into my heap, when, from the difficulty of separation, caused by his own folly, I would be entitled to the whole." Id. at 93 (opinion of Rossell, J.).

What does the proviso mean at the end of Locke's justification? When is there "enough, and as good left in common for others"? What should happen if there isn't?

4. Beyond these fundamental questions, what constitutes sufficient labor to justify awarding a property right in land? And to how much land should the laborer be entitled? Consider the Puritan argument, previously quoted at page 5, that Native Americans should not be able to claim title to millions of acres of land simply because they burned forests and engaged in nomadic hunting. See Robert Nozick, Anarchy, State, and Utopia 174–182 (1974); Carol Rose, Possession as the Origin of Property, 52 U. Chi. L. Rev. 73, 73–74 (1985).

The California Supreme Court faced this issue in Brumagim v. Bradshaw, 39 Cal. 24 (1870). The specific question was whether the plaintiff had gained the right to a sizable peninsula of land in San Francisco (what is today the Potrero district) by repairing a fence across the neck of the peninsula and pasturing livestock on the land. The court ruled against the plaintiff. According to the court, both "reason and authority" suggest that "the acts of ownership and dominion over land, which may be sufficient to constitute an actual possession, vary according to the condition, size, and locality of the tract." Id. at 44–45. The court illustrated this point with Santa Catalina, a 50,000–acre island off Southern California. Erecting a hut in the middle of the island, according to the court, would not entitle you to the entire island. But if you

> pastured large herds of cattle upon it, allowing them to roam all over it, or cultivate extensive fields on various portions of it, should prevent others from landing on it, should cut timber or open mines of quarries on many remote parts of it, there would probably be held to be such an act of dominion as to establish a *possessio pedis* of the whole.

Id. at 49–50.

5. A final question about Locke's labor theory of property: why should the mixing of labor and land entitle you to an *exclusive*, *longterm* right of dominion over the land? Recall that many Native American tribes recognized only a "usufructuary" right to land. A Southern New England Indian family enjoyed exclusive *use* of a planting field, so long as the family continued to use the field for planting, and exclusive rights to the *fruits* of the agricultural efforts. The family, however, could not exclude others from using the land in ways that did not interfere with the family's agricultural work. Moreover, the family held a claim to the land only so long as they farmed it. Europeans, by contrast, viewed private property as an exclusive and perpetual right. Isn't the concept of a "usufructuary" right more consistent than an exclusive and perpetual right with Locke's labor theory of property? Although the European view of property remains the prototypical property concept in the United States today, we award only nonexclusive usufructuary rights in some resources such as water. (We will look at water rights in Chapter 3 at pages 247–270).

6. **Utilitarian Theories of Property.** In contrast to John Locke, many other commentators have looked for instrumental justifications of private property rights. In the 18th century, David Hume provided a utilitarian justification: self-interest in our own happiness leads us to create and enforce property rights. As William Blackstone argued in his 1766 commentaries, early human societies had no need for exclusive property rights, although they recognized "a kind of transient property, that lasted so long as [an individual] was using it, and no longer." 2 William Blackstone, Commentaries on the Law of England *3 (1766).

> But when mankind increased in number, craft, and ambition, it became necessary to entertain conceptions of more permanent dominions; and to appropriate to individuals not the immediate *use* only, but the very *substance* of the thing to be used. Otherwise innumerable tumults must have arisen, and the good order of the world be continually broken and disturbed, while a variety of persons were striving who should get the first occupation of the same thing, or disputing which of them had actually gained it. As human life also grew more and more refined, abundance of conveniences were devised to render it more easy, commodious, and agreeable; as, habitations for shelter and safety, and raiment for warmth and decency. But no man would be at the trouble to provide either, so long as he had only an usufructuary property in

> them, which was to cease the instant that he quitted possession; if, as soon as he walked out of his tent, or pulled off her garments, the next stranger who came by would have a right to inhabit the one, and to wear the other.... It was [also] clear that the earth would not produce her fruits in sufficient quantities without the assistance of tillage; but who would be at the pains of tilling it, if another might watch an opportunity to seize upon and enjoy the product of his industry, art, and labor?....

Id. at *4 & *7.

7. Professor Robert Ellickson has described how private property benefitted early colonists. Some North American colonies such as Jamestown and Plymouth started with largely communal land systems, but quickly found that the awarding of individual property rights increased productivity. In Jamestown, for example, land

> was held as a collective asset. Although many settlers were bound to the Company by indentures, each was guaranteed an equal share of the common output regardless of the amount of work personally contributed. John Smith, the Colony's most effective leader, organized the settlers into work teams of a dozen or more to erect buildings and palisades, dig a well, and plant 100 acres of corn. When Smith was not in charge, however, the hallmark of the Jamestown colony was idleness. To the puzzlement of historians, the starving settlers shirked from catching fish and growing food. The most enduring image of Jamestown dates from May 1611, when Sir Thomas Dale found the inhabitants at "their daily and usuall workes, bowling in the streetes."
>
> The first settlers at Jamestown anticipated that land would eventually be parceled out to households, and this outcome was indeed gradually achieved over a period of a dozen years. Small gardens appeared within the first year or two. Then, in 1614, Governor Dale began assigning three-acre plots to settlers. According to Captain John Smith, this improved productivity at least sevenfold:
>
>> When our people were fed out of the common store, and laboured Jointly together, glad was he could slip from his labour, or slumber over his taske he cared not how, nay, the most honest among them would hardly take so much true paines in a weeke, as now for themselves they will doe in a day, neither cared they for the increase, presuming that howsoever the harvest prospered, the generall store must maintaine them, so that wee reaped not so much Corne from the labours of thirtie, as now three or foure doe provide for themselves. To prevent which, Sir Thomas Dale hath allotted every man three Acres of cleare ground. . . .

Robert C. Ellickson, Property in Land, 102 Yale L.J. 1315, 1336–37 (1993).

The Plymouth colonists similarly found that parcelization "had very good success; for it made all hands very industrious, so as much more corne was planted then other waise.... The women now wente willingly into the field, and tooke their lttle-ones with them to set corne, which before would aledg weaknes and inabilitie; whom to have compelled would have bene thought great tiranie and oppression." 1 William Bradford, History of Plymouth Plantation, 1620–1647, at 300–01 (Mass. Hist. Soc'y 1912). Professors Douglass North and Robert Thomas have argued that the advent of private property rights led to rapid economic growth throughout the western world. See Douglass C. North & Robert Paul Thomas, The Rise of the Western World (1973).

8. Does the utility of private property, and of different types of property rights (e.g., usufructuary versus exclusive), vary across cultures and time? Economists have long been interested in the differences in property systems among societies. According to economists, two factors can influence what type of property rights are economically efficient for a given society: the value of property rights (which depends on the scarcity of resources and other factors) and the obstacles to and costs of enforcing property rights (e.g., how easy it is to demarcate property rights and exclude others from the use of a resource). See Richard A. Posner, Economic Analysis of Law §§ 3.1–3.2 (6th ed. 2003).

Anthropological studies have shown that even aboriginal societies recognize forms of property rights, although in a more limited set of resources and to a more restricted extent than most modern societies. Based on his survey of anthropological studies, Professor Martin Bailey argues that the exact nature of property rights recognized in aboriginal societies depends in part on the nature of their economy. Hunting and fishing, for example, is often more effective when done as a group. In aboriginal societies, entire tribes, clans, or other groups therefore typically hunt or fish without regard to individual property rights in land, although each group generally enjoys exclusive rights to their collective territory. Private property, by contrast, is the norm where societies engage in horticulture or agriculture. In some cases, the property rights are merely usufructuary (as in the case of the New England tribes described earlier); in others, the rights are long term and even inheritable. Aboriginal societies typically recognize private property in food and personal items (although even here private property can give way to sharing during localized famines). Martin Bailey, Approximate Optimality of Aboriginal Property Rights, 35 J. L. & Econ. 183 (1992). See also Harold Demsetz, Toward a Theory of Property Rights, 57 Am. Econ. Rev. 347 (1967); Richard A. Posner, A Theory of Primitive Society, with Special Reference to Law, 23 J. L. & Econ. 1 (1980);

9. **Property, Freedom, & Democracy.** Since the formation of the United States, many political theorists also have argued that private property is important, perhaps essential, for freedom and democracy. Private property played a key role in the republican concept of government which inspired many of the early leaders of the United States. To Thomas

Jefferson, the importance of private property for republican government was tied to the cultivation of land. Farmers who owned their own land had exactly the virtues and independence needed to be valuable citizens; "they are tied to their country, and wedded to its liberty and interests, by the most lasting bonds." 8 The Papers of Thomas Jefferson 426 (J. Boyd ed. 1973). See generally Stanley N. Katz, Thomas Jefferson and the Right to Property in Revolutionary America, 19 J. L. & Econ. 467 (1976).

Modern writers have emphasized broader advantages to democracy and freedom. Economist Milton Friedman, for example, has argued that private property, by providing a voluntary means by which the economic decisions of separate individuals can be coordinated, reduces the need for central planning and thus enables greater freedom of activity. Milton Friedman, Capitalism and Freedom 7–32 (1962). Others have emphasized that private property can provide a useful buffer between the government and its citizens:

> In [a] sense, the ownership of private property is closely associated with the rule of law. Both of these create a realm of private autonomy in which the citizenry can operate without fear of public intrusion. That realm is indispensable to the public sphere itself. Only people with a degree of security from the state are able to participate without fear, and with independence, in democratic deliberations. In this sense, a sharp, legally-productive distinction between the private and the public can usefully serve the public sphere....
>
> A central point here is that in a state in which private property does not exist, citizens are dependent on the good will of government officials, almost on a daily basis. Whatever they have is a privilege and not a right. They come to the state as supplicants or beggars rather than as right holders. Any challenge to the state may be stifled or driven underground by virtue of the fact that serious challenges could result in the withdrawal of the goods that give people basic security. A right to private property, free from governmental interference, is in this sense a necessary basis for a democracy.

Cass R. Sunstein, On Property and Constitutionalism, 14 Cardoza L. Rev. 907, 914–15 (1993).

10. **Property and Personhood.** Beginning with Hegel, some philosophers and legal theorists have argued that property rights are important to enable people to achieve proper self-development. Hegel, Philosophy of Right §§ 41–70 (H. B. Nisbet trans. 1991). As elaborated by Professor Margaret Radin, who is the leading modern proponent of a "personhood" approach to property, "If an object you now control is bound up in your future plans or in your anticipation of your future self, and it is partly these plans for your own continuity that make you a person, then your personhood depends on the realization of these expectations." Margaret J. Radin, Property and Personhood, 34 Stan. L. Rev. 957, 968 (1982).

A personhood approach would not accord the same level of protection to all forms of property rights and would exclude recognition entirely to some. "If there is a traditional understanding that a well developed person must invest herself to some extent in external objects, there is no less a traditional understanding that one should not invest oneself *in the wrong way* or *to too great an extent* in external objects. Property is damnation as well as salvation, object-fetishism as well as moral groundwork." Id. at 961. See also Karl Marx, Capital, ch. 1 (1889) (arguing that market societies lead to the subordination of people to commodities).

11. **Anti–Property Arguments.** Marx is not the only one to have warned of problems in private property rights (at least as defined and awarded in western society). Henry George, Plato, Pierre–Joseph Proudhon, Jean Jacques Rousseau, and many early Christian philosophers also cautioned of property. Private property, it has been argued, inevitably creates a growing inequality of wealth which is morally unjustifiable and leads to social instability. Private property, it also has been urged, undermines good moral character. Recent scholars have argued that what some see as the advantages of private property can be disadvantages to others. In response to the argument that private property increases "the psychic good of certainty," for example, Professors Duncan Kennedy & Frank Michelman argue that "to enhance certainty for one person is to impair certainty for another. Under a property regime people are all certain that they and no one else will receive the fruits of their labor, but all are uncertain of access to the fruits of others' labor." Duncan Kennedy & Frank Michelman, Are Property and Contract Efficient?, 8 Hofstra L. Rev. 711 (1980). These arguments have led some to reject private property entirely and others to urge limitations on property rights (e.g., limits on the inheritability of property or on the quantity of property that any one can acquire). See Lawrence C. Becker, Property Rights: Philosophical Foundations 88–98 (1977).

12. **Origins of Private Property.** Whatever the arguments for private property, how do private property rights arise? Many have argued that private property can arise only from cooperative reflection and agreement among members of society—posing a problem for those who argue that private property is needed to avoid people's tendency to shirk responsibility and free ride on others. In response to Blackstone's argument that no one would till the fields if their harvest could be appropriated by others, Professor Carol Rose has asked:

> Now wait a minute: If nobody would be at pains of tilling unless they could capture the rewards, why should they be at pains of setting up a civil society? Why don't Blackstone's characters sit around waiting for [someone else to do the organizing work]?
>
> In short, there is a gap between the kind of self-interested individual who needs exclusive property to induce him to labor, and the kind of individual who has to be there to create, maintain, and protect a property regime. The existence of a property regime is not predictable from a starting point of rational self-interest....

Carol M. Rose, Property as Storytelling: Perspectives from Game Theory, Narrative Theory, Feminist Theory, 2 Yale J. L. & Humanities 37, 52 (1990).

B. A BRIEF HISTORY OF LAND ALLOCATION AND PROTECTION IN THE UNITED STATES

Johnson v. M'Intosh established that the right to allocate land ownership in the United States lay initially with the crown and later with the states and the national government. This section examines how these governments chose to allocate the land. The governments spent little time debating the niceties of the philosophical issues just surveyed, focusing instead on hard-edged political questions. Should land be sold to raise revenue for the government or given away to anyone willing to improve the land? Should large land holdings be permitted or prohibited? Should land use be carefully planned? Or should it be shaped by the cumulative choices of individual settlers? What lands, if any, should be held in public ownership?

Frequently skipped in basic property courses, the history of land allocation in the United States is essential to understand the land patterns that we see today. Many of the issues that underlay the allocation debates, moreover, remain important today even though the government long ago ceased allocating vacant lands to private parties. Whether some lands should be open to all members of the public, for example, finds echo in current debates over public access to privately owned beaches (an issue to which we return in later chapters). The choice of planned versus spontaneous development parallels today's debates over zoning (a controversy that Chapter 12 will cover).

Colonial Land Allocation

Although English colonies in North America adopted a wide variety of land systems, the colonists "exhibited an unrelenting drive to privatize land." Robert C. Ellickson, Property in Land, 102 Yale L.J. 1315, 1339 (1993). Perhaps the main differences between colonies lay in the degree to which they controlled where people settled and the amount of public lands retained.

The New England colonies favored careful planning and large common areas. Under the colonies' "township planting system," new settlers had to first obtain governmental permission to establish a town. The colonial legislature insisted settlements remain compact, making for easier governability and more intensive cultivation of available land. Compact settlement also was better suited to the harsher conditions of New England life, where bad weather and Native American resistance to settlement were more common than in the South. Each township cleared its land collectively and then divided it among all the settlers, with the group often retaining common grazing and meeting areas. Small farms were the norm.

In most of the other colonies, land was usually allocated through a "headright" system, under which each settler received the right to locate, survey, and patent a claim, usually 50 acres. Recipients could claim land wherever they chose, provided the land was not occupied. This system often resulted in scattered development patterns and multiple claims to the same piece of property. Headrights could also be traded for cash, permitting the accumulation of large plantations, especially in the southern colonies where agricultural practices rewarded large land ownership. The southern colonies were known for their "individualism," and common grazing and meeting areas were less common.

Property & the American Revolution

The Declaration of Independence listed as "Inalienable" only the rights to "Life, Liberty and the pursuit of Happiness." Thomas Jefferson believed that society must protect property, but that rights to property, unlike rights to life, liberty, and happiness, should be subject to restrictions in the interest of the public good. However, several state constitutions adopted during the revolutionary period elevated property to the same status as life, liberty, and the pursuit of happiness. The Pennsylvania Constitution of 1776, for example, provided that "All men are born equally free and independent, and have certain natural, inherent and inalienable rights, amongst which are the enjoying and defending of life and liberty, acquiring, possessing and protecting property, and pursuing and obtaining happiness and safety." Many state constitutions, including Pennsylvania's, still retain such declarations. See, e.g., Pa. Const., art. I, § 1.

Although "acquiring, possessing, and protecting property" was often a constitutionally recognized right, many states acted to eliminate perceived inequities in existing property entitlements. Immediately following the Declaration of Independence, a number of states confiscated the property of persons who remained loyal to the British. Although land was seized both for patriotic reasons (confiscation for treason was a well established British practice) and as a source of revenue, the confiscations also served to break up extensive landholdings, such as those of the Penn family in Pennsylvania. Virginia and several other states also abolished the "fee tail," under which ownership of land remained in the same family for generation after generation, and "primogeniture," under which land passed to the oldest son. (We will return briefly to this subject when we examine estates in land at pages 574–577.)

Many of the early leaders of the United States believed that widely diffused land ownership was critical to the success of government. In 1776, John Adams wrote that, because "power always follows property," the only way of "preserving the balance of power on the side of equal liberty and public virtue is to make the acquisition of land easy to every member of society, to make a division of land into small quantities, so that the multitude may be possessed of landed estates." 9 The Works of John Adams 375, 376 (C. Adams, ed. 1856). Repulsed by the concentrated land holdings that he encountered on his visit to France in the 1780s, Thomas

Jefferson wrote that, although "an equal division of property is impracticable . . . , legislators cannot invent too many devices for subdividing property." Indeed, "uncultivated lands and unemployed poor" in any country demonstrate that the country's property laws violate "natural right." 7 The Writings of Thomas Jefferson 33–36 (Paul L. Ford, ed. 1896). See Stanley N. Katz, Thomas Jefferson and the Right to Property in Revolutionary America, 19 J. L. & Econ. 467, 480 (1976).

Some proposals would have ensured very broad land ownership. Jefferson proposed both that the government allocate 50 acres of land to everyone who would work the land (borrowing from the earlier headright system) and that a progressive tax be imposed on property. Id. Thomas Paine argued for an inheritance tax to fund payments to each person reaching the age of majority.

Federal Land Acquisition

When the Articles of Confederation were signed, the new national government held virtually no property of its own and had no role in the allocation of property. Yet in less than a century, the national government would become the largest landholder in North America and oversee settlement in most of the nation.

The national government's role in land policy began with the acquisition of the Northwest territories. At the time of the revolution, seven of the newly formed states laid claim to land west of their present-day borders. This western territory was immense, and other states feared that the landed states would come to possess too much power in the new American nation as the lands were settled. The nonlanded states therefore urged that ownership and authority over the frontier lands be given to the national Congress. Reluctantly, the landed states ceded the disputed territory.[2]

The cession of the Northwest territories to the national government established a precedent for vast expansion of the federal public domain. In the Louisiana Purchase (made in 1803 from France), the Florida Purchase (1819 from Spain), the Oregon Compromise with Great Britain (1846), the cession and purchase of territory in the far Southwest following war with Mexico (1848 & 1853), and the purchase of Alaska (1867), the federal government gained ownership of nearly all the land newly acquired and not already privately owned.[3] Only Texas, which joined the union in 1845 after winning its independence from Mexico, was able to insist that non-private lands remain in the state's public domain. And even here, the federal government purchased from Texas a sizable land holding that ultimately formed parts of Colorado, Kansas, New Mexico, Oklahoma, and Wyoming.

2. This is how the United States came to own the property at issue in *Johnson v. M'Intosh*, initially part of Virginia.

3. The cessions and purchases typically guaranteed the property rights of private owners to whom former governments had granted land. This quantity of land—34 million acres in 19 states—was not minuscule.

Birth of the Township Survey

Debate inevitably erupted over how the United States should allocate its growing public domain. One of the first questions was whether to adopt the "headright" system of the southern states or the northern states' "township planting" system. Congress compromised on the Land Ordinance of 1785, which combined the northern emphasis on orderliness of settlement with the southern emphasis on individual choice.

The ordinance required Congressional appointment of surveyors who, following the extinguishment of Native American title to an area, would lay out "townships" of six-mile squares, divided into 36 "sections" of one square mile (640 acres) each. Land settlement prior to surveying was prohibited. After a township was surveyed, the United States would allocate available tracts of land. Congress hoped that the surveys would avoid confusion over land borders and ownership. By prohibiting settlement until land was surveyed, Congress also hoped to prevent the real estate market from becoming flooded and preserve the public domain as a steady source of revenue for the government.

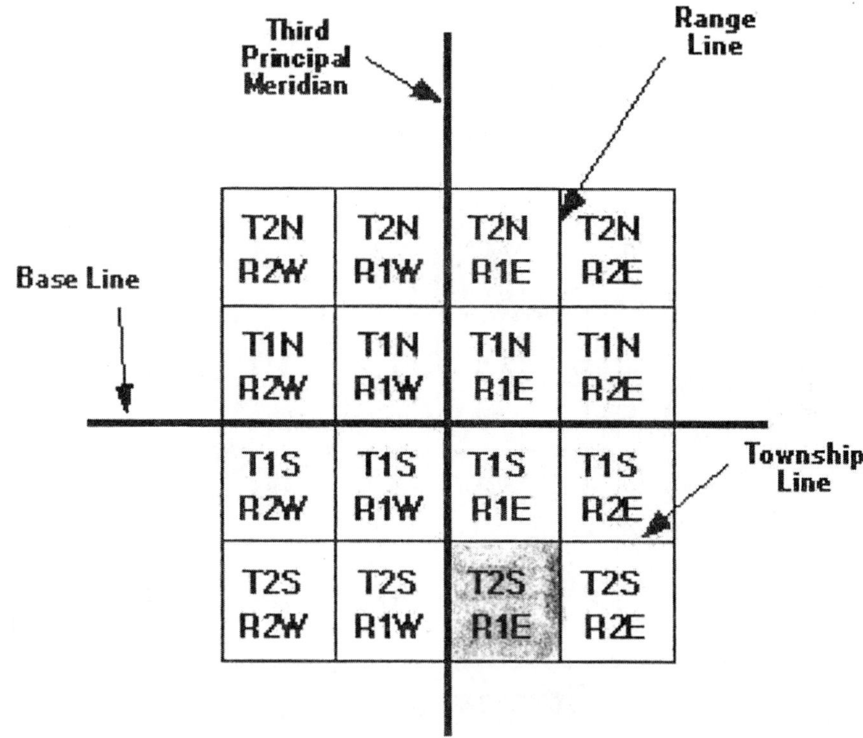

Figure 1–1

Although the United States government did not survey the original 13 colonies, it ultimately surveyed all of the West (except Texas) and much of the rest of the East. As described in Chapter 4, the survey is now the principal means by which land is identified and described in most states. (See pp. 386–397.) Anyone wishing to understand modern land titles and records thus must understand the system.

Figures 1–1 through 1–2 illustrate the surveying system. As shown in Figure 1–1, the government began by drawing imaginary lines approximately parallel to latitude and longitude lines and forming a grid of six-mile square boxes. For each area surveyed, there is a true or "principal" meridian and a true parallel of latitude known as a "base line." At six mile intervals east and west of the principal meridian, the government drew parallel "range lines." At six mile intervals north and south of the base line, the government drew "township lines."

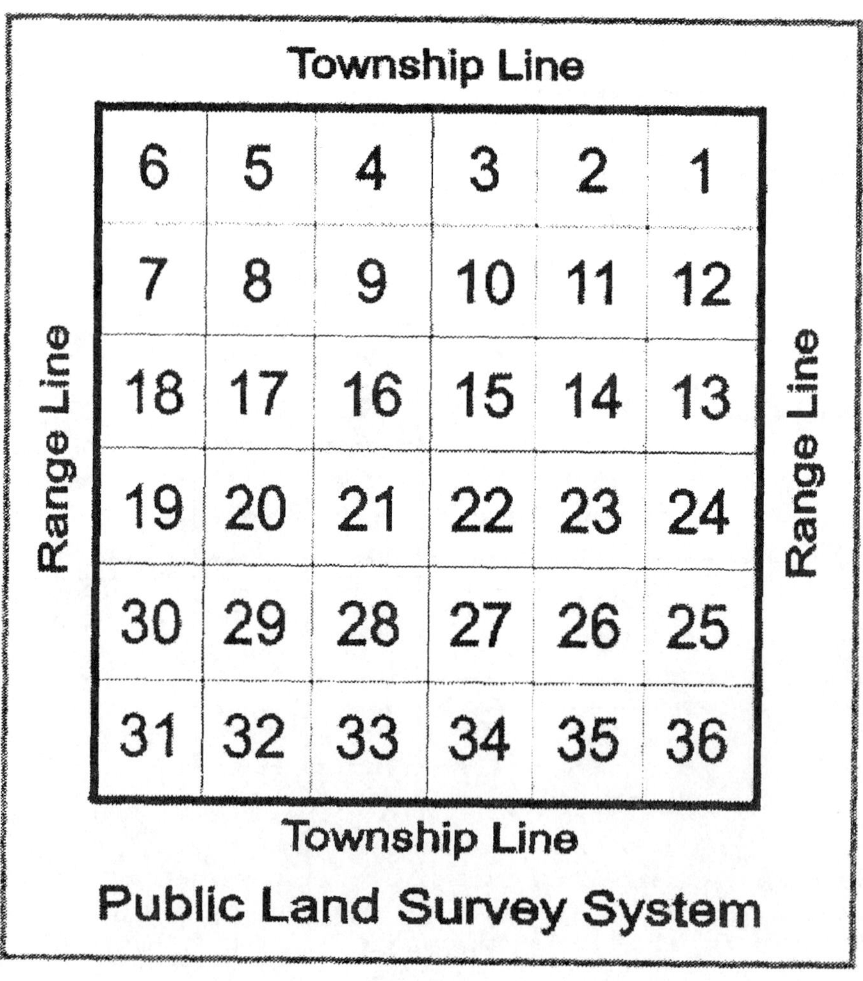

Figure 1–2

Each square in the grid is known as a "township" and can be identified by its location relative to the principal meridian and base line. In Figure 1–1, for example, the township that is darkened is "Township 2 South, Range 1 East of the Principal Meridian" for this grid.

As Figure 1–2 illustrates, townships are further divided into 640–acre tracts of land known as "sections." Each township is divided into 36 tracts, with tracts numbered consecutively, starting in the northeast corner of the township, running west, dropping down one row and running east, and then proceeding back and forth across the sections until reaching the 36th section in the southeast corner. Land within a section can be divided further into quarter sections (e.g., the Northwest quarter) or even smaller units.

Thomas Jefferson dreamt up the grid system and believed that it would help promote the republican society that he envisioned. In Jefferson's mind, townships would be divided into relatively small and uniform tracts of land that could be distributed to yeoman farmers eager to cultivate the land. One section in the center of each township would go to the state for erection of a public school—imitating the village commons of New England. Jefferson also contemplated that only alternate squares would be developed, with the remaining squares set aside as open space (although only Savanah, Georgia ultimately followed through on this concept). As anyone who has driven through many midwestern or western cities knows, the result was quite different than Jefferson contemplated: monotonous rectangular cities with little spacial beauty. The division of land into smaller units also did not prevent the accumulation of large tracts of land.

Allocating the Land

In the early years of the nation, the federal government took a variety of approaches to allocating the "public domain." Originally, Congress authorized the sale of surveyed tracts for one dollar per acre. In the Land Act of 1796, Congress provided for land auctions with a minimum price of two dollars per acre. To promote land sales, Congress began to liberalize credit terms. This, however, promoted speculation, which led to debt crises, which forced Congress to pass relief acts. Starting in 1820, Congress insisted on cash at the time of purchase. In the same year, Congress also provided that lands that were offered but not sold at auction would be opened for private entry at a lower price. Under the 1854 Graduation Act, land that had been offered but unclaimed for ten or more years would be reduced in price in proportion to the time unsold.

During this period, Congress also used land to promote various public policies. At several points, Congress paid off military veterans with land scrip. Beginning with the admission of Ohio to the Union in 1803, Congress also generally granted land to each new state for schools, internal improvements, and revenue. To encourage the construction of railroads, Congress either directly or through the states granted well over 100 million acres of odd-numbered sections of land to the railway companies in the mid–19th century.

What of the Lockean individual who went out into the wilderness and mixed his or her labor with the land? The federal government had no effective means of preventing people from "squatting" on unsurveyed land. But when the land was ultimately surveyed and offered for auction, squatters were often outbid by land speculators who commanded superior financial resources. Over time, political pressure increased to permit squatters who were willing to pay the minimum governmental price to "preempt" others who might want to bid for the land.

According to proponents of "preemption," settlers willing to stake a claim and work the frontier were entitled to their land. Settlers endured many costs to colonize the frontier, which benefitted the nation as a whole. As one group of squatters described the hardships, "we have left our homes, deprived ourselves of the many blessings and privileges of society, have born the expenses, and encountered the hardships of a perilous journey, advancing into a space beyond the bounds of civilization, and having the many difficulties and obstructions of a state of nature to overcome. . . ." 2 State Historical Society of Wisconsin, Collections 472–73 (1855).

In 1830, Congress passed the first preemption act. The legislation applied only retroactively and only for a limited time. For one year, squatters already occupying surveyed public domain lands could "enter," or claim, up to 160 acres at a price of $1.25 per acre. Many western members of Congress began to urge the adoption of a *prospective* preemption act that would allow settlers to move onto the public domain in the secure knowledge that, after improving a plot of land and living on it for a set period, they could purchase the land at the minimum government price. A general preemption statute, however, was opposed not only by land speculators, but by eastern politicians who did not want to lose public land revenues and viewed with alarm the prospect that eastern farmers would abandon their homes en masse for richer farmlands in the West. To some politicians, moreover, squatters were merely greedy land grabbers. Senator Henry Clay denounced squatters as a "lawless rabble" and preemption as "fraudulent, heartless, abominable speculation."

Despite his opposition, Clay would ultimately introduce the General Preemption Act of 1841 as part of a compromise measure that divided the proceeds from public land sales among the existing states in proportion to their Congressional representation. The law, which remained on the books until 1891, permitted prospective preemption of 160 acres so long as the preemptor made such improvements as the General Land Office decided were warranted and paid $1.25 per acre. Only citizens who owned less than 320 acres in other states or territories could take advantage of the law, and preemption was not permitted on Indian reservations or on lands that Congress had set aside for other purposes.

The 1841 General Preemption Act finally brought to life the Lockean concept of awarding property to individuals (so long as they were citizens) who mixed their labor with the land (and paid a modest tribute to the government). Yet preemption was subject to abuse. Many settlers were not satisfied with 160 acres, and many local land officials allowed settlers to lay preemptive claim to larger tracts, despite the Act's restrictions. Many settlers also tried to evade the requirement that land be improved—erecting laughable "dwellings" or falsifying affidavits. Some pioneers used the General Preemption Act to exploit natural resources on the public domain without ever intending to settle on the land. A common practice was to make a declaratory claim to a tract of land, strip it of all valuable resources (particularly timber), and then abandon the claim without payment. The General Land Office Commissioner in 1849 estimated that "not one in three" preemptive claims was pursued to awarding of the land.

Homesteading

By the middle of the 19th century, a number of policymakers urged that Congress nonetheless go further and provide land for free to those willing to work and "improve" the land. In eastern cities, immigration and industrialization were leading to severe unemployment and overcrowding. Much of the public domain simultaneously remained unclaimed, and state governments grew concerned that such lands might remain forever under federal ownership. To many western politicians, the awarding of property rights was essential to the frontier's development:

> Unless the government shall grant head rights . . . prairies, with their gorgeous growth of flowers, their green carpeting, their lovely lawns and gentle slopes, will for centuries continue to be the home of the wild deer and wolf, their stillness will be undisturbed by the jocund song of the farmer, and their deep and fertile soil unbroken by the plowshare. Something must be done to remedy this evil.

Cong. Globe, 28th Cong., 2d Sess. 52 (1845) (statement of Rep. Ficklin).

Opponents of "free soil" focused on practical concerns—although conservatives argued that free soil would, in the words of Professor Everett Dick, "destroy the people's self respect and noble spirit of independence." Everett Dick, The Lure of the Land 136 (1970). Land investors complained that free soil would make their investments worthless and strip the government of revenue. Eastern interests worried that free soil would drain the East of cheap labor and lower existing property values. The South worried that the territories settled would be anti-slavery and reduce the South's waning voting strength in Congress.

The concerns of southern states were enough to defeat passage of free soil legislation until the Civil War, but with their secession, a bill was finally approved and signed into law by President Abraham Lincoln in 1862. The Homestead Act provided that any person who was the head of a family or over 21 years of age, and was a citizen or had declared the intention of becoming one, could claim a standard allotment of federal public domain land open to preemption (160 acres in most cases, but 80 acres in some especially desirable areas) free of all but filing charges.

Within six months of application, the claimant was required to establish residence. Thereafter he or she was required to cultivate the land for a period of five years to receive a "patent" on the claim. Homesteaders could claim an additional 160 acres under the Preemption Act, but not simultaneously with their homesteading claims.

The Homestead Act, more than any other land law passed by Congress, provided the means by which the western United States was settled. By the turn of the 20th century, homesteading had created half a million farms on almost 100 million acres. Abuses, however, were again prevalent. The requirement that a claimant work his or her land for five years was intended to defeat speculators who sought land only for resale. Yet the preemption laws permitted speculators to easily avoid this requirement. Homesteaders could, after six months of occupancy, purchase their claims under the preemption laws, and speculators often provided homesteaders the money to do so in return for the homesteader's agreement to resell the land to the speculator at a low price. Other speculators perjured themselves to amass large landholdings under the Homestead Act. Those interested in stripping land of its natural resources used the Homestead Act just as they used the preemption laws to claim desirable lands only long enough to exploit the resources.

Reservation and Withdrawal

The vast abuses of federal land laws contributed to a rapacious exploitation of the nation's natural resources in the late 19th century, colloquially known as the "Great American Barbecue," and fueled calls for conserving portions of the federal public domain. Congress took one of the first steps to withdraw unique public lands from settlement in 1864 when it granted Yosemite Valley to the State of California on the sole condition that Yosemite be held for public use and recreation and never be sold. Beginning in 1872, Congress took a new tack for preserving unique public resources by creating Yellowstone National Park. In 1890, California returned ownership of Yosemite to the United States, and Congress declared Yosemite the nation's second National Park. In that same year, Congress established Sequoia and General Grant National Parks in California. By the end of the century, Congress had also set aside ("reserved" is the formal legal term) Mount Rainier National Park in Washington and Crater Lake National Park in Oregon.

Congress provided for far broader withdrawal of federal land in the Creative Act of 1891. There, for the first time, Congress authorized the President to "set apart and reserve . . . any part of the public lands wholly or in part covered with timber or undergrowth, whether of commercial value or not, as public reservations." Presidential exercise of this authority got off to a shaky start. When President Grover Cleveland in 1897 reserved almost 21 million acres of forest land in generally settled areas, westerners screamed in opposition to the "hasty and ill considered" action. Congress suspended the reservation and passed the Organic Administration Act of 1897 which provided for the establishment of national forests in specified circumstances. Yet by 1901, almost 50 million acres had been withdrawn for national forests; President Theodore Roosevelt quadrupled this amount. By 1904, most of the remaining public domain had been withdrawn from settlement under one law or another—effectively bringing to an end the allocation of the public domain. Today almost a third of the United States (virtually all in the West) remains in federal hands, as national parks or monuments, national forests, general public domain, or a variety of other forms of federal reservations.

Congress' multiple policies often clashed. Preemption and homesteading occasionally led pioneers to claim land that Congress wished to preserve for public purposes. Sometimes these conflicts were the result of a pioneer's effort to squeak out a living on the public domain; in other cases, speculators saw an opportunity for a quick buck.

Before Congress granted Yosemite Valley to California, a settler had entered the valley, built a house and outhouse, fenced about three acres of land, and cultivated the land. Six weeks before Congress granted the valley to California, James Mason Hutchings purchased the improvements from the settler for $400 in gold and moved onto the land with the intent to acquire title to 160 acres of land under the 1841 Preemption Act. At about the same time, Hutchings opened up one of the first hotels in Yosemite—a two-story, 28–room frame building known as The Hutchings House. When the State of California tried to take possession of his land, Hutchings refused to leave—leading to the following Supreme Court opinion.

Figure 1–3
Early stero view of the Hutchings House

The Yosemite Valley Case

Supreme Court of the United States, 1872.
82 U.S. 77.

MR. JUSTICE FIELD delivered the opinion of the Court:

The simple question presented for determination is whether a party, by mere settlement upon lands of the United States, with a declared intention to obtain a title to the same under the pre-emption laws, does thereby acquire such a vested interest in the premises as to deprive Congress of the power to divest it by a grant to another party. If such be the effect of mere settlement, with a view to pre-emption, upon the power of Congress to grant the lands occupied to another party, it must operate equally to deprive Congress of the power to reserve such lands from sale for public uses of the United States, though needed for arsenals, fortifications, light-houses, hospitals, custom-houses, court-houses, or for any other of the numerous public purposes for which property is used by the government. It would require very clear language in the acts of Congress before any intention thus to place the public lands of the United States beyond its control by mere settlement of a party, with a declared intention to purchase, could be attributed to its legislation.

The question here presented was before this court, and was carefully considered, in the case of Frisbie v. Whitney, [76 U.S. 187 (1869)]. And it was there held that under the pre-emption laws mere occupation and improvement of any portion of the public lands of the United States, with a view to pre-emption, do not confer upon the settler any right in the land occupied, as against the United States, or impair in any respect the power of Congress to dispose of the land in any way it may deem proper; and that the power of regulation and disposition, conferred upon Congress by the Constitution, only ceases when all the preliminary acts prescribed by those laws for the acquisition of the title, including the payment of the price of the land, have been performed by the settler. When these prerequisites have been complied with, the settler for the first time acquires a vested interest in the premises occupied by him, of which he cannot be subsequently deprived. He is then entitled to a certificate of entry from the local land officers, and ultimately to a patent for the land from the United States. Until such payment and entry, acts of Congress give to the settler only a privilege of pre-emption in the case the lands are offered for sale in the usual manner; that is, the privilege to purchase them in that event in preference to others. The United States by those acts enter into no contract with the settler, and incur no obligation to any one that the land occupied by him shall ever be put up for sale. They simply declare that in case any of their lands are thrown open for sale the privilege to purchase them in limited quantities, at fixed prices, shall be first given to parties who have settled upon and improved them. The legislation thus adopted for the benefit of settlers was not intended to deprive Congress of the power to make any other disposition of the lands before they are offered for sale, or to appropriate them to any public use.

The decision in *Frisbie v. Whitney* was pronounced by a unanimous court, and subsequent reflection has satisfied us of its entire soundness.... It is the only construction which preserves a wise control in the government over the public lands, and prevents a general spoliation of them under the pretence of intended settlement and pre-emption.... The whole difficulty in the argument of the defendant's counsel arises from his confounding the distinction made in all the cases, whenever necessary for their decision, between the acquisition by the settler of a legal right to the land occupied by him as against the owner, the United States; and the acquisition by him of a legal right as against other parties to be preferred in its purchase, when the United States have determined to sell. It seems to us little less than absurd to say that a settler or any other person by acquiring a right to be preferred in the purchase of property, provided a sale is made by the owner, thereby acquires a right to compel the owner to sell, or such an interest in the property as to deprive the owner of the power to control its disposition.

Judgment Affirmed.

Notes & Questions

1. Is the Supreme Court's opinion consistent with the policies that underlay the preemption laws? What impact do you believe *The Yosemite Valley Case* had on future settlers in the western United States (assuming they were aware of the Supreme Court's decision)? Would the impact have been good or bad?

2. Do you feel any sympathy for Hutchings? Under the various philosophical approaches to property discussed earlier, should Hutchings have won? Is Hutchings' claim stronger or weaker than that of Native American tribes who earlier European settlers encountered upon their arrival?

3. If Hutchings had taken every step prerequisite to getting a patent to a homestead (including payment and entry) but the government had not yet given him a patent, the Supreme Court suggests that he would then be entitled to demand a patent. Why? Why shouldn't the government always be entitled to change its mind before issuing a patent?

Cook v. United States, 42 Fed. Cl. 788 (1999), is a modern-day variant of *The Yosemite Valley Case*. The Mining Act of 1872, 30 U.S.C. §§ 22 et seq., entitles anyone who discovers a valuable mineral deposit on federal public land and pays a surprisingly small fee to obtain a mining patent from the United States. After several individuals had met all the statutory requirements for a patent to 23 placer mining claims but before the government had determined the validity of the application and issued the patent, Congress created the Jemez National Recreational Area and barred the government from issuing any new patents in the area of the claims. In a lawsuit by the miners, the Court of Federal Claims held that, because the miners had complied with all the statutory requirements, they had a "vested property interest" in the mining claims. See generally Sam Kalen, An 1872 Mining Law for the New Millennium, 71 U. Colo. L. Rev. 343 (2000) (discussing *Cook*, *The Yosemite Valley Case*, and the doctrine of vested rights).

4. *Hutchings* raises the more general issue of when, if ever, a government should be estopped from changing its mind about the allocation or use of property. Today, the issue frequently arises where a local government gives a developer a permit to build and then decides to change local zoning laws in a way that is inconsistent with construction. Under the doctrine of *vested rights*, the developer may have a right to build despite the zoning change. Chapter 11 examines this doctrine at pages 988–996.

5. As you will read in the next chapter, even if Hutchings had won, California could have condemned the land and taken title simply by paying Hutchings "just compensation" for the land. Would this have been fairer than the result that the Court reached? What would have been "just compensation" for a prime chunk of Yosemite Valley? (Despite losing in the United States Supreme Court, Hutchings continued to pursue his argument in the California state legislature, which ultimately agreed to pay Hutchings $24,000 for his buildings and improvements.)

6. Of what relevance to your analysis is the fact that *The Yosemite Valley Case* dealt with Congress' effort to protect a valley of immense natural beauty? Would you feel differently about the result if Congress had wanted to take the land from Hutchings and give it to a railroad for development? What if the case had dealt with an ordinary piece of property on which Hutchings had settled and started to farm?

7. The Supreme Court suggests that Hutchings' argument would undercut Congress ability to provide not only for public parks, but also for such "public uses" as arsenals, fortifications, lighthouses, hospitals, customhouses, and courthouses. Is the United States' interest in preserving the right to kick squatters off the public domain equally strong in all these cases? Yosemite was a unique natural resource, and various other uses mentioned by the Court (e.g., lighthouses and fortifications) often have to be built at specific locations. The government has more options in where it builds a courthouse or hospital. As a matter of policy, should this matter in defining the rights of a squatter?

8. The Supreme Court was not always so unsympathetic to squatters. Seven years after *The Yosemite Valley Case*, the Supreme Court held that prior occupancy by itself does sometimes give a superior right against latecomers, even where Congress later awards land to someone else for public purposes. Broder v. Natoma Water & Mining Co., 101 U.S. (11 Otto) 274 (1879), was a land dispute between a mining company and a railroad. In 1853, the Natoma Water and Mining Company completed a 15-mile canal across the federal public domain—without any statutory right to do so—at a cost of $200,000 and began appropriating water for mining, agriculture, and other uses. Twelve years later, Congress granted part of the land across which the canal ran to the Central Pacific Railroad Company, which later conveyed the land to Jacob Broder. Although Congress agreed in the Mining Act of 1866 to protect water canals against later land grants, the retroactivity of this provision was doubtful. The Supreme Court nonetheless held that the mining company had title superior to Broder:

> It is the established doctrine of this court that rights of miners, who had taken possession of mines and worked and developed them, and the rights of persons who had constructed canals and ditches to be used in mining operations and for purposes of agricultural irrigation, in the region where such artificial use of the water was an absolute necessity, are rights which the government had, by its conduct, recognized and encouraged and

> was bound to protect before the passage of the act of 1866. We are of opinion that [the Mining Act of 1866] was rather a voluntary recognition of a pre-existing right of possession, constituting a valid claim to its continued use, than the establishment of a new one.

Id. at 275.

Is *Broder* consistent with *The Yosemite Valley Case*? Assume that after *Broder*, a farmer had begun to homestead 160 acres of land in what would later become the Sequoia National Park in California; the homesteader also constructs a canal ten miles to a local river to supply his land with irrigation water. Before the homesteader is on her land for the required five years, Congress establishes the Sequoia National Park and orders the homesteader off the land. The case comes before the Supreme Court where you are a justice. How would you rule?

C. LIMITS TO PRIVATIZATION

Should some types of land remain public and open to everyone's use? Should the law prevent the government from turning some types of land over to private owners? For most of the United States' history, both the federal government and states assumed that they were free to turn over any of the land that they held to private owners. And many legislators argued that private ownership would best promote the nation's future. Yet the United States Supreme Court in 1892 suggested that some lands might be sufficiently important to the public to preclude private ownership.

Under the so-called "equal footing" doctrine, states upon admission to the Union acquire title to the beds and shores of navigable waterways within their jurisdiction. Pollard v. Hagan, 44 U.S. (3 How.) 212 (1842). In 1869, the Illinois legislature in turn granted most of the harbor of Chicago to the Illinois Central Railroad. The grant comprised a one square-mile parcel of land underlying Lake Michigan and was of immense value. The grant did not give the Illinois Central Railroad total control over the land. The grant required the railroad to hold the land in perpetuity; the railroad could not sell or convey the land to anyone else. The grant also proscribed the railroad from obstructing the harbor or otherwise impairing the public right of navigation. The railroad paid a significant sum for the land, but far less than the land was worth on the open market.

By 1873, the legislature had changed in political composition and decided to renege on the earlier grant. After repealing the 1869 grant, it brought a lawsuit to have the original grant declared invalid.

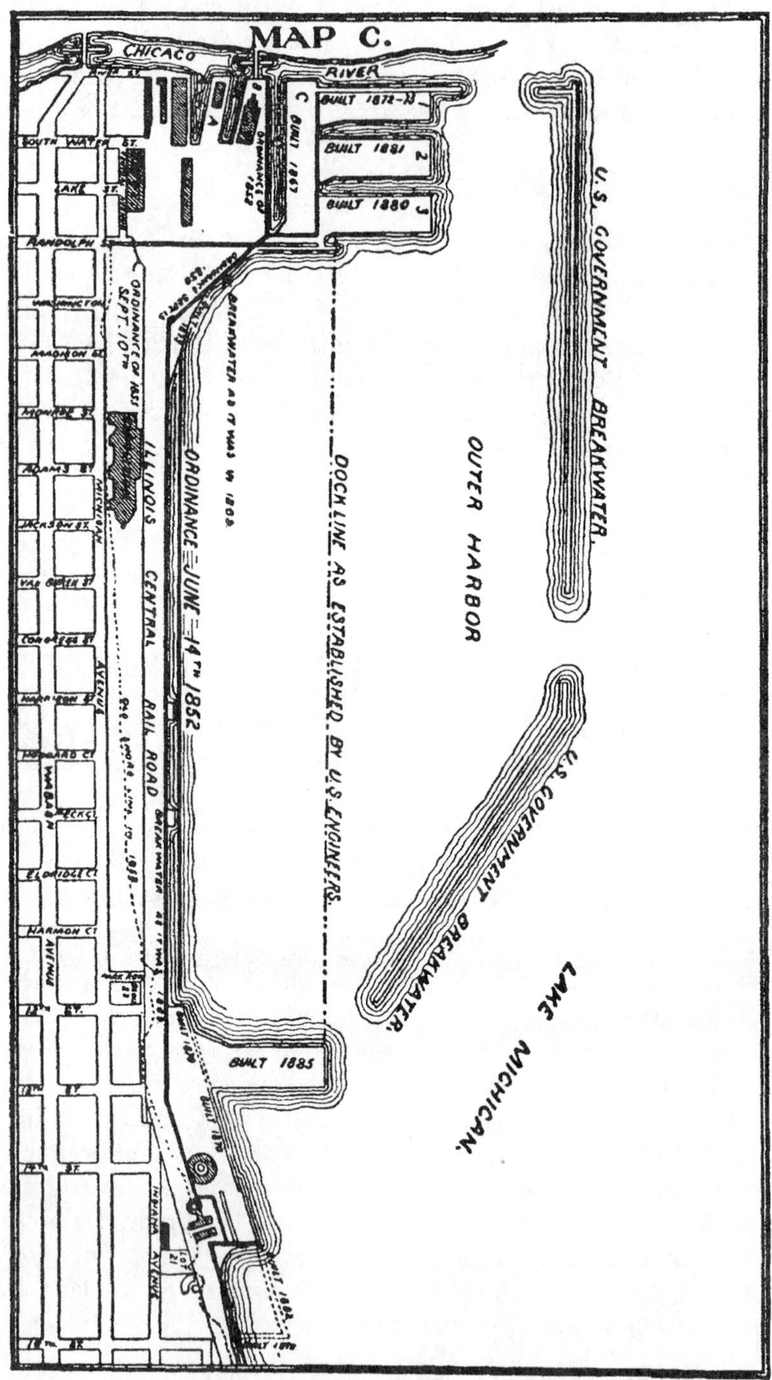
MAP C.
CHICAGO
RIVER
BUILT 1872-73
BUILT 1881
BUILT 1880
BUILT 1867
BUILT 1885
SOUTH WATER ST.
LAKE ST.
RANDOLPH ST.
MONROE ST.
ADAMS ST.
JACKSON ST.
ORDINANCE OF 1851 SEPT. 10TH
ILLINOIS CENTRAL RAIL ROAD
MICHIGAN AVENUE
WABASH AVENUE
INDIANA AVENUE
BREAKWATER AS IT WAS IN 1869
ORDINANCE JUNE 14TH 1852
DOCK LINE AS ESTABLISHED BY U.S. ENGINEERS.
OUTER HARBOR
U.S. GOVERNMENT BREAKWATER.
U.S. GOVERNMENT BREAKWATER.
LAKE MICHIGAN.

Figure 1–4

Illinois Central Railroad Co. v. Illinois

Supreme Court of the United States, 1892.
146 U.S. 387.

MR. JUSTICE FIELD delivered the opinion of the court.

. . .

The [initial 1869] act, if valid and operative to the extent claimed, placed under the control of the railroad company nearly the whole of the submerged lands of the harbor, subject only to the limitations that it should not authorize obstructions of the harbor or impair the public right of navigation, or exclude the legislature from regulating the rates of wharfage or dockage to be charged. With these limitations the act put it in the power of the company to delay indefinitely the improvement of the harbor ... or to construct as many docks, piers and wharves and other works as it might choose, and at such positions in the harbor as might suit its purposes, and permit any kind of business to be conducted thereon, and to lease them out on its own terms, for indefinite periods....

The circumstances attending the passage of the act through the legislature were on the hearing the subject of much criticism. As originally introduced, the purpose of the act was to enable the city of Chicago to enlarge its harbor and to grant to it the title and interest of the State to certain lands adjacent to the shore of Lake Michigan on the eastern front of the city, and place the harbor under its control, giving it all the necessary powers for its wise management. But during the passage of the act its purport was changed. Instead of providing for the cession of the submerged lands to the city, it provided for a cession of them to the railroad company....

The question, therefore, to be considered is whether the legislature was competent to thus deprive the State of its ownership of the submerged lands in the harbor of Chicago, and of the consequent control of its waters; or, in other words, whether the railroad corporation can hold the lands and control the waters by the grant, against any future exercise of power over them by the State.

That the State holds the title to the lands under the navigable waters of Lake Michigan, within its limits, in the same manner that the State holds title to soils under tide water, by the common law, we have already shown, and that title necessarily carries with it control over the waters above them whenever the lands are subjected to use. But it is a title different in character from that which the State holds in lands intended for sale. It is different from the title which the United States hold in the public lands which are open to preemption and sale. It is a title held in trust for the people of the State that they may enjoy the navigation of the waters, carry on commerce over them, and have liberty of fishing therein freed from the obstruction or interference of private parties. The interest of the people in the navigation of the waters and in commerce over them may be improved in many instances by the erection of wharves, docks and piers therein, for which purpose the State may grant parcels of the submerged lands; and, so long as their disposition is made for such purpose, no valid objections can be made to the grants. It is grants of parcels of land under navigable waters, that may afford foundation for wharves, piers, docks and other structures in aid of commerce, and grants of parcels which, being occupied, do not substantially impair the public interest in the lands and waters remaining, that are chiefly considered and sustained in the adjudged cases as a valid exercise of legislative power consistently with the trust to the public upon which such lands are held by the State. But that is a very different doctrine from the one which would sanction the abdication of the general control of the State over lands under the navigable waters of an entire harbor or bay, or of a sea or lake. Such abdication is not consistent with the exercise of that trust which requires the government of the State to preserve such waters for the use of the public. The trust devolving upon the State for the public, and which can only be discharged by the management and control of property in which the public has an interest, cannot be relinquished by a transfer of the property. The control of the State for the purposes of the trust can never be lost, except as to such parcels as are used in promoting the interests of the public therein, or can be disposed of without any substantial impairment of the public interest in the lands and waters remaining. It is only by observing the distinction between a grant of such parcels for the improvement of the public interest, or which when occupied do not substantially impair the public interest in the lands and water remaining, and a grant of the whole property in which the public is interested, that the language of the adjudged cases can be reconciled. General language sometimes found in opinions of the courts, expressive of absolute ownership and control by the State of lands under navigable waters, irrespective of any trust as to their use and disposition, must be read and construed with reference to the special facts of the particular cases. A grant of all the lands under the navigable waters of a State has never been adjudged to be within the legislative power; and any attempted grant of the kind would be held, if not absolutely void on its face, as subject to revocation. The State can no more abdicate its trust over property in which the whole people are interested, like navigable waters and soils under them, so as to leave them entirely under the use and control of private parties, except in the instance of parcels mentioned for the improvement of the navigation and use of the waters, or when parcels can be disposed of without impairment of the public interest in what remains, then it can abdicate its police powers in the administration of government and the preservation of the peace. In the administration of government the use of such powers may for a limited period be delegated to a municipality or other body, but there always remains with the State the right to revoke those powers and exercise them in a more direct manner. So with trusts connected with public property, or property of a special character, like lands under navigable waters, they cannot be placed entirely beyond the direction and control of the State.

The harbor of Chicago is of immense value to the people of the State of Illinois in the facilities it affords to its vast and constantly increasing commerce; and the idea that its legislature can deprive the State of control over its bed and waters and place the same in the hands of a private corporation created for a different purpose, one limited to transportation of passengers and freight between distant points and the city, is a proposition that cannot be defended.

The area of the submerged lands proposed to be ceded by the act in question to the railroad company embraces something more than a thousand acres, being, as stated by counsel, more than three times the area of the outer harbor, and not only including all of that harbor but embracing adjoining submerged lands which will, in all probability, be hereafter included in the harbor. It is as large as that embraced by all the merchandise docks along the Thames at London; is much larger than that included in the famous docks and basins at Liverpool; is twice that of the port of Marseilles, and nearly if not quite equal to the pier area along the water front of the city of New York. And the arrivals and clearings of vessels at the port exceed in number those of New York, and are equal to those of New York and Boston combined.... It is hardly conceivable that the legislature can divest the State of the control and management of this harbor and vest it absolutely in a private corporation. Surely an act of the legislature transferring the title to its submerged lands and the power claimed by the railroad company, to a foreign State or nation would be repudiated, without hesitation, as a gross perversion of the trust over the property under which it is held.... All the objections which can be urged to such attempted transfer may be urged to a transfer to a private corporation like the railroad company in this case.

. . .

We cannot, it is true, cite any authority where a grant of this kind has been held invalid, for we believe that no instance exists where the harbor of a great city and its commerce have been allowed to pass into the control of any private corporation. But the decisions are numerous which declare that such property is held by the State, by virtue of its sovereignty, in trust for the public. The ownership of the navigable waters of the harbor and of the lands under them is a subject of public concern to the whole people of the State. The trust with which they are held, therefore, is governmental and cannot be alienated, except in those instances mentioned of parcels used in the improvement of the interest thus held, or when parcels can be disposed of without detriment to the public interest in the lands and waters remaining.

This follows necessarily from the public character of the property, being held by the whole people for purposes in which the whole people are interested....

[The dissenting opinion of JUSTICE SHIRAS, with whom JUSTICE GRAY and JUSTICE BROWN joined, is omitted.]

Notes & Questions

1. The *Illinois Central* case is the most famous discussion in the United States of what is labeled the "public trust" doctrine: some lands are held by the government in trust for the public as a whole. Under the public trust doctrine, the state holds the tidelands (defined as those lands below the mean high tide) and the beds of navigable waterways in trust for the public.

For general discussions of the public trust doctrine and its history, see Molly Selvin, This Tender and Delicate Business: The Public Trust Doctrine in American Law and Economic Policy 1789–1920 (1987); Joseph D. Kearney & Thomas W. Merrill, The Origins of the Public Trust Doctrine: What Really Happened in *Illinois Central*, 71 U. Chi. L. Rev. 799 (2004); Joseph L. Sax, The Public Trust Doctrine in Natural Resource Law: Effective Judicial Intervention, 68 Mich. L. Rev. 471 (1970); William Drayton, Jr., The Public Trust in Tidal Areas: A Sometimes Submerged Doctrine, 79 Yale L.J. 762 (1970).

2. In an earlier case dealing with whether private individuals could claim property rights in the beds of navigable waterways, the New Jersey Supreme Court suggested that there are three basic forms of property: private property and two forms of public property—governmental (or "public domain") property and common property.

> Every thing susceptible of property is considered as belonging to the nation that possesses the country, and as forming the entire mass of its wealth. But the nation does not possess all those things in the same manner. By very far the greater part of them are divided among the individuals of the nation, and become *private property*. Those things not divided among the individuals still belong to the nation, and are called *public property*. Of these, again, some are reserved for the necessities of the state, and are used for the public benefit, and those are called *"the domain of the crown or of the republic"*; others remain common to all citizens who take of them and use them, each according to his necessities, and according to the laws which regulate their use, and are called *common property*. . . .
>
> The title of both these, for the greater order, and, perhaps, of necessity, is placed in the hands of the sovereign power, but it is placed there for different purposes. The citizen cannot enter upon the domain of the crown and apply it, or any part of it, to his immediate use. He cannot go into the king's forests and fall and carry away the trees, though it is the public property; it is placed in the hands of the king for a different purpose, it is the domain of the crown, a source of revenue; so neither can the king intrude upon the common property, thus understood, and appropriate it to himself, or to the fiscal purposes of the nation, the enjoyment of it is a natural right which cannot be infringed or taken away, unless by arbitrary power; and that, in theory at least, could not exist in a free government. . . .

Arnold v. Mundy, 6 N.J. Law 1, 71–73 (1821) (emphasis in original). See also Carol Rose, The Comedy of the Commons: Custom, Commerce, and Inherently Public Property, 53 U. Chi. L. Rev. 711, 720 (1986) (dividing property into private property, public property, and "inherently public property" where the public's rights are "independent of and indeed superior to the claims of any purported governmental manager").

According to Justice Fields, what type of property is the Chicago harbor? Does *Illinois Central Railroad* suggest a different typography of property than suggested in *Arnold v. Mundy*?

3. What exactly is the holding of the Supreme Court in *Illinois Central Railroad*? Was the original 1869 grant of land to the railroad invalid? Was the grant valid but subject to the inherent right of a future legislature to retake the land? What would have happened if the Illinois legislature had not repealed the 1869 grant, but the City of Chicago had sued to invalidate the grant?

In the seventeenth and early eighteenth centuries, many of the New England states granted much of their seaboard to private parties who promised to develop wharves and other navigational improvements (although no grant individually was ever as large as the grant at issue in *Illinois Central*). Are these grants invalid under Justice Fields' opinion?

4. Whatever the Court's holding, the legal basis for that holding is exceptionally opaque. The Court appears to limit the power of the legislature to alienate land. That would suggest that the Court relied on a constitutional provision or on federal statutory law, because neither common nor state statutory law can ordinarily bind state legislative policy. Yet the Court refers to no constitutional provision nor any federal statute. Are there any other possible bases for the Court's decision?

In *Arnold v. Mundy*, supra Note 2, the New Jersey Supreme Court suggested that states never received the right to give "common property" to private individuals. Under this theory, the King of England took possession of North American lands, through the "right of discovery," in his "sovereign capacity" and never acquired the right to "grant what is called the *common property* as to convert it into private property." Because New Jersey traced its title to navigable waterways through the Duke of York to the King, New Jersey enjoyed no greater power than the King held. Does this mean that there is no way ever to privatize "common property"? Is common property inherently held under a public trust that can never be changed—even by the public? Can the logic of *Arnold v. Mundy* apply to lands outside the boundaries of the original colonies?

For discussions of the potential legal basis for the public trust doctrine, see Michael C. Blumm, Renouncing the Public Trust Doctrine: An Assessment of the Validity of Idaho House Bill 794, 24 Ecology L.Q. 461 (1997); James R. Rasband, The Disregarded Common Parentage of the Equal Footing and Public Trust Doctrines, 32 Land & Water L. Rev. 1 (1997); Charles F. Wilkinson, The Headwaters of the Public Trust: Some Thoughts on the Source and Scope of the Traditional Doctrine, 19 Envt'l L. 425 (1989). For a critique of Justice Fields' opinion in *Illinois Central Railroad*, see Eric Pearson, *Illinois Central* and the Public Trust Doctrine in State Law, 15 Va. Envtl. L.J. 713 (1996).

5. Although the modern basis of the public trust doctrine might be unclear, the concept that tidelands and navigable waterways should be open to the general public has a relatively venerable legal history. Roman

authorities recognized that, as a matter of "natural" law, "air, running water, the sea, and consequently the seashore" were "common to all." Justinian, Institutes § 2.1.1 (4th ed. J.B. Moyle transl. 1889). No one was "forbidden access to the seashore, provided he abstains from injury to [improvements].... [A]ll rivers and harbours are public, so that all persons have a right to fish therein [and] everyone is entitled to bring his vessel to the bank...." Id. §§ 2.1.1–2.1.6.

6. As a policy matter, should there be limits on a state's authority to grant lands under navigable waterways to private entities? Professor Richard Epstein has suggested that navigable waterways should be common property because of the considerable difficulty that otherwise might confront someone interested in using the waterway for transportation or other commerce. Imagine that each segment of a waterway, including harbors, was owned by a different person. Anyone interested in traveling the waterway would have to negotiate with all the relevant owners, leading to high "transaction costs." Because no one could travel the waterway without getting the permission of all the owners, each owner would also enjoy a "natural monopoly" that he or she could exploit over the travel. Bargaining breakdowns with one owner could stymie travel along the entire waterway. See Richard A. Epstein, The Public Trust Doctrine, 7 Cato J. 411, 415 (1987).

Professor Carol Rose has suggested two other possible reasons why navigable waterways should be common property. First, until a waterway gets too crowded, society benefits by having more and more people use it. As Rose puts it, there is a "publicness" of commerce reflected in "increasing returns from greater participation." The state therefore has an interest in ensuring free access and not letting private owners "capture the rent created and enhanced by commerce itself." Second, Rose argues that 19th century commerce was a "socializing activity" that benefitted from open access to all members of society. See Rose, supra Note 2, at 766–777.

Are these justifications convincing? Do you see any other possible justifications?

7. To what property should the public trust doctrine extend? Although the traditional public trust extended to tidelands and the beds of navigable waterways, Justice Fields in *Illinois Central* suggests that the doctrine applies to a broader category of land. At one point, for example, he says that the "State can no more abdicate its trust over property in which the whole people are interested, *like* navigable waters and soils under them, ... then it can abdicate its police powers" (emphasis added). Should the public trust doctrine apply to: (a) Yosemite National Park, (b) the Gettysburg National Military Park, or (c) the last remaining habitat of an endangered woodpecker?

What test or tests should be used to determine whether a particular resource should be held by the state as "common property"? Consider the following potential tests:

(1) Would private ownership make it difficult to put the resource to its highest-valued use? This is the basis for Professor Richard

Epstein's argument that rivers and other highways of commerce should be commonly owned. (See Epstein, supra Note 6, at 414.)

(2) Is the resource either "so plentiful or so unbounded" that the problems of creating and enforcing private property in the resource would outweigh any benefits that a private property system could provide? Oceans and air are frequently listed examples. (See Rose, supra Note 2, at 717–718.)

(3) Is the property of such unique value to the public that a private owner would enjoy a "natural monopoly" and be inequitably enriched? An example here might be Yellowstone National Park. (See Rose, supra Note 2, at 718–720.)

(4) Is the property "most valuable when used by indefinite and unlimited numbers of persons—by the public at large"? In other words, is the property "ever more valuable as more participate"? (See Rose, supra Note 2, at 774.)

What forms of property would qualify under each of these various tests?

8. Although arguments can be made for extending the public trust doctrine to a wide variety of lands and other resources, most states still apply the doctrine only to tidelands and the beds of navigable waterways. In recent decades, however, a handful of states have expanded the reach of the doctrine in response to growing interest in public recreation and resource preservation. New Jersey, for example, has used the public trust doctrine to open public access to the dry-sand area of beaches. See Matthews v. Bay Head Improvement Ass'n, infra p. 94. California and Hawaii have invoked the doctrine to prevent water users from diverting water from streams to the detriment of the environment. See National Audubon Society v. Superior Court, infra p. 255; In re Water Use Permit Application for the Waiahole Ditch, 9 P.3d 409 (Haw. 2000).

Private property owners and others have criticized decisions expanding the public trust doctrine on the grounds that judicial intervention is unwise, an improper interference with private property rights, and an inappropriate assumption of legislative functions. For a sampling of criticisms of efforts to expand the public trust doctrine, see Lloyd R. Cohen, The Public Trust Doctrine: An Economic Perspective, 29 Cal. Western L. Rev. 239 (1992); James Huffman, A Fish Out of Water: The Public Trust Doctrine in a Constitutional Democracy, 19 Envtl. L. 527 (1989); Richard Lazarus, Changing Conceptions of Property and Sovereignty in Natural Resources: Questioning the Public Trust Doctrine, 71 Iowa L. Rev. 631 (1986).

D. A Brief Note on Public Lands

This book is primarily about private land. Federal, state, and local governments, however, still own a sizable portion of the land in the United States. The federal government owns over 600 million acres of land—or 28 percent of the nation's total acreage. The federal government owns an even higher percentage of the western United States, where it holds title to over half of the land in Alaska (67%), Idaho (62%), Nevada (83%), Oregon (52%), and Utah (64%). State governments own slightly less than 10 percent of total acreage in the United States. Those states governments holding particularly large amounts of land include Alaska (29%) and New York (37%). Federal and state governments together hold approximately 96 percent of the land in Alaska, 88 percent in Nevada, 75 percent in Utah, and 70 percent in Idaho.

A variety of agencies manage the federal government's land holdings. Within the federal Department of the Interior, for example, the National Park Service manages National Parks, National Monuments, and other historic and recreational lands. The U.S. Fish and Wildlife Service manages National Wildlife Refuges. And the nation's general public lands fall under the jurisdiction of the Bureau of Land Management (BLM). The U.S. Forest Service, within the Department of Agriculture, manages National Forests.

Public lands raise a large number of unique and often complex legal issues. A diverse set of laws and doctrines control how federal agencies use and manage the public lands. Congress, for example, requires that the U.S. Forest Service and BLM manage their lands for "multiple uses." National forests must be administered for "outdoor recreation, range, timber, watershed, and wildlife and fish purposes." 16 U.S.C. § 528. Congress has instructed the U.S. Forest Service to manage the national forests "so that they are utilized in the combination that will best meet the needs of the American people." Id. § 531(a). In the case of the general public domain, the BLM must administer lands for an open-ended list of uses, "including, but not limited to, recreation, range, timber, minerals, watershed, wildlife and fish, and natural scenic, scientific and historical values." 43 U.S.C. § 1702. BLM must ensure that the lands meet "the present and future needs of the American people" and not permanently impair either land productivity or environmental quality. Id.

In the case of other federal lands, Congress requires that federal agencies manage land for particular uses and outlaw incompatible uses. National Wildlife Refuges, for example, are to be used principally to protect and conserve wildlife. Other uses, such as public recreational use or grazing, are permitted only if "compatible" with a refuge's principal purposes. 16 U.S.C. § 668dd(d)(1). The National Park Service is charged with managing its land "to conserve the scenery and the natural and historic objects and wildlife therein and to provide for the enjoyment of the same in such manner and by such means as will leave them unimpaired for the enjoyment of future generations." 16 U.S.C. § 1.

Many of the largest land controversies today involve public rather than private lands. In recent years, for example, Congress has repeatedly debated whether to open the Arctic National Wildlife Refuge (ANWR) to petroleum development. While some members of Congress argue that oil from ANWR is essential in reducing the nation's dependence on foreign oil, others believe that ANWR is simply too pristine of wilderness to subject to the risks of oil development. The ANWR debate is just one instance of the larger debate whether to manage the federal public lands primarily for conservation and low-impact recreation such as hiking or, alternatively, to permit mining companies, ranchers, off-road vehicle users, and others to use the lands for higher-impact activities.

In the course of discussing property doctrines relevant to private land, the remaining chapters occasionally will take a quick digression to see whether and how these doctrines apply to public lands. In thinking about property issues in the private context, keep asking yourself whether the same rules should apply to public lands. Should public lands, for example, be subject to a different level of protection than private lands? Should the government enjoy greater powers over public lands than private property owners enjoy over their lands?

For an excellent treatise on federal public lands, see George Cameron Coggins, Charles Wilkinson, & John D. Leshy, Federal Public Land and Resources Law (5th ed. 2002).

CHAPTER 2

Some Basic Rights and Responsibilities of the Landowner

Property ownership is often described as a "bundle of sticks" or a "bundle of rights"—e.g., the right to use your land, the right to exclude other people from using your land, and the right to sell your land.[1] The metaphor has been criticized on numerous grounds. The metaphor, for example, suggests that property ownership consists only of rights, when ownership actually carries both rights and responsibilities. The metaphor also intimates that the sticks are all of similar nature and length, when in fact the rights and responsibilities of a property owner vary tremendously in both character and importance. The metaphor also implies that one can relatively easily separate the sticks, subtracting one or adding another, when the rights and responsibilities are often intimately bound together and gain new relevance when combined together.

The "bundle of sticks" metaphor, nonetheless, is valuable in emphasizing both that property ownership consists of an amalgamation of various legal relationships and that the exact set of rights and responsibilities that make up a property right can vary among situations. This Chapter examines some of the basic rights and responsibilities that make up the "bundle of sticks" for the owner of a "fee simple absolute." A fee simple absolute is the most common form of land ownership in the United States; most people who own a home or a parcel of commercial real estate own a fee simple absolute. A fee simple absolute is of infinite duration and carries the broadest set of rights permitted by the law. As you will see in Part III, there are various other forms of property interests. Some property interests, like leases, last only for a limited period of time. Other property interests, like easements, give the holder far fewer sticks than the fee simple absolute. But the rights and responsibilities of the owner of a fee simple absolute are common to many property interests, and they provide a good spot to begin our examination of property rights.

1. The lineage of this metaphor is unclear. Some attribute it to Supreme Court Justice Benjamin N. Cardozo; others to Professor Wesley Hohfield. One article traces the term to an 1888 treatise which stated that the "dullest individual among the people knows and understands that his property in anything is a bundle of rights." John Lewis, A Treatise on the Law of Eminent Domain in the United States 57 (1888). See Robert J. Goldstein, Green Wood in the Bundle of Sticks: Fitting Environmental Ethics and Ecology into Real Property Law 347, 366 (1998).

This Chapter does not try to provide an exhaustive overview of all the rights and responsibilities of a landowner. One modern effort to broadly categorize the incidents of ownership came up with over a dozen classifications. See Lawrence C. Becker, The Moral Basis of Property Rights, 22 Nomos 187, 190–191 (1980). This Chapter examines some of the major rights and responsibilities that figure into disputes among property owners or between property owners and other members of society, including a landowner's right to "exclusive possession," the mutual rights of landowners to use and enjoy their land, and the government's ability to "expropriate" private property for public use. Other chapters look in detail at other specific rights and responsibilities, such as the right to sell or dispose of property.

A. The Right to Exclude

Recall from page 1 that Blackstone claimed that nothing "engages the affections of mankind, as the right of property; or that *sole and despotic dominion* which one man claims and exercises over the external things of the world, *in total exclusion of the right of any other individual in the universe.*" 2 Commentaries on the Laws of England *2 (1766) (emphasis added). To many observers, the cornerstone of private property is the right to exclude anyone and anything from your property that you don't want on your property. Indeed, Professor Felix Cohen suggested that private property is anything to which the following warning could be attached: "To the world: Keep off X unless you have my permission, which I may grant or withhold." Felix Cohen, Dialogue on Private Property, 9 Rutgers L. Rev. 357, 374 (1954). Some have even suggested that eliminating the right to exclude would lead to the "destruction of property." See George M. Armstrong, Jr., From the Fetishism of Commodities to the Regulated Market: The Rise and Decline of Property, 82 Nw. U. L. Rev. 79, 96–97 (1987).

Yet the right to exclude other people and things from your property is not absolute. Both courts and legislatures have created a variety of exceptions to the general rule—and new exceptions continually arise. The means of enforcing the right to exclude also vary from context to context. In reading these materials, consider both why the right to exclude is considered a key element of private property and why the law has often limited the right.

1. Trespass—The Right to Exclude Others

If another person physically enters your land without your permission, the person is guilty of "trespass" and you can sue for relief. The right to eject trespassers is intrinsic to most people's idea of property and has been a right of landowners since the Code of Hammurabi and the Israelite's Covenant Code. See Robert C. Ellickson & Charles Thorland, Ancient Land Law: Mesopotamia, Egypt, and Israel, 71 Chi.-Kent L. Rev. 321, 342 (1995). The general disfavor with which the law views trespassing is reflected in the moral condemnation inherent in the very term "trespass" which is used generally in our society to denote any offense, sin, or wrong against an individual. Indeed, in many cases, the question is only how severe of punishment should be meted out to the trespasser.

Jacque v. Steenberg Homes, Inc.

Supreme Court of Wisconsin, 1997.
563 N.W.2d 154.

WILLIAM A. BABLITCH, J.

Steenberg Homes had a mobile home to deliver. Unfortunately for Harvey and Lois Jacque (the Jacques), the easiest route of delivery was across their land. Despite adamant protests by the Jacques, Steenberg plowed a path through the Jacques' snow-covered field and via that path, delivered the mobile home. Consequently, the Jacques sued Steenberg Homes for intentional trespass. At trial, Steenberg Homes conceded the intentional trespass, but argued that no compensatory damages had been proved, and that punitive damages could not be awarded without compensatory damages. Although the jury awarded the Jacques $1 in nominal damages and $100,000 in punitive damages, the circuit court set aside the jury's award of $100,000. The court of appeals affirmed, reluctantly concluding that it could not reinstate the punitive damages because it was bound by precedent establishing that an award of nominal damages will not sustain a punitive damage award. We conclude that when nominal damages are awarded for an intentional trespass to land, punitive damages may, in the discretion of the jury, be awarded. We further conclude that the $100,000 awarded by the jury is not excessive. Accordingly, we reverse and remand for reinstatement of the punitive damage award.

The relevant facts follow. Plaintiffs, Lois and Harvey Jacques, are an elderly couple, now retired from farming, who own roughly 170 acres near Wilke's Lake in the town of Schleswig. The defendant, Steenberg Homes, Inc. (Steenberg), is in the business of selling mobile homes. In the fall of 1993, a neighbor of the Jacques purchased a mobile home from Steenberg. Delivery of the mobile home was included in the sales price.

Steenberg determined that the easiest route to deliver the mobile home was across the Jacques' land. Steenberg preferred transporting the home across the Jacques' land because the only alternative was a private road which was covered in up to seven feet of snow and contained a sharp curve which would require sets of "rollers" to be used when maneuvering the home around the curve. Steenberg asked the Jacques on several separate occasions whether it could move the home across the Jacques' farm field. The Jacques refused....

On the morning of delivery, Mr. Jacque observed the mobile home parked on the corner of the town road adjacent to his property. He decided to find out where the movers planned to take the home. The movers, who were Steenberg employees, showed Mr. Jacque the path they planned to take with the mobile home to reach the neighbor's lot. The path cut across the Jacques' land. Mr. Jacque informed the movers that it was the Jacques' land they were planning to cross and that Steenberg did not have permission to cross their land.... [The] assistant manager asked Mr. Jacque how much money it would take to get permission. Mr. Jacque responded that it was not a question of money; the Jacques just did not want Steenberg to cross their land. Mr. Jacque testified that he told Steenberg to "Follow the road, that is what the road is for." Steenberg employees left the meeting without permission to cross the land.

At trial, one of Steenberg's employees testified that, upon coming out of the Jacques' home, the assistant manager stated: "I don't give a what [Mr. Jacque] said, just get the home in there any way you can." The other Steenberg employee confirmed this testimony and further testified that the assistant manager told him to park the company truck in such a way that no one could get down the town road to see the route the employees were taking with the home. The assistant manager denied giving these instructions, and Steenberg argued that the road was blocked for safety reasons.

The employees, after beginning down the private road, ultimately used a "bobcat" to cut a path through the Jacques' snow-covered field and hauled the home across the Jacques' land to the neighbor's lot. One employee testified that upon returning to the office and informing the assistant manager that they had gone across the field, the assistant manager reacted by giggling and laughing. The other employee confirmed this testimony. The assistant manager disputed this testimony.

When a neighbor informed the Jacques that Steenberg had, in fact, moved the mobile home across the Jacques' land, Mr. Jacque called the Manitowoc County Sheriff's Department. After interviewing the parties and observing the scene, an officer from the sheriff's department issued a $30 citation to Steenberg's assistant manager. The Jacques commenced an intentional tort action in Manitowoc County Circuit Court....

Steenberg argues that, as a matter of law, punitive damages could not be awarded by the jury because punitive damages must be supported by an award of compensatory damages and here the jury awarded only nominal and punitive damages. The Jacques contend that the rationale supporting the compensatory damage award requirement is inapposite when the wrongful act is an intentional trespass to land. We agree with the Jacques....

The general rule was stated in Barnard v. Cohen, 165 Wis. 417, 162 N.W. 480 (1917), where the question presented was: "In an action for libel, can there be a recovery of punitory damages if only nominal compensatory damages are found?" With the bare assertion that authority and better reason supported its conclusion, the *Barnard* court said no. *Barnard* continues to state the general rule of punitive damages in Wisconsin. The rationale for the compensatory damage requirement is that if the individual cannot show actual harm, he or she has but a nominal interest, hence, society has little interest in having the unlawful, but otherwise harmless, conduct deterred, therefore, punitive damages are inappropriate.

However, whether nominal damages can support a punitive damage award in the case of an intentional trespass to land has never been squarely addressed by this court. Nonetheless, Wisconsin law is not without reference to this situation. In 1854 the court established punitive damages, allowing the assessment of "damages as a punishment to the defendant for the purpose of making an example." McWilliams v. Bragg, 3 Wis. 377, 378 (1854). The *McWilliams* court related the facts and an illustrative tale from the English case of Merest v. Harvey, 128 Eng. Rep. 761 (C.P. 1814), to explain the rationale underlying punitive damages.

In *Merest*, a landowner was shooting birds in his field when he was approached by the local magistrate who wanted to hunt with him. Although the landowner refused, the magistrate proceeded to hunt. When the landowner continued to object, the magistrate threatened to have him jailed and dared him to file suit. Although little actual harm had been caused, the English court upheld damages of 500 pounds, explaining "in a case where a man disregards every principle which actuates the conduct of gentlemen, what is to restrain him except large damages?"

To explain the need for punitive damages, even where actual harm is slight, *McWilliams* related the hypothetical tale from *Merest* of an intentional trespasser:

> Suppose a gentleman has a paved walk in his paddock, before his window, and that a man intrudes and walks up and down before the window of his house, and looks in while the owner is at dinner, is the trespasser permitted to say "here is a halfpenny for you which is the full extent of the mischief I have done." Would that be a compensation? I cannot say that it would be....

Thus, in the case establishing punitive damages in this state, this court recognized that in certain situations of trespass, the actual harm is not in the damage done to the land, which may be minimal, but in the loss of the individual's right to exclude others from his or her property and, the court implied that this right may be punished by a large damage award despite the lack of measurable harm.... The Jacques argue that both the individual and society have significant interests in deterring intentional trespass to land, regardless of the lack of measurable harm that results. We agree with the Jacques. An examination of the individual interests invaded by an intentional trespass to land, and society's interests in preventing intentional trespass to land, leads us to the conclusion that the *Barnard* rule should not apply when the tort supporting the award is intentional trespass to land.

We turn first to the individual landowner's interest in protecting his or her land from trespass. The United States Supreme Court has recognized that the private landowner's right to exclude others from his or her land is "one of the most essential sticks in the bundle of rights that are commonly characterized as property." Dolan v. City of Tigard, 512 U.S. 374, 384 (1994) (quoting Kaiser Aetna v. United States, 444 U.S. 164 (1979)).... Harvey and Lois Jacque have the right to tell Steenberg Homes and any other trespasser, "No, you cannot cross our land." But that right has no practical meaning unless protected by the State. And, as this court recognized as early as 1854, a "halfpenny" award does not constitute state protection.

Society has an interest in punishing and deterring intentional trespassers beyond that of protecting the interests of the individual landowner. Society has an interest in preserving the integrity of the legal system. Private landowners should feel confident that wrongdoers who trespass upon their land will be appropriately punished. When landowners have confidence in the legal system, they are less likely to resort to "self-help" remedies. In *McWilliams*, the court recognized the importance of " 'preventing the practice of dueling, [by permitting] juries [ ] to punish insult by exemplary damages.' " *McWilliams*, 3 Wis. at 381. Although dueling is rarely a modern form of self-help, one can easily imagine a frustrated landowner taking the law into his or her own hands when faced with a brazen trespasser, like Steenberg, who refuses to heed no trespass warnings.

People expect wrongdoers to be appropriately punished. Punitive damages have the effect of bringing to punishment types of conduct that, though oppressive and hurtful to the individual, almost invariably go unpunished by the public prosecutor. The $30 forfeiture was certainly not an appropriate punishment for Steenberg's egregious trespass in the eyes of the Jacques. It was more akin to *Merest*'s "halfpenny." If punitive damages are not allowed in a situation like this, what punishment will prohibit the intentional trespass to land? Moreover, what is to stop Steenberg Homes from concluding, in the future, that delivering its mobile homes via an intentional trespass and paying the resulting Class B forfeiture, is not more profitable than obeying the law? Steenberg Homes plowed a path across the Jacques' land and dragged the mobile home across that path, in the face of the Jacques' adamant refusal. A $30 forfeiture and a $1 nominal damage award are unlikely to restrain Steenberg Homes from similar conduct in the future. An appropriate punitive damage award probably will....

[The court next took up the question of whether the punitive award was so high to be legally unsupportable and concluded that it was not.] The punitive award neither shocks our conscience, nor takes our breath away. On the contrary, it is the brazen conduct of Steenberg Homes that we find shocking, not the $100,000 punitive damages award....

Notes & Questions

1. Is it relevant in your view that Steenberg Homes used the Jacques' land for a commercial purpose—to deliver a mobile home to one of its purchasers? Should punitive damages be available if an individual intentionally trespasses across the Jacques' land to get to a favorite fishing lake in an adjoining national forest?

2. Landowners enjoy several remedies for trespass. One is damages. Even if a landowner suffers no actual damage, a court will award nominal damages against trespassers. Where actual damage occurs, the courts

generally will measure damages by the difference between the land's value before and after the trespass. In some states, however, damages are measured by the cost of repairing the damage if the trespass is not continuing, the injury is reparable, and the cost of repair is less than the diminution in the property's value. See, e.g., Kratze v. Independent Order of Oddfellows, 500 N.W.2d 115 (Mich. 1993). The landowner is also entitled to compensation for all injuries that naturally and proximately result from the trespass—including personal injuries (physical, mental or reputational) and injuries to personal property.

3. If the trespass is willful, wanton, or malicious, some courts may also award punitive damages as in *Jacques*. See, e.g., IMAC Energy, Inc. v. Tittle, 590 So. 2d 163, 169 (Ala. 1991) (a jury is warranted in awarding punitive damages if a trespass is attended by "rudeness, wantonness, recklessness or an insulting manner or is accompanied by circumstances of fraud and malice, oppression, aggravation, or gross negligence"). The Restatement (Second) of Torts supports the holding in *Jacques* that a landowner can collect punitive damages even though he is awarded only nominal compensatory damages. Most courts, however, will not award punitive damages in such circumstances. Which is the better position? Why should the law treat trespassers so harshly if the landowner has not suffered significant economic damage?

4. Many states, like Wisconsin, have also made trespass a crime. In New York, for example, trespassing can land you in jail for periods ranging from 15 days for a simple trespass, to three months for trespassing on fenced or otherwise enclosed premises, to seven years for trespassing in a building with a deadly weapon or explosives. See New York—McKinney's Penal Law §§ 140.05, 140.10, 140.15 & 140.17.

5. A landowner can obtain an injunction against a trespasser if she can demonstrate that damages are an "inadequate" remedy—typically because damages will not make her whole or will require a multiplicity of lawsuits. See, e.g., Mack v. Edens, 412 S.E.2d 431 (S.C. App. 1991). If the trespasser remains on the land, the landowner can sue to regain control of the land through a common law "ejectment" proceeding or through the far quicker statutory vehicle of "unlawful detainer" (to which we will return when we look at landlord-tenant relations in Chapter 8).

6. If someone ignores your fence and drags a mobile home across your land without permission, that person is pretty clearly a trespasser. But trespass law erects legal barriers that are higher and deeper than any fence. Courts historically have held that a possessor's rights extend not only to the surface of the land but also to the entire column of space below—*usque ad inferos*—and above—*usque ad coelum*. Landowners thus can typically enjoin others from digging under their property or intruding into underground caves. See, e.g., Harding v. Bethesda Regional Cancer Treatment Center, 551 So. 2d 299 (Ala. 1989) (extraction of roots from beneath property constitutes a trespass); Marengo Cave Co. v. Ross, 10 N.E.2d 917 (Ind. 1937) (cave). The only significant limit on the possessor's subsurface rights is the ancient "rule of capture" which, as we will see in

Chapter 3, permits a property owner to suck out and claim oil, gas, and water from underneath a neighbor's land, so long as the property owner does not drill under the neighbor's land (see pages 232–245).

With the growth of air travel, courts have retreated from the position that a plane flying over someone's property is automatically trespassing. See United States v. Causby, 328 U.S. 256 (1946). But a plane flying below administratively set minimum flight levels might still support a trespass action. See, e.g., Burnham v. Beverly Airways, Inc., 42 N.E.2d 575 (Mass. 1942). And a landowner who finds use of her land disrupted by flights might in some cases still be able to sue under nuisance law, discussed later at pages 128–167.

7. A trespass can occur not only where another person comes onto your property, but where that person intentionally places animals or other things on your property. As the following case discusses, however, state law varies regarding a landowner's right to damages where straying livestock damage her crops or land.

Maguire v. Yanke

Supreme Court of Idaho, 1978.
590 P.2d 85.

DONALDSON, Justice.

[Maguire farmed 82 acres of land near Hailey, Idaho. Yanke ran a ranch across the road, which in 1975, included a herd of 130 cows, 130 calves, and 8 bulls.]

On numerous occasions between mid-July 1975 and August 2, 1975, several of Yanke's cattle broke through the pasture fence and strayed onto Maguire's alfalfa land south of the road. On August 2, 1975, a major breakout of Yanke's cattle occurred, and approximately 137 head of cows and calves entered Maguire's hayfield. At the time, Maguire had baled hay in the field which was substantially damaged by the cattle. Substantial damage was also done to the growing second crop of hay. When Maguire learned of the breakout, Yanke was called and the cattle were promptly removed.

Maguire thereafter filed this action against Yanke for damages. Maguire sought $3,818 actual damages and $10,000 punitive damages. The district court awarded Maguire a judgment of $3,818 to compensate him for his actual damages. The district court refused to allow any punitive damages, finding that Yanke had not acted wilfully....

I

The trial court reasoned that ... it was Yanke's duty to keep his cattle fenced in because the land was situated in what was historically an area of enclosed lands and not in open range....

A review of the law relating to the liability of an owner of livestock for damage caused by his stock straying on another's land is necessary to the resolution of the issues presented in this case. At common law it was the duty of the owner of livestock to fence them in, and no duty was placed upon the adjoining landowner to fence them out. The owners of livestock were liable for the damage caused by their stock straying upon another's land whether the land was enclosed or not. An early English case stated the rule as follows: "[W]here my beasts of their own wrong without my will and knowledge break another's close I shall be punished, for I am the trespasser with my beasts . . . for I am held by the law to keep my beasts without their doing wrong to anyone." W. Prosser, Handbook of Law of Torts 496 (4th ed. 1971), *quoting* 12 Hen. VII, Keilwey 3b, 72 Eng. Rep. 156.

Western cattle states generally rejected the common law, holding that livestock roaming at large committed no trespass when they strayed on unenclosed private land. Idaho, concurring with the approach of its neighboring states, also rejected the common law rule.... However, one who willfully and deliberately drives his stock upon the lands of another, whether enclosed or unenclosed and grazes them upon such land without the permission of the owner, is liable in damages for the trespass.

In an effort to provide a remedy for landowners whose property was damaged by roaming cattle, most western states including Idaho passed fence laws. Idaho Code §§ 35–101 and 35–102 define what constitutes a legal fence, prescribing standards relating to height, length, number of rails and materials. Idaho Code § 25–2202 provides that a landowner who encloses his property with a legal fence has a cause of action against the owner of animals that break the enclosure. The United States Supreme Court, commenting on a Texas fence law, in Lazarus v. Phelps, 152 U.S. at 85, 14 S. Ct. at 478, states the object of such fence statutes:

> As there are, or were, in the state of Texas, as well as in the newer states of the west generally, vast areas of land, over which, so long as the government owned them, cattle had been permitted to roam at will for pasturage, it was not thought proper, as the land was gradually taken up by individual proprietors, to change the custom of the country in that particular, and oblige cattle owners to incur the heavy expense of fencing their land, or be held as trespassers by reason of their cattle accidentally straying upon the land of others.

The legal fence laws of the State of Idaho provide a remedy to the landowner whose property, although enclosed by a legal fence, is nonetheless damaged by roaming cattle.... [T]he legal fence laws of the State of Idaho are "fencing out" statutes. These legal fence statutes recognized the rancher's right to allow cattle to roam.

Although the "fence out" rule prevails in this state, there are some important legislative exceptions to the rule. Idaho and other western states provide for the creation of herd districts as an alternative to landowners who wish to protect their land from damage caused by roaming stock, but do not wish or cannot afford to fence their land. Idaho Code § 25–2401 *et seq.* permits districts within a county to petition for the creation of a herd district. If a majority of the landowners owning more than fifty percent of the land in the district vote to create a herd district, livestock are prohibited from running at large within the district, and a landowner may recover for damages caused by animals straying upon his property, regardless of whether it is enclosed by a legal fence. In essence the creation of a herd district in Idaho reinstates the English common law within that district, placing a duty on the livestock owner to fence in his stock and holding him liable for damages caused if his stock escapes onto another's land, regardless of whether that land is fenced or not.

In 1963, the Idaho Legislature amended the herd district law, I.C. § 25–2402, to not allow inclusion of open range in a herd district. Open range was defined as follows: "all uninclosed lands outside cities and villages upon which by custom, license or otherwise, livestock, excepting swine, are grazed or permitted to roam." The legislature also added to the section a provision that excepts from the application of herd district laws any livestock roaming or straying into the district from open range, unless the district is enclosed by a legal fence. . . .

II

The prior review of Idaho law reveals that there are two geographical areas other than cities and villages recognized in this state in relation to the liability of livestock owners for damage done by their stock to another's land. First, herd districts created pursuant to I.C. § 25–2401 *et seq.* where within the district the English common law rule of prohibiting livestock from running at large is reinstated. . . . The second area contains "open range" as defined by I.C. § 25–2402 and all other areas of the state not within cities, villages, or already created herd districts. . . . It is in this area where the rule that livestock owners are not required to fence their stock in and are not liable for damages caused by their stock to another's land unless the landowner's property is enclosed by a legal fence obtains.

The trial court held that it was the duty of Yanke to keep his cattle fenced in because the area was an area of enclosed lands and not located in open range. Testimony was received at trial that the area in question had been one of enclosed land where cattle were not permitted to roam for more years than any witness could remember to the contrary. It appears that the trial court relied on this testimony and the definitions of "open range" contained in I.C. § 25–2402 in determining the area was not in open range and thus placing a duty on Yanke to fence his livestock in. Maguire concurs with the trial court that the right of livestock to roam freely is restricted to "open range" and that the controlling definition of "open range" is contained in I.C. § 25–2402 . . ., which includes only land where historically livestock were grazed or permitted to roam.

This analysis, in essence, creates a third area relating to liability for damage caused by roaming livestock. This area would encompass all land which livestock by custom, license, lease, or permit are not permitted to roam at large or graze. In this region, a livestock owner would have a duty to fence his cattle in, and there would be no duty on a landowner to fence cattle out in order to recover damages caused by roaming livestock.

Yanke contends that the trial court erred in using the analysis above in determining he had a duty to fence his cattle in. Yanke argues that this Court's rejection of the English common law duty to keep one's livestock enclosed, and the adoption of the rule of no duty to fence in livestock in later cases, plus the enactment of fence laws by the Idaho Legislature, firmly establish that within this state there is no duty for a livestock owner to fence his cattle in. Yanke asserts that notwithstanding the fact that the area in question was not one where by custom livestock were grazed or permitted to roam, no liability attaches to a livestock owner for damage done by his stock straying onto another's land, unless the damaged landowner's property is enclosed with a legal fence. Yanke argues that the only method by which a landowner may relieve himself of his duty to fence livestock out and place upon the livestock owner the duty to fence his stock in is the creation of a herd district. We agree.

The trial court erred in restricting the right of livestock owners to roam stock to only those areas where by custom, license, or permit livestock are grazed or permitted to roam. The adoption of such a rule creates de facto herd districts in areas where by custom livestock have not been permitted to roam and thereby renders I.C. § 25–2401 *et seq.* unnecessary. The trial court, in effect, applied herd district rules relating to liability for roaming livestock to these areas without requiring the creation of a herd district. It is a general rule of statutory construction that courts should not nullify a statute or deprive a law of potency or force unless such course is absolutely necessary. It appears the intent of the legislature in enacting I.C. § 25–2401 *et seq.* was that for areas where the historical use has been one of enclosed lands, the landowners in that area must petition and vote to designate that area a herd district in order to change the Idaho law regarding liability for damage by roaming livestock.

.... Prior to 1963, herd districts could be created in any part of Idaho. It is clear the amendment of I.C. § 25–2402 by the inserting of a definition of "open range" was designed to protect the rights of livestock owners by prohibiting herd districts in areas where they historically grazed stock, rather than limiting the area where livestock owners were free to let their stock roam at large. Under our decision, herd districts may still be created in any area not within "open range" as defined in I.C. § 25–2402. The passage of I.C. §§ 25–2402 and 25–2118, with their accompanying definition of "open range" in terms of historical use, was not intended to and does not change the law of this state that with the exception of cities, villages, and herd districts, livestock may run at large and graze upon unenclosed lands in this state....

The trial court erred in holding that Yanke had a duty to fence his cattle in and that Maguire had no duty to fence the cattle out in order to recover for the damages occasioned by the cattle straying upon his land. The rule simply stated is that in all areas in this state, with the exception of herd districts, villages, and cities, there is no duty for a livestock owner to confine his cattle to his own land and that no liability attaches to that livestock owner for damage occasioned by his stock straying onto another's property, unless the damaged landowner's property is enclosed by a legal fence.

Judgment reversed.

McFADDEN and BISTLINE, JJ., concur. [The opinion of BAKES, J., concurring in the reversal, but dissenting in the disposition, is omitted.]

Notes & Questions

1. Beginning in the late 17th century, most states abandoned the common law "closed range" rule that imposed liability on the owner of straying livestock, in favor of an "open range" or "fence out" rule that required farmers and other landowners to protect their property by erecting fences. See, e.g., 1 Hen. Stat., Act LXIII (1631–32), at 176 (1823) (Va.) ("Every man shall enclose his ground with sufficient fences upon theire perill"); J. Crawford King, The Closing of the Southern Range: An Exploratory Study, 48 J. Southern Hist. 53 (1982). A few states nonetheless stuck with the common law. See, e.g., Bastian v. King, 661 P.2d 953 (Utah 1983) (holding rancher liable for damage to crops and pipes on neighboring farmland).

In recent decades, suburban encroachment into rural areas, along with a decline in the ranching industry, has ignited a trend back toward the common law rule. Many states like Idaho have authorized local voters to create herd districts or similar regional zones in which the common law rule applies. See, e.g., Ariz. Rev. Stat. Ann §§ 3–1421 to 3–1422. Other states have abandoned the open range rule entirely or restricted it to purely rural areas. See Terence J. Centner, Reforming Outdated Fence Law Provisions: Good Fences Make Good Neighbors Only If They Are Fair, 12 J. Envtl. L. & Litig. 267, 272 (1997).

2. Choices between property rules can implicate both economic efficiency (does the rule maximize economic value?) and equity (is the rule "fair"?). In *Maguire v. Yanke*, does the open range rule minimize the economic loss from farmer-rancher conflicts? Is the rule fair to Maguire? Do efficiency and equity argue for the same rule? If not, how should the tension be resolved?

3. **Externalities.** The conflict between farmers and ranchers, which is well illustrated in *Maguire v. Yanke*, is an example of an economic externality. An externality is a cost or benefit to third parties that a decision maker will ignore in making a decision because the cost or benefit does not affect him—hence, it's a cost or benefit "external" to his decision. For example, if Yanke decides to increase the size of his herd, he will be imposing a cost on Maguire (in the form of lost crops). But that cost will not hurt Yanke if he is not held liable for it, so he will not take it into account in deciding whether to expand his herd. This can lead to a misallocation of society's resources. The cost in lost hay might be far

greater than the value of raising more cattle, but Yanke may choose to raise the cattle no matter what the cost to Maguire. Looked at in a slightly different way, the private costs and benefits of a decision frequently diverge from the societal costs and benefits. The losses to Maguire are costs to society, but Yanke is interested only in the private costs and benefits to him.

Who is the cause of this externality? You might be tempted to say Yanke is the cause, because it is his decision to graze more cattle. But Yanke's cattle grazing would not impose an externality on Maguire if Maguire did not grow hay in an unenclosed area close to Yanke's cattle. In short, *both* Yanke's decision to graze cattle *and* Maguire's decision to grow hay in an unenclosed area right next door are causes of the externality. Thus although the concept of externalities helps us describe the problem in *Maguire*, it does not single out either Maguire or Yanke as the party "at fault."

4. **The Coase Theorem.** Does the concept of externalities point us to a particular solution. For many years, policy analysts argued that the law should impose the cost of the externality on decisionmakers like Yanke. If Maguire can sue Yanke for the lost value of his crops, Yanke will take this into account in deciding whether to expand his cattle herd. As a result, Yanke will not expand the herd if the cost to Maguire is greater than the value to Yanke. Liability, in short, will force Yanke to "internalize" all the costs of cattle grazing.

In 1960, however, Professor Ronald Coase wrote a now famous article in which he argued that, assuming "zero transaction costs" (i.e., no hidden information and costless negotiations) and "rational" decisionmakers, the legal rule in a case like *Maguire* will have no affect on how societal resources are used. The parties will always end up doing what's economically efficient—whether that's enclosing the cattle, building a fence around the crops, or reducing the size of (or eliminating entirely) the cattle herd. Ronald Coase, The Problem of Social Cost, 3 J.L. & Econ. 1 (1960).

To understand Coase's argument, consider a simple hypothetical built loosely on the *Maguire* case. Assume that if no fences are built, Yankee's cattle will stray and destroy Maguire's crops. As shown in Figure 2–1, the size of the crop loss depends on the size of the herd. The costs of fencing Yanke's and Maguire's property are $2000 and $1200 respectively.

Number in herd (steers)	Total Annual Crop Loss	Crop Loss Attributable to the Last "Marginal" Steer
1	$100	$100
2	$300	$200
3	$600	$300
4	$1000	$400
5	$1500	$500

Figure 2–1

If Yanke is responsible for any damages caused by his straying cattle, Yanke's actions will depend on the "marginal" profit of raising each additional cow. For example, if the profit of raising an additional cow (taking into account all variable costs, other than the expense of compensating Maguire for crop losses) is $350, Yanke will graze 3 cows. The third cow will bring in a profit of $350, but only cost Yanke $300 more in extra damages to Maguire; a fourth cow, however, would cost Yanke another $400 in damages—more than the $350 in added profits.

If the profit from each cow increases to $500, Yankee will raise five cows (because the profit of the fifth cow will now just offset the added damages). Rather than pay Maguire $1500 in damages, however, Yankee will pay Maguire up to $1499 to build a fence around his crops. Maguire will agree to build the fence for some sum between $1201 and $1499 (depending on which of the two neighbors is the better bargainer) because Maguire can make a profit by doing so.

In a world with no transaction costs and "rational" decisionmakers, will things be any different if Maguire must bear his own losses from the straying cattle? Coase argued "no." First consider how large a herd Yanke will choose. One might initially suspect that Yanke will continue to increase the size of his herd so long as the profit from an additional cow (after taking into account all variable costs) is greater than $0. But that assumes Maguire will not pay Yanke to limit the size of his herd (remember we're in a world where there's no secret information, people are economically "rational," and negotiations are effortless). If Yanke has three cows and is considering purchasing a fourth, Maguire will pay the cattle owner up to $400 not to add the fourth cow because that is the damage Maguire would suffer from the fourth cow. If $400 is greater than Yanke's marginal profit from a fourth cow, Yanke will agree not to buy the cow—the same result as when Yanke was liable for damages from his wandering herd. The choice of liability rule will also not affect if a fence is built. If the profit from cows is quite high and Yanke chooses to graze five cows, Maguire will build a fence because that will be less costly than incurring $1500 in crop damage.

5. How valid are the assumptions on which this analysis is based? Assume that in the actual *Maguire v. Yanke* dispute, the most efficient result was for Yanke to build a fence or to reduce the size of his herd. Once the court ruled for Yanke, how likely do you believe that it was that Maguire and Yanke would successfully bargain to that result? What obstacles might have stood in the way of a successful negotiation? For experimental tests of the Coase Theorem, see Elizabeth Hoffman & Matthew Spitzer, Experimental Tests of the Coase Theorem with Large Bargaining Groups, 15 J. Legal Stud. 149 (1986); Elizabeth Hoffman & Matthew L. Spitzer, Experimental Law and Economics: An Introduction, 85 Colum. L. Rev. 991 (1985); Elizabeth Hoffman & Matthew L. Spitzer, The Coast Theorem: Some Experimental Tests, 25 J.L. & Econ. 73 (1982). But see Mark Kelman, Comment on Hoffman and Spitzer's *Experimental Law and Economics*, 85 Colum. L. Rev. 1037 (1985) (critiquing the studies).

6. Are there legal approaches other than a strict open-range or closed-range rule that would do a better job of resolving potential conflicts between ranchers and other property owners? A number of states with either the open range or closed range rules have adopted mandatory cost-sharing statutes. Under these statutes, liability does not change, but rancher and neighbor must share the cost of building a fence. In an open range area, for example, a farmer must build a fence to protect his crops, but the farmer can demand that a neighboring rancher pay a specified portion of the cost. See, e.g., Kan. Stat. Ann. § 29–301; Neb. Rev. Stat. § 34–103; Ohio Rev. Code Ann. § 971.02. Is mandatory cost-sharing better from the standpoint of either efficiency or equity? Is there any downside?

7. **Environmental Considerations.** Professor Terence J. Centner argues that the open range rule encourages "the destruction of vegetation by livestock meandering near water sources, which, in turn, adversely affects the quality of fish habitats and sport activities." Centner, supra Note 1, at 275–76. Studies show that grazing along streams can kill trees that provide critical shade for the streams; water temperatures therefore rise, threatening native fish species. Id. at 279. Destruction of vegetation in the "riparian" zone bordering streams can also affect water quality, stream flows, and local flora and fauna. See Robert H. Smith, Livestock Production: The Unsustainable Environmental and Economic Effects of an Industry Out of Control, 4 Buff. Envtl. L.J. 45 (1996) (noting that over 90% of original riparian ecosystems in Arizona and New Mexico are gone); Richard H. Braun, Emerging Limits on Federal Land Management Discretion: Livestock, Riparian Ecosystems, and Clean Water Law, 17 Envtl. L. 43 (1986).

Does this change your analysis of which rule is better, the open-range rule or the closed-range rule? Is the environmental problem better addressed by a law that limits grazing in sensitive riparian zones, even where the riparian zones are on the rancher's property? In 1996, Oregon voters rejected a ballot initiative, known as the Clean Streams Initiative, that would have banned grazing within defined riparian zones up to one hundred feet of a stream. Centner, supra Note 1, at 278–79.

8. **Invasive Species.** An increasingly serious environmental problem around the world is "invasive species," also sometimes known as "exotic" or "alien" species. An invasive species is a species that is introduced into a new area or ecosystem and can cause harm to the native species or other parts of the local environment. The introduction of the Nile perch into Africa's Lake Victoria, for example, led to the extinction of 200 endemic fish species and the devastation of local communities that depended on the endemic fish species for subsistence. See Chris Bright, Life Out of Bounds: Bioinvasion in a Borderless World 86–92 (1998). Any type of species, including plants, viruses, birds, animals, and fish, can be invasive.

Assume that a home owner imports a type of ornamental plant for her backyard and that the plant spreads to a neighbors yard, overwhelming and destroying native vegetation that the neighbor particularly enjoys. Does the neighbor have an action in trespass against the home owner for "letting" her plant escape onto the neighbor's property? Is there any reason to treat invasive species any differently from cattle? See generally Justin Pidot, The Applicability of Nuisance Law to Invasive Plants: Can Common Law Liability Inspire Government Action?, 24 Va. Envt'l L.J. 183 (2005).

9. **Law versus Norms.** In the mid–1980s, Professor Robert Ellickson decided to put the Coase Theorem to a real world test by examining how rural neighbors in Shasta County, a rural California community, actually resolved cattle disputes. Robert C. Ellickson, Of Coase and Cattle: Dispute Resolution Among Neighbors in Shasta County, 38 Stan. L. Rev. 623 (1986). Shasta County looked like a good setting for testing the Coase Theorem because some parts were subject to an open range rule while others were subject to a closed range rule, permitting a direct check on whether the legal rule of liability made any difference to the final outcomes.

Ellickson discovered that Coase was right—the legal liability rule did not affect results—but not for the reasons discussed above. The legal liability rule did not affect decisions because everyone, whether in an open-range or closed-range area, ignored the law in favor of local norms. In fact, many farmers and cattle owners did not even know what the law was in their area; they just didn't care.

> In rural Shasta County, trespass conflicts are generally resolved not "*in* the shadow of the law" but, rather, *beyond* that shadow. Most rural residents are consciously committed to an overarching norm of cooperation among neighbors. In trespass situations, their salient lower-level norm, adhered to by all but a few deviants, is that an owner of livestock is responsible for the acts of his animals. Allegiance to this norm seems wholly independent of formal legal entitlements. Most cattlemen believe that a rancher should keep his animals from eating a neighbor's grass, regardless of whether the range is open or closed. . . .
>
> The norm that an animal owner should control his stock is modified by another norm that holds that a rural resident should "lump" minor damage stemming from isolated trespass incidents. The neighborly response to an isolated infraction is an exchange of civilities. A trespass victim should notify the animal owner that the trespass has occurred and assist the owner in retrieving the stray stock. Virtually all residents have telephones, the standard means of communication. A telephone report is regarded not as a form of complaint, but rather as a service to the animal owner, who, after all, has a valuable asset on the loose. Upon receiving a telephone report, a cattleman who is a good neighbor will quickly retrieve the animals (by truck if necessary), apologize for the occurrence, and thank the caller.

The Shasta County residents enforced these norms through a variety of informal mechanisms. If a rancher failed to abide by the norms, his neighbors would begin by spreading word about his or her unneighborliness. That typically worked since the community was small and people valued their reputations. If that didn't resolve the problem, people would resort to "tougher self-help sanctions." Victims of stray cattle, for example, sometimes herded up the cattle and moved them to a location extremely inconvenient for the owner. Occasionally victims issued violent threats—e.g., to turn a stray bull into a steer, or shoot the cattle. If such threats didn't work, some victims occasionally carried through on the threats. Lawsuits were a last resort. Indeed, according to Ellickson, one of the strongest "norms of neighborliness" in Shasta County was not to file legal actions. As one resident put it, "Being good neighbors means no lawsuits."

Do Ellickson's Shasta County findings mean that the law is irrelevant? In what situations would one believe that informal norms would be most important? The least important?

10. Testimony in *Maguire v. Yanke* indicated that ranchers around Hailey, Idaho, had historically enclosed their lands with fences, suggesting that the community maintained a "closed range" norm. What role should such norms play in setting property law for the community? Should the law try to parrot local norms? What impact is a decision such as *Maguire v. Yanke* likely to have on inconsistent community norms?

2. ENCROACHMENTS

Building on someone else's land is a trespass for which the landowner can obtain an injunction or other relief. But sometimes a structure is built on someone else's land either accidentally or intentionally without that landowner realizing it. The landowner might not live on the land or might not realize exactly where his property begins or ends. If the landowner later discovers that a structure is "encroaching" on his land, how should the law respond? Should the court permit the person who built the "encroachment" to use it, but require him to compensate the landowner for the value of the underlying land? Should it matter whether the person who built the encroachment made an innocent mistake? Should it matter how much it would cost to remove the encroachment? How much land it occupies? Should the landowner have the right to demand that the encroachment be removed? What should the court do if the encroachment actually increases the value of the property (e.g., where someone accidentally builds a swimming pool in a neighbor's yard)? Should the neighbor get to keep the pool without paying for it?

Peters v. Archambault

Supreme Judicial Council of Massachusetts, 1972.
278 N.E.2d 729.

CUTTER, J. The plaintiffs by this bill seek to compel the defendants (the Archambaults) to remove a portion of the Archambault house which encroaches on the plaintiffs' land in Marshfield. The plaintiffs and the Archambaults own adjoining ocean-front lots. . . .

The Archambaults' predecessor in title obtained a building permit in 1946 and built a house partly on their own lot and partly on the plaintiffs' lot, of which the total area is about 4,900 square feet. Each lot had a frontage of only fifty feet on the adjacent way. The encroachment contains 465 square feet, and the building extends fifteen feet, three inches, onto the plaintiffs' lot, to a depth of thirty-one feet, four inches. The trial judge found that it will be expensive to remove the encroaching portion of the Archambaults' building....

A final decree ordered the removal of the encroachment. The Archambaults appealed....

In Massachusetts a landowner is ordinarily entitled to mandatory equitable relief to compel removal of a structure significantly encroaching on his land, even though the encroachment was unintentional or negligent and the cost of removal is substantial in comparison to any injury suffered by the owner of the lot upon which the encroachment has taken place.... In rare cases, referred to in our decisions as "exceptional," courts of equity have refused to grant a mandatory injunction and have left the plaintiff to his remedy of damages, "where the unlawful encroachment has been made innocently, and the cost of removal by the defendant would be greatly disproportionate to the injury to the plaintiff from its continuation, or where the substantial rights of the owner may be protected without recourse to an injunction, or where an injunction would be oppressive and inequitable.... But these are the exceptions. What is just and equitable in cases of this sort depends very much upon the particular facts and circumstances disclosed."[2]....

The present record discloses no circumstances which would justify denial of a mandatory injunction for removal of an encroachment taking away over nine per cent of the plaintiffs' lot. The exceptions to the general Massachusetts rule, hitherto recognized as sufficient to justify denial of mandatory relief, have related to much less significant invasions of a plaintiff's land, or have involved circumstances not here present. The invasion of the plaintiff's lot is substantial and not de minimis. Photographs and maps in evidence, portraying the encroachment, show that the intrusion of the Archambaults' building on the plaintiffs' small lot greatly increases the congestion of that lot.[3]....

TAURO, C.J. (dissenting).... The plaintiffs do not seek money damages but rather a decree for the removal of the encroachment on their land which, in effect, would result in the destruction of the defendants' dwelling. The Superior Court made, and the majority today affirm, such a decree. I cannot agree with the opinion of the majority....

2. Such cases have been based upon estoppel; or on laches; or on the trivial nature of the encroachment or injury.

3. Our position avoids constitutional doubts which might arise were we to allow the Archambaults, at their option and as a result of the trespass of their predecessor in title, to expropriate part of the plaintiffs' land by essentially an informal exercise of private eminent domain.

... [T]he defendants occupied their dwelling for over twelve years peacefully and without complaint prior to the present lawsuit. They bought their property in June, 1954, apparently without knowledge that, in 1946, their predecessor in title had mistakenly built partially upon an adjoining lot. The defendants' house was in plain view when the plaintiffs acquired title to the adjoining lot in June, 1966. It seems likely that, before the plaintiffs took title, they viewed the property and were aware of the location of the defendants' house and its proximity (by approximately six feet) to the house they might purchase. It is reasonable to infer, either that they inquired and were told that the space between the dwellings marked the property line, or that they made this assumption. The plaintiffs have disclosed that they discovered the encroachment one month after taking title as the result of a survey undertaken by them for the purpose of constructing a retaining wall. Apparently there was nothing about the defendants' dwelling which was offensive to the plaintiffs or even aroused their suspicions at the time of purchase. It appears therefore that the plaintiffs were satisfied with their purchase and the proximity of the defendants' dwelling to their own until the survey and that, but for the fortuity of the survey, the encroachment might have continued undiscovered indefinitely as it had during the entire period 1946 to 1966.

The discovery of the encroachment in these circumstances is best characterized as an unexpected windfall[6] rather than an intentional injury. The defendants are innocent of any wrongdoing and are at most guilty of unknowingly continuing a long-standing encroachment. Nor can it be said that the defendants have deprived the plaintiffs of something which they believed they were entitled to at the time of their purchase. On the contrary, the plaintiffs could only have believed that they were acquiring exactly what they contemplated when they inspected the property. Subsequently, by virtue of the survey which they had made, the plaintiffs discovered they had purchased more than they had bargained for. At the same time, the defendants learned that what they had purchased in 1954 was less than they had bargained for. These circumstances should not pass unnoticed.

Moreover, removal would be a severe burden upon the defendants. As the trial judge indicated, it would "cost a lot of money, and [involve] a lot of inconvenience, and ... reduce ... [the defendants'] property value to a great extent." ...

In the totality of circumstances, I conclude that equity does not, in the exercise of our sound discretion, require us to grant injunctive relief. Removal imposes upon the defendants substantial cost and inconvenience which are entirely disproportionate to the injury to the plaintiffs. ...

6. The close proximity of the defendants' dwelling to the plaintiffs' dwelling was necessarily a factor in the purchase price. As a corollary, the plaintiffs' property would have been worth more, and the plaintiffs would have had to pay more, if the distance between the two dwellings had been greater. It would seem therefore that, because of the mistake of both parties and of their predecessors in title, the plaintiffs stand to obtain a windfall at the defendants' expense.

Hardship alone is of course not a ground for denial of injunctive relief, but this court should take relative hardship into account, if, as in the instant case, the owner of the encroaching structure is not guilty of an intentional trespass. The view I express is not only in accordance with our own case law but also in accordance with decisions in other jurisdictions....

If we were to refuse injunctive relief, common sense suggests that, in all probability, this dispute would be settled eventually without the need for the destruction of the defendants' dwelling. This could be accomplished through an agreement by the plaintiffs voluntarily to relocate their boundary line in return for payment by the defendants of an amount negotiated between them. The parties would then have their certificates of title reformed to reflect the agreement. In the alternative, the plaintiffs could bring an action at law and the court would make an impartial assessment of damages. The placing of the potent weapon of injunctive relief in the hands of the plaintiffs is hardly conducive to a fair and just settlement. In circumstances such as those in the instant case, the court in Christensen v. Tucker, 114 Cal. App. 2d 554, 563, said: "[The] injunction should be denied, otherwise, the court would lend itself to what practically amounts to extortion." I would dismiss the bill and relegate the plaintiffs to their remedy at law.

Somerville v. Jacobs

Supreme Court of West Virginia, 1969.
170 S.E.2d 805.

Haymond, President:

The plaintiffs, W.J. Somerville and Hazel M. Somerville, herein sometimes referred to as the plaintiffs, the owners of Lots 44, 45 and 46 in the Homeland Addition to the city of Parkersburg, in Wood County, believing that they were erecting a warehouse building on Lot 46 which they owned, mistakenly constructed the building on Lot 47 owned by the defendants, William L. Jacobs and Marjorie S. Jacobs, herein sometimes referred to as the defendants. Construction of the building was completed in January 1967 and by deed dated January 14, 1967 the Somervilles conveyed Lots 44, 45 and 46 to the plaintiffs Fred C. Engle and Jimmy C. Pappas who subsequently leased the building to the Parkersburg Coca-Cola Bottling Company, a corporation. Soon after the building was completed but not until then, the defendants learned that the building was on their property and claimed ownership of the building and its fixtures on the theory of annexation. The plaintiffs then instituted this proceeding for equitable relief in the Circuit Court of Wood County and in their complaint prayed, among other things, for judgment in favor of the Somervilles for $20,500.00 as the value of the improvements made on Lot 47, or, in the alternative, that the defendants be ordered to convey their interest in Lot 47 to the Somervilles for a fair consideration. The Farmers Building and Loan Association, a corporation, the holder of a deed of trust lien upon the land of the defendants, was on motion permitted to intervene and be made a defendant in this proceeding....

The controlling question for decision is whether a court of equity can award compensation to an improver for improvements which he has placed upon land not owned by him, which, because of mistake, he had reason to believe he owned, which improvements were not known to the owner until after their completion and were not induced or permitted by such owner, who is not guilty of any fraud or inequitable conduct, and require the owner to pay the fair value of such improvements or, in the alternative, to convey the land so improved to the improver upon his payment to the owner of the fair value of the land less the value of the improvements....

Though the precise question here involved has not been considered and determined in any prior decision of this Court, the question has been considered by appellate courts in other jurisdictions and though the cases are conflicting the decisions in some jurisdictions, upon particular facts, recognize and sustain the jurisdiction of a court of equity to award compensation to the improver to prevent unjust enrichment to the owner and in the alternative to require the owner to convey the land to the improver upon his payment to the owner of the fair value of the land less the improvements....

In Section 625, Chapter 11, Volume 2, Tiffany Real Property, Third Edition, the text contains this language:

> Since the rule that erections or additions made by one who has no rights to land are fixtures, and therefore not removable by him, even though he made them in the belief that he was the owner of the land, is calculated to cause hardship to an innocent occupant of another's land, by giving the benefit of his labor and expenditures to the landowner, the courts of this country, without either imputing fraud or requiring proof of it, hold it inequitable to allow one to be enriched under such circumstances by the labor and expenditures of another who acted in good faith and in ignorance of any adverse claim or title. Applying this doctrine of "unjust enrichment," a court of equity will, on the principle that he who seeks equity must do equity, refuse its assistance to the rightful owner of land as against an occupant thereof unless he makes compensation for permanent and beneficial improvements, made by the latter without notice of the defect in his title....

From the foregoing authorities it is manifest that equity has jurisdiction to, and will, grant relief to one who, through a reasonable mistake of fact and in good faith, places permanent improvements upon land of another, with reason to believe that the land so improved is that of the one who makes the improvements, and that the plaintiffs are entitled to the relief which they seek in this proceeding.

The undisputed facts, set forth in the agreed statement of counsel representing all parties, is that the plaintiff W.J. Somerville in placing the warehouse building upon Lot 47 entertained a reasonable belief based on the report of the surveyor that it was Lot 46, which he owned, and that the building was constructed by him because of a reasonable mistake of fact and in the good faith belief that he was constructing a building on his own property and he did not discover his mistake until after the building was completed. It is equally clear that the defendants who spent little if any time in the neighborhood were unaware of the construction of the building until after it was completed and were not at any time or in any way guilty of any fraud or inequitable conduct or of any act that would constitute an estoppel. In short, the narrow issue here is between two innocent parties and the solution of the question requires the application of principles of equity and fair dealing between them.

It is clear that the defendants claim the ownership of the building. Under the common law doctrine of annexation, the improvements passed to them as part of the land. This is conceded by the plaintiffs but they assert that the defendants can not keep and retain it without compensating them for the value of the improvements, and it is clear from the testimony of the defendant William L. Jacobs in his deposition that the defendants intend to keep and retain the improvements and refuse to compensate the plaintiffs for their value. The record does not disclose any express request by the plaintiffs for permission to remove the building from the premises if that could be done without its destruction, which is extremely doubtful as the building was constructed of solid concrete blocks on a concrete slab, and it is reasonably clear, from the claim of the defendants of their ownership of the building and their insistence that certain fixtures which have been removed from the building be replaced, that the defendants will not consent to the removal of the building even if that could be done.

In that situation if the defendants retain the building and refuse to pay any sum as compensation to the plaintiff W.J. Somerville they will be unjustly enriched in the amount of $17,500.00, the agreed value of the building, which is more than eight and one-half times the agreed $2,000.00 value of the lot of the defendants on which it is located, and by the retention of the building by the defendants the plaintiff W.J. Somerville will suffer a total loss of the amount of the value of the building. If, however, the defendants are unable or unwilling to pay for the building which they intend to keep but, in the alternative, would convey the lot upon which the building is constructed to the plaintiff W.J. Somerville upon payment of the sum of $2,000.00, the agreed value of the lot without the improvements, the plaintiffs would not lose the building and the defendants would suffer no financial loss because they would obtain payment for the agreed full value of the lot and the only hardship imposed upon the defendants, if this were required, would be to order them to do something which they are unwilling to do voluntarily. To compel the performance of such an act by litigants is not uncommon in litigation in which the rights of the parties are involved and are subject to determination by equitable principles. And the right to require the defendants to convey the lot to the plaintiff W.J. Somerville is recognized and sustained by numerous cases cited earlier in this opinion. Under the facts and circumstances of this case, if the defendants refuse and are not required to exercise their option either to pay W.J. Somerville the value of the improvements or to convey to him the lot on which they are located upon his payment of the agreed value, the defendants will be unduly and unjustly enriched at the expense of the plaintiff W.J. Somerville who will suffer the complete loss of the warehouse building which by bona fide mistake of fact he constructed upon the land of the defendants. Here, in that situation, to use the language of the Supreme Court of Michigan in Hardy v. Burroughs, 251 Mich. 578, 232 N.W. 200, "It is not equitable . . . that defendants profit by plaintiffs' innocent mistake, that defendants take all and plaintiffs nothing."

To prevent such unjust enrichment of the defendants, and to do equity between the parties, this Court holds that an improver of land owned by another, who through a reasonable mistake of fact and in good faith erects a building entirely upon the land of the owner, with reasonable belief that such land was owned by the improver, is entitled to recover the value of the improvements from the landowner and to a lien upon such property which may be sold to enforce the payment of such lien, or, in the alternative, to purchase the land so improved upon payment to the landowner of the value of the land less the improvements and such landowner, even though free from any inequitable conduct in connection with the construction of the building upon his land, who, however, retains but refuses to pay for the improvements, must, within a reasonable time, either pay the improver the amount by which the value of his land has been improved or convey such land to the improver upon the payment by the improver to the landowner of the value of the land without the improvements. . . .

CAPLAN, Judge, [with whom BERRY, J., joins], dissenting:

Respectfully, but firmly, I dissent from the decision of the majority in this case. Although the majority expresses a view which it says would result in equitable treatment for both parties, I am of the opinion that such view is clearly contrary to law and to the principles of equity and that such holding, if carried into effect, will establish a dangerous precedent. . . .

I am aware of the apparent alarmist posture of my statements asserting that the adoption of the majority view will establish a dangerous precedent. Nonetheless, I believe just that and feel that my apprehension is justified. On the basis of unjust enrichment and equity, the majority has decided that the errant party who, without improper design, has encroached upon an innocent owner's property is entitled to equitable treatment. That is, that he should be made whole. How is this accomplished? It is accomplished by requiring the owner of the property to buy the building erroneously constructed on his property or by forcing (by court edict) such owner to sell his property for an amount to be determined by the court.

What of the property owner's right? The solution offered by the majority is designed to favor the plaintiff, the only party who had a duty to determine which lot was the proper one and who made a mistake. The defendants in this case, the owners of the property, had no duty to perform and were not parties to the mistake. Does equity protect only the errant and ignore the faultless? Certainly not.

It is not unusual for a property owner to have long range plans for his property. He should be permitted to feel secure in the ownership of such property by virtue of placing his deed therefor on record. He should be permitted to feel secure in his future plans for such property. However, if the decision expressed in the majority opinion is effectuated then security of ownership in property becomes a fleeting thing. It is very likely that a property owner in the circumstances of the instant case either cannot readily afford the building mistakenly built on his land or that such building does not suit his purpose. Having been entirely without fault, he should not be forced to purchase the building.

In my opinion for the court to permit the plaintiff to force the defendants to sell their property contrary to their wishes is unthinkable and unpardonable. This is nothing less than condemnation of private property by private parties for private use. Condemnation of property (eminent domain) is reserved for government or such entities as may be designated by the legislature. Under no theory of law or equity should an individual be permitted to acquire property by condemnation. The majority would allow just that.

I am aware of the doctrine that equity frowns on unjust enrichment. However, contrary to the view expressed by the majority, I am of the opinion that the circumstances of this case do not warrant the application of such doctrine. It clearly is the accepted law that as between two parties in the circumstances of this case he who made the mistake must suffer the hardship rather than he who was without fault.

I would reverse the judgment of the Circuit Court of Wood County and remand the case to that court with directions that the trial court give the defendant, Jacobs, the party without fault, the election of purchasing the building, of selling the property, *or* of requiring the plaintiff to remove the building from defendant's property.

Notes & Questions

1. **Calabresi & Melamed.** In a seminal 1972 article, Professor, now Judge, Guido Calabresi and Douglas Melamed explained that courts in encroachment and other property cases must make two determinations. First, courts must decide which party to favor. In *Peters*, for example, should the court award the Peters an entitlement against encroachments on their property, or should it award the Archambaults an entitlement to innocently encroach on their neighbor's property? Second, how should the court enforce the entitlement? If the court awards the entitlement to the Peters, for example, should it issue an injunction ordering the encroachment removed, or should the court award damages equal to the decreased value of the Peters' property? Guido Calabresi & A. Douglas Melamed, Property Rules, Liability Rules, and Inalienability: One View of the Cathedral, 85 Harv. L. Rev. 1089 (1972).

According to Calabresi and Melamed, the latter choice is between enforcing entitlements through a *property rule* (injunctive relief) or through a *liability rule* (damages). Under a property rule, no one can take a right holder's entitlement "unless the holder sells it willingly and at the price at which he subjectively values the property." If the Archambaults wanted to keep their house on the Peters' property, they would have to pay the Peters whatever they demand for the right. Under a liability rule, the court permits a transfer of the entitlement for the court-determined value of the entitlement. The Archambaults could continue to encroach if they paid court-determined damages to the Peters.[1]

2. **General Law of Encroachments.** The entitlement question is clear in the typical encroachment case: the landowner has an entitlement against encroachments. The controversial issue, as *Peters* demonstrates, is how to enforce the entitlement. Historically courts stood ready to order the removal of any and all encroachments, no matter how little the structures encroached on the landowners' property and no matter how innocent the encroachers. Courts still issue injunctions where the encroachment is intentional or even, in most cases, negligent. See Seymour v. Harris Trust & Savings Bank, 636 N.E.2d 985 (Ill. App. 1994).

In the case of innocent encroachments, by contrast, courts today will typically "balance the equities" in determining whether to issue an injunction. "A mandatory injunction to compel the removal of buildings or other structures wrongfully placed on the land of another will not be granted when it will operate inequitably or oppressively, or where the encroachment is trifling and the result of an innocent mistake and the damage caused to defendant by removal would be greatly disproportionate to the interest which plaintiff claims." Stuttgart Electric Co. v. Riceland Seed Co., 802 S.W.2d 484, 487 (Ark. App. 1991) (refusing to order the removal of a warehouse which encroached 2.3 feet onto the plaintiff's property). In these cases, the landowner is relegated to compensatory damages. See Capodilupo v. Vozzella, 704 N.E.2d 534 (Mass. App. 1999) (refusing to enjoin a wall that encroached 3.6–4.8 inches); Kratze v. Independent Order of Oddfellows, 500 N.W.2d 115 (Mich. 1993) (refusing to enjoin a lodge building that encroached 1.2 feet); Szymczak v. LaFerrara, 655 A.2d 76 (N.J. Super. 1995) (refusing to enjoin a 19 foot encroachment where the land was vacant and held for future sale); Seid v. Ross, 853 P.2d 308 (Ore. App. 1993) (3 ½ inch encroachment).

Peters v. Archambault thus represents a distinctly minority view. The Massachusetts Supreme Judicial Council nonetheless continues to favor injunctive relief in encroachment cases. In Goulding v. Cook, 661 N.E.2d 1322 (Mass. 1996), the Cooks built a septic tank on a 2,998 square foot triangle of land that even the local assessor believed was the Cooks' property, but unfortunately belonged to the Gouldings. Reversing the appeals court, the Supreme Judicial Council ordered an injunction issued

1. Calabresi & Melamed also suggested that the law can protect an entitlement through *rules of inalienability*. Here the law "not only decides who is to own something and what price is to be paid for it if it is taken or destroyed, but also regulates its sale—by, for example, prescribing preconditions for a valid sale or forbidding a sale altogether."

even though the septic tank was entirely underground and would be costly to relocate. According to the court,

> It is commonplace today that property rights are not absolute, and that the law may condition their use and enjoyment so that the interests of the public in general or of some smaller segment of the public, perhaps even just immediate neighbors, are not unduly prejudiced.... But, except in "exceptional" cases, we draw the line at permanent physical occupations amounting to a transfer of a traditional estate in land.... [W]e are committed to maintaining it, because the concept of private property represents a moral and political commitment that a pervasive disposition to balance away would utterly destroy.

3. From a policy standpoint, what is wrong with issuing an injunction requiring encroachments to be removed? In *Peters*, the dissenting judge suggests two points. First, he argues that issuing the Peters an injunction "would result in the destruction of the defendants' dwelling," imposing "substantial cost and inconvenience which are entirely disproportionate to the injury to the plaintiffs." Does this argument overlook the opportunity for negotiations between the parties after the decision? If the cost of removing the encroachment is far greater than the injury to the Peters, won't the Archambaults offer to pay the Peters not to enforce the injunction? Won't the Peters and Archambaults find some mutually acceptable price? In a fascinating study, Professor Ward Farnsworth has found that parties to property disputes do not engage in post-injunction negotiations because of animosity and an antipathy for monetary bargaining involving rights. See Ward Farnsworth, Do Parties to Nuisance Cases Bargain After Judgment? A Glimpse Inside the Cathedral, 66 U. Chi. L. Rev. 373 (1999) (study of 20 nuisance cases). See also Ward Farnsworth, The Economics of Enmity, 69 U. Chi. L. Rev. 211 (2002); Peter H. Huang, Reasons Within Passions: Emotions and Intentions in Property Rights Bargaining, 79 Or. L. Rev. 435 (2000).

Second, the judge suggests that the injunction would give the Peters "an unexpected windfall" and involve the court in "what practically amounts to extortion." Doesn't that imply that there will be a transfer of the entitlement? Even assuming that the Peters hold out for a stiff price, why is that "extortion"? For considerations of these issues, see Barton H. Thompson, Jr., Injunction Negotiations: An Economic, Moral, and Legal Analysis, 27 Stan. L. Rev. 1563 (1975); Stewart E. Sterk, Neighbors in American Land Law, 87 Colum. L. Rev. 55 (1987).

4. On the other side of the equation, what's the harm in relegating landowners to damages in encroachment cases? Damage awards are typically based on the testimony of real estate appraisers as to the "fair market value" of an *easement*, or right to build, on the encroached portion of land.[2] Is there any reason to believe that such damage awards will systematically understate the actual damage to the landowner? Historically courts held

2. Easements are discussed in detail in Chapter 10.

that damages were an inadequate remedy in property cases because land is "unique" and not always replaceable with other land. Yet this principle "originated when land was the dominant form of wealth in society and when tract houses and condominiums did not exist." Douglas Laycock, The Death of the Irreparable Injury Rule, 103 Harv. L. Rev. 688, 703–705 (1990). Is property more fungible today? Should that make a difference in deciding whether damages are an adequate remedy?

5. Who is in a better position to protect themselves against the cost of encroachments—encroachers or their neighbors? Before building something, most people have their property surveyed to determine their property lines. If the surveyor fails to exercise reasonable care in preparing his report and plat of the property, the builder can sue for negligence. If the builder purchases a "guaranteed survey," he or she can proceed against the guarantee in case of error without even worrying about negligence. Should this influence the choice between injunctive relief and damages?

6. In *Peters v. Archambault*, should it have mattered that the Peters purchased their property *after* the Archambault's encroaching house had been built? Is the dissent correct that the encroachment necessarily would have been reflected in the purchase price that the Peters paid for their property?

7. **Improving Encroachments.** In improving encroachment cases, the owner of the land on which the encroaching structure stands generally wants to keep the structure, rather than have it removed. The common law historically held that improvements, whether made in good or bad faith, belonged to the owner of the land. The only significant exception was where the landowner knew of the mistake before the structure was built but failed to warn the encroacher. A few courts also awarded restitution to the encroacher for the value of the improvement where the landowner sought to quiet title to the land through equitable relief—"on the principle that he who seeks equity must do equity." John Henry Merryman, Improving the Lot of the Trespassing Improver, 11 Stan. L. Rev. 456 (1959).

Statutes in an overwhelming majority of states have modified the common law. Most statutes follow the approach taken in *Somerville,* entitling the true owner of the land to elect between paying for the improvement and selling the land to the encroacher. These "good faith improver" statutes typically require that the encroacher have acted in good faith and in reliance on a deed or other document that appeared to give the encroacher title to the relevant land. See, e.g., Utah Code Ann. §§ 57–6–1 to 57–6–3.

8. What do you think of the remedy proposed by Judge Caplan—giving Jacobs "the election of purchasing the building, of selling the property, *or* of requiring the plaintiff to remove the building from defendant's property"? Would the addition of the third option load the deck too heavily in Jacobs' favor? How might such an option affect any negotiations between the Somervilles and the Jacobs?

9. What if the Somervilles had accidentally built their warehouse on land owned by The Nature Conservancy? Should it make a difference if the owner of the property on which the encroachment is placed does not want her property developed?

10. **Personal Property: Accession.** Say that the Somervilles had found a stack of oak logs on lot 47; believing that the logs belonged to them—although in fact they belonged to the Jacobs—the Somervilles cut and fashioned the logs into wine casks. Who owns the casks—the Jacobs, who unwittingly contributed the raw material, or the Somervilles, who innocently contributed the labor? Under the common law of accession, the answer generally depends on the degree to which the innocent converter has transformed the raw materials and increased their value: the greater the increase, the more likely it is that the converter will be given title. For example, in Wetherbee v. Green, 22 Mich. 311 (1871), an innocent converter who increased the value of another's timber from $25 to nearly $700 by making it into barrel hoops, was held to have title in the hoops. Note, however, that this rule applies only to innocent converters. If the converter knows the raw materials are not hers, she must return them, as improved, to their owner.

Say that the converter adds not only her labor, but also her own raw materials, to another's chattels. For example, the Somervilles take possession of the Jacobs' pick-up truck, paint it, and replace its seat covers. The law of accession will give title to the owner of the "principal goods"—presumably, in this case, the Jacobs as owners of the truck. The most striking feature of this rule is that it is indifferent to the converter's state of mind. Thus, if the Somervilles knowingly stole paint and fabric from the Jacobs' garage in order to restore the Somerville family car, the Somervilles would retain title to the car *and* the paint and fabric.

3. LIMITS ON THE RIGHT TO EXCLUDE

Despite Blackstone's description of property rights as despotic, property owners have never enjoyed the absolute power to exclude anyone from their property whenever they want. The right to exclude sometimes clashes with other public values, forcing courts and legislatures to decide how best to balance the competing interests.

Brooks v. Chicago Downs Association, Inc.

United States Court of Appeals for the Seventh Circuit, 1986.
791 F.2d 512.

FLAUM, Circuit Judge.

This is a case of first impression on whether under Illinois law the operator of a horse race track has the absolute right to exclude a patron from the track premises for any reason, or no reason, except race, color, creed, national origin, or sex. We find that Illinois follows the common law rule and would allow the exclusion. The court below is thus affirmed.

I

Plaintiffs are citizens of Pennsylvania who have formed a Pennsylvania partnership whose sole purpose is to pool the assets of the partners in order to place bets at horse racing tracks throughout the country. The plaintiffs are self-proclaimed expert handicappers, even though on the approximately 140 days they have bet at various race tracks they have ended up with net losses on 110 of those days. This case is about a bet they were not allowed to make.

The defendant is a private Illinois corporation licensed by the State of Illinois to conduct harness racing at Sportsman's Park race track in Cicero, Illinois. At various times during the racing season, Sportsman's Park conducts a parimutual pool known as "Super Bet." In order to win the Super Bet pool, one must select the first two finishers of the fifth and sixth races and the first three finishers of the seventh race. The Super Bet pool is able to increase quickly and substantially because if the pool is not won on any given day, the total amount wagered is rolled over and added to the Super Bet purse for the next racing date. For example, in April of 1985 the plaintiffs, using their method for handicapping horses, placed bets on the Super Bet totalling $60,000. They picked the right horses and took home approximately $600,000.

In late July, 1985 the president of Chicago Downs ordered two of the plaintiffs (Jeffrey Yass and Kenneth Brodie) barred from Sportsman's Park just as they were seeking to place a $250,000 wager in the Super Bet. After the plaintiffs had been barred from Sportsman's Park, the Park's counsel informed them that they would be denied entry to all future racing dates at the Park. The plaintiffs then filed suit seeking injunctive relief that would prohibit the defendant from barring them from entering the race track premises. Sportsman's Park filed a motion to dismiss the complaint on the ground that under Illinois law the operator of a proprietary race track has the absolute right to exclude a patron from the track premises for any reason except race, creed, color, national origin, or sex. The trial court agreed with the defendants and granted their motion to dismiss, from which the plaintiffs now appeal. We affirm.

II

. . .

The parties do not contest the Illinois Supreme Court's holding that a race track operator has the right to exclude patrons for good cause. Phillips v. Graham, 86 Ill. 2d 274, 427 N.E.2d 550, 56 Ill. Dec. 355 (1981). But in this case, the race track argues that it should be able to exclude a patron absent any cause at all, as long as it does not do so on the basis of race, color, creed, national origin, or sex. Under the defendant's theory, because the race track is a privately owned place of amusement it may exclude someone simply for wearing a green hat or a paisley tie. It need give no reason for excluding the patron, under its version of the common law, because it is not a state-granted monopoly, but a state-regulated licensee operating on private property.

.... Illinois follows the common law rule regarding the exclusion of patrons.... Of the cases cited by the Illinois courts as demonstrating the common law rule, Madden v. Queens County Jockey Club, 296 N.Y. 249, 72 N.E.2d 697 (Ct. App.), cert. denied, 332 U.S. 761 (1947), is the most explicit and most cited. The plaintiff, "Coley" Madden, who claimed to be a professional "patron of the races," was barred from the defendant's Aqueduct Race Track under the mistaken belief that he was "Owney" Madden, reputed to be the fabled Frank Costello's bookmaker. Coley Madden brought suit for declaratory judgment and contended that as a citizen and taxpayer he had the right to enter the track and patronize the races.... The Court of Appeals framed the question: "Whether the operator of a race track can, without reason or sufficient excuse, exclude a person from attending its races." 72 N.E.2d at 698. Its answer: "In our opinion he can; he has the power to admit as spectators only those whom he may select, and to exclude others solely of his own [volition,] as long as the exclusion is not founded on race, creed, color or national origin." 72 N.E.2d at 698.

The court went on to explain the common law:

> At common law a person engaged in a public calling, such as innkeeper or common carrier, was held to be under a duty to the general public and was obliged to serve, without discrimination, all who sought service. On the other hand, proprietors of private enterprises, such as places of amusement and resort, were under no such obligation, enjoying an absolute power to serve whom they pleased. A race track, of course, falls within that classification.

72 N.E.2d at 698 (emphasis added)....

In holding that Illinois follows the traditional common law rule we are not unmindful that several other states have questioned that rule as a matter both of law and of policy.... We also choose not to follow the arguable—but not clear—abandonment of the common law rule in New Jersey in the case of Uston v. Resorts International Hotel, Inc., 89 N.J. 163, 445 A.2d 370 (1982). In 1959 the New Jersey Supreme Court decided Garifine v. Monmouth Park Jockey Club, 29 N.J. 47, 148 A.2d 1 (Sup. Ct. 1959), which was an appeal from the trial court's refusal to grant the plaintiff injunctive relief from his exclusion from Monmouth Park race track. The defendant race track, relying on *Madden*, moved to dismiss the complaint on the ground that it had "an absolute right" to exclude the plaintiff. On appeal, the plaintiff contended that the operator of a race track should not have the common law right to exclude a patron without reasonable cause and that under the New Jersey Civil Rights Act the operator did not have such authority. In a scholarly opinion the court traced the genesis of the right of race tracks to exclude patrons without justifying the exclusion:

> There was a time in English history when the common law recognized in many callings the duty to serve the public without

> discrimination. With the passing of time and the changing of conditions, the common law confined this duty to exceptional callings where the needs of the public urgently called for its continuance. Innkeepers and common carriers may be said to be the most notable illustrations of business operators who, both under early principles and under the common law today, are obliged to serve the public without discrimination. On the other hand, operators of most businesses, including places of amusement such as race tracks, have never been placed under any such common-law obligation, for no comparable considerations of public policy have ever so dictated....

148 A.2d at 6–7.

However, in 1982 the New Jersey Supreme Court decided *Uston* in which the plaintiff was a practitioner of a strategy of playing blackjack known as "card counting." The defendant operated a gambling casino licensed pursuant to the New Jersey Casino Control Act. The defendant excluded Uston from the blackjack tables in its casino because of Uston's strategy of "card counting." The New Jersey Supreme Court held that the Casino Control Act gave the Casino Control Commission the exclusive authority to exclude patrons based upon their strategies for playing licensed casino games and that any common law right the defendant may have had to exclude Uston for these reasons was abrogated by the Act and outweighed by Uston's right of access. *Uston*, 445 A.2d at 372.

In Marzocca v. Ferone, 93 N.J. 509, 461 A.2d 1133 (1983), the owner of a harness race horse was barred from racing that horse at Freehold Raceway in New Jersey. The appellate court determined that *Uston* overruled Garifine v. Monmouth Park Jockey Club, *sub silentio*, and remanded the case to the trial court to hear evidence as to whether the race track's exclusion was reasonable. The case was then appealed to the New Jersey Supreme Court, where the court clarified its decision in *Uston* and reversed the appellate court, stating:

> Notwithstanding the dicta in *Uston*, we must part company with the court below on the issue of Freehold's right to exclude. Without commenting on the status of the law in the amusement owner/patron context, we hold that the racetrack's common law right to exclude exists in the context of this case, i.e., where the relationship [is] between the track management and persons who wish to perform their vocational activities on the track premises.

461 A.2d at 1137. Therefore, it is clear that New Jersey has not *per se* abandoned the common law rule but has adapted it, in a limited fashion, to the particular needs of its casino industry....

However, the New Jersey decisions do paint the wider policy picture of which our decision today is a part. As a policy matter, it is arguably unfair to allow a place of amusement to exclude for any reason or no reason, and to be free of accountability, except in cases of obvious discrimination. In this case, the general public is not only invited but, through advertising, is encouraged to come to the race track and wager on the races' outcome. But the common law allows the race track to exclude patrons, no matter if they come from near or far, or in reasonable reliance on representations of accessibility. We may ultimately believe that market forces would preclude any outrageous excesses—such as excluding anyone who has blond hair, or (like the plaintiffs) who is from Pennsylvania, or (even more outrageous) who has $250,000 to spend in one day of betting. But the premise of the consumer protection laws that the New Jersey Supreme Court alluded to in *Uston* and *Marzocca* recognizes that the reality of an imperfect market allows numerous consumer depredations. Excluding a patron simply because he is named Adam Smith arguably offends the very precepts of equality and fair dealing expressed in everything from the antitrust statutes to the Illinois Consumer Fraud and Deceptive Business Practice Act. Ill. Rev. Stat. ch. 121 ½, ¶ ¶ 262–73.

But the market here is not so demonstrably imperfect that there is a monopoly or any allegation of consumer fraud. Consequently, there is no such explicit legislative directive in the context of patrons attending horse races in Illinois—so the common law rule, relic though it may be,[3] still controls. . . .

III

For the foregoing reasons the court below is affirmed.

Notes & Questions

1. **Common Law Privileges.** The common law has always recognized exceptions to a landowner's right to exclude others from his or her property. Indeed, the traditional *privileges* to trespass take up an entire chapter of the Restatement of Torts. See Restatement of Torts, Second, §§ 167–215. Public officials, such as police, fire fighters, and health inspectors, are privileged to trespass on others' property in the course of their official investigations—although constitutional restrictions on searches, seizures, and arrests limit the use of this common law privilege. Citizens also enjoy a privilege of "necessity" to trespass across another's land where necessary to put out a fire, avoid a nuisance, or get around a blocked highway.

What is the rationale for these traditional privileges? Professor Richard Epstein has argued that, absent these privileges, property owners would enjoy monopoly power that could end up thwarting valuable societal activity. According to Epstein, the market normally ensures that land is used in a reasonable fashion. "As long as there are many buyers and sellers, robust markets will emerge in which any abuse of discretion in the

3. As the New Jersey Supreme Court noted in *Uston*, the rise of the American common law right to exclude without cause alarmingly corresponds to the fall of the old segregation laws. However, that is clearly not an issue in this case because the legislature has justly limited the absolute right to exclude to cases not involving exclusion based on race, creed, color, national origin, or sex. *Uston*, 445 A.2d at 374 n.4.

exercise of rights is effectively restrained, not by the heavy-handed use of governmental power, but by the presence of alternative buyers and sellers." Richard A. Epstein, Rights & "Rights Talk," 105 Harv. L. Rev. 1106 (1992). But this is not the case where, for example, fire fighters have to cross private property to get to a fire or a motorist must cross the edge of someone's property to avoid a blocked highway. See Richard A. Epstein, Property & Necessity, 13 Harv. J.L. & Pub. Poly. 2 (1990).

2. Epstein believes that monopoly power also explains why the common law has long imposed a duty on innkeepers and "common carriers," such as trains, buses, and planes, to serve all members of the public without discrimination. See Richard A. Epstein, Takings, Exclusivity and Speech: The Legacy of *PruneYard v. Robins*, 64 U. Chi. L. Rev. 21 (1997). Are there other rationales for the common law duty to serve?

3. Why shouldn't the common law duty to serve be extended to amusement places like racetracks? As the Seventh Circuit observes in *Brooks*, the New Jersey Supreme Court extended the common law duty to casinos in Uston v. Resorts International Hotel, Inc., 445 A.2d 370 (N.J. 1982). In *Uston*, Resorts International tried to exclude Kenneth Uston, a known card counter, for playing at its blackjack tables. In deciding to extend to casinos the common law duty to serve the public, the court argued that "the more private property is devoted to public use, the more it must accommodate the rights which inhere in individual members of the general public who use that property." Id., quoting State v. Schmid, 423 A.2d 615, 629 (N.J. 1980). The court concluded that casinos can exclude people who threaten security or disrupt activities, but otherwise must serve all customers.

New Jersey remains alone among American jurisdictions in expanding the common law duty to places of amusement. See Uston v. Airport Casino, Inc., 564 F.2d 1216 (9th Cir. 1977) (refusing to extend the common law duty to casinos under Nevada law); Nation v. Apache Greyhound Park, Inc., 579 P.2d 580 (Ariz. App. 1978) (refusing to extend the duty to race tracks).

4. **Civil Rights Laws.** Building on the common law duty of common carriers, Congress and most state legislatures have enacted laws prohibiting businesses open to the public from discriminating on the basis of race, color, creed, national origin, sex, or disability. Title II of the Civil Rights Act of 1964 prohibits "discrimination or segregation on the ground of race, color, religion, or national origin" in any "place of public accommodation"—defined to include inns, restaurants, theaters, concert halls, sports arenas, and any "other place of exhibition or entertainment." 42 U.S.C. § 2000a.

Many state anti-discrimination laws are even more expansive, both in the types of discrimination that they preclude and the types of facilities covered. The California Civil Rights Act, for example, provides that "All persons within the jurisdiction of this state are free and equal, and no matter what their sex, race, color, religion, ancestry, national origin, disability, or medical condition are entitled to the full and equal accommodations, advantages, facilities, privileges, or services in all business establishments of every kind whatsoever." Cal. Civ. Code §§ 51–52.

5. Should rules against discrimination extend beyond what traditionally have been considered "public" facilities? Title II of the federal Civil Rights Act of 1964, for example, explicitly does not apply to a "private club or other establishment not in fact open to the public, except to the extent that the facilities of such establishment are made available to the customers or patrons of an establishment" otherwise within the scope of Title II. 42 U.S.C. § 2000a(e). The federal Civil Rights Act of 1866, 42 U.S.C. § 1981, and various state anti-discrimination laws, however, have been used to successfully challenge discrimination by at least some "private" clubs. See, e.g., Watson v. Fraternal Order of Eagles, 915 F.2d 235 (6th Cir. 1990) (Civil Rights Act of 1866 bars racial discrimination by Fraternal Order of Eagles); Gibbs–Alfano v. Ossining Boat & Canoe Club, 47 F. Supp. 2d 506 (S.D.N.Y. 1999) (Civil Rights Act of 1866 bars discrimination by boat club against interracial couple); Frank v. Ivy Club, 576 A.2d 241 (N.J. 1990) (New Jersey Law Against Discrimination prohibits sex discrimination by eating clubs at Princeton University).

6. For more on efforts under anti-discrimination laws to limit property owners' ability to exclude, see Joseph William Singer, No Right to Exclude: Public Accommodations and Private Property, 90 Nw. U.L. Rev. 1283 (1996); Edith M. Hofmeister, Women Need Not Apply: Discrimination and the Supreme Court's Intimate Association Test, 28 U.S.F. L. Rev. 1009 (1994); Steven Sutherland, Patron's Right of Access to Premises Generally Open to the Public, 1983 U. Ill. L. Rev. 533 (1983).

New Jersey Coalition Against War in the Middle East v. J.M.B. Realty Corp.

Supreme Court of New Jersey, 1994.
650 A.2d 757.

The opinion of the Court was delivered by WILENTZ, C.J.

The question in this case is whether the defendant regional and community shopping centers must permit leafletting on societal issues. We hold that they must, subject to reasonable conditions set by them. Our ruling is limited to leafletting at such centers, and it applies nowhere else. It is based on our citizens' right of free speech embodied in our State Constitution....

In the summer and fall of 1990 our government and our country were debating what action, if any, should be taken in response to Iraq's invasion of Kuwait.... Plaintiff—a coalition of numerous groups—opposed military intervention and sought public support for its views. For that purpose, plaintiff decided to conduct a massive leafletting campaign on November 9 and November 10, urging the public to contact Congress to persuade Senators and Representatives to vote against military intervention. The November 9 effort was aimed at commuter stops around the State. The

November 10 targets were shopping centers, the ten very large regional and community shopping centers whose owners are the defendants herein. . . .

On November 10 plaintiff's members and representatives went to the malls and requested permission to leaflet. Four of the defendant malls granted plaintiff permission to leaflet on their premises, and plaintiff did in fact leaflet at two of those malls. Monmouth Mall initially denied plaintiff's request, but later issued plaintiff a permit to use its community booth for two days in January, and even provided professional signs and displays for the group. Plaintiff used the booth on those days. The conditions imposed by mall management, however, made it difficult for plaintiff to reach the public. Among other restrictions, plaintiff was not allowed to approach passersby to offer them literature. The Mall at Mill Creek, Cherry Hill Mall, and Woodbridge Center granted plaintiff permission to use their community booths, but required that plaintiff obtain or show proof of liability insurance in the amounts of $1,000,000 for bodily injury and $50,000 to $1,000,000 for property damage. Plaintiff was unable to obtain the necessary insurance, and requested that the malls waive the requirement. Woodbridge Center waived the insurance requirements, allowing plaintiff to distribute leaflets from a table, while The Mall at Mill Creek and Cherry Hill Mall refused.

Although the six remaining malls refused permission, one of those malls—Hamilton—ultimately allowed plaintiff to leaflet. While it initially denied permission, asking plaintiff to leave the premises, it eventually allowed plaintiff to leaflet undisturbed for approximately three to four hours.

As a consequence of defendants' refusal to allow plaintiff access to the malls, and the restrictions imposed on such access where allowed, few of the thousands of people at those malls on November 10 learned of plaintiff's views. . . .

Each of the ten defendant shopping centers is very large. For instance, one defendant mall, Woodbridge Center, serves an area with a population of 1,400,000. On an average day in 1990, approximately 28,750 people shopped there. November 10, 1990, however, was not an average day. Not only was the tenth a Saturday, a day that is generally very busy for shopping malls, but it was also part of Veterans' Day weekend. Thus, presumably many more people visited malls on that day than on an average day. Indeed, plaintiff's witnesses testified that they sought to leaflet on that day because of the large expected turnout of shoppers during the holiday weekend.

Nine of the defendant shopping centers are "regional centers." . . . The regional centers involved in this case have from 93 to 244 tenants. . . . The acreage of the regional centers ranges from 31.44 to 238 acres.

The tenth defendant is a "community" shopping center. A community center is smaller than a regional center and lacks the variety of merchandise available at a regional mall. . . . The only community center involved in this case, the Mall at Mill Creek, covers twenty-seven acres. It has a discount department store, a supermarket, sixty-two smaller retail stores, and a seven-restaurant food court....

III

We shall briefly summarize the lengthy history of the law of free speech that underlies this case. The relevant historical starting point is Marsh v. Alabama, 326 U.S. 501 (1946). In *Marsh*, the United States Supreme Court held that the First Amendment's guarantee of free speech[a] was violated when the private owners of a company town prevented distribution of literature in its downtown business district. Finding that the company town had all the attributes of a municipality, the Court held that the private owner's action was "state action" for constitutional free speech purposes. In a democracy, the Court recognized, citizens "must make decisions which affect the welfare of community and nation. To act as good citizens they must be informed. In order to enable them to be properly informed their information must be uncensored." Id. at 508. The paramount right of the citizens to be informed overrode the rights of the property owners in the constitutional balance.

The question whether citizens may exercise a right of free speech at privately-owned shopping centers without permission of the owners has been litigated extensively. The first time the question came before the Supreme Court, the Court upheld the right of free speech at shopping centers. Amalgamated Food Employees Union Local 590 v. Logan Valley Plaza, 391 U.S. 308 (1968). Clearly relying on *Marsh*, the majority in *Logan Valley* ruled that shopping centers are the functional equivalent of downtown business districts and that the private owners could therefore not interfere with the exercise of the right of free speech. For First Amendment purposes that interference constituted "state action." The Court implied, but did not hold, that an unrestricted free speech right existed. *Logan Valley* was thereafter "limited" by Lloyd Corp. v. Tanner, 407 U.S. 551 (1972), which held that war protesters had no right of free speech at shopping centers. The Court distinguished *Logan Valley*, confining it to the situation in which the speech was related to shopping center activities—a labor dispute involving one of the center's tenants—and in which no alternative was available for the expression of views—such as the public sidewalks that surrounded the center in *Lloyd*.

The Court in Hudgens v. NLRB, 424 U.S. 507 (1976), reviewing both *Logan Valley* and *Lloyd*, concluded not only that the reasoning of the latter amounted to a total rejection of the former, but that even the limited right of free speech (namely, that relating to shopping center activities) approved in *Lloyd* did not exist. That view was reaffirmed in PruneYard Shopping Center v. Robins, 447 U.S. 74 (1980). Those cases, *Hudgens* and *Prune-*

a. Eds.—The First Amendment of the United States Constitution provides in relevant part that "Congress shall make no law ... abridging the freedom of speech, or of the press; or of the right of the people peaceably to assemble, and to petition the government for a redress of grievances."

Yard, essentially held that the First Amendment right found in *Marsh* was limited to a privately-owned factory town, an entity that performed substantially all of the functions of government. Its actions were therefore akin to "state action," thereby triggering First Amendment protection. Not so the actions of shopping centers, whose functional equivalence to a town was limited to the downtown business district.

It is now clear that the Federal Constitution affords no general right to free speech in privately-owned shopping centers, and most State courts facing the issue have ruled the same way when State constitutional rights have been asserted....

California, Oregon, Massachusetts, Colorado, and Washington, however, have held that their citizens have a right to engage in certain types of expressive conduct at privately-owned malls. Of those five, only California has held that its free speech clause protects citizens from private action as well as state action and grants issue-oriented free speech rights at a regional shopping center. Robins v. PruneYard Shopping Ctr., 592 P.2d 341, 347 (Cal. 1979), aff'd, 447 U.S. 74 (1980). [In giving citizens a right of access for expressive purposes, Massachusetts relied on its constitution's "free-and-equal elections" provision; Oregon and Washington relied on their constitutions' initiative provisions.]

IV

In New Jersey, we have once before discussed the application of our State constitutional right of free speech to private conduct.[b] In State v. Schmid, 423 A.2d 615 (N.J. 1980), appeal dismissed sub nom. Princeton University v. Schmid, 455 U.S. 100 (1982), we held that the right conferred by the State Constitution was secure not only from State interference but—under certain conditions—from the interference of an owner of private property even when exercised on that private property. Specifically, we held that Schmid, though lacking permission from Princetown University, had the right to enter the campus, distribute leaflets, and sell political materials. We ruled that the right of free speech could be exercised on the campus subject to the University's reasonable regulations....

A

We found in *Schmid* that Princeton University, in pursuit of its own educational mission, had invited the public to participate in the intellectual life of the University in various ways, including participation in discussions of current and controversial issues. The University not only underlined its interest in free speech in various statements of policy, but in the imperative of extending participation beyond the student body so that both different views and groups would be heard. We found that this invitation included participation in various formal meetings of committees and clubs, invitations to both specific individuals and groups outside of the University body, and on occasion general invitations to the public. We held that all of these

b. Eds.—Article I, paragraph 6, of the New Jersey Constitution provides that "No law shall be passed to restrain or abridge the liberty of speech or of the press."

factors had the effect of opening up Princeton's property to a limited public use and that the activity sought to be carried on by Schmid was consonant with that use....

Schmid set forth "several elements" to be considered in determining the existence and extent of the State free speech right on privately-owned property. The three factors mentioned in that opinion as the "relevant considerations," have been the focus of the argument before us. As we noted in that case:

> This standard must take into account (1) the nature, purposes, and primary use of such private property, generally, its "normal" use, (2) the extent and nature of the public's invitation to use that property, and (3) the purpose of the expressional activity undertaken upon such property in relation to both the private and public use of the property. This is a multi-faceted test which must be applied to ascertain whether in a given case owners of private property may be required to permit, subject to suitable restrictions, the reasonable exercise by individuals of the constitutional freedoms of speech and assembly.

...

B

...

The normal use of these properties and the nature and extent of the public's invitation to use them (the first two elements) are best considered together, for in this case they are most closely interrelated.... The predominant characteristic of the normal use of these properties is its all-inclusiveness. Found at these malls are most of the uses and activities citizens engage in outside their homes. That predominant characteristic is not at all changed by the fact that the primary purpose of the centers is profit and the primary use is commercial. Within and without the enclosures are not only stores of every kind and size, but large open spaces available to the public and suitable for numerous uses. There is space to roam, to sit down, and to talk. The public is invited to exercise by walking through the centers before the retail stores have opened for business. There are theaters, restaurants, professional offices, meeting rooms, and almost always a community table or booth where various groups can promote causes and different activities taking place within their local area.

The invitation to the public is simple: "Come here, that's all we ask. We hope you will buy, but you do not have to, and you need not intend to. All we ask is that you come here. You can do whatever you want so long as you do not interfere with other visitors."....

The almost limitless public use of defendants' property, its inclusion of numerous expressive uses, its total transformation of private property to the mirror image of a downtown business district and beyond that, a replica of the community itself, gives rise to an implied invitation of constitutional dimensions that cannot be obliterated by defendants' attempted denial of that invitation, an implied invitation that includes leafletting on controversial issues. The regional and community shopping centers have achieved their goal: they have become today's downtown and to some extent their own community; their invitation has brought everyone there for all purposes. Those purposes in fact—regardless of their clear subjective profit motive—go far beyond buying goods; they include not only expressive uses but so many different uses without any commonality other than the mix of uses that define a community, and in terms of the centers' motivation, almost anything that will bring people to the centers. This is the new, the improved, the more attractive downtown business district—the new community—and no use is more closely associated with the old downtown than leafletting. Defendants have taken that old downtown away from its former home and moved all of it, except free speech, to the suburbs. In a country where free speech found its home in the downtown business district, these centers can no more avoid speech than a playground avoid children, a library its readers, or a park its strollers....

The third factor, the relationship between "the purpose of the expressional activity ... to both the private and public use of the property," *Schmid*, supra, examines the compatibility of the free speech sought to be exercised with the uses of the property. We note preliminarily that where expressive activity is permitted and therefore compatible with those uses, presumptively so is leafletting, and the burden should fall on those who claim it is not. More importantly, we find that the more than two hundred years of compatibility between free speech and the downtown business district is proof enough of its compatibility with these shopping centers. The downtown business districts at one time thrived: no one has ever contended that free speech and leafletting hurt them....

These centers have full power to minimize whatever slight discordance might otherwise exist; full power to adopt rules and regulations concerning the time, place, and manner of such leafletting, regulations that will assure beyond question that the leafletting does not interfere with the shopping center's business while at the same time preserving the effectiveness of plaintiff's exercise of their constitutional right....

C

We decide this case not only on the basis of the three-pronged test in *Schmid*, but also by the general balancing of expressional rights and private property rights. The standard and its elements are specifically designed with that balancing in mind. A more general analysis of the balance provides a further test of the correctness of our determination.

The essence of the balance is fairly described by Justice Handler in *Schmid*:

> Private property does not "lose its private character merely because the public is generally invited to use it for designated purposes." Nevertheless, as private property becomes, on a sliding scale, committed either more or less to public use and enjoyment,

> there is actuated, in effect, a counterbalancing between expressional and property rights.

Id. at 561 (quoting Lloyd Corp. v. Tanner, 407 U.S. 551, 569 (1972)) (citations omitted)....

There is no doubt about the outcome of this balance. On one side, the weight of the private property owners' interest in controlling and limiting activities on their property has greatly diminished in view of the uses permitted and invited on that property. The private property owners in this case, the operators of regional and community malls, have intentionally transformed their property into a public square or market, a public gathering place, a downtown business district, a community; they have told this public in every way possible that the property is theirs, to come to, to visit, to do what they please, and hopefully to shop and spend; they have done so in many ways, but mostly through the practically unlimited permitted public uses found and encouraged on their property. The sliding scale cannot slide any farther in the direction of public use and diminished private property interests.

On the other side of the balance, the weight of plaintiff's free speech interest is the most substantial in our constitutional scheme. Those interests involve speech that is central to the purpose of our right of free speech....

We need not deal directly with plaintiff's common law contentions. However, in deciding the case on constitutional grounds, we draw on [multiple sources], including our common law. It lays a foundation that would vindicate the exercise of speech and assembly rights in this setting.

In State v. Shack, 277 A.2d 369 (N.J. 1971), we ruled, on common law grounds, that two employees of federally funded organizations had the right to enter private property of an operator of a migrant labor camp to aid two migrant workers who lived and worked there. The aid included an aspect of free speech, the right to give the workers information about assistance available to them under federal statutes. By bringing migrant workers to their property, the operators of these camps created a need for free speech there that could not be denied because of its private ownership. We recognized in *Shack* that in necessitous circumstances, private property rights must yield to societal interests and needs, that there must be an "accommodation between the right of the owner and the interests of the general public," that

> while society will protect the owner in his permissible interests in land, yet "... such an owner must expect to find the absoluteness of his property rights curtailed by the organs of society.... The current balance between individualism and dominance of the social interest depends not only upon political and social ideologies, but also upon the physical and social facts of the time and place under discussion."

Id. at 373 (quoting 5 Powell on Real Property (Patrick J. Rohan, ed., 1970)).

. . .

GARIBALDI, J., dissenting....

We should not lose sight of the fact that persons who own and operate shopping malls are merchants. As such they should not be required to provide forum, place, or occasion for speech making, petition signing, parades, or cracker barrels, to discuss local or global events. They are in business for business sake. They are not municipalities, states, or villages, and however romantic it may be to believe that the public repair to these galvanic places, of a Saturday morning, for more than bread and salt, they are not yet instruments of the state....

The majority's opinion ignores the basic commercial purpose of these private malls, ascribes to them the downfall of urban business districts, and delegates to them the responsibility to fulfill the role once, and arguably still, played by town squares. It does all of that without any legitimate or rational justification. Moreover, the Court places burdens on the private malls that they are ill-suited to handle. Ultimately, mall owners will pass those burdens on to the consumer. The private property owner and ultimately the consumer, the forgotten person in the majority opinion, will have to pay the increased costs that result from the expanded security and other expenses associated with the public's free access to the mall for expressional activities. Unlike the municipalities that the majority thinks the malls have supplanted, malls are not exempt from most tort claims....

Plaintiffs cannot claim that they have no means to express their opinion to the public other than by distributing pamphlets in shopping malls. No evidence shows that plaintiffs could not effectively distribute their pamphlets in other areas. Indeed, according to plaintiff's November 9, 1990, press release, they distributed their materials in at least thirty locations, including several downtown areas. They were able to distribute over 85,000 pamphlets in those locations during a three-day period. Plaintiffs do not need to use the malls, save for their own convenience. "Petitioners' convenience, however, does not create a constitutional rights of access to private property for political activity." Citizens for Ethical Gov't v. Gwinnett Place Assocs., 392 S.E.2d 8, 9 (Ga. 1990)....

Justice Clifford and Judge Michels join in this opinion.

Notes & Questions

1. Since *J.M.B. Realty*, the Minnesota Supreme Court has also held that the state's interest in free speech trumps the private property rights of shopping mall owners. See State v. Wicklund, 576 N.W.2d 753 (Minn. App. 1998).

2. Is *J.M.B. Realty* justified by the significant role that shopping centers play today as "public commons." Recall that concerns over monopo-

ly power helped animate the traditional common law privileges against trespass, as well as the duty of innkeepers and "common carriers" to serve all members of the public without discrimination. Is *J.M.B. Realty* simply a modern day extension of these doctrines?

3. Are there other rationales for restricting the property rights of shopping mall owners? One argument reflected in *J.M.B. Realty* is that, although property owners have a legitimate interest in being able to exclude others from their property, they should not be able to open their property to the public but then deny a right of entry based solely on a person's desire to speak out on public issues. But why? Although the shopping malls in *J.M.B. Realty* may have consented to people coming on their land to shop, they had not consented to people coming on their land to leaflet. And as Justice Garibaldi notes in his dissent, opening the mall to protestors may be costly: mall owners may need to incur additional administrative and security expense to oversee the expressional activity.

Professor Lillian BeVier has suggested that restrictions on mall owners may be necessary to overcome a collective action problem. According to BeVier, each individual shopping mall owner may be willing to open up his or her mall to protestors, but only if all other mall owners do the same. Otherwise, shoppers might flee to those malls that do not permit protestors. By requiring all mall owners to permit protestors, the government merely accomplishes what the mall owners are willing to do but cannot accomplish on their own. Lillian B. BeVier, Give and Take: Public Use as Due Compensation in *PruneYard*, 64 U. Chi. L. Rev. 71 (1997). Does BeVier's argument ring true? Should shoppers be forced to listen to protestors?

4. As noted in *J.M.B. Realty*, the New Jersey Supreme Court in 1971 held that a farmer does not have a common law right to prevent health care providers and legal service attorneys from coming onto his property to aid migrant workers living on the farm. State v. Shack, 277 A.2d 369 (N.J. 1971). According to the court, "Property rights serve human values. They are recognized to that end, and are limited by it." Id. at 304. Property rights are "not absolute"; they are "relative" and must accommodate the rights of others. Id. at 305. Noting that the law is "not static," the court went on to argue that a landowner

> must expect to find the absoluteness of his property rights curtailed by the organs of society, for the promotion of the best interests of others for whom these organs also operate as protective agencies. The necessity for such curtailments is greater in a modern industrialized and urbanized society than it was in the relatively simple American society of fifty, 100, or 200 years ago. The current balance between individualism and dominance of the social interest depends not upon political and social ideologies, but also upon the physical and social facts of the time and place under discussion.

Id. at 305, quoting 5 Powell, Real Property (1970) § 745, pp. 493–494.

5. How would you resolve the following cases?

• A citizen group seeks to distribute flyers door to door to homeowners in a private condominium complex. The condominium association refuses permission, even though it actively endorses candidates for political office by distributing flyers itself. See Guttenberg Taxpayers & Rentpayers Ass'n v. Galaxy Towers Condominium Ass'n, 688 A.2d 156 (N.J. Super. 1996) (citizen group has a constitutional right to distribute the flyers).

• Homeowners seek to prohibit a company that publishes a free community newspaper from throwing the newspaper onto the property of an unwilling recipient after having been notified not to do so. See Tillman v. Distribution Systems of America, Inc., 648 N.Y.S.2d 630 (App. 1996) (company blocked from distributing newspapers).

6. **The Public Trust Doctrine.** Another limit on the right to exclude is the public trust doctrine. Recall from Chapter 1 that the public trust doctrine originally stood for the proposition that state governments hold tidelands (i.e., lands subject to tidal ebbs and flows) and lands underlying navigable waterways in trust for the public. According to the United States Supreme Court in *Illinois Central Railroad*, p. 43, the public trust doctrine restricts, but does not totally preclude states from turning trust lands over to private owners. Where states do sell or give trust lands to private owners, the public often retains rights to use the lands. Some states have held that members of the public have only narrowly specified rights in the privately held lands. See, e.g., Bell v. Town of Wells, 557 A.2d 168 (Me. 1989) (rights only of fishing, fowling, and navigation); Opinion of the Justices, 313 N.E.2d 561 (Mass. 1974) (rights of fishing and navigation). Other states have held that the public retains the right to enter and use most of the lands for a broad set of purposes, including recreation. See, e.g., Marks v. Whitney, 491 P.2d 374 (Cal. 1971); Opinion of the Justices, 649 A.2d 604 (N.H. 1994); Borough of Neptune City v. Borough of Avon–By–The–Sea, 294 A.2d 47 (N.J. 1972).

To what extent should the public's right to use the tidelands also justify a right of access across private property to get to the tidelands? To use private land adjacent to the tidelands for incidental purposes such as sunbathing?

Matthews v. Bay Head Improvement Association

Supreme Court of New Jersey, 1984.
471 A.2d 355.

SCHREIBER, J. . . .

The Borough of Point Pleasant instituted this suit against the Borough of Bay Head and the Bay Head Improvement Association (Association), generally asserting that the defendants prevented Point Pleasant inhabitants from gaining access to the Atlantic Ocean and the beachfront in Bay

Head. The proceeding was dismissed as to the Borough of Bay Head because it did not own or control the beach. Subsequently, Virginia Matthews, a resident of Point Pleasant who desired to swim and bathe at the Bay Head beach, joined as a party plaintiff, and Stanley Van Ness, as Public Advocate, joined as plaintiff-intervenor. When the Borough of Point Pleasant ceased pursuing the litigation, the Public Advocate became the primary moving party. The Public Advocate asserted that the defendants had denied the general public its right of access during the summer bathing season to public trust lands along the beaches in Bay Head and its right to use private property fronting on the ocean incidental to the public's right under the public trust doctrine. The complaint was amended on several occasions, eliminating the Borough of Point Pleasant as plaintiff and adding more than 100 individuals, who were owners or had interests in properties located on the oceanfront in Bay Head, as defendants....

Facts

The Borough of Bay Head (Bay Head) borders the Atlantic Ocean. A beach runs along its entire length adjacent to the Atlantic Ocean. There are 76 separate parcels of land that border the beach. All except six are owned by private individuals. Title to those six is vested in the Association.

The Association was founded in 1910 and incorporated as a nonprofit corporation in 1932. Its certificate of incorporation states that its purposes are the improving and beautifying of the Borough of Bay Head, New Jersey, cleaning, policing and otherwise making attractive and safe the bathing beaches in said Borough, and the doing of any act which may be found necessary or desirable for the greater convenience, comfort and enjoyment of the residents. Its constitution delineates the Association's object to promote the best interests of the Borough and "in so doing to own property, operate bathing beaches, hire life guards, beach cleaners and policemen...."

Nine streets in the Borough, which are perpendicular to the beach, end at the dry sand. The Association owns the land commencing at the end of seven of these streets for the width of each street and extending through the upper dry sand to the mean high water line, the beginning of the wet sand area or foreshore. In addition, the Association owns the fee in six shore front properties, three of which are contiguous and have a frontage aggregating 310 feet. Many owners of beachfront property executed and delivered to the Association leases of the upper dry sand area. These leases are revocable by either party to the lease on thirty days' notice. Some owners have not executed such leases and have not permitted the Association to use their beaches.

The Association controls and supervises its beach property between the third week in June and Labor Day. It engages about 40 employees, who serve as lifeguards, beach police and beach cleaners....

Membership is generally limited to residents of Bay Head. Class A members are property owners. Class B are non-owners. Large families (six or more) pay $90 per year and small families pay $60 per year. Upon application residents are routinely accepted. Membership is evidenced by badges that signify permission to use the beaches. Members, which include local hotels, motels and inns, can also acquire badges for guests. The charge for each guest badge is $12. Members of the Bay Head Fire Company, Bay Head Borough employees, and teachers in the municipality's school system have been issued beach badges irrespective of residency.

Except for fishermen, who are permitted to walk through the upper dry sand area to the foreshore, only the membership may use the beach between 10:00 a.m. and 5:30 p.m. during the summer season. The public is permitted to use the Association's beach from 5:30 p.m. to 10:00 a.m. during the summer and, with no hourly restrictions, between Labor Day and mid-June.

No attempt has ever been made to stop anyone from occupying the terrain east of the high water mark. During certain parts of the day, when the tide is low, the foreshore could consist of about 50 feet of sand not being flowed by the water. The public could gain access to the foreshore by coming from the Borough of Point Pleasant Beach on the north or from the Borough of Mantoloking on the south.

Association membership totals between 4,800 to 5,000. The Association President testified during depositions that its restrictive policy, in existence since 1932, was due to limited parking facilities and to the overcrowding of the beaches. The Association's avowed purpose was to provide the beach for the residents of Bay Head.

The trial court held that the Association was not an arm of the Borough of Bay Head, that the Association was not a municipal agency, and that nothing in the record justified a finding that public privileges could attach to the private properties owned or leased by the Association. A divided Appellate Division affirmed. The majority agreed with the trial court that the Association was not a public agency or a public entity and that the action of the private owners through the Association established no general right in the public to the use of the beaches.

Judge Greenberg dissented. He argued that the Association's beaches are de facto public to a limited extent, being public to residents and visitors who stay in hotels. They are private to everyone else. He reasoned that Bay Head residents have the advantage of living in a municipality with public beaches, but are troubled by having their beaches made available to outsiders. Judge Greenberg concluded that the Association's beaches must be open to all members of the public. However, he would not preclude any lessor from terminating his lease with the Association and thereby eliminating the public right of access to that part of the beach.

II

The Public Trust

In Borough of Neptune City v. Borough of Avon-by-the-Sea, 294 A.2d 47 (N.J. 1972), Justice Hall alluded to the ancient principle "that land covered by tidal waters belonged to the sovereign, but for the common use of all the people." .... This underlying concept was applied in New Jersey in Arnold v. Mundy, 6 N.J.L. 1 (Sup. Ct.1821)....

In *Avon,* Justice Hall reaffirmed the public's right to use the waterfront as announced in Arnold v. Mundy. He observed that the public has a right to use the land below the mean average high water mark where the tide ebbs and flows. These uses have historically included navigation and fishing. In *Avon* the public's rights were extended "to recreational uses, including bathing, swimming and other shore activities." .... It has been said that "[h]ealth, recreation and sports are encompassed in and intimately related to the general welfare of a well-balanced state." N.J. Sports & Exposition Authority v. McCrane, 292 A.2d 580 (N.J. Super. 1971), aff'd, 292 A.2d 545 (N.J.), appeal dismissed sub nom. Borough of East Rutherford v. N.J. Sports & Exposition Authority, 409 U.S. 943 (1972). Extension of the public trust doctrine to include bathing, swimming and other shore activities is consonant with and furthers the general welfare. The public's right to enjoy these privileges must be respected.

In order to exercise these rights guaranteed by the public trust doctrine, the public must have access to municipally-owned dry sand areas as well as the foreshore. The extension of the public trust doctrine to include municipally-owned dry sand areas was necessitated by our conclusion that enjoyment of rights in the foreshore is inseparable from use of dry sand beaches. In *Avon* we struck down a municipal ordinance that required nonresidents to pay a higher fee than residents for the use of the beach. We held that where a municipal beach is dedicated to public use, the public trust doctrine "dictates that the beach and the ocean waters must be open to all on equal terms and without preference and that any contrary state or municipal action is impermissible." ....

III

Public Rights in Privately–Owned Dry Sand Beaches

In *Avon* ... our finding of public rights in dry sand areas was specifically and appropriately limited to those beaches owned by a municipality. We now address the extent of the public's interest in privately-owned dry sand beaches. This interest may take one of two forms. First, the public may have a right to cross privately owned dry sand beaches in order to gain access to the foreshore. Second, this interest may be of the sort enjoyed by the public in municipal beaches under *Avon* ..., namely, the right to sunbathe and generally enjoy recreational activities.

Beaches are a unique resource and are irreplaceable. The public demand for beaches has increased with the growth of population and improvement of transportation facilities. Furthermore, the projected demand for salt water swimming will not be met "unless the existing swimming capacities of the four coastal counties are expanded." Department of Environmental Protection, Statewide Comprehensive Outdoor Recreation Plan 200 (1977). The DEP estimates that, compared to 1976, the State's salt water swimming areas "must accommodate 764,812 more persons by 1985 and 1,021,112 persons by 1995." Id....

Exercise of the public's right to swim and bathe below the mean high water mark may depend upon a right to pass across the upland beach. Without some means of access the public right to use the foreshore would be meaningless. To say that the public trust doctrine entitles the public to swim in the ocean and to use the foreshore in connection therewith without assuring the public of a feasible access route would seriously impinge on, if not effectively eliminate, the rights of the public trust doctrine. This does not mean the public has an unrestricted right to cross at will over any and all property bordering on the common property. The public interest is satisfied so long as there is reasonable access to the sea. . . .

The bather's right in the upland sands is not limited to passage. Reasonable enjoyment of the foreshore and the sea cannot be realized unless some enjoyment of the dry sand area is also allowed. The complete pleasure of swimming must be accompanied by intermittent periods of rest and relaxation beyond the water's edge. The unavailability of the physical situs for such rest and relaxation would seriously curtail and in many situations eliminate the right to the recreational use of the ocean. This was a principal reason why in *Avon* . . . we held that municipally-owned dry sand beaches "must be open to all on equal terms. . . ." We see no reason why rights under the public trust doctrine to use of the upland dry sand area should be limited to municipally-owned property. It is true that the private owner's interest in the upland dry sand area is not identical to that of a municipality. Nonetheless, where use of dry sand is essential or reasonably necessary for enjoyment of the ocean, the doctrine warrants the public's use of the upland dry sand area subject to an accommodation of the interests of the owner. . . .

Precisely what privately-owned upland sand area will be available and required to satisfy the public's rights under the public trust doctrine will depend on the circumstances. Location of the dry sand area in relation to the foreshore, extent and availability of publicly-owned upland sand area, nature and extent of the public demand, and usage of the upland sand land by the owner are all factors to be weighed and considered in fixing the contours of the usage of the upper sand.

Today, recognizing the increasing demand for our State's beaches and the dynamic nature of the public trust doctrine, we find that the public must be given both access to and use of privately-owned dry sand areas as reasonably necessary. While the public's rights in private beaches are not co-extensive with the rights enjoyed in municipal beaches, private landowners may not in all instances prevent the public from exercising its rights under the public trust doctrine. The public must be afforded reasonable access to the foreshore as well as a suitable area for recreation on the dry sand.

V

The Beaches of Bay Head

. . .

Bay Head Improvement Association is a non-profit corporation whose primary purpose as stated in its certificate of incorporation is the "cleaning, policing and otherwise making attractive and safe the bathing beaches" in the Borough of Bay Head "and the doing of any act which may be found necessary or desirable for the greater convenience, comfort and enjoyment of the residents."....

The Association's activities paralleled those of a municipality in its operation of the beachfront. The size of the beach was so great that it stationed lifeguards at five separate locations.... When viewed in its totality—its purposes, relationship with the municipality, communal characteristic, activities, and virtual monopoly over the Bay Head beachfront—the quasi-public nature of the Association is apparent. The Association makes available to the Bay Head public access to the common tidal property for swimming and bathing and to the upland dry sand area for use incidental thereto, preserving the residents' interests in a fashion similar to *Avon*.

There is no public beach in the Borough of Bay Head. If the residents of every municipality bordering the Jersey shore were to adopt the Bay Head policy, the public would be prevented from exercising its right to enjoy the foreshore. The Bay Head residents may not frustrate the public's right in this manner. By limiting membership only to residents and foreclosing the public, the Association is acting in conflict with the public good and contrary to the strong public policy "in favor of encouraging and expanding public access to and use of shoreline areas." Gion v. City of Santa Cruz, 2 Cal.3d 29, 43, 465 P.2d 50, 59, 84 Cal. Rptr. 162, 171 (1970). Indeed, the Association is frustrating the public's right under the public trust doctrine. It should not be permitted to do so.

Accordingly, membership in the Association must be open to the public at large. In this manner the public will be assured access to the common beach property during the hours of 10:00 a.m. to 5:30 p.m. between mid-June and September, where they may exercise their right to swim and bathe and to use the Association's dry sand area incidental to those activities. Although such membership rights to the use of the beach may be broader than the rights necessary for enjoyment of the public trust, opening the Association's membership to all, nonresidents and residents, should lead to a substantial satisfaction of the public trust doctrine.... The Association may continue to charge reasonable fees to cover its costs of lifeguards, beach cleaners, patrols, equipment, insurance, and administrative expenses. The fees fixed may not discriminate in any respect between residents and nonresidents. The Association may continue to enforce its regulations regarding cleanliness, safety, and other reasonable measures concerning the public use of the beach....

The Public Advocate has urged that all the privately-owned beachfront property likewise must be opened to the public. Nothing has been developed on this record to justify that conclusion. We have decided that the Association's membership and thereby its beach must be open to the public. That area might reasonably satisfy the public need at this time. We are aware that the Association possessed, as of the initiation of this litigation, about 42 upland sand lots under leases revocable on 30 days' notice. If any of these leases have been or are to be terminated, or if the Association were to sell all or part of its property, it may necessitate further adjudication of the public's claims in favor of the public trust on part or all of these or other privately-owned upland dry sand lands depending upon the circumstances. However, we see no necessity to have those issues resolved judicially at this time since the beach under the Association's control will be open to the public and may be adequate to satisfy the public trust interests. We believe that the Association and property owners will act in good faith and to the satisfaction of the Public Advocate. Indeed, we are of the opinion that all parties will benefit by our terminating this prolonged litigation at this time.

The record in this case makes it clear that a right of access to the beach is available over the quasi-public lands owned by the Association, as well as the right to use the Association's upland dry sand. It is not necessary for us to determine under what circumstances and to what extent there will be a need to use the dry sand of private owners who either now or in the future may have no leases with the Association. Resolution of the competing interests, private ownership and the public trust, may in some cases be simple, but in many it may be most complex. In any event, resolution would depend upon the specific facts in controversy.

None of the foregoing matters were fully argued or briefed, the disputes concerning rights in and to private beaches having been most general. All we decide here is that private land is not immune from a possible right of access to the foreshore for swimming or bathing purposes, nor is it immune from the possibility that some of the dry sand may be used by the public incidental to the right of bathing and swimming.

We realize that considerable uncertainty will continue to surround the question of the public's right to cross private land and to use a portion of the dry sand as discussed above. Where the parties are unable to agree as to the application of the principles enunciated herein, the claim of the private owner shall be honored until the contrary is established....

Notes & Questions

1. To date, the New Jersey Supreme Court is the only court to hold that the public trust doctrine provides the public with limited rights of access across and use of private beaches immediately adjacent to trust lands. However, as discussed in Chapter 10 at pages 880–881, California, Oregon, and a handful of other states have used other property doctrines to open up at least some privately owned beaches to the public. See, e.g., Villa Nova Resort, Inc. v. State, 711 S.W.2d 120 (Tex. Ct. Civ. App. 1986) (using the doctrines of prescriptive easement and implied dedication); Gion v. City of Santa Cruz, 465 P.2d 50 (Cal. 1970) (implied dedication); State ex rel. Thornton v. Hay, 462 P.2d 671 (Ore. 1969) (doctrine of custom).

2. The dissenting judge in the court below had argued that the beaches of the Bay Head Improvement Association were "de facto public to a limited extent, being public to residents and visitors who stay in hotels," and therefore could not be closed to other members of the public. Would this have been a better approach to resolving *Matthews* than the broader ruling of the New Jersey Supreme Court? Why do you think that the New Jersey Supreme Court did not take the narrower approach?

3. Although *Matthews* holds that the public enjoys "access to and use of privately-owned dry sand areas as reasonably necessary," the Bay Head Improvement Association was a quasi-public entity. A case dealing with purely private property did not reach the New Jersey Supreme Court until Raleigh Ave. Beach Ass'n v. Atlantis Beach Club, 879 A.2d 112 (N.J. 2005). The Atlantis Beach Club was a private corporation that owned the dry-sand portion of the only beach in Lower Township, N.J. When the Beach Club ejected a local community member for trespassing on their land, a local neighborhood association sued. In concluding that the public had a right of horizontal and vertical access across the Beach Club's land, the New Jersey Supreme Court weighed four factors:

i. "Location of the dry sand area in relation to the foreshore." The court noted that the Beach Club was immediately adjacent to the high water line and easily reached by pedestrians from local streets.

ii. "Extent and availability of publicly-owned upland sand area." The court emphasized that Lower Township enjoyed no publicly-owned beach area.

iii. "Nature and extent of the public demand." The court observed that, not only were local residents concerned about beach access, but also the "enormous public interest in the New Jersey shore is well known."

iv. "Usage of the upland sand land by the owner." Here, the court emphasized two factors. First, the beach was open to public use prior to 1996. Second, the Atlantis Beach Club was a commercial enterprise that, pursuant to state anti-discrimination laws, allowed anyone to be a member upon payment of a fee.

Are all of these factors appropriate in deciding whether to open a private beach to public access? Should the New Jersey courts consider other factors?

4. Why shouldn't the law leave access to and use of beaches to the marketplace? Is there again a concern that landowners will enjoy a monopoly power that might be abused?

5. Are there disadvantages to giving all members of the public open access to beaches? In The Tragedy of the Commons, 168 Science 1243 (1968), Garrett Hardin argued that opening a resource to all members of the public can lead to overuse and destruction of the resource. In the beach context, more and more sun lovers will flock to the beach, leading to overcrowded beaches. Does this argue against opening private beaches to

the public? Should the government limit the number of people who can use any particular beach on any specific day? If so, how? Should the government set a cap on the number of people who can use a beach and turn people away after that number is exceeded? Should the government sell or auction off beach-going rights (in the same way that most states sell or auction off fishing or hunting rights)? Would *Matthews* permit the Bay Head Improvement Association to take these actions, so long as it did not discriminate in favor of local residents?

6. Should courts use the public trust doctrine to provide public access across private lands to other water-related resources, such as rivers with terrific stretches of white water perfect for kayaking or rafting, beautiful sailing lakes, or good fishing spots? If so, is there any reason to stop with water-related resources? Should courts use the public trust doctrine to provide the public with access to other lands with high recreation value, such as forests or mountain meadows? How should courts decide how far to take the public trust doctrine? See Scott W. Reed, The Public Trust Doctrine: Is It Amphibious?, 1 Envtl. L. & Litig. 107 (1986).

7. For a general discussion of the current scope and use of the public trust doctrine, see Jack Archer et al., The Public Trust Doctrine and the Management of America's Coasts (1994).

B. ADVERSE POSSESSION

As you have seen, property owners can order intruders off of their property and can sue to remove encroaching structures that others have built without permission on their land. What happens if they do not? The law has long held that, under some circumstances, someone can gain "adverse possession" to someone else's property by going onto and staying on the property for a long enough period of time. This section investigates why and when someone who starts out a trespasser should ever be rewarded with title to the property through adverse possession.

Ray v. Beacon Hudson Mountain Corporation

Court of Appeals of New York, 1996.
666 N.E.2d 532.

TITONE, J.

.... The property that is the subject of this adverse possession claim is a .357–acre parcel improved with a cottage on top of Mt. Beacon in the Town of Fishkill. This improved parcel sits amidst a 156–acre site that was once a thriving resort community comprised of 21 seasonal residences, a casino, a hotel and a power plant. All of the cottage's neighboring structures have since been destroyed by vandalism, fire or general neglect. Prior to 1960, all of the cottage owners occupied their parcels as lessees.

Rose Ray came into possession of the subject premises pursuant to the terms of a December 1, 1906 lease that was assigned to her as lessee on January 31, 1931. Under the terms of that agreement, Ray purchased the cottage located on the property and paid rent for use of the underlying realty. The lease agreement provided that upon termination of the tenancy, any structures erected on the property would pass to the lessor, and the lessor would pay the lessee the reasonable value of the improvements. The lease also required the lessee to pay all taxes assessed upon the property. In December 1952, the lease was extended for 25 years, unless sooner terminated by the lessor.

The lessor terminated the leases of all occupants of the community in 1960 pursuant to the option clause in the lease. The incline service and all utilities were terminated and all cottage owners, including Ray, were directed to remove their personal effects. In accordance with this directive, Ray removed her belongings from the cottage and departed from the premises along with all remaining residents. She died in October 1962, never having been paid the reasonable value of the cottage.

In June 1963, the entire 156–acre site was purchased by Mt. Beacon Incline Lands, Inc. The contract of sale provided that all land and structures thereon were to be conveyed to the purchaser. Approximately one week after the sale in June 1963, plaintiffs—Colonel Robert L. Ray and Margaret A. Ray, the son and daughter-in-law of Rose Ray—reentered the premises formerly inhabited by Rose Ray. Thereafter, plaintiffs occupied the property for about one month per year during each summer between 1963 and 1988, which was most of Colonel Ray's leave time from the United States Army. Plaintiffs continually paid taxes and maintained fire insurance on the parcel, installed telephone and electric service, and claimed the site as their voting residence during the period of adverse possession. Plaintiffs also took steps to prevent vandalism on the property by posting "no trespassing" signs and placing bars, shutters and padlocks on the doors and windows. On several occasions, plaintiffs apprehended vandals on the property and had them prosecuted.

Defendant Beacon Hudson Mountain Corporation[3] acquired the 156–acre parcel in 1978 after the entire parcel was taken from defendant's predecessor by Dutchess County for nonpayment of taxes. Plaintiffs continued to possess the disputed parcel after defendant Beacon Hudson acquired the property.

Plaintiffs commenced this adverse possession action against defendant in 1988, alleging that from 1963 through 1988 they occupied the property in question by adverse possession under a claim of title not written,[a] and that they were its lawful owners. Defendant counterclaimed, seeking to

3. On July 5, 1995, defendant Beacon Hudson executed a deed purporting to transfer its interests in the 156–acre parcel, including the .357 acre in question, to Scenic Hudson Land Trust, Inc. On plaintiffs' motion filed in this Court, Scenic Hudson was joined as a party defendant, and adopts the arguments of defendant Beacon Hudson.

a. Eds.—Sections 521 and 522 of the New York Real Property Actions and Proceedings Law establishes the statutory requirements for adverse possession where the eject plaintiffs from the land. Following a bench trial, and a personal visit by the court to the property, Supreme Court dismissed the counterclaim and held that plaintiffs were rightful owners of the property and entitled to an easement by prescription and right of way for ingress and egress. The court concluded that plaintiffs' occupancy of the property was "too apparent to be overlooked," having been "continuous and open, through more than twenty-five years of paying real estate taxes, maintaining fire insurance, repelling and arresting trespassers, claiming the site as their voting residence, maintaining the structure against the effects of wind and weather and the attacks of vandals and nailing up posters against trespassers." The court expressly found that the parcel is bounded on all sides and set apart from neighboring property by permanent stone paths, a terraced rock garden and other prominent natural objects. The court also concluded that plaintiffs had put defendant on notice of the boundaries and limits of their claim by the "constant and conspicuous use" which "made unnecessary its inclosure in fences, walls or hedges."

The Appellate Division reversed, and declared that plaintiffs have no right, title or interest in the disputed property. The Court noted that the element of continuous possession necessary to establish title by adverse possession could be satisfied by seasonal use of property, but concluded that plaintiffs' use for one month out of the four-month summer season was not sufficiently regular to give the owner notice of the adverse claim. We granted plaintiffs' motion for leave to appeal, and now reverse.

To acquire title to real property by adverse possession, common law requires the possessor to establish that the character of the possession is "hostile and under a claim of right, actual, open and notorious, exclusive and continuous" (Brand v. Prince, 35 NY2d 634, 636) for the statutory period of 10 years. "Reduced to its essentials, this means nothing more than that there must be possession in fact of a type that would give the owner a cause of action in ejectment against the occupier throughout the prescriptive period" (Brand v. Prince, 35 NY2d, at 636, supra). Since the acquisition of title to land by adverse possession is not favored under the law, these elements must be proven by clear and convincing evidence.

The element of continuity will be defeated where the adverse possessor interrupts the period of possession by abandoning the premises, where an intruder's presence renders the possession nonexclusive, or where the record owner acts to eject the adverse possessor. However, the hostile claimant's actual possession of the property need not be constant to satisfy the "continuity" element of the claim.

Rather, the requirement of continuous possession is satisfied when the adverse claimant's acts of possessing the property, including periods during

person in possession of the property does not have any written deed or document purporting to give them title to the property. Section 521 provides that "[w]here there has been an actual continued occupation of premises under a claim of title, exclusive of any other right, but not founded upon a written instrument or a judgment or decree, the premises so actually occupied, and no others, are deemed to have been held adversely." Section 522 provides that land is deemed to be "occupied" within the meaning of section 521 when "usually cultivated or improved" or "protected by a substantial inclosure."

which the claimant exercises dominion and control over the premises or is physically present on the land, are consistent with acts of possession that ordinary owners of like properties would undertake (Miller v. Rau, 193 AD2d 868, 869; 1 Warren's Weed, New York Real Property, Adverse Possession, § 5.05). In other words, "[t]he character of disputed property is crucial in determining what degree of control and what character of possession is required to establish adverse possession. Thus, wild and undeveloped land that is not readily susceptible to habitation, cultivation or improvement does not require the same quality of possession as residential or arable land, since the usual acts of ownership are impossible or unreasonable" (7 Powell, Real Property, Adverse Possession ¶ 1012[2])....

Here, defendant claims that plaintiffs' possession of the property was not continuous because they were physically present there for only one month out of the summer season. However, this argument fails to take into consideration plaintiffs' other acts of dominion and control over the premises that are indicative of their actual possession of an estate in land. Here, plaintiffs' installation of utilities and over-all preservation of the cottage, a permanent and substantial structure, in a veritable ghost town, for the duration of the statutory period demonstrates continuous, actual occupation of land by improvement. Thus, plaintiffs' actual summertime use for a full month each season, coupled with their repeated acts of repelling trespassers, improving, posting, padlocking and securing of the property in their absences throughout the statutory period, demonstrated their continuous dominion and control over, and thus possession of, the property.

Indeed, this exercise of dominion and control over the premises is inconsistent with an abandonment and certainly consistent with the type of "usual acts of ownership" that would be reasonably expected to be made by owners of a summer residence in a now-defunct seasonal resort area plagued by vandals. Such seasonal presence, coupled with plaintiffs' preservation of the premises for the statutory period of 10 years—which was made more obvious by the fact that all neighboring structures had collapsed due to vandalism and abandonment—was sufficient to place the record owner on notice of their hostile and exclusive claim of ownership. Because defendant was clearly placed on notice of plaintiffs' hostile claim of ownership, its failure to seek plaintiffs' ouster within the statutory period results in its disseisin.

Defendant's remaining contentions lack merit.

Accordingly, the order of the Appellate Division should be reversed, with costs, and the judgment of Supreme Court, Dutchess County, reinstated.

East 13th Street Homesteaders' Coalition v. Lower East Side Coalition Housing Development

Supreme Court of New York, 1996.
646 N.Y.S.2d 324.

Opinion.

The petitioners are occupants of 537, 539, 541, and 545 East 13th Street, who brought this suit to prevent the City from removing them from these buildings to implement a Federally subsidized plan to rehabilitate the buildings and create low-income housing units.... The narrow issue presently on appeal is whether the petitioners should be granted a preliminary injunction barring their eviction pending trial on the issue of whether legal title to the property passed to them through adverse possession.

A preliminary injunction is warranted only upon a showing of (1) a likelihood of success on the merits of the underlying claim; (2) irreparable injury absent granting the injunction; and (3) that a balancing of the equities weighs in favor of the injunction. Because it is a drastic remedy, injunctive relief is reserved for those cases presenting a clear legal right thereto.

Considering that the petitioners claim the apartment buildings upon a theory of adverse possession, they must show that they are likely to prove, by clear and convincing evidence that for a period of ten years they actually possessed the subject property at issue, and that their possession was open and notorious, exclusive, continuous, hostile, and under claim of right (Spiegel v. Ferraro, 73 N.Y.2d 622; Garrett v. Holcomb, 215 A.D.2d 884, 885; accord, City of Tonawanda v. Ellicott Cr. Homeowners Assn., 86 A.D.2d 118, 120, appeal dismissed 58 N.Y.2d 824).

Our review of the record reveals that petitioners are not likely to prove ten years of actual, continuous, open and notorious possession of the subject buildings (between 1984 and 1994, the period here in question). Since petitioners' claim of right is not supported by a written instrument, they must show actual, not constructive, possession to establish the requisite temporal element (Real Property Actions and Proceedings Law § 521; Van Valkenburgh v. Lutz, 304 N.Y. 95, 98; Birnbaum v. Brody, 156 A.D.2d 408). The record contains documentary and photographic evidence that the City sealed the buildings numerous times during the claimed period, and that the occupants had to break these seals, sometimes with a sledgehammer, to reenter the buildings.

The petitioners argue that there was a chain of possession of coalition members in all of the buildings during the requisite period to support the requirement of continuous ownership, but the record does not reveal that such successive possession was continued by an unbroken chain of privity such that it could be tacked for adverse possession purposes (Garrett v. Holcomb, 215 A.D.2d 884; Pegalis v. Anderson, 111 A.D.2d 796; Belotti v. Bickhardt, 228 N.Y. 296, 306). In fact, there is no evidence of privity between successive occupants of the apartments, nor is there evidence of any intended transfers. In addition, some of the apartments were vacant for some period, such that the vacating occupant and the new occupant apparently had no contact at all.

In sharp distinction, the claimant in *Ray v. Beacon Hudson Mtn. Corp. (88 N.Y.2d 154),* the case relied upon in the dissent, was the same person who had occupied the property there in issue from 1963 through 1988, a period of twenty-five years. Such is not the case here, where we are presented with an oft-interrupted number of unrelated occupants.

Since petitioners have failed to demonstrate ten years of continuous possession of the subject property, a condition precedent to a claim for adverse possession, the likely success of which is evaluated on this motion, and respondents have countered with proof which persuasively weighs against the petitioners' claims, the order appealed is reversed, and the motion for a preliminary injunction denied.

KUPFERMAN, J.P., dissenting.

I would affirm.

In the recent case of *Ray v. Beacon Hudson Mtn. Corp.* (88 N.Y.2d 154, 156), Judge Titone, speaking for a unanimous Court, stated: "In determining whether the common-law requirement of 'continuity of possession' has been met in an adverse possession claim to an estate in land, a court should consider not only the adverse possessor's physical presence on the land but also the claimant's other acts of dominion and control over the premises that would appropriately be undertaken by owners of properties of similar character, condition and location. Thus, we conclude that plaintiffs' occupancy of the summer cottage in a now-defunct resort town for one month during the summer, coupled with their regular efforts taken to secure and improve the premises and to eject trespassers during their absences for the 10-year statutory period while all neighboring structures collapsed due to vandalism or abandonment, satisfied the element of continuous actual possession."

This statement is, *mutatis mutandis*, substantially analogous to our current situation.

Further on in his opinion, Judge Titone states "[P]laintiffs' installation of utilities and over-all preservation of the cottage, a permanent and substantial structure, in a veritable ghost town, for the duration of the statutory period demonstrates continuous, actual occupation of land by improvement."

In the case at bar, there is no doubt that the plaintiffs made improvements and attempted to preserve the buildings involved in an area that could be considered the equivalent of a "ghost town." Moreover, as in the *Ray* case, where the occupation was for only one month during the summer, we have intermittent occupation by various people who are a part of a cohesive group.

In 1977 and 1978, by *in rem* proceedings, the City acquired title to the four buildings in question. As the IAS Court found at the hearing it conducted, by the early 1980's the buildings had become a "neighborhood hazard, housing drug activity, litter and trash." The City having defaulted on its obligation to maintain order and ensure tranquility, the plaintiffs moved into the vacant buildings.

The City now indicates that it is prepared to gut the buildings and rehabilitate the neighborhood with private funds and Federal tax credits after having failed to do so for many years. This may be a consummation to be wished but not necessarily a firm result. In the interim, the preliminary injunctive relief granted by the IAS Court should be continued, preventing a warrant of eviction, until such time as there can be a definitive conclusion as to the claim that the plaintiffs have adverse possession.

Notes & Questions

1. **Justifications for Adverse Possession.** Why should the law ever reward a lengthy trespass by giving the trespasser title to the property? Professor Thomas Merrill has observed that judicial opinions provide four possible rationales for adverse possession. See Thomas W. Merrill, Property Rules, Liability Rules, and Adverse Possession, 79 Nw. U. L. Rev. 1122 (1984–85). First, adverse possession may be designed to avoid the difficulty of resolving stale claims to land. The law assumes that the person who has occupied a parcel of land in recent years is the legitimate owner and refuses to let others argue that they are the real owners. The law frequently employs statutes of limitations to avoid trying old causes of action where key witnesses may be dead, memories have faded, and evidence has been lost. However, as Professor Merrill notes, the traditional argument for statutes of limitations is particularly weak in the adverse possession context because, as Chapter 4 discusses, states maintain records of property ownership that make it quite easy for true property owners to establish their title to property—no matter how many years have passed.

Second, adverse possession may make it easier to buy and sell property. Imagine that John Charles Fremont wishes to buy a home that Mary Austin has lived in for 35 years. When Fremont checks the property records, however, he discovers that Austin never owned the land; 35 years ago when Austin moved onto the property, Jedediah Smith owned the land. Buying the home from Smith may be difficult. No one may know where Smith now lives, or whether he is even still alive. If he has died, he may have left multiple heirs, all of whom would now own a portion of the property. To encourage land transfers, therefore, the law might want to award title to Austin, the current possessor. Although this rationale might justify protecting a bona fide purchaser of the property like Fremont from a later lawsuit by the original owner, should it protect Austin from a lawsuit by Smith prior to any sale?

Third, adverse possession might be designed to punish property owners who sleep on their rights. Under one version of this argument, the law is designed to reward those landowners who use their land. In *Beacon Hudson Mountain*, for example, the true owner of the land was making no active use of it during the period of adverse possession. The Rays, by contrast, did.

But should the law encourage active use of property? Professor John Sprankling, in a provocative article discussed further below, suggests not. As he observes, there is a growing movement to protect wild land such as forests, grasslands, and wetlands through private land preserves and other means. Indeed, the Scenic Hudson Land Trust acquired the property at issue in *Ray* while the lawsuit was pending, and the land is now part of a 220–acre hiking preserve. "American adverse possession law is inherently hostile to private preservation of these wild lands in both spirit and substance. Its ideology equates preservation with waste, reflecting an era when cleared land symbolized both civilization and progress." John G. Sprankling, An Environmental Critique of Adverse Possession, 79 Cornell L. Rev. 816, 856 (1994).

Finally, the doctrine of adverse possession might reflect the reliance interests that the possessor has developed over the years in the property. As Justice Oliver Wendell Holmes wrote over a century ago, "A thing which you have enjoyed and used as your own for a long time, whether property or an opinion, takes root in your being and cannot be torn away without your resenting the act and trying to defend yourself, however you came by it. The law can ask no better justification than the deepest instincts of man." Oliver Wendell Holmes, The Path of the Law 476–77 (1897). In a similar vein, Holmes wrote a decade later that "truth, friendship and the statute of limitations have a common root in time. The true explanation of title by prescription seems to me to be that man, like a tree in the cleft of a rock, gradually shapes his roots to his surroundings, and when the roots have grown to a certain size, can't be displaced without cutting at his life." Letter to William James, April 1, 1907, in 2 Ralph Barton Perry, The Thought and Character of Williams James 461–462 (1935).

Professor Margaret Radin makes the same point in terms of "fungible" and "personal" property. According to Professor Radin, property can be divided into fungible property (which we hold purely for its tradable value) and personal property (which, because of our personal use of the property, has become fused with our personhood). Although a piece of property might initially be fungible to an adverse possessor, the land "becomes more and more personal as time passes. At the same time, the titleholder's interest fades from personal to fungible and finally to nothingness." Margaret Jane Radin, Time, Possession, & Alienation, 64 Wash. U. L.Q. 739, 748–49 (1986).

Further supporting Holmes' intuition, psychologists have found that someone who has possession of a physical object attaches greater value to it than someone who does not—a phenomenon dubbed the "endowment effect." In a series of experiments, subjects who have been given pens, coffee mugs, or a variety of other personal items demand on average a higher price to part with the objects than others without the items are willing to pay for them. See Daniel Kahneman et al., The Endowment Effect, Loss Aversion, and Status Quo Bias, 5 J. Econ. Perspectives, Winter 1991, at 193.

For other interesting discussions of the potential justifications for adverse possession, see Jeffrey E. Stake, The Uneasy Case for Adverse Possession, 89 Geo. L.J. 2419 (2001); Thomas J. Miceli & C.F. Sirmans, An Economic Theory of Adverse Possession, 15 Intl. Rev. L. & Econ. 161

(1995); Stewart Sterk, Neighbors in American Law, 87 Colum. L. Rev. 55 (1987); Richard A. Epstein, Past and Future: The Temporal Dimension in the Law of Property, 64 Wash. U. L.Q. 667 (1986).

2. Even if the court awards title to the property to the adverse possessor, should the adverse possessor at least have to compensate the true owner for the value of the property? Wouldn't this be a fairer approach? See Merrill, supra note 1, at 1145–53 (arguing for compensation, at least where the claimant intentionally possessed someone else's property).

3. **The Adverse Possessor's State of Mind.** Are any of these arguments strong enough to justify permitting a person to *intentionally* gain title to someone else's property through adverse possession? Isn't that what the Rays did in *Beacon Hudson Mountain Corporation*, and what the East 13th Street Homesteaders' Coalition tried to do? Doesn't the law have a strong interest in deterring such behavior?

Most adverse possession cases involve negligence where a person occupies someone else's land believing that it is their own. A few American courts hold that no one can gain adverse possession of a parcel of land without a "good faith" belief that they have a right to enter onto the land. According to the Georgia Supreme Court, for example, "To enter upon the land without any honest claim of right to do so is but a trespass and can never ripen into prescriptive title." Halpern v. Lacy Investment Corp., 379 S.E.2d 519, 521 (Ga. 1989).

The vast majority of courts, however, hold that the possessor's state of mind does not matter. See, e.g., ITT Rayonier v. Bell, 774 P.2d 6 (Wash. 1989); Tioga Coal Co. v. Supermarkets General Corp., 546 A.2d 1 (Pa. 1988); Chaplin v. Sanders, 676 P.2d 431 (Wash. 1984). A handful of courts have gone to the opposite extreme and held that an adverse possessor cannot gain title to land unless he knows that he does not own the land and intends to oust the rightful owner. See, e.g., Ellis v. Jansing, 620 S.W.2d 569 (Tex. 1981).

Of these three approaches, which constitutes the best policy? Based on a survey of adverse possession opinions, Professor Richard Helmholz concludes that, no matter what courts say in their opinions, they normally will not award title "to the trespasser who knows what he is doing at the time he enters the land in dispute." Richard Helmholz, Adverse Possession and Subjective Intent, 61 Wash. U. L.Q. 331 (1983). The law in action, in other words, is very different than the law set down in the judicial reports. For a subsequent debate over the accuracy of Professor Helmholz's conclusion, see Roger A. Cunningham, Adverse Possession and Subjective Intent: A Reply to Professor Helmholz, 64 Wash. U. L.Q. 1 (1986) (arguing that the actual opinions do not support Professor Helmholz's conclusion); R.H. Helmholz, More on Subjective Intent: A Response to Professor Cunningham, 64 Wash. U. L.Q. 65 (1986) (rejoining that Cunningham misunderstands the cases); Roger A. Cunningham, More on Adverse Possession: A Rejoinder to Professor Helmholz, 64 Wash. U. L.Q. 1167 (1986).

4. **Tacking.** Why do the Rays win, but the East 13th Street Homesteaders' Coalition lose? The most straightforward legal explanation is that the Rays occupied their vacation home for the requisite statutory period, while different squatters occupied the buildings on East 13th Street at different times during the statutory period. No single squatter apparently occupied any building for the required period.

The question of "tacking" asks whether two or more consecutive adverse possessors can add together their periods of adverse possession for purposes of establishing that the property has been adversely held for the statutory period. As the New York Supreme Court observes in *East 13th Street Homesteaders' Coalition*, American courts generally permit "tacking" only where there has been an "unbroken chain of privity" between the successive possessors. Privity is normally established by a deed or other agreement purporting to transfer the property from one possessor to the next. For example, where someone buys a home from an adverse possessor, thinking that the possessor owns the property, most courts will permit the purchaser to count the prior period of possession toward satisfaction of the statutory period. See also Noel v. Jumonville Pipe & Machinery Co., 158 So. 2d 179 (La. 1963) (heirs may tack father's period of adverse possession).

Why should tacking depend on privity between the possessors? The Washington State Court of Appeals has suggested that the privity requirement is designed to differentiate between the squatter, on the one hand, and the honest property purchaser, on the other. The "requirement of 'privity' is no more than judicial recognition of the need for some reasonable connection between successive occupants of real property so as to raise their claim of right above the status of the wrongdoer or the trespasser." Howard v. Kunto, 477 P.2d 210, 215 (Wash. App. 1970). English courts historically have not required privity for purposes of tacking. See Robert Megarry & H.W.R. Wade, Real Property 1036 (5th ed. 1984). If the purpose of requiring privity in the United States is to deny adverse possession to the bad faith trespasser, why don't the courts simply require good faith of everyone? Why should good faith be an issue only for purposes of tacking? If one is concerned about rewarding the trespasser, is there any reason to differentiate between the Rays and the East 13th Street Homesteaders' Coalition?

Tacking also is relevant when the actual owners of a property change during the period of adverse possession. Assume, for example, that the statutory period for adverse possession is ten years. If Mary Austin adversely starts living on Jedediah Smith's property in 2000, and Smith sells the property to John Charles Fremont in 2009, Mary Austin will gain adverse possession of the property if she is still living on the land in 2010—even though Fremont has owned the land for only one year. Changes in ownership, in short, generally do not matter for purposes of adverse possession.

5. **Squatting.** Does the law's bias against "bad faith" possessors reflect a class bias? The Rays aside, it is usually the poor and the displaced who, in their quest for shelter, take possession of land without claim of

right. Although squatting patterns differ, their object—a roof over one's head—is always the same. Squatting is typically an urban phenomenon. According to one dated but conservative estimate, 45 percent of the population of Ankara, Turkey were squatters; 20 percent of Manilla, Philippines; 35 percent of Caracas, Venezuela; and 25 percent of Santiago, Chile. Charles Abrams, Man's Struggle for Shelter in an Urbanizing World 13 (1964).

Squatters have tried various legal means to cling to their homes. In addition to asserting adverse possession, squatters have tried to delay their expulsion by demanding that property owners follow the letter of eviction laws, which as discussed in Chapter 8 often require lengthy proceedings, in trying to remove the squatters. See John P. Nogues, Jr., Defects in the Current Forcible Entry and Detainer Laws of the United States and England, 25 U.C.L.A. L. Rev. 1067 (1978).

In a handful of cases, squatters have also raised constitutional issues. For example, in Amezquita v. Hernandez–Colon, 518 F.2d 8 (1st Cir. 1975), members of the Villa Pangola, a squatter group occupying part of a farm owned by the Land Authority of the Commonwealth of Puerto Rico, sued the Authority and the Commonwealth, claiming that the Authority's forcible removal of their structures violated their Due Process rights not to be evicted without prior judicial authorization. The district court held for the squatters and ordered "the defendants and their agents to refrain from violating the civil rights of [the] plaintiffs by destroying plaintiff's property and invading plaintiff's privacy without previously obtaining a judicial order to that effect." The Court of Appeals reversed, holding that the squatters had no constitutionally protected property interest:

> We turn to Commonwealth law to determine whether such a protected interest exists. Germane to this issue are two Puerto Rico statutes:
>
>> "He who builds, plants, or sows in bad faith on another's land, loses what he has built, planted or sown, without having any right to indemnity." 31 L.P.R.A. § 1165.
>>
>> "The owner of the land on which any one has built, planted or sown in bad faith, may exact the demolition of the work or the removal of the planting or sowing and the replacing of everything in its former condition, at the expense of the person who built, planted or sowed." Id. § 1166.
>
> These statutes preclude us from recognizing in the plaintiffs a "property" interest in the land which could not be disturbed without procedural preliminaries.

518 F.2d at 13.

Is there a need for a modern homesteading law that would permit the homeless to acquire rights in unused urban structures? For suggestions along these lines, see Brian Gardiner, Squatters' Rights and Adverse Possession: A Search for Equitable Application of Property Law, 8 Ind. Int'l & Comp. L. Rev. 119, 142–45 (1997); Christine L. Wilson, Urban Homesteading: A Compromise Between Squatters and the Law, 35 N.Y.L.S. L. Rev. 709 (1990).

6. **Uninterrupted Use.** Courts frequently state that adverse possession requires "continuous" or "uninterrupted" use by the adverse possessor for the statutory period. Why then did the Rays, who occupied the land in dispute in *Beacon Hudson Mountain* for only one month each year, win? Most courts today hold that possession need not be literally "continuous" if ordinary use of the type of property at issue would not be continuous. All that is required is that the plaintiff establish such use "as ordinarily marks the conduct of owners in general in holding, managing, and caring for property of like nature and condition." Whalen v. Smith, 167 N.W. 646, 647 (Iowa 1918). See, e.g., Howard v. Kunto, 477 P.2d 210 (Wash. App. 1970) (summer occupancy of vacation home for statutory period adequate to establish title by adverse possession); White v. Boydstun, 428 P.2d 747 (Idaho 1967) (same); Park v. Powers, 42 P.2d 75 (Cal. 1935) (use of grassland to graze cattle only during grazing period is sufficient). Similarly, an adverse possessor can temporarily leave the property as a result of vacations, military service, or even imprisonment and still be found to have maintained "continuous" possession. See, e.g., Helton v. Cook, 219 S.E.2d 505 (N.C. App. 1975).

Quarles v. Arcega

Court of Appeals of New Mexico, 1992.
841 P.2d 550.

MINZNER, J.

Defendant Theis Company appeals the trial court's decision after a bench trial quieting title in favor of Plaintiffs Quarles and Chavez.... For the reasons stated below, we affirm.

I. BACKGROUND

[The case involved a land dispute between the Theis Company, which owned a 55,000-acre ranch in North-Central New Mexico, and two neighboring land owners—Marie Quarles and Natividad Chavez. The dispute centered on a 67-acre area of land between the Chama River and a fence (the Sargent-Theis fence) constructed by Edward Sargent, the Theis' Company's predecessor in title, in the late 1930's or early 1940's. The fence stood at the top of a hill across the river from Quarles' and Chavez's main properties.

Surveys indicated that the disputed land belonged to the Theis Company. Both Quarles and Chavez, however, had long believed that the land belonged to them and had used the land to graze cattle and sheep. In Quarles' case, deeds that had been issued in 1912, 1917, and 1919 to her ancestors had all mistakenly described her land as extending to the "top of the hill" across the Chama River. Quarles testified that she always believed that the Sargent-Theis fence was therefore the boundary to her property.

Quarles paid taxes on the property and used it as grazing land for over ten years.

Prior deeds to Chavez's property also mistakenly described her land as extending to "the top of the hill or ridge." Like Quarles, Chavez testified that she had always believed that her land extended to the fence. Chavez paid taxes on the land and "occasionally pastured sheep and cattle in the disputed area" for over ten years.

Both of the plaintiffs testified that they had never intended to claim land that did not belong to them. Quarles stated that "she meant only to claim the land described in her deeds, and nothing beyond that." Chavez testified that "she was not claiming any land beyond her deed description."]

Various neighbors also testified and confirmed that it was commonly understood that the Sargent–Theis fence was the western border of the properties in question. One witness stated that the disputed area was used by everyone, and he considered it to belong to everyone, because that was community custom.

Mr. Theis testified that the Sargent–Theis fence was not a boundary fence, but an internal cross fence. Mr. Theis testified that it was not economically feasible to build a fence on the river's bank because it would wash out each spring. He stated that there were fences running east to west on the east side of the fence through the disputed area. Mr. Theis acknowledged that he was aware that Quarles's cattle were in the disputed area, but he had assumed that the cattle wandered in accidentally, and he told his employees to run them off. He further testified that he made no use of the land in question.

Theis Company's ranch foreman, George Shouse, testified that in his thirty years on the ranch, he saw cattle between the fence and the river around five or six times a year, and on each occasion, he would push them back across the river. He said that he never grazed cattle in the disputed area because he did not need the property to maintain the cattle he had, and he did not want to take a chance on the cattle wandering across the river. . . .

II. DISCUSSION

. . . . To establish title by adverse possession within a land grant, a party must prove actual, visible, exclusive, hostile, and continuous possession of the disputed property, under color of title, for a ten-year period. See N.M. Stat. Ann. § 37–1–21; Esquibel v. Hallmark, 92 N.M. 254, 256, 586 P.2d 1083, 1085 (1978); Hernandez v. Cabrera, 107 N.M. 435, 759 P.2d 1017 (Ct. App.1988). The statute, which originally had no tax payment requirement, was modified to include such a requirement in 1979. See 1979 N.M. Laws, ch. 354, § 1. The conclusions made for each tract correspond to these elements. . . .

Theis Company specifically contends that the trial court erred in determining that Plaintiffs proved ownership by adverse possession because

(1) Plaintiffs lacked the requisite intent; (2) their deeds do not describe all of the land they claim, and therefore Plaintiffs failed to establish color of title to the disputed area; and (3) Plaintiffs' use of the area was insufficient to establish actual, open, exclusive possession....

A. Mistake

Theis Company contends that Plaintiffs' statements that they only intended to claim what was in their deeds established that Plaintiffs lacked the necessary hostile intent to establish a claim for adverse possession because their claims arose due to a mistaken belief about their western boundaries. See Ward v. Rodriguez, 88 P.2d 277, 281 (N.M.) (one who claims property belonging to another, under the mistaken belief that his boundary line encompasses the property, does not claim adversely, because he merely intends to claim what is truly his), cert. denied, 307 U.S. 627 (1939). We interpret this argument as having two parts: (1) Plaintiffs conceded their lack of hostility; and (2) Plaintiffs were mistaken about the extent of the property described by their deeds.

Although both Quarles and Chavez stated that they only meant to claim to the extent their deeds entitled them, they also testified that they had always considered the disputed area their property. There was no evidence that Plaintiffs discontinued their use, even after Mr. Theis told Quarles his property included the disputed area. Theis Company presented no evidence, beyond Plaintiffs' statements on cross-examination, that Carlist's and Chavez's possession was based solely on the mistake, and, but for the mistake, they had no intent to occupy the land. These statements do not support reversal.

We agree with the analysis found in Hicks v. Flanagan, 782 S.W.2d 587 (Ark. App. 1990), in which the court cautioned against giving too much weight to statements, identical to those made by Plaintiffs in this case, in which the claimant denied that he was claiming anything beyond his entitlement. The court noted that:

> [A]n honest claimant, unless previously warned, might not think to qualify his answers so as to claim what he considered to be his own, but would state that he claimed only his own, at which point his claim would disappear. In arriving at the intent of a disseisor, [it is] "better to weigh the reasonable import of his conduct in the years preceding the litigation rather than rely on one remark made during the stress of cross-examination."

Id., 782 S.W.2d at 589–90 (quoting Rye v. Baumann, 329 S.W.2d 161, 164 (Ark. 1959)).

Ward is also distinguishable because its facts indicate that the claimants never intended to claim beyond their true boundary. One of them attempted to erect a fence on the true line and was not attempting to appropriate his neighbors' land; in fact, he maintained all along that the fence was the true line. The court then stated that there was no proof that the titleholders ever understood that claimants claimed beyond the true line. *Ward*, 88 P.2d at 281. Thus, the claim of adverse possession failed for lack of the necessary intent.

The Arkansas Court of Appeals distinguished the situation in which a person "takes possession of the land of another intending to claim only to the true boundary" and that in which "acting on a mistake as to the true boundary, he takes possession of the land of another *believing it to be his own*." *Hicks*, 782 S.W.2d at 590 (emphasis in original). In the first situation, the possession is not adverse; in the second, "the intent to retain possession under an honest belief of ownership is adverse possession." Id.

We believe that *Ward* is an illustration of the first situation; the present case is an illustration of the second, if Plaintiffs were mistaken about the true boundary. We also believe that both situations present factual issues for the trial court to resolve. We note in *Ward* that the appellate court affirmed the trial court's decision in favor of the titleholder.

In addition, we note that Plaintiffs are entitled to rely on the possession of their predecessors in title. See Romero v. Herrera, 203 P. 243, 244 (N.M. 1921). The trial court concluded that Plaintiffs' predecessors had been in possession under a claim of right made in good faith. Theis Company does not appear to challenge that determination.

For these reasons, we hold that *Ward* neither controls this case nor disposes of Plaintiffs' claims. We next address Theis Company's contention that Plaintiffs failed to prove color of title.

B. Color of Title

The relevant statute provides that the claimant must hold or claim "by virtue of a deed or deeds of conveyance, . . . purporting to convey an estate in fee simple." § 37–1–21. Under that statute and our cases, "color" of title means "apparent," not "actual" title. It is an element of a claim to non-record title. Only a few states impose such a requirement; it was not a requirement at common law. See III American Law of Property § 15.4(c), at 785 (1952). Color of title "affords good evidence of the hostility of the possession of the grantee and may lessen the notoriety and frequency of his acts of ownership from what would otherwise be required to show title in him by adverse possession." Id. Thus, it serves two purposes. We recognized the first purpose in *Hernandez* when we held, under a related statute, that to establish adverse possession one must prove "a good faith claim of right under color of title." 759 P.2d at 1018.

The statute itself only requires a deed that purports to convey a fee. See § 37–1–21. There is no doubt that both Plaintiffs have satisfied that requirement. In New Mexico, as a matter of case law, we have also required that there be a sufficient description to identify the property. Brylinski v. Cooper, 624 P.2d 522 (N.M. 1981). "But where the description in the deed, aided by extrinsic evidence, is insufficient to identify the property, the deed cannot serve as color of title." Id. at 525.

Theis Company argues that the "principal office of color of title is to define boundaries." Green v. Trumbull, 26 P.2d 1079, 1080 (N.M. 1933). However, as *Hernandez* indicates, color of title also serves the purpose of establishing the requisite intent. Further, while the definition of boundaries might be necessary to identify the property claimed, a claimant may extend his or her claim of adverse possession by showing color of title to an area greater than the area actually possessed. See Marquez v. Padilla, 426 P.2d 593, 595 (N.M. 1967). Thus, if a claimant established actual possession of a portion of property under color of title to a larger parcel, he or she was treated at common law as being in constructive possession of all of the property described by deed. *Marquez* seems to be an example of that common law principle. We address the application of that principle under Theis Company's argument that Plaintiffs failed to prove the element of actual possession. In this case, however, we conclude the same evidence suffices to satisfy the requirement of color of title whether the issue is intent, identity, or scope of actual possession.

The rule in New Mexico is that a party's color of title must be supported by a writing or conveyance of some kind that purports to convey the land that is in dispute. Currier v. Gonzales, 434 P.2d 66 (N.M. 1967).... Extrinsic evidence may be offered to aid the description of an ambiguous deed for purposes of the color of title requirement, and the evidence need not be referred to in the deed itself.... The heart of Theis Company's appellate challenge is that the trial court improperly relied on the fence....

In this case, the long-standing existence of the fence and its reputation in the community was evidence regarding the portion of the hill to which Plaintiffs' deeds refer. Compare Woodburn v. Grimes, 275 P.2d 850 (N.M. 1954) (evidence of plaintiffs' silent acquiescence in defendant's and his predecessors' occupation of the premises he claimed up to the old fence line was sufficient to show that the old fence was built on the true boundary line) with Sanchez v. Scott, 516 P.2d 666 (N.M. 1973) (where there is doubt or uncertainty regarding the true location of a boundary line, the parties may by oral agreement fix a line that will, when followed by possession with reference to the boundary, be conclusive on them and their grantees). Our cases say that a fence may be evidence of the true boundary. It is only logical that it may also provide evidence of the boundary for purposes of the color of title requirement. Our cases also say that the extrinsic evidence used to construe an ambiguous deed for purposes of color of title need not be referred to in the deed itself. See Williams v. Howell, 770 P.2d at 872. For these reasons, we see neither inconsistency nor impropriety in recognizing the fence as relevant evidence for purposes of construing Plaintiffs' deeds in the context of their claim based on adverse possession....

In this case, there was evidence that Plaintiffs and others in the community viewed the fence as a boundary line. Moreover, Quarles's surveyor said that the line on which the fence was erected had historically been used as the boundary line in deeds dating from the early 1900s. There was also evidence that the fence was used as the western boundary for the parcels that lay primarily on the east side of the river. Mr. Theis himself testified to the existence of east-west fences that ran to the Sargent–Theis fence. Based on this evidence, we believe that the trial court was entitled to find that the fence marked the portion of the hill to which the deeds referred. Therefore, we conclude that the deeds to the Barranca Tract contained a sufficient description to satisfy the element of color of title....

C. Actual, Exclusive, and Open Possession

Theis Company contends that Plaintiffs failed to establish exclusivity of use because other members of the community allowed their cattle to graze on the disputed tract. However, allowing neighbors the use of the disputed area as grazing land does not destroy a finding of exclusivity. A claimant may successfully prove exclusivity by demonstrating that his acts pertaining to the property were consistent with ownership. If one can show that he exercised dominion and control over the property, and consistent with that control permitted others to occasionally use the property, exclusivity is not destroyed. Hernandez v. Cabrera, 759 P.2d at 1019. Therefore, the trial court's finding of longtime permissive use by neighbors does not compel a finding that a claim of adverse possession was not proved.

Theis Company also claims that Plaintiffs did not occupy or use the property in such a way to put it on notice that someone else might be claiming its property. However, having established color of title, Plaintiffs were not required to occupy the entire area claimed. See Marquez v. Padilla, 426 P.2d at 595. It is enough that "visible and notorious acts of ownership are manifested." Id.

The evidence clearly illustrated that the only use for the disputed area was for grazing livestock. Plaintiffs used the land in the only way it could be used. We must consider the nature and situation of the property in order to determine whether a claimant has done enough to prove a claim of adverse possession. See Lopez v. Barboa, 455 P.2d 842 (N.M. 1969). Given the nature of the property at issue, we conclude that Plaintiffs' use of the property for grazing was sufficient to establish actual and visible, or open, possession over the disputed area.

III. CONCLUSION

The trial court's finding that Plaintiffs established each element of adverse possession is supported by substantial evidence, and accordingly we affirm....

Notes & Questions

1. *Quarles* illustrates the most common form of adverse possession case—a boundary dispute between neighboring property owners. Each year, thousands of such cases are filed seeking to move the legal boundary line to correspond to the line that one or both parties had long thought to be the correct one.

2. Although the specific requirements for adverse possession vary from state to state, a number of general rules can be plucked from the cases. Virtually all courts hold that a plaintiff must show at least five things to establish adverse possession: (1) actual possession of the property

that is (2) open and notorious, (3) adverse and under "claim of right," (4) exclusive, and (5) continuous for the statutory period. Jurisdictions differ in their applications of these requirements and often add other requirements. The most common addition is a requirement that the adverse possessor pay taxes on the property throughout the period of possession. A few jurisdictions like New Mexico also require the plaintiff to prove "color of title"—i.e., a deed or other document purporting to provide title to the plaintiff.

3. **Actual possession.** The foundational requirement of adverse possessing is actual possession and occupation of the land. But what should count as actual possession? Cultivation, planting, harvesting, and construction are clear indicia of possession. See, e.g., Smith v. Hayden, 772 P.2d 47 (Colo. 1989) (construction of garage); Cheek v. Wainwright, 269 S.E.2d 443 (Ga. 1980) (timber cutting). Should it be enough that the adverse possessor constructed a fence around the land, even if she did not use the land for any active purpose? See Smith v. Tippett, 569 A.2d 1186 (D.C. 1990) (construction of wall sufficient). That the adverse possessor posted a "No Trespassing" sign? See Nutting v. Herman Timber Co., 29 Cal. Rptr. 754 (Cal. App. 1963) (posting of sign and use of land surrounding the disputed tract not sufficient to establish adverse possession). What if the adverse possessor has made no use of the land, but enrolled it in a government soil bank program which paid the adverse possessor not to use the land? See Doty v. Chalk, 632 P.2d 644 (Colo. App. 1981) (sufficient to establish adverse possession where the plaintiff kept the land free of weeds in compliance with the soil bank program). What counts as actual possession may depend on the type of property involved and the ordinary use of that property.

4. **Open & Notorious.** Closely related to the requirement of actual possession is the requirement that the possession be "open and notorious." Indeed, according to some courts, the "essence of actual possession is use of the land to such an extent and in such a manner as to put the world on notice [of the adverse possession]. This notice is achieved when the use is so notorious as to attract the attention of every adverse claimant." Cheek v. Wainwright, 269 S.E.2d 443, 445 (Ga. 1980). The "open and notorious" requirement therefore requires an adverse possessor to use the land in an obvious and visible fashion, not surreptitiously.

Can a subterranean use ever be "open and notorious"? In Marengo Cave Co. v. Ross, 10 N.E.2d 917 (Ind. 1937), the defendant had opened a cavern to the paying public. The cavern began under the defendant's property but extended under lands of another property owner, 700 feet from the cave opening. Although the defendant had operated the cavern for more than the statutory period, the Indiana Supreme Court held that the adverse possession was not sufficiently open to put the true owner on notice. To begin with, the possession "was not visible. No one could see below the earth's surface and determine that appellant was trespassing upon appellee's lands. This fact could not be determined by going into the cave. Only by a survey could this fact be made known." Further, plaintiff's "possession was not notorious. Not even [plaintiff] itself nor any of its remote grantors knew that any part of the 'Marengo Cave' extended beyond its own boundaries, and they at no time even down to the time [plaintiff] instituted this action made any claim to appellee's lands." Id. at 922.

Was *Marengo* correctly decided? Is its holding consistent with any of the rationales underlying adverse possession? Most courts hold that it is not necessary that the true owner have actual notice of the adverse possession. See, e.g., Lobro v. Watson, 116 Cal. Rptr. 533 (Cal. App. 1974) (finding adverse possession even though actual owner did not know that she owned the property).

5. **Color of Title.** Adverse possession is impossible in some states, such as New Mexico, unless the adverse possessor has occupied the property under color of a deed or some other document purporting to give the adverse possessor title to the property. See, e.g., Lakeside Boating & Bathing, Inc. v. State, 344 N.W.2d 217 (Iowa 1984). Other jurisdictions reward an adverse possessor who has color of title by reducing the statutory period needed for adverse possession. See, e.g., Ala. Code § 6–5–200 (shortening statutory period from 20 to 10 years); Ill. Rev. Stat, ch. 83, ¶¶ 6–7 (shortening statutory period from 20 to 7 years).

The principal role of "color of title" in most jurisdictions, however, is in defining the boundaries of the parcel of land to which an adverse possessor gains title. In many cases, an adverse possessor has occupied only a portion of the property to which he seeks title. Where the adverse possessor holds a deed or other document purporting to give him title to the property, most courts will hold that he has "constructive possession" of all the property described in the document—even if he has been in actual possession of only part of the land. See, e.g., DeShon v. St. Joseph Country Club Village, 755 S.W.2d 265 (Mo. App. 1988); Macallister v. DeStefano, 463 N.E.2d 346 (Mass. App. 1984). If the adverse possessor does not hold color of title, he will gain adverse possession only of that portion of the land over which he has maintained actual possession or of land that he has enclosed if he occupied part of it. See DeClerk v. Johnson, 596 S.W.2d 359 (Ark. App. 1980).

6. **Hostile & Under Claim of Right.** Almost all states provide that possession cannot ripen into title if possession has been with the true owner's permission. Possession, in other words, must be "hostile" or "adverse." Where someone enters onto land with the permission of the true owner, courts presume that possession continues with permission. Only an explicit revocation of permission by the owner or a clear statement by the adverse possessor to the owner that she intends to dispossess the true owner will start the statutory period for adverse possession to run. See, e.g., Buic v. Buic, 7 Cal. Rptr. 2d 738 (Cal. App. 1992); Alford v. Alford, 372 S.E.2d 389 (Va. 1988).

A small handful of courts also hold that possession cannot ripen into title if the possessor did not have the intent to keep the land if the land turned out not to be his. In Ellis v. Jansing, 620 S.W.2d 569 (Tex. 1981), for example, one homeowner claimed a portion of his neighbor's property that he had occupied for the statutory period in the mistaken belief that it was part of his land. Because the homeowner testified that "he never claimed or intended to claim any property other than that described in his deed, or what he thought was contained in his deed, and he never intended to claim any property owned by the abutting property owners," the Texas Supreme Court held that there was no adverse possession. "No matter how exclusive and hostile to the true owner the possession may be in appearance, it cannot be adverse unless accompanied by the intent on the part of the occupant to make it so. The naked possession unaccompanied with any claim of right will never constitute a bar." Id. at 571. Does this reward intentional wrongdoing? Does it encourage the possessor to falsely assert on the witness stand that he had an intent to keep any land that was not his (even though he probably never thought about the subject prior to consulting a lawyer)?

In *Quarles*, the Theis Company argued that the plaintiffs, who testified that they intended to claim only the land to which they had title, "lacked the necessary hostile intent to establish a claim of adverse possession." What was the New Mexico Supreme Court's response? Is it convincing?

The vast majority of courts have rejected the view that plaintiffs in adverse possession cases must show that they had an intent to keep the land that they occupied even if they did not have title to the land. See, e.g., Chaplin v. Sanders, 676 P.2d 431 (Wash. 1984) (the " 'hostility/claim of right' element . . . requires only that the claimant treat the land as his own as against the world throughout the statutory period").

7. **Exclusive.** Adverse possession cannot ripen into title where the possessor shared use of the land with the actual owner during the statutory period. See, e.g., Dzuris v. Kucharik, 434 P.2d 414 (Colo. 1967). Most courts also hold that an individual's long-term use of land cannot ripen into title where others have been making similar use of the land. In Sanchez v. Taylor, 377 F.2d 733 (10th Cir. 1967), for example, the exercise of traditional grazing rights by several hundred Chicano ranchers was held not to constitute adverse possession under Colorado law because no one had exclusive possession of the land. Is there any rationale for rejecting group claims to adverse possession? Does it reflect the law's inability to think beyond the traditional private property right model? See Christine A. Klein, Treaties of Conquest: Property Rights, Indian Treaties, and the Treaty of Guadalupe Hidalgo, 26 N.M.L. Rev. 201 (1966) (criticizing the decision in *Sanchez v. Taylor*). Given the testimony in *Quarles* that "the disputed area was used by everyone . . . because that was community custom," why did the plaintiffs prevail?

8. **Continuous for the Statutory Period.** Adverse possession must continue for the statutory period to ripen into title. The limitations period for adverse possession varies significantly from state to state depending on the predilections of the local legislators. Limitation periods, however, are generally longer in the East (where they typically range from 15 to 30 years) and shorter in the West (where 10 years is the norm). In recent decades, there has been a distinct trend toward shortening the period. See

William G. Ackerman & Shane T. Johnson, Outlaws of the Past: A Western Perspective on Prescription and Adverse Possession, 31 Land & Water L. Rev. 79, 111–112 (1996); Richard Epstein, Past and Future: The Temporal Dimension in the Law of Property, 64 Wash. U. L.Q. 667, 681 (1986) (suggesting that the trend is the result of a combination of politics and the reduced difficulty of vigilantly protecting your property).

Determining whether continuous possession for the statutory period has been established often raises a number of technical issues. Previous notes have discussed the problems of determining what constitutes *continuous* use (see Note 6 on page 113) and of *tacking* periods of possession or ownership (see Note 4 on page 111).

9. **Disabilities.** Should the true owner be protected from loss of title if the true owner was under a disability that prevented him from learning that he had a cause of action for trespass or from pursuing a lawsuit? An English statute, 21 Jac. 1, ch. 16 (1623), provided that if the true owner was an infant, a married woman ("femme covert"), insane, imprisoned, or "beyond the seas," at the time the cause of action first accrued, the limitations period would be extended to compensate for the disability. American legislation generally follows the policy of the English statute but varies the definition of disability. Although infancy and insanity continue to be disabilities in America, the disability of "coverture" was lifted after married women gained the right to sue for invasion of their property rights. Some, but not all, American statutes make imprisonment and absence from the country a disability. Other statutes use the general term "legal disability" and leave it to the courts to determine what facts should constitute disability in any particular case.

States differ as well on the exact effect of a disability. Some provide that the statute of limitations will not begin to run until the disability ends. See, e.g., Ariz. Rev. Stat. § 12–528. Others toll the statute but prescribe a shortened limitations period within which a trespass action must be brought once the disability is removed. See, e.g., Iowa Code Ann. § 614.8. Others prescribe a maximum period beyond which the statute's period will not be extended even if the disability continues. See, e.g., Fla. Stat. Ann. § 95.051. And while some states provide that, for the statute to be suspended, the disability must exist when a cause of action for trespass first accrued, others provide that intervening disabilities will correspondingly extend the limitations period.

10. **Tax Payments as a Requirement of Adverse Possession.** In some cases, an adverse possessor cannot gain title unless she has paid taxes on the land throughout the limitations period. A few states, like California and New Mexico, make taxpaying a categorical requirement in all adverse possession cases. See, e.g., Cal. Civ. Code § 325. Other states require tax payments only in special circumstances—e.g., if the parcel is claimed under an abbreviated limitations period, Ariz. Rev. Stat. §§ 12–524 & 12.525, or is claimed other than in a boundary dispute, Minn. Stat. Ann. § 541.02.

What rationale underlies a requirement that the adverse possessor have paid property taxes on the land? In most states, legislatures added the requirement in the 19th century at the behest of railroads. The federal government had awarded railroads vast, unoccupied tracts of land to encourage railroad construction, and the railroads were concerned that much of the land could be lost through adverse possession to the ever present and perennially troublesome squatters. Although "color of title" and good faith requirements went far toward protecting the railroads from squatters' claims, the railroads believed that a tax payment requirement would do even better: where a squatter paid the taxes, the railroad could quickly find out by checking the tax records; where a squatter was not paying the taxes, there was no risk of adverse possession. See also Dutton v. Thompson, 19 S.W. 1026 (Tex. 1892) (suggesting that the tax requirement also provided evidence of good faith and ensured that the government got its taxes).

11. **Doctrine of Agreed Boundaries.** In some states, neighborly disputes over the correct property line can also trigger the related doctrine of "agreed boundaries." If both neighbors are uncertain over the location of the correct property line, orally agree on where the boundary line is, and then acquiesce to this agreement for a lengthy time, the doctrine binds the parties to the agreement even if later it turns out that the agreed line is not the true boundary. See, e.g., Grappo v. Mauch, 887 P.2d 740 (Nev. 1994).

Devins v. Borough of Bogota

Supreme Court of New Jersey, 1991.
592 A.2d 199.

POLLOCK, J., writing for a unanimous Court.

The primary issue on this appeal is whether adverse possession should apply to municipally-owned property not dedicated to or used for a public purpose....

The property is a 25 × 100 foot lot located on Fairview Avenue and identified as Lot 10, Block 98 on the municipal tax map. In 1962, Bogota acquired title to the property through an in rem foreclosure. At that time, the lot was vacant. Since then, Bogota has not improved or used the property, nor has it dedicated the property to public use.

In 1965, plaintiffs purchased from James and Jeanette Geraghty an adjacent single-family residence at 132 Fairview Avenue, identified as Block 98, Lots 11 and 11A on the municipal tax map ("the house lot"). At that time, the Geraghtys, who in 1958 had received a quitclaim deed to Lot 10 from their grantors, also executed a quitclaim deed for that lot. Sometime before 1958, a chain link fence had been erected around Lot 10. That fence matches a fence around the house lot, creating the appearance that the lots are commonly owned. A barbecue pit, which had been constructed before plaintiffs acquired the house lot, remains on Lot 10.

Since 1965, plaintiffs have used Lot 10 for parking, cookouts, lounging, and other recreational purposes. Plaintiffs installed a basketball backboard on the lot in the mid–1970s and erected a shed around 1980. Additionally, they have mowed the grass and otherwise maintained the lot. At some point, a portion of Lot 10 was paved to provide parking for the house lot. Before the institution of suit, Bogota had not challenged plaintiffs' use of the property.

For their part, plaintiffs have never paid taxes on Lot 10. In 1985, however, their attorney sent a letter to the Mayor and Council of Bogota requesting that the Borough concede that plaintiffs had acquired title to Lot 10 by twenty years' adverse possession. The Borough promptly denied plaintiffs' claim, asserting that adverse possession cannot run against a municipality.

Plaintiffs then filed this action seeking a declaration that they had acquired title by twenty years' adverse possession. Although the Chancery Division believed that plaintiffs had established facts that could constitute adverse possession, it ruled that "adverse possession will not run against a municipality." Consequently, the court granted summary judgment for the municipality. The Appellate Division affirmed. . . .

The restriction on the application of adverse possession to public property is rooted in the ancient doctrine that time does not run against the king, sometimes expressed in the latin phrase *nullum tempus occurrit regi*. The phrase, which is often shortened to "*nullum tempus*," means "time does not run against the king." Black's Law Dictionary 963 (5th ed. 1969). Although none of the New Jersey statutes of limitation expressly excepts governmental entities, courts have long ruled, in reliance on the principle of *nullum tempus*, that the statutes do not run against property owned by either the State or by a municipality. [New Jersey decisions applying this doctrine to government land], however, have all involved land dedicated to or used for a public purpose.

Our analysis leads us to conclude that the *nullum tempus* exception to adverse possession should not be extended to include land held by a municipality for non-governmental purposes. The original rationale supporting *nullum tempus* was that the king was too busy protecting the interests of his people to keep track of his lands and to bring suits to protect them in a timely fashion. A second reason was that the king established his own rules for litigation.

In New Jersey, *nullum tempus* developed primarily in the context of claims of adverse possession of public lands. As explained by the courts, the reasons for the rule include: first, the public should not suffer from the negligence of its agents; second, absent the express inclusion of the State, a statute of limitations should not be read to affect adversely the State's rights; third, the State holds public property in trust for the people, so only the Legislature can divest the State of title; and finally, possession of public lands by a third party constitutes a public nuisance that no period of acquiescence will justify.

Those reasons are subject to countervailing considerations. First, statutes of limitation allow repose and avoid adjudications based on stale evidence. Second, adverse possession promotes certainty of title, and protects the possessor's reasonable expectations. Third, allowing adverse possession promotes active and efficient use of land and "tends to serve the public interest by stimulating the expeditious assertion of public claims," Eureka Printing Co. v. Department of Labor & Indus., 21 N.J. 383, 388 (1956). Consistent with this last proposition, plaintiffs argue that permitting adverse possession of municipal property would encourage municipal efficiency and the return of property to the tax rolls.

Recent trends in contract and tort law have eroded the notion that government should be treated as fundamentally different from private parties. In both torts, Willis v. Department of Conservation & Economic Dev., 55 N.J. 534 (1970) (abolishing sovereign immunity in tort), and contracts, P.T. & L. Constr. Co. v. Commissioner, Dep't of Transp., 55 N.J. 341 (1970) (abolishing sovereign immunity in contract), first the courts and then the Legislature have reconsidered sovereign immunity, with the result that the State may be liable in tort or contract.

In other states, legislatures have exposed the State to adverse possession claims in limited circumstances. The statutes in some states simply permit adverse possession of "any real property" held by the State. N.C. Gen. Stat. § 1–35; N.D. Cent. Code § 28–01–01; Utah Code Ann. § 78–12–2. Similarly, a Wisconsin statute provides that real property of the State or its subdivisions "may be obtained by adverse possession." Wis. Stat. § 893.29. Yet another State provides that the statutes of limitation apply to actions by the State the "same as to actions by private persons." Ky. Rev. Stat. Ann. § 413.150.

Other States qualify the power to obtain public real estate through adverse possession. Massachusetts and Michigan both permit adverse possession of State land but protect certain types of land. Massachusetts permits no adverse possession of State land "held for conservation, open space, parks, recreation, water protection, wildlife protection, or other public purpose." Mass. Gen. L. ch. 260, § 31. Michigan imposes no time bar for actions by municipal corporations to recover "any public highway, street, alley, or any other public ground." Mich. Comp. Laws § 27A.5821. In sum, state legislatures have struck different balances when addressing the issue of adverse possession of publicly-owned real estate. The point for our purposes, however, is that those States have recognized that their legislatures are specially suited to strike that balance.

Some commentators have called for the rejection of *nullum tempus* in adverse possession actions. See Note, Developments in the Law: Statutes of Limitations, 63 Harv. L. Rev. 1177 (1950); Note, State's Immunity to the Statute of Limitations, 38 Ill. L. Rev. 418 (1944). Similarly, a congressional commission that studied adverse possession of federal lands has recommended that *nullum tempus* should be abolished and that all such lands be made subject to adverse possession. The commission concluded that the federal government has adequate resources to protect public land. See Public Land Law Review Commission, Recommendation 113, One Third of the Nation's Land: A Report to the President and to the Congress 260–62 (1970).

Ultimately, the issue is one of public policy. We believe the better rule concerning municipally-owned real property not dedicated to or used for a public purpose is to treat it like property owned by private owners. Underlying our belief is the perception that we are not imposing an undue burden on municipalities by expecting them to discover within the relevant period of limitations what property they own and who possesses it. That expectation will encourage municipalities to make efficient use of their property and return it to the tax rolls. Conversely, we are reluctant to adopt a policy that would encourage municipalities not to use, dedicate, or even identify their property.

We conclude that for municipally-owned real estate not dedicated to or used for a public purpose, *nullum tempus* is an anachronism. Our decision today is consistent with decisions from Connecticut and Maryland, which hold that municipal land not used for a public purpose is subject to adverse possession. [See Goldman v. Quadrato, 114 A.2d 687 (Conn. 1955); Siejack v. City of Baltimore, 313 A.2d 843 (Md. App. 1974).] . . .

The judgment of the Appellate Division is reversed, and the matter is remanded to the Chancery Division.

Notes & Questions

1. As noted in Chapter 1, governments own more than a third of all the land in the United States. The federal government holds over 600 million acres, or slightly less than 30 percent, of all lands—and more than half of the lands in the western United States where the federal public lands are concentrated. State and local governments hold about 7 percent of all lands. The vast majority, on the order of 90 percent, of governmental lands are undeveloped.

2. The federal government and most states still prohibit adverse possession against the government. See, e.g., 48 U.S.C. § 1489; Cal. Civ. Code § 1007. Those states that permit adverse possession against the government generally use significantly longer limitations period in cases involving government land than in those cases involving private land. See, e.g., N.C. Gen. Stat. § 1–35 (extending standard limitations periods of 7 and 20 years to 21 and 30 years respectively in case of government lands); N.D. Cent. Code § 28–01–01 (40–year limitation period).

See generally Paula R. Latovick, Adverse Possession Against the States: The Hornbooks Have It Wrong, 29 U. Mich. J.L. Ref. 939 (1996); Carl C. Risch, Encouraging the Responsible Use of Land by Municipalities, 99 Dick. L. Rev. 197 (1994)

3. As the New Jersey Supreme Court notes, the Public Land Law Review Commission in 1970 recommended that "the doctrine of adverse possession be made applicable against the United States where land has been occupied in good faith." U.S. Public Land Law Review Commission,

One Third of the Nation's Land 261 (1970). Recognizing that the "principle that the United States cannot lose title to its lands by adverse possession by a private party is treated as axiomatic by the courts," the Commission observed that

> private citizens do occupy public lands in technical trespass, but in good faith believe that the land is theirs. Often valuable improvements are placed upon such lands in ignorance of the Federal claim. Partly because of the protection the Government enjoys, including inapplicability of the doctrine of adverse possession, such occupancies, although known to the Government's agents, are sometimes permitted to exist until there is a Federal use for the lands. At other times they simply remain undiscovered until there is a Federal requirement for the lands.

Id. at 262. Should the governmental privilege against adverse possession be abolished outright? Should the privilege be limited to specific lands? If so, which lands? See Elmer M. Million, Adverse Possession Against the United States—A Treasure for Trespassers, 26 Ark. L. Rev. 467 (1973) (criticizing the recommendations of the Public Land Law Review Commission).

4. Recall *The Yosemite Valley Case*, p. 37, in which the United States Supreme Court ruled that James Hutchings could not claim part of Yosemite Valley under the 1841 Preemption Act. If Hutchings had made improvements and lived in Yosemite Valley for the requisite statutory period, should he have been entitled to that portion of Yosemite Valley by adverse possession? Why or why not?

5. How easy is to apply the "public use" test set out in *Devins* for determining which land is exempt from adverse possession? See American Trading Real Estate Properties, Inc. v. Town of Trumbull, 574 A.2d 796 (Conn. 1990) ("public use" test met if land is held for potential future use by municipality); Paula R. Latovick, Adverse Possession of Municipal Land: It's Time To Protect This Valuable Asset, 31 U. Mich. J.L. Ref. 475 (1998) (criticizing "public use" test as difficult to apply). Could New Jersey municipalities get around *Devins* simply by dedicating all their unoccupied land as "open space" until such time as they might have some other use for the land?

6. **Adverse Possession & the Environment.** Does *Devins* display an anti-environmental bias? According to the court, restricting the governmental privilege will encourage municipalities "to make efficient use of their property and return it to the tax rolls." Is this a good thing? What's wrong with a city deciding to leave land vacant? Do the other adverse possession opinions in this section also display a pro-development bias?

As noted earlier, Professor John Sprankling argues that adverse possession law encourages the development of the nation's remaining wild lands. See John G. Sprankling, An Environmental Critique of Adverse Possession, 79 Cornell L. Rev. 816 (1994). According to Spankling, adverse possession law encourages potential claimants to put undeveloped land to economic use by cutting timber, grazing cattle, and removing minerals.

Adverse possession law also encourages the current owner of vacant land to develop the land or put it to economic use so that the activities of any adverse possessor will not be "exclusive" and thus not ripen into title.

Sprankling proposes exempting "wild lands" from adverse possession. According to Sprankling, the exemption should apply

> to land which is in a *substantially* natural, undeveloped condition before adverse possession activity begins. Land that has suffered minor human intrusion, such as seasonal grazing, timber thinning or fence installation still supports largely undisturbed ecosystems. Land whose natural vegetation has been destroyed, however, does not; thus, the filled wetland, the bulldozed grassland and the chopped forest would remain susceptible to adverse possession.

Id. at 864. Do you favor Sprankling's proposal? Do environmental concerns about adverse possession outweigh the arguments for adverse possession discussed earlier?

Massachusetts provides that adverse possession does not ban "an action by or on behalf of a nonprofit land conservation corporation or trust for the recovery of land or interests in land held for conservation, parks, recreation, water protection, or wildlife protection purposes." Mass. Ann. Laws ch. 260, § 21. A separate provision precludes adverse possession of state lands held for similar purposes. Id. § 31. Do these provisions meet Sprankling's concerns? Should they be extended to other owners of undeveloped land?

C. THE RIGHT TO USE

1. PRIVATE NUISANCES

Under the common law, property owners enjoy the right not only to exclude others from their property, but to use their property generally as they want. By its very nature, however, the right to use land cannot be absolute, because one landowner's use of his property can frequently interfere with another landowner's use of her property. If a factory has the exclusive right to use its land as it pleases, for example, it would be free to belch thick black soot and smoke, even if this means fouling the air on a neighboring homeowner's parcel. If the neighboring homeowner has the absolute right to use her land as she pleases, she would be entitled to have the factory's pollution enjoined. The common law typically resolves these types of conflicts through the doctrine of "private nuisance."

How should the law allocate rights between the factory and the homeowner? Should the factory be given the right to pollute? Or should the homeowner be given the right to clean air? One answer, frequently offered by environmentalists, is that the factory should be liable for its emissions because smoke damage represents a cost—specifically a "social cost"—of running the factory that is properly borne not by the homeowner, but by the producer; imposing liability on the factory will force it to account for the full cost of its product and, as a result, the factory will probably pollute less than if it bore no liability for its emissions.

The argument that the factory rather than the homeowner should bear the cost of pollution rests on the premise that it is the factory that causes the harm. In fact, it is equally plausible to say that the homeowner causes the harm, for if the house were not there—if the lot were vacant or occupied by another factory—there would be no injury to residential use. The damage that attends the factory's and the homeowner's use of the atmosphere can thus be viewed either as a cost of manufacturing the factory's product or as a cost of living in a residence adjacent to the factory. Or, perhaps, more accurately, the damage can be viewed as a joint cost of the two activities. (Recall the earlier discussion of the Coase Theorem at pages 64–66.)

On what basis, then, are property rights to be assigned? As the following cases demonstrate, the law has not always found this an easy question.

McCarty v. Natural Carbonic Gas Co.

Court of Appeals of New York, 1907.
81 N.E. 549.

VANN, J.

This action was brought to restrain the defendant from so operating its manufactory as to cause smoke, soot and dust emitted from its chimneys to gather and settle about the dwelling house of the plaintiff to his annoyance and injury.

The trial court found the following facts in substance: For four years prior to the 13th of July, 1904, when this action was commenced, the plaintiff owned certain premises on South Broadway in the village of Saratoga Springs, consisting of a lot of land with a frame dwelling house thereon, known as the "Anna Therese." Said house is situated in a country district suitable for country homes, "although not as yet so appropriated by others than the plaintiff." The defendant is a foreign corporation engaged in the manufacture of carbonic acid gas in a semi-fluid form convenient for shipment to market by compressing the natural gas found on its premises, and for this purpose it maintains a plant containing machinery operated by steam, which is generated from two boilers with a capacity of 100 horse power. It has two smokestacks, each 90 feet high, situated 840 feet from the residence of the plaintiff. From two and one-half to four tons of soft coal are used daily by the defendant and its chimneys continuously pour forth "a thick black smoke, large in volume and larger, denser and thicker when the fires are freshened twice" every hour during the twenty-four that the plant is in operation, Sundays excepted.

When the wind is right the smoke blows down upon the plaintiff's house and comes upon and around it. When the atmosphere is dense "clouds of smoke proceeding from the defendant's chimneys gather and settle about the plaintiff's house, enveloping it and sometimes obscuring it from view." Said smoke "has caused the exterior of the house of the plaintiff to become discolored with soot and has caused plaintiff and his family much discomfort and annoyance and some financial injury." The defendant causes this damage and injury by the use of soft coal, yet by the use of anthracite coal it would obtain the same result in manufacturing although at a greater expense, and if the use of soft coal were abandoned the discomfort experienced by the plaintiff would be entirely avoided. "The present use of soft coal is not a necessary use for the practical management and running of its plant" and "under all the circumstances of the case the present discomfort of the plaintiff is not occasioned by any reasonable use by the defendant of its own property." The plaintiff had owned his property for several years before the defendant erected its factory. Another factory like the defendant's was located in the neighborhood before the plaintiff purchased, but as it uses anthracite coal it has never caused any annoyance. The rental value of the plaintiff's house has been injured by the use of soft coal by the defendant to the extent of $800, and he has incurred expense for cleaning rugs to the extent of $18 more.

The court, after repeating as conclusions of law its findings of fact in relation to reasonable and necessary use, further found as conclusions of law that "the defendant should be enjoined, restrained and forbidden from burning soft coal on its said plant in the village of Saratoga Springs, New York, for the purpose of generating steam," and that "the plaintiff herein is entitled to the sum of $818.00 damages and is also entitled to the costs of the action." Upon appeal to the Appellate Division the judgment was modified by deducting from the damages awarded the sum of $18.00 as of the date when the judgment was entered, and, as so modified, the judgment was unanimously affirmed.

The action of the courts below ... leaves but one question upon the merits for us to decide and that is whether the facts found support the conclusions of law? In other words, in a country district suitable for country homes, does the use of soft coal in a factory so situated that thick, black smoke therefrom, great in volume and dense in quality, envelopes and discolors a neighboring dwelling house, causing much discomfort and some financial loss to the occupants, constitute a nuisance, when such use of soft coal is not necessary for the practical running of the plant and is not a reasonable use of the manufacturer's property?

The principles governing the decision of that question are neither recent in origin nor doubtful in application. The ancient maxim of *sic utere tuo ut alienum non loedas* is the foundation of the well-established rule that no one may make an unreasonable use of his own premises to the material injury of his neighbor's premises, and if he does the latter has a right of action even if he is not driven from his dwelling, provided the enjoyment of life and property is materially lessened.

The law relating to private nuisances is a law of degree and usually turns on the question of fact whether the use is reasonable or not under all the circumstances. No hard and fast rule controls the subject, for a use that is reasonable under one set of facts would be unreasonable under another.... Whether the use of property by one person is reasonable, with reference to the comfortable enjoyment of his own property by another, generally depends upon many and varied facts; such as location, nature of the use, character of the neighborhood, extent and frequency of the injury, the effect on the enjoyment of life, health and property and the like. Such was the nature of the question in this case which, we think, is one of fact....

In the well-known case of Cogswell v. New York, N.H. & H.R. Co., 8 N.E. 537 (N.Y. 1886), a railroad company had erected an engine house near a dwelling house in a city and the smoke, cinders and coal dust, carried by the winds, filled the house, injured articles therein and rendered the air offensive and the house uncomfortable. It was held that the "engine house, as used, was within every definition a nuisance, for which, as between individuals, an action would lie for damages and for which a court of equity would afford a remedy by injunction." All the judges united with Judge Andrews in saying: "However necessary it may be for the defendant that its engine house should be located where it is, this constitutes no justification for the injury suffered by the plaintiff, nor is it any answer to the action that it exercises all practicable care in its management. It may have the right, which it claims, to acquire land by purchase for the accommodation of its business, but it must secure such a location as will enable it to conduct its operations without violating the just rights of others. Public policy, indeed, requires that in adjusting the mutual relations between railroads and individuals, courts should not stand upon the assertion of extreme rights for either side, but in this case the facts leave no room for doubt that the plaintiff has suffered a substantial and unauthorized injury."....

The leading authorities in all jurisdictions hold that the question is whether the defendant makes a reasonable ... use of his own property? Sometimes negligence is referred to as an element in the question. Judge Landon once pointedly said: "A lawful business negligently conducted is not a lawful business lawfully conducted," but, as the quotation implies, since a negligent use of one's own property to the injury of another is an unreasonable use, the ultimate question after all is whether the use is reasonable. Negligence, wrong business methods, improper appliances and the like may bear upon but do not control the question of reasonable use. If the use is reasonable there can be no private nuisance, but if the use is unreasonable and results in substantial injury, an actionable nuisance exists. Trifling results are disregarded, for the courts proceed with great caution and will not interfere with the use of property by the owner thereof unless such use is unreasonable, the injury material and actual, not fanciful or sentimental. *Lex non favet votis delicatorum.*

.... The extent more than the nature of the injury, the *quantum*, rather than the *damnum*, constitutes the nuisance. Some smoke is generally created by the natural and ordinary use of land near a village or city, and while this may sometimes be annoying to neighbors it is part of the price paid for living where there are neighbors. But when the smoke is so unusual and excessive as to materially interfere with the ordinary comfort of human existence, the trier of the facts, taking into account all the circumstances, such as public utility, locality, immediate surroundings and the like, may find the use unreasonable. This is not a case where the defendant cannot carry on its business without injury to neighboring property, for all damage can be avoided by the use of hard coal, as is done by one of its competitors in the same kind of business in the same locality, or possibly by the use of some modern appliance such as a smoke consumer, although either would involve an increase in expense. It is better, however, that profits should be somewhat reduced than to compel a householder to abandon his home, especially when he did not "come to the nuisance," but was there before. "The safety of property generally is superior in right to a particular use of a single piece of property by its owner. It renders the enjoyment of all property more secure by preventing such use of one piece by one man as may injure all his neighbors." (Sullivan v. Dunham, 55 N.E. 923 (N.Y. 1900).)

The use made of property may be unpleasant, unsightly or, to some extent, annoying and disagreeable to the occupants of neighboring property without creating a nuisance. When, however, it not only interferes materially with the physical comfort of persons in their own homes, but also causes some financial injury to the owner, it constitutes a nuisance. . . .

O'BRIEN, J. (dissenting). . . .

The [trial] court in its findings expressly negatived some facts which the plaintiff sought to establish. It is found that no injury has been occasioned by the use of soft coal by the defendant to the trees or shrubbery of the plaintiff; that the use of soft coal by the defendant has not caused any injury to the health of the plaintiff or his family for which damages could be recovered; that there is nothing to show that plaintiff's house would not by this time require washing and painting even if it had not been soiled by the smoke from the defendant's plant; that no permanent injury has been done by the use of soft coal by the defendant to the plaintiff's furniture or to the interior decorations of his house. . . .

. . . [T]he question is whether a person residing in a city, village or other locality where manufacturing is carried on by the use of steam power has the legal right to exemption from annoyance or discomfort resulting from the use of soft coal. The decisions of this court must be the guide in the solution of such a question. In *Cogswell*, Judge Andrews laid down the rule in these terms: "The compromises exacted by the necessities of the social state, and the fact that some inconvenience to others must of necessity often attend the ordinary use of property, without permitting which there could in many cases be no valuable use at all, have compelled the recognition, in all systems of jurisprudence, of the principle that each member of society must submit to annoyances consequent upon the ordinary and common use of property, provided such use is reasonable, both as respects the owner of the property and those immediately affected by the use, in view of time, place and other circumstances." In the earlier case of

Campbell v. Seaman, 63 N.Y. 568 (1876), the rule was stated by Judge Earl in language somewhat different, but to the same effect: "It is a general rule that every person may exercise exclusive dominion over his own property and subject it to such uses as will best subserve his private interests. Generally, no other person can say how he shall use or what he shall do with his property. But this general right of property has its exceptions and qualifications. *Sic utere tuo ut alienum non loedas* is an old maxim which has a broad application. It does not mean that one must never use his own so as to do any injury to his neighbor or his property. Such a rule could not be enforced in civilized society. Persons living in organized communities must suffer some damage, annoyance and inconvenience from each other. For these they are compensated by all the advantages of civilized society. If one lives in the city he must expect to suffer the dirt, smoke, noisome odors, noise and confusion incident to city life."

The contention of the plaintiff in the present case is that the defendant in the operation of its manufacturing plant should have used anthracite coal instead of soft coal. It is found that this change must involve an additional expense upon the defendant. The amount of that additional expense has not been found, but it is found that in order to conduct the defendant's business from two and one-half to four tons of coal per day must be burned. The defendant cannot carry on its business without observing due economy in its management. If it can be compelled by the plaintiff for his own comfort to impose additional burdens upon the business, the result may be the loss of reasonable profits, and it may be in the destruction of the business entirely. If the plaintiff can legally demand that the defendant must use anthracite coal instead of soft coal, there is no reason why he may not demand other changes that would enhance his own comforts or enjoyment of his property.... There is nothing in the record to show that the business which the defendant is conducting is a very profitable one. It may well be that the business has not yet produced any profit whatever, and such an increase in the expense might not only absorb the profits, but result in a loss. It has been said that the power to tax includes the power to destroy, and if the plaintiff or other parties similarly situated, armed with the decree of the court, can compel the defendant to make the changes suggested by the judgment in this case for his own comfort, the application of such a principle might go far to render the defendant's property and business worthless....

Notes & Questions

1. Professor William Prosser spoke for virtually everyone who has ever studied nuisance cases when he wrote that there "is perhaps no more" impenetrable jungle in the entire law than that which surrounds the "nuisance." It has meant "all things to all men." William Prosser, Nuisance Without Fault, 20 Tex. L. Rev. 399, 410 (1949) (also arguing that nuisance law is a "legal garbage can" packed full of "vagueness, uncertainty, and confusion"). As Justice Harry Blackmun said with only a touch of overstatement, "one searches in vain ... for anything resembling a princi-

ple in the common law of nuisance." Lucas v. South Carolina Coastal Council, 505 U.S. 1003, 1055 (1992) (Blackmun, J., dissenting).

2. The Restatement (Second) of Torts tries to bring some clarity to nuisance law. According to the Restatement, only conduct that invades an interest in the private use and enjoyment of land can constitute a private nuisance. If the defendant's conduct is *unintentional*, an injured landowner can prevail only if she can demonstrate that the conduct is negligent, reckless, or constitutes an abnormally dangerous activity. Restatement (Second) Torts § 822(b) (1979). If the defendant's conduct is *intentional*, as in *McCarty*, the landowner can prevail by demonstrating that the conduct was "unreasonable." Id. § 822(a).

The trick, of course, is defining what is "unreasonable." Section 826(a) of the Restatement provides that an intentional invasion is "unreasonable" if the "gravity of the harm outweighs the utility of the actor's conduct." Sections 827 and 828 list the factors to be weighed in determining, respectively, the gravity of harm and the utility of the actor's conduct:

§ 827. Gravity of Harm—Factors Involved

In determining the gravity of the harm from an intentional invasion of another's interest in the use and enjoyment of land, the following factors are important:

(a) The extent of the harm involved;

(b) the character of the harm involved;

(c) the social value that the law attaches to the type of use or enjoyment invaded;

(d) the suitability of the particular use or enjoyment invaded to the character of the locality; and

(e) the burden on the person harmed of avoiding the harm.

§ 828. Utility of Conduct—Factors Involved

In determining the utility of conduct that causes an intentional invasion of another's interest in the use and enjoyment of land, the following factors are important:

(a) the social value that the law attaches to the primary purpose of the conduct;

(b) the suitability of the conduct to the character of the locality; and

(c) the impracticability of preventing or avoiding the invasion.

Displaying a bit of schizophrenia, the Restatement also sets out two alternative tests for determining the "reasonableness" of challenged conduct. Under section 826(b), intentional conduct is unreasonable if the "harm caused by the conduct is serious and the financial burden of compensating for this and similar harm to others would not make the continuation of the conduct not feasible." Section 829A of the Restatement provides that an intentional "invasion" is unreasonable "if the harm resulting from the invasion is severe and greater than the plaintiff should be required to bear without compensation."

How would *McCarty* have been decided under each of the tests? Do any of the tests describe the approach of the majority in *McCarty*? The dissent?

3. If a court finds that an activity is causing serious harm to a neighbor's use of his or her property, should it matter whether the "gravity of the harm outweighs the utility of the actor's conduct"? As discussed below at pages 151–158, the utility of the actor's conduct might be relevant to whether the court should prohibit the conduct by issuing an injunction. But should the utility of the actor's conduct justify denying the neighbor all relief, including damages? Assume that the carbonic gas factory in *McCarty* had been the major employer in the region. Should that have made a difference?

This was the issue in Carpenter v. Double R Cattle Co., 701 P.2d 222 (Idaho 1985). A group of homeowners alleged that a neighboring feedlot for 9,000 cattle was a nuisance. According to the homeowners, the feedlot had led to the "spread and accumulation of manure, pollution of river and ground water, odor, insect infestation, increased concentration of birds, [and] dust and noise." Reversing a lower court decision, the Idaho Supreme Court concluded that the utility of the feedlot was a relevant consideration in deciding whether it was a nuisance. "The State of Idaho is sparsely populated and its economy depends largely upon the benefits of agriculture, lumber, mining and industrial development. To eliminate the utility of conduct and other facts listed by the trial court from the criteria to be considered in determining whether a nuisance exists ... would place an unreasonable burden upon these industries." Id. at 228.

Two justices dissented, urging that the court adopt the "more progressive" approach of section 826(b) of the Restatement, which provides a "method of compensating those who must suffer the invasion without putting out of business the source or cause of the invasion." Id. at 229 (Bistline & Huntley, JJ., dissenting).

> The majority's rule today suggests that part of the cost of industry, agriculture or development must be borne by those unfortunate few who have the fortuitous luck to live in the immediate vicinity of a nuisance producing facility. Frankly, I think this naive economic view is ridiculous in both its simplicity and its outdated view of modern economic society. The "cost" of a product includes not only the amount it takes to produce such a product but also includes the external costs: the damage done to the environment through pollution of air or water is an example of an external cost. In the instant case, the nuisance suffered by the homeowners should be considered an external cost of operating a feedlot and producing beef for public consumption. I do not believe that a few should be required to pay this extra cost of doing business by going uncompensated for a nuisance of this sort. If a feedlot wants to continue, I say fine, providing compensation is paid for the serious invasion (the odors, flies, dust, etc.) of the

> homeowner's interest. My only qualification is that the financial burden of compensating for this harm should not be such as to force the feedlot (or any other industry) out of business. The true cost can then be shifted to the consumer who rightfully should pay for the entire cost of producing the product he desires to obtain.
>
> .... [M]eat prices at the grocery store will undoubtedly go up. But, in my view it is far better that the cost of the nuisance be carried by the consumer of the product than by the unfortunate homeowners currently suffering under adverse conditions. Some compensation should be paid the homeowners for suffering the burden from which we all benefit.

Id. at 229–230. Do the dissenters overlook Coase's observation that both the feedlot and the homeowners jointly cause the conflict? If the homeowners lived somewhere else, there would be no external cost. Assuming the homeowners should not have to bear the cost of the feedlot as a matter of equity or economic efficiency, moreover, why should it matter if compensation would put the feedlot out of business?

4. Commentators have suggested a number of other tests for determining whether an activity is a nuisance. Professor Richard Epstein argues that an activity cannot constitute a private nuisance unless it results in the physical invasion of another person's property. Even physical invasions are not nuisances, however, in those situations where property owners as a whole enjoy roughly compensating benefits for allowing the activity. See Richard A. Epstein, Nuisance Law: Corrective Justice and Its Utilitarian Constraints, 8 J. Legal Stud. 49 (1979). Professor Robert Ellickson has alternatively proposed that nuisances should be judged by a standard of "neighborliness"—what type of activities are acceptable under local norms? See Robert C. Ellickson, Alternatives to Zoning: Covenants, Nuisance Rules & Fines as Land Use Controls, 40 U. Chi. L. Rev. 681 (1973). How would *McCarty* have been resolved under either of these two formulations? Is either preferable to the Restatement tests?

5. Smoke and other forms of air pollution have frequently been found to be nuisances. See, e.g., Thomsen v. Greve, 550 N.W.2d 49 (Neb. App. 1996) (smoke from wood-burning stove found to be a nuisance, even though stove used to save energy). Loud noises, strong odors, and bright lights also are recurring subjects of successful nuisance actions. See, e.g., Patterson v. Robinson, 620 So. 2d 609 (Ala. 1993) (noise from raceway was a nuisance); Rose v. Chaikin, 453 A.2d 1378 (N.J. Super. 1982) (noise from windmill constituted a nuisance, despite defendant's claim that the windmill provided valuable energy conservation); Padilla v. Lawrence, 685 P.2d 964 (N.M. App. 1984) (odors, dust, noise, and flies from manure processor).

6. **Trespass Revisited.** Could *McCarty* have been decided on a trespass rather than a nuisance theory? A homeowner bothered by the way in which a neighboring landowner is using his property might prefer suing under trespass rather than nuisance law for a variety of reasons. While nuisance requires a showing of substantial harm, trespass requires none beyond the rule *de minimis non curat lex*. While nuisance makes intention-

al invasions actionable only if they are unreasonable, trespass essentially is *per se* illegal. Procedural rules might also favor a trespass action. Trespass actions, for example, often enjoy longer statutes of limitation.

Historically, air pollution and other nuisances such as noise and lights were not considered trespasses. W. Page Keeton, et al., Prosser and Keeton on The Law of Torts § 13, at 71 (5th ed. 1984). As discussed earlier in this Chapter, trespass addressed violations of a property owner's right of exclusive possession. Pollution, loud noises, and bright lights interfered with a property owner's use and enjoyment of his or her land—the province of nuisance law, but did not interfere with the landowner's exclusive possession. Some courts still hold firmly to the view that air and noise pollution cannot amount to trespass. See, e.g., Adams v. Cleveland–Cliffs Iron Co., 602 N.W.2d 215 (Mich. Ct. App. 1999).

In recent decades, however, there has been a discernible trend to expand trespass doctrine to cover activities that formerly were the province of nuisance alone. The Oregon Supreme Court started the trend in Martin v. Reynolds Metals Co., 342 P.2d 790 (Ore. 1959), ruling that defendant's discharge of imperceptible fluoride gases and particulates onto plaintiff's land constituted a trespass entitling plaintiff to use the six-year statute of limitations for trespass rather than the two-year nuisance statute. Rejecting defendant's argument that, at most, the plaintiff stated a claim for nuisance, the court defined trespass as "any intrusion which invades the possessor's protected interest in exclusive possession, whether that intrusion is by visible or invisible pieces of matter, or by energy which can be measured only by the mathematical language of the physicist." Id. at 794. See also Stevenson v. E.F. DuPont De Nemours, 327 F.3d 400 (5th Cir. 2003) (air pollution); Mock v. Potlatch Corp., 786 F. Supp. 1545 (D. Ida. 1992) (noise pollution); Bradley v. American Smelting & Refining Co., 709 P.2d 782 (Wash. 1985) (air pollution).

In extending trespass law to air and noise pollution, however, courts have simultaneously heightened the requirements for proving a trespass. While courts historically inferred damages as a matter of law from a trespass itself, most courts that apply trespass to air and noise pollution require that the plaintiff prove actual and substantial damages. See, e.g., Mock v. Potlatch Corp., 786 F. Supp. at 1549–51. The principal reason is a fear that the courts otherwise would be inundated with trespass actions. "No useful purpose would be served by sanctioning actions in trespass by every land owner within a hundred miles of a manufacturing plant. Manufacturers would be harassed and a litigious few would cause the escalation of costs to the detriment of the many." Bradley v. American Smelting & Refining Co., 709 P.2d at 791.

How far can the notion of trespass be stretched? Can a homeowner bring a trespass action where her son-in-law, who lives next door, aims allegedly vile and obscene words and gestures at her from across the property line? See Wilson v. Parent, 365 P.2d 72, 75 (Or. 1961) ("the ether waves moving from the hands of the defendant to the eyes of plaintiff and the sound waves from his vocal chords to her ears do not constitute trespass to land")

7. **Interferences With Light, Air, or View.** Under the law of most states, a landowner generally has no nuisance action against a neighbor whose buildings or other improvements interfere with his light, air, or view. For example, in Fontainebleau Hotel Corp. v. Forty–Five Twenty–Five, Inc., 114 So. 2d 357 (Fla. App. 1959), the court held that the Fontainebleau Hotel on Miami Beach could build a new 14–story addition even though, during winter months, the building would block the sunlight to the neighboring Eden Roc Hotel's swimming pool for a substantial part of the day. However, increased interest in solar heating and power has led several courts to reconsider the traditional rule where a structure interferes with a neighbor's solar system.

Prah v. Maretti

Supreme Court of Wisconsin, 1982.
321 N.W.2d 182.

This appeal from a judgment of the circuit court for Waukesha county was certified to this court by the court of appeals, as presenting an issue of first impression, namely, whether an owner of a solar-heated residence states a claim upon which relief can be granted when he asserts that his neighbor's proposed construction of a residence (which conforms to existing deed restrictions and local ordinances) interferes with his access to an unobstructed path for sunlight across the neighbor's property. This case thus involves a conflict between one landowner (Glenn Prah, the plaintiff) interested in unobstructed access to sunlight across adjoining property as a natural source of energy and an adjoining landowner (Richard D. Maretti, the defendant) interested in the development of his land. . . .

According to the complaint, the plaintiff is the owner of a residence which was constructed during the years 1978–1979. The complaint alleges that the residence has a solar system which includes collectors on the roof to supply energy for heat and hot water and that after the plaintiff built his solar-heated house, the defendant purchased the lot adjacent to and immediately to the south of the plaintiff's lot and commenced planning construction of a home. The complaint further states that when the plaintiff learned of defendant's plans to build the house he advised the defendant that if the house were built at the proposed location, defendant's house would substantially and adversely affect the integrity of plaintiff's solar system and could cause plaintiff other damage. Nevertheless, the defendant began construction. The complaint further alleges that the plaintiff is entitled to "unrestricted use of the sun and its solar power" and demands judgment for injunctive relief and damages. . . .

Plaintiff's home was the first residence built in the subdivision, and although plaintiff did not build his house in the center of the lot it was built in accordance with applicable restrictions. Plaintiff advised defendant that if the defendant's home were built at the proposed site it would cause a shadowing effect on the solar collectors which would reduce the efficiency of the system and possibly damage the system. To avoid these adverse effects, plaintiff requested defendant to locate his home an additional several feet away from the plaintiff's lot line, the exact number being disputed. Plaintiff and defendant failed to reach an agreement on the location of defendant's home before defendant started construction. ...

We consider first whether the complaint states a claim for relief based on common law private nuisance. This state has long recognized that an owner of land does not have an absolute or unlimited right to use the land in a way which injures the rights of others. The rights of neighboring landowners are relative; the uses by one must not unreasonably impair the uses or enjoyment of the other. When one landowner's use of his or her property unreasonably interferes with another's enjoyment of his or her property, that use is said to be a private nuisance.

The private nuisance doctrine has traditionally been employed in this state to balance the conflicting rights of landowners, and this court has recently adopted the analysis of private nuisance set forth in the Restatement (Second) of Torts. The Restatement defines private nuisance as "a nontrespassory invasion of another's interest in the private use and enjoyment of land." Restatement (Second) of Torts § 821D (1977). The phrase "interest in the private use and enjoyment of land" as used in sec. 821D is broadly defined to include any disturbance of the enjoyment of property. The comment in the Restatement describes the landowner's interest protected by private nuisance law as follows:

> The phrase "interest in the use and enjoyment of land" is used in this Restatement in a broad sense. It comprehends not only the interests that a person may have in the actual present use of land for residential, agricultural, commercial, industrial and other purposes, but also his interests in having the present use value of the land unimpaired by changes in its physical condition. Thus the destruction of trees on vacant land is as much an invasion of the owner's interest in its use and enjoyment as is the destruction of crops or flowers that he is growing on the land for his present use. "Interest in use and enjoyment" also comprehends the pleasure, comfort and enjoyment that a person normally derives from the occupancy of land. Freedom from discomfort and annoyance while using land is often as important to a person as freedom from physical interruption with his use or freedom from detrimental change in the physical condition of the land itself.

Restatement (Second) of Torts § 821D, Comment b, p. 101 (1977).

Although the defendant's obstruction of the plaintiff's access to sunlight appears to fall within the Restatement's broad concept of a private nuisance as a nontrespassory invasion of another's interest in the private use and enjoyment of land, the defendant asserts that he has a right to develop his property in compliance with statutes, ordinances and private covenants without regard to the effect of such development upon the plaintiff's access to sunlight. In essence, the defendant is asking this court to hold that the private nuisance doctrine is not applicable in the instant case and that his right to develop his land is a right which is per se superior to his neighbor's interest in access to sunlight. This position is expressed in the maxim "*cujus est solum, ejus est usque ad coelum et ad infernos*," that is, the owner of land owns up to the sky and down to the center of the earth. The rights of the surface owner are, however, not unlimited.

The defendant is not completely correct in asserting that the common law did not protect a landowner's access to sunlight across adjoining property. At English common law a landowner could acquire a right to receive sunlight across adjoining land by both express agreement and under the judge-made doctrine of "ancient lights." Under the doctrine of ancient lights if the landowner had received sunlight across adjoining property for a specified period of time, the landowner was entitled to continue to receive unobstructed access to sunlight across the adjoining property. Under the doctrine the landowner acquired a negative prescriptive easement and could prevent the adjoining landowner from obstructing access to light.[8]

Although American courts have not been as receptive to protecting a landowner's access to sunlight as the English courts, American courts have afforded some protection to a landowner's interest in access to sunlight. American courts honor express easements to sunlight. American courts initially enforced the English common law doctrine of ancient lights, but later every state which considered the doctrine repudiated it as inconsistent with the needs of a developing country. Indeed, for just that reason this court concluded that an easement to light and air over adjacent property could not be created or acquired by prescription and has been unwilling to recognize such an easement by implication.

Many jurisdictions in this country have protected a landowner from malicious obstruction of access to light (the spite fence cases) under the common law private nuisance doctrine. If an activity is motivated by malice it lacks utility and the harm it causes others outweighs any social values....

This court's reluctance in the nineteenth and early part of the twentieth century to provide broader protection for a landowner's access to sunlight was premised on three policy considerations. First, the right of landowners to use their property as they wished, as long as they did not cause physical damage to a neighbor, was jealously guarded. Second, sunlight was valued only for aesthetic enjoyment or as illumination. Since artificial light could be used for illumination, loss of sunlight was at most a personal annoyance which was given little, if any, weight by society. Third, society had a significant interest in not restricting or impeding land development....

These three policies are no longer fully accepted or applicable. They reflect factual circumstances and social priorities that are now obsolete.

8. Pfeiffer, Ancient Lights: Legal Protection of Access to Solar Energy, 68 A.B.A.J. 288 (1982). No American common law state recognizes a landowner's right to acquire an easement of light by prescription.

First, society has increasingly regulated the use of land by the landowner for the general welfare. Second, access to sunlight has taken on a new significance in recent years. In this case the plaintiff seeks to protect access to sunlight, not for aesthetic reasons or as a source of illumination but as a source of energy. Access to sunlight as an energy source is of significance both to the landowner who invests in solar collectors and to a society which has an interest in developing alternative sources of energy. Third, the policy of favoring unhindered private development in an expanding economy is no longer in harmony with the realities of our society.

Courts should not implement obsolete policies that have lost their vigor over the course of the years. The law of private nuisance is better suited to resolve landowners' disputes about property development in the 1980's than is a rigid rule which does not recognize a landowner's interest in access to sunlight....

Private nuisance law, the law traditionally used to adjudicate conflicts between private landowners, has the flexibility to protect both a landowner's right of access to sunlight and another landowner's right to develop land. Private nuisance law is better suited to regulate access to sunlight in modern society and is more in harmony with legislative policy and the prior decisions of this court than is an inflexible doctrine of non-recognition of any interest in access to sunlight across adjoining land.

We therefore hold that private nuisance law, that is, the reasonable use doctrine as set forth in the Restatement, is applicable to the instant case. Recognition of a nuisance claim for unreasonable obstruction of access to sunlight will not prevent land development or unduly hinder the use of adjoining land. It will promote the reasonable use and enjoyment of land in a manner suitable to the 1980's. That obstruction of access to light might be found to constitute a nuisance in certain circumstances does not mean that it will be or must be found to constitute a nuisance under all circumstances. The result in each case depends on whether the conduct complained of is unreasonable.

Accordingly we hold that the plaintiff in this case has stated a claim under which relief can be granted....

WILLIAM G. CALLOW, J. (dissenting).... The majority has failed to convince me that the policies [underlying the Court's prior reluctance to hold that the blocking of sunlight to a neighbor's solar system can be a nuisance] are obsolete.... The right of a property owner to lawful enjoyment of his property should be vigorously protected, particularly in those cases where the adjacent property owner could have insulated himself from the alleged problem by acquiring the land as a defense to the potential problem or by provident use of his own property....

I would submit that any policy decisions in this area are best left for the legislature. "What is 'desirable' or 'advisable' or 'ought to be' is a question of policy, not a question of fact. What is 'necessary' or what is 'in the best interest' is not a fact and its determination by the judiciary is an exercise of legislative power when each involves political considerations." In re City of Beloit, 155 N.W.2d 633, 636 (Wis. 1968).

I examine with interest the definition of nuisance as set out in the Restatement (Second) of Torts and adopted in the majority opinion: "A private nuisance is a nontrespassory *invasion* of another's interest in the private use and enjoyment of land." Restatement (Second) of Torts § 821D (1977) (emphasis added). The majority believes that the defendant's obstruction of the plaintiff's access to sunlight falls within the broad definition of "use and enjoyment of land." I do not believe the defendant's "obstruction" of the plaintiff's access to sunlight falls within the definition of "invasion," as it applies to the private use and enjoyment of land. Invasion is typically synonymous with "entry," "attack," "penetration," "hostile entrance," "the incoming or spread of something unusually hurtful." Webster's Third International Dictionary 1188 (1966). Most of the nuisance cases arising under this definition involve noxious odors, smoke, blasting, flooding, or excessive light invading the plaintiff's right to the use of enjoyment of his property. Clearly, an owner who merely builds his home in compliance with all building code and municipal regulations is not "invading" another's right to the use and enjoyment of his property. To say so is to acknowledge that all construction may be an "invasion" because all construction has some restrictive impact on adjacent land. A "view," for example, is modified by any construction simply because it is there.

In order for a nuisance to be actionable in the instant case, the defendant's conduct must be "intentional and unreasonable." It is impossible for me to accept the majority's conclusion that Mr. Maretti, in lawfully seeking to construct his home, may be intentionally and unreasonably interfering with the plaintiff's access to sunlight. In addressing the "unreasonableness" component of the actor's conduct, it is important to note that "[t]here is liability for a nuisance only to those to whom it causes significant harm, of a kind that would be suffered by a normal person in the community or by property in normal condition and used for a normal purpose." Restatement (Second) of Torts § 821F (1979). The comments to the Restatement further reveal that "[if] normal persons in that locality would not be substantially annoyed or disturbed by the situation, then the invasion is not a significant one, even though the idiosyncracies of the particular plaintiff may make it unendurable to him." Id. comment d.

I conclude that plaintiff's solar heating system is an unusually sensitive use. In other words, the defendant's proposed construction of his home, under ordinary circumstances, would not interfere with the use and enjoyment of the usual person's property. "The plaintiff cannot, by devoting his own land to an unusually sensitive use, such as a drive-in motion picture theater easily affected by light, make a nuisance out of conduct of the adjoining defendant which would otherwise be harmless." William Prosser, Law of Torts § 87, at 579....[8] ...

8. Mr. Prah could have avoided this litigation by building his own home in the center of his lot instead of only ten feet from the Maretti lot line and/or by purchasing the

Because I do not believe that the facts of the present case give rise to a cause of action for private nuisance, I dissent.

Notes & Questions

1. In Sher v. Leiderman, 226 Cal. Rptr. 698 (Cal. App. 1986), a California appellate court refused to follow the approach adopted by the *Prah* majority. The court's principal concern was interfering with legislative efforts to mediate the relative interests of solar-powered homes and their neighbors. In *Sher*, a professor living on the Stanford University campus complained when trees on a neighbor's property grew so tall that they interfered with his passive solar home. The California legislature had already passed a Solar Shade Control Act dealing with these types of conflicts, and the court feared meddling in an area best left to legislative judgment.

2. Statutes now address a number of issues that historically have been the subject of nuisance law. Several states have followed California's lead in enacting solar access laws. See, e.g., N.M. Stat. §§ 47–3–1 et seq. (creating solar rights that are effective against neighbors that purchase land subsequent to the recording of the right). A wide range of federal and state environmental laws regulate air and water pollution. See, e.g., Clean Air Act, 42 U.S.C. §§ 7401 et seq.; Clean Water Act, 33 U.S.C. §§ 1251 et seq. As discussed in Chapter 11, local zoning laws often regulate what structures can be erected on a piece of property, where on the lot the structure can be built, and the appearance of the structure.

Are legislatures better equipped to deal with the tradeoffs involved in most nuisance actions? Should courts leave new issues, such as solar energy, to the legislatures?

What role should legislative judgments play in judicial determinations of whether something is a nuisance? Courts generally consider zoning laws as some evidence whether a particular use is reasonable. At least one state statute immunizes activities that are explicitly permitted by a local zoning ordinance. See Cal. Code Civ. Proc. § 731a (immunizing the property owner so long a there is no evidence of "the employment of unnecessary and injurious methods of operation").

Zoning laws have also affected nuisance doctrine in a more subtle way. Zoning ordinances typically divide a community's land into industrial, commercial, and residential areas. As a result of this segregation there are fewer conflicts between competing uses and thus fewer nuisance lawsuits. Also, by seeking to harmonize visual amenities and uses of light and air and other resources not traditionally covered by nuisance law, zoning ordinances have reduced the pressures for nuisance law to expand in new

adjoining lot for his own protection. Mr. Maretti has already moved the proposed location of his home over an additional ten feet to accommodate Mr. Prah's solar collector, and he testified that moving the home any further would interfere with his view of the lake on which the property faces.

directions. In light of these developments, what kinds of nuisance lawsuits are likely to arise today in communities that have been comprehensively zoned?

3. **Spite Fences.** Where a property owner erects a "spite fence" or other structure for the sole, or at least primary, purpose of obstructing the light, air, or view of a neighbor, a number of courts have created an exception to the general rule permitting such obstructions. See, e.g., DeCecco v. Beach, 381 A.2d 543 (Conn. 1977); Restatement (Second) of Torts § 829. These courts reason that spite fences are not productive uses of land and should not be protected. Other jurisdictions have outlawed spite fences by statute. See, e.g., Rev. Code Wash. § 7.40.030 (prohibiting fences or other structures erected maliciously); Wisc. Stats. § 844.10 (prohibiting fences, hedges, or other structures exceeding six feet in height and erected maliciously).

Some states, however, continue to refuse to forbid such obstructions as private nuisances even when erected maliciously. See, e.g., 44 Plaza, Inc. v. Gray–Pac Land Co., 845 S.W.2d 576 (Mo. App. 1992) (no nuisance where fireworks retailer erects signs and plants trees to block public view of a competitor's store). According to courts in these states, the proscription of "lawful, but malicious, acts would be controlling moral conduct, not protecting a legal right." Id. at 579. The courts also express concern that a spite fence exception would require courts to determine a property holder's motive each time the owner erects something on his or her property that a neighbor dislikes.

4. **Visually Offensive Uses.** Should particularly ugly or visually offensive structures that do not block a neighbor's light constitute nuisances? The general approach to visually offensive land uses has been to permit them. In Wernke v. Halas, 600 N.E.2d 117 (Ind. App. 1992), for example, the defendant had constructed a "privacy fence" between his house and his neighbor's property that included vinyl strips, orange plastic construction fencing, and a license plate. The defendant also mounted a toilet seat atop a post overlooking the neighbor's land. When the neighbor sued, alleging a nuisance, the court ruled for the defendant, holding that "it is well-settled throughout this country that, standing alone, unsightliness, or lack of aesthetic virtue, does not constitute a private nuisance." Id. at 122.

The *Wernke* court listed several reasons for its ruling. First, the court suggested that most visual offenses are "trifles" that do not justify legal relief. Mere "annoyance or inconvenience will not support an action for a nuisance because the damages resulting therefrom are deemed *damnum absque injuria* in recognition of the fact life is not perfect." Id. at 122. Second, the court worried that aesthetic values are "inherently subjective" and thus not an appropriate subject for nuisance law. Finally, the court noted that freedom of expression is often involved, and "it is a 'bedrock principle' underlying the First Amendment that the government may not prohibit the expression of an idea simply because society finds the idea itself offensive or disagreeable." Id. at 123, quoting Texas v. Johnson, 491 U.S. 397, 414 (1989).

Courts occasionally depart from the general rule. In Puritan Holding Co. v. Holloschitz, 372 N.Y.S.2d 500 (Sup. Ct. 1975), the court awarded nuisance damages against defendant, whose abandoned apartment building "had deteriorated, become unsightly and been taken over by derelicts. The building's condition has caused a deterioration in values on the block." Plaintiff's neighboring building had allegedly declined in value by $30,000 to $35,000 as a result. See generally Raymond Robert Coletta, The Case for Aesthetic Nuisance: Rethinking Traditional Judicial Attitudes, 48 Ohio St. L.J. 141 (1987); Stephen Woodbury, Aesthetic Nuisances: The Time Has Come To Recognize It, 27 Nat. Res. J. 877 (1987).

5. **Unusually Sensitive Plaintiffs.** The dissent in *Prah* would have denied relief in part on the theory that the plaintiff was "unusually sensitive." A generally recognized defense in nuisance cases is that the plaintiff would not have suffered significant injury if the plaintiff had not been "unusually sensitive." See, e.g., Jenkins v. CSX Transportation, Inc., 906 S.W.2d 460 (Tenn. Ct. App. 1995) (creosote fumes did not constitute a nuisance even though plaintiff had severe allergic reaction because people with normal sensitivity would not have had any reaction). Should the law protect people (and structures) with high sensitivity to neighboring activities? Should it matter whether the sensitivity is inherent (e.g., the plaintiff with an unusual allergic reaction) or was created by the plaintiff (e.g., the homeowner who installs solar panels on her house)? Should some property owners be held to a higher nuisance standard than others because they had the "bad luck" to have unusually sensitive neighbors?

2. PUBLIC NUISANCES & THE REGULATION OF POLLUTION

Public Nuisance Law. *McCarty* and *Prah* involved conflicts between neighboring landowners, which is the grist of *private* nuisances. Land uses that unreasonably interfere with the rights of the general public are challengeable as *public* nuisances. See Restatement (Second) of Torts § 821B (a public nuisance is "an unreasonable interference with a right common to the general public"). Examples of land uses that traditionally have been found to be public nuisances include houses of prostitution, the storage of explosives in the middle of a city, and polluting factories. Id.

It is often said that the "distinction between a public nuisance and a private nuisance is that the former affects the general public, and the latter injures one person or a limited number of persons only." Duff v. Morgantown Energy Associates, 421 S.E.2d 253, 257 (W. Va. 1992). But this is not accurate. A polluting factory may be a public nuisance even though it affects only a small group of people living in the neighborhood of the factory. The question is not the number of people injured, but whether the activity impacts general public rights, like the interest in a healthy environment, rather than a private interest in land. Restatement (Second) of Torts §§ 821B & 821C. An activity, moreover, can constitute both a private nuisance and a public nuisance. A factory that pollutes a river, for example, might be committing both a private nuisance (if downstream landowners are prevented from enjoying their riverfront properties) and a public nuisance (if the health of the general public is affected). Opinions often refer to such activities as "mixed nuisances." See Brenteson Wholesale, Inc. v. Arizona Public Serv. Co., 803 P.2d 930, 935 (Ariz. App. 1990).

Public Nuisance Law & Pollution. Prior to the advent of modern environmental statutes, private and public nuisance actions were one of the principal means of regulating pollution. See, e.g., New York v. New Jersey, 256 U.S. 296 (1921) (water pollution); State ex rel. Board of Health v. Annett, 62 A.2d 224 (N.J. Super. 1948) (air pollution); Columbia River Fishermen's Protective Union v. City of St. Helens, 87 P.2d 195 (Ore. 1939) (water pollution); People v. Selby Smelting & Lead Co., 124 P. 692 (Cal. 1912) (air pollution).

Attempts to control pollution through nuisance law, however, suffer from a number of problems. The first problem is getting into court. Only property owners, of course, can sue for private nuisances, and only if they can show that the pollution has substantially interfered with use of their property. Historically, the only people who could sue to stop public nuisances were (1) public officials and (2) private parties who had suffered special damage *different in kind* from that suffered by the public at large. A private party could not obtain standing to sue simply by showing that he had suffered greater damages than the general public; the damage had to be of a different nature or type. See Schlirf v. Loosen, 232 P.2d 928, 930 (Okla. 1951).

Virtually all states continue to limit standing for public nuisance actions to these two limited categories of plaintiffs. See, e.g., Harbor Beach Surf Club v. Water Taxi of Ft. Lauderdale, Inc., 711 So. 2d 1230 (Fla. App. 1998); Jamail v. Stoneledge Condo. Owners Ass'n, 970 S.W.2d 673 (Tex. App. 1998); Hostetler v. Ward, 704 P.2d 1193 (Wash. App. 1985). According to the courts, two rationales underlie this limitation. "First, it was meant to relieve defendants and the courts of the multiple actions that might follow if every member of the public were allowed to sue for a common wrong. Second, it was believed that a harm which affected all members of the public equally should be handled by public officials." Armory Park Neighborhood Ass'n v. Episcopal Community Services, 712 P.2d 914, 918 (Ariz. 1985).

The Restatement proposes that courts expand standing for public nuisances to include anyone injured by a public nuisance. Restatement (Second) Torts § 821C. To date, courts have not adopted the Restatement approach except in a few cases where state statutes have provided for broader standing. See, e.g., Kellner v. Cappellini, 516 N.Y.S.2d 827 (Civ. Ct. 1986). Some courts, however, appear to be interpreting the "special injury" requirement quite broadly in order to ease the barriers to public nuisance actions. Is there any reason today to retain the restrictive standing rules? If the principal concern is multiplicity of actions, are there other means by which courts could address this concern?

Assuming that a public nuisance action involving pollution is not dismissed for lack of standing, the plaintiff faces the often daunting task of proving that the pollution constitutes a nuisance. As seen, many courts in deciding a private nuisance action balance the costs of the pollution against the benefits of the economic activity that generates the pollution. Whether an activity constitutes a public nuisance also requires courts to determine whether the activity is "reasonable," which most courts believe calls for a harm-benefit balance.

Yet another major issue is whether courts will enjoin *prospective* nuisances or will insist on waiting until damage can actually be shown. Courts historically held that a prospective nuisance is enjoinable only if it is a nuisance *per se*—i.e., an action that would constitute a nuisance at all times and under any circumstances, regardless of location. See, e.g., Davis v. Miller, 96 S.E.2d 498 (Ga. 1957); Cooper v. Whissen, 130 S.W. 703 (Ark. 1910). In recent years, however, some courts have enjoined actions where the plaintiff can show that the action is practically certain to result in substantial damage. See, e.g., Commerce Oil Ref. Corp. v. Miner, 281 F.2d 465 (1st Cir. 1960); Central Theatres, Inc. v. State ex rel. Braren, 161 So. 2d 558 (Fla. App. 1964) ("reasonable certainty" of "imminent" danger). See generally Andrew H. Sharp, An Ounce of Prevention: Rehabilitating the Anticipatory Nuisance Doctrine, 15 B.C. Envtl. Aff. L. Rev. 627 (1988).

These are not the only perceived obstacles in trying to regulate pollution through public nuisance and other common law doctrines. Common law actions, because they address pollution on a case by case basis, often ignore the cumulative impact of numerous pollution sources. Pollution from a particular source might appear reasonable in isolation, but may contribute to unacceptably poor air or water quality when combined with the discharges of numerous other sources. Courts also have trouble ensuring that their injunctions are obeyed. Lacking an enforcement staff, courts rely on plaintiffs to discover and prosecute violations, yet plaintiffs often do not have the authority or resources to monitor defendants' emissions.

Modern Regulation of Pollution. For all these reasons, federal and state statutes today dominate the regulation of pollution.[1] At the national level, the Clean Air Act, 42 U.S.C. §§ 7401 et seq., regulates air pollution from factories, cars, and other sources. The Clean Water Act, 33 U.S.C. §§ 121 et seq., regulates discharges of pollutants into the nation's waterways, while the Safe Drinking Water Act, 15 U.S.C. §§ 1261 et seq., protects underground drinking water sources from contamination. The Resource Conservation & Recovery Act, 42 U.S.C. §§ 6901 et seq., regulates how the nation disposes of hazardous waste. The Comprehensive Environmental Response, Compensation, & Liability Act, 42 U.S.C. §§ 9601 et seq., also known as Superfund, provides for supervised cleanups of former hazardous waste disposal sites and other contaminated lands.

1. For more background on the major federal environmental statutes, see James Salzman & Barton H. Thompson, Jr., Environmental Law and Policy (2003).

These and other statutes remedy many of the perceived deficiencies of the common law approach to pollution. Virtually every federal environmental statute, for example, includes a "citizen suit" provision that permits any citizen to enjoin violations of its provisions (subject to constitutional standing requirements) if the government is not prosecuting the violation. See, e.g., Clean Water Act § 505, 33 U.S.C. § 1365. The citizen suit provisions also provide that courts can require defendants to compensate plaintiffs for their attorney fees and other court costs.

Most federal pollution-control statutes also eschew the type of cost-benefit comparisons called for by the Restatement nuisance rules. The Clean Air Act, for example, uses a health-based approach to set standards for the most common air pollutants. The federal Environmental Protection Agency (EPA) begins by setting national ambient air quality standards (NAAQSs) that are sufficient to "protect the public health" after "allowing an adequate margin of safety." Clean Air Act § 109(b)(1), 42 U.S.C. § 7409(b)(1). Each state then must develop a program for restricting emissions that is adequate to achieve the NAAQSs in the state. In setting the NAAQSs, EPA cannot consider their economic or technological feasibility. See Lead Industries Ass'n v. EPA, 647 F.2d 1130 (D.C. Cir. 1980).

The Clean Water Act starts with a technology-based approach to regulating water pollution. The amount of contaminants that "point sources," like factories and sewage treatment facilities, can discharge into waterways depends on what is technologically achievable. Where these limitations are not sufficient to ensure that the nation's waterways are fishable and swimmable, states must further ratchet down on pollution sources in order to achieve the tougher quality standards. The stated goal of the Clean Water Act is to eliminate *all* discharges of pollution into the nation's waterways.[2]

Not surprisingly, the minimal role that cost plays in federal pollution statutes has proven controversial. Consider the views of the National Water Commission, which shortly after passage of the Clean Water Act criticized the Act's no-discharge goal:

> The Commission believes adoption of "no discharge" as a national goal for water quality management is no more sound than would be the establishment of a "no development" goal for controlling land use.... [T]he no discharge policy assumes that restoration and preservation of natural water quality is of higher value than any other use of the resource.... Adoption of a no-discharge policy ... amounts to the imputation of an extravagant social value to an abstract concept of water purity, a value that the Commission is convinced the American people would not endorse if the associated costs and effect on other resources were fully appreciated and the policy alternatives clearly understood.

2. Actually, the Clean Water Act provides that all discharges were to be eliminated by 1985. Clean Water Act § 101(a)(2), 33 U.S.C. § 1251(a)(2). The nation is somewhat behind in meeting this goal.

Final Report of the National Water Commission, Water Policies for the Future 69–70 (1973). Do you agree? Which constitutes better policy—the Restatement's harm-benefit test for determining when something is a nuisance, or the absolute approaches of the Clean Air Act and Clean Water Act? Are there other approaches preferable to these?

One of the most active debates today in the environmental field is over the relative merits of "command and control" and market systems. Federal environmental statutes traditionally have regulated pollution through a command and control approach. The Environmental Protection Agency or a state environmental agency determines how much pollution a given facility can discharge, based on health, technological, or other criteria, and then commands the facility not to discharge more than this amount. Critics of this approach argue that such fixed mandates are often economically inefficient because the cost of reducing pollution can vary significantly from facility to facility. Critics also argue that such mandates do not give regulated industries an incentive to do better than the mandated standard or to develop new technology.

Critics have suggested several market alternatives. One market proposal long advocated by economists, but almost entirely ignored by policymakers, would be a pollution tax that would impose a fee on polluting facilities equal to the damage done by the pollution. Facilities would then be free to decide how much to pollute based on the comparative cost of the tax and of reducing pollution emissions. Another market approach that is now being used in a variety of settings is a tradeable emission allowance—what is often called a "cap and trade" system. Here the government decides how much pollution in total can be emitted but, rather than telling each facility how much it can pollute, the government allocates emission allowances among the various facilities (perhaps via an auction or based on how much each facility has polluted in the past) and then permits the facilities to trade the allowances among themselves or to other companies. The government sets the total amount of allowances based on the amount of pollution that the government will permit. A facility can pollute up to the number of allowances they hold, including allowances they purchase from others. Facilities that can readily reduce their pollution levels below their allotted allowances can sell their extra allowances to facilities that are finding it more expensive or difficult to reduce their emissions. Although the total amount of pollution remains the same, a system of tradeable emission allowances helps reduce the overall cost of meeting the pollution goals and, at least in theory, gives companies an incentive to develop new technology that they can use to further reduce their emissions, freeing up allowances that they can then sell. For discussions of the debate over market versus command and control systems, see Richard Stewart, United States Environmental Regulation: A Failing Paradigm, 15 J.L. & Com. 585 (1996); Lisa Heinzerling, Selling Pollution, Forcing Democracy, 14 Stan. Envtl. L.J. 459 (1995); John P. Dwyer, The Use of Market Incentives in Controlling Air Pollution: California's Marketable Permits Program, 20 Ecology L.Q. 103, 112–17 (1993); Robert W. Hahn & Robert N. Stavins, Incentive–Based Environmental Regulation: A New Era for an Old Idea?, 18 Ecology L.Q. 1,

13 (1991); Robert W. Hahn & Gorden L. Hester, Marketable Permits: Lessons for Theory and Practice, 16 Ecology L.Q. 361 (1989).

Despite the ascent of environmental statutes, public officials and individual citizens continue to file lawsuits alleging that various polluting activities constitute private or public nuisances. Indeed, practicing lawyers reported a "resurgence" in such lawsuits in the 1990s. See L. Mark Walker & Dale E. Cottingham, An Abridged Primer on the Law of Public Nuisance, 30 Tulsa L.J. 355 (1994). There are several reasons why nuisance law remains important. Federal and state environmental laws generally do not provide for compensation to injured members of the public. Damaged parties thus must look to common law actions for recovery. In addition, local public officials or citizens who are dissatisfied with statutory pollution standards can use public nuisance actions to try to block activities that administrative agencies have okayed.

Public Nuisance Law and NIMBYism. Residential neighborhoods sometimes use public nuisance law to try to prohibit activities in their neighborhoods that they view as offensive, worrisome, or inappropriate. For example, in Armory Park Neighborhood Ass'n v. Episcopal Church Servs., 712 P.2d 914 (Ariz. 1985), a local homeowners' association in Tucson, Arizona, sued to prevent an Episcopal charity from running a free meal facility in the neighborhood. Residents complained that the center attracted transients who lingered long after finishing their meals and sometimes urinated, defecated, drank, or littered. "Many residents were frightened or annoyed by the transients and altered their lifestyles to avoid them." 712 P.2d at 916. Although the Arizona Supreme Court acknowledged the social value of the food facility, it nonetheless held that it was a public nuisance. The facility's purposes were "entirely admirable" and "entitled to greater deference than pursuits of lesser intrinsic value." But "even admirable ventures may cause unreasonable interferences. We do not believe that the law allows the costs of a charitable enterprise to be visited in their entirety upon the residents of a single neighborhood. The problems of dealing with the unemployed, the homeless, and the mentally ill are also matters of community or governmental responsibility." Id. at 921. Efforts to keep activities such as soup kitchens, homeless shelters, group homes, or half-way houses for prisoners or drug addicts out of neighborhoods has become sufficiently widespread to pick up a nickname—"Not In My BackYard" or "NIMBYism." How should the courts deal with such lawsuits? Are activities such as soup kitchens more appropriate for some neighborhoods than others? If so, should courts be making the determination of which neighborhoods?

Legislatures have sometimes passed statutes to address the problem of locally unwanted land uses (or LULUs) such as waste facilities, group homes, and prisons. Under one statutory approach, the developer of a LULU must negotiate a plan with the local community to compensate the community for siting the facility within its borders; this approach often provides for binding arbitration in case of disagreement. See, e.g., Vicki Been, Compensated Siting Proposals: Is it Time to Pay Attention?, 21

Fordham Urb. L.J. 787 (1994); Michael Wheeler, Negotiating NIMBYs: Learning from the Failure of the Massachusetts Siting Law, 11 Yale J. Reg. 241 (1994). Another approach requires that LULUs be dispersed among communities, rather than concentrated in one area. See, e.g., N.Y. Mental Hyg. Law § 41.34(c)(1)(C) (permitting municipalities to refuse a group home if it would result in significant concentration of such facilities). If you were a legislator concerned about the problem of finding appropriate sites for LULUs, what approach would you suggest?

3. REMEDIES

Boomer v. Atlantic Cement Co., Inc.

Court of Appeals of New York, 1970.
257 N.E.2d 870.

BERGAN, JUDGE.

Defendant operates a large cement plant near Albany. These are actions for injunction and damages by neighboring land owners alleging injury to property from dirt, smoke and vibration emanating from the plant. A nuisance has been found after trial, temporary damages have been allowed; but an injunction has been denied.

The public concern with air pollution arising from many sources in industry and in transportation is currently accorded ever wider recognition accompanied by a growing sense of responsibility in State and Federal Governments to control it. Cement plants are obvious sources of air pollution in the neighborhoods where they operate.

But there is now before the court private litigation in which individual property owners have sought specific relief from a single plant operation. The threshold question raised by the division of view on this appeal is whether the court should resolve the litigation between the parties now before it as equitably as seems possible; or whether, seeking promotion of the general public welfare, it should channel private litigation into broad public objectives.

A court performs its essential function when it decides the rights of parties before it. Its decision of private controversies may sometimes greatly affect public issues. Large questions of law are often resolved by the manner in which private litigation is decided. But this is normally an incident to the court's main function to settle controversy. It is a rare exercise of judicial power to use a decision in private litigation as a purposeful mechanism to achieve direct public objectives greatly beyond the rights and interests before the court.

Effective control of air pollution is a problem presently far from solution even with the full public and financial powers of government. In large measure adequate technical procedures are yet to be developed and some that appear possible may be economically impracticable.

It seems apparent that the amelioration of air pollution will depend on technical research in great depth; on a carefully balanced consideration of the economic impact of close regulation; and of the actual effect on public health. It is likely to require massive public expenditure and to demand more than any local community can accomplish and to depend on regional and interstate controls.

A court should not try to do this on its own as a by-product of private litigation and it seems manifest that the judicial establishment is neither equipped in the limited nature of any judgment it can pronounce nor prepared to lay down and implement an effective policy for the elimination of air pollution. This is an area beyond the circumference of one private lawsuit. It is a direct responsibility for government and should not thus be undertaken as an incident to solving a dispute between property owners and a single cement plant—one of many—in the Hudson River valley.

The cement making operations of defendant have been found by the court at Special Term to have damaged the nearby properties of plaintiffs in these two actions. That court, as it has been noted, accordingly found defendant maintained a nuisance and this has been affirmed at the Appellate Division. The total damage to plaintiffs' properties is, however, relatively small in comparison with the value of defendant's operation and with the consequences of the injunction which plaintiffs seek.

The ground for the denial of injunction, notwithstanding the finding both that there is a nuisance and that plaintiffs have been damaged substantially, is the large disparity in economic consequences of the nuisance and of the injunction. This theory cannot, however, be sustained without overruling a doctrine which has been consistently reaffirmed in several leading cases in this court and which has never been disavowed here, namely that where a nuisance has been found and where there has been any substantial damage shown by the party complaining an injunction will be granted.

The rule in New York has been that such a nuisance will be enjoined although marked disparity be shown in economic consequence between the effect of the injunction and the effect of the nuisance.

The problem of disparity in economic consequence was sharply in focus in Whalen v. Union Bag & Paper Co., 208 N.Y. 1, 101 N.E. 805. A pulp mill entailing an investment of more than a million dollars polluted a stream in which plaintiff, who owned a farm, was "a lower riparian owner." The economic loss to plaintiff from this pollution was small. This court, reversing the Appellate Division, reinstated the injunction granted by the Special Term against the argument of the mill owner that in view of "the slight advantage to plaintiff and the great loss that will be inflicted on defendant" an injunction should not be granted. "Such a balancing of injuries cannot be justified by the circumstances of this case," Judge Werner noted. He continued: "Although the damage to the plaintiff may be slight as compared with the defendant's expense of abating the condition, that is not a good reason for refusing an injunction."

Thus the unconditional injunction granted at Special Term was reinstated. The rule laid down in that case, then, is that whenever the damage resulting from a nuisance is found not "unsubstantial," viz., $100 a year, injunction would follow. This states a rule that had been followed in this court with marked consistency....

Although the court at Special Term and the Appellate Division held that injunction should be denied, it was found that plaintiffs had been damaged in various specific amounts up to the time of the trial and damages to the respective plaintiffs were awarded for those amounts. The effect of this was, injunction having been denied, plaintiffs could maintain successive actions at law for damages thereafter as further damage was incurred.

The court at Special Term also found the amount of permanent damage attributable to each plaintiff, for the guidance of the parties in the event both sides stipulated to the payment and acceptance of such permanent damage as a settlement of all the controversies among the parties. The total of permanent damages to all plaintiffs thus found was $185,000....

This result at Special Term and at the Appellate Division is a departure from a rule that has become settled; but to follow the rule literally in these cases would be to close down the plant at once. This court is fully agreed to avoid that immediately drastic remedy; the difference in view is how best to avoid it.*

One alternative is to grant the injunction but postpone its effect to a specified future date to give opportunity for technical advances to permit defendant to eliminate the nuisance; another is to grant the injunction conditioned on the payment of permanent damages to plaintiffs which would compensate them for the total economic loss to their property present and future caused by defendant's operations. For reasons which will be developed the court chooses the latter alternative.

If the injunction were to be granted unless within a short period—e.g., 18 months—the nuisance be abated by improved methods, there would be no assurance that any significant technical improvement would occur.

The parties could settle this private litigation at any time if defendant paid enough money and the imminent threat of closing the plant would build up the pressure on defendant. If there were no improved techniques found, there would inevitably be applications to the court at Special Term for extensions of time to perform on showing of good faith efforts to find such techniques.

Moreover, techniques to eliminate dust and other annoying by-products of cement making are unlikely to be developed by any research the defendant can undertake within any short period, but will depend on the

* Respondent's investment in the plant is in excess of $45,000,000. There are over 300 people employed there.

total resources of the cement industry nationwide and throughout the world. The problem is universal wherever cement is made.

For obvious reasons the rate of the research is beyond control of defendant. If at the end of 18 months the whole industry has not found a technical solution a court would be hard put to close down this one cement plant if due regard be given to equitable principles.

On the other hand, to grant the injunction unless defendant pays plaintiffs such permanent damages as may be fixed by the court seems to do justice between the contending parties. All of the attributions of economic loss to the properties on which plaintiffs' complaints are based will have been redressed.

The nuisance complained of by these plaintiffs may have other public or private consequences, but these particular parties are the only ones who have sought remedies and the judgment proposed will fully redress them. The limitation of relief granted is a limitation only within the four corners of these actions and does not foreclose public health or other public agencies from seeking proper relief in a proper court.

It seems reasonable to think that the risk of being required to pay permanent damages to injured property owners by cement plant owners would itself be a reasonably effective spur to research for improved techniques to minimize nuisance.

The power of the court to condition on equitable grounds the continuance of an injunction on the payment of permanent damages seems undoubted. . . .

The orders should be reversed, without costs, and the cases remitted to Supreme Court, Albany County to grant an injunction which shall be vacated upon payment by defendant of such amounts of permanent damage to the respective plaintiffs as shall for this purpose be determined by the court.

JASEN, JUDGE (dissenting).

I agree with the majority that a reversal is required here, but I do not subscribe to the newly enunciated doctrine of assessment of permanent damages, in lieu of an injunction, where substantial property rights have been impaired by the creation of a nuisance.

It has long been the rule in this State, as the majority acknowledges, that a nuisance which results in substantial continuing damage to neighbors must be enjoined. To now change the rule to permit the cement company to continue polluting the air indefinitely upon the payment of permanent damages is, in my opinion, compounding the magnitude of a very serious problem in our State and Nation today.

In recognition of this problem, the Legislature of this State has enacted the Air Pollution Control Act declaring that it is the State policy to require the use of all available and reasonable methods to prevent and control air pollution.

The harmful nature and widespread occurrence of air pollution have been extensively documented. Congressional hearings have revealed that air pollution causes substantial property damage, as well as being a contributing factor to a rising incidence of lung cancer, emphysema, bronchitis and asthma.

The specific problem faced here is known as particulate contamination because of the fine dust particles emanating from defendant's cement plant. The particular type of nuisance is not new, having appeared in many cases for at least the past 60 years. It is interesting to note that cement production has recently been identified as a significant source of particulate contamination in the Hudson Valley. This type of pollution, wherein very small particles escape and stay in the atmosphere, has been denominated as the type of air pollution which produces the greatest hazard to human health. We have thus a nuisance which not only is damaging to the plaintiffs, but also is decidedly harmful to the general public.

I see grave dangers in overruling our long-established rule of granting an injunction where a nuisance results in substantial continuing damage. In permitting the injunction to become inoperative upon the payment of permanent damages, the majority is, in effect, licensing a continuing wrong. It is the same as saying to the cement company, you may continue to do harm to your neighbors so long as you pay a fee for it. Furthermore, once such permanent damages are assessed and paid, the incentive to alleviate the wrong would be eliminated, thereby continuing air pollution of an area without abatement....

I would enjoin the defendant cement company from continuing the discharge of dust particles upon its neighbors' properties unless, within 18 months, the cement company abated this nuisance.

It is not my intention to cause the removal of the cement plant from the Albany area, but to recognize the urgency of the problem stemming from this stationary source of air pollution, and to allow the company a specified period of time to develop a means to alleviate this nuisance.

I am aware that the trial court found that the most modern dust control devices available have been installed in defendant's plant, but, I submit, this does not mean that *better* and more effective dust control devices could not be developed within the time allowed to abate the pollution.

Moreover, I believe it is incumbent upon the defendant to develop such devices, since the cement company, at the time the plant commenced production (1962), was well aware of the plaintiffs' presence in the area, as well as the probable consequences of its contemplated operation. Yet, it still chose to build and operate the plant at this site.

In a day when there is a growing concern for clean air, highly developed industry should not expect acquiescence by the courts, but should, instead, plan its operations to eliminate contamination of our air and damage to its neighbors....

Accordingly, the orders of the Appellate Division, insofar as they denied the injunction, should be reversed, and the actions remitted to Supreme Court, Albany County to grant an injunction to take effect 18 months hence, unless the nuisance is abated by improved techniques prior to said date.

Notes & Questions

1. Virtually all courts today will "balance the equities" in determining whether to grant an injunction in a nuisance case. The rule that an injunction should issue only if the benefits of the injunction outweigh the costs is also known as the "relative hardship doctrine," "equitable hardship doctrine," or "balancing the conveniences."

2. Does balancing the equities make it easier for a court to decide that a challenged activity is a nuisance? Courts that are concerned about the economic impact of enjoining a business can address the concern either by denying liability (under the Restatement's benefit-harm test) or by finding liability but denying an injunction (under the relative hardship doctrine). If a legislature were to adopt an absolute rule that an injunction must be allowed once a nuisance is found, courts would have only one option. Would this be good or bad?

How does the Restatement's benefit-harm test for determining whether there is a nuisance differ, if at all, from the balance mandated in *Boomer*? Could a court that finds a private nuisance under the Restatement's benefit-harm rule ever conclude that an injunction is inappropriate? Conversely, if an injunction is inappropriate under *Boomer*, can there be a nuisance under the Restatement benefit-harm rule? See Copart Indus. v. Consolidated Edison Co., 362 N.E.2d 968 (N.Y. 1977) (finding no nuisance on facts almost identical to those of *Boomer*).

If courts should balance harm and utility, when should they do it—in determining liability, in choosing a remedy, or at both steps?

3. In deciding whether the balance of equities favored issuing an injunction, the court in *Boomer* suggested that the value of the injunction to the plaintiffs, but not to the public as a whole, should be balanced against the cost of closing the factory. Why? If the goal is to promote the public good, shouldn't all the benefits and costs of issuing an injunction be considered?

4. Would issuing an injunction in *Boomer* necessarily have led to the closing of the Atlantic Cement Company's plant? As discussed in connection with encroachments, Atlantic would have been free to "buy off" the injunction by paying the plaintiffs not to enforce the injunction. Assume, as the court suggests, that the *Boomer* plaintiffs suffered $185,000 in permanent damages as a result of Atlantic's operation, and that Atlantic would lose $10 million if its operations were enjoined and shut down. Couldn't Atlantic offer to pay the *Boomer* plaintiffs somewhere between $185,001 and $9,999,999 to avoid its shutdown? Would this result be fairer than

relegating the plaintiffs to damages? Would it risk "extortion"? Would it lead to a less productive use of land than a rule requiring Atlantic to pay only $185,000 to the plaintiffs? Under the facts of the case, are transaction costs or psychological barriers likely to prevent the parties from coming to an agreement? Compare Ward Farnsworth, Do Parties to Nuisance Cases Bargain After Judgment? A Glimpse Inside the Cathedral, 66 U. Chi. L. Rev. 373 (1999) (finding, in study of 20 nuisance cases, that animosity and distaste for cash bargaining over rights precluded post-judgment bargaining) with Gideon Parchomovsky & Peter Siegelman, Selling Mayberry: Communities and Individuals in Law and Economics, 92 Calif. L. Rev. 75 (2004) (relating the successful buyout of an entire town by the American Electric Power Company, probably as a means of avoiding nuisance actions).

5. Say that, after entry of the decree in *Boomer,* Atlantic doubled its emissions. Would the *Boomer* plaintiffs be entitled to a new award of permanent damages? After the decree, would Atlantic have any incentive to *reduce* its emissions? Say that, after the decree, the federal government enforced an ambient air standard requiring Atlantic to cut its emissions by half. Would Atlantic be entitled to a partial refund from the *Boomer* plaintiffs? Will *Boomer* encourage, discourage, or have no effect on, investment in research and development aimed at producing more effective pollution control devices? What effects, if any, are decisions like *Boomer* likely to have on decisions by industries and residents as to where they locate their factories and homes?

6. **Nuisance Damages.** The basic measure of damages for nuisance is the difference in the land's value before and after the nuisance. Special damages may be recovered for injury to crops or business operations as well as for physical suffering. Some courts have held that plaintiff may recover for mental suffering even absent physical injury: "It is settled that, regardless of whether the occupant of land has sustained physical injury, he may recover the damages for the discomfort and annoyance of himself and the members of his family and for mental suffering occasioned by fear for the safety of himself and his family when such discomfort and suffering has been proximately caused by a trespass or a nuisance." Lew v. Superior Court, 25 Cal. Rptr. 2d 42, 46 (Cal. App. 1993).

After the *Boomer* remand, two of three actions still pending against Atlantic were settled. In the third action, plaintiff argued for measuring damages against a more generous standard than fair market value—either "special market value" ("based on inflated prices paid by defendant for other properties in the neighborhood") or "contract price" ("the amount that a private corporation would have to pay where it needs such servitude to continue in operation as against a seller who was unwilling to sell his land"). In the court's view, "while the fair market value rule may not be the sole criterion, it does serve as a restraining influence on the possible excessiveness of the so-called 'special' market value, and as a sure check on the subjective and speculative nature of the so-called 'contract price.' " Finding that the value of plaintiff's land without the nuisance was

$265,000, and with the nuisance was $125,000, the court awarded $175,000 in damages—$140,000 for the diminished value of the property, and $35,000 in temporary damages for the period up to trial. Boomer v. Atlantic Cement Co., 340 N.Y.S.2d 97 (Sup. Ct., Albany Cty. 1972), affirmed sub nom Kinley v. Atlantic Cement Co., 349 N.Y.S.2d 199 (3d Dept. 1973).

7. For careful analyses of *Boomer* and the issues that it raises, see Daniel A. Farber, Reassessing *Boomer*: Justice, Efficiency, and Nuisance Law, in Property Law and Legal Education: Essays in Honor of John E. Cribbet 7 (Peter Hay & Michael H. Hoeflich eds., 1988); A. Mitch Polinsky, Resolving Nuisance Disputes: The Simple Economics of Injunctive and Damage Remedies, 32 Stan. L. Rev. 1075 (1980); Barton H. Thompson, Jr., Injunction Negotiations: An Economic, Moral, and Legal Analysis, 27 Stan. L. Rev. 1563 (1975).

Spur Industries, Inc. v. Del E. Webb Development Co.

Supreme Court of Arizona, 1972.
494 P.2d 700.

CAMERON, VICE CHIEF JUSTICE.

From a judgment permanently enjoining the defendant, Spur Industries, Inc., from operating a cattle feedlot near the plaintiff Del E. Webb Development Company's Sun City, Spur appeals. Webb cross-appeals. Although numerous issues are raised, we feel that it is necessary to answer only two questions. They are:

> 1. Where the operation of a business, such as a cattle feedlot is lawful in the first instance, but becomes a nuisance by reason of a nearby residential area, may the feedlot operation be enjoined in an action brought by the developer of the residential area?
>
> 2. Assuming that the nuisance may be enjoined, may the developer of a completely new town or urban area in a previously agricultural area be required to indemnify the operator of the feedlot who must move or cease operation because of the presence of the residential area created by the developer?

The facts necessary for a determination of this matter on appeal are as follows. The area in question is located in Maricopa County, Arizona, some 14 to 15 miles west of the urban area of Phoenix, on the Phoenix–Wickenburg Highway, also known as Grand Avenue. About two miles south of Grand Avenue is Olive Avenue which runs east and west. 111th Avenue runs north and south as does the Agua Fria River immediately to the west. [See Figures 2–2 and 2–3.]

Farming started in this area about 1911. In 1929, with the completion of the Carl Pleasant Dam, gravity flow water became available to the property located to the west of the Agua Fria River, though land to the east remained dependent upon well water for irrigation. By 1950, the only urban areas in the vicinity were the agriculturally related communities of

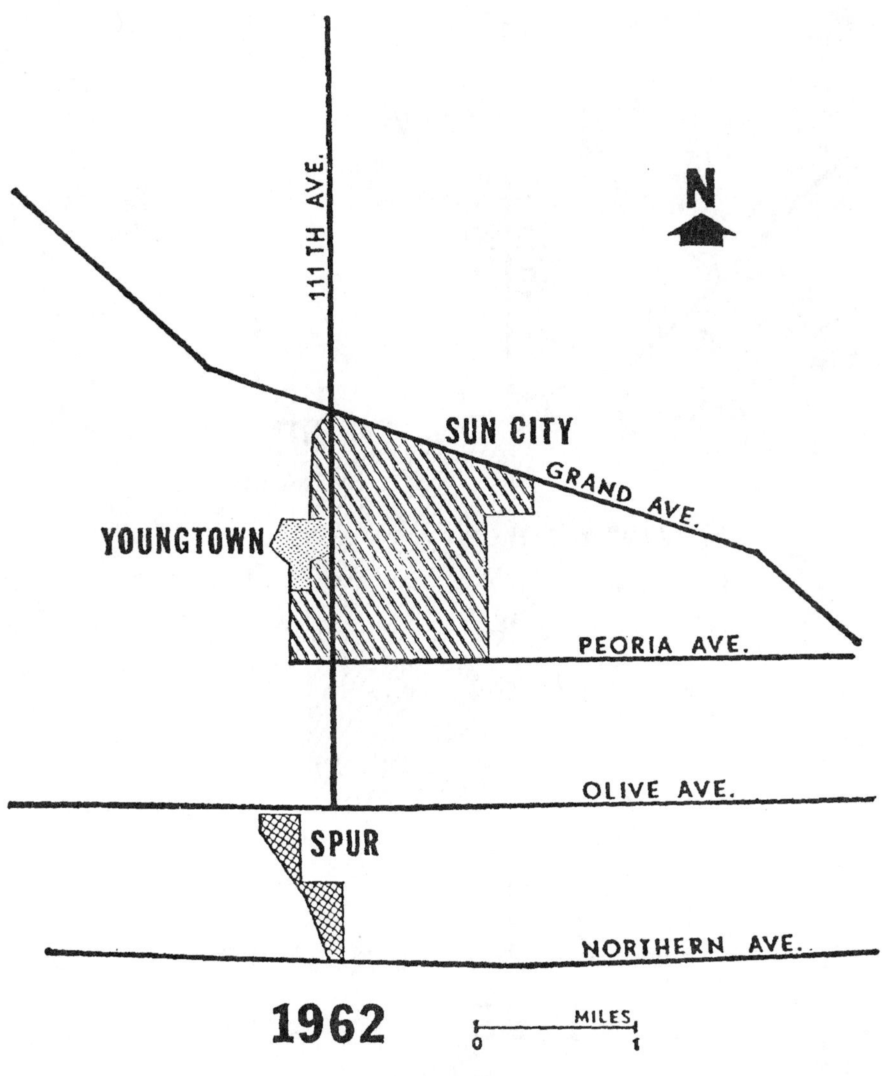

Figure 2–2

Peoria, El Mirage, and Surprise located along Grand Avenue. Along 111th Avenue, approximately one mile south of Grand Avenue and 1½ miles north of Olive Avenue, the community of Youngtown was commenced in 1954. Youngtown is a retirement community appealing primarily to senior citizens.

In 1956, Spur's predecessors in interest, H. Marion Welborn and the Northside Hay Mill and Trading Company, developed feedlots, about ½ mile south of Olive Avenue, in an area between the confluence of the usually dry Agua Fria and New Rivers. The area is well suited for cattle feeding and in 1959, there were 25 cattle feeding pens or dairy operations within a 7 mile radius of the location developed by Spur's predecessors. In April and May of 1959, the Northside Hay Mill was feeding between 6,000 and 7,000 head of

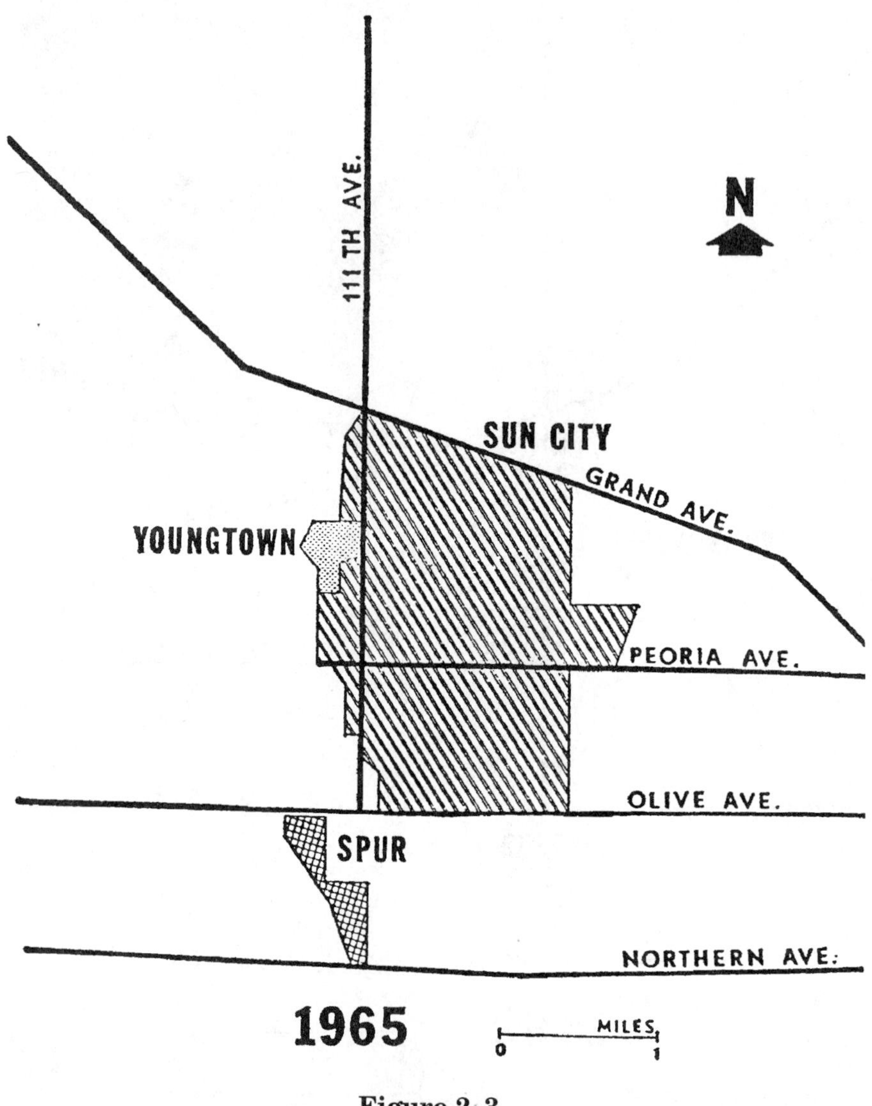

Figure 2–3

cattle and Welborn approximately 1,500 head on a combined area of 35 acres.

In May of 1959, Del Webb began to plan the development of an urban area to be known as Sun City. For this purpose, the Marinette and the Santa Fe Ranches, some 20,000 acres of farmland, were purchased for $15,000,000 or $750.00 per acre. This price was considerably less than the price of land located near the urban area of Phoenix, and along with the success of Youngtown was a factor influencing the decision to purchase the property in question.

By September 1959, Del Webb had started construction of a golf course south of Grand Avenue and Spur's predecessors had started to level ground for more feedlot area. In 1960, Spur purchased the property in question and began a rebuilding and expansion program extending both to the north and south of the original facilities. By 1962, Spur's expansion program was completed and had expanded from approximately 35 acres to 114 acres. See [Figure 2–2].

Accompanied by an extensive advertising campaign, homes were first offered by Del Webb in January 1960 and the first unit to be completed was south of Grand Avenue and approximately 2 ½ miles north of Spur. By May 1960, there were 450 to 500 houses completed or under construction. At this time, Del Webb did not consider odors from the Spur feed pens a problem and Del Webb continued to develop in a southerly direction, until sales resistance became so great that the parcels were difficult if not impossible to sell....

By December 1967, Del Webb's property had extended south to Olive Avenue and Spur was within 500 feet of Olive Avenue to the north. See [Figure 2–3]. Del Webb filed its original complaint alleging that in excess of 1,300 lots in the southwest portion were unfit for development for sale as residential lots because of the operation of the Spur feedlot.

Del Webb's suit complained that the Spur feeding operation was a public nuisance because of the flies and the odor which were drifting or being blown by the prevailing south to north wind over the southern portion of Sun City. At the time of the suit, Spur was feeding between 20,000 and 30,000 head of cattle, and the facts amply support the finding of the trial court that the feed pens had become a nuisance to the people who resided in the southern part of Del Webb's development. The testimony indicated that cattle in a commercial feedlot will produce 35 to 40 pounds of wet manure per day, per head, or over a million pounds of wet manure per day for 30,000 head of cattle, and that despite the admittedly good feedlot management and good housekeeping practices by Spur, the resulting odor and flies produced an annoying if not unhealthy situation as far as the senior citizens of southern Sun City were concerned. There is no doubt that some of the citizens of Sun City were unable to enjoy the outdoor living which Del Webb had advertised and that Del Webb was faced with sales resistance from prospective purchasers as well as strong and persistent complaints from the people who had purchased homes in that area....

It is noted, however, that neither the citizens of Sun City nor Youngtown are represented in this lawsuit and the suit is solely between Del E. Webb Development Company and Spur Industries, Inc.

MAY SPUR BE ENJOINED?

The difference between a private nuisance and a public nuisance is generally one of degree. A private nuisance is one affecting a single individual or a definite small number of persons in the enjoyment of private rights not common to the public, while a public nuisance is one affecting the rights enjoyed by citizens as a part of the public. To constitute a public nuisance, the nuisance must affect a considerable number of people or an entire community or neighborhood.

Where the injury is slight, the remedy for minor inconveniences lies in an action for damages rather than in one for an injunction. Moreover, some courts have held, in the "balancing of conveniences" cases, that damages may be the sole remedy. See Boomer v. Atlantic Cement Co., 257 N.E.2d 870 (N.Y. 1970).

Thus, it would appear from the admittedly incomplete record as developed in the trial court, that, at most, residents of Youngtown would be entitled to damages rather than injunctive relief.

We have no difficulty, however, in agreeing with the conclusion of the trial court that Spur's operation was an enjoinable public nuisance as far as the people in the southern portion of Del Webb's Sun City were concerned....

> .... [I]t hardly admits a doubt that, in determining the question as to whether a lawful occupation is so conducted as to constitute a nuisance as a matter of fact, the locality and surroundings are of the first importance. (citations omitted) A business which is not per se a public nuisance may become such by being carried on at a place where the health, comfort, or convenience of a populous neighborhood is affected.... What might amount to a serious nuisance in one locality by reason of the density of the population, or character of the neighborhood affected, may in another place and under different surroundings be deemed proper and unobjectionable.... [MacDonald v. Perry, 255 P. 494, 497 (Ariz. 1927).]

It is clear that as to the citizens of Sun City, the operation of Spur's feedlot was both a public and a private nuisance. They could have successfully maintained an action to abate the nuisance. Del Webb, having shown a special injury in the loss of sales, had standing to bring suit to enjoin the nuisance. The judgment of the trial court permanently enjoining the operation of the feedlot is affirmed.

MUST DEL WEBB INDEMNIFY SPUR?

A suit to enjoin a nuisance sounds in equity and the courts have long recognized a special responsibility to the public when acting as a court of equity....

In addition to protecting the public interest, however, courts of equity are concerned with protecting the operator of a lawfully, albeit noxious, business from the result of a knowing and willful encroachment by others near his business.

In the so-called "coming to the nuisance" cases, the courts have held that the residential landowner may not have relief if he knowingly came into a neighborhood reserved for industrial or agricultural endeavors and has been damaged thereby:

> Plaintiffs chose to live in an area uncontrolled by zoning laws or restrictive covenants and remote from urban development. In such an area plaintiffs cannot complain that legitimate agricultural pursuits are being carried on in the vicinity, nor can plaintiffs, having chosen to build in an agricultural area, complain that the agricultural pursuits carried on in the area depreciate the value of

their homes. The area being *primarily agricultural,* any opinion reflecting the value of such property must take this factor into account. The standards affecting the value of residence property in an urban setting, subject to zoning controls and controlled planning techniques, cannot be the standards by which agricultural properties are judged.

People employed in a city who build their homes in suburban areas of the county beyond the limits of a city and zoning regulations do so for a reason. Some do so to avoid the high taxation rate imposed by cities, or to avoid special assessments for street, sewer and water projects. They usually build on improved or hard surface highways, which have been built either at state or county expense and thereby avoid special assessments for these improvements. It may be that they desire to get away from the congestion of traffic, smoke, noise, foul air and the many other annoyances of city life. But with all these advantages in going beyond the area which is zoned and restricted to protect them in their homes, they must be prepared to take the disadvantages. [Dill v. Excel Packing Company, 331 P.2d 539, 548, 549 (Kan. 1958).]

.... Were Webb the only party injured, we would feel justified in holding that the doctrine of "coming to the nuisance" would have been a bar to the relief asked by Webb, and, on the other hand, had Spur located the feedlot near the outskirts of a city and had the city grown toward the feedlot, Spur would have to suffer the cost of abating the nuisance as to those people locating within the growth pattern of the expanding city:

The case affords, perhaps, an example where a business established at a place remote from population is gradually surrounded and becomes part of a populous center, so that a business which formerly was not an interference with the rights of others has become so by the encroachment of the population.... [City of Ft. Smith v. Western Hide & Fur Co., 239 S.W. 724, 726 (Ark. 1922).]

We agree, however, with the Massachusetts court that:

The law of nuisance affords no rigid rule to be applied in all instances. It is elastic. It undertakes to require only that which is fair and reasonable under all the circumstances. In a commonwealth like this, which depends for its material prosperity so largely on the continued growth and enlargement of manufacturing of diverse varieties, "extreme rights" cannot be enforced.... [Stevens v. Rockport Granite Co., 104 N.E. 371, 373 (Mass. 1914).]

There was no indication in the instant case at the time Spur and its predecessors located in western Maricopa County that a new city would spring up, full-blown, alongside the feeding operation and that the developer of that city would ask the court to order Spur to move because of the new city. Spur is required to move not because of any wrongdoing on the part of Spur, but because of a proper and legitimate regard of the courts for the rights and interests of the public.

Del Webb, on the other hand, is entitled to the relief prayed for (a permanent injunction), not because Webb is blameless, but because of the damage to the people who have been encouraged to purchase homes in Sun City. It does not equitably or legally follow, however, that Webb, being entitled to the injunction, is then free of any liability to Spur if Webb has in fact been the cause of the damage Spur has sustained. It does not seem harsh to require a developer, who has taken advantage of the lesser land values in a rural area as well as the availability of large tracts of land on which to build and develop a new town or city in the area, to indemnify those who are forced to leave as a result.

Having brought people to the nuisance to the foreseeable detriment of Spur, Webb must indemnify Spur for a reasonable amount of the cost of moving or shutting down. It should be noted that this relief to Spur is limited to a case wherein a developer has, with foreseeability, brought into a previously agricultural or industrial area the population which makes necessary the granting of an injunction against a lawful business and for which the business has no adequate relief.

It is therefore the decision of this court that the matter be remanded to the trial court for a hearing upon the damages sustained by the defendant Spur as a reasonable and direct result of the granting of the permanent injunction. Since the result of the appeal may appear novel and both sides have obtained a measure of relief, it is ordered that each side will bear its own costs.

Affirmed in part, reversed in part, and remanded for further proceedings consistent with this opinion.

Notes & Questions

1. Over four hundred property owners in Sun City had a lawsuit pending against Spur at the time the Arizona Supreme Court decided *Spur v. Webb*. After the decision in *Spur*, Spur filed a third party complaint against Webb demanding that Webb indemnify it for damages for which it might be held liable to the plaintiff property owners. See Spur Feeding Co. v. Superior Court of Maricopa County, 505 P.2d 1377 (Ariz. 1973) (holding that the previous ruling in *Spur v. Webb* was not *res judicata* as to whether Webb should be required to indemnify Spur as to any damages that the court might find that the plaintiffs are entitled to receive). After *Spur v. Webb*, should Spur recover in its third-party action against Webb? On what theory?

2. **Coming to the Nuisance.** Was *Spur* correct to give Del Webb an action even though it "came to the nuisance"? Section 840D of the Restatement (Second) of Torts, headed "Coming to the Nuisance," provides that "the fact that the plaintiff has acquired or improved his land after a nuisance interfering with it has come into existence is not in itself sufficient to bar his action, but it is a factor to be considered in determining whether the nuisance is actionable." According to Comment *b*, the Restatement thought that coming to the nuisance should not be an absolute bar

because otherwise "the defendant by setting up an activity or a condition that results in the nuisance could condemn all the land in his vicinity to a servitude without paying any compensation, and so could arrogate to himself a good deal of the value of the adjoining land." The vast majority of courts agree. See, e.g., Jacques v. Pioneer Plastics, Inc., 676 A.2d 504 (Me. 1996) (coming to the nuisance is "not a complete defense"); Weida v. Ferry, 493 A.2d 824 (R.I. 1985) (same). What are the likely effects of a "coming to the nuisance" defense on the first person's decision where to locate? On the decision of later individuals where to locate? See generally Donald Wittman, First Come, First Served: An Economic Analysis of "Coming to the Nuisance," 9 J. Legal Studies 557 (1980).

3. **Right-to-Farm Statutes.** Almost all states have now adopted "right-to-farm" statutes designed to protect farming operations from nuisance suits brought by offended suburban neighbors. Some of the laws provide for an absolute coming to the nuisance defense. Others bar any nuisance action against agricultural operations that meet statutorily specified standards, whether the agricultural operation predated neighboring homes or not. See Neil D. Hamilton, Right–To–Farm Laws Reconsidered: Ten Reasons Why Legislative Efforts to Resolve Agricultural Nuisances May Be Ineffective, 3 Drake J. Agric. L. 103 (1998); Alexander A. Reinert, The Right to Farm: Hog–Tied and Nuisance–Bound, 73 N.Y.U. L. Rev. 1694 (1998). Why should farmers be singled out for special protections?

Are right-to-farm statutes unconstitutional as a "taking" of property without just compensation? Do right-to-farm statutes take one of the central property rights of neighboring landowners—the right to be free of nuisances? Compare Bormann v. Board of Supervisors, 584 N.W.2d 309 (Iowa 1998) (state right-to-farm statute held unconstitutional) with Moon v. North Idaho Farmers Ass'n, 96 P.3d 637 (Idaho 2004) (statute overriding nuisance law where farmers burn grass held constitutional). Should legislatures have the right to redefine nuisance law in a manner that permits some property owners—i.e., farmers—to engage in some activities that were previously illegal as private nuisances?

4. On the assumption that *Spur* was correct to find a nuisance under the facts, was the court correct to charge Webb with the costs of Spur's relocation? If the court had found that Spur's activities did not constitute a nuisance as against Webb, what kind of bargain, if any, might Spur and Webb have struck between themselves? Would the likely terms of a bargain have differed from the terms that the court imposed in requiring Webb to indemnify Spur? Would they have been preferable?

5. Recall that property rights can be enforced through either a *property rule*, in which case the court will protect the right through an injunction, or a *liability rule*, in which case the right is protected through damages. See p. 75–76 supra. In 1972, Guido Calabresi and Douglas Melamed observed that, pairing the two possible liability outcomes (ruling for the plaintiff or for the defendant) with these two enforcement options, provides a court with four ways of resolving a dispute. Guido Calabresi & A. Douglas Melamed, Property Rules, Liability Rules, and Inalienability:

One View of the Cathedral, 85 Harv. L. Rev. 1089 (1972). As shown in Figure 2–4, a court can (1) rule for the plaintiff and issue an injunction; (2) rule for the plaintiff but relegate the plaintiff to damages (the result in *Boomer*); (3) rule for the defendant and deny the plaintiff all relief; or (4) rule for the defendant, but enjoin the defendant's activity only if the plaintiff will pay the defendant damages. At the time that Calabresi and Melamed wrote their article, they could find no example where a court had used the fourth option. Within a matter of months, however, the Arizona Supreme Court adopted the fourth option as its approach in *Spur*—without presumably knowing of the Calabresi and Melamed article.

		Method of Protecting the Entitlement	
		Property Rule	**Liability Rule**
Holder of Entitlement	**Plaintiff**	**1: Nuisance Enjoined.**	**2: Nuisance Allowed. Plaintiff Receives Damages.**
	Defendant	**3: Nuisance Allowed. No Damages.**	**4: Nuisance Enjoined. Defendant Receives Damages**

Figure 2–4

6. **Remedies for Public Nuisances.** In trying to remedy a public nuisance, public officials typically have three options. First, they can bring a regular civil action seeking to enjoin the nuisance or recover damages. Second, in most cases, they can bring a criminal action for the nuisance. Public nuisances originally arose as a concept of criminal law and so have long been recognized as offenses against the state. See Osborne M. Reynolds, Jr., Public Nuisance: A Crime in Tort Law, 318 Okla. L. Rev. 318 (1978); W. Page Keeton, Prosser and Keeton on the Law of Torts § 90, at 645 (5th ed. 1984). Finally, the state itself can abate the nuisance and then sue to recover for the cost.

A private plaintiff seeking to remedy a public nuisance, by contrast, has a choice between a civil action and abatement. Because private plaintiffs may bring a public nuisance action only if they have suffered special damages, most courts will limit a private plaintiff's remedies in a public nuisance action to his special injuries. Thus, private plaintiffs cannot recover for injuries to the general public or abate a public nuisance to a degree greater than is necessary to eliminate the special damages. See W. Page Keeton, supra, § 90, at 645; Fowler V. Harper, The Law of Torts § 1.18, at 59 & n.17 (2d ed. 1986).

7. Do you agree with *Spur*'s reasoning that Del Web had suffered special injury and therefore was entitled to bring a public nuisance action?

What was Webb's special injury? How can loss of sales—to individuals who, if they became home buyers would themselves have, at best, a private action against Spur—qualify as special injury?

D. Protecting Natural Services

Before development, land has various "natural" attributes. The land might be relatively arid, never seeing much water, or perhaps with a culvert that brings raging flood waters during the few occasional storms. Alternatively, a stream or river might run through the land; the stream might flow at a relatively constant volume or frequently flood. Or the land might be a perennial wetland. Turning to soil and typography, the land might be geologically stable, with little shifting or sliding of the soil. Or the land might be hilly and subject to periodic landslides. These and other conditions, in turn, help determine the land's ecosystem. Some lands will be desert, others coastal sagebrush, and yet others old growth forest.

The natural attributes of land can be important to all species living there, including humans. When someone develops a parcel of land, the development often alters those natural attributes to the potential detriment of neighboring property owners, the public generally, and plants, fish, and wildlife. By paving an area of land for a parking lot, for example, a property owner may change drainage patterns, sending a deluge of water onto a neighbor's land, or may pollute a nearby creek with oil and other runoff, harming the local fish population. Hillside development can destabilize the soils of neighboring lands and also pollute adjacent waterways.

How should the law deal with these types of impacts? Although courts use nuisance doctrine to handle many of these issues, courts have developed separate canons to address two specific types of harm—the alteration of natural drainage patterns, and the removal by one property owner of soil support for another property owner's land. In reading the materials that follow, ask yourself whether there is any reason why courts employ unique canons for these disputes, or whether courts could and should use standard nuisance doctrine to resolve them.

The common law concerns itself primarily with the impact of land development on neighboring property owners, not with the broader impact on fish, wildlife, and the environment in general. In recent years, however, a range of federal, state, and local laws have begun to address the environmental impacts. At the federal level, for example, section 404 of the Clean Water Act regulates the drainage and filling of wetlands. And the Endangered Species Act restricts the modification of land that serves as habitat for endangered or threatened species. Chapter 12 examines these laws. This section looks only at common law limitations on development.

Argyelan v. Haviland

Supreme Court of Indiana, 1982.
435 N.E.2d 973.

PRENTICE, J.

The facts of the instant case are not in material dispute. Plaintiffs are the owners of a residential lot improved with a house and two outbuildings.... Plaintiff, Mrs. Haviland, testified that prior to Defendants improving their lot, she had never seen surface water drain from the Defendants' lot onto their own and that no consequential amount of surface water had, theretofore, puddled or accumulated upon their lot....

Prior to 1970, Defendants' lot [which is immediately adjacent to plaintiffs' lot] was covered with grass and trees. In 1971, Defendants erected a commercial building on that portion of their lot adjacent to Washington Street; and in 1974, they built another commercial building along the foot of the "L" adjacent to and twenty (20) feet north of the Plaintiffs' north line. They also paved, for parking, that portion of the lot not built upon, except for the twenty foot strip adjacent to the Plaintiffs' north line. Some fill was used around the building; and, although it is not clear, it appears that Defendants also used substantial fill along the foot of the "L," increasing it as it extended to the toe.

The roof of the more recently constructed of Defendants' buildings is drained by means of three downspouts on the south side of the building. Two of these downspouts empty onto splash blocks at the corners of the building. The third one drains into an underground pipe which carries the water eastwardly to a point twenty feet north of the dividing line and fifty feet west of Plaintiffs' east line, if extended.

Following completion of Defendants' aforementioned improvements, Plaintiffs complained that surface water was draining from Defendants' property onto their property, pooling there and causing substantial damage. Defendants then erected a concrete curbing approximately one foot north of Plaintiffs' north line and extending approximately six inches above the finished grade of Defendants' lot.... Erection of the curbing, if it alleviated the Plaintiffs' surface problem, did not eliminate it. There was testimony that in a sustained rain, water would accumulate behind the curb but eventually flow over it.

Historically, two diametrically opposed but clear rules were consistently followed in the various states with respect to surface water, which must be distinguished from water flowing, even if not continuously, through established and defined channels. Through extensive modifications of both rules, a third doctrine emerged and has been adopted in approximately twenty of the states....

In its most simplistic and pure form the rule known as the "common enemy doctrine," declares that surface water which does not flow in defined channels is a common enemy and that each landowner may deal with it in such manner as best suits his own convenience. Such sanctioned dealings include walling it out, walling it in and diverting or accelerating its flow by any means whatever. The "civil law" doctrine, on the other hand, proscribes interfering with or altering the flow of surface water.

Both doctrines are harsh but have the common virtue of predictability. Under them, landowners know where they stand. They know what they may do and what they may not do without incurring severe risks. If at times the doctrines work to one's disadvantage, there are other times when he reaps its benefits.

Because of the harshness of both of these rules, various exceptions and limitations have been engrafted upon them in all jurisdictions of the United States. A substantial number of states have permitted but minor modifications, and in such jurisdictions the doctrines are still generally referred to as the "common law doctrine" and the "civil law doctrine," notwithstanding such modifications. Other jurisdictions, approximately twenty in number, have evolved to or adopted by express design the aforementioned third doctrine now referred to as the "Rule of Reasonable Use."

> The reasonable use rule was apparently first adopted in New Hampshire. Noting the inconvenience which would arise from adopting extreme rules that a landowner has either no right of drainage or an absolute right, the court in Bassett v. Salisbury Mfg. Co. (1862) 43 N.H. 569 (which was apparently primarily concerned with percolating waters) said that the sole ground of qualification of the landowner's right of drainage was the similar rights of others, the extent of the qualification being determined under the rule of reasonable use, and the rights of each landowner being similar and his enjoyment dependent upon the action of the other landowners, so that the rights must be valueless unless exercised with reference to each other.... [93 A.L.R.3d 1193 at 1216.]

The common enemy and civil law rules are grounded upon real property concepts. The modifications engrafted upon them resulted from the use of tort law concepts used to mitigate the harsh results of the property law doctrines. The doctrine of "reasonable use," however, goes much further and focuses upon the results of the action and the consequent interference with another's use of his land. Its advantage is flexibility. Its disadvantage, obviously, is its unpredictability.

Although Indiana doubtlessly would not permit a malicious or wanton employment of one's drainage rights under the common enemy doctrine, it appears that the only limitation upon such rights that we have thus far judicially recognized is that one may not collect or concentrate surface water and cast it, in a body, upon his neighbor.

Plaintiffs acknowledge the rule in Indiana [is the common enemy doctrine]. They appear to argue, however, that by a combination of erecting downspouts directed towards the property line, paving a substantial portion of their land and erecting the aforementioned curb or retaining wall along the property line, the defendants somehow exceed the limits of what is permissible in fending off the surface water. It requires no reweighing of the evidence to determine that the evidence does not bear them out. There is simply no evidence that any surface water was ever channeled from Defendants' land onto that of the Plaintiffs or cast in a body upon them.

Under the common enemy doctrine, it is not unlawful to accelerate or increase the flow of surface water by limiting or eliminating ground absorption or changing the grade of the land. These two things, we may concede, are shown by the evidence to have resulted from Defendants' improvements. However, the only evidence that water from the Defendants' premises entered those of the Plaintiffs' was testimony that, on occasions following sustained moderate to heavy rains, the water built up behind the wall and overflowed it. . . .

[In Rounds v. Hoelscher, 428 N.E.2d 1308 (Ind. App. 1981), the Third District Court of Appeals for Indiana held that the Common Enemy Doctrine should be abandoned.] Judge Hoffman, concurring in the result in *Rounds*, correctly noted that the case law in this area was not unsettled and that the majority had ignored stare decisis. "I cannot agree," he wrote, "that this court should in any respect presume to be a barometer of public opinion or the weathervane of social change. It is for the Legislature to establish the procedures for such change. The function of the Court of Appeals is to interpret the law and lay down general guidelines by which the lawyers and the trial courts of the State may make determinations upon which they can depend. This function cannot be fulfilled by summarily abandoning the common enemy rule and replacing it with a rule of reasonableness. No longer will lawyers be able to advise their clients with any degree of certainty. What may be reasonable to one person in the use of his property may be unreasonable to an adjacent landowner. Neither of these opinions may comport with what a trial judge might declare is reasonable. The majority opinion does nothing more than muddy the waters in this area of the law." 428 N.E.2d at 1318.

To Judge Hoffman's comments we add that although the Common Enemy Doctrine may, at times, inflict hardships, it is as fair to one as it is to another—a guiding precept of the law. Additionally, it has worked satisfactorily in this State from the beginning, and it is well understood. There has been no change in the forces that cause water to run down hill since the problems caused thereby were first considered and resolved in this State; and there is no basis for assuming that a change in the rules for coping with such problems would, over-all, reduce their number or make them any more palatable. Although courts should not be slow to respond to changing conditions, changes in the established law are not warranted simply because it is imperfect, and we should not feel compelled to join the ranks of greater numbers when it has not been demonstrated that their way is the better way.

We recognize no need to take the advantage, which must repose somewhere, away from the owner at the top of the hill simply to give it to the owner who was the first in the watershed to develop his land, or to the owner who has friends in high places or can engender the greater sympathy for his plight. Neither are we disposed to make drainage commissions of our already overburdened trial courts. These, we perceive to be some of the latent drawbacks to the so-called Rule of Reasonable Use. We, therefore, expressly disapprove the holding in *Rounds*, supra, to the extent that it purports to change the surface water law of this State....

HUNTER, J., dissenting.

I must respectfully dissent from the majority opinion.... As it is, this jurisdiction is today presented with a rule of law and result so inimical to any sense of justice, be it lay or legal, that it offends our system of jurisprudence. Lest the legal and factual nuances involved in this cause obscure the import of the majority's decision, its ramifications for the homeowners of this state should be recognized from the outset. In its simplest terms, the majority of this Court has held that a landowner, in seeking to use property for a commercial purpose, may so alter the ground surface and natural drainage pattern that an adjacent landowner's existing usage of his property for residential purposes is rendered impossible by virtue of the resultant accumulation and run-off of surface water.

That is a proposition out of step with time and judicial logic, one which, as the majority tacitly concedes, is not and would not be followed by any other jurisdiction in this nation. Our law of surface water is today reduced to the rule of the jungle, where "might makes right" and the race belongs to the person who is last in time, elevates his land the highest, and paves the greater portion of his lot surface. It requires no resort to hyperbole to recognize that the ramifications for the homeowners of this state are unconscionable. For that reason, the majority's opinion warrants an exacting scrutiny....

To understand and appreciate the import of the court's holding today, it is necessary to begin with an examination of all the evidence before us concerning the dispute between the Havilands, as plaintiffs, and the Argyelans, as defendants.... In 1948, Harold and Maxine Haviland purchased a lot and home at 807 South Auburn Street in Indianapolis, Indiana.... Then, in 1970, the two undeveloped lots to the north of the Havilands were purchased by Steve Argyelan. Through his efforts, the lot adjacent to the Havilands' property was rezoned from a residential to a business classification. By 1974, Argyelan had constructed two large commercial buildings on his property. In constructing the buildings, he removed all trees and grass and raised the level of his lots two to three feet with fill dirt and crushed stone. Argyelan then paved the vast portion of the two-acre ground surface not occupied by the business structures.

It is uncontradicted that prior to Argyelan's alterations of his property, the Havilands had no problem with flooding or standing water on their property. Both the Havilands and Argyelan acknowledged that when grass and trees occupied the two-acre parcel, the tract absorbed the surface water which fell upon it; it was agreed that Argyelan's alterations virtually eliminated the capacity of the parcel to absorb water.

In the spring of 1975, the Havilands began to experience severe drainage problems on a regular basis; standing water became a commonplace event, occurring after every moderate rainfall.... The water, which would commonly stand for periods up to twenty-four hours, oftentimes measured three to four inches in depth both in and about the Havilands' garage and utility shed, as was evidenced by testimony and photographs. The accumulation also regularly submerged the Havilands' garden area and portions of their driveway. To protect their garage and its contents, it became customary for the Havilands to battle the encroaching water with brooms during and after rainfalls....

It is hardly appropriate that our surface water law requires homeowners such as the Havilands, who have a long-standing property interest in their home and lot, not only to suffer the deluge of water, but also to share indirectly the expense of another's use of adjacent property for commercial gain. While the majority may suggest that a strict application of the common enemy doctrine "is as fair to one as it is to another," it should be recognized that it is rarely the residential property owner who so alters his property, either by the construction of large buildings or the installation of massive paved areas, that the absorption capacity of the land is virtually eliminated....

Eighteen jurisdictions, as well as the American Law Institute, today embrace outright the rule of reasonable use. These jurisdictions have rejected the civil law rule and the common enemy doctrine out of an unwillingness to countenance the unconscionable results which, like the Havilands endure here, follow from a strict application of either rule.... Virtually every other jurisdiction, also mindful of the harsh results engendered by a strict application of either the civil law or common enemy doctrines, has applied a significantly modified version of their respective rules in order to accommodate equity and achieve a proper allocation of the costs arising from an alteration of surface water drainage....

It has been recognized that the common enemy doctrine was born of an agrarian age, when it was a sacrosanct view of the law and the populace that a landowner could do whatever he wished with his property.... [T]he technological ability to pave massive areas of ground surface was not developed until after the inception of the common enemy doctrine; similarly, the ability to radically alter natural drainage patterns and ground surfaces has followed from the creation of massive earth-moving machines. Together with these developments, as well as refinements in the construction industry and changes in our shopping patterns, the last thirty years have yielded an urban landscape dotted with giant commercial structures and vast shopping malls and plazas. The paved parking areas necessary to serve the customers of these various business enterprises lie in tight geographical juxtaposition with high density residential housing. Major quantities of surface water from falling rain and melting snow, once absorbed into the ground, are now repelled from the vast roofs and parking lots and seek lower ground via unnatural drainage patterns....

The majority ought to examine ... Ind. Code § 34–1–52–1 (Burns 1973), where, 101 years ago ... our legislature defined its approach to questions such as that before us. The statute reads: "*Whatever* is injurious to health, or indecent, or offensive to the senses, or an obstruction to the free use of property, so as essentially to interfere with the comfortable enjoyment of life or property, is a nuisance, and the subject of an action" (emphasis added). Defined in the statute is an action to recover damages to the use and enjoyment of property under the theory of nuisance. Its applicability is not limited to injuries occasioned via particular mediums; the legislature stated that "whatever" caused the unlawful interference, the nuisance action could be employed by the victimized property owner. In addition, injury to the health or senses is not the sole gravamen of the statute. Rather, as the legislature also stated, the catalyst of the statute is "an obstruction" to the use and enjoyment of property.

Obviously, the statutory action of nuisance, though not pleaded here, is applicable to the victims of unreasonable alterations in surface water drainage such as the Havilands. They suffer a very real and serious obstruction in their use of their driveway, garden, garage, and utility shed. Consistency in our laws would deem that our common law surface water rules comport with our statutory nuisance-to-property principles and that the Havilands be permitted recovery, just as would be the case if they had proceeded under the statutory remedy also available to them.

In terms of fundamental principles of liability, there is no rational justification for distinguishing between interferences with the use of property occasioned by surface water, as opposed to other mediums such as pollution, sound, or vibration. Other jurisdictions have recognized that no rational distinction exists by which to exclude surface water from the realm of nuisance law and principles. See, e.g., Butler v. Bruno, 341 A.2d 735 (R.I. 1975) ("the invasion of one's property by surface waters can be a nuisance, no different from an invasion by noise, noxious vapors, or the like"); Deason v. Southern R. Co., 140 S.E. 575 (S.C. 1927) (common enemy doctrine expressly modified to comport with nuisance law).

As embodied within our case precedent and nuisance statute, our ultimate concern in any instance must continue to be whether the circumstances justify shifting the loss from the victimized property owner to the person responsible for the interference to the use and enjoyment of property. It is a question of reasonableness; the rule reflects respect for the Latin maxim expressly recognized in our property case law, *sic utere tuo ut alienum non laedas* (so use your property as not to injure the rights of another)....

In all this there is neither nothing new or extreme.... Absent recognition of the rule of reasonable use, this Court should adopt a modified version of the common enemy doctrine, as so many jurisdictions have done. Although the majority has not addressed this alternative, the doctrine could be modified to comport with Ind. Code § 34–1–52–1, or to require undue harm not be inflicted on adjacent landowners, or to impose a reasonable degree of care on urban landowners. Any of these alternatives would preclude the incredibly harsh results endured by the Havilands. Instead, the majority of this Court has reverted to an antiquated rule of law outside the pale of logic or legal authority, a rule so extreme that its doctrinaire application is shunned by all other jurisdictions of this nation....

Notes & Questions

1. Although the dissent in *Argyelan* suggests that only Indiana follows a strict version of the common enemy doctrine, several other courts also hold that landowners can develop their property in ways that redirect waters onto a neighbor's land unless the landowners unnecessarily collect and discharges the water at one place. See Halverson v. Skagit County, 983 P.2d 643 (Wash. 1999); Nu–Dwarf Farms, Inc. v. Stratbucker Farms, Ltd., 470 N.W.2d 772 (Neb. 1991); White v. Pima County, 775 P.2d 1154 (Ariz. App. 1989); Department of Highways v. Feenan, 752 P.2d 182 (Mont. 1988).

A handful of jurisdictions also continue to follow the civil law rule, known as the *natural flow rule*, under which landowners are strictly liable for any flood damage caused by development of their property. See, e.g., Powers v. Judd, 553 A.2d 139 (Vt. 1988); Fisher v. Space of Pensacola, 483 So. 2d 392 (Ala. 1986); Henrickson v. Wagners, 598 N.W.2d 507 (S.D. 1999). A growing number of jurisdictions, however, have abandoned these approaches in favor of a reasonable use test. For recent converts, see Heins Implement Co. v. Missouri Highway & Transp. Comm'n, 859 S.W.2d 681 (Mo. 1993); Westland Skating Center v. Gus Machado Buick, Inc., 542 So. 2d 959 (Fla. 1989); Morris Associates, Inc. v. Priddy, 383 S.E.2d 770 (W. Va. 1989).

2. When, if ever, are "absolute" rules like the common enemy doctrine or the natural flow rule preferable to balancing approaches like the harm-benefit test for nuisance set out in the Restatement? Is there any reason not to treat drainage cases as nuisance actions? How, if at all, does a case like *Argyelan* differ from a nuisance action where the defendant is polluting the plaintiff's property?

3. What social preferences regarding resource use underlie the common enemy doctrine or the natural flow rule? To the degree that social preferences change, does the law need to change? Or can landowners simply contract around the existing legal rule?

4. **Ecosystem Services.** Lands in their natural condition provide a variety of valuable services to humans—what ecologists have dubbed "ecosystem services." Wetlands and forests along a river, for example, can help protect downstream water quality, reduce downstream flood risks, and sequester carbon that otherwise might contribute to the warming of the atmosphere. Other lands might harbor pollinating insects that increase local crop yields. See generally Nature's Services: Societal Dependence on Natural Ecosystems (Gretchen C. Daily ed., 1997). Economists have estimated that these ecosystem services are of immense value. Indeed, one study placed a total price on the world's ecosystem services of $33 trillion (with a confidence interval from $16 to $54 trillion), slightly more than the approximately $30 trillion combined gross national product of all the

countries in the world in 2000. See Robert Constanza et al., The Value of the World's Ecosystem Services and Natural Capital, 387 Nature 253, 259 (1997).

5. To what degree, and how, should the law protect ecosystem services? As the dissent in *Argyelan* notes, for example, by paving over their property, the defendants "virtually eliminated the capacity of the parcel to absorb water." Land covered by trees and other vegetation often absorbs water that filters down into underground aquifers—natural underground water-storage systems upon which others can draw for drinking or irrigation water. When land is paved over for subdivisions, the water that would go into underground aquifers often ends up running down storm drains and is lost for consumptive use. One study by several environmental organizations estimated that the paving over of land as part of "suburban sprawl" has led to dramatic losses in groundwater in the United States. The study concludes, for example, that Atlanta, Georgia has lost between 56.9 and 132.8 billion gallons of water per year; Boston has lost between 43.9 and 102.5 billion gallons per year; Washington, D.C., between 23.8 and 55.6 billion gallons. See American Rivers, Natural Resources Defense Council, & Smart Growth America, Paving Our Way to Water Shortages: How Sprawl Aggravates the Effects of Drought (2002).

If the defendants' actions in *Argyelan* reduced total groundwater recharge, should that constitute a public nuisance? Should groundwater users have a right of action against subdividers if the groundwater users could show that the subdivisions reduced their groundwater supply? Should legislatures address this issue? See generally James Salzman, Barton H. Thompson, Jr., & Gretchen C. Daily, Protecting Ecosystem Services: Science, Economics, and Law, 20 Stan. Envtl. L.J. 309 (2001).

6. Land development also can accelerated soil erosion. In Hall v. Wood, 443 So. 2d 834 (Miss. 1983), a developer cleared his 20–acre parcel of property of trees and other vegetation in anticipation of commercial construction. Rain water flooded down the denuded property, scouring the land, and dumping up to 100 tons of sediment per year per acre into one end of a neighboring lake. The sediment destroyed valuable spawning habitat, leading to a decline in the recreational value of the lake. In a suit for damages brought by homeowners surrounding the lake, the Mississippi Supreme Court held that where development of a parcel of land presents a reasonable likelihood of damage to other property through erosion or drainage, the landowner is "required to do whatever is reasonable to minimize the damage." Id. at 840.

Could the landowners in *Hall* or a governmental official have brought a public nuisance action against the developer based on destruction of the spawning habitat? See People v. Truckee Lumber Co., 48 P. 374 (Cal. 1897) (holding that pollution from a sawmill and box factory that killed fish was a public nuisance).

7. How should courts resolve the following hypothetical cases? Why?

(a) Jedediah Smith cuts down a forest covering his property. The forest provided habitat for bees that were a natural source of pollinators to neighboring farmers, and the bees disappear with the forest. Lacking natural pollinators, the neighboring farmers must pay a beekeeper for artificial pollination. If the farmers sue Jedediah for the cost of the beekeeper, how should the court rule?

(b) The Pure River runs through Mary Austin's property. Wetlands along the river currently help to filter contaminants that otherwise would flow into the river and thus protect the river's water quality. Mary fills in the wetlands. The river's water quality deteriorates as a result, forcing a downstream water supplier to begin filtering the water that it pulls from the Pure River before delivering the water to its customers. What should a court rule if the water supplier sues Austin for the cost of the new filtration system?

(c) The wetlands on Mary Austin's property also helps prevent floods by helping to absorb storm surges. After Mary destroys the wetlands, a storm leads to downstream flooding of residential property. If the downstream property owners sue Mary for their damages and can show that the flooding would not have occurred if Mary had not filled in the wetlands, what should the court do?

Lateral and Subjacent Support

Lateral Support. A parcel of land may physically support the neighboring land surrounding it. If Jedidiah lives at the base of a hill and decides to remove part of the hill in order to have more level land on which to build, the excavation can lead the rest of the hill to collapse. If Mary is unlucky enough to live at the top of the hill, her house can suffer severe damage or be destroyed entirely. Similarly, if Jedidiah decides to construct an underground parking lot on his property, the excavation can damage neighboring property. The support that one parcel of land provides to other parcels is known as *lateral support*.

The law protects lateral support up to a degree:

> An adjacent landowner is strictly liable for acts of commission and omission on his part that result in the withdrawal of lateral support to his neighbor's property. This strict liability, however, is limited to land in its natural state; there is no obligation to support the added weight of buildings or other structures that land cannot naturally support. However, the majority of American jurisdictions hold that if land in its natural state would be capable of supporting the weight of a building or other structure, and such building or other structure is damaged because of the subsidence of the land itself, then the owner of the land on which the building or structure is constructed can recover damages for both the injury to his land and the injury to his building or structure.

Noone v. Price, 298 S.E.2d 218 (W. Va. 1982). Landowners also are liable for any damage to adjacent buildings or other structures resulting from the negligent withdrawal of support.

Why is strict liability for lateral support confined to land in its natural state and not extended to structures on land? Would a contrary rule encourage the overdevelopment of land by enabling each improving landowner to impose the cost of support on his neighbor?

The common law rules on lateral support developed during an era when the American economy was predominantly agrarian. Statutes in several states and many municipalities have altered the common law rules in an effort to encourage more productive land uses in urban land areas. New York City, for example, provides that anyone excavating down more than 10 feet deep must protect neighboring structures; the owners of neighboring land, however, must give the excavator permission to come onto their property for this purpose. Where the excavation is less than 10 feet deep, the owners of neighboring structures are responsible for protecting those structures, so long as the excavator gives them permission to come onto the excavation site for this purpose. New York City Admin. Code § C26–385.0. Why might New York draw this distinction?

Subjacent Support. Where minerals or water are extracted from beneath a parcel of land, an issue of *subjacent* support can arise. The issue most commonly arises in connection with subsurface mining operations. Subsurface minerals, such as coal, are often owned separately from the surface itself. If mining of the minerals causes the surface to subside, can the surface owner sue? Under the common law, surface owners had an absolute right to subjacent support. Surface owners, however, could waive this right and, when purchasing subsurface rights, most mining companies historically sought a waiver agreement from the surface owner. Concerns over the effect of such waivers have led to dozens of state and federal laws limiting the enforceability of such waivers or mandating some degree of surface support. See generally Robert E. Beck, Protecting the Public Interest or Surface Owners From Their Own Folly?: A Close Look at "Preventing" Subsidence Under the Surface Mining Control and Reclamation Act of 1977, 21 S. Ill. U.L.J. 391 (1997).

Groundwater pumping can also lead to significant subsidence of both the land on which the groundwater well is located and neighboring land. Courts vary tremendously in how they resolve lawsuits brought by neighbors trying to enjoin such pumping or seeking damages. Some courts will resolve the cases using groundwater law (discussed in Chapter 3 at pages 262–270). So long as the pumper is complying with the groundwater law, no liability arises. See, e.g., Finley v. Teeter Stone, Inc., 248 A.2d 106 (Md. 1968) (no liability for subsidence so long as groundwater used for reasonable use). Other courts, however, have turned to nuisance law or a similar tort approach in addressing at least some subsidence cases. See, e.g., Friendswood Development Co. v. Smith–Southwest Indus., Inc., 576 S.W.2d 21 (Tex. 1978) (holding that groundwater pumpers are liable if their manner of groundwater extraction is "negligent, willfully wasteful, or for the purpose of malicious injury"); Henderson v. Wade Sand & Gravel Co.,

388 So. 2d 900 (Ala. 1980) (applying nuisance law where groundwater is extracted not for the water itself, but to permit mining operations). See generally Susan M. Kincaid, Cities Supported by Sticks in the Mud: A Variation on the Settlement of Land and Structures Caused by Ground Water Removal, 15 B.C. Envtl. Aff. L. Rev. 349 (1988).

Remedies. The remedies for withdrawal of lateral and subjacent support are substantially similar. Injunctions are rarely granted. Damages are generally measured by the lesser of the diminution in the value of the injured land or the cost of restoring the land to its original condition. See, e.g., Knapp v. Cirillo, 133 N.Y.S.2d 356 (Sup. Ct. 1954). Is the remedy consistent with the purported absolute nature of the right being protected?

In Barr v. Smith, 598 So. 2d 438 (La. App. 1992), the plaintiff's home had been owned by his family since 1868. When a neighboring landowner leveled part of the hillside below the plaintiff's lot for the construction of commercial chicken houses, several trees and a considerable amount of dirt fell down from plaintiff's property and created a "significant drop-off." Testimony showed that the assessed market value of plaintiff's property before the collapse of the hillside was $6,800, and the assessed value of the 50–foot strip of plaintiff's land that was damaged was only $537.03, while the estimated cost of repairing the damage was between $18,000 and $20,000. In remanding the case to the trial court to see if the cost of restoration indeed exceeded the damage, the Louisiana Court of Appeal reiterated the traditional rule that where the cost of restoration is greater than the market value of the damaged property, the proper measure of damages is the lost market value. But the court suggested that, in a future case, it might find this measure of damages to be constitutionally inadequate.

> [T]o allow a defendant to simply pay for the extent of a neighbor's property which has been damaged may establish a poor precedent. Such a result would allow a property owner to do as he will with his property in order to reap major economic benefit, since any damage to neighboring property can be remedied by the payment of a sum that is relatively nominal when the gain involved is considered.

Id. at 442. Do you agree? What should be the appropriate remedy in such cases?

A few states will occasionally award both restoration expenses and an allowance for diminution in value. For example, the court in Grant v. Leith, 407 P.2d 157 (Wash. 1965), awarded plaintiff restoration costs, which far exceeded the original value of the property, as well as $5,600 to cover irreparable cracks in the foundations and walls of his home that reduced the value of the property.

E. PROTECTION FROM GOVERNMENTAL EXPROPRIATION

An individual cannot normally seize someone else's property, but the government can. Under the power of "eminent domain" or "expropriation,'' governments historically have enjoyed the right to take the property of individual citizens for public use. In the United States, the federal government's power of eminent domain is regulated by the Fifth Amendment to the Constitution which provides: ''nor shall private property be taken for public use without just compensation.'' The United States Supreme Court has held that this provision also applies to state exercises of eminent domain, through incorporation by the Fourteenth Amendment, and virtually every state constitution includes a similar limitation.

The constitutional restraints on eminent domain have generated three major sets of issues. First, what is a ''public use''? Courts have read the Fifth Amendment as prohibiting governments from taking property for private, rather than public use. The distinction between private and public uses, as you will see in a moment, is not as clear as you might expect. Second, what is ''just compensation'' when the government expropriates your property? Finally, when has the government ''taken'' your property? The latter question is relatively easy to answer when the government physically takes your property and builds something, like a highway, across it. But the courts also have held that the government sometimes ''takes'' your property when it regulates the property, whether or not the government takes title to or physical possession of the property. In the regulatory setting, courts have found it far more difficult to determine what is a ''taking.''

This section investigates the first two issues. The question of ''regulatory taking'' is reserved for Chapter 13, although you will encounter the issue throughout this book.

1. THE PUBLIC USE LIMITATION

Kelo v. City of New London

Supreme Court of the United States, 2005.
125 S.Ct. 2655.

JUSTICE STEVENS delivered the opinion of the Court.

In 2000, the city of New London approved a development plan that, in the words of the Supreme Court of Connecticut, was ''projected to create in excess of 1,000 jobs, to increase tax and other revenues, and to revitalize an economically distressed city, including its downtown and waterfront areas.'' 843 A.2d 500, 507 (Conn. 2004). In assembling the land needed for this project, the city's development agent has purchased property from willing sellers and proposes to use the power of eminent domain to acquire the remainder of the property from unwilling owners in exchange for just compensation. The question presented is whether the city's proposed disposition of this property qualifies as a ''public use'' within the meaning of the Takings Clause of the Fifth Amendment to the Constitution.

I

The city of New London (hereinafter City) sits at the junction of the Thames River and the Long Island Sound in southeastern Connecticut. Decades of economic decline led a state agency in 1990 to designate the City a "distressed municipality." In 1996, the Federal Government closed the Naval Undersea Warfare Center, which had been located in the Fort Trumbull area of the City and had employed over 1,500 people. In 1998, the City's unemployment rate was nearly double that of the State, and its population of just under 24,000 residents was at its lowest since 1920.

These conditions prompted state and local officials to target New London, and particularly its Fort Trumbull area, for economic revitalization. To this end, respondent New London Development Corporation (NLDC), a private nonprofit entity established some years earlier to assist the City in planning economic development, was reactivated. In January 1998, the State authorized a $5.35 million bond issue to support the NLDC's planning activities and a $10 million bond issue toward the creation of a Fort Trumbull State Park. In February, the pharmaceutical company Pfizer Inc. announced that it would build a $300 million research facility on a site immediately adjacent to Fort Trumbull; local planners hoped that Pfizer would draw new business to the area, thereby serving as a catalyst to the area's rejuvenation. After receiving initial approval from the city council, the NLDC continued its planning activities and held a series of neighborhood meetings to educate the public about the process. In May, the city council authorized the NLDC to formally submit its plans to the relevant state agencies for review. Upon obtaining state-level approval, the NLDC finalized an integrated development plan focused on 90 acres of the Fort Trumbull area.

The Fort Trumbull area is situated on a peninsula that juts into the Thames River. The area comprises approximately 115 privately owned properties, as well as the 32 acres of land formerly occupied by the naval facility (Trumbull State Park now occupies 18 of those 32 acres). The development plan encompasses seven parcels. Parcel 1 is designated for a waterfront conference hotel at the center of a "small urban village" that will include restaurants and shopping. This parcel will also have marinas for both recreational and commercial uses. A pedestrian "riverwalk" will originate here and continue down the coast, connecting the waterfront areas of the development. Parcel 2 will be the site of approximately 80 new residences organized into an urban neighborhood and linked by public walkway to the remainder of the development, including the state park. This parcel also includes space reserved for a new U.S. Coast Guard Museum. Parcel 3, which is located immediately north of the Pfizer facility, will contain at least 90,000 square feet of research and development office space. Parcel 4A is a 2.4–acre site that will be used either to support the adjacent state park, by providing parking or retail services for visitors, or to support the nearby marina. Parcel 4B will include a renovated marina, as well as the final stretch of the riverwalk. Parcels 5, 6, and 7 will provide land for office and retail space, parking, and water-dependent commercial uses.

The NLDC intended the development plan to capitalize on the arrival of the Pfizer facility and the new commerce it was expected to attract. In addition to creating jobs, generating tax revenue, and helping to "build momentum for the revitalization of downtown New London," the plan was also designed to make the City more attractive and to create leisure and recreational opportunities on the waterfront and in the park.

The city council approved the plan in January 2000, and designated the NLDC as its development agent in charge of implementation. The city council also authorized the NLDC to purchase property or to acquire property by exercising eminent domain in the City's name. The NLDC successfully negotiated the purchase of most of the real estate in the 90–acre area, but its negotiations with petitioners failed. As a consequence, in November 2000, the NLDC initiated the condemnation proceedings that gave rise to this case.

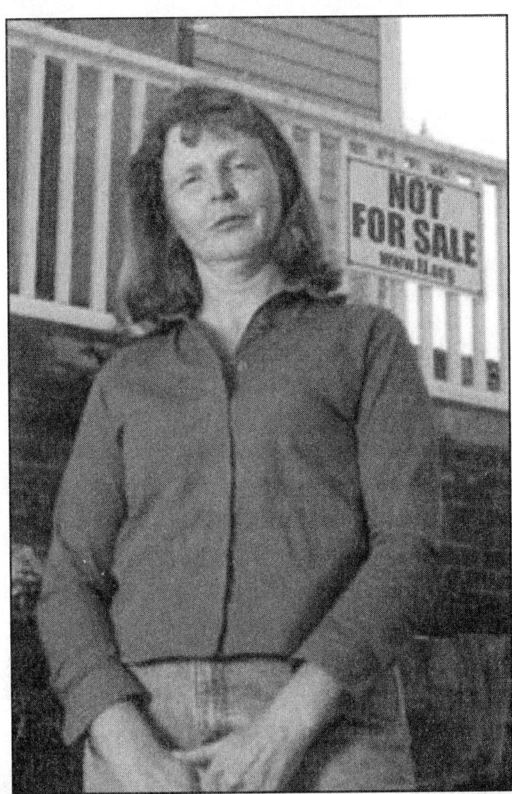

Figure 2–5
Susette Kelo and her home

Photo by Isaac Reese. Copyright © 2004 Institute for Justice.

II

Petitioner Susette Kelo has lived in the Fort Trumbull area since 1997. She has made extensive improvements to her house, which she prizes for its water view. Petitioner Wilhelmina Dery was born in her Fort Trumbull house in 1918 and has lived there her entire life. Her husband Charles (also a petitioner) has lived in the house since they married some 60 years ago. In all, the nine petitioners own 15 properties in Fort Trumbull—4 in parcel 3 of the development plan and 11 in parcel 4A. Ten of the parcels are occupied by the owner or a family member; the other five are held as investment properties. There is no allegation that any of these properties is blighted or otherwise in poor condition; rather, they were condemned only because they happen to be located in the development area.

In December 2000, petitioners brought this action in the New London Superior Court. They claimed, among other things, that the taking of their properties would violate the "public use" restriction in the Fifth Amendment....

We granted certiorari to determine whether a city's decision to take property for the purpose of economic development satisfies the "public use" requirement of the Fifth Amendment.

III

Two polar propositions are perfectly clear. On the one hand, it has long been accepted that the sovereign may not take the property of *A* for the sole purpose of transferring it to another private party *B*, even though *A* is paid just compensation. On the other hand, it is equally clear that a State may transfer property from one private party to another if future "use by the public" is the purpose of the taking; the condemnation of land for a railroad with common-carrier duties is a familiar example. Neither of these propositions, however, determines the disposition of this case.

As for the first proposition, the City would no doubt be forbidden from taking petitioners' land for the purpose of conferring a private benefit on a particular private party. See Hawaii Housing Authority v. Midkiff, 467 U.S. 229, 245 (1984) ("A purely private taking could not withstand the scrutiny of the public use requirement; it would serve no legitimate purpose of government and would thus be void"). Nor would the City be allowed to take property under the mere pretext of a public purpose, when its actual purpose was to bestow a private benefit. The takings before us, however, would be executed pursuant to a "carefully considered" development plan. 843 A.2d at 536. The trial judge and all the members of the Supreme Court of Connecticut agreed that there was no evidence of an illegitimate purpose in this case. Therefore, as was true of the statute challenged in *Midkiff,* 467 U.S. at 245, the City's development plan was not adopted "to benefit a particular class of identifiable individuals."

On the other hand, this is not a case in which the City is planning to open the condemned land—at least not in its entirety—to use by the general public. Nor will the private lessees of the land in any sense be required to operate like common carriers, making their services available to all comers. But although such a projected use would be sufficient to satisfy the public use requirement, this "Court long ago rejected any literal requirement that condemned property be put into use for the general public." Id., at 244. Indeed, while many state courts in the mid–19th century endorsed "use by the public" as the proper definition of public use, that narrow view steadily eroded over time. Not only was the "use by the public" test difficult to administer (*e.g.*, what proportion of the public need have access to the property? at what price?), but it proved to be impractical given the diverse and always evolving needs of society. Accordingly, when this Court began applying the Fifth Amendment to the States at the close of the 19th century, it embraced the broader and more natural interpretation of public use as "public purpose." See, e.g., Fallbrook Irrigation Dist. v. Bradley, 164 U.S. 112, 158–164 (1896). Thus, in a case upholding a mining company's use of an aerial bucket line to transport ore over property it did not own, Justice Holmes' opinion for the Court stressed "the inadequacy of use by the general public as a universal test." Strickley v. Highland Boy Gold Mining Co., 200 U.S. 527, 531 (1906). We have repeatedly and consistently rejected that narrow test ever since.

The disposition of this case therefore turns on the question whether the City's development plan serves a "public purpose." Without exception, our cases have defined that concept broadly, reflecting our longstanding policy of deference to legislative judgments in this field.

In Berman v. Parker, 348 U.S. 26 (1954), this Court upheld a redevelopment plan targeting a blighted area of Washington, D.C., in which most of the housing for the area's 5,000 inhabitants was beyond repair. Under the plan, the area would be condemned and part of it utilized for the construction of streets, schools, and other public facilities. The remainder of the land would be leased or sold to private parties for the purpose of redevelopment, including the construction of low-cost housing.

The owner of a department store located in the area challenged the condemnation, pointing out that his store was not itself blighted and arguing that the creation of a "better balanced, more attractive community" was not a valid public use. Writing for a unanimous Court, Justice Douglas refused to evaluate this claim in isolation, deferring instead to the legislative and agency judgment that the area "must be planned as a whole" for the plan to be successful. The Court explained that "community redevelopment programs need not, by force of the Constitution, be on a piecemeal basis—lot by lot, building by building." The public use underlying the taking was unequivocally affirmed:

> We do not sit to determine whether a particular housing project is or is not desirable. The concept of the public welfare is broad and inclusive.... The values it represents are spiritual as well as physical, aesthetic as well as monetary. It is within the power of the legislature to determine that the community should be beautiful as well as healthy, spacious as well as clean, well-balanced as well as carefully patrolled. In the present case, the Congress and its authorized agencies have made determinations that take into account a wide variety of values. It is not for us to reappraise them. If those who govern the District of Columbia decide that the Nation's Capital should be beautiful as well as sanitary, there is nothing in the Fifth Amendment that stands in the way.

In Hawaii Housing Authority v. Midkiff, 467 U.S. 229 (1984), the Court considered a Hawaii statute whereby fee title was taken from lessors and transferred to lessees (for just compensation) in order to reduce the concentration of land ownership. We unanimously upheld the statute and rejected the Ninth Circuit's view that it was "a naked attempt on the part of the state of Hawaii to take the property of A and transfer it to B solely for B's private use and benefit." Reaffirming *Berman*'s deferential approach to legislative judgments in this field, we concluded that the State's purpose of eliminating the "social and economic evils of a land oligopoly" qualified as a valid public use. Our opinion also rejected the contention that the mere fact that the State immediately transferred the properties to private individuals upon condemnation somehow diminished the public character of the taking. "It is only the taking's purpose, and not its mechanics," we explained, that matters in determining public use....

In that same Term we decided another public use case that arose in a purely economic context. In Ruckelshaus v. Monsanto Co., 467 U.S. 986 (1984), the Court dealt with provisions of the Federal Insecticide, Fungicide, and Rodenticide Act under which the Environmental Protection Agency could consider the data (including trade secrets) submitted by a prior pesticide applicant in evaluating a subsequent application, so long as the second applicant was paid just compensation for the data. We acknowledged that the "most direct beneficiaries" of these provisions were the subsequent applicants, but we nevertheless upheld the statute under *Berman* and *Midkiff*. We found sufficient Congress' belief that sparing applicants the time-consuming research eliminated a significant barrier to entry in the pesticide market and thereby enhanced competition.

Viewed as a whole, our jurisprudence has recognized that the needs of society have varied between different parts of the Nation, just as they have evolved over time in response to changed circumstances. Our earliest cases in particular embodied a strong theme of federalism, emphasizing the "great respect" that we owe to state legislatures and state courts in discerning local public needs. See Hairston v. Danville & Western R. Co., 208 U.S. 598, 606–607 (1908) (noting that these needs were likely to vary depending on a State's "resources, the capacity of the soil, the relative importance of industries to the general public welfare, and the long-established methods and habits of the people"). For more than a century, our public use jurisprudence has wisely eschewed rigid formulas and intrusive scrutiny in favor of affording legislatures broad latitude in determining what public needs justify the use of the takings power.

IV

Those who govern the City were not confronted with the need to remove blight in the Fort Trumbull area, but their determination that the area was sufficiently distressed to justify a program of economic rejuvenation is entitled to our deference. The City has carefully formulated an economic development plan that it believes will provide appreciable benefits to the community, including—but by no means limited to—new jobs and increased tax revenue. As with other exercises in urban planning and development, the City is endeavoring to coordinate a variety of commercial, residential, and recreational uses of land, with the hope that they will form a whole greater than the sum of its parts. To effectuate this plan, the City has invoked a state statute that specifically authorizes the use of eminent domain to promote economic development. Given the comprehensive character of the plan, the thorough deliberation that preceded its adoption, and the limited scope of our review, it is appropriate for us, as it was in *Berman*, to resolve the challenges of the individual owners, not on a piecemeal basis, but rather in light of the entire plan. Because that plan unquestionably serves a public purpose, the takings challenged here satisfy the public use requirement of the Fifth Amendment.

To avoid this result, petitioners urge us to adopt a new bright-line rule that economic development does not qualify as a public use. Putting aside the unpersuasive suggestion that the City's plan will provide only purely economic benefits, neither precedent nor logic supports petitioners' proposal. Promoting economic development is a traditional and long accepted function of government. There is, moreover, no principled way of distinguishing economic development from the other public purposes that we have recognized. In our cases upholding takings that facilitated agriculture and mining, for example, we emphasized the importance of those industries to the welfare of the States in question; in *Berman,* we endorsed the purpose of transforming a blighted area into a "well-balanced" community through redevelopment, 348 U.S. at 33; in *Midkiff*, we upheld the interest in breaking up a land oligopoly that "created artificial deterrents to the normal functioning of the State's residential land market," 467 U.S. at 242; and in *Monsanto*, we accepted Congress' purpose of eliminating a "significant barrier to entry in the pesticide market," 467 U.S. at 1014–1015. It would be incongruous to hold that the City's interest in the economic benefits to be derived from the development of the Fort Trumbull area has less of a public character than any of those other interests. Clearly, there is no basis for exempting economic development from our traditionally broad understanding of public purpose.

Petitioners contend that using eminent domain for economic development impermissibly blurs the boundary between public and private takings. Again, our cases foreclose this objection. Quite simply, the government's pursuit of a public purpose will often benefit individual private parties. For example, in *Midkiff*, the forced transfer of property conferred a direct and significant benefit on those lessees who were previously unable to purchase their homes. In *Monsanto*, we recognized that the "most direct beneficiaries" of the data-sharing provisions were the subsequent pesticide applicants, but benefiting them in this way was necessary to promoting competition in the pesticide market. The owner of the department store in *Berman* objected to "taking from one businessman for the benefit of another businessman," referring to the fact that under the redevelopment plan land would be leased or sold to private developers for redevelopment. Our rejection of that contention has particular relevance to the instant case: "The public end may be as well or better served through an agency of private enterprise than through a department of government—or so the Congress might conclude. We cannot say that public ownership is the sole method of promoting the public purposes of community redevelopment projects." 348 U.S. at 34.

It is further argued that without a bright-line rule nothing would stop a city from transferring citizen *A*'s property to citizen *B* for the sole reason that citizen *B* will put the property to a more productive use and thus pay more taxes. Such a one-to-one transfer of property, executed outside the confines of an integrated development plan, is not presented in this case. While such an unusual exercise of government power would certainly raise a suspicion that a private purpose was afoot, the hypothetical cases posited by petitioners can be confronted if and when they arise. They do not warrant the crafting of an artificial restriction on the concept of public use.[19] . . . .

In affirming the City's authority to take petitioners' properties, we do not minimize the hardship that condemnations may entail, notwithstanding the payment of just compensation. We emphasize that nothing in our opinion precludes any State from placing further restrictions on its exercise of the takings power. Indeed, many States already impose "public use" requirements that are stricter than the federal baseline. Some of these requirements have been established as a matter of state constitutional law, while others are expressed in state eminent domain statutes that carefully limit the grounds upon which takings may be exercised. As the submissions of the parties and their *amici* make clear, the necessity and wisdom of using eminent domain to promote economic development are certainly matters of legitimate public debate. This Court's authority, however, extends only to determining whether the City's proposed condemnations are for a "public use" within the meaning of the Fifth Amendment to the Federal Constitution. Because over a century of our case law interpreting that provision dictates an affirmative answer to that question, we may not grant petitioners the relief that they seek.

The judgment of the Supreme Court of Connecticut is affirmed.

JUSTICE KENNEDY, concurring.

I join the opinion for the Court and add these further observations. . . .

19. A parade of horribles is especially unpersuasive in this context, since the Takings Clause largely "operates as a conditional limitation, permitting the government to do what it wants so long as it pays the charge." Eastern Enterprises v. Apfel, 524 U.S. 498, 545 (1998) (Kennedy, J., concurring in judgment and dissenting in part). Speaking of the takings power, Justice Iredell observed that "it is not sufficient to urge, that the power may be abused, for, such is the nature of all power—such is the tendency of every human institution: and, it might as fairly be said, that the power of taxation, which is only circumscribed by the discretion of the Body, in which it is vested, ought not to be granted, because the Legislature, disregarding its true objects, might, for visionary and useless projects, impose a tax to the amount of nineteen shillings in the pound. We must be content to limit power where we can, and where we cannot, consistently with its use, we must be content to repose a salutory confidence." Calder v. Bull, 3 U.S. 386, 400 (1798) (opinion concurring in result).

A court applying rational-basis review under the Public Use Clause should strike down a taking that, by a clear showing, is intended to favor a particular private party, with only incidental or pretextual public benefits, just as a court applying rational-basis review under the Equal Protection Clause must strike down a government classification that is clearly intended to injure a particular class of private parties, with only incidental or pretextual public justifications. As the trial court in this case was correct to observe, "Where the purpose [of a taking] is economic development and that development is to be carried out by private parties or private parties will be benefited, the court must decide if the stated public purpose—economic advantage to a city sorely in need of it—is only incidental to the benefits that will be confined on private parties of a development plan."

A court confronted with a plausible accusation of impermissible favoritism to private parties should treat the objection as a serious one and review the record to see if it has merit, though with the presumption that the government's actions were reasonable and intended to serve a public purpose. Here, the trial court conducted a careful and extensive inquiry into "whether, in fact, the development plan is of primary benefit to . . . the developer [*i.e.*, Corcoran Jennison], and private businesses which may eventually locate in the plan area [*e.g.*, Pfizer], and in that regard, only of incidental benefit to the city." . . . .

The trial court concluded . . . that benefiting Pfizer was not "the primary motivation or effect of this development plan"; instead, "the primary motivation for [respondents] was to take advantage of Pfizer's presence." Likewise, the trial court concluded that "there is nothing in the record to indicate that . . . [respondents] were motivated by a desire to aid [other] particular private entities." Even the dissenting justices on the Connecticut Supreme Court agreed that respondents' development plan was intended to revitalize the local economy, not to serve the interests of Pfizer. This case, then, survives the meaningful rational basis review that in my view is required under the Public Use Clause. . . .

My agreement with the Court that a presumption of invalidity is not warranted for economic development takings in general, or for the particular takings at issue in this case, does not foreclose the possibility that a more stringent standard of review than that announced in *Berman* and *Midkiff* might be appropriate for a more narrowly drawn category of takings. There may be private transfers in which the risk of undetected impermissible favoritism of private parties is so acute that a presumption (rebuttable or otherwise) of invalidity is warranted under the Public Use Clause. This demanding level of scrutiny, however, is not required simply because the purpose of the taking is economic development.

This is not the occasion for conjecture as to what sort of cases might justify a more demanding standard, but it is appropriate to underscore aspects of the instant case that convince me no departure from *Berman* and *Midkiff* is appropriate here. This taking occurred in the context of a comprehensive development plan meant to address a serious city-wide depression, and the projected economic benefits of the project cannot be characterized as *de minimus*. The identity of most of the private beneficiaries were unknown at the time the city formulated its plans. The city complied with elaborate procedural requirements that facilitate review of the record and inquiry into the city's purposes. In sum, while there may be categories of cases in which the transfers are so suspicious, or the procedures employed so prone to abuse, or the purported benefits are so trivial or implausible, that courts should presume an impermissible private purpose, no such circumstances are present in this case.

For the foregoing reasons, I join in the Court's opinion.

JUSTICE O'CONNOR, with whom THE CHIEF JUSTICE, JUSTICE SCALIA, and JUSTICE THOMAS join, dissenting.

Over two centuries ago, just after the Bill of Rights was ratified, Justice Chase wrote:

> "An ACT of the Legislature (for I cannot call it a law) contrary to the great first principles of the social compact, cannot be considered a rightful exercise of legislative authority.... A few instances will suffice to explain what I mean.... [A] law that takes property from A. and gives it to B: It is against all reason and justice, for a people to entrust a Legislature with SUCH powers; and, therefore, it cannot be presumed that they have done it." Calder v. Bull, 3 U.S. 386 (1798) (emphasis deleted).

Today the Court abandons this long-held, basic limitation on government power. Under the banner of economic development, all private property is now vulnerable to being taken and transferred to another private owner, so long as it might be upgraded—i.e., given to an owner who will use it in a way that the legislature deems more beneficial to the public—in the process. To reason, as the Court does, that the incidental public benefits resulting from the subsequent ordinary use of private property render economic development takings "for public use" is to wash out any distinction between private and public use of property—and thereby effectively to delete the words "for public use" from the Takings Clause of the Fifth Amendment. Accordingly I respectfully dissent....

Where is the line between "public" and "private" property use? We give considerable deference to legislatures' determinations about what governmental activities will advantage the public. But were the political branches the sole arbiters of the public-private distinction, the Public Use Clause would amount to little more than hortatory fluff. An external, judicial check on how the public use requirement is interpreted, however limited, is necessary if this constraint on government power is to retain any meaning.

Our cases have generally identified three categories of takings that comply with the public use requirement, though it is in the nature of things that the boundaries between these categories are not always firm. Two are relatively straightforward and uncontroversial. First, the sovereign may transfer private property to public ownership—such as for a road, a hospital, or a military base. Second, the sovereign may transfer private property to private parties, often common carriers, who make the property available for the public's use—such as with a railroad, a public utility, or a stadium. But "public ownership" and "use-by-the-public" are sometimes too constricting and impractical ways to define the scope of the Public Use Clause. Thus we have allowed that, in certain circumstances and to meet certain exigencies, takings that serve a public purpose also satisfy the Constitution even if the property is destined for subsequent private use. See, e.g., Berman v. Parker, 348 U.S. 26 (1954); Hawaii Housing Authority v. Midkiff, 467 U.S. 229 (1984).

This case returns us for the first time in over 20 years to the hard question of when a purportedly "public purpose" taking meets the public use requirement. It presents an issue of first impression: Are economic development takings constitutional? I would hold that they are not. We are guided by two precedents about the taking of real property by eminent domain. In *Berman*, we upheld takings within a blighted neighborhood of Washington, D.C. The neighborhood had so deteriorated that, for example, 64.3% of its dwellings were beyond repair. It had become burdened with "overcrowding of dwellings," "lack of adequate streets and alleys," and "lack of light and air." Congress had determined that the neighborhood had become "injurious to the public health, safety, morals, and welfare" and that it was necessary to "eliminate all such injurious conditions by employing all means necessary and appropriate for the purpose," including eminent domain. Mr. Berman's department store was not itself blighted. Having approved of Congress' decision to eliminate the harm to the public emanating from the blighted neighborhood, however, we did not second-guess its decision to treat the neighborhood as a whole rather than lot-by-lot. See also *Midkiff*, 467 U.S. at 244 ("it is only the taking's purpose, and not its mechanics, that must pass scrutiny").

In *Midkiff*, we upheld a land condemnation scheme in Hawaii whereby title in real property was taken from lessors and transferred to lessees. At that time, the State and Federal Governments owned nearly 49% of the State's land, and another 47% was in the hands of only 72 private landowners. Concentration of land ownership was so dramatic that on the State's most urbanized island, Oahu, 22 landowners owned 72.5% of the fee simple titles. The Hawaii Legislature had concluded that the oligopoly in land ownership was "skewing the State's residential fee simple market, inflating land prices, and injuring the public tranquility and welfare," and therefore enacted a condemnation scheme for redistributing title.

In those decisions, we emphasized the importance of deferring to legislative judgments about public purpose. Because courts are ill-equipped to evaluate the efficacy of proposed legislative initiatives, we rejected as unworkable the idea of courts' " 'deciding on what is and is not a governmental function and ... invalidating legislation on the basis of their view on that question at the moment of decision, a practice which has proved impracticable in other fields.' " Likewise, we recognized our inability to evaluate whether, in a given case, eminent domain is a necessary means by which to pursue the legislature's ends.

Yet for all the emphasis on deference, *Berman* and *Midkiff* hewed to a bedrock principle without which our public use jurisprudence would collapse: "A purely private taking could not withstand the scrutiny of the public use requirement; it would serve no legitimate purpose of government and would thus be void." *Midkiff*, 467 U.S. at 245. To protect that principle, those decisions reserved "a role for courts to play in reviewing a legislature's judgment of what constitutes a public use . . . [though] the Court in *Berman* made clear that it is 'an extremely narrow' one." Id. at 240.

The Court's holdings in *Berman* and *Midkiff* were true to the principle underlying the Public Use Clause. In both those cases, the extraordinary, precondemnation use of the targeted property inflicted affirmative harm on society—in *Berman* through blight resulting from extreme poverty and in *Midkiff* through oligopoly resulting from extreme wealth. And in both cases, the relevant legislative body had found that eliminating the existing property use was necessary to remedy the harm. Thus a public purpose was realized when the harmful use was eliminated. Because each taking *directly* achieved a public benefit, it did not matter that the property was turned over to private use. Here, in contrast, New London does not claim that Susette Kelo's and Wilhelmina Dery's well-maintained homes are the source of any social harm. Indeed, it could not so claim without adopting the absurd argument that any single-family home that might be razed to make way for an apartment building, or any church that might be replaced with a retail store, or any small business that might be more lucrative if it were instead part of a national franchise, is inherently harmful to society and thus within the government's power to condemn.

In moving away from our decisions sanctioning the condemnation of harmful property use, the Court today significantly expands the meaning of public use. It holds that the sovereign may take private property currently put to ordinary private use, and give it over for new, ordinary private use, so long as the new use is predicted to generate some secondary benefit for the public—such as increased tax revenue, more jobs, maybe even aesthetic pleasure. But nearly any lawful use of real private property can be said to generate some incidental benefit to the public. Thus, if predicted (or even guaranteed) positive side-effects are enough to render transfer from one private party to another constitutional, then the words "for public use" do not realistically exclude *any* takings, and thus do not exert any constraint on the eminent domain power.

. . . . The Court protests that it does not sanction the bare transfer from A to B for B's benefit. It suggests two limitations on what can be taken after today's decision. First, it maintains a role for courts in ferreting out takings whose sole purpose is to bestow a benefit on the private transferee—without detailing how courts are to conduct that complicated inquiry. For his part, Justice Kennedy suggests that courts may divine illicit purpose by a careful review of the record and the process by which a legislature arrived at the decision to take—without specifying what courts should look for in a case with different facts, how they will know if they have found it, and what to do if they do not. Whatever the details of Justice Kennedy's as-yet-undisclosed test, it is difficult to envision anyone but the "stupid staffer" failing it. The trouble with economic development takings is that private benefit and incidental public benefit are, by definition, merged and mutually reinforcing. In this case, for example, any boon for Pfizer or the plan's developer is difficult to disaggregate from the promised public gains in taxes and jobs....

A second proposed limitation is implicit in the Court's opinion. The logic of today's decision is that eminent domain may only be used to upgrade—not downgrade—property. At best this makes the Public Use Clause redundant with the Due Process Clause, which already prohibits irrational government action. The Court rightfully admits, however, that the judiciary cannot get bogged down in predictive judgments about whether the public will actually be better off after a property transfer. In any event, this constraint has no realistic import. For who among us can say she already makes the most productive or attractive possible use of her property? The specter of condemnation hangs over all property. Nothing is to prevent the State from replacing any Motel 6 with a Ritz–Carlton, any home with a shopping mall, or any farm with a factory....

Any property may now be taken for the benefit of another private party, but the fallout from this decision will not be random. The beneficiaries are likely to be those citizens with disproportionate influence and power in the political process, including large corporations and development firms. As for the victims, the government now has license to transfer property from those with fewer resources to those with more. The Founders cannot have intended this perverse result. "That alone is a *just* government," wrote James Madison, "which *impartially* secures to every man, whatever is his *own*." For the National Gazette, Property, (Mar. 29, 1792), reprinted in 14 Papers of James Madison 266 (Rutland et al. eds. 1983).

I would hold that the takings in both Parcel 3 and Parcel 4A are unconstitutional, reverse the judgment of the Supreme Court of Connecticut, and remand for further proceedings.

JUSTICE THOMAS, dissenting.

.... Today's decision is simply the latest in a string of our cases construing the Public Use Clause to be a virtual nullity, without the slightest nod to its original meaning. In my view, the Public Use Clause, originally understood, is a meaningful limit on the government's eminent domain power. Our cases have strayed from the Clause's original meaning, and I would reconsider them.

The Fifth Amendment provides: ".... nor shall private property be taken for public use, without just compensation."....

The most natural reading of the Clause is that it allows the government to take property only if the government owns, or the public has a legal right to use, the property, as opposed to taking it for any public purpose or necessity whatsoever.... When the government takes property and gives it to a private individual, and the public has no right to use the property, it strains language to say that the public is "employing" the property, regardless of the incidental benefits that might accrue to the public from the private use. The term "public use," then, means that either the government or its citizens as a whole must actually "employ" the taken property....

Tellingly, the phrase "public use" contrasts with the very different phrase "general Welfare" used elsewhere in the Constitution. See Article 1, § 8 ("Congress shall have Power To ... provide for the common Defence and general Welfare of the United States"); preamble (Constitution established "to promote the general Welfare"). The Framers would have used some such broader term if they had meant the Public Use Clause to have a similarly sweeping scope. Other founding-era documents made the contrast between these two usages still more explicit. See Sales, Classical Republicanism and the Fifth Amendment's "Public Use" Requirement, 49 Duke L. J. 339, 368 (2000) (noting contrast between, on the one hand, the term "public use" used by 6 of the first 13 States and, on the other, the terms "public exigencies" employed in the Massachusetts Bill of Rights and the Northwest Ordinance, and the term "public necessity" used in the Vermont Constitution of 1786). The Constitution's text, in short, suggests that the Takings Clause authorizes the taking of property only if the public has a right to employ it, not if the public realizes any conceivable benefit from the taking....

The consequences of today's decision are not difficult to predict, and promise to be harmful. So-called "urban renewal" programs provide some compensation for the properties they take, but no compensation is possible for the subjective value of these lands to the individuals displaced and the indignity inflicted by uprooting them from their homes. Allowing the government to take property solely for public purposes is bad enough, but extending the concept of public purpose to encompass any economically beneficial goal guarantees that these losses will fall disproportionately on poor communities. Those communities are not only systematically less likely to put their lands to the highest and best social use, but are also the least politically powerful. If ever there were justification for intrusive judicial review of constitutional provisions that protect "discrete and insular minorities," United States v. Carolene Products Co., 304 U.S. 144, 152 (1938), surely that principle would apply with great force to the powerless groups and individuals the Public Use Clause protects. The deferential standard this Court has adopted for the Public Use Clause is therefore deeply perverse. It encourages "those citizens with disproportionate influence and power in the political process, including large corporations and development firms" to victimize the weak. *Ante* (O'Connor, J., dissenting).

Those incentives have made the legacy of this Court's "public purpose" test an unhappy one. In the 1950's, no doubt emboldened in part by the expansive understanding of "public use" this Court adopted in *Berman*, cities "rushed to draw plans" for downtown development. B. Frieden & L. Sagalayn, Downtown, Inc. How America Rebuilds Cities 17 (1989). "Of all the families displaced by urban renewal from 1949 through 1963, 63 percent of those whose race was known were nonwhite, and of these families, 56 percent of nonwhites and 38 percent of whites had incomes low enough to qualify for public housing, which, however, was seldom available to them." Id., at 28. Public works projects in the 1950's and 1960's destroyed predominantly minority communities in St. Paul, Minnesota, and Baltimore, Maryland. Id., at 28–29. In 1981, urban planners in Detroit, Michigan, uprooted the largely "lower-income and elderly" Poletown neighborhood for the benefit of the General Motors Corporation. J. Wylie, Poletown: Community Betrayed 58 (1989). Urban renewal projects have long been associated with the displacement of blacks; "in cities across the country, urban renewal came to be known as 'Negro removal.' " Pritchett, The "Public Menace" of Blight: Urban Renewal and the Private Uses of Eminent Domain, 21 Yale L. & Pol'y Rev. 1, 47 (2003). Over 97 percent of the individuals forcibly removed from their homes by the "slum-clearance" project upheld by this Court in *Berman* were black. 348 U.S. at 30. Regrettably, the predictable consequence of the Court's decision will be to exacerbate these effects....

Notes & Questions

1. Over a half century ago, a student writer concluded that the "Supreme Court has repudiated the doctrine of public use." Comment, The Public Use Limitation on Eminent Domain: An Advance Requiem, 58 Yale L.J. 599, 614 (1949). *Kelo* certainly appears to confirm this assessment. What would it take for a property owner to win a "public use" challenge after *Kelo*? Even before *Kelo*, property owners seldom won in federal court. In the past twenty years, only two published federal decisions have held that a taking of private property was unconstitutional because for private rather than public use. See Aaron v. Target Corp., 269 F. Supp. 2d 1162 (E.D. Mo. 2003), rev'd, 357 F.3d 768 (8th Cir. 2004); In re Persky, 134 B.R. 81 (Bankr. E.D.N.Y. 1991).

2. State courts, however, continue to wield the "public use" test to invalidate exercises of the eminent domain power that appear primarily to benefit private interests. A survey by Professor Thomas Merrill of "public use" challenges between 1954 (the year that the United States Supreme Court decided *Berman v. Parker*) and 1985 found that over 15 percent of the state public-use decisions invalidated the exercise of eminent domain. The state-court trend, moreover, was toward decreased deference to the legislature. Thomas J. Merrill, The Economics of Public Use, 72 Cornell L. Rev. 61 (1986). Why might state courts be more stringent than federal courts in their application of the "public use" requirement?

3. ***Poletown* and *Wayne County*.** To keep General Motors from moving it assembly operations from Detroit to the southern United States in the 1970s, the City of Detroit condemned a large tract of land in an area known as Poletown and conveyed it to General Motors for construction of a new assembly plant. The Michigan Supreme Court held that the condemna-

tion was for a "public use." Poletown Neighborhood Council v. City of Detroit, 304 N.W.2d 455 (Mich. 1981). According to the court, the city had condemned the land for the "essential public purposes of alleviating unemployment and revitalizing the economic base of the community"; the court dismissed the private benefit to General Motors as "merely incidental" to these more significant public purposes.

In County of Wayne v. Hatchcock, 684 N.W.2d 765 (Mich. 2004), the Michigan Supreme Court overruled *Poletown* and held that Wayne County's attempt to condemn private property for the construction of a 1300–acre business and technology park was unconstitutional. Adopting the dissenting opinion of Justice James L. Ryan in *Poletown*, the court held that condemnations involving a transfer of the condemned property to a private entity are for a "public use" only in three situations:

> First, condemnations in which private land [is] transferred by the condemning authority to a private entity [are constitutional if they involve] "public necessity of the extreme sort otherwise impracticable." The "necessity" that Justice Ryan identified in our pre–1963 case law is a specific kind of need:
>
> > The exercise of eminent domain for private corporations has been limited to those enterprises generating public benefits whose very *existence* depends on the use of land that can be assembled only by the coordination central government alone is capable of achieving.
>
> Justice Ryan listed "highways, railroads, canals, and other instrumentalities of commerce" as examples of this brand of necessity. A corporation constructing a railroad, for example, must lay track so that it forms a more or less straight path from point A to point B. If a property owner between points A and B holds out—say, for example, by refusing to sell his land for any amount less than fifty times its appraised value—the construction of the railroad is halted unless and until the railroad accedes to the property owner's demands. And if owners of adjoining properties receive word of the original property owner's windfall, they too will refuse to sell.
>
> The likelihood that property owners will engage in this tactic makes the acquisition of property for railroads, gas lines, highways, and other such "instrumentalities of commerce" a logistical and practical nightmare. Accordingly, this Court has held that the exercise of eminent domain in such cases—in which collective action is needed to acquire land for vital instrumentalities of commerce—is consistent with the constitutional "public use" requirement.
>
> Second, this Court has found that the transfer of condemned property to a private entity is consistent with the constitution's "public use" requirement when the private entity remains accountable to the public in its use of that property.... Thus, in the

common understanding of those sophisticated in the law at the time of ratification, the "public use" requirement would have allowed for the transfer of condemned property to a private entity when the public retained a measure of control over the property.

> Finally, condemned land may be transferred to a private entity when the selection of the land to be condemned is itself based on public concern. In Justice Ryan's words, the property must be selected on the basis of "facts of independent public significance," meaning that the underlying purposes for resorting to condemnation, rather than the subsequent use of condemned land, must satisfy the Constitution's public use requirement.
>
> The primary example of a condemnation in this vein is found in In re Slum Clearance, 50 N.W.2d 340 (Mich. 1951), a 1951 decision from this Court. In that case, we considered the constitutionality of Detroit's condemnation of blighted housing and its subsequent resale of those properties to private persons. The city's *controlling purpose* in condemning the properties was to remove unfit housing and thereby advance public health and safety; subsequent resale of the land cleared of blight was "incidental" to this goal. We concluded, therefore, that the condemnation was indeed a "public use," despite the fact that the condemned properties would inevitably be put to private use. *In re Slum Clearance* turned on the fact that the act of condemnation *itself*, rather than the use to which the condemned land eventually would be put, was a public use. Thus, as Justice Ryan observed, the condemnation was a "public use" because the land was selected on the basis of "facts of independent public significance"—namely, the need to remedy urban blight for the sake of public health and safety.

The court rejected the *Poletown* conclusion that the local economic benefits of the future use of the property could constitute a sufficient "public use":

> Every business, every productive unit in society, does ... contribute in some way to the commonweal. To justify the exercise of eminent domain solely on the basis of the fact that the use of that property by a private entity seeking its own profit might contribute to the economy's health is to render impotent our constitutional limitations on the government's power of eminent domain. *Poletown*'s "economic benefit" rationale would validate practically *any* exercise of the power of eminent domain on behalf of a private entity. After all, if one's ownership of private property is forever subject to the government's determination that another private party would put one's land to better use, then the ownership of real property is perpetually threatened by the expansion plans of any large discount retailer, "megastore," or the like....

4. Note that the United States Constitution does not explicitly prohibit the use of eminent domain for private purposes. Courts instead have implied a public use requirement from the Fifth Amendment's language,

"nor shall private property be taken for public use, without just compensation." Is this a reasonable reading of the language?

If so, what does the "public use" requirement mean? As the Court observes in *Kelo,* early courts often took the view that the public must actually use or at least have the right to use the condemned property. Lawrence Berger, The Public Use Requirement in Eminent Domain, 57 Or. L. Rev. 203, 205–209 (1978). In this century, by contrast, the United States Supreme Court has focused more on whether exercise of the eminent domain power could reasonably be viewed as benefitting the public. Yet once the focus shifts to the purposes that the government is trying to achieve, the "public use" inquiry begins to look very similar to the Due Process requirement that *any* governmental action, whether or not it uses the power of eminent domain, must be rationally related to a legitimate state purpose. See, e.g., Smithfield Concerned Citizens for Fair Zoning v. Town of Smithfield, 907 F.2d 239, 243–46 (1st Cir. 1990) (due process challenge to zoning regulation). Under *Kelo*, is there any difference in the inquiries? Should courts give the same, virtually total, deference to legislative judgments on "public use" that they give to legislative judgments under the Due Process Clause? If not, how would you distinguish the inquiries?

5. Professor Thomas Merrill has suggested that the "public use" test should focus, not on the *ends* sought to be achieved, but on whether the *means* of eminent domain are necessary to achieve the ends: Does the government need to use its condemnation power to achieve its stated goals? Or could the government easily purchase the land? See Merrill, supra Note 2.

How would *Kelo* be decided under Merrill's "public use" test? Is it relevant that private developers assembling sites for office buildings, industrial parks, and shopping centers, by following careful strategy and playing good poker, often manage to overcome holdout problems without the aid of eminent domain?

6. Given that the United States Constitution mandates that private property owners receive "just compensation" for their property, why does it matter whether the condemnation power is being used for a public use? One answer is that very few property owners receive what they believe is adequate compensation for their property. As discussed in the materials that follow, courts have almost universally interpreted "just compensation" to mean "fair market value"—the amount that a willing buyer would pay a willing seller in the market place. But condemnation does not involve a willing seller; at the time of condemnation, few property owners are interested in selling their property even at its current market value. Most condemnation awards, moreover, do not include relocation expenses and do not reflect the personal value that residents attach to their homes and neighborhoods. These uncompensated values are doubtless very high for many residents, forced out of a neighborhood in which they have lived for years. Consider, for example, Poletown, Michigan, where homes were condemned in the 1970s for a new General Motors plant. The condemned

neighborhood was a "tightly-knit residential enclave of first- and second-generation Americans, for many of whom their home was their single most valuable and cherished asset and their stable ethnic neighborhood the unchanging symbol of the security and quality of their lives." *Poletown*, supra Note 3, 304 N.W.2d at 470 (Ryan, J., dissenting).

7. **Delegation of Eminent Domain Authority.** Governments have long used their condemnation power to benefit private industry. In colonial times, eminent domain's two principal uses were for the construction of roads—often to connect private lands to public highways—and the construction of mills along waterways. Both forms of condemnation flourished after the Revolution, particularly the "Mill Acts" which legislatures eventually broadened to authorize the condemnation of dam sites for privately owned sawmills, paper mills, and other private industrial uses. Private companies, chartered by the state to build railroads, bridges, canals, turnpikes, and later, power and telephone lines, also received authority to condemn the land they needed. See generally Morton J. Horwitz, The Transformation of American Law, 1780–1860, at 63–66 (1977); Harry N. Scheiber, Property Law, Expropriation, and Resource Allocation by Government: The United States, 1789–1910, 33 J. Econ. Hist. 232 (1973). Does Justice Thomas ignore this early history in arguing for a narrow reading of the "public use" requirement in *Kelo*?

There is a modern trend to delegate the eminent domain power to institutions such as hospitals, universities, and cemetery associations which, though not public utilities or common carriers, are thought to have some special claim on the public interest. Can these delegations be justified in the usual terms of public use?

8. **Private Condemnation Provisions.** Several state constitutions include provisions like the first sentence of article I, section 16 of the Washington State Constitution: "Private property shall not be taken for private use, except for private ways of necessity, and for drains, flumes or ditches on or across the lands of others for agricultural, domestic, or sanitary purposes." Can these provisions, which effectively enable landlocked owners to condemn rights of way over their neighbors' parcels, be reconciled with the United States Constitution which contains no comparable authority for private condemnation? When, if at all, should private landowners be permitted to use the condemnation power?

9. **Condemnation of Private Businesses.** Can a city use the eminent domain power to condemn a local business—such as a computer software developer—that threatens to move its operations out of town? The Oakland Raiders professional football team announced plans to relocate in Los Angeles in the early 1980s. The City of Oakland responded by instituting a condemnation proceeding to acquire all property rights in the team. In City of Oakland v. Oakland Raiders, 646 P.2d 835 (Cal. 1982), the California Supreme Court rejected the team's claim that only real property, and not intangible business property, could be taken by eminent domain. Observing that condemnations of land for purposes of building ballparks have been upheld as satisfying the public use test, the court also ruled that,

as a matter of law, condemning a ball team could qualify as a "public use." The court remanded for a determination whether condemning the Oakland Raiders constituted a public use under the terms of the specific eminent domain statute at issue. A lower court later held that condemnation of a professional sports team would unconstitutionally interfere with interstate commerce in violation of the Commerce Clause, and the Raiders moved to Los Angeles. The Raiders, however, moved back to Oakland in 1995 after Oakland offered the Raiders a substantial set of economic incentives (much like Detroit offered General Motors in *Poletown*). See generally Steven R. Hobson, Preventing Franchise Flight: Could Cleveland Have Kept the Browns by Exercising its Eminent Domain Power?, 29 Akron L. Rev. 665 (1996); Charles Gray, Keeping the Home Team at Home, 74 Cal. L. Rev. 1329 (1986).

2. JUST COMPENSATION

United States v. 564.54 Acres of Land

Supreme Court of the United States, 1979.
441 U.S. 506.

MR. JUSTICE MARSHALL delivered the opinion of the Court.

At issue in this case is the proper measure of compensation when the Government condemns property owned by a private nonprofit organization and operated for a public purpose. In particular, we must decide whether the Just Compensation Clause of the Fifth Amendment requires payment of replacement cost rather than fair market value of the property taken.

I

Respondent, the Southeastern Pennsylvania Synod of the Lutheran Church in America, operates three nonprofit summer camps along the Delaware River. In June 1970, the United States initiated a condemnation proceeding to acquire respondent's land for a public recreational project. Before trial, the Government offered to pay respondent $485,400 as the fair market value of its property. Respondent rejected the offer and demanded approximately $5.8 million, the asserted cost of developing functionally equivalent substitute facilities at a new site. This substantial award was necessary, respondent contended, because the new facilities would be subject to financially burdensome regulations from which existing facilities were exempt under grandfather provisions....

II

In giving content to the just compensation requirement of the Fifth Amendment, this Court has sought to put the owner of condemned property "in as good a position pecuniarily as if his property had not been taken." Olson v. United States, 292 U.S. 246, 255 (1934). However, this principle of indemnity has not been given its full and literal force. Because of serious practical difficulties in assessing the worth an individual places on particular property at a given time, we have recognized the need for a relatively objective working rule. The Court therefore has employed the concept of fair market value to determine the condemnee's loss. Under this standard, the owner is entitled to receive "what a willing buyer would pay in cash to a willing seller" at the time of the taking.

Although the market-value standard is a useful and generally sufficient tool for ascertaining the compensation required to make the owner whole, the Court has acknowledged that such an award does not necessarily compensate for all values an owner may derive from his property. Thus, we have held that fair market value does not include the special value of property to the owner arising from its adaptability to his particular use. As Mr. Justice Frankfurter wrote for the Court in Kimball Laundry Co. v. United States, 338 U.S. 1, 5 (1949):

> The value of property springs from subjective needs and attitudes; its value to the owner may therefore differ widely from its value to the taker. Most things, however, have a general demand which gives them a value transferable from one owner to another. As opposed to such personal and variant standards as value to the particular owner whose property has been taken, this transferable value has an external validity which makes it a fair measure of public obligation to compensate the loss incurred by an owner as a result of the taking of his property for public use. In view, however, of the liability of all property to condemnation for the common good, loss to the owner of nontransferable values deriving from his unique need for property or idiosyncratic attachment to it, like loss due to an exercise of the police power, is properly treated as part of the burden of common citizenship.

In short, the concept of fair market value has been chosen to strike a fair "balance between the public's need and the claimant's loss" upon condemnation of property for a public purpose.

But while the indemnity principle must yield to some extent before the need for a practical general rule, this Court has refused to designate market value as the sole measure of just compensation. For there are situations where this standard is inappropriate. As we held in United States v. Commodities Trading Corp., 339 U.S. 121, 123 (1950):

> [When] market value has been too difficult to find, or when its application would result in manifest injustice to owner or public, courts have fashioned and applied other standards.... Whatever the circumstances under which such constitutional questions arise, the dominant consideration always remains the same: What compensation is "just" both to an owner whose property is taken and to the public that must pay the bill?

Hence, we must determine whether application of the fair-market-value standard here would be impracticable or whether an award of market value would diverge so substantially from the indemnity principle as to violate the Fifth Amendment.

The instances in which market value is too difficult to ascertain generally involve property of a type so infrequently traded that we cannot predict whether the prices previously paid, assuming there have been prior sales, would be repeated in a sale of the condemned property. This might be the case, for example, with respect to public facilities such as roads or sewers. But respondent's property does not fall in this category. There was a market for camps, albeit not an extremely active one. The Government's expert witness presented evidence concerning 11 recent sales of comparable facilities in the vicinity, and estimated that respondent's camps could have been sold within six months to a year after they were offered for sale.... The only remaining inquiry is whether such an award would impermissibly deviate from the indemnity principle.

Emphasizing that the primary value of the condemned property lies in the use to which it is put, respondent argues that compensating only for market value would be unjust in the present context. Because new facilities would bear financial burdens imposed by regulations to which the existing camps were not subject, an award of market value would preclude continuation of respondent's use. Respondent therefore concludes that such a recovery would be insufficient to indemnify for its loss.

However, it is not at all unusual that property uniquely adapted to the owner's use has a market value on condemnation which falls far short of enabling the owner to preserve that use. Such a situation may often arise, for example, where a family home has been built to the owner's tastes, but is old and deteriorated, or where property, like respondent's camps, is exempt from regulations applicable to new facilities. Yet the Court has previously determined that nontransferable values arising from the owner's unique need for the property are not compensable, and has found that this divergence from full indemnification does not violate the Fifth Amendment. We are unable to discern why a different result should obtain here. That respondent is a nonprofit organization may provide some basis for distinguishing it from business enterprises, since the uses to which commercial property is put can often be valued in terms of the capitalized earnings produced. But there is no reason to treat respondent differently from the many private homeowners and other noncommercial property owners who neither derive earnings from their property nor hold it for investment purposes. Unless the Just Compensation Clause mandates a Government subsidy for nonprofit organizations, a proposition we find patently implausible, respondent's nonprofit status does not require us to reject application of the fair-market-value standard.

Nor is it relevant in this case whether respondent's camps were reasonably necessary to the public welfare. In condemnations of property owned by public entities, lower courts have applied the reasonable-necessity standard to determine if the entity has an obligation to continue providing the facilities taken. If the condemnee has such a duty to replace the property, these courts have reasoned that only an award of the costs of developing requisite substitute facilities will compensate for the loss.

Whatever the merits of this reasoning with respect to public entities, it does not advance analysis here. For respondent is under no legal or factual obligation to replace the camps, regardless of their social worth. As a private entity, respondent is free to allocate its resources to serve its own institutional objectives, which may or may not correspond with community needs. Awarding replacement cost on the theory that respondent would continue to operate the camps for a public purpose would thus provide a windfall if substitute facilities were never acquired, or if acquired, were later sold or converted to another use....

In sum, we find no circumstances here that require suspension of the normal rules for determining just compensation. Respondent, like other private owners, is not entitled to recover for nontransferable values arising from its unique need for the property. To the extent denial of such an award departs from the indemnity principle, it is justified by the necessity for a workable measure of valuation. Allowing respondent the fair market value of its property is thus consistent with the "basic equitable principles of fairness," United States v. Fuller, 409 U.S. 488, 490 (1973), underlying the Just Compensation Clause.

The judgment of the Court of Appeals is

Reversed.

MR. JUSTICE POWELL took no part in the consideration or decision of this case.

MR. JUSTICE WHITE, concurring.

The Court rejects the claim that the measure of compensation in this case is the cost of substitute facilities rather than the fair market value of the taken property, here camps owned by a private, nonprofit corporation. I am in full agreement. The substitute-facilities doctrine is unrelated to fair market value and does not depend on whether fair market value is readily ascertainable; rather, it unabashedly demands additional compensation over and above market value in order to allow the replacement of the condemned facility. In those cases where it has been applied, primarily where public facilities have been condemned, the basic premise is that the condemnee is under some obligation to continue the functions performed on the taken property. But I do not understand how a duty to replace the condemned facility justifies paying more than market value. Obviously, replacing the old with a new facility will cost more than the value of the old, but the new facility itself will be more valuable and last longer. This is true with respect to condemnation of any facility, whether or not there is an obligation to reproduce it, and I had not understood the Just Compensation Clause to guarantee subsidies to either private or public projects. Similarly, if more demanding building codes or other regulations will enhance the cost of replacement, it is reasonable to assume that compliance itself will be of some benefit to the owner and hence need not be financed by the condemnor....

I thus agree with the Court that the Just Compensation Clause does not require payment of the cost of a substitute facility where the condemnee is a private organization, even if it could be said that such an owner is in some sense obligated to replace the property or that the public has a stake in the continuance of the function that is being conducted on the taken property. I also have substantial doubt that the Clause should be any differently construed and applied where public property is condemned, whether or not the function conducted on the property must be continued at another location. That issue, however, is not before the Court and is expressly put aside for another day.

Notes & Questions

1. As stated in *564.54 Acres*, the standard measure of just compensation is the fair market value of the property, or "what a willing buyer would pay in cash to a willing seller" at the time of the taking. This measure will rarely leave the condemnee as well off as if no condemnation had occurred. Typically it will leave him far worse off. Apart from the emotional jar of being required to move, a family whose home is taken by eminent domain will usually not be compensated for relocation costs, including moving expenses, carrying charges, and the possibly higher price and financing costs of a new home. As the Southeastern Pennsylvania Synod discovered, businesses and non-profit organizations do no better. A firm generally cannot recover either relocation expenditures or damages arising from destruction of its business, lost goodwill, or the diminished value of equipment that, if custom-built for the condemned site, will be less useful at some other site. (Although condemnors are not required to compensate for movable equipment, they must pay for fixtures and other improvements to the condemned parcel.)

Is there any good reason for government to be so stingy in condemnation cases? Courts and legislatures have moved toward providing more complete compensation. A number of judicial decisions and statutes, for example, now provide for compensation of at least some business losses. See, e.g., City of Minneapolis v. Schutt, 256 N.W.2d 260 (Minn. 1977) (going-concern value can be recovered where business cannot be practically relocated). A number of states also now provide at least partial compensation for relocation costs. See, e.g., Mass. Gen. Laws Ann. ch. 79, § 6A. But compensation awards still fail to provide complete indemnity.

2. Empirical studies, moreover, indicate that property owners sometimes receive substantially less than the "just compensation" required by constitutions and statutes. For example, a study of condemnation practices in Nassau County, New York, revealed that the process of determining compensation awards systematically understated the "fair market value" of condemned properties. One reason lay in the appraisal process. Typically the county would order one appraisal; since condemnees rarely obtained their own appraisals, this appraisal became the benchmark for all subsequent negotiations. Because these appraisals were infrequently tested in court, the appraiser had every opportunity to bias his result downward in order to favor the county, his regular employer. On those occasions when

the county did order a second appraisal, wide discrepancies appeared. Indeed, in one out of ten situations, the two appraisals varied by 50% or more. Curtis J. Berger & Patrick J. Rohan, The Nassau County Study: An Empirical Look into the Practice of Condemnation, 67 Colum. L. Rev. 430 (1967).

The settlement process also contributed to undercompensation in Nassau County. The first county official to contact the condemnee was a professional negotiator authorized to settle at a figure no higher than between 60% and 85% of the already understated first appraisal. If these negotiations failed, the matter was then turned over to a litigator on the county attorney's staff for further negotiation and, if these settlement efforts failed, for trial. Settlement agreements were reached for more than 85% of the parcels studied. According to the authors, "the condemnee who agreed to settle was shockingly underpaid. Only about one in six (15.7%) realized or bettered the County's low appraisal, a sum that an impartial observer might consider a *sine qua non* for 'just' compensation. Even regarding the next group of settlements—those between 90 and 99% of low appraisal—as within a tolerable range, nearly three claimants in five (56.9%) received under 90% of the County's low appraisal, and one in twelve (8.6%) received less than 50%!" Id. at 442–43.

A subsequent study of condemnation proceedings in a Chicago urban renewal program found that, while high-valued parcels received more than market value, low-valued parcels tended to receive less than market value. Patricia Munch, An Economic Analysis of Eminent Domain, 84 J. Pol. Econ. 473 (1976).

3. **Contaminated Property.** Assuming that property is contaminated by various toxic substances (e.g., oil or hazardous waste), should courts take the contamination into account in valuing the property? Should it matter whether the government also would have a later cause of action under federal or state law to sue the former property owner for the costs of cleaning up the property? See Housing Authority v. Suydam Investors, L.L.C., 826 A.2d 673 (N.J. 2003) (contamination should not be taken into account in valuation, but money should be placed in a trust fund that the government can utilize for cleaning up the property).

4. A property owner whose land loses value because a government project, such as a freeway or garbage facility, is built nearby generally is not entitled to compensation. Most states, however, have made an exception where a portion of the property owner's land has been condemned for the project. In this case, the property owner generally receives compensation not only for the part of the land taken, but also for damages to the part retained—what is often called "severance damages." See, e.g., State v. Weiswasser, 693 A.2d 864 (N.J. 1997) (loss of visibility from highway reduced value of remaining land). This special rule for severance damages often means that two property owners immediately next to each other will be treated differently. Even though Mary Austin and Jedediah Smith both find themselves living next to a noisy freeway, Mary will get compensation for this inconvenience if part of her land was needed to build the freeway,

while Jedediah will not if the government needed none of his land. Is the different treatment justified? Should the situations be treated the same? If so, should both Mary and Jedediah receive compensation? Should neither?

The next case considers the question of whether and when the *benefits* of being near a governmental project should be taken into account in determining severance damages.

Los Angeles County Metropolitan Transportation Authority v. Continental Development Corporation

Supreme Court of California, 1997.
941 P.2d 809.

WERDEGAR, J.

The taking of private property in eminent domain is constrained by the California Constitution, which provides in relevant part that "[p]rivate property may be taken or damaged for public use only when just compensation, ascertained by a jury unless waived, has first been paid to, or into court for, the owner." (Cal. Const., art. I, § 19; see also U.S. Const., Amends. V, XIV.) By statute, the owner of property acquired by eminent domain is entitled to the fair market value of the property taken. (Code Civ. Proc., § 1263.010, 1263.310.) When the property taken is part of a larger parcel, in addition to being compensated for the part taken, the owner is compensated for the injury, if any, to the remainder. (§ 1263.410, subd. (a).) Compensation for injury to the remainder is the amount of the damage to the remainder, or severance damages, reduced by the amount of benefit to the remainder. (§ 1263.410, subd. (b).)

In the early eminent domain case of Beveridge v. Lewis (1902) 137 Cal. 619 [70 P. 1083] (*Beveridge*), this court distinguished between different types of benefits to remainder property. We stated: "Benefits are said to be of two kinds, general and special. General benefits consist in an increase in the value of land common to the community generally, from advantages which will accrue to the community from the improvement.... Special benefits are such as result from the mere construction of the improvement, and are peculiar to the land in question." (Id. at pp. 623–624.) Only special benefits, we concluded, may be set off against severance damages. (Id. at p. 624.) Later cases have reiterated the distinction. (See, e.g., Pierpont Inn, Inc. v. State of California (1969) 70 Cal. 2d 282 [74 Cal. Rptr. 521, 449 P.2d 737] (Pierpont Inn).)

Here, the Los Angeles County Metropolitan Transportation Authority (the MTA) brought a condemnation action to acquire a narrow strip of land for an easement along one side of a parcel owned by Continental Development Corporation (Continental) for the construction of a portion of an elevated light rail line known as the Green Line. The Douglas Street Green Line station is located within a 10–minute walk from Continental's property.

In pretrial proceedings relating to Continental's severance damages claim, the MTA proffered evidence that the value of office buildings in other localities increased as a result of their proximity to public transit stations, as well as expert testimony that the value of Continental's property would increase by several million dollars as a result of the operation of the line. The trial court ruled the evidence inadmissible; the court reasoned that proximity to the transit station was not a special benefit because it was shared by numerous properties in the vicinity and, therefore, was not a feature peculiar or special to Continental's property. At the conclusion of the trial, the jury returned a verdict awarding Continental compensation for the property taken and for severance damages. On the MTA's appeal from the ensuing judgment, the Court of Appeal affirmed....

For the reasons discussed below, we conclude the distinction between general and special benefits no longer finds support in the reasons articulated at its inception. We further conclude this lack of support and the difficulties inherent in courts' efforts consistently to apply the distinction warrant overruling this aspect of *Beveridge* and its progeny. We therefore reverse the judgment and remand the case for a new trial on severance damages....

FACTS

Continental owned a 14–acre parcel of land that was divided into 3 lots.... On September 4, 1990, the Los Angeles County Transportation Commission, the predecessor of the MTA, brought an eminent domain proceeding to acquire three interests in a small part of the subject property. These three interests consist of an air rights easement for the area in which the Green Line guideway was constructed, a construction easement located under the air rights easement, and a small area taken in fee.[a] The easements run along the entire northeast side of the property, approximately five feet in average width. The area of the fee is 373 square feet, located entirely within the area covered by the easements. When this suit was filed, the property was unimproved, although by the time of trial Continental had constructed a four-story office building on the site. At the time of trial, the Green Line had not yet begun operation.

Prior to trial, the court conducted a hearing to determine whether the MTA would be permitted to present evidence on the issue of severance damages that proximity to the Douglas Street Station was a special benefit that enhanced the value of Continental's remaining property. The question was decided on the parties' memoranda and declarations; no testimony was taken. Continental's appraiser, Joseph A. Hennessey, averred there were

a. Eds.—Easements, which are covered in Chapter 10, are "non-possessory" interests in property that give the holder a right to use or restrict the use of a parcel of land while leaving title to the property in someone else. The "air rights easement" in this case, for example, gave MTA the right to use the air overlying Continental's land for its mass transit system; the related "construction easement" gave MTA the right to come onto Continental's land in order to construct the transit system. Continental, however, remained the owner of the land subject to these easements.

565 separate parcels of property located within 1,700 feet of the Douglas Street Station, of which 7 were being condemned for the construction of the Green Line. Attached to the Hennessey declaration were two reports prepared for the MTA by consultants SGM Group and Desmond, Marcello & Amster. The SGM report sets forth its analysis of the effect on rents and property values of modern elevated rail lines in other cities. SGM found that buildings within walking distance of San Francisco Bay Area Rapid Transit (BART) stations enjoyed, on average, 11 percent lower vacancy rates and 20 percent higher rents than comparable buildings located beyond walking distance from BART stations. SGM concluded that location of the Douglas Street Station within walking distance of Continental's property enhanced its value by $4.1 million. The Desmond report concluded the value of Continental's property was enhanced by $3,760,000 due to proximity to the station.

The trial court ruled, however, that "[t]he benefit of being within walking distance of a rail transit station is merely the benefit of access. As such it confers no peculiar or unique benefit upon defendant's property." . . . .

On the issue of compensation for the property taken, the MTA valued the fee and easements taken at $99,532; Continental introduced evidence they were worth $141,666. The jury awarded Continental a total of $106,356 for the taking; that award is not here at issue.

On the issue of severance damages, Continental sought recovery based on three factors: building redesign, noise mitigation, and visual impact.

Continental presented evidence it spent $23,123 to have plans redrawn to resite the building farther from the elevated line. The MTA essentially did not dispute that claim. Continental also presented evidence that, to soundproof the portion of the building facing the elevated line, Continental laminated the windows on the northeast side and incurred related expenses. The parties disputed whether further soundproofing would ultimately be needed; the MTA contended the existing lamination would suffice, but Continental introduced evidence it would need to install double windowpanes at a cost of over $400,000.

The major contested issue at trial was Continental's claimed damages stemming from the effect of the elevated line on views from offices on the northeast side of the building. Hennessey, Continental's appraiser, testified he believed those offices would command lower rents; he capitalized the projected lower rents to arrive at an opinion the property would lose $1,038,300 in value from the visual impact of the Green Line. The MTA presented the testimony of Lawrence Goldstein, who had studied the economic effects of urban transit lines on real estate values. Goldstein testified he compared rents for properties within 90 feet of elevated rail lines in Washington, D.C., and in areas served by the BART system in the San Francisco Bay Area, with rents of comparable properties located substantially farther from the lines. He concluded commercial office buildings located next to modern elevated rail lines suffered no decrease in rents.

The jury's total severance damages award was $1,015,793. Because the trial court denied the MTA's request for a special verdict form that would have required the jury to state separately the amounts awarded for different elements of severance damages, no such allocation was made. Nevertheless, assuming the jury awarded Continental the full amount it sought for noise mitigation ($416,604), it is clear a substantial part of the award represented damages for visual impact. . . .

DISCUSSION

Just Compensation: Offset of Benefits Against Severance Damages

. . . . [The] *Beveridge* court introduced into California decisional law for the first time the principle that benefits, to be eligible for setoff, must be "special" or "peculiar" to the remainder property. . . . The court commenced its analysis by returning to what might be termed the first principle of takings law, that a landowner must receive "just compensation" for a taking. The court noted that a compensation law, to be valid, must at the least fully compensate the owner, it must apply uniformly, and it must compensate in money, rather than "conjectured advantage."

Against this background, in particular the prohibition against compensation in the form of "conjectured advantage," the *Beveridge* court turned its attention to the distinction between general and special benefits. "Benefits are said to be of two kinds, general and special," the court observed. "General benefits consist in an increase in the value of the land common to the community generally, from advantages which will accrue to the community from the improvement. They are conjectural and incapable of estimation. They may never be realized, and in such case the property-owner has not been compensated save by the sanguine promise of the promoter." Special benefits, by contrast, are "such as result from the mere construction of the improvement," or, in other words, "reasonably certain to result from the construction of the work," and are "peculiar to the land in question." . . . .

The difficulty of determining whether a particular benefit is special or general, and the resulting inconsistency among published decisions on the subject, is clear in a comparison of the present case with earlier cases in which the benefit was that of enhanced access to the property. In City of Hayward v. Unger (1961) 194 Cal. App. 2d 516 [15 Cal. Rptr. 301], for example, the city widened a street in the block on which the subject property was located. In rejecting the landowner's contention the ensuing improvement of access to the property was a general benefit as a matter of law, the Court of Appeal cited expert testimony establishing that the widening of the street increased the flow of traffic past the property, and thus specially benefited it. Likewise, in Los Angeles v. Marblehead Land Co. (1928) 95 Cal. App. 602, 614–615 [273 P. 131], the Court of Appeal concluded the evidence supported the trial court's finding of special benefits for enhanced access resulting from the construction of a highway through the subject property. In Pierpont Inn, Inc. v. State of California (1969) 70 Cal. 2d 282 [74 Cal. Rptr. 521, 449 P.2d 737], by contrast, we upheld a finding of no special benefit for enhanced access resulting from the construction of a freeway and offramp in the vicinity of the subject property, and, of course, the lower courts in the present case came to the same conclusion regarding the enhanced access to Continental's property from proximity to the Douglas Street station....

The just compensation clause is primarily aimed at making a landowner whole for any governmental taking or damage to his or her property. Indeed, certain language in opinions arising under this provision suggests that as long as Continental is fully compensated for the taking of its property and for loss in property value resulting from the project, it can have no complaint. As acknowledged in S.F., A. & S.R.R. Co. v. Caldwell (1866) 31 Cal. 367, "Just compensation requires a full indemnity and nothing more."....

The United States Supreme Court has written to the same effect in Bauman v. Ross, (1897) 167 U.S. 548, stating, "The just compensation required by the Constitution to be made to the owner is to be measured by the loss caused to him by the appropriation. He is entitled to receive the value of what he has been deprived of, and no more. To award him less would be unjust to him; to award him more would be unjust to the public." And in McCoy v. Union Elevated R. R. Co. (1918) 247 U.S. 354, the high court said:

> The fundamental right guaranteed by the Fourteenth Amendment is that the owner shall not be deprived of the market value of his property under a rule of law which makes it impossible for him to obtain just compensation. There is no guarantee that he shall derive a positive pecuniary advantage from a public work whenever a neighbor does. It is almost universally held that in arriving at the amount of damage to property not taken allowance should be made for peculiar and individual benefits conferred upon it—compensation to the owner in that form is permissible. And we are unable to say that he suffers deprivation of any fundamental right when a State goes one step further and permits consideration of actual benefits—enhancement in market value—flowing directly from a public work, although all in the neighborhood receive like advantages. In such case the owner really loses nothing which he had before; and it may be said, with reason, there has been no real injury.

Yet these principles may be said to collide with another value implicit in the just compensation clause. We have recognized that the policy underlying the just compensation clause is to ensure that the owner of damaged property is not forced to "contribute more than his proper share to the public undertaking"; in other words, the clause aims "to distribute throughout the community the loss inflicted upon the individual by the making of the public improvements...." (Locklin v. City of Lafayette (1994) 7 Cal. 4th 327, 365 [27 Cal. Rptr. 2d 613, 867 P.2d 724].) Arguably, if setoff against severance damages is permitted of all benefits flowing from the project, the landowner does suffer a loss of his or her expectation, shared with neighboring owners and which they retain, of appreciation in the property's value stemming from the public work. In considering whether to adopt a rule that would permit offset against severance damages of all reasonably certain enhancement in the value of the property, as the MTA urges, we therefore must ask whether Continental would thereby be forced to contribute more than its proper share to the construction and operation of the transit project.

In examining this question, we are forced to confront an obdurate fact: Applying existing rules, to distribute the cost of this project across the community with perfect equality is impossible. If Continental is subjected to setoff of general benefits resulting from proximity to the Douglas Street station, one might say it pays more than its proper share of the cost of this transit project because it loses an expectation of gain that other property owners, from whom no land is taken, are allowed to keep. If, on the other hand, Continental is permitted both to recover severance damages and to retain the general enhancement in the value of its property, one could with equal validity say it thereby pays less than its proper share of the project cost vis-a-vis those property owners from whom no property is taken, and who cannot recover damages for the diminution in the value of their property resulting from the operation of the transit line, when those effects are not sufficiently deleterious to support an action in inverse condemnation or nuisance. The law has no mechanism by which to ensure an absolutely fair distribution of costs and benefits across the entire community. We must instead search for the rule of greatest relative fairness, or least unfairness.

One general principle relevant to this determination is that taxpayers should not be required to pay more than reasonably necessary for public works projects. Stated another way, compensation for taking or damage to property must be just to the public as well as to the landowner. (United States v. Commodities Corp. (1950) 339 U.S. 121, 123.) A rule permitting setoff against severance damages of all reasonably certain and nonspeculative benefits minimizes the cost of public works projects in two respects: Certain offsets would be permitted that presently are disallowed, and transaction costs would be reduced due to the new rule's greater clarity and certainty.

Another question we might ask is whether the landowner's expectancy interest in the increased value of remainder property is entitled to the same protection under the just compensation clause as his or her more tangible property rights. The very exercise of the power of eminent domain in effect defeats a landowner's expectation of holding onto the condemned property and reaping any eventual enhancement in its value, since just compensation requires only that the owner be paid the fair market value of the property, measured on the date of valuation. (§ 1263.320, subd. (a).) In this regard, we note that if the government condemns an entire tract of land, the fair market value of the property in general does not include any increase in the value of the property that is attributable to the project for which the property is taken. (§ 1263.330; see Merced Irrigation Dist. v.

Woolstenhulme (1971) 4 Cal. 3d 478, 495 [93 Cal. Rptr. 833, 483 P.2d 1] [exception for "project enhanced value" of lands not originally expected to be within the scope of the project].)

A rule permitting offset of all reasonably certain, immediate and nonspeculative benefits has the virtue of treating benefits and severance damages evenhandedly. Continental was entitled to, and did, present evidence that the effects of the Green Line operation on perceptions of view, light and noise within its building would lower expected future rents. Contrary to a suggestion in Continental's brief, the increase in rental value that the MTA sought to prove appears to be no more speculative or uncertain, and no less immediate, than the decrease in rental value that Continental was permitted to prove. Continental insists the existing *Beveridge* rule does treat benefits and severance damages equally because "only damage that is special to the defendant's property is compensable." The contention is surely incorrect if the term "special" retains any connotation of singularity, uniqueness or peculiarity, inasmuch as the Green Line obviously will affect views, light and noise levels of other properties in the neighborhood of Continental's, property as to some of which no compensation will be paid....

We acknowledge that the rule we adopt today is not the majority view in the United States. (See 3 Nichols on Eminent Domain (rev. 3d ed. 1992) § 8A.03, pp. 8A–26 to 8A–31 and cases cited therein.) In adopting this rule, however, we join a quite respectable minority. (Ill. State Toll Hwy. v. Am. Nat. Bank, (1994) 162 Ill. 2d 181 [642 N.E.2d 1249]; Brand v. State (1964) 21 A.D.2d 727 [250 N.Y.S.2d 158]; State v. Atchison, Topeka And Santa Fe Railway Co. (1966) 76 N.M. 587 [417 P.2d 68, 70]; Michigan State Highway Commission v. Frederick (1971) 32 Mich. App. 236 [188 N.W.2d 193]; see also N.C. Gen. Stat. § 136–112 [when North Carolina State Board of Transportation exercises power of eminent domain to condemn private property for public use, both general and special benefits may be deducted from owner's condemnation award]; Strouds Creek & M. R. Co. v. Herold (1947) 131 W.Va. 45 [45 S.E.2d 513, 519–522].) Like our sister minority jurisdictions, we are persuaded the rule we announce today is ultimately the most workable and the most fair to all parties concerned....

KENNARD, J., concurring and dissenting.

Without any good reason for doing so, the majority abandons California's adherence to a long-established rule of American law followed by most other states....

There is no substantial justification for abandoning the distinction between special and general benefits. In resolving the statutory question of how broadly to interpret the term "benefit to the remainder" (§ 1263.410, subd. (b), 1263.430), one should keep in mind that it implements the just compensation provision of the California Constitution. The goal of that constitutional provision is to ensure that the landowner is compensated for the value of what has been taken or damaged by the government and does not "contribute more than his proper share to the public undertaking."

(Clement v. State Reclamation Board (1950) 35 Cal. 2d 628, 642 [220 P.2d 897].)

This purpose is furthered by deducting only special and not general benefits from the damages to the remainder, for that rule produces a fairer determination of just compensation in the circumstances of a partial taking. As our statutory scheme recognizes, when a portion of a larger parcel is taken, the landowner's loss is not limited to the value of that portion. The landowner loses the synergistic value of the parcel—the extent to which its value as a whole exceeds the separate values of the portion taken and the remainder (because, as noted, a larger parcel offers more opportunities for development and use). The general benefits to the remainder, however, would have been the landowner's even in the absence of any taking. It is unfair to the landowner who has suffered a severance of his or her property to reduce his or her compensation by offsetting general benefits to the remainder against the severance and other damages to the remainder. All properties in the locality of the project receive those general benefits, yet only the landowner whose property has been in part physically taken is made, by forgoing compensation for his or her other losses, to pay for those general benefits.

As we stated almost a century ago in *Beveridge v. Lewis*, supra, 137 Cal. at page 625: "The chance that land will increase in value as population increases and new facilities for transportation and new markets are created is an element of value quite generally taken into consideration in the purchase of land in estimating its present market value. This chance for gain is the property of the land-owner. If a part of his property is taken for the construction of the [project], he stands in reference to the other property not taken like similar property-owners in the neighborhood. His neighbors are not required to surrender this prospective enhancement of value in order to secure the increased facilities which the [project] will afford."

The preeminent commentary on eminent domain law puts it similarly: "General benefits may not be used to offset damages because the owner whose land is taken would be placed in a worse position than his neighbor whose estate lies outside the path of the improvement and who shares in the increased value without any pecuniary loss. . . . The condemnee pays in taxation for his share of general benefits, just as other members of the public, and therefore, is entitled to receive his fair portion of the general advantages brought about by a public improvement." (3 Nichols on Eminent Domain, supra, § 8A.05, pp. 8A–57 to 8A–58.) . . .

Finally, the majority takes the position that it is fairer to deduct general benefits as well as special benefits. The majority asserts that the landowner may obtain compensation for damages from the project that are generally shared throughout the locality as well as special damages peculiar to the property severed, and therefore offsetting only special benefits results in an unfair overcompensation to landowners. The premise of the majority's argument is erroneous, for the damages that a landowner may recover are more limited than the majority acknowledges. A landowner may not recover for damages to the remainder that are "general to all property owners in the neighborhood, and not special to [the landowner]." (City of Berkeley v. Von Adelung (1963) 214 Cal. App. 2d 791, 793 [29 Cal. Rptr. 802]; accord, People v. Gianni (1933) 130 Cal. App. 584, 588–589 [20 P.2d 87].) The examples of compensable damages listed by this court in *Pierpont Inn, Inc. v. State of California*, supra, 70 Cal. 2d 282, 295, and repeated by the majority are ones that typically will arise out of some direct and unique relationship (often the relationship of contiguity) between the remainder of the severed property and the project and will not be shared generally by all properties in the vicinity served by the project: deprivation of access, impairment of light and air, impairment of view, invasion of privacy. Because only special and not general damages are compensable, only special and not general benefits should be deductible. . . .

BAXTER, J., concurred.

Notes & Questions

1. Note that California permits the government to offset benefits against any severance damages, but not against the value of any land actually condemned by the government. Should benefits such as being near a subway station also be offset against the value of any land condemned? If the government in *Continental* was correct that the landowner's property would increase in value by several million dollars because of its proximity to a light rail station, why should the landowner have received $106,356 in compensation for the land that was condemned—an award that was not challenged? Wouldn't an award of even $106,356 be a windfall to Continental?

2. States use two principal formulae for compensating partial takings: the *value plus damages* formula employed in California, and the *before and after* formula (where compensation is measured by the difference between the fair market value of the entire parcel before the taking and the value of the remainder after the taking). While most states use one formula to the exclusion of the other, some allow the condemnee to elect between them. See, e.g., Merrill Trust Co. v. State, 417 A.2d 435 (Me. 1980). And although the *value plus damages* formula has historically been preferred by courts, the *before and after* test is increasing in popularity. What is the difference, if any, between the *before and after* approach and the approach adopted by the California Supreme Court in *Continental*? Which approach is fairer—the traditional *value plus damages* formula, the *Continental* approach, or the *before and after* test? Which is most efficient?

3. Return to an earlier question: should the law compensate property owners when none of their land is condemned but the land loses value because of a nearby public project like a freeway? Some courts have held that such property owners can obtain compensation on an "inverse condemnation" theory if they can show substantial and unique injury to their land. For example, in Varjabedian v. City of Madera, 572 P.2d 43 (Cal. 1977), the California Supreme Court held that a farmer could claim inverse

condemnation by reason of an adjacent, noisome municipal sewage plant even though they could show no physical invasion of their parcel. Although "fears that 'compensation ... will seriously impede, if not stop' the beneficial construction of sewage treatment plants might be realized if courts were to award compensation for every objectionable odor," the "direct, substantial, and peculiar" nature of the burden imposed on the property owner triggered the "policy favoring distribution of the resulting loss of market value" through governmental compensation while lessening the concern that compensation would impede necessary public construction.

4. For jurisdictions following the traditional rule that only property owners who have part of their property condemned are entitled to compensation for losses in the value of the remainder, an important issue often is what lands can be considered to be part of the remainder. For example, if *A* owns two separate lots immediately next to each other and one is condemned, can *A* recover for any reduction in the value of the other lot? What if the two lots are a block apart?

Traditionally, in order to recover severance damages, a condemnee was required to show unity of title (i.e., that both properties were owned by the condemnee), unity of use (i.e., that both properties were used for the same purpose), and physical contiguity between the land taken and the land retained. Although common ownership is still required, courts have begun to relax the earlier insistence on technical unity of title under which someone who owned one lot but only leased a neighboring lot could not collect severance damages. See, e.g., Symms v. Nelson Sand & Gravel, 468 P.2d 306 (Idaho 1970) (permitting recovery of severance damages to adjacent parcel held under lease). And, although many states still require strict physical contiguity, most now permit recovery if the parcels are proximate and there is either current or reasonably probable future unity of use. See, e.g., City of San Diego v. Neumann, 863 P.2d 725 (Cal. 1993). Unity of use continues to be required everywhere.

CHAPTER 3

PROPERTY OTHER THAN LAND

Most of this casebook focuses on land. Yet the United States recognizes property rights in a variety of tangible and intangible resources, including some that are connected with land and thus typically classified as "real property" (e.g., water and petroleum) and many that are not. As Professor Tom Grey has observed, "most property in a modern capitalist economy is intangible. Consider the common forms of wealth: shares of stock in corporations, bonds, various kinds of commercial paper, bank accounts, insurance policies—not to mention more arcane intangibles such as trade-marks, patents, copyrights, franchises, and business goodwill." All of these are forms of property. Thomas Grey, The Disintegration of Property, 22 Nomos 69, 70–71 (1980).

This Chapter briefly explores private rights in six types of valuable resources—fish and wildlife, oil and gas, water, news and ideas, cyberspace, and human cells. This excursion provides yet another opportunity to scrutinize the rationales for private property and to examine the issues involved in shaping and awarding those rights. The excursion also gives us a glimpse of some alternative ways to approach property questions encountered in Chapters 1 and 2.

A. FISH & WILDLIFE

First consider to whom, if anyone, the law should award private property rights in fish and wildlife. Fishing and hunting for wildlife were long the major source of human sustenance (and are still critical to many societies around the world). As societies have grown more affluent, fishing and hunting also have become major recreational activities. Competition among hunters and fishers for limited supplies of animals, in turn, has sometimes generated disputes over who has the right to capture or keep a particular animal.

The principal American judicial decision to address private rights to wildlife, and one of the classic nuggets of property law, dealt with an early nineteenth century hunting dispute over a dead fox.

Pierson v. Post

Supreme Court of New York, 1805.
3 Cai. R. 175, 2 Am. Dec. 264.

This was an action of trespass on the case commenced in a justice's court, by the present defendant against the now plaintiff.

The declaration stated that Post, being in possession of certain dogs and hounds under his command, did, "upon a certain wild and uninhabited, unpossessed and waste land, called the beach, find and start one of those noxious beasts called a fox," and whilst there hunting, chasing and pursuing the same with his dogs and hounds, and when in view thereof, Pierson, well knowing the fox was so hunted and pursued, did, in the sight of Post, to prevent his catching the same, kill and carry it off.... [The lower court held that the fox's pelt belonged to Post.]

TOMPKINS, J., delivered the opinion of the court.

This cause comes before us on a return to a *certiorari* directed to one of the justices of Queens county.

The question submitted by the counsel in this cause for our determination is, whether Lodowick Post, by the pursuit with his hounds in the manner alleged in his declaration, acquired such a right to, or property in, the fox, as will sustain an action against Pierson for killing and taking him away.

The cause was argued with much ability by the counsel on both sides, and presents for our decision a novel and nice question. It is admitted that a fox is an animal *ferae naturae*, and that property in such animals is acquired by occupancy only. These admissions narrow the discussion to the simple question of what acts amount to occupancy, applied to acquiring right to wild animals.

If we have recourse to the ancient writers upon general principles of law, the judgment below is obviously erroneous. Justinian's Institutes and Fleta adopt the principle, that pursuit alone vests no property or right in the huntsman; and that even pursuit, accompanied with sounding, is equally ineffectual for that purpose, unless the animal be actually taken. The same principle is recognised by Bracton.

Puffendorf defines occupancy of beasts *ferae naturae*, to be the actual corporal possession of them, and Bynkershoek is cited as coinciding in this definition. It is indeed with hesitation that Puffendorf affirms that a wild beast mortally wounded, or greatly maimed, cannot be fairly intercepted by another, whilst the pursuit of the person inflicting the wound continues. The foregoing authorities are decisive to show that mere pursuit gave Post no legal right to the fox, but that he became the property of Pierson, who intercepted and killed him.

It therefore only remains to inquire whether there are any contrary principles, or authorities, to be found in other books, which ought to induce a different decision. Most of the cases which have occurred in England, relating to property in wild animals, have either been discussed and decided upon the principles of their positive statute regulations, or have arisen between the huntsman and the owner of the land upon which beasts *ferae naturae* have been apprehended; the former claiming them by title of occupancy, and the latter *ratione soli*. Little satisfactory aid can, therefore, be derived from the English reporters.

Barbeyrac, in his notes on Puffendorf, does not accede to the definition of occupancy by the latter, but, on the contrary, affirms, that actual bodily seizure is not, in all cases, necessary to constitute possession of wild animals. He does not, however, *describe* the acts which, according to his ideas, will amount to an appropriation of such animals to private use, so as to exclude the claims of all other persons, by title of occupancy to the same animals; and he is far from averring that pursuit alone is sufficient for that purpose. To a certain extent, and as far as Barbeyrac appears to me to go, his objections to Puffendorf's definition of occupancy are reasonable and correct. That is to say, that actual bodily seizure is not indispensable to acquire right to, or possession of, wild beasts; but that, on the contrary, the mortal wounding of such beasts, by one not abandoning his pursuit, may, with the utmost propriety, be deemed possession of him; since, thereby, the pursuer manifests an unequivocal intention of appropriating the animal to his individual use, has deprived him of natural liberty, and brought him within his certain control. So also, encompassing and securing such animals with nets and toils, or otherwise intercepting them in such a manner as to deprive them of their natural liberty, and render escape impossible, may justly be deemed to give possession of them to those persons who, by their industry and labour, have used such means of apprehending them. Barbeyrac seems to have adopted and had in view of his notes, the more accurate opinion of Grotius, with respect to occupancy.... The case now under consideration is one of mere pursuit, and presents no circumstances or acts which can bring it within the definition of occupancy by Puffendorf, or Grotius, or the ideas of Barbeyrac upon that subject.

.... We are the more readily inclined to confine possession or occupancy of beasts *ferae naturae*, within the limits prescribed by the learned authors above cited, for the sake of certainty, and preserving the peace and order in society. If the first seeing, starting, or pursuing such animals, without having so wounded, circumvented, or ensnared them, so as to deprive them of their natural liberty, and subject them to the control of their pursuer, should afford the basis of actions against others for intercepting and killing them, it would prove a fertile source of quarrels and litigation.

However uncourteous or unkind the conduct of Pierson towards Post, in this instance, may have been, yet his act was productive of no injury or damage for which a legal remedy can be applied. We are of opinion the judgment below was erroneous, and ought to be reversed.

LIVINGSTON, J.

My opinion differs from that of the court. Of six exceptions, taken to the proceedings below, all are abandoned except the third, which reduces the controversy to a single question.

Whether a person who, with his own hounds, starts and hunts a fox on waste and uninhabited ground, and is on the point of seizing his prey, acquires such an interest in the animal, as to have a right of action against another, who in view of the huntsman and his dogs in full pursuit, and with knowledge of the chase, shall kill and carry him away?

This is a knotty point, and should have been submitted to the arbitration of sportsmen, without poring over Justinian, Fleta, Bracton, Puffendorf, Locke, Barbeyrac, or Blackstone, all of whom have been cited; they would have had no difficulty in coming to a prompt and correct conclusion. In a court thus constituted, the skin and carcass of poor *reynard* would have been properly disposed of, and a precedent set, interfering with no usage or custom which the experience of ages has sanctioned, and which must be so well known to every votary of Diana. But the parties have referred the question to our judgement, and we must dispose of it as well as we can, from the partial lights we possess, leaving to a higher tribunal, the correction of any mistake which we may be so unfortunate to make. By the pleadings it is admitted that a fox is a "wild and noxious beast." Both parties have regarded him, as the law of nations does a pirate, "*hostem humani generis*," and although "*de mortuis nil nisi bonum*," be a maxim of our profession, the memory of the deceased has not been spared. His depredations on farmers and on barn yards have not been forgotten; and to put him to death wherever found is allowed to be meritorious, and of public benefit. Hence it follows, that our decision should have in view the greatest possible encouragement to the destruction of an animal, so cunning and ruthless in his career. But who would keep a pack of hounds; or what gentleman, at the sound of the horn, and at peep of day, would mount his steed, and for hours together, "*sub jove figido*," or a vertical sun, pursue the windings of this wily quadruped, if, just as night came on, and his stratagems and strength were nearly exhausted, a saucy intruder, who had not shared in the honours or labours of the chase, were permitted to come in at the death, and bear away in triumph the object of pursuit? Whatever Justinian may have thought of the matter, it must be recollected that his code was compiled many hundred years ago, and it would be very hard indeed, at the distance of so many centuries, not to have a right to establish a rule for ourselves. In his day, we read of no order of men who made it a business, in the language of the declaration in this cause, "with hounds and dogs to find, start, pursue, hunt, and chase," these animals, and that, too, without any other motive than the preservation of Roman poultry; if this diversion had been then in fashion, the lawyers who composed his institutes would have taken care not to pass it by, without suitable encouragement. If any thing, therefore, in the digests or pandects shall appear to militate against the defendant in error, who, on this occasion, was the foxhunter, we have only to say *tempora mutantur*; and if men themselves change with the times, why should not laws also undergo an alteration?

It may be expected, however, by the learned counsel, that more particular notice be taken of their authorities. I have examined them all, and feel great difficulty in determining, whether to acquire dominion over a thing, before in common, it be sufficient that we barely see it, or know where it is, or wish for it, or make a declaration of our will respecting it; or whether, in the case of wild beasts, setting a trap, or lying in wait, or starting, or pursuing, be enough; or if an actual wounding, or killing, or bodily tact and occupation be necessary. Writers on general law, who have favoured us with their speculations on these points, differ on them all; but, great as is the diversity of sentiment among them, some conclusion must be adopted on the question immediately before us. After mature deliberation, I embrace that of Barbeyrac, as the most rational, and least liable to objection. If at liberty, we might imitate the courtesy of a certain emperor, who, to avoid giving offence to the advocates of any of these different doctrines, adopted a middle course, and by ingenious distinctions, rendered it difficult to say (as often happens after a fierce and angry contest) to whom the palm of victory belonged. He ordained, that if a beast be followed by *large dogs and hounds*, he shall belong to the hunter, not the chance occupant; and in like manner, if he be killed or wounded with a lance or sword; but if chased with *beagles only*, then he passed to the captor, not to the first pursuer. If slain with a dart, a sling, or a bow, he fell to the hunter, if still in chase, and not to him who might afterwards find and seize him.

Now, as we are without any municipal regulations of our own, and the pursuit here, for aught that appears on the case, being with dogs and hounds of *imperial stature*, we are at liberty to adopt one of the provisions just cited, which comports also with the learned conclusion of Barbeyrac, that property in animals *ferae naturae* may be acquired without bodily touch or manucaption, provided the pursuer be within reach, or have a *reasonable* prospect (which certainly existed here) of taking, what he has *thus* discovered an intention of converting to his own use.

When we reflect also that the interest of our husbandmen, the most useful of men in any community, will be advanced by the destruction of a beast so pernicious and incorrigible, we cannot greatly err, in saying, that a pursuit like the present, through waste and unoccupied lands, and which must inevitably and speedily have terminated in corporal possession, or bodily *seisin*, confers such a right to the object of it, as to make any one a wrongdoer, who shall interfere and shoulder the spoil. The justice's judgment ought, therefore, in my opinion, to be affirmed.

Notes & Questions

1. Does this strike you as a pretty silly lawsuit? Lodowick Post was 26 years old, the son of a relatively wealthy Dutch country gentleman. Jesse Pierson was 23 years old, the son of a wealthy English farmer and ex-army officer. The fathers financed the lawsuit. Each side of the dispute reportedly spent over £1,000 litigating the matter—a very large sum for the time. See Dale D. Goble & Eric T. Freyfogle, Wildlife Law 121 (2002).

2. **Constructive Possession.** The events in *Pierson* took place, as the court emphasized, "upon a certain wild and uninhabited, unpossessed and waste land." If Pierson had shot the fox on Smith's property, should the pelt have belonged to Smith? Under the common law, a landowner is viewed as having "constructive possession" of any wild animals found on his or her property. Under the doctrine of *ratione soli* or *ratione privilegii*, the landowner has a superior right to such animals, and trespassers have no right to take them. See William Blackstone, Commentaries on the Laws

of England *393 (1766); Dean Lueck, Property Rights and the Economic Logic of Wildlife Institutions, 35 Nat. Resources J. 630, 631 (1995). Once the animal wanders off the property, however, the landowner loses constructive possession.

3. Should Pierson's motives in shooting the fox have mattered? Should it have mattered whether Post was fox hunting for pleasure or for commercial profit? In Keeble v. Hickeringill, 103 Eng. Rep. (Q.B. 1707), the defendant fired shots at flying ducks in order to purposefully scare them away from the plaintiff's commercial duck pond. The court held that the defendant's actions constituted unlawful interference with the plaintiff's use of his land. According to the court, "where a violent or malicious act is done to a man's occupation, profession, or way of getting a livelihood, there an action lies in all cases." The court, however, suggested that the defendant was free to construct his own duck pond, even if that attracted ducks away from the plaintiff's land.

4. Both the majority and dissenting opinions in *Pierson* suggest that their respective rules would promote important policy goals. The majority, for example, claims that it is acting "for the sake of certainty, and preserving peace and order in society." Does the majority's rule provide certainty? When exactly does a pursuer deprive an animal of its "natural liberty" and bring the animal "within [the pursuer's] certain control"? Are these terms the grist of certainty?

More importantly, does the search for "certainty" ignore other important legal goals. As Professor Carol Rose has observed, courts can address property issues by announcing relatively hard-edged rules of entitlement (e.g., whoever first sets his hands on the fox gets it), which Professor Rose labels "crystals," or by using relatively fuzzy and ambiguous standards (e.g., whoever deserves the fox gets it), which she dubs "mud." See Carol A. Rose, Crystals and Mud in Property Law, 40 Stan. L. Rev. 577 (1988). Each approach has its advantages and disadvantages. Crystalline rules provide greater certainty (and thus permit greater advance planning) and are less subject to arbitrary, even prejudiced application. But crystalline rules do not permit courts to consider all of the factors that they might find relevant in a particular case. As a result, crystalline rules often hit too broad of the mark, failing to block some unwanted behavior and deterring some desirable actions. Muddy standards, by contrast, permit judges to consider and weigh the multitude of factors that may go into an informed judgment about the equity of any particular dispute. Should courts favor crystalline rules in hunting disputes like *Pierson*? Or would a muddy standard be better? What advantages and disadvantages to each do you see in this context?

5. In his dissent, Justice Livingston argues that the law should promote the destruction of "pernicious beasts," and that his rule would do this more effectively than the majority's rule. How does he determine that the law should promote the destruction of foxes? Given that foxes eat small rodents such as gophers and rats, might foxes actually be beneficial to

humans? Even if the goal is to destroy foxes, is Livingston correct that his rule would promote that goal better than the majority's approach?

6. Both the majority and dissent assume that they have to rule for one party or the other. Were there other options open to them? Could they have split the fox between Pierson and Post? Would this have been a better result than ruling for either Pierson or Post?

7. Should wildlife, or any animals, be the subject of private property? Do animals have rights that are inconsistent with treating them as chattel? See generally David Favre, Equitable Self–Ownership for Animals, 50 Duke L.J. 473 (2000); Steven M. Wise, Hardly a Revolution: The Eligibility of Nonhuman Animals for Dignity—Rights in a Liberal Democracy, 22 Vt. L. Rev. 793 (1998).

8. What role should local norms have played in the resolution of *Pierson*? According to Professor Richard Epstein, "it appeared from the record [in the case] that all hunters in the region regarded hot pursuit as giving rights to take an unimpeded first possession." Richard A. Epstein, Possession as the Root of Title, 13 Ga. L. Rev. 1221, 1231 (1979). Do you believe that farmers like Pierson might have had different norms than the hunters? Recall the earlier discussion of norms in connection with the choice between open-range and closed-range rules for straying cattle (pp. 67–68 supra). When should the law defer to norms? If norms are relevant, how should the courts determine what the appropriate norms are?

Ghen v. Rich

United States District Court, District of Massachusetts, 1881.
8 Fed. 159.

NELSON, DISTRICT JUDGE.

This is a libel to recover the value of a fin-back whale. The libellant lives in Provincetown and the respondent in Wellfleet. The facts, as they appeared at the hearing, are as follows:

> In the early spring months the easterly part of Massachusetts bay is frequented by the species of whale known as the fin-back whale. Fishermen from Provincetown pursue them in open boats from the shore, and shoot them with bomb-lances fired from guns made expressly for the purpose. When killed they sink at once to the bottom, but in the course of from one to three days they rise and float on the surface. Some of them are picked up by vessels and towed into Provincetown. Some float ashore at high water and are left stranded on the beach as the tide recedes. Others float out to sea and are never recovered. The person who happens to find them on the beach usually sends word to Provincetown, and the owner comes to the spot and removes the blubber. The finder usually receives a small salvage for his services. Try-works are established in Provincetown for trying out the oil. The business is of considerable extent, but, since it requires skill and experience,

> as well as some outlay of capital, and is attended with great exposure and hardship, few persons engage in it. The average yield of oil is about 20 barrels to a whale. It swims with great swiftness, and for that reason cannot be taken by the harpoon and line. Each boat's crew engaged in the business has its peculiar mark or device on its lances, and in this way it is known by whom a whale is killed.
>
> The usage in Cape Cod, for many years, has been that the person who kills a whale in the manner and under the circumstances described, owns it, and this right has never been disputed until this case. The libellant has been engaged in this business for ten years past. On the morning of April 9, 1880, in Massachusetts bay, near the end of Cape Code, he shot and instantly killed with a bomb-lance the whale in question. It sunk immediately, and on the morning of the 12th was found stranded on the beach in Brewster, within the ebb and flow of the tide, by one Ellis, 17 miles from the spot where it was killed. Instead of sending word to Provincetown, as is customary, Ellis advertised the whale for sale at auction, and sold it to the respondent, who shipped off the blubber and tried out the oil. The libellant heard of the finding of the whale on the morning of the 15th, and immediately sent one of his boat's crew to the place and claimed it. Neither the respondent nor Ellis knew the whale had been killed by the libellant, but they knew or might have known, if they had wished, that it had been shot and killed with a bomb-lance, by some person engaged in this species of business.

The libellant claims title to the whale under this usage. The respondent insists that this usage is invalid. It was decided by Judge Sprague, in Taber v. Jenny, 1 Sprague 315, that when a whale has been killed, and is anchored and left with marks of appropriation, it is the property of the captors; and if it is afterwards found, still anchored, by another ship, there is no usage or principle of law by which the property of the original captors is diverted, even though the whale may have dragged from its anchorage....

In Bartlett v. Budd, 1 Low. 223, the facts were these: The first officer of the libellant's ship killed a whale in the Okhhotsk sea, anchored it, attached a waif to the body, and then left it and went ashore at some distance for the night. The next morning the boats of the respondent's ship found the whale adrift, the anchor not holding, the cable coiled round the body, and no waif or irons attached to it. Judge Lowell held that, as the libellants had killed and taken actual possession of the whale, the ownership vested in them. In his opinion the learned judge says:

> A whale, being *ferae naturae*, does not become property until a firm possession has been established by the taker. But when such possession has become firm and complete, the right of property is clear, and has all the characteristics of property.

He doubted whether a usage set up but not proved by the respondent, that a whale found adrift in the ocean is the property of the finder, unless the first taker should appear and claim it before it is cut in, would be valid, and remarked that "there would be great difficulty in upholding a custom that should take the property of A. and give it to B., under so very short and uncertain a substitute for the statute of limitations, and one so open to fraud and deceit." Both the cases cited were decided without reference to usage, upon the ground that the property had been acquired by the first taker by actual possession and appropriation.

In Swift v. Gifford, 2 Low. 110, Judge Lowell decided that a custom among whalemen in the Arctic seas, that the iron holds the whale, was reasonable and valid. In that case a boat's crew from the respondent's ship pursued and struck a whale in the Arctic ocean, and the harpoon and the line attached to it remained in the whale, but did not remain fast to the boat. A boat's crew from the libellant's ship continued the pursuit and captured the whale, and the master of the respondent's ship claimed it on the spot. It was held by the learned judge that the whale belonged to the respondents. It was said by Judge Sprague, in Bourne v. Ashley, an unprinted case referred to by Judge Lowell in Swift v. Gifford, that the usage for the first iron, whether attached to the boat or not, to hold the whale was fully established; and he added that, although local usages of a particular port ought not to be allowed to set aside the general maritime law, this objection did not apply to a custom which embraced an entire business, and had been concurred in for a long time by every one engaged in the trade.

In Swift v. Gifford, Judge Lowell also said:

> The rule of law invoked in this case is one of very limited application. The whale fishery is the only branch of industry of any importance in which it is likely to be much used, and if a usage is found to prevail generally in that business, it will not be open to the objection that it is likely to disturb the general understanding of mankind by the interposition of an arbitrary exception.

I see no reason why the usage proved in this case is not as reasonable as that sustained in the cases cited. Its application must necessarily be extremely limited, and can affect but a few persons. It has been recognized and acquiesced in for many years. It requires in the first taker the only act of appropriation that is possible in the nature of the case. Unless it is sustained, this branch of industry must necessarily cease, for no person would engage in it if the fruits of his labor could be appropriated by any chance finder. It gives reasonable salvage for securing or reporting the property. That the rule works well in practice is shown by the extent of the industry which has grown up under it, and the general acquiescence of a whole community interested to dispute it. It is by no means clear that without regard to usage the common law would not reach the same result. That seems to be the effect of the decisions in Taber v. Jenny and Bartlett v. Budd. If the fisherman does all that it is possible to do to make the animal his own, that would seem to be sufficient. Such a rule might well be applied in the interest of trade, there being no usage or custom to the contrary. But be that as it may, I hold the usage to be valid, and that the property in the whale was in the libellant. . . .

Notes & Questions

1. Why does the court defer to the industry custom in *Ghen*? Should courts defer? Are there circumstances where a court should not defer to an industry custom in resolving a dispute involving the industry? If so, what are those circumstances?

2. Professor Robert Ellickson has argued that norms developed by closely knit groups to govern everyday matters, such as the whaling custom at issue in *Ghen*, generally serve to maximize the aggregate economic welfare of the members of the groups. Do you believe that the whaling custom at issue in *Ghen* was "welfare maximizing"? Do you agree with Professor Ellickson that the workaday norms of closely knit groups are likely to be welfare maximizing? If so, why is that likely to be the case? See generally Robert C. Ellickson, Order Without Law: How Neighbors Settle Disputes (1991); Robert C. Ellickson, A Hypothesis of Wealth–Maximizing Norms: Evidence from the Whaling Industry, 5 J. Law, Econ. & Org. 83 (1989). For criticism of Ellickson's claim, see Lewis A. Kornhauser, Are There Cracks in the Foundations of Spontaneous Order?, 67 N.Y.U. L. Rev. 647 (1992).

3. **Cheyenne Customs.** The late Professor Karl Llewellyn investigated the legal customs that the Cheyenne Indians followed in the 19th century before being confined to reservations. When groups of Cheyennes went on horse raids,

> the spoils were individually divided. Unless it was agreed otherwise beforehand, each horse went to the man who first struck a coup on it. This gave great advantage to the man with a fast horse. To equalize this, the Cheyennes often agreed before the raid to divide equally, in which event the leader of the raid took first choice, then named the succession of choice for the rest of the party. There was no notion of the spoils belonging technically to the leader, to be shared with the others because ethics of generosity demanded it. . . . [I]n the absence of the equality distribution, scouts out on duty who missed out on the take, missed out on the booty! Nor did the cooks receive any special preference for their labors.

Karl N. Llewellyn & E. Adamson Hoebel, The Cheyenne Way 223 (1941). Llewellyn suggested that awarding horses to "the man who first struck a coup on it" was "queerly out of keeping with the general utilitarianism of Cheyenne law." Id. Do you agree that the basic Cheyenne rule for horse raids was not "utilitarian"? Why do you believe that the Cheyennes adopted this particular rule?

The Cheyennes employed a nuanced set of norms for rights in horses that varied from setting to setting. When a group was not on a horse raid, for example, "the person first to sight the tracks of a stray horse laid claim to the animal. He stopped his companions and called their attention to the tracks." Id. at 224. Yet another set of rules applied where a horse stolen by enemy raiders was recovered:

> If horses were recovered in pursuit, before the enemy getaway was complete, they went back to their owners. However, the owners of many horses, if generous, gave at least one horse to the recoverer for his pains. If the theft was successful, the title passed to the enemy, so that whosoever recovered a stolen horse became its full owner. But a personal bond lending a moral right was recognized. The former owner of a recaptured horse, if it was a favorite, went to its new captor with a good blanket or other bundle. Placing the bundle on the ground before him he said, "Friend, I love that horse. Pray, will you give him to me again?".... Since the blanket or goods were not usually so valuable as the horse, a residue of proprietary right where sentimental attachment existed was recognized. There was no seizing a bargaining advantage in the former owner's desire to recover.

Id. at 225.

The Tragedy of the Commons and the Decline of the World's Fisheries

Judge Nelson in *Ghen v. Rich* assumed that the major policy goal should be to encourage the hunting and capturing of animals. In this century, however, the concern has shifted to protecting animals from over-hunting and extinction.

One major cause of over-hunting is the "tragedy of the commons"—a phrase first coined by Garrett Hardin in his aptly famous article by that name in 168 Science 1243 (1968). Ocean fishing illustrates the problem. Most ocean fisheries are "commons," much like the uninhabited wasteland of *Pierson v. Post*, where fish belong to the first person who catches them. The predictable result is that fishermen rush to catch fish with little apparent concern for the long term viability of the fisheries. As Professor C. Scott Gordon wrote in an early description of the problem, "Wealth that is free for all is valued by no one because he who is foolhardy enough to wait for its proper time of use will only find that it has been taken by another.... The fish in the seas are valueless to the fisherman, because there is no assurance that they will be there for him tomorrow if they are left behind today." C. Scott Gordon, The Economic Theory of a Common–Property Resource: The Fishery, 62 J. Pol. Econ. 124, 135 (1954).

The consequences for the world's fisheries have been nothing short of catastrophic. As fishermen rushed to catch more and more fish in some fisheries, the catch ultimately exceeded the fisheries' natural regeneration rate—leading to a decline in the number of fish and, despite further increases in fishing efforts, eventually to a decline in the number of fish caught. Since 1992, the major fishing regions of the Atlantic Ocean, Pacific Ocean, and Mediterranean and Black Seas have all seen significant declines in average yearly catch; in the Southeast Atlantic, the decline has exceeded 50 percent. Governments have temporally had to close some of the world's most important fishing grounds, including Grand Banks and Georges Bank off the East Coast of North America. Worldwide, the catch of wild fish appears to have peaked in 1989 and either declined or stagnated ever since. See Carl Safina, The World's Imperiled Fish, Scientific American, Nov. 1995.

How can the law try to overcome the tragedy of the commons? One approach is regulation. The International Whaling Commission, for example, currently bans all commercial whaling. Fishing within the jurisdiction of the United States is governed by the Fishery Conservation and Management Act of 1976, 16 U.S.C. §§ 1801 et seq. (generally known as the Magnuson–Stevens Act). Under the Act, eight "Regional Fishery Management Councils" are charged with developing fishery management plans for any fishery that "requires conservation and management." Id. § 1852(h)(1). The plans are supposed to "prevent overfishing and rebuild overfished stocks, and to protect, restore, and promote the long-term health and stability of the fishery." Id. § 1853(a)(1)(A). Regional councils have used a variety of tools to try to reduce fishing, including quotas on the total allowable catch, limits on the length of the fishing season, and various technological requirements designed to make catching fish more difficult and expensive.

Most observers agree that the Magnuson–Stevens Act has not been very effective in avoiding the tragedy of the commons. Because fisheries remain a common resource, fishermen have an economic incentive to find ways around the regulations and catch more fish. Fishing regulations therefore often seem to be chasing their own tail. As fishermen find ways around one regulation, regulators have to come up with a new rule to repair the crack in the regulatory structure. But fishermen then find a way around the new rule, requiring yet another regulation. Soon fisheries are awash in a sea of regulations, but overfishing nonetheless continues.

Faced by significant scientific uncertainty and immense opposition from the fishing industry, moreover, few of the fishery management plans have imposed meaningful constraints. Fishermen often have invested huge sums in their boats and equipment, and they need to maintain and sometimes expand their catches in order to pay off their debts and survive. Most fishermen therefore oppose any significant interference with their occupation.

> Fishery law expert Eldon Greenberg has observed that although "[t]he Magnuson Act, as envisioned by its sponsors, was primarily a conservation-oriented statute, focused upon the biological aspects of managing fish stocks, . . . the focus of managers has

> been on the social and economic interests of the users."[279] In some fisheries, there has been "a history of lack of willingness to impose significant, biological conservation measures."[280].... The Regional Council system, innovative as it was in 1976, has been criticized for "institutionaliz[ing] special interests in fishery management," resulting in allowable catch quotas that are not biologically based but instead attempt to satisfy all those who want to fish.[282]

Michael J. Bean & Melanie J. Rowland, The Evolution of National Wildlife Law 191–192 (1997).

Another potential solution to the tragedy of the commons is private property. Where a resource is owned by one person, the owner need not race to harvest the resource for fear someone else will otherwise get to the resource first. In some cases, awarding private property rights in a fishery may be both feasible and effective. The Gulf and Atlantic Coast oyster industries employ two different property right regimes. Most oyster beds are set aside as common fisheries for anyone to enjoy. Some oyster beds, however, are leased by states to private parties for exclusive oystering. A 1975 study of the oyster industry found that the communal beds suffered from both too many oystermen and over exploitation, just as the tragedy of the commons would predict. See Richard J. Agnello & Lawrence P. Donnelley, Property Rights and Efficiency in the Oyster Industry, 18 J. L. & Econ. 521 (1975). As more and more people have been attracted to the communal beds, and oyster populations have declined, income levels have also declined in the local fisheries. Although the government has tried to reduce congestion and over-exploitation through regulation, the regulations have been relatively ineffective.

The private oyster beds have not suffered from the same problems. According to the authors of the 1975 study, "if all coastal states had relied entirely on private property in oyster harvesting in 1969, [the shift in property regimes would have led to] an increase in average oystermen's incomes of around $1300 or almost fifty percent of 1969 average income." Id. at 533. The authors suggest that, given the benefits of a private property system, "one can conclude that considerations other than economic efficiency are used by states relying on common property for the oyster industry." Id. What might those considerations be? Do you believe that they outweigh the benefits of private property in terms of both fishing conservation and economic efficiency?

Even if private ownership of fisheries were an unequivocally good idea, many fisheries would be difficult, if not impossible, to privatize. Many fish, unlike oysters, migrate often lengthy distances. Although the right to fish for a species within a set geographic area could be awarded to a single individual or group, a tragedy of the commons could still develop if the fish

279. Eldon V.C. Greenberg, The Magnuson Act After Fifteen Years: Is It Working? at B–9 (paper presented at the 1992 National Fishery Law Symposium, Washington, D.C., October 15–16, 1992).

280. Id. at B–6.

282. Global Marine Biological Diversity 263 (Elliott Norse ed., 1993).

migrated between several private fishing grounds since each owner would have an incentive to catch the fish before they migrated to the next person's territory.

Another approach to creating private property in fisheries is to assign tradable rights to catch a certain amount of fish every season. Several regional fishery management plans, as well as a number of foreign jurisdictions such as New Zealand, have successfully used "individual transferable quotas" or ITQs to limit fishing. A quota is first set on the total amount of fish that can be caught. This quota is then divided up into ITQs that are allocated to individual fishermen based on factors such as prior catch and investment in the fishery. Once assigned, ITQs can be traded like most other forms of private property. What potential advantages might ITQs have over simply imposing a quota on the total amount of fish each fisherman can catch? For an exhaustive analysis of ITQs conducted at the request of Congress and favoring their (cautious) use in fishing management, see National Research Council, Sharing the Fish: Toward a National Policy on Individual Fishing Quotas (1999).

A third approach to reducing overfishing is the creation of group property rights that can be policed through group norms. Maine lobstermen, for example, historically divided themselves into informal groups based on the harbor from which they fished. Membership in such "harbor gangs"

> controls entry into the industry. To go lobster fishing, a man must first become a member of a harbor gang. Once he has gained admission, he can go fishing only in the territory "owned" communally by members of that gang. Fishermen who place their traps in the territory of another gang can expect swift retribution, normally the purposeful destruction of their gear....
>
> [Within a harbor gang, a fisherman] is expected to keep his distance from other fishermen and not "dump" his traps on top of another's, where they can become entangled. Fishermen with traps in a saturated location have usufructuary rights; others cannot enter until someone leaves. The older, more skilled fishermen are likely to have their traps prepositioned in the best locations. When lobsters do appear, those who have "camped out" in good spots have monopolized all or most of the available space. Younger fishermen—particularly those who have joined the gang recently—are well advised to stay out of the way of men with status in the hierarchy of skills and prestige. Men of lower status can lose a great deal by coming into conflict with highliners.

James M. Acheson, The Lobster Gangs of Maine 48–49, 76 (1988).

Which of these various approaches to the tragedy of the commons (regulation, private property, or group norms) is preferable? Does the relative attractiveness of the approaches differ from fishery to fishery? If so, what determines the relative attractiveness of the approaches in any particular fishery? Are there other potential solutions that might work better than the three identified here?

Endangered Species

In recent decades, the rate at which species are going extinct has increased dramatically. Although estimates of extinction rates are largely educated guesses, even conservative estimates of the increase in the extinction rate pegs the current rate of extinction to be three to four times the historic average. Some scientists estimate that, at the current rate of extinction, only half of the world's current species will survive to the end of the 21st century.

Overexploitation. World species face multiple threats. One is overexploitation. As just explained, overfishing has led to significant declines in many of the world's fisheries. Overhunting has also been a major reason for declines in the populations of various species of alligators, buffalos, elephants, rhinoceroses, and other commercially prized animals. Here, as with fisheries, a root cause is open access. Because non-domesticated animals are *ferae naturae* and capturable by anyone when not on private property, no one recognizes the full benefit of conservation and everyone tries to bag their prize before someone else does. The traditional open access regime for wild animals can lead to the extinction of a species where the consumptive value of the species is greater than the costs of catching the species even at low population levels, and the species' natural population growth is inadequate to offset losses to hunting.

What role can private property play in trying to protect species from overexploitation? Some economists have argued that giving landowners property rights in those species that are found on their property (the common law doctrine of "constructive possession" (see p. 218)) provides landowners with an incentive to protect species from overexploitation and other threats. Imagine, for example, an endangered species that hunters like to track and shoot. As the species becomes rarer, the species will become more valuable to hunters and to other people such as ecotourists. If landowners have a property right to any members of the species found on their property, the owners of viable habitat will have an incentive to conserve the species on their property for limited hunting, ecotourism, and other uses. Landowners will not want to overexploit the species to the point of extinction because they then will receive no profits whatsoever. Although landowners are likely to permit some hunting (because it's profitable), they will protect the species from going extinct. The problem, in the view of many economists, arises where law or custom treats wildlife as a common resource, available to anyone to trap or kill. In this situation, no one has an incentive to protect the species from overexploitation because, if one person takes steps to conserve a species, others will still be free to trap or kill the species. Thus, no one has an incentive to try to protect the species. See generally Terry L. Anderson & Donald R. Leal, Enviro–Capitalists: Doing

Good While Doing Well (1997); Robert K. Davis, A New Paradigm in Wildlife Conservation: Using Markets to Produce Big Game Hunting, in Wildlife in the Marketplace 107 (Terry L. Anderson & Peter J. Hill eds., 1995)

Not everyone agrees. To some, permitting landowners to own and exploit wildlife on their properties inevitably threatens the wildlife. According to one wildlife manager, "markets in dead wildlife reward its killing" and therefore "a global luxury market in wildlife is compatible with neither conservation nor good economics." Valerius Geist, Wildlife Conservation as Wealth, 368 Nature 491 (1994).

Rather than rely on property rights, most governments have responded to the problem of overexploitation by directly regulating the hunting and capturing of wild animals. Since the late nineteenth century, state fish and game commissions have limited the hunting of particular species to specified seasons, required hunters to obtain licenses, and imposed quotas and "bag limits" on how many members of particular species can be captured or killed. Although initially fish and game commissions merely tried to conserve enough animals for future hunting seasons, commissions have responded to more recent concerns over species preservation by, in some cases, imposing complete moratoria on species at risk of extinction.

In the United States today, the Endangered Species Act (ESA) plays the principal role in attempting to protect species from extinction. 16 U.S.C. §§ 1531 et seq. The federal government begins by listing species that are "endangered" (defined as in danger of extinction throughout all or a significant portion of their range) or "threatened" (defined as likely to become endangered within the foreseeable future). As of September 2005, 993 domestic species were listed as endangered, and an additional 275 domestic species were listed as threatened. Internationally, another 563 species were listed as endangered or threatened.

The ESA helps protect species against overexploitation by prohibiting the hunting, shooting, wounding, killing, trapping, or capturing of an endangered or threatened species. The ESA also prohibits the sale of an endangered or threatened species, even if the species was killed or captured legally before passage of the ESA or before the species was listed as endangered or threatened. Why does the ESA need to prohibit the sale of listed species if it already bans the killing or capturing of such species? Even if a prohibition of sales is necessary, why should the prohibition extend to species that were killed or captured legally?

Does the ban on the sale of a listed species that someone legitimately owns constitute a "taking of property" for which the owner is entitled to compensation under the Fifth Amendment of the United States Constitution? No, according to the courts. See United States v. Kepler, 531 F.2d 796 (6th Cir. 1976); United States v. Hill, 896 F. Supp. 1057 (D. Colo. 1995). In Andrus v. Allard, 444 U.S. 51 (1979), the Supreme Court rejected a similar challenge to the federal Eagle Protection Act, 11 U.S.C. §§ 668 et seq., that bans commercial transactions in bald or golden eagles or any parts of such birds, whether acquired before or after passage of the act. The government had prosecuted two owners of Indian artifacts that predated the act but included eagle feathers, after which the owners brought a takings challenge. The Court concluded that the government had not taken the Indian artifacts but merely restricted the rights that the owners of the artifacts enjoyed. Although the owners could not sell the artifacts, the owners still possessed the artifacts and could donate them to others or exhibit them. "At least where an owner possesses a full 'bundle' of property rights, the destruction of one 'strand' of the bundle is not a taking, because the aggregate must be viewed in its entirety." 444 U.S. at 65–66.

At the international level, the Convention on International Trade in Endangered Species of Wild Fauna and Flora (CITES) restricts trade in endangered species. If species are "threatened with extinction" and "are or may be affected by trade," CITES prohibits international trade except where "scientific authorities" of the relevant countries have decided that the trade will not be "detrimental to the survival" of that species. The ESA similarly prohibits anyone from importing an endangered or threatened species into the United States except in limited situations.

Habitat Destruction. Overexploitation, however, is only one of the threats that is leading to species extinction. On land, loss of habitat is a far more important cause of species loss. Species often depend on relatively undisturbed habitat. Owners of that habitat, however, typically find that the benefits of using their land for residential or commercial purposes far exceed the direct benefits, if any, to them of preserving the land for species habitat. As more and more habitat is lost to human use, the species that are reliant on that habitat can face extinction.

Only a few endangered species provide any potential for profit to landowners who preserve the species' habitat, and that profit is typically small. Although some biologists have touted the potential genetic value of endangered species for medicinal and other purposes, only one in 25,000 species, at best, are projected to produce commercially valuable genetic discoveries. One economic study estimated that pharmaceutical companies are unlikely to pay more than about $20 per hectare (2.47 acres) to protect species-rich habitat in western Ecuador; payments drop to around $1 per hectare in prime habitat regions of Asia and Africa. R. David Simpson, Roger A. Sedjo, & John W. Reid, Valuing Biodiversity for Use in Pharmaceutical Research, 104 J. Pol. Economy 163 (1996). A few species produce potential tourism income, but the vast majority are insufficiently charismatic to attract tourists (e.g., more clams than mammals are endangered in the United States).

Endangered species, however, provide significant societal value on which the owners of their habitat cannot capitalize. Biodiversity, for example, increases the overall productivity of ecosystems (e.g., by promoting plant growth or nutrient retention) and helps ecosystems both recover from environmental shocks such as droughts and storms and adjust to long-term environmental change. See generally Gretchen C. Daily, ed., Nature's Services: Societal Dependence on Natural Ecosystems (1997); John M. Gowdy, The Value of Biodiversity, 73 Land Econ. 25 (1997).

Many members of our society also value protecting species, even if the species do not provide us with any immediate economic benefit. To some, the "existence" value of a species is immeasurable. Economists, nonetheless, have attempted to attach some numbers to this value by asking random samples of the population how much they would be willing to pay to preserve species with little or no commercial value. Annual willingness-to-pay amounts have ranged from $5–10 per household for some lesser known fish such as the striped shiner to $95 per household for the northern spotted owl. See John B. Loomis & Douglas J. White, Economic Benefits of Rare and Endangered Species: Summary and Meta–Analysis, 18 Ecological Econ. 197, 199 (1996).

For these reasons, the ESA prohibits landowners from significantly modifying the habitat of endangered species if the modification "actually kills or injures [protected] wildlife by significantly impairing essential behavioral patterns, including breeding, feeding, or sheltering." Chapter 12 examines in more detail the ESA's restrictions on private land development. To ensure that federal agencies do not engage in activities (e.g., the construction of a dam or the leasing of public land for grazing) that would harm an endangered species' habitat, the ESA also prohibits federal agencies from taking any action, including the authorization of funding of private actions, that might "jeopardize the continued existence" of a listed species or "result in the destruction or adverse modification" of the species' critical habitat.

Invasive Species. The least addressed threat to endangered species, but a significant and growing threat, is competition from invasive species. Some conservation biologists estimate that invasive species have led to the decline of over a third of the species currently listed as endangered or threatened under the ESA. See, e.g., David S. Wilcove et al., Quantifying Threats to Imperiled Species in the United States, 48 BioScience 607 (1998) (invasive species contributing factor in listing of 35–46% of species). Invasive species not only threaten native species but can be exceptionally expensive to the local economy. One set of researchers estimate that invasive species cost the U.S. economy over $135 billion every year.

There is no easy legal solution to the problem of invasive species. Invasive species enter the country through multiple means; although people introduce some invasive species intentionally, many invasive species enter the country covertly in the ballast water of ships, the luggage compartment of airplanes, or the undercarriage of people's cars. In 1999, President Bill Clinton took an initial step to address the problem by issuing Executive Order 13,112, 64 Fed. Reg. 6183 (Feb. 3, 1999). The Executive Order directs "each federal agency ... to the extent practicable and permitted by law" to use its programs and authority to respond to harmful invasive species. The Executive Order created a cabinet-level Invasive Species Council and directed it to develop an Invasive Species Management Plan. In 2001, the Invasive Species Council issued its first management plan, which proposed a number of specific actions, including:

- developing a "risk-based comprehensive screen system for evaluating first-time intentionally introduced non-native species,"
- identifying "the pathways by which invasive species move, rank[ing] them according to their potential for ecological and economic impacts, and develop[ing] mechanisms to reduce movement of invasive species," and
- interdicting "pathways that are recognized as significant sources for the unintentional introduction of invasive species."

National Invasive Species Council, Meeting the Invasive Species Challenge: Management Plan (2001). For useful background on legal approaches to the problem of invasive species, see Harmful Invasive Species: Legal Responses (Marc L. Miller & Robert N. Fabian eds., 2004).

B. OIL & GAS

Petroleum, a liquid mixture of hydrocarbons found under current or prehistoric oceans, and natural gas, a gaseous mixture of hydrocarbons often found in conjunction with petroleum deposits, provide approximately 60 percent of the energy used in the United States today. (Coal provides approximately a quarter, with nuclear and various renewable energy sources providing the remaining energy.) Petroleum and its raw constituents are used to make transportation fuels and a variety of petrochemical products, including plastics and medicines. Natural gas is one of the most common fuels for heating homes and cooking. Power plants use both natural gas and petroleum to produce electricity. Although the United States is now a net importer of both petroleum and natural gas, it is still one of the world's major producers; indeed, it is the second leading producer in the world, following Russia, of natural gas.

The nation's oil industry dates from the successful drilling by "Colonel" Edwin Drake, a former railroad conductor, of a well in Titusville, Pennsylvania in 1859. Drake's well was supported by money from eastern investors, including a Yale chemistry professor.

A decline in the regional whale population drove early interest in petroleum. During the first half of the nineteenth century, whales provided the very best oil for illumination. But as overexploitation led to a decline in whale populations and a consequential increase in the price of whale oil, entrepreneurs responded by developing first oil shale (in Scotland in 1847) and then coal liquefaction (in the 1850s in England and in the U.S.). Both involved chemical processes to produce a liquid from crushed rock. The coal process proved more successful, and its product was called "kerosene" (liquid wax). By 1856 there were more than 50 kerosene refineries in the United States.

But some people, including Benjamin Silliman, a chemistry professor at Yale, thought there might be an easier source of kerosene—petroleum (or "rock oil"). Petroleum seeps had been known from ancient times and had been used for the tar or pitch they produced. In America, petroleum also acquired a reputation as a medicinal tonic and was produced for that purpose in small quantities from some creeks and wells in western New York and Pennsylvania. One creek in western Pennsylvania was known as "Oil Creek" because seeping petroleum usually formed a slick on its surface. The Silliman group backed Drake to dig a well in that region of Western Pennsylvania. The area was already known for brine deposits, used to produce salt, so there was some expertise in drilling. Drake adapted a brine lease for petroleum and set to work drilling. When his well reached 69 feet, it began to fill with a pool of oil. The world's first oil boom was on.

Western Pennsylvania rapidly filled with people seeking to get rich quick with this black gold. Prices for oil started as high as $25 per "barrel" (a unit of measure equal to 42 gallons, probably taken from the wooden barrels used initially to transport oil and allowing for two gallons of leakage). By 1861, tens of thousands of barrels of oil were being produced, every kerosene refinery in America had converted to oil or had gone out of business, and the price of oil had fallen to under $2 per barrel—the first of many boom and bust cycles in oil production.

Hundreds of wells were drilled throughout western Pennsylvania in the 1860s. Within several decades, both petroleum and natural gas production would become major industries in the United States.[1] Who owned the oil and natural gas that flowed out of the mushrooming number of wells? In most countries, then and now, this would not be a relevant question, because only one "person" would have the right to drill a well into a reservoir: the sovereign. Even in England, the source of the common law adage for describing land ownership rights, *ad coelum et ad infernos* (from the heavens to hell), the Crown retained all rights to subsurface oil. The United States, Imperial Russia, and Canada have been the only significant oil producing nations that, now or ever, have recognized private property rights in oil.

Initially courts in the United States held that oil belonged to the owner of the surface of the land below which it was found, based on the *ad coelum* principle. But the *ad coelum* rule quickly proved unworkable. Oil moves. By pumping from beneath his land, one landowner can attract and capture oil from beneath a neighbor's property. Under the *ad coelum* doctrine, the neighbor technically would have a right to sue for *conversion* of the lost oil.

1. Petroleum production grew much faster than natural gas production in the 19th century. Some towns in Western New York State were using natural gas for street lighting as early as 1825. But for most of the nineteenth century, "gas" was "city gas," produced by controlled combustion of coal in gas works on the outskirts of town. This city gas was made up of roughly equal parts of methane and carbon monoxide. It had about half the heating and lighting power of methane gas and was much more poisonous. It was not until the 1910s that production of "natural" gas, so called to distinguish it from the artificial "city gas," became important, mainly in the Appalachian regions. Most, but not all, of the early case law therefore dealt with petroleum rather than natural gas production. Yet the property law for the two resources is largely the same—not surprisingly given that natural gas production historically was usually the byproduct of oil production or exploration.

But it was impossible for the courts to determine where particular quantities of petroleum had originated. The *ad coelum* rule thus threatened to sink the infant petroleum industry under a flood of lawsuits and unanswerable proof questions.

The courts responded by switching to a *rule of capture*, under which any person who reduces oil to surface possession through a well on her property owns it. As the Pennsylvania Supreme Court said with respect to a dispute over natural gas wells,

> Water and oil, and still more strongly gas, may be classed by themselves, if the analogy be not too fanciful, as minerals *ferae naturae*. In common with animals, and unlike other minerals, they have the power and the tendency to escape without the volition of the owner. Their "fugitive and wandering existence within the limits of a particular tract was uncertain.". . . . They belong to the owner of the land, and are part of it, so long as they are on or in it, and are subject to his control; but when they escape, and go into other land, or come under another's control, the title of the former owner is gone. Possession of the land, therefore, is not necessarily possession of the gas. If an adjoining, or even a distant, owner drills his own land, and taps your gas, so that it comes into his well and under his control it is no longer yours, but his. . . . [T]he one who controls the gas—has it in his grasp, so to speak—is the one who has possession in the legal as well as the ordinary sense of the word.

Westmoreland & Cambria Nat. Gas Co. v. DeWitt, 18 A. 724 (Pa. 1889).

Although all oil-bearing states adopted a rule of capture, their courts reached this result by two different theories. Under an *ownership-in-place* theory adopted by some states, a landowner holds title to any oil and gas underneath his land, but loses title to it if it migrates to beneath someone else's property. The just-quoted excerpt from the Pennsylvania Supreme Court's decision in *DeWitt* reflects the "ownership in place" doctrine. Under the alternative *exclusive-right-to-take* theory, no one holds title to the oil when it sits underground; landowners gain title to oil only by pumping it from the ground and thus "capturing" it.

Should it matter *how* a landowner is producing oil and natural gas from wells on his property? The method by which one landowner produces hydrocarbons from a reservoir can affect the total production of the field. For example, early releases of natural gas or water found in a hydrocarbon field can reduce the amount of oil that is economically capturable. While natural gas always flows up under its own pressure, oil is frequently pumped and always needs some pressure to move to the surface. In some fields, the pressure comes from the natural gas found in the field; in others, water lying underneath the petroleum pushes it up. If the pressure is unnecessarily dissipated by producing all the "gas cap" first or pumping large amounts of water, petroleum production will suffer.

Some courts, including the Louisiana Supreme Court, concluded that the rule of capture was absolute. Even if one person's operations "wasted" oil or gas, he was not liable to other landowners overlying the hydrocarbon field. See, e.g., McCoy v. Arkansas Natural Gas Co., 165 So. 632 (La. 1936); McCoy v. Arkansas Natural Gas Co., 143 So. 383 (La. 1932); Louisiana Gas & Fuel Co. v. White Bros., 103 So. 23 (La. 1925). Other courts, however, had second thoughts about an absolute rule of capture.

Elliff v. Texon Drilling Co.

Supreme Court of Texas, 1948.
210 S.W.2d 558.

Folley, J.

This is a suit by the petitioners, Mrs. Mabel Elliff, Frank Elliff, and Charles C. Elliff, against the respondents, Texon Drilling Company, a Texas corporation, Texon Royalty Company, a Texas corporation, Texon Royalty Company, a Delaware corporation, and John L. Sullivan, for damages resulting from a "blowout" gas well drilled by respondents in the Agua Dulce Field in Nueces County.

The petitioners owned the surface and certain royalty interest in 3054.9 acres of land in Nueces County, upon which there was a producing well known as Elliff No. 1. They owned all the mineral estate underlying the west 1500 acres of the tract, and an undivided one-half interest in the mineral estate underlying the east 1554.9 acres. Both tracts were subject to oil and gas leases, and therefore their royalty interest in the west 1500 acres was one-eighth of the oil or gas, and in the east 1554.9 acres was one-sixteenth of the oil and gas.[a]

It was alleged that these lands overlaid approximately fifty percent of a huge reservoir of gas and distillate and that the remainder of the reservoir was under the lands owned by Mrs. Clara Driscoll, adjoining the lands of petitioners on the east. Prior to November 1936, respondents were engaged in the drilling of Driscoll–Sevier No. 2 as an offset well at a location 466 feet east of petitioners' east line. On the date stated, when respondents had reached a depth of approximately 6838 feet, the well blew out, caught fire and cratered. Attempts to control it were unsuccessful, and huge quantities of gas, distillate and some oil were blown into the air, dissipating large quantities from the reservoir into which the offset well was drilled. When the Driscoll–Sevier No. 2 well blew out, the fissure or opening in the

a. Eds.—Fee simple interests in land can be divided into a variety of separate interests. Land, for example, can be divided into a mineral estate (which entitles the holder to extract valuable minerals from the land) and a surface estate (which entitles the holder to use the surface of the land for residential or other purposes, subject to the right of the holder of the mineral estate to extract the minerals). In many cases, the holder of a valuable mineral estate will contract with a third party to actually extract, refine, and market the minerals; in return the holder of the mineral estate may receive an upfront cash payment, lease payments, and/or a "royalty" share in the value of the extracted minerals.

ground around the well gradually increased until it enveloped and destroyed Eliff No. 1. The latter well also blew out, cratered, caught fire and burned for several years. Two water wells on petitioners' land became involved in the cratering and each of them blew out. Certain damages also resulted to the surface of petitioners' lands and to their cattle thereon. The cratering process and the eruption continued until large quantities of gas and distillate were drained from under petitioners' land and escaped into the air, all of which was alleged to be the direct and proximate result of the negligence of respondents in permitting their well to blow out....

The jury found that respondents were negligent in failing to use drilling mud of sufficient weight in drilling their well, and that such negligence was the proximate cause of the well blowing out. It also found that petitioners had suffered $4,620.00 damage to sixty acres of the surface, and $1,350.00 for the loss of 27 head of cattle. The damages for the gas and distillate wasted "from and under" the lands of petitioners, due to respondents' negligence, was fixed by the jury at $78,580.46 for the gas, and $69,967.73 for the distillate. These figures were based upon the respective fractional royalty interests of petitioners in the whole amount wasted under their two tracts of land, and at a value, fixed by the court without objection by the parties, of two cents per 1,000 cubic feet for the gas and $1.25 per barrel for the distillate....

.... [O]ur attention will be confined to the sole question as to whether the law of capture absolves respondents of any liability for the negligent waste or destruction of petitioners' gas and distillate, though substantially all of such waste or destruction occurred after the minerals had been drained from beneath petitioners' lands.

We do not regard as authoritative the three decisions by the Supreme Court of Louisiana to the effect that an adjoining owner is without right of action for gas wasted from the common pool by his neighbor, because in that state only qualified ownership of oil and gas is recognized, no absolute ownership of minerals in place exists, and the unqualified rule is that under the law of capture the minerals belong exclusively to the one that produces them.... Moreover, from an examination of those cases it will be seen that the decisions rested in part on the theory that "the loss complained of was, manifestly, more a matter of uncertainty and speculation than of fact or estimate." In the more recent trend of the decisions of our state, with the growth and development of scientific knowledge of oil and gas, it is now recognized "that when an oil field has been fairly tested and developed, experts can determine approximately the amount of oil and gas in place in a common pool, and can also equitably determine the amount of oil and gas recoverable by the owner of each tract of land under certain operating conditions." Brown v. Humble Oil & Refining Co., 126 Texas 296, 83 S.W. (2d) 935, 940, 87 S.W. (2d) 1069, 99 A.L.R. 1107, 101 A.L.R. 1393.

In Texas, and in other jurisdictions, a different rule exists as to ownership. In our state the landowner is regarded as having absolute title in severalty to the oil and gas in place beneath his land. The only qualification of that rule of ownership is that it must be considered in connection with the law of capture and is subject to police regulations. The oil and gas beneath the soil are considered a part of the realty. Each owner of land owns separately, distinctly and exclusively all the oil and gas under his land and is accorded the usual remedies against trespassers who appropriate the minerals or destroy their market value.

The conflict in the decisions of the various states with reference to the character of ownership is traceable to some extent to the divergent views entertained by the courts, particularly in the earlier cases, as to the nature and migratory character of oil and gas in the soil. In the absence of common law precedent, and owing to the lack of scientific information as to the movement of these minerals, some of the courts have sought by analogy to compare oil and gas to other types of property such as wild animals, birds, subterranean waters, and other migratory things, with reference to which the common law had established rules denying any character of ownership prior to capture. However, as was said by Professor A. W. Walker, Jr., of the School of Law of the University of Texas: "There is no oil or gas producing state today which follows the wild-animal analogy to its logical conclusion that the landowner has no property interest in the oil and gas in place." 16 Tex. L. Rev. 371. In the light of modern scientific knowledge these early analogies have been disproven, and courts generally have come to recognize that oil and gas, as commonly found in underground reservoirs, are securely entrapped in a static condition in the original pool, and, ordinarily, so remain until disturbed by penetrations from the surface. It is further established, nevertheless, that these minerals will migrate across property lines towards any low pressure area created by production from the common pool. This migratory character of oil and gas has given rise to the so-called rule or law of capture. That rule simply is that the owner of a tract of land acquires title to the oil or gas which he produces from wells on his land, though part of the oil or gas may have migrated from adjoining lands. He may thus appropriate the oil and gas that have flowed from adjacent lands without the consent of the owner of those lands, and without incurring liability to him for drainage. The nonliability is based upon the theory that after the drainage the title or property interest of the former owner is gone. This rule, at first blush, would seem to conflict with the view of absolute ownership of the minerals in place, but it was otherwise decided in the early case of Stephens County v. Mid–Kansas Oil & Gas Co., 113 Texas 160, 254 S.W. 290, 29 A.L.R. 566 (1923). Mr. Justice Greenwood there stated:

> The objection lacks substantial foundation that gas or oil in a certain tract of land cannot be owned in place, because subject to appropriation, without the consent of the owner of the tract, through drainage from wells on adjacent lands. If the owners of adjacent lands have the right to appropriate, without liability, the gas and oil underlying their neighbor's land, then their neighbor has the correlative right to appropriate, through like methods of drainage, the gas and oil underlying the tracts adjacent to his own.

Thus it is seen that, notwithstanding the fact that oil and gas beneath the surface are subject both to capture and administrative regulation, the fundamental rule of absolute ownership of the minerals in place is not affected in our state. In recognition of such ownership, our courts, in decisions involving well-spacing regulations of our Railroad Commission, have frequently announced the sound view that each landowner should be afforded the opportunity to produce his fair share of the recoverable oil and gas beneath his land, which is but another way of recognizing the existence of correlative rights between the various landowners over a common reservoir of oil or gas.

It must be conceded that under the law of capture there is no liability for reasonable and legitimate drainage from the common pool. The landowner is privileged to sink as many wells as he desires upon his tract of land and extract therefrom and appropriate all the oil and gas that he may produce, so long as he operates within the spirit and purpose of conservation statutes and orders of the Railroad Commission. These laws and regulations are designed to afford each owner a reasonable opportunity to produce his proportionate part of the oil and gas from the entire pool and to prevent operating practices injurious to the common reservoir. In this manner, if all operators exercise the same degree of skill and diligence, each owner will recover in most instances his fair share of the oil and gas. This reasonable opportunity to produce his fair share of the oil and gas is the landowner's common law right under our theory of absolute ownership of the minerals in place. But from the very nature of this theory the right of each land holder is qualified, and is limited to legitimate operations. Each owner whose land overlies the basin has a like interest, and each must of necessity exercise his right with some regard to the rights of others. No owner should be permitted to carry on his operations in reckless or lawless irresponsibility, but must submit to such limitations as are necessary to enable each to get his own.

While we are cognizant of the fact that there is a certain amount of reasonable and necessary waste incident to the production of oil and gas to which the non-liability rule must also apply, we do not think this immunity should be extended so as to include the negligent waste or destruction of the oil and gas. . . .

In 85 A.L.R. 1156, in discussing the case of Hague v. Wheeler, 27 A. 714 (Pa. 1893), the annotator states:

> The fact that the owner of the land has a right to take and to use gas and oil, even to the diminution or exhaustion of the supply under his neighbor's land, does not give him the right to waste the gas. His property in the gas underlying his land consists of the right to appropriate the same, and permitting the gas to escape into the air is not an appropriation thereof in the proper sense of the term.

In like manner, the negligent waste and destruction of petitioners' gas and distillate was neither a legitimate drainage of the minerals from beneath their lands nor a lawful or reasonable appropriation of them.

Consequently, the petitioners did not lose their right, title and interest in them under the law of capture. At the time of their removal they belonged to petitioner, and their wrongful dissipation deprived these owners of the right and opportunity to produce them. That right is forever lost, the same cannot be restored, and petitioners are without an adequate legal remedy unless we allow a recovery under the same common law which governs other actions for damages and under which the property rights in oil and gas are vested. This remedy should not be denied.

In common with others who are familiar with the nature of oil and gas and the risks involved in their production, the respondents had knowledge that a failure to use due care in drilling their well might result in a blowout with the consequent waste and dissipation of the oil, gas and distillate from the common reservoir. In the conduct of one's business or in the use and exploitation of one's property, the law imposes upon all persons the duty to exercise ordinary care to avoid injury or damage to the property of others. Thus under the common law, and independent of the conservation statutes, the respondents were legally bound to use due care to avoid the negligent waste or destruction of the minerals imbedded in petitioners' oil and gas-bearing strata. This common-law duty the respondents failed to discharge. For that omission they should be required to respond in such damages as will reasonably compensate the injured parties for the loss sustained as the proximate result of the negligent conduct. The fact that the major portion of the gas and distillate escaped from the well on respondents' premises is immaterial. Irrespective of the opening from which the minerals escaped, they belonged to the petitioners and the loss was the same. They would not have been dissipated at any opening except for the wrongful conduct of the respondents. Being responsible for the loss they are in no position to deny liability because the gas and distillate did not escape through the surface of petitioners' lands.

Notes & Questions

1. The rule of capture is a judicially imposed commons with all the tragic consequences attendant thereto. Under a strict rule of capture, all property owners overlying a petroleum reservoir have an incentive to extract the resource as quickly as possible—before their neighbors do. In the early years of oil production, the rule of capture led to exactly the type of overexploitation that one would expect.

As *Ellis* illustrates, overexploitation is not the only problem with treating oil and gas as commons. A strict rule of capture can also lead to what Professor Elinor Ostrom has labeled "provision problems." See Elinor Ostrom, Ray Gardner, & James Walker, Rules, Games, and Common–Pool Resources 9 (1994). In deciding what type of technology to use and how careful to be, a well driller like the Texon Drilling Company will take into account the costs and benefits to it, but not to others. Because the cost of slipshod drilling will be borne in part by other property owners, each well driller will tend to underinvest in safety. Similarly, if one landowner could increase total production from the field by reducing her pumping (for example, because her property overlies the natural gas or water that provides the pressure needed to drive production), the benefits would be split among all producers, so the landowner may well decide that it is in her individual best interest to continue pumping at full speed.

The history of the Spindletop field in Texas provides a vivid illustration of both overexploitation and provision problems:

> On January 10, 1901, near Beaumont, Texas, Captain Anthony F. Lucas and his drilling team struck oil after drilling more than 1,000 feet into the Spindletop salt dome. The "black plume" that shot into the sky rose to twice the derrick height. This initial Spindletop well produced 800,000 barrels of oil in its first nine days, a world record. A hysteria of speculation followed, "with wells being drilled as close together as physically possible." By the end of 1901, 440 wells had been drilled on the 125–acre hill where Spindletop was located. The disastrous effects of this "oil rush" were manifest in the rapidly diminishing production returns. In 1904, only 100 of the 1,000 wells that had been drilled around Spindletop were producing at least 10,000 barrels per day. When Captain Lucas returned to Spindletop in 1904, he noted, "The cow was milked too hard, and moreover she was not milked intelligently."

Rance L. Craft, Of Reservoir Hogs and Pelt Fiction: Defending the Ferae Naturae Analogy Between Petroleum and Wildlife, 44 Emory L.J. 697, 701 (1995).

2. If the rule of capture makes so little sense, why did courts adopt it? And why have they largely stuck with it? Would any alternative private property regime work better?

3. **The Correlative Rights Doctrine.** *Elliff* softens the rule of capture by adding a reasonableness requirement. The *Elliff* approach, also known as the correlative rights doctrine, provides landowners overlying a hydrocarbon field with rights against a variety of actions by their neighbors that could harm the field. As shown in *Ellis*, landowners have a right against spoilage of the reservoir through negligence. Landowners can enjoin pumping that unreasonably threatens a field's pressure (e.g., by prematurely depleting natural gas). See Manufacturers' Gas & Oil Co. v. Indiana Natural Gas & Oil Co., 57 N.E. 912 (Ind. 1900). The correlative rights doctrine also encompasses a "fair share principle." As the Texas Supreme Court announced in Halbouty v. Railroad Commission, 357 S.W.2d 364, 374 (Tex. 1962), "if in a common reservoir one tract owner is allowed to produce many times more gas than underlies his tract he is denying to some other landowner in the reservoir a fair chance to produce the gas underlying his land."

How effective do you believe courts can be under the correlative rights doctrine in avoiding the problems of the commons? Although the correlative rights doctrine smooths some of the roughest edges off the rule of capture, overlying landowners still retain an incentive to find means of maximize their own income even if it harms their neighbors. Avoiding the problems of the commons thus may require micromanagement of pumping activities. Are courts the best governmental institutions for regulating pumping? Are legislatures and administrative agencies better equipped to regulate pumping? For a more thorough discussion of the correlative rights doctrine and its limitations, see David Edward Pierce, Coordinated Reservoir Development—An Alternative to the Rule of Capture for the Ownership and Development of Oil and Gas, 4 J. Energy L. & Policy 1 (1983).

4. **Administrative Regulation.** Most state legislatures have responded to the problems of the commons by regulating oil and gas production through administrative agencies such as Texas' Railroad Commission. Under so-called "conservation laws," states limit total production within their borders and then prorate the allowable production among the state's various fields and wells. States also employ well spacing regulations that require a minimum distance between wells and between wells and property lines. Well spacing both prevents well operations from unnecessarily interfering with each other and serves as an indirect restriction on overdrilling.

Although these regulations address some of the problems created by the commons, most observers do not believe that they come close to optimizing oil and gas production in the United States. According to Professor David Pierce, current state regulations fail to encourage production techniques that will yield the maximum recovery. Indeed, "many operate directly against maximizing recovery by failing to deal with the rule of capture as the basic property law of oil and gas." Pierce, supra note 3, at 78. Prorationing, for example,

> has no relation to geology or good reservoir engineering. Prorationing does not consider whether a well *should* be produced; it only determines how much it can produce under the applicable allocation formula. For example, if the well is bottomed in a gas cap, it should not be produced at all.... However, if a well is given a certain allowable [production], ... the rule of capture will in most cases result in maximum permissible production without regard for damage to the reservoir.

Id. at 71.

5. **Unitization.** The most direct solution to the tragedy of the commons is to eliminate the commons. Landowners overlying a hydrocarbon field can eliminate the commons by "unitizing" their operations. Under unitization, landowners choose a single firm, known as the unit operator, to develop and operate the field as a whole. Net revenues from this operation are then apportioned among all landowners according to a negotiated formula. The unit operator, unlike individual landowners, has the incentive to maximize total income from the field. Some industry sources have estimated that unitization, by comparison to an unconstrained commons, increases recovery from a field by two to five fold. See Gary D. Libecap, Contracting for Property Rights 95 (1989).

Disagreements among landowners over how to allocate the unit revenue, however, have kept voluntary unitization to a minimum. As Professor Howard Williams has noted, "there is a certain amount of gamblers' instinct to be overcome; some [owners] may be inclined to rely on the possibility that their interests lie in the most favorable part of the producing structure and to take their chances that the entire production from their land will be more valuable than an undivided interest in production from a much larger unitized tract." Howard R. Williams, Conservation of Oil and Gas, 65 Harv. L. Rev. 1155 (1952). As a result, some states have adopted "compulsory unitization" laws that permit a majority of landowners, weighted generally by acreage, to compel unitization of the field.

6. **Storage.** Because production of natural gas from a hydrocarbon field cannot always be timed to coincide with market demand, producers sometimes store natural gas for later sale. The removal of natural gas from a field sometimes creates storage capacity that can be used for this purpose. Who, if anyone, owns this storage capacity?

Hammonds v. Central Kentucky Natural Gas Co.

Supreme Court of Kentucky, 1934.
75 S.W.2d 204.

STANLEY, COMMISSIONER. The case seems to be one of first impression. About 1919 the appellee exhausted the gas from a field of about 15,000 acres in Menifee and adjoining counties, most of which it had under lease. Thereafter it brought in vast quantities of gas from distant fields and put it by force through its previously drilled wells into the vacated underground reservoir, withdrawing it as desired. In recent rate litigation the company valued these holdings at $2,000,000....

The appellee owns 54 acres within this boundary which was never leased to the company. It is not disputed that this geological dome or basin underlies her land. She brought this suit to recover a large sum for use and occupation under the idea of trespass, it being charged that the gas was placed in or under his property without her knowledge or consent. Judgment went for the defendant. The decision must rest upon the character and nature of property in natural gas....

[In an omitted passage, the Court recounts how early courts, analogizing oil and gas to wild animals, adopted the rule of capture.].... [Oil and gas] belong to the owner of the land as a part of it so long as [the oil and gas] are on it or subject to his control; when they are gone, his title is gone....

If they escape into the land of another, they become his property in like degree or manner. So it is declared that oil and gas are not the property of any one until reduced to actual possession by extraction, although by virtue of his proprietorship the owner of the surface, or his grantee of the severed mineral estate, has the exclusive right of seeking to acquire and of appropriating the oil and gas directly beneath. This theory of ownership or, perhaps more accurately speaking, lack of ownership is practically universally recognized. . . .

When gas is thus severed and brought under dominion and into actual possession at the surface, it, of course, becomes the personal property of the one who has extracted it under a right so to do. The appellee acquired such title to the gas here involved. The question is whether that gas, having once been reduced to possession and absolute ownership having vested, was restored to its original wild and natural status by being replaced in a similar reservoir of nature, taking the place of other gas which once occupied that same subterranean chamber.

In seeking for an analogous condition in the law, the courts . . . have compared natural gas and oil to that of animals *ferae naturae*. The analogy, as we have seen, formed the basis of the all but universal doctrine of property in these wandering minerals. So we may look to that analogous law. From the beginning, wild animals have been regarded as quasi property of the entire human race. It is the recognition of land titles rather than of any individual property in the game that prevents its pursuit, and, barring all questions of trespass, exclusive property in birds and wild animals becomes vested in the person capturing or reducing them to possession. But unless killed, this is a qualified property, for when restored to their natural wild and free state, the dominion and individual proprietorship of any person over them is at an end and they resume their status as common property. So, too, are fish collective property so long as they remain unconfined in their natural element in a public stream, and not even the owner of the soil over which the stream flows owns the fish therein, although he may have the exclusive right of fishing in the stream where it runs over his land. And, as in the case of wild game, a qualified property in an individual may be acquired by catching and confining fish within a private pond so they cannot escape. If, however, the fish escape and are found at large in their proper element, they again become public property and are subject to appropriation by the first person who takes them.

If one capture a fox in a forest and turn it loose in another, or if he catch a fish and put it back in the stream at another point, has he not done with that migratory, common property just what the appellee has done with the gas in this case? Did the company not lose its exclusive property in the gas when it restored the substance to its natural habitat?

Another analogue to the moving deposits of oil and gas is subterranean and percolating water which also have a similarity of relation though not of identity, the substantial difference being only that oil and gas are vanishing products while water may be perpetually supplied by nature. One may draw water and it becomes his when placed in his own receptacle. He may appropriate water from a running stream to turn his mill or to irrigate his land and the property therein may be said to exist in him so long as it remains under his control. But once the water is restored to the earth or to the running stream that exclusive, individual title is lost. . . .

We are of the opinion, therefore, that if in fact the gas turned loose in the earth wandered into the plaintiff's land, the defendant is not liable to her for the value of the use of her property, for the company ceased to be the exclusive owner of the whole of the gas—it again became mineral *ferae naturae*.

Accordingly, the judgment is affirmed.

Notes & Questions

1. Should it matter to the liability question whether the Central Kentucky Natural Gas Company still owns the natural gas after they put it into the field? If the Central Kentucky Natural Gas Company had discharged a flood of water onto Ms. Hammonds property, should it matter to liability whether the company "owned" the water? If the company had intentionally released a large pack of foxes, and the foxes had eaten Ms. Hammonds' livestock, should it matter that the company did not "own" the foxes? Is it relevant that Ms. Hammonds was suing for the storage value of the reservoir under her land rather than for physical damage? What if the natural gas had seaped to the surface and exploded on her property, causing significant damage?

2. If you were Ms. Hammonds, what would you do in response to the court's opinion? In protecting the Central Kentucky Natural Gas Company from liability to overlying property owners, did the court create an even bigger problem for natural gas companies interesting in storing natural gas in underground reservoirs?

3. When the owners of land overlying a petroleum reservoir have tried to extract natural gas stored in the reservoir by a third party, courts of other jurisdictions have often rejected the logic of *Hammonds* and held that the third party retains ownership of the natural gas even after it has been pumped into the reservoir. See, e.g., White v. New York State Natural Gas Corp., 190 F. Supp. 342 (W.D. Pa. 1960); Lone Star Gas Co. v. Murchison, 353 S.W.2d 870 (Tex. Civ. App. 1962). But see Anderson v. Beech, 699 P.2d 1023 (Kan. 1985) (holding that stored gas is subject to rule of capture). In 1987, the Kentucky Supreme Court itself overruled *Hammonds* and held that gas injected into a geographically well-defined reservoir remains the property of the injector. See Texas American Energy Corp. v. Citizens Fidelity Bank & Trust Co., 736 S.W.2d 25 (Ky. 1987). Does this mean that overlying owners can sue the injector for trespass? Can a court consistently hold both that the natural gas belongs to the injector and that there is no trespass? How?

Many petroleum states have dealt with the issue of underground gas storage through statute. The statutes typically provide that the gas remains the property of the injector, but that the injector must either reach an agreement with the overlying owner concerning storage or pay a statutorily dictated amount. See, e.g., Mo. Rev. Stat. § 393.500; Okla. Stat. Ann. Tit. 52, § 36.6.

4. **Ownership of Groundwater Aquifer Capacity.** A similar issue has arisen in connection with groundwater aquifers. In the western United States, significant quantities of water must be stored to meet domestic, agricultural, and industrial needs during lengthy dry seasons and droughts. Surface storage in large manmade reservoirs raises a number of problems, including construction expense, environmental damage, evaporation loss, and the risk of dam failure. In recent years, large water distributors therefore have become increasingly interested in the option of storing water in underground "aquifers" (essentially natural groundwater reservoirs) that have storage capacity due to prior groundwater pumping.

Only a handful of courts have yet dealt with objections by overlying landowners to such storage. In Central Nebraska Public Power & Irrigation Dist. v. Abrahamson, 413 N.W.2d 290 (Neb. 1987), the Nebraska Supreme Court rejected a landowner's argument that state approval of a public storage project "took" their property without compensation because the landowner failed to present evidence that the project interfered with use of their property. "A statute cannot deprive a person of property unless it prevents him from doing an act which he desires to do or diminishes the enjoyment or profit which he would otherwise derive from his property." Id. at 299. See also Board of Commr's v. Park Cty. Sportsmen's Ranch, 45 P.3d 693 (Colo. 2002) (holding that overlying landowners cannot object to groundwater storage); Niles Sand & Gravel Co. v. Alameda County Water Dist., 112 Cal. Rptr. 846 (Cal. App. 1974) (rejecting challenge by landowner who found his gravel mining operation flooded by a local groundwater storage project).

A Brief Note on Fossil Fuels & Climate Change

No discussion of oil and gas would be complete today without at least a brief discussion of the unfortunate environmental side effects of fossil fuels. Perhaps the most important side effect today is that, when burned, they emit carbon dioxide (CO_2), methane, and NO_x into the atmosphere. And the increasing atmospheric concentrations of these gases are threatening global climate change.

Climate change looms as a defining issue of the 21st century, pitting our fossil-fuel economy against the potential disruption of our global climate system. CO_2, methane, and NO_x are *greenhouse gases* that let sunlight pass through our atmosphere while trapping heat from the earth's surface. (The other major man-made greenhouse gases are chlorofluorocarbons.) Atmospheric concentrations of CO_2, methane, and NO_x have increased approximately 30%, 145%, and 15%, respectively, during the industrial era. Fossil fuels are the major anthropogenic source of greenhouse gases today. Petroleum and natural gas, for example, produce over 60 percent of the CO_2 emissions in the United States.

The potential impact of increasing greenhouse gas concentrations on the planet's climate system is enormous. Long-term climate data suggest that the planet's average surface air temperature already has increased since the late 19th century by about 0.6° Celsius.

> Although legitimate and important areas of uncertainty still exist with respect to the ultimate impacts of climate change, the range of uncertainty is narrowing over time. Perhaps most important, a global consensus now exists among the international scientific community that we are witnessing discernible impacts on our climate and natural systems due to human activities. The Second Assessment [of the Intergovernmental Panel on Climate Change (IPCC)] concluded in 1995 that the observed warming trend was "unlikely to be entirely natural in origin" and that the balance of evidence suggested a "discernible human influence" on the Earth's climate.... The IPCC compiled and released its Third Assessment in 2001, which concluded that "most of the warming observed over the last 50 years is likely to have been due to the increase in greenhouse gas concentrations" attributable to human activities.
>
> According to the IPCC, failure to mitigate greenhouse gases will result in a projected increase of between 1.4 to 5.8° Celsius by the year 2100. Such a rate of warming is apparently without precedent for at least the last 10,000 years. Temperatures over land and particularly over the northern hemisphere are anticipated to increase even more than these global averages. The expected impact of climate change include not only an increase in global temperature but a rise in the "energy" of storms and weather patterns, sea level rise, water availability, disease, and loss of biodiversity. The range of possible impacts is so broad and severe that many observers believe climate change to be the most significant long-term environmental problem facing the planet.

James Salzman & Barton H. Thompson, Jr., Environmental Law and Policy 113–114 (2003).

The dangers of global climate change brought calls for international action as early as the 1970s. In 1992, over 150 nations, including the United States, signed a Framework Convention on Climate Change. The Convention called for the stabilization of atmospheric greenhouse gas concentrations "at a level that would prevent dangerous anthropogenic interference with the climate system," but did not set any numeric targets. After the IPCC released its Second Assessment, the parties to the Convention negotiated the Kyoto Protocol to the Climate Change Convention setting binding reduction targets for the United States and other developed countries. Although most of the developed nations have now ratified the Kyoto Protocol, two major nations—the United States and Australia—have refused to ratify it. Even if the United States and Australia were to ratify and comply with the Kyoto Protocol, moreover, the reductions mandated by the protocol would be only a first step toward solving the problem of global climate change. International debates and discussions therefore continue over how to solve the problem.

Recall the law of private and public nuisance from Chapter 2. See pp. 128–167. Assuming that the owners of ocean-front property a number of decades from now could show that increasing sea levels had damaged their property and were most likely the result of greenhouse gas emissions, could they bring a private nuisance action against major petroleum companies and major electric utilities? Could governmental officials sue these companies today for public nuisance? What types of issues would such suits raise, and how should courts resolve them? In 2004, the attorney generals from nine U.S. states filed public nuisance actions in federal district court against the top five domestic emitters of CO_2. In September 2005, the district court dismissed the complaints on the ground that they presented "non-justiciable political questions that are consigned to the political branches, not the judiciary." According to the court, resolution of the issues presented by the public nuisance action would require "identification and balancing of economic, environmental, foreign policy, and national security interests," which would call for exactly the types of policy determinations that are non-justiciable. State of Connecticut v. American Electric Power Co., 406 F. Supp. 2d 265 (S.D.N.Y. 2005). The case is now on appeal. See generally David A. Grossman, Warming Up to a Not–So–Radical Idea: Tort–Based Climate Change Litigation, 28 Colum. J. Envtl. L. 1 (2003).

C. WATER

Along with air, water is the world's most crucial natural resource. Humans obviously need water to survive, but the two quarts of water we drink each day are just the start. Today the average American uses about 100 gallons a day at home. Farms, industries, and commercial establishments require another 300 billion gallons of freshwater each day—or 1300 gallons per day for each American. (To understand why these figures are so large, consider that, counting the water needed to grow the feed, it takes about 3.5 million gallons of water to raise a 1000–pound steer—or over 3500 gallons per steak.)

The United States, like the world at large, also suffers from a considerable imbalance in water supplies. Historic storm patterns, for example, guarantee significant rainfall to most of the nation east of the 100th meridian. By contrast, the western flatlands are parched, leading early cartographers to label the area "The Great American Desert." These differences in precipitation are reflected in river variations. The four largest American rivers are the Mississippi, the Columbia, the Ohio, and the St. Lawrence. The Colorado River, which dominates the Southwest's geography, ranks only 25th nationally and carries about 3 percent of the water in the Mississippi.

How does the law allocate property rights in scarce water resources among competing users? The law varies considerably from state-to-state, particularly between the eastern United States and the West, and also depends on what type of water is being allocated. Water resources are divided into two main categories. The first category is surface water which consists of rivers, lakes, streams, and other waterways found above ground. The second category is groundwater which is found underneath in aquifers. Eighty percent of all the water currently used in the United States comes from surface waterways. Groundwater, however, is extremely important in many regions and sectors. Indeed, groundwater provides roughly a third of the water used for domestic needs in the nation.

1. Surface Water

The Riparian Doctrine. States use two principal doctrines to allocate surface water. States east of the 100th meridian (which runs roughly down the middle of the continental United States) use the *riparian doctrine*. Only water users who own "riparian" land (i.e., land through which or tangential to which a waterway flows) have a common-law right to withdraw water from that waterway.

Courts originally held that every riparian was entitled to the natural flow of the waterway; upstream users could not divert or diminish the water that would otherwise go downstream except to meet domestic uses. Because the *natural flow rule* proved unworkable in a growing economy, eastern states later abandoned the natural flow rule in favor of a *reasonable use rule* which permits each riparian to use a "reasonable" quantity of water. As the Georgia Supreme Court explained in Price v. High Shoals Mfg. Co., 64 S.E. 87, 88 (Ga. 1909), every riparian

> is entitled to a reasonable use of the water in the stream. If the general rule that each riparian owner could not in any way interrupt or diminish the flow of the stream were strictly followed, the water would be of but little practical use to any proprietor, and the enforcement of such rule would deny, rather than grant, the use thereof. Every riparian owner is entitled to a reasonable use of the water. Every such proprietor is also entitled to have the stream pass over his land according to its natural flow, subject to such disturbances, interruptions, and diminutions as may be necessary and unavoidable on account of the reasonable and proper use of it by other riparian proprietors. Riparian proprietors have a common right in the waters of the stream, and the necessities of the business of one can not be the standard of the rights of another, but each is entitled to a reasonable use of the water with respect to the rights of others.

Courts look to a variety of factors in determining whether a particular use of water is reasonable, including the purpose and value of the use, the suitability of the use to the watershed, the extent and amount of harm caused to other riparians, the availability of alternative water supplies, and "the protection of existing values of water uses, land, investments, and enterprises." Restatement (Second) of Torts § 850A (1979). Historically, riparians were not permitted to divert water for use on lands that were not riparian to the waterway. Cities usually obtained water supplies for their residents, most of whom were not riparian to the source of the cities' water supply, by condemning the water through their power of eminent domain.

In more recent years, however, states have begun to loosen the riparian restriction and permit uses on non-riparian lands, so long as the use is reasonable.

What do you see as the advantages of allocating water by the riparian doctrine? The disadvantages? Assume that you are advising a riparian who is interested in starting a farm or building a factory on his property for which the riparian will need to invest significant capital. Prior to investing money in the enterprise, the riparian would like to know how much water she is entitled to under the riparian doctrine. What would you tell the riparian? How much certainty does the riparian doctrine provide? In this regard, note that what is "reasonable" can change over time as local needs and conditions change. Would the riparian doctrine work very well where water is exceptionally scarce, as in most of the western United States?

The Prior Appropriation System. Western states have largely rejected the riparian doctrine in favor of the *prior appropriation system.* Under prior appropriation, rights to water are separated from the ownership of riparian land. Anyone, riparian or nonriparian, is entitled to "appropriate," or divert, water from a river or lake for use even scores of miles away so long as the water is not already being used by someone else. The West thus allocates water on a first-come, first-served basis. If you are the first one to take water out of a river, you have the first priority to that amount of water for as long as you continue to use the water. If in a drought year there is only enough water to meet your right, no one else can take any water from the stream.

There are various limits on prior appropriation rights that make them look quite different from other property rights that you have seen. First, you are entitled to water only if you put the water to a "reasonable and beneficial" use. No one is entitled to take water for speculative purposes or for uses that courts have decided are unimportant (e.g., to drown gophers). Nor can an appropriator take more water than she reasonably needs. Second, if you stop using water (or do not put the water to a reasonable and beneficial use) for a lengthy enough period of time, you lose your right to the water. "Use it or lose it" is a key tenet of the prior appropriation system.

Permit Systems. Eastern and western states also administer their surface water systems in very different ways. Because western water users need highly secure water rights, state water agencies (often known as "state engineers," "water boards," or "departments of water resources") carefully oversee the prior appropriation system. Anyone wishing to divert water from a stream must apply for an appropriation permit from the state agency, which will check to ensure that unappropriated water is available in the stream and that the applicant plans to use the water for a "reasonable and beneficial" purpose. A growing number of western states also require the administrative agency to determine whether issuing a water permit is in the "public interest." See, e.g., Alaska Stat. § 46.15.080. If the applicant meets all the requirements, the state agency will issue an appropriation permit certifying the water right.

The East's vast natural supplies of water historically generated few disputes. Courts resolved the occasional dispute that arose. As water demand has grown, however, some eastern states also have set up administrative permit systems to track water use and resolve the mounting number of disputes. See Robert Abrams, Water Allocation by Comprehensive Permit Systems in the Eastern United States: Considering a Move Away from Orthodoxy, 9 Va. Envtl. L.J. 255 (1990); George Sherk, Eastern Water Law: Trends in State Legislation, 9 Va. Envtl. L.J. 287 (1990).

The Problems of Conservation & Instream Flow. Two issues that currently confront all of the United States, but particularly the arid West, are how to encourage water conservation and how to put more water back into our rivers for the benefit of fish, wildlife, and the general environment. As the nation's population continues to grow, means must be found to conserve on existing water uses to make water available for new uses. The nation historically did not worry much about water use, even in water scarce regions. Cities and agricultural communities that faced local water shortages simply turned to distant watershed for supplemental supplies. Today a variety of economic and environmental constraints make this approach unworkable.

At the same time that the nation is trying to stretch its available water supplies, the nation must also find a way of restoring an environmental balance to its waterways. Many of the water development projects in the 20th century caused serious environmental harm. For example, the first major federal reclamation project, the Newlands Project in the Great Basin of Nevada, siphoned water from the few natural water bodies found in the region, dramatically reducing the water level of Pyramid Lake and totally drying up Lake Winnemucca. Changes to Pyramid Lake have led to the extinction of the native stock of Lahontan cutthroat trout and to the listing as an endangered species of the only other migratory fish native to the lake, the Cui-ui. The project also significantly reduced flows into Nevada's Stillwater Marsh.

Western water law historically tried to regulate waste through the "reasonable and beneficial use" doctrine. See Janet C. Neuman, Beneficial Use, Waste, and Forfeiture: The Inefficient Search for Efficiency in Western Water Use, 28 Envtl. L. 919 (1998). As explained earlier, appropriators are not entitled to divert an unreasonable quantity of water for their uses. Any amount of water that is wasted is not being put to a reasonable and beneficial use and is thus subject to forfeiture by the appropriator. As the next case shows, however, courts have been reticent to require appropriators to conserve water at their own expense—even when appropriators are using what appear to be extreme quantities of water.

Erickson v. Queen Valley Ranch Co.

California Court of Appeals, 1971.
99 Cal. Rptr. 446.

FRIEDMAN, ACTING PRESIDING JUSTICE

Plaintiffs own 240 acres of ranch lands in Mono County. They seek to quiet title to the water of Morris Creek. In the early part of the century, plaintiffs' properties were owned by John Pedro, who established an appropriative right to the entire flow of Morris Creek. . . .

The headwaters of the creek are located in Nevada. In a state of nature the creek flowed into California, although John Pedro's ranch was not riparian to it. Commencing in 1902, Pedro acquired appropriative rights and built a diversion dam, which is located about one-half mile east of the present California–Nevada state line. From the dam he built a stone-lined diversion ditch, which conducted the entire flow of the creek by gravity to his ranch, about 2½ miles distant. The ditch was about 2 feet deep and 2 feet wide. John Pedro died in 1916. The ranch was held by his widow and three sons until 1966, when it was sold to plaintiffs.

Some years after John Pedro's death, and over the protests of the Pedro family, defendants were issued appropriative permits by the Nevada state authorities, allowing them to transport up to five second/feet of Morris Creek by pipeline to irrigate Nevada property. The permits were expressly subordinated to any preexisting rights found by a court. At one point a contractor employed by defendants stopped the flow of water into the diversion ditch. Plaintiffs' protests caused partial restoration of the flow. Plaintiffs then instituted this action.

After considering evidence, the trial court found that John Pedro and his successors had continually put to beneficial use for irrigation and domestic purposes all the water of Morris Creek diverted to the land; that the Pedro family never abandoned or forfeited any right to the water; that, except for occasional storm runoffs, there is no surplus or unappropriated water; that evapotranspiration losses occurred during the 2½ miles of flow but these losses were not unreasonable and were similar to the custom or practice prevailing in the locality. The court entered a judgment quieting the title to plaintiffs as appropriative owners of all the water of Morris Creek diverted at the upper end of the ditch.

Generally, an appropriative water right is forfeited by force of statute and reverts to the public if the appropriator fails to put it to beneficial use during a three-year period. (Water Code, §§ 1240–1241.) . . .

As defendants view the evidence, there was no beneficial use of the water reaching the Pedro ranch during the nine years from 1956 to 1965. [During this period, the Pedro family used its water only for domestic use, watering of personal poultry and livestock, and irrigation of a family orchard. Defendants contend that, because the water was used for noncommercial and family use, it was not being used "beneficially."] . . . . Agriculture is a beneficial use of water even if it does not result in profit. Domestic use, irrigation of pasture, irrigation of a garden and fruit trees and watering of livestock, are all beneficial uses of water. Watering of barnyard animals not kept for profit is a beneficial domestic use. . . .

[Defendants also argue that the Pedro family wasted water, and thus did not make beneficial use of its entire appropriation, because its 2½-mile diversion canal was unpaved, leading to considerable amounts of leakage.] Here we find reversible error. Plaintiffs' existing appropriative right is measured not by the flow originally appropriated and not by the capacity of the diversion ditch, but by the amount of water put to beneficial use at the delivery point plus such additional flow as is reasonably necessary to deliver it....

An appropriator cannot be compelled to divert according to the most scientific methods; he is entitled to make a reasonable use of the water according to the general custom of the locality, so long as the custom does not involve unnecessary waste. The trial court's finding included a formulary statement designed to satisfy this rule, declaring that evapotranspiration losses in the course of the 2½ miles of conveyance by ditch "are not unreasonable and are similar to the custom or practice of the locality."

According to measurements taken in August 1963, the Pedro ditch contained a flow of 2.585 cubic feet per second at a point 100 yards below the diversion dam, while only 0.424 cubic feet per second was delivered at the Pedro ranch. The major part, that is, five-sixths of the flow, was lost en route to the point of use. Although the evidence includes no later flow data, it supplies no ground for believing that the transmission loss is any less now than it was in 1963. Inferably, absorption into the sandy desert soil is a major loss factor, evaporation a relatively minor factor.

Article XIV, section 3, of the California Constitution declares the state's policy to achieve maximum beneficial use of water and prevention of waste, unreasonable use and unreasonable method of use.[a] The constitutional policy applies to every water right and every method of diversion. It imposes upon trial courts an affirmative duty to fashion a decree which will simultaneously protect the paramount right of the established appropriator and prevent waste.

The findings and decree in this case fail to accomplish the second of these objectives. By holding that transmission losses amounting to five-sixths of the flow are reasonable and consistent with local custom, the court effectually placed the seal of judicial approval on what appears to be an inefficient and wasteful means of transmission. Such a holding is not in conformity with the demands of article XIV, section 3.

It is doubtless true that water in the arid desert areas of Mono County is frequently transported by open ditch; also, that much of the flow may be lost by absorption and evaporation. Moreover, an appropriator who has for many years conveyed water by earth ditches may not be compelled at his own expense to install impervious conduit. Nevertheless, an excessive diversion of water for any purpose is not a diversion for beneficial use. Water of Morris Creek which is presently wasted becomes excess water

a. Eds.—The California constitutional provision, which has been renumbered as Article X, § 2, provides that the "right to water or to the use or flow of water in or from any natural stream or water course ... is and shall be limited to such water as shall be reasonably required for the beneficial use to be served, and such right does not and shall not extend to the waste or unreasonable use or unreasonable method of use or unreasonable method of diversion of water."

available for appropriation. (See Water Code, §§ 1201, 1202, 1241; Stevinson Water Dist. v. Roduner, 36 Cal. 2d 264, 270 [223 P.2d 209]; Meridian, Ltd. v. San Francisco, 13 Cal. 2d 424, 445–446 [90 P.2d 537, 91 P.2d 105].) Another would-be appropriator may be willing to invest in a more efficient conveyance system in order to capture and use the water now lost en route....

Some enlightenment dehors the record turned up at oral argument. The attorneys were in apparent general agreement on the unrecorded circumstances; these circumstances do not affect our decision to reverse; their consideration may assist the trial court and parties. It appears that the 2½ miles of ditch traverses land under the jurisdiction of the United States Forest Service. Over the years leakage from the ditch has generated vegetation. The water and vegetation support a population of deer and quail. Plaintiffs sought permission to replace the ditch with a pipeline but the Forest Service declined for the sake of the animal and bird life. As we pointed out earlier, plaintiffs are under no legal compulsion to install a pipe. Defendants, on the other hand, are under some economic compulsion, for their ability to segregate a surplus flow available for appropriation may depend upon a physical means of preventing transmission loss. Defendants may be able and willing to work out a solution with the Forest Service. Whether the federal agency has any proprietary interest in the water leakage is outside the present scope of this lawsuit. If a three-way extrajudicial solution is impossible, a three-way lawsuit in an appropriate forum may be necessary to resolve the problem. As between the present parties, in any event, the trial court is obliged to fashion findings and a judgment consistent with the constitutional policy of water conservation.

Judgment reversed.

Notes & Questions

1. What is the holding of the court? The court states that an "excessive diversion of water for any purpose is not a diversion for beneficial use" and that excess water becomes "available for appropriation," but then concludes that "plaintiffs are under no legal compulsion to install a pipe" and suggests that the defendants must pay for a new diversion system if they want any water. If the plaintiffs' method of diversion was unreasonable, shouldn't they have lost the right to divert the water?

2. In 1903, the Nevada Supreme Court similarly said, "If waste by seepage and evaporation can be prevented ... by substituting improved methods of conveying water ... the desired improvement should be made at the expense of the subsequent [junior] appropriator who desires to utilize the water thereby to be saved." Tonkin v. Winzell, 73 P. 593, 595 (Nev. 1903). Why should the junior appropriator have to pay the water "waster"?

3. In *Erickson*, the California Court of Appeal does not resolve the question of whether the United States Forest Service has a "proprietary interest" in the water that is leaking from the plaintiffs' ditch and on

which local vegetation relies. Should anyone have a right to insist that water "waste" be continued? Does the vegetation suggest that the water seeping from the plaintiffs' earthen canal may not really be "wasted"?

4. Although the prior appropriation doctrine technically prohibits "wasteful" water use, courts have historically been reticent to order appropriators to reduce their water use except in the most egregious cases. Many courts look to community norms in determining whether particular water uses are unreasonable. If most farms use unlined ditches, courts hold that the use of unlined ditches is not unreasonable. See, e.g., McDonald v. Montana, 722 P.2d 598, 605–07 (Mont. 1986); A–B Cattle Co. v. United States, 589 P.2d 57, 69 (Colo. 1978). Although a few courts have become more aggressive in recent years, it is still extremely rare to find judicial decisions ordering conservation measures. See generally Steven J. Shupe, Waste in Western Water Law: A Blueprint for Change, 61 Or. L. Rev. 483 (1982).

5. **Water Markets.** The law does not generally worry about land being "wasted." Nuisance law limits land uses that may impact neighboring land, but there is no law that requires landowners to make "reasonable and beneficial" use of their land. Instead, the law generally relies on the market to ensure that land is not wasted. If a current landowner is not maximizing the economic value of her land, she can profit by selling it to someone who will—creating a compelling economic incentive to maximize the land's economic value. Why shouldn't the law similarly rely on the market to encourage water conservation? Rather than resorting to a lawsuit, couldn't the defendants in *Erickson* simply have paid the plaintiffs to conserve water?

For years, many western states prohibited the purchase and sale of appropriation rights. The prohibitions grew in part from fears that water markets would encourage people to appropriate more water than they needed so that they could sell it. Some policymakers also objected that water markets would permit individuals to profit from a free public resource and could lead to water monopolies. As an early opponent of water markets wrote at the start of the twentieth century:

> If water is to be bartered and sold, then the public should not give streams away, but should auction them off to the highest bidder.... The doctrine that air, water, and sunshine are gifts from God should not be lightly set aside even in arid lands.... The growth and danger of monopolies in oil, copper, coal, and iron afford a warning of the greater danger of permitting monopolies in water....
>
> In monarchies streams belong to the crown, and in the early history of irrigation in Italy and other parts of Europe, favorites of the rulers were rewarded with grants of streams. But in a republic they belong to the people, and ought forever to be kept as public property for the benefit of all who use them, and for them alone, such use to be under public supervision and control.

Elwood Mead, Irrigation Institutions 264 & 365–66 (1903).

Today all western states permit appropriation rights to be traded to at least some degree. But various legal constraints still make water transfers difficult. An intense debate, moreover, still rages over water markets. Rural communities, in particular, fear that unrestricted water markets would permit large cities to buy up all the water from their area and "dry up" their communities.

For more on water markets and the controversies surrounding them, see Barton H. Thompson, Jr., Water Markets & the Problem of Shifting Paradigms, in Water Marketing: The Next Generation (1997); Eric T. Freyfogle, Water Rights and the Common Wealth, 26 Envtl. L. 27 (1996); Barton H. Thompson, Jr., Institutional Perspectives on Water Policy and Markets, 81 Calif. L. Rev. 671 (1993).

National Audubon Society v. Superior Court

Supreme Court of California, 1983.
658 P.2d 709.

BROUSSARD, JUSTICE

Mono Lake, the second largest lake in California, sits at the base of the Sierra Nevada escarpment near the eastern entrance to Yosemite National Park. The lake is saline; it contains no fish but supports a large population of brine shrimp which feed vast numbers of nesting and migratory birds. Islands in the lake protect a large breeding colony of California gulls, and the lake itself serves as a haven on the migration route for thousands of Northern Phalarope, Wilson's Phalarope, and Eared Grebe. Towers and spires of tufa on the north and south shores are matters of geological interest and a tourist attraction.

Although Mono Lake receives some water from rain and snow on the lake surface, historically most of its supply came from snowmelt in the Sierra Nevada. Five freshwater streams—Mill, Lee Vining, Walker, Parker and Rush Creeks—arise near the crest of the range and carry the annual runoff to the west shore of the lake. In 1940, however, the Division of Water Resources, the predecessor to the present California Water Resources Board, granted the Department of Water and Power of the City of Los Angeles (hereafter DWP) a permit to appropriate virtually the entire flow of four of the five streams flowing into the lake. DWP promptly constructed facilities to divert about half the flow of these streams into DWP's Owens Valley aqueduct. In 1970 DWP completed a second diversion tunnel, and since that time has taken virtually the entire flow of these streams.

As a result of these diversions, the level of the lake has dropped; the surface area has diminished by one-third; one of the two principal islands in the lake has become a peninsula, exposing the gull rookery there to coyotes and other predators and causing the gulls to abandon the former island. The ultimate effect of continued diversions is a matter of intense dispute, but there seems little doubt that both the scenic beauty and the ecological values of Mono Lake are imperiled.

Plaintiffs filed suit in superior court to enjoin the DWP diversions on the theory that the shores, bed and waters of Mono Lake are protected by a public trust....

This case brings together for the first time two systems of legal thought: the appropriative water rights system which since the days of the gold rush has dominated California water law, and the public trust doctrine which, after evolving as a shield for the protection of tidelands, now extends its protective scope to navigable lakes. Ever since we first recognized that the public trust protects environmental and recreational values (Marks v. Whitney (1971) 6 Cal. 3d 251 [98 Cal. Rptr. 790, 491 P.2d 374]), the two systems of legal thought have been on a collision course. They meet in a unique and dramatic setting which highlights the clash of values. Mono Lake is a scenic and ecological treasure of national significance, imperiled by continued diversions of water; yet, the need of Los Angeles for water is apparent, its reliance on rights granted by the board evident, the cost of curtailing diversions substantial....

1. Background and history of the Mono Lake litigation.

[In 1940, DWP applied to the California Water Board] for permits to appropriate the waters of the four tributaries. At hearings before the board, various interested individuals protested that the city's proposed appropriations would lower the surface level of Mono Lake and thereby impair its commercial, recreational and scenic uses.

The board's primary authority to reject that application lay in a 1921 amendment to the Water Commission Act of 1913, which authorized the board to reject an application "when in its judgment the proposed appropriation would not best conserve the public interest." (Stats. 1921, ch. 329, § 1, p. 443, now codified as Water Code, § 1255.) The 1921 enactment, however, also "declared to be the established policy of this state that the use of water for domestic purposes is the highest use of water" (id., now codified as Water Code, § 1254), and directed the Water Board to be guided by this declaration of policy. Since DWP sought water for domestic use, the board concluded that it had to grant the application notwithstanding the harm to public trust uses of Mono Lake....

As noted above, Mono Lake has no outlets. The lake loses water only by evaporation and seepage. Natural salts do not evaporate with water, but are left behind. Prior to commencement of the DWP diversions, this naturally rising salinity was balanced by a constant and substantial supply of fresh water from the tributaries. Now, however, DWP diverts most of the fresh water inflow. The resultant imbalance between inflow and outflow not only diminishes the lake's size, but also drastically increases its salinity.

Plaintiffs predict that the lake's steadily increasing salinity, if unchecked, will wreck havoc throughout the local food chain. They contend that the lake's algae, and the brine shrimp and brine flies that feed on it, cannot survive the projected salinity increase. To support this assertion, plaintiffs point to a 50 percent reduction in the shrimp hatch for the spring of 1980 and a startling 95 percent reduction for the spring of 1981. These reductions affirm experimental evidence indicating that brine shrimp populations diminish as the salinity of the water surrounding them increases. DWP admits these substantial reductions, but blames them on factors other than salinity.

DWP's diversions also present several threats to the millions of local and migratory birds using the lake. First, since many species of birds feed on the lake's brine shrimp, any reduction in shrimp population allegedly caused by rising salinity endangers a major avian food source. The report of the Interagency Task Force on Mono Lake considered it "unlikely that any of Mono Lake's major bird species . . . will persist at the lake if populations of invertebrates disappear." (Cal. Dept. Water Resources, Report of the Interagency Task Force on Mono Lake (Dec. 1969), p. 20.) Second, the increasing salinity makes it more difficult for the birds to maintain osmotic equilibrium with their environment.

The California gull is especially endangered, both by the increase in salinity and by loss of nesting sites. Ninety-five percent of this state's gull population and 25 percent of the total species population nests at the lake. (Task Force Report at p. 21.) Most of the gulls nest on islands in the lake. As the lake recedes, land between the shore and some of the islands has been exposed, offering such predators as the coyote easy access to the gull nests and chicks. In 1979, coyotes reached Negrit Island, once the most popular nesting site, and the number of gull nests at the lake declined sharply. In 1981, 95 percent of the hatched chicks did not survive to maturity. Plaintiffs blame this decline and alarming mortality rate on the predator access created by the land bridges; DWP suggests numerous other causes, such as increased ambient temperatures and human activities, and claims that the joining of some islands with the mainland is offset by the emergence of new islands due to the lake's recession.

Plaintiffs allege that DWP's diversions adversely affect the human species and its activities as well. First, as the lake recedes, it has exposed more than 18,000 acres of lake bed composed of very fine silt which, once dry, easily becomes airborne in winds. This silt contains a high concentration of alkali and other minerals that irritate the mucous membranes and respiratory systems of humans and other animals. While the precise extent of this threat to the public health has yet to be determined, such threat as exists can be expected to increase with the exposure of additional lake bed. DWP, however, claims that its diversions neither affect the air quality in Mono Basin nor present a hazard to human health.

Furthermore, the lake's recession obviously diminishes its value as an economic, recreational, and scenic resource. Of course, there will be less lake to use and enjoy. The declining shrimp hatch depresses a local shrimping industry. The rings of dry lake bed are difficult to traverse on foot, and thus impair human access to the lake, and reduce the lake's substantial scenic value. Mono Lake has long been treasured as a unique scenic, recreational and scientific resource, but continued diversions threaten to turn it into a desert wasteland....

To abate this destruction, plaintiffs filed suit for injunctive and declaratory relief in the Superior Court for Mono County on May 21, 1979....

2. The Public Trust Doctrine in California.

. . .

Early English decisions generally assumed the public trust was limited to tidal waters and the lands exposed and covered by the daily tides; many American decisions, including the leading California cases, also concern tidelands. It is, however, well settled in the United States generally and in California that the public trust is not limited by the reach of the tides, but encompasses all navigable lakes and streams.

This question was considered in two venerable California decisions. The first, People v. Gold Run D. & M. Co. (1884) 66 Cal. 138 [4 P. 1152], is one of the epochal decisions of California history, a signpost which marked the transition from a mining economy to one predominately commercial and agricultural. The Gold Run Ditch and Mining Company and other mining operators used huge water cannons to wash gold-bearing gravel from hillsides; in the process they dumped 600,000 cubic yards of sand and gravel annually into the north fork of the American River. The debris, washed downstream, raised the beds of the American and Sacramento Rivers, impairing navigation, polluting the waters, and creating the danger that in time of flood the rivers would turn from their channels and inundate nearby lands.

Although recognizing that its decision might destroy the remains of the state's gold mining industry, the court affirmed an injunction barring the dumping. The opinion stressed the harm to the navigability of the Sacramento River, "a great public highway, in which the people of the State have paramount and controlling rights." (P. 146.) Defendant's dumping, the court said, was "an unauthorized invasion of the rights of the public to its navigation." (P. 147.) Rejecting the argument that dumping was sanctioned by custom and legislative acquiescence, the opinion asserted that "the rights of the people in the navigable rivers of the State are paramount and controlling. The State holds the absolute right to all navigable waters and the soils under them.... The soil she holds as trustee of a public trust for the benefit of the people; and she may, by her legislature, grant it to an individual; but she cannot grant the rights of the people to the use of the navigable waters flowing over it...." (Pp. 151–152.)

In the second decision, People v. Russ (1901) 132 Cal. 102 [64 P. 111], the defendant erected dams on sloughs which adjoined a navigable river. Finding the sloughs nonnavigable, the trial court gave judgment for defendant. We reversed, directing the trial court to make a finding as to the effect of the dams on the navigability of the river. "Directly diverting waters in material quantities from a navigable stream may be enjoined as a public nuisance. Neither may the waters of a navigable stream be diverted in substantial quantities by drawing from its tributaries.... If the dams upon these sloughs result in the obstruction of Salt River as a navigable stream, they constitute a public nuisance." (P. 106.)

DWP points out that the *Gold Run* decision did not involve diversion of water, and that in *Russ* there had been no finding of impairment to navigation. But the principles recognized by those decisions apply fully to a case in which diversions from a nonnavigable tributary impair the public trust in a downstream river or lake. "If the public trust doctrine applies to constrain fills which destroy navigation and other public trust uses in navigable waters, it should equally apply to constrain the extraction of water that destroys navigation and other public interests. Both actions result in the same damage to the public interest." (Johnson, Public Trust Protection for Stream Flows and Lake Levels (1980) 14 U.C. Davis L. Rev. 233, 257–258; see Dunning, The Significance of California's Public Trust Easement for California Water Rights Law (1980) 14 U.C. Davis L. Rev. 357, 359–360.)

We conclude that the public trust doctrine, as recognized and developed in California decisions, protects navigable waters from harm caused by diversion of nonnavigable tributaries. . . .

4. The relationship between the Public Trust Doctrine and the California Water Rights System.

As we have seen, the public trust doctrine and the appropriative water rights system administered by the Water Board developed independently of each other. Each developed comprehensive rules and principles which, if applied to the full extent of their scope, would occupy the field of allocation of stream waters to the exclusion of any competing system of legal thought. Plaintiffs, for example, argue that the public trust is antecedent to and thus limits all appropriative water rights, an argument which implies that most appropriative water rights in California were acquired and are presently being used unlawfully. Defendant DWP, on the other hand, argues that the public trust doctrine as to stream waters has been "subsumed" into the appropriative water rights system and, absorbed by that body of law, quietly disappeared; according to DWP, the recipient of a board license enjoys a vested right in perpetuity to take water without concern for the consequences to the trust.

We are unable to accept either position. In our opinion, both the public trust doctrine and the water rights system embody important precepts which make the law more responsive to the diverse needs and interests involved in the planning and allocation of water resources. To embrace one system of thought and reject the other would lead to an unbalanced structure, one which would either decry as a breach of trust appropriations essential to the economic development of this state, or deny any duty to protect or even consider the values promoted by the public trust. Therefore, seeking an accommodation which will make use of the pertinent principles of both the public trust doctrine and the appropriative water rights system, and drawing upon the history of the public trust and the water rights system, the body of judicial precedent, and the views of expert commentators, we reach the following conclusions:

a. The state as sovereign retains continuing supervisory control over its navigable waters and the lands beneath those waters. This principle, fundamental to the concept of the public trust, applies to rights in flowing waters as well as to rights in tidelands and lakeshores; it prevents any party from acquiring a vested right to appropriate water in a manner harmful to the interests protected by the public trust.

b. As a matter of current and historical necessity, the Legislature, acting directly or through an authorized agency such as the Water Board, has the power to grant usufructuary licenses that will permit an appropriator to take water from flowing streams and use that water in a distant part of the state, even though this taking does not promote, and may unavoidably harm, the trust uses at the source stream. The population and economy of this state depend upon the appropriation of vast quantities of water for uses unrelated to in-stream trust values.[26] California's Constitution (see art. X, § 2), its statutes (see Water Code, §§ 100, 104), decisions (see, e.g., Waterford Irrigation Dist. v. Turlock Irrigation Dist. (1920) 50 Cal. App. 213, 220 [194 P. 757]), and commentators (e.g., Hutchins, The Cal. Law of Water Rights, p. 11) all emphasize the need to make efficient use of California's limited water resources: all recognize, at least implicitly, that efficient use requires diverting water from in-stream uses. Now that the economy and population centers of this state have developed in reliance upon appropriated water, it would be disingenuous to hold that such appropriations are and have always been improper to the extent that they harm public trust uses, and can be justified only upon theories of reliance or estoppel.

c. The state has an affirmative duty to take the public trust into account in the planning and allocation of water resources, and to protect public trust uses whenever feasible. Just as the history of this state shows that appropriation may be necessary for efficient use of water despite unavoidable harm to public trust values, it demonstrates that an appropriative water rights system administered without consideration of the public trust may cause unnecessary and unjustified harm to trust interests. As a matter of practical necessity the state may have to approve appropriations despite foreseeable harm to public trust uses. In so doing, however, the state must bear in mind its duty as trustee to consider the effect of the taking on the public trust, and to preserve, so far as consistent with the public interest, the uses protected by the trust.

Once the state has approved an appropriation, the public trust imposes a duty of continuing supervision over the taking and use of the appropriated water. In exercising its sovereign power to allocate water resources in the public interest, the state is not confined by past allocation decisions which may be incorrect in light of current knowledge or inconsistent with current needs.

26. In contrast, the population and economy of this state does not depend on the conveyance of vast expanses of tidelands or other property underlying navigable waters....

The state accordingly has the power to reconsider allocation decisions even though those decisions were made after due consideration of their effect on the public trust. The case for reconsidering a particular decision, however, is even stronger when that decision failed to weigh and consider public trust uses. In the case before us, the salient fact is that no responsible body has ever determined the impact of diverting the entire flow of the Mono Lake tributaries into the Los Angeles Aqueduct. This is not a case in which the Legislature, the Water Board, or any judicial body has determined that the needs of Los Angeles outweigh the needs of the Mono Basin, that the benefit gained is worth the price. Neither has any responsible body determined whether some lesser taking would better balance the diverse interests. Instead, DWP acquired rights to the entire flow in 1940 from a water board which believed it lacked both the power and the duty to protect the Mono Lake environment, and continues to exercise those rights in apparent disregard for the resulting damage to the scenery, ecology, and human uses of Mono Lake. . . .

It is clear that some responsible body ought to reconsider the allocation of the waters of the Mono Basin. No vested rights bar such reconsideration. We recognize the substantial concerns voiced by Los Angeles—the city's need for water, its reliance upon the 1940 board decision, the cost both in terms of money and environmental impact of obtaining water elsewhere. Such concerns must enter into any allocation decision. We hold only that they do not preclude a reconsideration and reallocation which also takes into account the impact of water diversion on the Mono Lake environment. . . .

Notes & Questions

1. The bottom line of *National Audubon* is that the public trust doctrine must be balanced against the value of water diversions in deciding whether water can be appropriated from California rivers and lakes. However, no such balance is employed in deciding whether the state can grant private parties the right to own and use *lands* invested with the public trust. See Illinois Central Railroad Co. v. Illinois, supra, p. 43; Marks v. Whitney, 491 P.2d 374 (Cal. 1971) (holding that the owner of tidelands cannot fill and develop them). Why should land be more constrained than water? Does it reflect a concern that, because all navigable waters are subject to the public trust, strict application of the trust in the water context might bring western economies to a halt? By contrast, only some land is subject to the public trust, so a strict application to land may have less of an economic impact.

2. Other states generally have not followed California's lead in using the public trust doctrine to limit diversions of surface water. In a case predating *National Audubon*, however, the North Dakota Supreme Court held that the public trust doctrine requires state officials deciding whether to issue a *new* appropriation permit to determine, at a minimum, "the potential effect of the allocation of water on the present water supply and

future water needs" of the state. United Plainsmen Ass'n v. North Dakota State Water Conservation Comm'n, 247 N.W.2d 457 (N.D. 1976). The Hawaii Supreme Court has not only agreed that the public trust doctrine protects water resources, but has extended the trust to all water (including non-navigable waterways and groundwater) and ruled that the state must apply the "precautionary principle" in protecting water resources. In re Water Use Permit Applications for the Waiahole Ditch, 9 P.3d 409 (Haw. 2000). According to the court, the state need not "wait for full scientific certainty in fulfilling its duty toward the public interest in minimum instream flows." Id. at 467.

3. Are diversions that harm fish or wildlife "reasonable and beneficial"? Would this have been a better legal basis for the California Supreme Court's decision in *National Audubon*?

4. Could Los Angeles' diversions have been challenged as a public nuisance? (See the earlier discussion of public nuisance at pages 145–151.) How does the public trust balance required by *National Audubon* differ from the Restatement's balancing test for nuisances, discussed supra at page 134? Why might an environmental organization like the National Audubon Society prefer suing under the public trust doctrine rather than public nuisance law?

5. Environmental groups have also successfully used federal and state environmental laws to restrict diversions that threaten fish or other wildlife dependent on instream flows. See, e.g., James City County v. Environmental Protection Agency, 12 F.3d 1330 (4th Cir. 1993) (upholding EPA's veto of a permit that the county had to obtain under section 404 of the Clean Water Act to construct a dam and reservoir across Ware Creek); United States v. Glenn–Colusa Irrigation District, 788 F. Supp. 1126 (E.D. Cal. 1992) (finding that pumping of water from the Sacramento River violated the federal Endangered Species Act); United States v. State Water Resources Control Board, 227 Cal. Rptr. 161 (Cal. App. 1986) (holding that the state board could restrict diversions to meet water quality laws).

6. For more on the public trust doctrine's relevance to water rights, see Michael Blumm & Thea Schwartz, Mono Lake and the Evolving Public Trust in Western Water, 37 Ariz. L. Rev. 701 (1995); Symposium: The Public Trust and the Waters of the American West: Yesterday, Today and Tomorrow, 19 Envtl. L. 425 (1989); Harrison Dunning, The Significance of California's Public Trust Easement for California's Water Rights, 14 U.S.C. L. Rev. 357 (1980).

2. GROUNDWATER

States vary considerably in how they allocate groundwater. Originally, most states allocated groundwater under a rule of capture known as *absolute ownership*. Under the absolute ownership rule, everyone overlying an aquifer is entitled to pump as much water as they want from wells on their property—creating exactly the type of tragedy of the commons that one would expect. The quantity of groundwater in an aquifer consists of both *annual recharge* (the quantity of water which seeps into the aquifer each year from overlying precipitation or waterways) and *fossil water* (the quantity of water that has found its way into the aquifer over thousands of years without being withdrawn). Groundwater pumpers can withdraw the annual recharge each year without draining or "overdrafting" the aquifer. Under a rule of capture, however, groundwater users have no incentive to limit themselves to the annual recharge and often extract the depletable fossil water.

Such *groundwater overdrafting* generates severe problems. First, the fossil water will ultimately run out, forcing overlying owners to either find alternative supplies or dramatically reduce their water use. Second, groundwater overdrafting lowers the water table, forcing overlying owners to pump the groundwater from greater depths, using more energy and costing more money. As the water table drops below root bottoms, plants on the surface can also die. Third, if an aquifer consists of poorly consolidated materials (like sand or gravel), overlying land can subside. As a result of groundwater overdrafting, the Shipping Channel area of Houston, Texas dropped six inches per year in the late 1960s and early 1970s, resulting in millions of dollars in property damage. Finally, falling pressure in the aquifer can lead to destructive groundwater contamination. Overdrafting of coastal aquifers, for example, often pulls salt water into the aquifer from the ocean, destroying the usefulness of the aquifer.

Given the problems of an absolute ownership rule, most states have moved to a *reasonable use rule* under which landowners can pump as much water as they want from wells on their property, but only for a "reasonable use" and only for use on land overlying the aquifer. Although the reasonable use rule does not prohibit groundwater overdrafting, the rule reduces the amount of water that is likely to be taken from an aquifer.

A growing number of states now limit the total amount of water that can be withdrawn from many aquifers to the aquifers' annual recharge. Many western states allocate the annual recharge among competing pumpers through the same *prior appropriation system* that they use for surface water. Under the *correlative rights doctrine*, a number of other states apportion annual recharge by awarding each overlying landowner a reasonable and fair share of the recharge. The Restatement of Torts takes an ambiguous position on groundwater overdrafting; according to the Restatement, each overlying land is entitled to a "reasonable share of the annual supply *or* total store of ground water." Restatement (Second) of Torts § 858 (emphasis added).

As the 20th century came to a close, Texas was the only state that still followed the absolute ownership rule to resolve disputes among groundwater users.

Sipriano v. Great Spring Waters of America, Inc.

Supreme Court of Texas, 1999.
1 S.W.3d 75.

JUSTICE ENOCH delivered the opinion for a unanimous Court.

For over ninety years, this Court has adhered to the common-law rule of capture in allocating the respective rights and liabilities of neighboring landowners for use of groundwater flowing beneath their property. The rule of capture essentially allows, with some limited exceptions, a landowner to pump as much groundwater as the landowner chooses, without liability to neighbors who claim that the pumping has depleted their wells. We are asked today whether Texas should abandon this rule for the rule of reasonable use, which would limit the common-law right of a surface owner to take water from a common reservoir by imposing liability on landowners who "unreasonably" use groundwater to their neighbors' detriment. Relying on the settled rule of capture, the trial court granted summary judgment against landowners who sued a bottled-water company for negligently draining their water wells. The court of appeals affirmed. Because we conclude that the sweeping change to Texas's groundwater law Sipriano urges this Court to make is not appropriate at this time, we affirm the court of appeals' judgment.

Henderson County landowners Bart Sipriano, Harold Fain, and Doris Fain (Sipriano) sued Great Spring Waters of America, Inc., a/k/a Ozarka Natural Spring Water Co., for negligently draining their water wells. According to Sipriano's allegations, which we take as true for summary judgment purposes, Ozarka, in 1996, began pumping about 90,000 gallons of groundwater per day, seven days a week, from land near Sipriano's. Soon after the pumping began, Sipriano's wells were severely depleted. Sipriano sought injunctive relief, as well as actual and punitive damages for Ozarka's alleged nuisance, negligence, gross negligence, and malice. . . .

This Court adopted the common-law rule of capture in 1904 in *Houston & Texas Central Railway Co. v. East.*[4] The rule of capture answers the question of what remedies, if any, a neighbor has against a landowner based on the landowner's use of the water under the landowner's land. Essentially, the rule provides that, absent malice or willful waste, landowners have the right to take all the water they can capture under their land and do with it what they please, and they will not be liable to neighbors even if in so doing they deprive their neighbors of the water's use. Rooted in English common law, the rule of capture was perhaps first enunciated in 1843 in Acton v. Blundell:

> That person who owns the surface may dig therein, and apply all that is there found to his own purposes at his free will and pleasure; and that if, in the exercise of such right, he intercepts or drains off the water collected from underground springs in his neighbor's well, this inconvenience to his neighbor falls within the description *damnum absque injuria* [an injury without a remedy] which cannot become the ground of an action.[6]

In *East*, this Court faced a choice between the rule of capture and its counterpart, the rule of reasonable use. No constitutional or statutory

4. 81 S.W. 279 (Tex. 1904).

6. 152 Eng. Rep. 1223, 1235 (Ex. Ch. 1843), quoted in *East*, 81 S.W. at 280.

considerations guided or constrained our selection at that time. Articulating two public-policy reasons, we chose the rule of capture. First, we noted that the movement of groundwater is "so secret, occult, and concealed that an attempt to administer any set of legal rules in respect to [it] would be involved in hopeless uncertainty, and would, therefore, be practically impossible."[8] And second, we determined that "any ... recognition of correlative rights would interfere, to the material detriment of the commonwealth, with drainage and agriculture, mining, the construction of highways and railroads, with sanitary regulations, building, and the general progress of improvement in works of embellishment and utility."[9] Thus, we refused to recognize tort liability against a railroad company whose pumping of groundwater under its own property allegedly dried the neighboring plaintiff's well.

After droughts in 1910 and 1917, the citizens of Texas voted in August 1917 to enact section 59 of article 16 of the Texas Constitution, which placed the duty to preserve Texas's natural resources on the State: "The conservation and development of all of the natural resources of this State ... and the preservation and conservation of all such natural resources of the State are each and all hereby declared public rights and duties; and the Legislature shall pass all such laws as may be appropriate thereto."[12] This constitutional amendment, proposed and passed after our common-law decision in *East*, made clear that in Texas, responsibility for the regulation of natural resources, including groundwater, rests in the hands of the Legislature.

By 1955, this Court recognized that what was "secret [and] occult" to us in 1904—the movement of groundwater—was no longer so.[13] But in *City of Corpus Christi v. City of Pleasanton* we continued to adhere to the rule of capture.[14] ....

In 1978, in *Friendswood Development Co. v. Smith–Southwest Industries, Inc.*,[21] we were again invited to abandon the rule of capture and adopt the rule of reasonable use. Again, we declined. But ... we recognized that the rule of capture is not without exception. Specifically, we "agreed that some aspects of the ... common law rule as to underground waters are harsh and outmoded, and [that] the rule had been severely criticized since its reaffirmation by this Court in 1955."[22] Thus, we used *Friendswood* to "discard an objectionable aspect of the court-made ... rule [of capture] as it relates to subsidence."[23] Specifically, we recognized an exception to the rule for a landowner's negligence that proximately causes the subsidence of another's land.

8. *East*, 81 S.W. at 281 (quoting Frazier v. Brown, 12 Ohio St. 294, 311 (1861)).

9. Id. (quoting *Frazier*, 12 Ohio. St. at 311).

12. Tex. Const. art. XVI, § 59(a).

13. See *City of Corpus Christi*, 276 S.W.2d at 805–06 (Wilson, J., dissenting).

14. See 276 S.W.2d at 801.

21. 576 S.W.2d 21.

22. 576 S.W.2d at 28–29.

23. Id. at 30.

Now, Sipriano asks us to fundamentally alter the common-law framework within which Texas has operated since the 1904 *East* decision. That common-law framework existed in 1917 when the citizens of Texas charged the Legislature with the constitutional duty to preserve groundwater through regulation. It persisted through our decisions in *City of Corpus Christi* in 1955 and *Friendswood* in 1978.... Like the voters who passed the 1917 constitutional amendment, this Court has consistently recognized "the need for legislative regulation of water."[29] Today, again, we reiterate that the people have constitutionally empowered the Legislature to act in the best interest of the State to preserve our natural resources, including water. We see no reason, particularly because of the 1917 constitutional amendment, for the Legislature to feel constrained from taking appropriate steps to protect groundwater....

With the allocation of responsibility for groundwater regulation contemplated by the 1917 amendment in mind, it is important that this case comes to us on the heels of Senate Bill 1,[31] which has been described as a "comprehensive water management bill."[32] Passed in June 1997, Senate Bill 1 revamped significant parts of the Water Code and other Texas statutes in an attempt to improve on this State's water management. Perhaps most relevant to our decision today is the Legislature's efforts to streamline the process for creating groundwater conservation districts and to make them more effective in the water management process. Indeed, the Legislature expressly stated that "groundwater conservation districts ... are the state's preferred method of groundwater management."[33]

The Legislature first exercised its constitutional authority to create groundwater conservation districts in 1949. And since then the Legislature has repeatedly revisited and modified the operation of groundwater conservation districts. Now, with Senate Bill 1, the Legislature has given more authority to locally-controlled groundwater conservation districts for establishing requirements for groundwater withdrawal permits and for regulating water transferred outside the district. Senate Bill 1 also revised the "critical area" designation process to require the Texas Natural Resource Conservation Commission and the Texas Water Development Board to identify areas anticipated to experience critical groundwater problems, and streamlined the process by which the TNRCC or the Legislature can create a district in these areas. Senate Bill 1 also included various provisions calling for more comprehensive and coordinated water planning. While the efficacy of the groundwater management methods the Legislature chose and implemented through Senate Bill 1 has been a matter of considerable debate, as the amicus briefs filed in this case reflect, we cannot say at this

29. Barshop v. Medina County Underground Water Conservation Dist., 925 S.W.2d 618, 626 (1996); see also *Friendswood*, 576 S.W.2d at 30; *City of Corpus Christi*, 276 S.W.2d at 803.

31. See Senate Bill 1, Act of June 1, 1997, 75th leg., R.S., ch. 1010, 1997 Tex. Gen. Laws 3610.

32. Senator J.E. "Buster" Brown, Senate Bill 1: We've Never Changed Texas Water Law This Way Before, 28 St. B. Tex. Envtl. L.J. 152, 153 (1998).

33. Tex. Water Code § 36.0015.

time that the Legislature has ignored its constitutional charge to regulate this natural resource.

By constitutional amendment, Texas voters made groundwater regulation a duty of the Legislature. And by Senate Bill 1, the Legislature has chosen a process that permits the people most affected by groundwater regulation in particular areas to participate in democratic solutions to their groundwater issues. It would be improper for courts to intercede at this time by changing the common-law framework within which the Legislature has attempted to craft regulations to meet this state's groundwater-conservation needs. Given the Legislature's recent actions to improve Texas's groundwater management, we are reluctant to make so drastic a change as abandoning our rule of capture and moving into the arena of water-use regulation by judicial fiat. It is more prudent to wait and see if Senate Bill 1 will have its desired effect, and to save for another day the determination of whether further revising the common law is an appropriate prerequisite to preserve Texas's natural resources and protect property owners' interests.

We do not shy away from change when it is appropriate. We continue to believe that "the genius of the common law rests in its ability to change, to recognize when a timeworn rule no longer serves the needs of society, and to modify the rule accordingly."[43] And Sipriano presents compelling reasons for groundwater use to be regulated. But unlike in *East*, any modification of the common law would have to be guided and constrained by constitutional and statutory considerations. Given the Legislature's recent efforts to regulate groundwater, we are not persuaded that it is appropriate today for this Court to insert itself into the regulatory mix by substituting the rule of reasonable use for the current rule of capture. Accordingly, we affirm the court of appeals' judgment.

JUSTICE HECHT, joined by JUSTICE O'NEILL, concurring.

The people of Texas have given the Legislature, in article XVI, section 59 of the Texas Constitution, not only the power but the duty to "pass all such laws as may be appropriate" for the conservation, development, and preservation of the State's natural resources, including its groundwater. The Legislature has concluded that local "groundwater conservation districts ... are the state's preferred method of groundwater management."[2] Actually, such districts are not just the preferred method of groundwater management, they are the only method presently available. Yet in the fifty years since the Legislature first authorized the creation of groundwater conservation districts, the record in this case shows that only some forty-two such districts have been created, covering a small fraction of the State. Not much groundwater management is going on.

The reason is not lack of groundwater. Twenty-nine aquifers underlie eighty-one percent of the State. Nor is the reason lack of use. In 1992, groundwater sources supplied fifty-six percent of all water used in the

43. Gutierrez v. Collins, 583 S.W.2d 312, 317 (Tex. 1979).

2. Tex. Water Code § 36.0015.

State, including sixty-nine percent of agricultural needs and forty-one percent of municipal needs. Nor is the reason lack of need of management. Over twenty-five years ago the Texas Senate's Interim Committee on Environmental Affairs warned of severe, impending problems with municipal groundwater use and called for comprehensive regulation. The predicted problems have in fact occurred. The comprehensive revision of the Water Code in 1997 was motivated by what the Lieutenant Governor's general counsel has called "the seriousness of the situation": recurring droughts, expansive population growth, and dwindling water supplies.

What really hampers groundwater management is the established alternative, the common law rule of capture, which entitles a landowner to withdraw an unlimited amount of groundwater for any purpose other than willful waste or malice, and as long as he is not negligent in causing subsidence of nearby property. When this Court adopted the rule of capture as a common-law rule ninety-five years ago in *Houston & Texas Central Railway Co. v. East*, we believed it to have been adopted in England and by the court of last resort in every state in this country except New Hampshire. Thirty-five years later only eleven of the eighteen western states still followed the rule of capture; after two more decades, only three western states still followed the rule. Now there is but one lone holdout: Texas....

Neither respondent nor any of the more than a dozen *amici curiae* who have appeared in support of respondent's position attempt a principled argument for retaining the rule of capture. They focus instead on pragmatics. First, they say, the rule should not be abandoned because it has been the rule for a long time. The oft-cited wisdom of Justice Holmes is sufficient to rebut this argument: "It is revolting to have no better reason for a rule of law than that so it was laid down in the time of Henry IV. It is still more revolting if the grounds upon which it was laid down have vanished long since, and the rule simply persists from blind imitation of the past."[3]

Second, respondent and its supporters argue that abandoning the rule of capture would be disruptive. To some extent they are right, of course, but the cost of such disruption must be balanced against the danger that the State's water supply will be threatened because of a lack of reasoned water planning. Studies on the subject seem rather uniformly to indicate that the balance tilts against the rule of capture. Finally, respondent argues that water regulation is the Legislature's responsibility under the Constitution, and that the Court should not venture into the area. I agree that this argument has merit, at least since 1917 when article XVI, section 59 was adopted, but it comes ninety-five years too late: the Court entered the area of water regulation in *East* when it adopted the rule of capture. Does the Court intrude on the Legislature's constitutional responsibility and duty by maintaining the rule of capture or by abandoning it? It is hard to see how maintaining the rule of capture can be justified as deference to the

3. Oliver Wendell Holmes, Jr., The Path of the Law, 10 Harv. L. Rev. 457, 469 (1897).

Legislature's constitutional province when the rule is contrary to the local regulation that is the Legislature's "preferred method of groundwater management."

Dissenting in *City of Corpus Christi v. City of Pleasanton*, Justice Will Wilson cautioned in 1955 that this Court would not forever use deference to the Legislature to justify maintaining the rule of capture in the face of changing circumstances. After all, even if the Court abandoned the rule of capture as part of the common law, the Legislature could adopt the rule by statute—although given its stated regulatory preference, presumably it would not do so. Petitioners make a strong case for replacing the rule of capture with the beneficial purpose doctrine set out in section 858 of the Restatement (Second) of Torts.[a] ... While neither section 858 nor any other common law rule of water regulation is preferable to almost any effective legislative solution, absent such a solution, section 858 is preferable to the rule of capture.

Nevertheless, I am persuaded for the time being that the extensive statutory changes in 1997, together with the increasing demands on the State's water supply, may result before long in a fair, effective, and comprehensive regulation of water use that will make the rule of capture obsolete. I agree with the Court that it would be inappropriate to disrupt the processes created and encouraged by the 1997 legislation before they have had a chance to work. I concur in the view that, for now—but I think only for now—*East* should not be overruled.

Notes & Questions

1. *Sipriano* raises institutional questions of repeated importance in the law. What is the relative competence of courts and legislatures in addressing social questions? When should courts act to try to resolve a social problem, and when should they defer to the legislature? How would you answer these questions in the groundwater context?

All the members of the Texas Supreme Court appear to have doubts about the continuing wisdom of the rule of capture, so why should the court wait to modify the rule? If the court had abandoned the rule of capture in favor, for example, of a reasonable use rule, how could that have interfered with legislative actions to encourage the formation of groundwater conservation districts or pursue other groundwater controls? By retaining the rule of capture, might the Texas Supreme Court actually have made it more difficult to solve groundwater problems? If the Texas legislature threatens to restrict groundwater pumping, current and potential groundwater users are likely to argue (whether or not they can win the argument) that any restrictions would constitute an unconstitutional "taking" of their right to pump as much water as they want under the rule of capture. (See

a. Eds.—Section 858 of the Restatement provides that a landowner is liable to a neighbor if the landowner "unreasonably causes harm" to the neighbor by "lowering the water table or reducing artesian pressure" or by withdrawing more than the landowner's "reasonable share of the annual supply or total store of ground water."

the earlier discussion at pages 178–213 of the constitutional takings restrictions.) Such takings arguments often prove politically quite powerful. A reasonable use rule would weaken the takings argument because the state could argue that any pumping in excess of the regulated amount would be "unreasonable."

2. **Takings Challenges.** To date, takings challenges to legislative restrictions on groundwater extraction have proven singularly unsuccessful in court. In rejecting taking challenges, courts have frequently emphasized the limited nature of most common law groundwater rights and the importance to a state's welfare of husbanding its water resources. See, e.g., Bamford v. Upper Republican Natural Resources Dist., 512 N.W.2d 642 (Neb. 1994); Town of Chino Valley v. City of Prescott, 638 P.2d 1324 (Ariz. 1981); Village of Tequesta v. Jupiter Inlet Corp., 371 So. 2d 663 (Fla. 1979); Peterson v. Department of Ecology, 596 P.2d 285 (Wash. 1979). None of these challenges, however, arose in a state following a rule of capture. Professor Dan Tarlock, however, has suggested that the rule of capture, which permits one landowner to capture all of the groundwater from under a neighbor's property, does not provide a sufficient enough expectation in future groundwater extraction to provide the basis for a viable takings claim. Because each groundwater user's ability to extract groundwater is "subject to complete destruction by a more powerful overlying pumper," his "expectation of exclusive use of groundwater [is] close to illusory." A. Dan Tarlock, Law of Water Rights and Resources ¶ 4.09[1] (1986).

3. Legislatures nationwide have taken a growing interest in the problem of groundwater mining. Approaches have been as varied as the legislative imagination. Some states like Texas have authorized local groundwater users to form groundwater districts with broad powers to regulate and sometimes tax groundwater use. Other states have mandated that anyone wishing to pump groundwater, at least from aquifers that the states determine are in critical danger, must obtain a permit from a state or local agency with the authority to restrict groundwater extraction. Yet other states have imposed conservation measures on groundwater users. Legislative change, however, has been slow, and groundwater mining remains a serious problem in many parts of the United States.

For discussions of various states' approaches to groundwater extraction, see Jeffrey S. Ashley & Zachary C. Smith, Groundwater Management in the West (1999); Kevin L. Patrick & Kelly E. Archer, A Comparison of State Groundwater Laws, 30 Tulsa L.J. 123 (1994); Paula K. Smith, Coercion and Groundwater Management: Three Case Studies and a "Market" Approach, 16 Envtl. L. 797 (1986).

D. INTELLECTUAL PROPERTY

The United States Constitution grants Congress the power to protect writings and inventions in Article I, section 8, clause 8:

> The Congress shall have power . . . to promote the progress of science and useful arts, by securing for limited times to authors and inventors the exclusive right to their respective writings and discoveries.

Congress has exercised this power by enacting patent protection for useful inventions and copyright protection for maps, charts, and books. The history of patent protection has been related by the United States Supreme Court:

> Congress quickly responded to the bidding of the Constitution by enacting the Patent Act of 1790 during the second session of the First Congress. It created an agency in the Department of State headed by the Secretary of State, the Secretary of the Department of War and the Attorney General, any two of whom could issue a patent for a period not exceeding 14 years to any petitioner that "hath . . . invented or discovered any useful art, manufacture, . . . or device, or any improvement therein not before known or used" if the board found that "the invention or discovery (was) sufficiently useful and important. . . ." 1 Stat. 110. This group, whose members administered the patent system along with their other public duties, was known by its own designation as "Commissioners for the Promotion of Useful Arts."
>
> Thomas Jefferson, who as Secretary of State was a member of the group, was its moving spirit and might well be called the "first administrator of our patent system." He was not only an administrator of the patent system under the 1790 Act, but was also the author of the 1793 Patent Act. In addition, Jefferson was himself an inventor of great note. His unpatented improvements on plows, to mention but one line of his inventions, won acclaim and recognition on both sides of the Atlantic. Because of his active interest and influence in the early development of the patent system, Jefferson's views on the general nature of the limited patent monopoly under the Constitution, as well as his conclusions as to conditions for patentability under the statutory scheme, are worthy of note.
>
> Jefferson, like other Americans, had an instinctive aversion to monopolies. It was a monopoly on tea that sparked the Revolution and Jefferson certainly did not favor an equivalent form of monopoly under the new government. His abhorrence of monopoly extended initially to patents as well. From France, he wrote to Madison (July 1788) urging a Bill of Rights provision restricting monopoly, and as against the argument that limited monopoly might serve to incite "ingenuity," he argued forcefully that "the benefit even of limited monopolies is too doubtful to be opposed to that of their general suppression," V Writings of Thomas Jefferson, at 47 (Ford ed., 1895). His views ripened, however, and in another letter to Madison (Aug. 1789) after the drafting of the Bill

of Rights, Jefferson stated that he would have been pleased by an express provision in this form:

> "Art. 9. Monopolies may be allowed to persons for their own productions in literature, & their own inventions in the arts, for a term not exceeding—years, but for no longer term & no other purpose." Id. at 113.

. . .

Jefferson's philosophy on the nature and purpose of the patent monopoly is expressed in a letter to Isaac McPherson (Aug. 1813).... He rejected a natural-rights theory in intellectual property rights and clearly recognized the social and economic rationale of the patent system. The patent monopoly was not designed to secure to the inventor his natural right in his discoveries. Rather, it was a reward, an inducement, to bring forth new knowledge. The grant of an exclusive right to an invention was the creation of society—at odds with the inherent free nature of disclosed ideas—and was not to be freely given. Only inventions and discoveries which furthered human knowledge, and were new and useful, justified the special inducement of a limited private monopoly. Jefferson did not believe in granting patents for small details, obvious improvements, or frivolous devices. His writings evidence his insistence upon a high level of patentability.

Graham v. John Deere Co., 383 U.S. 1, 6–9 (1966).

Today's inventors submit applications for patents to the Patent and Trademark Office, rather than a cabinet-level Commission for the Promotion of Useful Arts. See Patent Act of 1952, 35 U.S.C. §§ 100 et seq. Patent examiners then review applications to decide whether they meet the four requirements for a patent: patentable subject matter, novelty, usefulness, and non-obviousness. In most cases, the last two requirements are the decisive ones—and the most difficult ones to define. If the applicant is granted a patent, he receives the exclusive right to make, use, and sell his invention for twenty years from the date of his application. At the end of twenty years, the invention passes into the public domain, available for all to make, use, and sell.

Congress protects literary and artistic works through the federal Copyright Act, 17 U.S.C. §§ 1 et seq. While the range of protected works is broad—from poetry to movies to computer programs—copyright protects only the author's expression of ideas, not the ideas themselves. The holder of a copyright receives a variety of exclusive rights in the copyrighted work for the life of the author plus 70 years (or, in the case of an institutional copyright holder, 95 years from the date of the work's publication). The exclusive rights include the rights to reproduce the work, to distribute copies to the public, and to prepare derivative works. Anyone, however, can make limited, "fair use" of the work; thus, for example, the author of a book review in *The New York Times* can quote short passages from the book without obtaining permission of the author. Unlike in the case of patents, the government does not require applications to be submitted and reviewed before granting them copyrights (although an author must register her work with the Copyright Office before suing for infringement).[1]

Creators of intellectual goods sometimes ask courts to use their common law powers to give "property" protection to plaintiffs' creations. One of the most famous cases involved a lawsuit in which one news service sought to stop another from poaching its reported news.

International News Service v. Associated Press

United States Supreme Court, 1918.
248 U.S. 215.

MR. JUSTICE PITNEY delivered the opinion of the court.

The parties are competitors in the gathering and distribution of news and its publication for profit in newspapers throughout the United States. The Associated Press, which was complainant in the District Court, is a cooperative organization, incorporated under the Membership Corporations Law of the State of New York, its members being individuals who are either proprietors or representatives of about 950 daily newspapers published in all parts of the United States.... Complainant gathers in all parts of the world, by means of various instrumentalities of its own, by exchange with its members, and by other appropriate means, news and intelligence of current and recent events of interest to newspaper readers and distributes it daily to its members for publication in their newspapers. The cost of the service, amounting approximately to $3,500,000 per annum, is assessed upon the members and becomes a part of their costs of operation, to be recouped, presumably with profit, through the publication of their several newspapers. Under complainant's by-laws each member agrees upon assuming membership that news received through complainant's service is received exclusively for publication in a particular newspaper, language, and place specified in the certificate of membership, that no other use of it shall be permitted, and that no member shall furnish or permit anyone in his employ or connected with his newspaper to furnish any of complainant's news in advance of publication to any person not a member. And each member is required to gather the local news of his district and supply it to the Associated Press and to no one else.

Defendant is a corporation organized under the laws of the State of New Jersey, whose business is the gathering and selling of news to its customers and clients, consisting of newspapers published throughout the United States, under contracts by which they pay certain amounts at stated times for defendant's service. It has wide-spread news-gathering agencies; the cost of its operations amounts, it is said, to more than $2,000,000 per annum; and it serves about 400 newspapers located in the various cities of

1. For more background on the patent and copyright systems, see Robert Meyer et al., Intellectual Property in the New Technology Age (1997); Paul Goldstein, Copyright's Highway: From Gutenberg to the Celestial Highway (rev. ed. 2003).

the United States and abroad, a few of which are represented, also, in the membership of the Associated Press.

The parties are in the keenest competition between themselves in the distribution of news throughout the United States; and so, as a rule, are the newspapers that they serve, in their several districts....

The bill was filed to restrain the pirating of complainant's news by defendant in three ways: First, by bribing employees of newspapers published by complainant's members to furnish Associated Press news to defendant before publication, for transmission by telegraph and telephone to defendant's clients for publication by them; Second, by inducing Associated Press members to violate its by-laws and permit defendant to obtain news before publication; and Third, by copying news from bulletin boards and from early editions of complainant's newspapers and selling this, either bodily or after rewriting it, to defendant's customers.

The District Court, upon consideration of the bill and answer, with voluminous affidavits on both sides, granted a preliminary injunction under the first and second heads; but refused at that stage to restrain the systematic practice admittedly pursued by defendant, of taking news bodily from the bulletin boards and early editions of complainant's newspapers and selling it as its own. The court expressed itself as satisfied that this practice amounted to unfair trade, but as the legal question was one of first impression it considered that the allowance of an injunction should await the outcome of an appeal....

The only matter that has been argued before us is whether defendant may lawfully be restrained from appropriating news taken from bulletins issued by complainant or any of its members, or from newspapers published by them, for the purpose of selling it to defendant's clients. Complainant asserts that defendant's admitted course of conduct in this regard both violates complainant's property right in the news and constitutes unfair competition in business. And notwithstanding the case has proceeded only to the stage of a preliminary injunction, we have deemed it proper to consider the underlying questions, since they go to the very merits of the action and are presented upon facts that are not in dispute. As presented in argument, these questions are: 1. Whether there is any property in news; 2. Whether, if there be property in news collected for the purpose of being published, it survives the instant of its publication in the first newspaper to which it is communicated by the news-gatherer; and 3. Whether defendant's admitted course of conduct in appropriating for commercial use matter taken from bulletins or early editions of Associated Press publications constitutes unfair competition in trade.

.... Complainant's news matter is not copyrighted.... No doubt news articles often possess a literary quality, and are the subject of literary property at the common law; nor do we question that such an article, as a literary production, is the subject of copyright by the terms of the act as it now stands.... But the news element—the information respecting current events contained in the literary production—is not the creation of the writer, but is a report of matters that ordinarily are *publici juris*; it is the history of the day. It is not to be supposed that the framers of the Constitution, when they empowered Congress "to promote the progress of science and useful arts, by securing for limited times to authors and inventors the exclusive right to their respective writings and discoveries" (Const., Art I, § 8, par. 8), intended to confer upon one who might happen to be the first to report a historic event the exclusive right for any period to spread the knowledge of it.

We need spend no time, however, upon the general question of property in news matter at common law, or the application of the copyright act, since it seems to us the case must turn upon the question of unfair competition in business. And, in our opinion, this does not depend upon any general right of property analogous to the common-law right of the proprietor of an unpublished work to prevent its publication without his consent; nor is it foreclosed by showing that the benefits of the copyright act have been waived. We are dealing here not with restrictions upon publication but with the very facilities and processes of publication. The peculiar value of news is in the spreading of it while it is fresh; and it is evident that a valuable property interest in the news, as news, cannot be maintained by keeping it secret. Besides, except for matters improperly disclosed, or published in breach of trust or confidence, or in violation of law, none of which is involved in this branch of the case, the news of current events may be regarded as common property. What we are concerned with is the business of making it known to the world, in which both parties to the present suit are engaged. That business consists in maintaining a prompt, sure, steady, and reliable service designed to place the daily events of the world at the breakfast table of the millions at a price that, while of trifling moment to each reader, is sufficient in the aggregate to afford compensation for the cost of gathering and distributing it, with the added profit so necessary as an incentive to effective action in the commercial world. The service thus performed for newspaper readers is not only innocent but extremely useful in itself, and indubitably constitutes a legitimate business. The parties are competitors in this field; and, on fundamental principles, applicable here as elsewhere, when the rights or privileges of the one are liable to conflict with those of the other, each party is under a duty so to conduct its own business as not unnecessarily or unfairly to injure that of the other.

Obviously, the question of what is unfair competition in business must be determined with particular reference to the character and circumstances of the business. The question here is not so much the rights of either party as against the public but their rights as between themselves. And although we may and do assume that neither party has any remaining property interest as against the public in uncopyrighted news matter after the moment of its first publication, it by no means follows that there is no remaining property interest in it as between themselves. For, to both of them alike, news matter, however little susceptible of ownership or dominion in the absolute sense, is stock in trade, to be gathered at the cost of enterprise, organization, skill, labor, and money, and to be distributed and sold to those who will pay money for it, as for any other merchandise.

Regarding the news, therefore, as but the material out of which both parties are seeking to make profits at the same time and in the same field, we hardly can fail to recognize that for this purpose, and as between them, it must be regarded as quasi property, irrespective of the rights of either as against the public....

The peculiar features of the case arise from the fact that, while novelty and freshness form so important an element in the success of the business, the very processes of distribution and publication necessarily occupy a good deal of time. Complainant's service, as well as defendant's, is a daily service to daily newspapers; most of the foreign news reaches this country at the Atlantic seaboard, principally at the City of New York, and because of this, and of time differentials due to the earth's rotation, the distribution of news matter throughout the country is principally from east to west; and, since in speed the telegraph and telephone easily outstrip the rotation of the earth, it is a simple matter for defendant to take complainant's news from bulletins or early editions of complainant's members in the eastern cities and at the mere cost of telegraphic transmission cause it to be published in western papers issued at least as early as those served by complainant. Besides this, and irrespective of time differentials, irregularities in telegraphic transmission on different lines, and the normal consumption of time in printing and distributing the newspaper, result in permitting pirated news to be placed in the hands of defendant's readers sometimes simultaneously with the service of competing Associated Press papers, occasionally even earlier.

Defendant insists that when, with the sanction and approval of complainant, and as the result of the use of its news for the very purpose for which it is distributed, a portion of complainant's members communicate it to the general public by posting it upon bulletin boards so that all may read, or by issuing it to newspapers and distributing it indiscriminately, complainant no longer has the right to control the use to be made of it; that when it thus reaches the light of day it becomes the common possession of all to whom it is accessible; and that any purchaser of a newspaper has the right to communicate the intelligence which it contains to anybody and for any purpose, even for the purpose of selling it for profit to newspapers published for profit in competition with complainant's members.

The fault in the reasoning lies in applying as a test the right of the complainant as against the public, instead of considering the rights of complainant and defendant, competitors in business, as between themselves. The right of the purchaser of a single newspaper to spread knowledge of its contents gratuitously, for any legitimate purpose not unreasonably interfering with complainant's right to make merchandise of it, may be admitted; but to transmit that news for commercial use, in competition with complainant—which is what defendant has done and seeks to justify—is a very different matter. In doing this defendant, by its very act, admits that it is taking material that has been acquired by complainant as the result of organization and the expenditure of labor, skill, and money, and which is salable by complainant for money, and that defendant in appropriating it and selling it as its own is endeavoring to reap where it has not sown, and by disposing of it to newspapers that are competitors of complainant's members is appropriating to itself the harvest of those who have sown. Stripped of all disguises, the process amounts to an unauthorized interference with the normal operation of complainant's legitimate business precisely at the point where the profit is to be reaped, in order to divert a material portion of the profit from those who have earned it to those who have not; with special advantage to defendant in the competition because of the fact that it is not burdened with any part of the expense of gathering the news. The transaction speaks for itself, and a court of equity ought not to hesitate long in characterizing it as unfair competition in business....

The contention that the news is abandoned to the public for all purposes when published in the first newspaper is untenable. Abandonment is a question of intent, and the entire organization of the Associated Press negatives such a purpose. The cost of the service would be prohibitive if the reward were to be so limited. No single newspaper, no small group of newspapers, could sustain the expenditure. Indeed, it is one of the most obvious results of defendant's theory that, by permitting indiscriminate publication by anybody and everybody for purposes of profit in competition with the news-gatherer, it would render publication profitless, or so little profitable as in effect to cut off the service by rendering the cost prohibitive in comparison with the return....

It is to be observed that the view we adopt does not result in giving to complainant the right to monopolize either the gathering or the distribution of the news, or, without complying with the copyright act, to prevent the reproduction of its news articles; but only postpones participation by complainant's competitor in the processes of distribution and reproduction of news that it has not gathered, and only to the extent necessary to prevent that competitor from reaping the fruits of complainant's efforts and expenditure, to the partial exclusion of complainant, and in violation of the principle that underlies the maxim *sic utere tuo*, etc....

The decree of the Circuit Court of Appeals will be Affirmed.

MR. JUSTICE CLARKE took no part in the consideration or decision of this case.

MR. JUSTICE HOLMES.

When an uncopyrighted combination of words is published there is no general right to forbid other people repeating them—in other words there is no property in the combination or in the thoughts or facts that the words express....

Fresh news is got only by enterprise and expense. To produce such news as it is produced by the defendant represents by implication that it has been acquired by the defendant's enterprise and at its expense. When it comes from one of the great news-collecting agencies like the Associated Press, the source generally is indicated, plainly importing that credit; and that such a representation is implied may be inferred with some confidence from the unwillingness of the defendant to give the credit and tell the truth. If the plaintiff produces the news at the same time that the defendant does, the defendant's presentation impliedly denies to the plaintiff the credit of collecting the facts and assumes that credit to the defendant. If the plaintiff is later in western cities it naturally will be supposed to have obtained its information from the defendant. The falsehood is a little more subtle, the injury a little more indirect, than in ordinary cases of unfair trade, but I think that the principle that condemns the one condemns the other. It is a question of how strong an infusion of fraud is necessary to turn a flavor into a poison. The does seems to me strong enough here to need a remedy from the law. But as, in my view, the only ground of complaint that can be recognized without legislation is the implied misstatement, it can be corrected by stating the truth; and a suitable acknowledgment of the source is all that the plaintiff can require. I think that within the limits recognized by the decision of the Court the defendant should be enjoined from publishing news obtained from the Associated Press for hours after publication by the plaintiff unless it gives express credit to the Associated Press; the number of hours and the form of acknowledgment to be settled by the District Court.

MR. JUSTICE MCKENNA concurs in this opinion.

MR. JUSTICE BRANDEIS, dissenting.

. . . . News is a report of recent occurrences. The business of the news agency is to gather systematically knowledge of such occurrences of interest and to distribute reports thereof. The Associated Press contended that knowledge so acquired is property, because it costs money and labor to produce and because it has value for which those who have it not are ready to pay; that it remains property and is entitled to protection as long as it has commercial value as news; and that to protect it effectively the defendant must be enjoined from making, or causing to be made, any gainful use of it while it retains such value. An essential element of individual property is the legal right to exclude others from enjoying it. If the property is private, the right of exclusion may be absolute; if the property is affected with a public interest, the right of exclusion is qualified. But the fact that a product of the mind has cost its producer money and labor, and has a value for which others are willing to pay, is not sufficient to ensure to it this legal attribute of property. The general rule of law is, that the noblest of human productions—knowledge, truths ascertained, conceptions, and ideas—become, after voluntary communication to others, free as the air to common use. . . .

The great development of agencies now furnishing country-wide distribution of news, the vastness of our territory, and improvements in the means of transmitting intelligence, have made it possible for a news agency or newspapers to obtain, without paying compensation, the fruit of another's efforts and to use news so obtained gainfully in competition with the original collector. The injustice of such action is obvious. But to give relief against it would involve more than the application of existing rules of law to new facts. It would require the making of a new rule in analogy to existing ones. The unwritten law possesses capacity for growth; and has often satisfied new demands for justice by invoking analogies or by expanding a rule or principle. This process has been in the main wisely applied and should not be discontinued. Where the problem is relatively simple, as it is apt to be when private interests only are involved, it generally proves adequate. But with the increasing complexity of society, the public interest tends to become omnipresent; and the problems presented by new demands for justice cease to be simple. Then the creation or recognition by courts of a new private right may work serious injury to the general public, unless the boundaries of the right are definitely established and wisely guarded. In order to reconcile the new private right with the public interest, it may be necessary to prescribe limitations and rules for its enjoyment; and also to provide administrative machinery for enforcing the rules. It is largely for this reason that, in the effort to meet the many new demands for justice incident to a rapidly changing civilization, resort to legislation has latterly been had with increasing frequency....

A legislature, urged to enact a law by which one news agency or newspaper may prevent appropriation of the fruits of its labors by another, would consider such facts and possibilities and others which appropriate enquiry might disclose. Legislators might conclude that it was impossible to put an end to the obvious injustice involved in such appropriation of news, without opening the door to other evils, greater than that sought to be remedied. Such appears to have been the opinion of our Senate which reported unfavorably a bill to give news a few hours' protection; and which ratified, on February 15, 1911, the convention adopted at the Fourth International American Conference; and such was evidently the view also of the signatories to the International Copyright Union Of November 13, 1908; as both these conventions expressly exclude news from copyright protection.

Or legislators dealing with the subject might conclude, that the right to news values should be protected to the extent of permitting recovery of damages for any unauthorized use, but that protection by injunction should be denied, just as courts of equity ordinarily refuse (perhaps in the interest of free speech) to restrain actionable libels, and for other reasons decline to protect by injunction mere political rights; and as Congress has prohibited courts from enjoining the illegal assessment or collection of federal taxes. If a legislature concluded to recognize property in published news to the extent of permitting recovery at law, it might, with a view to making the remedy more certain and adequate, provide a fixed measure of damages, as in the case of copyright infringement.

Or again, a legislature might conclude that it was unwise to recognize even so limited a property right in published news as that above indicated; but that a news agency should, on some conditions, be given full protection of its business; and to that end a remedy by injunction as well as one for damages should be granted, where news collected by it is gainfully used without permission. If a legislature concluded ... that under certain circumstances news-gathering is a business affected with a public interest, it might declare that, in such cases, news should be protected against appropriation, only if the gatherer assumed the obligation of supplying it, at reasonable rates and without discrimination, to all papers which applied therefor. If legislators reached that conclusion, they would probably go further, and prescribe the conditions under which and the extent to which the protection should be afforded; and they might also provide the administrative machinery necessary for ensuring to the public, the press, and the news agencies, full enjoyment of the rights so conferred.

Courts are ill-equipped to make the investigations which should precede a determination of the limitations which should be set upon any property right in news or of the circumstances under which news gathered by a private agency should be deemed affected with a public interest. Courts would be powerless to prescribe the detailed regulations essential to full enjoyment of the rights conferred or to introduce the machinery required for enforcement of such regulations. Considerations such as these should lead us to decline to establish a new rule of law in the effort to redress a newly-disclosed wrong, although the propriety of some remedy appears to be clear.

Notes & Questions

1. In *International News Service*, a central issue once again is the relative competence of the legislature and courts. Are there any responses to Brandeis' argument that Congress was the better body to decide whether to create a property right in the news?

Given the takings protections of the Constitution, should courts leave the recognition of new property rights to the legislature? If the courts create a new property right, any effort by Congress to overrule the court would raise takings issues. If the courts refuse to recognize a new property right, however, Congress arguably can legislatively create a right without constitutional concern.

2. Why does Justice Pitney in the majority opinion say that news must be regarded as "quasi property" rather than just "property"? How is "quasi property" different from "property"? How do the rights that the Court awards to news differ from other property rights that you have encountered so far in this book?

3. Despite *International News Service*, lower courts have not rushed to extend common law protection in other contexts where business enterprises have resorted to copying from their competitors. In Cheney Bros. v. Doris Silk Corp., 35 F.2d 279 (2d Cir. 1929), the Court of Appeals held that a fabric manufacturer could copy the design of a competitor's more expensive silk fabrics. With obvious sympathy for Justice Brandeis' dissent in *International New Service*, the court suggested that courts should leave to Congress the decision whether to grant a "monopoly" in ideas and inventions. Indeed, the court suggested that the Constitution allows only Congress to create such a monopoly. Similarly in Smith v. Chanel, Inc., 402 F.2d 562 (9th Cir. 1968), the Court of Appeals rejected an effort by Chanel

to keep another perfume company from marketing their perfume as identical to Chanel No. 5. According to the court, "imitation is the life blood of competition. It is the unimpeded availability of substantially equivalent units that permits the normal operation of supply and demand to yield the fair price society must pay for a given commodity." Id. at 567, quoting American Safety Table Co. v. Schreiber, 269 F.2d 255, 272 (2d Cir. 1959). Are these cases distinguishable from *International News Service*?

4. **The Right of Publicity.** A major issue in recent years is the degree to which courts and legislatures should provide individuals with a right to their name and likeness, either as a matter of property or privacy. One of the earliest cases dealt with baseball cards. In Haelan Laboratories v. Topps Chewing Gum, 202 F.2d 866 (2d Cir. 1953), the court held that a baseball player who had entered into an exclusive contract with one chewing gum company could prevent his picture from being used by a competitor. According to the court,

> a man has a right in the publicity value of his photograph, i.e., the right to grant the exclusive privilege of publishing his picture, and that such a grant may validly be made "in gross," i.e., without an accompanying transfer of a business or of anything else. Whether it be labeled a "property" right is immaterial; for here, as often elsewhere, the tag "property" simply symbolizes the fact that courts enforce a claim which has pecuniary worth.
>
> The right might be called a "right of publicity." For it is common knowledge that many prominent persons (especially actors and ball-players), far from having their feelings bruised through public exposure of their likenesses, would feel sorely deprived if they no longer received money for authorizing advertisements, popularizing their countenances, displayed in newspapers, magazines, busses, trains and subways. This right of publicity would usually yield them no money unless it could be made the subject of an exclusive grant which barred any other advertiser from using their picture.

Is there any reason to grant a "right of publicity"? What is the law trying to accomplish in doing so?

Even if a card company obtains a license from a baseball player to use his picture, the company might not be home free. It would still have to worry about the rights of the photographer—copyright law protects photographs.

5. Is there a danger of giving people too many rights over their "publicity"? In White v. Samsung Electronics America, Inc., 971 F.2d 1395 (9th Cir. 1992), a panel of the federal Court of Appeals for the Ninth Circuit held that Vanna White, the wheel spinner on Wheel of Fortune, was entitled to a trial on her claim that Samsung had violated her "right of publicity" by running an advertisement starring a robot dressed in a wig, gown, and jewelry reminiscent of White and posed next to a Wheel-of-

Fortune-like game board. In dissenting from the Ninth Circuit's refusal to rehear the case *en banc*, Judge Alex Kozinksi wrote:

> Saddam Hussein wants to keep advertisers from using his picture in unflattering contexts. Clint Eastwood doesn't want tabloids to write about him. Rudolf Valentino's heirs want to control his film biography. The Girl Scouts don't want their image soiled by association with certain activities. George Lucas wants to keep Strategic Defense Initiative fans from calling it "Star Wars." Pepsico doesn't want singers to use the word "Pepsi" in their songs. Guy Lombardo wants an exclusive property right to ads that show big bands playing on New Year's Eve. Uri Geller thinks he should be paid for ads showing psychics bending metal through telekinesis. Paul Prudhomme, that household name, thinks the same about ads featuring corpulent bearded chefs. And scads of copyright holders see purple when their creations are made fun of.
>
> Something very dangerous is going on here. Private property, including intellectual property, is essential to our way of life. It provides an incentive for investment and innovation; it stimulates the flourishing of our culture; it protects the moral entitlements of people to the fruits of their labors. But reducing too much to private property can be bad medicine. Private land, for instance, is far more useful if separated from other private land by public streets, roads, and highways. Public parks, utility rights-of-way, and sewers reduce the amount of land in private hands, but vastly enhance the value of the property that remains.
>
> So too it is with intellectual property. Overprotecting intellectual property is as harmful as underprotecting it. Creativity is impossible without a rich public domain. Nothing today, likely nothing since we tamed fire, is genuinely new: Culture, like science and technology, grows by accretion, each new creator, building on the works of those who came before. Overprotection stifles the very creative forces it's supposed to nurture.
>
> The panel's opinion is a classic case of overprotection. Concerned about what it sees as a wrong done to Vanna White, the panel majority erects a property right of remarkable and dangerous breadth: Under the majority's opinion, it's now a tort for advertisers to remind the public of a celebrity. Not to use a celebrity's name, voice, signature, or likeness; not to imply the celebrity endorses a product; but simply to evoke the celebrity's image in the public's mind. This Orwellian notion withdraws far more from the public domain than prudence and common sense allow. It conflicts with the Copyright Act and the Copyright Clause. It raises serious First Amendment problems. It's bad law, and it deserves a long, hard second look.
>
> .... [C]onsider the moral dimension [of the panel's opinion.] Saying Samsung "appropriated" something of White's begs the question: Should White have the exclusive right to something as

> broad and amorphous as her "identity"? Samsung's ad didn't simply copy White's shtick—like all parody, it created something new.... Why is Vanna White's right to exclusive for-profit use of her persona—a persona that might not even be her own creation, but that of a writer, director, or producer—superior to Samsung's right to profit by creating its own inventions?....

White v. Samsung Electronics America, Inc., 989 F.2d 1512 (9th Cir. 1993) (Kozinsky, J., dissenting).

6. In intellectual property cases, one question is what to protect; another is how long to extend the protection. Patents, as noted earlier, last 20 years; copyrights last much longer. How long should someone have a "publicity right" in his name and likeness? In one of the first cases to address this issue, the Georgia Supreme Court held that the right survives the death of the celebrity and is both inheritable and devisable:

> Recognition of the right of publicity rewards and thereby encourages effort and creativity. If the right of publicity dies with the celebrity, the economic value of the right of publicity during life would be diminished because the celebrity's untimely death would seriously impair, if not destroy, the value of the right of continued commercial use. Conversely, those who would profit from the fame of a celebrity after his or her death for their own benefit and without authorization have failed to establish their claim that they should be the beneficiaries of the celebrity's death. Finally, the trend since the early common law has been to recognize survivability, notwithstanding the legal problems which may thereby arise.

Martin Luther King, Jr., Center for Social Change v. American Heritage Products, 296 S.E.2d 697, 705 (Ga. 1982). Is the court suggesting that people will be less creative if the right of publicity ends with death? Is it unfair to let others exploit someone's "publicity" value after her death? For legislative answers to the question of how long the right of publicity should last, see Cal. Civil Code § 3344.1 (70 years after death); Tenn. Code Ann. § 47–25–1104 (for 10 years after death or as long as the right is actively used for commercial purposes, whichever is longer).

7. **Software Protection.** In recent years, another important question has been the appropriate protection for computer software. Lawmakers commonly greet the arrival of a new kind of information product with two questions: Should the product be protected by intellectual property? If so, should protection be under state law, as happened with the right of publicity, or federal law, which is the increasingly dominant source of protection? Software producers initially relied on state contract and trade secret law as a stopgap while they waited to see whether and to what extend federal copyright and patent law would protect their computer programs. While varying from state to state, trade secret law provides some degree of protection for business information that is not generally known and is subject to reasonable efforts to protect confidentiality.

State trade secret law continues today to protect not only custom-made computer programs, but also the treasured source code of more widely distributed, off-the-shelf programs. Although patents, with their focus on functional subject matter, might have seemed the logical choice for federal law protection of software, the high threshold for protection (patent subject matter must, among other things, be novel and nonobvious) and the often protracted patent examination process discouraged many innovators in this essentially incremental but fast-paced environment, as did a Supreme Court decision, Gottschalk v. Benson, 409 U.S. 63 (1972), that effectively questioned patent law's suitability for protecting programs. It was copyright law, which has a low threshold for protection (a copyrighted work need only be original and expressive) and requires no governmental examination, that became the most popular form of intellectual property protection for computer programs over the course of the 1980's. As soon became clear, however, the problem with copyright as a vehicle for protecting software is that, because it protects only expression, not ideas, it gives software designers scant incentive to invest in developing new ideas. By the end of the 20th century, software developers, encouraged by a more compliant Patent and Trademark Office, looked to patents for protection once again.

In light of the deficiencies in existing law—trade secret law's requirement of secrecy, patent law's high standards and long delays, and copyright's low level of protection—would it make sense for Congress (or state legislatures) to enact a new intellectual property law designed specifically for computer software? There is no shortage of such proposals for so-called *sui generis* regimes. See, e.g., Pamela Samuelson et al., A Manifesto Concerning the Legal Protection of Computer Programs, 94 Colum. L. Rev. 2307 (1994); Elmer Galbi, Proposal for New Legislation to Protect Computer Programming, 17 Bull. Copyright Soc'y 280 (1970). What questions would you ask in designing such a regime?

8. **Enforcement Problems.** Enforcement is rarely a problem in real property disputes. Trespasses to land, and even nuisances, are relatively easy to detect and their perpetrators—usually small in number—are relatively easy to track down. Enforcement of rights in intellectual property can be far more difficult and, indeed, may even be futile, such as when a sound recording is uploaded onto the Internet for downloading by uncounted millions of users around the world, none paying any consideration to the copyright owner. Although there are disputes about the precise impact of such free uses on the revenues earned by copyright owners through traditional retail channels—and indeed through licensed uses on the Internet—there is little doubt that free use has some impact on the willingness of individuals and entertainment companies to invest in creating, producing, and distributing these goods.

It is a central precept of real property law that property rights are more efficient than fences in excluding unauthorized users. Is the same true of intellectual property law?

E. CYBERSPACE

Intel Corp. v. Hamidi

Supreme Court of California, 2003.
30 Cal. 4th 1342.

WERDEGAR, J.

Intel Corporation (Intel) maintains an electronic mail system, connected to the Internet, through which messages between employees and those outside the company can be sent and received, and permits its employees to make reasonable nonbusiness use of this system. On six occasions over almost two years, Kourosh Kenneth Hamidi, a former Intel employee, sent e-mails criticizing Intel's employment practices to numerous current employees on Intel's electronic mail system. Hamidi breached no computer security barriers in order to communicate with Intel employees. He offered to, and did, remove from his mailing list any recipient who so wished. Hamidi's communications to individual Intel employees caused neither physical damage nor functional disruption to the company's computers, nor did they at any time deprive Intel of the use of its computers. The contents of the messages, however, caused discussion among employees and managers.

On these facts, Intel brought suit, claiming that by communicating with its employees over the company's e-mail system Hamidi committed the tort of trespass to chattels.[a] The trial court granted Intel's motion for summary judgment and enjoined Hamidi from any further mailings. A divided Court of Appeal affirmed.

After reviewing the decisions analyzing unauthorized electronic contact with computer systems as potential trespasses to chattels, we conclude that under California law the tort does not encompass, and should not be extended to encompass, an electronic communication that neither damages the recipient computer system nor impairs its functioning. Such an electronic communication does not constitute an actionable trespass to personal property, i.e., the computer system, because it does not interfere with the possessor's use or possession of, or any other legally protected interest in, the personal property itself. . . .

a. Eds.—The basic doctrine of trespass, examined in Chapter 2 at pages 53–68, applies only to real property. Two other doctrines apply to personal property. The doctrine of "trespass to chattels," with which this case deals, prohibits intentional interferences with someone else's personal property. The related doctrine of "conversion," which is the subject of Moore v. Regents of the University of California, p. 297, bars the wrongful exercise of dominion over someone else's personal property. The distinction between the two doctrines is not always clear. According to Prosser, a trespass to chattels is an interference with someone else's personal property that is "not sufficiently important to be classed as conversion." Prosser & Keeton § 14, at 85–86 (5th ed. 1984).

Hamidi, a former Intel engineer, together with others, formed an organization named Former and Current Employees of Intel (FACE–Intel) to disseminate information and views critical of Intel's employment and personnel policies and practices. FACE–Intel maintained a Web site (which identified Hamidi as Webmaster and as the organization's spokesperson) containing such material. In addition, over a 21–month period Hamidi, on behalf of FACE–Intel, sent six mass e-mails to employee addresses on Intel's electronic mail system. The messages criticized Intel's employment practices, warned employees of the dangers those practices posed to their careers, suggested employees consider moving to other companies, solicited employees' participation in FACE–Intel, and urged employees to inform themselves further by visiting FACE–Intel's Web site. The messages stated that recipients could, by notifying the sender of their wishes, be removed from FACE–Intel's mailing list; Hamidi did not subsequently send messages to anyone who requested removal.

Each message was sent to thousands of addresses (as many as 35,000 according to FACE–Intel's Web site), though some messages were blocked by Intel before reaching employees. Intel's attempt to block internal transmission of the messages succeeded only in part; Hamidi later admitted he evaded blocking efforts by using different sending computers. When Intel, in March 1998, demanded in writing that Hamidi and FACE–Intel stop sending e-mails to Intel's computer system, Hamidi asserted the organization had a right to communicate with willing Intel employees; he sent a new mass mailing in September 1998.

The summary judgment record contains no evidence Hamidi breached Intel's computer security in order to obtain the recipient addresses for his messages; indeed, internal Intel memoranda show the company's management concluded no security breach had occurred. Hamidi stated he created the recipient address list using an Intel directory on a floppy disk anonymously sent to him. Nor is there any evidence that the receipt or internal distribution of Hamidi's electronic messages damaged Intel's computer system or slowed or impaired its functioning. Intel did present uncontradicted evidence, however, that many employee recipients asked a company official to stop the messages and that staff time was consumed in attempts to block further messages from FACE–Intel. According to the FACE–Intel Web site, moreover, the messages had prompted discussions between "[e]xcited and nervous managers" and the company's human resources department.

Intel sued Hamidi and FACE–Intel, pleading causes of action for trespass to chattels and nuisance, and seeking both actual damages and an injunction against further e-mail messages. Intel later voluntarily dismissed its nuisance claim and waived its demand for damages. The trial court entered default against FACE–Intel upon that organization's failure to answer. The court then granted Intel's motion for summary judgment, permanently enjoining Hamidi, FACE–Intel, and their agents "from sending unsolicited e-mail to addresses on Intel's computer systems." Hamidi appealed; FACE–Intel did not. . . .

[The California Supreme Court began its opinion by discussing the doctrine of "trespass to chattels." The court held that trespass to chattels "lies where an intentional interference with the possession of personal injury *has proximately caused injury*." There is no actionable trespass absent "some actual injury." Quoting section 218 of the Restatement (Second) of Torts, the court noted that "one who intentionally intermeddles with another's chattel is subject to liability only if his intermeddling is harmful to the possessor's materially valuable interest in the physical condition, quality, or value of the chattel, or if the possessor is deprived of the use of the chattel for a substantial time, or some other legally protected interest of the possessor is affected . . ."]

The dispositive issue in this case, therefore, is whether the undisputed facts demonstrate Hamidi's actions caused or threatened to cause damage to Intel's computer system, or injury to its rights in that personal property, such as to entitle Intel to judgment as a matter of law. To review, the undisputed evidence revealed no actual or threatened damage to Intel's computer hardware or software and no interference with its ordinary and intended operation. Intel was not dispossessed of its computers, nor did Hamidi's messages prevent Intel from using its computers for any measurable length of time. Intel presented no evidence its system was slowed or otherwise impaired by the burden of delivering Hamidi's electronic messages. Nor was there any evidence transmission of the messages imposed any marginal cost on the operation of Intel's computers. In sum, no evidence suggested that in sending messages through Intel's Internet connections and internal computer system Hamidi used the system in any manner in which it was not intended to function or impaired the system in any way. . . .

Relying on a line of decisions, most from federal district courts, applying the tort of trespass to chattels to various types of unwanted electronic contact between computers, Intel contends that, while its computers were not damaged by receiving Hamidi's messages, its interest in the "physical condition, quality or value" (Rest.2d Torts, § 218, com. e, p. 422) of the computers was harmed. We disagree. The cited line of decisions does not persuade us that the mere sending of electronic communications that assertedly cause injury only because of their contents constitutes an actionable trespass to a computer system through which the messages are transmitted. Rather, the decisions finding electronic contact to be a trespass to computer systems have generally involved some actual or threatened interference with the computers' functioning.

In Thrifty–Tel, Inc. v. Bezenek, 46 Cal. App. 4th 1559 (1996), the California Court of Appeal held that evidence of automated searching of a telephone carrier's system for authorization codes supported a cause of action for trespass to chattels. The defendant's automated dialing program "overburdened the [plaintiff's] system, denying some subscribers access to phone lines," showing the requisite injury.

Following *Thrifty–Tel*, a series of federal district court decisions held that sending UCE [unsolicited commercial bulk e-mail] through an ISP's

[Internet service provider's] equipment may constitute trespass to the ISP's computer system.... In each of these spamming cases, the plaintiff showed, or was prepared to show, some interference with the efficient functioning of its computer system. In CompuServe, Inc. v. Cyber Promotions, Inc., 962 F. Supp. 1015 (S.D. Ohio 1997), the plaintiff ISP's mail equipment monitor stated that mass UCE mailings, especially from nonexistent addresses such as those used by the defendant, placed "a tremendous burden" on the ISP's equipment, using "disk space and drain[ing] the processing power," making those resources unavailable to serve subscribers. Similarly, in Hotmail Corp. v. Van$ Money Pie, Inc., 1998 WL 388389 (N.D. Cal. 1998), the court found the evidence supported a finding that the defendant's mailings "fill[ed] up Hotmail's computer storage space and threaten[ed] to damage Hotmail's ability to service its legitimate customers."....

Building on the spamming cases, in particular *CompuServe*, three even more recent district court decisions addressed whether unauthorized robotic data collection from a company's publicly accessible Web site is a trespass on the company's computer system.[4] The two district courts that found such automated data collection to constitute a trespass relied, in part, on the deleterious impact this activity could have, especially if replicated by other searchers, on the functioning of a Web site's computer equipment.

In the leading case, eBay, Inc. v. Bidder's Edge, Inc., 100 F. Supp. 2d 1058 (N.D. Cal. 2000), the defendant Bidder's Edge (BE), operating an auction aggregation site, accessed the eBay Web site about 100,000 times per day, accounting for between 1 and 2 percent of the information requests received by eBay and a slightly smaller percentage of the data transferred by eBay. The district court rejected eBay's claim that it was entitled to injunctive relief because of the defendant's unauthorized presence alone, or because of the incremental cost the defendant had imposed on operation of the eBay site, but found sufficient proof of *threatened* harm in the potential for others to imitate the defendant's activity: "If BE's activity is allowed to continue unchecked, it would encourage other auction aggregators to engage in similar recursive searching of the eBay system such that eBay would suffer irreparable harm from reduced system performance, system unavailability, or data losses." Again, in addressing the likelihood of eBay's success on its trespass to chattels cause of action, the court held the evidence of injury to eBay's computer system sufficient to support a preliminary injunction: "If the court were to hold otherwise, it would likely encourage other auction aggregators to crawl the eBay site, potentially to the point of denying effective access to eBay's customers. If preliminary injunctive relief were denied, and other aggregators began to crawl the eBay site, there appears to be little doubt that the load on eBay's

4. Data search and collection robots, also known as "Web bots" or "spiders," are programs designed to rapidly search numerous Web pages or sites, collecting, retrieving, and indexing information from these pages. Their uses include creation of searchable databases, Web catalogues and comparison shopping services.

computer system would qualify as a substantial impairment of condition or value." . . . .

Intel connected its e-mail system to the Internet and permitted its employees to make use of this connection both for business and, to a reasonable extent, for their own purposes. In doing so, the company necessarily contemplated the employees' receipt of unsolicited as well as solicited communications from other companies and individuals. That some communications would, because of their contents, be unwelcome to Intel management was virtually inevitable. Hamidi did nothing but use the e-mail system for its intended purpose—to communicate with employees. The system worked as designed, delivering the messages without any physical or functional harm or disruption. These occasional transmissions cannot reasonably be viewed as impairing the quality or value of Intel's computer system. We conclude, therefore, that Intel has not presented undisputed facts demonstrating an injury to its personal property, or to its legal interest in that property, that support, under California tort law, an action for trespass to chattels.

We next consider whether California common law should be *extended* to cover, as a trespass to chattels, an otherwise harmless electronic communication whose contents are objectionable. We decline to so expand California law. Intel, of course, was not the recipient of Hamidi's messages, but rather the owner and possessor of computer servers used to relay the messages, and it bases this tort action on that ownership and possession. The property rule proposed is a rigid one, under which the sender of an electronic message would be strictly liable to the owner of equipment through which the communication passes—here, Intel—for any consequential injury flowing from the *contents* of the communication. The arguments of amici curiae and academic writers on this topic, discussed below, leave us highly doubtful whether creation of such a rigid property rule would be wise.

Writing on behalf of several industry groups appearing as amici curiae, Professor Richard A. Epstein of the University of Chicago urges us to excuse the required showing of injury to personal property in cases of unauthorized electronic contact between computers, "extending the rules of trespass to real property to all interactive Web sites and servers." The court is thus urged to recognize, for owners of a particular species of personal property, computer servers, the same interest in inviolability as is generally accorded a possessor of land. In effect, Professor Epstein suggests that a company's server should be its castle, upon which any unauthorized intrusion, however harmless, is a trespass.

Epstein's argument derives, in part, from the familiar metaphor of the Internet as a physical space, reflected in much of the language that has been used to describe it: "cyberspace," "the information superhighway," e-mail "addresses," and the like. Of course, the Internet is also frequently called simply the "Net," a term, Hamidi points out, "evoking a fisherman's chattel." A major component of the Internet is the World Wide "Web," a descriptive term suggesting neither personal nor real property, and "cyberspace" itself has come to be known by the oxymoronic phrase "virtual reality," which would suggest that any real property "located" in "cyberspace" must be "virtually real" property. Metaphor is a two-edged sword.

Indeed, the metaphorical application of real property rules would not, by itself, transform a physically harmless electronic intrusion on a computer server into a trespass. That is because, under California law, intangible intrusions on land, including electromagnetic transmissions, are not actionable as trespasses (though they may be as nuisances) unless they cause physical damage to the real property. Since Intel does not claim Hamidi's electronically transmitted messages physically damaged its servers, it could not prove a trespass to land even were we to treat the computers as a type of real property. Some further extension of the conceit would be required, under which the electronic signals Hamidi sent would be recast as tangible intruders, perhaps as tiny messengers rushing through the "hallways" of Intel's computers and bursting out of employees' computers to read them Hamidi's missives. But such fictions promise more confusion than clarity in the law.

The plain fact is that computers, even those making up the Internet, are—like such older communications equipment as telephones and fax machines—personal property, not realty. Professor Epstein observes that "[a]lthough servers may be moved in real space, they cannot be moved in cyberspace," because an Internet server must, to be useful, be accessible at a known address. But the same is true of the telephone: to be useful for incoming communication, the telephone must remain constantly linked to the same number (or, when the number is changed, the system must include some forwarding or notification capability, a qualification that also applies to computer addresses). Does this suggest that an unwelcome message delivered through a telephone or fax machine should be viewed as a trespass to a type of real property? We think not.... [T]he contents of a telephone communication may cause a variety of injuries and may be the basis for a variety of tort actions (e.g., defamation, intentional infliction of emotional distress, invasion of privacy), but the injuries are not to an interest in property, much less real property, and the appropriate tort is not trespass.

More substantively, Professor Epstein argues that a rule of computer server inviolability will, through the formation or extension of a market in computer-to-computer access, create "the right social result." In most circumstances, he predicts, companies with computers on the Internet will continue to authorize transmission of information through e-mail, Web site searching, and page linking because they benefit by that open access. When a Web site owner does deny access to a particular sending, searching, or linking computer, a system of "simple one-on-one negotiations" will arise to provide the necessary individual licenses.

Other scholars are less optimistic about such a complete propertization of the Internet. Professor Mark Lemley ..., writing on behalf of an amici curiae group of professors of intellectual property and computer law, observes that under a property rule of server inviolability, "each of the hundreds of millions of [Internet] users must get permission in advance from anyone with whom they want to communicate and anyone who owns a server through which their message may travel." The consequence for e-mail could be a substantial reduction in the freedom of electronic communication, as the owner of each computer through which an electronic message passes could impose its own limitations on message content or source. As Professor Dan Hunter of the University of Pennsylvania asks rhetorically: "Does this mean that one must read the 'Terms of Acceptable Email Usage' of every email system that one emails in the course of an ordinary day? If the University of Pennsylvania had a policy that sending a joke by email would be an unauthorized use of its system, then under the logic of [the lower court decision in this case], you would commit 'trespass' if you emailed me a . . . cartoon." (Hunter, Cyberspace as Place and the Tragedy of the Digital Anticommons (2003) 91 Cal. L. Rev. 439, 508–509.)

Web site linking, Professor Lemley further observes, "would exist at the sufferance of the linked-to party, because a Web user who followed a 'disapproved' link would be trespassing on the plaintiff's server, just as sending an e-mail is trespass under the [lower] court's theory." Another writer warns that "[c]yber-trespass theory will curtail the free flow of price and product information on the Internet by allowing website owners to tightly control who and what may enter and make use of the information housed on its Internet site." (Chang, Bidding on Trespass: *eBay, Inc. v. Bidder's Edge, Inc.* and the Abuse of Trespass Theory in Cyberspace Law (2001) 29 AIPLA Q.J. 445, 459.) A leading scholar of Internet law and policy, Professor Lawrence Lessig of Stanford University, has criticized Professor Epstein's theory of the computer server as quasi-real property, previously put forward in the *eBay* case, on the ground that it ignores the costs to society in the loss of network benefits: "eBay benefits greatly from a network that is open and where access is free. It is this general feature of the Net that makes the Net so valuable to users and a source of great innovation. And to the extent that individual sites begin to impose their own rules of exclusion, the value of the network as a network declines. If machines must negotiate before entering any individual site, then the costs of using the network climb." (Lessig, The Future of Ideas: The Fate of the Commons in a Connected World (2001) p. 171.)

We discuss this debate among the amici curiae and academic writers only to note its existence and contours, not to attempt its resolution. Creating an absolute property right to exclude undesired communications from one's e-mail and Web servers might help force spammers to internalize the costs they impose on ISP's and their customers. But such a property rule might also create substantial new costs, to e-mail and e-commerce users and to society generally, in lost ease and openness of communication and in lost network benefits. In light of the unresolved controversy, we would be acting rashly to adopt a rule treating computer servers as real property for purposes of trespass law.

The Legislature has already adopted detailed regulations governing UCE. (Bus. & Prof. Code §§ 17538.4, 17538.45.) It may see fit in the future also to regulate noncommercial e-mail, such as that sent by Hamidi, or other kinds of unwanted contact between computers on the Internet, such as that alleged in *eBay.* But we are not persuaded that these perceived problems call at present for judicial creation of a rigid property rule of computer server inviolability. We therefore decline to create an exception, covering Hamidi's unwanted electronic messages to Intel employees, to the general rule that a trespass to chattels is not actionable if it does not involve actual or threatened injury to the personal property or to the possessor's legally protected interest in the personal property. No such injury having been shown on the undisputed facts, Intel was not entitled to summary judgment in its favor....

BROWN, J., dissenting.

Candidate A finds the vehicles that candidate B has provided for his campaign workers, and A spray paints the water soluble message, "Fight corruption, vote for A" on the bumpers. The majority's reasoning would find that notwithstanding the time it takes the workers to remove the paint and the expense they incur in altering the bumpers to prevent further unwanted messages, candidate B does not deserve an injunction unless the paint is so heavy that it reduces the cars' gas mileage or otherwise depreciates the cars' market value. Furthermore, candidate B has an obligation to permit the paint's display, because the cars are driven by workers and not B personally, because B allows his workers to use the cars to pick up their lunch or retrieve their children from school, or because the bumpers display B's own slogans. I disagree.

Intel Corporation has invested millions of dollars to develop and maintain a computer system. It did this not to act as a public forum but to enhance the productivity of its employees. Kourosh Kenneth Hamidi sent as many as 200,000 e-mail messages to Intel employees. The time required to review and delete Hamidi's messages diverted employees from productive tasks and undermined the utility of the computer system. "There may ... be situations in which the value to the owner of a particular type of chattel may be impaired by dealing with it in a manner that does not affect its physical condition." (Rest.2d Torts, § 218, com. h, p. 422.) This is such a case.

The majority repeatedly asserts that Intel objected to the hundreds of thousands of messages solely due to their content, and proposes that Intel seek relief by pleading content-based speech torts. This proposal misses the point that Intel's objection is directed not toward Hamidi's message but his use of Intel's property to display his message. Intel has not sought to prevent Hamidi from expressing his ideas on his Web site, through private mail (paper or electronic) to employees' homes, or through any other means like picketing or billboards. But as counsel for Intel explained during oral argument, the company objects to Hamidi's using Intel's property to advance his message.

Of course, Intel deserves an injunction even if its objections are based entirely on the e-mail's content. Intel is entitled, for example, to allow employees use of the Internet to check stock market tables or weather forecasts without incurring any concomitant obligation to allow access to pornographic Web sites. A private property owner may choose to exclude unwanted mail for any reason, including its content. (Rowan v. U.S. Post Office Dept. (1970) 397 U.S. 728, 738; Tillman v. Distribution Systems of America Inc. (App. Div. 1996) 224 A.D.2d 79.)....

... [E]ven if Hamidi's interference did not affect the server's utility to Intel, it would still amount to a trespass. Intel has poured millions of dollars into a resource that Hamidi has now appropriated for his own use. As noted above, "the appropriation of another's property to one's own use, even for a temporary purpose, constitute[s] [a] trespass[]." (Speiser et al., American Law of Torts (1990) Trespass § 23:23, p. 667.) The use by one party of property whose costs have been paid by another amounts to an unlawful taking of those resources—even if there is no unjust enrichment by the trespassing party.

MOSK, J., dissenting.

.... In my view, the repeated transmission of bulk e-mails by appellant Kourosh Kenneth Hamidi (Hamidi) to the employees of Intel Corporation (Intel) on its proprietary confidential e-mail lists, despite Intel's demand that he cease such activities, constituted an actionable trespass to chattels. The majority fail to distinguish open communication in the public "commons" of the Internet from unauthorized intermeddling on a private, proprietary intranet. Hamidi is not communicating in the equivalent of a town square or of an unsolicited "junk" mailing through the United States Postal Service. His action, in crossing from the public Internet into a private intranet, is more like intruding into a private office mailroom, commandeering the mail cart, and dropping off unwanted broadsides on 30,000 desks. Because Intel's security measures have been circumvented by Hamidi, the majority leave Intel, which has exercised all reasonable self-help efforts, with no recourse unless he causes a malfunction or systems "crash." Hamidi's repeated intrusions did more than merely "prompt[] discussions between '[e]xcited and nervous managers' and the company's human resources department"; they also constituted a misappropriation of Intel's private computer system contrary to its intended use and against Intel's wishes.

The law of trespass to chattels has not universally been limited to physical damage. I believe it is entirely consistent to apply that legal theory to these circumstances—that is, when a proprietary computer system is being used contrary to its owner's purposes and expressed desires, and self-help has been ineffective. Intel correctly expects protection from an intruder who misuses its proprietary system, its nonpublic directories, and its supposedly controlled connection to the Internet to achieve his bulk mailing objectives—incidentally, without even having to pay postage....

The majority agree that an impairment of Intel's system would result in an action for trespass to chattels, but find that Intel suffered no injury. As did the trial court, I conclude that the undisputed evidence establishes that Intel was substantially harmed by the costs of efforts to block the messages and diminished employee productivity....

The Restatement explains that the rationale for requiring harm for trespass to a chattel but not for trespass to land is the availability and effectiveness of self-help in the case of trespass to a chattel. "Sufficient legal protection of the possessor's interest in the mere inviolability of his chattel is afforded by his privilege to use reasonable force to protect his possession against even harmless interference." (Rest.2d Torts, § 218, com. (e), p. 422.) Obviously, "force" is not available to prevent electronic trespasses. As shown by Intel's inability to prevent Hamidi's intrusions, self-help is not an adequate alternative to injunctive relief.

The common law tort of trespass to chattels does not require physical disruption to the chattel. It also may apply when there is impairment to the "quality" or "value" of the chattel. (Rest.2d Torts, § 218, subd. b, p. 420.).... Here, Hamidi's deliberate and continued intermeddling, and threatened intermeddling, with Intel's proprietary computer system for his own purposes that were hostile to Intel, certainly impaired the quality and value of the system as an internal business device for Intel and forced Intel to incur costs to try to maintain the security and integrity of its server—efforts that proved ineffective.... All of these costs to protect the integrity of the computer system and to deal with the disruptive effects of the transmissions and the expenditures attributable to employee time constitute damages sufficient to establish the existence of a trespass to chattels, even if the computer system was not overburdened to the point of a "crash" by the bulk electronic mail....

The majority suggest that Intel is not entitled to injunctive relief because it chose to allow its employees access to e-mail through the Internet and because Hamidi has apparently told employees that he will remove them from his mailing list if they so request. They overlook the proprietary nature of Intel's intranet system; Intel's system is not merely a conduit for messages to its employees. As the owner of the computer system, it is Intel's request that Hamidi stop that must be respected. The fact that, like most large businesses, Intel's intranet includes external e-mail access for essential business purposes does not logically mean, as the majority suggest, that Intel has forfeited the right to determine who has access to its system. Its intranet is not the equivalent of a common carrier or public communications licensee that would be subject to requirements to provide service and access. Just as Intel can, and does, regulate the use of its computer system by its employees, it should be entitled to control its use by outsiders and to seek injunctive relief when self-help fails....

As discussed above, I believe that existing legal principles are adequate to support Intel's request for injunctive relief. But even if the injunction in this case amounts to an extension of the traditional tort of trespass to chattels, this is one of those cases in which, as Justice Cardozo suggested, "[t]he creative element in the judicial process finds its opportunity and power" in the development of the law. (Cardozo, Nature of the Judicial Process (1921) p. 165.)

The law has evolved to meet economic, social, and scientific changes in society. The industrial revolution, mass production, and new transportation and communication systems all required the adaptation and evolution of legal doctrines.

The age of computer technology and cyberspace poses new challenges to legal principles. As this court has said, "the so-called Internet revolution has spawned a host of new legal issues as courts have struggled to apply traditional legal frameworks to this new communication medium." (Pavlovich v. Superior Court (2002) 29 Cal. 4th 262, 266.) The court must now grapple with proprietary interests, privacy, and expression arising out of computer-related disputes. Thus, in this case the court is faced with "that balancing of judgment, that testing and sorting of considerations of analogy and logic and utility and fairness" that Justice Cardozo said he had "been trying to describe." (Cardozo, Nature of the Judicial Process, supra, pp. 165–166.) Additionally, this is a case in which equitable relief is sought. As Bernard Witkin has written, "equitable relief is *flexible and expanding*, and the theory that 'for every wrong there is a remedy' [Civ. Code, § 3523] may be invoked by equity courts to justify the invention of new methods of relief for new types of wrongs." (11 Witkin, Summary of Cal. Law, supra, Equity, § 3, p. 681.) That the Legislature has dealt with some aspects of commercial unsolicited bulk e-mail (Bus. & Prof. Code, §§ 17538.4, 17538.45) should not inhibit the application of common law tort principles to deal with e-mail transgressions not covered by the legislation....

Notes & Questions

1. *Hamidi* yet again raises the question of the appropriate role of courts in creating new forms of property. Even if the majority had been convinced that permitting Intel to exclude Hamidi from its electronic mail system was good public policy, should it have deferred to the legislature and refused to find a trespass to chattel?

2. As the court in *Hamidi* emphasizes, trespasses to chattels generally require that the defendant either damage the chattel or dispossess the plaintiff of use or enjoyment of the property. Is there a good reason why actions for trespass to real property do not require a showing of injury (see Jacque v. Steenberg Homes, Inc., p. 54 supra), but actions for trespass to chattels requires some showing of either injury or dispossession? As Justice Mosk notes in his dissent, the Restatement of Torts explains the difference on the ground that people can use self-help to protect their personal property. Even if true, should this make a difference?

3. Although agreeing with the California Supreme Court that trespasses to chattels require either damage or dispossession, most courts that have dealt with trespasses in cyberspace have readily found the requisite damage. In addition to the cases cited in *Hamidi*, see Register.com, Inc. v. Verio, Inc., 356 F.3d 393 (2d Cir. 2004) (unauthorized accessing of a web site by automated software performing multiple successive queries diminished the "condition, quality, or value" of the computer system and risked leading to a server crash). Was the California Supreme Court wrong in concluding that there was no damage in *Hamidi*? For interesting observa-

tions on *Hamidi* and similar cases, see David McGowan, The Trespass Trouble and the Metaphor Muddle, 1 J.L. Econ. & Pol'y 109 (2005).

4. **Spam.** A majority of states have now adopted some form of anti-spam legislation. The federal CAN–SPAM Act, 15 U.S.C. §§ 7701 et seq. (more fully known as the "Controlling the Assault of Non–Solicited Pornography and Marketing Act"), outlaws the sending of spam to recipients who request not to receive any spam from the sender. See generally Lily Zhang, The CAN–SPAM Act: An Insufficient Response to the Growing Spam Problem, 2005 Berkeley Tech. L.J. 301; Roger Allan Ford, Preemption of State Spam Law by the Federal CAN–SPAM Act, 72 U. Chi. L. Rev. 355 (2005); Daniel L. Mayer, Attacking a Windmill: Why the CAN–SPAM Act is a Futile Waste of Time and Money, 31 J. Legis. 177 (2004).

5. **Domain Names.** Are Internet domain names protected property? Should they be? In Kremen v. Cohen, 337 F.3d 1024 (9th Cir. 2003), the plaintiff, Gary Kremen, acquired the domain name "sex.com" from Network Solutions, the exclusive registrar of domain names. When Network Solutions later mistakenly transferred the domain name to a con-man named Stephen Cohen, Kremen sued for conversion. The court had little trouble concluding that domain names are property and that Kremen had a legitimate claim for conversion:

> Property is a broad concept that includes "every intangible benefit and prerogative susceptible of possession or disposition." Downing v. Mun. Court, 88 Cal. App. 2d 345, 350, 198 P.2d 923 (1948) (internal quotation marks omitted). We apply a three-part test to determine whether a property right exists: "First, there must be an interest capable of precise definition; second, it must be capable of exclusive possession or control; and third, the putative owner must have established a legitimate claim to exclusivity." G.S. Rasmussen, 958 F.2d at 903 (footnote omitted). Domain names satisfy each criterion. Like a share of corporate stock or a plot of land, a domain name is a well-defined interest. Someone who registers a domain name decides where on the Internet those who invoke that particular name—whether by typing it into their web browsers, by following a hyperlink, or by other means—are sent. Ownership is exclusive in that the registrant alone makes that decision. Moreover, like other forms of property, domain names are valued, bought and sold, often for millions of dollars, and they are now even subject to in rem jurisdiction.
>
> Finally, registrants have a legitimate claim to exclusivity. Registering a domain name is like staking a claim to a plot of land at the title office. It informs others that the domain name is the registrant's and no one else's. Many registrants also invest substantial time and money to develop and promote websites that depend on their domain names. Ensuring that they reap the benefits of their investments reduces uncertainty and thus encourages investment in the first place, promoting the growth of the Internet overall.

Kremen therefore had an intangible property right in his domain name, and a jury could find that Network Solutions "wrongfully disposed of" that right to his detriment by handing the domain name over to Cohen. . . .

The district court was worried that "the threat of litigation threatens to stifle the registration system by requiring further regulations by [Network Solutions] and potential increases in fees." Given that Network Solutions's "regulations" evidently allowed it to hand over a registrant's domain name on the basis of a facially suspect letter without even contacting him, "further regulations" don't seem like such a bad idea. And the prospect of higher fees presents no issue here that it doesn't in any other context. A bank could lower its ATM fees if it didn't have to pay security guards, but we doubt most depositors would think that was a good idea.

The district court thought there were "methods better suited to regulate the vagaries of domain names" and left it "to the legislature to fashion an appropriate statutory scheme." The legislature, of course, is always free (within constitutional bounds) to refashion the system that courts come up with. But that doesn't mean we should throw up our hands and let private relations degenerate into a free-for-all in the meantime. We apply the common law until the legislature tells us other-wise. And the common law does not stand idle while people give away the property of others.

What does the court mean when it says that the legislature is always free to refashion the property system that the courts devise "within constitutional bounds"? If Congress responded to the *Kremen* case by passing legislation that abolished property rights in domain names, would that constitute an unconstitutional "taking" for which the federal government would have to pay compensation?

F. HUMAN CELLS

Moore v. Regents of the University of California

Supreme Court of California, 1990.
793 P.2d 479.

EDWARD A. PANELLI, JUSTICE.

We granted review in this case to determine whether plaintiff has stated a cause of action against his physician and other defendants for using his cells in potentially lucrative medical research without his permission. Plaintiff alleges that his physician failed to disclose preexisting research and economic interests in the cells before obtaining consent to the medical procedures by which they were extracted. The superior court sustained all defendants' demurrers to the third amended complaint, and the Court of Appeal reversed. We hold that the complaint states a cause of action for breach of the physician's disclosure obligations, but not for conversion.

Our only task in reviewing a ruling on a demurrer is to determine whether the complaint states a cause of action. Accordingly, we assume that the complaint's properly pleaded material allegations are true.... For these purposes we briefly summarize the pertinent factual allegations of the 50–page complaint.

The plaintiff is John Moore (Moore), who underwent treatment for hairy-cell leukemia at the Medical Center of the University of California at Los Angeles (UCLA Medical Center). The five defendants are: (1) Dr. David W. Golde (Golde), a physician who attended Moore at UCLA Medical Center; (2) the Regents of the University of California (Regents), who own and operate the university; (3) Shirley G. Quan (Quan), a researcher employed by the Regents; (4) Genetics Institute, Inc. (Genetics Institute); and (5) Sandoz Pharmaceuticals Corporation and related entities (collectively Sandoz).

Moore first visited UCLA Medical Center on October 5, 1976, shortly after he learned that he had hairy-cell leukemia. After hospitalizing Moore and "withdraw[ing] extensive amounts of blood, bone marrow aspirate, and other bodily substances," Golde confirmed that diagnosis. At this time all defendants, including Golde, were aware that "certain blood products and blood components were of great value in a number of commercial and scientific efforts" and that access to a patient whose blood contained these substances would provide "competitive, commercial, and scientific advantages."

On October 8, 1976, Golde recommended that Moore's spleen be removed. Golde informed Moore "that he had reason to fear for his life, and that the proposed splenectomy operation ... was necessary to slow down the progress of his disease." Based upon Golde's representations, Moore signed a written consent form authorizing the splenectomy.

Before the operation, Golde and Quan "formed the intent and made arrangements to obtain portions of [Moore's] spleen following its removal" and to take them to a separate research unit. Golde gave written instructions to this effect on October 18 and 19, 1976. These research activities "were not intended to have ... any relation to [Moore's] medical ... care." However, neither Golde nor Quan informed Moore of their plans to conduct this research or requested his permission. Surgeons at UCLA Medical Center, whom the complaint does not name as defendants, removed Moore's spleen on October 20, 1976.

Moore returned to the UCLA Medical Center several times between November 1976 and September 1983. He did so at Golde's direction and based upon representations "that such visits were necessary and required for his health and well-being, and based upon the trust inherent in and by virtue of the physician-patient relationship...." On each of these visits

Golde withdrew additional samples of "blood, blood serum, skin, bone marrow aspirate, and sperm." On each occasion Moore traveled to the UCLA Medical Center from his home in Seattle because he had been told that the procedures were to be performed only there and only under Golde's direction.

"In fact, [however,] throughout the period of time that [Moore] was under [Golde's] care and treatment, ... the defendants were actively involved in a number of activities which they concealed from [Moore]. ..." Specifically, defendants were conducting research on Moore's cells and planned to "benefit financially and competitively ... [by exploiting the cells] and [their] exclusive access to [the cells] by virtue of [Golde's] on-going physician-patient relationship...."

Sometime before August 1979, Golde established a cell line from Moore's T-lymphocytes. On January 30, 1981, the Regents applied for a patent on the cell line, listing Golde and Quan as inventors. "[B]y virtue of an established policy ..., [the] Regents, Golde, and Quan would share in any royalties or profits ... arising out of [the] patent." The patent issued on March 20, 1984, naming Golde and Quan as the inventors of the cell line and the Regents as the assignee of the patent.

The Regents' patent also covers various methods for using the cell line to produce lymphokines. Moore admits in his complaint that "the true clinical potential of each of the lymphokines ... [is] difficult to predict, [but] ... competing commercial firms in these relevant fields have published reports in biotechnology industry periodicals predicting a potential market of approximately 3.01 Billion Dollars by the year 1990 for a whole range of [such lymphokines]...."

With the Regents' assistance, Golde negotiated agreements for commercial development of the cell line and products to be derived from it. Under an agreement with Genetics Institute, Golde "became a pair consultant" and "acquired the rights to 75,000 shares of common stock." Genetics Institute also agreed to pay Golde and the Regents "at least $330,000 over three years, including a pro-rata share of [Golde's] salary and fringe benefits, in exchange for ... exclusive access to the materials and research performed" on the cell line and products derived from it. On June 4, 1982, Sandoz "was added to the agreement," and compensation payable to Golde and the Regents was increased by $110,000....

A. Breach of Fiduciary Duty and Lack of Informed Consent

Moore repeatedly alleges that Golde failed to disclose the extent of his research and economic interests in Moore's cells before obtaining consent to the medical procedure by which the cells were extracted. These allegations, in our view, state a cause of action against Golde for invading a legally protected interest of his patient. This cause of action can properly be characterized as the breach of a fiduciary duty to disclose facts material to the patient's consent or, alternatively, as the patient's informed consent.

Our analysis begins with three well-established principles. First, "a person of adult years and in sound mind has the right, in the exercise of control over his own body, to determine whether or not to submit to lawful medical treatment." Second, "the patient's consent to treatment, to be effective, must be an informed consent." Third, in soliciting the patient's consent, a physician has a fiduciary duty to disclose all information material to the patient's decision. . . .

Accordingly, we hold that a physician who is seeking a patient's consent for a medical procedure must, in order to satisfy his fiduciary duty and to obtain the patient's informed consent, disclose personal interests unrelated to the patient's health, whether research or economic, that may affect his medical judgment. . . .

B. Conversion

Moore also attempts to characterize the invasion of his rights as a conversion—a tort that protects against interference with possessory and ownership interests in personal property. He theorizes that he continued to own his cells following their removal from his body, at least for the purpose of directing their use, and that he never consented to their use in potentially lucrative medical research. Thus, to complete Moore's argument, defendants' unauthorized use of his cells constitutes a conversion.[a] As a result of the alleged conversion, Moore claims a proprietary interest in each of the products that any of the defendants might ever create from his cells or the patented cell line. . . .

1. Moore's Claim Under Existing Law

. . . . Since Moore clearly did not expect to retain possession of his cells following their removal, to sue for their conversion he must have retained an ownership interest in them. . . . Moore relies, as did the Court of Appeal, primarily on decisions addressing privacy rights. One line of cases involved unwanted publicity. These opinions hold that every person has a proprietary interest in his own likeness and that unauthorized, business use of a likeness is redressible as a tort. . . .

. . . . Moore . . . argues that "[i]f the courts have found a sufficient proprietary interest in one's persona, how could one not have a right in one's own genetic material, something far more profoundly the essence of one's human uniqueness than a name or a face?" However, . . . the goal and result of defendants' efforts has been to manufacture lymphokines. Lymphokines, unlike a name or a face, have the same molecular structure in every human being and the same, important functions in every human being's immune system. Moreover, the particular genetic material which is responsible for the natural production of lymphokines, and which defendants use to manufacture lymphokines in the laboratory, is also the same in every person; it is no more unique to Moore than the number of vertebrae in the spine or the chemical formula of hemoglobin. . . .

a. Eds.—As discussed on p. 285 note a, "conversion" is the wrongful exercise of dominion or control over someone else's personal property.

The next consideration that makes Moore's claim of ownership problematic is California statutory law, which drastically limits a patient's control over excised cells [by regulating disposal of human tissues to protect public health and safety].... By restricting how excised cells may be used and requiring their eventual destruction, the statute eliminates so many of the rights ordinarily attached to property that one cannot simply assume that what is left amounts to "property" or "ownership" for purposes of conversion law....

Finally, the subject matter of the Regent's patent—the patented cell line and the products derived from it—cannot be Moore's property. This is because the patented cell line is both factually and legally distinct from the cells taken from Moore's body. Federal law permits the patenting of organisms that represent the product of "human ingenuity," but not naturally occurred organisms. Diamond v. Chakrabarty, 447 U.S. 303, 309–310 (1980). Human cell lines are patentable because "[l]ong-term adaptation and growth of human tissues and cells in culture is difficult—often considered an art ...," and the probability of success is low. It is this inventive effort that patent law rewards, not the discovery of naturally occurring raw materials. Thus, Moore's allegations that he owns the cell line and the products derived from it are inconsistent with the patent, which constitutes an authoritative determination that the cell line is the product of invention....

2. Should Conversion Liability Be Extended?

As we have discussed, Moore's novel claim to own the biological materials at issue in this case is problematic, at best. Accordingly, his attempt to apply the theory of conversion within this context must frankly be recognized as a request to extend that theory. While we do not purport to hold that excised cells can never be property for any purpose whatsoever, the novelty of Moore's claim demands express consideration of the policies to be served by extending liability rather than blind deference to a complaint alleging as a legal conclusion the existence of a cause of action.

There are three reasons why it is inappropriate to impose liability for conversion based upon the allegations of Moore's complaint. First, a fair balancing of the relevant policy considerations counsels against extending the tort. Second, problems in this area are better suited to legislative resolution. Third, the tort of conversion is not necessary to protect patients' rights. For these reasons, we conclude that the use of excised human cells in medical research does not amount to a conversion.

Of the relevant policy considerations, two are of overriding importance. The first is protection of a competent patient's right to make autonomous medical decisions.... This policy weighs in favor of providing a remedy to patients when physicians act with undisclosed motives that may affect their professional judgment. The second important policy consideration is that we not threaten with disabling civil liability innocent parties who are engaged in socially useful activities, such as researchers who have no reason to believe that their use of a particular cell sample is, or may be, against a donor's wishes....

Research on human cells plays a critical role in medical research. This is so because researchers are increasingly able to isolate naturally occurring, medically useful biological substances and to produce useful quantities of such substances through genetic engineering. These efforts are beginning to bear fruit. Products developed through biotechnology that have already been approved for marketing in this country include treatments and tests for leukemia, cancer, diabetes, dwarfism, hepatitis-B, kidney transplant rejection, emphysema, osteoporosis, ulcers, anemia, infertility, and gynecological tumors, to name but a few.

The extension of conversion law into this area will hinder research by restricting access to the necessary raw materials. Thousands of human cell lines already exist in tissue repositories, such as the American Type Culture Collection and those operated by the National Institutes of Health and the American Cancer Society. These repositories respond to tens of thousands of requests for samples annually. Since the patent office requires the holders of patents on cell lines to make samples available to anyone, many patent holders place their cell lines in repositories to avoid the administrative burden of responding to request. At present, human cell lines are routinely copied and distributed to other researchers for experimental purposes, usually free of charge. This exchange of scientific materials, which still is relatively free and efficient, will surely be compromised if each cell sample becomes the potential subject matter of a lawsuit.

To expand liability by extending conversion law into this area would have a broad impact. The House Committee on Science and Technology of the United States Congress found that "49 percent of the researchers at medical institutions surveyed used human tissues or cells in their research." Many receive grants from the National Institute of Health for this work. In addition, "there are nearly 350 commercial biotechnology firms in the United States actively engaged in biotechnology research and commercial product development and approximately 25 to 30 percent appear to be engaged in research to develop a human therapeutic or diagnostic reagent.... Most, but not all, of the human therapeutic products are derived from human tissues and cells, or human cell lines or cloned genes."....

If the scientific users of human cells are to be held liable for failing to investigate the consensual pedigree of their raw materials, we believe the Legislature should make that decision. Complex policy choices affecting all society are involved, and "[l]egislatures, in making such policy decisions, have the ability to gather empirical evidence, solicit the advice of experts, and hold hearings at which all interested parties present evidence and express their views...." ...

For these reasons, we hold that the allegations of Moore's third amended complaint state a cause of action for breach of fiduciary duty or lack of informed consent, but not conversion.

ARMAND ARABIAN, JUSTICE, concurring.

.... Plaintiff has asked us to recognize and enforce a right to sell one's own body tissue for profit. He entreats us to regard the human vessel—the single most venerated and protected subject in any civilized society—as equal with the basest commercial commodity. He urges us to commingle the sacred with the profane. He asks much. . . .

I share Justice Mosk's sense of outrage [in his dissenting opinion reproduced below], but I cannot follow its path. His eloquent paean to the human spirit illuminates the problem, not the solution. Does it uplift or degrade the "unique human persona" to treat human tissue as a fungible article of commerce? Would it advance or impede the human condition, spiritually or scientifically, by delivering the majestic force of the law behind plaintiff's claim? I do not know the answers to these troubling questions, nor am I willing—like Justice Mosk—to treat them simply as issues of "tort" law, susceptible of judicial resolution.

Where then shall a complete resolution be found? Clearly the Legislature, as the majority opinion suggests, is the proper deliberative forum. . . .

STANLEY MOSK, JUSTICE, dissenting.

. . . . [T]he concept of property is often said to refer to a "bundle of rights" that may be exercised with respect to that object—principally the rights to possess the property, to use the property, to exclude others from the property, and to dispose of the property by sale or by gift. . . . But the same bundle of rights does not attach to all forms of property. For a variety of policy reasons, the law limits or even forbids the exercise of certain rights over certain forms of property. For example, both law and contract may limit the right of an owner of real property to use his parcel as he sees fit. Owners of various forms of personal property may likewise be subject to restrictions on the time, place, and manner of their use. Limitations on the disposition of real property, while less common, may also be imposed. Finally, some types of personal property may be sold but not given away,[9] while others may be given away but not sold,[10] and still others may neither be given away nor sold.[11]

In each of the foregoing instances, the limitation or prohibition diminishes the bundle of rights that would otherwise attach to the property, yet what remains is still deemed in law to be a predictable property interest. "Since property or title is a complex bundle of rights, duties, powers and immunities, the pruning away of some or a great many of these elements does not entirely destroy the title. . . ." (People v. Walker (1939) 33 Cal. App. 2d 18, 20 [90 P.2d 854] [even the possessor of contraband has certain property rights in it against anyone other than the state].) [Even if the majority is correct that California law limits a patient's control over excised cells, Moore] at least had the right to do with his own tissue whatever the

9. A person contemplating bankruptcy may sell his property at its "reasonably equivalent value," but he may not make a gift of the same property.

10. A sportsman may give away wild fish or game that he has caught or killed pursuant to his license, but he may not sell it. (Fish & Game Code §§ 3039, 7121.) The transfer of human organs and blood is a special case that I discuss below.

11. E.g., a license to practice a profession, or a prescription drug in the hands of the person for whom it is prescribed.

defendants did with it: i.e., he could have contracted with researchers and pharmaceutical companies to develop and exploit the vast commercial potential of his tissue and its products. Defendants certainly believe that their right to do the foregoing ... is a significant property right.... The Court of Appeal summed up the point by observing that "Defendants' position that plaintiff cannot own his tissue, but that they can, is fraught with irony." It is also legally untenable....

[The majority's argument that the patent on the cell line precludes plaintiff's conversion claim is also wrong.] To be sure, the patent granted defendants the exclusive right to make, use, or sell the invention for a period of 17 years. But Moore does not assert any such right for himself. Rather, he seeks to show that he is entitled, in fairness and equity, to some share in the profits that defendants have made and will make from their commercial exploitation of the Mo cell line. I do not question that the cell line is primarily the product of defendants' inventive effort. Yet likewise no one can question Moore's crucial contribution to the invention—an invention named ironically, after him: but for the cells of Moore's body taken by defendants, there would have been no Mo cell line....

[E]very individual has a legally predictable property interest in his own body and its products. First, our society acknowledges a profound ethical imperative to respect the human body as the physical and temporal expression of the unique human persona. One manifestation of that respect is our prohibition against direct abuse of the body by torture or other forms of cruel or unusual punishment. Another is our prohibition against indirect abuse of the body by its economic exploitation for the sole benefit of another person. The most abhorrent form of such exploitation, of course, was the institution of slavery. Lesser forms, such as indentured servitude or even debtors' prison, have also disappeared. Yet their specter haunts the laboratories and boardrooms of today's biotechnological research-industrial complex. It arises wherever scientists or industrialists claim, as defendants claim here, the right to appropriate and exploit a patient's tissue for their sole economic benefit—the right, in other words, to freely mine or harvest valuable physical properties of the patient's body: ".... Such research tends to treat the human body as a commodity—a means to a profitable end. The dignity and sanctity with which we regard the human whole, body as well as mind and soul, are absent when we allow researchers to further their own interests without the patient's participation by using a patient's cells as the basis for a marketable product." Danforth, Cells, Sales, & Royalties: The Patient's Right to a Portion of the Profits, 6 Yale L. & Pol'y Rev. 179, 190 (1988).

A second policy consideration adds notions of equity to those of ethics. Our society values fundamental fairness in dealings between its members, and condemns the unjust enrichment of any member at the expense of another. This is particularly true when, as here, the parties are not in equal bargaining positions. We are repeatedly told that the commercial products of the biotechnological revolution "hold the promise of tremendous profit." In the case at bar, for example, the complaint alleges that the market for the kinds of proteins produced by the Mo cell line was predicted to exceed $3 billion by 1990. These profits are currently shared exclusively between the biotechnology industry and the universities that support that industry....

There is, however, a third party to the biotechnology enterprise—the patient who is the source of the blood or tissue from which all these profits are derived. While he may be a silent partner, his contribution to the venture is absolutely crucial: ... but for the cells of Moore's body taken by defendant there would have been no Mo cell line at all. Yet defendants deny that Moore is entitled to any share whatever in the proceeds of his cell line. This is both inequitable and immoral....

[The concurring and dissenting opinion of Justice Allen Broussard is omitted.]

Notes & Questions

1. The Connecticut Supreme Court has reached a similar result in Cornelio v. Stamford Hospital, 717 A.2d 140 (Conn. 1998), holding that a patient did not have a property right to her cells contained in pap smear specimen slides.

2. **The Tragedy of the Anticommons.** Can the law sometimes create too much property? In *Moore*, the majority argues against awarding the plaintiff a property right in his excised cells on the ground in part that it could interfere with scientific research. According to the court, the exchange of scientific materials "will surely be compromised if each cell sample becomes the potential subject matter of a lawsuit." In an important article, Professor Michael Heller has argued more generally that, just as the lack of property can lead to tragedy (the "tragedy of the commons," see p. 224), the creation of too many property rights can also lead to tragic consequences (the tragedy of the anticommons). Michael A. Heller, The Tragedy of the Anticommons: Property in the Transition from Marx to Markets, 111 Harv. L. Rev. 621 (1998). Professor Heller illustrates the tragedy of the anticommons by observing that many Moscow storefronts are bare despite market reforms. The reason, according to Professor Heller, is that too many people have rights over the storefronts. "Transition regimes have often failed to endow any individual with a bundle of rights that represents full ownership of storefronts or other scarce resources.... In a typical Moscow storefront, one owner may be endowed initially with the right to sell, another to receive sale revenue, and still others to lease, receive lease revenue, occupy, and determine use. Each owner can block the others from using the space as a storefront. No one can set up shop without collecting the consent of all of the other owners." Id. at 623

3. Justice Panelli argues that, because California statutory law regulates the use and disposal of human tissue, so few rights remain that "one cannot simply assume that what is left amounts to 'property' or 'ownership' for purposes of conversion law" (supra page 301). Does "property" require a certain set or quantum of rights? If so, what are the rights? As

you have already seen (and will discover again in Chapters 7–10), real property interests do not always include every right included in a fee simple absolute. Even if the California Supreme Court had simply held that an individual has a right to preclude others from using any cells excised from his body without his permission, wouldn't this "right to exclude"—perhaps the core interest of property rights (see page 53 supra)—be sufficient to constitute a property right?

4. **The Sale of Body Parts.** What are the consequences of calling something "property"? If the California Supreme Court had recognized a personal property interest in excised cells, would it have had to acknowledge a right in each person to sell her cells? What might be the practical consequences of awarding a property right in human cells but not the right to sell the property?

Policymakers have long debated whether to permit sales of blood and human organs. Some have argued that blood sales dilute altruism and erode community. See, e.g, Richard Titmuss, The Gift Relationship: From Human Blood To Social Policy (1997); Thomas H. Murray, On the Human Body as Property: The Meaning of Embodiment, Markets, and the Meaning of Strangers, 20 J. Legal Reform 1055 (1987). Others have argued that sales of blood and other body parts undermine human dignity. See, e.g., Stephen R. Munzer, An Uneasy Case Against Property Rights in Body Parts, Soc. Phil. & Pol'y, Summer 1994, at 259. Others argue that markets in human biological materials are for all practical purposes unavoidable and not inherently troubling. See Julia D. Mahoney, The Market for Human Tissue, 86 Va. L. Rev. 163 (2000).

The National Organ Transplant Act of 1984 makes it a criminal offense for "any person to knowingly acquire, receive, or otherwise transfer any human organ for valuable consideration for use in human transplantation if the transfer affects interstate commerce." 42 U.S.C. § 274e. And about half the states have similar laws. See, e.g., Fla. Stat. Ann. § 873.01 (prohibiting the sale or purchase of human organs or tissues for valuable consideration); S.D. Codified Laws § 34–26–44 (prohibiting the acquisition or transfer of human organs for valuable consideration for use in a transplant). Yet most states do permit blood, sperm, and eggs to be bartered on the market. A few states authorize limited transfers of human organs for valuable consideration. See, e.g., Miss. Code Ann. § 41–39–9 (permitting contracts for the use of human organs after death). And everyone has the right to pick and choose who, if anyone, will benefit from their body parts by donating body parts while they are alive or devising them in their will. See Uniform Anatomical Gift Act, 8A U.L.A. 99 (1993).

5. **Property Rights in Dead Bodies.** The spouses and family of decedents have raised property claims in an effort to prevent hospitals and others from using corneas, eye balls, and other organs from the decedents without permission. In Brotherton v. Cleveland, 923 F.2d 477 (6th Cir. 1991), for example, the court held that a widow held limited property interests in her dead husband's body and that the state's removal of his corneas for transplants constituted an unconstitutional taking of the prop-

erty without compensation. See also Mansaw v. Midwest Organ Bank, 1998 WL 386327 (W.D. Mo. 1998) (parents of dead child have constitutionally protected property interest in the child's organs and must consent to their removal); Whaley v. County of Tuscola, 58 F.3d 1111 (6th Cir. 1995) (relatives have constitutionally protected property interest in corneas and eye balls of the deceased). But see Florida v. Powell, 497 So. 2d 1188 (Fla. 1986) (next of kin does not possess property interest in decedent's body and thus could not object to removal of corneas); Georgia Lions Eye Bank, Inc. v. Lavant, 335 S.E.2d 127 (Ga. 1985) (no constitutionally protected property in corneas from dead bodies).

6. **Property Rights in Stored Sperm & Frozen Embryos.** Advances in medical science during the latter decades of the 20th century have led to a number of cases involving rights to stored sperm and frozen embryos. Courts have split on whether to decide such cases based on traditional property concepts. In Hecht v. Superior Court, 59 Cal. Rptr. 2d 222 (Cal. App. 1996), for example, the former girlfriend and two adult children of a man who had committed suicide battled over the dead man's frozen sperm. The girlfriend claimed them based on the man's will, while the children relied on a settlement agreement dividing the residual assets of the man's estate. After earlier deciding that the sperm were property and subject to the jurisdiction of the probate court, the California Court of Appeal backed away from a pure property approach. As the court explained, the sperm might have been the property of the man, but

> the genetic material involved here is a unique form of "property." It is not subject to division through an agreement among the decedent's potential beneficiaries which is inconsistent with decedent's manifest intent about its disposition. A man's sperm or a woman's ova or a couple's embryos are not the same as a quarter of land, a cache of cash, or a favorite limousine. Rules appropriate to the disposition of the latter are not necessarily appropriate for the former.

Because the man clearly intended the sperm to go to his girlfriend, the court ruled in her favor on largely privacy grounds. See also York v. Jones, 717 F. Supp. 421 (E.D. Va. 1989) (applying property law to adjudicate a dispute over a frozen embryo); Davis v. Davis, 842 S.W.2d 588 (Tenn. 1992) (using privacy rather than property concepts to resolve a divorced couple's dispute over frozen embryos).

7. **Property Rights in a Woman's Womb.** Over half of the states currently have laws that prevent doctors from removing life-support systems from incompetent pregnant women, even if they have made their wish known through a living will or designated proxy not to have their life sustained by artificial means. See, e.g., Conn. Gen. Stat. Ann. § 19A–574; Tex. Health & Safety Code Ann. § 672.019. Do such laws violate the property rights of the women? See Radhika Rao, Property, Privacy, and the Human Body, 80 B.U.L. Rev. 359, 409–414 (2000) (such laws "literally 'take' the bodies of incompetent pregnant women, treating them as chattel that may be drafted into service as fetal incubators for the state").

8. The relevance of property concepts for these issues has produced an outpouring of legal analysis. For a sampling, see E. Richard Gold, Body Parts: Property Rights and the Ownership of Human Biological Materials (1996); Rao, supra Note 7; Mahoney, supra note 3; Munzer, supra Note 4; Stephen R. Munzer, Kant and Property Rights in Body Parts, 6 Can. J.L. & Juris. 319 (1993).

PART II

LAND TRANSFER AND FINANCE

One of the most important rights in the ownership of real property is the right to transfer the property to someone else. Land changes hands every day as people move, their needs change, and new, economically more valuable uses of land arise. The free alienability of real property permits ownership to continually evolve in response to these changes, providing property owners with valuable flexibility and encouraging economically more efficient use of land.

Effective markets in land depend upon a high degree of certainty regarding the rights that are being traded and upon low transaction costs. People will be more hesitant to purchase land if they are unsure whether the seller really owns the property rights that she claims to have. Most people are risk averse and avoid buying pigs in a poke. Property transfers will also decline if the costs of negotiating and concluding the purchase are high. Land transfers, however, can be extremely complex, generate significant transaction costs, and raise significant uncertainties. One dimension for evaluating the effectiveness of a legal system is how well it performs in minimizing the transaction costs and uncertainties that accompany transactions in land.

Why are land transfers so complex? Why can a transfer of land not be accomplished as simply as the sale of a light bulb or a pound of butter? One reason is that a single parcel of real property is almost infinitely divisible into separate ownership—mining rights, surface rights and air rights, easements for rights of way or public utility lines, and security for mortgage loans, taxes, and judgments. The buyer must, before closing, uncover each such interest that will encumber his ownership. Since, unlike most other objects of ownership, land endures, these interests endure as well and, accumulating over time, increase a buyer's costs of search and negotiation as each day goes by.

Another reason for complexity is historical. Conveyancing rules were originally designed to meet needs quite different from those that dominate today's real estate marketplace, and law reform has not always kept pace with economic and social change. Early English conveyancing law required—if this can be imagined—an actual, physical delivery of the land itself. The principal method of land transfer in feudal times was feoffment with livery of seisin: *A* and *B,* transferor and transferee, would travel to the land to be conveyed and, in the presence of assembled neighbors, *A* would orally convey title and possession to *B,* symbolizing the transfer by handing over a twig or clump of earth. If the land was particularly valuable, or the terms of the transfer complex, the conveyance might also be evidenced by a written charter or deed, but a writing was neither necessary nor sufficient to accomplish the conveyance.

The Statute of Uses, enacted in 1535, made it possible for *A* to convey title to *B* by a written instrument alone, thus avoiding the inconvenience of feoffment with livery of seisin. The Statute of Frauds, enacted in 1677, made it *mandatory* for *A* to use a written instrument. Thus, by the late seventeenth century, execution and delivery of a deed replaced the ceremony of livery of seisin as the central requirement for land transfers in England.

The American colonists drew selectively from English conveyancing practice, adapting some elements, discarding others, to fit the needs of a society in which land was viewed as an item of commerce and not as a dynastic base, and in which free and easy transfers were preferred to highly formalized ceremonies. Although land in America was sometimes conveyed by feoffment with livery of seisin, transfer by delivery of a written deed was by far the more common practice. And, over time, the deeds themselves took increasingly shorter and more simplified forms.

The evolution of conveyancing practice, both in England and America, produced an almost total dependence on written instruments, and on the paper record of those instruments, as the basis for land transfer. Although this new reliance on documentary evidence of title succeeded in adapting transfer formalities to post-feudal commercial needs, it also produced several new problems. Paper is cheap and easily transmitted—attributes that facilitate not only legitimate land transfers but unintended or unauthorized transfers as well. New formalities—seal, acknowledgment, delivery—were adopted to minimize the risk of a forged or other unintended transfer.

A still greater problem created by the new reliance on documentary transfers was that it enabled secret, multiple conveyances of the same piece of land to unsuspecting conveyees. Given several blank deed forms and a disposition to fraud, *A,* who had once conveyed Greenacre to *B,* could subsequently convey it, all over again, to *C, D, E* and countless others. In England, the Statute of Enrollments, enacted at the same time as the Statute of Uses, sought to reduce fraud by exposing conveyances on the public record; however, large loopholes in the statute doomed it to failure. Recording acts adopted in the New England colonies were far more successful and set the pattern for recording systems that, used in all American states today, almost entirely eliminate the opportunity for fraudulent or mistaken multiple transfers.

The recording acts, in turn, created yet another conveyancing dilemma. Because the efficacy of the recording system depends on the permanence of its underlying records, land titles will over time become tangled and encrusted with records of transactions dating back decades and even centuries; as a result, the speed and security of title searches declined as each year passed.

This Part examines the role of the law in promoting the alienability of land. Chapter 4 examines the typical land sale and the legal issues that arise in negotiating and consummating a sale. Chapter 5 then turns to the methods that states and private institutions have adopted to provide assurance to purchasers that the sellers have satisfactory title to the land they are transferring. Chapter 6 finally takes a brief look at the means by which purchasers finance their land acquisitions. Throughout these materials, ask yourself the purpose behind the various requirements imposed by the law, whether the requirements serve a valuable social goal, and whether that goal could be accomplished at a lower cost.

CHAPTER 4

LAND SALES

Buying land, as already noted, is no simple matter. Whether it is a one-family house or a 200–store shopping center, buyer and seller will typically find it necessary to execute several documents and to employ the services of many specialists. All purchase transactions, residential or commercial, rest on the same fundamental principles and usually follow roughly the same steps.

Consider, as an example, the typical steps involved in the sale of a home. As an initial step, the owner who wishes to sell her home will usually hire a real estate broker who, in return for a commission on sale—commonly 5% to 7% of the sale price—will agree to show the property to prospective buyers. Often this broker will enlist the aid of other brokers in the community to solicit buyers and to help close the transaction.

Once a willing buyer has been found and the terms of the purchase have been negotiated, the parties will execute a sales contract obligating the seller to convey title, and obligating the buyer to pay the purchase price, on the closing date, typically 30 to 60 days from the date the contract was signed. Many sales contracts today are form contracts that the broker will fill in on behalf of the parties. The seller's performance under the contract will usually be conditioned only on the buyer's payment of the purchase price. The buyer, however, will typically condition his performance on the seller's ability to convey clear title and on the availability of a mortgage loan to finance his purchase. When the sales contract is executed, the buyer generally will also pay a small down payment toward the ultimate purchase of the house.

During the contract's executory period, the buyer will pursue the applications and inquiries required by the contract conditions. Often he will rely on the real estate broker to help him arrange the needed financing with a local institutional lender such as a bank or savings and loan association. In some locales the buyer's lawyer will order a search of local land title records, review the search report, and then advise the buyer on whether the seller has good title; in other locales, the buyer will ask a title insurance company to perform the title search and, if the search discloses that title is good, to issue an insurance policy to that effect.

If the institutional lender refuses to make the requested loan, or if the title search reveals that the seller's title is not good, the buyer will be excused from performing the contract. If, however, all conditions have been met, the buyer will tender the purchase price and the seller will tender a deed conveying title to the property. The contract will close when the seller receives the money and the buyer receives the deed which he will then promptly record in the county recorder's office. (As part of the closing, the institutional lender will simultaneously receive a note or bond and mortgage or deed of trust from the buyer, and will promptly record the mortgage or deed of trust.)

A. The Role of Real Estate Brokers and Lawyers

1. Brokers

Quintin Johnstone, Land Transfers: Process and Processors

22 Val. U. L. Rev. 493, 494–98 (1988).

The major services provided by real estate brokers are bringing buyers and sellers together, assisting them to make informed decisions on whether or not to enter into sales contracts, and assisting them with the terms of any such arrangements. Most brokered real estate sales are of single family residences and one or both parties to these sales agreements usually know little about land transfer procedures and often know little about the housing market. Furthermore, the buyers usually have a limited capacity to evaluate the merits of the properties being purchased. Thus, in these residential transactions, brokers commonly assume important educational and advisory roles in relation to the parties. In sales of commercial, industrial, large multi-unit residential, and most large agricultural land parcels, the parties normally are far more knowledgeable. While brokers in these transactions also may have educational and advisory roles, they operate in a context of far greater buyer and seller expertise. Although most real estate sales are made with the assistance of brokers, a small, but possibly growing minority are made by owners without the participation of brokers. . . .

Real estate brokers for their sales work almost universally are paid on a commission basis, commonly six percent of the contract price, and estimates indicate that gross commissions nationally can total as much as $10 billion per year. The commission is earned only if a willing buyer is found, a contract to purchase is entered into, or the sales transaction is closed and a deed delivered. The broker's contract with his principal, usually the seller, often expressly states how far the transaction must proceed before the broker's commission is earned. Irrespective of how much time and money the broker invests in trying to effectuate a sale, the broker normally receives nothing for his efforts unless a qualified buyer is produced and a sale is made or some other specified stage in the transaction is reached. Real estate brokers' commission rates are not set by statute or government regulation, but by contract between brokers and their principals. . . .

In most communities, marketing of single-family residences is greatly enhanced by a form of cooperative venture among brokers, the multiple listing service (MLS). The MLS device, well-established in the United States since at least the 1920s, is a pooled marketing arrangement, functioning somewhat like a stock or commodities exchange, in which listing of properties for sale made with are participating broker are circulated to all other brokers participating in the scheme. Prospective buyers who contract any participating broker then are informed of the types of available properties that are listed through the exchange. If a listed property is sold, the sales commission is split between the listing broker, the one with whom the property was originally listed, and the so-called selling broker, the one who finds a buyer....

Compared to many occupations, real estate brokers are not extensively regulated by government. Real estate brokers are licensed, although license acquisition is relatively easy to obtain; and real estate brokers are, of course, subject to the limitations of antitrust law and to laws restricting performance of many law-related services to lawyers. There are few other significant regulatory restrictions on them of much significance. Every state licenses brokers, but the requirements vary somewhat from state to state. Generally, an examination is required along with evidence of good moral character. Licenses are subject to revocation for improper conduct. Some classes of persons may engage in real estate brokerage activities without being licenses; commonly, persons selling properties they own, lawyers, and financial institutions acting as fiduciaries. Salespersons, those persons working for a broker as employees or independent contractors, are separately licensed, although the examination and other prerequisites for these license ordinarily are less demanding than for broker licenses. A high percentage of licensed salespersons work only apart-time at selling real estate. Many hold other jobs full-time and moonlight at selling real estates. Some are housewives or retired persons without other employment. In periods when sales activity is slow, there is a tendency for the part-timers to put in less effort on their real estate work or to withdraw entirely pending market revival. The usual compensation of salespersons, both full- and part-time, is a portion of the sales commission going to the broker....

Notes & Questions

1. **Real Estate Brokers.** As Johnstone notes, real estate brokers are almost always the agents of, and paid by, the seller. As explained below in Note 5, however, the listing broker in many cases also represents the buyer. About 80 percent of home sellers use brokers to market their homes, and 90 percent of the home sales negotiated through a broker are listed with one or more of the multiple listing services described by Johnstone. Although brokerage firms were historically local and relatively small, many have developed into nationwide organizations through mergers, franchising, and referral networks. Real estate brokers have also begun to expand the services that they provide to include home finance, insurance, and escrow and other closing services.

Computer technology has doubtless spurred the geographic expansion of brokerage firms. Today a person moving from one coast to the other can access a nationwide listing service on the internet and call up current housing listings from the area to which she is moving. The same computer-communications technologies have also helped to nationalize and shorten the otherwise local and protracted search for financing. Several computer databases now give brokers continuously updated lists of mortgage lenders and itemize the availability and terms of loans. Some services will also evaluate the borrower's creditworthiness, process the loan documents, and even commit the funds.

2. **Brokerage Agreements.** Brokers use four basic types of agreements in listing and marketing houses for sellers: *exclusive right to sell*, *exclusive agency*, *open*, and *net*. *Exclusive right to sell* contracts are the most favorable to the listing broker, giving her the right to a commission if the property is sold by anyone, even the owner, during the term of the listing agreement. *Exclusive agency* contracts entitle the broker to a commission if she or any other broker sells the property, but not if the property is sold through the efforts of the owner. In an *open,* or *nonexclusive,* listing agreement, the broker is entitled to a commission only if she is the first to procure a ready, willing, and able buyer; if the owner, or anyone else for that matter, finds a buyer first, the broker has no claim. In a *net* listing contract, the owner agrees to accept a specific price for the property and the broker receives any amount paid in excess of that price.

3. **Interpreting Brokerage Agreements.** Most brokers encourage sellers to sign pre-printed agreements drafted by broker associations. Even the most commonly used broker-drafted forms, however, are not free from ambiguity, and courts are sometimes called on to resolve a number of questions. Courts generally construe ambiguous agreements against the broker on the ground that brokers have superior bargaining power, greater expertise, and are responsible for selecting the form of listing agreement.

One question that occasionally arises is what type of listing agreement broker and seller have made. For example, in Holiday Homes of St. John, Inc. v. Lockhart, 678 F.2d 1176 (3d Cir.1982), the form agreement specified an "Exclusive Right to Sell Basis," but also provided that the commission would be payable only upon the broker's procurement of a ready, willing and able buyer. The court seized on this ambiguity to hold that an exclusive right to sell agreement had not been created. See also Bourgoin v. Fortier, 310 A.2d 618 (Me. 1973) (ambiguous agreements should be read to create an exclusive agency listing, rather than an exclusive right to sell listing).

A more frequent question is when has a "sale" occurred entitling the broker to his commission. What happens, for example, if the broker produces a buyer ready, willing, and able to buy on the terms fixed by the seller, but for some reason the sale never takes place? The traditional rule is that a broker is entitled to a commission when the broker produces a "ready, willing, and able" buyer who is accepted by the seller, whether or not the sale is later consummated. See, e.g., Ladd v. Coldwell Banker, 563

N.Y.S.2d 255 (App. Div. 1990); Sticht v. Shull, 543 So. 2d 395 (Fla. App. 1989). A growing minority of jurisdictions, however, have held that brokers are not entitled to a commission unless and until a sale closes (except where the failure to complete the sale is the result of a wrongful act or interference by the seller). See Margaret H. Wayne Trust v. Lipsky, 846 P.2d 904 (Idaho 1993); Tristram's Landing, Inc. v. Wait, 327 N.E.2d 727 (Mass. 1975); Ellsworth Dobbs, Inc. v. Johnson, 236 A.2d 843 (N.J. 1967).

A related question is what constitutes a sale. An exchange of property usually constitutes a sale for purposes of exclusive right to sell listings. See, e.g., Donlon v. Babin, 44 So. 2d 134 (La. App. 1950). But the government's exercise of eminent domain does not. See, e.g., Lundstrom, Inc. v. Nikkei Concerns, Inc., 758 P.2d 561 (Wash. App. 1988).

4. **Broker's Duties to Seller.** A broker's duties to the listing seller are governed by a fiduciary standard. The standard is usually applied strictly. For example, in Cogan v. Kidder, Mathews & Segner, Inc., 648 P.2d 875 (Wash. 1982), the broker's failure to inform the seller that it was acting as a dual agent, and also represented the buyer, was held to bar the broker from recovering the $19,000 commission that seller had agreed to pay, even though the nondisclosure caused seller no more than $660 damages.

Is it realistic to apply such a strict fiduciary standard to the broker's relationship with the seller? What implications does this standard have for the broker's behavior in presenting to the seller an offer that falls below the seller's asking price? Is it relevant that, because the broker will characteristically be working on a commission basis and will be paid only if a deal is concluded, she will be inclined to favor a sure deal at a lower price over the risk of no deal at the listing price?

5. **Broker's Duties to Buyer.** Because it is the seller who retains the listing broker, under traditional doctrine the broker is the seller's agent and consequently has no duties, fiduciary or otherwise, to the buyer. See, e.g., Richard Brown Auction & Real Estate, Inc. v. Brown, 583 So. 2d 1313 (Ala. 1991) (no obligation to disclose title defects to buyer); Andrie v. Chrystal–Anderson & Associates Realtors, Inc., 466 N.W.2d 393 (Mich. App. 1991) (broker under no duty to convey buyer's offer to seller). Traditional doctrine also holds that a member of a multiple listing service ("MLS") who shows a house listed by the seller's broker acts as the subagent of the listing broker and is thus under the same fiduciary duties to the seller as is the listing broker. See Stortroen v. Beneficial Finance Co., 736 P.2d 391 (Colo. 1987).

Traditional doctrine obviously ignores the new realities and expectations created by multiple listing services. A prospective buyer commonly approaches a broker who may have been recommended to him and describes his housing needs and financial capabilities to the broker. This broker will show the buyer listings in the current MLS book (including housing for which he is the listing broker), take him on a tour of possibly interesting properties and, eventually, present the buyer's offer and negotiate on his behalf for the chosen property. After all this, what reasonable buyer will not assume that the broker is *his* agent and expect the broker to represent *his* interests in the negotiations? And what seller can comfortably rely on the undivided loyalty of the broker in this position?

A handful of courts have begun to move away from the traditional rule. In Cashion v. Ahmadi, 345 So. 2d 268 (Ala.1977), for example, the buyer, on discovering a periodic water problem in the basement, abandoned the house and sued the seller and the two real estate firms that had brokered the transaction, claiming that all had known of the defect. While ruling for the seller and the listing broker on strict *caveat emptor* grounds, the Alabama Supreme Court reversed the judgment for the broker chosen by the buyer, holding that, as to him, a jury might find an agency relationship with the buyer and, consequently, a duty to disclose his knowledge of the defect. Among the facts to be considered on remand were whether the broker's statements indicated a belief that he was primarily representing buyer or seller. See also Lewis v. Long & Foster Real Estate, Inc., 584 A.2d 1325 (Md. App. 1991) (question for jury whether agency relationship arose between buyer and broker).

Even in the vast majority of jurisdictions where the broker's fiduciary duties are still limited exclusively to the seller, an injured buyer is not entirely without remedy. Buyers, for example, can sue the broker for fraud where the broker intentionally conceals material information from the buyer. See, e.g., Roberts v. Estate of Barbagallo, 531 A.2d 1125 (Pa. Super. 1987) (failure to reveal presence of hazardous urea formaldehyde foam insulation). Legislation in California requires brokers involved in residential sales to "conduct a reasonably competent and diligent visual inspection" and to disclose to the buyer facts uncovered by the investigation which materially affect the "value or desirability of the property." Cal. Civ. Code § 2079(a).

Other theories are available to the buyer who is unable to meet the requirements of common law fraud. One theory is to imply a private right of action for damages against a broker violating disclosure and self-dealing provisions of state broker licensing statutes. See, e.g., Sawyer Realty Group, Inc. v. Jarvis Corp., 432 N.E.2d 849 (Ill. 1982). At least one court has found a broker liable to buyers under a "general duty not to negligently cause them harm" Gerard v. Peterson, 448 N.W.2d 699 (Iowa App. 1989) (broker negligently advised buyers that a mortgage contingency clause was not necessary in a sales contract).

6. **Buyer's Duties to Broker.** Do the new realities and expectations created by multiple listing services also give brokers rights against buyers who have maneuvered them out of their commissions or prevented the deal from closing? Traditionally, brokers had little need for such rights since their client—seller—was liable for the commission at the moment the broker presented a ready, willing and able buyer. But with a growing number of courts holding that a commission is not due until the sale is consummated, brokers are increasingly looking to defaulting buyers for relief.

In Ellsworth Dobbs, Inc. v. Johnson, 236 A.2d 843 (N.J. 1967), the New Jersey Supreme Court sought to protect the broker by enlarging the occasions for buyer liability: "when a prospective buyer solicits a broker to find or to show him property which he might be interested in buying, and the broker finds property satisfactory to him which the owner agrees to sell at the price offered, and the buyer knows the broker will earn a commission for the sale from the owner, the law will imply a promise on the part of the buyer to complete the transaction with the owner." Id. at 859.

The New Jersey Supreme Court itself limited *Ellsworth Dobbs* in Rothman Realty Corp. v. Bereck, 376 A.2d 902 (N.J. 1977). Buyers in that case suffered a sudden stock market reversal, making it impossible for them to come up with the cash needed to close the purchase of a house. The court held that buyers' "implied promise to the broker to complete the transaction did not encompass a failure to close where they had acted in good faith, and the inability to consummate the deal ... was due to a circumstance beyond their control." The court distinguished *Ellsworth Dobbs* on the ground that the buyer there was engaged in a commercial enterprise; the "bargaining power and expertise of such buyers are far superior to those of the average home purchaser." Id. at 908–09.

7. **Housing Discrimination.** As gatekeepers to their communities, real estate brokers have in the not distant past contributed to racially discriminatory patterns of home ownership. Probably the most notorious practice was blockbusting, in which brokers stimulated sales by representing to fearful home owners that the racial composition of their neighborhood was about to change and real estate values about to plummet. State and local governments have enacted criminal and civil prohibitions against blockbusting. The practice has also been outlawed by Title VIII of the Civil Rights Act of 1968. Title VIII provides in part that it shall be unlawful "[f]or profit, to induce or attempt to induce any person to sell or rent any dwelling by representations regarding the entry or prospective entry into the neighborhood of a person or persons of a particular race, color, religion, sex, handicap, familial status, or national origin." 42 U.S.C. § 3604(e).

Title VIII of the 1968 Civil Rights Act has also been interpreted to prohibit racial steering, another discriminatory practice, in which the broker directs white buyers to white neighborhoods, and minority buyers to minority or mixed neighborhoods. As late as 1950, the National Association of Real Estate Boards (now the National Association of Realtors) expressly encouraged racial steering. The Association's Code of Ethics provided that "A realtor should never be instrumental in introducing into a neighborhood ... members of any race or nationality, or any individual whose presence would be clearly detrimental to property values in that neighborhood." Today the Association endorses the principle that brokers "have the responsibility to offer equal service to all clients and prospects without regard to race." National Association of Realtors, Realtors' Guide to Practice Equal Opportunity in Housing 5 (1973).

Apart from general statutory sanctions, a broker who participates in racially discriminatory practice may lose her license. In a small number of states, licensing statutes specifically make discriminatory practices a ground for suspension or revocation. Other states discipline brokers on more general and traditional grounds. In New York, the Secretary of Sate has disciplined brokers on the ground that discriminatory practices constitute "untrustworthy" behavior. See, Kamper v. Department of State, 238 N.E.2d 914 (N.Y. 1968). But see Ford v. Wisconsin Real Estate Examining Board, 179 N.W.2d 786 (Wis. 1970) (discriminatory practices do not constitute "incompetency," "improper dealing," or "untrustworthiness" as those terms are used in the state's license revocation statute).

8. **Antitrust Concerns.** The brokerage industry has been subject to significant antitrust scrutiny. In the mid–20th century, the real estate industry used mandatory commission schedules. Although the United States Supreme Court held that such schedules violated the Sherman Antitrust Act in United States v. National Ass'n of Real Estate Boards, 339 U.S. 485 (1950), commission rates remain amazingly uniform. A 1979 survey by the Federal Trade Commission ("FTC") found that "85 percent of the sellers surveyed alleged they were quoted a rate either of 6 or 7 percent by the broker whom they used, and ultimately 78 percent paid either 6 or 7 percent." Staff Report by the Los Angeles Regional Office of the Federal Trade Commission, The Residential Real Estate Brokerage Industry 15, 19 (Dec. 1983).

The FTC report sought to explain this puzzling uniformity. Interdependency among brokers, facilitated by multiple listing services, appeared to be the cause. Most homes are now listed on multiple listing services, and listing brokers depend on the services to help find buyers. While "brokers might attract many listings by advertising low commission fees, those brokers might encounter problems in cooperatively selling their listings. Cooperating brokers usually are compensated by the listing broker's splitting his or her commission with the cooperating brokers. 'Discount' or 'alternative' brokers may offer potential cooperating brokers substantially less compensation than that provided by 'traditional' brokers. For this reason (and also because a cooperating traditional broker who charges the higher prevailing commission rate will be a competitor of the listing discount broker for future listings) many traditional brokers are alleged to quite understandably steer potential buyers to homes listed by brokers charging the prevailing commission rate and offering the prevailing split." Id. at 17–19.

2. LAWYERS

Quintin Johnstone, Land Transfers: Process and Processors

22 Val. U. L. Rev. 500–03 (1988).

Historically, land transfer servicing was one of the principal types of work performed by American lawyers, and although of less overall significance to contemporary lawyers than to their predecessors, it is still of tremendous importance to many in practice today. This phase of the practice also is referred to as conveyancing, settlement, or closing work. Small private law firms and solo practitioners in the general practice of law are particularly active in sales of single-family residences and family farmers, with larger law firms concentrating on sales of more expensive properties, such as large apartment buildings, hotels, office buildings, and industrial properties. Legal work required in connection with the ordinary single-family home sale tends to be a routine procedure including preparation of the contact of sale; title search, title examination, and perhaps clearing of title defects; drafting or review of a mortgage; drafting of a deed; preparation of a closing statement showing expenses and receipts; and a final closing session in which the seller is paid and the deed delivered to the buyer Supplemental steps often are involved, such as ordering a survey and reviewing the surveyor's report, and ordering and approving a title insurance policy. The period between the contract of sale and closing usually is eight or ten weeks, during which time the buyer ordinarily arranges for financing and the necessary title work is performed. Added problems, of course, may emerge in connection with the sale transaction which lawyers may be asked to resolve, such as controversies over the broker's commission or deed covenant compliance. In sales of properties for large sums of money, a much wider range of legal problems typically exists, including intricate financing arrangements, complicated income tax considerations, zoning and other land use control issues, and frequently construction problems, as these sales often are tied into major development projects.

In the sale of a single-family residence, the buyer and seller each may be represented by a different lawyer; or to save expense, the same lawyer may represent both, only one may be represented by a lawyer, or neither may be represented. Also, in single family residence sales, there are considerable variations in lawyers' roles depending on the geographic area. In many places, lawyers do not become involved in such sale transactions until after the contract of sale has been signed because brokers commonly prepare the sales contracts. In some areas, lawyers in private practice do little or no title work unless title curing litigation is necessary; title insurers, relying on their private title plants and their own staff, perform the requisite search and examination tasks. In still other areas, lay abstracters do most of the title searching, and lawyers' title work is restricted largely to legal evaluation of titles based on summaries of public title records prepared by the abstracters. Similarly, lawyers do not have a monopoly on final closings in many regions. In many communities, title companies, lenders, brokers, or escrows companies have taken over much of the final closing or settlement work. Lawyers in larger firms often refuse to do single-family residence closings or will do them only as an accommodation for their better clients. Overhead of these firms is such that they claim closing work of this kind is unprofitable. . . .

Mortgage lenders are usually represented by lawyers who make certain that in individual transactions the lenders' interests are adequately protected. Some home buyers do not retain their own counsel because they are willing to gamble that transaction approval by the lenders' lawyers sufficiently protects the buyers' generally similar, but in some respects quite different, interests....

Compared to most occupations, lawyers are extensively regulated with the focus heavily on the individual lawyer. Licensing requirements are demanding in their education and bar examination prerequisites, and professional behavior after licensing is subject to comprehensive controls, principally by the courts. The most detailed post-admission regulations are two sets of ethical standards of conduct, the Model Code of Professional Responsibility and the more recent Model Rules of Professional Conduct. These standards were drafted and approved by the American Bar Association, and, with the exception of California, one or the other set is in effect in every state.[14] Violations can subject lawyers to disciplinary sanctions, imposed generally by the courts, varying from judicial censure to disbarment. Relative to land transfer servicing, there are several respects in which the standards are of particular importance: in particular, they severely restrict the conflict of interest situations in which an individual lawyer or law firm may become involved, and they permit lawyer advertising but prohibit in-person solicitation of prospective clients. The conflict of interest proscriptions do not prevent a lawyer from representing both the buyer and seller or borrower and lender in the same real estate sale transaction, provided that neither party is likely to be harmed thereby and both parties consent. However, some lawyers consider the possibilities of conflict so serious that they will never represent both parties to a real estate transaction; and there is case law which indicates that when such dual representation occurs the consents must be knowing and based on full and timely disclosure.[17] Lawyers may, and a considerable number do, advertise that they will perform land transfer services, but questions have arisen about the validity of direct mail advertising of such services. The prohibition of in-person solicitation of potential clients outlaws such possible means of generating land transfer legal work as lawyers or their agents making solicitation calls in person or by telephone on persons who are actively seeking to buy a home or who have contracted to do so.

For many years, lawyers and their professional associations were generally believed to be exempt from the federal antitrust laws, but in a 1975 opinion, *Goldfarb v. Virginia State Bar*,[19] the United States Supreme Court corrected this view. In the *Goldfarb* case, the Court held that bar association minimum fee schedules and their implementation violated the Sherman Act. The complained-of fee fixing in the *Goldfarb* case pertained to real property title examinations, but the *Goldfarb* opinion obviously applies to most services the prices of which are set by bar association minimum fee schedules. Such schedules, at the time of the Supreme Court ruling, were in effect in much of the United States and set extensively

14. California has its own set of rules that in many respects resembles the ABA Model Code or Model Rules....

17. Two cases in which lawyers were sanctioned for inadequate client disclosure when simultaneously representing buyers and sellers real estate transactions are In re Dolan, 384 A.2d 1076 (N.J. 1978) and In re Robertson, 624 P.2d 603 (Or. 1981).

19. 421 U.S. 773 (1975).

adhered-to prices for many services performed by lawyers for their clients. . . .

In re Opinion No. 26 of the Committee on the Unauthorized Practice of Law

Supreme Court of New Jersey, 1993.
654 A.2d 1344.

PER CURIAM.

We again confront another long-simmering dispute between realtors and attorneys concerning the unauthorized practice of law. Title companies are also involved. . . . The question before us is whether brokers and title company officers, who guide, control and handle all aspects of residential real estate transactions where neither seller nor buyer is represented by counsel, are engaged in the unauthorized practice of law. That many aspects of such transactions constitute the practice of law we have no doubt, including some of the activities of these brokers and title officers. Our power to prohibit those activities is clear. We have concluded, however, that the public interest does not require such a prohibition. Sellers and buyers, to the extent they are informed of the true interests of the broker and title officer, sometimes in conflict with their own interests, and of the risks of not having their own attorney, should be allowed to proceed without counsel. The South Jersey practice, for it is in that part of the state where sellers and buyers are most often unrepresented by counsel in residential real estate transactions, may continue subject to the conditions set forth in this opinion. By virtue of this decision, those participating in such transactions shall not be deemed guilty of the unauthorized practice of law so long as those conditions are met. Our decision in all respects applies not only to South Jersey, but to the entire state.

Under our Constitution, this Court's power over the practice of law is complete. N.J. Const. art. 6, § 2, ¶ 3. We are given the power to permit the practice of law and to prohibit its unauthorized practice. We have exercised that latter power in numerous cases.

The question of what constitutes the unauthorized practice of law involves more than an academic analysis of the function of lawyers, more than a determination of what they are uniquely qualified to do. It also involves a determination of whether non-lawyers should be allowed, in the public interest, to engage in activities that may constitute the practice of law. As noted later, the conclusion in these cases that parties need not retain counsel to perform limited activities that constitute the practice of law and that others may perform them does not imply that the public interest is thereby advanced, but rather that the public interest does not require that those parties be deprived of their right to proceed without counsel. We reach that conclusion today given the unusual history and experience of the South Jersey practice as developed in the record before us. . . .

The South Jersey Practice

Although the variations are numerous, the South Jersey practice complained of typically involves residential real estate closings in which neither buyer nor seller is represented by counsel, and contrasts most sharply with the North Jersey practice if one assumes both parties are represented there. Obviously, that is not always the case: the record shows that about sixty percent of the buyers and about sixty-five percent of the sellers in South Jersey are not represented by counsel. In North Jersey, only one half of one percent of buyers, and fourteen percent of sellers, proceed without counsel.

In North Jersey, when both seller and buyer are represented by counsel, they sign nothing, agree to nothing, expend nothing, without the advice of competent counsel. If, initially without counsel, they sign a contract of sale prepared by the broker, they ordinarily then retain counsel who can revoke that contract in accordance with the three-day attorney review clause. They are protected, and they pay for that protection. The seller in North Jersey spends on average $750 in attorney fees, and the buyer in North Jersey spends on average $1,000. The buyer in South Jersey who chooses to proceed without representation spends nothing. The South Jersey seller whose attorney does no more than prepare the deed and affidavit of title, usually without even consulting with the seller, spends about $90. South Jersey buyers and sellers who are represented throughout the process, including closing, pay an average of $650 and $350, respectively.[2] Savings obviously do not determine the outcome of this case; they are but one factor in the mix of competing considerations.

The typical South Jersey transaction starts with the seller engaging a broker who is ordinarily a member of the multiple listing system. The first broker to find an apparently willing buyer gets in touch with the seller and ultimately negotiates a sale price agreeable to both. The potential buyer requires financing arrangements which are often made by the broker. Before the execution of any sales contract the broker puts the buyer in touch with a mortgage company to determine if the buyer qualifies for the needed loan. At this preliminary stage, no legal obligations of any kind are likely to have been created, except for those that arise from the brokerage relationship itself.

Assuming the preliminary understanding between the seller and buyer remains in effect, the broker will present the seller with the standard form of contract used in that area (usually a New Jersey Association of Realtors Standard Form of Real Estate Contract). That form includes, pursuant to our opinion in New Jersey State Bar Association v. New Jersey Association of Realtor Boards, 93 N.J. 470, 461 A.2d 1112 (1983), notice that the attorney for either party can cancel the contract within three business days. If the seller signs the contract, and does not within three days retain

2. It is suggested that although the parties under the South Jersey practice save the cost of counsel, the savings may be offset to some extent because they nonetheless pay others for services attorneys in North Jersey customarily provide.

counsel, the seller will have become legally bound to perform numerous obligations without the benefit of any legal advice whatsoever, some of which may turn out to be onerous, some costly, some requiring unanticipated expense, and some beyond the power of the seller to perform, with the potential of substantial liability for such nonperformance. Many sellers will not understand just what those obligations are, and just what the risks are. Not only has the seller not retained a lawyer, the only person qualified to explain those risks. Worse yet, the only one the seller has had any contact with in the matter is the broker, whose commission depends entirely on consummation of the transaction, and whose interest is primarily—in some cases it is fair to say exclusively—to get the contract signed and the deal closed.

After the seller signs the contract, the broker delivers it to the buyer for execution. The buyer may not know if the description of the property is precisely that assumed to be the subject of the purchase. The buyer may have no idea if the title described in the contract is that with which he would be satisfied, no sound understanding of what the numerous obligations on the part of the seller mean, and no fair comprehension of whether all of the possible and practical concerns of a buyer have been addressed by the contract. No lawyer is present to advise or inform the buyer; indeed, there is no one who has the buyer's interest at heart, only the broker, whose interests are generally in conflict with the buyer's. Although the record does not dispose of the issue, and although Judge Miller explicitly left it undecided, he noted concern that the broker, through his or her actions, may lead the buyer to believe that the broker is looking out for the buyer's interests. Therefore, without independent advice, the buyer signs the contract. If no attorney is retained within three days, the buyer is bound by all of its terms.

For both seller and buyer, it is that contract that substantially determines all of their rights and duties. Neither one of them can be regarded as adequately informed of the import of what they signed or indeed of its importance. At that point the broker, who represents only the seller and clearly has an interest in conflict with that of the buyer (the broker's interest is in consummation of the sale, the buyer's in making certain that the sale does not close unless the buyer is fully protected) performs a series of acts on behalf of the buyer, and is the only person available as a practical matter to explain their significance to the buyer. The broker orders a binder for title insurance, or a title commitment to make sure that the buyer is going to get good title. The buyer has no idea, and hopefully never will have, whether the broker ordered the right kind of title search, a fairly esoteric question that only an experienced attorney can determine.

The broker also orders numerous inspection and other reports, all primarily of interest to the buyer, to make certain that not only is the title good, but that there are no other problems affecting the premises, the house and their use. Those reports can have substantial legal consequences for both seller and buyer. For example, at what threshold dollar amount of required repairs should the seller (or the buyer) be able to cancel the contract? At what dollar amount should the buyer ignore the repairs? At what dollar amount should the buyer be able to compel the seller to make the repairs, and within what time frame? At this stage of the transaction the help of a lawyer could be invaluable, and the advice of a broker problematic.

The seller in the meantime is happy to hear from no one, for it suggests there are no problems. Eventually, the seller is told that a deed will be arriving drafted by an attorney selected by the broker, the instrument that our decisions clearly require may be drafted only by the seller's attorney. Of course, the purpose of that ruling was to assure competent counsel in the drafting of such a uniquely legal document, but "competent" always meant counsel who understood the entire transaction. In South Jersey, the attorney selected by the broker, while theoretically representing the seller, may be primarily interested in the broker, the source of the attorney's "client" and the likely source of future "clients," and consequently primarily interested in completing the sale. That attorney is likely to prepare a deed satisfactory to the title company—in fact that attorney often does not even contact the seller. He or she may have no idea of anything in the contract of sale other than the description of the land and the fact that a certain kind of deed is required. No advice on the substance of the transaction comes from such an attorney even though the seller may get the impression that, since an attorney drafted the deed, the seller's interests are somehow being protected. In fact, the only protection those interests ever received, other than those that happened to appear in the form contract, is in the numbers inserted in that contract, the total purchase price, the down payment, and the closing date, for those are probably the only terms of that contract fully understood by the seller.

The buyer's position is even worse when the closing occurs. The seller will at least know that he or she got paid. Legal training is not required for that fact, even though there is no practical assurance that the seller will not thereafter be sued. The buyer, on the other hand, wants something that is largely incomprehensible to almost all buyers, good and marketable title, one that will not result in problems in the future. What the buyer gets before closing is a "title binder," a piece of paper that may suggest something about the quality of the seller's title, but that is very much in need of explanation for any substantial understanding of its meaning. The title company is required to mail to the unrepresented buyer notice of any exceptions or conditions associated with the title insurance policy. This notice, which must be sent five days prior to the closing, must also notify the buyer of the right to review the title commitment with an attorney. If the buyer chooses not to retain an attorney, there is no one to give the buyer that understanding other than the broker and the title agent. The broker's knowledge will often be inadequate, and the conflicting interest apparent. The title company similarly has a conflicting interest, for it too is interested in completion of the transaction, the sine qua non of its title premium. But the title company is also interested in good title, for it is guaranteeing that to the mortgage company, as well as to the buyer. "Good title", however, may be one on which the title company and the mortgagee are willing to take a risk, but one on which a buyer might or should not be willing to, if the buyer knew what the risk was. Again, there is no one to tell the buyer what those risks are, and in some cases the explicit exceptions found in a title policy, those matters that the title company will not guarantee, are of the greatest importance. The significance of those matters is conceded by all to be something that only attorneys can give advice on, and it is contended by all that they never give such advice. Yet such exceptions exist, and title still closes, and the buyer is totally unrepresented by counsel. One must assume that somewhere, somehow, the buyer is satisfied that there is nothing to worry about, leading to the inescapable conclusion that either the broker or the title officer provides some modicum of assurance or explanation.

The day for closing arrives and everyone meets, usually at the offices of the title company. Seller and buyer are there, each without an attorney; the broker is there, and the title officer is there, representing both the title company and the mortgagee. The funds are there. And the critical legal documents are also on hand: the mortgage and the note, usually prepared by the mortgagee; the deed, along with the affidavit of title, prepared by the attorney selected by the broker or by the title company; the settlement statement, usually prepared by the title company, indicating how much is owed, what deductions should be made for taxes and other costs and what credits are due; and the final marked-up title binder, which evidences the obligation of the title company to issue a title policy to the buyer, and which at that point is probably practically meaningless to the buyer. All are executed and delivered, along with other documents, and the funds are delivered or held in escrow until the title company arranges to pay off prior mortgages and liens.

It would take a volume to describe each and every risk to which the seller and buyer have exposed themselves without adequate knowledge. But it takes a very short sentence to describe what apparently occurs: the deal closes, satisfactory to buyer and seller in practically all cases, satisfactory both at the closing and thereafter.

The Unauthorized Practice of Law

As noted above, this transaction in its entirety, the sale of real estate, especially real estate with a home on it, is one that cannot be handled competently except by those trained in the law. The most important parts of it, without which it could not be accomplished, are quintessentially the practice of law. The contract of sale, the obligations of the contract, the ordering of a title search, the analysis of the search, the significance of the title search, the quality of title, the risks that surround both the contract and the title, the extent of those risks, the probability of damage, the obligation to close or not to close, the closing itself, the settlement, the documents there exchanged, each and every one of these, to be properly understood must be explained by an attorney. And the documents themselves to be properly drafted, must be drafted by an attorney. Mixed in with these activities are many others that clearly do not require an attorney's knowledge, such as the ordering of inspection and other reports, and the price negotiation. But after that, even though arguably much can be accomplished by others, practically all else, to be done with full understanding, requires the advice of counsel.

As this Court's prior treatment of the subject shows, the prohibition against non-lawyers engaging in activities that are the practice of law is not automatic. Having answered the question whether the practice of law is involved, we must decide whether the public interest is served by such prohibition. Not every such intrusion by laymen into legal matters disserves the public: this Court does not wear public interest blinders when passing on unauthorized practice of law questions. We have often found, despite the clear involvement of the practice of law, that non-lawyers may participate in these activities, basing our decisions on the public interest in those cases in allowing parties to proceed without counsel. . . .

In what is undoubtedly the clearest example of the dominating influence of the public interest in this area, we decided in *New Jersey Association of Realtor Boards*, supra, that real estate brokers may draft contracts for the sale of residential property if the contract contains a prominent clause informing the parties of their right, through counsel, to cancel it within three days. While our decision took the form of the approval of a settlement reached between the brokers and the bar, our approval was explicitly based on a finding by Justice Sullivan, sitting as the trial judge, that the settlement was in the public interest, a finding with which we concurred. . . . He concluded that "the settlement is in the public interest" and that the three-day cancellation clause "affords adequate protection to purchasers and sellers of residential real estate or lessors and lessees thereof." In so concluding, he noted that it had been asserted "without contradiction that 'no State in the Country has prohibited Brokers from completing form contracts in connection with residential property sales.' " The record in this case also demonstrates that the conduct in question is permitted in many other states. . . .

In this case, the record clearly shows that the South Jersey practice has been conducted without any demonstrable harm to sellers or buyers, that it apparently saves money, and that those who participate in it do so of their own free will presumably with some knowledge of the risk; as Judge Miller found, the record fails to demonstrate that brokers are discouraging the parties from retaining counsel, or that the conflict of interest that pervades the practice has caused material damage to the sellers and buyers who participate in it. Given that record, and subject to the conditions mentioned hereafter, we find that the public interest will not be compromised by allowing the practice to continue. . . .

Of decisive weight in our determination is the value we place on the right of parties to a transaction to decide whether or not they will retain counsel. We should not force them to do so absent persuasive reasons. Given the importance in our decision of the assumption that the parties have chosen not to retain counsel, and without coercion have made that decision, we have attached a condition to the conclusion that the South

Jersey practice does not constitute the unauthorized practice of law. [Before signing a sales contract, the buyer and seller both must sign a statement, found at the end of this decision, informing them of their right to an attorney and the risks of not doing so.] The condition is designed to assure that the decision is an informed one. If that condition is not met, the brokers (and title officers, if aware of the fact) are engaged in the unauthorized practice of law, and attorneys with knowledge of that fact who participate are guilty of ethical misconduct. . . .

We do not here adopt a "consumerism" that invariably requires that services be made available at the lowest price no matter how great the risk. The record suggests that despite their conflict of interest, brokers' ethical standards have resulted in some diminishment of those risks. Unlike prior cases, there is no finding here, for instance, that brokers are discouraging retention of counsel, no suggestion that title companies are paying rebates to referring brokers. Today's public, furthermore, not only has the benefit of the attorney review clause, but is presumably better educated about the need for counsel, the function of attorneys, and the legal aspects of the sale of the home. The public continues, in South Jersey, to choose not to be represented. We assume that the public has simply concluded that the perceived advantages are worth those risks. . . .

There is a point at which an institution attempting to provide protection to a public that seems clearly, over a long period, not to want it, and perhaps not to need it—there is a point when that institution must wonder whether it is providing protection or imposing its will. It must wonder whether it is helping or hurting the public.[5] We have reached that point in this case. Although we have strong doubts, the evidence against our doubt requires that we allow this practice to continue with some form of added protection, recognizing, however, that like the attorney-review clause, the added protection may not be effective.

Conclusion and Conditions

We premise our holding on the condition that both buyer and seller be made aware of the conflicting interests of brokers and title companies in these matters and of the general risks involved in not being represented by counsel. We shall ask the Civil Practice Committee to recommend to us practical methods for achieving those aims. Presumably, that Committee will want to form a subcommittee including those who have been involved with this problem for many years. Obviously, the best way to achieve the goal is to have a knowledgeable disinterested attorney sit down with both buyer and seller and carefully explain both the conflict factor and the risk factor, but we doubt if that would be practical. Pending the report of that Committee and our action on it, we have decided to adopt an interim notice

5. We note that in Arizona, after its Supreme Court prohibited brokers from preparing real estate sales contracts, the people approved a constitutional amendment that provided that licensed real estate brokers "shall have the right to draft or fill out and complete" real estate documents, including deeds, mortgages, and contracts of sales. Ariz. Const. art. XXVI, § 1.

requirement that the broker must comply with. If that notice is not given, the broker will be engaged in the unauthorized practice of law. Furthermore, anyone who participates in the transaction, other than buyer and seller, knowing that the notice has not been given when and as required, will also be engaged in the unauthorized practice of law. As for any attorney who, under the same circumstances, continues to participate in the transaction, that attorney will also be subject to discipline for unethical conduct. At the commencement of the closing or settlement, the title officer in charge shall inquire of both buyer and seller whether, how, and when, the notice was given, and shall make and keep a record of the inquiry and the responses at that time....

Appendix A

NOTICE

To Buyer and Seller:

You Must Read This Notice Before Signing the Contract

The Supreme Court of New Jersey requires real estate brokers to give you the following information before you sign this contract. It requires us to tell you that you must read all of it before you sign. Here is the information for both buyer and seller:

(1) I am a real estate broker. I represent the seller. I do not represent the buyer. The title company does not represent either the seller or the buyer. Furthermore, both the seller and the buyer should know that it is in my financial interest that the house be sold and that the closing be completed. My fee is paid only if that happens. The title company has the same interest, for its insurance premium is paid only if that happens.

(2) I am not allowed, and I am not qualified, to give either the seller or the buyer any legal advice. Neither the title company nor any of its officers are allowed to give either the seller or buyer any legal advice. Neither of you will get any legal advice at any point in this transaction unless you have your own lawyer. If you do not hire a lawyer, no one will represent you in legal matters either now, or at the closing. I will not represent you and the title company and its officers will not represent you in those matters.

(3) The contract attached to this notice is the most important part of the sale. It determines your rights, your liabilities, and your risks. It becomes final when you sign it—unless it is cancelled by your lawyer within three days—and when it does become final you cannot change it, nor can any attorney you may hire thereafter change it in any way whatsoever.

(4) The buyer especially should know that if he or she has no lawyer, no one will be able to advise him or her what to do if problems arise in connection with your purchasing this property. Those problems may be about various matters, including the seller's title to the property. They may affect the value of the property. If either the broker or title company sees that there are problems and that because of them you need your own lawyer, they should tell you. However, it is possible that they may not

recognize the problems or that it may be too late for a lawyer to help. Also, they are not your lawyers, and they may not see the problem from your point of view.

(5) Whether you, seller or buyer, retain a lawyer is up to you. It is your decision. The purpose of this notice is to make sure you have some understanding of the transaction, the risks, who represents whom, and what their interests are, when you make that decision. The rules and regulations concerning brokers and title companies prohibit each of them from suggesting that you are better off without a lawyer. If anyone makes that suggestion to you, you should carefully consider whose interest they are serving. The decision whether to hire a lawyer to represent your interests is yours and yours alone.

Notes & Questions

1. The experience of South Jersey, where most parties to residential home sales do not consult an attorney, is probably closer to the national norm than the experience of North Jersey. An American Bar Foundation study conducted in the early 1970s revealed that buyers of homes consult a lawyer in only 40% of the estimated 5.5 million residential purchases made every year. Barbara A. Curran, Survey of the Public's Legal Needs, 64 A.B.A.J. 848, 850 (1978). Of the other 60 percent, some buyers may rely on the work done by a seller's lawyer, but much of the time neither buyer nor seller will retain an attorney, depending instead on the expertise and services of brokers, title insurers, financial institutions, and escrow companies.

2. Even when parties to a real estate transaction consult a lawyer, they are not guaranteed good representation. A survey of eight law firms conducted by the Wall Street Journal in 1980 to determine the ability of lawyers to spot several defects in a proposed residential real estate sale contract produced some unsettling results. In the judgment of the Journal's panel of real estate experts, none of the eight attorneys spotted every defect he or she should have. Two of the lawyers did "dangerously bad" jobs and four got "low marks" on either or both of the major problem areas. Hal Lancaster, Rating Lawyers: If Your Legal Problems Are Complex, a Clinic May Not Be the Answer, Wall St. J., July 31, 1980, at 1. These survey results should, however, be kept in perspective. The survey was "admittedly unscientific." Six of the eight firms were "advertised as, or appeared to be," legal clinics. And, probably most important, the survey was conducted in California where lawyers only rarely represent parties to residential transactions and thus have little of the experience that is so common to general practitioners elsewhere in the country. (Inexperience does not, however, excuse bad advice. As one member of the panel observed, the correct approach for several of these attorneys would have been to refer the client to a real estate specialist.)

3. As the New Jersey Supreme Court notes, the Arizona Supreme Court took an unusually hard line against the unauthorized practice of law

in real estate transactions, ruling that brokers may not advise or assist in the preparation of documents that affect, alter, or define legal rights. State Bar of Arizona v. Arizona Title & Trust Co., 366 P.2d 1 (Ariz. 1961). The court's proscription encompassed even the filling in of blanks on printed forms. In response, brokers obtained 107,420 signatures on an initiative petition for an amendment to the state constitution giving real estate brokers and salespeople the right "to draft or fill out and complete, without charge, ... preliminary purchase agreements ... deeds, mortgages, leases ... contracts of sale." The proposed amendment passed by a margin of almost 4 to 1. See Ariz. Const. art. XXVI, § 1.

The brokers' victory in Arizona was not costless. In 1976 an Arizona appellate court ruled that the constitutional amendment created not only new rights, but also new duties, and held that a broker breached his duty to seller by failing to explain the possible consequences of accepting buyer's promissory note in which one key phrase—"This note is secured by a mortgage on real property"—had been stricken. The action was precipitated by the buyer's default on the note. Morley v. J. Pagel Realty & Insurance, 550 P.2d 1104 (Ariz. App. 1976).

4. For recent articles exploring the diminishing role of lawyers in residential real estate transactions and what constitutes the unauthorized practice of law by other professionals, see Alice M. Noble–Allgire, Attorney Approval Clauses in Residential Real Estate Contracts—Is Half a Loaf Better Than None?, 48 Kan. L. Rev. 339 (2000); Joyce Palomar, The War Between Attorneys and Lay Conveyancers—Empirical Evidence Says "Cease Fire!," 31 Conn. L. Rev. 423 (1999); Michael Braunstein, Structural Change and Inter–Professional Competitive Advantage: An Example Drawn From Residential Real Estate Conveyancing, 62 Mo. L. Rev. 241 (1997); Michael Braunstein & Hazel Genn, Odd Man Out: Preliminary Findings Concerning the Diminishing Role of Lawyers in the Home–Buying Process, 52 Ohio St. L.J. 469 (1991).

B. THE CONTRACT OF SALE

The Standard Form Purchase & Sale Agreement that begins on the next page illustrates many of the provisions found in the modern contract of sale for real property. Standard contract forms vary from region to region, depending on local legal requirements, issues, and traditions.

GREATER BOSTON REAL ESTATE BOAR

STANDARD FORM PURCHASE & SALE AGREEMENT

From the Office of:__________________________

This____________________ day of__________________, 20________

1. PARTIES AND MAILING ADDRESSES *(fill in)*

hereinafter called the SELLER, agrees to SELL and

hereinafter called the BUYER or PURCHASER, agrees to BUY, upon the terms hereinafter set forth, the following described premises:

2. DESCRIPTION *(fill in and include title reference)*

3. BUILDINGS, STRUCTURES, IMPROVEMENTS, FIXTURES *(fill in or delete)*

Included in the sale as a part of said premises are the buildings, structures, and improvements now thereon, and the fixtures belonging to the SELLER and used in connection therewith including, if any, all wall-to-wall carpeting, drapery rods, automatic garage door openers, venetian blinds, window shades, screens, screen doors, storm windows and doors, awnings, shutters, furnaces, heaters, heating equipment, stoves, ranges, oil and gas burners and fixtures appurtenant thereto, hot water heaters, plumbing and bathroom fixtures, garbage disposers, electric and other lighting fixtures, mantels, outside television antennas, fences, gates, trees, shrubs, plants and, ONLY IF BUILT IN, refrigerators, air conditioning equipment, ventilators, dishwashers, washing machines and dryers; and

but excluding

4. TITLE DEED *(fill in)* **Include here by specific reference any restrictions, easements, rights and obligations in party walls not included in (b), leases, municipal and other liens, other encumbrances, and make provision to protect SELLER against BUYER's breach of SELLER's covenants in leases, where necessary.*

Said premises are to be conveyed by a good and sufficient quitclaim deed running to the BUYER, or to the nominee designated by the BUYER by written notice to the SELLER at least seven __________________ days before the deed is to be delivered as herein provided, and said deed shall convey a good and clear record and marketable title thereto, free from encumbrances, except

a. Provisions of existing building and zoning laws;
b. Existing rights and obligations in party walls which are not the subject of written agreement;
c. Such taxes for the then current year as are not due and payable on the date of the delivery of such deed;
d. Any liens for municipal betterments assessed after the date of this agreement;
e. Easements, restrictions and reservations of record, if any, so long as the same do not prohibit or materially interfere with the current use of said premises;

*f.

5. PLANS

If said deed refers to a plan necessary to be recorded therewith the SELLER shall deliver such plan with the deed in form adequate for recording or registration.

6. PURCHASE PRICE *(fill in)* space is allowed to spell out the amounts if desired

The agreed purchase price for said premises is $

dollars, of which

$ have been paid as a deposit this day and
$
$ are to be paid at the time of delivery of the deed in cash, or by certified, cashier's,check(s).

$____________________
$ TOTAL

This form has been made available through the courtesy of the Greater Boston Real Estate Board and is protected by the copyright laws.

7. REGISTERED TITLE	In addition to the foregoing, if the title to said premises is registered, said deed shall be in form sufficient to entitle the BUYER to a Certificate of Title of said premises, and the SELLER shall deliver with said deed all instruments, if any, necessary to enable the BUYER to obtain such Certificate of Title.
8. TIME FOR PERFORMANCE; DELIVERY OF DEED *(fill in)*	Such deed is to be delivered at____________o'clock (am/pm)_______on the____________day of_________________________20 , at the____________________________________ Registry of Deeds, unless otherwise agreed upon in writing. It is agreed that time is of the essence of this agreement.
9. POSSESSION and CONDITION of PREMISE *(attach a list of exceptions, if any)*	Full possession of said premises free of all tenants and occupants, except as herein provided, is to be delivered at the time of the delivery of the deed, said premises to be then (a) in the same condition as they now are, reasonable use and wear thereof excepted, and (b) not in violation of said building and zoning laws, and (c) in compliance with the provisions of any instrument referred to in clause 4 hereof. The BUYER shall be entitled personally to enter said premises prior to the delivery of the deed in order to determine whether the condition thereof complies with the terms of this clause.
10. EXTENSION TO PERFECT TITLE OR MAKE PREMISES CONFORM *(Change period of time if desired).*	If the SELLER shall be unable to give title or to make conveyance, or to deliver possession of the premises, all as herein stipulated, or if at the time of the delivery of the deed the premises do not conform with the provisions hereof, then any payments made under this agreement shall be forthwith refunded and all other obligations of the parties hereto shall cease, and this agreement shall be void without recourse to the parties hereto, unless the SELLER elects to use reasonable efforts to remove any defects in title, or to deliver possession as provided herein, or to make the said premises conform to the provisions hereof, as the case may be, in which event the SELLER shall give written notice thereof to the BUYER at or before the time for performance hereunder, and thereupon the time for performance hereof shall be extended for a period of thirty __________________ days.
11. FAILURE TO PERFECT TITLE OR MAKE PERMISES CONFORM, etc.	If at the expiration of the extended time the SELLER shall have failed so to remove any defects in title, deliver possession, or make the premises conform, as the case may be, all as herein agreed, or if at any time during the period of this agreement or any extension thereof, the holder of a mortgage on said premises shall refuse to permit the insurance proceeds, if any, to be used for such purposes, then any payments made under this agreement shall be forthwith refunded and all other obligations of the parties hereto shall cease and this agreement shall be void without recourse to the parties hereto.
12. BUYER's ELECTION TO ACCEPT TITLE	The BUYER shall have the election, at either the original or any extended time for performance, to accept such title as the SELLER can deliver to the said premises in their then condition and to pay therefore the purchase price without deduction, in which case the SELLER shall convey such title, except that in the event of such conveyance in accord with the provisions of this clause, if the said premises shall have been damaged by fire or casualty insured against, then the SELLER shall, unless the SELLER has previously restored the premises to their former condition, either a. pay over or assign to the BUYER, on delivery of the deed, all amounts recovered or recoverable on account of such insurance, less any amounts reasonably expended by the SELLER for any partial restoration, or________________________________ b. if a holder of a mortgage on said premises shall not permit the insurance proceeds or a part thereof to be used to restore the said premises to their former condition or to be so paid over or assigned, give to the BUYER a credit against the purchase price, on delivery of the deed, equal to said amounts so recovered or recoverable and retained by the holder of the said mortgage less any amounts reasonably expended by the SELLER for any partial restoration.
13. ACCEPTANCE OF DEED	The acceptance of a deed by the BUYER or his nominee, as the case may be, shall be deemed to be a full performance and discharge of every agreement and obligation herein contained or expressed, except such as are, by the terms hereof, to be performed after the delivery of said deed.
14. USE OF MONEY TO CLEAR TITLE	To enable the SELLER to make conveyance as herein provided, the SELLER may, at the time of delivery of the deed, use the purchase money or any portion thereof to clear the title of any or all encumbrances or interests, provided that all instruments so procured are recorded simultaneously with the delivery of said deed.

15. INSURANCE
Insert amount (list additional types of insurance and amounts as agreed)

Until the delivery of the deed, the SELLER shall maintain insurance on said premises as follows:

Type of Insurance	*Amount of Coverage*
a. Fire & Extended Coverage	*$
b.	*$
c.	*$

16. ADJUSTMENTS
(list operating expenses, if any, or attach schedule)

Collected rents, mortgage interest, water and sewer use charges, operating expenses (if any) according to the schedule attached hereto or set forth below, and taxes for the then current fiscal year, shall be apportioned and fuel value shall be adjusted, as of the day of performance of this agreement and the net amount thereof shall be added to or deducted from, as the case may be, the purchase price payable by the BUYER at the time of delivery of the deed. Uncollected rents for the current rental period shall be apportioned if and when collected by either party.

17. ADJUSTMENT OF UNASSESSED AND ABATED TAXES

If the amount of said taxes is not known at the time of the delivery of the deed, they shall be apportioned on the basis of the taxes assessed for the preceding fiscal year, with a reapportionment as soon as the new tax rate and valuation can be ascertained; and, if the taxes which are to be apportioned shall thereafter be reduced by abatement, the amount of such abatement, less the reasonable cost of obtaining the same, shall be apportioned between the parties, provided that neither party shall be obligated to institute or prosecute proceedings for an abatement unless otherwise herein agreed.

18. BROKER's FEE
(fill in fee with dollar amount or percentage;also name of Brokerage firm(s))

A Broker's fee for professional services of____________________
is due from the SELLER to____________________

the Broker(s) herein, but if the SELLER pursuant to the terms of clause 21 hereof retains the deposits made hereunder by the BUYER, said Broker(s) shall be entitled to receive from the SELLER an amount equal to one-half the amount so retained or an amount equal to the Broker's fee for professional services according to this contract, whichever is the lesser.

19. BROKER(S) WARRANTY
(fill in name)

The Broker(s) named herein____________________
warrant(s) that the Broker(s) is (are) duly licensed as such by the Commonwealth of Massachusetts.

20. DEPOSIT
(fill in name)

All deposits made hereunder shall be held in escrow by____________________
as escrow agent subject to the terms of this agreement and shall be duly accounted for at the time for performance of this agreement. In the event of any disagreement between the parties, the escrow agent may retain all deposits made under this agreement pending instructions mutually given in writing by the SELLER and the BUYER.

21. BUYER's DEFAULT; DAMAGES

If the BUYER shall fail to fulfill the BUYER's agreements herein, all deposits made hereunder by the BUYER shall be retained by the SELLER as liquidated damages unless within thirty days after the time for performance of this agreement or any extension hereof, the SELLER otherwise notifies the BUYER in writing.

22. RELEASE BY HUSBAND OR WIFE

The SELLER's spouse hereby agrees to join in said deed and to release and convey all statutory and other rights and interests in said premises.

23. BROKER AS PARTY

The Broker(s) named herein join(s) in this agreement and become(s) a party hereto, insofar as any provisions of this agreement expressly apply to the Broker(s), and to any amendments or modifications of such provisions to which the Broker(s) agree(s) in writing.

24. LIABILITY OF TRUSTEE, SHAREHOLDER, BENEFICIARY, etc.

If the SELLER or BUYER executes this agreement in a representative or fiduciary capacity, only the principal or the estate represented shall be bound, and neither the SELLER or BUYER so executing, nor any shareholder or beneficiary of any trust, shall be personally liable for any obligation, express or implied, hereunder.

25. WARRANTIES AND REPRESENTATIONS
(fill in) if none, state "none"; if any listed, indicate by whom each warranty or representation was made

The BUYER acknowledges that the BUYER has not been influenced to enter into this transaction nor has he relied upon any warranties or representations not set forth or incorporated in this agreement or previously made in writing, except for the following additional warranties and representations, if any, made by either the SELLER or the Broker(s):

26. CONTINGENCY CLAUSE
(omit if not provided for in Offer to Purchase)

In order to help finance the acquisition of said premises, the BUYER shall apply for a conventional bank or other institutional mortgage loan of $________________ at prevailing rates, terms and conditions. If despite the BUYER's diligent efforts a commitment for such loan cannot be obtained on or before________________, 20________, the BUYER may terminate this agreement by written notice to the SELLER and/or the Broker(s), as agent(s) for the SELLER, prior to the expiration of such time, whereupon any payments made under this agreement shall be forthwith refunded and all other obligations of the parties hereto shall cease and this agreement shall be void without recourse to the parties hereto. In no event will the BUYER be deemed to have used diligent efforts to obtain such commitment unless the BUYER submits a complete mortgage loan application conforming to the foregoing provisions on or before________________, 20________.

27. CONSTRUCTION OF AGREEMENT

This instrument, executed in multiple counterparts, is to be construed as a Massachusetts contract, is to take effect as a sealed instrument, sets forth the entire contract between the parties, is binding upon and enures to the benefit of the parties hereto and their respective heirs, devisees, executors, administrators, successors and assigns, and may be cancelled, modified or amended only by a written instrument executed by both the SELLER and the BUYER. If two or more persons are named herein as BUYER their obligations hereunder shall be joint and several. The captions and marginal notes are used only as a matter of convenience and are not to be considered a part of this agreement or to be used in determining the intent of the parties to it.

28. LEAD PAINT LAW

The parties acknowledge that, under Massachusetts law, whenever a child or children under six years of age resides in any residential premises in which any paint, plaster or other accessible material contains dangerous levels of lead, the owner of said premises must remove or cover said paint, plaster or other material so as to make it inaccessible to children under six years of age.

29. SMOKE DETECTORS

The SELLER shall, at the time of the delivery of the deed, deliver a certificate from the fire department of the city or town in which said premises are located stating that said premises have been equipped with approved smoke detectors in conformity with applicable law.

30. CARBON MONOXIDE DETECTORS

For properties sold or conveyed after March 30, 2006, the Seller shall provide a certificate from the fire department of the city or town in which the premises are located, either in addition to or incorporated into the certificate described above, stating that the premises have been equipped with carbon monoxide detectors in compliance with M.G.L. c. 148 § 26F1/2 or that the Premises are otherwise exempted the Statute.

31. ADDITIONAL PROVISIONS

The initialed riders, if any, attached hereto, are incorporated herein by reference.

FOR RESIDENTIAL PROPERTY CONSTRUCTED PRIOR TO 1978, BUYER MUST ALSO HAVE SIGNED LEAD PAINT "PROPERTY TRANSFER NOTIFICATION CERTIFICATION"

NOTICE: This is a legal document that creates binding obligations. If not understood, consult an attorney.

SELLER:________________	BUYER:________________
Print Name:________________	Print Name:________________
Taxpayer ID/Social Security No.________________	Taxpayer ID/Social Security No.________________
SELLER (or Spouse):________________	BUYER:________________
Print Name:________________	Print Name:________________
Taxpayer ID/Social Security No.________________	Taxpayer ID/Social Security No.________________

____

BROKER(S)

This form has been made available through the courtesy of the Greater Boston Real Estate Board and is protected by the copyright laws.

1. THE STATUTE OF FRAUDS

Baliles v. Cities Service Co.

Supreme Court of Tennessee, 1979.
578 S.W.2d 621.

COOPER, JUSTICE.

This is an action for specific performance of a contract for the sale of real property or, in the alternative, for damages for its breach....

In July 1974, the respondent Cities Service Company orally agreed to sell one of its employees, Dewey M. Newman, Jr., lots 99 and 100 in the Cherokee Hills Subdivision. It became necessary for Mr. Newman to borrow money from the local bank to cover costs of the construction planned for lots 99 and 100. An official of the bank requested a letter from respondents setting forth its commitment to sell lots 99 and 100 to Mr. Newman. On July 23, 1974, respondent sent the following letter to the bank, addressed to Mr. Newman:

> Cities Service Company has agreed to sell to you lots 99 and 100 in Cherokee Hills for residential purposes. As soon as residences are well under construction deeds to these lots will be delivered to you.

On receipt of the letter, the bank loaned Mr. Newman $5,000.00. Mr. Newman then began construction of a residence on lot 100. He completed the foundation and the outer walls of the ground-level basement before encountering financial difficulties.

In the summer of 1975, being in financial difficulty and realizing that he had no chance to build a second house, Mr. Newman went to respondent's offices and released lot 99 to respondent. It also appears that he requested a deed to lot 100, but was refused "until the house was in the dry."

On August 25, 1975, Mr. Newman assigned his interest in lots 99 and 100 to petitioner, Billy D. Baliles, for $6,500.00, the approximate value of the labor and materials expended in improving lot 100.

The chancellor found the memorandum of the agreement for the sale of lots 99 and 100 met the requirements of the statute of frauds....

The applicable section of the statute of frauds, T.C.A. § 23–201, provides that:

> No action shall be brought: ... (4) upon a contract for the sale of lands ... [u]nless the promise or agreement upon which such action shall be brought or some memorandum or note thereof, shall be in writing, and signed by the party to be charged therewith, or some other person by him thereunto lawfully authorized.

The purpose of the statute of frauds "is to reduce contracts to a certainty, in order to avoid perjury on the one hand and fraud on the other." Price v. Tennessee Products & Chemical Corporation, 53 Tenn. App. 624, 385 S.W.2d 301 (1964). Consequently, to comply with the statute of frauds, a memorandum of an agreement to sell must show, with reasonable certainty, the estate intended to be sold.

> Where the instrument is so drawn that upon its face it refers necessarily to some existing tract of land, and its terms can be applied to that one tract only, parol evidence may be employed to show where the tract so mentioned is located. But, where the description employed is one that must necessarily apply with equal exactness to any one of an indefinite number of tracts, parol evidence is not admissible to show that the parties intended to designate a particular tract by the description.

Dobson v. Litton, 45 Tenn. 616. See also Dry Goods Co. v. Hill, 135 Tenn. 60, 185 S.W. 723 (1916).

The memorandum relied on by petitioner as written evidence of the agreement to sell, and which is set out above, does not locate the Cherokee Hills Subdivision by county or state. Neither does it contain any information which would tend to locate the subdivision. Further, the description of the specific property that is the subject of the oral agreement is by lot numbers only. There is no recorded plat to show the location of lot 100 within the subdivision, nor its dimensions or calls.

In Kirshner v. Feigenbaum, 180 Tenn. 476, 176 S.W.2d 806 (1944), it is pointed out that a memorandum of an agreement for the transfer of an interest in real property which fails to designate the county and state where the land is located is insufficient under the statute of frauds, unless the description of the property as set out in the memorandum is otherwise so definite and exclusive that "it does not reasonably appear that the description given would fit equally any other tract, then parol proof is admissible to locate and designate the tract intended."

We think it evident, and we agree with the Court of Appeals, that the description in the memorandum does not describe the tract of land with reasonable certainty, that the description is of no material aid in locating the property that is the subject of the agreement to sell, and consequently does not satisfy the requirements of the statute of frauds.

Petitioner insists that even though the memorandum of the agreement to sell is insufficient to meet the requirements of the statute of frauds, the agreement should be enforced on the basis of part performance, or by the application of the doctrine of estoppel.

The appellate courts of this state consistently have refused to enforce an oral contract for the sale of land on the basis of part performance alone. And, it is now a rule of property in this state that part performance of a parol contract for the sale of land will not take the agreement out of the statute of frauds. The harshness of this rule has been mitigated by the application of the doctrine of equitable estoppel in exceptional cases where to enforce the statute of frauds would make it an instrument of hardship and oppression, verging on actual fraud.

> Equitable estoppel, in the modern sense, arises from the "conduct" of the party, using that word in its broadest meaning, as including his spoken or written words, his positive acts, and his silence or negative omission to do any thing. Its foundation is justice and good conscience. Its object is to prevent the unconscientious and inequitable assertion or enforcement of claims or rights which might have existed, or been enforceable by other rules of law, unless prevented by an estoppel; and its practical effect is, from motives of equity and fair dealing, to create and vest opposing rights in the party who obtains the benefit of the estoppel.

Evans v. Belmont Land Co., 92 Tenn. 348, 365, 21 S.W. 670, 673–674 (1893).

We think this is such a case. In dealing with Mr. Newman, respondent not only placed him in possession and permitted him to construct improvements on lot 100, but took affirmative action thereafter to aid Mr. Newman to secure a $5,000.00 loan—this latter action being taken with the knowledge that the proceeds of the loan were to be used in the construction of a dwelling on lot 100. In the face of this affirmative action by respondent, to allow it to set up the statute of frauds as bar to enforcement of the agreement to sell lot 100 to Mr. Newman, and thus secure to itself the improvements on lot 100 would be a gross injustice and moral fraud on Mr. Newman.

Petitioner had no direct dealings with respondent relative to lot 100, except to give notice of the assignment executed by Mr. Newman. However, by virtue of the assignment, petitioner acquired all the rights and remedies possessed by Mr. Newman under the agreement to sell, and took the contract subject to the same restrictions, limitations, and defenses as it had in the hands of Mr. Newman. It follows that since it is unconscionable to allow respondent to set up the statute of frauds as a bar to enforcement of the agreement to sell lot 100 to Mr. Newman, it would be unconscionable to permit the defense to be interposed in this action brought by Mr. Newman.

Respondent argues that the agreement to sell lot 100 was not assignable—that it was a special kind of contract entered into only with respondent's employees. We find nothing in the record to indicate that the agreement was not assignable. To the contrary, the representative of respondent who made the agreement testified that there was nothing to prevent an employee from taking a lot, putting up a house, and then selling it to someone who was not an employee.

The Court of Appeals pointed out in its opinion that even if the agreement to sell lot 100 is enforceable, respondent [sic] is not now entitled to a deed to the property because a condition precedent to receiving a deed—that is, to have the residence under roof—has not been met. The chancellor also recognized that the condition precedent had not been met by petitioner at the time of trial of the cause. He also noted the practical difficulty, or dilemma, faced by petitioner in expending additional monies on the residence to place it under roof in the face of the insistence of respondent that Mr. Newman's rights in lot 100 were not assignable, and absent a judicial declaration of the efficacy of the agreement between Mr. Newman and respondent. In resolving this dilemma, the chancellor pointed out that the action brought by petitioner "conforms to a certain extent to a declaratory judgment." The chancellor then undertook to declare the rights of the parties in the agreement. He held the agreement to sell was enforceable, the assignment was valid, and that petitioner would be entitled to a deed to lot 100 when he had the residence under roof. We think the chancellor's findings were correct and that his declaration of petitioner's right to a deed to lot 100, when the condition precedent is met, was timely and proper. . . .

Hickey v. Green

Appeals Court of Massachusetts, 1982.
442 N.E.2d 37.

CUTTER, J.

This case is before us on stipulated facts. . . . Mrs. Gladys Green owns a lot (Lot S) in the Manomet section of Plymouth. In July, 1980, she advertised it for sale. On July 11 and 12, Hickey and his wife discussed with Mrs. Green purchasing Lot S and "orally agreed to a sale" for $15,000. Mrs. Green on July 12 accepted a deposit check of $500, marked by Hickey on the back, "Deposit on Lot ... Massasoit Ave. Manomet ... Subject to Variance from Town of Plymouth." Mrs. Green's brother and agent "was under the impression that a zoning variance was needed and [had] advised ... Hickey to write" the quoted language on the deposit check. It turned out, however, by July 16 that no variance would be required. Hickey had left the payee line of the deposit check blank, because of uncertainty whether Mrs. Green or her brother was to receive the check and asked "Mrs. Green to fill in the appropriate name." Mrs. Green held the check, did not fill in the payee's name, and neither cashed nor endorsed it. Hickey "stated to Mrs. Green that his intention was to sell his home and build on Mrs. Green's lot."

"Relying upon the arrangements ... with Mrs. Green," the Hickeys advertised their house on Sachem Road in newspapers on three days in July, 1980, and agreed with a purchaser for its sale and took from him a deposit check for $500 which they deposited in their own account. On July 24, Mrs. Green told Hickey that she "no longer intended to sell her property to him" but had decided to sell to another for $16,000. Hickey told Mrs. Green that he had already sold his house and offered her $16,000 for Lot S. Mrs. Green refused this offer.

The Hickeys filed this complaint seeking specific performance. Mrs. Green asserts that relief is barred by the Statute of Frauds contained in G.L. c. 259, § 1. The trial judge granted specific performance. Mrs. Green has appealed.

The present rule applicable in most jurisdictions in the United States is succinctly set forth in Restatement (Second) of Contracts § 129 (1981).

The section reads: "A contract for the transfer of an interest in land may be specifically enforced notwithstanding failure to comply with the Statute of Frauds if it is established that the party seeking enforcement, *in reasonable reliance on the contract* and on the continuing assent of the party against whom enforcement is sought, *has so changed his position that injustice can be avoided only by specific enforcement*" (emphasis supplied).[6] The earlier Massachusetts decisions laid down somewhat strict requirements for an estoppel precluding the assertion of the Statute of Frauds. Frequently there has been an actual change of possession and improvement of the transferred property, as well as full payment of the full purchase price, or one or more of these elements.

It is stated in Park, Real Estate Law § 883, at 334, that the "more recent decisions ... indicate a trend on the part of the [Supreme Judicial C]ourt to find that the circumstances warrant specific performance." This appears to be a correct perception. See Fisher v. MacDonald, 332 Mass. 727, 729 (1955), where specific performance was granted upon a showing that the purchaser "was put into possession and ... [had] furnished part of the consideration in money and services"; Orlando v. Ottaviani, 337 Mass. 157, 161–162 (1958), where specific performance was granted to the former holder of an option to buy a strip of land fifteen feet wide, important to the option holder, and the option had been surrendered in reliance upon an oral promise to convey the strip made by the purchaser of a larger parcel of which the fifteen-foot strip was a part.

The present facts reveal a simple case of a proposed purchase of a residential vacant lot, where the vendor, Mrs. Green, knew that the Hickeys were planning to sell their former home (possibly to obtain funds to pay her) and build on Lot S. The Hickeys, relying on Mrs. Green's oral promise, moved rapidly to make their sale without obtaining any adequate memorandum of the terms of what appears to have been intended to be a quick cash sale of Lot S. So rapid was action by the Hickeys that, by July 21, less than ten days after giving their deposit to Mrs. Green, they had accepted a deposit check for the sale of their house, endorsed the check,

6. Comments a and b to ¶ 129 read (in part): "a.... This section restates what is widely known as the 'part performance doctrine.' Part performance is not an accurate designation of such acts as taking possession and making improvements when the contract does not provide for such acts, but such acts regularly bring the doctrine into play. The doctrine is contrary to the words of the Statute of Frauds, but is was established by English courts of equity soon after the enactment of the Statute. Payment of purchase-money, without more, was once thought sufficient to justify specific enforcement, but a contrary view now prevails, since in such cases restitution is an adequate remedy.... Enforcement has ... been justified on the ground that repudiation after 'part performance' amounts to a 'virtual fraud.' A more accurate statement is that courts with equitable powers are vested by tradition with what in substance is a dispensing power based on the promisee's reliance, *a discretion to be exercised with caution* in light of all the circumstances.... [emphasis added].

"B.... Two distinct elements enter into the application of the rule of this Section: first, the extent to which the evidentiary function of the statutory formalities is fulfilled by the conduct of the parties; second, the reliance of the promise, providing a compelling substantive basis for relief in addition to the expectations created by the promise."

and placed it in their bank account. Above their signatures endorsing the check was a memorandum probably sufficient to satisfy the Statute of Frauds under A.B.C. Auto Parts, Inc. v. Moran, 359 Mass. 327, 329–331 (1971). At the very least, the Hickeys had bound themselves in a manner in which, to avoid a transfer of their own house, they might have had to engage in expensive litigation. No attorney has been shown to have been used either in the transaction between Mrs. Green and the Hickeys or in that between the Hickeys and their purchaser.

There is no denial by Mrs. Green of the oral contract between her and the Hickeys. This, under § 129 of the Restatement, is of some significance. There can be no doubt (a) that Mrs. Green made the promise on which the Hickeys so promptly relied, and also (b) she, nearly as promptly, but not promptly enough, repudiated it because she had a better opportunity. The stipulated facts require the conclusion that in equity Mrs. Green's conduct cannot be condoned. This is not a case where either party is shown to have contemplated the negotiation of a purchase and sale agreement. If a written agreement had been expected, even by only one party, or would have been natural (because of the participation by lawyers or otherwise), a different situation might have existed. It is a permissible inference from the agreed facts that the rapid sale of the Hickeys' house was both appropriate and expected. These are not circumstances where negotiations fairly can be seen as inchoate.

We recognize that specific enforcement of Mrs. Green's promise to convey Lot S may well go somewhat beyond the circumstances considered in the *Fisher* case, 332 Mass. 727 (1955), and in the *Orlando* case, 337 Mass. 157 (1958), where specific performance was granted.... We recognize also the cautionary language about granting specific performance in comment a to § 129 of the Restatement (see note 6, *supra*). No public interest behind G. L. c. 259, § 1, however, in the simple circumstances before us, will be violated if Mrs. Green fairly is held to her precise bargain by principles of equitable estoppel, subject to the considerations mentioned below....

Notes & Questions

1. Most American statutes of frauds are closely patterned after the original English Statute of Frauds, 29 Car. II c. 3 (1677), and require not only that deeds conveying an interest in land be in writing and signed by the grantor, but also that land sale contracts be in writing and signed by the parties. Should the writing requirement for contracts be applied less stringently than the writing requirement for deeds? Note that deeds form links in a parcel's chain of title that must be relied upon to identify the parcel and its owner decades, even centuries, later, when all witnesses to the transaction have disappeared and a prospective buyer is seeking to determine whether his seller has good title. Sales contracts, by contrast, have short lives—typically 60 days at most—and are rarely recorded; once the executory period expires, they are not relied on by anyone for any

purpose. Cf. Patrick M. McFadden, Oral Transfers of Land in Illinois, 1988 U. Ill. L. Rev. 667 (arguing for recognition of oral conveyances and maintaining that recording laws could adequately protect third parties).

2. **Signed Writing.** While a formally executed contract of sale meets the requirements of the statute of frauds, other pieces of paper generated during the sales process may also suffice. See, e.g., Hessenthaler v. Farzin, 564 A.2d 990 (Pa. Super. 1989); George W. Watkins Family v. Messenger, 766 P.2d 1267 (App. 1988), aff'd, 797 P.2d 1385 (Idaho 1990) (initials, rather than signature, on contract were adequate). Although a faxed copy of a signed contract probably suffices under the statute of frauds, the imprinting of the sender's name and address at the top of each page does not substitute for a signature. See Parma Tile Mosaic & Marble Co. v. Estate of Short, 663 N.E.2d 633 (N.Y. 1996).

The Electronic Signatures in Global and National Commerce Act, 15 U.S.C. §§ 7001 et seq., signed into law in 2000, provides:

> Notwithstanding any statute, regulation, or other rule of law ... with respect to any transaction in or affecting interstate or foreign commerce—
>
> (1) a signature, contract, or other record relating to such transaction may not be denied legal effect, validity, or enforceability solely because it is in electronic form; and
>
> (2) a contract relating to such transaction may not be denied legal effect, validity, or enforceability solely because an electronic signature or electronic record was used in its formation.

The sale, lease, exchange or other disposition of an interest in land are defined as "transactions" covered by the Act. 15 U.S.C. § 7006(13)(B).

A real estate contract can thus be valid even though it is in electronic form, and an "electronic signature" will be valid if it is a "symbol ... attached to or logically associated with the intent to sign the record." 15 U.S.C. § 7006(5). As Professor Patrick A. Randolph, Jr., suggests:

> So, for instance, if you sent me an e-mail that said: "I'll buy your property at 450 W. Meyer in Chicago for $50,000," and I typed at the top of this message "OK" and hit "return," it is quite likely that we would have a binding real estate contract. All you would have to show is that the typing of the word "OK" indicated my intent to express agreement. The fact that I did not type out my name would not matter, because I "attached" an "electronic symbol" (i.e., the word "OK") to a contract.

Patrick A. Randolph, Jr., Has E–Sign Murdered the Statute of Frauds?, Probate & Prop., July/Aug. 2001, at 23, 24.

3. **Adequacy of Description.** *Baliles* lies somewhere between the two polar American views on the adequacy of descriptions in land sale contracts. At one pole, some courts treat contract descriptions far more liberally than deed descriptions. See, e.g., Stachnik v. Winkel, 213 N.W.2d 434 (App. 1973), rev'd on other grounds 230 N.W.2d 529 (Mich. 1975)

(contract for "your [seller's] property located in Glen Arbor Twp. Lee Lanau Co. situated on Wheeler Rd." is sufficiently definite because external evidence showed that this was the only property that the sellers owned in Lee Lanau County). At the other extreme, a few courts insist that the contract description contain all of the detail required for deeds. See, e.g., Martin v. Seigel, 212 P.2d 107 (Wash. 1949) (specific performance refused even though contract identified parcel by street address, city, county and state, and even though parol evidence further provided the parcel's lot and block numbers).

4. **Exceptions.** *Baliles* and *Hickey* illustrate the two principal exceptions to the statute of frauds: part performance, and estoppel. Why do courts recognize any exceptions? See Michael Braunstein, Remedy, Reason, and the Statute of Frauds: A Critical Economic Analysis, 1989 Utah L. Rev. 383 (arguing that exceptions to the statute of frauds are applied not because they provide satisfactory evidence of an agreement but because adherence to the statute in such cases would sanction economically wasteful behavior).

5. **Part Performance.** Was *Baliles* overly rigorous in holding that part performance alone will not take an oral contract out of the statute of frauds? Many courts are less exacting. Some hold that the buyer's entry onto the parcel under an oral contract will suffice. Others require possession accompanied by some payment to the seller. Others require possession and the construction of valuable improvements. And still others require possession and proof that removal will cause irreparable injury. See 3 American Law of Property § 11.7 (A.J. Casner ed. 1952).

6. **The Uniform Land Transactions Act.** Are there better devices than the present statutes of frauds "to avoid perjury on the one hand and fraud on the other"? The Uniform Land Transactions Act, approved in 1975 by the National Conference of Commissioners on Uniform State Laws but not yet adopted by any state over a quarter of a century later, represents a comprehensive effort to harmonize, simplify and modernize state law governing land transactions. Its provisions paralleling the statutes of frauds appear in § 2–201:

> (a) Notwithstanding agreement to the contrary and except as provided in subsection (b), a contract to convey real estate is not enforceable by judicial proceeding unless there is a writing signed by the party against whom enforcement is sought or by the party's representative which:
>
> (1) contains a description of the real estate that is sufficiently definite to make possible an identification of the real estate with reasonable certainty;
>
> (2) except as to an option to renew a lease, states the price or a method of fixing the price;[a] and
>
> (3) is sufficiently definite to indicate with reasonable certainty that a contract to convey has been made by the parties.

a. Eds.—What *was* the agreed-on price in *Baliles*?

(b) A contract not evidenced by a writing satisfying the requirements of subsection (a), but which is valid in other respects, is enforceable if:

(1) it is for the conveyance of real estate for one year or less;

(2) the buyer has taken possession of the real estate, and has paid all or part of the contract price;

(3) the buyer has accepted a deed from the seller;

(4) the party seeking to enforce a contract, in reasonable reliance upon the contract and upon the continuing assent of the party against whom enforcement is sought has changed his position to his detriment to the extent that an unjust result can be avoided only by enforcing the contract; or

(5) the party against whom enforcement is sought admits in his pleading, testimony, or otherwise in court that the contract for conveyance was made.

Commissioners' Comment 4 adds that "Failure to satisfy the requirements of this section does not render the contract void for all purposes, but merely prevents it from being judicially enforced in favor of a party to the contract. For example, a buyer who takes possession of real estate as provided in an oral contract which the seller has not meanwhile repudiated, is not a trespasser. Nor would the statute of frauds provisions of this section be a defense to a third person who wrongfully induces a party to refuse to perform an oral contract, even though the injured party cannot maintain an action for damages against the party so refusing to perform."

For a discussion of why states have not adopted the U.L.T.A., see Marion W. Benfield, Jr., Wasted Days and Wasted Nights: Why the Land Act Failed, 20 Nova L. Rev. 1037 (1996).

2. CONDITIONS

The typical land sale contract contains several conditions, some express, others implied, that must be met or waived for the sale to close. Conditions are essentially substitutes for information—information about the home finance market, the quality of title and of the premises, and local government regulations. Conditions postpone contract performance until a time when that information can be obtained—through a lender's response to a loan application, a title report, a housing inspection, an environmental audit, and a land use review.

a. FINANCING

Bushmiller v. Schiller

Court of Appeals of Maryland, 1977.
368 A.2d 1044.

MELVIN, JUDGE.

The dispute in this case is over which of the parties to a real estate contract is entitled to a $13,000 deposit initially received by the seller (appellant) from the buyer (appellee) as part payment of the $130,000 purchase price for a residential property located in Baltimore County. By suit and counter-suit, each party sought judgment against the other for the amount of the deposit. After a bench trial in the Circuit Court for Baltimore County (Proctor, J.), the buyer and original plaintiff, Mrs. Eunice Myrta Schiller, emerged victorious with a judgment for $13,000 against the seller and original defendant, Mr. Joseph Bushmiller. Judgment was also entered against Mr. Bushmiller in his counter-suit. Aggrieved by the results, Mr. Bushmiller has appealed to us to set aright what he perceives as a wrong decision by the trial court.

The dispute over the deposit had its genesis when Mrs. Schiller won "a million dollar lottery" in the Maryland State Lottery, entitling her to receive $50,000 a year for 20 years. Not long after this fortuitous happening, she entered into a written contract with Mr. Bushmiller, dated 25 July 1975, to purchase his house for $130,000. The contract provided for the payment of a deposit of $13,000 to be applied as part payment of the purchase price. Settlement was to be within 45 days and "[i]f the Purchaser ... fail[ed] to make full settlement," the deposit was to be "forfeited at the option of the Seller, in which event the Purchaser shall be relieved from further liability...."

The contract further provided that,

> This contract is subject to the ability of the Purchaser to secure [within 10 days], a written commitment for ... [a] first mortgage secured on said premises in the amount of $100,000, for a term of Twenty (20) years, and bearing interest at the rate of prevailing per annum [sic].
>
> Purchaser utilizing a loan agrees to make application immediately and file all necessary papers that are required to complete processing, including resubmission and appeal where necessary, and agrees that failure so to do shall give the Seller the right to declare the deposit forfeited....

In her suit to recover the deposit Mrs. Schiller alleged that she "was unable to obtain the necessary financing and advised the Defendants and each of them and demanded the refund of the deposit monies and ... Defendants have failed and refused to return said monies." The gravamen of Mr. Bushmiller's counter-suit was that Mrs. Schiller "was obligated under the terms of the aforesaid Contract to act in good faith in securing a written commitment for a first mortgage within ten (10) days from the date of the Contract, and said Counter–Defendant wholly failed and refused to act in good faith to secure the said mortgage commitment, notwithstanding that mortgage monies on the terms required under the contract were readily available to the Counter–Defendant." By a "Stipulation of Counsel" filed prior to trial, Mr. Bushmiller's damages against Mrs. Schiller were "limited to the sum of Thirteen Thousand Dollars ($13,000.00)," the amount of the deposit that had been paid into court by Bushmiller's agent who had originally received it from Mrs. Schiller.

The Evidence

The pertinent facts as found by the trial judge can be summarized as follows:

Mrs. Schiller became interested in buying Mr. Bushmiller's property. Before submitting an offer she telephoned the Equitable Trust Bank on Wednesday 23 July 1975 to inquire about the possibility of a mortgage loan. She talked to a Mrs. Davis who was a mortgage loan officer for Equitable. Mrs. Davis advised her that a mortgage loan would in all probability be favorably considered on the basis of a 20–year mortgage with "ballooning" at the end of five years. Mrs. Schiller did not understand what the term "ballooning" meant and at that time made no effort to find out. The next day, 24 July, Mrs. Schiller filled out a formal application for a mortgage loan of $97,500.00, to be repaid in "300 months" (25 years). On the same day, Mrs. Schiller signed an undated contract of sale prepared by her agent, a Mr. Collins of Century 21, a real estate brokerage firm. Mrs. Schiller then left the Baltimore area to visit her sister in Connecticut.

On Friday, 25 July 1975, Mr. Collins submitted the contract offer to Mr. Bushmiller. As prepared by Mr. Collins, the contract provided that the time within which the purchaser was to secure a written commitment for the mortgage loan was 30 days. Mr. Bushmiller wanted that time period reduced to 10 days. Mr. Collins telephoned Mrs. Schiller in Connecticut and Mrs. Schiller agreed to the change by a telegram dated 25 July 1975. The change was made in the contract itself and initialed by Mr. Collins as agent for Mrs. Schiller. As thus amended, the contract was dated and executed by Mr. Bushmiller on 25 July 1975.

On Sunday 27 July, Mrs. Schiller left Connecticut and went to New Hampshire to visit her son. As found by the trial judge, "when she gets to her son's her eyes are opened, first, as to what balloon mortgage financing means, and secondly, as to the problems involved in a large expensive house. She immediately calls off the Equitable Trust Company loan, and then does nothing more." The record shows that Mrs. Schiller telephoned Equitable from New Hampshire on either 28 July, 29 July, or 30 July (probably 29 July) and cancelled her loan application. There is no indication in the record that she notified Mr. Bushmiller of the cancellation.

Mrs. Schiller returned to Baltimore in the late evening of 5 August, eleven days after the date the contract was executed. On 6 August, Mr. Bushmiller's agent contacted Mrs. Schiller. The agent's testimony (which the trial court found to be uncontradicted) concerning her conversation with Mrs. Schiller was as follows:

> Then Mrs. Schiller told me that when she was in New Hampshire and talked to her son, he told her that it was unwise for her to buy this house. She said, "I cannot afford it; this is ridiculous. He's shown me that I will have to pay capital gains on my house,"

which was not true because she was reinvesting the money; and I tried to explain this to her. She said, "[W]ell, it doesn't—I just can't afford the house"; and she said "[I]t doesn't matter." And when we mentioned the means of financing that we had available and the fact that it was savings and loans money available at the terms that she wanted, she said "[T]hat doesn't matter, I'm not interested in buying the house; I can't afford it; my son has advised me against it."

It appears that on 6 August, the day after her return to Baltimore, Mrs. Schiller also contacted Mrs. Davis of Equitable and told her she did not want a "balloon" mortgage. On 7 August Mrs. Davis wrote to Mrs. Schiller as follows:

> Dear Mrs. Schiller:
>
> Pursuant to our telephone conversation of August 6, 1975, I must issue a letter of decline in answer to your mortgage request.
>
> When I was first approached by Mrs. Spilman of Piper & Co. concerning financing for you, I told her that it would appear Equitable Trust would help you based on a $100,000.00 loan written for 5 years based on a 20 year payout. The interest rate would be determined when the loan was presented for approval. Since, on your application, you have specifically requested a straight 25 year mortgage loan and are not willing to consider a five year loan with a balloon payment, I must decline your loan request.
>
> Thank you for the opportunity to be of service to you.
>
> Very truly yours,
>
> /s/Verna Q. Davis
> Mortgage Officer

Also on 7 August, Mrs. Schiller's attorney wrote to Mr. Bushmiller's agent and to Mr. Collins as follows:

> Dear Sir & Madam:
>
> Our office represents E. Myrta Schiller and have had referred to it, for attention, the contract for the captioned property dated July 25, 1975.
>
> As both of you know, Mrs. Schiller promptly made application for a mortgage loan with The Equitable Trust Company in the amount of $100,000.00 for a term of twenty years, repayable in monthly installments of principal and interest only.
>
> We regret to advise that The Equitable Trust Company has turned down the application and was only willing to grant a 20 year amortization plan with a 5 year balloon.

As the balloon provision is unacceptable, I must advise that the purchaser was unable to secure a written commitment for the first mortgage described in the contract within ten days from the date of the contract.

Please, therefore, promptly return the $13,000.00 being held by you to the writer.

If there are any further negotiations to be conducted under a new contract between the seller and my client, I would appreciate your clearing the same through this office. I am enclosing herewith, for your records, a copy of the letter received from The Equitable Trust Company indicating that they would only write the mortgage loan under a balloon clause.

Very truly yours,
Theodore C. Denick.

The record reveals no further contact between the parties until 13 October 1975. On that date Mr. Bushmiller's attorney wrote to Mrs. Schiller's attorney as follows:

Dear Mr. Denick:

As you know, this office represents Joseph Bushmiller, the owner and seller of the property known as 401 Falls Road. The seller's position remains unchanged, in that he is still ready, willing and able to convey the property to Mrs. Schiller under the contract of sale dated July 25, 1975.

It is our belief that Mrs. Schiller's failure to consummate this contract constitutes a breach of the contract; and we intend to hold Mrs. Schiller's deposit of $13,000.00, and we further intend to hold her liable for any damages which we sustain on resale of the property. We presently have two buyers who have offered $100,000.00 for the purchase of the property. Although we feel the property is worth more than $100,000.00, neither of the prospective buyers will offer more. Accordingly, we may be constrained to accept a $100,000.00 offer and look to Mrs. Schiller for the balance. The market conditions continue to deteriorate because of tight money and the approaching winter months. The seller has a second mortgage which falls due in early November and we have been advised that foreclosure proceedings will be instituted immediately if the entire mortgage balance is not paid when due.

If Mrs. Schiller is willing to proceed under her contract, I am confident that we can obtain financing for her at the prevailing interest rates. Please let me hear from you if Mrs. Schiller is willing to proceed with the contract; however, I shall notify you in any event of the execution of a new contract by the seller.

Very truly yours,

J. Earle Plumhoff

Mrs. Schiller's response to this letter was her suit, filed 24 October 1975, to recover the $13,000 deposit.

Decision

It is clear that the requirement of obtaining mortgage financing as a condition in a contract for the sale of realty must be given effect unless the condition has been altered by the parties or waived by the one for whose benefit the condition was made. In this case, the obligations of Mrs. Schiller to buy and Mr. Bushmiller to sell were each conditioned upon Mrs. Schiller's ability to secure within ten (10) days of the contract date (July 25, 1975) a written commitment for a mortgage loan in the amount of $100,000, for a term of twenty (20) years at the "prevailing" interest rate. The burden of satisfying this condition was placed squarely upon Mrs. Schiller. By the terms of the contract she was obligated "to make application immediately and file all necessary papers that are required to complete processing, including resubmission and appeal where necessary." To these express requirements are added the further implied requirement that she take "bona fide, reasonable and prompt action to obtain the financing specified." Traylor v. Grafton, 332 A.2d 651, 675 (Md. 1975).

The trial judge found that Mrs. Schiller did not know what "balloon" financing meant when she discussed the subject of a mortgage with Mrs. Davis of Equitable on 24 July and that it was not until Sunday 27 July when she visited her son in New Hampshire that she learned the meaning of the term. We cannot say that these factual findings were clearly erroneous. Nor do we find erroneous the judge's finding that upon learning the meaning of a "balloon" mortgage and upon being persuaded by her son "as to the problems involved in a large expensive house, [s]he immediately calle[d] off the Equitable Trust Company loan, and then does nothing more." We do not agree, however, that the inaction on her part satisfied the requirement of good faith efforts to obtain the financing specified by the contract. The judge felt that her inaction was justified and comported with good faith because " . . . even if she had probably made up her mind that she still wanted the house, it would almost certainly have been impossible for her in that very brief period of time to arrange for a written commitment for a loan in the amount of $100,000."

While it is undoubtedly true that it may have been difficult to obtain a loan commitment within the ten-day limitation, patently it would not have been "impossible." In any event, we cannot equate "no" efforts with "reasonable" efforts to obtain the specified financing. Moreover, there is no indication in the record that Mrs. Schiller's failure to proceed with further efforts to obtain financing within the allotted time was due in the slightest degree to any thought or knowledge on her part that it could not be obtained within the ten-day period. The conclusion is inescapable that after talking with her son on 27 July she decided she no longer wanted Mr. Bushmiller's "large expensive house," that she could not afford it, and that she wanted "out" of her contractual obligations, and that it was for these reasons alone that she ceased any further efforts to obtain the necessary financing. This conclusion is fortified by her refusal to even consider the offer of Mr. Bushmiller's agent to obtain financing for her that was "available at the terms that she wanted." It is true that this offer was made after the ten-day period, and had Mrs. Schiller made good faith efforts within the 10–day period to obtain financing and been unsuccessful, she would have been justified in not accepting the offer. Under the circumstances here, however, we think the refusal of the offer has significance as bearing on the question of Mrs. Schiller's good faith efforts to satisfy the condition precedent in the contract.

In the circumstances we hold that the trial judge was clearly erroneous in his finding that Mrs. Schiller's efforts to obtain financing were made in good faith. It follows that the judgments below must be reversed and the case remanded for entry of judgment for costs in favor of Mr. Bushmiller in the original suit filed by Mrs. Schiller, and for entry of a judgment for $13,000, plus costs and interest from date of entry in his counter-suit against Mrs. Schiller.

Notes & Questions

1. *Bushmiller* graphically illustrates the pitfalls that surround real estate contract conditions. However carefully they are drafted, and however explicitly the parties' duties respecting their fulfillment are prescribed, contract conditions can still be used as an escape hatch, enabling buyer or seller to renege for reasons totally unrelated to the condition—at least if he or she is more circumspect than Mrs. Schiller about revealing the true motives for backing out of the contract. (Representing Mrs. Schiller, and with the benefit of hindsight, could you have improved on Mr. Denick's effort, in his August 7 letter, to state Mrs. Schiller's position in a noncompromising manner?)

One problem in drafting contract conditions is coming up with the right degree of specificity. If conditions are drafted with excessive detail, they give the buyer considerable opportunity to renege for reasons totally unrelated to the conditions. For example, a financing condition that prescribes a twenty year, level payment mortgage at an interest rate of 8.75%, with no points and no prepayment penalties after five years, can easily be employed to excuse performance if interest rates move up a fraction or if market conditions operate to vary some other term. Yet, if the parties seek to close this loophole by phrasing the financing condition more generally—for example, "buyer must be able to obtain financing at prevailing market terms"—they run the risk that the contract will be held too indefinite to be enforced. See, e.g., Anand v. Marple, 522 N.E.2d 281 (Ill. App. 1988). And if fulfilling the condition is left to the exclusive control of one of the parties there is the added problem of illusoriness or lack of mutuality of obligation.

2. **"Reasonableness" and "Good Faith."** To what extent can concepts of reasonableness and good faith be used to patch over the inherent difficulty in drafting real estate contract conditions? Courts will sometimes fill in incomplete financing clauses by looking to the circumstances surrounding the contract, including the prevailing money market conditions, that presumably reflect the parties' original expectations. See, e.g., Hunt v. Shamblin, 371 S.E.2d 591 (W. Va. 1988). Most courts also require a good faith effort on the part of the buyer to meet conditions in the sales contract. See, e.g., Greer Properties, Inc. v. LaSalle National Bank, 874 F.2d 457 (7th Cir. 1989).

Did Mrs. Schiller act in bad faith by applying for a 25–year mortgage for $97,500 when the contract specified a 20–year mortgage for $100,000? Did the contract condition contemplate a fully amortized mortgage and, if so, would the proffered "balloon" feature have been sufficient to excuse her performance? Under a fully amortized mortgage, the borrower completely repays the principal—here, $100,000—over the mortgage term—here, 20 years. Under a balloon mortgage, no principal payments are made until the end of the term, when the entire principal—the "balloon"—becomes payable. The instrument offered by Equitable Trust to Mrs. Schiller was a hybrid: for the first five years, the mortgage would be amortized on the basis of a 20–year term; but, at the end of five years, the entire remaining principal would be fully payable.

3. **Specification of the Financing Institution.** If the financing condition in a land sale contract specifies not only the terms of an acceptable mortgage loan but also the particular institution that is to make the loan, will the buyer be excused if the specified institution rejects the loan application, but some other institutional lender agrees to make the loan on the terms specified? What if no institutional lender will make the loan, but the seller agrees to finance the transaction herself?

In Kovarik v. Vesely, 89 N.W.2d 279 (Wis. 1958), buyers' performance was conditioned on financing through a "$7,000 purchase money mortgage from the Fort Atkinson Savings and Loan Ass'n." One week after unsuccessfully applying to Fort Atkinson Savings & Loan, the buyers were told that the sellers would be willing to take back a purchase money mortgage on the terms and conditions specified in the buyers' application to Fort Atkinson. The buyers declined and brought suit to recover their down payment. Holding for the sellers, the court agreed with the trial court's finding that the "buyers were interested in financing a Seven Thousand Dollar mortgage and not in any particular loaning agency." It rejected buyers' argument that, because their contract specified Fort Atkinson Savings & Loan, good faith did not require them to accept financing from the sellers.

Was *Kovarik* correctly decided? Why should a buyer care about the source of his funds? Justice Fairchild, dissenting, offered two possible reasons: "the buyer will feel more confident of his own judgment of the price he is to pay if a lending institution is willing to make a loan" and "the buyer would rather have the matter, in the event of default, in the hands of an established lending institution than in the hands of an individual who might be less able, if not less willing, to adjust matters reasonably." Id. at 286. For a case reaching a result opposite to *Kovarik*, see Gardner v. Padro, 517 N.E.2d 1131 (Ill. App. 1987).

4. **Whose Condition Is It?** It is sometimes unclear whether the parties intended a particular condition to benefit buyer, seller, or both. The question of who was intended to benefit from a particular condition is obviously important because only the intended beneficiary can waive the condition. Nonetheless, even well-counseled buyers and sellers often fail to indicate which of them was intended to benefit from the specified conditions.

In *Bushmiller*, which party—buyer or seller—was the intended beneficiary of the financing condition? Of the ten-day time limit on performance of the condition? In a similar case, Loda v. H.K. Sargeant & Associates, Inc., 448 A.2d 812 (Conn. 1982), the Connecticut Supreme Court upheld a lower court finding that the financing condition was intended to benefit the buyer while the time limit on performance was intended to benefit the seller who did not wish to keep his property tied up by a buyer who had no prospects of obtaining the needed financing. Note, though, that in discussing the offer by seller Bushmiller to obtain financing for buyer Schiller after the ten-day performance period had expired, the court observed that "had Mrs. Schiller made good faith efforts within the 10–day period to obtain financing and been unsuccessful, she would have been justified in not accepting the offer." 368 A.2d at 1049.

Should a buyer be able to waive a financing condition and pay the seller in cash? In Dale Mortgage Bankers Corp. v. 877 Stewart Avenue Associates, 518 N.Y.S.2d 411 (1987), the court strictly applied a contingency clause that said either party could void the sale if the purchaser could not obtain financing and held that the buyer therefore could not pay cash over the seller's objections. Did the court correctly decide the case? Why do you think the seller wanted the condition? Was the seller asserting the cancellation right in order to renegotiate the contract or find a better price if the buyer could not obtain financing? Or did the seller just want to be able to avoid the delay of waiting until closing to find out that the buyer would not be able to perform?

b. TITLE

Conklin v. Davi

Supreme Court of New Jersey, 1978.
388 A.2d 598.

MOUNTAIN, J.

Plaintiffs contracted to sell and convey to defendants a residential property in Ridgewood. The purchasers refused to consummate the sale, alleging defects in title and misrepresentations on the part of the sellers. Plaintiffs instituted an action for specific performance; defendants counterclaimed for rescission. Before the trial commenced, plaintiffs abandoned their claim for specific performance, and the case proceeded solely as an action on the counterclaim of the defendants-purchasers, seeking rescission, in effect to secure the return of the down payment....

It would appear that the validity of the title to a portion of the premises in question is sought to be sustained by the sellers upon a claim of adverse possession. The purchasers take the position that this being so, they were justified in repudiating the agreement; that the sellers could not force such a title upon them, but should have perfected the record title prior to the date of closing. This, they add, should have been done either by securing a deed from the present record title holder, or by means of an action to quiet title. While we readily concede that the sellers would have been well advised to have followed such a course, we do not agree that their failure to do so imperiled their position to the extent urged by the purchasers.

When a prospective seller's title is grounded upon adverse possession, or contains some apparent flaw of record, he has a choice of options. He may at once take whatever steps are necessary to perfect the record title, including resort to an action to quiet title, an action to cancel an outstanding encumbrance, or whatever other appropriate step may be necessary to accomplish the purpose. In the alternative he may, believing his title to be marketable despite the fact that it rests on adverse possession or is otherwise imperfect of record, choose to enter into a contract of sale, hoping to convince the purchaser or, if necessary, a court, that his estimate of the marketability of his title is justified. That is the course the sellers seem to have followed here. It must be borne in mind that this latter course is available only where the contract of sale does not require the vendor to give a title valid of record, but provides for a less stringent requirement, such as marketability or insurability. Such is the case here. Of course "[a] buyer is entitled to the kind of title stipulated for in the contract of sale." Friedman, Contracts and Conveyances of Real Property (3rd ed. 1975) § 4.2, p. 259; Lounsbery v. Locander, 25 N.J. Eq. 554 (E. & A.1874). Here the contract contained the following provision:

> Title to be conveyed shall be marketable and insurable, at regular rates, by any reputable title insurance company licensed to do business in the State of New Jersey, subject only to the encumbrances hereinabove set forth.

It will be seen at once that while the title for which the purchasers have contracted must be marketable and insurable, there is no requirement that it be a perfect title of record. Many titles, imperfect of record, are nonetheless marketable. Justice Cardozo, then Chief Judge of the New York Court of Appeals, observed:

> The law assures to a buyer a title free from reasonable doubt, but not from every doubt.... If "the only defect in the title" is "a very remote and improbable contingency," a "slender possibility only," a conveyance will be decreed. ...

Norwegian Evangelical Free Church v. Milhauser, 252 N.Y. 186, 169 N.E. 134, 135 (1929). Incidentally, the law will imply that title must be marketable, even where the contract is silent upon the point. The purchasers are accordingly in error in insisting that nothing less than a good record title will suffice. A title that is marketable and insurable, though imperfect of record, will meet the terms of the contract....

Notes & Questions

1. **Marketable Title.** Courts in all states will imply a covenant or condition of marketable title into contracts for the sale of land. The definitions they give for marketable title are almost invariably circular and thus of little help in predicting results: "A marketable title has been defined as one that may be freely made the subject of resale. It is one which can be readily sold or mortgaged to a person of reasonable prudence, the test of the marketability of a title being whether there is an objection thereto such as would interfere with a sale or with the market value of the property." Regan v. Lanze, 354 N.E.2d 818, 822 (N.Y. 1976). Or a marketable title is one "which at all times, and under all circumstances, may be forced upon an unwilling purchaser." Pyrke v. Waddington, 10 Hare 1, 68 Eng. Rep. 813 (Chancery 1852). Yet another definition is that a marketable title is one that can be held quietly without fear of litigation to determine its validity.

No contract condition has produced more litigation or confusion than marketable title. The main reason for the confusion is that courts employ the concept to encompass two essentially different problems affecting marketability—*chain of title defects* and *encumbrances*.

Chain of title defects affect ownership. For example, the seller or one of the seller's predecessors in title may have obtained title through a fraudulent transfer. There may have been an irregularity in the conduct of a mortgage foreclosure, tax sale, or probate proceeding, or a technical error or omission in a prior conveyance, such as a misspelling in the name of a party, a misdescription of the parcel, or the omission of a proper acknowledgment.

Every state has remedial statutes aimed at curing chain of title defects—curative acts, statutes of limitations, and marketable title acts. These remedial statutes can be consulted to distinguish with some confidence between those title defects that have been cured with the passage of time and those that continue to impair title. While these statutes are not directly concerned with resolving contract disputes over marketable title, they do provide an independent and objective basis for determining the sort of title that seller *A* may be allowed to force upon buyer *B* and, by implication, the sort of title that buyer *B* will in the future be allowed to force upon his buyer *C*. A title with a defect that has been cured by passage of the statutory period, or by the occurrence of the statutorily-prescribed events, is not only good in some abstract sense; it is also marketable in the sense that, as a matter of public policy, the legislature has determined that in acquiring this title a buyer should feel confident that he can later sell it without fear that it will then be held unmarketable.

Encumbrances reduce the value of land in ways that fall short of breaks in the chain of title. Mainly they take the form of security interests, possessory interests and nonpossessory interests. Mechanics liens, mortgage liens and judgment liens are typical security interests. Leases typify possessory encumbrances. Right of way or utility easements and restrictive covenants prohibiting specified land uses are typical nonpossessory encumbrances.

Unlike chain of title defects, for which remedial statutes provide an objective benchmark of marketability, encumbrances must be measured on an entirely subjective, case-by-case basis. Whether and to what extent a right of way impairs a parcel's value will vary from time to time, from parcel to parcel, and from owner to owner. A restrictive covenant prohibiting the parcel's use for commercial purposes will be of no great concern to *A* who plans to put the parcel to residential use, but it will be of great concern to *B* who wants to operate a gas station on the parcel. As a result, the correct resolution between one buyer and seller may not be the correct resolution between another buyer and seller or, more important, between the present buyer and some future buyer from him.

See generally, Milton R. Friedman, Contracts and Conveyances of Real Property 600–615 (5th ed. 1991).

2. **Marketable Title, Record Title, and Insurable Title Compared.** Marketable title can be compared to two other forms of title conditions sometimes obtained by buyers as an alternative, or in addition, to marketable title. *Record title* is title, typically in fee simple absolute, that can be proved by reference to the record alone and without resort to collateral proceedings such as a quiet title action brought to establish seller's title by adverse possession. Perfect record title does not necessarily constitute perfect title. A title that, from the record, appears to be perfect may in fact be entirely invalid because of fraud, nondelivery, or a wild deed somewhere in the chain of title.

Insurable title is title that a title insurance company is willing to insure as valid. Insurable title need not be good record title. For example, a title insurer may decide that, because seller's adverse possession appears to be incontrovertible, it will insure seller's title to the adversely claimed land even though seller has no record title to it. Also insurable title may not be marketable title, for the title policy may except defects or encumbrances that make the title unmarketable.

3. Was *Conklin* correctly decided? One effect of the decision is to require buyers who have not contracted for record title to keep the funds for their share of the purchase price liquid, and to keep their institutional

lender's commitment to finance the remainder of the purchase price alive, throughout the months and possibly years that it will take for litigation to resolve the status of seller's title. As a practical matter it will be virtually impossible for a residential buyer to persuade an institutional lender to extend its financing commitment indefinitely. Commercial buyers may have greater success in obtaining extensions, but at considerable expense.

Obviously, the buyer can protect himself against these consequences if he is aware of the *Conklin* rule *and* if in the negotiations leading up to the contract of sale he can get the seller to agree to convey valid title of record on the date of closing. Is it fair or efficient to place this negotiating burden on the buyer? As between seller and buyer who is better placed to acquire information respecting title expeditiously? To resolve adverse possession claims?

Absent an implied condition of good record title, and absent a willingness on the part of sellers to promise good record title expressly, the parties may compromise by agreeing on insurable title. Will a buyer always be better off with insurable title than with marketable title? Say that, although some defect makes title unmarketable, a title company is willing to insure against the defect because the company determines that it is unlikely that a claim based on the defect will ever be made. By accepting title insurance instead of marketable title, the buyer is effectively accepting a promise of cash payment from the title company as a substitute for the land itself in the event the claim is ever made.

4. **Zoning and Other Land Use Controls.** Say that *B* contracts to buy an undeveloped parcel, Greenacre, from *A*, intending to build and operate a gas station on the parcel. After executing the contract, but before the closing, *B* discovers that a local zoning ordinance bars commercial uses such as gas stations in the neighborhood. Absent a specific provision in the contract governing the point, can *B* rescind the contract and recover his deposit? (If it were not a zoning ordinance, but rather a restrictive covenant, that barred *B*'s commercial use, *B* might be able to rescind on the ground that title was unmarketable.)

In deciding whether to excuse contract performance on the ground that a preexisting public land use regulation such as a zoning ordinance will interfere with buyer's plans, courts almost universally reject the analogy to private land use controls such as easements and covenants. As a general rule, "building and zoning laws in existence at the time a land contract is signed are not treated as encumbrances, and the purchaser has no recourse against the vendor by virtue of restrictions imposed by such laws on the use of the property purchased." Dover Pool & Racquet Club, Inc. v. Brooking, 322 N.E.2d 168, 169 (Mass. 1975). See also Rosique v. Windley Cove, Ltd., 542 So. 2d 1014 (Fla. App. 1989). The position apparently rests on the rule that contracts are subject to all laws in force at the time they are made.

Courts divide on whether land use ordinances enacted *during* the executory period should be treated similarly. *Dover Pool* excused buyer performance in this situation. Other courts take the view that buyers should bear the risk of changes in the law. See, e.g., Felt v. McCarthy, 922 P.2d 90 (Wash. 1996).

Courts also split on whether the buyer should be excused when the land use being made at the time the contract of sale is signed violates an applicable regulation. One line of authority treats these violations like encumbrances and places their burden on seller. For example, in Lohmeyer v. Bower, 227 P.2d 102 (Kan. 1951), buyers were granted rescission when, after signing the contract, they discovered that the house violated not only deed restrictions but also a local zoning ordinance. For the opposing view, that existing violations do not excuse buyer performance, see Gnash v. Saari, 267 P.2d 674 (Wash. 1954).

c. THE TIME SPECIFIED FOR CLOSING

Virtually all sales contract specify that the contract shall close on a particular date. If on the date set for closing seller fails to tender a deed, or buyer fails to tender the purchase price, is the other party discharged from the obligation to perform? The answer will turn on whether the action is in law or in equity. When a legal remedy is sought, performance on the closing date will be considered essential unless the contract discloses a contrary intent. In actions for an equitable remedy, time is not of the essence unless the contract or surrounding circumstances indicate that it should be. These rules apply not only to closing dates, but also to other deadlines specified in the contract such as the deadline for obtaining a financing commitment. See Kakalik v. Bernardo, 439 A.2d 1016 (Conn. 1981).

In Limpus v. Armstrong, 322 N.E.2d 187 (Mass. App. 1975), the contract of sale, dated September 16, called for a closing on or before November 25. After a series of missed telephone calls between buyer and seller, and buyer's failure to perform by November 25, seller on November 29 wrote buyer that the contract was no longer in force and that his $100 deposit was forfeited. Reversing a decision for seller, the court ruled that plaintiff buyer was entitled to specific performance. "The mere fact that the agreement specified a date for closing did not make time of the essence." Further, the court noted, both parties had it within their power to make time of the essence even after they entered into the contract of sale. "Since both the plaintiff and the defendants had failed to perform within the time specified for conveyance, either, by notice to the other upon unreasonable or unnecessary delay by the latter, might have been assigned a reasonable time for the completion of the transaction, thereby making performance within that time of the essence of the contract." Id. at 190.

The Uniform Land Transactions Act goes beyond present law by rejecting the rule that time is of the essence in actions at law, and substituting for it a rule under which one party's delay in performance past a specified date discharges the other only if the delay amounts to a "material breach." U.L.T.A. § 2–302(b)(1). The provision is, however, hedged by limitations. For example, one party, by giving notice to the other before the date set for closing, can "specify effectively that failure to perform on the specified date will discharge him from his own duties under the contract." Id. § 2–302(d). Under section 2–302(a), if the contract does not specify a closing date, the time for performance is "a reasonable time after the making of the contract." Further, "either party may fix a time for performance if the time is not unreasonable and is fixed in good faith."

3. REMEDIES

A buyer whose seller has breached their contract for the sale of land has four possible remedies. The buyer can obtain a decree of specific performance, ordering seller to convey title to him in return for payment of the purchase price. He can obtain damages measured by the difference between the parcel's market value at the date of breach and the contract price, together with any incidental expenses and losses incurred. He can obtain rescission and recover any deposits made. Finally—although this remedy is not much used—the buyer has a lien (called a "vendee's lien") on seller's legal title, securing the seller's obligation to refund the buyer's deposit in the event the seller breaches; the lien can be foreclosed and the land sold to satisfy this obligation if the seller fails to refund the deposit.

A seller whose buyer has breached their contract for the sale of land also has four possible remedies, each paralleling the remedies available to buyer. The seller can obtain a decree of specific performance requiring buyer to pay the purchase price in return for the seller's conveyance of title. The seller can obtain damages measured by the difference between the contract price and the parcel's market value at the date of breach, together with incidental expenses and losses. She can obtain rescission, entitling her to retain any deposits made by the buyer on account. Finally, seller has a lien (called a "vendor's lien") on buyer's equitable title, securing the buyer's obligation to pay the purchase price; if buyer fails to perform, the lien can be foreclosed and the land sold to satisfy the buyer's obligation.

In seeking relief, a buyer or seller must elect between those remedies that affirm the contract and those that disaffirm it. The affirming remedies of specific performance and damages may not be sought together with rescission, which disaffirms.

The cases that follow consider the availability and contours of specific performance and damages in particular contexts. The notes that follow explore each of the principal remedies more closely.

Centex Homes Corp. v. Boag

Superior Court of New Jersey, Chancery Division, 1974.
320 A.2d 194.

GELMAN, J.S.C.

Plaintiff Centex Homes Corporation (Centex) is engaged in the development and construction of a luxury high-rise condominium project in the Boroughs of Cliffside Park and Fort Lee. The project when completed will consist of six 31–story buildings containing in excess of 3,600 condominium apartment units, together with recreational buildings and facilities, parking garages and other common elements associated with this form of residential development. . . .

On September 13, 1972 defendants Mr. and Mrs. Eugene Boag executed a contract for the purchase of apartment unit No. 2019 in the building under construction and known as "Winston Towers 200." The contract purchase price was $73,700, and prior to signing the contract defendants had given Centex a deposit in the amount of $525. At or shortly after signing the contract defendants delivered to Centex a check in the amount of $6,870 which, together with the deposit, represented approximately 10% of the total purchase of the apartment unit. Shortly thereafter Boag was notified by his employer that he was to be transferred to the Chicago, Illinois, area. Under date of September 27, 1972 he advised Centex that he "would be unable to complete the purchase" agreement and stopped payment on the $6,870 check. Centex deposited the check for collection approximately two weeks after receiving notice from defendant, but the check was not honored by defendants' bank. On August 8, 1973 Centex instituted this action in Chancery Division for specific performance of the purchase agreement or, in the alternative, for liquidated damages in the amount of $6,870. The matter is presently before this court on the motion of Centex for summary judgment. . . .

Centex urges that since the subject matter of the contract is the transfer of a fee interest in real estate, the remedy of specific performance is available to enforce the agreement under principles of equity which are well-settled in this state. The principle underlying the specific performance remedy is equity's jurisdiction to grant relief where the damage remedy at law is inadequate. The text writers generally agree that at the time this branch of equity jurisdiction was evolving in England, the presumed uniqueness of land as well as its importance to the social order of that era led to the conclusion that damages at law could never be adequate to compensate for the breach of a contract to transfer an interest in land. Hence specific performance became a fixed remedy in this class of transactions. See 11 Williston on Contracts (3d ed. 1968), § 1418A; 5A Corbin on Contracts § 1143 (1964). The judicial attitude has remained substantially unchanged and is expressed in 1 Pomeroy, Equity Jurisprudence § 221(b) (5th ed. 1941), as follows:

> in applying this doctrine the courts of equity have established the further rule that in general the legal remedy of damages is inadequate in all agreements for the sale or letting of land, or of any estate therein; and therefore in such class of contracts the jurisdiction is always exercised, and a specific performance granted, unless prevented by other and independent equitable considerations which directly affect the remedial right of the complaining party. . . .

While the inadequacy of the damage remedy suffices to explain the origin of the vendee's right to obtain specific performance in equity, it does not provide a *rationale* for the availability of the remedy at the instance of the vendor of real estate. Except upon a showing of unusual circumstances or a change in the vendor's position, such as where the vendee has entered into possession, the vendor's damages are usually measurable, his remedy at law is adequate and there is no jurisdictional basis for equitable relief. But see Restatement, Contracts § 360, comment c.[2] The early English precedents suggest that the availability of the remedy in a suit by a vendor was an outgrowth of the equitable concept of mutuality, *i.e.*, that equity would not specifically enforce an agreement unless the remedy was available to both parties. See the discussion in Stoutenburgh v. Tompkins, 9 N.J. Eq. 332, 342–346 (Ch. 1853); 4 Pomeroy, Equity Jurisprudence § 1405 (5th ed. 1941).

So far as can be determined from our decisional law, the mutuality of remedy concept has been the prop which has supported equitable jurisdiction to grant specific performance in actions by vendors of real estate....

Our present Supreme Court has squarely held, however, that mutuality of remedy is not an appropriate basis for granting or denying specific performance. Fleischer v. James Drug Stores, 1 N.J. 138 (1948); see also Restatement, Contracts § 372; 11 Williston, Contracts § 1433 (3d ed. 1968).... The disappearance of the mutuality of remedy doctrine from our law dictates the conclusion that specific performance relief should no longer be automatically available to a vendor of real estate, but should be confined to those special instances where a vendor will otherwise suffer an economic injury for which his damage remedy at law will not be adequate, or where other equitable considerations require that the relief be granted. As Chancellor Vroom noted in King v. Morford, 1 N.J. Eq. 274, 281–282 (Ch. Div. 1831), whether a contract should be specifically enforced is always a matter resting in the sound discretion of the court and " ... considerable caution should be used in decreeing the specific performance of agreements, and ... the court is bound to see that it really does the complete justice which it aims at, and which is the ground of its jurisdiction."

Here the subject matter of the real estate transaction—a condominium apartment unit—has no unique quality but is one of hundreds of virtually identical units being offered by a developer for sale to the public. The units are sold by means of sample, in this case model apartments, in much the same manner as items of personal property are sold in the market place. The sales prices for the units are fixed in accordance with schedule filed by Centex as part of its offering plan, and the only variance as between apartments having the same floor plan (of which six plans are available) is

2. The Restatement's reasoning, as expressed in § 360, comment c, amounts to the inconsistent propositions that (1) because the vendor may not have sustained any damage which is actionable at law, specific performance should be granted, and (2) he would otherwise sustain damage equal to the loss of interest on the proceeds of the sale. Yet loss of interest is readily measurable and can be recovered in an action at law, and to the extent that the vendor has sustained no economic injury, there is no compelling reason for equity to grant to him the otherwise extraordinary remedy of specific performance. At the end of the comment, the author suggests that the vendor is entitled to specific performance because that remedy should be mutual, a concept which is substantially rejected as a decisional basis in §§ 372 and 373 of the Restatement.

the floor level or the building location within the project. In actuality, the condominium apartment units, regardless of their realty label, share the same characteristics as personal property.

From the foregoing one must conclude that the damages sustained by a condominium sponsor resulting from the breach of the sales agreement are readily measurable and the damage remedy at law is wholly adequate. No compelling reasons have been shown by Centex for the granting of specific performance relief and its complaint is therefore dismissed as to the first count.

Centex also seeks money damages pursuant to a liquidated damage clause in its contract with the defendants. It is sufficient to note only that under the language of that clause (which was authored by Centex) liquidated damages are limited to such moneys as were paid by defendant at the time the default occurred. Since the default here consisted of the defendant's stopping payment of his check for the balance of the down-payment, Centex's liquidated damages are limited to the retention of the "moneys paid" prior to that date, or the initial $525 deposit. Accordingly, the second count of the complaint for damage relief will also be dismissed.

Kuhn v. Spatial Design, Inc.

Superior Court of New Jersey, Appellate Division, 1991.
585 A.2d 967.

R.S. COHEN, J.A.D.

Plaintiffs John and Marlene Kuhn contracted to buy a home from defendant Spatial Design, Inc. The sale was contingent on the Kuhns' obtaining a mortgage to finance the purchase. They applied to Prudential Home Mortgage Company through a mortgage broker, defendant Sterling National Mortgage Company, Inc., with the help of Sterling employees, defendants Ellberger and Wolf. Prudential issued a mortgage commitment but later withdrew it. The Kuhns then sought to void their purchase contract with Spatial Design for failure of the mortgage contingency. When they did not get their deposit back, they started suit. Spatial Design counterclaimed for damages for breach of contract. Judge Patrick J. McGann, Jr., heard the matter and found that the Kuhns had breached. He therefore denied their claim and awarded Spatial Design damages on the counterclaim. We affirm substantially for the reasons expressed in Judge McGann's oral opinion of March 22, 1990, in which he meticulously and thoroughly expressed his findings of fact and conclusions of law. There are two matters, however, on which we feel it would be useful to express our own views.

Judge McGann concluded on compelling evidence that the Kuhns and Sterling's people purposely submitted a mortgage application that presented a materially false picture of the Kuhns' income and assets, because they knew that revealing their true financial situation would not produce the loan they sought. The judge further found that the Kuhns and Sterling were encouraged to submit such an application by Prudential's dependably credulous way of dealing with income and asset information submitted to it.

The Kuhns knew that their application showed that Kuhn was an Air Force colonel, but did not reveal that he had already been approved for retirement; that Mrs. Kuhn had a substantial income from "Plants–R–You," a florist business which existed only in the minds of the Kuhns and Sterling's people; that the fictitious business had assets of $50,000, which did not exist at all; that the $50,000 deposit on the purchase came from savings, when in fact it was borrowed on a second mortgage on the Kuhns' present home, and that the Kuhns had jewelry, antiques, stamps and the like worth $123,000, which Kuhn actually thought would fetch some $47,000.

Kuhn knew that his true current income and assets would not support the mortgage application. He and his wife also knew that Wolf had left some figures blank in the application they signed. Wolf had said they were not going to be "boy scouts" in the matter. Predictably, Sterling's president, Ellberger, who knew what numbers it took to make the application viable, supplied some impressive ones. They showed bank balances of some $240,000 instead of the real $10,000, and total family income of some $218,000 instead of the real $65,000 or even the fictitious $95,000 that earlier appeared. Not surprisingly, Prudential issued a commitment for a $300,000 mortgage for the $515,000 purchase.

All of this was possible because the Kuhns were making a "no documentation" loan application. That meant that Prudential would probably not check to see if the represented facts showing the career Air Force officer's improbably comfortable financial situation were true.[3]

Colonel Kuhn expected the whole business to be ultimately supported by a high-salaried but not-yet-identified private sector job he hoped to find before he retired. The $30,000 in income he thought was going to be attributed to "Plants–R–You" (Ellberger eventually settled on $9400 per month.) was really his Air Force pension. The $65,000 he thought he showed as service income (Ellberger made it $8800 per month.) would be covered by the private sector job he had not yet sought.

When Kuhn put the present home up for sale and looked for a private sector job, he found both the real estate market and the job market unwelcoming. He heard that Spatial Design might have sold the house across the street from their new one for much less than they were paying. He therefore decided to climb down from the shaky limb he was on.[4] He

3. It is impossible to tell from the evidence if Prudential greeted improbable information in "no documentation" applications with a knowing wink, and counted on ever-rising property values to pick up the slack.

4. The Kuhns' purchase was not conditional on the sale of their home. Instead, Spatial Design had agreed to provide a bridge loan of $185,000. The Kuhns could therefore have ended up with two homes, the Prudential mortgage, the bridge loan, and the first and second mortgages on their unsold other house, all to be satisfied out of a $30,000 pension.

telephoned Prudential and wrote to Sterling, stating that he had decided to retire from the Air Force, and would thus lose some $40,000 in annual income. He inquired innocently if that would affect the mortgage commitment.

Almost simultaneously, Kuhn wrote to the Air Force to withdraw his approved retirement, thus falsifying the sole expressed basis of his communications with Prudential and Sterling. Prudential withdrew its commitment on the basis of the new information. It had retained the right to withdraw "if any material facts appear that have not previously been revealed by [the applicant]." Kuhn then unsuccessfully tried to cancel the purchase contract on the thesis that the mortgage contingency was not satisfied.

The Kuhns sued Spatial Design, which counterclaimed for the deposit and damages. They then sued Sterling, Wolf and Ellberger for indemnification against the counterclaim. Spatial Design crossclaimed against Sterling, Wolf and Ellberger for fraud, tortious interference, conspiracy and negligence.

After a bench trial, Judge McGann found in favor of Spatial Design and against the Kuhns, and assessed damages at almost $100,000, less the retained deposit of $50,000. He denied the Kuhns' indemnification claim and Spatial Design's damage claim against the mortgage brokers.

Spatial Design has not cross appealed from the denial of its damage claim against the mortgage brokers. We therefore do not comment on it.[5] In all respects material to this appeal, however, Judge McGann's findings and conclusions on the conduct of the parties are supported by compelling evidence. . . .

Now, as to damages. The contract price was $515,000, subject to a real estate commission of 5% or $25,750. The house was eventually sold, free of commission, for $434,000. In the interim, there were carrying charges for taxes and interest. There was no reason suggested by the evidence to doubt the reasonableness either of the time it took to resell the house or the sale price obtained.

Damages arose from two different sources. The first was the decreasing value of the house due to general market conditions. The second was the cost of holding the house until it could be resold. The holding costs are not the subject of this appeal. The Kuhns have two arguments, however, about the loss-of-value damages.

The first argument is that the true measure of a seller's damages for breach of contract by a buyer of real estate is the difference between the contract price and the market value at the time of the breach, less credit for any deposit retained by the seller. . . . They point out that if values were steadily declining, as the judge found, they had declined very little in the

5. We do note *N.J.S.A.* 17:11B–14g, which prohibits material misrepresentations, circumventions and concealments by mortgage brokers, and *N.J.S.A.* 17:11B–17, which makes willful violations third-degree crimes. We do not say whether these statutes create a cause of action, or whether the disappointed seller would have standing to sue.

few months between contract and breach, and certainly much less than at the time of resale, many months later. Thus, the Kuhns argue, it was error to measure Spatial Design's damages by the difference between the two contract prices.

Neither of the cases cited by the Kuhns involved the assessment of damages resulting from a breach in a falling market. In such circumstances, two basic rules must be consulted. One is that contract damages are designed to put the injured party in as good a position as if performance had been rendered as promised. The other, from Hadley v. Baxendale, 156 Eng. Rep. 145 (Ex. 1854), is that damages should be such as may fairly be considered either arising naturally, *i.e.*, according to the usual course of things, from the breach, or such as may reasonably be supposed to have been in the contemplation of both parties, at the time they contracted, as the probable result of the breach.

In the usual course of things, a $515,000 house cannot be resold the instant a contract buyer breaches, and a reasonable time for resale must therefore be allowed. In addition, it is not uncommon for property values to experience a general fall-off after a period of intense run-up. In a falling market, buyers take longer to find, and they buy at reduced prices.

A rule that restricts damages for breach of a contract to buy real estate to the difference between contract price and value at the time of breach (plus expenses) works fairly only in a static market. A damage rule works fairly in a declining market only if it takes account of slowing sales and falling values. In such cases, where the seller puts the property back on the market and resells, the measure is not contract price less value at the time of breach, but rather the resale price, if it is reasonable as to time, method, manner, place and terms. These are matters for the factfinder, who may or may not conclude from the evidence that what actually occurred after breach by way of resale was reasonable and thus provides an accurate measure of damages. Judge McGann found that it did here, on sufficient credible evidence.

We adopt,[6] for these purposes, the essence of the sellers' damage rules provided for sellers of goods in the Uniform Commercial Code, N.J.S.A. 12A:2–706 and 708, and adapted for sellers of real estate in §§ 504–507 of the Uniform Land Transactions Act (ULTA), which New Jersey has not adopted. We adopt these rules because they take account of the effect of changing market conditions in sound ways which New Jersey's reported decisions have not yet taken into account.

Where a buyer of real estate wrongfully rejects, repudiates or materially breaches as to a substantial part of the contract, the seller may resell in a manner that is reasonable as to method, manner, time, place and terms. The defaulting buyer must have reasonable notice of the time after which

6. The Kuhn contract did not contain a liquidated damage clause, either forfeiting the deposit on the buyer's breach without proof of damages, or limiting liability of the buyer to the amount of the deposit. We do not intend by this opinion to affect the applicability or enforceability of such provisions.

resale will take place. If the resale is a public sale, the defaulting buyer must have notice of the time and place, and may buy. The seller may then recover the amount by which the unpaid contract price and any incidental and consequential damages exceed the resale price, less expenses avoided because of the buyer's breach. See ULTA § 2–504, 13 U.L.A. 552 (1977); N.J.S.A. 12A:2–706.

A seller's incidental damages include any reasonable out-of-pocket expenses incurred because of the buyer's breach. A seller's consequential damages include any loss the buyer knew or at the time of contracting had reason to know would result from the buyer's breach and which reasonably could not be avoided by the seller. See ULTA § 507, 13 U.L.A. 555 (1977).

The case may be different where the seller does not put the property back on the market. In such a case, the measure of the seller's damages is the amount by which the unpaid contract price and any incidental and consequential damages exceed the fair market value of the property at the time of breach, less expenses avoided because of the buyer's breach. See ULTA § 2–505(a), 13 U.L.A. 553 (1977) (using the value at the time set for conveyance instead of at the time of breach); see also N.J.S.A. 12A:2–708(1). Without a resale, value at the time of breach is used, even in a declining market, because the choice of any other time would be so speculative. We need not explore application of the exceptions made by ULTA 2–505(b) and N.J.S.A. 12A:2–708(2) for situations in which the difference between contract price and fair market value is inadequate to put the seller in as good a position as performance would have.

[The court proceeded to consider how real estate commissions should be treated in calculating damages, concluding that it did not have enough information to make a determination at this time.]

Notes & Questions

1. **Specific Performance.** Both buyer and seller are typically entitled as a matter of course to a decree of specific performance in the event of default by the other. Buyer is entitled to a decree requiring seller to convey title to him in return for payment of the purchase price. Seller is entitled to a decree requiring buyer to pay the purchase price in return for the conveyance of title. However, courts frequently find reasons to refuse specific performance to buyer or seller. Unfairness, inadequate consideration, unconscionability, and overreaching are just a few of the reasons that have been given.

2. **Should Buyers Receive Specific Performance?** The standard rationale for giving buyers specific performance is that land is unique; having bargained for a specific parcel, the buyer is entitled to be made whole through a decree ordering its conveyance to him. But is land really unique? Should courts award specific performance to a buyer when the property in question—a new tract home in a subdivision containing hundreds of identical houses—has few if any unique attributes? If the buyer, rather than the seller, had sought specific performance in *Centex*, should

the result have been the same—no specific performance? See Suchan v. Rutherford, 410 P.2d 434 (Idaho 1966) (refusing to award specific performance in a case involving irrigated farmland that the court concluded was not unique).

Why should land's uniqueness justify the buyer remedy of specific performance? After all, a parcel's unique appeal to a particular buyer can always be reduced to dollars and cents—specifically, the amount the buyer would accept to give up his right to the parcel. The real reason courts order specific performance as a matter of course in land contract cases may well be the concern that juries making damage awards will systematically refuse to compensate buyers for losses based on valuations substantially in excess of "reasonable market value."

See generally Lawrence V. Berkowich, To Pay or Convey?: A Theory of Remedies for Breach of Real Estate Contracts, 1995 Ann. Survey Am. L. 319 (criticizing the grant by courts of specific performance rather than damages).

3. **Should Sellers Receive Specific Performance?** The standard rationale for giving sellers specific performance, as *Centex* explains, is mutuality of remedy. Are there better rationales? Consider three possible justifications. First, land may possess unique *dis*advantages for the seller, such as exposure to liability for dangerous conditions on the land. Second, where the buyer is also asserting a cause of action, the buyer's suit may make it impossible for the seller to dispose of the property elsewhere so long as the claim is outstanding. Finally, "in the absence of some objective indicator of the land's market price, such as value established by frequent sales or condemnation proceedings of substantially similar land, it is apparent that the vendor may in fact not have an adequate remedy at law." Comment, 48 Temp. L.Q. 847, 851–52 (1975).

4. **Damages.** A land buyer whose seller has breached their contract is typically entitled to recover the difference between the market value of the property at the time of breach and the agreed-upon purchase price, together with consequential damages, if any, and the return of any deposit paid on account. A seller whose buyer has breached is typically entitled to recover the difference between the contract price and the market value of the property at the time of breach, less any amounts paid by buyer on account, together with consequential damages and incidental expenses, if any, incurred in mitigating damages.

A handful of cases, such as *Kuhn*, as well as commentators, have criticized the typical rule for seller's damages that measures seller's damages from the date of buyer's breach rather than from the date of resale for failing to account for the difficulties and delay in reselling land. See, e.g., Gerald Korngold, Seller's Damages from a Defaulting Buyer of Realty: The Influence of the Uniform Land Transactions Act on the Court, 20 Nova L. Rev. 1069 (1996) (analyzing *Kuhn* and criticizing the traditional rule). The Uniform Land Transactions Act would also measure damages as the difference between the contact price and the resale price and any incidental and consequential damages, less expenses avoided because of the buyer's breach. U.L.T.A. § 2–504. Despite the criticism of the traditional rule, *Kuhn* is an atypical case and a majority of the courts continue to measure damages as of the date of the buyer's breach. See Milton R. Friedman, Contracts and Conveyances of Real Property 1031–37 (5th ed. 1991).

Is it relevant that land sellers have alternative remedies at their disposal—remedies not generally available to sellers of fungible goods? The land seller who faces a long delay in a declining market before resale can try to make herself whole by obtaining a specific performance decree requiring the buyer to pay the full contract price. Possibly, just by reminding the buyer of the disadvantages of specific performance to the buyer, the seller will be able to persuade the buyer to settle on a compromise sufficient to make the seller whole. And, even resale in a declining market will often make the seller whole: the resale price is good, and sometimes *prima facie,* evidence of the land's value at the time of breach, particularly if the sale was made at arm's length and shortly after the breach. See Costello v. Johnson, 121 N.W.2d 70 (Minn. 1963). Consequential damages will also help to make the seller whole if she can introduce evidence that the land's value at the time of breach was depressed by the dissemination of information about the broken contract. Further, the seller can collect for maintenance expenses incurred between breach and resale. Finally, in many cases, seller's retention of the buyer's deposit will more than compensate her for her loss.

The argument against the traditional damage measure would appear to be strongest when one or another of these alternative remedies is not available to the seller. For example, measuring damages from the time of breach rather than resale might very well be unfair to the seller if she is in a jurisdiction that, following *Centex*, would deny her specific performance. In many cases like *Kuhn*, moreover, specific performance may be available but impracticable. If a buyer does not close because he lacks the funds to do so, what real effect—and strategic leverage—can a specific performance decree have? (The court will not imprison the buyer for nonpayment of the price.)

5. **The Rule of *Flureau v. Thornhill*.** Beginning with Flureau v. Thornhill, 96 Eng. Rep. 625 (1776), a number of courts have refused to award buyers "benefit of the bargain" damages (i.e., the difference between the market value of the property at the time of the breach and the agreed upon purchase price) unless the seller's breach is in bad faith. Instead, courts following the *Flureau* rule relegate the buyer to any out-of-pocket losses. Approximately fifteen jurisdictions expressly follow the *Flureau* rule, and many other states effectively adopt its result by treating marketable title as a condition rather than as a covenant.

What is the justification for not awarding benefit-of-the-bargain damages in cases of good faith breaches? "Good faith" breaches characteristically arise from title defects. At the time *Flureau* was decided, land records were in such poor condition that it was thought to be unfair to burden a seller with damages unless she in fact knew that her title was defective. Does it make sense to continue following *Flureau* when contemporary

American title institutions have dramatically improved the quality of title records and reduced the costs of searching them? There is a discernible trend away from the *Flureau* rule and toward the "American" rule that awards buyers benefit-of-the-bargain damages in all case. See, e.g., Donovan v. Bachstadt, 453 A.2d 160 (N.J. 1982) (rejecting the *Flureau* rule as outdated); Smith v. Warr, 564 P.2d 771 (Utah 1977).

6. **Earnest Money Deposits and Liquidated Damages.** It is customary on the execution of a land sale contract for buyer to give seller an earnest money deposit securing his performance. The deposit, which commonly ranges from 1% to 10% of the purchase price, may be held by the seller, the broker or the escrow agent. The question that these deposits most frequently raise is whether the seller may retain the earnest money in the event of the buyer's breach, or must return it in whole or in part. The rule in most states is that the seller may keep a breaching buyer's deposit even though the contract nowhere expressly entitles her to do so and even though the forfeited sum exceeds the seller's provable damages. See generally Milton R. Friedman, Contracts and Conveyances of Real Property 1043–60 (5th ed. 1991).

A few jurisdictions allow the land seller to keep only as much of the deposit as is necessary to cover her damages, and require her to return the surplus to the buyer. Because, however, the buyer has the heavy burden of proving that the deposit exceeds seller's damages, sellers will, even in these states, probably be able to retain the entire deposit. For an example of the difficulties buyers encounter in discharging this burden of proof, see Zirinsky v. Sheehan, 413 F.2d 481 (8th Cir.1969).

Sellers can also try to forestall claims that they will be unjustly enriched if allowed to retain buyer's deposit by characterizing the deposit as liquidated damages. This might also serve the buyer's interest since earnest money leaves the seller free to pursue the full range of remedies, while liquidated damages bar compensatory damages. But liquidated damages clauses have their own requirements. To be upheld, the liquidated sum must be reasonably proportioned to the contract price and must represent a reasonable forecast of compensation for the harm caused by the breach. Further, the harm caused by the breach must be of the sort that is difficult to estimate accurately. Compare Johnson v. Carman, 572 P.2d 371 (Utah 1977) (to allow the seller to retain $34,596.10 paid by buyer when seller's actual damages were only $25,650.00 would be "grossly excessive and disproportionate to any possible loss") and Colonial at Lynnfield, Inc. v. Sloan, 870 F.2d 761 (1st Cir. 1989) (liquidated damages of $200,000 on contract price of $3,375,000 were denied when seller resold property for $251,000 more than buyers agreed to pay since actual damages turned out to be easily ascertainable and liquidated damages were grossly disproportionate to the "loss") with Vines v. Orchard Hills, Inc., 435 A.2d 1022 (Conn. 1980) ("A liquidated damages clause allowing the seller to retain 10 percent [$7,880] of the contract price as earnest money is presumptively a reasonable allocation of the risks associated with default").

6. **Rescission.** Mutual rescission doubtless represents the most common resolution of land sale contract breaches, at least in the residential setting. By agreeing on rescission, buyer and seller can avoid the expense, delay and uncertainty of litigation and can, through the seller's return of part or all of the buyer's down payment, reach some rough justice between themselves. Mutual rescission creates problems only in retrospect, when one side tries to avoid the asserted rescission, and a court must determine whether rescission has in fact occurred. (*B* writes to *S*, "this whole deal is really a bad idea"; *S* responds, "I guess you could say so".) And even if a court can piece together an intent to rescind from ambiguous words and conduct, the question remains how the *status quo ante* is to be restored.

Unilateral rescission, in which buyer or seller declares that the other's conduct constitutes grounds for terminating the contract, contains more than the usual hazards of self-help. Pitfalls surround the requirements that the rescission be effected by notice and that the notice be timely. (What constitutes effective notice? At what point does notice become untimely?) There is also the risk that the asserted misconduct does not in fact constitute ground for termination. A seller wishing to rescind when her buyer fails to perform on the closing date must consider the possibility that time will be held not of the essence. A buyer who wishes to rescind when his seller contracts to sell the land to someone else must consider the possibility that the subsequent buyer will be held not to qualify as a bona fide purchaser who can defeat the original buyer's claims. An added cost of guessing wrong about the effect of the other side's conduct may be a finding that the rescinding party anticipatorily repudiated the contract.

4. RISK OF LOSS

Skelly Oil Co. v. Ashmore

Supreme Court of Missouri, 1963.
365 S.W.2d 582.

HYDE, JUDGE.

This suit for specific performance was transferred by Division Two to the Court en Banc because of the dissent of one of the Judges....

This is a suit by the purchaser, Skelly Oil Company, a corporation, against the vendors, Tom A. Ashmore and Madelyn Ashmore, husband and wife, in two counts. Count One is for the specific performance of a contract to sell the north half of a certain described southwest corner lot (fronting 97 ½ feet on Main and 195 feet on 42nd Streets) in that part of Joplin lying in Newton County. Count Two seeks an abatement in the purchase price of $10,000, being the proceeds received by the vendors under an insurance policy on a building on the property, which building was destroyed by fire in the interim between the execution of the contract of sale and the time for closing of said sale by the exchange of the $20,000 consideration for the deed to the property. The case was tried in Jasper County upon a change of venue granted from Newton County. The trial court found the issues in favor of the purchaser, decreed specific performance, and applied the $10,000 insurance proceeds on the $20,000 purchase price. The vendors have appealed.

The vendors acquired this property about 1953, and operated a grocery store in the concrete block building, with fixtures and furniture, and a one story frame "smoke house" thereon. Deeds of trust on the property, securing notes of the vendors to the Bank of Neosho were of record. At all times here material and up to September 30, 1961, the property was leased to Don Jones at a rental of $150 a month. The vendors had a fire insurance policy, with a standard mortgage clause in favor of the Bank of Neosho attached, on the buildings and fixtures, issued February 8, 1958, for a term of one year.

Joe Busby, of the Kansas City office of the Skelly Oil Company real estate department, and Mr. Ashmore conducted the negotiations resulting in the contract of sale. The Ashmores lived in Lawton, Oklahoma. Mr. Ashmore had engaged in the real estate business since 1951. Busby secured the execution of a Skelly printed form of option by the vendors, dated July 31, 1957, for Skelly "to purchase" for the sum of $20,000, "payable in cash upon delivery of deed" said property, "together with the buildings, driveways, and all construction and equipment thereon, at any time before" August 31, 1957. The words "and equipment" were "x-ed" out on said option. The option provided in typewriting (referring to the Jones lease): "Purchaser agrees to honor present lease on above property until expiration." The option originally lapsed August 31, 1957. Busby had an agreement for the mutual cancellation of the lease prepared by Skelly's legal department for execution by the Ashmores and Jones, and on August 20 took up securing a cancellation of the lease and possession with Ashmore and his lawyer, Mr. Foulke. Mr. Foulke did not know how long this would take and the option was extended to January 1, 1958. Busby knew Ashmore filed an ejectment suit against Jones, was "patiently waiting" to hear from Mr. Foulke, and on trips to Joplin would inquire if any headway was being made on securing possession. On December 30, the option was extended to March 1, 1958. Skelly's legal department concluded this lease entitled Jones to possession until September 30, 1961. Skelly acquired the property immediately south of the Ashmore property, continued the operation of a service station thereon, and decided to go ahead and exercise the Ashmore option with Jones in possession under his lease and later combine the two properties and erect a service station that required more area than the Ashmore property.

Busby and Ashmore met in Joplin on February 25. Busby informed Ashmore Skelly had decided to purchase under its option with Jones in possession under his lease. The parties orally agreed to certain details, some being mentioned hereinafter in connection with the contract of sale. Busby also informed Ashmore Skelly could not complete the transaction by March 1, and the Ashmores extended the option from March 1 to March 10, 1958. No consideration passed for any extension of the option.

The Bank of Neosho forwarded the abstract of title to Skelly.

The option provided it could be accepted "by giving written notice" to the vendors. By letter to the Ashmores under date of March 4, 1958, Skelly explicitly stated: "This letter is to inform you that Skelly Oil Company does hereby exercise its option to purchase the above described property for the sum of $20,000.00, subject to all the terms and conditions of the above referred to option, and with" further understandings, among others, to the effect: The fixtures and equipment in the store building were to remain the property of the Ashmores; the Ashmores were to assign the Jones lease to Skelly and Skelly was to remit to the Ashmores $5.00 a month for Jones' use of said fixtures and equipment; the Ashmores were to remove said fixtures and equipment within sixty days after the termination of said lease by lapse of time or otherwise, Skelly assuming no responsibility for the repair or physical condition of said fixtures and equipment. The letter also stated that upon approval of the title and the obtaining of necessary permits "we will get in touch with you further toward closing." Immediately following the signature of the purchaser on said letter appears: "ACKNOWLEDGED and AGREED TO This 7th day of March, 1958, Tom A. Ashmore Madelyn Ashmore." The vendors mailed the original thereof to the purchaser.

The latter part of March Busby telephoned to Ashmore in Lawton and they agreed to meet in Joplin on April 16, 1958, to close the transaction.

The concrete block building, furniture and fixtures were destroyed by fire on April 7, 1958, without fault of either party.

Skelly's Kansas City headquarters advised Busby, who was in St. Joseph, on April 7 of the fire. The next day Busby telephoned Ashmore from Kansas City. In this conversation Ashmore said he had insurance on the building and fixtures, naming the company in Kansas City carrying it. Asked on cross-examination whether he told Ashmore the fire would have no effect on the deal, Busby answered: "I told him absolutely not, we would go through with our deal. Q. Just like it was? A. Sure, just like this contract, sir, we're obligated, we can't get out of it." Busby called the insurance company and was informed there was $10,000 insurance on the building and $4,000 on the fixtures. He reported this to the purchaser's legal department. Then, after research, the legal department concluded that Skelly was entitled to have the insurance on the building applied on the purchase price. The closing papers were prepared accordingly.

The closing of the transaction was considered by the parties on April 15, 16 and 17. Busby and Ashmore met on the evening of the 15th. Mr. Winbigler of Skelly's legal department arrived on the 16th. They informed Ashmore they were there to close the purchase of the property; that Skelly thought it was entitled to the insurance proceeds on the building and would like an assignment of the insurance proceeds. When Ashmore disagreed, they informed him Skelly would close the deal and pay him the contract price but would not waive its rights to the insurance proceeds in so doing. Ashmore would not agree to this. They then went to Mr. Foulke's office and informed him of the situation. Mr. Foulke told them he needed time to check into the matter before he could advise his client. Busby and Winbigler returned to Kansas City.

By letter dated April 26, 1958, the Ashmores notified Skelly that the "option agreement" was rescinded "because it was given without consideration and is therefore not binding on us and for the further reason that you have refused to complete the purchase unless we reduce the agreed price, which constitutes a breach of the terms of the agreement."

A month or so later the Phoenix Insurance Company, under the standard mortgage clause, paid the Bank of Neosho the balance due on the vendors' notes, $7,242.46, and $2,757.54, the balance of the $10,000 insurance on the building, to the vendors, and also paid the vendors the $4,000 insurance carried on the furniture and fixtures.

This purchaser's claims are founded on the contract of sale in its letter of March 4, 1958, and the option therein referred to, which letter was "acknowledged and agreed to" by the vendors. Said claims are not based on a mere option to purchase where the improvements on the property were damaged prior to the purchaser's exercise of the option.

The vendors say that the letter and option were prepared by the purchaser and ambiguities and doubts therein are to be resolved in favor of the vendors; that the purchaser paid no consideration for the option or the three extensions; that specific performance will result in inequity, hardship or loss to vendors and that the trial court's decree of specific performance constitutes an abuse of discretion. It is stated that, since there was no binding contract between the parties prior to the letter of March 4, this letter was only an offer to purchase under the terms and conditions in the original option and said letter, which vendors could accept or reject; that the vendors retained possession and the option contained four or more conditions and the letter added others, and because of these "suspensive conditions" the plain intention of the parties was that the purchaser was not to be bound until all these contingencies were met and no specifically enforceable contract existed on April 7, the date of the fire.

We are not impressed with the vendors' broad position that no valid enforceable contract ever existed. The principal suspensive conditions under the option authorized the purchaser to withdraw its acceptance of the option "before the consummation of purchase by payment of the full purchase price" if, sufficiently stated, the purchaser be unable to secure the proper licenses, consents or permits for the erection, maintenance and operation of a service station of a type and according to a ground plan of its choice on the premises, or if any such licenses, consents or permits be revoked, or if the purchaser be enjoined from erecting and operating a service station on said premises. The option called for an abstract showing a merchantable title in the vendors, and the letter of March 4 stated: "Upon approval of title by our Legal Department and our obtaining all necessary permits, we will get in touch with you further toward closing." There was no objection to this condition in the letter and the parties made it definite by orally agreeing the last part of March upon April 16 for the closing date. Under the mentioned suspensive conditions, as well as others of less importance, when the vendors "acknowledged and agreed to" the contract of sale, the purchaser could not act arbitrarily, capriciously or in bad faith in invoking said provisions of the contract; and in consideration of the mutual promises a mutually enforceable contract of sale arose. None of the suspensive conditions entered into the vendors' failure to close the sale on April 16 or their rescission of the contract on April 26. The vendors' only objection to completing the transaction was, as stated in their letter of rescission, "that you have refused to complete the purchase unless we reduce the agreed price," which, of course, refers to the purchaser's claim to the $10,000 insurance proceeds. Mr. Ashmore testified that the only thing that held up the closing of the transaction was Skelly Oil Company's claim to the insurance proceeds. . . .

The contract of sale here involved contained no provision as to who assumed the risk of loss occasioned by a destruction of the building, or for protecting the building by insurance or for allocating any insurance proceeds received therefor. When the parties met to close the sale on April 16, the purchaser's counsel informed vendors and their attorney he was relying on Standard Oil Co. v. Dye, 223 Mo. App. 926, 20 S.W.2d 946, for purchaser's claim to the $10,000 insurance proceeds on the building. Purchaser made no claim to the $4,000 paid vendors for the loss of the furniture and fixtures. It is stated in 3 American Law of Property, § 11.30, p. 90, that in the circumstances here presented at least five different views have been advanced for allocating the burden of fortuitous loss between vendor and purchaser of real estate. We summarize those mentioned: (1) The view first enunciated in Paine v. Meller (Ch. 1801, 6 Ves. Jr. 349, 31 Eng. Reprint 1088, 1089) is said to be the most widely accepted; holding that from the time of the contract of sale of real estate the burden of fortuitous loss was on the purchaser even though the vendor retained possession. (2) The loss is on the vendor until legal title is conveyed, although the purchaser is in possession, stated to be a strong minority. (3) The burden of loss should be on the vendor until the time agreed upon for conveying the legal title, and thereafter on the purchaser unless the vendor be in such default as to preclude specific performance, not recognized in the decisions. (4) The burden of the loss should be on the party in possession, whether vendor or purchaser, so considered by some courts. (5) The burden of loss should be on the vendor unless there is something in the contract or in the relation of the parties from which the court can infer a different intention, stating "this rather vague test" has not received any avowed judicial acceptance, although it is not inconsistent with jurisdictions holding the loss is on the vendor until conveyance or jurisdictions adopting the possession test.

We do not agree that we should adopt the arbitrary rule of Paine v. Meller, supra, and Standard Oil Co. v. Dye, supra, that there is equitable conversion from the time of making a contract for sale and purchase of land and that the risk of loss from destruction of buildings or other substantial part of the property is from that moment on the purchaser. . . . We take the view stated in an article on Equitable Conversion by Contract, 13 Columbia Law Review 369, 386, Dean Harlan F. Stone, later Chief Justice Stone, in which he points out that the only reason why a contract for the sale of land by the owner to another operates to effect conversion is that a court of equity will compel him specifically to perform his contract. He further states:

> A preliminary to the determination of the question whether there is equitable ownership of land must therefore necessarily be the determination of the question whether there is a contract which can be and ought to be specifically performed *at the very time when the court is called upon to perform it.* This process of reasoning is, however, reversed in those jurisdictions where the "burden of loss" is cast upon the vendee. The question is whether there shall be a specific performance of the contract, thus casting the burden on the vendee, by compelling him to pay the full purchase price for the subject matter of the contract, a substantial part of which has been destroyed. The question is answered somewhat in this wise: equitable ownership of the vendee in the subject matter of the contract can exist only where the contract is one which equity will specifically perform. The vendee of land is equitably entitled to land, therefore the vendee may be compelled to perform, although the vendor is unable to give in return the performance stipulated for by his contract. The *non sequitur* involved in the proposition that performance may be had because of the equitable ownership of the land by the vendee, which in turn depends upon the right of performance, is evident. The doctrine of equitable conversion, so far as it is exemplified by the authorities hitherto considered, cannot lead to the result of casting the burden of loss on the vendee, since the *conversion depends upon the question whether the contract should in equity be performed.* In all other cases where the vendee is treated as the equitable owner of the land, it is only because the contract is one which equity first determines should be specifically performed.
>
> Whether a plaintiff, in breach of his contract by a default which goes to the essence, as in the case of the destruction of a substantial part of the subject matter of the contract, should be entitled to specific performance, is a question which is answered in the negative in every case except that of destruction of the subject matter of the contract. To give a plaintiff specific performance of the contract when he is unable to perform the contract on his own part, violates the fundamental rule of equity that ... *equity will not compel a defendant to perform when it is unable to so frame its decree as to compel the plaintiff to give in return substantially what he has undertaken to give* or to do for the defendant.
>
> The rule of casting the "burden of loss" on the vendee by specific performance if justifiable at all can only be explained and justified upon one of two theories: first, that since equity has for most purposes treated the vendee as the equitable owner, it should do so for all purposes, although *this ignores the fact that in all*

> *other cases the vendee is so treated only because the contract is either being performed or in equity ought to be performed;* or, second, which is substantially the same proposition in a different form, the specific performance which casts the burden on the vendee is an incident to and a consequence of an equitable conversion, whereas in all other equity relations growing out of the contract, the equitable conversion, if it exists, is an incident to and consequence of, a specific performance. Certainly nothing could be more illogical than this process of reasoning. (Emphasis ours.)

For these reasons, we do not agree with the rule that arbitrarily places the risk of loss on the vendee from the time the contract is made. Instead we believe the Massachusetts rule is the proper rule. It is thus stated in Libman v. Levenson, 236 Mass. 221, 128 N.E. 13, 22 A.L.R. 560: When "the conveyance is to be made of the whole estate, including both land and buildings, for an entire price, and the value of the buildings constitutes a large part of the total value of the estate, and the terms of the agreement show that they constituted an important part of the subject matter of the contract ... the contract is to be construed as subject to the implied condition that it no longer shall be binding if, before the time for the conveyance to be made, the buildings are destroyed by fire. The loss by the fire falls upon the vendor, the owner; and if he has not protected himself by insurance, he can have no reimbursement of this loss; but the contract is no longer binding upon either party. If the purchaser has advanced any part of the price, he can recover it back. If the change in the value of the estate is not so great, or if it appears that the buildings did not constitute so material a part of the estate to be conveyed as to result in an annulling of the contract, specific performance may be decreed, *with compensation for any breach of agreement,* or relief may be given in damages." (Emphasis ours.)

An extreme case, showing the unfairness of the arbitrary rule placing all loss on the vendee, is Amundson v. Severson, 41 S.D. 377, 170 N.W. 633, where three-fourths of the land sold was washed away by the Missouri River (the part left being of little value) and the vendor brought suit for specific performance. Fortunately for the vendee, he was relieved by the fact that the vendor did not have good title at the time of the loss, although the vendor had procured it as a basis for his suit. However, if the vendor had then held good title even though he did not have the land, the vendee would have been required to pay the full contract price under the loss on the purchaser rule. (Would the vendee have been any better off if the vendor had good title from the start but did not have the land left to convey?) The reason for the Massachusetts rule is that specific performance is based on what is equitable; and it is not equitable to make a vendee pay the vendor for something the vendor cannot give him.

However, the issue in this case is not whether the vendee can be compelled to take the property without the building but whether the vendee is entitled to enforce the contract of sale, with the insurance proceeds substituted for the destroyed building. We see no inequity to defendants in such enforcement since they will receive the full amount ($20,000.00) for which they contracted to sell the property. Their contract not only described the land but also specifically stated they sold it "together with the buildings, driveways and all construction thereon." While the words "Service Station Site" appeared in the caption of the option contract and that no doubt was the ultimate use plaintiff intended to make of the land, the final agreement made by the parties was that plaintiff would take it subject to a lease of the building which would have brought plaintiff about $6,150.00 in rent during the term of the lease. Moreover, defendants' own evidence showed the building was valued in the insurance adjustment at $16,716.00 from which $4,179.00 was deducted for depreciation, making the loss $12,537.00. Therefore, defendants are not in a very good position to say the building was of no value to plaintiff. Furthermore, plaintiff having contracted for the land with the building on it, the decision concerning use or removal of the building, or even for resale of the entire property, was for the plaintiff to make. Statements were in evidence about the use of the building and its value to plaintiff made by its employee who negotiated the purchase but he was not one of plaintiff's chief executive officers nor possessed of authority to bind its board of directors. The short of the matter is that defendants will get all they bargained for; but without the building or its value plaintiff will not.

We therefore affirm the judgment and decree of the trial court.

[The opinion of STORCKMAN, J., dissenting is omitted.]

Notes

1. **Allocation of Risk of Loss.** The rule of Paine v. Meller, 6 Ves. Tr. 349 (Ch.1801), making buyer bear the risk of loss during the executory interval, made practical sense in the early agrarian environment that spawned it. Because in an agrarian economy it was land, not buildings, that presumably formed the object of sale, fortuitous destruction of the buildings would not prevent the buyer from getting what he had bargained for and, so it was thought, should not be allowed to excuse his performance.

Although the rule of Paine v. Meller represents the majority position in the United States today, there is a growing trend to replace it with a rule that allocates risk of loss to the party—whether seller or buyer—in possession at the time the premises are destroyed. The technical rationale for this newer rule is almost as formalistic as the rationale given for the traditional rule: "the purchaser in possession is substantial owner of the property and should bear the burdens of ownership, while the purchaser out of possession is not substantial owner." 3 American Law of Property § 11.30 (A.J. Casner, ed. 1952). The better reason for the rule is that the party in possession is best placed to guard against the hazards of destruction, to insure the premises, and to conserve any evidence bearing on destruction.

Which of these two rules—majority or minority—makes more sense today? Should the answer depend on whether urban or rural land is involved? On whether the contract involves commercial or residential property? Whichever rule is adopted, should it be applied differently depending on whether the loss arose from destruction of the premises by natural causes, such as fire, or arose from government's condemnation of the land under the eminent domain power?

The most striking aspect of both the majority and minority rules is that there should be any need for them at all. They are rules of implication, not rules of law, and can be easily altered by contract terms expressly allocating the risk of loss. ("Buyer shall not be obligated to perform if, during the executory period and before Buyer takes possession, the premises are substantially or entirely destroyed by natural causes or if, during the executory period, and without regard to whether Buyer was in possession, the premises are substantially or entirely taken by eminent domain.") Why do you suppose residential buyers and sellers, and their lawyers and brokers, are so reluctant to address and resolve the question of losses during the executory term? Even if the issue is raised, will the drafted language be adequate to express the parties' intent? See Bryant v. Willison Real Estate Co., 350 S.E.2d 748 (W. Va. 1986) (clause stating that the "owner is responsible for said property until the Deed has been delivered to said purchaser" placed risk on seller despite "as is" clause and provision requiring the buyer to insure). See generally Banks McDowell, Insurable Interest in Property Revisited, 17 Cap. U. L. Rev. 165 (1988).

For background on equitable conversion and allocation of risk of loss during the executory interval, see Robert L. Flores, A Comparison of the Rules and Rationales for Allocating Risks Arising in Realty Sales Using Executory Sale Contracts and Escrows, 59 Mo. L. Rev. 307 (1994); Linda S. Hume, Real Estate Contracts and the Doctrine of Equitable Conversion in Washington: Dispelling the Ashford Cloud, 7 U. Puget Sound L. Rev. 233 (1984); Allison Dunham, Vendor's Obligation as to Fitness of Land for a Particular Purpose, 37 Minn. L. Rev. 108 (1953).

2. **Allocation of Insurance Proceeds.** American courts, which have widely followed the English rule of Paine v. Meller on risk of loss during the executory interval, have not followed the English position on a related question: who is entitled to the proceeds paid on the seller's insurance policy? The English rule, formulated in Rayner v. Preston, 18 Ch. Div. 1 (1881), is that the seller is entitled to retain the proceeds free of any claim by the buyer. American courts generally hold that the buyer is entitled to the insurance proceeds, chiefly to avoid giving the seller a windfall (the full purchase price plus the full insurance proceeds). See, e.g., Hillard v. Franklin, 41 S.W.3d 106 (Tenn. App. 2000). Moreover, the proceeds have been held transferrable to the buyer despite a prohibition in the insurance contract against assignment. See, e.g., Smith v. Buege, 387 S.E.2d 109 (W. Va. 1989). It would appear to follow under the American approach that if a state adopts the minority rule on risk of loss and, as a consequence, allocates that risk to seller rather than to buyer, the seller will be entitled to retain the insurance proceeds. See generally West Bend Mutual Insurance Co. v. Salemi, 511 N.E.2d 785 (Ill. App. 1987) (allowing

seller to proceed against buyer's insurer where buyer agreed to insure for seller's benefit).

The English rule rests on the perception that the insurance policy is strictly a personal contract between the seller and her insurer, and its benefits do not pass with the land into the buyer's hands. American courts justify their position on three closely connected grounds: the insurance proceeds are held by the seller in trust for the purchaser; since, under equitable conversion, the buyer is considered to be equitable owner of the land, he should also be considered the equitable owner of the insurance proceeds which stand in place of the land; and since insurance is customarily considered to be for the benefit of the property rather than the person insured the proceeds should go with the land. 3 American Law of Property § 11.31 (A.J. Casner, ed. 1952).

3. Did the court in Skelly v. Ashmore in fact do what it claimed to have done—reject the Paine v. Meller rule which "arbitrarily places the risk of loss on the vendee from the time the contract is made"? Can the court's holding be explained by any rule *other* than Paine v. Meller? Recall that the American rule allocating seller's insurance proceeds to buyer rests entirely on the assumption that buyer bears the risk of loss; if seller bears the risk of loss, the American rule will give the insurance proceeds to seller rather than to buyer. The Massachusetts rule, which the court purported to adopt, squarely places risk of loss on seller, rather than buyer; it thus offers no basis for the court's decision awarding the insurance proceeds to the buyer.

Nor can the court's result be rationalized in terms of the Massachusetts rule that if the destruction is not great and "the buildings did not constitute so material a part of the estate as to result in an annulling of the contract, specific performance may be decreed, with compensation for any breach of agreement, or relief may be given in damages." As Judge Storckman observed in his dissent, "defendants' evidence tended to prove that the real estate was worth more as a site for a service station after the fire than before and that the value of the real estate after the fire was in excess of $20,000." 365 S.W.2d 582. As a result, Skelly apparently suffered no damages that could be set off against the purchase price.

4. **The UVPRA and the ULTA.** The Uniform Vendors and Purchasers Risk Act would alter the majority American rule by placing risk of loss from destruction or condemnation on buyer only if he has taken possession or title; otherwise seller bears the risk. The brain child of Professor Samuel Williston, the UVPRA was promulgated by the National Conference of Commissioners on Uniform State Laws in 1935. At last count, the Act has been adopted in twelve states. See Cal. Civ. Code § 1662; Haw. Rev. Stat. § 508–1; 29 Ill. Comp. Stat. §§ 8.1–8.3; Mich. Comp. Laws §§ 565.701–.703; Nev. Rev. Stat. §§ 113.030–.050; N.Y. Gen. Oblig. Law § 5–1311; N.C. Gen. Stat. §§ 39–36 through 39–39; Okla. Stat., tit. 16, §§ 201–203; Oregon Rev. Stat. §§ 93.290–.300; S.D. Laws §§ 43–26–5 through 43–26–8; Tex. Prop. Code Ann. § 5.007; Wis. Stat. § 706.12.

Almost all these statutes track the language of the original Uniform Act. The Illinois version differs in one detail—assigning special consequence to passage of title through escrow. The New York act makes two changes. It states that its terms are not intended to deprive the seller or buyer of any right to recover damages against the other for breach of contract occurring prior to the destruction or condemnation. And it provides that if buyer has taken neither possession nor title, and an "immaterial part" is destroyed or taken, neither seller nor buyer "is thereby deprived of the right to enforce the contract; but there shall be, to the extent of the destruction or taking, an abatement of purchase price."

The Uniform Land Transactions Act would modify the approach taken by the UVPRA. Section 2–406(c)(2) adopts the Illinois rule on sales closed through escrow, and section 2–406(b)(2)(I) incorporates the New York approach respecting abatement of purchase price for nonmaterial diminutions in value. Also, in the event "the loss or taking results in a substantial failure of the real estate to conform to the contract," section 2–406(b)(1) gives the buyer the option of cancelling the contract and recovering any down payment or enforcing the contract and accepting the property with a "reduction of the contract price for the loss or taking." Can you think of situations in which it would be unfair to require the seller to give up her property in return for a sharply reduced price?

C. CLOSING THE CONTRACT: THE DEED

There is a modern trend to simplify the form and content of real property deeds. Many states have enacted short form deed statutes, prescribing language that eliminates many of the customary redundancies and flourishes. The deed shown on the next page reflects the contemporary trend toward simplification. Even so, the deed contains all of the basic elements that have traditionally been employed since the earliest English deeds.

The portion of the deed beginning with "This indenture ..." and ending with the line, "Together with ...," constitutes the *premises* of the deed—the names of grantor and grantee; the words of grant; background facts and purposes; consideration; and the legal description of the parcels conveyed.

The next portion of the deed, beginning with the line, "To have and to hold," and ending with the third covenant, is the *habendum*, which describes the interest taken by the grantee, any conditions on the grant and any covenants of title (these last are sometimes said to comprise the *warranty clause*).

The *execution clause* begins with the phrase, "In Witness Whereof," and contains the grantors' signatures, their seal, and the date of the deed. (In states that require the deed to be witnessed, the signatures of the witnesses would also appear in the execution clause.) Finally, beneath the grantors' signatures is the *acknowledgment*, in which a public officer, typically a notary, attests to the execution.

WARRANTY DEED

Warranty Deed with Lien Covenant
Laws of 1917, Chap. 681, Laws of 1954 — 880½ — David F. Williamson Co., Inc., Publishers, Buffalo, New York

This Indenture,

Made the 1st *day of* September *, Nineteen Hundred and* eighty-three (1983)

Between Robert W. Jones and Mary Ruth Jones, his wife, residing at 23 Oak Street, Amherst, New York 14221

Grantor(s), and

John J. Smith and Katherine Ann Smith, his wife, residing at 49 Willow Street, Buffalo, New York 14202

Witnesseth, *that the said Grantor(s), in consideration of* ------------------------------------ ---------------------ONE & MORE------------------------- *Dollars* ($1.00 & More ----------) *lawful money of the United States, paid by the Grantee(s), do hereby grant and release unto the Grantee(s),* their heirs *and assigns forever.*

All that Tract or Parcel of Land, situate in the Town of Amherst, County of Erie and State of New York, being part of Lot Number 45, Township 11 and Range 7 of the Holland Land Company's Survey and according to a Subdivision Map filed in the Erie County Clerk's Office under Cover Number 922 is known and distinguished as Subdivision Lot Number 117.

TOGETHER *with the appurtenances and all the estate and rights of the Grantor(s) in and to the said premises.*

TO HAVE AND TO HOLD, *the above granted premises unto the said Grantee(s).*

AND *the said Grantor(s) do covenant with said Grantee(s) as follows:*

FIRST.—*That the Grantee(s) shall quietly enjoy the said premises.*

SECOND.—*That the Grantor(s) will forever* **WARRANT** *the title to said premises.*

THIRD.—*Subject to the trust fund provisions of section thirteen of the lien law.*

IN WITNESS WHEREOF, *The said Grantor(s) have hereunto set* their *hands and seals the day and year first above written.*

IN PRESENCE OF

______________________ [L.S.] ______________________ [L.S.]
ROBERT W. JONES MARY RUTH JONES

______________________ [L.S.] ______________________ [L.S.]

STATE OF NEW YORK) ss. On this 1st day of September,
COUNTY OF ERIE) Nineteen Hundred and eighty-three (1983)

before me, the subscriber(s), personally appeared Robert W. Jones and Mary Ruth Jones, his wife,

to me personally known and known to me to be the same persons described in and who executed the within instrument, and they acknowledged to me that they executed the same.

____
notary public

STATE OF NEW YORK) ss. On this day of
COUNTY OF) Nineteen Hundred and

before me, the subscriber(s), personally appeared

to me personally known and known to me to be the same person described in and who executed the within instrument, and he acknowledged to me that he executed the same.

Formalities Required. Apart from a written instrument signed by the grantor, most states today require few formalities for a deed to be effective. The deed must name the grantor and grantee; it must contain express words of grant; and it must describe the parcel conveyed to the exclusion of all other parcels in the world.

Formalities Not Required. *Consideration.* Although consideration is required for the grantee to be a "purchaser for value," and thus protected under the recording acts, it is not required for the deed to be effective as between the parties. Nonetheless, deeds will commonly refer to the consideration given, frequently in some such mysterious terms as "One and More Dollars," or "Ten Dollars and other Valuable Consideration." Why the secrecy? One reason is that deeds, once recorded, are public documents, and a recital of the owner's true purchase price might give an undesired bargaining advantage to some future purchaser from the owner. (Prospective purchasers will sometimes try to pierce this veil and calculate the seller's purchase price by counting the documentary tax stamps affixed to the deed; since, at the time of purchase the owner is required to buy stamps in proportion to the actual purchase price of the parcel, the number of stamps might be thought to indicate the purchase price. But sellers are clever, too, and, anticipating the future purchaser's strategy, will sometimes buy more stamps than are required, thus indicating a higher price than was actually paid.)

Seal. It was once commonly required that for a deed to be effective it had to be sealed—stamped with the grantor's mark. Most states have since eliminated the requirement. And, even in those states that still impose the requirement, it is easily met—through use of the written word, "Seal," or, as in the Jones–Smith deed, through use of the initials "L.S.," (signifying *locus sigilli*, or "the place of the seal").

Acknowledgment. Only a small number of states require an acknowledgment for a deed to be effective as between the parties. Acknowledgment is, however, required for a deed to be legally recorded. Acknowledgment has traditionally conferred two other benefits. It makes the deed admissible into evidence without further proof of execution, and it creates a presumption that the deed is genuine. For an exhaustive analysis of acknowledgment requirements and related formalities see Robert D. Brussack, Reform of American Conveyancing Formality, 32 Hastings L.J. 561 (1981).

The Cost of Formalities. One obvious and oft-lamented cost of formal requirements is that, by invalidating imperfect transfers, they penalize grantors and grantees who retained inept lawyers or no lawyers at all. Formal rules respecting deed drafting, descriptions and delivery, considered in the pages that follow, can have a similarly harsh effect.

Formal requirements have another, possibly more substantial cost. By inducing grantees and grantors to reduce their transactions to writing and to have these writings acknowledged, delivered and recorded, the American conveyancing system also induces future grantees to rely on the paper record as perfectly evidencing the current state of title. Unfortunately, even the most perfect-appearing paper record is sometimes flawed. A swindler can easily forge a deed conveying Greenacre from the current record owner to himself. By forging a notarial seal and acknowledgment, he can also easily record the deed and, once having recorded it, can sell the land to some unsuspecting buyer. In the late 1980s, at least one title company encountered a significant and growing number of forged deeds. See Reuben, Real Estate Title Forgeries Seen Increasing, Los Angeles Daily J., May 11, 1987, at 5, col. 1 (reporting title company's experience that forgery claims rose from 3.8 percent to 12.9 percent of total claims between 1970 and 1985).

Can you think of ways to reduce the incidence or cost of fraud without sacrificing the efficiencies of a paper record? See generally Roger W. Andersen, Conveyancing Reform: A Great Place to Start, 25 Real Prop. Probate & Trust J. 333 (1990).

1. Deed Construction

Courts called on to construe real property deeds typically start from the proposition that "the intention of the grantor or grantors must be gathered from the whole instrument and every part thereof given effect." Beveridge v. Howland, 271 S.E.2d 910, 913 (N.C. 1980). If, however, the deed contains "conflicting provisions which are irreconcilable," courts will employ one or more standard interpretational canons to resolve the conflict or ambiguity. Id.

For example, if there is an irreconcilable conflict between the granting clause and the habendum, it is generally said that the granting clause will control. And, "so long as they do not conflict, written and printed parts are of equal force; when inconsistent, printed parts must give way to typed or written words, and, between the latter two, written words give a stronger indication of intention than typed words. When contradictory, general words must usually give way to specific words. Where a recital and an operative part of the deed come in conflict, it is the latter which prevails. And it is a general rule, subject to all those just noted, that when two repugnant clauses cannot be reconciled, the earlier of the two will stand. Another rule, not to be applied until all others fail to reconcile a conflict, and only when there is a real ambiguity or uncertainty, is that a deed will be construed most strongly against the grantor, or against the grantee when the instrument was drafted by him." 3 American Law of Property § 12.90 (A.J. Casner ed. 1952). See also Tevis Herd, Deed Construction and the "Repugnant to the Grant" Doctrine, 21 Tex. Tech. L. Rev. 635 (1990).

It is the rare deed dispute in which some of these canons cannot be asserted on one side, and some on the other. Would these canons help you in giving a title opinion on an ambiguous deed executed thirty or forty years earlier? Consider whether you would feel more or less comfortable with your opinion, knowing that, in addition to these canons of construction, a court interpreting the deed will often look to "all the attendant circumstances as to situation of the parties, relationship, object of the conveyance, person who drew the deed, and all surrounding situations which may throw light on the meaning which the parties attached to ambiguous or inconsistent portions of the instruments. And unless forbidden by some rule of law, the courts will follow the construction given a deed by the parties themselves as shown by their subsequent admissions or conduct." 3 American Law of Property § 12.91 (A.J. Casner ed. 1952).

Given a choice, is it preferable for a court construing a deed to attempt to discern the actual, subjective intent of the original grantor and grantee, or to refuse to look outside the deed's four corners? Which rule will better promote certainty among title examiners and their clients over the long term?

2. DELIVERY

A deed does not effectively transfer title to an interest in land unless and until it is delivered.[1] Delivery is a term of art and means something more than physical transfer of a deed from grantor to grantee. In its ideal form, delivery requires both physical transfer and a present intent by the grantor to transfer an interest in the property to the grantee. Thus, if the transferor hands a deed to the transferee, delivery will not occur if the requisite intent is missing (e.g., "I am giving you this deed to hold for safekeeping in the event I later decide to give Greenacre to you"). See Jorgensen v. Crow, 466 N.W.2d 120 (N.D. 1991) (where transferee picked up deed at closing but grantors lacked intent to transfer, no delivery occurred). If, however, the intent is clear, courts will often find delivery without physical transfer, through devices such as symbolic, constructive, or agency delivery (e.g., "I am presently transferring Greenacre to you, but I will hold the deed for you until you reach 18"). Intent is thus pivotal.

Obviously a system that rests title on something so ephemeral as intent can hardly be expected to promote faith in the paper record or in land transactions generally. Thus, it is no surprise that in the example just given courts have developed presumptions bringing delivery rules into line with the reasonable expectations of title searchers. Thus, while physical transfer does not constitute delivery, it is widely held to create a presumption of delivery. Conversely, failure to transfer the deed creates a presumption of nondelivery. Other acts creating a presumption of delivery are recordation of the deed and the deed's acknowledgment. See generally Richard R. Powell, Powell on Real Property § 81A.04[2](a) (Michael Allan Wolf ed., 2005).

Acceptance. In order for a deed to be effectively delivered, the grantee must accept the delivery. In most cases, because the grant will benefit the grantee, acceptance will be presumed. However, courts will not presume acceptance if the conveyance might be disadvantageous to the grantee. And, even if the conveyance will be advantageous, courts will allow the presumption of acceptance to be rebutted by evidence that the grantee did not in fact wish to accept title to the land.

1. A will does not effectively transfer title to an interest in land until the death of the individual who made the will.

In Hood v. Hood, 384 A.2d 706 (Me. 1978), plaintiff grantor, in her mid-eighties, had entered a hospital for surgery "from which she believed she might not recover." While in the hospital, she executed a deed to her farm, upon which she and her son Kenneth lived, to Kenneth. The attorney who drew up the deed recorded it the next day. According to the facts, "Kenneth E. Hood had no knowledge of the transaction until sometime later, when he visited his mother in the hospital. After she told him what she had done, her son informed her he wanted no part of the property, and he requested his mother to 'take it right back' to herself. Mrs. Hood subsequently attempted to contact the attorney who had drawn the deed, but was unsuccessful because he was on vacation. Kenneth E. Hood died on May 9, 1974, holding record title to the farm."

Mrs. Hood subsequently brought an action against Kenneth's surviving daughters, and their husbands, to declare the conveyance void. The Maine Supreme Court affirmed the trial court's judgment for Mrs. Hood. Rejecting defendants' argument that "delivery was completed when the Plaintiff gave the deed to the attorney for recording, thus relinquishing the right to recall the deed," the court observed that "Maine has traditionally followed what appears to be the majority rule that delivery of a deed is a consensual act. Thus, effective delivery of a deed requires the correlative act of acceptance by the grantee. The rationale for such a rule is that an estate cannot be thrust upon a person against his will, even if done gratuitously."

Do you think that the court would—or should—have reached the same result if Kenneth had survived his mother? What sentiments do you suppose prompted Kenneth's remark to his mother that "he wanted no part of the property," and his request that she "take it right back" to herself?

Wiggill v. Cheney

Supreme Court of Utah, 1979.
597 P.2d 1351.

MAUGHAN, JUSTICE.

This case involves the disposition of certain real property located in Weber County, State of Utah. The judgment before us invalidated a Warranty Deed, because of no valid delivery. We affirm. No costs awarded.

The material facts are undisputed. Specifically, on the 25th day of June, 1958, Lillian W. Cheney signed a deed to certain real property located in the city of Ogden, Utah, wherein the defendant, Flora Cheney, was named grantee. Thereafter Lillian Cheney placed this deed in a sealed envelope and deposited it in a safety deposit box in the names of herself and the plaintiff, Francis E. Wiggill. Following the deposition of the deed, Lillian Cheney advised plaintiff his name was on the safety deposit box and instructed plaintiff that upon her death, he was to go to the bank where he would be granted access to the safety deposit box and its contents. Lillian

Cheney further instructed, "in that box is an envelope addressed to all those concerned. All you have to do is give them that envelope and that's all." At all times prior to her death, Lillian Cheney was in possession of a key to the safety deposit box and had sole and complete control over it. Plaintiff was never given the key to the safety deposit box.

Following the death of Lillian Cheney, plaintiff, after gaining access to the safety deposit box, delivered the deed contained therein to Flora Cheney, the named grantee.

The sole issue presented here on appeal is whether or not the acts of plaintiff constitute a delivery of the deed such as will render it enforceable as a valid conveyance.

The rule is well settled that a deed, to be operative as a transfer of the ownership of land, or an interest or estate therein, must be delivered. It was equally settled in this and the vast majority of jurisdictions that a valid delivery of a deed requires it pass beyond the control or domain of the grantor. The requisite relinquishment of control or dominion over the deed may be established, notwithstanding the fact the deed is in possession of the grantor at her death, by proof of facts which tend to show delivery had been made with the intention to pass title and to explain the grantor's subsequent possession. However, in order for a delivery effectively to transfer title, the grantor must part with possession of the deed or the right to retain it.

The evidence presented in the present case establishes Lillian Cheney remained in sole possession and control of the deed in question until her death. Because no actual delivery of the deed occurred prior to the death of the grantor, the subsequent manual delivery of the deed by plaintiff to defendant conveyed no title to the property described therein, or any part thereof, or any of its contents.[5]

Notes & Questions

1. Delivery is frequently an issue in donative transfers like the one involved in *Wiggill* and, as a consequence, raises problems for any buyer whose chain of title has a gift as one of its links.

Say that, upon receiving the deed from Francis Wiggill, Flora Cheney recorded it and then conveyed her interest, for value, to a buyer relying on her apparently good record title. How could the buyer have protected himself against the finding that Flora in fact had no title to convey?

5. Concerning the contention that the grantor intended title to pass, the applicable rule was explained in *Singleton v. Kelly*, supra, at 66, where this court stated, "that is true (the courts will carry out the grantor's intention whenever this is possible), but without any evidence of delivery, it can be of no importance whatever what the intentions of the grantor in this case were. One may have an intention to convey his property to another, but unless the deed is delivered to the grantee, or someone for him, title cannot pass, and the undelivered deed is a nullity."

Obviously, record title and possession in the seller—the traditional indicia of ownership—are insufficient to ensure that the seller has anything to convey. Would a standard policy of title insurance offer sufficient protection? Would the buyer eventually gain title by adverse possession?

2. **Escrows.** In some parts of the country, buyer and seller will close their contract through *escrow*, an arrangement under which a third party—the "escrow holder"—holds the deed from seller and the purchase money from buyer and buyer's lender pending fulfillment of the contract conditions. If all conditions are fulfilled, the escrow holder will on the date set for closing deliver and record the deed and mortgage to buyer and lender respectively, deliver the note to the lender, and deliver the purchase money to the seller. If, however, one or more of the contract conditions is not fulfilled, the escrow holder will return the documents and funds to the appropriate parties. This type of escrow arrangement is used both where the contract of sale provides for a short executory period and where the purchase is being made under a long term installment contract. Practices vary from region to region as to who serves the escrow function: lawyer, broker, lender, title insurance company or independent escrow company. Overall closing costs may vary as a result.

The use of escrows has virtually eliminated delivery as an issue when land is being transferred for consideration. Yet, escrows themselves are not problem-free. When problems arise it is usually because the parties have failed to be sufficiently explicit or objective in drafting the escrow instructions. Since an escrow agent should act strictly as an automaton and without discretion, escrow instructions will be inadequate if they fail to specify the agent's conduct under every conceivable contingency.

3. Description of the Land Conveyed

To be valid, a deed must adequately describe the property conveyed. The clear trend has been away from punctilio and toward a minimal requirement that the description enable location of the parcel to the exclusion of all others—essentially the standard imposed for land descriptions in contracts. See generally 3 American Law of Property § 12.98 (A.J. Casner ed. 1952).

A deed can employ any one or more of three principal techniques to describe the land conveyed: *metes and bounds* (typically using courses and distances), *references to government survey*, and *reference to a recorded instrument* (typically a subdivision map). The lawyer counseling a buyer or seller in a real estate transaction should be familiar with all three techniques to ensure not only that the proposed deed description complies with the statute of frauds, but also that it is accurate and that the buyer will get precisely the land he thinks he is getting. The excerpts in this section describe these three land description techniques.

Curtis M. Brown, Boundary Control and Legal Principles*

9–11, 14–17 (2d ed. 1969).

1.6. Written Perimeter Descriptions

Land can be described by a sequence of courses, and where the sequence of courses has a direction of travel around a perimeter and has calls for adjoiners, the description is said to be by *metes and bounds*. *Mete* means to measure or to assign by measure, and *bounds* means the boundary of the land or the limits and extent of a property. Within the generally accepted usage of the term metes and bounds it is not necessary to recite measures of a property as implied by the word metes. A parcel of land can be described without a single measurement being given: "Beginning at an oak tree blazed on the north; thence to a large boulder located on the bank of Lake Washington; thence along the lake to . . ., etc." Usually metes and bounds descriptions are described by successive courses, said courses being fixed by adjoiners, monuments, direction, distance, or all four.

Bounds descriptions are perimeter descriptions, but they do not have a direction of travel: "All of that land bounded on the north by Thelma Lane; bounded on the south by Rodger River; bounded on the west by the land of Thomas L. Brown; and bounded on the east by the land of Ruth Almstead." The sequence of reciting the bounds is immaterial; the description has no mandatory direction of travel.

Metes descriptions are perimeter descriptions described by measurements, have a direction of travel, and recite no bounds (adjoiners). Often a metes description is included within the common usage of the term metes and bounds. . . .

1.9. Calls in Descriptions

In litigation and in surveying the terms *deed calls* and *running out the calls* are commonly used. According to *Websters International Dictionary* in American land law a call is a "reference to, or statement of, an object, course (meaning direction), distance, or other matter of description in a survey or grant. . . ." The calls of a surveyor's field notes are for the objects and measurements noted. A call, as commonly used, can be a phrase in a land description: "thence to a blazed oak tree." This call tells the surveyor to go thence (from the last place mentioned) in a straight line to a blazed oak tree. Other examples of calls are N 10° 15° E, 327.62, along Red River, due north, along the center line of B Street, to the Santa Fe Railroad tracks. . . .

Direction of Travel

True metes and bounds descriptions and many quasi-metes and bounds descriptions have a direction of travel. A bearing may be stated in either of two directions on a map or plat but only one can be used in a written perimeter description. In Figure [4–1], starting at the point of beginning, the direction of travel is to the southeast, making the first written bearing in the description S 45° 00 E, not N 45° 00 W. Because the relationship of one line to another is shown by the plotting of the lines in Figure [4–3], it is immaterial whether the bearing on the plat is written S 45° 00 E or N 45° 00 W.

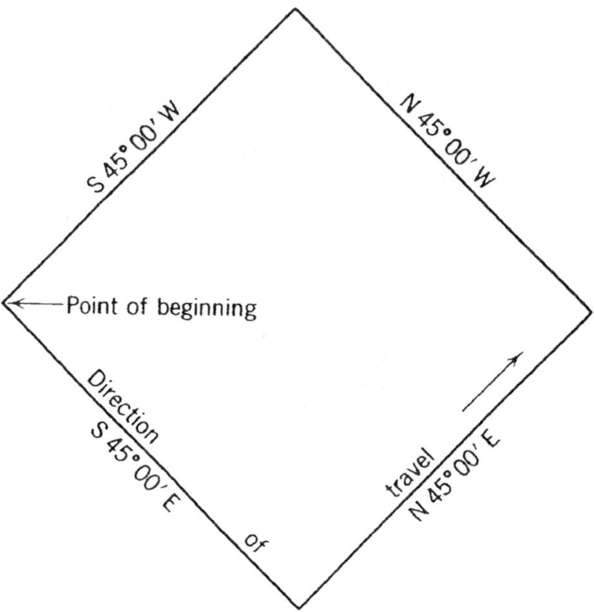

Figure 4–1

Monuments

Monuments are classified as either *natural, artificial, record,* or *legal.* Naturally occurring monuments such as rivers, lakes, oceans, bays, sloughs, cliffs, trees, hills, and large boulders are permanent objects found on the land as they were placed by nature and are usually considered controlling over *artificial monuments* (man-made) such as iron stakes, wooden stakes, rock mounds, stones, and wooden fences, but, if the writings clearly indicate a contrary intent, especially where the lines of a survey are called for, the control might be reversed. Some man-made monuments, because of the certainty of location, visibility, stability, and permanence, are considered equal in rank to natural monuments. In this classification would fall sidewalks, street paving, curbs, wells, canals, concrete buildings, and concrete fences.

Record Monuments or Boundaries

These exist because of a reference to them in a deed or legal description; thus, "to Brown's property line" is a call for a record monument

(Brown's property). Record monuments may or may not be marked upon the ground by artificial or natural monuments. Where a deed reads "to the side line of the street," the call is for the boundary of a record monument (street) which could be marked by stakes, improvements, fences, or all three, or not marked at all. A call for any record monument is a call for all the monuments, or considerations, that establish the location of the record monument. If a monument is controlling in a legal description, it is often classified as a *legal monument.* "To a stone" is a call for a legal artificial monument; "to Brown's property line" is a call for a legal record monument. The words record monument and legal monument are sometimes used synonymously. Because of the confusion over the various meanings of the term "legal," the words legal monument should be avoided.

Courts may refer to record monuments as natural monuments. The boundaries of a street are marked by man, but the dirt composing the street is naturally occurring, and, in this sense, the street is a natural monument. It is an unfortunate classification. In the order of importance of conflicting elements within deeds, natural monuments are normally considered superior to artificial monuments. A call for a record monument, where no senior right is interfered with, is normally subordinate to a call for an artificial monument. If record monuments are classified as natural monuments, the statement that natural monuments control artificial monuments is not exactly true.

Adjoiners, streets, and parcels of land differ from rivers, lakes, and the like, in that man marks and defines these boundary divisions. Waters and creeks always have visible boundaries, whereas a parcel of land may not be physically marked at all. A deed call for an adjoiner is a call for a monument in the form of a parcel of land that has size, shape, and location, but there is poor foundation for classifying the monument as a natural monument. Since the limits of a parcel of land must be marked by man, why not classify the call for an adjoiner as a call for an artificial monument? Because adjoiners to a conveyance are mainly dependent upon the record for their existence and because they may have invisible lines marking their limits, the classification "record monument" is preferred. The term "natural monument" as used herein is exclusive of record monuments.

Properties of Monuments

A good monument should possess the quality of being easily visible, certain of identification, stable in location, permanent in character, and nondependent upon measurement for its location. An artificial monument possesses the qualities of a natural monument to a lesser degree. Thus a stake placed in the ground will rust or rot with time and is less permanent than a naturally occurring large boulder. A stake is easier to move than a boulder and is therefore less stable. The visibility of record monuments is wholly dependent upon the natural or artificial monuments (fences, stakes, cultivation, plantings, and the like) that mark the limits of the record monument.

Straight Lines

A line in a description is assumed to be the shortest horizontal distance between the points called for unless the contrary is indicated by the writings. To be absolutely correct, a straight line curves with the surface of the earth; but the curvature is so slight that it is not considered in land descriptions. A line to be identified must have a definition of its start, direction, and length. *Free lines* are not terminated by an adjoiner or monument as "beginning at a 2–inch iron pipe; thence N 60° 00 W, 200.00 feet." If the same phrase were reworded "beginning at a 2–inch iron pipe; thence N 60° 00 W, 200.00 feet to a blazed sycamore tree," the terminus of the line is fixed by the tree; the line is not free. Many of the lines described in deeds are dependent upon monuments and are not free lines.

A bearing quoted for a line defines it as a straight line. If a line is defined by monuments, without bearing or distance, the words "in a straight line" or "in a direct line" are sometimes added to emphasize the presumed fact that the line is straight.

Direction

As commonly practiced in this country, direction is defined by either a call for monuments or a bearing; but azimuth, deflection angle, or coordinate may be used. If a deed is written "commencing at a blazed sycamore tree located approximately 100 feet west of Jones' well; thence to a blazed white oak, etc.," the direction is clearly defined. It is very desirable to quote the bearing of the line for plotting purposes, but it is not essential to the legality of the conveyance. Bearings are always read in degrees and minutes (plus seconds if fractions of a minute are involved) from the *north* point or from the *south* point. *Never* from the east or west points.... The direction of a line is dependent upon [at] which end of the line you are standing; thus on a northwesterly line the direction would be SE if you were at the northerly terminus of a line, whereas it would be NW if you were at the southerly terminus of the same line. On a map it is immaterial which bearing you write, since the drawing shows the relationship of one line to another; but in a written metes and bounds description the exact direction of travel of the line being described must be stated.

Wilkie Cunnyngham, Making Land Surveys and Preparing Descriptions to Meet Legal Requirements*

19 MO. L. REV. 234, 236–238 (1954).

The following [metes and bounds] description of a tract of land in Missouri is copied from a deed written in 1903:

> A tract of land situated in the County of Ste. Genevieve, on the waters of the Establishment Creek, and being part of Survey No. 2088, confirmed to Jean Bte Valle, to-wit—beginning at the

> Southwest corner of a tract of land sold by the said Felix Valle to Louis Lalumondiere, containing sixty arpents and from thence North 55° West along and with the said Lalumondiere line 35 chains and 60 links, to said Lalumondiere's corner stone and continuing said line to 53 09/100 chains set a Flower stone 18 × 6 × 3 inches for a corner stone from said stone a Post Oak tree 7 inches in diameter bears S. 70° W. 17 ½ links distant and a Post oak 8 inches in diameter bears S. 27° E. 17 links distant. Thence S. 35° W. 16.14/100 chains intersecting the line sold by said Felix Valle to Charles Carsow, set a corner stone 18 × 6 × 4 inches for a corner stone, and from said stone a Black oak Tree 10 inches in diameter bears S. 55° E. 22 links distant, and a Black oak tree, four inches in diameter bears N. 22° E. 37 links distant, and from thence S. 55° E, with the line of said Carsow 53.00 chains and 9 links to the Establishment Creek, and from thence down said Establishment Creek with the meanders thereof to the place of beginning, containing 103 arpents and 90/100 of an arpent, more or less. Excepting and reserving 1.69/100 acres in the N.W. corner of said tract conveyed to John Kertz in January 1888. Also all that part of U.S. Survey No. 2088 described as follows, begin at most Eastern corner on Establishment Creek, of land belonging to John Kertz at a stone from which a sycamore 14 in. in diameter bears N. 60° W. 60 links distant and a Burr Oak 7 in. in diameter bears N. 8° W. 72 links distance; thence N. 55° W. 11.37/100 chains to a stone for corner; thence S. 18° E. 5.00/100 to a point on said Establishment Creek from which a hickory 7 in. in diameter bears N. 10° E. 23 links and an Elm 7 in. in diameter bears N. 60° W. 22 links distant, thence down and with the meanders of said creek to the beginning corner containing one 69/100 acres, more or less.

One of these descriptions might not only become very long, but involve tracking down innumerable descriptions in long chains of title to the ancient sources of many boundary tracts. Yet this is the method used in most of the world, including 19 of the American States (Texas, and the states in, or carved out of the original Thirteen Colonies—Maine, New Hampshire, Vermont, Massachusetts, Rhode Island, Connecticut, New York, Pennsylvania, New Jersey, Delaware, Maryland, Virginia, West Virginia, Kentucky, North Carolina, Tennessee, South Carolina, and Georgia).

Land descriptions in the other 29 states are generally much simpler. Most of the lands in these states were at one time owned by the Federal Government. The disposition of such a vast acreage presented a major problem in identification and description. The fertile imagination and inventive genius of Thomas Jefferson worked out a plan for dividing the public lands into a gigantic checkerboard of uniform square tracts each measuring one mile (80 chains) on its sides, and containing 640 acres. These "sections" are divided into "quarters" of 160 acres each, ½ mile (40 chains) on a side; and may be still further subdivided into "quarter-quarter-sections" (1/16–section) of 40 acres, 1/4 mile on each side etc. The boundaries of these sections were to be a series of parallel north-south lines one mile apart, and east-west lines, also one mile apart. ...Under this system it should be possible to describe almost any tract in the 29 states so surveyed.[a] ....

However, in actual practice and for many reasons, sections will not always be found to fit into such a scheme with perfect uniformity. If two lines, drawn exactly one mile apart at the Base Line, are projected due north, they must approach closer together each mile as they proceed north, until they will have merged into a single point at the North Pole.

There are also mechanical and human surveying errors in determining bearings and distances in the east-west, as well as the north-south, lines. We should remember that some of the first surveys were made 150 years ago through almost impenetrable wildernesses, over wild land of little value, ... by contract surveyors sometimes interested only in collecting their pay for as little time and effort as possible, using crude instruments and methods (e.g., reputedly measuring distance by counting revolutions of a cartwheel with a rag tied around the rim or by a hemp rope dragged on horse back). Even with the most modern transit, the magnetic needle is not supported to a point toward true north, but toward a "magnetic" north which is continually shifting and changing the magnetic "declination". Local ore deposits, metal objects, and power lines affect the needle. "It (the magnetic compass) is an instrument helpful for finding general directions but not reliable when accuracy is required, nor is it used except for checking purposes in surveys."[4] When using the transit for turning angles from a base line, the finest gradation on the horizontal circle may be one degree, or on the more expensive instruments with vernier attachments, one-half minute.

Curtis M. Brown, Boundary Control and Legal Principles*

10–11, 27–29 (2d ed. 1969).

1.8. Descriptions by Reference

The simplest form for writing a land description is by reference to a map or plat as: Lot 1, Block 49 of La Jolla Park, City of San Diego, California. See Figure [4–2]. ...

1.13. Subdivision Descriptions

If a map of parcels of land is filed with a public agency and the parcels thereon are designated by number or letters, the map is commonly referred to as a subdivision map. The precise meaning of the term subdivision varies from state to state, and the meaning within a given state is whatever the

a. Eds.—Chapter 1 describes the government survey system in more detail at pages 31–33.

4. Henrie v. Hyer, 70 P.2d 154, 158 (Utah 1937).

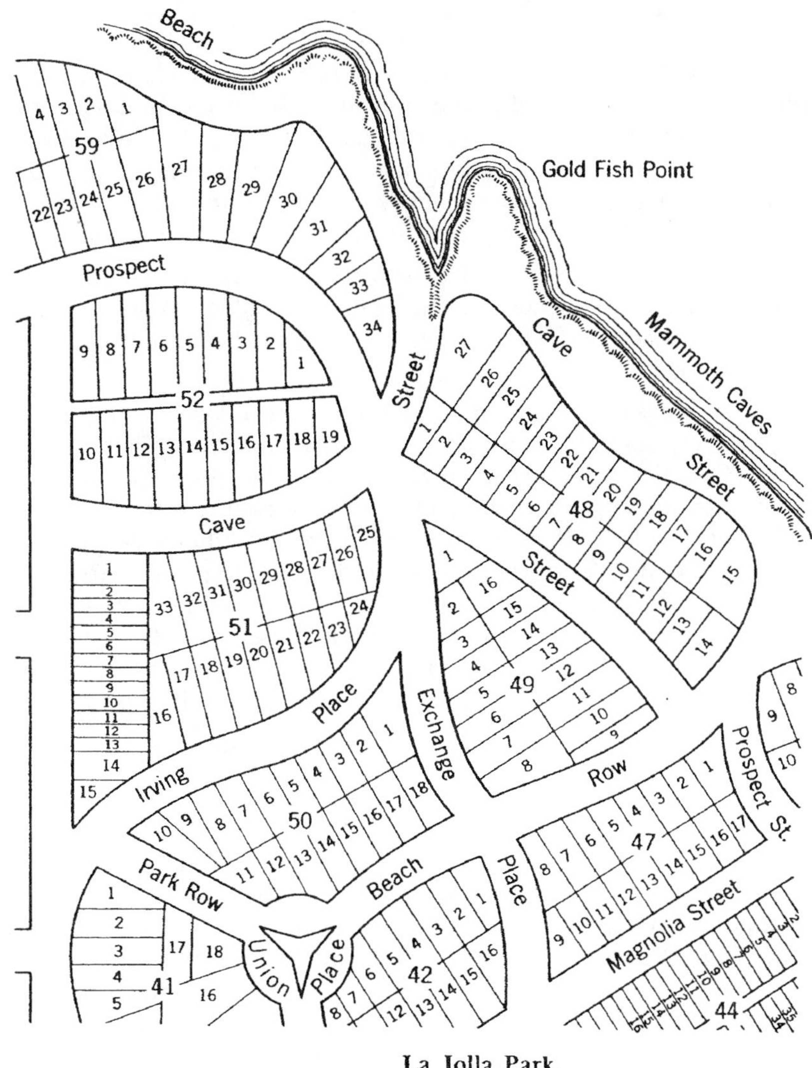

La Jolla Park.

Figure 4–2

law defines it as being within that state. In a number of states the law authorizing preparation of subdivision maps is sometimes called a *platting* act instead of *subdivision* act. . . .

From the standpoint of the retracement surveyor the important features of a map are the following

1. What monuments were set or found?
2. What are the record sizes and locations of the lots and blocks?

From the standpoint of the scrivener, subdivision maps offer the simplest means of describing land since they present the maximum of information and the minimum of words. "Lot 40 of La Mesa Colony, according to Map 346 as filed in the Office of the Recorder, San Diego County, Calif." or "Sec. 16, T15N, R20E, Principal Meridian" or "Lot 2 according to the partition map filed in Superior Court Case 17632" form complete descriptions of land that can be identified from all other parcels of land. The simplicity of the title wording does not mean that a lot and block description of a section of land is easier to survey than is a parcel of land described by a metes and bounds conveyance. Certainty and ease of location are totally unrelated to the length of the deed describing the land.

Most subdivision laws require that, previous to filing a map, survey markers must be established on the land. Many older maps, made before the passage of such laws, were "office maps" made from the record without benefit of survey. . . .

Early subdivisions executed by private interests were poorly regulated by law, and any sheet of paper presented as a subdivision map to the land or recorder's office was filed upon payment of the filing fee. Occasionally, maps failed to show street widths, lot sizes, and what was being subdivided. The map of La Jolla Park was compiled with undimensioned lots and undimensioned curved streets laid out with a varying radius french curve (see Figure [4–2]). On old maps the surveyor or engineer rarely made a statement describing what monuments he found or set. How could a later surveyor, ignorant of what markers were originally set, retrace a subdivision? Most modern subdivisions are regulated by rigid laws, which have corrected many of the conditions mentioned. . . .

1.14. Parcels Created by Protraction

Parcels of land or lots drawn upon a subdivision map but not monumented on the ground by an original survey are said to be created by protraction. If a surveyor divides a parcel of land into blocks 200 × 300 feet by setting monuments at each block corner and then draws 12 lots in each block of his map, the lots are said to be protracted. In the sectionalized land system sections are created by prior survey and monumentation; parts of sections are created by protraction (SW1/4 of NE1/4 of Section 10). The words "protracted lots" or "protracted parcels" imply "created on paper without the benefit of an original survey." If several parcels or lots are protracted on the same map, all are simultaneously created at the moment of approval of the map; no parcel or lot has senior rights over an adjoiner. In New York the date of sale determines prior rights; this is an exception to the general rule.

Notes & Questions

1. **Ambiguous Descriptions in Deeds.** Traditionally, for a deed to be valid it had to describe the parcel conveyed to the exclusion of all other parcels in the world. Contemporary courts have relaxed this requirement somewhat by resorting to parol evidence—oral statements, extrinsic writings, the physical condition of the land and improvements—in order to cure omissions or ambiguities within the deed's four corners.

Colman v. Butkovich, 556 P.2d 503, 504–505 (Utah 1976), typifies the modern trend. In an action to quiet title, the question arose whether a deed description—"All unplatted land in this Block (29 P.C.) and all land West of this Blk: and Pt. Lot 1: Pt. Lot A"—was sufficient. Upholding the deed, the court observed:

> It is not to be questioned that in order to be valid, a deed must contain a sufficiently definite description to identify the property it conveys.... The problem lies in ascertaining the intent with which it was executed. It should be resolved, if possible, by looking to the terms of the instrument itself and any reasonable inferences to be drawn therefrom; and if there then remains any uncertainty or ambiguity, it can be aided by extrinsic evidence. If from that process the property can be identified with reasonable certainty, the deed is not invalid for uncertainty.

Doubtless the main reason courts are reluctant to invalidate deeds like the one in *Colman* is that the grantor, although she may have been less than clear in describing the parcel conveyed, has been crystal clear in expressing an intent to convey *something* to the grantee; if parol evidence will resolve the ambiguity and make the deed enforceable, it should be admitted.

Which will better serve an efficient conveyancing system: a rule that validates the deed by focusing on buyer's and seller's actual intent or one that invalidates the deed if that intent has not been expressed clearly in the written instrument? Is the threat of invalidation likely to spur buyers and sellers to draft clear descriptions? For some thoughtful reflections along these lines, see Linda Little Carloni, The Use of Extrinsic Evidence to Interpret Real Property Conveyances: A Suggested Limitation, 65 Calif. L. Rev. 897 (1977).

2. **Construing Deed Descriptions.** Ambiguity, even though not fatal to a real property deed, must still be cured if the deed is to be given force as between two or more neighbors, each of whom claims that the ambiguity should be resolved in favor of enlarging his parcel. Although parol evidence can help to resolve ambiguity, it will not always be available or, when available, dispositive. Thus, courts construing ambiguous or conflicting descriptions will often resort to any one or more of at least ten canons of construction. See John E. Cribbet & Corwin W. Johnson, Principles of the Law of Property 210–12 (3d ed. 1989).

Some of these canons can be quite helpful in divining the seller's and buyer's intent. One canon states that, in case of a conflict between the various indicators and measures used in a description, "monuments control distances and courses; courses control distances; and quantity is the least reliable guide of all." The canon presumably corresponds with the expectations of seller and buyer: "most monuments would be difficult to mistake so they are probably identified correctly. A course, 'northerly at a 90° angle' is more certain than a distance 'thence 80 ft.,' since most people cannot measure distances with any degree of accuracy with the naked eye." Distance is also subject to the hazards of uneven terrain.

Another helpful canon is that, when "a tract of land is bounded by a monument which has width, such as a highway or a stream, the boundary line extends to the center, provided the grantor owns that far." Again, the canon presumably reflects the parties' original expectations—in this case, that the grantee would receive the grantor's entire interest in the parcel. To mark the boundary at the near edge of the highway or stream would mean that if the highway is later abandoned, or the stream diverted, the grantor would have title to the strip between the edge and the center. *Id.*

As Professors Cribbet and Johnson acknowledge, however, other canons are simply conclusional, explaining rather than predicting results. Among these are, "extrinsic evidence will be allowed to explain a latent ambiguity but a patent ambiguity must be resolved within the four corners of the deed." (What is patent? What is latent?) "Useless or contradictory words may be disregarded as mere surplusage." (Which of two conflicting words is "useless"? Which of two antithetical terms is "contradictory"?) And, "particular descriptions control over general descriptions, although a false particular may be disregarded to give effect to a true general description." (Huh?) See also Student Symposium, Operation and Construction of Deeds, 6 St. Mary's L.J. 806 (1975).

3. **Surveyor Malpractice.** Increasingly, surveyors are being held to account for their errors. Breach of contract, the traditional ground for recovery on a faulty survey or description, has now been joined by the tort of negligent misrepresentation. Because it is a tort, and has no privity requirement, negligent misrepresentation can give relief to distant purchasers as well as to the buyer or developer who first contracted with the surveyor. Liability is also being extended by the "discovery" rule under which the statute of limitations for negligent misrepresentation does not begin to run until the misrepresentation has been, or should have been, discovered.

Rozny v. Marnul, 250 N.E.2d 656 (Ill. 1969), reflects the modern trend. Defendant had prepared an inaccurate parcel survey for a builder. A legend appearing on the face of the survey stated that the "survey carries our absolute guarantee for accuracy." Plaintiffs, who bought the parcel from the builder, sought damages when they discovered that, relying on markers placed in accordance with the faulty survey, they had constructed improvements that encroached on an adjacent lot. Holding for plaintiffs, the Illinois Supreme Court reversed the appellate court's decision that plaintiffs' action was barred for lack of contractual privity. The Supreme Court chose instead to follow the warranty theory adopted in the Restatement of Torts, Second § 402B (1965): "The Restatement uses the language of misrepresentation to make it clear that the basis of liability is tort and expressly states that the privity of contract requirement is not applicable."

The court rejected the claim that its ruling would expose surveyors to unlimited liability. First, since defendant "admitted he knew the plats were customarily used by lending agencies and others," he could have reasonably foreseen that the plat would be "relied on to his damage by a third party [plaintiffs] in connection with the financing and purchase of the surveyed property." Second, the situation is "not one fraught with such an overwhelming potential liability as to dictate a contrary result, for the class of persons who might foreseeably use this plat is rather narrowly limited, if not exclusively so, to those who deal with the surveyed property as purchasers or lenders. Injury will ordinarily occur only once and to the one person then owning the lot." 250 N.E.2d at 662.

Finally, the court rejected defendant's contention that the five year statute of limitations period began to run when the plat was delivered to the builder who ordered it or, at the latest, from the time the plaintiffs relied on the guarantee. Instead, the court held that the statute of limitations should not begin to run until the misrepresentation had been, or should have been, discovered: "Where the passage of time does little to increase the problems of proof, the ends of justice are served by permitting plaintiff to sue within the statutory period computed from the time at which he knew or should have known of the existence of the right to sue." 250 N.E.2d at 664.

4. WARRANTY OF TITLE

Before paying the purchase price and accepting seller *A*'s deed, buyer *B* will want assurance that *A*'s title is good—that no fraud or formal defect clouds her ownership and that there are no outstanding conditions or encumbrances that might interfere with *B*'s ownership or use of the land. *B* can get this assurance in part by searching *A*'s record title and updating this search down to the moment of closing. If the search discloses a material defect, the covenant of marketable title in the parties' contract will excuse *B* from performing and entitle him to the return of his deposit. But, if the search discloses no such defect *B* will, as required by the contract, accept *A*'s deed and pay the price.

Since some title defects will not be disclosed by a record search, *B* may want additional assurances that *A*'s title is good. One form that these assurances commonly take is covenants—promises—respecting title made by *A* and incorporated in her deed to *B*. Title covenants can be shaped to meet any specific need—that title is good as against a neighbor claiming adverse possession, that a disputed mortgage has been paid off, or that a troublesome relative in fact has no interest in the land. In addition to such custom-crafted covenants are six standard title covenants that have been in common use since at least the seventeenth century in England:

> *Covenant of Seisin*. This covenant is the grantor's promise that she owns at least the interest in land that she is purporting to convey to the grantee. (Thus, if *A*'s deed purports to give *B* complete ownership of Greenacre, but at the time of the conveyance *A* had only a twenty-year lease to Greenacre, the covenant would be breached.)
>
> *Covenant of the Right to Convey*. Here the grantor covenants that she has full power to transfer the interest that the deed purports to convey. This covenant substantially overlaps the cove-

nant of seisin, but provides protection in occasional circumstances where the covenant of seisin does not. For example, the fact that *X* is in adverse possession of Greenacre at the time *A* conveys to *B* does not affect *A*'s ownership of the parcel and, thus, does not breach her covenant of seisin; it would, however, give *B* an action against *A* for breach of the covenant of the right to convey.

Covenant Against Encumbrances. This is the grantor's promise that no outstanding encumbrances affect ownership or use of the land. Mortgages, leases, unpaid taxes and judgment liens are typical encumbrances affecting ownership. Easements, building restrictions and rights in third parties to remove minerals or other resources from the land are typical encumbrances affecting use.

Covenant of Warranty. This is the single most frequently used covenant in the United States. It obligates the grantor to compensate the grantee for any losses when the title conveyed falls short of the title that the deed purports to convey. A covenant of *general warranty* encompasses all defects in title and shortages in the area conveyed, regardless of the reason for the defect or shortage. Covenants of *special warranty* limit the defects covered; they may, for example, cover only those defects that arose while the grantor owned the land.

Covenant of Quiet Enjoyment. Under this covenant, the grantor promises that the grantee's possession will not be disrupted either by the grantor or by anyone with a lawful claim superior to the grantor. (The covenant does not, however, protect against intrusions by trespassers.) Courts in the United States generally treat the covenant for quiet enjoyment as equivalent to the covenant of warranty.

Covenant for Further Assurances. Rarely used in the United States, the covenant for further assurances obligates the grantor to take such further reasonable steps as are necessary to cure defects in the grantee's title. For example, the grantor might be required to obtain the release of an encumbrance or to buy off an adverse possessor. Unlike the covenant of warranty, which gives the grantee damages for the land he has lost, the covenant for further assurances enables the grantee to remain in possession of the land—a particularly valuable right when the land has substantially appreciated in value.

The first three covenants—seisin, right to convey and freedom from encumbrances—are commonly called *present covenants* because they make representations respecting the condition of title at the time the deed is delivered to the grantee. As a consequence, these covenants are breached only if the defect they cover exists at the time of delivery, and the statute of limitations for breach begins to run from that time. The second set of three covenants—warranty, quiet enjoyment and further assurances—are called *future covenants* because they protect against interferences with possession occurring at some future time, and obligate the grantor to take steps to correct the interference at that time. As a consequence, the statute of limitations for their breach begins to run not from the moment of delivery, but rather from the moment at which the grantee or his successor is first evicted from possession.

Deeds sometimes spell out each of the agreed-upon covenants in detail. Many states, however, have eliminated the need for full explication by providing that a deed's use of a single key word or phrase will automatically incorporate specified covenants in the deed unless the deed expressly excludes them. For example, in Alabama use of the word "grant," "bargain" or "sell" will imply covenants of seisin, freedom from encumbrances created by the grantor, and quiet enjoyment. Ala. Code 1975 § 35–4–271.

Brown v. Lober

Supreme Court of Illinois, 1979.
389 N.E.2d 1188.

UNDERWOOD, JUSTICE.

Plaintiffs instituted this action in the Montgomery County circuit court based on an alleged breach of the covenant of seisin in their warranty deed. The trial court held that although there had been a breach of the covenant of seisin, the suit was barred by the 10–year statute of limitations in section 16 of the Limitations Act (Ill. Rev. Stat. 1975, ch. 83, par. 17). Plaintiffs' posttrial motion, which was based on an alleged breach of the covenant of quiet enjoyment, was also denied. A divided Fifth District Appellate Court reversed and remanded. We allowed the defendant's petition for leave to appeal.

The parties submitted an agreed statement of facts which sets forth the relevant history of this controversy. Plaintiffs purchased 80 acres of Montgomery County real estate from William and Faith Bost and received a statutory warranty deed containing no exceptions, dated December 21, 1957. Subsequently, plaintiffs took possession of the land and recorded their deed.

On May 8, 1974, plaintiffs granted a coal option to Consolidated Coal Company (Consolidated) for the coal rights on the 80–acre tract for the sum of $6,000. Approximately two years later, however, plaintiffs "discovered" that they, in fact, owned only a one-third interest in the subsurface coal rights. It is a matter of public record that, in 1947, a prior grantor had reserved a two-thirds interest in the mineral rights on the property. Although plaintiffs had their abstract of title examined in 1958 and 1968 for loan purposes, they contend that until May 4, 1976, they believed that they were the sole owners of the surface and subsurface rights on the 80–acre tract. Upon discovering that a prior grantor had reserved a two-thirds interest in the coal rights, plaintiffs and Consolidated renegotiated their agreement to provide for payment of $2,000 in exchange for a one-third interest in the subsurface coal rights. On May 25, 1976, plaintiffs filed this action against the executor of the estate of Faith Bost, seeking damages in the amount of $4,000.

The deed which plaintiffs received from the Bosts was a general statutory form warranty deed meeting the requirements of section 9 of "An Act concerning conveyances" (Ill. Rev. Stat. 1957, ch. 30, par. 8). That section provides:

> Every deed in substance in the above form, when otherwise duly executed, shall be deemed and held a conveyance in fee simple, to the grantee, his heirs or assigns, with covenants on the part of the grantor, (1) that at the time of the making and delivery of such deed he was lawfully seized of an indefeasible estate in fee simple, in and to the premises therein described, and had good right and full power to convey the same; (2) that the same were then free from all incumbrances; and (3) that he warrants to the grantee, his heirs and assigns, the quiet and peaceable possession of such premises, and will defend the title thereto against all persons who may lawfully claim the same. And such covenants shall be obligatory upon any grantor, his heirs and personal representatives, as fully and with like effect as if written at length in such deed. [Ill. Rev. Stat.1957, ch. 30, par. 8.]

The effect of this provision is that certain covenants of title are implied in every statutory form warranty deed. Subsection 1 contains the covenant of seisin and the covenant of good right to convey. These covenants, which are considered synonymous assure the grantee that the grantor is, at the time of the conveyance, lawfully seized and has the power to convey an estate of the quality and quantity which he professes to convey.

Subsection 2 represents the covenant against incumbrances. An incumbrance is any right to, or interest in, land which may subsist in a third party to the diminution of the value of the estate, but consistent with the passing of the fee by conveyance.

Subsection 3 sets forth the covenant of quiet enjoyment, which is synonymous with the covenant of warranty in Illinois. By this covenant, "the grantor warrants to the grantee, his heirs and assigns, the possession of the premises and that he will defend the title granted by the terms of the deed against persons who may lawfully claim the same, and that such covenant shall be obligatory upon the grantor, his heirs, personal representatives, and assigns." Biwer v. Martin (1920), 294 Ill. 488, 497, 128 N.E. 518, 522.

Plaintiffs' complaint is premised upon the fact that "William Roy Bost and Faith Bost covenanted that they were the owners in fee simple of the above described property at the time of the conveyance to the plaintiffs." While the complaint could be more explicit, it appears that plaintiffs were alleging a cause of action for breach of the covenant of seisin. This court has stated repeatedly that the covenant of seisin is a covenant *in praesenti* and, therefore, if broken at all, is broken at the time of delivery of the deed.

Since the deed was delivered to the plaintiffs on December 21, 1957, any cause of action for breach of the covenant of seisin would have accrued on that date. The trial court held that this cause of action was barred by the statute of limitations. No question is raised as to the applicability of the 10–year statute of limitations (Ill. Rev. Stat. 1975, ch. 83, par. 17). We conclude, therefore, that the cause of action for breach of the covenant of seisin was properly determined by the trial court to be barred by the statute of limitations since plaintiffs did not file their complaint until May 25, 1976, nearly 20 years after their alleged cause of action accrued.

In their post-trial motion, plaintiffs set forth as an additional theory of recovery an alleged breach of the covenant of quiet enjoyment. The trial court, without explanation, denied the motion. The appellate court reversed, holding that the cause of action on the covenant of quiet enjoyment was not barred by the statute of limitations. The appellate court theorized that plaintiffs' cause of action did not accrue until 1976, when plaintiffs discovered that they only had a one-third interest in the subsurface coal rights and renegotiated their contract with the coal company for one-third of the previous contract price. The primary issue before us, therefore, is when, if at all, the plaintiffs' cause of action for breach of the covenant of quiet enjoyment is deemed to have accrued.

This court has stated on numerous occasions that, in contrast to the covenant of seisin, the covenant of warranty or quiet enjoyment is prospective in nature and is breached only when there is an actual or constructive eviction of the covenantee by the paramount titleholder.

The cases are also replete with statements to the effect that the mere existence of paramount title in one other than the covenantee is not sufficient to constitute a breach of the covenant of warranty or quiet enjoyment: "[T]here must be a union of acts of disturbance and lawful title, to constitute a breach of the covenant for quiet enjoyment, or warranty... ." (Barry v. Guild (1888), 126 Ill. 439, 446, 18 N.E. 759, 761.) "[T]here is a general concurrence that something more than the mere existence of a paramount title is necessary to constitute a breach of the covenant of warranty." (Scott v. Kirkendall (1878), 88 Ill. 465, 467.) "A mere want of title is no breach of this covenant. There must not only be a want of title, but there must be an ouster under a paramount title." Moore v. Vail (1855), 17 Ill. 185, 189.

The question is whether plaintiffs have alleged facts sufficient to constitute a constructive eviction. They argue that if a covenantee fails in his effort to sell an interest in land because he discovers that he does not own what his warranty deed purported to convey, he has suffered a constructive eviction and is thereby entitled to bring an action against his grantor for breach of the covenant of quiet enjoyment. We think that the decision of this court in Scott v. Kirkendall (1878), 88 Ill. 465, is controlling on this issue and compels us to reject plaintiffs' argument.

In *Scott*, an action was brought for breach of the covenant of warranty by a grantee who discovered that other parties had paramount title to the land in question. The land was vacant and unoccupied at all relevant times.

This court, in rejecting the grantee's claim that there was a breach of the covenant of quiet enjoyment, quoted the earlier decision in Moore v. Vail (1855), 17 Ill. 185, 191:

> "Until that time, (the taking possession by the owner of the paramount title,) he might peaceably have entered upon and enjoyed the premises, without resistance or molestation, which was all his grantors covenanted he should do. They did not guarantee to him a perfect title, but the possession and enjoyment of the premises." [88 Ill. 465, 468]

Relying on this language in *Moore*, the *Scott* court concluded:

> We do not see but what this fully decides the present case against the appellant. It holds that the mere existence of a paramount title does not constitute a breach of the covenant. That is all there is here. There has been no assertion of the adverse title. The land has always been vacant. Appellant could at any time have taken peaceable possession of it. He has in no way been prevented or hindered from the enjoyment of the possession by any one having a better right. It was but the possession and enjoyment of the premises which was assured to him, and there has been no disturbance or interference in that respect. True, there is a superior title in another, but appellant has never felt "its pressure upon him." [88 Ill. 465, 468–69]

Admittedly, *Scott* dealt with surface rights while the case before us concerns subsurface mineral rights. We are, nevertheless, convinced that the reasoning employed in *Scott* is applicable to the present case. While plaintiffs went into possession of the surface area, they cannot be said to have possessed the subsurface minerals. "Possession of the surface does not carry possession of the minerals.... To possess the mineral estate, one must undertake the actual removal thereof from the ground or do such other act as will apprise the community that such interest is in the exclusive use and enjoyment of the claiming party." Failoni v. Chicago & North Western Ry. Co. (1964), 30 Ill.2d 258, 262, 195 N.E.2d 619, 622.

Since no one has, as yet, undertaken to remove the coal or otherwise manifested a clear intent to exclusively "possess" the mineral estate, it must be concluded that the subsurface estate is "vacant." As in *Scott*, plaintiffs "could at any time have taken peaceable possession of it. [They have] in no way been prevented or hindered from the enjoyment of the possession by any one having a better right." (88 Ill. 465, 468.) Accordingly, until such time as one holding paramount title interferes with plaintiffs' right of possession (*e.g.*, by beginning to mine the coal), there can be no constructive eviction and, therefore, no breach of the covenant of quiet enjoyment.

What plaintiffs are apparently attempting to do on this appeal is to extend the protection afforded by the covenant of quiet enjoyment. However, we decline to expand the historical scope of this covenant to provide a remedy where another of the covenants of title is so clearly applicable. As this court stated in Scott v. Kirkendall (1878), 88 Ill. 465, 469:

> To sustain the present action would be to confound all distinction between the covenant of warranty and that of seizin, or of right to convey. They are not equivalent covenants. An action will lie upon the latter, though there be no disturbance of possession. A defect of title will suffice. Not so with the covenant of warranty, or for quiet enjoyment, as has always been held by the prevailing authority.

The covenant of seisin, unquestionably, was breached when the Bosts delivered the deed to plaintiffs, and plaintiffs then had a cause of action. However, despite the fact that it was a matter of public record that there was a reservation of a two-thirds interest in the mineral rights in the earlier deed, plaintiffs failed to bring an action for breach of the covenant of seisin within the 10–year period following delivery of the deed. The likely explanation is that plaintiffs had not secured a title opinion at the time they purchased the property, and the subsequent examiners for the lenders were not concerned with the mineral rights. Plaintiffs' oversight, however, does not justify us in overruling earlier decisions in order to recognize an otherwise premature cause of action. The mere fact that plaintiffs' original contract with Consolidated had to be modified due to their discovery that paramount title to two-thirds of the subsurface minerals belonged to another is not sufficient to constitute the constructive eviction necessary to a breach of the covenant of quiet enjoyment.

Finally, although plaintiffs also have argued in this court that there was a breach of the covenant against incumbrances entitling them to recovery, we decline to address this issue which was argued for the first time on appeal. It is well settled that questions not raised in the trial court will not be considered by this court on appeal.

Accordingly, the judgment of the appellate court is reversed, and the judgment of the circuit court of Montgomery County is affirmed.

Notes & Questions

1. Was it fair in *Lober* for plaintiffs' action on the covenant of seisin to be barred by the statute of limitations? For plaintiffs' action on the covenant of quiet enjoyment to be dismissed on the ground that the covenant had not yet been breached? What, if anything, could plaintiff have done to precipitate a constructive eviction and hence a breach of the covenant of quiet enjoyment? How would you advise a client caught between one title claim that is not yet ripe and another that is overripe? Can you draft a covenant that would cover the situation that arose in *Lober*?

Should plaintiffs have been barred on the alternative ground that, at the time they accepted delivery they knew or should have known of the outstanding mineral interest? As a general rule, a buyer's actual or constructive knowledge of a title defect or encumbrance will not defeat his action on a covenant that covers the defect or encumbrance. See Jones v. Grow Investment & Mortgage Co., 358 P.2d 909 (Utah 1961) ("The very purpose of the covenant is to protect a grantee against defects and to hold that one can be protected only against unknown defects would be to rob the covenant of most of its value. If from the force of the covenant it is desired to eliminate known defects, or to limit the covenant in any way, it is easy to do so.").

2. **Coverage Limitations.** Because deed covenants protect only against defects in title, there can be no action on the warranty on the ground that the configuration of the property does not comply with zoning requirements. See, e.g., Barnett v. Decatur, 403 S.E.2d 46 (Ga. 1991). Similarly, title covenants do not warrant the physical quality of the premises. See Casenote, 51 Mont. L. Rev. 205 (1990).

3. **Statutory Short Forms and Presumptions.** Covenants of title may be present in a deed even absent express covenant language. Under statutes in some jurisdictions, the use of a seemingly innocuous term in a deed will imply certain covenants of title. See, e.g., Mont. Code Ann. § 70–20–304 ("grant" imports covenant against encumbrances created by grantor). As Brown v. Lober indicates, statutes also may authorize short forms of deeds where the use of one phrase may create covenants. See, e.g., Ohio Rev. Code § 5302.06 ("general warranty covenants" creates covenants of seisin, right to convey, absence of encumbrances, and general warranty). A lawyer must for this reason be familiar with local statutes and presumptions in evaluating deeds. For an excellent discussion of this issue, see Robert G. Natelson, Modern Law of Deeds to Real Property 60–62, 332–37 (1992).

D. Fitness of the Premises

Traditionally, a buyer disappointed with the quality of the property he purchased was out of luck. Under the doctrine of caveat emptor, buyers got what they bought. In recent years, however, buyers have enjoyed some, albeit limited, success in attacking the doctrine of caveat emptor. Some courts have held that sellers and various professionals involved in land transfers have a duty to disclose known and material deficiencies. Other courts have held that land sales include an implied warranty of the fitness of the property. Statutes have also come to the aid of disgruntled buyers. Many of the cases, as you will see, have involved environmental issues—typically pollutants present on the property.

1. Duty to Disclose

Strawn v. Canuso

Supreme Court of New Jersey, 1995.
657 A.2d 420.

O'Hern, J.

Because this case arises from a motion for summary judgment, we must view the facts that may be inferred from the pleadings and discovery in the light most favorable to plaintiffs. In that light, the issue in this case is whether a builder-developer of new homes and the brokers marketing those homes have a duty to disclose to prospective buyers that the homes have been constructed near an abandoned hazardous-waste dump. The Appellate Division held that such a duty exists. We agree and affirm the judgment of the Appellate Division primarily for the reasons stated in its opinion.

The facts of the case are set forth in the reported opinion of the Appellate Division. The case concerns the claims of more than 150 families seeking damages because the new homes that they bought in Voorhees Township, New Jersey, were constructed near a hazardous-waste dump site, known as the Buzby Landfill. The complaint named as defendants John B. Canuso, Sr., and John B. Canuso, Jr., and their companies: Canetic Corporation and Canuso Management Corporation. Fox & Lazo Inc. (Fox & Lazo), the brokerage firm that was the selling agent for the development, was also named as a codefendant.

Plaintiffs base their claims on common-law principles of fraud and negligent misrepresentation, and the New Jersey Consumer Fraud Act, N.J.S.A. 56:8–1 to–66. The twenty-six plaintiff-families filed a class-action lawsuit on behalf of all of the purchasers of the homes in the development sold by defendants. Those families purchased their homes between 1984 and 1987.

The Buzby Landfill consists of two tracts of property, a nineteen-acre portion owned by RCA and a contiguous thirty-seven-acre parcel now owned by Voorhees Township. Those two tracts were the site of a landfill from 1966 to 1978. Although the Buzby Landfill was not licensed to receive liquid-industrial or chemical wastes, large amounts of hazardous materials and chemicals were dumped there. The landfill was also plagued by fires.

Toxic wastes dumped in the Buzby Landfill began to escape because it had no liner or cap. Tests done by the New Jersey Department of Environmental Protection and Energy (DEPE) revealed that leachate was seeping from the landfill into a downstream lake. The DEPE estimated that half of the landfill material was submerged in ground water, thereby contaminating the ground water with hazardous substances. Additional tests indicated the presence of hazardous waste in ground water, in marsh sediments taken from the landfill, and in lakes southeast of the landfill.

RCA installed a system at the landfill to vent excessive levels of methane gas at the site. DEPE's site manager discovered gas leaks in that venting system. Those leaks released contaminants, including benzene and other volatile organic compounds. In 1986, methane gases, which naturally accumulate in landfills, emanated from the dump site. Reports of the federal Environmental Protection Agency (EPA) confirm that residents' complaints about odors and associated physical symptoms are consistent with expected reactions to exposure to gases from the landfill. EPA recommended that the site be considered for a Superfund cleanup.

Plaintiffs allege that the developers knew of the Buzby Landfill before they considered the site for residential development. Plaintiffs contend that although defendants were specifically aware of the existence and hazards of the landfill, they did not disclose those facts to plaintiffs when they bought their homes. A 1980 EPA report warned: "The proposed housing development on land adjacent to the site has all the potential of developing into a future Love Canal if construction is permitted." A copy of the EPA report was in the Canuso defendants' files. Those defendants also met with a DEPE employee to discuss the prospects of building homes near the landfill. (Later reports of regulatory agencies tempered those earlier reports, one of which described any risk as "indeterminate." We also note that such reports may contain hearsay and, therefore, may be inadmissible at trial.)

In addition, one of Fox & Lazo's marketing directors urged his firm and the individual Canuso defendants to disclose the existence of the Buzby Landfill to home buyers. Each refused that request and instead followed a policy of nondisclosure. That policy continued even after early purchasers complained about odors. Defendants' representatives were instructed never to disclose the existence of the Buzby Landfill, even when asked about such conditions. Later, some prospective home buyers, having independently learned about the Buzby Landfill, refused to convert their initial nonbinding deposits into enforceable agreements of sale.

John Canuso, Jr., who personally supervised the sales force, instructed his sales manager to ascertain what information DEPE was providing to people who asked about the landfill. The sales manager spoke with a DEPE representative, who again warned defendants of the problems of building a large development near the landfill. The sales manager repeated in a memorandum the warnings given to her by the DEPE employee and placed the memorandum with related papers in a "hazardous waste" file that the Canuso defendants maintained. John Canuso, Jr. discussed this memorandum with his father, John Canuso, Sr., who refused to disclose to home buyers the proximity of the landfill....

Only gradually has the law of real property assimilated other principles of law. One commentator observed that "the law offers more protection to a person buying a dog leash than it does to the purchaser of a house." John H. Scheid, Jr., Note, Mandatory Disclosure Law: A Statute for Illinois, 27 J. Marshall L. Rev. 155, 160 (1993) (citing Paul G. Haskell, The Case for an Implied Warranty of Quality in Sales of Real Property, 53 Geo. L.J. 633 (1965)). For years, "courts continued to cling to the notion that a seller had no duty whatsoever to disclose anything to the buyer." Ibid. That attitude endured, though the purchase of a home "is almost always the most important transaction [one] will ever undertake." In re Opinion No. 26 of the Committee on the Unauthorized Practice of Law, 128 N.J. 114, 607 A.2d 962 (1995).

The lack of protection afforded to purchasers of real property remained even though principles of commercial marketability had long since been infused into most business transactions.... However, in the field of real property, the doctrine of caveat emptor survived into the first half of the twentieth century. Generally speaking, "the principle of caveat emptor dictates that in the absence of express agreement, a seller is not liable to the buyer or others for the condition of the land existing at the time of transfer." T & E Indus., Inc. v. Safety Light Corp., 123 N.J. 371, 387, 587 A.2d 1249 (1991) (citing Restatement (Second) of Torts, § 352 comment a (1977)). Legal historians will continue to debate whether the doctrine of caveat emptor was the creation of laissez-faire judges or merely a rule of legal convenience reflecting the fact that most land transactions involved vacant land. Professor Morton Horwitz believes that it was the former. Morton J. Horwitz, The Transformation of American Law, 1780–1860, at 102, 107–08 (1977). Professor Cornelius Moynihan has suggested a less sinister origin. He explained that after the Norman Conquest, the King became the owner of all land and transferred some of it to soldiers for payment of military duties and, as such, the grantees were unlikely to complain about any defects. Cornelius J. Moynihan, A Preliminary Survey of the Law of Real Property, 3–4 (1940).

Whatever its origins or purposes, "the rule of caveat emptor has not retained its original vitality. With time, and in differing contexts, we have on many occasions questioned the justification for the rule." *T & E Indus., Inc.*, supra, 123 N.J. at 388. In Michaels v. Brookchester, Inc., 26 N.J. 379, 382, 140 A.2d 199 (1958), this Court recognized that the doctrine of caveat emptor no longer applied to leasehold interests in property. We stated: "This principle [caveat emptor], suitable for the agrarian setting in which it was conceived, lagged behind changes in dwelling habits and economic realities." Ibid. (citing 1 America Law of Property § 3.78 (1952)).

Exceptions to the broad immunity of caveat emptor inevitably developed in the sale of land. In Schipper v. Levitt & Sons, Inc., 44 N.J. 70, 207 A.2d 314 (1965), the Court held that a builder-developer of real estate gave an implied warranty that the structure it built would be properly constructed—a warranty of its habitability. The Court said:

> The arguments advanced by [the builder] in opposition to the application of warranty or strict liability principles appear to us to lack substantial merit. Thus its contention that caveat emptor should be applied and the deed viewed as embodying all the rights and responsibilities of the parties disregards the realities of the situation. Caveat emptor developed when the buyer and seller were in an equal bargaining position and they could readily be expected to protect themselves in the deed. Buyers of mass produced development homes are not on an equal footing with the builder vendors and are no more able to protect themselves in the deed than are automobile purchasers in a position to protect themselves in a bill of sale. [Id. at 91–92.]

In McDonald v. Mianecki, 79 N.J. 275, 298, 398 A.2d 1283 (1979), the Court extended the principles of *Schipper*, supra, 44 N.J. 70, to a small-scale builder of new homes and held that an implied warranty of habitability included a potable water supply. The Court used the occasion to note that the doctrine of caveat emptor "as applied to new houses is an anachronism patently out of harmony with modern home buying practices." Id. at 290 (quoting Humber v. Morton, 426 S.W.2d 554, 562 (Tex. 1968)).

Finally, in Weintraub v. Krobatsch, 64 N.J. 445, 455–56, 317 A.2d 68 (1974), the Court ruled that a seller of real estate had an obligation to disclose the existence of roach infestation unknown to the buyers. The Court noted that in certain circumstances " 'silence may be fraudulent.' " Id. at 449 (quoting Keen v. James, 39 N.J. Eq. 527, 540 (E. & A. 1885)). Further, "relief may be granted to one contractual party where the other suppresses facts," ibid., that he or she "under the circumstances, is bound in conscience and duty to disclose to the other party, and in respect to which he cannot, innocently, be silent." Conover v. Wardell, 22 N.J. Eq. 492, 498–99 (E. & A. 1871).

In short, "caveat emptor, the early rule, no longer prevails in New Jersey." Berman v. Gurwicz, 189 N.J. Super. 89, 93, 458 A.2d 1311 (Ch. Div. 1981) (citing Weintraub, supra, 64 N.J. at 455), aff'd, 189 N.J. Super. 49, 458 A.2d 1289 (App. Div.), certif. denied, 94 N.J. 549 (1983).

Other jurisdictions have limited the doctrine of caveat emptor. In California, when the seller knows of facts materially affecting the value or desirability of property and the seller also knows that such facts are not known to, or within the reach of the diligent attention and observation of the buyer, the seller is subject to a duty to disclose those facts to the buyer. Lingsch v. Savage, 213 Cal. App. 2d 729, 29 Cal. Rptr. 201, 209 (Dist. Ct. App. 1963); see also Easton v. Strassburger, 152 Cal. App. 3d 90, 199 Cal. Rptr. 383 (Ct. App. 1984) (imposing duty on broker to inspect property listed for sale to determine whether settlement or erosion problems are likely to occur and to disclose such information to prospective purchasers). . . .

One author has noted:

> California and Colorado courts have taken the lead in imposing on sellers affirmative obligations to disclose matters materially affecting the value of the property. This information disclosure obligation applies broadly and includes defects in construction and soil conditions as well as matters wholly external to the property that appreciably affect its value. . . .
>
> Sellers generally need disclose only matters of which they have some degree of personal knowledge. Thus, the complicated issue of a seller's knowledge remains a major matter of dispute. Sellers, moreover, need only disclose matters not reasonably ascertainable by the buyer, a limit that denies relief to buyers who should have known the relevant information. Under some formulations of the duty the seller must also know or suspect that the buyer is acting in ignorance. Different jurisdictions limit relief in other ways. Wisconsin, for example, only imposes disclosure duties on professional sellers. [Eric T. Freyfogle, Real Estate Sales and

the New Implied Warranty of Lawful Use, 71 Cornell L. Rev. 1, 25–28 (1985) (footnotes omitted).]

Other jurisdictions have imposed duties on brokers through consumer-protection legislation. See Buzzard v. Bolger, 117 Ill. App. 3d 887, 453 N.E.2d 1129, 73 Ill. Dec. 140 (Ill. App. Ct. 1983) (buyer may sue broker under consumer-fraud and deceptive-trade-practices statutes for broker's misstatement as to condition of premises); Strauss v. Latter and Blum, Inc., 431 So. 2d 9 (La. Ct. App.) (broker liable for nondisclosure under state deceptive-trade-practices statute if defect known to broker), cert. denied, 438 So. 2d 572 (La. 1983); Mongeau v. Boutelle, 10 Mass. App. Ct. 246, 407 N.E.2d 352 (Mass. App. Ct. 1980) (broker's failure to disclose material fact that might influence buyer is actionable under state deceptive-practices statute).

We need not debate the outer limits of the duty to disclose. Some courts have gone well beyond the confines of this case. In Reed v. King, 145 Cal. App. 3d 261, 193 Cal. Rptr. 130 (Ct. App. 1983), the court imposed a duty on the seller to disclose that a property had been the scene of a mass murder several years earlier. And in New York's so-called "poltergeist case," the purchaser argued that the presence of such spirits in his new home was a material element of the sale that should have been disclosed. The court agreed and imposed a duty on the seller to disclose that the property had been haunted. Stambovsky v. Ackley, 169 A.D.2d 254, 572 N.Y.S.2d 672 (App. Div. 1991).[1]

As of 1988, the courts of only California, New Mexico, and Utah had "advanced the law of real estate beyond fraud to simple negligence by establishing an affirmative duty to buyers to investigate the property for material defects." Sarah Waldstein, A Toxic Nightmare on Elm Street: Negligence and the Real Estate Broker's Duty in Selling Previously Contaminated Residential Property, 15 B.C. Envtl. Aff. L. Rev. 547, 551 (1988). Several jurisdictions have responded to such developments with statutory amendments. California and Illinois have adopted mandatory disclosure laws. Cal. Civ. Code §§ 1102 to 1102.15; Ill. Ann. Stat. ch. 765, ¶ 77/1 to /99. Other states have similar laws. See Scheid, supra, 27 J. Marshall L. Rev. at 156, 187. Codification of the limits of disclosure is a difficult task. For example, in California the form in use requires disclosure of whether the seller is aware of "fill (compacted or otherwise) on the property or any portion thereof" or "neighborhood noise problems or other nuisances." Cal. Civ. Code § 1102.6. If this case were to arise in California, an issue would

1. *Stambovsky* and *Reed* involved "stigmatized property," which has been defined as "property psychologically impacted by an event which occurred or was suspected to have occurred on the property, such event being one that has no physical impact of any kind." National Association of Realtors, Study Guide: Stigmatized Property 2 (1990), quoted in Robert M. Morgan, The Expansion of the Duty of Disclosure in Real Estate Transactions: It's Not Just For Sellers Anymore, Fla. B.J., Feb. 1994, at 31. Some states have enacted legislation to provide guidance regarding the types of nonphysical or emotional defects that are material. See, e.g., Fla. Stat. Ann. § 689.25. New Jersey has no such legislation, and we do not address the materiality of such conditions.

be whether an abandoned hazardous-waste site in the neighborhood constitutes a nuisance.

In the absence of such legislation or other regulatory requirements affecting real estate brokers, the question is whether our common-law precedent would require disclosure of off-site conditions that materially affect the value of property. By its favorable citation of California precedent, *Weintraub*, supra, 64 N.J. at 454–55, establishes that a seller of real estate or a broker representing the seller would be liable for nondisclosure of on-site defective conditions if those conditions were known to them and unknown and not readily observable by the buyer. Such conditions, for example, would include radon contamination and a polluted water supply. Whether and to what extent we should extend this duty to off-site conditions depends on an assessment of the various policies that have shaped the development of our law in this area.

As noted, the principal factors shaping the duty to disclose have been the difference in bargaining power between the professional seller of residential real estate and the purchaser of such housing, and the difference in access to information between the seller and the buyer. Those principles guide our decision in this case.

The first factor causes us to limit our holding to professional sellers of residential housing (persons engaged in the business of building or developing residential housing) and the brokers representing them. Neither the reseller of residential real estate nor the seller of commercial property has that same advantage in the bargaining process. Regarding the second factor, professional sellers of residential housing and their brokers enjoy markedly superior access to information. Hence, we believe that it is reasonable to extend to such professionals a similar duty to disclose off-site conditions that materially affect the value or desirability of the property. . . .

[As the New Jersey Superior Court stated in *Berman*, supra, 189 N.J. Super. at 94]

> The fact that no affirmative misrepresentation of a material fact has been made does not bar relief. The suppression of truth, the withholding of the truth when it should be disclosed, is equivalent to the expression of falsehood. The question under those circumstances is whether the failure to volunteer disclosure of certain facts amounts to fraudulent concealment, or, more specifically, whether the defendant is bound in conscience and duty to recognize that the facts so concealed are significant and material and are facts in respect to which he [or she] cannot innocently be silent. Where the circumstances warrant the conclusion that [the seller] is so bound and has such a duty, equity will provide relief.
>
> . . . .

Is the nearby presence of a toxic-waste dump a condition that materially affects the value of property? Surely, Lois Gibbs would have wanted to know that the home she was buying in Niagara Falls, New York, was within one-quarter mile of the abandoned Love Canal site. See Lois M. Gibbs, Love Canal: My Story (1982) (recounting residents' political struggle concerning leaking toxic-chemical dump near their homes). In the case of on-site conditions, courts have imposed affirmative obligations on sellers to disclose information materially affecting the value of property. There is no logical reason why a certain class of sellers and brokers should not disclose off-site matters that materially affect the value of property.

We know that the physical effects of abandoned dump sites are not limited to the confines of the dump. For example, in Ayers v. Township of Jackson, 106 N.J. 557, 525 A.2d 287 (1987), toxic pollutants from a landfill contaminated the water supply of residents of nearby homes. . . .

In short, our precedent and policy offer reliable evidence that the value of property may be materially affected by adjacent or nearby landfills. Professional sellers in southern New Jersey could not help but have been aware of the potential effects of such conditions. In December 1983, the Real Estate Commission wrote to the Camden County Board of Realtors, stating that "because of the potential effects on health, and because of its impact on the value of property, location of property near a hazardous waste site is a bit of information that should be supplied to potential buyers. Difficulties in selling such property should be disclosed to potential sellers." . . .

The duty that we recognize is not unlimited. We do not hold that sellers and brokers have a duty to investigate or disclose transient social conditions in the community that arguably affect the value of property. In the absence of a purchaser communicating specific needs, builders and brokers should not be held to decide whether the changing nature of a neighborhood, the presence of a group home, or the existence of a school in decline are facts material to the transaction. Rather, we root in the land the duty to disclose off-site conditions that are material to the transaction. That duty is consistent with the development of our law and supported by statutory policy.

We note that in some instances the Legislature has required disclosure of information to certain classes of home buyers. See e.g., N.J.S.A. 45:22A–1 to–56. However, we have previously acted in this field absent a specific legislative mandate. The Legislature will often refine the contours of a judicially-imposed duty, as it did with The New Home Warranty and Builders' Registration Act, N.J.S.A. 46:3B–1 to–20.

We hold that a builder-developer of residential real estate or a broker representing it is not only liable to a purchaser for affirmative and intentional misrepresentation, but is also liable for nondisclosure of off-site physical conditions known to it and unknown and not readily observable by the buyer if the existence of those conditions is of sufficient materiality to affect the habitability, use, or enjoyment of the property and, therefore, render the property substantially less desirable or valuable to the objectively reasonable buyer. Whether a matter not disclosed by such a builder or broker is of such materiality, and unknown and unobservable by the buyer, will depend on the facts of each case.

We realize that there is considerable debate regarding the nature and extent of the hazard imposed by the Buzby Landfill. For example, defendants note that the Buzby Landfill has never been on the Superfund list or the New Jersey Priority List both of which delineate toxic landfill sites; that much of the information on which plaintiffs rely postdates their purchase of the property; that Fox & Lazo was involved in only a portion of the sales (those between 1985 and 1986); and that some of the plaintiffs have already sold their homes at a profit. Those and other facets of the case will bear on its final resolution.

Ultimately, a jury will decide whether the presence of a landfill is a factor that materially affects the value of property; whether the presence of a landfill was known by defendants and not known or readily observable by plaintiffs; and whether the presence of a landfill has indeed affected the value of plaintiffs' property. Location is the universal benchmark of the value and desirability of property. Over time the market value of the property will reflect the presence of the landfill. Professional builders and their brokers have a level of sophistication that most home buyers lack. That sophistication enables them better to assess the marketability of properties near conditions such as a landfill, a planned superhighway, or an office complex approved for construction. With that superior knowledge, such sellers have a duty to disclose to home buyers the location of off-site physical conditions that an objectively reasonable and informed buyer would deem material to the transaction, in the sense that the conditions substantially affect the value or desirability of the property....

Notes & Questions

1. A growing number of jurisdictions impose a disclosure obligation on the seller. In the case of a breach of the obligation, buyers can rescind the sales contract or seek damages equal to the reduction in the value of the property attributable to the information that was not disclosed.

2. Why should sellers have a disclosure obligation? *Strawn* emphasizes one of the principal reasons given for a disclosure obligation—the relative access of buyer and seller to pertinent information. Other courts have argued that changing moral standards require abandonment of the traditional nondisclosure, *caveat emptor* rule. See, e.g., Ollerman v. O'Rourke Co., 288 N.W.2d 95 (Wis. 1980).

What is the likely impact of a disclosure rule on a current homeowner's incentive to obtain information about the condition of her property? See Anthony T. Kronman, Mistake, Disclosure, Information, and the Law of Contracts, 7 J. Legal Stud. 1 (1978) (arguing that there will be a disincentive to obtain information if one must disclose it without compensation, but maintaining that information acquired without much cost should be disclosed).

See generally Richard M. Jones, Risk Allocation and the Sale of Defective Used Housing in Ohio—Should Silence Be Golden, 20 Capital U.L. Rev. 215 (1991); Frona M. Powell, The Seller's Duty to Disclose in Sales of Commercial Property, 28 Am. Bus. L.J. 245 (1990).

3. **Extent of Disclosure.** What facts must a seller disclose? There are several dimensions to this question. First, how serious must potential problems be before the buyer has a duty to disclose? The West Virginia Supreme Court has written that a vendor must disclose "defects of conditions which substantially affect the value or habitability of the property." Thacker v. Tyree, 297 S.E.2d 885, 888 (W. Va. 1982). Is this too strict? Does this standard reflect a belief that a seller might not remember lesser problems and that all buyers of used housing should reasonably expect some minor defects? Most courts speak instead in terms of what information would be material to a reasonable person deciding whether to buy the property.

Second, what type of defects must be disclosed? *Strawn* concludes that off-site problems must be revealed if they affect the value of the property being sold. See also Haberstick v. Gundaker Real Estate Co., 921 S.W.2d 104 (Mo. App. 1996) (duty to disclose possible hazardous waste on neighboring land). But see McMullen v. Joldersma, 435 N.W.2d 428 (Mich. App. 1988) (no liability for failure to disclose that a project would divert traffic from the store being sold). For an excellent discussion of the issues raised by offsite environmental contamination, see Serena M. Williams, When Daylight Reveals Neighborhood Nightmares: The Duty of Builders and Developers to Disclose Off–Site Environmental Conditions, 12 J. Nat. Resources & Envtl. L. 1 (1997).

Must information be disclosed that does not concern the physical condition of the property or even the neighborhood, but that might be a source of emotional concern? *Strawn* mentions two famous disclosure cases that involved "stigmatized property"—Stambovsky v. Ackley, 572 N.Y.S.2d 672 (1991), involving a house that was widely reputed to be possessed by poltergeists, and Reed v. King, 193 Cal. Rptr. 130 (Ct. App. 1983), involving a home where a murder had occurred. Should courts be concerned with such issues? Does the court's intervention "permit the camel's nose of unrestrained irrationality admission to the tent." *Reed*, 193 Cal.Rptr. at 132. See also *Stambovsky*, 572 N.Y.S.2d at 678 (Smith, J., dissenting: "if the doctrine of caveat emptor is to be discarded, it should be for a reason more substantive than a poltergeist. The existence of a poltergeist is no more binding upon the defendants than it is upon this court."). A number of jurisdictions have passed statutes relieving sellers from disclosing various nonphysical facts such as prior murders, suicides, or felonies that occurred on the premises or that a prior occupant had AIDS. See, e.g., Cal. Civ. Code § 1710.2 (partially superseding *Reed*); Conn. Gen. Stat. Ann. § 20–329cc; N.M. Ann. Stat. § 47–13–2; Or. Rev. Stat. § 93.277 (1991); Tenn. Code Ann. § 66–5–110. See generally Ronald Benton Brown & Thomas H. Thurlow, III, Buyers Beware: Statutes Shield Real Estate Brokers and Sellers Who Do Not Disclose That Properties Are Psychologically Tainted, 49 Okla. L. Rev. 625 (1996); Paula C. Murray, AIDS, Ghosts, Murder: Must Real Estate Brokers and Sellers Disclose?, 27 Wake Forest L. Rev. 689 (1992).

Must sellers disclose information about permissible land uses—e.g., zoning ordinances or restrictive covenants—that might be of interest to the seller? Most courts hold no, perhaps on the theory that buyers can readily obtain such information. See, e.g., Equity Capital Corp. v. Kreider Transp. Serv. Inc., 967 F.2d 249 (7th Cir. 1992).

4. **Buyer's Disclosure Obligation.** Most courts hold that a buyer has no duty to disclose facts concerning the property's value even if the facts might significantly raise the price that the seller is currently asking for the property. See, e.g., Nussbaum v. Weeks, 263 Cal. Rptr. 360 (Cal. App. 1989) (buyer who was general manager of local water district did not disclose to seller that property was subject to a new water policy that would make it more valuable); Noss v. Abrams, 787 S.W.2d 834 (Mo. App. 1990). In Zaschak v. Traverse Corp. 333 N.W.2d 191 (Mich. App. 1983), the seller of mineral interests asserted that the buyer had failed to tell him of information regarding oil and gas activity in the area that affected the value of the property. The court rejected the lawsuit:

> Plaintiff Robert Zaschak testified by deposition that defendant Faith, in response to questioning regarding the property, told plaintiffs that he was unaware of any oil and gas exploration activity in the area. Because Faith possesses a graduate degree in geology and undoubtedly had information regarding oil and gas exploration activity in the area of plaintiff's land, we have little doubt that Faith could have concealed material facts from plaintiff. However, Michigan law dictates that a prospective purchaser is under no duty to disclose facts or possible opportunities within his knowledge which materially affect the value of the property. Michigan courts have not yet recognized a duty on the part of a vendee to disclose facts relevant to the value of the real estate in question even when specifically asked. We decline to promulgate such a duty on the facts of this case. Although plaintiffs claim that they would not have sold the mineral rights absent Faith's alleged concealment of facts, the record discloses that plaintiffs received what was then the accepted value for the rights, $200 per acre. Moreover, rather than obtain an independent appraisal of the property's mineral potential, plaintiffs relied upon [defendant] Francisco, with whom they have previously settled, who assured them that $200 was the going rate for mineral rights.

Id. at 192–93. Do the arguments for imposing a disclosure duty on sellers also extend to buyers? What are a buyer's and seller's incentives if the buyer has no duty to disclose? If the buyer has a duty to disclose?

5. **Statutory Provisions.** Some state legislation mandates disclosure of various categories of problems by sellers. See, e.g., Cal. Civil Code § 1102 et seq. (requiring specified disclosure statement and providing damages remedy). See Katherin A. Pancak et al., Residential Disclosure Laws: The

Further Demise of Caveat Emptor, 24 Real Est. L.J. 291 (1996); Robert M. Washburn, Residential Real Estate Condition Disclosure Legislation, 44 DePaul L. Rev. 281 (1995). For an excellent critique of the disclosure legislation, see Alan M. Weinberger, Let the Buyer Be Well Informed?—Doubting the Demise of Caveat Emptor, 55 Md. L. Rev. 387 (1996) (arguing that disclosure statutes "constitute a brake on the erosion of the doctrine of caveat emptor".)

A growing number of state statutes attempt to address transfers of property that might be contaminated by hazardous substances. Some states require disclosure of environmental contamination before the land is transferred. See, e.g., Cal. Health & Safety Code §§ 25230(a)(2), 25359.7; Pa. Stat. Ann. tit. 35, § 6018.405. New Jersey's Industrial Site Recovery Act, N.J.S.A. §§ 13:1K–6 et seq., takes a different approach, requiring that before the transfer of an "industrial establishment" (defined as any place of business used for storage, manufacture, or disposal of hazardous waste), the owner must notify the state of the proposed transfer and obtain approval of a declaration that there have been no discharges of hazardous wastes or that any discharges have been removed. If the land is still contaminated, the owner must receive approval of a cleanup plan. Penalties for failure to comply with the Act include the voiding of the sale.

The federal government also requires disclosure of environmental contamination in some limited situations. The federal Residential Lead–Based Paint Hazard Reduction Act of 1992, 42 U.S.C. §§ 4852 et seq., for example, requires a seller of housing built prior to 1978 to provide the buyer with a brochure on lead paint hazards, disclose any known lead paint problems, and give the buyer a one-day opportunity before the buyer becomes obligated under the sales contract to inspect for lead paint conditions.

6. **"As–Is" Clauses.** Most courts hold that clauses in real estate contracts stating that the buyer is acquiring the property "as is" do not bar recovery based on fraud. See, e.g., Stemple v. Dobson, 400 S.E.2d 561 (W. Va. 1990); Weintraub v. Krobatsch, 317 A.2d 68 (N.J. 1974). Some courts have dismissed lawsuits where buyers able to assess the risks of such clauses have freely negotiated them See, e.g., Van Gessel v. Folds, 569 N.E.2d 141 (Ill. App. 1991); Shapiro v. Hu, 233 Cal. Rptr. 470 (Cal. App. 1986). Why would buyers ever waive their right against fraud? Should the courts ever permit such waivers?

2. WARRANTY OF FITNESS

Wawak v. Stewart

Supreme Court of Arkansas, 1970.
449 S.W.2d 922.

GEORGE ROSE SMITH, JUSTICE.

The defendant-appellant Wawak, a house builder, bought a lot in North Little Rock in the course of his business, built a house on it, and sold it to the appellees Stewart for $28,500. The heating and air-conditioning ductwork had been embedded in the ground before the concrete-slab floor was poured above that ductwork. Some months after the Stewarts moved into the house a serious defect manifested itself, in that heavy rains caused water and particles of fill to seep into the ducts and thence through the floor vents into the interior of the house, with consequent damage that need not be described at the moment.

The Stewarts brought this action for damages. The great question in the case, overshadowing all other issues, is whether there is any implied warranty in a contract by which the builder-vendor of a new house sells it to its first purchaser. The trial court sustained the theory of implied warranty and awarded the Stewarts damages of $1,309.

The trial court was right. Twenty years ago one could hardly find any American decision recognizing the existence of an implied warranty in a routine sale of a new dwelling. Both the rapidity and the unanimity with which the courts have recently moved away from the harsh doctrine of caveat emptor in the sale of new houses are amazing, for the law has not traditionally progressed with such speed.

Yet there is nothing really surprising in the modern trend. The contrast between the rules of law applicable to the sale of personal property and those applicable to the sale of real property was so great as to be indefensible. One who bought a chattel as simple as a walking stick or a kitchen mop was entitled to get his money back if the article was not of merchantable quality. But the purchaser of a $50,000 home ordinarily had no remedy even if the foundation proved to be so defective that the structure collapsed into a heap of rubble....

In the past decade six states have recognized an implied warranty—of inhabitability, sound workmanship, or proper construction—in the sale of new houses by vendors who also built the structures. Carpenter v. Donohoe, 388 P.2d 399 (Colo. 1964); Bethlahmy v. Bechtel, 415 P.2d 698 (Idaho 1966); Schipper v. Levitt & Sons, 207 A.2d 314 (N.J. 1965); Waggoner v. Midwestern Dev. Co., 154 N.W.2d 803 (S.D. 1967); Humber v. Morton, 426 S.W.2d 554 (Tex. 1968); House v. Thornton, 457 P.2d 199 (Wash. 1969). The near unanimity of the judges in those cases is noteworthy. Of the 36 justices who made up the six appellate courts, the only dissent noted was that of Justice Griffin in the Texas case, who dissented without opinion.

A few excerpts from those recent opinions will illustrate what seems certain to be the accepted rule of the future. In the *Schipper* case the New Jersey court had this to say:

> The law should be based on current concepts of what is right and just and the judiciary should be alert to the never-ending need for keeping its common law principles abreast of the times. Ancient distinctions which make no sense in today's society and tend to discredit the law should be readily rejected.... We consider

that there are no meaningful distinctions between Levitt's [a large-scale builder-seller] mass production and sale of homes and the mass production and sale of automobiles and that the pertinent overriding considerations are the same. . . .

Caveat emptor developed when the buyer and seller were in an equal bargaining position and they could readily be expected to protect themselves in the deed. Buyers of mass produced development homes are not on an equal footing with the builder vendors and are no more able to protect themselves in the deed than are automobile purchasers in a position to protect themselves in the bill of sale. Levitt expresses the fear of "uncertainty and chaos" if responsibility for defective construction is continued after the builder vendor's delivery of the deed and its loss of control of the premises, but we fail to see why this should be anticipated or why it should materialize any more than in the products liability field where there has been no such result.

A similar point of view was expressed in the *House* case by the Washington Supreme Court:

As between vendor and purchaser, the builder-vendors, even though exercising reasonable care to construct a sound building, had by far the better opportunity to examine the stability of the site and to determine the kind of foundation to install. Although hindsight, it is frequently said, is 20–20 and defendants used reasonable prudence in selecting the site and designing and constructing the building, their position throughout the process of selection, planning and construction was markedly superior to that of their first purchaser-occupant. To borrow an idea from equity, of the innocent parties who suffered, it was the builder-vendor who made the harm possible. If there is a comparative standard of innocence, as well as of culpability, the defendants who built and sold the house were less innocent and more culpable than the wholly innocent and unsuspecting buyer. Thus, the old rule of caveat emptor has little relevance to the sale of a brand-new house by a vendor-builder to a first buyer for purposes of occupancy.

We apprehend it to be the rule that, when a vendor-builder sells a new house to its first intended occupant, he impliedly warrants that the foundations supporting it are firm and secure and that the house is structurally safe for the buyer's intended purpose of living in it. Current literature on the subject overwhelmingly supports this idea of an implied warranty of fitness in the sale of new houses. . . .

As might be expected, we have been presented with the timeworn, threadbare argument that a court is legislating whenever it modifies common-law rules to achieve justice in the light of modern economic and technological advances. That same argument was doubtless made in a famous case that parallels this one: MacPherson v. Buick Motor Co., 111 N.E. 1050 (N.Y. 1916). There the court, with respect to the sale of automobiles, abolished a requirement of privity of contract that was just as firmly embedded in the common law as is the rule that we are now re-examining. Yet the doctrine of the *MacPherson* case is now accepted as commonplace throughout the nation. We have no doubt that the modification of the rule of *caveat emptor* that we are now considering will be accepted with like unanimity within a few years....

[Wawak also] insists that all warranties, express, or implied, were negatived by this paragraph in the offer-and-acceptance agreement that preceded the execution of a warranty deed when the sale was consummated:

> Buyer certifies that he has inspected the property and he is not relying upon any warranties, representations or statements of the Agent or Seller as to age or physical condition of improvements.

Even if we assume that the preliminary contract was not merged in the warranty deed, we think it plain that the quoted paragraph did not exclude an implied warranty with respect to the particular defect now in question, which lay beneath the concrete floor and could not possibly have been discovered by even the most careful inspection. The quoted paragraph does not purport to exclude all warranties. It merely states that he buyer has inspected the property and is not *relying* on any warranties as to the age or physical condition of the improvements. Construing the printed contract against the seller, who evidently prepared it, we hold that the clause applies only to defects that might reasonably have been discovered in the course of an inspection by a purchaser of average experience in such matters....

Nichols v. R.R. Beaufort & Associates, Inc.

Supreme Court of Rhode Island, 1999.
727 A.2d 174.

FLANDERS, JUSTICE.

This case requires us to determine for the first time whether the buyers of a latently defective home can maintain an action against the house builder—with whom they lack any contractual privity—for the builder's alleged breach of implied warranties of habitability and workmanlike quality....

In 1983, Beaufort built the Nichols' home on Kimberly Lane in Cranston and immediately sold it to his cousin, Debra Cronin, and her husband (the Cronins). Within two to three months after purchasing their home, the Cronins noticed large cracks in the cement floor of the garage. Beaufort described the cracks as "pretty good size[d]," "larger than normal," and "larger than what would be acceptable" for industry standards. Beaufort attempted to correct this problem by pouring a new garage floor in late 1983.

Approximately a year and a half later, in June 1985, the Nichols purchased the property from the Cronins and thereafter built a 16′ × 24′ addition to the existing house. The record is silent concerning whether the Cronins informed the Nichols about the garage-floor cracks. Moreover, it fails to indicate whether the Nichols conducted any pre-purchase inspection of the house or whether such an inspection would have revealed the defects about which the Nichols now complain. In any event, in 1988, some three years after the purchase of the house, the garage floor caved in. Subsequently, in 1991, Mr. Nichols noticed cracks in the walls of the addition, the kitchen, and the garage. At this point, the Nichols hired Geisser Engineering Corporation (Geisser) to investigate these problems. They soon learned that, according to Geisser, Beaufort had constructed the home's foundation on unstable soil containing voids and organic materials that had decomposed over time. These voids eventually subsided, causing the walls in the various parts of the house to crack and the garage floor to collapse.

In February 1994, the Nichols filed this action in Superior Court charging Beaufort with negligent construction, breach of implied warranties, and negligent violation of certain building-code provisions when he built the house in 1983. . . .

The Nichols argue that under the circumstances of this case, the implied warranties of habitability and workmanlike quality that the law imposes upon a builder-vendor in connection with the sale of a new home should extend to protect subsequent purchasers of that home. In Padula v. J. J. Deb–Cin Homes, Inc., 298 A.2d 529, 531 (R.I. 1973), we held that when a builder-vendor sells a new house or one that is under construction, "he [or she] implicitly warrants that the construction has been or will be done in a workmanlike manner and that the dwelling will be reasonably fit for human habitation." Thereafter, we extended the application of these implied warranties to a situation where a builder-vendor first created a one-year intervening tenancy and then sold what could have been characterized as a "used" house to the plaintiff-purchaser. See Casavant v. Campopiano, 327 A.2d 831 (R.I. 1974). We determined that, notwithstanding the intervening tenancy, the house was still relatively "new" and that the one-year tenancy "was [not] of such [an] extended duration as to make an application of the [implied] warranties unreasonable." Id. at 833.

The thrust of the above-cited cases was to afford protection to new home buyers from any latently defective work and possible overreaching by knowledgeable builder-vendors. However, we refused to extend the application of these implied warranties to protect used-home buyers in a suit against a vendor who was not also the builder of the house. See Sousa v. Albino, 388 A.2d 804 (R.I. 1978). There, the Court reasoned as follows:

> The applicability of the implied warranty is based upon the premise that, with respect to the sale of new homes, the purchaser has little choice but to rely upon the integrity and professional competence of the builder-vendor. The public interest dictates that if the construction of a new house is defective, its repair cost should be borne by the responsible builder-vendor who created the

> defect and is in a better economic position to bear the loss, rather than by the ordinary purchaser who justifiably relied upon the builder's skill. . . .
>
> On the resale of used housing the vendor usually has no greater skill relevant to determining the quality of a house than the purchaser. . . .
>
> In order for [the] plaintiffs to successfully invoke the doctrine, they should allege that the house, in question, is new and that it was purchased from a builder-vendor.

Id. at 805–06. The Nichols assert that the principles enunciated in Padula and Casavant should apply here and that Sousa is distinguishable because, unlike the situation in that case, the Nichols are suing only the original builder and are not trying to hold a non-builder vendor liable for the latent defects in the house.

Recently, in answering a certified question from the United States District Court for the District of Rhode Island, this Court affirmed the need for contractual privity in a commercial setting. See Boston Investment Property #1 State v. E.W. Burman, Inc., 658 A.2d 515 (R.I. 1995) (*Burman*). In *Burman*, the plaintiff was the second owner of a commercial property known as One State Street. The plaintiff claimed that the building on the property had developed leaky windows and that its parking lot suffered from erosion problems. In addition to suing the original owner and vendor for breach of contract and breach of express and implied warranties, the plaintiff also sued the builder, E.W. Burman, Inc., for negligence. Relying on our reasoning in Hydro–Manufacturing., Inc. v. Kayser–Roth Corp., 640 A.2d 950 (R.I. 1994) (addressing risk allocation in commercial real-estate transactions), we noted that the plaintiff, a sophisticated commercial buyer of real estate, had the option to inspect the property and to investigate any possible defects before it decided to close on such a purchase, thereby enabling it to negotiate a fair price. As a result, we concluded as follows: "An extension of tort liability for economic damages to subsequent purchases of commercial property is unwarranted. In the case of sophisticated commercial entities in the commercial real estate market, contract law is the proper device to allocate economic risk." *Burman*, 658 A.2d at 518. Accordingly, in *Burman*, we held that in the absence of any privity of contract with the builder, a subsequent purchaser of a commercial building in Rhode Island was not entitled to recover economic damages resulting from the general contractor's alleged negligence in constructing the building.

Here, however, the Nichols argue that *Burman* is distinguishable because it involved a commercial real-estate transaction between sophisticated business entities rather than, as in this situation, a purchase by consumers of residential housing. They argue that this Court would not have reached the same result in *Burman* if the plaintiff there had been a consumer who had purchased a home containing latent defects. They point out that in reaching our decision, we were careful to anticipate this distinction when we noted "that it is appropriate for sophisticated commercial entities to utilize contract law to protect themselves from economic damages." *Burman*, 658 A.2d at 517. n3.

Another case that sheds more light on this situation is Davis v. New England Pest Control Co., 576 A.2d 1240 (R.I. 1990). There, home buyers sued a pest-exterminating company hired by the sellers for negligently inspecting their home. Although reversing on other grounds, we upheld the Superior Court's ruling that an implied contractual obligation ran from the pest-exterminating company to the home buyers. We reasoned that when one party for valuable consideration engages another to act for the benefit of a foreseeable third party, that third party may maintain an action for breach of an implied contractual obligation to perform the job in a workmanlike manner. Indeed, we noted that: "as a general rule there is implied in every contract for work or services a duty to perform it skillfully, carefully, and diligently and in a workmanlike manner, and a negligent failure to observe any of those conditions is a tort as well as a breach of contract." Id. at 1242. Here, the Nichols argue that, like the plaintiffs in *Davis* they too were foreseeable beneficiaries of the original contract and the implied warranties that arose from that contract. Although Beaufort never knew their identity nor communicated with them in any way, the Nichols claim that Beaufort should have foreseen that the Cronins were not likely to be the home's only owners during the ten-year-statute-of-repose period. Accordingly, the Nichols argue that, like the plaintiffs in *Davis* they ought to be able to maintain an action for breach of implied warranties against the responsible home contractor despite their lack of contractual privity with this defendant. For the reasons discussed below, we are persuaded that the absence of contractual privity in these circumstances should not bar the Nichols' claims for breach of implied warranties.

Joining those "numerous jurisdictions [that] have now found privity of contract unnecessary for [maintaining a lawsuit based upon an] implied warranty," Lempke v. Dagenais, 547 A.2d 290, 293 (N.H. 1988), this Court now holds that "the privity requirement should be abandoned in suits by subsequent purchasers [of homes] against a builder or contractor for breach of an implied warranty of good workmanship for latent defects." Id. at 294. Our reasons for doing so are as follows:

(1) "To require privity between the contractor and the home owner in such a situation would defeat the purpose of the implied warranty of good workmanship and could leave innocent homeowners without a remedy. . . ." Id. (quoting Aronsohn v. Mandara, 484 A.2d 675, 680 (N.J. 1984)).

(2) "The essence of implied warranty is to protect innocent buyers. As such, this principle, which protects first purchasers . . . is equally applicable to subsequent purchasers." *Lempke*, 547 A.2d at 294.

(3) "No reason has been presented to us whereby the original owner should have the benefits of an implied warranty [for] recovery . . . and the next owner should not simply because there has been a transfer. Such intervening sales, standing by themselves, should not, by any standard of reasonableness, effect an end to an implied warranty or, in that matter, a right of recovery on any other ground, upon manifestation of a defect. The

builder always has available the defense that the defects are not attributable to him." Id. (quoting Moxley v. Laramie Builders, Inc., 600 P.2d 733, 736 (Wyo. 1979)).

(4) "Common experience teaches that latent defects in a house will not manifest themselves for a considerable period of time . . . after the original purchaser has sold the property to a subsequent unsuspecting buyer." *Lempke*, 547 A.2d at 295 (quoting Terlinde v. Neely, 275 S.C. 395, 271 S.E.2d 768, 769 (S.C. 1980)).

(5) "We are an increasingly mobile people; a builder-vendor should know that a house he builds might be resold within a relatively short period of time and should not expect that the warranty will be limited by the number of days that the original owner holds onto the property." *Lempke*, 547 A.2d at 295 (quoting Redarowicz v. Ohlendorf, 441 N.E.2d 324, 330 (Ill. 1982)).

(6) "Like an initial buyer, the subsequent purchaser has little opportunity to inspect and little experience and knowledge about construction." *Lempke*, 547 A.2d at 295. "Consumer protection demands that those who buy homes are entitled to rely on the skill of a builder and that the house is constructed so as to be reasonably fit for its intended use." Id. (quoting *Moxley*, 600 P.2d at 735).

(7) Pursuant to *Padula* and *Boghossian*, home builders and contractors are already under a legal duty in this jurisdiction to construct habitable houses in a workmanlike manner. Moreover, following a new home's construction and sale, it is foreseeable that there may be more than one set of owners and inhabitants of the house during the ten-year-statute-of-repose period for the filing of tort claims against the builder. Given the existing contractual and implied-warranty liability of home builders under *Padula* and *Boghossian* to the home's original owners—a liability that can extend well beyond the expiration of the ten-year-statute-of-repose period for the filing of tort claims—allowing subsequent owners to maintain a similar cause of action (subject to their satisfaction of reasonable time limitations for doing so) will not drastically enlarge this basic obligation of the home builder. Thus, it is not unfair to the builder/contractor to extend the implied warranties of habitability and workmanlike quality to subsequent purchasers like the Nichols who not only discover latent defects in their home within ten years of the home's substantial completion, but who then file suit thereon within a reasonable period of time after discovering such defects.

(8) "Interposing a first purchaser as a bar to recovery 'might encourage sham first sales to insulate builders from liability.' " *Lempke*, 547 A.2d at 295 (citing Richards v. Powercraft Homes, Inc., 678 P.2d 427, 430 (Ariz. 1984)). Here, Beaufort sold the house initially to the Cronins, who in turn resold it to the Nichols less than two years after Beaufort completed the home's construction. The mere fact that this initial transfer was a related-party sale (Mrs. Cronin was a first cousin of Beaufort) does not necessarily destroy its arms-length nature. But if implied warranties ended after the first sale, then unscrupulous builder-vendors, without much difficulty,

could arrange for straw buyers or for transient, related-party sales as a means to limit their liability.

(9) "By virtue of superior knowledge, skill, and experience in the construction of houses, a builder-vendor is generally better positioned than the purchaser to ... evaluate and guard against the financial risk posed by a [latent defect]. . . ." *Lempke*, 547 A.2d at 295 (quoting George v. Veach, 313 S.E.2d 920, 923 (N.C. App. 1984)). Thus, allowing subsequent owners to sue builder-vendors recognizes that, as a society, we have evolved from an era when *caveat emptor* ruled the legal world to one where, at least in consumer transactions, *caveat venditor* is the heir apparent to this crown.

(10) "Not only do policy and economic reasons convince us that a privity requirement in this situation is unwarranted, but analogous situations show us the soundness of this extension. Public policy has compelled a change in the law of personal property and goods, as witnessed by the adoption of the UCC. The logic which compelled this change is equally persuasive for real property." *Lempke*, 547 A.2d at 295. . . .

In allowing purchasers who are not in privity with the builder-vendor of a house to hold such a party responsible for economic damages caused by the home's latent defects, we recognize that some limitations must be imposed on the scope of this otherwise potentially unlimited liability. "As with any rule, there must be built-in limitations, which in this case would act as a barrier to the possibility of unlimited liability. Therefore, our extension of the implied warranty of workmanlike quality is not unlimited; it does not force the builder to act as an insurer, in all respects, to a subsequent purchaser." *Lempke*, 547 A.2d at 297. Thus, we limit the extension of implied-warranty liability to home buyers who are not in privity with the builder to latent defects existing at the time of the home's original sale that were not known to or were not reasonably discoverable by the buyer when he or she purchased the house, and "which become manifest after the subsequent owner's purchase and which were not discoverable had a reasonable inspection of the structure been made prior to the purchase." Id. (quoting Richards, 678 P.2d at 430).

Second, to avoid exposing builders, architects, engineers, and other home contractors to the specter of a virtually unlimited period of potential liability, we restrict the coverage of the implied warranties of habitability and of workmanlike quality to those latent defects that subsequent owners discover within a reasonable period of time after these home contractors have substantially completed their work on the improvement at issue. Informed by the ten-year repose period established by § 9–1–29 for tort claims, we deem a period of ten years after substantial completion of the improvement in question to be a reasonable period of time within which subsequent owners should be able to discover any latent defects in the home for their implied-warranty claims to be actionable. In this case, the Nichols discovered the latent defects during the ten-year period after Beaufort had substantially completed the construction of the house. Although "the length of time for latent defects to surface, so as to place subsequent purchasers on equal footing should be controlled by the standard of reasonableness and not an arbitrary time limit created by the court,'' id. (quoting *Terlinde*, 271 S.E.2d at 769), we do not believe it would be arbitrary to hold the builder responsible for latent defects that subsequent buyers of the home discover within the ten-year-statute-of-repose period for tort claims and then sue upon thereafter within a reasonable time frame. Given the existing three-year statute of limitations for malpractice suits filed against, inter alia, real-estate agents, see § 9–1–14.1, and given the close similarities between such malpractice claims and those alleging a breach of the builder's implied warranties of habitability and workmanlike quality, we are of the opinion that such claims have been timely filed when subsequent owners initiate breach-of-implied-warranty claims, as here, within three years of the date when they discover any latent defects or within three years of the date when, in the exercise of due diligence, they should have discovered such defects.

Finally, the subsequent-owner plaintiffs have the burden to show that the builder's faulty workmanship caused any latent defects. Such claims also shall be subject to whatever other defenses the builder may have, including, for example, ''that the defects were not attributable to him, that they are the result of age or ordinary wear and tear, or that previous owners have made substantial changes.'' *Lempke*, 547 A.2d at 297 (quoting *Richards*, 678 P.2d at 430).

Notes & Questions

1. **Incidence of Housing Defects.** A somewhat dated government study, based on a sample of new housing built in 1977 and 1978, revealed that 79 percent of new housing buyers had at least one complaint about housing quality. Seventy-five percent of the problems were discovered in the first six months of ownership, and 93 percent in the first year. On receiving complaints, builders were most ready to correct defects in plumbing, cooling and heating systems, in major appliances and in interior electrical work. Builders were less willing to correct problems with yard drainage, roofs, foundations and driveways and improperly fitted doors and windows. Seven percent of buyers reported that they consulted a lawyer about the problem and four percent retained lawyers. U.S. Dept. of Housing & Urban Development and Federal Trade Commission, A Survey of Homeowner Experience with New Residential Housing Construction iii-viii, 10–29 (1980).

2. **Warranty of New Housing.** The implied warranty of fitness represents the main avenue today for buyers of defective housing to recover from their builder-sellers. With roots in both contract and tort theory, the warranty of fitness has made substantial inroads on *caveat emptor*, giving disappointed buyers an easier and more complete remedy than fraud or negligence. Colorado became the first state to recognize an implied an implied warranty in Carpenter v. Donohoe, 388 P.2d 399 (Colo. 1964). By 1980, over 40 states had implied a warranty into new housing sales, variously calling it a warranty of ''quality,'' ''habitability,'' ''good work-

manship," or "fitness." See Peter J. Shedd, The Implied Warranty of Habitability: New Implications, New Applications, 8 Real Estate L.J. 291 (1980).

For an excellent analysis of the history and doctrinal implications of seller liability for housing defects, see E.G. Roberts, The Case of the Unwary Home Buyer: The Housing Merchant Did It, 52 Cornell L.Q. 835 (1967).

3. **What is the Standard?** What must a plaintiff show to establish a breach of the implied warranty? Most appellate courts have been relatively unspecific, leaving the issue up to lower courts and juries. In Samuelson v. A.A. Quality Const., Inc., 749 P.2d 73 (Mont. 1988), the Montana Supreme Court adopted an unusually strict standard, limiting the warranty to "defects which are so substantial as reasonably to preclude the use of the dwelling as a residence." In *Samuelson,* the court concluded that the warranty had not been breached even though water seepage had affected a guest bedroom, storage area, recreation area, and crawl space, necessitating removal of furniture, carpeting, and sheetrock and the use of floor heaters and pumps. The buyers had to pay more than $11,000 to remedy the problem, even though the house cost only $155,000. What justification is there for taking such a cramped view of the implied warranty?

4. **Disclaimers.** Most courts that have implied a warranty of fitness into the sale of new housing have also suggested that sellers and buyers can contract around the implied warranty. Yet there is a general disposition to construe disclaimers and "as is" provisions against builder-sellers. *Wawak* is typical in holding that, strictly construed, the disclaimer clause did not exclude an implied warranty with respect to latent defects—"the clause applies only to defects that might reasonably have been discovered in the course of an inspection made by a purchaser of average experience in such matters." Other courts have reached the same result by holding that, to be enforced, a disclaimer clause must be expressed in clear and unambiguous language and that seller has the burden of proving that buyer knowingly made the disclaimer. See, e.g., Crowder v. Vandendeale, 564 S.W.2d 879, 881 n.4 (Mo. 1978).

Some courts have held that any disclaimer is void as against public policy. See, e.g., Buchanan v. Scottsdale Envtl. Constr. & Dev. Co., 787 P.2d 1081 (Ariz. App. 1989). See also Ind. Code § 34–4–20.5 (builder-vendor can disclaim implied warranties, but only by providing specified express warranties including a 10–year warranty against any defects in the structure).

For discussion of the law on disclaimers, see Frona Powell, Disclaimers of Implied Warranty in the Sale of New Homes, 34 Vill. L. Rev. 1123 (1989); David L. Abney, Disclaiming the Implied Real Estate Common–Law Warranties, 17 Real. Est. L.J. 141 (1988).

5. **Warranty of Used Housing.** Most residential sales involve used rather than new housing. Should buyers of used housing be able to recover for latent defects against either the original builder or their immediate seller? Suits against the original builder were initially unsuccessful. Tort

actions based on a strict liability theory were usually fruitless because most courts required a showing of personal injury, not just economic damages. Warranty actions brought against homebuilders by second and subsequent buyers were usually dismissed for lack of privity.

The barriers to recovery by distant buyers against the original builder, however, are breaking down. Product liability law's requirement that plaintiff demonstrate personal injury in order to recover was the first barrier to crumble. In Kriegler v. Eichler Homes, Inc., 74 Cal. Rptr. 749 (Cal. App. 1969), the court imposed strict liability for defects causing economic injury. Eichler's faulty installation of a radiant heating system in a house that plaintiff had bought from its original buyer eventually caused the system to fail, reducing the value of the house by over $5,000. Holding for plaintiff homeowners, the court noted that "at the time of the installation of the heating system in the Kriegler home," the building industry "had knowledge of methods by which the injury could reasonably have been avoided." A short while later, another California court relied on *Eichler* to impose strict liability for damages to a house and lot caused by the improper compaction of fill and other errors in the developer's preparation of the soil. Avner v. Longridge Estates, 77 Cal. Rptr. 633 (Cal. App. 1969).

More recently, as *Nichols* illustrates, the privity bar to warranty actions has begun to give way. The Indiana Supreme Court was the first court to extend the warranty to subsequent purchasers. See Barnes v. Mac Brown & Co., 342 N.E.2d 619 (Ind. 1976). Over a dozen states have since followed suit. See Sean M. O'Brien, Caveat Venditor: A Case for Granting Subsequent Purchasers a Cause of Action Against Builder–Vendors for Latent Defects in the Home, 20 J. Corp. L. 525, 534 (1995); Robert L. Cherry, Jr., Builder Liability for Used Home Defects, 18 Real Est. L.J. 115, 138 (1989). Some courts, however, have refused to extend the warranty to permit subsequent purchasers to sue the original builder. See, e.g., Haygood v. Burl Pounders Realty, Inc., 571 So. 2d 1086 (Ala. 1990).

Are there any good reasons for *not* extending the warranty to subsequent purchasers? Can a developer protect herself against warranty liability to second and successive purchasers by obtaining from her immediate buyer an express disclaimer of any implied warranties? How long should the implied warranty last? Although *Nichols* establishes a set period of time, most courts have held that the implied warranty lasts for a "reasonable period of time." See, e.g., Blagg v. Fred Hunt Co., Inc., 612 S.W.2d 321, 322 (Ark. 1981). Is indeterminate liability likely to induce developers to build houses that are more durable—and probably more expensive—than their immediate buyers might desire?

6. **Commercial Transactions.** As discussed in *Nichols*, the Rhode Island Supreme Court has held that privity is necessary in commercial transactions. See Boston Investment Property #1 State v. E.W. Burman, Inc., 658 A.2d 515 (R.I. 1995). Is *Burman* convincing in its arguments for requiring privity in commercial transactions? Should a warranty of fitness apply even in the acquisition of new commercial buildings?

7. **Actions Against Other Parties.** A homeowner who has discovered latent defects in his residence may try to seek relief not only against the original builder, but also against the seller, in cases where the seller is not the original builder, and against others involved in the construction of the house such as lenders or architects. To date, however, such actions have not met with much success.

Sellers. As suggested in *Nichols*, most courts have refused to hold that sales from one homeowner to another include an implied warranty of fitness. See, e.g., Stevens v. Bouchard, 532 A.2d 1028 (Me. 1987); Sousa v. Albino, 388 A.2d 804 (R.I. 1978). Why should warranties only be implied against builders and not other sellers?

Courts occasionally stretch the definition of who is a builder. In Callander v. Sheridan, 546 N.E.2d 850 (Ind. App. 1989), a homeowner who was not a professional builder acted as his own general contractor in building his house, obtaining and modifying plans, hiring and supervising subcontractors, and buying construction materials. The court held that his subsequent sale of the house included an implied warranty. "Apparently [the original homeowner] felt he was qualified to act as a general contractor. Since he undertook this responsibility he must also accept the attached liability of a builder-vendor to a subsequent buyer." Do the reasons that *Wawak* and *Nichols* give for an implied warranty apply in this situation? Compare Oliver v. Superior Court, 259 Cal. Rptr. 160 (Cal. App. 1989) (holding that a person who built only two homes was not a builder for purposes of strict liability recovery for defective housing).

Lenders. Although actions against lenders have generally been unavailing, buyers enjoy occasional success where the lender has played a significant role in construction of the residence. For example, in Connor v. Great Western Savings & Loan Association, 447 P.2d 609, 617 (Cal. 1968), a lender that had not only financed a housing development, but also exercised substantial control over its construction and design, was held liable to homebuyers for damages resulting from faulty foundations: "privity of contract is not necessary to establish the existence of a duty to exercise ordinary care not to injure another, but such duty may arise out of a voluntarily assumed relationship if public policy dictates the existence of such a duty." *Connor* has since been substantially limited by statute in California (see Cal. Civ. Code § 3434) and has been rejected or distinguished in other states. See, e.g., Ex parte Farmers Exchange Bank, 783 So. 2d 24 (Ala. 2000) (no liability for failure to disclose termite problem, even though it was alleged that bank prepared legal documents in the transaction, told borrower that she did not need a lawyer, and gave borrower the termite certificate but not the underlying report disclosing the damage).

Architects. Architects have only recently been made liable to third parties injured as a consequence of negligently prepared plans. Until the middle 1950's the general rule was that an architect's liability to individuals other than his client evaporated at the moment the client accepted the completed building. There were early exceptions to the rule—for willful negligence and latent, dangerous conditions—but the rule itself did not begin to collapse until the 1950's. Architects are now widely held liable for design defects ranging from soil and foundation failures to improper windows, insulation and roofing. For the question of whether privity is necessary, compare Beachwalk Villas Condominium Ass'n v. Martin, 406 S.E.2d 372 (S.C. 1991) (homeowner association can assert negligence action against architect despite absence of privity) with Floor Craft Floor Covering, Inc. v. Parma Community Gen. Hosp. Ass'n, 560 N.E.2d 206 (Ohio 1990) (contractor cannot sue architect in absence of privity).

8. **Statutory Warranties.** State warranty legislation ranges from statutes like Maryland's Code of Real Property §§ 10–201 et seq., and New York's General Business Law § 777, which follow the general contours of the common law implied warranty, to New Jersey's far more ambitious New Home Warranty and Builder's Registration Act, N.J. Stat. Ann. § 46:3B–1 et seq.

The Maryland statute implies into sales of improved residential real property a warranty that the improvement (defined as a newly constructed private dwelling unit), is habitable, free from faulty materials and constructed according to sound engineering standards in a workmanlike manner. The warranty lasts for one year after closing and excludes any defect that inspection by a reasonably diligent first buyer would have disclosed. The warranty may be waived or modified only through a writing signed by the purchaser that specifically describes the warranty waived and the terms of the new agreement. The statute implies a warranty of fitness for a particular purpose, and also provides that an express warranty is created by a written affirmation of fact or promise, a written description of the improvement, or a sample model that is part of the basis of the bargain.

The New York statute makes the seller liable for one year for failure to build in a "skillful manner," for two years for defects in major systems (e.g., heat and electrical), and for six years for certain specified "material defects." See Amy L. McDaniel, The New York Housing Merchant Warranty Statute: Analysis and Proposals, 75 Cornell L. Rev. 754 (1990).

The New Jersey statute directs the Commissioner of the Department of Community Affairs to prescribe home warranties incorporating quality standards for construction materials and methods. The warranty's duration will depend on its subject matter—one year for defects caused by a specified class of faulty installation of plumbing, electrical, heating and cooling systems, and ten years for major construction defects including damages due to soil subsidence. The builder's liability extends not only to the initial buyer but also to any subsequent buyer whose claim arises during the applicable warranty period. The ceiling on liability is the purchase price of the home in the first good faith sale.

A builder must register with the Department to build houses in New Jersey. One condition of registration is that the builder participate in a warranty security fund, established by the Act, or an approved alternative fund. The fund provides a back-up source of compensation when fund participants have not themselves made good on valid homeowner claims. Before making a claim against the fund, a homeowner must notify the builder of the defects and allow a reasonable time for their repair. Once a claim is made against the fund, it is reviewed through a conciliation or arbitration procedure administered by the Department. If a defect is found, the builder is ordered to correct it and, failing that, the owner is allowed to recover from the fund. While the Act does not preempt private law remedies, it does require the homeowner to elect between statutory and common law relief.

E. THE RISK OF ENVIRONMENTAL LIABILITY

The growth of environmental laws and regulations over the last several decades has exposed participants in real estate transactions to potentially sizable liability. This new source of legal risk substantially affects the way buyers, sellers, lenders, brokers, and others do business. Although participants in commercial property transactions are at the greatest risk, even participants in residential transactions must be aware of the issues.

Of the many environmental regulations that touch real estate transactions, the key statute is the federal Comprehensive Environmental Response, Compensation, and Liability Act, 42 U.S.C. §§ 9601 et seq., commonly referred to as "CERCLA" or "Superfund." Congress passed CERCLA in 1980 following national publicity about Love Canal. In the mid–20th century, Hooker Chemical and Plastics Corporation had dumped a variety of hazardous chemicals, including carcinogens, at a 16–acre site near Niagara Falls, New York. After covering the chemicals with a layer of clay, Hooker sold the site to the Niagara Falls Board of Education for one dollar. After a school and scores of homes were built on the site, heavy rains in 1978 led a toxic brew to seep into the basements of a number of homes. The area was evacuated, homes were demolished, and Congress began debating how to deal with the hundreds of sites around the country like Love Canal that posed potential health hazards to nearby residents.

CERCLA established a superfund of $1.6 billion to help pay for the cleanup of such sites. Under the statute, the federal Environmental Protection Agency ("EPA") can use the superfund to *remove* hazardous wastes from a site and then *remediate* any remaining contamination. Although EPA can engage in a removal action on any site that it believes poses an imminent threat to health or the environment, it must evaluate and place sites on the *National Priority List* ("NPL") before engaging in remediation. Today there are over 1400 sites on the NPL.

Congress recognized that the superfund would not be sufficient to clean up all sites. Nor did Congress believe that it was fair to impose the cleanup burden on the general taxpayer. Section 107 of CERCLA therefore authorizes EPA to seek reimbursement for cleanup costs from four categories of *potentially responsible parties* ("PRPs"):

(1) current owners and operators of the sites,

(2) owners and operators of the sites at the time hazardous substances were left at them,

(3) persons who arranged for the disposal or treatment of the hazardous substances (i.e., the generators of the hazardous substances), and

(4) transporters who chose to take the hazardous substances to the site.

For purposes of real estate transactions, the main cause of concern is the first category. Because current owners are liable, anyone purchasing a site at which hazardous waste might be found runs the risk of being held liable for cleanup expenses. Moreover, negligence, intent, and comparative fault are irrelevant in determining CERCLA liability. A current owner may be held strictly liable even though the owner had no role in the discharge, did not benefit from it, and did not own the land at the time the discharge occurred. Liability under CERCLA also is generally joint and several. A current landowner therefore may be held liable for the full cost of a cleanup unless the owner meets the difficult burden of showing that the harm is divisible or is successful in suing other PRPs for contribution.

The potential liability can be staggeringly large. According to the Environmental Protection Agency, the cost of a CERCLA cleanup through 1986 averaged approximately $14 million per site. See 52 Fed. Reg. 2495 (Jan. 22, 1987), discussed in Mark P. Fitzsimmons & Jeffrey K. Sherwood, The Real Estate Lawyer's Primer (And More) to Superfund: The Environmental Hazards of Real Estate Transactions, 22 Real Prop. Prob. & Tr. J. 765, 770 (1987).

To protect purchasers with no culpability whatsoever for the contamination, Congress amended CERCLA in 1986 to provide an *innocent purchaser defense*. As discussed in the following case, the innocent purchaser defense is a specific application of a more general defense for defendants who can show that the release of hazardous substances was entirely the result of the acts of third parties.

United States v. A & N Cleaners

United States District Court for the Southern District of New York, 1994.
854 F.Supp. 229.

ROBERT W. SWEET, DISTRICT JUDGE.

Plaintiff United States of America (the "Government") brought this action to hold defendants Jordan W. Berkman ("Berkman"), John A. Petrillo ("Petrillo"), and Joseph and Mario Curto (the "Curtos") (collectively, the "Berkman Defendants") liable under CERCLA § 107(a), 42 U.S.C. § 9607(a), of the Comprehensive Environmental—Response, Compensation, and Liability Act of 1980 ("CERCLA"), for costs incurred and to be incurred by the Government at the Brewster Wellfield Site (the "Well Field" or "Site") in Putnam County, New York, and elsewhere, in response to a release or threatened release of hazardous substances from real estate owned by the Berkman Defendants located at the intersection of Routes 6 and 22 in the Town of Southeast, Putnam County, New York (the "Property").

[The question is whether the Berkman Defendants can claim any of the CERCLA affirmative defenses and, in particular, the "innocent landowner" defense.] I regretfully find that the Berkman Defendants are unable to claim the protection of [the] defenses.

Findings of Fact

This action arises out of the Government's investigation of and remedial actions relating to contamination at the Site.... Berkman and Petrillo each hold a one-third interest and the Curtos together hold a one-third interest in the Property, which is located at the intersection of Routes 6 and 22 in the Town of Southeast, Putnam County, New York. The Berkman Defendants purchased the Property on March 2, 1979, and own it as tenants-in-common. The Berkman Defendants knew that a dry cleaning business [A & N Cleaners & Launderers ("A & N")] was located on the Property prior to March 2, 1979. [A & N continued to lease a portion of the Property from the Berkman Defendants after they purchased the Property.]

Berkman is an attorney admitted to practice in New York State who specializes in real estate law. He was the Town Attorney for the Village of Brewster from 1975 through 1990. Petrillo is a builder engaged in the construction business. The Curtos are retired individuals. Ben Forcucci is the sole shareholder, officer, and director of A & N Cleaners and Launderers, Inc., a/k/a Alben Cleaners & Launderers ("A & N"). At all relevant times, he alone was responsible for the day-to-day operation of the dry cleaning machines at A & N and the disposal of waste.

The Property consists of a one-story brick building (the "Building") akin to a shopping mall, which is surrounded by a parking lot and adjacent grassy area on a total of approximately 1.8 acres. The Building occupies 12,500 square feet. A floor drain (the "Floor Drain") traverses the entire length of the interior of the Building and emptied into a dry well (the "Dry Well") under the parking lot in the rear of the Property until August of 1991....

The Well Field has been in operation since 1954. Over the years, the Well Field's configuration and utilization has changed as wells have been installed and replaced. These wells have generally extracted between 300,000 and 400,000 gallons of water per day from the aquifer. The presence of volatile halogenated organic compounds ("VHO's") [including PCE and TCE] was first detected in the ground water at the Well Field in 1978. In December 1982, the Well Field was placed on the National Priorities List ("NPL")....

Forcucci's dry cleaning process resulted in the production of a waste stream associated with his drying machines (the "Dryer Condensate"), which was contaminated with PCE and TCE. In addition, Forcucci's dry cleaning process resulted in the production of a waste stream associated with his ironing machines (the "Ironing Machine Condensate").

Prior to March 1, 1979, Forcucci disposed of the Dryer Condensate down the Floor Drain.... At trial, Forcucci was able to fix the date at which he stopped disposing of Dryer Condensate down the Floor Drain by reference to the receipt of a letter from the NYDEC dated March 1, 1979, informing him that the NYDEC disapproved of his disposal practices. Forcucci testified with certainty that, by the time he received this letter, he had stopped disposing of the Dryer Condensate down the drain. This testimony established by a preponderance of the evidence that Forcucci stopped disposing of Dryer Condensate down the Floor Drain prior to the Berkman Defendants' purchase of the Property on March 2, 1979.

Forcucci disposed of Ironing Machine Condensate down the Floor Drain until 1991. On December 12, 1985, David Sands, the geologist [involved in determining the nature and extent of contamination at the site], visited A & N for the purpose of, among other things, testing the Ironing Machine Condensate. Sands testified at trial that Forcucci pointed out the vessel that collected the Ironing Machine Condensate, and that Sands personally took a sample of the Condensate from the vessel to which he was directed (the "1985 Sample"). The 1985 Sample contained PCE at 117 ug/l.... [Other evidence, however, cast doubt on whether the vessel from which Sands took his sample was the vessel that held the Ironing Machine Condensate.]

In September 1978, the Putnam County Health Department published a notice informing village of Brewster residents of the Well Field contamination and advising them to boil their water. Berkman knew about the boil water notice at or about the time it was issued. Newspaper articles in September 1978 discussed the Well Field contamination and specifically described the source of the contamination as "tetrachloroethylene—commonly used as a spot remover or solvent." Press coverage relating to the Well Field contamination continued in the fall and winter of 1978 and in 1979....

From 1979 until 1988, the Berkman Defendants made no contact with Forcucci with regard to his waste disposal practices, or his use of his floor drain. [In December 1979, Berkman signed an access agreement with environmental agencies giving them permission to come onto the property "for the purpose of determining the source of contamination of the Village well fields."] After he signed the access agreement in December 1979, Berkman did not ask Forcucci any questions about his waste disposal practices, nor did he ask [the environmental agencies] about the results of any tests performed on the Property.

Statutory Framework

Congress enacted CERCLA in 1980 because then-existing laws ... were inadequate to respond to the problems raised by hazardous waste produced and abandoned in the past.... While the perceived problem of contaminated sites in this country was large at the time of CERCLA's passage, further study revealed this problem's staggering proportions. It is estimated that between 130,000 and 380,000 sites are potential candidates for government-initiated response actions under CERCLA. Evan Bogart Westerfield, When Less is More: A Significant Threat Threshold for CERCLA Liability, 60 U. Chi. L. Rev. 697, 697 n.4 (1993). It will probably take until the year 2003 to begin construction on the sites that are currently on the NPL, and the EPA estimates that it expects to add sites to the NPL at the rate of 75 to 100 per year. William K. Reilly, Administrator, EPA, A Management Review of the Superfund Program, reprinted in 18 Chem. Waste Litig. 400, 406 (1990).

Estimates of the costs of this cleanup are nearly as staggering as the estimates of the contamination to be addressed. See, e.g., Office of Technology Assessment, Assessing Contractor Use in Superfund, reprinted in 17 Chem. Waste Litig. Rep. 715, 715 (1989) (cleanup costs under CERCLA estimated at $500 billion dollars, excluding the costs of cleaning up Department of Energy facilities); John T. Ronan III, A Clean Sweep on Cleanup, The Recorder, Sept. 30, 1992, at 10 (CERCLA cleanup costs could be as high as $750 billion dollars)....

Under CERCLA, the Government may take response action whenever there is a release or threatened release of "hazardous substances," and then sue certain persons for reimbursement of the cleanup costs ("Response Costs"). Private parties are also entitled, and encouraged, to implement remedial action under CERCLA. These parties may thereafter sue to recover their Response Costs.

To establish liability, a plaintiff must demonstrate that (1) there has been a "release" or a "substantial threat of release" of a "hazardous substance"; (2) from a "facility"; (3) which caused the plaintiff to incur Response Costs; and (4) each of the defendants fits within one of the categories of potentially responsible parties ("PRPs") identified under CERCLA § 107(a). Among the four classes of PRPs under CERCLA § 107(a) are the current "owner and operator" of the facility.

Absent a showing by a preponderance of the evidence that one of the affirmative defenses contained in CERCLA § 107(b), has been satisfied, PRPs' potential liability for Response Costs is strict. Where the environmental harm is indivisible, liability is also joint and several.

Under the "Third–Party Defense" set forth in CERCLA § 107(b)(3), a defendant is not liable if it establishes that the release or threatened release was caused solely by:

> (3) an act or omission of a third party other than an employee or agent of the defendant, or than one whose act or omission occurs in connection with a contractual relationship, existing directly or indirectly, with the defendant ... if the defendant establishes by a preponderance of the evidence that (a) he exercised due care with respect to the hazardous substance concerned, taking into consideration the characteristics of such hazardous substance, in light of all relevant facts and circumstances [the "Due Care

> Requirement"], and (b) he took precautions against foreseeable acts or omissions of any such third party and the consequences that could foreseeably result for such acts or omissions [the "Precautionary Requirement"].

The second defense relevant to this case, the "Innocent Landowner Defense," is actually a special case of the Third–Party Defense. In 1986 Congress created an exception to the "no contractual relationship" requirement of the Third–Party Defense, thereby making it available to some owners who acquired the relevant property after the disposal or placement of hazardous substances occurred. CERCLA § 101(35)(A) defines "contractual relationship" for purposes of CERCLA § 107(b)(3) as including "land contracts, deeds or other instruments transferring title or possession," unless:

> the real property on which the facility concerned is located was acquired by the defendant after the disposal or placement of the hazardous substance on, in, or at the facility and ... at the time the defendant acquired the facility the defendant did not know and had no reason to know that any hazardous substance which is the subject of the release or threatened release was disposed of on, in, or at the facility.

To qualify as an Innocent Landowner under CERCLA § 101(35)(A), one must have undertaken "all appropriate inquiry into the previous ownership and uses of the property, consistent with good commercial or customary practice" at the time of transfer. CERCLA § 101(35)(B). "Good commercial or customary practice" is not defined in the statute, and the relevant legislative history is vague, indicating that "a reasonable inquiry must have been made in all circumstances, in light of best business and land transfer principles." H.R. Conf. Rep. No. 962, 99th Cong., 2d Sess., at 187 (1986). In deciding whether a defendant has complied with this standard, courts consider any specialized knowledge or expertise the defendant has, whether the purchase price indicated awareness of the presence of a risk of contamination, commonly known or reasonable information about the property, the obviousness of the presence of contamination at the property, and the ability to detect such contamination by appropriate inspection. CERCLA § 101(35)(B).

Landowners who meet the requirements of CERCLA § 101(35)(A) will not be found to be in a "contractual relationship" with the party responsible for the release of hazardous substances at the property. To obtain the protection of the Innocent Landowner Defense, they must also meet the Due Care and Precautionary Requirements of CERCLA § 107(b)(3)(a) and (b).

The Due Care Requirement, also undefined in the statute, has been interpreted as requiring that a defendant demonstrate that it took necessary steps to prevent foreseeable adverse consequences arising from the pollution on the site. Kerr–McGee Chem. Corp. v. Lefton Iron & metal Co., 14 F.3d 321 (7th Cir. 1994); (due care not established when PRP took no affirmative measures to clean site); United States v. DiBiase Salem Realty

Trust, 1993 U.S. Dist. LEXIS 20031 (D. Mass. Nov. 19, 1993) (CERCLA's affirmative defenses not available when defendant took no steps to prevent harm from hazardous substances); H.R. Rep. No. 1016, 96th Cong., 2d Sess., pt 1, at 34 (1980) ("to establish that he exercised due care, the defendant must demonstrate that he took all precautions with respect to the particular waste that a similarly situated reasonable and prudent person would have taken"); H.R. Rep. No. 253, 99th Cong., 2d Sess. 187 (1986) (due care "would include those steps necessary to protect the public from a health or environmental threat"); cf. Lincoln Props. v. Higgins, 823 F. Supp. 1528, 1543 (E.D. Cal. 1992) (defendant exercised due care by taking contaminated wells out of service and destroying them in manner intended to prevent further contamination); In re Sterling Steel Treating, Inc., 94 Bankr. 924, 930 (Bankr. E.D. Mich. 1989) (defendant exercised due care after discovering hazardous waste on property when it took immediate steps to properly dispose thereof). The Precautionary Requirement is satisfied by taking precautionary action against the foreseeable actions of third parties responsible for the hazardous substances in question.

Both the Third-Party Defense and the Innocent Landowner Defense are affirmative defenses, requiring the defendant to prove each of the required elements by a preponderance of the evidence. A defendant's failure to meet its burden on any one of the required elements precludes application of the defense....

CERCLA's liability scheme was intended to ensure that those who were responsible for, and who profited from, activities leading to property contamination, rather than the public at large, should be responsible for the costs of the problems that they had caused. In addition, Congress intended CERCLA's liability scheme to provide incentives for private parties to investigate potential sources of contamination and to initiate remediation efforts.

The imposition of strict liability solely on the basis of property ownership, however, does something other than cause handlers of dangerous substances to be responsible for the hazards they create. It transfers the costs of the national problem of remediating abandoned contaminated sites onto the shoulders of individuals involved in real estate transactions, many of whom had never violated any environmental regulation, thereby negating Congress' intention of making those responsible for causing contamination pay for its remediation. The Second Circuit has noted that:

> In passing CERCLA Congress faced the unenviable choice of enacting a legislative scheme that would be somewhat unfair to generators of hazardous substances or one that would unfairly burden the taxpaying public. The financial burdens of toxic cleanup had been vastly underestimated—in 1980 when CERCLA was enacted $1.8 billion was thought to be enough. In 1986 when the Superfund Amendments and Reauthorization Act of 1986 (SARA), Pub. L. No. 99–499, 100 Stat. 1613 (1986), was passed, $100 billion was held to be needed. It may well be more today. It is of course the public-at-large that is already bearing the economic brunt of

> this enormous national problem. There may be unfairness in the legislative plan, but ... we still must take this statute as it is.

United States v. Alcan Aluminum Corp., 990 F.2d 711, 716–17 (2d Cir. 1993).

Alcan involved a generator of hazardous wastes who knowingly sent contaminated waste to a site for disposal and treatment. If imposing CERCLA liability on such defendants is "unfair," it is immeasurably more so to impose CERCLA liability on unwitting owners of contaminated property that have played no part in the activities leading to the contamination. But see United States v. Price, 577 F. Supp. 1103, 1114 (D.N.J. 1983) ("Though strict liability may impose harsh results on certain defendants, it is the most equitable solution in view of the alternative—forcing those who bear no responsibility for causing the damage, the tax payers, to shoulder the full cost of the clean up.").

CERCLA's narrow affirmative defenses do little to alleviate the unfairness of the statute's liability scheme, particularly in cases where liability is predicated solely on property ownership. By restricting the application of the Defenses to those that have complied with a series of ill-defined due care and investigatory requirements, CERCLA in practice imposes the costs of the public problem of ferreting out contaminated sites onto the private individuals involved in real estate transactions and ownership without even providing reasonable guidance on what these property owners must do to meet their obligations.

The assignment of the burden of proof on causation to defendants pleading the third-party defense also leads to unjust results. While it is true that "traditional tort law has ... imposed strict liability while recognizing a causation defense," New York v. Shore Realty Corp., 759 F.2d 1032, 1044 (2d Cir. 1985), this doctrine often applies when each of the defendants engaged in blameworthy activity, or where the defendants have superior access to relevant information. The only blameworthy activity that many property owners facing CERCLA liability have engaged in is the failure to comply with the host of amorphous and undefined due care requirements necessary for establishing CERCLA's affirmative defenses. Also, as demonstrated by the present case, the Government's access to the highly technical information necessary to identify contamination is often superior to that of the ordinary landowner. Rather than preventing blameworthy defendants from escaping liability, shifting the burden of proof of causation to defendants merely helps ensure that the Government will recoup their Response Costs, "at the cost of imposing liability upon some individual defendants who caused no harm, but are unable to prove it by a preponderance of the evidence." Developments, Toxic Waste Litigation, 99 Harv. L. Rev. 1458, 1544 (1986).

In addition to its unfairness, the liability structure of CERCLA is counter-productive. PRPs faced with disproportionate liability litigate tenaciously, prolonging or postponing remediation of contaminated sites and increasing dramatically the costs of remediation. See 140 Cong. Rec. S3965, S3965 (daily ed. March 25, 1994) (statement of Sen. Smith) (50% of costs at most Superfund sites are legal and other transaction costs); Frona M. Powell, Insuring Environmental Cleanup, 71 Neb. L. Rev. 1194, 1196 (1992) (noting 1992 RAND Institute for Civil Justice study finding that only 12% of CERCLA-related monies paid by insurance companies went to actual cleanup, while 78% went to legal and other non-cleanup related transaction costs).

Uncertainty over what investigatory steps property owners must take to avoid CERCLA liability has cast a pall over the real estate market, with unfortunate effects on the general economy. Douglas F. Rohrman & Michael J. Hoffman, Environmental Audits: Assessing Environmental Liability in Real Estate Transactions, 77 Ill. B.J. 690 (1989); H. Glenn Boggs, Real Estate Environmental Damage, The Innocent Residential Purchaser and Federal Superfund Liability, 22 Envtl. L. 977, 978–79, 986 (1992).[12]

If Congress must shift the costs of ferreting out contamination from the general public to those involved in real estate transactions it should, at a minimum, define the scope of the required investigation. See James McNerney, Innocence is a Virtue Seldom Found in a Landowner, 342 PLI/Real 379 (1989) ("The question that has caused the greatest loss of sleep is: 'Am I an innocent purchaser?' Following that as natural corollaries for the insomniac are: 'Have I done a thorough investigation?'; 'How much is enough?' "). Were the Berkman Defendants to have had a clear, intelligible mandate from Congress or the EPA regarding the investigation they should have conducted prior to purchasing the Property and the monitoring that they should have conducted since its purchase, it is doubtful that they would be before the Court at this time. By imposing a standard of diligence which the Government itself can neither meet nor define, CERCLA has imbued the conduct of business with unnecessary peril, and has made the current Defendants liable for our collective failure to fashion a reasonable response to the problems of chemical contamination.

Conclusions of Law

.... The Berkman Defendants have demonstrated by a preponderance of the evidence that Forcucci stopped dumping the Dryer Condensate prior to the time that they purchased the Property. The Berkman Defendants have shed considerable doubt on the Government's tests of the Ironing Machine Condensate.... However, since the Berkman Defendants' liability is predicated on their unwitting ownership of contaminated property, rather than on any disposal of waste which might have occurred on the Property since they purchased it, they bear the burden of showing that a

12. This uncertainty concerning what must be done to qualify for CERCLA's affirmative defenses may even discourage investigation. Environmental audits can be enormously expensive. One Florida environmental auditing firm, for example, charges up to $3,500 per acre for environmental audits, and possibly much more, depending on the characteristics of the site. Boggs, supra, at 984–85, and investigation imposes delays on the transfer of property, and can trigger reporting or remediation obligations that would not have been incurred if the contamination had not come to light. An uncertain chance of qualifying for the innocent purchaser defense may be seen as insufficient to justify these costs and risks.

totally unrelated third party is the sole cause of the release of hazardous substances in question. As it is equally likely that the Ironing Machine Condensate is contaminated or that it is not contaminated, and since Forcucci disposed of the Ironing Machine Condensate down the Floor Drain until 1991, the Berkman Defendants have failed in this burden. This conclusion precludes the application of either of the Defenses to the Berkman Defendants.

Both the Third–Party Defense and the Innocent Landowner Defense also require that a defendant establish by a preponderance of the evidence that he or she fulfilled the Due Care Requirement and the Precautionary Requirement. Willful or negligent ignorance about the presence of or threats associated with hazardous substances does not excuse a PRP's non-compliance with either of these requirements. In this action, this Court has previously held that:

> Given the [existence of various] newspaper articles, Berkman's consent to have the Village of Brewster take borings on the Property "for the purpose [**48] of determining the source of contamination in the Village well fields," and the extent of investigative activity that apparently was taking place at the Property, the Berkman Defendants were sufficiently aware that they should have made inquiry of the various subtenants.

788 F. Supp. at 1329.

In addition to inquiring as to Forcucci's disposal practices, the Berkman Defendants should have made inquiries to environmental officials regarding the status of the Property and the legality of their tenants' and subtenants' disposal practices. In the exercise of due care, this inquiry should have been made in 1979 or soon thereafter, following Berkman's signing of the access agreement, and while he was in receipt of information regarding investigations into the contamination of the Well Field.

Even if, after proper investigation, the Berkman Defendants were told that Forcucci was no longer improperly disposing of hazardous substances, they would have learned that he had disposed of hazardous substances down the Floor Drain prior to 1979. After making this discovery, due care would have required that they take some steps to ascertain the nature of any environmental threats associated with this disposal. Such steps could have included hiring an engineer to test the soil on their property, . . . contacting EPA [and state environmental agencies] to discuss a the problem, cleaning up the Property themselves and thereafter seeking recovery of their response costs, or taking such other actions which, in light of a full evaluation of the relevant facts and circumstances, were appropriate. The Berkman Defendants were prevented from considering these options by their failure to inquire into Forcucci's disposal practices.

Under the circumstances of this case, where the Berkman Defendants had reason to inquire of Forcucci and the relevant environmental officials regarding Forcucci's disposal practices, the failure to so inquire was itself a lack of due care with respect to the hazardous substances which were later found on the Property. It is no defense to insist that, in the course of its ongoing testing, the Government should have notified the Berkman Defendants that there was a problem on the Property, since Congress has seen fit to shift the public responsibility of locating contamination onto the shoulders of individual property owners....

For the reasons discussed above, the Berkman Defendants are not entitled to rely on the Innocent Purchaser or Third–Party Defenses.

Notes & Questions

1. The court in *A & N Cleaners* expresses doubt about the wisdom of holding current landowners responsible for cleanups stemming from hazardous waste disposal that occurred prior to their ownership of the site. Why do you believe Congress included current landowners as PRPs? Was it simply an effort to reach as many "deep pockets" as possible? Is it fair to hold new purchasers liable if they were not responsible for the disposal of hazardous waste on the property? What incentives are created by holding current landowners liable? What incentives would be created by holding landowners liable only if they owned the property at the time of disposal?

2. **The Innocent Landowner Defense.** As *A & N Cleaners* suggests, landowners have found it extremely difficult to establish an "innocent purchaser" defense—more frequently referred to as an "innocent landowner" defense. A handful of reported decisions, however, have upheld the defense. In State of New York v. Lashins Arcade Co., 91 F.3d 353 (2d Cir. 1996), for example, Lashins Arcade Company purchased a shopping center in 1987, nine years after the county and state had found contamination in the groundwater in the area and begun remediation. Lashins knew of the contamination before it purchased but was told by a water service contractor that it was due to an area-wide groundwater problem probably created by a nearby gasoline station. After the purchase closed, the state identified the source of contamination as a dry cleaning business that operated in the shopping center prior to 1971. The court held that Lashins satisfied the innocent landowner defense. Should Lashins have made more of an inquiry?

The greatest obstacle for most landowners is establishing that they "did not know and had no reason to know that any hazardous substance" had been disposed of on, in, or at the site. CERCLA § 101(35)(A)(i). To meet this requirement, CERCLA requires a landowner to prove that she undertook,

> at the time of acquisition, all appropriate inquiry into the previous ownership and uses of the property consistent with good commercial or customary practice in an effort to minimize liability. For purposes of the preceding sentence the court shall take into account any specialized knowledge or experience on the part of the defendant, the relationship of the purchase price to the value of the property if uncontaminated, commonly known or reasonably ascertainable information about the property, the obviousness of

> the presence or likely presence of contamination at the property, and the ability to detect such contamination by appropriate inspection.

Id. § 101(35)(B).

Many environmental practitioners believe that the "appropriate inquiry" requirement effectively eviscerates the innocent landowner defense. They argue that if a potential buyer performs an "appropriate inquiry," he will find the hazardous substance, reject the property, and consequently never need to rely on the defense. If, however, the buyer makes an inquiry, does not find the contamination, and buys the property, the court will likely determine that the inquiry was not "appropriate" as it did not uncover the problem. See, e.g., Mary E. Hitt, Desperately Seeking SARA: Preserving the Innocent Landowner Defense to Superfund Liability, 18 Real. Est. L.J. 3 (1989); William A. Anderson, II, Will The Meek Even Want the Earth?, 38 Mercer L. Rev. 535 (1987). The due diligence necessary to claim the innocent landowner defense is often based on an environmental audit of the property conducted by the buyer before purchase or closing. For descriptions of the steps that buyers can take to try to avoid CERCLA liability, see Ram Sundar & Bea Grossman, The Importance of Due Diligence in Commercial Transactions: Avoiding CERCLA Liability, 7 Fordham Envtl. L.J. 351 (1996); Geoffrey P. Patterson, A Buyer's Catalogue of Prepurchase Precautions to Minimize CERCLA Liability in Commercial Real Estate Transactions, 15 U. Puget Sound L. Rev. 469 (1992). Should Congress spell out specific steps that, if a buyer takes them, would automatically qualify as "appropriate inquiry"?

Even if someone engages in all appropriate inquiry and purchases property with no knowledge of hazardous substances, she still might not qualify for the innocent landowner defense if she fails to take precautions to prevent damage after acquiring the property. See, e.g., Kerr–McGee Chem. Corp. v. Lefton Iron & Metal Co., 14 F.3d 321 (7th Cir. 1994).

3. **Governmental Ownership, Inheritance, Bequests, & Gifts.** The innocent landowner defense also covers governmental entities that acquire a site "by escheat, or through any other involuntary transfer or acquisition, or through the exercise of eminent domain authority by purchase or condemnation" and persons who acquire ownership of a site "by inheritance or bequest." Although such PRPs do not have to establish that they were unaware prior to acquiring ownership of any disposal of hazardous waste on the site, they must still show that after acquiring ownership they "exercised due care with respect to" hazardous substances found on the site. See CERCLA §§ 101(35), 107(b)(3).

What of people who acquire land by gift? In United States v. Pacific Hide & Fur Depot, Inc., 716 F. Supp. 1341 (D. Idaho 1989), the founder of a corporation that ran a recycling facility gave his children shares in the corporation. Because the children were young and did not have knowledge of the hazardous waste problems when they received their shares in the corporation, the court found that the children were innocent landowners and thus not responsible for the costs of removing hazardous substances from the site. In the course of its decision, the court suggested that landowners who receive their interest by gift are more likely to succeed in meeting the innocent landowner requirements—even though they must show ignorance of the hazardous waste problem:

> [The] legislative history [of the 1986 amendments to CERCLA] establishes a three-tier system: Commercial transactions are held to the strictest standard; private transactions are given a little more leniency; and inheritances and bequests are treated the most leniently of these three situations. The present case is actually more like an inheritance than a private transaction. Certainly these three defendants did not obtain their interest in an arms-length private sales transaction—they obtained their initial interest by familial gift and their ultimate interest by a corporate event beyond their control. All of this occurred when they were barely out of their teenage years. This is precisely the situation designed to be covered by the innocent landowner defense.

Id. at 1348.

4. **Liability of Prior Owners.** Superfund holds two categories of landowners potentially liable: (1) the current owner of the site, and (2) the "person who at the time of disposal of any hazardous substance" owned the site. Are landowners liable if they purchase land after hazardous waste has been disposed of on the property but then sell the land before it becomes a Superfund site? Does it matter if the hazardous waste was leaking out of containers, which might well be buried and not known to the landowner, while the landowner owned the property? Some courts have held that such leakage constitutes passive disposal of hazardous waste and therefore makes the landowner potentially liable as a person who owned the site at the time that hazardous waste was disposed of there. See, e.g., Nurad, Inc. v. William E. Hooper & Sons Co., 966 F.2d 837 (4th Cir. 1992). According to the court in *Nurad*, any other holding would permit landowners who know of hazardous waste on their property but take no steps to control it to escape liability so long as they did not own the land at the time of the waste's initial disposal and sold it before it became a Superfund site. The court also noted that CERCLA broadly defines "disposal" to mean the "discharge, deposit, injection, dumping, spilling, leaking, or placing" of a hazardous waste "into or on any land or water." 42 U.S.C. §§ 1004(3), 9601(29).

Other courts have disagreed with the Fourth Circuit's view in *Nurad*. See, e.g., United States v. CDMG Realty, 96 F.3d 706 (3d Cir. 1996); United States v. Petersen Sand & Gravel, Inc., 806 F. Supp. 1346 (N.D. Ill. 1992). The court in *Petersen Sand & Gravel* quoted approvingly from Edward Hines Lumber Co. v. Vulcan Materials Co., 861 F.2d 155, 157 (7th Cir. 1988):

> We are enforcing a statute rather than modifying rules of common law.... To the point that courts could achieve "more" of the legislative objectives by adding to the lists of those responsible, it is enough to respond that statutes have not only ends but also

> limits. Born of compromise, laws such as CERCLA ... do not pursue their ends to their logical limits. A court's job is to find and enforce stopping points no less than to implement other legislative choices.

Given the broad language of CERCLA and, in particular, its definition of "disposal," is it clear where liability "ends"?

In jurisdictions that follow the *Nurad* rule and hold landowners liable if they owned the site during a period of "passive disposal," can the landowners try to assert an "innocent purchaser" defense? Section 101(35) of CERCLA, which sets out the defense, is limited to those situations where the site "was acquired by the defendant *after* the disposal or placement of the hazardous substance on, in, or at" the site. Can a current landowner assert an "innocent purchaser" defense under *Nurad* if hazardous waste is currently leaking at the site? Since the hazardous waste is often leaking at Superfund sites, would *Nurad* thus eviscerate the "innocent purchaser" defense?

5. **Indemnification of Buyers.** Courts differ on the enforceability of clauses that attempt to shift CERCLA liability. Two issues control: Is the indemnification language sufficient to show an intent to shift CERCLA costs? And does CERCLA permit the parties to shift liability? See generally Joseph A. Sevack, Passing the Big Bucks: Contractual Transfers of Liability Between Potentially Responsible Parties Under CERCLA, 75 Minn. L. Rev. 1571 (1991); Penny L. Parker & John Slavich, Contractual Efforts to Allocate the Risk of Environmental Liability: Is There A Way To Make Indemnities Worth More Than the Paper They Are Written On?, 44 Sw. L.J. 1349 (1991). Should buyers be able to shift their liability back to the seller through contract? Does this undermine any of the potential purposes of holding current landowners liable in the first place?

6. **A Buyer's Other Potential Remedies.** The buyer of contaminated property may also turn to a variety of state law theories in an effort to hold the seller responsible for any CERCLA costs the buyer must pay. Buyers sometimes succeed, on theories such as abnormally dangerous activities, see, e.g., T & E Industries, Inc. v. Safety Light Corp., 587 A.2d 1249 (N.J. 1991) (permitting buyer to maintain action against owner earlier in chain of title that discarded radioactive materials on the site in the course of manufacturing activities); public and private nuisance, see, e.g., Westwood Pharmaceuticals, Inc. v. National Fuel Gas Distribution Corp., 737 F. Supp. 1272 (W.D.N.Y. 1990), aff'd, 964 F.2d 85 (2d Cir. 1992); mutual mistake, see, e.g., Garb–Ko v. Lansing–Lewis Services, Inc., 423 N.W.2d 355 (Mich. App. 1988) (seller permitted to rescind contract where neither seller nor buyer knew of underground gasoline tanks); and builder-vendor warranty, see Frona M. Powell, Builder–Vendor Liability for Environmental Contamination in the Sale of New Residential Property, 58 Tenn. L. Rev. 231 (1991).

Buyers have enjoyed less success in claiming that the presence of hazardous materials breached express or implied promises relating to title. See, e.g., HM Holdings, Inc. v. Rankin, 70 F.3d 933 (7th Cir. 1995) (no violation of implied warranty of marketable title); United States v. Allied Chemical Corp., 587 F. Supp. 1205 (N.D. Cal. 1984) (hazardous waste was not "encumbrance" within seller's covenant that land was free from encumbrances).

7. **Contribution.** A buyer who is held liable under CERCLA can then sue other PRPs for contribution. In determining the amount of recovery in contribution actions, moreover, most courts will consider the relative contribution of the parties to the hazardous waste problem that led to the cleanup. See, e.g., United States v. Monsanto Co., 858 F.2d 160, 168 n.13 (4th Cir. 1988) ("[t]he site owners' relative degree of fault would, of course, be relevant" in applying equitable contribution); Alcan–Toyo America v. Northern Illinois Gas Co., 881 F. Supp. 342 (N.D. Ill. 1995) (contaminating former owner liable for ninety percent of response costs and non-contaminating buyer liable for ten percent since it failed to inspect property before buying).

8. **Buyer Lawsuit Under CERCLA.** Purchasers of property sometimes find that CERCLA is their friend, not their enemy. Where a landowner discovers hazardous substances on his property and spends money to remove the substances and clean up the property, the landowner may be able to sue prior owners, as well as generators and transporters of the waste, for the cost. See CERCLA § 107(a)(4)(B) (PRPs liable for any "necessary costs of response incurred" by any person "consistent with the national contingency plan").

9. **The Lawyer's Ethical Obligation.** If a seller's attorney learns of hazardous wastes buried on the property, must he or she reveal this knowledge to the buyer or to the appropriate governmental official? The answer requires a difficult balancing of the attorney's duty to maintain confidentiality against the obligation to refrain from assisting the client's commission of fraudulent or criminal acts and the potential statutory duty to report environmental hazards. See David Richman & Donald B. Bauer, Responsibilities of Lawyers and Engineers to Report Environmental Hazards and Maintain Client Confidences: Duties in Conflict, 5 Toxics L. Rep. 1458 (1991); Ilona L. Dotterrer, Attorney–Client Confidentiality: The Ethics of Toxic Dumping Disclosure, 35 Wayne L. Rev. 1157 (1989).

10. **Lender Liability.** Because a lender holding a mortgage on a CERCLA site might be considered an owner or operator under some state laws, Congress has specified that the lender is not a PRP if the lender holds "indicia of ownership primarily to protect a security interest" without "participating in management." In light of United States v. Fleet Factors, 901 F.2d 1550 (11th Cir. 1990) concluding that "participation in management" includes the "ability to control" managerial decisions, Congress in 1996 passed the Asset Conservation, Lender Liability, and Deposit Insurance Protect Act of 1996 defining participation to mean "actually participating in the management or operational affairs [of the site] ... and does not include merely having the capacity to influence, or the unexercised right to control ... operations [at the site]." CERCLA § 101(20)(F).

Is a lender liable if it forecloses on the property? The 1996 amendments also provide that a foreclosing lender does not become a PRP if, after foreclosing, it seeks to sell or otherwise divest itself of the property at the earliest practicable, commercially reasonable time, on commercially reasonable terms in light of market conditions. Id. § 101(20)(E). How comfortable do the 1996 amendments make you as a lender? How clear are the protections? Even if you do not become a PRP by foreclosing on the property, who is going to buy it? And at what price? See Joseph M. Macchione, Lender Liability Under CERCLA in Light of the Asset Conservation, Lender Liability and Deposit Insurance Protection Act of 1996: Does the Act Spell Lender Relief or Continued Heartburn?, 16 Temp. Envtl. L. & Tech. J. 81 (1997).

11. **Brownfields.** Policymakers have grown increasingly concerned that CERCLA and similar state cleanup statutes might discourage the redevelopment of contaminated inner-city sites, frequently referred to as "Brownfields" (in contrast to the greenbelts outside the cities where development is otherwise likely to occur). In response, both the federal and state governments have taken steps to try to encourage developers to acquire and develop Brownfields sites. The federal EPA, for example, will enter into agreements with prospective purchasers that may include a limited covenant not to sue where the purchaser is not responsible for the contamination and undertakes to perform a supervised cleanup or help defray the costs of a governmental cleanup. See EPA, Guidance on Agreements with Prospective Purchasers of Contaminated Property and Model Prospective Purchaser Agreements, 60 Fed. Reg. 34792 (1995).

For articles analyzing the many issues raised by Brownfields initiatives, see Frona M. Powell, Amendments to CERCLA to Encourage the Redevelopment of Brownfields: Issues, Concerns, and Recommendations, 53 Wash. U.J. Urb. & Contemp. L. 113 (1998); Joel B. Eisen, "Brownfields of Dreams"? Challenges and Limits of Voluntary Cleanup Programs and Incentives, 1996 U. Ill. L. Rev. 883 (1996); Terry J. Tondro, Reclaiming Brownfields to Save Greenfields: Shifting the Environmental Risks of Acquiring and Reusing Contaminated Land, 27 Conn. L. Rev. 789 (1995).

12. For articles on CERCLA's general relevance to land transactions, see Michael J. Gergen, The Failed Promise of the "Polluter Pays" Principle: An Economic Analysis of Landowner Liability for Hazardous Waste, 69 N.Y.U. L. Rev. 624 (1994); H. Glenn Boggs, Real Estate Environmental Damage, The Innocent Residential Purchaser, and Federal Superfund Liability, 22 Envtl. L. 977 (1992); Mark P. Fitzsimmons & Jeffery K. Sherwood, The Real Estate Lawyer's Primer (And More) to Superfund: The Environmental Hazards of Real Estate Transactions, 22 Real Prop. Prob. & Tr. J. 765 (1987).

CHAPTER 5

TITLE ASSURANCE

A. THE RECORD SYSTEM

The aim of the record system in America is to protect a buyer of land against the possibility that his seller, or some predecessor in interest to his seller, previously conveyed away all or part of the interest that the buyer has contracted to buy.

At early common law, when land was transferred by the ceremony of feoffment with livery of seisin, the possibility of such multiple transfers was small. The required presence of witnesses disciplined landowners from trying to sell the same parcel twice. But with the growth of documentary transfers after the Statute of Uses, and with the proliferation of interests such as covenants, easements, and tax and mortgage liens that could simultaneously coexist in a single parcel, it became increasingly probable that a scheming or forgetful grantor would fail to inform her grantee of some prior, adverse transfer respecting the land. Covenants of title partially protected grantees who obtained less than they bargained for. Covenantors could not always be found, however, and, if found, often lacked the resources to make good on their promises. A rule was needed to determine the rights of competing grantees fairly and efficiently.

The common law responded with a simple rule for determining who should prevail when grantor *A* conveyed the same interest in land to two grantees, *B* and *C*: *first in time, first in right*. The rule worked fairly and efficiently when the first grantee, *B*, went into immediate possession of the land. A quick inspection by *C* before accepting and paying for the deed from *A*, would disclose that someone other than *A* was in possession. *C*'s inquiry of *B* as to why *B* rather than *A* was in possession would disclose that *B*'s possession was under a prior deed from *A*. *C* could then rescind the contract with *A* and recover any deposit paid. But the rule of first in time, first in right was neither efficient nor fair when, as often happened, *B* did not go into possession. *C*, seeing either *A* or no one in possession, would have no reason to inquire into the possibility that anyone other than *A* had title. *C*, having paid the purchase price, would then lose his interest when *B* later asserted his prior rights.

The first recording acts were passed to resolve this shortcoming. The American acts replaced the common law rule of first in time, first in right with an equally simple, but fairer and more efficient prescription: *first to record, first in right*. By providing a place to record instruments effecting transfers of real property—typically county recorders' offices—and by providing that an instrument of transfer will be valid as against subsequent, competing instruments only if it is recorded, the American record system provided a comparatively cheap and certain method for *C* not only to determine whether *A* was conveying good title to him, but also to assure himself that title, once conveyed, would not be lost to any subsequent competing grantee.

The system enabled *C* to determine the status of *A*'s title by conducting a record search in the county where the land was situated. Under the system, if prior grantee, *B*, was not in possession, *C* would nonetheless discover the conveyance to *B* if *B* had recorded it. The title search would fail to disclose the *A* to *B* transfer only if *B* had failed to record the instrument. But, if *B* had failed to record, his interest would be invalid against *C* under a first to record, first in right regime—so long as *C* promptly recorded his instrument of transfer. And by promptly recording, *C* would gain priority not only over all earlier grantees who failed to record, but against all grantees subsequent to him who, by definition, will have recorded later.

The genius of the American recording system is that it operates almost entirely on individual initiative. A buyer who follows the steps prescribed by the system can almost always assure himself of good title. Although American recording acts take different forms, all assure the buyer that his interest will be secure as against both earlier and later grantees if he follows the standard operating procedure of searching title down to the moment of closing, rejecting title at that point if it is unmarketable, and, if title is marketable, recording his own interest at the moment of closing.

Because recording acts of one kind or another have been enacted in every state, and because they so completely dominate the conveyancing system, it is easy to overlook the fact that the recording acts have only partially preempted the common law rule of first in time, first in right, with the result that, in situations to which the recording acts do not apply, the common law priorities still govern in every state.

When will the common law priority, rather than the recording act priority apply? Almost all states today hold that if subsequent purchaser *C* acquired with notice of the prior transfer to *B*, he will not be protected by the recording act and will thus lose out to *B* even though *B* has not recorded. Also, *C* will lose out to adverse possessor *B* even though *C*'s diligently conducted title search would not uncover rights acquired by adverse possession. Nor would a search disclose the fact that a deed in the chain of title was forged, undelivered, or executed by an incompetent. See, e.g., Lloyd v. Chicago Title Ins. Co., 576 So. 2d 310 (Fla. App. 1990) (mortgagee who relied on a recorded, but forged satisfaction of the first mortgage is junior to the first mortgage). For a hair-raising catalogue of extra-record risks to title, see Ralph L. Straw, Jr., Off–Record Risks for Bona Fide Purchasers of Interests in Real Property, 72 Dick. L. Rev. 35 (1967).

Should recording acts be revised to completely preempt the common law priority and be conclusive as to the current state of title? If you were a residential tenant under a short term lease, would you be happy knowing that, under such a regime, your lease could be terminated at any time by a grantee from your landlord unless you had recorded it? Will your answer depend on how easily and cheaply recording can be accomplished?

For a provocative analysis of some of these points, see Douglas G. Baird & Thomas H. Jackson, Information, Uncertainty and the Transfer of Property, 13 J. Legal Stud. 331 (1984).

1. TYPES OF RECORDING ACTS

Corwin W. Johnson, Purpose and Scope of Recording Statutes

47 Iowa L. Rev. 231–233 (1962).

A basic policy question is whether emphasis should be upon penalizing those who fail to record or upon protecting those who deserve protection. Conceivably, strict adherence to the penalty approach could lead to requiring recordation as essential to the validity of a deed, even as to the grantor, in addition to the requirements of delivery and writing. On the other hand, it would be consistent with the protection approach to regard unrecorded deeds void only as to those who actually examine the records and who substantially change their positions in reliance thereon. No modern recording act (excluding Torrens acts [discussed below at pages 521–523]) goes to either of these extremes. Rather, the impact of both policies—penalty and protection—may be observed in the acts now in force. How these seemingly inconsistent policies have been accommodated is a major question to be considered in this review of the salient features of land recording acts.

1. BASIC TYPES OF STATUTES

Recording acts typically are classified as (1) race, (2) notice, or (3) race-notice. If conveyees are allowed a specified period of time within which to record—a feature which may be added to any of the above types of acts but which is not common today—the statute is also categorized as a "period of grace" act. A recent survey placed the recording acts of only two states, Louisiana and North Carolina, in the race category generally, and those of three other states in that category as to some instruments—mortgages in Arkansas, Ohio, and Pennsylvania (except for purchase money) and oil and gas leases in Ohio. Most states have acts either of the notice or race-notice type, each type having about an equal following.

Of these types, the race statute is most consistent with the penalty principle. The North Carolina act provides: "No conveyance of land . . . shall be valid to pass any property, as against lien creditors or purchasers for a valuable consideration . . . but from the time of registration thereof. . . ."[1] Under this act, as construed, an unrecorded conveyance is void even as to a subsequent purchaser who knew of its existence, and a subsequent bona fide purchaser gains no priority over the earlier unrecord-

1. N.C. Gen. Stat. § 47–18 (Supp. 1959).

ed instrument unless he records first. Thus, priority is determined by a race to the records. Of course, an unrecorded conveyance would be valid as to the grantor, his heirs, devisees, donees, and anyone else other than "lien creditors or purchasers for a valuable consideration." The North Carolina act is very similar to the Colonial prototypes. While there are many factors which may have shaped the early acts, it has been asserted that the most significant was a desire to provide a substitute for the publicity afforded by livery of seisin, which had been discarded as a mode. of conveyance. In this context there would be a tendency to look upon recording acts as an additional conveyancing formality and to emphasize what was to be required of the grantor rather than what should be the qualifications of those to be protected. Subsequently, probably as a result of experience with actual cases, attention shifted to the latter and to "the view generally accepted in America today that the Recording Acts are an extension of the equitable doctrine of notice."[7]

In some of its applications the race statute seems unfair and out of harmony with the stated objectives of recordation. But instances in which bad faith purchasers are benefited and good faith purchasers are harmed are probably infrequent, and can be almost eliminated by prompt recording. Indeed, the threat of such dire consequences may provide added incentive to prompt recordation. The best argument in favor of the race statute, however, is that it enables the title searcher to rely upon the records without the substantial risk under other types of acts that one will have constructive notice of unrecorded instruments.

A representative "notice" type act is the Iowa statute, which provides: "No instrument affecting real estate is of any validity against subsequent purchasers for a valuable consideration, without notice, unless filed in the office of the recorder of the county in which the same lies, as hereinafter provided."[8] California's act is an example of the "race-notice" type: "Every conveyance of real property ... is void as against any subsequent purchaser or mortgagee of the same property, or any part thereof, in good faith and for a valuable consideration, whose conveyance is first duly recorded. . . ."[9] Both acts give priority over unrecorded instruments to subsequent purchasers only if they are without notice, and the California act also requires the bona fide purchaser to record first. The latter is an obvious compromise of the objectives of penalizing non-recordation and protecting those who are likely to rely upon the records. By withholding protection from one who has not himself obeyed the statutory mandate to record, the race-notice act may be thought to have the merit of fairness and to encourage recording to a greater extent than would the notice act. But the seeming fairness of putting beyond the pale of the act both non-recorders is quite superficial, since only one has caused harm. It is also extremely doubtful that recording is actually stimulated by acts of the race-notice type, since even in a state

7. Bordwell, Recording of Instruments Affecting Land, 2 Iowa L. Bull. 51, 52 (1916).

8. Iowa Code § 558.41 (1958).

9. Cal. Civ. Code § 1214.

having a notice type statute failure to record makes those protected by the act vulnerable to subsequent claims.

Taylor Mattis, Recording Acts: Anachronistic Reliance

23 Real. Prop. Prob. & Tr. J. 17, 95–96, 98–100 (1990).

The next step is to determine which type of statute, notice or race-notice, better protects the reliance interest and achieves this fairness goal without unacceptable costs.... The prototypical example is that of an earlier instrument recorded after payment for and delivery of a later instrument, but before the recording of the later instrument. Chronologically: (1) *O* conveys or mortgages to *A*. (2) *O* conveys or mortgages to *B*, who is without notice. (3) *A* records before *B* records. In notice jurisdictions priorities are determined at step (2), and *B* prevails. In race-notice jurisdictions priorities are determined at step (3), and *A* prevails.

Both types of statutes withhold protection from a subsequent taker with notice. Both are fair to *A* in that regard, unlike the amoral pure race statutes. *B*, upon finding *A* in a vulnerable position, holding an unrecorded interest, cannot wilfully divest *A* by obtaining a deed or mortgage from *O* for value and winning a race with *A* to the courthouse. Only the pure notice statute, however, is fair to *B*, where *B* has taken her interest without notice of *A* but then lost the race to the courthouse. Once step (2) has happened, loss to one or the other of *A* or *B* is inevitable. There was never anything that *B* could have done to avoid it. *A* could have. To punish the one that did not cause the loss and reward the one who did, on the basis of an event irrelevant to the cause of the loss (step (3)), is unfair.

.... Efficiency arguments for race-notice might be that by requiring *B* to record before *A* to get protection from *A*: (1) extrinsic evidence about who is the prior and who is the subsequent taker is avoided, and (2) recording is encouraged generally by punishing *B* for not recording before *A*....

To only a limited degree, then, race-notice is more efficient than notice in avoiding extrinsic evidence about which instrument was delivered first in the rare instances when such a controversy might arise. In the great majority of cases the presumption that an instrument was delivered on the date of the instrument is sufficient without extrinsic evidence. The unfairness in the more usual situations when race-notice produces a result different from notice outweighs this small advantage....

The race-notice methodology for inducing recording is overkill. No person knows at the time of acquiring an interest in Blackacre whether in a future controversy that person will be cast in the role of the prior or the subsequent taker. Relativity is a central tenet of property. To protect *B*, who has not recorded, from an unrecorded claim of *A* is not to concede protection to *B* as against a potential *C*. If *B* records after *A*, she is vulnerable to *C* because *B*'s out-of-chain recording should not be deemed constructive notice to *C*. *B* can now notify potential subsequent takers only by a lawsuit. The peril of *B*'s losing to *C* is quite sufficient to induce *B* to get it right the first time by recording in the chain of title, before *A*. The additional threat of loss to an unknown *A* is unnecessary.

Notes & Questions

1. Although race statutes and notice statutes rest on sharply divergent conceptual bases, their practical operation is much the same. Whether Greenacre is in a race or a notice jurisdiction, *B*, who is about to acquire the parcel, will be well advised to conduct a thorough title search before paying *A* and accepting a deed. In a race jurisdiction, only a title search can inform *B* whether there is an outstanding interest adverse to his that has been recorded first. In a notice jurisdiction, a title search will inform *B* of any recorded, adverse interest that will operate to defeat his title under the doctrine of constructive notice. Similarly, once *B* acquires Greenacre, he is well advised, whether in a race or notice jurisdiction, to record his instrument promptly—in a race jurisdiction, in order to win the race to the recorder's office as against any subsequent grantee; in a notice jurisdiction, to give any subsequent grantee constructive notice of his claim.

As a practical matter, race and notice systems differ only in the additional search burden that notice statutes impose on the buyer. Under a race statute, *B* need do no more than search record title. In a notice jurisdiction, *B* must not only search title, but must also inspect Greenacre for physical evidence of title defects or encumbrances, such as possession by someone other than *A*, putting him on inquiry notice of an adverse claim.

2. Which system, race or notice, do you believe is more efficient? More fair? As a legislator forced to choose between the two, which would you pick? Do race-notice statutes offer a desirable compromise, or do they only compound the individual defects of race and notice systems?

For additional thoughts on the theory and polices of the recording acts, see Dan S. Schecter, Judicial Lien Creditors Versus Prior Unrecorded Transferees of Real Property: Rethinking the Goals of the Recording System and Their Consequences, 62 S. Cal. L. Rev. 105 (1988); Bernard Berger, An Analysis of the Doctrine that "First in Time is first in Right," 64 Neb. L. Rev. 349 (1985); Menachem Mautner, "The Eternal Triangles of the Law": Toward a Theory of Priorities in Conflicts Involving Remote Parties, 90 Mich. L. Rev. 95 (1991).

2. STATUTORY CONDITIONS OF PROTECTION

a. PURCHASER WITHOUT NOTICE

Three forms of notice will operate to defeat subsequent purchasers of an interest in land under notice and race-notice statutes:

(a) Actual notice (the notice given by the subsequent purchaser's actual knowledge of the prior transfer);

(b) Inquiry notice, sometimes called implied actual notice (the notice given by the subsequent purchaser's actual knowledge of facts that, if reasonably inquired into, would produce actual knowledge of the prior transfer);

(c) Constructive notice (the notice given by the recording of the prior transfer in the public title records in such a way that the subsequent purchaser, conducting a reasonable title search, would obtain actual knowledge of the transfer).

These three forms of notice effectively prescribe the standard operating procedure that a purchaser in notice and race-notice jurisdictions should follow before paying the purchase price and accepting a deed: (a) search files, desk drawers, and memory for any facts or communications that might have given actual knowledge; (b) inspect the land for physical evidence of an interest in someone other than the immediate seller; and (c) conduct a title search for documentary evidence of an interest in someone other than the immediate seller. (A purchaser in a race jurisdiction need only conduct a title search to determine whether anyone has beaten him, or any predecessor in title, to the recorder's office.)

There is some interplay between the three forms of notice. For example, it is generally held that the recording of an unrecordable instrument, such as an unacknowledged deed, will not give constructive notice of the instrument's contents. See, e.g., Metropolitan Nat'l Bank v. United States, 901 F.2d 1297 (5th Cir. 1990). Yet the instrument will give actual notice to a title examiner who comes upon the recording in the course of his or her search. As a matter of standard operating procedure, buyers will almost invariably order title searches before paying the purchase money. Thus, as a practical matter a buyer will, in the course of reviewing his examiner's title report, obtain actual notice of recorded, but unrecordable, instruments. Would you ever advise a client not to order a title search on the off-chance that he can thus avoid learning of an earlier transaction embodied in a recorded but unrecordable instrument?

Recording rules differ considerably among states as to what can be recorded and in what form they should be recorded. The following case deals with the recording rules in Massachusetts that govern leases of more than seven years. Massachusetts requires the lessee to record either a copy of the lease or a "notice of lease" satisfying various statutory requirements. The relevant statutory provision provides:

A conveyance of an estate in fee simple, fee tail or for life, or a lease for more than seven years from the making thereof, or an assignment of rents or profits from an estate or lease, shall not be valid as against any person, except the grantor or lessor, his heirs and devisees and persons having actual notice of it, unless it, or an office copy . . ., or, with respect to such a lease or an assignment of rents or profits, a notice of lease or a notice of assignment of rents or profits, as hereinafter defined, is recorded in the registry of deeds for the county or district in which the land to which it relates lies. A "notice of lease", as used in this section, shall mean

> an instrument in writing executed by all persons who are parties to the lease of which notice is given and shall contain the following information with reference to such lease:—the date of execution thereof and a description, in the form contained in such lease, of the premises demised, and the term of such lease, with the date of commencement of such term and all rights of extension or renewal....

Mass. Gen. Laws ch. 183, § 4.

Mister Donut of America, Inc. v. Kemp

Supreme Court of Massachusetts, 1975.
330 N.E.2d 810.

BRAUCHER, JUSTICE.

The principal question before us is whether a "notice of lease" recorded in a registry of deeds under G.L. c. 183, § 4, must refer to an option to purchase contained in the lease. We hold that such an option is not a right of "extension or renewal" and need not be referred to in the notice of lease. The recorded notice in this case was therefore in statutory form and was sufficient to give constructive notice of the option to the defendants, as persons not having "actual notice" of it.

The plaintiff lessee, Mister Donut of America, Inc., is the assignee of a lease made by Ernest Webby, Joseph E. Webby, and John J. Webby as lessors. The lease contains an option to purchase, and the lessee seeks specific performance of the option against the defendants Kemp, a grantee of the lessors, and Plymouth–Home National Bank, a mortgagee from Kemp. The facts are stipulated except as to the defendants' actual notice of the option, which was the subject of testimony. A judge of the Superior Court filed a memorandum of findings, rulings and order for decree granting specific performance, but after further hearing he vacated that memorandum and filed a second memorandum ordering a decree for the defendants. A decree was entered dismissing the bill in equity, and the plaintiff appealed to the Appeals Court. We granted the plaintiff's application for direct appellate review pursuant to G.L. c. 211A, § 10(A).

We summarize the judge's second memorandum, which he adopted as a report of material facts. The lease ran for twenty years from March 22, 1961, and was not recorded. Paragraph eleven gave the lessee the option to purchase the premises during the sixth to twentieth year for $53,000. A pasted overlay strip containing a substitute paragraph ten, unless lifted, hid most of paragraph eleven from view. A notice of lease in statutory form, recorded March 31, 1966, included the following: "Rights of extension and renewal, if any: None."

On July 15, 1971, Kemp and the Webbys and attorneys for them and for the bank were present in the office of the bank's attorney when Kemp took title to the premises from the Webbys. The Webbys told Kemp the original of the lease had been stolen, and gave him a photocopy and a written representation and warranty that the lease was as shown on the copy. The copy contained a legible reproduction of a portion of the option paragraph, containing clues pointing to a passage of title to real estate. Kemp acted in good faith; the bank attorney knew of the recorded notice but did not read the photocopy. Neither Kemp nor the bank had actual knowledge of the option. They were put on sufficient notice to warrant further inquiry, which would have revealed the option, but the circumstances were not sufficient to constitute "actual notice" under the statute.

1. *Actual notice.* Under G.L. c. 183, § 4, "actual notice" is ordinarily a question of fact, and a person claiming that another is not a good faith purchaser has the burden of proof. Knowledge of facts which would ordinarily put a party on inquiry is not enough. We are not prepared to relax our strict construction of the requirement, and therefore we uphold the judge's finding that the defendants had no actual notice of the option.

2. *Constructive notice.* The judge ruled "that a fair reading of the statute would require reference to the option in the notice following the legend 'rights of extension or renewal' in order to give constructive notice of the option to Kemp and the Bank," citing for comparison Universal Container Corp. v. Cambridge, 278 N.E.2d 727 (1972). In that case we said (278 N.E.2d at 729) "The recorded notice of lease is in the statutory form, and is sufficient to give the city constructive notice of the petitioner's interest." The interest in question was the tenant's right to share in damages for a taking by eminent domain; it depended in part on a provision of the lease not referred to in the statutory form.

Rights of "extension or renewal" have a settled meaning. Mutual Paper Co. v. Hoague–Sprague Corp., 297 Mass. 294, 299, 8 N.E.2d 802, 806 (1937): "An option for renewal implies the giving of a new lease upon the same terms as the old lease, whereas an option for extension contemplates a continuance of the old lease for a further period." Under our decisions such rights affect "the term during which the land which a purchaser had bought could be kept from his possession by the holder of an unrecorded lease." Toupin v. Peabody, 162 Mass. 473, 477, 39 N.E. 280, 281 (1895). An option to purchase is quite different; it does not contemplate either the giving of a new lease or the continuance of the old one. The statute does not require the notice of lease to refer to an option to purchase.

The plain object of the statute is to place recording of a notice of lease in statutory form on the same footing as recording of the entire lease, and to place both on the same footing as actual notice of the lease. If recording of a notice of lease were given a lesser effect, its utility would be largely lost, since those concerned would be well advised not to use it. The prospective purchaser of the lessor's interest can fully protect himself by examining the original lease or by consulting the lessee. Hence we hold that the defendants had constructive notice of the plaintiff's option to purchase.

3. *Consequences of notice.* The parties have assumed that if the defendants had actual or constructive notice of the lessee's option to purchase they took subject to it. No contention is made that the option was independent of the lease rather than incidental to it.

4. *Disposition*. The decree is reversed and the case is remanded to the Superior Court for further proceedings consistent with this opinion.

Gagner v. Kittery Water District

Supreme Court of Maine, 1978.
385 A.2d 206.

McKusick, Chief Justice.

The Kittery Water District (District), a defendant in the action below, appeals from the York County Superior Court's ruling that it has no valid easement as against the plaintiffs for maintenance of a water main claimed by the District. We sustain the appeal.

In 1969 Warren's Realty, Inc. (Realty) conveyed to the plaintiffs, Raymond and Beatrice Gagner, by warranty deed, certain realty abutting Route 1 in Kittery, Maine. The Gagners commenced the present action against their seller in 1971 for breach of covenant of warranty against encumbrances, having discovered shortly after taking the deed that a water main, owned by the District and serving the Portsmouth Naval Shipyard, traversed the property. Realty then brought a third-party complaint against the plaintiffs' attorney, who, in addition to having represented both the Gagners and Realty in the land transfer, had also searched the title for the plaintiffs and certified it to be free and clear of all encumbrances.[1] The plaintiffs later amended their complaint to join the District as an additional party defendant. With the case thus postured, the Superior Court issued a pre-trial order severing for hearing the issue of the validity of the District's easement. After a hearing limited to that issue, the Superior Court ruled that "there is no valid easement as against plaintiffs in this case for the maintenance of the water main claimed by the Kittery Water District." The District appealed the final judgment entered against it below.

The validity of the District's unrecorded water pipe easement as against the Gagners depends upon our applying to the facts of this case the governing Maine recording statute, 33 M.R.S.A. § 201 (1964), providing in pertinent part that:

> *[n]o conveyance* of an estate in fee simple, fee tail or for life, or lease for more than 2 years or for an indefinite term is *effectual against any person except* the grantor, his heirs and devisees, and *persons having actual notice thereof unless* the deed or lease is acknowledged and *recorded* in the registry of deeds within the county where the land lies.... (Emphasis added).

This court has in the past had occasion to define the term "actual notice" as used in the recording act.

1. At the time of the attorney's title search in 1969, the District owned an unrecorded water pipe easement over the property that the Gagners purchased. The easement was not recorded until December 13, 1973. All parties agree that the District's act of recordation has no bearing upon the outcome of the present litigation.

> Actual notice and actual knowledge are not necessarily synonymous expressions. Actual notice is that which gives actual knowledge, or the means to such knowledge. It is a warning brought directly home to one whom it concerns to know. Actual notice may be either express or implied. It is express when established by direct proof. It is implied when inferable as a fact by proof of circumstances. "Express actual notice" is, perhaps, its own best definition. Implied actual notice is that which one who is put on a trail is in duty bound to seek to know, even though the track or scent lead to knowledge of unpleasant and unwelcome facts.

Hopkins v. McCarthy, 121 Me. 27, 29, 115 A. 513, 515 (1921). Elaborating more particularly on the concept of "implied actual notice," we earlier said in Knapp v. Bailey, 79 Me. 195, 204, 9. A. 122, 124 (1887), that:

> The doctrine of actual notice implied by circumstances (actual notice in the second degree) necessarily involves the rule that a purchaser before buying, should clear up the doubts which apparently hang upon the title, by making due inquiry and investigation. If a party has knowledge of such facts as would lead a fair and prudent man, using ordinary caution, to make further inquiries, and he avoids the inquiry, he is chargeable with notice of the facts which by ordinary diligence he would have ascertained. He has no right to shut his eyes against the light before him. He does a wrong not to heed the "signs and signals" seen by him. It may be well concluded that he is avoiding notice of that which he in reality believes or knows. Actual notice of facts which, to the mind of a prudent man, indicate notice is proof of notice.

The Superior Court found in the present case that the plaintiffs had no notice, actual or implied, of the existence of the Kittery Water District's water line crossing their property. To the contrary, we conclude that in the circumstances of this case the plaintiffs, through their attorney and title searcher, were put on inquiry notice of the District's easement, but the inquiries made by them did not, as a matter of law, constitute the due diligence required to prevent the enforcement of the District's unrecorded easement against them.[3]

While examining the chain of title to the property at the York County Registry of Deeds in 1969, the Gagners' attorney noticed language in several earlier deeds, first appearing in 1922, stating that the conveyance was made "subject to the rights of the Kittery Water District to maintain a line of water pipes across said premises, as set forth in [a release from Joseph H. Blaisdell] to said Water District." The attorney searched the Registry records for the above-mentioned release, but, as it was then yet unrecorded, he found no such instrument. From the face of the deeds, the attorney also learned that the property which the Gagners desired to purchase had once formed part of a single larger parcel. In 1943 Warren

3. In view of our conclusion that the facts in this case add up to actual notice, we need not in addition inquire whether "constructive," or record, notice also existed.

Wurm and his wife had purchased that parcel "subject to" the rights of the District. In 1953 and 1958, the Wurms by two separate conveyances transferred title to the entire parcel to Realty, the Wurms' corporation. Only that part of the land conveyed by the 1953 deed was, however, conveyed "subject to" the rights of the District. Realty later conveyed that first parcel to a third party by a deed containing no reference to any rights of the Kittery Water District. The parcel that the Gagners purchased was identical to that which the Wurms had conveyed to Realty in 1958 without any "subject to" language.

At the hearing the Gagners' attorney acknowledged that what he actually saw in the deeds put him on inquiry as to the existence of the District's water line. Thus alerted, he contacted Warren Wurm representing Realty, the seller, and asked him whether the District owned any rights in the property. Wurm assured him in the negative. As the attorney testified:

> Mr. Wurm was very anxious to close, have a closing as soon as possible, and I had to go back a second time to the Registry of Deeds because of my concern about this easement. To my best recollection, Mr. Wurm came into my office, I believe it was in my office, he came in a couple of times regarding the closing and selling this parcel to Mr. Gagner, and I asked him about the water, the water easement, which was mentioned, and he assured me that it did not concern the Gagner parcel.

In addition, Mr. Gagner personally inspected the property prior to the purchase and was told by Warren Wurm that a water hydrant located immediately adjacent to the highway supplied water to the property. Mr. Gagner's inspection of the premises revealed no evidence of any other water main crossing the property. According to the attorney's testimony,

> At the time, not finding any recorded easement, and being assured by Mr. Wurm that it did not affect the premises, coupled with the fact that the deed, the prior deed of the premises being conveyed, made no mention of the right of way, it seemed to me I had done as much as was necessary....

The foregoing summary represents the sum total of the steps taken by the plaintiffs, through their attorney, to determine whether the District in fact owned any interest in the property they were purchasing. At no time was any attempt made to contact the District to inquire of it whether any such interest existed. In view of all the facts the plaintiffs are charged with knowing, the failure to do so constituted a fatal omission in executing their duty of reasonable inquiry.

The plaintiffs' attorney knew from the record that Joseph H. Blaisdell had once given a release to the District to maintain a line of water pipes at some location across the larger tract of which the Gagners were buying a portion. He admitted that the clause in the deeds put him on notice of a possible claim of the District in the property. What inquiry of the seller will satisfy the purchaser's duty of due diligence is in every case a question of fact. When the facts known to the purchaser cast doubt upon the very existence of the seller's title, he is bound to inquire of him whether he has any real title or not. The plaintiffs, by their attorney, recognized a duty to inquire of the seller, but upon receiving a false answer did nothing to check with the Kittery Water District, the named holder of the unrecorded interest. *Knapp v. Bailey*, supra, cannot be read to hold that inquiry of the seller will in all instances satisfy a purchaser's duty to inquire. Clearly, more could easily have been done here, and equally clearly, the true facts would have then been revealed.

The District, named as grantee of the interest, had its office in the same town where the subject property was located, and, as an active public utility, could be expected to maintain at a readily available office comprehensive maps and records relating to the easements for its mains. Under these circumstances, the purchasers were bound to inquire of the District, as the most reliable source of information, whether it still claimed the rights referred to in the deeds. Under all the circumstances, the failure to seek an explanation beyond that given by Warren Wurm, who, as the principal of the corporate seller, had an obvious interest in nondisclosure, can only be viewed as a failure of due inquiry. The Gagners are "chargeable with notice of the facts which by ordinary diligence [they] would have ascertained." *Knapp v. Bailey*, supra, 79 Me. at 204, 9 A. at 124.

Judgment reversed.

Miller v. Green

Supreme Court of Wisconsin, 1953.
58 N.W.2d 704.

CURRIE, JUSTICE.

Defendants Hines claim that their title under their deed is superior to the land contract interest of the plaintiffs inasmuch as their deed was recorded first. Section 235.49, Stats., provides as follows:

> Every conveyance of real estate within this state hereafter made (except patents issued by the United States or this state, or by the proper officers of either) which shall not be recorded as provided by law shall be void as against any subsequent purchaser in good faith and for a valuable consideration of the same real estate or any portion thereof whose conveyance shall first be duly recorded.

The question at issue on this appeal is whether the defendants Hines qualify under the foregoing statute as subsequent purchasers "in good faith." Plaintiffs contend that the defendants Hines do not so qualify because the plaintiffs were in possession of the premises on November 29, 1950, when the defendant W.E. Hines paid Mrs. Green $500 toward the purchase price of the farm, and that such possession constituted constructive notice of the plaintiffs' rights under their land contract. This makes it necessary to review the evidence bearing on such possession by the plaintiffs, or either of them.

Approximately 40 acres of the 63–acre tract was cultivated land and the remainder was pasture and woods. The buildings on the farm consisted of a small log house, a barn, and some sheds, which were in a dilapidated condition; the house was unlivable; and such buildings had not been used for many years. The plaintiff Eugene M. Miller had leased the entire 63–acre tract for the crop season of 1950 and had grown crops on the cultivated 40 acres and had grazed livestock on the remaining portion. The crop had been harvested prior to November, 1950, and the livestock had been removed when cold weather came about November 22, 1950. However, starting November 4, 1950 (the date that the Millers contracted to purchase this farm tract), Miller's father, in behalf of the Millers, hauled between 59 and 60 loads of manure to the farm. First the manure was spread over the land, but then after a snowstorm came it was piled on a pile about 100 feet from the road, such pile being about 60 feet long and several feet high. Such hauling of manure was taking place on November 29, 1950 (the date that the defendants Hines made the $500 down payment on the purchase price), and continued until about December 8 or 9, 1950. Also in November, prior to the snowstorm, approximately 2 acres of land had been plowed by Miller, which plowed land was plainly visible from the abutting highway before the snowstorm.

The Hines farm was located about one half mile from this 63–acre tract, although the distance by highway was about one and one half miles. Part of the tract was visible from the Hines home. The defendant W.E. Hines testified that he knew that the plaintiff Eugene M. Miller had leased the tract for the crop season of 1950, but denied that he drove past the tract on the abutting highway during November, 1950, and denied having seen the plowing of the land, the hauling of the. manure, or the manure pile on the land, although he admitted finding the manure pile there the following spring.

The general rule is that possession of land is notice to the world of whatever rights the possessor may have in the premises. The reason underlying this rule is well stated in Pippin v. Richards, 1911, 146 Wis. 69, 74, 130 N.W. 872, 874:

> The theory of the law is th at the person in possession may be asked to disclose the right or title which he has in the premises, and the purchaser will be chargeable with the actual notice he would have received, had he made inquiry. In Frame v. Frame, 32 W.Va. [463], at page 478, 9 S.E. [901] at page 907, the court said: "The earth has been described as that universal manuscript, open to the eyes of all. When, therefore, a man proposes to buy or deal with realty, his first duty is to read this public manuscript; that is, to look and see who is there upon it, and what are his rights there. And, if the person in possession has an equitable title to it, he is as much bound to respect it, as if it was a perfect legal title evidenced by a deed duly recorded."

An apt statement of this general principle of possession being constructive notice is stated in State v. Jewell, 1947, 250 Wis. 165, at page 171, 26 N.W.2d 825, at page 828, 28 N.W.2d 314:

> The possession of real estate is generally considered constructive notice of rights of the possessor, whether the possession is sought to be used for the purpose of charging a purchaser with notice of an outstanding equity, or whether it is sought to charge a subsequent purchaser with notice of an unrecorded instrument and thereby defeat his right to protection under the recording acts. It is so held in the United States courts and in 28 states of the Union.

The rule with respect to possession of a tenant constituting notice of any rights claimed by such tenant is stated in 5 Tiffany, Real Property, Third Ed., p. 73, sec. 1291:

> It has been decided in a number of states that, by the possession of a tenant under a lease, a purchaser is chargeable with notice, not only of the tenant's rights under the lease, but also of any right which he may have not under the lease, as, for instance, under an agreement by the lessor to sell the property to him.

The authorities generally hold that in order that possession may constitute constructive notice such possession must be "open, visible, exclusive and unambiguous." Ely v. Wilcox, 20 Wis. 523; Wickes v. Lake, 25 Wis. 71. It will thus be seen that the requirements as to the type of possession that will constitute constructive notice are practically identical with the requirements of the type of possession necessary to constitute adverse possession. In view of the fact that the farm buildings were unusable, the plowing of the 2 acres of land after November 4, 1950, and the hauling of the manure practically every day throughout November were acts which not only were "open and visible", but also "exclusive and unambiguous." They were the customary acts of possession which could be exercised as to unoccupied farm lands at such time of year. Surely they would have been sufficient to have constituted acts of adverse possession, and it would appear that the rule as to acts of possession necessary to constitute constructive notice to a purchaser is no more strict. *Wickes v. Lake*, supra, is authority for the principle that actual residence on the land is not required in order to have sufficient possession to constitute constructive notice.

In George v. Stansbury, 1922, 90 W.Va. 593, Ill S.E. 598, both the plaintiff and defendants claimed title to a city lot. The plaintiff, during 1919, had maintained a garden on the lot, and the following year, although he did not have a garden there, he permitted the owner of a nearby lot who was excavating for a building to haul a large quantity of dirt from the excavation and dump it on the lot so as to fill a low place. It was during this second year that the defendants purchased the premises and obtained a deed which they recorded, while the plaintiff's title was not recorded. The West Virginia court held that the gardening during the one season, followed by the permitting of the dirt to be hauled in and dumped the second year, constituted sufficient possession to be constructive notice to the defendants of plaintiff's rights, and plaintiff was held to have the superior title. If hauling dirt onto a vacant lot constitutes sufficient possession to be constructive notice to a subsequent purchaser, surely hauling manure onto farm land, as in the instant case, should be held to be equally effective to constitute constructive notice.

In Lyman v. Russell, 1867, 45 111. 281, plaintiff purchased some farm land but did not record his deed. The defendants claimed under a subsequent mortgage executed by plaintiff's vendor. The question was whether there was such "actual, open, notorious and visible possession" of the lands by plaintiff as to constitute constructive notice to the subsequent mortgagees. Plaintiff's act of possession consisted of plowing some of the land in view of all who passed along the adjoining highway. The Illinois court held that the plaintiff's possession was sufficient notice to put a subsequent purchaser on inquiry, and should operate as notice of plaintiff's rights.

The learned trial court in the instant case apparently was of the opinion that, in order for the plaintiff Eugene M. Miller's possession of the premises to have been constructive notice to the defendants Hines that Miller claimed rights of ownership therein, there must have been some change in the type of his possession after November 4, 1950 (the date the Millers entered into the contract to purchase), and his possession prior thereto. This is very apparent from finding No. 5 of the findings of fact made by the trial court, such finding reading as follows:

> That the plaintiff, Eugene M. Miller, continued in possession of said premises, and continued to pasture livestock thereon until about November 22, 1950, when it was necessary to remove them because of the weather, and continued to make such use of the tillable land on said premises as the weather permitted during the month of November, 1950. That the defendant, W.E. Hines knew at that time of the oral lease between the plaintiff, Eugene M. Miller, and the defendant, Mary Green, for the 1950 season. That there was nothing in the use to which the land was put by the plaintiff, Eugene M. Miller, to indicate to the defendant, W.E. Hines, that there had been a change in the status of said plaintiff with relation to said land.

In other words the trial court found that there was possession of the premises by Millers from November 4, 1950, through to the end of that month, but there was no change in the type of possession. Apparently it was the theory of the trial court that the defendants Hines could assume, because of such lack of change in the character of possession, that the possession after November 4, 1950, was that of a tenant and not of a purchaser. The authorities, however, clearly establish that no such change in the character of possession is necessary.

8 Thompson on Real Property (Permanent Edition), p. 413, sec. 4516, states:

> If the tenant changes his character by taking an agreement to purchase, or he has this right under his lease and exercises his option to purchase, his possession amounts to notice of his equitable title as purchaser.

To the same effect see Anderson. v. Brinser, 1889, 129 Pa. 376, 404, 11 A. 809, 18 A. 520, 521, 6 L.R.A. 205, wherein the Pennsylvania court stated:

> Knowledge of the existence of a lease will, of course, give constructive notice of all its provisions; but the possession, apart from the lease, we think, should be treated as notice of the possessor's claim of title, whatever that claim may be, for the lease may be but the first of two or more successive rights acquired by the tenant. While in the occupancy under a lease for years, the tenant may have purchased under articles, and entitled himself to an equity; or, indeed, he may have purchased the legal estate in fee, and failed to record his deed. Would it be supposed that a knowledge of the precedent, lease would dispense with the duty of inquiry, and entitle a subsequent grantee to the protection of an innocent purchaser?.... In Sugden on Vendors, (volume 1, 6th Amer., from 10th London, Ed., p. 265, § 22,) it is expressly stated, and numerous authorities are cited in support of the statement, that if a tenant, during his tenancy, changes his character by having agreed to purchase the estate, his possession amounts to notice of his equitable title as purchaser.

It is our considered judgment that the acts of possession on the part of the plaintiff Eugene M. Miller throughout the remainder of the month of November, 1950, following the purchase of the tract by the Millers on November 4, 1950, constituted constructive notice to all the world which required a subsequent purchaser to make inquiry as to what rights, if any, the plaintiff Eugene M. Miller claimed to have in the premises. Subsequent purchasers could not safely assume, without inquiry, as did the defendants Hines, that, because Miller had theretofore been a tenant for the season, there had been no subsequent change in his rights from that of a tenant to that of a purchaser.

Judgment reversed and cause remanded with directions to, enter judgment as prayed for in plaintiffs' complaint.

GEHL, Justice (dissenting).

The majority say in effect that as a matter of law any entry upon land and its occupation, no matter that the acts of entry may be infrequent and the occupation may be for short interrupted periods, constitutes such possession as to put a purchaser upon inquiry as to the rights of the person so occupying; that possession, regardless of its nature or extent, serves as notice to put the prospective buyer upon inquiry.

That is erroneous. Possession to constitute notice is that which is *required by law*, and is defined in Ely v. Wilcox, 20 Wis. 523:

> The next question is, whether there was such possession by Ely at the date of the deed to the appellant as to be constructive notice to him of the plaintiff's title. The burden of proof was on the plaintiff to prove such possession. He has failed to prove that either he or any one under him was in actual possession of the premises or any part of them at the date of the deed. The rule is, that possession, to be notice, must be open, visible, exclusive, and unambiguous; not liable to be misunderstood or misconstrued. The plaintiff had no such possession.

In Wickes v. Lake, 25 Wis. 71, the court restated the rule in the same language. Both cases have been considered and cited by this court numerous times.

Not all of the latter cases have dealt with the precise question here involved; they are referred to only as indicating that it is quite likely that the court has not overlooked the rule there stated. It has never, so far as I have been able to find, been held by this court that possession to be constructive notice, may be of a nature different from that there defined. The majority cite a number of cases dealing with situations similar to that presented in the instant case. The court in those cases described the possession upon which the party relied in opposition to the contention of one claiming as *bona fide* purchaser in terms different from those used by the court in the two earlier cases. But a reading of those cases will disclose that the possession there found was such as to meet the requirements of the earlier definition.

The rule as it is stated in the *Ely* case, supra, and the *Wickes* case is in substance identical with that stated in 55 Am. Jur. 1090:

> In order that possession of real estate may constitute notice to a purchaser of the rights of the party in possession or by virtue of which the possession is held, such possession must be visible, open, clear, full, notorious, unequivocal, unambiguous, inconsistent with or adverse to the title or interest of the vendor, and not likely to be misunderstood or misconstrued, but, to the contrary, sufficient to put the purchaser on his guard.

The issue presented is one of fact, and the court's finding should not be disturbed. That a finding has force is indicated quite clearly in First Nat. Bank v. Savings L. & T. Co., 207 Wis. 272, 240 N.W. 381, 384, a case involving similar issues where the court in discussing a finding that one claiming to be a *bona fide* purchaser did not have sufficient notice to put him upon inquiry said, "It is not at all clear that this court could have disturbed a contrary finding. . . ."

It was the burden of the plaintiffs to establish that Hines was not a bona fide purchaser. The court found that they had not met the burden. The fact that some of the land had been plowed, that a water tank and a pile of manure were left upon the farm (neither of which circumstances is evidence of possession inconsistent with the right of possession of Mrs. Green, and neither of which is a circumstance which would necessarily suggest that Miller rather than Mrs. Green or some one else acting for or under her had left the tank and manure upon the premises and had plowed the land), considered with the fact that the buildings were unoccupied and that the crop season for which period Miller had rented the farm had ended, are not such as to permit us to hold that the court's findings are contrary to the great weight and clear preponderance of the evidence. Certainly we should not say that under those circumstances the court erred in its finding that plaintiffs had failed to meet the burden to establish that their possession of the farm was "open, visible, exclusive and unambiguous; not liable to be misunderstood or misconstrued."

The trial judge made no specific finding that the possession of Miller was not that required by law to put Hines on inquiry. He did find that "there was nothing in the use to which the land was put by the plaintiff Eugene M. Miller, to indicate to the defendant W.E. Hines that (there had) been a change in the status of said plaintiff with relation to said land," which I construe as a finding that Miller's occupancy of the land was not such as is required by law to put Hines on inquiry. In any event, the omission, if there were such, to make the specific finding, one which is necessary to support the judgment, is equivalent to a finding against the contention of the plaintiffs.

I am authorized to state that Broadfoot and Brown, JJ., join in this dissent.

Notes & Questions

1. **Inquiry Notice Based on Inspection of Records.** To what extent will a recorded instrument trigger a duty of further inquiry? The question arises when a recorded instrument has obviously been altered or phrased in an unusual manner, or when a title search reveals only a partial conveyance to the purchaser's grantor or some predecessor in title, and no indication as to whether, or to whom, the other parts were conveyed. Courts generally hold purchasers to notice of all facts that they could have discovered through reasonable inquiry into the discrepancy.

The same question arises when an instrument that is disclosed by the title search refers to an instrument that is not disclosed, as happens when a deed recites that the property is subject to a mortgage and the mortgage is unrecorded. Here, too, courts impose a duty of reasonable inquiry. Many legislatures, however, have acted to relax the duty. Massachusetts, for example, requires that a reference be "definite" in order to put purchasers on notice. An "indefinite reference" is one that recites interests created by unrecorded or improperly recorded documents, ambiguous descriptions of the interest, indications that the holder of the interest is a "trustee" when the trust is not of record, or any references that do not disclose where the instrument is recorded. Mass. Gen. Laws ch. 184, § 25.

Is the Massachusetts Supreme Court opinion in *Kemp* consistent with these principles? After *Kemp*, would you ever allow a client to buy land subject to a lease without first obtaining and reading the entire lease? Say your client is planning to buy a large shopping center or apartment house occupied by 250 tenants. Will it be necessary to review each of the 250 leases?

2. **Inquiry Notice Based on Inspection of Land.** One fact that is universally held to put a purchaser on inquiry notice is possession by someone other than his seller. Often in these circumstances the possessor will be a tenant, and the purchaser will thus be placed on notice not only of the tenant's rights under its lease, but of any other rights, such as an option to purchase the property. Vitale v. Pinto, 500 N.Y.S.2d 283 (App. Div. 1986). Occasionally the possessor will claim ownership of the land through adverse possession or through a prior deed from the present seller or some other owner. See Bump v. Dahl, 133 N.W.2d 295 (Wis. 1965) (grading, sodding, planting, and landscaping of parcel gave subsequent purchaser inquiry notice of prior purchaser's possessory claim).

Nonpossessory interests are more problematic. As you will see in Chapter 10, nonpossessory interests are rights to use, or dictate the use of, land that is owned in fee or leased by someone else. The Water District in *Gagner*, for example, held an easement to run a water pipe across the Gagners' property; Gagner owned the land, but the Water District held the right to put the water pipe on the property. Because the use of easements is not always as obvious as possession of land, inquiry notice becomes a more complex question. Will manhole covers, for example, suffice to put a purchaser on inquiry notice of an easement for an underlying sewer line? Compare Lake Meredith Development Co. v. City of Fritch, 564 S.W.2d 427 (Tex. Civ. App. 1978) (yes) with Fanti v. Welsh, 161 S.E.2d 501 (W. Va. 1968) (no). Wolek v. Di Feo, 159 A.2d 127 (N.J. Super. 1960), found no basis for inquiry notice against an easement holder's argument that "in the quiet hours of the evening" the purchaser "must have heard the rush of water through the underground pipes." Even nonpossessory interests offering more clearly visible clues, such as power lines and support poles installed pursuant to a public utility easement, have been treated differently within the same jurisdiction. Compare Florida Power & Light Co. v. Rader, 306 So. 2d 565 (Fla. App. Dist. 1975) with McDaniel v. Lawyers' Title Guaranty Fund, 327 So. 2d 852 (Fla. App. Dist. 1976). For an in depth analysis, see Joel Eichengrun, The Problem of Hidden Easements and the Subsequent Purchaser Without Notice, 40 Okla. L. Rev. 3 (1987).

Do you agree with the result in Miller v. Green? Can a buyer avoid inquiry notice by simply not viewing the land? The answer, obviously, is that he cannot. All purchasers are presumed to have inspected the land they are about to buy, and to have seen all inquiry-provoking facts that such an inspection would have disclosed.

3. **Actual Knowledge by Agency Attribution.** Information uncovered in the course of a title search will give actual notice to the client who ordered the search, either because the searcher will communicate the information to the client or, absent such communication, because the agency relationship between searcher and client will impute the searcher's knowledge to the client. This latter rule is a frequent source of problems.

For example, in Farr v. Newman, 199 N.E.2d 369 (N.Y. 1964), plaintiff, who had entered into, but not recorded, a contract to purchase a parcel for $3,000, sought specific performance against defendant who purchased the parcel for $4,000 before plaintiff's contract was to close, but not before plaintiff informed defendant's attorney of plaintiff's outstanding contract. Holding for plaintiff, the court of appeals noted first that "[e]ven if the plaintiff had not affirmatively relied upon the agency of the attorney by giving notice, and the attorney had merely discovered plaintiff's equity in the course of his title investigation, the principal would still be bound by such knowledge. A conflict of interest does not avoid the imputation of knowledge." 199 N.E.2d at 373.

Did the attorney who represented both buyer and seller in Gagner v. Kittery Water District properly resolve the potential conflict of interest arising from that dual representation? What kind of disclosure should the attorney have made to buyer and seller? How could the attorney have properly served the interests of these two clients once having been told by seller's representative, Warren Wurm, that the Water District had no rights in the property and knowing also that "Mr. Wurm was very anxious to close" and that a far more reliable answer could be provided by the District?

4. What policies would be served—and disserved—if states were to drop the inquiry notice bar? The actual notice bar? Representing a buyer, how comfortable would you feel knowing that every tramped-down footpath or half-remembered conversation could later form the basis for a finding of inquiry or actual notice? In terms of fairness or efficiency, what is wrong with a pure race regime?

b. PURCHASER FOR VALUE

Daniels v. Anderson

Supreme Court of Illinois, 1994.
642 N.E.2d 128.

JUSTICE FREEMAN delivered the opinion of the court:

[In March 1977, the plaintiff, William L. Daniels, purchased two lots (the "Daniels Property") from James Anderson and Stephen Jacula, who jointly owned the land]. The written contract consisted of a preprinted form and a rider, which provided [for an easement of ingress and egress to the Daniels Property] and also provided:

> *Right to Purchase Additional Land.* Seller agrees that he shall grant Purchaser the first right to purchase (on the same terms and conditions, and for the same price, as any bona-fide offer in writing made to Seller) a tract of land approximately two acres in area [the "Contiguous Parcel"], being that piece adjacent to [the Daniels Property].... Said right shall be personal to Purchaser, shall not run with the land and shall terminate upon any transfer

of title by Purchaser other than a transfer resulting in ownership by Purchaser and his then spouse as joint tenants.

Daniels and his wife moved into the single-family home on the Daniels Property when they entered into the 1977 sales contract. In March 1979, the Daniels Property closed and the Danielses received a deed. This deed did not mention Daniels' easement or his right of first refusal of the Contiguous Parcel. Daniels did not record the 1977 sales contract at this time.

In June 1979, Jacula and his wife acquired sole ownership of the Contiguous Parcel.... In September 1985, Zografos contracted with the Jaculas to buy the Contiguous Parcel for $60,000. Daniels never received an offer to buy the Contiguous Parcel. Since Daniels had not recorded the 1977 contract by this time, a title search for this sale to Zografos reflected that Daniels did not have any interest in the Contiguous Parcel. Pursuant to the 1985 contract, Zografos paid the Jaculas $10,000 initially and delivered to them a judgment note on the balance. On February 18, 1986, Zografos paid $15,000 and, on March 22, he paid another $15,000. [In June 1986, Daniels' wife informed Zografos of Daniels' right of first refusal. Zografos nonetheless went forward with the purchase of the property.] At the closing on August 22, Zografos paid the remaining $20,000. Shortly after that date, Zografos recorded a warranty deed to the Contiguous Parcel....

Daniels brought this action in December 1989. Daniels sought the specific performance of his right of first refusal of the Contiguous Parcel.... At the close of a hearing, the trial court found as follows. Daniels' right of first refusal of the Contiguous Parcel, as provided by the 1977 sales contract, was legally enforceable. Zografos had actual notice of Daniels' right prior to Zografos' purchase of that parcel. Therefore, Zografos was not a *bona fide* purchaser of the Contiguous Parcel and he took title thereto subject to Daniels' right....

Based on these findings, the trial court entered a judgment that provided as follows. Zografos was ordered to convey the Contiguous Parcel to Daniels on the same terms and conditions as Zografos received the property, including the easement rights that he received from the Jaculas. Daniels was ordered to pay Zografos the full purchase price and reimburse him for approximately $11,000 in property taxes that Zografos had paid on the Contiguous Parcel during his ownership....

A contractual right of first refusal is a valuable prerogative. A landowner is under a duty not to sell to any third person without first offering the land to the promisee. The promisee has an enforceable right to such forbearance. If the owner offers or accepts an offer to sell the land to a third person, thereby breaching the contract, the promisee may obtain specific performance. This would compel the owner to convey to the promisee on the same terms as with the third person, *"as long as there is no contract with an innocent purchaser."* (Emphasis added.) 5A A. Corbin, Corbin on Contracts § 1197, at 377–78 (1964).

Zografos raises the defense that he was an innocent, or *bona fide,* purchaser. A *bona fide* purchaser is a person who takes title to real property in good faith for value without notice of outstanding rights or interests of others. A *bona fide* purchaser takes such title free of any interests of third persons, except such interests of which he has notice.

Zografos testified that he did not know of Daniels' right of first refusal until Daniels' wife told him in June 1986. By that time, Zografos had already contracted to buy the Contiguous Parcel and had paid $40,000 of the $60,000 purchase price. The trial court found that Zografos was not a *bona fide* purchaser based solely on this June 1986 notice.

In the appellate court, Zografos contended that he was a *bona fide* purchaser of the Contiguous Parcel despite his June 1986 notice of Daniels' interest. Zografos invoked the doctrine of equitable conversion in support of his *bona fide* purchaser defense. He argued that although he did not take legal title to the Contiguous Parcel until August 1986, he became the equitable owner of the Contiguous Parcel in September 1985, when he entered into the contract. Thus, Zografos reasoned, he became a *bona fide* purchaser because he took equitable title prior to receiving the June 1986 notice of Daniels' interest. The appellate court concluded that Zografos waived this theory. 252 Ill. App. 3d at 299.

Zografos repeats this theory before this court. We agree with the appellate court that Zografos did not assert this theory in any pleading, memorandum, argument, or post-trial motion in the trial court. Rather, Zografos raised this theory for the first time on appeal. "It has frequently been held that the theory upon which a case is tried in the lower court cannot be changed on review, and that an issue not presented to or considered by the trial court cannot be raised for the first time on review." Kravis v. Smith Marine, Inc. (1975), 60 Ill. 2d 141, 147, 324 N.E.2d 417.... We uphold the appellate court's finding that Zografos has waived application of the doctrine of equitable conversion.

We must next address, absent consideration of the equitable conversion doctrine, the issue of when during the executory stages of a real estate installment contract does the buyer become a *bona fide* purchaser. Zografos contends that, during this executory period, the buyer can rely solely on the public records and ignore even actual notice of an outstanding, unrecorded interest.

This contention is erroneous. The legal principles are quite established. As we earlier noted, a *bona fide* purchaser, by definition, takes title to real property *without notice* of the interests of others. A buyer who, prior to the payment of *any* consideration receives notice of an outstanding interest, pays the consideration at his or her peril with respect to the holder of the outstanding interest. Such a buyer is not protected as a *bona fide* purchaser and takes the property bound by the outstanding interest. The law reasons that consummation of the purchase, after notice of the outstanding interest, is a fraud upon the holder of that interest.

Where a buyer receives notice of an outstanding interest subsequent to paying *some,* but prior to paying the full purchase price, authorities differ on whether the buyer is a *bona fide* purchaser. As the appellate court noted, some of the authorities state that partial payment of the consideration is insufficient to render the buyer a *bona fide* purchaser. However, a majority of jurisdictions have relaxed this harsh rule. Instead, they apply a *pro tanto* rule, which protects the buyer to the extent of the payments made prior to notice, but no further. This court recognized this *pro tanto* rule in *dicta* in Redden v. Miller (1880), 95 Ill. 336, 346.

Courts have identified at least three methods to apply this *pro tanto* protection. First, the most common method is to award the land to the holder of the outstanding interest and award the buyer the payments that he or she made. The second method is to award the buyer a fractional interest in the land proportional to the amount paid prior to notice. The third method is to allow the buyer to complete the purchase, but to pay the remaining installments to the holder of the outstanding interest. Courts exercise considerable latitude in these cases, taking into account the relative equities of the parties.

In the present case, the trial court ordered Zografos to convey the Contiguous Parcel to Daniels and ordered Daniels to pay Zografos the full purchase price. The trial court also ordered Daniels to reimburse Zografos for the property taxes that Zografos had paid on the property. We agree with the appellate court that the trial court's disposition of this issue, between Daniels and Zografos, satisfied these well-settled principles of equity. We cannot say that the trial court abused its discretion. . . .

Notes & Questions

1. Almost all states today require that, to be protected, a subsequent grantee must be a purchaser for value. In most states the requirement appears in the recording act. In a few it has been added by judicial gloss. Courts generally agree that the required value need not approximate the property's market value but must represent more than merely nominal consideration. See generally 14 Richard R. Powell, Powell on Real Property § 82.01[2] (Michael Allan Wolf ed., 2005).

What interests does the purchaser for value requirement serve? Do the requirement's benefits outweigh the costs created by uncertainty respecting whether a purchaser gave the requisite value? How should the requirement be applied when someone first discovers the prior transfer after having partially paid for the property, as in *Daniels*?

2. In Lown v. Nichols Plumbing & Heating, Inc., 634 P.2d 554 (Alaska 1981), Walter Reams owned a parcel of land 26 miles west of Juneau. In 1965, Reams mortgaged the property. The mortgagee recorded the deed of trust in the wrong jurisdiction and did not correctly record the deed until May 1967. Shortly after mortgaging the property, Reams gave the property to J.J. Lown "to induce him to build a lodge on it, so that the surrounding parcels retained by Reams would be saleable as cabin sites." In June 1967, Lown started construction of the lodge. Lown did not learn of

the mortgage until December 1967. The Alaska Supreme Court ruled that Lown took the property subject to the mortgage. Lown initially was merely a donee and thus was not protected from unrecorded interests. Although Lown "arguably" became a "purchaser in good faith for a valuable consideration" in June 1967 when he began construction of the lodge, the May 1967 recording of the deed of trust by then had placed him on "constructive notice."

Chief Justice Rabinowitz dissented. Rabinowitz conceded that Lown would not have been protected from the earlier mortgage if he had received actual notice before investing in the property, but objected to denying him protection based on constructive notice:

> [In some] transfers of land, including this one, consideration is conveyed over a long period of time. The general rule is that when the purchaser receives actual notice of a third party's prior unrecorded interest, the purchaser has the status of "innocent purchaser in good faith for a valuable consideration" only to the extent of payments made before he becomes "infected" with notice, and is entitled only to a lien on the land as security for reimbursement for those payments. Were this rule extended to constructive notice, a purchaser would have to re-check the title records before each and every payment to insure that he was still "in good faith" in making that payment. I regard this as unduly burdensome.
>
> A less restrictive rule would require an additional search only before the initial transfer of consideration. However, I see no valid reason for imposing such a duty absent unusual circumstances. Where, as here, a third party tardily records an instrument between the time of delivery of the subsequent purchaser's deed and the first transfer of consideration under that subsequent conveyance, I think it is more reasonable to place the burden on that third party to provide the purchaser with actual notice, thereby destroying the purchaser's status as an "innocent purchaser in good faith for a valuable consideration," rather than requiring that purchaser to re-check for constructive notice.

Id. at 559–60. How should cases such as *Lown* be resolved? Who was better placed to discover the other's interest—the mortgagee, when it re-recorded in Juneau in May 1967, or Lown, when he began construction in June 1967?

B. THE SYSTEM AT WORK: THE TITLE SEARCH

1. THE INDICES

Note, The Tract and Grantor–Grantee Indices

47 IOWA L. REV. 481 (1962).

A practical and convenient means of locating records which an owner of property must rely upon to prove his title and which a prospective purchaser must depend upon when making a title search is an indispensable part of a workable system of recordation. Therefore, it is not surprising to discover that statutory provisions providing for some system of indexing which affords a history of the ownership of land and which discloses instruments or encumbrances affecting title to real property have been enacted in every state. There are currently two types of indices in use: (1) the grantor-grantee index, and (2) the tract index. This should not be interpreted as meaning that a dual system of indexing has always been present in the United States, for under the land owned by the English, French, Mexican, and Spanish governments on the North American Continent, there were no numbered tract systems in existence which could serve as a basis for land description. This was, of course, directly related to the fact that a competent survey had never been made of the land owned by these countries. Under these circumstances, even tax levies had to be against the owners of the land rather than against the land itself. Therefore, it was only logical that when some system of indexing was finally adopted the alphabetical or grantor-grantee system of indexing was selected. Nevertheless, even after the United States Government acquired the land formerly held by foreign countries in what is now the United States and adequate Government surveys had been undertaken and completed, the grantor-grantee system of indexing was still retained as the basis of land description. However, it was gradually discovered that the grantor-grantee system of indexing was inadequate in many respects. This led several states to enact statutes establishing a tract or numerical system of indexing. Nevertheless, even those states which adopted the tract system of indexing retained the alphabetical system of indexing which they had established at an earlier date.

Under the grantor-grantee or alphabetical index, pages are assigned in the index to each letter of the alphabet. As an instrument is received at the recorder's office, it is first recorded and then indexed under the name of the granting party on the appropriate page of the index. In addition, the county recorder is usually required to make notations on the grantor's page which disclose the name of the other party to the transaction, the book and page of the record where this particular transaction can be found, a description of the property, the date when the instrument was executed, the date when the instrument was filed for recordation, and the nature of the instrument. These same notations are then made as the transaction is indexed under the name of the grantee or the receiving party. After both steps have been completed, the instrument is considered to have been properly indexed.

Under the tract indexing system each parcel of land in a certain area is assigned a separate page in the index and every subsequent transaction affecting this property will be noted thereon. Under the tract system of indexing, a "parcel of land" means any geographical unit of land which has been surveyed and platted, such as sections, blocks, and lots. In addition to describing the property, the tract index also discloses the character of the instrument which affects the title to the property, the date of the execution of the instrument, the date of the filing of the instrument for recordation, and the names of the parties to the transaction. Under this system, therefore, all the instruments which affect the title to a particular parcel of realty will be noted on one page of the index. For this reason and innumerable others, the uniform adoption of the tract index has been urged by many legal scholars. However, the reaction of the respective state legislatures to this proposal apparently has not been enthusiastic.

Edward S. Bade, Cases and Materials on Real Property and Conveyancing

237–238 (1954).

INDICES OF RECORDS

The most widely required forms of indices for real estate records are grantor and grantee indices. In the grantor index, all conveyances are indexed alphabetically and chronologically under the initial letter of the grantor's surname. In the grantee index, a like index is made of conveyances under the initial letter of the grantee's surname. In running these indices the title searcher may begin with a known owner, *A*, at a stated time. He traces this name in the grantor index from the time *A* became an owner until he finds *A* made a conveyance of his title to another—*B*. The index will give the name of the grantee and other particulars such as the date of the instrument, date of recording, kind of instrument, and place where recorded in extenso. At this point he drops *A* and turns to *B* in the grantor index and traces *B*'s name from the *date of the deed* to him (not from the date of recording) until he finds a conveyance of the title from *B* to *C*. He repeats this operation for each successive owner in the chain of title. The grantor-index search for each is bounded in time by the date of *acquisition* and the date of *record* of his conveyance out.

Normally, the title search begins with the grantee index. *Z*, who claims to be the fee owner, is proposing to sell the land to a prospective purchaser. The intending buyer, or his agent, will go to the grantee index and beginning in point of time *presently* where the page is still blank, he will trace back in point of time to see when, if ever, *Z* became a grantee of the land. If he finds *Z*'s name, the index will tell him the name of *Z*'s grantor, *Y*, the date of recording, the date of the deed together with the same information contained in the grantor index.

The title searcher now drops his search for *Z* in the grantee index and turns to *Y*. He now searches the grantee index to see when *Y* became a grantee. In point of time, the search for *Y* as a grantee begins at the date of *the record* of the deed to *Z* and proceeds backward in time until *Y*'s name is found. In this way the title is traced back link by link. Both indices must be traced to complete the search.

To illustrate the matter for one step or link. When the searcher finds *Y* was the grantor of *Z* the searcher will then trace the grantee index to find when *Y* became a grantee. He will then want to know whether *Y* at any time since the *date of the deed* (not the date of its record) to him, made any conveyance out. Hence he traces *Y* in the grantor index from the *date of the deed* to *Y* down to the point where *Y* granted all his interest in the land to *Z*. The search at this point continues to the *date of record* of the deed from *Y* to *Z*. This is done because if *Z* did not record promptly, in notice and notice-race jurisdictions, *Y* may have made a subsequent conveyance to a bona fide purchaser for value who may have recorded his conveyance first, cutting off *Z*'s rights. In notice jurisdictions, of course, *Z*'s rights could be cut off without a prior recording.

In following this procedure, it will be apparent that if *Y* made a conveyance of the land before the date of the deed to him and which was recorded before the date of the deed to him, it would not be found. It will be outside the chain of title. So also it will be evident that a serious discrepancy in the name of a person who is a grantor and grantee or a misdescription of the property may break the thread of search.

The other type of index is variously known as a tract index, block index, and numerical index; most commonly as a tract index. Under this type of index a line or column is assigned to conveniently sized tracts. It may be a section, quarter section, platted blocks or lots. Under that land description, every conveyance of any interest in that land is indexed chronologically. Hence all conveyances affecting the title to that land will appear there. It will appear there no matter who made it, whether he is a stranger to the title or not. Consequently, if a tract index is a required record, purchasers should be, and usually are charged with constructive notice of all conveyances indexed there.

Most abstractors prepare abstracts of title from tract indices. If an abstract so prepared refers to a conveyance outside the chain of title, and is examined by the prospective purchaser or by his agent or attorney, is he put on inquiry even though a trat-t index is not a required index in the jurisdiction?

Howard Savings Bank v. Brunson

Superior Court of New Jersey, Chancery Division, 1990.
582 A.2d 1305.

MARGOLIS, J.S.C.

This matter involves cross motions for summary judgment on a priority dispute between mortgage holders. The essential facts are undisputed.

In January 1986, defendant Burl Brunson (Brunson) purchased a parcel of property in Newark, New Jersey. The deed for the property was properly recorded pursuant to N.J.S.A. 46:21–1 and indexed pursuant to N.J.S.A. 46:20–4 on January 24, 1986. In March 1986, Brunson borrowed $50,000 from plaintiff Howard Savings Bank (Howard) secured by a mortgage which was properly recorded on May 1, 1986. This mortgage was *not* properly indexed until February 3, 1988.

Brunson subsequently executed two mortgages to defendant Rols Capital Company (Rols) on April 11, 1986 and on May 14, 1986. On May 20,

1986, Brunson executed and delivered a mortgage on the property to Myron Pokross (Pokross). On the same day, Brunson executed and delivered a deed for the property to Pokross which was recorded in the office of the register of Essex County on July 7, 1988.

On October 6, 1987, Brunson executed and delivered a deed for the property to defendants Jesus Ijalba and Celeste Ijalba (Ijalba), which deed was properly recorded in the office of the register of Essex County on November 4, 1987. On October 6, 1987, Ijalba executed and delivered a mortgage covering the subject premises to defendant Chrysler First Financial Services Corporation (Chrysler). This mortgage was also properly recorded on November 4, 1987.

On the basis of a thorough title search and an affidavit of title executed by Brunson on October 5, 1987, representing that he had not allowed any legal interest to be created which would affect the ownership or use of the property, defendant Chicago Title Insurance Company (Chicago Title) issued a title insurance policy to Chrysler.

On May 19, 1988, Howard brought a foreclosure action against Chrysler and Ijalba, claiming that the proceeds of Brunson's sale of the premises to Ijalba were not applied to the mortgage held by Howard, and that its mortgage had priority over all subsequent encumbrancers of the property. The disposition of the claims, if any, arising from the interests of Rols and Pokross in the property are not before this court; therefore, this opinion is limited to a ruling on the priority between Howard and defendants Chrysler and Ijalba.

The central issue before the court is whether Howard's prior interest in the property, which was recorded but misindexed, has priority over the interests of Ijalba and Chrysler, subsequent lienors who failed to discover Howard's interest due to the misindexing.

Our inquiry begins with the New Jersey Recording Act. N.J.S.A. 46:21–1 provides:

> Except as otherwise provided herein, whenever any deed or instrument of the nature or description set forth in section 46:16–1 of this title, which shall have been or shall be duly acknowledged or proved and certified, shall have been or shall be duly recorded or lodged for record with the county recording officer of the county in which the real estate or other property affected thereby is situate or located such record shall, from that time, be notice to all subsequent judgment creditors, purchasers and mortgagees of the execution of the deed or instrument so recorded and of the contents thereof.

Howard contends that, because its mortgage from Brunson was properly recorded pursuant to the Recording Act, its interest has priority over all subsequent encumbrancers. Plaintiff further argues that valid recordation of a mortgage *alone* serves as constructive notice to interested parties; thus, defendants had constructive notice of Howard's interest because the mortgage was properly recorded over 17 months before defendants obtained an interest in the property.

N.J.S.A. 46:20–1 and–4 provide in pertinent part:

> The county recording officer of each county shall provide, at the expense of their respective counties, a book or books, and shall, in case it is not already done, make and therein enter indexes, in alphabetical order, to all the various books of record, called and backed "deeds" and called and backed "mortgages," heretofore or hereafter recorded in their respective offices, distinguishing the book in which each deed or mortgage is recorded.
>
> The indexes herein required to be kept shall contain the names of the several grantors and grantees of deeds, and the names of the several mortgagors of mortgages. . . .
>
> The county recording officer of each county shall keep, in addition to the daily entries of the same, an alphabetical index of all the names of the grantors in deeds, parties to instruments and mortgagors in mortgages that may be presented to him for record, which alphabetical index shall be made of all such deeds and instruments by the county recording officer on the same day, or on the day following, that they are received for record.

Plaintiff discounts the significance of N.J.S.A. 46:20–1, the indexing statute, arguing that although it imposes a duty on the county register to maintain an alphabetized index of the chronological record, it places no duty upon the mortgagee with regard to providing notice to subsequent parties in interest because it is not part of the record. Howard relies on Semon v. Terhune, 40 N.J. Eq. 364, 2 A. 18 (Ch. 1885) and its progeny in support of its argument. *Semon*, like the case at bar, involved the effect of misindexing a mortgage on a subsequent purchaser's constructive notice of its existence. The court held that the misindexing had no effect on the initial party's priority because only the record is necessary to provide notice and the index is not a part of that record. Id. at 367, 2 A. 18.

Defendants maintain that N.J.S.A. 46:21–1 must be read in conjunction with the indexing statute in order that the spirit and intent of the Recording Act be met. Chief among the cases and articles cited to support their argument is Jones, "The New Jersey Recording Act—A Study of its Policy," 12 Rutgers L. Rev. 328 (1957). In an exhaustive and definitive treatment of the subject, Jones discusses the history and intent of the Recording Act.

> An historical study of the [Recording] Act, as well as an analysis of the cases interpreting it, leads to the conclusion that it was designed to compel the recording of instruments affecting title, for the ultimate purpose of permitting purchasers to rely upon the record title and to purchase and hold title to lands within this state with confidence. [*Id.* at 329–330]

Clearly, the fundamental purpose of the Recording Act is to provide notice to subsequent parties in interest and "the protection of purchasers and encumbrancers of real property against undisclosed titles and liens." Solomon v. Canter, 113 N.J. Eq. 43, 45, 166 *A.* 158 (E. & A.1933). Once a mortgagee provides notice, a corresponding protection against subsequent titles and liens arises, ensuring that he may safely rely upon the statutes to establish the validity and priority of his mortgage. The issue which this court faces is whether the requisite notice is achieved through the mere recordation of a mortgage or whether notice is achieved only if the mortgage is also properly indexed.

Jones points out that *Semon* was decided in 1885, before a legislative requirement even existed for a mortgage index. At that time, mortgage entries were few and infrequent, and title searchers were able to thumb through the record books to ascertain the contents with little trouble. As the number of entries grew, however, there also grew a practical need for indices to the mortgage books to provide the means for efficient title searches. This need was codified in essentially its present form in 1898, but the Legislature has not since amended the recording statute or the indexing statute to reflect the extraordinary changes that have occurred in the custom and practice of title searching since then. Yet the New Jersey Supreme Court, in Palamarg Realty Co. v. Rehac, 80 N.J. 446, 404 *A.*2d 21 (1979), emphasized the fact that "title searching, upon which so much of our conveyancing practice rests, has been created in very large part without the aid of legislation," and that an investigation of the custom and practice of title searching is essential to determine current disputes in that area of law. See id. at 461, 404 *A.*2d 21.

For these reasons, and because this court is not bound by courts of equal jurisdiction, this court chooses to reexamine the *Semon* rule that the index is not considered in practice to be a part of the record. For purposes of this analysis, it is necessary to determine, from the evidence currently before the court, whether the current custom and practice of title searching require that the index be interpreted to be an integral part of the record.

In this regard, this court has had the benefit of the uncontroverted certification of Lawrence J. Fineberg, resident vice-president and associate regional counsel of defendant Chicago Title, an attorney fully familiar with the custom, practice and procedure of title searching in New Jersey. Fineberg states that the "customary period for title searching is to go back 60 years to a warranty deed" in order to establish an unbroken chain of title for the premises in question. Once the searcher has gone back at least 60 years, he "adverses" each successive owner in the chain of title for the time period during which that owner held title in order to discover liens, restrictions, conveyances to third parties and the like which would encumber title. In performing the adversing task, Fineberg continues, "[i]t has long been the practice of New Jersey title searchers to check the alphabetical indices under the name of each owner of record to see whether he executed any instruments which would create adverse interests in the particular property." Furthermore, "the only way to perform a search *without* relying on the indices is to turn each page of each record book in the county during the entire period of time that each individual appeared of record to be the owner until one discovers a particular instrument creating an adverse interest.... [T]here are literally thousands of record books in each county ... [and] [e]ach Mortgage Book contains at least 1,000 pages." Emphasis supplied.

Fineberg's certification unequivocally supports the title searchers' practice of relying solely upon the statutorily required alphabetical indices in performing title searches. This practice, and the resulting necessity of considering the index to be a part of the record so as to protect title searchers who rely upon it, is discussed favorably by several commentators. See Jones, supra at 340 ("[T]oday the index *must* be considered as part of the record, and ... an instrument which is not properly indexed is not 'duly recorded.' "). Cunningham & Tischler explain: "A mortgage can hardly be deemed 'duly recorded' unless it is properly indexed, if we are to take seriously the many statements by New Jersey courts to the effect that the object of the recording statutes is to prevent imposition upon subsequent bona fide purchasers and mortgagees; for without an index, searching for a mortgage in the public records would be like looking for the proverbial needle in a haystack." Cunningham & Tischler, Law of Mortgages, 29 N.J. Practice 106....

As Jones pointed out, "what is reasonable under the circumstances existing in one generation may be unreasonable under those existing in a subsequent generation." Jones, supra at 330. It would be *unreasonable* to saddle a purchaser with the obligation of thumbing through every page of every record book in the county register's office, representing the entire period of time that an individual appeared of record to be the owner, in order to overcome the risk of improper indexing, given the enormous number of real estate transactions which occur and are recorded daily in our state. Id. at 343. A rule prohibiting title searchers from depending upon the alphabetical index would unduly hinder the commercial transactions in the State: lengthy title searches would cost more and would cause unreasonably long closings; potential purchasers, mortgagors and lenders would hesitate to be involved in commercial transactions where they could not be confident that a reasonable search of the record would reveal prior interests or where they feared being held liable for a clerk's misindexing error; and the cost of title insurance would increase.

The solution is that the recording and indexing statutes must be read *in pari materia* such that they are "construed together as a unitary and harmonious whole in order that each may be fully effective." See Clifton v. Passaic County Bd. of Taxation, 28 N.J. 411, 421, 147 *A.*2d 1 (1958). The indices must be construed to be part of the record so as to reflect the current custom and practice of title searching and to provide stability and certainty in real estate transactions so that subsequent parties in interest may safely rely upon the record.

Obviously, one effect of finding a duty in the mortgagee to see that his instrument is properly indexed will be that the mortgagee will be required to conduct "run down" searches or to employ some other similar mechanism for ensuring that his interest is properly indexed. Yet such a practice is seen as making good business sense anyway. Furthermore, placing the burden upon the mortgagee to ensure that the requisite notice has been given is not out of step with the equitable maxim that where a loss must be borne by one of two innocent parties, equity will impose the loss on the party whose first act would have prevented the loss....

For the reasons set forth above, the court is satisfied that defendants made a *reasonable* search of the chain of title by searching the indices alone, the deed and mortgage of Ijalba and Chrysler have priority over Howard's lien, and defendants' cross motion for summary judgment is granted.

Skelton v. Martin

Court of Appeal of Florida, 1996.
673 So. 2d 877.

ALTENBERND, JUDGE.

Roy C. Skelton appeals a final judgment in an action to quiet title. The judgment invalidates his tax deed and upholds a subsequently recorded deed from Ernest Martin to Sandy K. Perry. We reverse.

Ernest Martin owned Lot 6, Block 13, of the replat of Pine City Subdivision in Pinellas County. He failed to pay the 1990 property tax on this lot. On May 22, 1991, the Pinellas County Tax Collector issued a tax certificate to Bank Atlantic for unpaid taxes. When Mr. Martin failed to redeem the certificate by August 25, 1993, Bank Atlantic requested a tax deed sale pursuant to section 197.502, Florida Statutes (1991).

The clerk of court scheduled a tax deed sale for January 19, 1994, and sent Mr. Martin the statutory notice to owner warning him of that sale. The clerk also notified the mortgagees of record. Public notice of the sale was published in the Pinellas County Review on December 17, 24, 31, 1993, and January 7, 1994. Mr. Skelton purchased the property for $23,500 at the scheduled sale. The tax deed was recorded on January 20, 1994.

Meanwhile, Mr. Martin entered into an agreement to sell this same property to Sandy K. Perry for $43,000. If there is a written contract of sale between these two parties, it is not in this record and was not recorded. Equity Title Southeast (Equity Title) performed a title search in connection with this sale in early January 1994. Equity Title did not send an abstractor to the courthouse and it did not examine the notices published in the Pinellas County Review. Instead, its title abstractor used a computer to connect with the "Pinellas County Computer Dial–Up System." The abstractor testified that he examined the current tax year screen for this parcel. In addition to information about current taxes, this screen normally indicates if there are delinquent taxes on the property from prior years. The screen did not so indicate in this instance, and the abstractor did not check the delinquent tax screen to determine whether it showed any tax certificates or delinquent taxes.

Because Equity Title did not discover a problem with Mr. Martin's title to the property and because Mr. Martin executed the no lien affidavit without disclosing the unpaid taxes, Ms. Perry purchased this property at a closing on January 7, 1994. Thus, the closing occurred twelve days before the tax deed sale and the same day as the last publication of public notice in the Pinellas County Review. As part of the closing, Equity Title paid the 1993 property taxes with a check that the tax collector deposited on January 11, 1994. However, no one paid the delinquent taxes. The deed to Ms. Perry was not recorded until January 25, 1994, a week after the tax deed sale and five days after Mr. Skelton's deed was recorded.

.... The evidence in this case is interesting because it demonstrates a serious variance between the statutory method for the maintenance of public records and the electronic means by which most private and public records are now retrieved. Technology has clearly jumped ahead of the traditional methods of public record-keeping. Equity Title understandably wishes to rely on more efficient technology, but legal title is still governed by statutes.

Section 28.222, Florida Statutes (1991), requires the clerk of circuit court, as the county recorder, to maintain a "general alphabetical index, direct and inverse, of all instruments filed for record," including deeds, mortgages, and tax certificates. These documents are recorded in "one general series of books called 'Official Records.' " The Pinellas County Computer Dial–Up System allows remote users to review an electronic version of the official records.

The current tax screen on the dial-up system is clearly not the "general alphabetical index" required by statute. Ms. Perry does not dispute that the tax certificate is properly recorded in the official record and adequately indexed as required by the statutes. Thus, Ms. Perry did not suggest that the tax certificate was void for a statutory reason or that the tax deed sale departed from the statutory requirements. Instead of raising a statutory challenge, Ms. Perry contended that her constitutional due process rights had been violated because she had not received adequate notice of the existence of the tax lien. In essence, Ms. Perry maintained that the current tax screen on the dial-up computer misled Equity Title, and that she would have learned of the tax sale but for this mistake.

For purposes of this opinion, we accept as true that an error existed on the current year tax screen and that such an omission would cause many abstractors not to further examine the computerized files. The question remains whether this error deprived Ms. Perry of constitutional notice of either the tax certificate or of the pending sale.

The tax certificate was recorded in the manner required by statute. Ms. Perry did not even prove that the delinquent tax screen on the dial-up computer omitted this information. The ability to retrieve government documents on the computerized information superhighway is a new tool that streamlines title searches and makes many transactions more economical. Nevertheless, there is no present statutory right to accurate government information on the Internet. At this point in history, such computerized data is not a form of notice constitutionally guaranteed by article I, section 9, of the Florida Constitution, or by the Fourteenth Amendment to the United States Constitution.[6]

Concerning notice of the tax deed sale, Ms. Perry had taken no step that would have placed the clerk on notice of her interest in the property. Although Ms. Perry purchased the property several days before the sale, she had no recorded interest in this lot that would have required the clerk of court to send her notice of the tax deed sale. See, e.g., Mennonite Bd. of Missions v. Adams, 462 U.S. 791, 103 S. Ct. 2706, 77 L. Ed. 2d 180 (1983) (recorded mortgagee entitled to notice of sale). Thus, she was only entitled to the same notice provided to other members of the public, including Mr. Skelton. Any error in the dial-up computer did not prevent her from reading the Pinellas County Review nor did it result in defective notice of this sale. Statutes may someday require notices of public sale to be posted on the Internet, but Ms. Perry has no due process right to that notice today.

Accordingly, we reverse the final judgment. On remand, the trial court shall enter a judgment validating Mr. Skelton's tax deed and permit Ms. Perry to pursue a claim against Mr. Martin, including a claim for the excess funds derived from the sale to Mr. Skelton.

Notes & Questions

1. **Indexing Errors.** If a grantee delivers an instrument to the recorder who fails to index it properly, most jurisdictions as in *Brunson* hold that a subsequent purchaser does not have constructive notice of the instrument. A minority of jurisdictions, however, hold that a recorded grant provides constructive notice to subsequent purchasers, even if the original grantee knew that the grant was not properly indexed. See, e.g., Frank v. Storer, 517 A.2d 1098 (Md. 1986). Which rule is preferable? Which party can best prevent the loss from improper indexing?

Can the party that bears the loss sue the recorder for incorrect indexing? See Siefkes v. Watertown Title Co., 437 N.W.2d 190 (S.D. 1989) (denying negligence action against recorder by title company seeking indemnification for improper indexing).

2. Some form of indexing is obviously required by the tremendous volume of recorded instruments. A 1973 study found that approximately 7,000 instruments were recorded each month in Suffolk County, Massachusetts (Boston), about 15,000 documents were recorded each month in Cook County, Illinois (Chicago), and 5,000–6,000 instruments were recorded each day in Los Angeles. Paul E. Basye, A Uniform Land Parcel Identifier—Its Potential for All Our Land Records, 22 Am. U.L. Rev. 251 (1973).

Even the best official indexing systems are incomplete. One limitation of contemporary indexing systems is that they do not tell title examiners

6. We do not need to determine whether such an error can create liability for the clerk of court.

how far back in a chain of title they must search in order to identify an indisputable source of title. This limitation is not particularly burdensome when a tract index is used because the tract index accumulates all transactions, including the first, on consecutive pages. The limitations can, however, prove costly when only grantor and grantee indices are available, particularly if the searcher must trace title all the way back to the original grant from the sovereign.

Many transactions affecting title will be revealed by neither the grantor-grantee index nor the tract index, no matter how far back title is traced. An examiner searching title must consult, among other sources, the indices of wills and administration of decedents' estates in the office of the county surrogate, the index of bankrupts in local federal court, local judgment dockets, and dockets of federal tax liens. One limitation of these other sources is that they were designed for purposes other than facilitating title searches. For example, because neither grantor-grantee nor tract indices refer to land transfers effected by will or intestacy, a title examiner will quickly conclude that if these indices reveal a gap in ownership it is because the land at that point passed by devise or descent. But it will take considerable sleuthing to bridge that gap since probate registers are indexed alphabetically by the name of the decedent and not by the name of the estate's recipient—the only name that the examiner knows.

Although tract indices suffer many of the same limitations in breadth as grantor-grantee indices, they are clearly superior on other relevant criteria: depth, speed and accuracy of search. Why, then, have tract indices not been widely adopted across the country? The simple answer is that they have—although not as official public indices, but rather as unofficial private indices maintained as "title plants" by examiners, abstracters, and title insurance companies. Recognizing the superiority of tract indices, title examiners long ago began compiling them on their own. Each time an examiner searched title to a parcel, she would place a copy of the search in her files, indexed by reference to the parcel; the next time the examiner was retained to search title to that parcel, she had only to pull the relevant file and update her last search to the present. Title plants represent valuable assets and many, if not most, have been purchased by title insurance companies, enabling them quickly to establish themselves and their services in new locales.

3. On computerization of land records, see John L. McCormack, Torrens and Recording: Land Title Assurance in the Computer Age, 18 Wm. Mitchell L. Rev. 61 (1992).

2. Extent of Search

Morse v. Curtis

Supreme Court of Massachusetts, 1885.
2 N.E. 929.

MORTON, C.J.

This is a writ of entry. Both parties derive their title from one Hall. Hall mortgaged the land to the demandant, August 8, 1872. On September

7, 1875, Hall mortgaged the land to one Clark, who had notice of the earlier mortgage. The mortgage to Clark was recorded January 31, 1876. The mortgage to the demandant was recorded September 8, 1876. On October 4, 1881, Clark assigned his mortgage to the tenant, who had no notice of the mortgage to the demandant. The question is, which of these titles has priority?....

.... The earliest registry law provides that no conveyance of land shall be good and effectual in law "against any other person or persons but the grantor or grantors, and their heirs only, unless the deed or deeds thereof be acknowledged and recorded in manner aforesaid." St.1783, c. 37, § 4. Under this statute the court, at an early period, held that the recording was designed to take the place of the notorious act of livery of seizin, and that though by the first deed the title passed out of the grantor as against himself, yet he could, if such deed was not recorded, convey a good title to an innocent purchaser who received and recorded his deed. But the court then held that a prior unrecorded deed would be valid against a second purchaser who took his deed with a knowledge of the prior deed, thus ingrafting an exception upon the statute. 3 Mass. 575; Marshall v. Fisk, 6 Mass. 24. This exception was adopted on the ground that it was a fraud in the second grantee to take a deed if he had knowledge of the prior deed. As Chief Justice Shaw forcibly says in Lawrence v. Stratton, 6 Cush. 163, the rule is "put upon the ground that a party with such notice could not take a deed without fraud; the objection was not to the nature of the conveyance, but to the honesty of the taker, and therefore, if the estate had passed through such taker to a bonafide purchaser without fraud, the conveyance was held valid." This exception by judicial exposition was afterwards ingrafted upon the statute, and somewhat extended by the legislature. Rev. St. 59, p. 28; Gen. St. c. 59, § 31; Pub. St. c. 120, § 4. It is to be observed that in each of these revisions it is provided that an unrecorded prior deed is not valid against any person except the grantor, his heirs and devisees, "and persons having actual notice of it." The reason why the statutes require actual notice to a second purchaser, in order to defeat his title, is apparent; its purpose is that his title shall not prevail against the prior deed if he has been guilty of a fraud upon the first grantee, and he could not be guilty of such fraud unless he had actual notice of the first deed.

Now, in the case before us, it is found as a fact that the tenant had no actual knowledge of the prior mortgage to the demandant at the time he took his assignment from Clark. But it is contended that he had constructive notice, because the demandant's mortgage was recorded before such assignment. It was held in Connecticut v. Bradish, 14 Am. 296, that such record was evidence of actual notice, but was not of itself enough to show actual notice, and to charge the assignee of the second deed with a fraud upon the holder of the first unrecorded deed. This seems to us to accord with the spirit of our registry laws, and the uniform understanding of and practice under them by the profession. These laws not only provide that deeds must be recorded, but they also prescribe the method in which the records shall be kept and indexes prepared for public inspection and examination. There are indexes of grantors and grantees, so that, in searching a title, the examiner is obliged to run down the list of grantors or run backward through the list of grantees. If he can start with an owner who is known to have a good title, as in the case at bar he could start with Hall, he is obliged to run through the index of grantors until he finds a conveyance by the owner of the land in question. After such conveyance the former owner becomes a stranger to the title, and the examiner must follow down the name of the new owner to see if he has conveyed the land, and so on. It would be a hardship to require an examiner to follow in the index of grantors the name of every person who at any time, through, perhaps, a long chain of title, was the owner of the estate.

We do not think this is the practical construction which lawyers and conveyancers have given to our registry laws. The inconvenience of such a construction would be much greater than would be the inconvenience of requiring a person who has neglected to record his prior deed for a time, to record it, and to bring a bill in equity to set aside the subsequent deed, if it was taken in fraud of his rights. The better rule, and the least likely to create confusion of titles, seems to us to be that if a purchaser, upon examining the registry, finds a conveyance from the owner of the land to his grantor which gives him a perfect record title, complete by what the law at the time it is recorded regards as equivalent to a livery of seizin, he is entitled to rely upon such recorded title, and is not obliged to search the record afterwards made, to see if there has been any prior unrecorded deed of the original owners.

This rule of property, established by the early case of Connecticut v. Bradish, supra, ought not to be departed from unless conclusive reasons therefor can be shown. We are therefore of opinion that in the case at bar the tenant has the better title. Verdict set aside.

Sabo v. Horvath

Supreme Court of Alaska, 1976.
559 P.2d 1038.

BOOCHEVER, CHIEF JUSTICE.

This appeal arises because Grover C. Lowery conveyed the same five-acre piece of land twice—first to William A. Horvath and Barbara J. Horvath and later to William Sabo and Barbara Sabo. Both conveyances were by separate documents entitled "Quitclaim Deeds." Lowery's interest in the land originates in a patent from the United States Government under 43 U.S.C. § 687a (1970) ("Alaska Homesite Law"). Lowery's conveyance to the Horvaths was prior to the issuance of patent, and his subsequent conveyance to the Sabos was after the issuance of patent. The Horvaths recorded their deed in the Chitna Recording District on January 5, 1970; the Sabos recorded their deed on December 13, 1973. The transfer to the Horvaths, however, predated patent and title, and thus the Horvaths' interest in the land was recorded "outside the chain of title." Mr.

Horvath brought suit to quiet title, and the Sabos counterclaimed to quiet their title.

In a memorandum opinion, the superior court ruled that Lowery had an equitable interest capable of transfer at the time of his conveyance to the Horvaths and further said the transfer contemplated more than a "mere quitclaim"—it warranted patent would be transferred. The superior court also held that Horvath had the superior claim to the land because his prior recording had given the Sabos constructive notice for purposes of AS 34.15.290. The Sabos' appeal raises the following issues:

1. Under 43 U.S.C. § 687a (1970), when did Lowery obtain a present equitable interest in land which he could convey?

2. Are the Sabos, as grantees under a quitclaim deed, "subsequent innocent purchaser[s] in good faith"?

3. Is the Horvaths' first recorded interest, which is outside the chain of title, constructive notice to Sabo?

issues

We affirm the trial court's ruling that Lowery had an interest to convey at the time of his conveyance to the Horvaths. We further hold that Sabo may be a "good faith purchaser" even though he takes by quitclaim deed. We reverse the trial court's ruling that Sabo had constructive notice and hold that a deed recorded outside the chain of title is a "wild deed" and does not give constructive notice under the recording laws of Alaska.[2]

The facts may be stated as follows. Grover C. Lowery occupied land in the Chitna Recording District on October 10, 1964 for purposes of obtaining Federal patent. Lowery filed a location notice on February 24, 1965, and made his application to purchase on June 6, 1967 with the Bureau of Land Management (BLM). On March 7, 1968, the BLM field examiner's report was filed which recommended that patent issue to Lowery. On October 7, 1969, a request for survey was made by the United States Government. On January 3, 1970, Lowery issued a document entitled "Quitclaim Deed" to the Horvaths; Horvath recorded the deed on January 5, 1970 in the Chitna Recording District. Horvath testified that when he bought the land from Lowery, he knew patent and title were still in the United States Government, but he did not rerecord his interest after patent had passed to Lowery.

Following the sale to the Horvaths, further action was taken by Lowery and the BLM pertaining to the application for patent and culminating in issuance of the patent on August 10, 1973.

Almost immediately after the patent was issued, Lowery advertised the land for sale in a newspaper. He then executed a second document also entitled "quitclaim" to the Sabos on October 15, 1973. The Sabos duly recorded this document on December 13, 1973.

2. Because we hold Lowery had a conveyable interest under the Federal statute, we need not decide issues raised by the parties regarding after-acquired property and the related issue of estoppel by deed.

Luther Moss, a representative of the BLM, testified to procedures followed under the Alaska Homesite Law. After numerous steps, a plat is approved and the claimant notified that he should direct publication of his claim. In this case, Lowery executed his conveyance to the Horvaths after the BLM field report had recommended patent.

The first question this court must consider is whether Lowery had an interest to convey at the time of his transfer to the Horvaths. Lowery's interest was obtained pursuant to ... the "Alaska Homesite Law." Since Lowery's title to the property was contingent upon the patent ultimately issuing from the United States Government and since Lowery's conveyance to the Horvaths predated issuance of the patent, the question is "at what point in the pre-patent chain of procedures does a person have a sufficient interest in a particular tract of land to convey that land by quitclaim deed." Willis v. City of Valdez, 546 P.2d 570, 575 (Alaska 1976)....

In Willis v. City of Valdez, supra at 578, we held that one who later secured a patent under the Soldiers' Additional Homestead Act had an interest in land which was alienable at the time that he requested a survey. Here, Lowery had complied with numerous requirements under the Homesite Law including those of occupancy, and the BLM had recommended issuance of the patent. Since 43 U.S.C. § 687a (1970) does not prohibit alienation, we hold that at the time Lowery executed the deed to the Horvaths he had complied with the statute to a sufficient extent so as to have an interest in the land which was capable of conveyance.

Since the Horvaths received a valid interest from Lowery, we must now resolve the conflict between the Horvaths' first recorded interest and the Sabos' later recorded interest.

The Sabos, like the Horvaths, received their interest in the property by a quitclaim deed. They are asserting that their interest supersedes the Horvaths under Alaska's statutory recording system. AS 34.15.290 provides that:

> A conveyance of real property ... is void as against a subsequent innocent purchaser ... for a valuable consideration of the property ... whose conveyance is first duly recorded. An unrecorded instrument is valid ... as against one who has actual notice of it.

Initially, we must decide whether the Sabos, who received their interest by means of a quitclaim deed, can ever be "innocent purchaser[s]" within the meaning of AS 34.15.290. Since a "quitclaim" only transfers the interest of the grantor, the question is whether a "quitclaim" deed itself puts a purchaser on constructive notice. Although the authorities are in conflict over this issue, the clear weight of authority is that a quitclaim grantee can be protected by the recording system, assuming, of course, the grantee purchased for valuable consideration and did not otherwise have actual or constructive knowledge as defined by the recording laws. We choose to follow the majority rule and hold that a quitclaim grantee is not precluded from attaining the status of an "innocent purchaser."

In this case, the Horvaths recorded their interest from Lowery prior to the time the Sabos recorded their interest. Thus, the issue is whether the Sabos are charged with constructive knowledge because of the Horvaths' prior recordation. Horvath is correct in his assertion that in the usual case a prior recorded deed serves as constructive notice pursuant to AS 34.15.290, and thus precludes a subsequent recordation from taking precedence. Here, however, the Sabos argue that because Horvath recorded his deed prior to Lowery having obtained patent, they were not given constructive notice by the recording system. They contend that since Horvaths' recordation was outside the chain of title, the recording should be regarded as a "wild deed."

It is an axiom of hornbook law that a purchaser has notice only of recorded instruments that are within his "chain of title." If a grantor (Lowery) transfers prior to obtaining title, and the grantee (Horvath) records prior to title passing, a second grantee who diligently examines all conveyances under the grantor's name from the date that the grantor had secured title would not discover the prior conveyance. The rule in most jurisdictions which have adopted a grantor-grantee index system of recording is that a "wild deed" does not serve as constructive notice to a subsequent purchaser who duly records.

Alaska's recording system utilizes a "grantor-grantee" index. Had Sabo searched title under both grantor's and grantee's names but limited his search to the chain of title subsequent to patent, he would not be chargeable with discovery of the pre-patent transfer to Horvath.

On one hand, we could require Sabo to check beyond the chain of title to look for pretitle conveyances. While in this particular case the burden may not have been great, as a general rule, requiring title checks beyond the chain of title could add a significant burden as well as uncertainty to real estate purchases. To a certain extent, requiring title searches of records prior to the date a grantor acquired title would thus defeat the purposes of the recording system. The records as to each grantor in the chain of title would theoretically have to be checked back to the later of the grantor's date of birth or the date when records were first retained.

On the other hand, we could require Horvath to rerecord his interest in the land once title passes, that is, after patent had issued to Lowery. As a general rule, rerecording an interest once title passes is less of a burden than requiring property purchasers to check indefinitely beyond the chain of title.

It is unfortunate that in this case due to Lowery's double conveyances, one or the other party to this suit must suffer an undeserved loss. We are cognizant that in this case, the equities are closely balanced between the parties to this appeal. Our decision, however, in addition to resolving the litigants' dispute, must delineate the requirements of Alaska's recording laws.

Because we want to promote simplicity and certainty in title transactions, we choose to follow the majority rule and hold that the Horvaths' deed, recorded outside the chain of title, does not give constructive notice to the Sabos and is not "duly recorded" under the Alaskan Recording Act, AS 34.15.290. Since the Sabos' interest is the first duly recorded interest and was recorded without actual or constructive knowledge of the prior deed, we hold that the Sabos' interest must prevail. The trial court's decision is accordingly.

Reversed.

Notes & Questions

1. Would and should the result in Morse v. Curtis have been different if demandant had gone into possession of the property? If the Massachusetts legislature had mandated use of an official tract index? If Massachusetts had a race-notice statute? A race statute? The rule of Morse v. Curtis has been rejected in a minority of states. See, e.g., Woods v. Garnett, 16 So. 390 (Miss. 1894). As a title examiner in one of these minority jurisdictions, is it likely that the cost of your search will be much higher than it would be in a majority jurisdiction? Needlessly so? Will your answer depend on whether you have ready access to a private title plant indexing all land transfers in your county by reference to the tract involved?

In 1983, a federal bankruptcy court questioned the continuing validity of *Morse* in light of modern search techniques:

> The validity of the *Morse* holding—that one does not have to check the grantor index beyond the period of ownership—might be questioned in view of the fact that its decision was primarily based upon the customary practices of conveyancers in 1886. Today, it is customary to run the grantor's name in the grantor index for a longer period of time than the period of ownership because a lien for real estate taxes arises upon assessment and does not dissolve until three years and nine months after the first of January in the year of assessment, if there has been a conveyance by a recorded instrument during that time.... Thus, it could arguably be said that a modern conveyancer's title search would disclose the second conveyance by the Trust and thus a bona fide purchaser from the Debtor would be considered to have constructive knowledge of its content.

In re Dlott, 43 B.R. 789, 795 (Bankr. Mass. 1983).

2. After the decision in Sabo v. Horvath, would the Horvaths have an action against Lowery to recover the value they paid for the land? Note that, although the Lowery–Horvath conveyance was by quitclaim deed, the trial court found that "the transfer contemplated more than a 'mere quitclaim'—it warranted patent would be transferred."

3. **Estoppel by Deed.** If Lowery had not subsequently executed a deed to the Sabos, the Horvaths would clearly have prevailed in a quiet title action against Lowery under the venerable doctrine of "estoppel by deed." This doctrine holds that if *A*, not owning Greenacre, purports to convey

Greenacre to *B* by warranty deed, then if *A* later acquires title to Greenacre, her title will automatically pass to *B* under the terms of the deed. The rationale for the doctrine is that *A*, as grantor under a deed to *B*, is representing that she owns the land, and thus will be estopped from later denying the effectiveness of that deed.

What effect will estoppel by deed have on a subsequent purchaser *C* who had no notice of the *A* to *B* deed? Although the *Sabo* court expressly sidestepped consideration of the issue, other courts have confronted it directly. In Breen v. Morehead, 136 S.W. 1047 (Tex. 1911), McKelligon, who had possession of, but not title to, a piece of land, deeded the property to Breen, who promptly recorded. About two years later, McKelligon acquired title to the parcel from the state and subsequently deeded it to Kern who had no knowledge of the earlier transfer to Breen. Other things being equal, the doctrine of estoppel by deed would have given title to Breen. But, of course, other things were not equal, for Kern, a bona fide purchaser for value, had intervened. The Texas Supreme Court held for Kern on the ground that if he were required to look beyond the origin of the title under which he was purchasing, "there could be no limit short of the vendor's life, and such requirement of purchasers would involve land titles in such uncertainty that it would be impracticable to rely on any investigation." Id. at 1049.

The court concluded: "We believe that the rule stated above that the date when the title originated in McKelligon marked the limit of investigation for previous sales or encumbrances of that tract of land by McKelligon should be applied here. It would be unreasonable to suppose that a man who had just received a title from the state had previously made a transfer of that land. That ordinary care and caution which the subsequent purchaser must exercise would not suggest an investigation for conveyances made before acquisition of title. It follows that the record of Breen's deed in El Paso county gave no notice to the subsequent purchasers from McKelligon who had no actual notice and paid a valuable consideration for the land." Id.

A few states reject the rule followed in Breen v. Morehead. See, e.g., Tefft v. Munson, 57 N.Y. 97 (1874). After Morse v. Curtis, would you expect Massachusetts to follow or to reject the rule? The surprising answer is that Massachusetts has rejected the rule. See Knight v. Thayer, 125 Mass. 25 (1878). Can you reconcile Knight v. Thayer with Morse v. Curtis?

C. ABSTRACTS, OPINIONS, AND TITLE INSURANCE

Using the public records or his own title plant, a title examiner will first search back to a parcel's root of title—when the parcel was last made the subject of an undisputed transfer—and he then will search forward, tracing all subsequent transfers to the present. The examiner will then prepare an abstract of title summarizing all transfers beginning with the first and indicating all other matters of record affecting the title. Characteristically, the abstract will conclude with the examiner's certification respecting the periods and records covered by his search.

Next, the abstract will be analyzed. Cancelled mortgages and other liens will be eliminated as will interests barred by the statute of limitations, reducing the abstract to the few surviving interests that continue to encumber or otherwise affect title. This analysis may be performed by a lawyer and embodied in a lawyer's opinion on title rendered to the buyer. Alternatively, a title insurance company may perform the analysis, stating the results in a policy of title insurance that guarantees good title except with respect to specified encumbrances or defects. (The lawyer's opinion will commonly read, "I have examined the abstract of title attached hereto, and from it find that on said date marketable title of record was vested in seller, free from encumbrances or defects, except as follows. . . ." The title company's guarantee will typically read, "The following estates, interests, defects, objections to title, liens and encumbrances and other matters are excepted from the coverage of this policy. . . .")

Although the steps from search to abstract to title opinion or title policy might seem entirely mechanical, they in fact often call for the most meticulous judgment. "Such questions as the following may be involved: whether a recorded conveyance should be questioned which does not have a notary's seal, or does not have a statement of the date on which the notary's commission expires; or, if a conveyance is made by a corporation, whether it should be questioned because there is no resolution on record showing the action of the corporation to make the conveyance, or showing whether the people who executed it as officers were in fact such officers at the time. As to these matters some title examiners may reach one conclusion and others the opposite conclusion. . . . If the practice of conveyancers is not uniform, the tendency always is for the standards of the overmeticulous conveyancer to determine the standards of all conveyancers. Lawyer *A* feels that a title should be passed even though there are certain defects in the recorded acknowledgment, and he realizes that the majority of experienced, competent conveyancers would agree with him. But he also knows that Lawyer *B* would refuse to pass the title and would require a quiet title suit. Since Lawyer *A* is aware that his client may some day wish to sell the land to someone who employs Lawyer *B* to pass on the title, he will be inclined to impose the same overmeticulous standard as Lawyer *B*. Like Gresham's law, the result will be that bad title standards drive out good standards." Lewis M. Simes & Clarence B. Taylor, Model Title Standards 2–3 (1960).

The sources of title services have changed dramatically over the past one hundred years. Originally lawyers conducted the title searches, prepared the abstract, and rendered the opinion based on the abstract. Although, in some places, lawyers continue to discharge all these functions, they have in most communities been partially or completely displaced by abstract and title companies. An abstract company may perform the search and compile the abstract while a lawyer selected by the buyer will review and opine on the abstract. Increasingly, title insurance companies are serving all these functions—conducting the search, preparing the abstract, and issuing a title policy insuring the accuracy of the search. Lawyers in many communities have responded to these incursions by setting up title insurance companies of their own. "By 1976, over 10,000 lawyers in nineteen states were organized in nine separate bar-related companies, with assets in excess of $18 million." H. Lee Roussel & Moses K. Rosenberg, Lawyer–Controlled Title Insurance Companies: Legal Ethics and the Need for Insurance Department Regulation, 48 Fordham. L. Rev. 25, 28 (1979).

1. ABSTRACTS AND LAWYERS' OPINIONS

Williams v. Polgar

Supreme Court of Michigan, 1974.
215 N.W.2d 149.

WILLIAMS, JUSTICE.

While important, the issue in this case is a relatively narrow one.

Michigan already permits a buyer of property who has relied on a faulty abstract to his detriment to recover from the abstracter, even though there is no clear contractual privity between them, if the abstracter in fact knew the buyer would rely on the abstract.

This case presents the issue whether a faulty abstracter should likewise be liable to a buyer he should have foreseen would rely on the abstract as well as to the buyer he knew would rely on it. The question boils down to whether there should be liability for foreseeable as well as known reliance.

This Court has answered that question affirmatively in a related fact situation, and in categorical terms relieved Michigan jurisprudence of the restrictions of "privity." In this opinion, we reaffirm our general decision eliminating privity and specifically apply it to abstracters. . . .

Plaintiffs Williams purchased certain property situated in the City of Warren, Macomb County, from defendants Polgar on a land contract dated August 1, 1959. At the time of purchase, as provided in the land contract, defendants furnished to plaintiffs an abstract of title certified to July 15, 1959 by Abstract and Title Guaranty Company. This abstract was originally issued on February 4, 1926 by the Macomb County Abstract Company and was extended by said company in 1936, 1937, 1943, 1944, 1945, 1946, 1948, 1951, and 1952. Defendant American Title Insurance Company is the successor in interest to Macomb County Abstract Company.

The abstract of title failed to include a deed dated May 1, 1926 which was recorded on May 24, 1926 in Liber 242 of Deeds at page 174 of Macomb County records. This deed conveyed the southerly 60 feet of the property in question to the Macomb County Board of Road Commissioners.

After execution of the land contract on August 1, 1959, plaintiffs learned, allegedly for the first time, of the existence of this omitted deed. As the result thereof, plaintiffs claim they were required to completely remove a building and that certain other damages were incurred.

Plaintiffs filed this action on April 21, 1971. All defendants filed motions for accelerated judgment based on the statute of limitations. The trial court held that plaintiffs' cause of action accrued no later than the execution of the land contract on August 1, 1959. Thus accelerated judgment was granted defendants. Plaintiffs were nonsuited. The Court of Appeals reversed and remanded. Defendant American Title Insurance Company requested leave to appeal to this Court which was granted on December 12, 1972. . . .

Where there is a person negligently injured by another, normally there is recovery therefor. *Ubi injuria, ibi remedium.*

Defendant title company here, however, seeks immunity from liability for the injury-it caused plaintiff buyers, pleading two defenses. First, defendant pleads it is immune from suit because it is not in contractual privity with plaintiffs. Second, defendant pleads it is immune from suit because of the statute of limitations. We disagree.

DEFENSE OF PRIVITY

A. *Cessante Ratione Legis, Cessat et Ipsa Lex*

The early common law rule restricting liability to those in contractual privity with an abstracter was based on a system where abstracts would only be used by real estate owners.

As time went on the actual usage of abstracts and the class of people relying on them expanded. . . .

Responding to the actual change in use of abstracts and the additional classes of persons relying on them, at least six general court-created exceptions have been grafted onto the supposed common law requirement of strict contractual privity. These exceptions include:

(1) abstracter's fraud or collusion,

(2) theory of third-party beneficiary contracts,

(3) theory of foreseeability of use by a third-party,

(4) actual knowledge or notice of third-party,

(5) agent for disclosed or undisclosed principal contracting with an abstracter, and

(6) re-issuance or recertification of an abstract.

Whereas the common law rule limiting abstracter liability provided immunity from all who were injured by a faulty abstract except those in actual contractual privity, of the 35 jurisdictions (outside of Michigan) addressing themselves to this matter only seven retain a rule of strict contractual privity: Arizona, California, Florida, Illinois, Ohio, Texas and

Wisconsin. On the other hand, 11 extend liability to known third-parties relying thereon: Alabama, District of Columbia, Hawaii, Idaho, Indiana, Maryland, Missouri, New Jersey, New York, Pennsylvania and Tennessee. Two jurisdictions have allowed recovery by undiscovered principals: Iowa and Washington. Fourteen purport to extend liability by statute to "any person" relying on the abstract: Arkansas, Colorado, Kansas, Minnesota, Montana, Nebraska, Nevada, New Mexico, North Dakota, Oklahoma, Oregon, South Dakota, Utah and Wyoming. And one jurisdiction extends liability to foreseeable relying third-parties by court decision: Louisiana.

B. Michigan Has Abolished Privity Requirement

Michigan ended the last century and began this one firmly wed to the rule of contractual privity immunizing abstracters. By the end of the second decade it reluctantly broke away from strict privity in favor of a known third-party beneficiary. Beckovsky v. Burton Abstract & Title Co., 208 Mich. 224, 175 N.W. 235 (1919). Michigan thereby joined a category of 11 other jurisdictions just noted who had opened recovery to parties the abstracter knew would rely on the abstract. In *Beckovsky*, the plaintiff buyer actually accompanied the seller to the office of defendant title company and said he wanted an abstract but the contract in all truth was between the seller and the title company with the seller paying the title company for its work, although in order to avoid the title company's defense of privity, the trial court graciously put that question to the jury.

So *Beckovsky* extends liability to the faulty abstracter who knows a third-party beneficiary will rely on its abstract. The question remains, will liability likewise apply to the faulty abstracter who can reasonably foresee reliance by a third-party....

C. Privity Conclusion

Michigan's own jurisprudence records the categorical elimination of privity. This Court had previously extended abstracter liability consonant with the historical growth in reliance and use of abstracts and the corresponding changes in the law to known relying third-parties. Confronted now as of first impression with the question of abstracter liability to foreseeable, relying third-parties, we have but to apply our own persuasive precedent of categorical elimination of privity to an analogous situation, and we do so.

ABSTRACTER LIABILITY IN TORT FOR NEGLIGENT MISREPRESENTATION

With respect to the particular type of tort action arising from breach of an abstracter's contractual duty, we hold it to be an action in negligent misrepresentation. Numerous cases and law review articles have debated the precise tort cause of action most appropriate in this context. The theories of fraud, deceit, warranty, and strict liability have all been the subject of extensive discussion with respect to professional misrepresentations of this sort. None of these theories has been found to adequately deal with this particular problem; negligent misrepresentation, on the other hand, precisely fits this situation.

The obvious difficulty with a fraud or deceit action is the requisite element of scienter. The issue we are dealing with in the instant case does not, on the pleadings, involve intentional misrepresentation. To supply the element of intent constructively is to do great violence to existing law on the subject of fraud.

Further, to treat this cause of action as sounding in warranty or strict liability might serve to extend an abstracter's duty beyond the duty anticipated by the original contract. It is important to repeat that the tort cause of action created by an abstracter's nonfeasance or misfeasance stems from the contractual duty originally imposed and does not render an abstracter liable for action beyond such contractually-imposed duty, i.e., to perform in a diligent and reasonably skillful workmanlike manner.

Thus, we adopt the tort action of negligent misrepresentation in this context. It should be noted that this action is premised on negligence in title search; an abstracter is not converted into a title insurer by virtue of our decision today. We repeat that the only liability an abstracter has to an injured third-party is with respect to negligent performance of his or her contractual duty....

This cause of action arising from breach of the abstracter's contractual duty runs to those persons an abstracter could reasonably foresee as relying on the accuracy of the abstract put into motion. The particular expert-client relationship accruing to a professional contract to certify the condition of the record of title reposes a peculiar trust in an abstracter which runs not only to the original contracting party. There is a clearly foreseeable class of potential injured persons which would obviously include grantees where his or her grantor or any predecessor in title of the grantor has initiated the contract for abstracting services with the abstracter.

[The dissenting opinion of COLEMAN, J., is omitted.]

Notes & Questions

1. Abstracters and lawyers are liable for defects in their work product—abstracters for errors and omissions in compiling the abstract, lawyers for errors in analyzing the abstract and opining on title. Although buyers can pursue both contract and tort theories against the lawyer who represented them, tort theory represents their primary route for recovery against an abstracter with whom they will commonly not be in contractual privity.

Should buyers have a tort action against abstracters? If *Polgar* had gone the other way, is it likely that Michigan buyers would in the future protect themselves against title defects by insisting that their sellers give them warranty deeds? (Note that if a buyer recovers against his seller on a title covenant, the seller can then proceed on a contract theory against the abstracter with whom she will be in privity.) Is there any material difference in the damages a buyer will recover by proceeding against the seller under a covenant theory and proceeding against the abstracter under a tort theory? If, as often happens, the property appreciates in value between the time the buyer acquires it and the time he discovers the title defect, which theory—tort or contract—is more likely to make the buyer whole?

2. **Abstracter Licensing.** Many states, most of them situated west of the Mississippi, have enacted licensing laws for abstracters and abstracting firms. Among the statutory requirements are, maintenance of an adequate title plant and bonding to cover liability for errors and omissions in compiling abstracts. See, e.g., Colo. Rev. Stat. §§ 12–1–101 et seq. Most of these states require abstracting companies to employ at least one licensed abstracter who has successfully completed a state-administered exam.

3. **Lawyer Liability.** Lawyers who search or analyze title for their clients are held to the traditional negligence standard of reasonable care and skill. Malpractice claims most often involve the failure to note an encumbrance or to determine the property's true owner or proper location. Good faith errors in judgment are excused, and the lawyer is not considered to have guaranteed that title is perfect—unless, of course, he or she specifically makes such a guarantee.

While reasonable care will be measured by the skills possessed, and the customs ordinarily followed, by lawyers in the community, custom will not excuse grossly unreliable practices. In Gleason v. Title Guarantee Co., 300 F.2d 813 (5th Cir.1962), a title company sued for damages arising from defendant attorney's erroneous opinion that certain titles were clear when in fact they were encumbered by outstanding mortgages. The attorney had certified to having made a personal examination of the relevant records but had in fact reviewed neither the records nor the abstracts, relying instead on information received by telephone from the abstract company. In response to the attorney's argument that this method of obtaining title information was standard practice in that part of Florida, the court held that an improper custom, no matter how widely practiced, could not reduce the attorney's duty of care. Damages were awarded for the losses suffered by the title company.

4. **Lawyer Disclaimer.** How much liability can a lawyer disclaim? In Owen v. Neely, 471 S.W.2d 705 (Ky. 1971), defendant attorney, employed to "do the title work," gave plaintiffs a certificate of clear and merchantable title containing the standard disclaimer that the certificate was "subject to any information that would be revealed by an accurate survey...." In making the certificate, the attorney had used a description prepared by a surveyor. The lawyer later admitted that he had noticed discrepancies between the deed description and the survey description. In fact, the survey was erroneous, and the house the clients thought they were buying was not situated on the land that they bought. Acknowledging that reservations and disclaimers expressly set forth in the certificate of title will generally be enforced, the court ruled that if an attorney examining title receives

information that would give him or her grounds to suspect a defect, the attorney owes the client a duty of investigation that cannot be disclaimed.

5. **Lawyer Liability to Third Parties.** Courts divide on whether a lawyer, retained to examine title by a seller or a bank issuing a mortgage loan, can be held liable to the buyer for errors appearing in the lawyer's title report to his or her client. Most courts refuse to extend liability, on the ground that such an extension could create a conflict with the lawyer's responsibility to the client. See, e.g., Page v. Frazier, 445 N.E.2d 148 (Mass. 1983) (noting, in a suit against a bank-mortgagee's attorney, that some title defects would "not make the property unsatisfactory as a security but . . . would concern a buyer"). Courts also note that the buyer can always engage an attorney of his own choice to represent his interests. A few jurisdictions, however, have broken with traditional privity rules and held that buyers can sue attorneys for other parties to the transaction. See, e.g., Century 21 Deep South Properties, Ltd. v. Corson, 612 So. 2d 359 (Miss. 1992) (permitting buyer to sue sellers' attorney for malpractice based on failure to discover several title defects). Other courts finesse the privity issue by finding that an attorney-client relationship existed with the buyer. See, e.g., Westport Bank & Trust Co. v. Corcoran, Mallin & Aresco, 605 A.2d 862 (Conn. 1992) (where mortgagee sent letter requesting title search to law firm representing mortgagors in title matters, law firm had taken on dual representation to which mortgagors had impliedly consented).

2. Title Insurance

D. Barlow Burke, Jr., Law of Title Insurance

1:1–1:8, 2:1, & 2:9–2:10 (2d ed. 1993).

To protect against . . . defects in real property titles, American abstractors and attorneys well over 100 years ago devised the original forms of title insurance. Title insurance is an exclusively American invention. It involves the issuance of an insurance policy promising that if the state of the title is other than as represented on the face of the policy, and if the insured suffers losses as a result of the difference, the insurer will reimburse the insured for that loss and any related legal expenses, up to the face amount of the policy. As Professor Quintin Johnstone wrote many years ago in his still seminal law review article on this type of insurance, it is "a means of protecting against some defects of title and by insuring against potential losses from others."[3]

. . . . The first title insurance company was formed in Pennsylvania as early as 1853 and was known as the "Law Property Assurance and Trust Society."[5] However, it is an 1868 Pennsylvania case holding an abstractor

3. Johnstone, Title Insurance: A Primer for Attorneys, 14 Real Prop., Prob., & Tr. J. 608, 610 (1957).

5. E. Roberts et al., Public Regulation of Title Insurance Companies and Abstractors 1 (1961).

liable for negligence in the course of a title search that many writers have credited with giving impetus to the industry.[6]....

Some writers add that this genesis is an example of an industry created by the need to protect the insurer rather than the insured—to protect abstractors and lay conveyancers against their own legal liabilities. This is only part of the story, however, because while title insurers have, from the beginning of the industry, performed a title search as the basis for the policy and as a means of preventing claims and losses under the policy, they have also provided insurance against title defects that cannot be ascertained from the records used in the course of a title search, but that may nonetheless be asserted in the future. These are so-called off-record risks. Insuring against this type of risk is closer to "pure insurance"—protecting the insured against a future event—but the title search and review, as a precondition to the issuance of the policy, distinguishes title insurance from most other forms of insurance.

A plan for insuring title and mortgages was published in Pennsylvania in 1871, and three years later that state enacted the first statutes authorizing this type of insurance. The Lawyers' Title Insurance Corporation was formed under this type of statute in 1876. The corporation is still doing business today. By 1887, title insurance companies were established in some of the major urban centers in the eastern United States, including Philadelphia, Washington, D.C., New York City, and Baltimore.

On the West Coast as well, title insurance companies were formed in the 1880s. Part of the impetus to establish companies in this region was the confusion over California land titles, deriving as they did from Mexican land grants, Land Office patents, and sometimes squatter's rights. Large landowners and landlords had for several decades been concerned both about squatters and about the high, unpredictable costs of title searches and litigation needed to quiet and maintain their titles. In both northern and southern California, title insurance was a method for both reducing costs and rendering those costs predictable....

In the first two or three decades of the twentieth century, title insurance competed in many states with land title registration systems [discussed below at pages 521–523] that were still enjoying increased popularity. However, it became clear during this period that title insurance would prevail in this country as title insurers made a national market for their policies between the two World Wars of the century.

The insurers found that, as homeownership was increasingly financed through mortgage (and deed of trust) loans, their product complemented the growth of a nationwide market for residential mortgages. Third-party commercial lenders of this period became convinced that title insurance was a necessary ancillary service for the financing of residential properties. During the 1920s mortgagees of such property became convinced that title insurance was a held to those of their number who wanted to do a high-

6. Roberts, Title Insurance: State Regulation and the Public Perspective, 39 Ind. L.J. 1, 5–7 (1963), recites the history of this case, Watson v. Muirhead, 57 Pa. 161 (1868).

volume business in this form of finance. They could use the insurance policy to standardize their own product in order to sell the mortgage at a discount in the then developing national secondary for such mortgages....

As a consequence of these factors, mortgage lenders began to require title insurance as a part of many real estate transactions. In residential transactions, its presence often became routine in many regions and urban areas of the country, and in large commercial transactions title insurance became the norm.

For individual owners purchasing title insurance, the policy of title insurance was sold as a substitute for the warranties in the vendor's deed. After all, a vendor could die, become insolvent, or otherwise judgment proof—and the warranties would be useless to a purchaser. This rationale for owners' policies is particularly evident in New York cases, but it persists, there and elsewhere, to this day.

By the end of World War II, title insurance was the predominant (in number of transactions) form of title assurance in the country.... Iowa is the only jurisdiction in which title insurance is not written. In that state title insurance is prohibited by statute—a statute whose passage probably was encouraged by the state bar association.[25]....

Title insurance is a one-premium agreement to indemnify a policy-holder for losses caused by both on-record and off-record defects found in the title or interest to an insured property in amounts not exceeding the face amount of the policy and that are in existence on the date on which the policy is issued.

If the policy-holder does not "own" the property and so does not have title to it or possession of it, an insurer may nonetheless issue a policy. It will insure the priority of his lien or any other less-than-fee interest in real property. Title insurance thus may be held by both owners of and lenders on real property, and indeed the most common forms of title insurance policies are owner's and lender's policies....

Title insurance is unlike other types of insurance in at least two significant ways. First, it is not based on the prediction of a future event by an actuary or statistician, as is life or accident insurance. Title insurance is based in large part on the work of an abstractor, one who searches the public records of interests in real property to ascertain if defects already exist. The abstractor searches for preexisting defects, arising in past transactions, which may be asserted in the future. This search for past events with future consequences is hardly what most people see as the work of insurance companies. Indeed, if the abstractor's work is accurate and competent, the claims and loss rate for defects in title recorded on those records should be very low indeed, in fact, approaching zero. If any defect is found on the records, it comes the basis for an exception from coverage written into the policy—and the number of claims based on such

25. Iowa Code Ann. § 515.48(10), upheld in Chicago Title Ins. Co. v. Huff, 256 N.W.2d 17 (Iowa 1977).

defects will still approach zero. Title insurance is issued after the completion of work intended to reduce the number of claims—for a title insurer is in the unique position of being able, through its own work, to eliminate many claims. In contrast, a life insurance company knows that sooner or later it will have to pay the face amount of the policy.

Second, a title insurance policy is paid for all at once with only one premium and the coverage lasts for as long as the insured has some liability for a title defect, whether as the present owner or possessor, or as a vendor and warrantor of the state of the title upon some later sale.

Title insurance insures not only on-record defects in title, but also covers defects not revealed by an abstractor's search of the public records related to real property. Such defects are known to title insurers as "off-record risks" and not even the most thorough and competent title search will identify them. Included in any listing of off-record risks are:

(1) the misindexing or misfiling of a document by the recorder,

(2) matters pertaining to the identity of the parties to a document,

(3) its delivery to the transferee....

White v. Western Title Insurance Co.

Supreme Court of California, 1985.
710 P.2d 309.

BROUSSARD, JUSTICE.

Plaintiffs Brian and Helen White filed suit against defendant Western Title Insurance Company for breach of contract, negligence, and breach of implied covenants of good faith and fair dealing. A jury found for plaintiffs, awarding damages of $8,400 for breach of contract and negligence, and an additional $20,000 for breach of the covenants of good faith and fair dealing. We affirm the judgment.

In 1975, William and Virginia Longhurst owned 84 acres of land on the Russian River in Mendocino County. The land was divided into two lots, one unimproved, the other improved with a ranchhouse, a barn and adjacent buildings. It contained substantial subsurface water.

On December 29, 1975, the Longhursts executed and delivered an "Easement Deed for Waterline and Well Sites," conveying to River Estates Mutual Water Corporation an "easement for a right-of-way for the construction and maintenance of a water pipeline and for the drilling of a well or wells within a defined area and an easement to take water, up to 150 [gallons per minute], from any wells within said defined area." The deed was recorded the following day.

In 1978 plaintiffs agreed to purchase the property from the Longhursts. Plaintiffs, who were unaware of the water easement, requested preliminary title reports from defendant. Each report purported to list all easements, liens and encumbrances of record, but neither mentioned the recorded water easement.

Plaintiffs and the Longhursts opened two escrows, one for each lot. Upon close of escrow defendant issued to plaintiffs two standard CLTA title insurance policies, for which plaintiffs paid $1,467.55. Neither policy mentioned the water easement.

The title insurance policies provided:

> Subject to Schedule B and the Conditions and Stipulations Hereof, Western Title Insurance Company ... insures the insured ... against loss or damage, ... and costs, attorneys' fees and expenses ... incurred by said insured by reason of:
>
> 1. Title to the estate or interest described in Schedule A being vested other than as stated therein;
>
> 2. Any defect in or lien or encumbrance on such title....

"Schedule B" provided in part that

> [this] policy does not insure against loss or damage ... which [arises] by reason of the following: ...
>
> 3. Easements, liens or encumbrances, or claims thereof, which are not shown by the public records....
>
> 5. (a) Unpatented mining claims; (b) reservations or exceptions in patents or in Acts authorizing the issuance thereof; (c) *water rights, claims or title to water*." (Italics added.)

About six months after the close of escrow, River Estates Mutual Water Corporation notified plaintiffs of its intention to enter their property to implement the easement. Plaintiffs protested, and River Estates filed an action to quiet title to the easement. Plaintiffs notified defendant, who agreed to defend the proceeding. Plaintiffs, however, declined defendant's offer, preferring representation by an attorney who was then representing them in an unrelated action. River Estates eventually decided not to enforce its easement and dismissed the suit.

Plaintiffs' appraiser estimated the loss in value of their lots resulting from the potential loss of groundwater at $62,947. Plaintiffs then made a demand on defendant for that sum. Defendant acknowledged its responsibility for loss of value due to the easement (the loss attributable to the occupation of plaintiffs' land by wells and pipes, and to the water company's right to enter the property for construction and maintenance). It maintained, however, that any loss in value attributable to loss of groundwater was excluded by the policy, and since plaintiffs' claim of loss was based entirely on diminution of groundwater, declined to pay their claim....

1. Liability Under the Terms of the Insurance Contracts.

The insurance policies purport to insure a "fee" interest, free from any defect in title or any lien or encumbrance on title, subject to the exceptions listed in schedule B of the policies. A fee interest includes appurtenant water rights. Thus the only question is whether coverage under the present case is excluded by schedule B.

Schedule B contains two parts. Part two lists specific exceptions, generally encumbrances of record discovered by the title company and therefore excluded from coverage under the policy. The easement of River Estates Mutual Water Corporation was not listed in part two. Part one describes nine kinds of title defects excluded generally from coverage.[3] The first four paragraphs describe interests which should have been, but were not, recorded; item 3, for example, excludes coverage of "[easements], liens, or encumbrances ... which are not shown by the public records...." The remaining five paragraphs exclude interests of a type which are ordinarily not recorded, including, in paragraph 5, "(a) Unpatented mining claims; (b) reservations or exceptions in patents or in Acts authorizing the issuance

3. Schedule B, part one, reads in full as follows:

"This policy does not insure against loss or damage, nor against costs, attorneys' fees or expenses, any or all of which arise by reason of the following:

"Part One:

"1. Taxes or assessments which are not shown as existing liens by the records of any taxing authority that levies taxes or assessments on real property or by the public records.

"Proceedings by a public agency which may result in taxes or assessments, or notices of such proceedings, whether or not shown by the records of such agency or by the public records.

"2. Any facts, rights, interests or claims which are not shown by the public records but which could be ascertained by an inspection of the land or by making inquiry of persons in possession thereof.

"3. Easements, liens or encumbrances, or claims thereof, which are not shown by the public records.

"4. Discrepancies, conflicts in boundary lines, shortage in area, encroachments, or any other facts which a correct survey would disclose, and which are not shown by the public records.

"5. (a) Unpatented mining claims; (b) reservations or exceptions in patents or in Acts authorizing the issuance thereof; (c) water rights, claims or title to water.

"6. Any right, title, interest, estate or easement in land beyond the lines of the area specifically described or referred to in Schedule C, or in abutting streets, roads, avenues, alleys, lanes, ways or waterways, but nothing in this paragraph shall modify or limit the extent to which the ordinary right of an abutting owner for access to a physically open street or highway is insured by this policy.

"7. Any law, ordinance or governmental regulation (including but not limited to building and zoning ordinances) restricting or regulating or prohibiting the occupancy, use or enjoyment of the land, or regulating the character, dimensions or location of any improvement now or hereafter erected on the land, or prohibiting a separation in ownership or a reduction in the dimensions or area of the land, or the effect of any violation of any such law, ordinance or governmental regulation.

"8. Rights of eminent domain or governmental rights of police power unless notice of the exercise of such rights appears in the public records.

"9. Defects, liens, encumbrances, adverse claims, or other matters (a) created, suffered, assumed or agreed to by the insured claimant; (b) not shown by the public records and not otherwise excluded from coverage but known to the insured claimant either at Date of Policy or at the date such claimant acquired an estate or interest insured by this policy or acquired the insured mortgage and not disclosed in writing by the insured claimant to the Company prior to the date such insured claimant became an insured hereunder; (c) resulting in no loss or damage to the insured claimant; (d) attaching or created subsequent to Date of Policy; or (e) resulting in loss or damage which would not have been sustained if the insured claimant had been a purchaser or encumbrancer for value without knowledge."

thereof; (c) water rights, claims or title to water." Defendant relies on this last exclusion to avoid coverage in the present case.

Construction of the policy, however, is controlled by the well-established rules on interpretation of insurance agreements. As described most recently in Reserve Insurance Co. v. Pisciotta (1982) 30 Cal. 3d 800, 807–808: " '[Any] ambiguity or uncertainty in an insurance policy is to be resolved against the insurer and ... if semantically permissible, the contract will be given such construction as will fairly achieve its object of providing indemnity for the loss to which the insurance relates.' The purpose of this canon of construction is to protect the insured's reasonable expectation of coverage in a situation in which the insurer-draftsman controls the language of the policy. Its effect differs, depending on whether the language to be construed is found in a clause providing coverage or in one limiting coverage. 'Whereas coverage clauses are interpreted broadly so as to afford the greatest possible protection to the insured ... exclusionary clauses are interpreted narrowly against the insurer.' " (Citations omitted.)

The Court of Appeal in Jarchow v. Transamerica Title Ins. Co. (1975) 48 Cal. App. 3d 917, 941, reiterated these rules in the title insurance context: "In determining what benefits or duties an insurer owes his insured pursuant to a contract of title insurance, the court may not look to the words of the policy alone, but must also consider the reasonable expectations of the public and the insured as to the type of service which the insurance entity holds itself out as ready to offer. Stated in another fashion, the provisions of the policy, '*must be construed so as to give the insured the protection which he reasonably had a right to expect, ...*' " (Original italics.) (Gray v. Zurich Insurance Co., 65 Cal.2d 263, 270, fn. 7).

In the present context, these rules require coverage of water rights shown in public records within the scope of an ordinary title search. The structure of the policy itself creates the impression that coverage is provided for claims of record, while excluded for unrecorded claims. This impression is reinforced by the specific language of the policy. Paragraph 3, by excluding easements, liens, and encumbrances "not shown by public records," implies inclusion of such interests when recorded. Paragraph 5, the exclusion of water rights on which defendant relies, joins that exclusion with exclusion of unpatented mining claims and exceptions in patents or authorizing legislation—interests which would not appear in the records ordinarily searched by a title company.[5]

Coverage of claims of record also accords with the purpose of the title policies and the reasonable expectations of the insured. This standard CLTA policy is a policy based upon an inspection of records and, unlike more expensive policies, does not involve inspection of the property. The purchaser of such a policy could not reasonably expect coverage against

5. Water rights may arise by appropriation, prescription, or by virtue of ownership of riparian land. Often such rights do not appear of record, or if recorded do not clearly refer to the property whose title is under investigation, or appear in the recorded chain of title to that property. The same is true of unpatented mining claims and other interests mentioned in paragraph 5.

unrecorded claims, but he could reasonably expect that the title company had competently searched the records, disclosed all interests of record it discovered and agreed to protect him against any undisclosed interests. Nothing in the policy makes it clear that there may be interests of record undisclosed by the policy yet excluded from coverage.[7]

We conclude that the title insurance policies here in question, construed to carry out their purpose of protecting against undisclosed recorded interests, provide coverage for water rights which appear of record within the scope of the ordinary title search. . . .

2. Liability for Negligence.

Plaintiffs' cause of action for negligence rests on long-established principles concerning the duties of a title insurer. As explained in Jarchow v. Transamerica Title Ins. Co., supra, 48 Cal. App. 3d 917, 938–939: "When a title insurer presents a buyer with both a preliminary title report and a policy of title insurance, two distinct responsibilities are assumed. In rendering the first service, the insurer serves as an abstractor of title—and must list *all* matters of public record regarding the subject property in its preliminary report. The duty imposed upon an abstractor of title is a rigorous one: 'An abstractor of title is hired because of his professional skill, and when searching the public records on behalf of a client he must use the degree of care commensurate with that professional skill. . . . [The] abstractor must report all matters which could affect his client's interests and which are readily discoverable from those public records ordinarily examined when a reasonably diligent title search is made.' Similarly, a title insurer is liable for his negligent failure to list recorded encumbrances in preliminary title reports." These principles find support in the numerous cases cited in *Jarchow*, and also in the more recent decision of Wilkinson v. Rives (1981) 116 Cal. App. 3d 641, 650, where the court said that "[when] a title insurer furnishes a preliminary title report to a prospective buyer, the insurer serves as an abstractor of title and has a duty to list all matters of public record regarding the subject property in its preliminary report."

It is undisputed that the preliminary title report failed to list the recorded easement of River Estates Mutual Water Corporation. The failure of a title company to note an encumbrance of record is prima facie negligent. Defendant has made no attempt to rebut this inference of negligence.

7. Defendant quotes Miller and Starr, who after noting that some water rights are duly recorded in the chain of title, state that "the exclusion in the standard coverage policy is not limited merely to *unrecorded* rights. The policy apparently also intends to exclude liability arising out of recorded water interests. Therefore, a subsequent purchaser or encumbrancer is not protected by his title policy against prior interests in water on the property, whether recorded or unrecorded." (2 Miller & Starr, Current Law of Cal. Real Estate, *supra*, § 12.31.)

It may well be that the policy was intended to exclude recorded water rights, even those in the chain of title which would be discovered during the ordinary search incident to preparation of a standard title policy. Construction of the policy, however, depends not on the intent of the drafter but on the reasonable expectations of the insured.

Defendant relies instead on the language of the preliminary title reports and on the enactment of Insurance Code section 12340.11. Each report states that it "is issued solely for the purpose of facilitating the issuance of a policy of title insurance and no liability is assumed thereby." This statement, however, appears in the report itself, not in a contract under which defendant agreed to prepare that report. Moreover, even if we viewed the title report as a contract, the quoted provision would be ineffective to relieve defendant of liability for negligence. A title company is engaged in a business affected with the public interest and cannot, by an adhesory contract, exculpate itself from liability for negligence.

Insurance Code section 12340.11, effective January 1, 1982, provides: " 'Preliminary report', 'commitment', or 'binder' are reports furnished in connection with an application for title insurance and are offers to issue a title policy subject to the stated exceptions set forth in the reports and such other matters as may be incorporated by reference therein. The reports are not abstracts of title, nor are any of the rights, duties or responsibilities applicable to the preparation and issuance of an abstract of title applicable to the issuance of any report. Any such report shall not be construed as, nor constitute, a representation as to the condition of title to real property, but shall constitute a statement of the terms and conditions upon which the issuer is willing to issue its title policy, if such offer is accepted."

Whatever the effect of this statute upon preliminary title reports prepared after January 1, 1982, it has no effect upon the present case. " 'It is a general rule of construction . . . that, unless the intention to make it retrospective clearly appears from the act itself, a statute will not be construed to have that effect.' " (Western Pioneer Ins. Co. v. Estate of Taira (1982) 136 Cal. App. 3d 174, 180–181.) . . . .

Defendant finally argues that the trial court refused to permit it to introduce evidence of plaintiffs' contributory negligence. Defendant offered only to prove that plaintiffs by diligent investigation could have discovered the water easement. Since plaintiffs had no duty to investigate, but were entitled to rely on the preliminary title report, such evidence is insufficient to show contributory negligence. Defendant did not offer to prove that plaintiffs had actual knowledge of the easement.

3. Liability for Breach of the Covenant of Good Faith and Fair Dealing.

A covenant of good faith and fair dealing is implied in every insurance contract, including title insurance contracts. The jury found defendant breached the covenant, and awarded compensatory damages of $20,000. Defendant argues on appeal that . . . no substantial evidence supports the verdict finding a breach of the covenant of good faith and fair dealing. However, reading the record most favorably to the judgment below, it reveals that although defendant failed to disclose an easement of record on its preliminary title reports and its title insurance policies, it denied any liability for loss of value in water rights attributable to the easement. When plaintiffs filed suit, defendant responded with a motion for summary judgment. After losing that motion, defendant was faced with both a ruling of the trial court rejecting its narrow reading of the policy and a unanimous body of case law establishing liability for negligence. Defendant nevertheless offered only nuisance-value settlements, and made no attempt to appraise plaintiffs' loss until the issue of liability had been tried and decided in plaintiffs' favor.

The entire pattern of conduct shows a clear attempt by defendant to avoid responsibility for its obvious failure to discover and report the recorded easement of River Estates Mutual Water Corporation. We conclude that the evidence is sufficient to permit the jury to find a breach of the covenant of good faith and fair dealing. . . .

Haw River Land & Timber Co. v. Lawyers Title Insurance Corp.

United States Court of Appeals for the Fourth Circuit, 1998.
152 F.3d 275.

Niemeyer, Circuit Judge.

After Haw River Land & Timber Company, Inc., and George W. Riddle (collectively hereafter, "Haw River Timber") purchased the timber rights to 712 acres of land in Wake County, North Carolina, it learned that 179 acres lay within an environmental buffer zone created by a municipal ordinance which effectively prohibited timbering. Contending that the ordinance rendered title to the 179 acres of timber "unmarketable," Haw River Timber sued the title insurance company which insured against the "unmarketability of title" to the timber rights. The district court entered summary judgment in favor of the title company on the ground that the title was marketable and the economic value of the timber was irrelevant to the question.

Because the adverse economic impact of a municipal ordinance does not render title to timber legally unmarketable, we conclude that the loss sustained by Haw River Timber because of restrictions imposed by the municipal ordinance is not covered by the title insurance policy. Accordingly, we affirm.

I.

On September 13, 1995, Haw River Timber purchased "all the merchantable timber of all kinds and descriptions" standing on 712 acres of real property in Garner, North Carolina, from R.B. and Ida Mae Barefoot. The timber deed granted title to the standing timber together with the right to "pass and repass," at its option, on the underlying land to cut and remove the timber for a period of three years. Haw River Timber paid $800,000 for these timber rights.

In connection with the timber purchase, Haw River Timber purchased title insurance from Lawyers Title Insurance Corporation which issued a standard form American Land Title Association (ALTA) policy. The policy insured Haw River Timber's fee simple title to the merchantable timber for up to $800,000 against loss or damage suffered by reason of (1) title to timber being vested in another party; (2) any defect in or lien or encumbrance on the title to the timber; (3) unmarketability of title to the timber; or (4) lack of a right of access to the timber. The policy expressly excluded from coverage any loss or damage resulting from an ordinance, zoning law, or environmental protection legislation regulating the use of land "except to the extent that a notice of enforcement thereof or a notice of a defect, lien or encumbrance resulting from a violation or alleged violation affecting the land has been recorded in the public records at Date of Policy."

After Haw River Timber began harvesting timber on a portion of the 712–acre tract, it was informed by the Town of Garner that some of the property adjacent to Swift Creek was subject to municipal ordinances passed in 1988, 1989, and 1994 to preserve the vegetation in that area. The ordinances were enacted in response to a recommendation of the North Carolina Department of Natural Resources and Community Development that the Swift Creek watershed be upgraded for environmental purposes. The Town of Garner's ordinances preserve a buffer zone within an area 500 feet from the center of the creek or the 100–year flood plain plus 50 feet, effectively prohibiting timber harvesting within the buffer zone. Of the total 712–acre tract of which Haw River Timber held the timber rights, 179 acres fell within the buffer zone. Haw River Timber has valued the timber in the buffer zone, after cutting and hauling, at $374,769.

In its brief on appeal, Haw River Timber represents that it had a title search performed prior to closing, which did not reveal the existence of the conservation ordinances. In addition, it states that the ordinances were not cross-indexed in the Wake County Register of Deeds with the sellers or previous land owners in the chain of title.

Faced with a $375,000 loss attributed to the impact of Garner's municipal ordinances, Haw River Timber made a series of claims against Lawyers Title under differing theories for a reimbursement of the loss. . . .

II.

Haw River Timber contends that the scope of the Lawyers Title policy, insuring its title to the timber rights on 712 acres, covers the loss it sustained from the zoning ordinance that prohibits it from cutting and removing the timber to which it had title. It argues that since it bought only the timber rights and not the underlying property, its use of the timber was dependent on its right to remove the timber from the property. It maintains that its title was worthless if it could not remove the timber; that title to unremovable timber is essentially no title at all because it could not market, sell, or transfer its title to timber with the restrictions against timbering imposed by the ordinances.

While this argument has substantial appeal on a practical level, it fails to recognize any distinction between marketable title and marketable property and to comprehend the risks insured by the Lawyers Title policy. . . .

Title refers to the legal ownership of a property interest so that one having title to a property interest can withstand the assertion of others claiming a right to that ownership. But title to property does not characterize the property itself as valuable, merchantable, or even usable. Thus, while title to property may be unassailable, the property itself may have no value and may even constitute a burden to its owner. For these reasons, an insurance policy insuring legal title covers only the right of the owner to assert ownership against others claiming ownership or an interest in that ownership....

While it is true that the Town of Garner's zoning ordinances have effectively frustrated Haw River Timber's expectation of timbering 179 of the 712 acres granted under the timber deed, thereby substantially reducing the economic value of the interest purchased, Haw River Timber raises no issue about whether it received legal title to the timber from the grantors. And the Lawyers Title policy insuring marketable title under the timber deed only guarantees Haw River Timber a title that could be enforced in a suit for specific performance, not the economic value of the timber purchased. Indeed, the explicit definition of marketable title provided in the policy limits any more expansive notion by insuring against only those title defects that would entitle a purchaser "to be released from the obligation to purchase by virtue of a contractual condition requiring the delivery of marketable title." The ordinances on which Haw River relies as a title defect do not impair the grantor's ability to convey a timber deed....

III.

Should any doubt remain about whether an ALTA standard form title policy insures against economic loss occasioned by a town ordinance, that doubt is put to rest by an applicable policy exclusion which excludes coverage for any loss or damage arising by reason of:

> Any law, ordinance, or governmental regulation (including but not limited to building and zoning laws, ordinances or regulations) restricting, regulating, prohibiting, or relating to (I) the occupancy, use, or enjoyment of land; ... or (iv) environmental protection, or the effect of any violation of these laws, ordinances or governmental regulations, except to the extent that a notice of enforcement thereof or a notice of a defect, lien or encumbrance resulting from a violation or alleged violation affecting the land has been recorded in the public records at Date of Policy.

The ordinances enacted by the Town of Garner during the period from 1988 through 1994 establish an environmental buffer zone consisting of 500 feet on either side of Swift Creek, in which vegetation is preserved. They effectively prohibit Haw River Timber from cutting and removing its timber from this zone. Haw River Timber concedes that these ordinances fall within the language of the policy exclusion and that any loss occasioned by them is excluded from coverage of the policy unless coverage for the loss is provided by the last clause of exclusion—an exception to the exclusion—

providing coverage for a loss caused by an ordinance "to the extent that a notice of enforcement thereof or a notice of a defect, lien or encumbrance resulting from a violation ... has been recorded in the public records." Haw River Timber argues that in this case the exception has been met because the Town of Garner ordinances were "recorded at the local register of deeds office" in minute books and that "the recording of the Ordinances is 'notice of enforcement' " as would be covered by the policy.

Thus, the language of the policy's exclusion concededly denies coverage for the adverse economic impact caused by any ordinance or environmental protection enactment unless (1) a "notice of enforcement" of the ordinance or a "notice of [an] encumbrance resulting from a violation" has been issued and (2) such a notice has been "recorded in the public records." The policy defines public records to mean "records established under state statutes at Date of Policy for the purpose of imparting constructive notice of matters relating to real property to purchasers for value and without knowledge." In short, the adverse impact of ordinances is excluded from the scope of a standard ALTA title policy unless a notice of enforcement or of a violation is recorded in records established to put purchasers of real property on constructive notice of matters about the property. Stated otherwise, the risk transferred to the insurance company by the policy is the risk of not conducting an adequate title search among the records established by the state for searching titles to real property.

North Carolina law requires that the county commissioners of each county "provide for the register of deeds" in a "book, to be called Registration of Titles." See N.C. Gen. Stat. § 43–13. Since conveyances of land, contracts and options to convey land, leases over three years, and mortgages and deeds of trusts are required to be recorded in the Registration of Titles book in order to be effective against lien creditors or purchasers for value, see N.C. Gen. Stat. §§ 47–18, 47–20, the book establishes a chain of title on which purchasers can rely....

While the Registration of Titles book constitutes the "sole and conclusive legal evidence of title," N.C. Gen. Stat. § 43–22, liens, encumbrances, and other matters affecting specific parcels of real property may be recorded against the property in accordance with state statute and thereby put purchasers of that property on constructive notice also about them. For example, North Carolina provides for a "Record of Lis Pendens," see N.C. Gen. Stat. § 1–117; a "judgment docket" or book, see N.C. Gen. Stat. §§ 1–234 through 1–237, 1–208.1, 43–45; and a "Book of Wills," see N.C. Gen. Stat. § 31–20.

Thus, in order to be contained in the "public records," as used in the ALTA title policy, a notice of enforcement or of an encumbrance would have to be recorded in one of these public records designed to put purchasers of real property on constructive notice about matters affecting title to the property which they are purchasing.

This interpretation of the title insurance policy language is consistent with the principles of marketable title discussed above. Since the purpose of title insurance is to insure that there are no defects in the legal title to the real property interests being insured, the adverse impact of zoning ordinances and regulations would be covered only if they somehow affected title to specific property as it appeared in state established records putting persons on legal notice about matters affecting that property. Thus, in North Carolina as elsewhere, zoning or environmental laws of general application, which are not recorded against specific parcels of property, are generally excluded from standard-form ALTA title insurance policies.

We now turn to determine (1) whether a notice of enforcement or notice of violation of the Town of Garner's ordinances ever issued, and (2) whether the notices were recorded in public records established by North Carolina for the purpose of imparting constructive notice of matters relating to real property to purchasers of such property for value and without knowledge.

First, there is no evidence that any enforcement proceeding was ever initiated or "notice" given to enforce the buffer zone established by Garner's ordinances. Nor is there any indication that a notice of a violation of that buffer zone was ever issued. This is not surprising because until Haw River Timber was granted the timber deed, no one had apparently attempted to harvest the timber on the 179 acres adjacent to Swift Creek.

Second, there is no evidence that any notice of an enforcement action or a violation of an ordinance was recorded in the Record of Lis Pendens, the judgment docket, or the Registration of Titles book maintained in Wake County where the property was located. Indeed, there is no evidence that the ordinances themselves were ever so recorded. While the ordinances may have been on file in minute books maintained in the office of the register of deeds, this does not satisfy the requirements of North Carolina statutes adopted to put purchasers on constructive notice about matters affecting the real property that they are purchasing. Were we to hold, contrary to the language of the title policy in question, that the inclusion of the town ordinances of general application maintained in minute books located in the office of the register of deeds would have the same effect as matters recorded against specific property, we would frustrate not only the intent of the title insurance policy but also North Carolina policy that purchasers have a "reliable means for purchasers to determine the state of the title to real estate." Stegall v. Robinson, 344 S.E.2d 803, 804 (N.C. Ct. App. 1986).

For the reasons given, the judgment of the district court is AFFIRMED.

Hamilton, Circuit Judge, dissenting.

The majority rejects Haw River's claim seeking title insurance coverage on two alternative theories. First, the majority concludes that Haw River's title to the 179 acres of land lying within the environmental buffer zone is not "unmarketable" and, therefore, the ALTA policy's coverage provision for "unmarketability of the title" does not apply. Second, the majority concludes that even if Haw River's title to the timber is unmarketable, the exception to the zoning ordinance exclusion does not apply and, therefore, the ALTA policy provides no coverage for the loss. In my view, both of these conclusions rest on unpersuasive reasoning. The former conclusion is inconsistent with the North Carolina Supreme Court's decision in Marriott Financial Serv. v. Capitol Funds, Inc., 217 S.E.2d 551 (N.C. 1975). The latter conclusion is inconsistent with the North Carolina rule that if an insurance contract term is capable of one or more interpretations, the one most favorable to the insured applies. Because I believe Haw River suffered a loss covered by the ALTA policy and that the exception to the zoning ordinance exclusion does apply, I respectfully dissent.

I.

In *Marriott*, the plaintiff purchased land near a bridge in a heavily traveled area of Raleigh, North Carolina. Because of the high traffic flow, the Raleigh City Council adopted a policy to deny all driveway permit applications within 200 feet of the bridge. The policy was not embodied in an ordinance and therefore was not recorded at the county courthouse. When the plaintiff subsequently sought to subdivide the tract, which required separate driveways for each new lot, the permit request was denied because of the Raleigh City Council's policy. Marriott brought suit against the title insurance carrier contending that the loss in the value of the property caused by the government-created restriction on access was a covered risk under the title insurance policy issued to the plaintiff. The policy issued to the plaintiff insured against, among other things, losses due to "the lack of a right of access to and from land." Id. at 564.

The North Carolina Court of Appeals held that the policy provisions insuring against the lack of access applied only when the landowner had no right of access to and from the land. According to the North Carolina Court of Appeals, even pedestrian access to the property was sufficient to preclude coverage under the title insurance policy.

On appeal, the North Carolina Supreme Court rejected the North Carolina Court of Appeals' view that the presence of pedestrian access was sufficient to preclude coverage. Instead, the North Carolina Supreme Court adopted a reasonable insured approach. The North Carolina Supreme Court held "that when an insurer contracts to insure against lack of access to property, it must be deemed to have insured against the absence of access which, given the nature and location of the property, is reasonable access under the circumstances." Id. at 565.

Applying this reasonable insured approach, the North Carolina Supreme Court found coverage. In reaching this conclusion, the North Carolina Supreme Court stated that "it would strain credulity beyond reasonable limits to hold that the parties to this [insurance] contract understood that the insurance as to access could be satisfied by pedestrian access." The North Carolina Supreme Court reasoned that the "insured must have contemplated insurance protection against lack of vehicular access." Id.

Marriott instructs us to ask, given the circumstances surrounding the insurance contract at issue, whether Haw River contemplated that the "unmarketability of the title" provision would cover losses arising from a zoning ordinance filed in the Register of Deeds Office which rendered the timber economically unmarketable. If we answer this question in the affirmative then coverage attaches.

In this case, an insured in the same position as Haw River would have understood the ALTA policy to cover losses due to a zoning ordinance filed in the Register of Deeds Office that rendered the timber economically unmarketable. People acquire title to timber to market the harvested timber. Such is the nature of a timber deed. A timber deed holder cannot build on the property or otherwise use it in a recreational sense. In essence, the insured enjoys no use or enjoyment of the timber other than the ability to market it. Because the sole purpose behind the acquisition of a timber deed is to harvest and sell the timber, it follows that a reasonable insured would understand "unmarketability of the title" as insuring against the risk of loss due to the existence of a recorded local ordinance which rendered the timber economically unmarketable.

II.

The ALTA policy contains a general exclusion for, inter alia, zoning ordinances relating to environmental protection. There is, however, an exception to the zoning ordinance exclusion. The exception applies when "notice of the enforcement [of the ordinance] . . . has been recorded in the public records." Although the term "notice of enforcement" is not defined in the ALTA policy, the term "public records" is defined. That term is defined as "records established under state statutes . . . for the purpose of imparting constructive notice of matters relating to real property to purchasers for value and without knowledge." In this case, the public records is the Register of Deeds of Wake County. The majority concludes that the exclusion applies, but the exception does not. Although I agree the exclusion applies, as the ordinances at issue are zoning ordinances relating to environmental protection, the exception to the exclusion applies as well. In this case, the provision "notice of enforcement" is ambiguous. The term could be construed as applying when a violation of an ordinance is recorded in the public records. Alternatively, the term could be construed as applying when the ordinance is recorded in the public records.

Under North Carolina law, if an insurance contract term is capable of one or more interpretations, the one most favorable to the insured applies. Here, the interpretation most favorable to the insured is that the notice of enforcement provision applies when the zoning ordinance is recorded in the public records. It follows that because the zoning ordinances at issue were filed in the Register of Deeds of Wake County on the date the policy was issued to Haw River, the exception to the exclusion applies. . . .

Notes & Questions

1. **Standard Form Policies.** Most title insurance policies today are based on standard forms. The principal forms are those approved by the American Land Title Association ("ALTA"). However, not every state's title insurers use the ALTA forms. The California Land Title Association

("CLTA"), for example, has its own forms that are used in a large number of transactions, although ALTA forms are still used in many California transactions. New York and Texas insurers also often use alternative forms. Despite the use of standard forms, considerable room still exists for the knowledgeable attorney to negotiate additional protections for his or her client, by persuading the insurer to delete one or more exceptions or by purchasing additional coverage through endorsements designed to resolve particular title problems.

2. **Title Insurance and Title Warranties Compared.** Many titles are doubly assured, through title warranties given by the seller and title insurance from an institutional insurer. Although title warranties and title insurance overlap at many points, each also offers distinctive protection. A buyer who cannot get his title insurance company to delete an exception from its policy's coverage may turn to his seller and insist that she cover the exception by a deed warranty. Also, there are many defects, including off-record risks, that title insurance may not cover. And while the damages recoverable under a title policy are limited to the face amount of the policy, additional damages may be recovered under a warranty deed.

Why would a buyer want title insurance instead of, or in addition to, warranties? Title policies offer a degree of flexibility unattainable through warranties. Endorsements can be obtained to cover off-record risks and to increase the policy's coverage so that it keeps pace with inflation and with the value of improvements put on the premises. The protection of title policies can in certain instances be made to "run" to distant transferees through endorsements insuring assignments. Title companies also offer institutional advantages—basically, an available, solvent, and knowledgeable defendant. Probably most important is the fact that title insurance is not issued on a casualty basis. The insurer's title search is aimed at flushing out any possible flaws in title and at reducing the possibility that an insured will someday have to yield his home to a prior claimant and be relegated to the cold comfort of a monetary award.

For more on this subject, see Samuel Freshman, The Warranty Deed: Where and When to Use It, 51 L.A.B.J. 186 (1975); Jerome J. Curtis, Jr., Title Assurance in Sales of California Residential Realty: A Critique of Title Insurance and Title Covenants with Suggested Reforms, 7 Pac. L.J. 1 (1976).

3. **Tort Actions.** *White* follows the majority rule in permitting a buyer to sue his title insurance company for negligently conducting a title search. A substantial and growing minority of states, however, limit the buyer to the terms of the insurance contract. In Horn v. Lawyers Title Insurance Corp., 557 P.2d 206, 208 (N.M. 1976), the court held that the "rights and duties of the parties are fixed by the contract of title insurance.... Hence, any duty on the part of defendant to search the records must be expressed in or implied from the policy of title insurance.... Defendant clearly had no duty under the policy to search the records, and any search it may have actually undertaken, was undertaken solely for its own protection as indemnitor against losses covered by its policy." See also

Somerset Savings Bank v. Chicago Title Ins. Co., 649 N.E.2d 1123 (Mass. 1995); Walker Rogge, Inc. v. Chelsea Title & Guar. Corp., 562 A.2d 208 (N.J. 1989). State legislatures are also getting into the act. Some impose a duty on insurers to make a reasonable search (see, e.g., Tenn. Code Ann. § 56–35–129) while others expressly reject liability for negligent searches (see, e.g., Cal. Ins. Code §§ 12340.10–.11).

When will a buyer prefer tort to contract theory in an action against a title insurer? If the land has appreciated in value, tort recovery will be more likely to make the buyer whole than will recovery limited to the face amount of the policy. Also, tort theory enables recovery of consequential damages. And, of course, if the buyer relied on his seller's title insurance policy, rather than on a title policy he purchased for himself, tort will be the only available theory of recovery.

See generally James Bruce Davis, More Than They Bargained For: Are Title Insurance Companies Liable in Tort for Undisclosed Title Defects?, 45 Cath. U.L. Rev. 71 (1995); Joyce Dickey Palomer, Title Insurance Companies' Liability for Failure to Search Title and Disclose Record Title, 20 Creighton L. Rev. 455 (1987) (arguing that liability would force insurers to search more carefully and eliminate the need for a wasteful second search).

4. **State Regulation.** As title insurance companies have grown and expanded into new territories they have inevitably encountered state regulation. Although patterns vary from state to state, two concerns predominate: the price and quality of insurance, and the insurer's solvency. In Washington, for example, title insurers must file their rates with the state insurance commissioner who "may order the modification of any premium rate or schedule of premium rates found by him after a hearing to be excessive, or inadequate, or unfairly discriminatory." Wash. Rev. Code § 48.29.140(3).

Most states require specified reserve funds and capitalization levels to ensure the ability of title companies to pay off claims against them. New York, with one of the more extensive and detailed statutes, calls, among other things, for a "loss reserve at least equal to the aggregate estimated amounts due or to become due on account of all such unpaid losses and claims...." N.Y. Ins. Law § 6405(b). Some states require a cash deposit with the insurance commissioner and prohibit the issuance of any policy exposing the insurer to loss liability for more than fifty percent of its total capital and surplus. See, e.g., Hawaii Rev. Stat. § 431:20–112.

5. **Marketability of Title.** Most courts, like the North Carolina Supreme Court in *Haw River*, draw a distinction between marketable title and marketable property. See also Hocking v. Title Ins. & Trust Co., 234 P.2d 625 (Cal. 1951) (no liability where title insurer failed to identify municipal code violation because the violation did not "affect the marketability of [the buyer's] *title* to the land, but merely impaired the *value* of the property").

6. For an excellent treatise on title insurance, see D. Barlow Burke, Jr., Law of Title Insurance (2d ed. 1993). On title insurance generally, see

A.B.A., Title Insurance: The Lawyer's Expanding Role (1985); Theodore Taub, Rights and Remedies Under a Title Policy, 15 Real Prop., Prob., & Tr. J. 422 (1980).

D. Reforming the Title Assurance System

1. Marketable Title Acts, Statutes of Limitations, and Curative Acts

Lewis M. Simes & Clarence B. Taylor, Improvement of Conveyancing by Legislation

3–5, 17–19, 317, & 41–43 (1960).

MARKETABLE TITLE ACTS

No other remedial legislation which has been enacted or proposed in recent years for the improvement of conveyancing offers as much as the marketable title act. It may be regarded as the keystone in the arch which constitutes the structure of a modernized system of conveyancing.

Without doubt the chief impetus for such legislation has been the increasing length of the record of instruments which must be examined before a land title can be approved. As is well known, the practice still prevails in a very large number of states to trace title back to a grant from the United, States or from a state. The period of search thus becomes longer and longer as time goes on; and eventually this practice will have to be abandoned and the period restricted.

There is, of course, nothing new about limiting the period of search to a certain number of years. Obviously, in England, where there is no such thing as tracing land titles back to the government, the practice has long obtained of a vendee requiring title deeds to show a chain of title only for a fixed period of years. In some way this period seems to have been found by using the analogy of the longest period named in statutes of limitations with respect to actions for the recovery of real property. At the present time the period accepted is thirty years, and this practice is embodied in a statute. Similar practices have developed in some of the eastern states, where chains of title may be centuries long and are not traceable to the government.

But these practices of the bar in which titles are traced back only for an agreed period of years are unlike marketable title acts in one important respect. The bar practices leave the risk of loss, by reason of a defect in the title prior to the named period, on the purchaser. But under a marketable title act defects in the title prior to the named period are, by operation of the statute, extinguished.

Sometimes the modern American marketable title act is phrased like a statute of limitations; sometimes it may be analogized to a curative act. But in fact it is neither; and indeed it is definitely unique. Instead of interests being cut off because a claimant failed to sue, as would be the case if a statute of limitations were involved, the claimant's interest is extinguished because he failed to file a notice. In a sense the marketable title act may impose upon an owner a small additional burden, analogous to the burden of recording which was imposed when recording acts were first passed. Thus, before the recording acts, a prior conveyance from an owner of land was unimpeachable. But under recording acts, the grantee in the prior conveyance may lose his if he fails to record. Likewise, under a marketable title act, a claimant under a recorded deed may be required to file a notice in order to protect his title.

The essence of the Model Marketable Title Act which follows is simply this: If a person has a record chain of title for forty years, and no one else has filed a notice of claim to the property during the forty-year period, then all conflicting claims based upon any title transaction prior to the forty-year period are extinguished.

In one sense, the operation of the statute is all inclusive. It cuts off all interests, subject to a few exceptions unlikely to be encountered, which arise from title transactions prior to the forty-year period. It can extinguish ancient mortgages, servitudes, easements, titles by adverse possession, interests which are equitable as well as legal, future as well as present.

Yet in another sense, as a practical matter, the statute will probably cut off nothing at all, because there are no valid outstanding claims. It has been the experience of states with long-term marketable title acts that few if any notices of claim are ever filed, thus indicating that few claims actually exist. Indeed, the very fact that in some states title examination for only a thirty-or forty-year period is commonly accepted, without any legislation so providing indicates that there are in fact no enforceable claims adverse to the thirty-or forty-year chain of title.

It must not be assumed that the enactment of the Model Marketable Title Act will necessarily usher in an era of forty-year abstracts of title. The very fact that there are exceptions in the statute means that a title examiner will have to look back of the forty-year period to find instruments which may include the exceptions. But a competent title examiner will be able to see at a glance that most of the instruments do not concern the exceptions, and thus his task will be definitely lightened.

An important feature of the operation of the statute, however, is its curative effect. Ancient defects, which do not in fact give rise to substantial claims, but which may be the basis of a refusal to approve a title, are completely wiped out if they appear in the record more than forty years back. Even though the title examiner looks at the entire record from the government down to the present time, he is still greatly aided by the fact that he can ignore ancient defects. . . .

CURATIVE ACTS

A curative act is one which reaches back and corrects an error made in the past. As applied to conveyancing, it provides that certain prior failures to comply with the requirements for the execution or recording of an instrument, or for the transfer of an interest in land, shall be disregarded. Thus, a statute may provide that, after a defectively acknowledged instrument has been on record for two years, it shall be treated for all purposes as if it had been properly acknowledged at the time of its recording.

The permissible scope of curative legislation obviously is limited. Courts have said that one person's property may not be taken away from him and given to another as of a prior date. In general, curative statutes may be said to deal with matters of a formal character and to carry out the intentions of the parties which may otherwise have been frustrated by their failure to comply with formal requirements. Since the legislature could do away with such requirements, and since, quite commonly, the parties could be relieved of the requirements in the particular case by a judicial proceeding, retroactive statutes may be passed relieving the parties of these formal requirements as of a prior time.

In spite of their limitations, curative acts have been in operation since colonial times. They have dealt with a variety of situations, such as the following: absence of a seal; defective acknowledgments; failure to include any acknowledgment; defective conveyances under powers of attorney; defectively executed deeds of corporations; defective records of judicial sales.

The rational basis for the curative act may be stated as follows: Since human nature is fallible, people do make mistakes in executing legal instruments. There is no way to keep mistakes from creeping into the conveyancing process. But after defective instruments have been left standing for a certain period of time, justice is generally secured by providing that the defects are then to be ignored. Thus, the basic intent of the parties will be effectuated. Just where the line is to be drawn between those objectives which can be accomplished by curative acts and those which cannot, will be discussed more fully in connection with the subject of constitutionality of such legislation. Certainly no single formula can be found which will enable us to draw the line. We must, however, recognize that curative legislation has traditionally been approved in certain areas, that it tends to further the intent of the parties, and that it will not be approved to deprive innocent third parties of their property.

If the error to be corrected by curative legislation is of sufficiently long standing, it can equally well be corrected by a marketable title act. The great advantage of having curative acts in addition to a marketable act is that the curative acts become operative, in justice to all concerned, at the expiration of a much shorter period of time than the period of a marketable title act. Hence, curative legislation, when it is used at all to clear land titles, should provide for. a relatively short period after which the defect is cured.

A curative statute may take at least three possible forms. First, it may have a continuous and delayed operation, so that it will continue to cure the named defects after a certain period has elapsed. An example has already been given of a statute which continues to cure defective acknowledgments after they have been on record for two years. Second, the statute may name a particular date in the past, and be designed to cure defects in all instruments executed or recorded prior to that date. Thus, a statute might provide that all defectively acknowledged instruments which were recorded prior to January 1, 1954, shall be treated for all purposes, as if properly acknowledged at the time of their recording. The disadvantage of such a form of statute is that, as time passes, the period prior to which instruments are cured becomes longer, and it soon is necessary to enact a new statute naming a later date.

This second form of statute may, however, be desirable when it accompanies a change in legislative policy. Thus, the legislature may have repealed a requirement that instruments of conveyance be sealed. Thereafter, a statute may be enacted curing all unsealed instruments executed prior to the date of the repeal. Thus, the curative provision merely has the effect of making retroactive the statute abolishing the use of seals on instruments of conveyance. The policy in this legislation is not merely to correct the frailty of human nature, but to make retroactive a change of legislative policy.

Or, third, there may be a change in legislative policy with respect to certain formal requirements for conveyancing, and as a part of this legislation, or contemporaneous with it, a curative statute is enacted, immediately effective as to all instruments. Thus, in connection with the abolition of the requirement of a seal for instruments of conveyance, it may be enacted that, from and after the effective date of the act, all instruments of conveyance heretofore executed shall be valid without being sealed. . . .

STATUTES OF LIMITATIONS

Essentially, statutes of limitations fix a time beyond which ancient disputes, claims and matters can no longer be brought forth for judicial determination. Simply by withdrawing the privilege to litigate and denying the aid of the courts in asserting claims and interests of ancient origin, they effectuate a number of important public policies. Further, although the application of a rigidly fixed time limitation in a particular case may appear arbitrary, no one doubts that, in general, they tend to promote justice as between parties to controversies. But they also perform other important functions, entirely apart from affecting the course of any actual litigation; and nowhere are such functions more important than in the law of conveyancing. . . .

Statutes limiting recovery of real property commonly have three weaknesses as devices to cure defective titles: (1) the time when the period ends is uncertain due to provisions for extension by reason of disabilities and other facts; (2) adverse possession for the statutory period is outside the record and is often difficult to prove; (3) the statutes do not bar future interests. An ideal statute should go as far as possible to obviate these weaknesses.

As to disabilities, the type of statute which merely states an additional period after disabilities have terminated is undesirable. If the disability is insanity, there is no way to determine how long the period may last. It is preferable to name an overall period, which is the maximum regardless of disabilities. Thus, in the model statute the periods are extended by disabilities, but in no case are they extended beyond twenty years from the time the right of recovery first accrued. Furthermore, if the person subject to the disability is under guardianship, it is provided that there is no extension for disability during the period of guardianship. All these provisions as to disabilities are based on precedents in existing legislation, as is indicated in the comment....

It is important, however, to have provisions in the statute naming a short period where there is color of title of record. This results in the clearing of a record title, and does not lead to a title based solely on extrinsic facts. It is here, no doubt, that the statute will have its greatest value for the title man. The Model Act states a period of five years for title by adverse possession with color of title consisting of recorded instruments.

However, we still are faced with the question: How do we prove adverse possession for the statutory period? Various attempts have been made by legislation to avoid the necessity of direct proof of possession. Thus, in some states payment of taxes for the statutory period is made the equivalent of possession for that period. One difficulty with that solution is that payment of taxes is a matter to be determined by tax records and not by title records, and also, tax records may not show who paid the taxes or be available for the requisite period. If it cannot be determined that the person claiming adversely paid the taxes, the payment is of uncertain significance. On the other hand, there is no reason why payment of taxes for the statutory period may not constitute prima facie evidence of adverse possession, and the Model Act so provides. It also provides that present possession together with a recorded instrument of title for the statutory period is prima facie evidence of adverse possession.

Marshall v. Hollywood, Inc.

Supreme Court of Florida, 1970.
236 So. 2d 114.

CARLTON, JUSTICE.

We now review an application of the Marketable Record Titles to Real Property Act, Chapter 712, Florida Statutes.... The District Court held, in effect, that the Act confers marketability to a chain of title arising out of a forged or a wild deed, so long as the strict requirements of the Act are met. We affirm this decision.

The complex facts involved in this case have been presented extensively and with clarity in the opinion of the District Court. We will only briefly summarize these facts. In 1912 Mathew Marshall and Carl Weidling owned a large tract of land in South Florida. In 1913 they organized and incorporated the Atlantic Beach Company. They transferred their property interests in the large tract to the Company, and in return they received two-thirds and one-third, respectively, of the Company's total authorized and issued stock, in direct proportion to their initial ownership interests in the tract. Marshall and Weidling were the sole officers of the Company and they alone participated in its stock.

Mr. Marshall died in December 1923, leaving Louise Marshall as his widow and sole surviving heir. Mrs. Marshall was totally unaware of her husband's interests in the Company, and within a month after his passing, she left the State without ever returning. After her departure, a man named Frank M. Terry, apparently aided and abetted by certain associates, set into motion a clever scheme calculated to defraud the Marshall estate of all interests in the Company and its property. Although there is some question as to exactly who played what part in this scheme, for purposes of this opinion we shall ascribe all responsibility to Mr. Terry.

Within a few days after Mrs. Marshall's departure, Terry forged her name to an Application for Letters of Administration concerning Mathew Marshall's estate. Letters were subsequently issued by the County Judge, Dade County, to Mrs. Marshall and Terry received them. About this same time, Terry wrote up certain "Minutes of Dissolution of Atlantic Beach Company" and he also prepared a deed conveying all of the Company's property to himself and others residing out of the State, who were alleged in the spurious Minutes to be the remaining stockholders of the Company. Thereafter, these Minutes were purportedly acknowledged, and the deed conveying all of the Company's property, was executed by those who were alleged to be the stockholders.

Next, Terry prepared a petition seeking an Order dissolving the Company which was then filed in Circuit Court, Broward County, along with the Minutes of Dissolution. The Court granted the petition since it appeared in order, and a decree dissolving the Company was entered in February 1924. The day before this petition was filed, Terry and the other grantees under the deed from the Company joined in executing a deed conveying the tract to Hollywood Realty Company, a Florida corporation. This deed was recorded in April 1924. In August 1924 Hollywood Realty in turn executed a deed conveying this same property to Homeseekers Realty Company, which was recorded August 22, 1924.

All of the foregoing transactions are alleged by petitioner to have been part of a scheme to defraud the Mathew Marshall estate. The record is silent as to why Carl Weidling, initially owner of a one-third undivided interest in the tract, and subsequently holder of one-third of the Atlantic Beach Company stock, never raised any objections or questions. Mr. Weidling died in 1963; his interests are not represented in this suit. Mrs. Marshall died in 1945 without ever having learned of her husband's interests in the Company. The Company itself was never legally dissolved until September 14, 1936, when it was dissolved by proclamation of the Governor on account of failure to pay capital stock tax.

Homeseekers Realty Company disposed of approximately one third of the initial Atlantic Beach Company tract through sales before it lost its control over the remainder by forced sheriff's sale in 1929. In that year, the

Highway Construction Company of Ohio, Inc., obtained a judgment against Homeseekers and caused the sale at which Highway purchased the remaining unsold two-thirds of the initial tract. A sheriff's deed evidencing the judgment sale was recorded December 30, 1930. Highway Construction Company then conveyed its interests in the tract to respondent Hollywood, Inc., and this deed was recorded on February 21, 1931.

Respondent Hollywood, Inc., still retains title to the two-thirds of the original Atlantic Beach tract which was conveyed to it as a result of the forced sheriff's sale. The other respondents are those numerous persons, or their successors, who derived title to parcels on the one-third portion of the original tract from Homeseekers Realty prior to the 1929 judgment sale. Diagramed, the chain of title to the property involved in this suit, insofar as it is relevant to the issues involved here, looks like this:

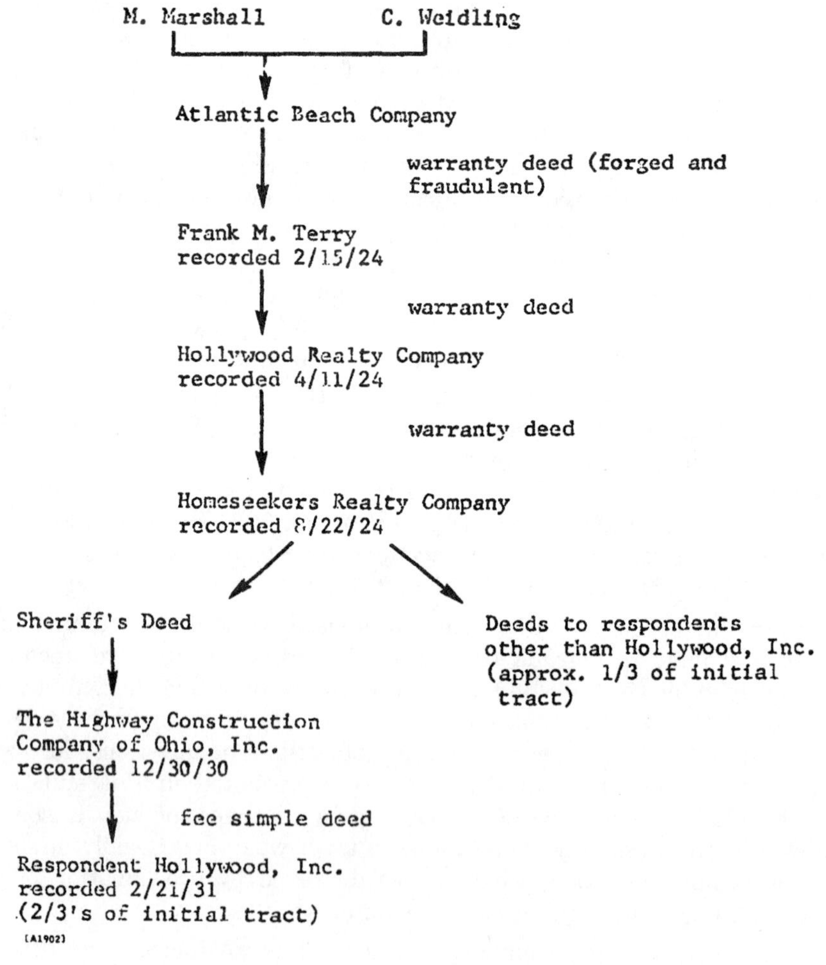

It was not until November 1966, that petitioner, a brother of Mathew Marshall, uncovered Terry's actions. Petitioner obtained appointment as Administrator of the Marshall estate, and subsequently, in his capacity as Administrator, he filed his initial complaint on July 13, 1967. An amended complaint was filed on April 5, 1968. The amended complaint sought a decree establishing the equitable interest of petitioner in the tract initially belonging to the Atlantic Beach Company, confirmation of the ownership of Atlantic Beach stock by petitioner, and also the appointment of a trustee for the Company who could convey legal title to the interest in the original tract to the heirs of Marshall.

Upon respondents' motion, the amended complaint was dismissed by final judgment with prejudice. The order of dismissal stated that petitioner's amended complaint failed to state a cause of action because the estate's claims were barred by operation of the Marketable Record Title Act, Ch. 712, F.S. The dismissal was appealed to the District Court. The issue framed on appeal was whether or not the Act applied to the claim of title asserted in petitioner's amended complaint in a manner which would extinguish the claim....

.... The most persuasive argument of petitioner is that the Marketable Record Title Act preserves case law which is inconsistent with dismissal of petitioner's amended complaint. F.S. § 712.07, F.S.A. states:

> Nothing contained in this Act shall be construed to extend the period for the bringing of an action or for the doing of any other act required under any statute of limitations or to affect the operation of any statute governing the effect of the recording or the failure to record any instrument affecting land. This law shall not vitiate any curative act.

Petitioner asserts that by preserving the operation of statutes of limitations, and curative and recording acts, the Legislature intended that the Act must be construed in a manner consistent with these previous, enactments and all case law interpreting them. In cases dealing with wild or forged deeds under these various acts, it has consistently been held, according to petitioner, that such deeds are void and of no effect even though they may have been recorded. Therefore petitioner suggests that the Act cannot bar a complaint which demonstrates that the chain of title involved in a cause initiated out of a forgery or a wild deed, even though the forgery or the wild deed came into being more than thirty years before marketability was being determined.

The answer to this argument is simply that the Act in question goes beyond previous enactments and is in a category of its own. We quote with approval the following commentary. Boyer & Shapo, Florida's Marketable Title Act: Prospects and Problems, 18 U. Miami L. Rev. 103, 104:

> The Marketable title concept is simple, although it has fathered many variations in draftsmanship. The idea is to extinguish all claims of a given age (thirty years in the Florida Statute) which conflict with a record chain of title which is at least that old. The act performs this task by combining several features, which gener-

> ally, are singly labeled as "statutes of limitations," "curative acts," and "recording acts."
>
> The new act is in fact all of these: It declares a marketable title on a recorded chain of title which is more than thirty years old, and it nullifies all interests which are older than the root of title. This nullification is subject to a group of exceptions—including interests which have been filed for record in a prescribed manner.
>
> The act is also more: It goes beyond the conventional statute of limitations because it runs against persons under disability. It is broader than the kind of legislation generally described as a curative act, because it actually invalidates interests instead of simply "curing" formal defects. It also differs from a recording act by requiring a rerecording of outstanding interests in order to preserve them.
>
> . . . .

In view of the special nature of this Act and its special purpose the assertion that its construction and application must be bound by precedents relating to less comprehensive acts does not make good sense and cannot make good law. The clear Legislative intention behind the Act, as expressed in F.S. § 712.10, F.S.A., was to simplify and facilitate land title transactions by allowing persons to rely on a record title as described by F.S. § 712.02, F.S.A., subject only to such limitations as appear in F.S. § 712.03, F.S.A. To accept petitioner's arguments would be to disembowel the Act through a case dealing with a factual situation of a nature precisely contemplated and remedied by the Act itself. This we cannot do.

In summary, although the Atlantic Beach Company/Terry deed initiating the chain of title involved here was forged, this deed formed but one link in the chain coming *before* the effective roots of title in this case as defined by the Act, i.e., transactions with either The Highway Construction Company or the Homeseekers Realty Company as grantors. Claims arising out of transactions, whether based upon forgeries or not, predating the effective roots of title are extinguished by operation of the Act unless claimants can come in under any of the specified exceptions to the Act. In this case, petitioner fails to qualify under any of the exceptions to the Act, and therefore, petitioner's claims are barred.

The certified question involved in this cause was, in effect, whether the Marketable Record Titles to Real Property Act, Ch. 712, F.S., confers marketability to a chain of title arising out of a forged or wild deed, so long as the strict requirements of the Act are met. This question is answered in the affirmative.

The decision of the appellate court here reviewed having properly affirmed the decree of the lower court, the writ heretofore issued in this cause should be and it is hereby discharged.

Notes & Questions

Approximately twenty states have now adopted marketable title acts. A number of other states require holders of various types of property interests to rerecord their interests every set number of years, frequently 30. If the holders fail to rerecord their interests, the interests expire. Are such rerecordation statutes unconstitutional "takings" of private property? Can they be applied to preexisting property owners who might not be aware of the rerecordation requirement? See Texaco v. Short, 454 U.S. 516 (1982) (holding that a statute requiring the rerecording of mineral interests was not unconstitutional even though property owners only had two years after passage of the statute to rerecord their interests and received no formal notice of the requirement).

2. Title Registration

Clinton P. Flick, Abstract and Title Practice

Vol. 1, pp. 188–190, 192–194 (2d ed. 1958).

The certificate system is in world-wide use for the purpose of showing ownership of merchant vessels. Every ship is listed in a national registry. A page in the Register is devoted to each ship and on that page there appears its name and description, the name of the owner, and any encumbrances. A duplicate of this page in the form of a certificate is given to the owner and is his evidence of ownership no matter where he may be. It is usually kept on the ship and accordingly is frequently spoken of in literature as the "ship's papers." Any lien or claim against a ship is required to be noted on the original register page so that it is possible for any interested person to tell at a glance exactly the condition of the title. To make a transfer, the owner assigns the certificate which he has and takes it to the registry office whereupon the old certificate is cancelled, the old page is closed, a new page is opened, and a duplicate certificate of the new page is given to the new owner.

In fact the Torrens system grew out of the fact that its originator, Robert R. Torrens, had been connected with the shipping industry for a number of years before he was appointed Registrar General of the Province of South Australia and given charge of registering all instruments affecting the title to real estate in that province. His experience in his former office led him to speculate on the subject of why the title to a tract of land could not be registered with the same simplicity as the title to a ship. He demonstrated that this was entirely possible and the system for which he drafted the law in Australia has proven to be a very efficient method of keeping track of the ownership of real property and of simplifying every transaction concerned with transferring the title or of using that type of property as security.

Torrens Acts have been passed in [a number of states.].... Upon each voluntary transfer by deed, and upon each involuntary transfer by deed, decree, descent, devise, or otherwise when accompanied by a court order directing it, the registrar cancels the old certificate and its duplicate and enters a new certificate and delivers an owner's duplicate to the new owner—all much the same as in the case of a transfer of corporation stock. It is the registration of a conveyance which is the operative act of transfer to a new owner. Prior to registration, a deed of registered land, like a fulfilled contract for a deed under the recording system, creates merely a right to the title as between the parties and is of no effect as to a bona fide purchaser from the registered owner.

From the foregoing it will be apparent that a report as to ownership may be made, and can only be made, from an examination, direct or indirect, of the original certificate of title on file in the office of the registrar. The certificate will usually be found to be in such definite and certain terms that no construction is required; when this is not the case the principles which govern the construction of deeds also apply to certificates of title. The reliability of an examiner's report will necessarily depend upon the conclusiveness of the certificate of title. This may vary slightly in the different states, but the variation is confined almost entirely to the difference in periods of limitation and periods allowed for appeal, or to reopen, as to a case upon the final order in which a certificate depends. After allowing for these, and for such exceptions as are expressly provided for in the registration statutes, the certificate creates an indefeasible title in the registered owner as against every one else, free from all claims and incumbrances except those noted on the certificate of title. Examination of the certificate alone is all that is necessary to determine ownership of the legal title.

Loss or destruction of duplicates occasionally occurs, and the registration acts all make provision for issuance of a new duplicate. In some states this is only after notice and hearing by the court, in others upon proof of loss and identity to the registrar, but in all states under very careful safeguards. Neither the public nor the owner is subject to any danger of loss from forged deeds so long as the latter safeguards his duplicate with the same care that he keeps any other valuable paper. If he is careless in the matter of to whom he entrusts it, there exists, except for the owner's signature card on file with the registrar, the same danger that exists with unregistered titles—with the loss, however, if not payable from an assurance fund, upon the negligent owner rather than upon an innocent purchaser or mortgagee.

In furtherance of the theory that everything regarding a present title should be ascertainable from the certificate on file in the office of the Registrar of Titles, the statutes provide that no title to registered land in derogation of that of the registered owner may be acquired by prescription or by adverse possession and, in the main, that the time-honored doctrine in most states of constructive notice by reason of occupancy does not prevail. This is the only change in substantive principles, though there are necessarily some changes in purely statutory principles, such as the nonapplicability of the recording act, the inception of judgment liens and other matters.

Notes & Questions

1. Although as many as twenty-one states at one time authorized the registration of title to real property, the number has since dwindled to ten—Colorado, Georgia, Hawaii, Massachusetts, Minnesota, North Carolina, Ohio, Pennsylvania, Virginia, and Washington. See Ted J. Fiflis, English Registered Conveyancing: A Study in Effective Land Transfer, 59 Nw. U. L. Rev. 468 (1964). And, even in these states, landowners only infrequently resort to title registration. According to Fiflis, "In Hawaii, perhaps one-third of all transactions are under the title registration system. In Cook County, Illinois, about 15% of all transactions are in registered land. Except in these states, and Massachusetts, Minnesota and perhaps Ohio, the system is virtually unused." Id. n.1. Illinois repealed its Torrens Act in 1992, effective as of July 1, 2037; in the meantime, no new land can be registered under the act. The history of state adoption of Torrens is summarized in 14 Richard R. Powell, Powell on Real Property § 83.01 (Michael Allan Wolf, ed. 2005).

2. This general rejection of title registration contrasts sharply with the claims for its superiority made in the literature. See, e.g., Joseph T. Janczyk, An Economic Analysis of the Land Title Systems for Transferring Real Property, 6 J. Legal Stud. 213, 215 (1977) ("The results of this paper indicate that the cost of transferring a title in the Torrens [system] is approximately $100 less than in the recording system, and further, that Cook County could save $76 million by adopting the Torrens system; some other counties could also realize a substantial savings.").

3. Why has title registration failed to take hold in the United States? Blame is most commonly placed on the title insurance companies: "The chief, major, proximate, and direct cause of the non-use of, or of the public 'disinclination' to use, the Torrens system has been the bitter, multi-form opposition—lobbying against any reform, wounding statutes when enactment is inevitable, conspiring with lending agencies, spreading adverse publicity, and so forth—of title companies and title lawyers." Myres S. McDougal & John W. Brabner–Smith, Land Title Transfer: A Regression, 48 Yale L.J. 1125, 1147 (1939). Why have title companies opposed title registration? Why should industry opposition alone have succeeded in sinking the concept? What reasons do consumers have to switch from title insurance to title registration, which is initially more costly?

4. The fight over title registration has produced some of the sharpest scholarly debates in real property law. Compare Richard R. Powell, Registration of the Title to Land in the State of New York (1938) with Myres S. McDougal & John W. Brabner–Smith, supra. Proposals for the adoption of title registration continue to be made. See, e.g., Barry Goldner, The Torrens System of Title Registration: A New Proposal for Effective Implementation, 29 U.C.L.A. L. Rev. 661 (1982) (also contains footnote references to most of the major literature in the area); Martin Lobel, A Proposal for a Title Registration System for Realty, 11 U. Rich. L. Rev. 471 (1977).

See generally Blair C. Shick & Irving H. Plotkin, Torrens in the United States (1978); John L. McCormack, Torrens and Recording: Land Title Assurance in the Computer Age, 18 Wm. Mitchell L. Rev. 61 (1992).

CHAPTER 6

LAND FINANCE

Virtually every developed piece of land in America has, at one time or another, been pledged as security for a loan. The pledge may have taken one of several forms. It may have taken the form of a *mortgage* given by the landowner, as *mortgagor*, to the lender, as *mortgagee*, to secure the landowner's obligation to pay a debt, evidenced by a bond or *promissory note*. It may have taken the form of a *deed of trust*, executed by landowner, as *trustor* to some third party as *trustee*, to hold title for the benefit of lender, as *beneficiary*, to secure payment of a bond or note. Or it may have taken the form of an *installment land contract*, structured much like the usual land sale contract but having a much longer executory period—20 or 30 years rather than 30 or 60 days—so that, during the executory period, the buyer in possession who makes monthly payments to the seller is effectively the homeowner, and the seller is effectively the lender, with the, contract itself representing both the security instrument and the promise to pay.

These land finance arrangements can be used for many purposes. They can be used to finance the acquisition of a house or an undeveloped parcel of land, in which case the instrument is typically called a *purchase money mortgage* or a *purchase money deed of trust*. They may be used to finance the construction of improvements on land, or activities totally unconnected to land, such as a vacation trip or a child's college education. Land finance is not limited to the needs of residential homeowners. Every day, loans for millions of dollars are given on the security of shopping centers, apartment houses and office buildings. Both residential and commercial real estate loans come from a variety of sources—savings and loan associations, savings banks, commercial banks, life insurance companies, pension funds, real estate investment trusts, and from the sellers themselves.

Because land is such a central and productive asset in American life, the law and institutions of land finance unavoidably mirror the nation's economic and social history. The cycles of agricultural bust and boom throughout the nineteenth century can be traced in laws enacted in the farming states, first enlarging the rights of farmer-mortgagors to redeem their property from foreclosing bank-mortgagees and then, when farming conditions improved, reducing mortgagors' redemption rights in order to stimulate increased lending activity.

The depression of the 1930's produced even more dramatic upheavals in the law and practice of land finance. The principal change was the federal government's effort, through direct intervention in land finance markets, to increase the opportunities for financing housing purchases and to create a national market for the purchase and sale of mortgage loans. The Federal Housing Administration, created by the National Housing Act in 1934, was given authority to insure home mortgage loans made by private lenders. The FHA not only stimulated private lending but also, through its underwriting requirements, effectively altered the prevailing real estate loan from a short term instrument with the principal fully payable at maturity, to far more affordable and stable long-term instruments—typically 25—or 30–year mortgages, with principal repayments, or amortization, spread out over the entire period. The Federal National Mortgage Association was chartered by the FHA in 1938 to create a secondary market for FHA-insured mortgages, buying these instruments when credit was tight and selling them when funds for housing finance were abundant. The Federal Home Loan Bank System, created by the Federal Home Loan Bank Act in 1932 and modeled after the Federal Reserve System, was intended to give credit to member institutions engaged in mortgage lending, taking some of the members' mortgages as collateral.

Spiraling inflation and a credit crunch in the 1970's and 1980's tested the ability of land finance institutions to respond to a different social and economic development: the collapse of the American dream that anyone who worked hard enough could, in time, afford the down payment and monthly installments needed to acquire a home. The private and governmental responses were mixed. Government lifted usury limits, reopening finance markets that had frozen shut once interest rates exceeded the statutory ceiling. To combat higher interest costs, many state courts outlawed due-on-sale clauses by which institutional lenders prohibited borrowers from passing on their old, low-interest loans to their buyers. Lenders offered a new array of mortgage instruments designed to reconcile consumer needs with the capacities of capital markets. Many of the new instruments were only dressed-up versions of pre-Depression devices, but all got snappy new names—variable rate mortgages, renegotiable rate mortgages, reverse annuity mortgages and shared appreciation mortgages, to name just a few.

What effect does a mortgage have on title to the underlying land? Many states continue to follow the "title theory" of mortgages, clinging to the early common law view that the mortgagee holds title from the moment the mortgage is executed to the time that the underlying obligation is paid or the mortgage is foreclosed. A majority of states, however, now follow the "lien theory," under which the mortgagee has only a lien on the property to secure the mortgagor's performance.

The basic distinction between the two theories lies in the right to possession. In title theory states the mortgagee has the right, rarely exercised, to possess the land from the moment the mortgage is given. In lien theory states the mortgagor has the right to possession unless and until foreclosure occurs. In a third group of states, following the "intermediate theory," the mortgagor has the right to possession until default on the underlying obligation.

Though much written about, the distinctions between these three theories have little practical consequence since title and intermediate states effectively clothe the mortgagor with virtually all of the attributes of ownership. Further, the distinctions are easily circumvented by agreement between borrower and lender.

The materials in this section touch only on the fundamentals of land finance. They focus almost exclusively on home finance, rather than on more complex commercial land transactions, and leave to other courses and other casebooks consideration of the intricate planning strategies that pervade land finance. See, e.g., Gerald Korngold & Paul Goldstein, Real Estate Transactions: Cases and Materials on Land Transfer, Development and Finance (4th ed. 2002). The standard treatise in this field is Grant S. Nelson & Dale A. Whitman, Real Estate Finance Law (4th ed. 2001).

A. THE FORMS OF LAND FINANCE

Bernard Rudden & Hywel Moseley, An Outline of the Law of Mortgages

34, 8 (1967).

1. THE MORTGAGE AT COMMON LAW

Mortgages of land were made in England long before there was any system of law common to the whole country. There are records of mortgages in Anglo–Saxon days, and at the period immediately after the Conquest when Domesday Book was being compiled. But there was no effective common law over the whole of England until the first half of the 12th century, and it is therefore impossible to state the doctrines of the law concerning mortgages before that time. Even then the practice is obscure, but it is clear that lending money at interest was both amoral wrong and a crime against the usury laws. Even a feudal economy, however, could not flourish without some means of financing development, and so the earliest transactions had to provide both security to the lender and some means of enabling him to obtain a return on his loan in lieu of the forbidden interest. So the lender took a lease of the land, went into possession, and farmed or otherwise managed it, using the profits to pay off the principal—in which case the transaction was called a "live pledge" (in Norman French, *vif gage*). Alternatively, in the harsher type of deal, the lender used the profits of the land for his own gain, leaving the principal advance still owing. This was the "dead pledge" or *mort gage*. The disadvantage of this situation from the point of view of the lender was that, being a mere tenant, he was not, at that time, well protected by the courts. In particular, if he were evicted, his only remedy was damages; so the whole value of the arrangement was lost to him, as he could not be sure of keeping his hands on the land itself. To be absolutely secure he had to be able to show that he was a *freeholder*. Consequently, by the end of the 15th century, most lenders insist that the land be conveyed to them *in fee simple*, in return for the loan. The transaction is still a mortgage, of course, not an out-and-out sale, and so the fee simple is transferred subject to a condition that, if the loan is repaid on the date agreed, the borrower may re-enter the land and claim the fee simple. As a further precaution, and to provide documentary evidence that the borrower has repaid the loan and redeemed the land, the lender covenants that, on repayment, he will re-convey the fee simple.

This gives the lender a great deal of security and, as the usury laws after 1545 allowed interest to be charged (subject to maximum rates), there was not the same need for the lender to go into possession to disguise interest as profits. Consequently, the practice grew of leaving the borrower in possession. In a case in 1620 we find a proviso "that the mortgagee, his heirs and assigns shall not intermeddle with the actual possession of the premises or perception of the rents until default of payment" and after the Restoration this practice became a commonplace.

The lender could afford to leave the borrower in possession since, from the former's point of view, the transaction is simply an investment of money and since he could, if necessary, evict the borrower at once.

Thus the later mortgage at common law consisted of a conveyance of his estate by the borrower (who was, and is, called the mortgagor) to the lender (the mortgagee) as security for the debt or loan owing to or advanced by the latter. The conveyance was a transfer of the fee simple, as a vendor might convey it to a purchaser; but it contained the "proviso for redemption," i.e., a stipulation that, if the mortgagor should repay the debt with a certain rate of interest upon it, *at an agreed date* (usually six months hence) the mortgagee would reconvey the fee simple to the mortgagor.

The common law enforced strictly the proviso for redemption—after all, said the judges, that was what the parties had agreed. Consequently the borrower had one chance *and one only* to redeem his property—on the agreed date. If he did not do so then, at common law, the lender's estate was absolute and could never be redeemed. The transaction was regarded primarily as a bargain between the parties; and, as in the case of any other bargain, the law would enforce it according to its terms....

The above is a description of the classical form of the mortgage—a form which it retained until 1925, a form which determines the present appearance of a mortgage deed, and a form which is one long lie. The reason for this is the intervention of equity.

2. THE MORTGAGE IN EQUITY

We have seen that the mortgagor whose date for redemption had passed could not approach the common law courts and ask them to make the lender re-convey the land on receipt of the money. But if the mortgagor petitioned the Court of Chancery he might well succeed....

It will be obvious that the mortgage was a fertile field for the growth of the Chancellor's powers. Up to the early 17th century, he would give relief only in special cases as where there was some fraud on the part of the lender, or the borrower's inability to repay on the exact date arose through some accident. After that time, however, Chancery took the view that *all* mortgages were no more than a borrowing upon security, and it became settled that the mortgagor was entitled to redeem at any time, notwithstanding that the date on which he had promised to do so was long past. If the lender refused to allow redemption, Chancery would order him to reconvey the estate . . . .

It is most important—even today—to understand this dual nature of the mortgage, which resulted from the fact that the transaction could come before two separate courts. The common law court would do nothing unless the borrower repaid the loan on the agreed date; and, since the lender already had the fee simple conveyed to him by the mortgage, on default in repayment by the mortgagor he was, at common law, the absolute owner. Equity, however, would still intervene, treating the *borrower* as the owner, and confining the mortgagee's rights to those necessary to secure his advance. This affected profoundly the rights of the parties. The practice grew of stipulating in the mortgage deed that the loan should be repaid in six months' time. Usually, of course, both parties expected the loan to be outstanding for a much longer time—after all, it is an investment by the lender. The date was put in, however, so that the mortgagee could, if necessary, call in his loan at any time thereafter; and, as will be shown, he has several remedies to enforce his right to the money. As far as the borrower is. concerned, he has two rights to redeem: the *contractual right* on the date specified in the deed, and the *equitable right* to redeem *at any time* thereafter, on paying principal, interest and costs and giving proper notice to the mortgagee.

This equitable right to redeem could be ended by the court itself in an application by the mortgagee—for what the Chancellor had created, he could end. This process of curtailing the equitable right to redeem and so leaving the mortgagee with a fee simple absolute both at law and in equity, is known as *foreclosure*.

Sebastian v. Floyd

Supreme Court of Kentucky, 1979.
585 S.W.2d 381.

AKER, JUSTICE.

This case presents the question whether a clause in an installment land sale contract providing for forfeiture of the buyer's payments upon the buyer's default may be enforced by the seller.

The movant, Jean Sebastian, contracted on November 8, 1974, to buy a house and lot situated in Covington, Kentucky, from Perl and Zona Floyd, respondents in this motion for review. Sebastian paid $3,800.00 down and was to pay the balance of the $10,900.00 purchase price, plus taxes, insurance, and interest at the rate of 8½% per annum, in monthly installments of $120.00. A forfeiture clause in the contract provided that if Sebastian failed to make any monthly payment and remained in default for 60 days, the Floyds could terminate the contract and retain all payments previously made as rent and liquidated damages.

During the next 21 months, Sebastian missed seven installments. Including her down payment, she paid the Floyds a total of $5,480.00, rather than the $6,320.00 which was called for by the terms of the contract. Of this amount, $4,300.00, or nearly 40% of the contract price, had been applied against the principal.

The Floyds brought suit in the Kenton Circuit Court against Sebastian in August, 1976, seeking a judgment of $700.00 plus compensation for payments for taxes and insurance, and seeking enforcement of the forfeiture clause. Sebastian admitted by her answer that she was in default but asked the court not to enforce the forfeiture clause. Sebastian counterclaimed for all payments made pursuant to the contract. On advice of counsel, Sebastian ceased to make payments after the institution of this law suit.

The case was referred to a master commissioner for hearing. The commissioner recommended termination of the land sale contract and enforcement of the forfeiture clause. The Kenton Circuit Court entered a judgment adopting the commissioner's recommendations. On appeal, the Court of Appeals affirmed. We granted discretionary review to consider the validity of the forfeiture clause. We reverse.

When a typical installment land contract is used as the means of financing the purchase of property, legal title to the property remains in the seller until the buyer has paid the entire contract price or some agreed-upon portion thereof, at which time the seller tenders a deed to the buyer. However, equitable title passes to the buyer when the contract is entered. The seller holds nothing but the bare legal title, as security for the payment of the purchase price.

There is no practical distinction between the land sale contract and a purchase money mortgage, in which the seller conveys legal title to the buyer but retains a lien on the property to secure payment. The significant feature of each device is the seller's financing the buyer's purchase of the property, using the property as collateral for the loan.

Where the purchaser of property has given a mortgage and subsequently defaults on his payments, his entire interest in the property is not forfeited. The mortgagor has the right to redeem the property by paying the full debt plus interest and expenses incurred by the creditor due to default. In order to cut off the mortgagor's right to redeem, the mortgagee must request a court to sell the property at public auction. From the proceeds of the sale, the mortgagee recovers the amount owed him on the mortgage, as well as the expenses of bringing suit; the mortgagor is entitled to the balance, if any.

The modern trend is for courts to treat land sale contracts as analogous to conventional mortgages, thus requiring a seller to seek a judicial sale of the property upon the buyer's default. It was stated in Skendzel v. Marshall, 261 Ind. 226, 301 N.E.2d 641, 648 (1973):

> A conditional land contract in effect creates a vendor's lien in the property to secure the unpaid balance owed under the contract. This lien is closely analogous to a mortgage—in fact, the vendor is commonly referred to as an "equitable mortgagee." . . . In view of this characterization of the vendor as a lienholder, it is only logical that such a lien be enforced through foreclosure proceedings.

We are of the opinion that a rule treating the seller's interest as a lien will best protect the interests of both buyer and seller. Ordinarily, the seller will receive the balance due on the contract, plus expenses, thus fulfilling the expectations he had when he agreed to sell his land. In addition, the buyer's equity in the property will be protected.

This holding comports with our decision in Real Estate and Mortgage Co. of Louisville v. Duke, 251 Ky. 385, 65 S.W.2d 81 (1933), wherein it was stated at page 82 of 65 S.W.2d:

> The forfeiture clause was intended simply as a security for the payment of the purchase price. In these circumstances the forfeiture provided for by the contract will be disregarded. . . .

Respondents contend the preponderance of Kentucky cases permits enforcement of forfeiture clauses in land sale contracts. However, installment land contracts were not involved in two of the cases cited in respondents' brief. In Ward Real Estate v. Childers, 223 Ky. 302, 3 S.W.2d 601 (1928), and Graves v. Winer, Ky., 351 S.W.2d 193 (1961), this court permitted retention by the sellers of "earnest money" deposited pursuant to an executory deposit receipt agreement. The ordinary short-term real estate contract presents a situation very different from the case at bar. Such an agreement generally provides that in the event the buyer fails to perform the contract, the seller may retain the down payment (usually no more than ten per cent of the contract price) as liquidated damages. In *Ward*, supra, and *Graves*, supra, the sum specified as liquidated damages clearly bore a reasonable relation to the actual damages suffered by the seller, which damages would be difficult to ascertain. Our holding therefore has no bearing on the typical earnest money deposit. . . .

The judgment of the trial court and the opinion of the Court of Appeals are reversed and the case remanded for further proceedings consistent with this opinion.

Koenig v. Van Reken

Court of Appeals of Michigan, 1979.
279 N.W.2d 590.

V.J. BRENNAN, PRESIDING JUDGE.

In October of 1974, plaintiff Helen Koenig brought suit in Oakland County Circuit Court to have a warranty deed executed by her to defendants Van Reken declared an equitable mortgage. The original complaint was later supplemented to add a count against the defendants for unjust enrichment. The defendants moved for a summary judgment under GCR 1963, 117.2(1) claiming that the plaintiff failed to state a claim upon which relief could be granted. The plaintiff appeals by right the lower court's granting of the defendants' motion, but contests only the dismissal of the equitable mortgage count. Our review is thus limited to the question of whether the trial court under GCR 1963, 117.2(1) properly dismissed the action regarding the imposition of an equitable mortgage....

In 1970, plaintiff owned a home in Oakland County with a market value of $60,000 that was encumbered by three mortgages totaling $25,933.26. The real estate taxes on plaintiff's home had become delinquent and foreclosure proceedings had begun on one of the mortgages. Plaintiff was then approached by defendant, Stanley Van Reken, who proposed that for a fee of 10% he would "service" the mortgages and pay the delinquent taxes. Subsequently, on June 16, 1970, plaintiff and defendant Stanley Van Reken executed three documents that form the basis of this action.

The first of these documents, entitled "AGREEMENT," stated that plaintiff desired to prevent the loss of her home and provided that defendant Stanley Van Reken purchase the property, redeem it from tax sale and mortgage foreclosure, and give plaintiff an exclusive right to repurchase according to the terms of a lease-option agreement that was also executed between the parties.

The second document was a warranty deed which conveyed the property from plaintiff to defendants for a stated consideration of $28,600. Plaintiff alleges that the deed was silent as to consideration when she signed it, that the figure of $28,600 was added subsequently, and that she never received any such consideration.

The third document provided that Stanley Van Reken was to lease the premises to plaintiff for a 3-year period at a fixed monthly rent of $300. Plaintiff was also to receive an exclusive option to repurchase the premises during the term of the lease for a price of $32,318.79, with a downpayment of $3,500 and monthly payments of $300 which were to include taxes, insurance, principal and interest.

At no time during the negotiations that led to the execution of these documents was. plaintiff represented by an attorney, and all three documents were prepared by Stanley Van Reken.

The parties operated under the lease from June 16, 1970, to February, 1972, and during this time plaintiff made total payments of $5,800. In February, 1972, plaintiff defaulted in a monthly rental payment. Plaintiff was thereupon evicted from the home.

The defendants argue on appeal that the subject transaction cannot be deemed to create an equitable mortgage since it has not been alleged that the deed was given to secure an obligation owed by the plaintiff to the defendants. The defendants contend that the "obligation owed" is a necessary requisite to establish an equitable mortgage "as a matter of law."

The defendants' argument not only shows a lack of understanding of the nature and purpose of equitable relief but overlooks well-established Michigan case law on point. The court of equity protects the necessitous by looking through form to the substance of the transaction. Although no set criterion has been established, the controlling factor in determining whether a deed absolute on its face should be deemed a mortgage is the intention of the parties. Such intention may be gathered from the circumstances attending the transaction including the conduct and relative economic positions of the parties and the value of the property in relation to the price fixed in the alleged sale. Under Michigan law, it is well settled that the adverse financial condition of the grantor, coupled with the inadequacy of the purchase price for the property, is sufficient to establish a deed absolute on its face to be a mortgage. Ellis v. Wayne Real Estate Co., 357 Mich. 115, 97 N.W.2d 758 (1959).

In *Ellis*, supra, the plaintiffs initially sought a loan from defendant to save their home from forfeiture. After hurried negotiations, the plaintiffs executed a quit claim deed to defendant and simultaneously entered into a land contract under which the plaintiffs were to repurchase the property. The defendant then satisfied a default and paid the delinquent taxes. In noting the discrepancy between the price paid by the defendant and the value of the property, the Court held that the transaction constituted a loan by defendant secured by a mortgage on the property.

In taking the plaintiff's well-pleaded facts in the present case as true, there is a close parallel with *Ellis*, supra. Here the plaintiff, while in financial distress, sought help from the defendants in saving her home from foreclosure. Although plaintiff was not desirous of selling her home, she entered into a transaction which conveyed her equity worth over $30,000 for less than $4,000. While financial embarrassment of the grantor and inadequacy of consideration do not provide an infallible test, they are an indication that the parties did not consider the conveyance to be absolute. We note that the lease-back arrangement entered into by the parties effectively circumvented the right to redeem, which is designed to protect purchasers such as plaintiff in times of financial crisis. In applying these facts to the aforementioned case law, it could be found without difficulty that the subject transaction constituted a mortgage to secure a loan in the amount of defendants' initial expenditure.

We reverse the order granting summary judgment in favor of the defendant on the equitable mortgage count and remand for trial on this issue.

Notes & Questions

1. A financing arrangement arises any time one person provides part or all of the capital needed to support another's activities in return for repayment of the capital, plus consideration, over a period of time. Al-

though mortgages and deeds of trust are the instruments most popularly associated with land finance, many other arrangements also qualify. Installment land contracts like the one in *Sebastian* are often used to finance the acquisition of housing or of undeveloped land. Leases are also financing arrangements. The leased premises represent the asset lent by the landlord to the tenant; in return, the tenant pays rent for use of the premises. (If, as sometimes happens, the lease gives the tenant an option to buy the premises at the end of the term at a specified price, the lease begins to look much more like an installment land contract or even a purchase money mortgage or deed of trust given by buyer to seller.)

Lawyers structuring real estate transactions help select the financing form that will best accommodate the parties' interests. One pitfall to be avoided is the ever-present risk that the form the parties select will later be judicially recast into some other form, as happened in both *Sebastian* and *Koenig*. Judicial recharacterization of a financing arrangement will obviously disrupt the expectations of the immediate parties; it may unsettle the expectations of third parties as well. If Van Reken had recorded his putative deed from Koenig and then sold the premises to a third party who had no notice of the underlying transaction, would—and should—the third party be bound by the deed's later recharacterization as an equitable mortgage? For a court to protect the third party purchaser in this situation will only encourage grantee-lenders to record and dispose of their putative interests as quickly as they can, leaving the original grantor with only a personal action. See generally Roger A. Cunningham & Saul Tischler, Disguised Real Estate Security Transactions as Mortgages in Substance, 26 Rutgers L. Rev. 1 (1972).

2. Probably the most important distinction between the different forms of real property security is their contemplated method of foreclosure and sale. Unless a mortgage provides otherwise, the mortgagee must resort to judicial proceedings in order to foreclose the mortgagor's equity of redemption and obtain a sale of the property to satisfy the debt. However, if the mortgage contains a *power of sale*, expressly giving the mortgagee the power to conduct the foreclosure sale herself, and if local statutes do not bar this self help procedure, judicial proceedings are unnecessary and the mortgagee can foreclose simply by public sale after notice to all interested parties.

Lenders in several states have traditionally preferred the deed of trust to the mortgage with power of sale. Like the mortgage with power of sale, the deed of trust enables sale of the encumbered property without resort to judicial process. The deed of trust differs in that, where the mortgage involves two parties—mortgagor and mortgagee—the deed of trust involves three: the borrower ("trustor") conveys title to a third party ("trustee") as security for the trustor's performance of its debt obligation to the lender ("beneficiary"). If the trustor defaults, and if the beneficiary so requests, the trustee will arrange a public nonjudicial sale of the land to satisfy the debt.

For lenders, the original advantage of the deed of trust over the mortgage with power of sale was the freedom that it gave them to bid at the foreclosure sale. Since the sale under a mortgage with power of sale was conducted by the mortgagee, courts and legislatures, concerned about the possibility of self-dealing, barred mortgagees from bidding at their own sales. Because the sale under a deed of trust was conducted by a third party trustee, lawmakers saw no conflict of interest. (This clearly represents form triumphing over substance: more often than not, the third party trustee is the nominee or alter ego of the beneficiary.) Statutes today have eliminated most of the differences between deeds of trust and mortgages with power of sale, and have generally removed the restriction on the mortgagee's ability to bid at her own foreclosure sale. The two forms of security are for this reason treated interchangeably throughout this chapter.

3. **The "Credit Quartet."** All land finance arrangements can be reduced to four variables: interest rate, rate of amortization (the rate at which the loan principal is paid off), length of loan term, and loan-to-value ratio (the ratio between the amount of the loan and the value of the property securing it; thus an $80,000 loan on a property appraised at $100,000 has an 8:10 loan to value ratio, sometimes simply called an 80% loan to value ratio). Each variable can be adjusted to meet the particular needs of borrower and lender. For example, a borrower might agree to a shorter loan term, thereby reducing the lender's exposure and risk, in return for a lower interest rate, a slower amortization rate, or a higher loan to value ratio.

The most dramatic, systemic shift in the orientation of these four variables occurred as a result of the Depression of the 1930s. The standard pre-Depression mortgage instrument had a short-term (typically 5 years), low loan to value ratio (typically 50%), and no amortization (the entire principal was payable as a "balloon" at the end of the term). New Deal programs introduced a strikingly different instrument and encouraged its adoption with the lure of FHA insurance. The new instrument had a much longer term (20 to 30 years), a higher loan to value ratio (typically 80%), and complete amortization over the life of the loan. Most instruments of this period were so-called "level payment" mortgages, calling for an identical monthly payment covering interest and reduction in principal throughout the loan term. Level payment mortgages are still widely used. In the loan's early years, most of the level payment goes toward interest payments and only a small amount toward reduction of principal. But, as principal is reduced, the interest payments on the principal outstanding become smaller and reductions in principal become consequently larger, producing still smaller interest payments and still larger reductions in principal, until the loan is completely paid off.

4. **Alternatives to Fixed Rate Mortgages.** By the mid–1970's, the long-term fixed rate mortgage had become increasingly unattractive to lenders and borrowers alike. With interest rates constantly rising, lenders were reluctant to tie up their capital over a long period at interest rates that they believed would soon fall short of their own cost of capital.

Borrowers disliked the higher interest rates, shorter terms, and lower loan to value ratios that lenders began to require in return for their own diminished prospects. This shared dilemma produced a burst of "creative financing" that often resembled, and bore many of the hazards of, pre-Depression real estate finance.

Among the more prominent arrangements proffered were adjustable rate mortgages ("ARMs"). In an ARM, the interest rate paid by the borrower varies over the life of the loan according to a designated index reflecting current market rates. Since the common wisdom during the 1970's was that interest rates would rise over the long term, ARMs were attractive to lenders because they protected against inflation, and were attractive to borrowers who might thus obtain a lower initial interest rate than under a fixed rate mortgage. Borrowers' concerns that interest increases might exceed increases in their income, thus jeopardizing their ability to make the monthly mortgage payment, were assuaged by legislated limits on the frequency and amount by which interest rates could be increased.

For discussion of the various alternatives to fixed rate mortgages, see Christopher Caswell, The New Mortgages: A Functional Legal Analysis, 10 Fla. St. U. L. Rev. 95 (1982); Stanley Izeman, Alternative Mortgage Instruments: Their Effect on Residential Financing, 10 Real Est. L.J. 3 (1981).

B. Creditor Protections

First Indiana Federal Savings Bank v. Hartle

Indiana Court of Appeals, 1991.
567 N.E.2d 834.

Hoffman, P.J.

Plaintiff-appellant First Indiana Federal Savings Bank appeals the trial court's grant of summary judgment in favor of the Hartles, defendants-appellees....

This controversy centers around a 1963 note and mortgage and a subsequent warranty deed. The mortgage note was executed on October 28, 1963 by Loell and Bonnie Good and payable to Pendleton Loan Association [predecessor in interest to First Indiana]. It was for the sum of $13,600.00 to be paid in monthly installments for 20 years. The note provided that it was secured by a certain real estate mortgage. The mortgage, in turn, specifically provided that it was:

> .... to secure the repayment of a loan made by the association to the mortgagors as evidenced by their promissory note of even date herewith in the principal sum of $13,600.00, payable in installments with interest and attorney's fees, the last installment being due and payable 20 years after date....

> The mortgagors covenant and agree with the association that they will:
>
> (1) pay said note according to its terms....
>
> In June, 1971, Sarah Vilcsek was the owner of the real estate by warranty deed. Ms. Vilcsek then conveyed the real estate by warranty deed to William and Joyce Hartle. The deed provided that the Hartles were taking the real estate:
>
> Subject to a mortgage to Pendleton Loan Association dated October 28, 1963, and recorded on October 30, 1963, in Mortgage Record 475, page 583, Records of Madison County, Indiana, which mortgage the Grantees herein hereby assume and agree to pay.

Joyce argues that First Indiana may not seek personal liability against them on the note. First Indiana avers that the covenant in the deed is sufficient to confer personal liability to the Hartles for repayment of the note.

Joyce asserts that Ind. Code § 32–8–11–2 prevents First Indiana from pursuing them. However this section only states that a mortgage will not be construed as implying a covenant for the payment of a sum intended to be secured. An action for personal liability is maintainable where an express covenant for payment is contained in the mortgage.[1] This Court in Warner v. Webber Apartments, Inc. (1980), Ind. App., 400 N.E.2d 1180, 1181, quoted the rule on covenants in mortgages imparting personal liability:

> It is the general rule, except where statutes provide otherwise, that if the mortgage contains a covenant to pay the debt secured, the mortgagor is personally liable and an action in debt will lie on the covenant....

While the covenant in this case is not an example of model draftmanship in that it could have been more specific as to the note, it is an express covenant nonetheless to pay the mortgage indebtedness. The Hartles did not take the real estate simply subject to the mortgage; through the covenant, the Hartles did "assume and agree" to pay the mortgage indebtedness. Hancock v. Fleming (1885), 103 Ind. 533, 3 N.E. 254.

While it is true that the covenant states that grantees would assume and agree to pay the "mortgage," it has long been held that a mortgage is merely security for the payment of a debt. Reasoner v. Edmundson (1854), 5 Ind. 393. After all, it is possible to give a mortgage to secure a debt without assuming personal liability for that debt. However, in this case, when the Hartles assumed and agreed to pay the mortgage through the assumption clause in the warranty deed, they were clearly assuming and agreeing to pay the mortgage indebtedness....

SULLIVAN, J., dissenting.

1. In the absence of an express agreement to pay, a mortgagee's remedy is confined to foreclosure only. Ind. Code § 32–8–11–2; Maloney v. Home Loan & Trust Co. (1933), 97 Ind. App. 564, 186 N.E. 897, mandate modified 97 Ind. App. 564, 187 N.E. 682.

I fully agree that the Hartles contracted with Vilcsek to pay the "mortgage indebtedness" and that such agreement could have been enforced directly against the Hartles by the Bank. I further agree that a mortgage is security for payment of a debt. Additionally, I agree that "it is possible to give a mortgage to secure a debt without assuming personal liability for that debt." This is precisely why I believe assumption of a mortgage does not also assume the underlying debt unless specifically stated.

The "mortgage indebtedness" is the indebtedness set forth in the mortgage. It recites a principal amount and it sets forth the manner in which that "mortgage indebtedness" is to be paid. The person assuming that mortgage indebtedness assumes only the mortgage obligation, not the underlying obligation which, in the mortgage, the mortgagor may have separately and independently agreed to pay. The obligations are certainly interrelated, but they are not identical. If the "mortgage indebtedness" and the obligation upon the underlying promissory note were one and the same, there would be no need to include in the original mortgage instrument a specific and severable promise upon the part of the mortgagor to "pay said note according to its terms." Here, as in Warner v. Webber Apartments, Inc. (1980) 3rd Dist., Ind. App., 400 N.E.2d 1180, the original mortgagor agreed to pay, not only the mortgage indebtedness, but the underlying obligation as well. Without question, in *Warner*, as here, the original mortgagor was bound upon both obligations. That does not mean that a subsequent mortgage assumption carries with it both obligations and the *Warner* case does not so hold. . . .

Notes & Questions

1. A mortgagee typically has two avenues of relief against a defaulting mortgagor. She may proceed against the mortgagor personally on his promise, embodied in his note or bond, to repay the mortgage debt. And she may proceed against the land securing the promise by foreclosure and sale, using the sale proceeds to satisfy the personal debt.

Relief becomes a bit more complicated when the mortgagor has transferred the encumbered land. If the transferee has *taken subject to* the mortgage, the mortgagee will have no recourse against the transferee personally but can, as before, obtain relief against the mortgagor personally or against the land through foreclosure. If the mortgagee chooses to proceed against the mortgagor personally, the mortgagor, once having paid the debt, becomes subrogated to the mortgagee's rights against the land and can thus obtain reimbursement from the land itself through foreclosure, sale and satisfaction of the debt out of the sale proceeds.

If, by contrast, the transferee has *assumed* the mortgagor's personal liability for the debt, the mortgagee will be able to obtain relief not only from the mortgagor and from the land, but also from the transferee personally. If the mortgagee elects to proceed against the mortgagor personally, the mortgagor can obtain reimbursement by proceeding both against the transferee on his promise and against the land, which remains the primary security for the debt. See generally Grant S. Nelson & Dale A. Whitman, Real Estate Finance Law ¶¶ 5.1–5.20 (4th ed. 2001).

2. Why does the mortgagee care whether later purchasers of secured property assume personal liability on the property? In some cases, the secured property is worth less than the unpaid loan, often because the property has declined in value, and the original mortgagor has little money.

3. **Due on Sale Clauses.** Lenders frequently seek to limit the mortgagor's freedom to transfer the mortgaged property through "due on sale" clauses that make the loan fully payable upon the property's transfer. One traditional justification for due on sale clauses is that they protect the lender against the possibility that the new owner will be less creditworthy or less inclined to maintain the premises than the original borrower, thus increasing the prospect of default and impairing the security for the loan.

The dramatically increasing interest rates of the 1970's supplied an additional reason for due on sale clauses: by enforcing a due on sale clause and requiring the original borrower to pay off a loan that had been made when interest rates were low, the lender could recapture funds for relending at the higher, prevailing market rates. (As a lender, how would you have felt about holding a 30–year, $100,000 note with fixed interest of 6% and 20 years to run, in a market in which interest rates were 12% and rising?) Sellers obviously disliked due on sale clauses because, without one, a seller could transfer her property subject to a mortgage bearing a below market interest rate and obtain from her buyer, as additional consideration for the property, the capitalized value of the difference between the low interest rate on her mortgage and the interest that the buyer would have had to pay at current market rates. (As a buyer, how much would you have paid your seller for the right to have $100,000 for 20 years at 6% interest rather than obtain a new loan at 12% interest?)

This economic conflict between lenders and borrowers inevitably led to a rash of litigation challenging due on sale clauses. Courts in several states invalidated the clauses in whole or in part on the ground that, by inhibiting the original borrower's ability to sell her property, they constituted an unlawful restraint on alienation. (For more on the general rule against restraints on alienation, see pages 621–634 below.) For example, in Wellenkamp v. Bank of America, 582 P.2d 970 (Cal. 1978), the California Supreme Court rejected the "contention that the lender's interest in maintaining its loan portfolio at current interest rates justifies the restraint imposed by exercise of a due-on clause upon transfer of title in an outright sale," and held that "a due-on clause contained in a promissory note or deed of trust cannot be enforced upon the occurrence of an outright sale unless the lender can demonstrate that enforcement is reasonably necessary to protect against impairment to its security or the risk of default." Id. at 976–977.

The wave of controversy surrounding the due on sale issue carried it into both the Supreme Court and the Congress. In Fidelity Federal Savings & Loan Association v. de La Cuesta, 458 U.S. 141 (1982), the Court held that a regulation promulgated by the Federal Home Loan Bank Board permitting federal savings and loan associations to exercise due on sale clauses in their mortgages preempted conflicting state law. And in the Garn–St. Germain Depository Institutions Act of 1982, 12 U.S.C. § 1701j–3, Congress generally preempted state law prohibitions of due on sale clauses for transfers occurring after October 15, 1982. Under the Act, the rights and remedies of lender and borrower are governed exclusively by the terms of the loan instrument.

For a comprehensive discussion of the history of due on sale clauses, see Grant S. Nelson & Dale A. Whitman, Congressional Preemption of Mortgage Due–On–Sale Law: An Analysis of the Garn–St. Germain Act, 35 Hastings L.J. 241 (1983).

4. **Waste.** Before agreeing to make a home loan, an institutional lender will typically examine the borrower's resources and job prospects in order to assure itself that the borrower will be able to make the mortgage payments over the life of the loan. The lender will also appraise the house and land to assure itself that, in the event of default, the property will, on foreclosure, produce sufficient cash to pay off the outstanding debt. Once the loan is made, there is obviously little the lender can do to keep the borrower gainfully employed. However, the lender can, by appropriate provisions in the mortgage instrument, require that the house and land be kept in good condition so that the loan security remains unimpaired.

Absent an express agreement on the subject between mortgagor and mortgagee, courts will impose a duty on the mortgagor not to waste the premises. (The common law of waste generally is considered at pages 634–646 below.) Does the availability of relief for waste, and the fact that mortgagor and mortgagee can by contract increase the mortgagor's duties respecting maintenance of the premises, remove one justification—avoiding impairment of the security—that lenders commonly give for insisting on due on sale clauses?

See generally David A. Leipziger, The Mortgagee's Remedies for Waste, 64 Calif. L. Rev. 1086 (1976).

C. DEFAULT

Cornelison v. Kornbluth

Supreme Court of California, 1975.
542 P.2d 981.

SULLIVAN, JUSTICE.

In this action for damages for the breach of covenants contained in a deed of trust and for damages for waste, brought by the beneficiary against the trustors and their successors in interest, plaintiff Mary Cornelison appeals from a summary judgment entered in favor of defendant John Kornbluth and against plaintiff. As will appear, we have concluded that upon the record presented, the summary judgment was properly granted and should be affirmed.

On July 15, 1964, plaintiff sold a single-family dwelling in Van Nuys, California, to Maurice and Leona Chanon, taking back a promissory note in the sum of $18,800 secured by a first deed of trust on the property. The deed of trust, recorded on August 21, 1964, contained the following covenants: that the Chanons would pay the real property taxes and assessments against the property; that they would care for and maintain the property; and that if they resold the property, the entire unpaid balance would become immediately due and payable.

On December 10, 1964, the Chanons conveyed the property to defendant by grant deed. On September 6, 1968, defendant sold the property to Richard Larkins. In January 1969 the county health department condemned the house as unfit for human habitation. The Chanons being in default on the promissory note, plaintiff caused the property to be sold at a trustee's sale. Plaintiff purchased the property at the sale for the sum of $21,921.42, that being an amount equal to the balance due on the note plus foreclosure costs.

Plaintiff then brought the instant action for damages, her amended complaint (hereafter "complaint") filed March 24, 1970, setting forth two causes of action, one for breach of contract and one for damages for waste. The first cause of action alleged in substance that defendant "agreed in writing to be bound by and to perform all of the covenants contained in the Note and Deed of Trust theretofore executed by defendants Maurice L. Chanon and Leona Chanon"; and that defendants breached these covenants (a) by selling the property to Larkins, (b) by failing to pay property taxes, (c) by failing to make payments on the note, and (d) by failing to properly care for and maintain the premises.

The second cause of action, after incorporating by reference the material allegations of the first cause of action, alleged in substance that defendant owed a duty to properly and adequately care for the property and that defendant negligently failed to fulfill this duty, thereby causing plaintiff to be damaged in specified particulars and amounts by reason of the loss of improvements to the real property as well as by reason of the loss of its use. On the first cause of action plaintiff prayed for damages in the sum of $18,169.66, and on the second cause of action for damages in the sum of $20,000 plus the reasonable rental of the property, and in addition for $45,000 punitive damages.

Defendant's answer admitted that he purchased the property from the Chanons and sold it to Larkins, but denied all other allegations for lack of information or belief. Defendant then moved for summary judgment. His declaration in support of the motion states in substance that he purchased the subject real property from the Chanons, that at the time of the purchase he knew it was encumbered by the deed of trust in favor of plaintiff as beneficiary, that he never assumed either orally or in writing the indebtedness secured by the deed of trust, and that no such assumption was contained in the deed conveying the property to him. The declaration attaches and incorporates by reference a copy of the grant deed which confirms the last statement. . . .

. . . . [W]e are satisfied that defendant's declaration is sufficient to support a summary judgment on the first cause of action for breach of contract. As previously stated, the basic theory of this cause of action is that defendant had a duty to comply with the covenants contained in the deed of trust given plaintiff by the Chanons since the document was recorded and its covenants ran with the land. Plaintiff's legal premise is completely erroneous. Upon the transfer of real property covered by a mortgage or deed of trust as security for an indebtedness, the property remains subject to the secured indebtedness but the grantee is not personally liable for the indebtedness or to perform any of the obligations of the mortgage or trust deed unless his agreement to pay the indebtedness, or some note or memorandum thereof, is in writing and subscribed by him or his agent or his assumption of the indebtedness is specifically provided for in the conveyance. Defendant's declaration states positively that he never assumed either orally or in writing the indebtedness secured by the Chanon deed of trust and that no such assumption was contained in the deed by which the Chanons conveyed the property to him. An examination of a copy of the deed attached to the declaration confirms this. Plaintiff filed no counterdeclaration denying these allegations and as a consequence raised no triable issue of fact. . . .

We now proceed to determine whether defendant's declarations are sufficient to support the summary judgment on the second stated cause of action for waste. On this issue we may outline the positions of the parties as follows: Defendant contends that since, as set forth in his attorney's declaration, plaintiff purchased the property for a full credit bid an action for waste is thereby precluded both by reason of the antideficiency legislation (Code Civ. Proc., §§ 580b, 580d) and by reason of the extinguishment of the security interest through a full credit bid at the trustee's sale. Plaintiff on the other hand contends that an action for waste may be maintained independently of the antideficiency provisions of sections 580b and 580d of the Code of Civil Procedure.

In order to resolve this issue it is necessary to first define, and trace the history of an action for waste and secondly to analyze the impact of the antideficiency legislation induced by the depression of the 1930's upon this traditional action.

Section 2929 of the Civil Code provides: "*Waste.* No person whose interest is subject to the lien of a mortgage may do any act which will substantially impair the mortgagee's security." This section, enacted in 1872, codified a portion of the common law action for waste, as developed in England and adopted in earlier California cases. . . . The action for waste originated in the early common law sometime during the 12th century. Initially, it was designed to protect owners of succeeding estates of inheritance from the improper conduct of the person in possession which harmed the property. As the action evolved during the ensuing development of the common law, it was broadened so as to afford protection to concurrent holders of interests in land who were out of possession (e.g., mortgagees) from harm committed by persons who were in possession (e.g., mortgagors). Recognition of this enlarged purpose of the remedy was given in the United States in the leading case of Van Pelt v. McGraw (1850) 4 N.Y. (4 Comst.) 110 where the court held that a holder of a mortgage on lands had an action on the case against the mortgagor for acts of waste committed by the latter with knowledge that the value of the security would thereby be injured. *Van Pelt* clearly set forth the measure of damages: "Now this action is not based upon the assumption that the plaintiff's [mortgagee's] land has been injured, but that his mortgage as a security has been impaired. His damages, therefore, would be limited to the amount of injury to the mortgage, however great the injury to the land might be." (Id., at p. 112.)

Section 2929 of the Civil Code . . . imposes a duty not to commit waste upon any "person whose interest is subject to the lien." Although a nonassuming grantee of mortgaged property is not personally liable on the debt, his interest in the property is subject to the lien and therefore he is under a duty not to impair the mortgagee's security. Defendant as a nonassuming grantee of the property subject to plaintiff's deed of trust was under a duty not to commit waste.

Defendant contends, however, that assuming arguendo that he was under a duty not to commit waste and that his acts or omissions constituted waste by so materially impairing the value of the property as to render it inadequate security for the mortgage debt, nevertheless plaintiff is not entitled to recover because such recovery for waste would amount to a deficiency judgment proscribed by sections 580b[5] and 580d[6] of the Code of Civil Procedure. In order to resolve this contention it is necessary to briefly summarize the array of legislation in the field of secured transactions in real property spawned by the depression of the 1930's.

Prior to 1933, a mortgagee of real property was required to exhaust his security before enforcing the debt or otherwise to waive all right to his security. However, having resorted to the security, whether by judicial sale or private nonjudicial sale, the mortgagee could obtain a deficiency judg-

5. Section 580b provides in relevant part: "No deficiency judgment shall lie in any event after any sale of real property for failure of the purchaser to complete his contract of sale, or under a deed of trust, or mortgage, given to the vendor to secure payment of the balance of the purchase price of real property, or under a deed of trust, or mortgage, on a dwelling for not more than four families given to a lender to secure repayment of a loan which was in fact used to pay all or part of the purchase price of such dwelling occupied, entirely or in part, by the purchaser."

6. Section 580d provides: "No judgment shall be rendered for any deficiency upon a note secured by a deed of trust or mortgage upon real property hereafter executed in any case in which the real property has been sold by the mortgagee or trustee under power of sale contained in such mortgage or deed of trust.

"The provisions of this section shall not apply to any deed of trust, mortgage or other lien given to secure the payment of bonds or other evidences of indebtedness authorized or permitted to be issued by the Commissioner of Corporations, or which is made by a public utility subject to the provisions of the Public Utilities Act."

ment against the mortgagor for the difference between the amount of the indebtedness and the amount realized from the sale. As a consequence during the great depression with its dearth of money and declining property values, a mortgagee was able to purchase the subject real property at the foreclosure sale at a depressed price far below its normal fair market value and thereafter to obtain a double recovery by holding the debtor for a large deficiency. In order to counteract this situation, California in 1933 enacted fair market value limitations applicable to both judicial foreclosure sales (§ 726)[7] and private foreclosure sales (§ 580a)[8] which limited the mortgagee's deficiency judgment after exhaustion of the security to the difference between the fair value of the property at the time of the sale (irrespective of the amount actually realized at the sale) and the outstanding debt for

7. Section 726 provides in part: "In the event that a deficiency is not waived or prohibited and it is decreed that any defendant is personally liable for such debt, then upon application of the plaintiff filed at any time within three months of the date of the foreclosure sale and after a hearing thereon at which the court shall take evidence and at which hearing either party may present evidence as to the fair value of the property or the interest therein sold as of the date of sale, the court shall render a money judgment, against such defendant or defendants for the amount by which the amount of the indebtedness with interest and costs of sale and of action exceeds the fair value of the property or interest therein sold as of the date of sale; provided, however, that in no event shall the amount of said judgment, exclusive of interest from the date of sale and of costs exceed the difference between the amount for which the property was sold and the entire amount of the indebtedness secured by said mortgage or deed of trust."

8. Section 580a provides: "Whenever a money judgment is sought for the balance due upon an obligation for the payment of which a deed of trust or mortgage with power of sale upon real property or any interest therein was given as security, following the exercise of the power of sale in such deed of trust or mortgage, the plaintiff shall set forth in his complaint the entire amount of the indebtedness which was secured by said deed of trust or mortgage at the time of sale, the amount for which such real property or interest therein was sold and the fair market value thereof at the date of sale and the date of such sale. Upon the application of either party made at least ten days before the time of trial the court shall, and upon its own motion the court at any time may, appoint one of the inheritance tax appraisers provided for by law to appraise the property or the interest therein sold as of the time of sale. Such appraiser shall file his appraisal with the clerk and the same shall be admissible in evidence. Such appraiser shall take and subscribe an oath to be attached to the appraisal that he has truly, honestly and impartially appraised the property to the best of his knowledge and ability. Any appraiser so appointed may be called and examined as a witness by any party or by the court itself. The court must fix the compensation of such appraiser, not to exceed five dollars per day, and expenses for the time actually engaged in such appraisal, which may be taxed and allowed in like manner as other costs. Before rendering any judgment the court shall find the fair market value of the real property, or interest therein sold, at the time of sale. The court may render judgment for not more than the amount by which the entire amount of the indebtedness due at the time of sale exceeded the fair market value of the real property or interest therein sold at the time of sale with interest thereon from the date of the sale; provided, however, that in no event shall the amount of said judgment, exclusive of interest after the date of sale, exceed the difference between the amount for which the property was sold and the entire amount of the indebtedness secured by said deed of trust or mortgage. Any such action must be brought within three months of the time of sale under such deed of trust or mortgage. No judgment shall be rendered in any such action until the real property or interest therein has first been sold pursuant to the terms of such deed of trust or mortgage, unless such real property or interest therein has become valueless."

which the property was security. Therefore, if, due to the depressed economic conditions, the property serving as security was sold for less than the fair value as determined under section 726 or section 580a, the mortgagee could not recover the amount of that difference in his action for a deficiency judgment.

In certain situations, however, the Legislature deemed even this partial deficiency too oppressive. Accordingly, in 1933 it enacted section 580b (see fn. 5, ante) which barred deficiency judgments altogether on purchase money mortgages. "Section 580b places the risk of inadequate security on the purchase money mortgagee. A vendor is thus discouraged from overvaluing the security. Precarious land promotion schemes are discouraged, for the security value of the land gives purchasers a clue as to its true market value. If inadequacy of security results, not from overvaluing, but from a decline in property values during a general or local depression, section 580b prevents the aggravation of the downturn that would result if defaulting purchasers were burdened with large personal liability. Section 580b thus serves as a stabilizing factor in land sales." (Roseleaf Corp. v. Chierighino (1963) 59 Cal. 2d 35, 42, 27 Cal. Rptr. 873, 378 P.2d 97.)

Although both judicial foreclosure sales and private nonjudicial foreclosure sales provided for identical deficiency judgments in nonpurchase money situations subsequent to the 1933 enactment of the fair value limitations, one significant difference remained, namely property sold through judicial foreclosure was subject to the statutory right of redemption (§ 725a), while property sold by private foreclosure sale was not redeemable. By virtue of sections 725a and 701, the judgment debtor, his successor in interest or a junior lienor could redeem the property at any time during one year after the sale, frequently by tendering the sale price. The effect of this right of redemption was to remove any incentive on the part of the mortgagee to enter a low bid at the sale (since the property could be redeemed for that amount) and to encourage the making of a bid approximating the fair market value of the security. However, since real property purchased at a private foreclosure sale was not subject to redemption, the mortgagee by electing this remedy, could gain irredeemable title to the property by a bid substantially below the fair value and still collect a deficiency judgment for the difference between the fair value of the security and the outstanding indebtedness.

In 1940 the Legislature placed the two remedies, judicial foreclosure sale and private nonjudicial foreclosure sale on a parity by enacting section 580d (see fn. 6, ante). Section 580d bars "any deficiency judgment" following a private foreclosure sale. "It seems clear ... that section 580d was enacted to put judicial enforcement on a parity with private enforcement. This result could be accomplished by giving the debtor a right to redeem after a sale under the power. The right to redeem, like proscription of a deficiency judgment, has the effect of making the security satisfy a realistic share of the debt. By choosing instead to bar a deficiency judgment after private sale, the Legislature achieved its purpose without denying the creditor his election of remedies. If the creditor wishes a deficiency judgment, his sale is subject to statutory redemption rights. If he wishes a sale resulting in nonredeemable title, he must forego the right to a deficiency judgment. In either case the debtor is protected." (Roseleaf Corp. v. Chierighino, supra, 59 Cal. 2d 35, 43–44.)

In the case at bench, we are now called upon to determine the effect of this antideficiency legislation upon the statutory action for waste. It will be recalled that damages in an action for waste are measured by the amount of injury to the security caused by the mortgagor's acts, that is by the substantial harm which "[impairs] the value of the property subject to the lien so as to render it an inadequate security for the mortgage debt." (Robinson v. Russell (1864) 24 Cal. 467, 473.) A deficiency judgment is a personal judgment against the debtor-mortgagor for the difference between the fair market value of the property held as security and the outstanding indebtedness. (§ 726.) It is clear that the two judgments against the mortgagor, one for waste and the other for a deficiency, are closely interrelated and may often reflect identical amounts. If property values in general are declining, a deficiency judgment and a judgment for waste would be identical up to the point at which the harm caused by the mortgagor is equal to or less than the general decline in property values resulting from market conditions. When waste is committed in a depressed market, a deficiency judgment, although reflecting the amount of the waste, will of course exceed it if the decline of property values is greater. However, when waste is committed in a rising market, there will be no deficiency judgment, unless the property was originally overvalued; in this event, there would be no damages for waste unless the impairment due to waste exceeded the general increase in property values.

Mindful of the foregoing, we now proceed to arrive at an assessment of the effect of sections 580b and 580d upon an action for waste. First, we examine the 580b proscription of a deficiency judgment after any foreclosure sale, private or judicial, of property securing a purchase money mortgage. The primary purpose of section 580b is "in the event of a depression in land values, to prevent the aggravation of the downturn that would result if defaulting purchasers lost the land and were burdened with personal liability." (Bargioni v. Hill (1963) 59 Cal. 2d 121, 123, 28 Cal. Rptr. 321, 378 P.2d 593.) It is clear that allowing an action for waste following a foreclosure sale of property securing purchase money mortgages may often frustrate this purpose. Damages for waste would burden the defaulting purchaser with both loss of land and personal liability and the acts giving rise to that liability would have been caused in many cases by the economic downturn itself. For example, a purchaser caught in such circumstances may be compelled in the normal course of events to forego the general maintenance and repair of the property in order to keep up his payments on the mortgage debt. If he eventually defaults and loses the property, to hold him subject to additional liability for waste would seem to run counter to the purpose of section 580b and to permit the purchase money lender to obtain what is in effect a deficiency judgment. It is of course true that not all owners of real property subject to a purchase money mortgage commit waste solely or primarily as a result of the economic pressures of a market depression; indeed many are reckless, intentional, and at times even malicious despoilers of property. In these latter circumstances to which we shall refer for convenience as waste committed in bad faith, the purchase money lender should not go remediless since they do not involve the type of risk intended to be borne by him in promoting the objectives of section 580b alluded to above.

Accordingly, we hold that section 580b should apply to bar recovery in actions for waste following foreclosure sale in the first instance but should not so apply in the second instance of "bad faith" waste. We further hold that it is within the province of the trier of fact to determine on a case by case basis to what, if any, extent the impairment of the mortgagee's security has been caused (as in the first instance) by the general decline of real property values and to what, if any, extent (as in the second instance) by the bad faith acts of the mortgagor, such determination, in either instance, being subject to review under the established rule of appellate review.

We now turn to assess the effect upon an action for waste of section 580d which applies to a nonpurchase money mortgage. We are satisfied that a different analysis must be pursued. It will be recalled from our earlier discussion that the Legislature intended to establish parity between judicial foreclosure and private foreclosure by denying a deficiency judgment subsequent to a private sale. Under a judicial foreclosure, the mortgagee is entitled to a deficiency judgment, but must bear the burden of a statutory redemption; under a private sale the mortgagee need not bear the burden of redemption, but cannot recover any deficiency judgment. If following a nonjudicial sale the mortgagee were allowed to obtain a judgment for damages for waste against the mortgagor, he would have the double benefits of an irredeemable title to the property and a personal judgment against the mortgagor for the impairment of the value of the property. This would essentially destroy the parity between judicial foreclosure and private foreclosure in all instances where the waste is actually caused by general economic conditions, since as we have explained, such recovery is in effect a deficiency judgment. If, however, the recovery is limited to waste committed in "bad faith," then the personal judgment would be entirely independent of the problems encompassed by the antideficiency legislation and would not affect the parity of remedies. Accordingly, we hold that in situations arising under section 580d, recovery for waste against the mortgagor following nonjudicial foreclosure sale is barred by the section's proscription against deficiency judgments when the waste actually results from the depressed condition of the general real estate market but not when the waste is caused by the "bad faith" acts of the mortgagor. . . .

While our foregoing conclusion may expose defendant to liability on the basis of having committed "bad faith" waste, the question need not be resolved. We have further concluded that even assuming that defendant is liable on such basis, nevertheless plaintiff cannot recover since she purchased the subject property at the trustee's sale by making a full credit bid.

As stated previously, the measure of damages for waste is the amount of the impairment of the security, that is the amount by which the value of the security is less than the outstanding indebtedness and is thereby rendered inadequate. The point of defendant's argument is that the mortgagee's purchase of the property securing the debt by entering a full credit bid establishes the value of the security as being equal to the outstanding indebtedness and ipso facto the nonexistence of any impairment of the security. As applied to the factual context of the instant case, the argument is that the purchase by plaintiff-vendor-beneficiary of the property covered by the purchase money deed of trust pursuant to a full credit bid made and accepted at the nonjudicial foreclosure sale resulted in a total satisfaction of the secured obligation. We agree.

.... If the beneficiary or mortgagee at the foreclosure sale enters a bid for the full amount of the obligation owing to him together with the costs and fees due in connection with the sale, he cannot recover damages for waste, since he cannot establish any impairment of security, the lien of the deed of trust or mortgage having been theretofore extinguished by his full credit bid and all his security interest in the property thereby nullified. If, however, he bids less than the full amount of the obligation and thereby acquires the property valued at less than the full amount, his security has been impaired and he may recover damages for waste in an amount not exceeding the difference between the amount of his bid and the full amount of the outstanding indebtedness immediately prior to the foreclosure sale....

To recapitulate, we conclude that the trial court properly granted summary judgment in favor of defendant and against plaintiff (1) as to the first cause of action for breach of contract since defendant at no time assumed the underlying indebtedness; and (2) as to the second cause of action for waste since, although defendant as a nonassuming grantor could be held liable for waste if proved to have been committed in bad faith, nevertheless plaintiff can establish no impairment of security, having acquired the property at the foreclosure sale by making a full credit bid.

Murphy v. Financial Development Corp.

Supreme Court of New Hampshire, 1985.
495 A.2d 1245.

DOUGLAS, J.

The plaintiffs brought this action seeking to set aside the foreclosure sale of their home, or, in the alternative, money damages. The Superior Court ... entered a judgment for the plaintiffs in the amount of $27,000 against two of the defendants, Financial Development Corporation and Colonial Deposit Company (the lenders).

The plaintiffs purchased a house in Nashua in 1966, financing it by means of a mortgage loan. They refinanced the loan in March of 1980, executing a new promissory note and a power of sale mortgage, with

Financial Development Corporation as mortgagee. The note and mortgage were later assigned to Colonial Deposit Company.

In February of 1981, the plaintiff Richard Murphy became unemployed. By September of 1981, the plaintiffs were seven months in arrears on their mortgage payments, and had also failed to pay substantial amounts in utility assessments and real estate taxes. After discussing unsuccessfully with the plaintiffs proposals for revising the payment schedule, rewriting the note, and arranging alternative financing, the lenders gave notice on October 6, 1981, of their intent to foreclose.

During the following weeks, the plaintiffs made a concerted effort to avoid foreclosure. They paid the seven months' mortgage arrearage, but failed to pay some $643.18 in costs and legal fees associated with the foreclosure proceedings. The lenders scheduled the foreclosure sale for November 10, 1981, at the site of the subject property. They complied with all of the statutory requirements for notice.

At the plaintiffs' request, the lenders agreed to postpone the sale until December 15, 1981. They advised the plaintiffs that this would entail an additional cost of $100, and that the sale would proceed unless the lenders received payment of $743.18, as well as all mortgage payments then due, by December 15. Notice of the postponement was posted on the subject property on November 10 at the originally scheduled time of the sale, and was also posted at the Nashua City Hall and Post Office. No prospective bidders were present for the scheduled sale.

In late November, the plaintiffs paid the mortgage payment which had been due in October, but made no further payments to the lenders. An attempt by the lenders to arrange new financing for the plaintiffs through a third party failed when the plaintiffs refused to agree to pay for a new appraisal of the property. Early on the morning of December 15, 1981, the plaintiffs tried to obtain a further postponement, but were advised by the lenders' attorney that it was impossible unless the costs and legal fees were paid.

At the plaintiffs' request, the attorney called the president of Financial Development Corporation, who also refused to postpone the sale. Further calls by the plaintiffs to the lenders' offices were equally unavailing.

The sale proceeded as scheduled at 10:00 a.m. on December 15, at the site of the property. Although it had snowed the previous night, the weather was clear and warm at the time of the sale, and the roads were clear. The only parties present were the plaintiffs, a representative of the lenders, and an attorney, Morgan Hollis, who had been engaged to conduct the sale because the lenders' attorney, who lived in Dover, had been apprehensive about the weather the night before. The lenders' representative made the only bid at the sale. That bid of $27,000, roughly the amount owed on the mortgage, plus costs and fees, was accepted and the sale concluded.

Later that same day, Attorney Hollis encountered one of his clients, William Dube, a representative of the defendant Southern New Hampshire

Home Traders, Inc. (Southern). On being informed of the sale, Mr. Dube contacted the lenders and offered to buy the property for $27,000. The lenders rejected the offer and made a counter offer of $40,000. Within two days a purchase price of $38,000 was agreed upon by Mr. Dube and the lenders, and the sale was subsequently completed.

The plaintiffs commenced this action on February 5, 1982. The lenders moved to dismiss, arguing that any action was barred because the plaintiffs had failed to petition for an injunction prior to the sale. The master denied the motion. After hearing the evidence, he ruled for the plaintiffs, finding that the lenders had "failed to exercise good faith and due diligence in obtaining a fair price for the subject property at the foreclosure sale. . . ."

The master also ruled that Southern was a bona fide purchaser for value, and thus had acquired legal title to the house. That ruling is not at issue here. He assessed monetary damages against the lenders equal to "the difference between the fair market value of the subject property on the date of the foreclosure and the price obtained at said sale."

Having found the fair market value to be $54,000, he assessed damages accordingly at $27,000. He further ruled that "[t]he bad faith of the 'Lenders' warrants an award of legal fees." The lenders appealed.

[The court first decides that the plaintiffs were free to bring their action despite failing to seek a pre-foreclosure sale injunction.]

The second issue before us is whether the master erred in concluding that the lenders had failed to comply with the often-repeated rule that a mortgagee executing a power of sale is bound both by the statutory procedural requirements *and* by a duty to protect the interests of the mortgagor through the exercise of good faith and due diligence. See, e.g., Carrols Equities Corp. v. Della Jacova, 126 N.H. 116, 489 A.2d 116 (1985); Lakes Region Fin. Co. v. Goodhue Boat Yard, Inc., 118 N.H. 103, 382 A.2d 1108 (1978); Wheeler v. Slocinski, 82 N.H. 211, 131 A. 598 (1926). We will not overturn a master's findings and rulings "unless they are unsupported by the evidence or are erroneous as a matter of law." Summit Electric, Inc. v. Pepin Brothers Const., Inc., 121 N.H. 203, 206, 427 A.2d 505, 507 (1981).

The master found that the lenders, throughout the time prior to the sale, "did not mislead or deal unfairly with the plaintiffs." They engaged in serious efforts to avoid foreclosure through new financing, and agreed to one postponement of the sale. The basis for the master's decision was his conclusion that the lenders had failed to exercise good faith and due diligence in obtaining a fair price for the property.

This court's past decisions have not dealt consistently with the question whether the mortgagee's duty amounts to that of a fiduciary or trustee. Compare Pearson v. Gooch, 69 N.H. 208, 209, 40 A. 390, 390–91 (1897) and Merrimack Industrial Trust v. First Nat. Bank of Boston, 121 N.H. 197, 201, 427 A.2d 500, 504 (1981) (duty amounts to that of a fiduciary or trustee) with Silver v. First National Bank, 108 N.H. 390, 391, 236 A.2d 493, 494–95 (1967) and Proctor v. Bank of N.H., supra at 400, 464 A.2d at 266 (duty does not amount to that of a fiduciary or trustee). This may be an inevitable result of the mortgagee's dual role as seller and potential buyer at the foreclosure sale, and of the conflicting interests involved.

We need not label a duty, however, in order to define it. In his role as a seller, the mortgagee's duty of good faith and due diligence is essentially that of a fiduciary. Such a view is in keeping with "[t]he 'trend . . . towards liberalizing the term [fiduciary] in order to prevent unjust enrichment.' " Lash v. Cheshire County Savings Bank, Inc., 124 N.H. 435, 438, 474 A.2d 980, 981 (1984) (quoting Cornwell v. Cornwell, 116 N.H. 205, 209, 356 A.2d 683, 686 (1976)).

A mortgagee, therefore, must exert every reasonable effort to obtain "a fair and reasonable price under the circumstances," Reconstruction & c. Corp. v. Faulkner, 101 N.H. 352, 361, 143 A.2d 403, 410 (1958), even to the extent, if necessary, of adjourning the sale or of establishing "an upset price below which he will not accept any offer." Lakes Region Fin. Corp. v. Goodhue Boat Yard, Inc., 118 N.H. at 107, 382 A.2d at 1111.

What constitutes a fair price, or whether the mortgagee must establish an upset price, adjourn the sale, or make other reasonable efforts to assure a fair price, depends on the circumstances of each case. Inadequacy of price alone is not sufficient to demonstrate bad faith unless the price is so low as to shock the judicial conscience.

We must decide, in the present case, whether the evidence supports the finding of the master that the lenders failed to exercise good faith and due diligence in obtaining a fair price for the plaintiffs' property.

We first note that "[t]he duties of good faith and due diligence are distinct. . . . One may be observed and not the other, and any inquiry as to their breach calls for a separate consideration of each." Wheeler v. Slocinski, 82 N.H. at 213, 131 A. at 600. In order "to constitute bad faith there must be an intentional disregard of duty or a purpose to injure." Id. at 214, 131 A. at 600–01.

There is insufficient evidence in the record to support the master's finding that the lenders acted in bad faith in failing to obtain a fair price for the plaintiffs' property. The lenders complied with the statutory requirements of notice and otherwise conducted the sale in compliance with statutory provisions. The lenders postponed the sale one time and did not bid with knowledge of any immediately available subsequent purchaser. Further, there is no evidence indicating an intent on the part of the lenders to injure the mortgagor by, for example, discouraging other buyers.

There is ample evidence in the record, however, to support the master's finding that the lenders failed to exercise due diligence in obtaining a fair price. "The issue of the lack of due diligence is whether a reasonable man in the [lenders'] place would have adjourned the sale," id. at 215, 131 A. at 601, or taken other measures to receive a fair price.

In early 1980, the plaintiffs' home was appraised at $46,000. At the time of the foreclosure sale on December 15, 1981, the lenders had not had the house reappraised to take into account improvements and appreciation.

The master found that a reasonable person in the place of the lenders would have realized that the plaintiffs' equity in the property was at least $19,000, the difference between the 1980 appraised value of $46,000 and the amount owed on the mortgage totaling approximately $27,000.

At the foreclosure sale, the lenders were the only bidders. The master found that their bid of $27,000 "was sufficient to cover all monies due and did not create a deficiency balance" but "did not provide for a return of any of the plaintiffs' equity."

Further, the master found that the lenders "had reason to know" that "they stood to make a substantial profit on a quick turnaround sale." On the day of the sale, the lenders offered to sell the foreclosed property to William Dube for $40,000. Within two days after the foreclosure sale, they did in fact agree to sell it to Dube for $38,000. It was not necessary for the master to find that the lenders knew of a specific potential buyer before the sale in order to show lack of good faith or due diligence as the lenders contend. The fact that the lenders offered the property for sale at a price sizably above that for which they had purchased it, only a few hours before, supports the master's finding that the lenders had reason to know, at the time of the foreclosure sale, that they could make a substantial profit on a quick turnaround sale. For this reason, they should have taken more measures to ensure receiving a higher price at the sale.

While a mortgagee may not always be required to secure a portion of the mortgagor's equity, such an obligation did exist in this case. The substantial amount of equity which the plaintiffs had in their property, the knowledge of the lenders as to the appraised value of the property, and the plaintiffs' efforts to forestall foreclosure by paying the mortgage arrearage within weeks of the sale, all support the master's conclusion that the lenders had a fiduciary duty to take more reasonable steps than they did to protect the plaintiffs' equity by attempting to obtain a fair price for the property. They could have established an appropriate upset price to assure a minimum bid. They also could have postponed the auction and advertised commercially by display advertising in order to assure that bidders other than themselves would be present.

Instead, as Theodore DiStefano, an officer of both lending institutions, testified, the lenders made no attempt to obtain fair market value for the property but were concerned *only* with making themselves "whole." On the facts of this case, such disregard for the interests of the mortgagors was a breach of duty by the mortgagees.

Although the lenders *did* comply with the statutory requirements of notice of the foreclosure sale, these efforts were not sufficient in this case to demonstrate due diligence. At the time of the initially scheduled sale, the extent of the lenders' efforts to publicize the sale of the property was publication of a legal notice of the mortgagees' sale at public auction on November 10, published once a week for three weeks in the Nashua Telegraph, plus postings in public places. The lenders did not advertise, publish, or otherwise give notice to the general public of postponement of the sale to December 15, 1981, other than by posting notices at the plaintiffs' house, at the post office, and at city hall. That these efforts to advertise were ineffective is evidenced by the fact that no one, other than the lenders, appeared at the sale to bid on the property. This fact allowed the lenders to purchase the property at a minimal price and then to profit substantially in a quick turnaround sale.

We recognize a need to give guidance to a trial court which must determine whether a mortgagee who has complied with the strict letter of the statutory law has nevertheless violated his additional duties of good faith and due diligence. A finding that the mortgagee had, or should have had, knowledge of his ability to get a higher price at an adjourned sale is the most conclusive evidence of such a violation. See Lakes Region Fin. Corp. v. Goodhue Boat Yard, Inc., 118 N.H. at 107–08, 382 A.2d at 1111.

More generally, we are in agreement with the official Commissioners' Comment to section 3–508 of the Uniform Land Transactions Act:

> The requirement that the sale be conducted in a reasonable manner, including the advertising aspects, requires that the person conducting the sale use the ordinary methods of making buyers aware that are used when an owner is voluntarily selling his land. Thus an advertisement in the portion of a daily newspaper where these ads are placed or, in appropriate cases such as the sale of an industrial plant, a display advertisement in the financial sections of the daily newspaper may be the most reasonable method. In other cases employment of a professional real estate agent may be the more reasonable method. It is unlikely that an advertisement in a legal publication among other legal notices would qualify as a commercially reasonable method of sale advertising.

13 Uniform Laws Annotated 704 (West 1980). As discussed above, the lenders met neither of these guidelines.

While agreeing with the master that the lenders failed to exercise due diligence in this case, we find that he erred as a matter of law in awarding damages equal to "the difference between the fair market value of the subject property . . . and the price obtained at [the] sale."

Such a formula may well be the appropriate measure where *bad faith* is found. See Danvers Savings Bank v. Hammer, 122 N.H. 1, 5, 440 A.2d 435, 438 (1982). In such a case, a mortgagee's conduct amounts to more than mere negligence. Damages based upon the *fair market value*, a figure in excess of a *fair* price, will more readily induce mortgagees to perform their duties properly. A *fair* price may or may not yield a figure close to *fair market value*; however, it will be that price arrived at as a result of due diligence by the mortgagee.

Where, as here, however, a mortgagee fails to exercise due diligence, the proper assessment of damages is the difference between a fair price for the property and the price obtained at the foreclosure sale. We have held, where lack of due diligence has been found, that " 'the test is not "fair market value" as in eminent domain cases nor is the mortgagee bound to give credit for the highest possible amount which might be obtained under different circumstances, as at an owner's sale.' " Silver v. First National Bank, 108 N.H. 390, 392, 236 A.2d 493, 495 (1967) (quoting Reconstruction & c. Corp. v. Faulkner, 101 N.H. 352, 361, 143 A.2d 403, 410 (1958)). Accordingly, we remand to the trial court for a reassessment of damages consistent with this opinion . . . .

BROCK, J., dissenting.

I agree with the majority that a mortgagee, in its role as seller at a foreclosure sale, has a fiduciary duty to the mortgagor. I also agree with the majority's more specific analysis of that duty, including its references to the commissioners' comment to the Uniform Land Transactions Act, as well as those to *Wheeler* and other decisions of this court.

On the record presently before us, however, I cannot see any support for the master's finding that the lenders here failed to exercise due diligence as we have defined that term. I would remand the case to the superior court for further findings of fact.

Specifically, the master made no findings regarding what an "owner . . . voluntarily selling his land" would have done that the lenders here did not do, in order to obtain a fair price. The master's report stated that the lenders "did not establish an upset price or minimum bid," and that they "did not cause the property to be reappraised," but there is nothing in the record to show that an owner conducting a voluntary sale would have done these things.

Nor is there anything to indicate what an appropriate upset price would have been under the conditions present here. The master correctly noted that "[a] foreclosure sale . . . usually produces a price less than the property's fair market value," so it is virtually certain that any upset price would have been less than that amount.

I also cannot accept the majority's statement that the lenders' offer to sell the house for $40,000 constitutes support for a finding that they "should have taken more measures to ensure receiving a fair price at the sale." The offer was certainly relevant to the question of what the lenders knew about the house's value. Standing alone, however, it says nothing about what a reasonable person in the lenders' position would have done to ensure a fair price under the circumstances of this particular sale.

The master, in fact, found that the lenders "did not mislead or deal unfairly with the plaintiffs" until the sale itself. He did not find, as the majority appears to assume, that the lenders should have adjourned the sale a second time. Although the report nowhere states specifically *what* the lenders should have done, its clear implication is that they should have made a higher bid at the foreclosure sale.

There is no authority for such a conclusion. The mortgagee's fiduciary duty extends only to its role as a *seller*. Once the mortgagee has exerted every reasonable effort to obtain a fair price (which may sometimes include setting an upset price and adjourning the sale if no bidder meets that price), it has no further obligation in its role as a potential buyer.

As the majority notes, a low price is not of itself sufficient to invalidate a foreclosure sale, unless the price is "so low as to shock the judicial conscience." The price here was clearly not that low. Cf. Shipp Corp., Inc. v. Charpilloz, 414 So. 2d 1122, 1124 (Fla. Dist. Ct. App. 1982) (bid of $1.1 million was not grossly inadequate compared to a market value of between $2.8 and $3.2 million).

Because it is unclear whether the master applied the correct standard regarding the mortgagees' duty, and because the record as presently constituted cannot support a determination that the lenders violated that standard, I respectfully dissent.

United States v. Chappell

United States District Court for the District of New Hampshire, 2000.
2000 WL 1507431.

STEVEN J. MCAULIFFE, DISTRICT JUDGE.

The United States, through the Farm Service Agency ("FSA"), a successor to the Farmers Home Administration ("FmHA"), seeks a deficiency judgment against defendants Ronald and Susan Chappell, after having foreclosed on defendants' dairy farm. The government has moved for summary judgment, saying it is entitled to judgment as a matter of law in the amount of approximately $140,000, plus accumulating interest. Defendants, who are proceeding pro se, object and have themselves moved for summary judgment, asking that "all monies collected from offset by [the government] be returned."

Background

Briefly stated, the material facts appear as follows. In 1982, the FmHA extended financing to defendants so that they might purchase a dairy farm in Colebrook, New Hampshire. The FmHA secured its $92,000 loan to defendants through a mortgage deed on the property.

Almost immediately after purchasing the property, defendants encountered numerous unanticipated problems, including seriously ill cattle, structural problems with the barn, plumbing and electrical problems with the house and barn, and a non-functioning septic system. With financial assistance from the FmHA, they sued the people from whom they purchased the farm and apparently settled their claims short of trial. Nevertheless, those problems, combined with a decline in the profitability of dairy farming in the area, a high mortality rate in their herd, and low milk output, caused defendants to incur substantial cash flow difficulties and apparently prevented them from paying approximately nine years' worth of state real estate taxes. The record suggests that the government assisted defendants by making tax payments on their behalf (averaging between $2,500 and $3,000 per year). Monies used to satisfy defendants' state tax obligations were added to their total indebtedness to the FmHA.

In 1985, the FmHA refinanced defendants' loan to help them stay current. Then, in 1986, and again in 1987, the FmHA extended defendants additional credit, in the form of a $1,000 and then a $4,000 dollar loan. In 1988, defendants' obligations to the FmHA were secured by a new mortgage deed. On November 22 of that year, however, defendants again stopped making payments on their obligations to the government. Approximately three and one-half years later, in March of 1992, the FSA accelerated defendants' obligations, essentially demanding that they immediately pay the full amount owed to the government. Defendants apparently remained in default and made no further payments. Roughly one year later, in May of 1993, defendants abandoned the property.

More than 18 months after defendants abandoned the property, and more than six years after they defaulted, FSA finally foreclosed on the farm. The foreclosure sale yielded $40,000. Notwithstanding the fact that defendants paid in excess of $90,000 for the farm in 1982, and made substantial improvements to it, the government says the relatively modest amount received at the foreclosure sale was reasonable due to several factors, including a downturn in the local economy and real estate market, a decline in the profitability of dairy farms in the area, waste and mismanagement by defendants, and the general deterioration of the property since defendants abandoned it in 1993.

The government now seeks the balance of the sums owed by defendants, which, as of December 9, 1998, it calculates to be $138,616.58, with interest accumulating at the rate of about $13.17 per day. That sum represents defendants' total indebtedness to the government, less the $40,000 obtained at foreclosure.

Although defendants do not directly challenge the procedural aspects of the foreclosure sale, they do interpose several objections to the government's motion for summary judgment. None of defendants' objections appears to have much legal merit, but then defendants are not schooled in the law and the case no doubt appears complex to them. Nevertheless, the court concludes that several unresolved legal and factual matters apparent in the record preclude the entry of judgment as a matter of law in favor of the government, at least at this point.

Discussion

The record suggests that the FmHA and FSA made an effort over the years to assist defendants in making their dairy farm profitable. The affidavit submitted by Patrick Freeman, the Farm Loan Chief of the FSA, summarizes some of those efforts:

> The FSA did not simply give up on this family and cut off their financing; instead it worked with them to resolve their problems through additional funding, rewriting loans, and advancing money for nine years' worth of real estate taxes to save the farm from being sold at tax sale. FSA also assisted the family through forbearance. For example, payments due FSA through a milk assignment were returned to them, while other creditors were

> being paid as agreed; FSA accepted interest payments only on new loans to help the family build up their operation; FSA made new loans to the family after protective advances were made to buy feed for cows which the Chappells could not afford to buy.

While there appears little doubt that defendants are, in fact, obligated to repay at least a portion of the outstanding amount claimed by the government, the precise amount owed remains uncertain. That uncertainty arises from issues concerning the timing of some of the government's actions in this case. For example, the following question presents itself: Whether the government had an obligation to preserve the value of the assets securing defendants' obligations (i.e., the farm, structures, equipment, cattle, and related assets) by acting in a more timely fashion to foreclose upon those assets.

Defendants defaulted on their obligations to the government in 1988 and yet the government did not foreclose on the farm until more that six years later. In the interim, the local real estate market suffered an enormous downturn, causing the failure of several major New Hampshire banks. More significantly, defendants abandoned the property, which appears to have been left unattended for at least 18 months prior to the foreclosure sale. That, in turn, appears to have caused the property to deteriorate substantially and may well have contributed substantially to the low price at which defendants' farm was eventually sold at foreclosure.

One might reasonably posit that if the government foreclosed on the property within a reasonable time after defendants defaulted in 1988, or after defendants' obligations were accelerated in 1992, or, at a minimum, after defendants abandoned the farm in 1993, the sums recovered at a foreclosure sale (which would have been conducted prior to any deterioration suffered during the 18 month period during which the property was unattended) would likely have been much higher than the $40,000 eventually recognized. That, in turn, would have reduced the outstanding obligations owed by defendants.

To be sure, there may be entirely plausible, reasonable, and even laudatory reasons why the government did not foreclose on the farm sooner. On that point, however, the record is silent. And, the record does not disclose what obligation (if any) the government might have had to act in a more speedy manner, aimed at preserving the value of the loan's security, particularly as time went on and it became apparent that New Hampshire was plunging into a severely depressed real estate market, and in light of the fact that, despite the best efforts of defendants and the government, it certainly appeared that defendants would never be able to make the farm self-sustaining.

Under New Hampshire law, a foreclosing "mortgagee's duty of good faith and due diligence is essentially that of a fiduciary.... A mortgagee, therefore, must exert every reasonable effort to obtain a 'fair and reasonable price under the circumstances.'" Murphy v. Financial Development Corp., 126 N.H. 536, 541, 495 A.2d 1245 (1985). The precise point in time at which that duty attaches is unclear. It is undeniable that it attaches once a mortgagee decides to foreclose on any asset(s) pledged as security for an underlying loan. It is, however, conceivable that the government had some obligation (perhaps short of a fiduciary duty) to protect the value of that security even before it decided to foreclose. That is to say, if a reasonable lender would have reasonably concluded, say in 1988 (when defendants defaulted) or even 1993 (when defendants abandoned the property), that defendants were unlikely to ever make the farm self-sustaining, the government might well have been obligated to conduct the foreclosure at or about that time. Had the government done so, it would have foreclosed on defendants' farm while it was still occupied or, at a minimum, before it had been left abandoned for 18 months. Certainly a larger sum would probably have been realized at the foreclosure sale if it had occurred before 18 months of neglect ran its course. . . .

In light of the foregoing, the court concludes that existence of genuine issues of material fact precludes it from entering judgment as a matter of law in favor of the government. According, its motion for summary judgment is denied, without prejudice. Likewise, defendants' motion for summary judgment is denied, without prejudice.

Notes & Questions

1. **Remedies on Default.** Mortgagees have historically been able to terminate the defaulting mortgagor's interest, and recover the land or its cash equivalent, through one or more of four methods.

The oldest method, *strict foreclosure*, was commonly employed in England and the American colonies through the end of the seventeenth century. Strict foreclosure simply terminated the mortgagor's equity of redemption and, without a sale or further proceeding, vested title to the property in the mortgagee. The mortgagee would enjoy a windfall—and the mortgagor would suffer a loss—to the extent that the value of the land exceeded the amount of the debt outstanding. Strict foreclosure has been abolished in all but a small handful of states. See, e.g., Conn. Gen. Stat. § 49–15; Vt. Stat. Ann. tit. 12, § 4531. Illinois, the only other state allowing strict foreclosure, imposes three requirements designed to safeguard the mortgagor and prevent unjust enrichment to the mortgagee: the property's value cannot exceed the debt; a deficiency judgment cannot be recovered; and the mortgagor must be insolvent. See Ill. Comp. Stat. § 5/15–1403; Great Lakes Mortgage Corp. v. Collymore, 302 N.E.2d 248 (Ill. App. 1973).

By the early nineteenth century, courts in England and courts and legislatures in the United States had replaced strict foreclosure with *judicial foreclosure*. Although judicial foreclosure eliminated the possibility of unjust enrichment by requiring that the excess of the property's value over the outstanding debt be returned to the mortgagor, the method could benefit mortgagees in another respect: if the value of the property fell below the amount of the debt, the mortgagee could as part of the foreclosure proceeding obtain a judgment against the mortgagor for the difference. Then, as now, the "number of steps necessary to consummate foreclosure by court process naturally results in delay, considerable court costs and a fairly large attorney's fee"; the typical proceeding "involves a preliminary title search, to determine all parties in interest; the filing of a lis pendens, summons or complaint; service of the process; a time for a hearing, if necessary; the decree or judgment; the delivery to the sheriff of papers authorizing him to self; notice of sale and service of notice; the actual sale and the issuance of a certificate of sale; and the sheriffs report." Robert H. Skilton, Developments in Mortgage Law and Practice, 17 Temp. U. L.Q. 315, 320 (1943).

By the last quarter of the nineteenth century, mortgagees commonly resorted to *nonjudicial foreclosure*, authorized by their deeds of trust or mortgages with power of sale, in order to avoid the expense and delay of judicial foreclosure. Nonjudicial foreclosure required only two steps: notice and sale. One observer, writing in 1877, noted that the use of deeds of trust and mortgage with power of sale "has rapidly extended, so that in some states the use of any other form is exceptional. The validity of these powers of sale is everywhere recognized, and the use of them, either in mortgages or trust deeds, is becoming general." Jones, Power of Sale Mortgages and Trust Deeds, 3 S.L. Rev. 703, 708 (1877). Does nonjudicial foreclosure deprive mortgagors of property without due process of law? Most federal and state courts reviewing power of sale foreclosures have found no violation of due process guarantees, principally because they could find no state action. See, e.g., Levine v. Stein, 560 F.2d 1175 (4th Cir. 1977). But see Turner v. Blackburn, 389 F. Supp. 1250 (W.D.N.C.1975).

When it is clear to the mortgagor that a foreclosure sale will not yield proceeds in excess of the debt, and it is clear to the mortgagee that an action on the note will either be barred by antideficiency rules or unavailing because the mortgagor has no resources, the two may agree on *a deed in lieu of foreclosure* under which the mortgagor simply conveys the land to the mortgagee. Although this simple solution may be best for both sides, it is surrounded by legal pitfalls. Courts will invalidate the transfer if there is any hint of fraud or overreaching by the mortgagee, and will sometimes recharacterize the deed as an equitable mortgage.

2. California's foreclosure scheme, outlined in *Cornelison*, embodies virtually all of the techniques that states across the country employ to protect mortgagors from price inadequacy in mortgage foreclosure sales. In addition to an outright prohibition on deficiency judgments, a state may limit mortgagor liability by imposing fair value restrictions, statutory redemption periods or procedural safeguards on sale. The California scheme is unusual only in that it combines so many rules and policies in a single system.

When, if ever, would it make sense for a California institutional lender, foreclosing on a loan it had made for a home purchase, to proceed by judicial rather than nonjudicial foreclosure, with its added delay, expense and the hurdle of statutory redemption? To be sure, section 580d of the California Code of Civil Procedure prohibits deficiency judgments after nonjudicial foreclosure. But will section 580b allow the lender to obtain a deficiency judgment in these circumstances after judicial foreclosure?

Cornelison also exposes the variety of policies that lie behind these various debtor-protection schemes. One policy is to protect homeowners against the immediate burdens of economic collapse. Another is to spread the risk of decline in real property values between property owners and secured lenders. Do you agree with these policies? Do you agree with the more specific policies behind section 580b—for example, prohibiting deficiency judgments when the seller has financed the purchase? Does it make sense to apply section 580b's bar not only to financing sellers but also to third-party lenders?

3. **Statutory Right to Redeem.** In nearly half of the thirty-three states that provide for statutory redemption periods, the debtor is unconditionally allowed to remain in possession of the land. In others, he is allowed to stay on only under special conditions, such as that the land is a homestead or is used for farming. See, e.g., Wash. Rev. Code § 6.23.110. In a few states, the purchaser is allowed to occupy the land during the redemption period but is generally required to credit any rents received against the amount the debtor must pay to redeem. See, e.g., N.H. Rev. Stat. Ann. § 529:26.

Ironically, the statutory right to redeem—ostensibly a debtor-protection provision—will effectively depress the price obtained at a foreclosure sale since during a redemption period, which may be as long as a year or more, it clouds the purchaser's title with the prospect that the mortgagor will retake his title through redemption.

4. **One–Action Rules.** Can an undersecured mortgagee circumvent a state's fair value or antideficiency rule by proceeding first against the mortgagor personally on the note and then, to the extent the personal judgment is unsatisfied, by foreclosing on the real property security and applying the sales proceeds to the remainder of the debt?

This strategy affronts the notion, held by some state legislatures, that creditors who seek collateral for their loan should be required to proceed first against the collateral. Five states require the mortgagee to proceed against the real property securing the debt before obtaining a final judgment in a personal action on the note. Cal. Code Civ. Proc. § 726; Idaho Code § 6–101; Mont. Code Ann. § 71–1–222; Nev. Rev. Stat. § 40.430; Utah Code Ann. § 78–37–1. If the mortgagor fails to raise the requirement as a defense on the note, he will suffer a personal judgment. He can, however, later prevent a foreclosure proceeding against the real property on the ground that, by proceeding first on the note, the mortgagee effectively elected that as his exclusive remedy.

5. For thoughtful explorations of issues involved in foreclosures, see James B. Hughes, Jr., Taking Personal Responsibility: A Different View of Mortgage AntiDeficiency and Redemption Statutes, 39 Ariz. L. Rev. 117 (1997); Lawrence D. Jones, Deficiency Judgments and the Exercise of the Default Option in Home Mortgage Loans, 36 J.L. & Econ. 115 (1993); Michael H. Schill, An Economic Analysis of Mortgagor Protection Laws, 77 Va. L. Rev. 489 (1991); Robert M. Washburn, The Judicial and Legislative Response to Price Inadequacy in Mortgage Foreclosure Sales, 53 S. Cal. L. Rev. 843 (1980).

*

PART III

DIVIDING LAND OWNERSHIP

Recall that property is often referred to as a "bundle of rights" or "bundle of sticks." The law permits landowners, within closely guarded restraints, to divide and repackage these rights or sticks and allocate them to different people. First, landowners can divide up rights across time by creating various forms of current and future "estates" in land. Eliza Farnham, for example, might choose to rent or lease her property to Meriwether Lewis for a year while retaining the right to occupy the property after the lease expires.

A landowner may decide to divide up her land over time for various reasons. Eliza, for example, might not have any personal use for her land at the moment and wish to rent it for a period in order to make money, yet retain future possession of the property as an investment. Alternatively, a landowner might wish to control the ownership and use of her property after she dies. Eliza, for example, might want to leave her land initially to her children but to provide that the land will go to her grandchildren when they turn 21. Eliza can typically accomplish these goals by the artful division of her property into current and future estates. Such divisions, however, can sometimes reduce the marketability of land and give one generation the ability to dictate ownership in future generations. The law therefore, has developed a number of doctrines to promote marketability and protect the discretion of future generations.

Chapter 7 discusses the various forms of present and future possessory interests in land and the rules that govern them. We save a more detailed look at the most common form of division across time, the landlord-tenant relationship, for Chapter 8. Because the typical landlord-tenant relationship is commercial, rather than personal, it raises legal concerns and issues that are quite different from other forms of estates.

Land can also be owned at a given point in time by multiple individuals. Individuals may wish to own property together, sharing in the various rights and responsibilities, for personal, financial, and other reasons. Husbands and wives, for example, frequently own property together. Shared ownership can raise a number of legal issues. Must the parties agree on how to use and manage the property, or can each owner act unilaterally? What happens if the parties cannot agree on how to use or manage the property? Can the owners sell their interests separately, or must they agree on a sale? If one of the owners occupies the property by herself, what obligations does she owe to the other? How can the parties terminate their joint ownership? What happens when one of the owners dies? Chapter 9 examines these and other questions arising from shared ownership.

Finally, in some cases, a landowner may want to give someone limited rights in her property without making the other person a co-owner. Eliza, for example, might want to permit Meriwether to lay an underground water pipe across a portion of her property. Or Eliza might want to give The Nature Conservancy the right to prevent her and future owners from developing her property. The law enables landowners to do this through a system of nonpossessory interests known as easements, covenants, and servitudes. Chapter 10 examines how these interests are created, terminated, and governed.

CHAPTER 7

DIVIDING OWNERSHIP ACROSS TIME

The common law has developed an elaborate system of *estates* that permit landowners, if they want, to divide ownership of their land across time. As explained in Part I of this casebook, most landowners hold a *fee simple absolute*, entitling them to possess their land forever. The owner, Eliza, of a fee simple can part with possession of her land for a specified period—e.g., by renting the land to Meriwether for ten years—and retain the right to repossess the land at the end of this period. Using the terminology of the estates system, Meriwether would then hold a *leasehold* estate (more specifically a type of leasehold estate known as a *term of years*) and Eliza would retain a *future interest* known as a *reversion* in fee simple absolute. Eliza alternatively could convey present possession to her husband for his lifetime, with possession to pass upon his death to their child. In this case, Eliza's husband would hold a *life estate*, and their child would hold a future interest known as a *remainder* in fee simple absolute.

The number of legally recognized estates is limited to a bare handful, and each estate has its own attributes. Although private choice is thereby somewhat constrained, the estates system aims to promote certainty and simplicity by limiting transfers to a few well-established forms with well-established consequences.

All of this just skims the surface, though, because the modern system of estates in land represents only the most recent phase in an evolutionary process that dates back more than nine hundred years and that, doubtless, still has some distance to go. The relationship between landlord and tenant today offers only the faintest reflection of the bonds of blood, loyalty, and service that tied tenant to lord in feudal England. Yet our current estate system arose out of that feudal system. Several doctrines that were first shaped to resolve the peculiar tensions of feudal society have survived to the present, and the law of estates is unfortunately still in the process of shedding anachronistic encumbrances.

Estates in land are unknown outside the common law system. In the civil law world, encompassing most of western Europe, Central and South America, and parts of Asia and Africa, private ownership is indivisible: one, and only one, person can at any time be said to own a particular piece of land. Thus, in Italy, a typical civil law jurisdiction, it would be unthinkable to say that the transfer "Eliza to Meriwether for life" gives an estate to Meriwether equal in dignity to Eliza's reversion. Rather, Eliza alone would be said to own the land, subject to an "usufrutto," giving Meriwether certain rights, but no part of the land's ownership. Similarly, a lease from Eliza to Meriwether in Italy gives Meriwether general contract rights but no property interest; Eliza remains the exclusive owner.

As a general matter, the civil law concept of indivisible ownership offers the landowner less flexibility in carving up his interests than does the common law. The differences between civil and common law systems should not, however, be exaggerated. Similar economic and social pressures in both systems often produce results that in practice are much alike. Thus, there are many more similarities than differences between the actual positions of a life tenant and the holder of an usufrutto for life.

A. A SHORT HISTORY OF THE ESTATES SYSTEM

To understand the current system of estates employed in the United States, it is useful to understand its history. The often peculiar contours of current estates are more comprehensible with a little bit of historical background.

1. THE FEUDAL TENURE SYSTEM

One of the first steps that William of Normandy took after the victory at Hastings in 1066 established his right to the Crown of England was to position himself as the sole owner of all land in the country. He then conveyed vast tracts of land to those of his followers willing to pay the price—cash, needed services, and a vow of loyalty to the King. The genius of William's system was that each grantee held his land not as an outright owner but rather as a tenant whose continued possession depended upon his loyalty and delivery of prescribed services to the King.

Another striking feature of the system was that it readily lent itself to replication. The tenants who held directly of the King (tenants in chief, or *in capite*) parceled out some of their lands to other tenants, who in turn conveyed some of their lands to still other tenants. Through this process of *subinfeudation*, a tenant in chief whose right to possession was conditioned on providing military service to the King might divide his land into several parcels, occupying one and granting the others to tenants who would agree to render military service or other consideration such as food or labor. These tenants would then make conditional transfers to other tenants, and these to others. At the bottom of the pyramid was the tenant *in demesne*. Above the tenant in demesne were the *mesne* lords and at the very top, of course, was the King.

Three features dominated each level of this hierarchy. One was the personal bond between a tenant and the tenant's "land lord," expressed in the ceremony of doing homage. According to Littleton's 15th century treatise, *Of Tenures*:

> When the tenant shall make homage to his lord, he shall be ungirt, and his head uncovered, and his lord shall sit, and the tenant shall kneel before him on both his knees, and hold his

> hands jointly together between the hands of his lord, and shall say thus: I become your man from this day forward [of life and limb, and of earthly worship], and unto you shall be true and faithful, and bear to you faith for the tenements that I claim to hold of you, saving the faith that I owe unto our sovereign lord the king; and then the lord, so sitting, shall kiss him.

Book II, ch. 1 (1481). The second major feature of the feudal hierarchy was the requirement that the tenant render specified services to his lord in return for possession of the land and for the lord's protection. The third feature was the payment of incidents—essentially feudal taxes. It was these last two features, services and incidents, that eventually gave shape to the common law system of estates.

Free Tenures.

Services. William and his successors needed three things to keep government going. On earth they needed the security offered by a standing army. In heaven they needed the support of the Church. And at their meal tables, they needed the supplies provided by agricultural production. The so-called "free tenures" were devised to secure these needs. They were, respectively, the military tenures, the frankalmoign (or religious) tenure, and the socage (or economic) tenure, each with its own form of required service.

- *Military Tenures.* Of the military tenures, the tenancy by knight service was the most important. The service required the tenant to provide a designated number of knights for a specified period, sometimes as brief as forty days each year. Although the King could assemble as many as 5,000 knights this way, their service was discontinuous, making the army far less effective than a full time army of mercenaries. But, to hire mercenaries, the King needed money. By 1166 he was encouraging his tenants in chief to substitute money payments (called *scutages*, or shield money) for their fixed quota of warriors. The tenants in chief raised this money by exacting scutages from their tenants, and these tenants by exacting scutages from theirs.
- *Frankalmoign (or Religious Tenure).* Frankalmoign tenure involved the grant of lands to religious institutions or officials in return for their performance of spiritual—and occasionally more worldly—services on behalf of the grantor.
- *Socage (or Economic Tenures).* Socage was the great residual class of free tenures. If a free tenure was not a military tenure or frankalmoign tenure, it was considered to be socage tenure. The services required under socage tenure usually involved the provision of labor or agricultural goods or, eventually, their money equivalent. Sometimes the service was only nominal, such as giving a peppercorn or a rose at midsummer, designed to evidence that the land was held of the lord.

Although tenures were divided into these three types, each with its form of required service, the specific services required of tenants varied widely to meet each lord's needs or whims. In addition to the services just described were such services as training hounds and hawks for the lord's use on hunts, assisting the King when travel across the Channel made him seasick and, as in the case of one unfortunate tenant, the obligation every Christmas day to make "altogether, and once, a leap, a whistle and a fart" for the amusement of the King. All these services had two things in common: all served to document the fact that the land was held of a lord, and virtually all—including the synchronous leap, whistle, and fart—were converted over time into money obligations.

The Development of Heritability. Tenants initially held their estates only for their life times. William's primary concern was ensuring that his tenants, particularly those who held by knight service, be loyal and able, and he wanted to ensure that a tenant could not pass his land on to an heir whose loyalty and ability to discharge his father's obligations were unknown. So he provided that estates ended upon the tenant's death. Tenants in chief and mesne lords imposed the same limit on their grants of land.

In most cases, nonetheless, land lords allowed the land to pass from tenant to heir upon the heir's payment of a reasonable sum, known as a *relief*. Over time, many lords began to recognize an advance obligation to consent to the inheritance of a tenant's land by the tenant's son. Heirs pressed for legal recognition of this customary claim and, by 1100, a hereditary principle was recognized for lands held by tenants in chief and, soon after, for lands held of mesne lords, again subject to the payment of a relief.

Incidents. Each form of tenure except frankalmoign also carried specified incidents. Among the more important were *aids* (money contributions to the lord at times of financial emergency, including the knighting of the lord's eldest son, the marriage of his eldest daughter, and a demand for ransom if the lord was captured by enemies), *relief* (as just described, a payment by the tenant's heir on the tenant's death), and *escheat* (the land's reversion to the lord if the tenant died without heirs or was convicted of a felony).

The military tenures also carried the incidents of *wardship* and *marriage*. If a tenant died and his heir was a minor, wardship gave the lord custody of the heir and of the tenant's lands, entitling the lord to receive, and not be accountable for, their rents and profits. Marriage gave the same lord the right to choose his ward's marriage partner—and the right to compensation from a ward who, unhappy with the lord's choice, decided to look elsewhere for a spouse. Although these incidents might not sound very valuable today when most parents live to see their children turn 21, illnesses, warfare, and other forms of violence made that a far less likely event in feudal England. A lord could expect, on average, to enjoy the incidents of wardship and marriage 25 percent of the time (assuming that the lord himself lived long enough to enjoy them).

Incidents flourished long after most other elements of the feudal system lost their substance and value. Reliefs effectively became inheritance taxes. Wardships and marriage, with their guaranteed stream of income, were traded like securities. The principal reason for the continued vitality of incidents for several centuries was that, unlike services, which had a fixed value, incidents were essentially inflation-proof, fluctuating with the value of the land to which they were annexed.

Unfree Tenures (or Copyholds)

This elaborate feudal edifice, with all of its channels of duty, privilege, and protection, could not obviate the need for someone to work the land. The task fell to *villeins*, agricultural laborers who lived on the lord's manor, providing food for the lord and his entourage for a week or a month every year, receiving in return shelter and use of the parcel for their own family needs. Unlike those who held free tenure, the villein held his land at the will of his lord and did not receive protection from the king's courts. (The modern word, "villain," derives from this early feudal term and reflects the low esteem with which the class-conscious English viewed the agricultural yeoman.)

Over time, the villein's economic position improved. By the fourteenth century, fixed money payments, which the lord used to employ hired help, replaced the obligation to provide food and labor. By the sixteenth century, the real value of these fixed payments had slipped substantially due to inflation, and many tenants were paying lump sums to buy out their rental obligations. The villein's legal position also improved dramatically over this period, from a status in which he held at the will of his lord to one approximating outright ownership. At first, villeins were given a copy of manorial court records reflecting not only their obligations to the lord but also their rights (giving rise to the term "copyholder" to describe villeins). These rights were gradually expanded and solidified to reflect the custom of the manor and, by the fifteenth century, copyholders had gained access to the King's courts for protection against the lord's infringement of their rights. One opinion of the period went so far as to suggest that a lord who wrongfully ejected his copyholder could be sued for trespass. By the middle of the seventeenth century, copyhold tenure had come to possess the security and dignity of socage tenure in virtually all respects.

2. THE RISE OF THE FEE & THE EVOLUTION OF THE ESTATE SYSTEM

The history of tenures and estates in England reflects virtually continual evolution toward freer marketability of land. During the first two centuries of the feudal estate system, tenants found it difficult to transfer their lands during their lifetimes. First, a tenant needed the consent of his lord. Second, after the hereditary principle was recognized, the tenant also needed the consent of his heir apparent. But growth in England's rural population during the 13th century increased both the demand for and the value of land. Tenants began to seek the right to transfer land to whomever they wanted without permission of either lord or heir apparent.

In 1225, D'Arundel's Case, Bracton's Notebook, pl. 1054, lifted the latter constraint, holding that a tenant could make a transfer during his lifetime, an *inter vivos* transfer, free of his heir's claims. After D'Arundel's Case, an heir inherited land only if his predecessor died without having transferred it in his lifetime.

Tenants also found a means around the first constraint. Tenants could transfer their estates either by *substitution* or *subinfeudation*. Assume that *B* was the tenant of *A* and wished to transfer his estate to *C*. In a transfer by substitution, *B* would substitute *C* as the tenant of *A*. Because the services to *A* would now be owed by someone other than his original tenant, *A*'s consent to the transfer was required. By contrast, *A*'s consent was generally not required for subinfeudation, in which *C* would become the tenant of *B*, while *B* remained the tenant of *A*, thus adding another level to the feudal hierarchy Although subinfeudation would not disturb the services that *B* owed to *A*, it could substantially undermine the value of the incidents. Incidents, as noted, varied in value in proportion to *B*'s estate. If *B* conveyed to *C* a portion of his land in return for a substantial monetary payment and the periodic delivery of a peppercorn, the incidents that *B* owed *A* in the event of escheat, relief, wardship, or marriage were seriously diminished. If *B* died and left an heir under 21, for example, *A* would gain wardship control only of *B*'s remaining land, if any, and the periodic peppercorn.

To get rid of subinfeudation, the lords ultimately gave into the free transferability of property. In 1290, Parliament passed the *Statute Quia Emptores* which prohibited transfers by subinfeudation in fee simple, but permitted free transfers by substitution without any requirement of the lord's consent. *Quia Emptores* represented a major turning point in the development of the principle of free marketability and, as it turned out, in the decline of the feudal system. Once land became freely alienable, the personal relationship between tenant and lord that had characterized the feudal system disappeared. Services and incidents remained, but they were essentially economic—a form of taxes. Over time, with escheats and forfeitures, many mesne lordships disappeared, substantially collapsing the feudal structure. However, the feudal system did not disappear immediately. It was not until 1660 that the military tenures, and with them the bulk of feudal incidents, were abolished.

Quia Emptores and other contemporaneous developments also helped promote a diversity of estates. *Quia Emptores* applied only to transfers of fee simples. After *Quia Emptores*, a tenant could transfer a fee simple during his lifetime only by substitution; if the tenant did not transfer his estate during his lifetime, it passed to his heirs upon his death. But there were a variety of other estates that could be transferred by subinfeudation. These included the life estate, the fee tail (in which land would pass from generation to generation to a tenant's lineal descendants, each of whom would enjoy a life estate, but nothing more), the term of years (which gave land to someone for a set number of years), and various "defeasible" fees (which lasted only so long as the tenant complied with specific conditions).

As the importance of these various types of estates grew, the law began to insist that grantors use precise wording to express their intent. After

D'Arundel's Case and *Quia Emptores, A*'s conveyance "to *B and his heirs*" created a fee simple in *B*. After the passage in 1285 of another piece of Edwardian legislation, *De Donis Conditionalibus, A* had to transfer his land "to *B and the heirs of his body*" to create a fee tail. Failure to use the formulaic language "and his heirs" or "heirs of his body" meant that *B* would acquire no more than a life estate.

The fee simple, life estate, fee tail, and defeasible fees were called *freehold* estates, signaling their normal use within the traditional feudal tenures, and distinguishing them from villeinage and copyhold as well as from the term of years which originated as a device for evading the prohibition against usury. (To the medieval mind, these latter estates were inferior to the freehold estates even though the tenant's possession might last longer—a term of years, for example, frequently outlasted a life estate.) The principal distinction between nonfreehold and freehold estates was that the owner of a nonfreehold estate was entitled to occupancy, while the owner of a freehold estate was entitled to something subtly greater—*seisin*, meaning very roughly, possession. The distinction made a difference in terms of the remedies available to the possessor against intruders on his land.

3. The Estate System's History in America

By the time England settled the American colonies, the feudal tenures were clearly in decline. Yet, as William Vance has observed, "The first royal grants of vacant lands in the New World were made during the critical period when the Stuarts were struggling to re-establish the waning feudal powers of the Crown." Subinfeudation of the fee simple, outlawed in England, was expressly permitted in the colonies. And it "was but natural that patents were in feudal form, the land to be held in free and common socage, reserving some nominal services, like the annual render of two beaver skins or 'an Indian arrow of these parts.' " William R. Vance, The Quest for Tenure in the United States, 33 Yale L.J. 248, 256 (1924). Services also often involved money payments, called quit rents, and these, with their implicit message of subordination to the sovereign's will, angered the colonists. Not surprisingly, quit rents quickly disappeared almost everywhere when the Revolution ended all tenurial ties to the Crown.

Holding title to a vast, vacant domain, the new federal government faced the same challenge and opportunity as William of Normandy seven centuries earlier: to dispose of its land in a way that would best secure the interests of the sovereign. As described in Chapter 1, the objects and methods that the United States chose contrasted sharply with William's. Instead of subordinating landholders to state ownership, the government sought through its sales and grants of land to promote economic and political independence among its settlers and to encourage various economic and social activities such as the construction of railroads, the development of schools and agricultural colleges, and settlement of the western United States.

Although the tenurial system never obtained a substantial or lasting hold in America, the English system of estates did. *De Donis Conditionali-*

bus, *Quia Emptores*, and the distinctions between freehold and nonfreehold estates were received into state law almost everywhere. The validity and efficacy of the fee simple, life estate, and fee tail were widely acknowledged. Although some doubt was expressed about the validity of defeasible fees, these too were soon accepted into American practice.

4. THE LEGACY OF TENURES AND ESTATES

The long history of tenures and estates in England reveals a driving force toward the freer marketability of land. The commutation of services into cash obligations and free trade in feudal incidents were the beginnings of a trend. *D'Arundel's Case*, freeing tenants from the claims of their heirs, and *Quia Emptores*, freeing them from the claims of their lord, were perhaps the most salient milestones along the way. The development of various forms of estates and judicially-evolved rules of interpretation also pressed in the same direction. As you will soon see, American courts were quick to pick up the trend, amplifying it and eventually elevating it to an explicit, overarching, and operative policy favoring the free marketability of land.

Interestingly, England, the birthplace of the estates system, has to a significant degree become its final resting place as well. The 1925 Law of Property Act, 15 & 16 Geo. V, c. 20, abolished all *legal* estates other than the fee simple absolute and term of years. Grantees of any other interest, such as life tenancies or defeasible fees, hold them only as *equitable* estates: legal title to the land is vested in a trustee, with the holder of the equitable estate having only the right to enjoy and use the property during the period of the estate.

The principal aim of the 1925 Law of Property Act was to increase the marketability of land titles by enabling a single, readily identifiable person—the trustee—to convey fee title unencumbered by a diversity of future interests. Before the Act, if *B* held only a life estate in Greenacre with a remainder interest in *B*'s surviving children, Greenacre would have been unmarketable in *B*'s lifetime because a buyer could not possibly have determined which children would survive *B* and thus could not have bought out their interests. The only interest that an interested purchaser could have bought would have been *B*'s life estate, for which there often would not have been much of a market. Now after the Act, a trustee (which might be *B* or an independent trustee) holds legal title to the land in fee simple absolute and thus can freely sell or otherwise dispose of the land. If the land is sold, the trustee will hold the proceeds for distribution according to the terms of the original conveyance—interest income to *B* for life, and principal to the equitable remaindermen who survive her.

B. PRESENT INTERESTS IN LAND

The United States ultimately recognized a number of different *present* interests in land, shown in Figure 7–1 along with their respective *future* interests. The law, moreover, continues to evolve. Most states, for example, no longer recognize the fee tail. And a number of commentators, as well as a draft Restatement of Property produced by the American Law Institute, has called for simplification of the remaining estates.

Present Interest	Future Interest in Grantor	Future Interest in a Third Party
Fee Simple Absolute		
Fee Tail	Reversion	Remainder
Life Estate	Reversion	Remainder
Fee Simple Determinable	Possibility of Reverter	
Fee Simple Subject to a Condition Subsequent	Right of Entry (or Power of Termination)	
Fee Simple Subject to an Executory Limitation		Executory Interest
Leasehold: **Term of Years** **Periodic Tenancy** **Tenancy at Will** **Tenancy at Sufferance**	Reversion	Remainder

Figure 7–1
Present and Future Interests in Land

Note that most present interests are paired with one or more future interests. The only exception is the fee simple absolute, which lasts forever. Because each of the other present interests may terminate at some point in the future, the law pairs them with a future interest that specifies who will receive the property if and when the present interest ends. Depending on the type of present interest, the future interest can be held by the original grantor or by a third party (known as a *transferee*). In most cases, the grant of the present interest will state the future interest. If the grant does not specify the future interest, courts typically will hold that the grantor implicitly retained a future interest in herself to fill the void.

Standard form language has evolved for the creation of each of these present and future interests, and litigation involving freehold estates focuses principally on determining the intent of grantors who failed to use the prescribed words. The answer can be crucial, for the attributes of one interest can differ substantially from those of another. In describing the language used to create an estate in land, courts and lawyers often talk about *words of purchase* and *words of limitation*. Words of purchase identify *who* takes the estate. Words of limitation identify *what* type of estate (e.g., fee simple absolute or life estate) is created.

This section provides a brief introduction to the basic estates in land. The remaining sections explore in more depth some of the issues raised by today's estate system.

1. THE FEE SIMPLE ABSOLUTE

The *fee simple absolute* (sometimes known just as a *fee simple*) is the greatest estate in land recognized by the law. The fee simple absolute lasts forever, and the owner has virtually complete discretion over who will succeed him as owner. The owner of a fee simple absolute can sell his estate *inter vivos* (i.e., during her lifetime) or give it away. If the owner does not transfer the estate during his lifetime, the fee simple will pass upon his death according to the specifications of his will or, if he leaves no will, to his common law heirs. Subject to due process restrictions, the owner's creditors can seize and sell the fee to satisfy the owner's outstanding debts. All other types of estates and interests in land represent mere divisions of the fee simple absolute into a smaller set of rights.

Words of Limitation. At common law, it was essential to the creation of a fee simple absolute by inter vivos transfer that the conveyance be worded

[7.1] "to *B* and his [or her] heirs."

Form prevailed over *A*'s express statements of intent, so that transfers such as

[7.2] "*A* to *B* to hold forever," or even

[7.3] "*A* to *B* in fee simple absolute"

did not create fee simples. Failure to use the talismanic words "and his heirs" meant that *B* received only a life estate and that *A* or his heirs regained the property upon *B*'s death.[1] The rule was not, however, applied to transfers by will (known as *testamentary* transfers). Wills were held to transfer fee simple absolutes even absent the "and his heirs" language so long as the testator's intent to create a fee simple absolute was evident.

Most states have abolished the "and his heirs" requirement by statute, with the result that both *Examples 7.2* and *7.3* would today be held to transfer a fee simple absolute. See, e.g., Cal. Civ. Code § 1072; N.Y. Real Prop. Law § 240(1); Dennen v. Searle, 176 A.2d 561 (Conn. 1961). Statutes in these states also typically go one step further, providing that every conveyance of land is presumed to transfer a fee simple estate absent clear evidence to the contrary. See, e.g., Cal. Civ. Code § 1105; N.Y. Real Prop. Law § 245. Thus, a conveyance of land using the simple language

[7.4] "*A* hereby conveys to *B*"

will generally create a fee simple absolute unless it is clearly demonstrated that *A*'s intent was to transfer some lesser estate.

Inheritance. What happens if the owner of a fee simple absolute dies? When someone dies owning property, the first question is whether the

1. In City of Manhattan Beach v. Superior Court, 914 P.2d 160, 172 n.15 (Cal. 1996), the California Supreme Court jokingly provided the following grant of a fee simple absolute as an example of good legal drafting: "I, John of Gaunt Do give and do grant To Sir John Burgoyne And the heirs of his loin Both Sutton and Potton Till the world goes rotten."

owner died with a valid will, in which case the property will pass to whomever the owner specified in her will. That person is known as a *devisee* (if real property is involved) or a *legatee* (in the case of personal property). If the owner died *intestate* (i.e., without a valid will), the property will go to the owner's *heirs* as specified by the applicable state's *statute of descent*.

The prescribed order of descent varies from state to state, but most states follow a relatively common order. See Figure 7–2 below. First, the law will look to see if the deceased owner (known as the *intestate*) has a surviving spouse or descendants (children, grandchildren, and so on). If

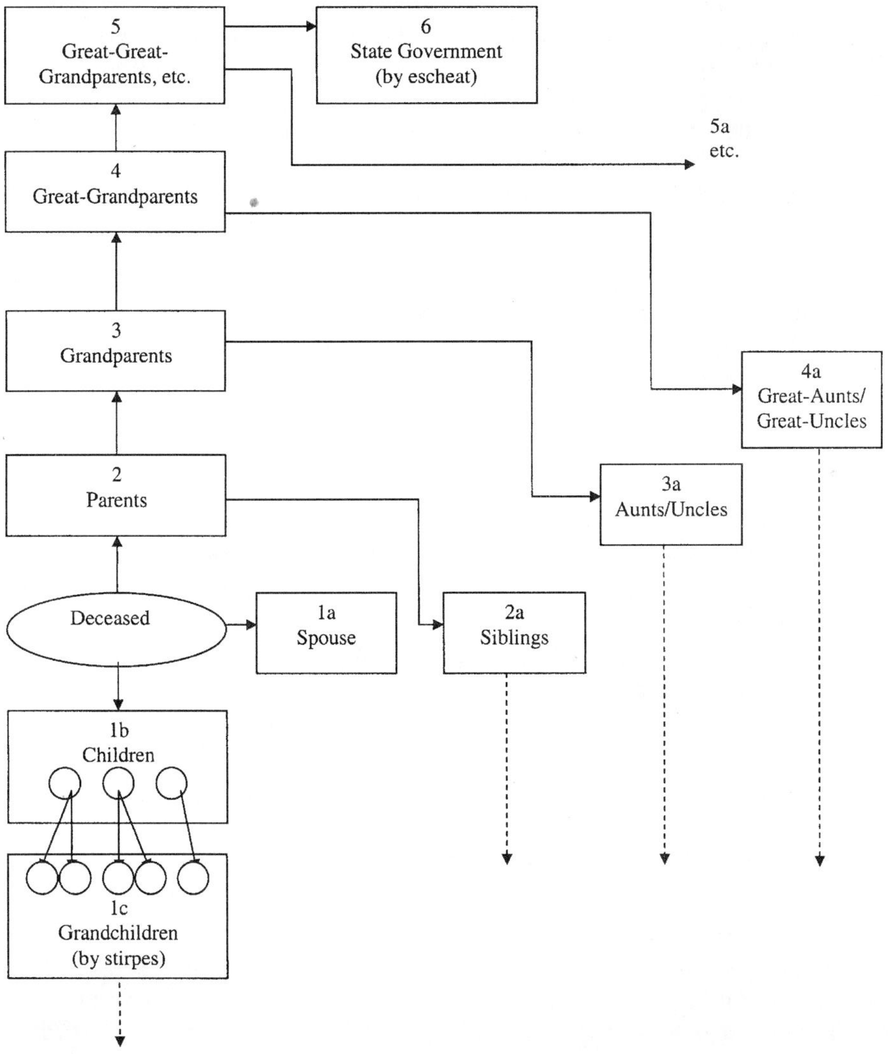

Figure 7–2
Illustrated Rules of Intestate Succession

there is a spouse but no descendants, the spouse will typically get the entire property (although some states require the spouse to split the property with an intestate's surviving parents). If there is both a spouse and descendants, the law will divide the property among the spouse and descendants. In most states, the surviving spouse will receive half of the property, with the remainder going to the descendants, but a few states will relegate the spouse to a lower percentage, particularly where there are multiple descendants. The descendants will generally share in the property *per stirpes* (meaning "by the stocks"): the descendants' percentage of the property will be divided up equally among the intestate's children and, if any child has died before the intestate, that child's share will go to her own children by right of representation (and so on down the generations if a grandchild or great-grandchild has died before the intestate).

At common law, children born out of wedlock could not inherit property. Over time, most states passed statutes that permitted children born out of wedlock to inherit from their mother, but not from their father unless paternity was acknowledged by the father. In Trimble v. Gordon, 430 U.S. 762 (1977), the Supreme Court held that such statutes violated the equal protection provisions of the United States Constitution. According to the court, the refusal to permit a child born out of wedlock to inherit from the father except where the father acknowledged paternity did not bear a rational relationship to a legitimate state purpose. Most states have responded to *Trimble* by providing that a child born out of wedlock can also inherit from someone who has been adjudged by a court to be the child's father.

If there is no surviving spouse or descendant, the property will generally go

- first to the intestate's parents,
- if the parents are both dead, to the intestate's brothers and sisters, or to the descendants of the brothers and sisters per stirpes,
- if none of these survives, then to the intestate's grandparents and their descendants per stirpes,
- if none of these survives, then to great-grandparents and to their descendants per stirpes, and
- finally to the intestate's nearest remaining kindred (such as cousins many times removed).

What if there are no heirs at all? In that case, the intestate's property typically passes—or *escheats* (borrowing from the feudal terminology)—to the state in which the property is situated.

2. THE FEE TAIL

Although the law has generally tried to encourage free marketability by eliminating historic restrictions that hindered transfers, many landowners have tried to find ways to evade this policy and to restrict the future ownership of their land. At times, they have succeeded. One of the most powerful motivations has been a landowner's desire to keep his land "in the family" by preventing his descendants from selling the land or losing it to creditors through financial mismanagement. This was the purpose of the *fee tail*, which, reflecting the law's bias toward free marketability, has now been abolished in most states.

English History. The history of the fee tail began in 1225 with *D'Arundel's Case* which, as you will recall, struck a blow for free marketability by holding that the holder of a fee simple could transfer the land inter vivos, free of any claims by future heirs. After *D'Arundel's Case*, a landowner, *A*, could not ensure that his land remained within the family by granting the land to his son, *B*, and "his heirs." Shortly after, landowners therefore began to use the phrase

[7.5] "to *B* and the heirs of his body"

to signify their intent that the land should pass from generation to generation to *B*'s lineal descendants. So long as the law imposed the doctrine of "primogeniture," this meant that the land would go to the eldest surviving son in each succeeding generation. If and when the line of descent failed, the land would return to the original landowner, *A*, or his heirs.

The courts tried to strike another blow for free marketability by interpreting the phrase, "and the heirs of his body," as imposing merely a condition that *B* have issue. The new estate was known as a *fee simple conditional*. Upon the birth of a child, *B* could transfer a fee simple, free of any claims by either his heirs or by *A*. If *B* did not transfer the land during his lifetime, his heirs would inherit a fee simple conditional. But each generation could freely market the land as a fee simple absolute so long as that generation had children. If the current holder of a fee simple conditional died without children, the land would revert to *A* or his heirs.

English barons did not appreciate the effort to increase the marketability of their land because it permitted the future breakup of their estates rather than ensuring that the land remained perpetually in the family. In response to a petition from large landowners, Parliament effectively overturned the fee simple conditional in *De Donis Conditionalibus*, 13 Edw. I, c. 1 (1285), which required courts to enforce these conveyances according to the grantor's original intent,

> so that they to whom the land was given under such condition shall have no power to alien the land so given, but that it shall remain unto the issue of them to whom it was given after their death, or shall revert unto the giver or his heirs if issue fail either by reason that there is no issue at all, or if any issue be, it fail by death, the heir of such issue failing.

The estate soon became known as a fee tail (from the French, "tailler," meaning to cut up or to carve), reflecting the grantor's intent to carve out a series of succeeding life estates.

The holder of a fee tail—the *tenant in tail*—often did not want to leave the land to his heirs, preferring to sell or transfer the land inter vivos. By the late 15th century, English lawyers had figured out a complex process, known as *common recovery*, by which a tenant in tail could convert his fee tail into a fee simple absolute. See Taltarum's Case, Y.B. 12 Edw. IV, 19 (1472) (permitting common recovery). In 1833, Parliament eliminated the need for common recovery by passing the Fines and Recoveries Act, 3 & 4 Will. IV, c. 74, which provided that a tenant in tail could convert his estate into a fee simple absolute simply by conveying his estate to another person. Thus, *B*, holding as a tenant in tail, could, by conveying "to *Z* and his heirs," give *Z* a fee simple. If the parties desired, *Z* could then reconvey the fee simple absolute to *B*.

History and Abolition in the United States. In the United States, abolition of the fee tail began at the time of the American Revolution. To Thomas Jefferson and many other Americans, the ability to pass land down from generation to generation to the eldest son was an unwanted vestige of England's hereditary aristocracy. At Jefferson's urging, the Virginia legislature abolished both the fee tail and the concept of primogeniture in 1776. Over time, virtually every other state also abolished the fee tail. Only four states—Delaware, Maine, Massachusetts, and Rhode Island—currently recognize fee tails (and, even in those states, they are seldom seen). As in England, these states allow a tenant in tail to convert his estate into a fee simple absolute simply by conveying it to someone else.

States have taken three approaches to eliminating the fee tail.[2]

(1) Many states provide that the language, "*A* to *B* and the heirs of his body," creates a fee simple absolute in *B*, and no interest at all in the issue. See, e.g., Cal. Civ. Code § 763.

(2) Some states have simply abolished the fee tail, without providing guidance on how to interpret deeds or wills that use the language "*A* to *B* and the heirs of his body." See, e.g., Texas Const. Art. I, § 26. What is the effect in these jurisdictions of such language? The apparent constructional preference is to find a fee simple in *B*. See Restatement of Property § 104 (1936).

(3) Other states preserve the fee tail for one generation by interpreting the phrase "*A* to *B* and the heirs of his body" as giving a fee tail to *B* and a fee simple to *B*'s issue. See, e.g., Conn. Stat. Ann. § 47–3 (1978). In these states, if *B* dies without issue, the estate reverts to *A*. If *B* dies with issue, however, the issue receive a fee simple.

Is one of these three approaches preferable to the others? Which approach comes closest to reflecting the intentions of the grantor? Which approach best supports the free marketability of land? How should any conflict between these potential goals be resolved? Given that fee tails

2. South Carolina technically never even recognized the fee tail. Because South Carolina never accepted *De Donis Conditionalibus*, use of the phrase "to *B* and the heirs of his body" in South Carolina creates a fee simple conditional. As in England before 1285, *B* can transfer a fee simple absolute upon the birth of his first child. If *B* does not transfer the land during his lifetime, his heirs receive a fee simple conditional. If *B* dies without heirs, the land reverts to the original grantor or his heirs (or to a third party if the original grantor so specified).

today can be converted into fee simples merely by conveying the land, is there any reason for abolishing the fee tail?

Even though the fee tail was abolished long ago in most states, it can still surface in modern property disputes. For example, in Robins Island Preservation Fund, Inc. v. Southold Development Corp., 959 F.2d 409 (2d Cir. 1992), a conservation group attempting to preserve Robins Island in the Peconic Bay of Long Island purchased three quarters of the island from someone claiming to be the heir to Joseph Parker Wickham. In 1715, Joseph Wickham, Sr., had purchased Robins Island, and twenty years later he had devised the land to his son Joseph Wickham, Jr., "and to the male heirs of his body lawfully begotten or to be begotten forever." Under this fee tail, the island passed first to Joseph Wickham, Jr., and then upon Joseph, Jr.'s death, to his son, Parker Wickham. Parker was a "loyalist" during the Revolutionary War and, as punishment, New York passed a law in 1779 seizing all the property "owned" by Parker (as well as 58 other loyalists). The Robins Island Preservation Fund argued that this law seized only a life estate from Parker (since that's all he possessed under the fee tail), and that Parker's son, Joseph Parker Wickham, gained a fee tail upon his father's death—which became a fee simple absolute under New York's Act to Abolish Entails of 1782, which converted fee tails into fee simple absolutes. The Preservation Fund thus claimed that they now owned most of the island. A great theory (someone was paying attention during property class!), but the Second Circuit decided that the 1779 law seized all interest in the land, not just Parker's life interest in the land.

3. THE LIFE ESTATE

Another form of estate by which a current landowner can try to control future ownership is the *life estate*, which gives the life tenant the right to possess the property only for his lifetime. If *A* wishes to give *B* possession of Greenacre during *B*'s life, but would like the property on *B*'s death to go to *C* and his family, *A* can grant the land

[7.6] "to *B* for life, then to *C*."

This grant will give *B* a life estate and *C* a *remainder* in fee simple absolute. Alternatively, *A* might want to give *B* a life estate and, upon *B*'s death, have the property revert to *A* and her heirs. *A* can accomplish this by granting the land simply

[7.7] "to *B* for life."

Here, *B* will have a life estate, and *A* will hold an implicit *reversion interest* in fee simple absolute.

Life estates are transferable inter vivos. *B*, who holds a life estate under either of the grants just described, can sell, lease, mortgage, or otherwise dispose of her estate—*if* she can find someone to pay for an interest that will end on her death. If *B* conveys her interest to *X*, *X* has the right to possess Greenacre until *B*'s death. *X*'s interest is called a life estate *pur autre vie* (i.e., an estate measured by another's life). What happens if *X* dies before *B* dies? *X*'s heirs or devisees receive the life estate pur autre vie entitling them to possess the property until *B* dies.

Because life estates are far less marketable than fee simples, courts today typically presume that a will or conveyance creates a fee simple unless it is clear from the language and context that a life estate is intended. Indeed, courts often seem to bend over backward to find a fee simple rather than a life estate. In Williamson v. Williamson, 2002 WL 1302473 (Ky. App. 2002), Camilla Williamson willed her "farm to Elias Williamson for his lifetime to use as he sees fit." She also provided that if "anything happens to Elias," two other relatives were to have the right to "work the farm," and that if "neither of them want to work the farm," the property was to be sold and the money distributed to various parties. The Kentucky Court of Appeals held that Elias Williamson received a fee simple absolute, not a life estate. According to the court, the language was not so clear "as to defeat the law's clear preference for a fee over a life estate." The court also noted that the will gave Elias the right to sell the farm—"a sure badge of a fee simple absolute." One member of the court, Judge Emberton, dissented:

> The court's task is to determine from the language of the will what the testator intended, not to create a devise she did not intend to create. Notwithstanding that fee simple estates are in some instances preferred over life estates, it is important we not lose sight of the fact that the concept of a life estate fits the needs and wishes of many a testator, and we must not make the creation of such an estate so difficult we deny them an opportunity to make the disposition of their preference.

4. DEFEASIBLE FEES

A defeasible estate terminates, and the land passes to the holder of the future interest, if and when an event specified in the creation of the defeasible fee occurs. If that event never occurs, the defeasible fee lasts forever, just like a fee simple absolute. Landowners find defeasible fees valuable in several situations. First, a landowner might want someone to possess her property only under specific circumstances. A mother, for example, might want Greenacre to go to her son only if the son reaches the age of 21. Second, a landowner might want to control how her property is used in the future. For example, the landowner might want Greenacre to go to The Nature Conservancy but only if The Nature Conservancy preserves the land in its natural condition. Subject to important restrictions discussed later, a landowner can use defeasible fees to accomplish either goal.

Fee Simple Determinable. Defeasible fees come in three forms. A *fee simple determinable* (also sometimes called a *fee simple on a special limitation*) automatically ends, or "determines," upon the occurrence of a specified event. Thus, if *A* conveys Greenacre

[7.8] "to *B* so long as the land is maintained in its natural condition, otherwise to revert to *A*"

B or his successors will automatically lose the estate if and when the land is developed. Because the fee simple determinable is a property interest and not a contract, the prohibition on developing the land binds not only *B*, but also anyone who subsequently acquires the estate by purchase, gift, inheritance, or devise. If the property is developed at any point, the land will automatically revert to *A* or her successors.

Durational language, like "so long as," is usually accepted as evidence that the grantor intended to create a fee simple determinable. Other durational terms commonly used to signify a fee simple determinable are "until," "while," and "during." Courts thus would generally find that each of the following conveyances creates a fee simple determinable:

[7.9] "to *B* so long as *B* does not subdivide the property"

[7.10] "to *X* while *X* continues to live on the property"

The future interest that follows a fee simple determinable is always held by the grantor and her successors and is called a *possibility of reverter*. Where *A* conveys Greenacre to

[7.11] "*B* so long as the land is maintained in its natural condition,"

A has implicitly created a possibility of reverter in herself even though the grant does not explicitly refer to a possibility of reverter in *A*.

Fee Simple Subject to Condition Subsequent. The fee simple subject to condition subsequent differs from the fee simple determinable only in that the former does not automatically terminate upon the specified condition. Instead, the original grantor or her successors have a right to retake possession of the property if and when the condition is breached. *A*, for example, might grant Greenacre

[7.12] "to *B* on the condition that the land is maintained in its natural condition, and in the event the land is developed, then *A* may enter and retake the premises."

Here, if *B* develops the property, *B*'s estate would not automatically terminate, but *A* or her successors could exercise their right to enter and claim ownership of the property for breach of the condition.

Conditional rather than durational language usually signals the intent to create a fee simple subject to condition subsequent. "On the condition that," or "on the express condition that," are two examples. Other language that a court would typically hold creates a fee simple subject to a condition subsequent would include:

[7.13] "to *X*, but if *X* uses the property for commercial purposes, then *A* may enter and retake the premises"

[7.14] "to *B*, provided, however, that *B* continues to use the property as a horse ranch"

In practice, as you will see in a moment, distinguishing between a fee simple determinable and a fee simple subject to condition subsequent is not easy.

The future interest that follows a fee simple subject to condition subsequent is again held by the grantor and her successors, and is called a *right of entry* (or sometimes a *power of termination*). In many cases, including *Examples 7.12* and *7.13*, the right of entry is explicitly reserved in the grant. If the grantor fails to reserve the right of entry expressly, the court will imply one. Thus, in *Example 7.14* above, a court would typically hold that the original grantor implicitly reserved a right of entry in herself or her successors. By not expressly creating a right of entry, however, the grantor has clouded the issue of whether she intended to create a fee simple subject to condition subsequent.

Are there any practical differences between a fee simple determinable and a fee simple subject to condition subsequent? In most situations, the differences, if any, between the two defeasible fees are inconsequential, and the differences are becoming less significant over time. No matter what type of defeasible fee is involved, for example, the holder of the future interests must generally bring an action to take possession of the property after the specified condition is violated. Although the fee simple determinable in theory terminates automatically, the holder of a possibility of reverter must still generally bring an action to obtain possession.

Possibilities of reverter historically differed from rights of entry in how fast the holder had to act to recover the property after the condition in the defeasible fee was violated. Because a fee simple determinable terminates automatically, the statute of limitations for purposes of adverse possession begins to run as soon as the condition is violated. If the holder of a possibility of reverter does nothing for the statutory period, the holder of the fee simple determinable may gain a fee simple absolute by adverse possession. The holder of a right of entry, by contrast, historically could take as long as he wanted to exercise the right—without worrying about adverse possession or any other adverse legal consequences.

Today, however, that has changed in most states. Legislatures in some states have adopted explicit statutes of limitation for the exercise of rights of entry. See, e.g., Cal. Civ. Code § 885.070 (5-year statute of limitations). Courts in other states use the equitable doctrines of laches or waiver to bar future interest holders from exercising rights of entry an unreasonable length of time after the violation of the condition. See, e.g., Martin v. City of Seattle, 765 P.2d 257 (Wash. 1988) (laches); Sligh v. Plair, 569 S.W.2d 58 (Ark. 1978). Even where the holder of a right of entry must exercise that right within a given period of time, however, the length of time within which he must act may differ from the adverse possession period for a possibility of reverter.

Fee Simple Subject to Executory Limitation. Like the fee simple determinable, and unlike the fee simple subject to condition subsequent, the *fee simple subject to executory limitation* (also sometimes called a *fee simple subject to an executory interest*) terminates automatically upon the occurrence of a specified event. Unlike the first two defeasible fees, however, the fee simple subject to executory limitation is followed by a future interest—called an *executory interest*—in someone other than the grantor. Thus, if *A* conveys Greenacre

[7.15] "to *B* so long as the land is maintained in its natural condition, and then to C," or

[7.16] "to *B*, but if the land is developed, then to *C*,"

B's interest in Greenacre is a fee simple subject to an executory limitation and would terminate automatically if the land is developed. *C* and her successors would hold an executory interest in Greenacre and would gain possession of the property if and when *B* or his successors develop the property.

Covenants. Mere promises, or *covenants*, must be distinguished from defeasible fees. Someone might buy a piece of property and promise the seller to use or not use the property in specified ways. Such covenants can bind not only the original purchasers but also all successors in interest to the land. But covenants differ from defeasible fees in that they do not affect ownership of the land. If a purchaser violates a covenant, the seller can sue the purchaser to enforce the covenant, but the purchaser remains owner of the property.

Marhenholz v. County Board of School Trustees

Appellate Court of Illinois, 1981.
417 N.E.2d 138.

JONES, J. delivered the opinion of the court....

On March 18, 1941, W. E. and Jennie Hutton executed a warranty deed in which they conveyed certain land, to be known here as the Hutton School grounds, to the trustees of School District No. 1, the predecessors of the defendants in this action. The deed provided that "this land to be used for school purpose only; otherwise to revert to Grantors herein." W. E. Hutton died intestate on July 18, 1951, and Jennie Hutton died intestate on February 18, 1969. The Huttons left as their only legal heir their son Harry E. Hutton.

The property conveyed by the Huttons became the site of the Hutton School. Community Unit School District No. 20 succeeded to the grantee of the deed and held classes in the building constructed upon the land until May 30, 1973. After that date, children were transported to classes held at other facilities operated by the District. The District has used the property since then for storage purposes only.

Earl and Madeline Jacqmain executed a warranty deed on October 9, 1959, conveying to the plaintiffs over 390 acres of land in Lawrence County and which included the 40–acre tract from which the Hutton School grounds were taken. When and from whom the Jacqmains acquired the land is not shown and is of no consequence in this appeal. The deed from the Jacqmains to the plaintiffs [purported to convey the future interest originally held by the Huttons.]

On May 7, 1977, Harry E. Hutton, son and sole heir of W. E. and Jennie Hutton, conveyed to the plaintiffs all of his interest in the Hutton School land. This document was filed in the recorder's office of Lawrence County on September 7, 1977. On September 6, 1977, Harry Hutton disclaimed his interest in the property in favor of the defendants. The disclaimer was in the form of a written document entitled "Disclaimer and Release." It contained the legal description of the Hutton School grounds and recited that Harry E. Hutton disclaimed and released any possibility of reverter or right of entry for condition broken, or other similar interest, in favor of the County Board of School Trustees for Lawrence County, Illinois, successor to the Trustees of School District No. 1 of Lawrence County, Illinois. The document further recited that it was made for the purpose of releasing and extinguishing any right Harry E. Hutton may have had in the "interest retained by W.E. Hutton and Hennie Hutton ... in that deed to the Trustees of School District No. 1, Lawrence County, Illinois dated March 18, 1941, and filed on the same date...."....

The basic issue presented by this appeal is whether the [plaintiffs could] have acquired any interest in the school property from the Jacqmains or from Harry Hutton. Resolution of this issue must turn upon the legal interpretation of the language contained in the March 18, 1941, deed from W. E. and Jennie Hutton to the Trustees of School District No. 1: "this land to be used for school purpose only; otherwise to revert to Grantors herein." In addition to the legal effect of this language we must consider the alienability of the interest created and the effect of subsequent deeds.

The parties appear to be in agreement that the 1941 deed from the Huttons conveyed a defeasible fee simple estate to the grantee, and gave rise to a future interest in the grantors, and that it did not convey a fee simple absolute, subject to a covenant. The fact that provision was made for forfeiture of the estate conveyed should the land cease to be used for school purposes suggests that this view is correct.

The future interest remaining in this grantor or his estate can only be a possibility of reverter or a right of re-entry for condition broken. As neither interest may be transferred by will nor by inter vivos conveyance (Ill. Rev. Stat. 1979, ch. 30, ¶ 37b), and as the land was being used for school purposes in 1959 when the Jacqmains transferred their interest in the school property to the plaintiffs, the trial court correctly ruled that the plaintiffs could not have acquired any interest in that property from the Jacqmains by the deed of October 9, 1959.

Consequently this court must determine whether the plaintiffs could have acquired an interest in the Hutton School grounds from Harry Hutton. The resolution of this issue depends on the construction of the language of the 1941 deed of the Huttons to the school district. As urged by the defendants, and as the trial court found, that deed conveyed a fee simple subject to a condition subsequent, followed by a right of re-entry for condition broken. As argued by the plaintiffs, on the other hand, the deed conveyed a fee simple determinable followed by a possibility of reverter. In either case, the grantor and his heirs retain an interest in the property which may become possessory if the condition is broken. We emphasize here that although section 1 of "An Act relating to Rights of Entry or Re-entry for breach of condition subsequent and possibilities of reverter" effective July 21, 1947 (Ill. Rev. Stat. 1979, ch. 30, ¶ 37b) provides that rights of re-entry for condition broken and possibilities of reverter are neither alienable nor devisable, they are inheritable. The type of interest held governs the mode of reinvestment with title if reinvestment is to occur. If the grantor had a possibility of reverter, he or his heirs become the owner of the property by operation of law as soon as the condition is broken. If he has a right of re-entry for condition broken, he or his heirs become the owner of the property only after they act to retake the property.

It is alleged, and we must accept, that classes were last held in the Hutton School in 1973. Harry Hutton, sole heir of the grantors, did not act to legally retake the premises but instead conveyed his interest in that land to the plaintiffs in 1977. If Harry Hutton had only a naked right of re-entry for condition broken, then he could not be the owner of that property until he had legally re-entered the land. Since he took no steps for a legal re-entry, he had only a right of re-entry in 1977, and that right cannot be conveyed inter vivos. On the other hand, if Harry Hutton had a possibility of reverter in the property, then he owned the school property as soon as it ceased to be used for school purposes. Therefore, assuming (1) that cessation of classes constitutes "abandonment of school purposes" on the land, (2) that the conveyance from Harry Hutton to the plaintiffs was legally correct, and (3) that the conveyance was not pre-empted by Hutton's disclaimer in favor of the school district, the plaintiffs could have acquired an interest in the Hutton School grounds if Harry Hutton had inherited a possibility of reverter from his parents.

The difference between a fee simple determinable (or determinable fee) and a fee simple subject to a condition subsequent, is solely a matter of judicial interpretation of the words of a grant.... A fee simple determinable may be thought of as a limited grant, while a fee simple subject to a condition subsequent is an absolute grant to which a condition is appended. In other words, a grantor should give a fee simple determinable if he intends to give property for so long as it is needed for the purposes for which it is given and no longer, but he should employ a fee simple subject to a condition subsequent if he intends to compel compliance with a condition by penalty of a forfeiture....

We believe that a close analysis of the wording of the original grant shows that the grantors intended to create a fee simple determinable followed by a possibility of reverter. Here, the use of the word "only" immediately following the grant "for school purpose" demonstrates that the Huttons wanted to give the land to the school district only as long as it was needed and no longer. The language "this land to be used for school purpose only" is an example of a grant which contains a limitation within the granting clause. It suggests a limited grant, rather than a full grant subject to a condition, and thus, both theoretically and linguistically, gives rise to a fee simple determinable.

The second relevant clause furnishes plaintiffs' position with additional support. It cannot be argued that the phrase "otherwise to revert to grantors herein" is inconsistent with a fee simple subject to a condition subsequent. Nor does the word "revert" automatically create a possibility of reverter. But, in combination with the preceding phrase, the provisions by which possession is returned to the grantors seem to trigger a mandatory return rather than a permissive return because it is not stated that the grantor "may" re-enter the land. . . .

[Cases cited by the defendant are distinguishable from the facts here.] The estate created in Latham v. Illinois Central R.R. Co. (1912), 253 Ill. 93, 97 N.E. 254, was held to be a fee simple subject to a condition subsequent. Land was conveyed to a railroad in return for the railroad's agreement to erect and maintain a passenger depot and a freight depot on the premises. The deed was made to the grantee, "their successors and assigns forever, for the uses and purposes hereinafter mentioned, and for none other." Those purposes were limited to "railroad purposes only." The deed provided "that in case of non-user of said premises so conveyed for the uses and purposes aforesaid, that then and in that case the title to said premises shall revert back to [the grantors], their heirs, executors, administrators and assigns.". . . . The estate in *Latham* may be distinguished from that created here in that the former was a grant "forever" which was subjected to certain use restrictions while the Hutton deed gave the property to the school district only as long as it could use it.

In Northwestern University v. Wesley Memorial Hospital (1919), 290 Ill. 205, 207, 125 N.E. 13, a conveyance was "made upon the express condition that said Wesley Hospital, the grantee herein, shall erect a hospital building on said lot . . . and that on the failure of said Wesley Hospital to carry out these conditions the title shall revert to Northwestern University." This language cannot be interpreted as creating anything but a fee simple subject to a condition subsequent, and the court so held.

The defendants also direct our attention to the case of McElvain v. Dorris (1921), 298 Ill. 377, 131 N.E. 608. There, land was sold subject to the following condition: "This tract of land is to be used for mill purposes, and if not used for mill purposes the title reverts back to the former owner." When the mill was abandoned, the heirs of the grantor brought suit in ejectment and were successful. The Supreme Court of Illinois did not mention the possibility that the quoted words could have created a fee simple determinable but instead stated,

> Annexed to the grant there was a condition subsequent, by a breach of which there would be a right of re-entry by the grantor or her heirs at law. A breach of the condition in such a case does not, of itself, determine the estate, but an entry, or some act equivalent thereto, is necessary to revest the estate, and bringing a suit in ejectment is equivalent to such re-entry.

It is urged by the defendants that *McElvain v. Dorris* stands for the proposition that the quoted language in the deed creates a fee simple subject to a condition subsequent.... To the extent that *McElvain* holds that the quoted language establishes a fee simple subject to a condition subsequent, it is contrary to the weight of Illinois and American authority. A more appropriate case with which to resolve the problem presented here is North v. Graham (1908), 235 Ill. 178, 85 N.E. 267. Land was conveyed to trustees of a church under a deed which stated that "said tract of land above described to revert to the party of the first part whenever it ceases to be used or occupied for a meeting house or church." Following an extended discussion of determinable fees, the court concluded that such an estate is legal in Illinois and that the language of the deed did in fact create that estate.

North v. Graham, like this case, falls somewhere between those cases in which appears the classic language used to create a fee simple determinable and that used to create a fee simple subject to a condition subsequent....

We hold, therefore, that the 1941 deed from W. E. and Jennie Hutton to the Trustees of School District No. 1 created a fee simple determinable in the trustees followed by a possibility of reverter in the Huttons and their heirs .... We refrain from deciding the following issues: (1) whether the 1977 conveyance from Harry Hutton was legally sufficient to pass his interest in the school property to the plaintiffs, (2) whether Harry Hutton effectively disclaimed his interest in the property in favor of the defendants by virtue of his 1977 disclaimer, and (3) whether the defendants have ceased to use the Hutton School grounds for "school purposes."....

Reversed and remanded.

Notes & Questions

1. On remand, how would you resolve the question of whether the school district's use of the property for storage purposes violated the provision that the property be used "for school purposes only"? In Mahrenholz v. County Bd. of School Trustees, 544 N.E.2d 128 (Ill. App. 1989), the Appellate Court of Illinois held there was no violation, so the school district ended up keeping the property in any case.

2. **Presumption Against Forfeiture.** If there is doubt whether an instrument establishes a fee simple determinable or a fee simple subject to condition subsequent, most courts resolve the doubt in favor of the fee simple subject to condition subsequent. See Restatement of Property, Present and Future Interests § 45 cmt. m. This presumption is one of several that seek to avoid the forfeiture of fee interests in order to promote their freer marketability. At least at the time the policy against forfeitures was being formulated, the fee simple subject to condition subsequent was the less forfeitable of the two estates since the failure to exercise a right of entry could eventually bar the right through equitable estoppel or laches, allowing the possessory estate to ripen into a fee simple absolute.

If there is a question whether an instrument establishes a condition subsequent or a covenant, most courts prefer the latter, which poses no risk of forfeiture at all. Similarly, faced with a choice between a covenant that binds not only *B* but also his successors to Greenacre, and a contract that binds *B* only, courts prefer the contract. And given a choice between a contractual undertaking and a precatory indication of purpose with no operative consequence at all, courts prefer the latter. See, e.g., Station Associates, Inc. v. Dare County, 513 S.E.2d 789 (N.C. 1999).

3. *Mahrenholz* demonstrates the unexpected but significant consequences that can sometimes attend the difference between a fee simple determinable and a fee simple subject to a condition subsequent. As the Illinois Appellate Court correctly observes, neither a possibility of reverter (which follows a fee simple determinable) nor a right of entry (which follows a fee simple subject to a condition subsequent) historically were transferable inter vivos or by will, but were only inheritable. W.E. and Jennie Hutton therefore could not have transferred their future interest in the Hutton School grounds during their lifetimes, and the Jacqmains, who claimed to have purchased the future interest from the Huttons, could not have acquired the future interest. Instead, upon the death of his parents, Harry Hutton inherited their future interest in the school grounds. If the future interest was a possibility of reverter, Harry would have gained a fee simple absolute in the school grounds as soon as the condition was violated, and the fee simple would have been transferable. But if the future interest was a right of entry, Harry would not have received a fee simple absolute unless and until he exercised that right. Should the effect of Harry's transfer depend on whether the Huttons originally created a fee simple determinable rather than a fee simple subject to a condition subsequent? Do you think that the Huttons ever contemplated this issue at the time of the original grant? How do you think that the Huttons would have wanted the dispute in *Mahrenholz* resolved?

4. Most states today permit inter vivos transfers of both possibilities of reverter and rights of entry. A few states, however, permit inter vivos transfers of possibilities of reverter, but still prohibit the transfer of rights of entry (and indeed sometimes hold that any effort to transfer a right of entry inter vivos destroys it). And a few states still prohibit inter vivos transfers of both rights of entry and possibilities of reverter.

Even in states that prohibit inter vivos transfers of such future interests, the holder of the future interest can "release" his interest to the holder of the present possessory estate, thereby terminating the future interest. For example, in South Carolina Dept. of Parks v. Brookgreen Gardens, 424 S.E.2d 465 (S.C. 1992), Archer Huntington had given Brookgreen Gardens a fee simple determinable in coastal land to be maintained in its natural state for the exhibition and preservation of South Carolina flora and fauna. After Huntington's death, his wife and sole heir executed a "Deed of Real Estate, and Release" in which she conveyed, released, and discharged "all rights she had as a possibility of reverter or as a right of re-entry, which might then exist or arise in favor of herself individually or as the sole heir of her husband." The South Carolina Supreme Court held that the release served "to eliminate the condition on the fee simple determinable estate, rendering the possessory interest a fee simple absolute." Should heirs have the ability to eliminate conditions on the use of property by the mere expediency of conveying their future interest to the holder of the possessory interest? Could Archer Huntington have taken any other steps to ensure that Brookgreen Gardens was used for a nature preserve as he intended?

5. Is there any reason to continue to distinguish between fee simples determinable and fee simples subject to a condition subsequent? In most cases, the distinction makes no difference. But where it makes a difference, as in *Mahrenholz*, the difference can be significant and often unexpected. Two states, California and Kentucky, have abolished the fee simple determinable; where the language of a fee simple determinable is used, the interest is interpreted as a fee simple subject to a condition subsequent. See Cal. Civ. Code § 885.020; Ky. Rev. Stat. § 381.218.

5. LEASEHOLDS

The nonfreehold interest held by villeins ultimately evolved into today's leasehold estates. Leases, and the legal rights of lessors (landlords) and lessees (tenants), are examined in Chapter 8. Leaseholds have always held an uncertain place in real property law. Although leaseholds are today recognized as possessory estates, leases were once viewed as personal contracts between lessors and lessees. Courts today still draw as much on contract principles as on real property law in interpreting leases and in resolving disputes between the parties to the lease.

Leaseholds fall into four different categories. The most common is the *term of years tenancy* which has a fixed duration such as ten years or six months. At the end of the specified term, the lease automatically expires. Also common is the *periodic tenancy* which provides for the continual renewing of the lease at the end of a specified period unless and until the lessor or lessee terminates the tenancy by giving the other party prior notice. Under a month-to-month periodic tenancy, for example, the lease automatically continues at the end of each month unless the lessor or lessee has provided advance notice that she intends to end the lease at the conclusion of the current month. The other leasehold estates are the *tenancy at will* (which lasts until either the lessor or lessee terminates the lease) and the *tenancy at sufferance* (which arises automatically when someone in lawful possession of real property wrongfully continues in possession after his right to be there has ended).

Under all leaseholds, the lessee holds a present possessory estate in the property. Because the leasehold is only a temporary estate, it must be followed by a future interest. As with future interests following a life estate, future interests following a leasehold can be held either by the original lessor (in which case it is a *reversion* interest) or by a third party (in which case it is a *remainder* interest).

C. FUTURE INTERESTS

As you have seen, every present possessory interest other than the fee simple absolute is accompanied by one or more future interests. See Figure 7–3, below. The future interest may be reserved to the grantor ("*A* to *B* for life, then back to *A*"); it may be created in someone other than the grantor ("*A* to *B* for life, then to *C*"); or it may be divided between the two ("*A* to *B* for life, remainder to *C* if she survives *B*, otherwise back to *A*"). The grantor also may retain present possession to himself while creating a future interest in another ("*A* to *B, B* to take possession on the occasion of her graduation from law school").

Present Interest	Future Interest in Grantor	Future Interest in a Third Party
Fee Simple Absolute		
Fee Tail	**Reversion**	**Remainder**
Life Estate	**Reversion**	**Remainder**
Fee Simple Determinable	**Possibility of Reverter**	
Fee Simple Subject to a Condition Subsequent	**Right of Entry (or Power of Termination)**	
Fee Simple Subject to an Executory Limitation		**Executory Interest**
Leasehold: Term of Years Periodic Tenancy Tenancy at Will Tenancy at Sufferance	**Reversion**	**Remainder**

Figure 7–3
Future Interests in Land

1. CLASSIFICATION OF FUTURE INTERESTS

Correct classification of future interests is crucial because the rules governing the validity, transferability, and enforceability of future interests often vary from one interest to another. *Mahrenholz*, supra at page 579, illustrates the potentially important distinction, for example, between a possibility of reverter and a right of entry.

Future Interests Retained by the Grantor. As summarized in Figure 7–3, grantors can retain three different types of future interests. Where the grantor creates a life estate, fee tail, or leasehold, any future interest that the grantor retains is a *reversion*. Reversion interests vary depending on what type of estate the grantor held at the outset. If *A* owns a fee simple absolute and grants *B* a leasehold, *A* retains a *reversion in fee simple absolute*. By contrast, if *A* owns a life estate and gives *B* a leasehold, *A* retains a *reversion in a life estate*. As these examples show, the reversion interest is what remains of the grantor's original estate after the grantor has transferred a lesser estate to someone else.

The other two types of future interests retained by grantors are the *possibility of reverter* and the *right of entry.* As discussed earlier, the possibility of reverter follows a fee simple determinable, while the right of entry follows a fee simple subject to a condition subsequent. Unlike reversions, the possibility of reverter and the right of entry do not guarantee that the grantor or his successors will ever regain possession of the property. If the condition in the prior estate is never violated, the prior estate can continue out into time indefinitely. Because of this, the common law permitted inter vivos transfers of a reversion, but not of a possibility of reverter or a right of entry. Possibilities of reverter and rights of entry were viewed as too insubstantial or speculative to qualify as true interests in land that were capable of transfer. Today, as discussed at pages 584–585, most states permit inter vivos transfers of both.

Future Interests in Transferees. The law subclassifies future interests in a transferee into *remainders* and *executory interests.* A future interest in a transferee is a remainder only if it follows an interest or interests that inevitably will end. Thus, in the conveyance,

[7.17] "*A* to *B* for life, then to *C* and his heirs,"

C's interest is a remainder because it follows *B*'s life estate, which is certain to end with *B*'s death.

If the transferee's future interest does not qualify as a remainder, it is an executory interest. Executory interests *divest*, or cut short, an earlier estate. Thus in the conveyance,

[7.18] "*A* to *B* so long as no house over two stories is built on the premises, then to *C*,"

C's interest is an executory interest because it divests B's preceding fee estate. Another way to put the proposition is that if a transferee's future interest follows a defeasible fee (i.e., a fee simple determinable or a fee simple subject to a condition subsequent), it must be an executory interest.

Complex Estates. A grantor can create multiple future interests. *A*, for example, might grant land

[7.19] "to *B* for life, then to *C* for life, then to *D* so long as the property is used for residential purposes."

In this example, *B* would hold a life estate. *C* would enjoy a remainder interest for life. *D* would enjoy a remainder interest in a fee simple determinable. Because *D*'s fee simple determinable could terminate, and the grantor did not specify a future interest to fill the remaining gap, the court would hold that *A* implicitly retained a possibility of reverter.

Consider what type of present and future interests are created in the following examples. Answers are found at the bottom of the page (but try to figure out the answers before you peak).

Example 7–20: "*A* to *B* for ten years, then to *C* for life, then to my heirs."[a]

Example 7–21: "*A* to *B* for life, then to *C* on the condition that the land not be developed, and if the land is developed, then to *D* and his heirs."[b]

2. THE HISTORY OF FUTURE INTERESTS

a. EXECUTORY INTERESTS AND THE STATUTE OF USES

The early common law permitted fewer classes of future interests than the law recognizes today. Courts, in particular, did not recognize future interests in third parties that could cut short, or divest, a preceding estate. Thus, in *A*'s conveyance, "to my oldest son *B* and his heirs, but if *B* acquires more than 100 acres of my other lands at any time, then to my second son, *C* and his heirs," *C*'s interest (which today would be an executory interest) would have been invalid on the ground that it was a *shifting interest* in a stranger that unlawfully cut short *B*'s freehold estate. *B* would have held a fee simple absolute. Similarly, in the conveyance, "*A* to *X* and his heirs upon *X*'s marriage to *A*'s daughter, *D*," *X*'s future interest (which again today would be an executory interest) would have been invalidated on the ground that it was an unlawful *springing interest,* a freehold estate intended to spring up out of the grantor at some point in the future.

The common law's refusal to recognize shifting and springing interests hampered early efforts at estate planning and commercial transactions. *A*, for example, might have wanted to avoid the effects of primogeniture by having his second son, *C*, take *A*'s land in the event that *A*'s death left the oldest son, *B*, adequately provided for. Or *A*, whose daughter was planning to marry *X*, might not have wanted *X* to have control of the marriage parcel until the knot was actually tied. As early as the twelfth century, grantors sought to avoid the common law rule by leaving the legal fee title intact, and charging the title with a protected interest known as a *use*. Thus, in the last example, *A* (the *feoffor*) would convey legal fee title to *T*, a trusted friend of both *A* and *X*, "to the use of *X* and his heirs when *X* should marry *A*'s daughter, *D*." *A* would continue in possession until the marriage, at which point *T*, the *feoffee to uses,* would convey legal title to *X*.

Since common law courts would not enforce uses, only *T*'s steadfastness guaranteed his performance. Soon, though, grantors looked to the Court of Equity (also known as the Court of Chancery) to enforce uses as a matter of moral obligation. By the mid-fifteenth century, grantors regularly turned for relief to Chancery, with its burgeoning jurisdiction, its sweeping equitable powers of injunction and imprisonment, *and* its freedom from the common law rules against shifting and springing interests. Although the

a. *B* holds a *term of years* leasehold. *C* holds a *remainder interest for life. A*'s heirs hold a *remainder interest* in a fee simple absolute.

b. *B* holds a *life estate. C* holds a *remainder interest* in a fee simple subject to an executory limitation. *D* holds an *executory interest* in a fee simple absolute.

Chancellor could not render judgment on legal title—which was strictly a matter for the common law courts—he could, by recognizing equitable interests, carry out the grantor's plans. Thus, Chancery would hold that even if the conveyance, "*A* to *T* and his heirs to the use of *X* and his heirs when *X* should marry *D*," gave *T* *legal title* in fee simple absolute, *A* held *equitable title* in fee simple subject to an *equitable executory interest* in *X*. *T* could enforce his interest at law, and *A* and *X* could enforce their interests at equity.

Uses enabled more than just the circumvention of common law rules against shifting and springing interests. Grantors could also employ uses to avoid the common law requirement that freehold estates be transferred only through an elaborate public ceremony, called *livery of seisin*, requiring *A*, as seller, and *B*, as buyer, to travel to the parcel where *A* would convey title and possession by handing a twig or a clod of earth to *B* while speaking the words of conveyance. To avoid this bother and the attendant publicity, *A* and *B* might instead enter into a bargain and sale agreement which, if it recited consideration paid by *B*, would be treated by Chancery as vesting equitable title in *B* on the theory that equity views as done that which should be done. The agreement effectively made *A* a feoffee to the use of *B*. *A* still had legal title and *B* had equitable title in fee simple absolute.

Uses were probably most popular as a vehicle for testamentary transfers. *A* was not at this time allowed to transfer a common law estate in land by will. But, through the device of the use, *A* could in his lifetime convey legal title to *T* in fee simple, "to be held by *T* to *A*'s use in fee simple, and on *A*'s death, *T* to convey legal title to such persons, in such proportions, as *A* shall designate by will." If *T* failed to perform, *A*'s devisees could petition the Chancellor to order the conveyance according to the terms of the use and the will. Alternatively, since uses—unlike legal estates—were devisable, *A* could simply devise the use to the objects of his desires.

Shifting and springing interests, secret conveyances, and testamentary transfers of land—all made possible by the use—substantially undercut the common law scheme. Even more unsettling, particularly to the King, was the extent to which the use enabled landowners to avoid the important, revenue-raising feudal incidents—wardship, marriage, relief—that became due when property descended on death. The principal tax avoidance technique was for *A* to enfeoff a large number of feoffees as joint tenants to the use of *A*. On *A*'s death, the use would pass by will or intestacy. Since it was an equitable, not a legal, interest that passed, there was no occasion for the assessment of feudal incidents. At the same time, the death of any one or more of the joint tenants holding legal title would not result in the imposition of incidents because, under the rules applicable to joint tenancies, the interest of one joint tenant accrues on his death to the remaining joint tenants and does not descend to his heirs. When the number of surviving joint tenants began to dwindle, it was easy enough for the equitable titleholder to ask the remaining feoffees to enfeoff additional younger joint tenants. The effect was that legal title never descended and the feudal incidents never came due.

Although piecemeal efforts were made to correct the situation, it was left to a financially strapped Henry VIII to end the charade entirely in 1535 with the *Statute of Uses*, 27 Hen. VIII, c. 10. The Statute provided that whenever one or more individuals (*T*) are seised to the use of another (*A*), the beneficiary of the use (*A*) shall have a legal estate of the same character as the equitable estate that he held under the use. Simply put, the Statute transformed ("executed") equitable estates into their corresponding legal estates. Thus, the effect of the Statute on the conveyance, "*A* to *T* and his heirs to the use of *A* and his heirs," was to convert *A*'s equitable title in fee simple absolute into legal title in fee simple absolute, and to deprive *T* of any title at all.

Although it might at first appear that the Statute did little more than place *A* back in his original position, the consequences were in fact enormous:

Executory Interests. "*A* to *T* and his heirs to the use of *X* and his heirs upon *X*'s marriage to *D*." The Statute converted *A's* equitable fee simple subject to a springing executory interest into a legal fee simple subject to a springing executory interest and converted *X*'s equitable springing executory interest into a legal springing executory interest. In a word, the Statute validated legal executory interests. (Because the Statute only executed uses, and did not directly validate executory interests, it was necessary, in order to create a legal executory interest, to couch the conveyance in terms of a use that could then be executed. This extra step is unnecessary today and, under modern practice, *A* would simply convey "to *X* upon the occasion of his marriage to *D*.")

Inter Vivos Transfers. The Statute's effect on bargain and sale agreements between *A* as seller and *B* as buyer was to convert *B*'s equitable title into legal title and to convert *A*'s legal title into no title at all. Thus, in a stroke, the Statute enabled the transfer of legal title without resort to the cumbersome and public formalities of livery of seisin. The change also facilitated secret transfers, and it was to prevent these that Parliament enacted the Statute of Enrollments, 27 Hen. VIII c. 16 (1536), providing that a freehold conveyance would be ineffective unless it was recorded—enrolled—in one of the King's courts of record within six months of its execution. Although the Statute of Enrollments was poorly drawn and was quickly circumvented by ingenious lawyers, it was the precursor of the modern recording acts in force and universally honored throughout the United States.

Testamentary Transfers. However great a boon it was to *inter vivos* transfers, the Statute of Uses appeared to eliminate testamentary land transfers entirely, forcing estate planners back to the unsatisfactory, pre-use alternatives of inter vivos transfers or reliance on the laws of descent. Strong public pressure for change led to the Statute of Wills, 32 Hen. VIII c. 1 (1540), permitting landowners to devise two-thirds of any land held in knight service and all lands held in socage tenure. Devisees were, however, liable for the feudal incidents to the same extent as if they had taken by descent.

b. TRUSTS

The Statute of Uses did not execute all uses. Doubtless the most significant exception carved out by courts involved the so-called *active use* in which *A* conveyed to *T* for the use of *B*, imposing on *T* the duty to actively manage the property for the benefit of *B*. The active use was the direct forerunner of the modern *trust* in which *A* transfers real property, personal property, or both to *T*, as trustee, to hold and manage for the trust beneficiary, *B*. As in the use, *T* has *legal title* to the trust assets and *B* has *equitable title*.

The trust is a very useful instrument. Assume that Eliza Farnham wishes to give her sister an investment property, Greenacre, in life estate with remainder interests to her sister's children. She also wishes to give one person—perhaps herself or her sister, but often a third party—the authority to manage the property on behalf of all the interest holders, as well as the freedom to sell Greenacre and reinvest the proceeds if that would be prudent. Eliza can do this by creating a trust and giving the trust legal title to Greenacre. Under the terms of the trust, she would instruct the manager of the trust, known as the *trustee*, to pay the income from the property to her sister for life and then to deliver the land to her sister's children upon the sister's death. Eliza's sister would hold an *equitable life estate* in the trust and her children would hold *equitable remainder interests*. Eliza would also give the trustee the power to sell Greenacre and invest the proceeds in other property if appropriate.

The trustee's basic obligation is to manage the trust assets faithfully and prudently according to the terms of the trust and applicable local law—selling the trust assets when appropriate, reinvesting the proceeds, and paying income to beneficiaries. If the trustee believes that bonds would be a better investment than Greenacre, for example, the trustee can sell Greenacre and invest the proceeds in bonds. The bonds then become the property of the trust. The sister would enjoy the income from the property during her lifetime, and the children would receive the proceeds of the trust upon their mother's death.

c. THE RULE IN SHELLEY'S CASE

Uses were just one technique through which landowners sought to avoid the imposition of feudal incidents. Another ploy was to take advantage of the fact that incidents were payable not on death but on descent. If *A* conveyed to *B* in fee simple absolute, and *B* died intestate, *B*'s heirs would be liable for the feudal incidents. But if *A* conveyed "to *B* for life, remainder to the heirs of *B*," *A* could hope to get the land into the heirs' hands without the payment of incidents since the heirs would succeed to *B*'s estate by transfer rather than descent. Similarly, instead of *A* conveying "to *B* for life," leaving *A* with a reversion in fee that would pass to *A*'s heirs by descent, *A* could convey "to *B* for life, remainder to the heirs of *A*."

Courts were quick to stymie both these efforts at medieval tax avoidance. At least as early as 1324, courts held that the conveyance, "*A* to *B* for life, remainder to the heirs of *B*," gave *B* not only a life estate, but the remainder in fee as well, thus effectively recasting the conveyance as, "to *B* for life, remainder to *B* in fee simple." Abel's Case, Y.B. 18 Edw. 2, f.577 (1324). This rule later became known as the *Rule in Shelley's Case*, reflecting its most famous exposition in Wolfe v. Henry Shelley, 1 Co. Rep. 93b (K.B.1581). Because the life estate and the remainder were held by a single individual, *B*, the doctrine of merger converted them into a single fee simple absolute in *B*'s hands. If *B* died without having disposed of the fee inter vivos, it would descend to his heirs who would then become liable for the feudal incidents.

Although American common law early adopted the Rule in Shelley's Case, the rule has since been abolished by statute or judicial decision in virtually every state. Lawyers in those states that have not abolished the rule or have only recently abrogated it, however, must still know of its existence. See, e.g., City Bank & Trust Co. v. Morrissey, 454 N.E.2d 1195 (Ill. App. 1983) (applying rule to a 1952 will); Smith v. Wright, 779 S.W.2d 177 (Ark. 1989) (continuing to recognize the rule).

d. THE DOCTRINE OF WORTHIER TITLE

Courts also attempted to frustrate the medieval efforts to avoid payment of incidents through the *Doctrine of Worthier Title* (also called the *Rule Forbidding Remainders to the Grantor's Heirs*). Under this doctrine, courts held that, in the conveyance, "*A* to *B* for life, remainder to the heirs of *A*," the grantor's attempt to create a remainder in her own heirs was void, thus leaving an implied reversion in the grantor. As a result, if *A*'s heirs took at all, they took by descent rather than as purchasers. (The doctrine got its name—its misnomer, really—from a connected rule that, if *A* attempts to devise by will the same freehold estate that the devisee would have taken by descent if *A* had died intestate, then the estate passes by descent, rather than by devise, because descent represents the source of "worthier title.")

A majority of states have abolished the Doctrine of Worthier Title. A handful of states, however, still follow the doctrine as a rule of construction rather than as a rule of law. In Doctor v. Hughes, 122 N.E. 221 (N.Y. 1919), Judge Cardozo pioneered the doctrine's use as a rule of construction, holding that in the conveyance, "*A* to *B* for life, then to the heirs of *A*," *A* will be presumed to have retained a reversion in herself, and it is up to the heirs to prove affirmatively that *A* intended them to have a remainder. Commentators have criticized Judge Cardozo's effort to preserve the doctrine as a rule of construction, however, noting that the doctrine provides little guidance on a grantor's likely intent. See, e.g., T.P. Gallanis, The Future of Future Interests, 60 Wash. & Lee L. Rev. 513 (2003) (calling for the outright abolition of the doctrine).

3. VESTING OF FUTURE INTERESTS

In classifying and enforcing future interests in transferees, it often becomes important to determine whether the interest is *vested.* A future interest is vested if

(a) there is no contingency that must be met before the interest can become presently possessory (other than the natural termination of the preceding estate), and

(b) the person or persons who will be entitled to possession are immediately ascertainable.

If a future interest is not vested, it is *contingent.*

Under this definition, executory interests are typically not vested because some contingency must be met before they can become possessory. Thus, in the conveyance,

[7.22] "*A* to *B* so long as the land is not developed, otherwise to *C*,"

C's executory interest is not vested because it is not certain that the land will ever be developed, and thus it is uncertain that *C*, his assigns, devisees, or heirs will ever take possession.

When will a remainder be vested in interest? In the conveyance,

[7.23] "*A* to *B* for life, remainder to *C*,"

C's remainder is vested because (a) *C's* interest is certain to become possessory (*B* must die at some point), and (b) an ascertainable person—*C*—will be entitled to possession. (It doesn't matter that *C* might die before *B*. If *C* dies before *B*, the property will go to *C*'s heirs or devisees upon *B*'s death.) By contrast, in the conveyance,

[7.24] "*A* to *B* for life, then to the heirs of *C*,"

the remainder in *C*'s heirs is not vested if *C* is alive because the heirs are not ascertainable in her lifetime. Similarly, in the conveyance,

[7.25] "*A* to *B* for life, then to *C* if she survives *B*,"

C's remainder, if *B* is still alive, is a contingent, rather than a vested, remainder because it is subject to the condition that *C* survive *B*. In both of the last two examples, the future interest is thus a *contingent remainder.*

In the conveyance,

[7.26] "*A* to *B* for life, then to *C* if she survives *B*, otherwise to *D*,"

both *C* and *D* have contingent remainders. As in the last example, *C*'s remainder is contingent, rather than vested, because it is subject to the condition that *C* survive *B*. *D*'s interest is also contingent because it is subject to the condition that *C* not outlive *B*. Because *D* will not gain possession of the land if *C* does, and vice-versa, the two future interests in this example are known as *alternative contingent remainders.*

Most vested remainders are *indefeasibly vested,* meaning that they are not only certain of becoming possessory in the future but cannot be divested. But that is not always the case. In the conveyance,

[7.27] "*A* to *B* for life, then to *C*, but if *C* does not survive *B*, then to *A*,"

C holds a *vested remainder subject to complete defeasance*. Is *Example 7.27* any different from the following conveyance?

[7.28] "*A* to *B* for life, then to *C* if she survives *B*"

Substantively, *C's* remainder in the two conveyances might appear to be identical, but in *Example 7.28*, *C* holds a contingent remainder. In the second conveyance, the condition is part of the language creating the remainder; *C* outliving *B* thus is a condition precedent to *C*'s taking the land. In the first conveyance, the condition appears *after* the language creating the remainder, indicating that, upon *B*'s death, *C* automatically gains possession of the land but then loses possession if, as a condition subsequent, she has not survived *B*.

How does vesting work where a future interest is created in a class of individuals, some of whom become identifiable before others? Assume, for example, that *A* conveys land to

[7.29] "*B* for life, then to *B*'s children."

If *B* has no children at the time the conveyance is made, the future interest in *B*'s children is contingent because there is no currently ascertainable owner. If *B* has one child—*C*—at the time of the grant, *C* holds a vested remainder interest *subject to partial divestment* if additional children are born. If no other children are born, *C* will receive a full fee simple absolute in the land. But if an additional child is born, *C* will receive only a 50% interest in a fee simple absolute. Because *B*'s children will share equally, *C*'s interest shrinks each time another child is born. Hence, *C*'s remainder interest, while vested, is "subject to partial divestment." Remainders that are vested subject to partial divestment are also sometimes called *vested subject to open*.

Browning v. Sacrison

Supreme Court of Oregon, 1974.
518 P.2d 656.

O'CONNELL, CHIEF JUSTICE.

This is a suit in which plaintiff seeks to have a provision in the will of Kate Webb construed. The question presented is whether the remainder devised to plaintiff's husband, Franklin Browning, now deceased, and his brother, Robert Sacrison, the defendant, was vested or contingent at the time of Mrs. Webb's death. The trial court found the remainder to be contingent. Plaintiff appeals.

Kate Webb was the maternal grandmother of Franklin Browning and Robert Sacrison. Her will, executed in 1943, when Franklin was 20 and Robert 13, contained the following provision (paragraph III):

> I give and devise to my daughter, Ada W. Sacrison, a life estate for the term of her natural life in and to all real property belonging to me at the time of my death, excepting only the

> residence property at Pilot Rock described in paragraph II of this will, with remainder over at the death of the said Ada W. Sacrison, share and share alike, to my grandsons, Francis Marion Browning[1] and Robert Stanley Browning,[2] or, if either of them be dead, then all to the other, subject to a like condition as to the use of the same or any portion of the proceeds thereof for Clyde Browning, as mentioned in paragraph II of this my last will.[3]

Kate Webb died in 1954. She was survived by her daughter, Ada, and grandchildren Franklin and Robert. At the time of her death, Mrs. Webb owned 960 acres of farmland in Umatilla County. This is the land devised by paragraph III of the will. Franklin died in 1972 without issue. He did not survive the life tenant Ada, who is still alive.

Plaintiff takes the position that the language in paragraph III of the will, creating an interest in the two grandsons "or, if either of them be dead, then all to the other" refers to the death of the testatrix not the death of their mother Ada, the life tenant. Thus, she argues the estate vested at the time of Mrs. Webb's death.

Conversely, defendant contends that the grandsons each took a remainder contingent upon surviving the life tenant.

Plaintiff relies upon the constructional preference favoring the early vesting of estates. It cannot be denied that there is considerable case support, including our own cases, for the view that the law favors the early vesting of estates. And it is clear that at an earlier day the rule was widely, if not universally accepted. The policy reason for this preference is that it "quickens commerce in the ownership of property by facilitating alienability to a considerable degree."[6] But with the passage of time the rule was eroded by exceptions and by a closer analysis of the rationale for the early vesting preference, until today that constructional preference probably no longer represents the prevailing view. The most severe criticism of the constructional preference for vesting is found in V American Law of Property, § 21.3 at 130 (Casner ed. 1952), where it is said:

> The preference for vested interests undoubtedly originated in connection with conveyances of interests in land and at a time in feudal England when contingent interests in land had not attained a dignified stature. Under such conditions, it may be reasonable to attribute to a transferor the intention to give the transferee an estate of recognized quality. Today, however, unfortunate tax consequences may follow a determination that an interest is vested and most transferors who consider all the consequences which attach to a vested interest are inclined to postpone vesting until

1. Francis Marion Browning is the same person as Franklin M. Browning.

2. Robert Stanley Browning is the same person as Robert Stanley Sacrison.

3. This condition was "that no portion of the property or proceeds thereof shall ever go to or be used for the benefit of their father, Clyde Browning." For further discussion of the effect of this condition see infra.

6. Dean et al. v. First Nat'l Bank et al., 217 Or. 340 at 361, 341 P.2d 512 at 522 (1959).

the time set for enjoyment of the interest in possession. Thus continued adherence to this preference in modern times is at least of doubtful validity in many situations.

The foregoing critique has in turn been criticized for being a "harsh, unbalanced assessment of the rule, ... as unfortunate as the more common tendency to accept the rule uncritically."[9] Thus a middle position has evolved which urges that "what is needed is a more discriminating evaluation rather than outright rejection of the rule."[10]

We adopt this latter approach. It is true that the reasons which prompted the creation of the rule favoring early vesting no longer obtain. Nevertheless, early vesting still may be desirable for other reasons which have application today.[11] On the other hand, the factors supporting early vesting must compete against other factors favoring the postponement of vesting. All of the factors "must be given their respective weights in the ultimate determination of the judicially ascertained intent of the conveyor."[12]

In the present case, competing with the constructional preference for early vesting is the preference for that construction which conforms more closely to the intent commonly prevalent among conveyors similarly situated than does any other possible construction. In modern law it is felt that when a devise is made to a life tenant with a remainder conditioned upon an ambiguous form of survivorship, the intent "commonly prevalent among conveyors similarly situated"[14] is deemed to require that the remainderman survive the life tenant rather than the testator. The application of this constructional preference would make Franklin's interest subject to the condition that he survive his mother Ada, as the trial court held.

The trial court based its decision in part upon a comparison of the language in other parts of the will with the language in paragraph III. For example, paragraph II provided as follows:

> I give and devise to my grandsons, Francis Marion Browning and Robert Stanley Browning, share and share alike, the real property owned by me in the Town of Pilot Rock, in Umatilla County, Oregon, subject to the condition that no portion of said property or the proceeds thereof shall ever go to or be used for the benefit of their father, Clyde Browning, and if either of said

9. Rabin, The Law Favors the Vesting of Estates: Why?, 65 Colum. L. Rev. 467, 479 (1965).

10. Ibid.

11. "... Nevertheless the early vesting of interests is still regarded as very desirable from the viewpoint of public interest. Construing an interest as vested may reduce the number of persons having interests in the affected thing and thus makes it easier to secure a conveyance of the ownership of such thing. Also such construction tends to reduce the uncertainties as to the created interest and hence results in a readier market for it. Thus earlier vesting still facilitates alienability to a considerable degree. Furthermore the rule against perpetuities operates more destructively as to interests subject to a condition precedent than as to interests vested subject to complete defeasance." 3 Restatement, Property, § 243 at 1217–18 (1940).

12. 3 Restatement, Property, § 243 at 1209 (1940).

14. Ibid.

> grandchildren be not living at the time of my death, then the other shall take all of such property, subject to said condition.

In this paragraph the testatrix expressly designates that the time for vesting of the Pilot Rock property in the survivor shall be "at the time of my death." The trial court reasoned that "it must be assumed that when these specific words were not used [in paragraph III] after the estate of Ada Sacrison, but the words, 'or, if either of them be dead, then to the other,' the testatrix intended that the interest become vested at the time of the death of the life tenant, and not at the date of her death."

The principle employed by the trial court is well recognized as one of the canons of construction. However, it loses some of its force here because the disposition in paragraph II, being directly to the devisees or the survivor without the intervention of a life estate, would necessarily have to vest, if it were going to vest at all, upon the death of the testatrix and therefore the survivorship provision could not relate to any other person's death insofar as it affected the vesting of the estate. This factor, standing alone, therefore would not justify the trial court's decision.

The trial court did, however, point to another factor which we think is more significant in ascertaining the testatrix's intent. The trial court noted that "all provisions of the will specifically excluded Clyde Browning from sharing in any interest in the estate." The court then concluded that "[i]f the construction propounded by the plaintiff were to be followed, the grandsons of Kate Webb would have had a vested transferable interest at the death of Kate Webb, and had they died intestate without issue prior to the death of the life tenant, their father, Claude (sic) Browning would have shared in his interest to the estate of Kate Webb as an heir of his child, contrary to the testatrix' specific wishes."

To strengthen this conclusion, the trial court could have pointed out that at the time the will was executed in 1943 Robert was only 13, Franklin was 20, and neither of them was married. (Indeed, neither had married by 1954 when the testatrix died.) There was, then, at least in the case of Robert, a rather long period of time during which a beneficiary might die intestate and before marriage and/or the birth of issue could divert the estate from vesting in whole or in part in Clyde Browning. It must be noted, of course, that even if the estate is regarded as vesting only upon the death of Ada, the life tenant, the survivor who outlived Ada might not have married or had issue, in which case Clyde would share in the estate upon his son's death. Moreover, if a grandson did have issue and predeceased the life tenant, treating the vesting event as the death of Ada would result in the disinheritance of the grandson's issue. However, we can only indulge in assumptions as to her possible objectives. We think that the assumption made by the trial court, supported by the preference for the construction which more closely conforms to the intent commonly prevalent among testators similarly situated, is the most reasonable.

The decree of the trial court is affirmed.

Notes & Questions

1. **Preference for Early Vesting.** In contrast to *Browning*, many courts still employ a strong preference for early vesting of contingent remainders. For example, in Usry v. Farr, 553 S.E.2d 789 (Ga. 2001), Watson Usry left a will providing for successive life estates:

> I will, bequeath and devise all of the land, with improvements thereon, which I may own at my death to my Wife, LUCILLE, to be hers for and during her lifetime; and at her death same is to go to my children who may survive my wife, and to my grandchildren with restrictions as follows: Any of my children taking land under this Item shall have a life interest therein, share and share alike, with any grandchildren who take hereunder taking the part which their father or mother would have taken. Upon the death of my last surviving child title in fee simple to said lands shall vest in my grandchildren, per stirpes and not per capita.

Despite the final sentence of this provision, the Georgia Supreme Court held that the remainder interest in the grandchildren vested upon Usry's death, not on "on the death of [his] last surviving child." According to the court, this interpretation was consistent with the Georgia rule "favoring vesting of title as of the time of the testator's death." Three justices dissented, arguing that this preference was inconsistent with the clear language of Usry's will. How would you interpret Watson Usry's will? To what factors should a court look in deciding when an interest vests?

2. **Transferability of Contingent Remainders.** As *Browning* demonstrates, the time at which an interest vests can determine who holds the interest. Vesting used to have other legal significance, although the importance of vesting has shrunk over time. Contingent remainders, for example, traditionally were inalienable; remainders could be sold only once they had vested.

The vast majority of states, however, now permit the sale of contingent remainders. A handful of states allow the sale of future interests that are contingent on an event (e.g., "to A if she reaches the age of 21") but not as to the person who will hold the interest (e.g., "to my grandchildren," where some of the grandchildren may not have been born yet). Several other states still prohibit the sale of contingent interests. See T.P. Gallanis, The Future of Future Interests, 60 Wash. & Lee L. Rev. 513, 516–521 (2003). Even in states that do not permit transfers of any contingent remainders, holders of contingent future interests frequently can find ways to sell them—e.g., by entering into a contract to sell the future interest once it vests.

3. **Destruction of Contingent Remainders.** Under the common law, courts also destroyed contingent remainders in two situations. First, the common law destroyed a contingent remainder if it had not vested at the time the preceding freehold estate terminated. For example, in the conveyance,

[7.30] "*A* to *B* for life, then to *C* when she turns 21,"

C's remainder would be destroyed if *C* had not yet reached 21 when *B* died. In this situation, *C* took no interest at all—even if she subsequently turned 21; instead, the next vested estate (in this case *A's* implied reversion) would become possessory immediately upon *B's* death.

Second, a contingent remainder could be destroyed through "merger." The doctrine of merger provided that when a person holding one interest in land acquired another interest in the same land, the two interests merged if no other interest stood between them. For example, if after the conveyance in *Example 7.30*, *A* conveyed his reversion to the life tenant, *B*, before *C* reached 21, *A's* estate and *B's* would be held to merge, giving *B* a fee simple absolute. What of *C's* interest? Since it had not vested at the time of *A's* transfer of his reversion to *B*, it was not sufficiently strong to stave off merger and was thus destroyed. If *C* had already turned 21, however, *C* would hold a vested remainder interest and *A*'s and *B*'s interests would not merge. See Abo Petroleum Corp. v. Amstutz, 600 P.2d 278 (N.M. 1979).

Does either of these two rules make any practical sense? Only a handful of states, if any, still follow the common law rules respecting the destructibility of contingent remainders. Gallanis, supra Note 2, at 530–534. In these states, the rules illustrate yet another important distinction between vested and contingent remainders and between remainders and other forms of future interests. Only contingent remainders are destructible. Vested remainders, executory interests, and future interests retained by the grantor are all categorically exempt.

4. Vesting is also important in two other contexts. First, as discussed next, contingent remainders are subject to the Rule Against Perpetuities, which invalidates future interests that may not vest until far in the future. Second, some states do not permit the holder of contingent remainders to sue where the owner of the current possessory estate is taking actions that might reduce the value of the future interest. The holder of a vested remainder, by contrast, can sue the current possessory owner for *waste* (a subject to which we turn later in this Chapter at pages 634–646).

D. RULES PROMOTING ALIENABILITY AND MARKETABILITY

1. THE RULE AGAINST PERPETUITIES

To what degree should a current owner of a piece of property be able to dictate future title to property scores of years down the road? Assume that Meriwether Lewis is making out his will. Should Meriwether be able to dictate in his will not only that his land should go to his widow for life and then to his children for their lives, but also that his land should then go to his grandchildren (whoever they might be) for their lives and then to his great-grandchildren? This is the subject of the "Rule Against Perpetuities," perhaps one of the most confusing doctrines for any law student studying property law.

The Rule Against Perpetuities originated in the Duke of Norfolk's Case, 3 Ch. Cas. 1, 22 Eng. Rep. 931 (1682). For a fascinating discussion of the history of and motivations behind the original development of the rule, see George Haskins, Extending the Grasp of the Dead Hand: Reflections on the Origins of the Rule Against Perpetuities, 126 U. Pa. L. Rev. 19 (1977). Today, virtually all states follow the Rule Against Perpetuities in at least some form and in at least some contexts. As discussed later, however, most states have adopted significant reforms to the Rule Against Perpetuities, and a growing number have abolished the rule entirely in the case of trusts that give the trustee the power to sell the trust property. See pp. 613–615. These reforms have significantly reduced the importance of the Rule in many states. Before turning to these reforms, however, it is important to understand the traditional common law rule.

The traditional formulation of the Rule reads: *No interest is good unless it must vest, if at all, not later than twenty-one years after some life in being at the creation of the interest.* John C. Gray, The Rule Against Perpetuities § 201 (3rd ed. 1915). Put more plainly: *An interest is void if there is any possibility that it will not vest within twenty-one years after the end of some life in being at the creation of the interest.*

Unfortunately, it is one thing to state the rule, quite another to apply it. As a starting point, it is important to bear in mind that the rule is concerned with *possibilities*, not *probabilities*. Thus, in the conveyance, "*A* to *B* until it next rains in Seattle, Washington, and then to *C*," *C*'s interest is invalid because it is possible—even though improbable—that the defeasing event will first occur, and *C*'s interest will first vest, hundreds of years in the future and outside the period of the Rule.

Second, the Rule is concerned with the possibility that a future interest will *vest* outside the prescribed period, not with the possibility that it will become *possessory* outside the period. So, for example, in the conveyance, "*A* to *B* for seventy years, then to *C* and her heirs," *C*'s interest is valid under the rule because *C*'s interest is vested at the very moment of the conveyance, thus excluding any possibility that it will first vest outside the period. The immediate vesting satisfies the Rule even though *C*'s interest may become *possessory* more than twenty-one years after lives in being at the time of its creation.

Finally, it is necessary to parse the Rule. Which "interests" are covered by the Rule, and which fall outside its scope? What is the consequence of finding that an interest is "void" under the Rule? How rigorous is the Rule when it speaks of "any possibility"? What lives qualify as "lives in being"?

Hagemann v. National Bank & Trust Co.

Supreme Court of Virginia, 1977.
237 S.E.2d 388.

POFF, JUSTICE.

In this appeal, we are asked to construe a will to determine whether the residuary clause violates the rule against perpetuities.

The will of Mildred Hart Woodward, executed January 15, 1971, was admitted to probate on March 16, 1971 and National Bank and Trust Company, the trustee named in the will, qualified as administrator. The testatrix was survived by her children, Anne Mutter Woodward Hagemann, Fletcher D. Woodward, Jr., and Malcolm P. Woodward, her sole heirs at law, all of whom were named as beneficiaries in her will.

Article Eight, the residuary clause of the will, creates two equal trust funds, one for Fletcher and his descendants and the other for Malcolm and his descendants. The clause contains eight paragraphs. Paragraph 1 provides that the son will receive the income so long as he lives and has living children under the age of 25 years and that, upon the son's death, the income shall be paid to his surviving wife and children for their "support, comfort and education"; paragraph 2 authorizes the trustee to invade the corpus for such purposes. Paragraph 3 provides:

> 3. When the youngest living child of such son of mine has reached age twenty-five years, that trust shall end and the fund shall be divided one-third to such son of mine and two-thirds equally to his then living descendants, *per stirpes*. Should such son of mine not then be living, the whole of the fund shall go to his then living descendants, *per stirpes*.

Under paragraph 4, if the last surviving child of one of the testatrix's sons dies before attaining the age of 25 years, the corpus will be paid on that date to that son, if living, and if not, will be added to the corpus of the other trust fund. Paragraphs 5, 6, and 7 are irrelevant to the issue at bar. The provisions of paragraph 8, however, considered in context with those of paragraph 3, are of crucial relevance:

> 8. Notwithstanding the foregoing, if any portion of my estate is in any contingency capable of being held in trust for a longer period than is permitted by the law of the state of my domicile, or if in any such contingency the vesting of any interest hereunder may occur after the expiration of such permissive period, then upon the happening of any such contingency such portion of my estate shall not be held in further trust, but shall rather be paid over absolutely to the person or persons to whom, and in the proportions in which, such portion would ultimately go under the provisions hereof.

Anne and Fletcher, complainants, filed a bill of complaint seeking construction of the will. The administrator-trustee, Malcolm, and infant beneficiaries, now born or as yet unborn, were named respondents. The chancellor appointed a guardian *ad litem* to represent the infant respondents and later joined Katherine D. Woodward, one of Fletcher's children who had attained her majority, as a party-respondent. Complainants prayed that the residuary clause "be declared null and void and of no effect as violating the rule against perpetuities, and that as a consequence thereof it be declared that the testatrix died intestate as to her residuary estate." . . . .

On appeal, all parties agree that under the rule against perpetuities as applied in this Commonwealth, the remainder interests granted the children (or descendants) of the testatrix's sons by paragraph 3 are void unless "saved" by paragraph 8. Complainants contend that paragraph 8 "saves" none of the interests granted by paragraph 3 and that the residuary estate must pass by the laws of descent and distribution in equal shares to the three children of the testatrix. Respondents argue that paragraph 8 "saves" the residuary clause in its entirety, or, in the alternative, that the rule invalidates only the remainder interests of the children (or descendants) of the sons but not the income or remainder interests of the sons.

The rule against perpetuities in Virginia voids a contingent remainder or executory interest, created *inter vivos* or by will, which may, by some possibility, however unlikely that possibility may be, vest beyond a life or lives in being at the effective date of the instrument creating the interest, plus 21 years and 10 months.

The effective date of the Woodward will is the date of Mrs. Woodward's death. In paragraph 3, she disposes of two-thirds of each of the two funds there created to the descendants of her sons living when the youngest living child of a son attains 25 years. The words "then living" create an express condition that a descendant, as a member of the class of descendants, must survive to the time at which the youngest child of the son attains 25 years of age. A contingent remainder is created in the class of "descendants."

By the familiar rule in Leake v. Robinson, 2 Mer. 363, 35 Eng. Rep. 979 (1817), generally followed in the United States and discussed in detail in Simes and Smith, The Law of Future Interests § 1265 (2d ed.1956), a class must stand or fall as a unit when the rule against perpetuities is applied. If the interest of one member of that class could vest beyond the time permitted by the rule, the interests of all members of that class fail for remoteness. Here, it is possible that the sons could die survived by a child in gestation or by a child under the age of three years and two months. In such case the interest of descendants of the testatrix would vest upon the 25th birthday of that child which is beyond the time permitted by the rule. It is not *actuality* or *probability* but *possibility,* viewed from the effective date of the will, that actuates the rule against perpetuities . . . .

In support of their position that the residuary clause is valid in its entirety, respondents rely upon two rationales. First, they urge us to approve the chancellor's holding that all residuary interests are saved by his construction of the clause as modified by paragraph 8; second, they ask us to construe the residuary clause "in a manner which upholds its validity while allowing a 'wait and see attitude' as to whether or not the savings clause has to be applied." We address the latter rationale first.

As respondents point out, these contingent remainders *could* vest before expiration of the term permitted by the rule upon the happening of any of several events. For example, the rule *could* be satisfied if the testatrix's son should die survived by children, none of whom are under the age of three years and two months and none of whom are in gestation at his death. There are other possibilities, even probabilities, of valid vesting. Respondents say, in effect, that we should so construe the will that the trustee will be allowed to "wait and see" whether any such future event occurs, and if not, then "upon the happening of any such contingency" which violates the rule, the trustee will be allowed to terminate the trust and distribute the corpus.

A statute embodying the "wait and see" doctrine has been adopted in England, Perpetuities and Accumulations Act, 1964, c. 55, § 3(1), and in some of the states, see, e.g., Ky. Rev. Stat. § 381.216 (1972), Vt. Stat. Ann. Tit. 27, § 501 (1975). But a majority of the states, including Virginia, apply the common law rule in its orthodox form. As respondents tacitly acknowledge, the "wait and see" rule is actuated by the possibility of timeliness. The common law rule is actuated by the possibility of remoteness. Burruss v. Baldwin, 199 Va. at 887, 103 S.E.2d at 252. Absent statutory mandate, we reject the "wait and see" rule and adhere to the common law rule.

Turning to respondents' first rationale, we examine the chancellor's ruling that paragraph 8 "saved" the residuary clause.

The rule against perpetuities "is a rule adopted in furtherance of public policy to prevent excessive restraints or limitations upon the alienation of an estate." Burruss v. Baldwin, supra. The language of the Woodward will leaves nothing ambiguous about the possibility of remoteness or the thrust of testamentary intent. The testatrix intended to forbid alienation of her residuary estate until her youngest grandchild, living at the time of her death or later born, reached the age of 25 years. Nor can there be any doubt that she attempted to do so knowing that what she attempted posed the possibility of remoteness and constituted a violation of the rule as applied "in the state of [her] domicile." She knew, too, that what she attempted would succeed so long as her will was not challenged in court.

Against the hazard of such a challenge, she added a "savings clause." That clause provides that if "the vesting of any interest hereunder may occur after the expiration of ... [the period permitted by the rule], then upon the happening of any such contingency such portion of my estate shall not be held in further trust but shall be paid over absolutely." Manifestly, the testatrix's deliberate purpose was to violate but, if possible, evade the effect of the rule against perpetuities, and if the rule were ever invoked, to rewrite the rule so that it would be actuated only upon the "happening" of an event which made remoteness an inevitability. But, as we have said, the rule is actuated by the *possibility* of remoteness, and that possibility must be determined as of the date of the testatrix's death.

The savings clause was patterned after a model form found in Rabkin & Johnson, 3 Current Legal Forms, Form 8.24(30). Indeed, with one exception, the language was identical. The Woodward clause provided that, upon the happening of a contingency that violated the rule against perpetuities, the corpus would be paid "to the person or persons to whom, and in the proportions in which, such portion would ultimately go under the provisions hereof"; the model form provided that in such event the corpus would be paid to those to whom "the income therefrom was then payable." While we do not decide what impact the model form might have had if its exact language had been employed in the Woodward will, we do note that the effect of such language is to fix the date for determining the remaindermen at a time within the term permitted by the rule against perpetuities. The language of the Woodward will, on the other hand, fixes the date at a time which could fall beyond the end of that term, for it identifies the remaindermen as those to whom the corpus "would ultimately go under the provisions hereof." Under the provisions of paragraph 3, the interests of the grandchild-remaindermen would be void for remoteness. A "savings clause" cannot save a void interest by adopting the very provisions which make it void. . . .

Respondents cite several cases decided in other jurisdictions which uphold savings clauses. Those clauses and the testamentary gifts to which they were applied are wholly unlike those before us, and we neither endorse nor reject the reasoning applied or the result reached in those cases.

Nor do we intend to imply that all savings clauses are inherently ineffectual in Virginia. If the language of a will leaves it ambiguous whether there is a possibility of remoteness, then a savings clause may be effective. But where, as here, the language reasonably permits no construction but that remoteness is a possibility, the use of a savings clause only reinforces the conclusion that the paramount testamentary intent was to violate the very rule which condemns such intent.

Accordingly, we hold that paragraph 8 of the residuary clause in the Woodward will did not save the remainder interests granted by paragraph 3 to the children (or descendants) of the testatrix's sons.

Finally, we consider whether the failure of these interests caused the other interests created by the residuary clause to fail. . . . The cases discovered in our research are conflicting, but the conflicts result not so much from jurisprudential differences as from factual, syntactical, and statutory diversity. We have concluded that the most succinct exposition of the general rule is that found in 28 A.L.R. Prior Estate—Remainder Void for Remoteness 375, supp. 75 A.L.R. 124, 168 A.L.R. 321:

> The general rule is that a remainder which is void because in violation of the rule against perpetuities does not necessarily render invalid the prior estate, but that the latter will be sustained notwithstanding the invalidity of the ulterior estate, where the two are not inseparable and dependent parts of a general testamentary scheme, and to uphold the one without the other would not defeat the primary or dominant purpose of the testator. . . .

Unless infected by the invalidity of the ulterior estates, the anterior estates created by the residuary clause of the Woodward will are valid: the income interest of the son will vest, if at all, within his lifetime; the income interests of the "surviving wife" of the son and his children will vest, if at all, not later than the death of the son; and the son's interest in the corpus will vest, if at all, within his lifetime. Under the rule quoted above, these anterior estates are not infected by the invalidity of the ulterior estates when "the two are not inseparable and dependent parts of a general testamentary scheme, and to uphold the one without the other would not defeat the primary or dominant purpose" of the testatrix.

As reflected in the will as a whole, the testatrix's "general testamentary scheme" was to make roughly equivalent provision for her three children and their descendants. In Article Seven, she created a specific trust for the benefit of her daughter and her daughter's children, and in Article Eight she created residuary trusts for her two sons and their descendants. If the invalidity of the ulterior interests infects the anterior interests, the entire residuary estate will pass by intestacy. In such case, the daughter would receive a portion of the estate intended for the sons and their descendants. This would effectively thwart the general testamentary scheme and defeat what we perceive to be the primary or dominant purpose of the testatrix. Clearly, with respect to her residuary estate, the testatrix's dominant purpose was to make available, during the critical period her grandchildren were to be reared and educated, not only the income from the trust but also such portion of the corpus as might be necessary for "support, comfort and education." Only after the expiration of that critical period was the corpus to be distributed and, then, only what had not been consumed.

We are of opinion that the anterior and ulterior estates were not "inseparable and dependent parts" of the general testamentary scheme and that to uphold the former would not defeat but, rather, would substantially promote the "primary or dominant purpose" of the testatrix.

We hold, therefore, that the anterior estates which, as we have said, will vest, if at all, within the term permitted by the rule against perpetuities, are not infected by the invalidity of the ulterior estates. We will reverse the final decree insofar as it upholds the remote remainders and affirm the final decree insofar as it upholds the other estates created by the residuary clause. And this cause will be remanded with instructions to restore it to the docket and enter a new decree consistent with this opinion.

Reversed in part, affirmed in part, and remanded.

Notes & Questions

1. Why did Anne and Fletcher bring suit in *Hagemann*? What were they trying to accomplish? Who "wins" in the case? What interests do the various parties hold at the conclusion of the litigation?

2. **"An interest . . ."** Consider in more detail the importance of each of the various elements of the Rule Against Perpetuities: *An interest is void if there is any possibility that it will not vest within twenty-one years after*

the end of some life in being at the creation of the interest. Start with the subject of the Rule. Although, taken literally, the Rule Against Perpetuities covers all interests, only future interests run the risk of violating the Rule. Interests that become presently possessory at the moment of the transfer are always valid under the Rule because they are immediately *vested in possession,* thus removing any possibility that they will first vest outside the perpetuities period. In both of the following conveyances, for example, *B* has a present possessory interest and thus does not need to worry about the Rule.

[7.31] "*A* to *B* for life, remainder to *C*"

[7.32] "*A* to *B* so long as the land is preserved as open space, otherwise to *C*"

The Rule also excepts future interests held by the grantor or his successors—reversions, possibilities of reverter, and rights of entry—on the theory that, though not vested in possession, they are inherently *vested in interest* from the moment of the transfer. Consider, for example, the conveyance:

[7.33] "*A* to *B* so long as the land is preserved as open space"

A holds a possibility of reverter that is inherently vested in interest and thus valid.

Can this exception be employed to circumvent the Rule's application to future interests created in transferees? For example, could you, using two pieces of paper instead of one, have employed this exception to effectuate the grantor's intent in *Hagemann*? Is there any functional reason to except grantor future interests from the operation of the Rule? See Jesse Dukeminier, A Modern Guide to Perpetuities, 74 Calif. L. Rev. 1867, 1906–07 (1986); Verner F. Chaffin, Reverters, Rights of Entry, and Executory Interests: Semantic Confusion and the Tying Up of Land, 31 Fordham L. Rev. 303 (1962).

3. **"... is void ..."** The effect of a finding that an interest is void under the Rule Against Perpetuities is to strike the interest from the conveyance and to treat the conveyance as if the interest had never been created.

What is the effect of an interest's invalidation on the remaining, otherwise valid interests? In part, the answer turns on the grantor's intent. If, as in *Hagemann,* enforcement of the remaining interests will not violate the grantor's overall purpose, they will be left intact. If, however, the voided interests were integral to the grantor's plan, the entire transfer will be voided. The answer also depends on the nature of the stricken interests and of the preceding estates. In the conveyance,

[7.34] "*A* to *B* for life, remainder to such of *B*'s children as shall reach 25,"

the remainder will be stricken for violating the Rule, and the preceding life estate will be kept intact, with a reversion following the life estate implied in *A* and his successors. See Lovering v. Worthington, 106 Mass. 86 (1870).

What if an interest following a defeasible fee is stricken? The answer can rest on very technical differences. Contrast the following two conveyances:

[7.35] "*A* to *B* so long as no building is erected on the parcel, then to *C*"

[7.36] "*A* to *B* on the express condition that no building be erected on the parcel, and in that event to *C*"

Although the two provisions have the same general purpose, Massachusetts courts have held that they have very different consequences under the Rule Against Perpetuities. In the first conveyance, *C*'s interest would be stricken, *B* would be held to have a fee simple determinable, and *A* and her successors would be held to have an implied possibility of reverter. See, e.g., First Universalist Society of North Adams v. Boland, 29 N.E. 524 (Mass. 1892). By contrast, in the second conveyance, *C*'s interest would be stricken, and *B*'s interest would be characterized as a fee simple absolute with no future interest implied in *A* or her successors. See, e.g., Brattle Square Church v. Grant, 69 Mass. (3 Gray) 142 (1855). Why should *B* have a fee simple determinable under the first conveyance and a fee simple absolute under the second? The technical reason given is that in the first conveyance the determining event is part of the fee and remains with it when the executory interest is stricken, while in the second conveyance the condition subsequent is part of the executory interest, rather than the preceding fee, with the result that, when the executory interest falls, the condition falls with it. Does the distinction make any sense? Does it give proper effect to the general principle that, apart from the Rule's effect on proscribed interests, the grantor's intent is to be honored?

4. **"... if there is any possibility ..."** If, at the time an interest is created, there is *any* possibility that the interest will vest outside the perpetuities period, the interest is void even though it probably would vest or—viewed in retrospect—actually did vest within the period. Assume that *A* makes the following gift of Greenacre:

[7.37] "*A* to *B* for life, remainder to that son of *B* who first reaches the age of 30"

If at the time of the gift, *B* has no son who has reached 30, the remainder is invalid—even though at the time of the gift *B* has a son who is only one day short of his thirtieth birthday, even though the son will in all probability reach his thirtieth birthday, and even though, in retrospect, when the gift is litigated, the son is over 30 years old.

In the case of an *inter vivos* gift or other conveyance, the validity of an interest is determined at the time of the gift or other conveyance. In the case of a will, the validity of an interest is determined at the death of the decedent.

The Rule's rigorous insistence on considering even the most ludicrous possibilities in determining an interest's validity has been the object of widespread criticism and occasional reform. It has also produced some common law oddities—fertile octogenarians, unborn widows, and slothful executors:

The Fertile Octogenarian. *A* and *B* are a married couple who are in their 80's and have three living children. *A* dies and leaves Greenacre as follows:

[7.38] "*A* to my wife *B* for life, then to *B*'s children for their lives, remainder in fee to the children of *B*'s children then living"

In this example, the remainder to the grandchildren is invalid because the possibility exists that *B* will have yet another child—who, unborn at the time of *A*'s death, when *A*'s will first becomes effective, cannot be used as a measuring life—and the interest of this child's children could thus vest more than twenty-one years after the death of everyone alive at the time of *A*'s death. See Jee v. Audley, 1 Cox Eq. Cases 324, 29 Eng. Rep. 1186 (Ch. 1787).

The Unborn Widow. *A* dies and leaves Greenacre to his brother, *B*, who is sixty years old, married, with grown children. The will reads:

[7.39] "to *B* for life, then to *B*'s widow for her life, remainder in fee to the children of *B* then living"

The children's remainder is invalid because *B* might remarry and his new wife might not have been born yet at the time of *A*'s devise, thus disqualifying her as a life in being. The children's interest, since it is contingent on their surviving *B*'s widow, may thus vest outside the perpetuities period. (The widow's life estate is valid because it will inevitably vest or fail upon *B*'s death.)

The Slothful Executor. *A* dies and devises Greenacre as follows:

[7.40] "to *B* and her heirs on the admission of this will to probate"

B's executory interest is invalid because probate may still be incomplete over twenty-one years after the death of *A*, *B*, and any other lives in being at the time of the devise, due to the executor's slowness. See Miller v. Weston, 189 P. 610 (Colo. 1920).

In each of the three examples just given, how could *A* have redrafted his will to avoid problems under the Rule?

5. **"... that the interest will not vest ..."** An interest can vest either *in possession* or *in interest*. An interest *vests in possession* when the person holding the interest first becomes entitled to possess the land. Thus, in the transfer

[7.41] "*A* to *B* for life, remainder to *C* in fee,"

B's interest vests in possession at the moment of the conveyance; it is valid under the Rule since there is no possibility that it will first vest at some later point, outside the perpetuities period.

An interest *vests in interest* at the moment it is held by an ascertained person with no condition precedent to enjoyment of the interest. See page 595 above. In the transfer,

[7.42] "*A* to *B* for life, remainder to *C* in fee,"

C's interest vests in interest at the moment of the transfer since there is doubt neither about the identity of the interest holder—*C*—nor about the fact that *C*'s interest will at some point vest in possession—since *B* will certainly die and her life estate end. *C*'s interest is thus valid under the Rule since there is no possibility that it will vest outside the perpetuities period. Similarly, in the devise from *A*

[7.43] "to *B* for life, then to *B*'s children for their lives, remainder to *C* in fee,"

C's interest is valid even though it may not become possessory within the perpetuities period. *B* may have a child subsequent to the devise with the result that *C* may not take possession for more than twenty-one years following all lives in being at the time of the devise. *C*'s interest is valid, however, because it vested in interest at the moment of the devise; at that point, *C* was identifiable as the taker, and it was certain that he or his estate would take the land at some future point upon the death of all of *B*'s children.

When is an interest *not* presently vested in interest? Consider the following transfer:

[7.44] "*A* to *B* for life, then to *B*'s first-born child in fee"

If *B* has no children at the time of the conveyance, the child's interest is not presently vested because the child is not ascertained at the moment of the transfer. The child's interest—a contingent remainder—is valid under the Rule, however, because she will become identifiable no later than *B*'s death (which is inside the period of the Rule).

In the transfer

[7.45] "*A* to *B* for life, remainder to the first child of *B* to complete nursing school,"

the child's interest is not presently vested because there is a condition precedent to her enjoying the interest. Because the condition precedent may first be met—and the presently unborn child's interest may first vest—outside the perpetuities period, the child's interest is invalid. Also, in the transfer

[7.46] "*A* to *B* so long as the land is used for school purposes, then to *C*,"

C's executory interest is invalid because of the possibility that the condition precedent—use for other than school purposes—will occur too remotely.

6. **". . . within 21 years after some life in being at the creation of the interest."** At common law, and sometimes by statute, the twenty-one year period is extended to include periods of gestation. The importance of this extension is illustrated by the following transfer:

[7.47] "*A* to my brother *B* for life, remainder to such children of *B* as shall reach the age of twenty-one"

The children's remainder technically is invalid under the traditional Rule because *B*'s wife might give birth to his child after his death, with the result that the child's interest would vest, if at all, more than twenty-one years after the end of all relevant lives in being. When periods of gestation are annexed to the rule's twenty-one year period, however, the gift over is valid.

Who can be counted as a life in being? Technically anyone alive at the time the interest was created can count as a *measuring life* to determine whether the interest satisfies the Rule. In practice, however, you generally need only look at people who are mentioned in the transfer or intervening generations. See generally Jesse Dukeminier, Perpetuities: The Measuring Lives, 85 Colum. L. Rev. 1648 (1985).

7. **Purposes of the Rule.** Now that you have a sense for how the Rule works, what purposes does the Rule play? Defenders of the Rule have identified at least three purposes. First, the Rule limits the ability of current property owners to dictate future ownership of the land so far into the future that they are unable to reasonably anticipate needs and conditions. The perpetuities period developed from the notion that family patriarchs could judge the competency of their children and often their grandchildren, but not of generations beyond the perpetuities period. Second, the Rule limits the ability of one generation to dictate land ownership in future generations. Finally, the Rule helps promote the marketability of land. While land remains divided up into multiple present and future interests, it can be very hard to sell the property.

For interesting discussions of the Rule and its potential justifications, see Thomas P. Gallanis, The Rule Against Perpetuities and the Law Commission's Flawed Philosophy, 59 Cambridge L.J. 284 (2000); Jeffrey E. Stake, Darwin, Donations and the Illusions of Dead Hand Control, 64 Tul. L. Rev. 705 (1990).

8. **Modification and Abolition of the Rule.** Virtually all states have today partially blunted the rule's rigorous application through decision and statute. One technique is to construe ambiguous language to comply with the Rule. Even John Chipman Gray, the most ardent advocate of the Rule's remorseless application, allowed that, "When the expression which a testator uses is really ambiguous, and is fairly capable of two constructions, one of which would produce a legal result, and the other a result that would be bad for remoteness, it is a fair presumption that the testator meant to create a legal rather than an illegal interest." John Chipman Gray, The Rule Against Perpetuities § 633 (3rd ed. 1915).

Cy pres. A handful of states take the somewhat more dramatic approach, known as *cy pres* or *equitable reformation*, of reforming otherwise invalid interests so that they comply with the Rule. For example, in Berry v. Union National Bank, 262 S.E.2d 766 (W. Va. 1980), the testatrix created a private educational trust to last for twenty-five years after her death, with the principal to then go to certain named beneficiaries. Although the court concluded that the future interest clearly violated the Rule, the court nonetheless validated the future interest by using its equitable powers to modify the will, reducing the 25–year period to 21 years. The court announced strict limits on the doctrine of equitable reformation, requiring that four conditions be met before an instrument will be modified: "(1) the testator's intent is expressed in the instrument or can readily be determined by a court; (2) the testator's general intent does not violate the rule against perpetuities; (3) the testator's particular intent, which does violate the rule, is not a critical aspect of the testamentary scheme; and (4) the proposed modification will effectuate the testator's general intent, will avoid the consequences of intestacy, and will conform to the policy considerations underlying the rule." 262 S.E.2d at 771.

Wait & See Doctrine. By far the most dramatic inroad on the Rule is the *wait-and-see approach*, adopted by the American Law Institute in the Restatement (Second) of Property, Donative Transfers § 1.4 (1983). The wait-and-see approach validates interests that, *in fact,* vest within the perpetuities period even though, at the time of their creation, some possibility existed that they would vest too remotely. Thus, in the conveyance,

[7.48] "*A* to *B* so long as the land is used for school purposes, then to *C*,"

C's executory interest is void under a strict application of the Rule. "Wait-and-see" would defer the determination of validity for twenty-one years after the death of all lives in being at the creation of the interest and if, within that period, the land ceases to be used for school purposes, *C*'s interest would be valid because it actually vested within the perpetuities period.

Uniform Statutory Rule. The Uniform Statutory Rule Against Perpetuities (USRAP) permits future interests that either satisfy the traditional Rule or that in fact vest within 90 years of their creation. If an interest fails both the traditional Rule and the 90–year wait-and-see test, USRAP provides that courts should reform the future interest to come as close as possible to meeting the intent of the creator while vesting within the 90–year period. Approximately half of the states, and the District of Columbia, have now adopted USRAP, including Arizona, California, Colorado, Connecticut, Florida, Georgia, Hawaii, Indiana, Kansas, Massachusetts, Michigan, Minnesota, Montana, Nebraska, Nevada, New Mexico, North Carolina, North Dakota, Oregon, South Carolina, Tennessee, Utah, Virginia, and West Virginia. For discussions of the USRAP and its 90–year period, see Lawrence W. Waggoner, The Uniform Statutory Rule Against Perpetuities: The Rationale of the 90–Year Waiting Period, 73 Cornell L. Rev. 157 (1988); Jesse Dukeminier, The Uniform Statutory Rule Against Perpetuities: Ninety Years in Limbo, 34 UCLA L. Rev. 1023 (1987); Ira M. Bloom, Perpetuities Refinement: There Is an Alternative, 62 Wash. L. Rev. 23 (1987).

Abolition. A handful of states have abolished the Rule entirely. See, e.g., N.J. Stat. § 46:2F–9; R.I. Gen. Laws § 34–11–38; S.D. Codified Laws § 43–5–8. A few have abolished it for personal property. See, e.g., Idaho Code § 55–111; Va. Code Ann. § 55–13.3(C).

9. **Perpetual Trusts.** Should the Rule Against Perpetuities apply to trusts, like those created by Mildred Woodward in *Hagemann*? Modern trustee typically have not only the power, but also the duty, to manage the trust assets productively. Since the trustee enjoys the full power of trans-

fer, and since unidentified or contingent future interest holders do not have to join to convey good title, the Rule does not play any valuable role in advancing the marketability of the trust property.

A growing number of states now permit trusts to last forever (or for a very long time) if the trustee has the power to sell the property. See, e.g., 765 Ill. Comp. Stat. 305/1 et seq.; S.D. Laws §§ 43–5–1 & 43–5–8; Wis. Stat. § 700.16. The Rule still applies to future interests outside of trusts, but very few people create such interests today; most people who divide title to land into multiple interests over time do so through trusts. Federal estate tax law has made perpetual trusts up to a limited size a particularly appealing method of estate planning. Recognizing the demand for perpetual or "dynasty" trusts, states have been racing to pass statutes freeing trusts within their jurisdiction from the Rule and thus attracting trust monies into the state. See Robert H. Sitkoff & Max Schanzenbach, Jurisdictional Competition for Trust Funds: An Empirical Analysis of Perpetuities and Taxes, 115 Yale L.J. 356 (2005) (finding that trust assets increase 20% in states permitting perpetual trusts relative to other states); Stewart E. Sterk, Jurisdictional Competition to Abolish the Rule Against Perpetuities: R.I.P. for the R.A.P., 24 Cardoza L. Rev. 2097 (2003); Joshua C. Tate, Perpetual Trusts and the Settlor's Intent, 53 U. Kan. L. Rev. 595 (2005); Verner F. Chaffin, Georgia's Proposed Dynasty Trust: Giving the Dead Too Much Control, 35 Ga. L. Rev. 1 (2000).

While the growth in perpetual trusts might not reduce the marketability of property, does it undermine the other goals of the Rule—preventing one generation from dictating the ownership of land for future generations and so far into the future that uncertainty is huge? Do perpetual trusts deprive each generation of an equal opportunity to control property? As the late Professor Jesse Dukeminier and Professor James Krier have noted, perpetual trusts might also create other problems:

> Equal opportunity aside, there is an argument that trusts concentrate economic power in the rich or, more accurately, in the trustees for the rich. In the case of trusts, the trustees, not the beneficiaries, have the power of investment. They decide where the trust capital is to be invested....
>
> Consider finally the argument that the certainty of receiving trust income makes beneficiaries lazy and unproductive. Alexander Hamilton is reported to have said that "we do not want a large leisure class in this country; we want to give people an incentive to work." This nicely encapsulates the thinking of Franklin, Jefferson, and Adams as well. When the Republic was established, England had a "leisure class," composed of nobles and country gentlemen who lived off their land rents and inheritances and refrained from something as low as work.... But this country has never had a leisure class like England's. We have no sense of inherited hierarchy. Our work ethic, deeply imbedded from the times of the Puritans, has spared us a class of great drones.

Jesse Dukeminier & James E. Krier, The Rise of the Perpetual Trust, 50 UCLA L. Rev. 1303, 1324–1325 (2003).

10. **Charitable Exception.** The Rule Against Perpetuities generally does not apply to future interests where all interests, both current and future, are held by charitable organizations. See, e.g., United States v. Cerio, 831 F. Supp. 530 (E.D. Va. 1993). If someone leaves their property to "Princeton, so long as Princeton teaches courses on animal rights, otherwise to Stanford," Stanford's future interest would be valid even though it would violate the Rule absent the charitable exception.

Coulter & Smith, Ltd. v. Russell

Court of Appeals of Utah, 1996.
925 P.2d 1258.

WILKINS, JUDGE.

Coulter & Smith, Ltd. (Coulter) challenges the trial court's summary judgment in favor of Roger Russell, Roger Richards, and Kristen Russell (Russell). We affirm.

Coulter owned a parcel of undeveloped real estate in an unincorporated area of Salt Lake County. Russell controlled about 3.67 acres (Russell property) several hundred yards north of Coulter's property. Between Coulter's and Russell's properties were four parcels owned by four unrelated parties. Independent of each other, Coulter and Russell made plans to develop subdivisions on their respective properties.

Discovering their similar development plans, Coulter and Russell discussed joint development of their properties and the possibility of Coulter buying the Russell property. Coulter hoped to buy the intervening properties and develop all the properties together as a single subdivision. Based on their negotiations, Coulter prepared an option agreement on its letterhead memorializing Russell's offer to sell subdivision lots to be developed by Coulter on the Russell property. On April 27, 1991, Russell signed the following option agreement:

Dear Dr. Russell:

> In response to your request for a written proposal to purchase your lots west of 1700 East at 10800 South, I submit the following offer which you may accept by signing below:
>
>> Price: $26,500 per lot during the 1st month following completion of the lots; price of each lot to increase $100 per lot each month thereafter until each lot is closed.
>
>> Upon completion of the subdivision development we offer to pay you $1,500 per lot; the balance of the purchase price ($25,000 at the outset) to be paid upon closing of each lot. We understand that the cost of the land and lot improvements will be paid upon closing of each lot.

The enclosed Work Exchange Agreement will initiate our cooperative efforts. We will proceed posthaste to annex and develop our tracts jointly. I believe that working in concert will greatly facilitate zoning and all other development concerns.

Respectfully,
/s/Nathan Coulter

Coulter & Smith Ltd. is hereby granted an option to purchase lots as per terms detailed above. This option terminates 2 years from the date of completion of the subdivision.

/s/Roger Russell 4–27–91 1991

The last sentence was inserted above Russell's signature line and was handwritten, in contrast to the rest of the document which was typed. In his affidavit, Russell asserts it was not on the document he signed. Meanwhile, Nathan Coulter states in his affidavit: "At Russell's request before the Option Agreement was signed, and for his benefit, I added the handwritten language at the bottom of the Option Agreement indicating that the option was to terminate 2 years from the date of completion of the subdivision."....

At the time Russell signed the option agreement, no lots existed on the Russell property. Further, the parties did not know how many lots could eventually be developed on the property because they had not yet attempted to annex the property to Sandy City and obtain zoning.

Although the parties believed the development could be finished by the spring of 1992, by that time Coulter had not substantially progressed toward completion—e.g., Coulter had not yet submitted a formal annexation petition, bought the four intervening parcels, or worked on the Russell property itself. Even so, Coulter had been laying groundwork for the development by negotiating to buy the four intervening parcels, hiring an engineering firm to design a subdivision including the Russell property, and enlarging a master drain system on the Coulter property to accommodate development on the Russell property. However, having failed to meet the parties' time expectations, Coulter began regularly reporting to Russell regarding Coulter's efforts to overcome several obstacles to the development.

[By September 1994, Coulter was still trying to remove various obstacles to its development of the properties. When Russell threatened to sell his property to a competing developer, Coulter sued for specific performance of the option agreement. The trial court granted judgment for Russell on several grounds, including that there was no consideration for the option agreement and that the option agreement violated the rule against perpetuities.

[In the first part of its appellate opinion, the Utah Supreme Court concluded as a matter of contract law that there was sufficient consideration for the option agreement:] In the letter, Coulter promised to "proceed posthaste to annex and develop our tracts jointly." His promise to do something he was not otherwise required to do supplied the consideration necessary to support the contract to leave the offer open. Accordingly, we reverse the trial court's determination regarding consideration.

We next consider Coulter's contentions that the trial court should not have applied the rule against perpetuities to invalidate the option agreement and should not have determined on summary judgment that a reasonable time had already passed for exercise of the option. These issues stem from the fact that the option agreement does not explicitly provide a deadline for Coulter to fulfill its promise to jointly develop the properties and thus does not provide a deadline by which Coulter must exercise its option following development.

An option to buy land is an interest in real estate, Coombs v. Ouzounaian, 24 Utah 2d 39, 465 P.2d 356 (1970), which is invalidated by the rule against perpetuities "unless it must vest, if at all, not later than twenty-one years after some life in being at the creation of the interest." Clark v. Shelton, 584 P.2d 875, 876 (Utah 1978) (quoting John C. Gray, The Rule Against Perpetuities § 201 (4th ed. 1942))....

There is a well recognized contract rule that "when a provision in a contract requires an act to be performed without specifying the time, the law implies that it is to be done within a reasonable time under the circumstances." Cooper v. Deseret Fed. Sav. & Loan Ass'n, 757 P.2d 483, 485 (Utah App. 1988) (quoting Bradford v. Alvey & Sons, 621 P.2d 1240, 1242 (Utah 1980)). This rule has been applied by Utah courts in cases involving interests in land, and even in cases which also consider the application of the rule against perpetuities. See Fredericksen v. Knight Land Corp., 667 P.2d 34, 38 (Utah 1983) (land option); Catmull v. Johnson, 541 P.2d 793, 795 (Utah 1975) (royalties option); Cummings v. Nielson, 42 Utah 157, 168, 129 P. 619, 622 (1912) (land option). However, in none of these cases, nor in any other case of record, has this general rule of contract construction been applied to defeat the operation of the rule against perpetuities....

In the present case, the language of the option agreement, even considered with the handwritten language alleged by Coulter to have been part of the agreement, does not expressly require the transfer of the interests in land to be completed, if at all, within the period of lives in being plus twenty-one years, as required by the rule. Admittedly, the agreement between Coulter and Russell requires Coulter to begin the development process "posthaste" and "immediately," but it expresses no completion date. The process of development is expressly made a precondition to transfer. Arguably, this process could take a longer period of time than allowed by the rule, despite the best efforts of all concerned. Regulatory, economic, geologic, or other concerns could interfere with the expeditious completion of the development.

The rule against perpetuities mandates that for an option agreement to be enforceable, the interests in land contemplated "must vest, if at all" within the period of the rule. Such is not the case here, although it is certainly possible that such vesting could occur. With or without the addition of the handwritten provision by which the option expires two years after the completion of the development, the rule is not satisfied and the agreement is void.

JACKSON, JUDGE (dissenting):

I respectfully dissent. The majority opinion regarding the rule against perpetuities is contrary to Utah law, the policies underlying the rule, and the great weight of authority in this country. I would hold that based on the language of the option agreement and the circumstances surrounding this transaction the law implies a reasonable time within which Coulter may exercise the option. Thus, the option agreement should not be deemed void from its inception as the majority has decided; instead, we should remand to the trial court for the factual determination of a reasonable time. Then, only if the reasonable time exceeds the perpetuities period would this contract be void under the rule against perpetuities....

"The rule against perpetuities is not merely a technical rule to be mechanically applied. The rule was created by judges to serve important considerations of public policy, and should be applied with those policies in mind." Cambridge Co. v. East Slope Inv. Corp., 700 P.2d 537, 540 (Colo. 1985). The rule is said to be based on policies prohibiting remoteness of vesting, restraint on alienation, and restraint on improvements. George T. Dunlap III & Fredric G. Levin, Note, Options & the Rule Against Perpetuities, 13 U. Fla. L. Rev. 214, 217 (1960); accord Restatement (Second) of Property, Div. 1, Part I, at 8–10 (1981). "The purposes behind the rule against remoteness are to curtail dead hand domination and to facilitate marketability." Dunlap & Levin, supra, at 217–18. The analysis I suggest allows these important policy considerations to remain intact while also honoring the parties' intent. If the fact finder decides on a reasonable time that is within the perpetuities period, then the agreement does not tie up the land long enough to violate any of the above policies. Likewise, if the fact finder decides on a reasonable time that exceeds the perpetuities period, the rule would void the option agreement in observation of its policy underpinnings.

As an aside, my research shows the application of the rule to options, and to commercial transactions in general, has been roundly criticized by courts and commentators alike. A good example of the tone of this criticism follows:

> The application of the Rule Against Perpetuities to options was a step of doubtful wisdom....
>
> The Common–Law period of perpetuities—lives in being plus twenty-one years—is well adapted to keeping family gift transactions within reasonable bounds. But neither lives in being nor a period of twenty-one years, nor both together, have any significance in commercial dealings. The dividing line between reasonable and unreasonable options should be based upon the realities

> of commerce in land, not upon a borrowing from the law of family settlements . . . .
>
> The self-interest of the parties can be relied upon to see that long-term options are kept well within the limits of public convenience. An owner of land will not be likely to give such an option where development of the land is a real possibility; and if such an option is given, the self-interest of the option holder will lead him to exercise the option and develop the land as soon as such action offers an opportunity for profit. . . .
>
> The trouble with a prohibitory rule not supported by a real public need is that it invalidates reasonable transactions, deprives one party (the option holder) of the benefit of his bargain when it proves profitable, and gives to the other party (the option giver) a loophole by which to evade his undertaking. An examination of the cases in which options have been invalidated will reveal a series of episodes in which lawyers have enabled owners to escape obligations freely assumed; they will not reveal cases in which the performance of these obligations would have caused any detriment to the public.

6 American Law of Property § 24.56, at 141, 142, 144–45 (Casner ed. 1952). . . .

Notes & Questions

1. On appeal, the Utah Supreme Court reversed and adopted the position of Judge Jackson's dissent in the Court of Appeals. The court held that commercial options were subject to the Rule against Perpetuities, but that the option in this case should be interpreted to place a restriction on the length of the option. "[W]e conclude that the court of appeals erred in applying the rule against perpetuities to the option without first employing the ordinary rules of contract construction to determine the scope of the interest created by the option. Applying those rules, we find that the parties expressly agreed to proceed expeditiously in developing and subdividing their properties and we will, therefore, infer from their agreement a reasonable time constraint within which Coulter must exercise the option. Thus, the option will be valid under the rule against perpetuities so long as a trier of fact determines that a reasonable time in this case is less than twenty-one years." Coulter & Smith, Ltd. v. Russell, 966 P.2d 852, 858–59 (Utah 1998).

2. If Russell had died before selling his property, could Coulter have exercised the option against Russell's heirs or devisees? Note that the option agreement says nothing about binding heirs or successors. If the option was enforceable only against Russell, wasn't it valid under the Rule against Perpetuities? Russell was a life in being at the time that the option was created, and the option would have to vest, if at all, during his lifetime.

3. **Options.** A majority of courts today hold that options are subject to the Rule against Perpetuities, despite the criticism quoted in Judge Jackson's dissenting opinion in *Russell*. See, e.g., The Symphony Space, Inc. v. Pergola Properties, Inc., 669 N.E.2d 799 (N.Y. 1996); Ferraro Constr. Co. v. Dennis Rourke Corp., 536 A.2d 1137 (Md. 1988). The Uniform Statutory Rule Against Perpetuities would exempt options and other commercial transactions from the Rule.

4. **Lease Options.** Should a lessee's option to purchase the leased premises be treated differently from other options? According to the late Professor Leach:

> In England it was held that an option to purchase by a lessee stood on the same footing as an option to purchase in gross: it was void if it could be exercised beyond the period of perpetuities. Thus an option to purchase at any time during a lease for 30 years failed. It was not observed that the situation was the exact opposite of that which exists where there is an option in gross. The improvement of the land is stimulated, not retarded, by the existence of an option in the lessee. If the lessee has an option to purchase he can safely improve; for, by the exercise of the option, he can preserve to himself the benefit of the improvement. If he has no option to purchase he can economically make an improvement which will still have a substantial value at the termination of the lease. Thus, a rule which invalidates options in lessees for the full term of their leases defeats the policy favoring free alienation and full use of property which the Rule against Perpetuities was designed to further. Several American jurisdictions have recognized this fact and have held valid such options; but the English cases still have some following in the United States.

W. Barton Leach, Perpetuities in a Nutshell, 51 Harv. L. Rev. 638, 661 (1938). See Citgo Petroleum Corp. v. Hopper, 429 S.E.2d 6 (Va. 1993) (holding the Rule inapplicable to lease options); Texaco Refining & Marketing, Inc. v. Samowitz, 570 A.2d 170 (Conn. 1990) (same).

4. Options are not the only trap that the Rule sets for the unwary business lawyer. Is a building lease, whose ten-year term is to commence "upon the completion of the building," valid under the Rule? The California Supreme Court ruled that it is. Wong v. Di Grazia, 386 P.2d 817 (Cal. 1963). But unlike the Utah Court of Appeals, the California court, recognizing the Rule's literal application might invalidate the lease, ruled that the "nature of the circumstances shows that the contemplated building was to be completed within a reasonable time and that such reasonable time was less than twenty-one years, hence the interest would either vest or fail within the statutory period." Id. at 819. Could the lease also have been validated on the ground that, although not vested in possession, it had vested in interest at the moment of its execution?

2. STATUTORY LIMITATIONS ON REVERTERS & RIGHTS OF ENTRY

As noted in the last section, the Rule Against Perpetuities does not apply to possibilities of reverter and rights of entry because they are held by grantors. Is there any reason to worry about future interests in third parties but not future interests in grantors? A number of states have passed statutes that cut off possibilities of reverter and rights of entry after a set period of time. Massachusetts and Nebraska, for example, cut off possibilities of reverter and rights of entry after thirty years. Mass. Gen Laws Ann. Ch. 184A, § 7; Neb. Rev. Stat. § 76–107. North Carolina doubles that period and does not cut off the future interests for sixty years. N.C. Gen. Stat. § 4–32. Other states have passed *marketable title statutes* that require the holders of future interests to re-record their interests periodically with the local recorder's office; if they are not re-recorded, the future interests lapse. See, e.g., Iowa Code § 614.24; pp. 512–521 supra

Can the legislature constitutionally limit the period during which a possibility of reverter or right of entry is valid? Is this an unconstitutional taking of the future interest for which the state must pay compensation? In Board of Education of Central School District No. 1 v. Miles, 207 N.E.2d 181 (N.Y. 1965), the Court of Appeals invalidated portions of N.Y. Real Prop. Law § 345 that made rights of entry and possibilities of reverter unenforceable unless a declaration of intention to preserve the future interest was recorded and renewed within prescribed periods after the condition or restriction was created. The court concluded that section 345 was an unconstitutional impairment of contract and also took the property of the future interest holder without due process of law. Most courts, however, have upheld provisions limiting the life of possibilities of reverter and rights of entry. According to the Illinois Supreme Court, such future interests are "no more than an expectation—a possibility that an interest in property may accrue in the future." Trustees of Schools of Township v. Batdorf, 130 N.E.2d 111, 114 (Ill. 1955). As a result, they are not protected from legislative limitation. See also Walton v. City of Red Bluff, 3 Cal. Rptr. 2d 275 (Cal. App. 1991); Ludington & Northern Ry. v. The Epworth Assembly, 468 N.W.2d 884 (Mich. App. 1991); Presbytery of Southeast Iowa v. Harris, 226 N.W.2d 232 (Iowa 1975).

3. RESTRAINTS ON ALIENATION

The common law also frowns on attempts by a current land owner to restrain the ability of future owners to sell or otherwise "alienate" their property. The next three cases illustrate the current application of the Rule Against Restraints on Alienation.

Alsup v. Montoya

Supreme Court of Tennessee, 1972.
488 S.W.2d 725.

ERBY L. JENKINS, SPECIAL JUSTICE.

This is an action brought by devisees under the will of W. C. Alsup to have certain lands devised under the will sold and the proceeds reinvested for the benefit of the life tenants and contingent remaindermen.

W. C. Alsup died, and his will was probated, in 1920. By that will he devised to each of his three daughters, for and during their lives, a farm of approximately two hundred acres. The will further provided that:

> These tracts of land I devise to my daughters for and during the periods of their natural lives, and after their deaths, they are to go to their children, or the heirs of any child who may then be dead, the heirs of any child who may then be dead to represent its parent and take his or her share of said land. If either of my daughters should die leaving no children and no issue of their bodies, then the tract of land herein devised to her will go to her sisters, or the heirs of any sister who may then be dead, said heirs to represent said sister and take her share of said lands.
>
> The land herein devised to my daughters shall not be sold or alienated *during their lives* and no court shall sell the same for reinvestment or alter the situation of said land as it exists today, it being my purpose that it shall not be sold in any way whatever. [Emphasis ours.]

The complainants in this case are the three daughters of W. C. Alsup. Also joined as complainants are the two adult children of one daughter, Mrs. Martha Virginia Alsup Ritland. The other two daughters, Susan Rebecca Alsup and Miriam Katherine Alsup, now sixty-two and fifty-seven years old respectively, are unmarried and have no issue. Joined as defendants are the minor children of Mrs. Ritland's daughters. The defendants are sued individually and as representatives of the class of possible remaindermen under the will.

The theory of the original complaint is that "due to material change in conditions, the restraint upon alienation . . . should be abrogated and set aside" under the inherent powers vested in a court of equity. By an amended complaint it is also contended that the restraint upon alienation was void ab initio.

The case was tried in the Chancery Court upon stipulations of fact. As fairly summarized in the complainants' brief, the stipulations show that since 1924 the entire family has lived in California. The family did not inherit the testator's agricultural love. The land has been rented out or share-cropped for more than fifty years. For a long time a benevolent Federal Government had it in the "Soil Bank," allowing it to lie fallow, paying yearly "rent" thereon, a questionable practice not only for the economy of the country but also the morale of the people. The buildings are antiquated and would require extensive repair, and some of the fences are in need of rebuilding. Some of the land has been heavily cropped over the years and has deteriorated in fertility and productivity. The farms are located in a strictly agricultural section of the county and would sell, even in their present condition, for an amount considerably in excess of $100,000.00. The income to the life tenants is considerably less than a reasonable return based on the present market value of the land.

Upon hearing of the cause the Chancellor found there had been a material change in conditions which could not have been foreseen by Mr. Alsup at the time the will was executed; that due to this material change it was in the best interest of all the parties, especially the ultimate remaindermen, that the land be sold for reinvestment, and that, accordingly, this restraint on alienation was no longer valid. From the Chancellor's decree ordering a sale of the land the defendants bring this appeal.

The defendants, by their guardian ad litem, make essentially three contentions on appeal. First, that the restraint on alienation is valid; second, that the Chancery Court had no power to remove the restraint because of a change in conditions, or because it might be in the best interests of the life tenants or remaindermen; and, third, that there was in any event no evidence or stipulation of fact that the removal of the restraint on alienation would be in the best interest of the contingent remaindermen. . . .

While there is no case in Tennessee directly passing upon the validity of a restraint upon alienation annexed to a legal life estate, the law generally is clear that any restraint which undertakes to wholly remove the power of a life tenant to alienate his estate is absolutely void.

We can see no reason to depart from this nearly unanimous view of the law. A testator, or the settlor of a nontestamentary trust, if he so desires, may still through the medium of a trust restrict the power of his trustee to sell or otherwise alienate the property which he has devised or given. And, in such a case, the devise or gift is subject to the constant supervision of courts of equity, which are empowered, if conditions so warrant, to decree a sale of the property when necessary to effectuate the intention of the testator.

The overriding issue is, what did the creator of this estate wish? What were his desires when the will was made, and what would his desires be under the conditions as exist today?

Although we do not necessarily concur, it has been written that "The only authentic evidence . . . which we have of the survival of life after death is the ability of the judges to read the intention of the testator long after he has been buried," and it may come to pass that a group of ghosts of dissatisfied testators may wait on the other side of the River Styx or on the Golden Shore to "receive" this and other courts who have construed their wills; however, under the circumstances, we cannot permit the writing of a dead hand of over fifty years, from the silent tomb, to control the action of this Court in this case.

When this will was made, the testator had three daughters, and three farms. His paramount desire, no doubt, as is the desire of so many men of wealth, was to protect his loved ones insofar as he could do so. But in trying he went too far. He could not look into the future and envision the changed conditions of over half a century. He desired to protect his children from all who descend upon those who come into wealth. He had made his living by farming and he felt that they would live on these farms, raise their children who would also be farmers.

Let us for a moment, in our mind's eye, witness his reaction to this situation, if he could be "materialized and view the present situation on his return to earth."

First of all, he would no doubt be disappointed that they all had forsaken the land and moved to far-away California, a place he had heard of, but probably never seen. Then, as he rides over his once fertile acres and takes a look at his once proud farms in their run-down condition, he probably would want to remake his will, but he cannot do that now. He sees once lush producing acres now grown up and cropped up to death, stately beautiful houses and great barns, falling in decay and disrepair. If he were not a very devout man, we can imagine some of his torrid words and exclamations.

Then, too, it would be hard for him, a rugged individualist, to understand the philosophy of a paternalistic government that pays a farmer not to farm under the guise of a soil bank, the only bank he ever heard of being one where money is kept.

And we can imagine, after surveying all that had happened, the condition that the land and the buildings are in, he would say, "Judge, times have changed. Do the best you can under the changed circumstances. I tried and made a mistake." And then, taking a last look around, he would mount his horse, and ride into the sunset and the great beyond, a land to where we are all hastening and where he has spent over half of a century, and as he rides off, we can hear him say, "I am better here."

We, therefore, hold the restraint upon alienation in his case to be invalid.

Although such a holding makes it unnecessary to discuss the other assignments of error made by the defendants, it cannot fully dispose of the case. The restraint being void, the life tenants are, of course, free to sell their estates. But the complainants have sought by this suit the sale of the entire fee, and not the sale of the life interests only.

Our law is clear, however, that a chancery court has wide discretion and the inherent power to order a sale for reinvestment, such as is being sought here, provided that the sale is manifestly advantageous to the interests of all the parties.

Although the chancellor's decree below was concerned with the avoidance of the restraint upon alienation, it was based on his finding that a sale of the property was "to the manifest interest of the parties and especially to the manifest interest of the ultimate remaindermen. . . ." This finding is in our opinion fully supported by the stipulated facts which were summarized above.

We, therefore, find that the decree for sale and reinvestment was proper, and the case must be in all respects affirmed.

Notes & Questions

1. The validity of direct restraints on the sale or other transfer of real property depends on three factors: the scope of the restraint, the method by which the restraint is enforced, and the nature of the interest restrained. See Figure 7–4.

Scope of the Restraint. The restraint may be *total* or *partial*. While a total restraint prohibits all transfers, a partial restraint limits transfers for a specific period of time ("*A* conveys Greenacre to *B*, but *B* shall not transfer Greenacre until she reaches the age of 21" or "*A* to *B*, but *B* shall not transfer for 5 years"), prohibits particular manners of transfers ("*A* to *B*, but *B* may not transfer other than by warranty deed"), or precludes transfers to particular people ("*A* to *B*, but *B* may not convey Greenacre to any member of the Grubb family").

Method of the Restraint. Disabling restraints withhold the power of alienation ("*A* to *B*, and any attempted transfer by *B* shall be void and of no effect"). *Forfeiture* restraints provide that the grantee will lose her interest if she attempts to transfer the property ("*A* to *B* so long as *B* does not convey"). *Promissory* restraints expose the grantee to contract remedies in the event of an attempted transfer ("*A* to *B*, and *B* promises never to convey the lands").

Nature of the Interest Restrained. The last factor considered by the courts is what type of estate is restrained—e.g., a fee simple or a life estate.

Courts generally hold that restraints on the alienation of fee interests are invalid. However, the restraint has some chance of being upheld if it is only partial and promissory. Restraints on life estates will generally be upheld if they are promissory or forfeiture restraints, but not if they are disabling restraints. And all forms of restraints are generally allowed in leases. Even in the case of leases, however, courts will try to construe the language of the restraint to permit alienability (e.g., by holding that the restraint is promissory rather than disabling).

Type of Restraint	Fee Simple	Life Estate	Leasehold
Disabling	**Invalid**	**Prohibited**	**Okay**
Forfeiture	**Invalid**	**Okay**	**Okay**
Promissory	**Possibly okay if partial and reasonable**	**Okay**	**Okay**

Figure 7–4
Validity of Direct Restraints on Alienation

2. What was the nature of the interest restrained in Alsup v. Montoya? What was the scope of the restraint? The method of the restraint? Reasoning backwards from the result in the case, it would appear that the court viewed the restriction as a disabling restraint since forfeiture and promissory restraints on life estates are generally permitted.

3. *Montoya* raises an interesting procedural issue. When a disabling, rather than a forfeiture or promissory restraint is created, who has standing to enforce the restraint? Who were the likely successors, if any, to W.C. Alsup's interest in enforcing the restriction? Did the defendants have standing to enforce the disabling restraint? These questions are important because another way that a property owner might free his interest from a disabling restraint is to buy off anyone with the standing to enforce the restraint. If you were advising the daughters in *Montoya*, what would you have advised them to do? Was a lawsuit inevitable?

4. **Agricultural Easements.** Do you agree with the court that W.C. Alsup would have wanted the court to permit his daughters to sell the property given the downswing in farming and the changed times? Note that his will is not only emphatic that the land should not be sold during his daughters' lifetimes, but he also provides that "no court shall sell the same for reinvestment or alter the situation of said land as it exists today." Was the Tennessee Supreme Court's decision in *Alsup* driven by concerns for Alsup's intent or by a desire to maximize the marketability of land? What if, rather than prohibiting the sale of the farm, W.C. Alsup had simply required that the property be used as a farm during his daughters' lifetimes? Should courts also void restrictions on use?

A growing number of farmers are imposing *agricultural easements*, also known as *farm easements*, on their properties. Under these easements, farmers agree, both on their own behalf and on behalf of all future owners of the properties, that the properties will be used forever as farms. Farmers use agricultural easements to help protect their farmland from urban conversion. As of 2003, more than 1.8 million acres of agricultural land, involving several thousand farms, were subject to such easements. Farmers who create agricultural easements receive federal tax benefits. (See the discussion in Chapter 10 of conservation easements, p. 927.) More than half of the states, moreover, now have programs in which the government pays farmers to create agricultural easements. See Center for Agriculture in the Environment & American Farmland Trust, The National Assessment of Agricultural Easement Programs (Sept. 2003).[1] Should the law permit current farmers to impose their farming preference on future generations? Shouldn't future generations be able to choose for themselves how to use the land? Should the government encourage farm easements through tax incentives and other public policies? Was W.C. Alsup just ahead of his time? Consider the next two cases in connection with the legality of agricultural easements.

Mountain Brow Lodge No. 82 v. Toscano

Court of Appeal of California, 1967.
64 Cal. Rptr. 816.

GARGANO, JUSTICE.

This action was instituted by appellant, a nonprofit corporation, to quiet its title to a parcel of real property which it acquired on April 6, 1950,

1. Available at http://www.aftre search .org/PDRdatabase/NAPidx.htm.

by gift deed from James V. Toscano and Maria Toscano, both deceased. Respondents are the trustees and administrators of the estates of the deceased grantors and appellant sought to quiet its title as to their interest in the land arising from certain conditions contained in the gift deed....

The controversy between the parties centers on the language contained in the habendum clause of the deed of conveyance which reads as follows:

> Said property is restricted for the use and benefit of the second party, only; and in the event the same fails to be used by the second party or in the event of sale or transfer by the second party of all or any part of said lot, the same is to revert to the first parties herein, their successors, heirs or assigns.

Respondents maintain that the language creates a fee simple subject to a condition subsequent and is valid and enforceable. On the other hand, appellant contends that the restrictive language amounts to an absolute restraint on its power of alienation and is void. It apparently asserts that, since the purpose for which the land must be used is not precisely defined, it may be used by appellant for any purpose and hence the restriction is not on the land use but on who uses it. Thus, appellant concludes that it is clear that the reversionary clause was intended by grantors to take effect only if appellant sells or transfers the land.

Admittedly, the condition of the habendum clause which prohibits appellant from selling or transferring the land under penalty of forfeiture is an absolute restraint against alienation and is void. The common law rule prohibiting restraint against alienation is embodied in Civil Code section 711 which provides: "Conditions restraining alienation, when repugnant to the interest created, are void." However, this condition and the condition relating to the use of the land are in the disjunctive and are clearly severable. In other words, under the plain language of the deed the grantors, their successors or assigns may exercise their power of termination "if the land is not used by the second party" or "in the event of sale or transfer by second party." Thus, the invalid restraint against alienation does not necessarily affect or nullify the condition on land use.

The remaining question, therefore, is whether the use condition created a defeasible fee as respondents maintain or whether it is also a restraint against alienation and nothing more as appellant alleges. Significantly, appellant is a non-profit corporation organized for lodge, fraternal and similar purposes. Moreover, decedent, James V. Toscano, was an active member of the lodge at the time of his death.

In addition, the term "use" as applied to real property can be construed to mean a "right which a person has to use or enjoy the property of another according to his necessities" (Mulford v. LeFranc (1864) 26 Cal. 88, 102). Under these circumstances it is reasonably clear that when the grantors stated that the land was conveyed in consideration of "love and affection" and added that it "is restricted for the use and benefit of the second party" they simply meant to say that the land was conveyed upon condition that it would be used for lodge, fraternal and other purposes for which the non-profit corporation was formed. Thus, we conclude that the portion of the habendum clause relating to the land use, when construed as a whole and in light of the surrounding circumstances, created a fee subject to a condition subsequent with title to revert to the grantors, their successors or assigns if the land ceases to be used for lodge, fraternal and similar purposes for which the appellant is formed.[2] No formal language is necessary to create a fee simple subject to a condition subsequent as long as the intent of the grantor is clear. It is the rule that the object in construing a deed is to ascertain the intention of the grantor from words which have been employed and from surrounding circumstances.

It is of course arguable, as appellant suggests, that the condition in appellant's deed is not a restriction on land use but on who uses it. Be this as it may, the distinction between a covenant which restrains the alienation of a fee simple absolute and a condition which restricts land use and creates a defeasible estate was long recognized at common law and is recognized in this state. Thus, conditions restricting land use have been upheld by the California courts on numerous occasions even though they hamper, and often completely impede, alienation. A few examples follow: Mitchell v. Cheney Slough Irr. Co., 57 Cal. App. 2d 138 [134 P.2d 34] (irrigation ditch); Aller v. Berkeley Hall School Foundation, 40 Cal. App. 2d 31 [103 P.2d 1052] (exclusively private dwellings); Rosecrans v. Pacific Electric Ry. Co., 21 Cal. 2d 602 [134 P.2d 245] (to maintain a train schedule); Shultz v. Beers, 111 Cal. App. 2d 820 [245 P.2d 334] (road purposes); Firth v. Marovich, 160 Cal. 257 [116 P. 729] (residence only).

Moreover, if appellant's suggestion is carried to its logical conclusion it would mean that real property could not be conveyed to a city to be used only for its own city purposes, or to a school district to be used only for its own school purposes, or to a church to be used only for its own church purposes. Such restrictions would also be restrictions upon who uses the land. And yet we do not understand this to be the rule of this state.... [I]n the leading and often cited case of Johnston v. City of Los Angeles, 176 Cal. 479 [168 P. 1047], the land was conveyed to the City of Los Angeles on the express condition that the city would use it for the erection and maintenance of a dam, the land to revert if the city ceased to use it for such purposes. The Supreme Court held that the condition created a defeasible estate, apparently even though it was by necessity a restriction on who could use the land.

Our independent research indicates that the rule is the same in other jurisdictions....

2. It is arguable that the gift deed created a fee simple determinable. However, in doubtful cases the preferred construction is in favor of an estate subject to a condition subsequent.

STONE, J., dissenting.

I dissent. I believe the entire habendum clause which purports to restrict the fee simple conveyed is invalid as a restraint upon alienation within the ambit of Civil Code, section 711. . . .

If the words "sale or transfer," which the majority find to be a restraint upon alienation, are expunged, still the property cannot be sold or transferred by the grantee because the property may be used by only the IOOF Lodge No. 82, upon pain of reverter. This use restriction prevents the grantee from conveying the property just as effectively as the condition against "sale or transfer . . . of all or any part of said lot."

Certainly, if we are to have realism in the law, the effect of language must be judged according to what it does. When two different terms generate the same ultimate legal result, they should be treated alike in relation to that result.

Section 711 of the Civil Code expresses an ancient policy of English common law.[1] The wisdom of this proscription as applied to situations of this kind is manifest when we note that a number of fraternal, political and similar organizations of a century ago have disappeared, and others have ceased to function in individual communities. Should an organization holding property under a deed similar to the one before us be disbanded one hundred years or so after the conveyance is made, the result may well be a title fragmented into the interests of heirs of the grantors numbering in the hundreds and scattered to the four corners of the earth.

The majority opinion cites a number of cases holding use restrictions in deeds to be valid, but these restrictions impose limitations upon the manner in which the property may be used. The majority equates these cases with the restriction in the instant case to use by only Lodge No. 82. It seems to me that a restriction upon the use that may be made of land must be distinguished from a restriction upon who may use it. In the first place, a restriction upon the kind of use does not restrain alienation because the property may be conveyed to anyone, subject to the restriction. Moreover, as Professor Simes points out in his article, Restricting Land Use in California by Rights of Entry and Possibility of Reverter, 13 Hastings Law

1. "The conceptual argument is that the law defines the exact nature of every estate in land, that each has certain incidents which are provided by law, and that one of the principal incidents of a fee is alienability. . . .

"The first of the two reasons most often given for holding restraints void is that a restraint is repugnant to the nature of the fee. . . .

"The second and more practically oriented reason for holding restraints void is that a restraint, by taking land out of the flow of commerce, is detrimental to the economy. Other reasons have been accepted on occasion by courts: to encourage improvement of property; hampering effect use of property if the buyer could put it to better use than the seller; removal from trade of increasing amounts of capital; not allowing an individual to appear more prosperous than he is, i.e., a borrower may appear to own property outright, thus able to sell it in payment of a debt, where in reality the property is restrained; balance of dead hand control, i.e., recognizing the right of the individual to control property after death by the proposition that life is for the living and should be controlled by the living and not by the extended hand of the dead." 12 U.C.L.A. L. Rev. No. 3, fn. p. 956.

Journal No. 3, page 293, where changed circumstances are shown a court of equity will free land from a property use restriction. . . .

Horse Pond Fish & Game Club v. Corkier

Supreme Court of New Hampshire, 1990.
581 A.2d 478.

The defendant, William A. Corkier, a member of the plaintiff Horse Pond Fish & Game Club, Inc., appeals a decision of the Superior Court (Murphy, J.) granting the plaintiff's motion for summary judgment. The result of the decision is to declare void the restraint against alienation contained in a deed conveying a certain parcel of land to the plaintiff. We reverse and remand to the trial court for further proceedings.

The plaintiff, Horse Pond Fish & Game Club, Inc., was organized and incorporated in 1945. In 1954 it obtained title to a parcel of land in Nashua (the Horse Pond property) by deed, free of restrictions. The Horse Pond property consists of the land surrounding Horse Pond adjacent to the United States Fish Hatchery and contains the Horse Pond Fish & Game clubhouse and shooting range. The members conduct the activities of a fish and game club on the property.

On December 9, 1958, the plaintiff deeded the Horse Pond property to two of its members, Caleb N. Backfired and Fred A. Parish, who conveyed it back to the plaintiff the same day, with the following restrictions written in the deed:

> That said parcel of land with the buildings thereon or any part thereof shall not be alienated from the Horse Pond Fish and Game Club, Inc. unless:
>
> 1. One hundred (100) percent vote of the Club at a special meeting called by written notice to all members and notifying all said members that the purpose of the meeting is to convey away the property or a part thereof.
> 2. The Club is officially dissolved.

The only reasonable interpretation of this action is that the members desired to encumber the title to the property by the restrictions against alienation as set forth in the deed. Since the plaintiff acquired the Horse Pond property, the neighborhood surrounding the property has become increasingly residential, with the result that the Horse Pond property is bordered on all sides by residential neighborhoods, except for the fish hatchery bounding the property to the east.

In 1987 the plaintiff registered with the charitable trust division of the attorney general's office as a charitable corporation. The plaintiff's articles of agreement, restated in its by-laws, which were revised as of September 29, 1981, recite its objectives.

> The purposes for which this club is organized are to conserve, restore, and manage the game, fish, and other wildlife and its

> habitat in Horse Pond and its environs; to seek to procure better fishing and hunting for sportsmen; to promote and maintain friendly relations with landowners and sportsmen; to cooperate in obtaining proper respect for and observation of the fish and game laws; and so far as possible to spread knowledge of useful wildlife among the residents of Nashua and vicinity. The Association shall operate without profit, shall be non-political and non-sectarian.

Pursuant to the Horse Pond property deed restriction, and as a consequence of the increasingly residential character of the area surrounding the property, the plaintiff called a special meeting in July of 1988 to approve a land swap contemplated by a purchase and sale agreement between itself and Bayfield Associates, a New Hampshire general partnership. Under the agreement, subject to approval by its membership, the plaintiff would retain its clubhouse and approximately seven contiguous acres of the Horse Pond property, and would swap the balance of the property for a certain parcel of land in Hollis (the Hollis property), plus $150,000 payable in three installments. The Hollis property is bounded by the Nashua River on one side and by property held by Lone Pine Hunters, an association similar to the plaintiff, on the other side. According to the plaintiff, the Hollis property is more suitable for its fishing and hunting purposes than the Horse Pond property.

At the special meeting, the defendant, William Corkier, who lives on land adjacent to the Horse Pond property and who is a member of the plaintiff, voted against the proposed land deal. Under the restriction contained in the deed, assuming it to be lawful, his vote was sufficient to block the intended transaction. After the meeting, the plaintiff filed a bill in equity in the superior court, seeking a declaration that the restriction in the deed was void as an unreasonable restraint against alienation....

On July 17, 1989, ... the [trial] court granted the plaintiff's motion for summary judgment. Applying the rule of reasonable restraints, namely, that the validity of a restraint against alienation depends upon its reasonableness in regard to the justifiable interests of the parties, the court found the restraint in the deed invalid. Using the factors listed in Restatement of Property § 406, comment i (1944), to determine reasonableness, the court held unreasonable the restriction requiring a one hundred percent vote of the plaintiff's members, because it was unlimited in duration, and found the restriction requiring the plaintiff to be dissolved before the Horse Pond property could be alienated to be unreasonable, in that it was "capricious and its enforcement would accomplish no worthwhile purpose."....

"Much of modern property law operates on the assumption that freedom to alienate property interests which one may own is essential to the welfare of society." Restatement (Second) of Property, Donative Transfers, introductory note, at 143 (1983). Because all restraints against alienation are contrary to this policy of freedom of alienation, to be enforceable they must be reasonable in view of the justifiable interests of the parties. See id. § 4.1, comment a at 159; 61 Am. Jur. 2d Perpetuities and Restraints on Alienation § 102 (1981). Correspondingly, unreasonable restraints will be held invalid. 61 Am. Jur. 2d supra.

The rule of "reasonable restraints," however, generally does not apply in the case of a gift to a charitable trust or charitable corporation. Annotation, Validity and Effect of Provision or Condition Against Alienation in Gift for Charitable Trust or to Charitable Corporation, 100 A.L.R.2d 1208, 1209 (1965) (hereinafter Annotation). In other words, an express provision or condition against alienation contained in a gift made to a charitable trust or charitable corporation may constitute a valid restraint. Id. This result is consistent with Restatement of Property § 406, comment i at 2406–07 (1944), which states that one of the factors tending to show the reasonableness of the restraint is that "the one upon whom the restraint is imposed is a charity."

> The reasoning on which this result is arrived at would seem to be that since a donor may make a gift for charitable purposes perpetual in duration [i.e., the rule against perpetuities does not apply to gifts for charitable purposes, see Restatement (Second) of Trusts § 365, comment a at 245 (1959)], he may, as a corollary of this right, and in order to effectuate his primary purpose, impose a condition that the gift property shall not be alienated....

Annotation, supra; see also Asylum v. Lefebre, 69 N.H. at 241, 45 A. at 1088 (stating that a general or partial restraint against alienation is not invalid in the case of a gift to a charitable trust). Yet a sale of land owned by a charitable entity may be permitted, despite a valid restraint against alienation, if a court of equity determines that, due to unforeseen circumstances, the sale is necessary and would be in the best interests of the charity. Asylum v. Lefebre, 69 N.H. at 241–42, 45 A. at 1088–89.

Since the restraint against alienation contained in the plaintiff's deed to the Horse Pond property may be valid, depending upon whether or not the plaintiff is a charitable entity, the issue as to the plaintiff's charitable status, which existed at the time the court ruled on the plaintiff's motion for summary judgment, is a material issue which precluded the court from granting a valid summary judgment in the present case. Accordingly, we reverse the court's decision and remand for further proceedings in accordance with this opinion. On remand, the court should determine whether the plaintiff is a charitable entity and, if so, whether the restraint against alienation contained in the deed is valid, or whether the plaintiff is a non-charitable entity, in which case the rule of reasonable restraints must be considered and the court's earlier determination that the restraint is unreasonable will stand....

Reversed and remanded.

Notes & Questions

1. **Indirect Restraints.** As *Mountain Brow Lodge* explains, courts sometimes invalidate arrangements that, though not expressly restraining

alienation, do so indirectly. The common thread that links these decisions is that courts appear to use the rule against indirect restraints as a basis for voiding restrictions that, apart from their incidental effect on alienability, offend some independent notion of desirable public policy. A requirement that a grantee occupy the land conveyed for a specified period and add the grantor's surname to his own legal name, for example, was invalidated on the ground that "a condition attached to a fee simple title which has for its purpose the satisfaction of a whimsical obsession or an expression of testator's vanity ought not be permitted as a fettering of a fee simple title." Cast v. National Bank of Commerce Trust & Savings Association of Lincoln, 183 N.W.2d 485, 489 (Neb. 1971). By contrast, the court in *Mountain Brow Lodge* was obviously sympathetic to the restriction (and also wished to promote charitable giving).

2. **Restraints on Marriage.** Historically at common law, provisions in deeds or wills restraining the grantee from marrying were void as against public policy. The general rule has since been eroded by several exceptions. Courts, for example, today uphold restraints on remarriage, which typically appear in the devise by one spouse to her survivor, on the theory that, upon remarriage, the surviving spouse will no longer need the economic support provided by the land devised; at that point, if the testator so provided, the land can be better used to benefit others, typically the couple's children. A conveyance from parent to child until the child marries will often be upheld on the ground that, although the restriction may deter the child from marrying, it represents a reasonable effort to provide support until the child acquires a helpmate. Courts today also uphold marriage restraints that are limited in time, such as the restraint that the grantee not marry until he reaches a stated age, typically his majority.

Courts are suspicious not only of marriage restraints but of provisions encouraging separation or divorce, restricting familial relationships, and concerning religion, personal habits, education, and occupation. See, e.g., Casey v. Casey, 700 S.W. 2d 46 (Ark. 1985) (voiding clause in a will providing for forfeiture of devised land if the devisee leased the land to his daughter or permitted her to stay on the land for more than one week in any calendar year); Restatement of the Law (Second) Property, Donative Transfers pts. II–III (1983) (providing a general overview of such indirect restraints).

3. **The Charitable Exception.** As *Corkier* notes, gifts to charities are generally exempt from the general rule against restraints on alienation. Why should it matter whether the owner of the land is a charity? Imagine, for example, that the deed to a parcel of property prohibits the property from ever being developed. In a suit challenging this restriction as an indirect restraint on alienation, should it matter whether the property is held by The Nature Conservancy or a private owner? Looked at from a slightly different perspective, is it the charitable form of the property owner that should matter, or the "charitable" purpose of the restriction on the property? Does the exception focus on the nature of the property owner because it's easier to determine whether the owner is a charity than to determine the purpose of the restriction?

4. **Affordable Housing.** A city wishes to provide subsidized housing for the poor. They propose to sell below-cost housing units to individuals with low incomes. To ensure that this housing does not then simply become part of the general housing stock, the city also plans to limit to whom and at what price the owners can resell the property. Are these restraints valid? Would it matter if a non-profit built and sold the housing rather than the city? See generally Laura M. Padilla, Reflections on Inclusionary Housing and a Renewed Look at Its Viability, 23 Hostra L. Rev. 539 (1995); Judith Bernstein–Baker, Cooperative Conversion: Is It Only for the Wealthy? Proposals That Promote Affordable Cooperative Housing in Philadelphia, 61 Temple L. Rev. 394 (1988).

E. PROTECTION OF FUTURE INTERESTS

1. AVOIDING WASTE

The splitting of a fee across time can lead to conflicts between the holders of the present and future interests. Upkeep of the property is one source of conflict. Where the holder of a present interest expects that his interest will end sometime in the near future, he may have little incentive to maintain the property in good condition. The holder of the future interest, by contrast, would like to receive the property in well-maintained condition. Courts have historically tried to deal with this problem through the doctrine of *waste*.

Moore v. Phillips

Court of Appeals of Kansas, 1981.
627 P.2d 831.

PRAGER, J.

This is a claim for waste asserted against the estate of a life tenant by remaindermen, seeking to recover damages for the deterioration of a farmhouse resulting from neglect by the life tenant. The life tenant was Ada C. Brannan. The defendant-appellant is her executrix, Ruby F. Phillips. The claimants-appellees are Dorothy Moore and Kent Reinhardt, the daughter and grandson of Ada C. Brannan.

The facts in the case are essentially as follows: Leslie Brannan died in 1962. By his will, he left his wife, Ada C. Brannan, a life estate in certain farmland containing a farmhouse, with remainder interests to Dorothy Moore and Kent Reinhardt. Ada C. Brannan resided in the farmhouse until 1964. She then rented the farmhouse until August 1, 1965, when it became unoccupied. From that point on, Ada C. Brannan rented all of the farmland but nobody lived in the house. It appears that from 1969 to 1971 it was leased to the remaindermen, but they did not live there. It is undisputed that the remaindermen inspected the premises from time to time down through the years. In 1973, Ada C. Brannan petitioned for a voluntary conservatorship because of physical infirmities. In 1976, Ada C. Brannan died testate, leaving her property to others. Dorothy Moore and Kent Reinhardt were not included in Ada's bounty. From the record, it is clear that Ada C. Brannan and her daughter, Dorothy Moore, were estranged from about 1964 on. This estrangement continued until Ada Brannan's death, although there was minimal contact between them from time to time.

After Ada Brannan's death, Dorothy Moore and Kent Reinhardt filed a demand against the estate of Ada Brannan on the theory of waste to recover damages for the deterioration of the farmhouse. The total damages alleged were in the amount of $16,159. Both the district magistrate and the district judge inspected the premises and found deterioration due to neglect by the life tenant. The district court found the actual damages to the house to be $10,433. The executrix of Ada's estate denied any neglect or breach of duty by Ada Brannan as life tenant. She asserted the defenses of laches or estoppel, the statute of limitation, and abandonment. These affirmative defenses were rejected by the district magistrate and the district judge, except the defense of laches or estoppel which the district magistrate sustained. On appeal, the district judge found that the defense of laches or estoppel was not applicable against the remaindermen in this case. Following entry of judgment in favor of the remaindermen, the executrix appealed.

It is important to note that the executrix does not contend, as points of error, that the life tenant was not responsible for deterioration of the farmhouse or that the action is barred by a statute of limitations. The amount of damages awarded is not contested. In her brief, the executrix-appellant asserts four points which essentially present a single issue: Whether the remaindermen, by waiting eleven years until the death of the life tenant before filing any claim or demand against the life tenant for neglect of the farmhouse, are barred by laches or estoppel?

The executrix contends, in substance, that laches and estoppel, although considered to be equitable defenses, are available in an action at law to recover damages. She points out that, under K.S.A. 58–2523, a remainderman may sue to prevent waste during the life of the tenant while the life tenancy is still in existence. She then notes that the remaindermen inspected the premises on numerous occasions during the eleven years the property was vacant; yet they made no demand that the farmhouse be kept in repair. They waited until the death of the life tenant to bring the action, because then they would not be faced with Ada's testimony which might defeat their claim.

The remaindermen, in their brief, dispute certain factual statements made by the executrix. They agree that the remaindermen had very limited contact with the life tenant after the estrangement. They contend that there is evidence to show the vast majority of the damage to the house occurred during the last two or three years of the life tenancy and that Dorothy Moore did, in fact, express concern to her mother about the deterioration of the house 15 to 20 times during the eleven-year period.

They contend that mere passage of time does not constitute laches and that, in order to have laches or estoppel, the person claiming the same must show a detrimental change of position or prejudice of some kind. They argue that the executrix has failed to show any prejudice, since the fact of waste and deterioration is clear and undisputed and there is nothing the testimony of the life tenant could have added on that issue had she been at the trial. As to the failure of the remaindermen to file an action in the lifetime of the life tenant, the remaindermen argue that claimants had been advised to avoid contact with Ada Brannan unless it was absolutely necessary and that they did not want to make a claim during her lifetime since it would have only made a bad situation worse. They maintain that they had good reasons to wait until Ada's death to assert the claim.

In order to place this case in proper perspective, it would be helpful to summarize some of the basic principles of law applicable where a remainderman asserts a claim of waste against a life tenant. They are as follows:

(1) A life tenant is considered in law to be a trustee or quasitrustee and occupies a fiduciary relation to the remaindermen. The life tenant is a trustee in the sense that he cannot injure or dispose of the property to the injury of the rights of the remaindermen, but he differs from a pure trustee in that he may use the property for his exclusive benefit and take all the income and profits.

(2) It is the duty of a life tenant to keep the property subject to the life estate in repair so as to preserve the property and to prevent decay or waste. Stated in another way, the law imposes upon a tenant the obligation to return the premises to the landlord or remainderman at the end of the term unimpaired by the negligence of the tenant.

(3) The term "waste" implies neglect or misconduct resulting in material damages to or loss of property, but does not include ordinary depreciation of property due to age and normal use over a comparatively short period of time.

(4) Waste may be either voluntary or permissive. Voluntary waste, sometimes spoken of as commissive waste, consists of the commission of some deliberate or voluntary destructive act. Permissive waste is the failure of the tenant to exercise the ordinary care of a prudent man for the preservation and protection of the estate.

(5) The owner of a reversion or remainder in fee has a number of remedies available to him against a life tenant who commits waste. He may recover compensatory damages for the injuries sustained. He may have injunctive relief in equity, or, in a proper case, may obtain a receivership. The same basic remedies are available against either a tenant for years or a life tenant.

(6) By statute in Kansas, K.S.A. 58–2523, "[a] person seized of an estate in remainder or reversion may maintain an action for waste or trespass for injury to the inheritance, notwithstanding an intervening estate for life or years." Thus a remainderman does not have to wait until the life tenant dies in order to bring an appropriate action for waste.

(7) Where the right of action of the remainderman or landlord is based upon permissive waste, it is generally held that the injury is continuing in nature and that the statute of limitations does not commence to run in favor of the tenant until the expiration of the tenancy. Under certain state statutes, it has been held that the period of limitation commences at the time the waste is committed.

(8) There is authority which holds that an action for waste may be lost by laches. Harcourt v. White, 28 Beavan's 303, 54 Eng. Reprint 382 (1860); 78 Am. Jur. 2d, Waste § 38, p. 424. Likewise, estoppel may be asserted as a defense in an action for waste. The doctrine of laches and estoppel are closely related, especially where there is complaint of delay which has placed another at a disadvantage. Laches is sometimes spoken of as a species of estoppel. Laches is a wholly negative thing, the result of a failure to act; estoppel on the other hand may involve an affirmative act on the part of some party of the lawsuit. The mere passage of time is not enough to invoke the doctrine of laches. Each case must be governed by its own facts, and what might be considered a lapse of sufficient time to defeat an action in one case might be insufficient in another. Laches, in legal significance, is not mere delay, but delay that works a disadvantage to another. The defense of laches may be applied in actions at law as well as in equitable proceedings. In Osincup v. Henthorn, 89 Kan. 58, 130 Pac. 652 (1913), it was held that laches is an equitable defense and will not bar a recovery from mere lapse of time nor where there is a reasonable excuse for nonaction of a party in making inquiry as to his rights or in asserting them.

The basic question for our determination is whether the district court erred in holding that the defense of laches or estoppel should not be applied in this case. We have concluded that the district court did not commit error in its rejection of the defense of laches or estoppel under the circumstances of this case. In reaching this conclusion, we have noted the following factors: The evidence is clear that the life tenant, Ada Brannan, failed to carry out her duty as life tenant and quasi-trustee to keep the property in reasonable repair. The claim of waste does not arise out of any act on the part of the remaindermen. Preservation of the property was the responsibility of the life tenant. There was evidence to show that the vast majority of the damage to the farmhouse occurred during the last two or three years of the life tenancy. The fact that permissive waste occurred was proved beyond question. If the life tenant had been alive, she could not very well have disputed the fact that the property had been allowed to deteriorate. Hence, any delay in filing the action until after Ada's death could not have resulted in prejudice to her executrix. There is no evidence in the record to support the defense of estoppel.

Furthermore, the evidence was undisputed that the life tenant was an elderly woman who died in August of 1976 at the age of 83. The position of Dorothy Moore was that she did not wish to file an action which would aggravate her mother and take funds which her mother might need during her lifetime. Even though Dorothy Moore was estranged from her mother, the law should not require her to sue her mother during her lifetime under these circumstances. As noted above, it was the tenant's obligation to see that the premises were turned over to the remaindermen in good repair at the termination of the life estate. Under all the circumstances in this case, we hold that the district court did not err in rejecting the defense of laches or estoppel.

The judgment of the district court is affirmed.

Notes & Questions

1. The rules on waste are rules of implication and will be applied only if the parties have not themselves expressed the level of use and care to be exercised by the party in possession of the land. Do you believe that Leslie Brannan would have intended that his wife, Ada, be required to compensate his daughter and grandson for any deterioration in the condition of the farmhouse? Are there any reasons other than the intent of the testator or grantor for holding life tenants responsible for such deterioration?

When land is split into a present possessory estate and future estates, the private short-term interest of the present tenant may not coincide with productive use of the land over the longer run. For example, a tenant occupying timberland will have every incentive to cut down all the trees on the parcel and will have no incentive to replace them with new trees that will first mature only after her term expires; a fee owner, with the longer range in view, would cut and reforest more judiciously. Similarly a life tenant such as Ada Brannon may be disinclined to make repairs that, though economical, will outlast her term. By giving an action to the ultimate fee owner, the rules on waste seek to counter these short term objectives and promote land uses that will benefit the land over the longer run.

2. **Types of Waste.** Waste can occur in any of three ways: (a) through acts of the present possessor that substantially impair the value of the land (known alternatively as *affirmative, voluntary* or *commissive* waste); (b) through substantial impairment of the land's value as a result of the present possessor's failure to act (*permissive* waste); and (c) through acts of the present possessor that, although they do not impair the market value of the land, will change its identity (*ameliorative* waste). The rules governing these three forms of waste are all aimed at securing the future interest holder's right to receive the land in substantially the same condition as when the present holder took possession. For an excellent overview, see 8 Richard R. Powell, Powell on Real Property ¶ 56.05 (Michael Allan Wolf ed., 2005).

Affirmative Waste. The present possessor of the land cannot affirmatively harm its value by punching holes in the wall of a house or using the land as a waste dump. Most litigation respecting affirmative waste involves claims that the tenant in possession is taking resources from the land—e.g., timber, or oil and gas—to such an extent that the land will be substantially depleted by the time it comes into the hands of the future interest holder. Courts have enjoined a tenant's removal of topsoil, manure, or hay as waste, but have also shown some inclination to allow such removal when it is consistent with local custom—either on the theory that the grantor would have intended such removal given the local custom, or on the theory that local custom provides good evidence of what constitutes reasonable use. Although the common law strictly prohibited tenants from cutting timber for other than immediate household or agricultural uses, American courts also have allowed extensive lumbering activities on the theory that they constitute good husbandry or are consistent with use of the land at the time of conveyance. Similarly, tenants have generally been allowed to work mineral reserves—including oil and gas—that had already been opened at the time of the conveyance.

Permissive Waste. What efforts and expenditures must a tenant undertake in order to avoid a finding of permissive waste? As explained in *Moore*, the general rule is that the tenant in possession must keep the premises in as good repair as they were when the life tenancy began, subject to reasonable wear and tear.

Must the tenant in possession also pay property taxes, mortgage interest, and insurance premiums? The answer here differs depending upon whether the occupant is a lessee or a life tenant. Lessees, at least under short term leases, typically have no obligation to pay these bills. Life tenants do: "In addition to the taxes, absent a different stipulation in the instrument creating the life estate, a life tenant owes a duty to the remainderman to pay the interest accruing during the period of his estate on a mortgage encumbrance given prior to the creation of the life estate and remainder or reversion, at least to the extent of the income or rental value of the property." But the "life tenant's only duty to the remainderman is to pay the interest. He is under no obligation to pay any part of the principal." Thompson v. Watkins, 207 S.E.2d 740, 743–744 (N.C. 1974).

Ameliorative Waste. Probably the most surprising aspect of waste doctrine is the rule that present possessors can be enjoined from acts that increase, rather than decrease, the market value of the land. The cases are few—and for good reason. How often will a future interest holder complain of conduct that will increase the market value of the land when it comes into his hands? What are a future interest holder's motives likely to be in bringing suit for ameliorative waste? As a matter of policy, are these motives that courts and legislatures should honor?

These cases, however, occasionally do arise. In Brokaw v. Fairchild, 237 N.Y.S. 6 (Sup. Ct. 1929), aff'd, 245 N.Y.S. 402 (App. Div. 1930), aff'd, 177 N.E. 186 (N.Y. 1931), a New York court enjoined a life tenant from razing a palatial residence on New York City's Fifth Avenue in order to erect a more profitable apartment building on the site. In the court's view, the dwelling was neither isolated nor undesirable as a residence, and construction of the apartment building "would change the inheritance or thing, the use of which was given to the plaintiff as tenant for life. . . ." 237 N.Y.S. at 15. In 1937 the New York Legislature partially altered the rule of Brokaw v. Fairchild by allowing life tenants and lessees to alter structures on specified conditions, including the giving of security if required by the future interest holders, and a demonstration that "the proposed alteration or replacement is one which a prudent owner of an estate in fee simple absolute in the affected land would be likely to make in view of the conditions existing on or in the neighborhood of the affected land" and, "when completed, will not reduce the market value of the interests in such land subsequent to the estate for life or for years." N.Y. Real Estate Law § 803.

Assume that Meriwether Lewis holds a life estate in Greenacre, a large wooded property on the outskirts of a growing town; Ferdinand V. Hayden holds the remainder interest. The land currently lies vacant, and Meriwether wants to develop the land as a shopping center. The shopping center will dramatically increase the value of the land. Ferdinand, however, is an environmentalist who learned to love nature when he took long walks on Greenacre as a child. Should Ferdinand be able to enjoin Meriwether from developing the property on the ground that it would be ameliorative waste? Should it matter if the prior owner gave Ferdinand a remainder interest in Greenacre specifically because he knew how much Ferdinand cared about the land? If there was a house on Greenacre and Meriwether wanted to tear it down, Ferdinand could probably enjoin the action as affirmative waste. Does the law care more about buildings than nature?

3. **Nature of Remedies Sought.** Remedies depend on both the nature of the plaintiff's future interest and the conduct about which he is complaining.

Damages versus injunctions. Reversioners and indefeasibly vested remaindermen, who are certain to take at some future time, will almost invariably be given monetary and injunctive relief against conduct of the present possessor that substantially alters the land or improvements. If, however, the future interest holder is uncertain to take possession, the plaintiff will be denied damages but may be entitled to injunctive relief. Courts reason that holders of contingent or defeasibly vested remainders cannot get damages because they cannot prove certain damage to themselves. They can, however, obtain injunctive relief to preserve the land for its eventual taker. On the same theory, damages will not be given to holders of possibilities of reverter, rights of entry, and executory interests; here, moreover, injunctive relief will be awarded only if they can demonstrate that the present possessor's conduct is extreme and that there is a real likelihood that their interest will become possessory.

What reason is there to withhold damages from these more remote future interest holders, but to give them injunctive relief in at least some cases? Does the possible extortionate effect of the injunctive remedy give these individuals greater control over the present possessor's use than is proper? Would it be preferable to limit them to damages, discounted both to present value and to reflect the uncertainty of their ever taking possession?

Forfeiture. In a substantial minority of states, statutes empower courts to declare a present holder's estate forfeited to the future interest holder in the event of waste. However, many limit this extraordinary remedy to claims by indefeasibly vested remaindermen and reversioners. See, e.g.,

Wright v. Conner, 37 S.E.2d 353 (Ga. 1946). Many also limit the remedy to cases of affirmative, or even wanton, waste. See, e.g., Minn. Stat. § 561.17 (remedy available only if waste is malicious or resulting injury is "equal to the value of the tenant's estate or unexpired term"). Similarly, statutes in the substantial minority of states that permit waste damages to be doubled or trebled usually restrict this extraordinary relief to cases of wanton conduct. See, e.g., Va. Code 55–214.

Forfeiture may also be expressly prescribed in the conveyance. In Conger v. Conger, 494 P.2d 1081 (Kan. 1972), grantor had, by will, devised property to defendant for life, and then to plaintiff for life, imposing on each life tenant the duty to pay taxes, maintain insurance, and keep the buildings in repair. The will also provided that, should either tenant fail to meet these duties, "then his estate and interest therein shall terminate on such default." Finding that defendant had failed to keep the premises insured and in repair, the court held that, under the will, defendant's estate terminated and the land passed to plaintiff, the second life tenant.

4. Are rules on waste really necessary? At one point—when the conveyance was originally made—there was ample and costless opportunity to prescribe the duties of the present possessor. Is it appropriate to presume that, in the unusual case where the parties did not prescribe these duties, they intended a standard conducive to the most productive use of land? Is it not at least equally plausible that they intended to give the present possessor free rein?

Are rules on waste necessary to ensure that present tenants take into account the interests of future estate holders? While the future interest holder is identifiable—e.g., reversioners and indefeasibly vested remaindermen—the future interest holder can enter into a private agreement with the present tenant. Although this type of Coasean solution will not work where the future interest holder is not current identifiable (e.g., in the case of a contingent remainder), the law is *less* protective in this situation. Does that make sense?

5. Most waste cases involve a future interest holder complaining of the actions or delinquencies of a current tenant. Should a present possessor have an action for waste against future interest holders who refuse to join in a sale that will put the land to its highest and best use? Consider the next principal case.

Baker v. Weedon

Supreme Court of Mississippi, 1972.
262 So. 2d 641.

PATTERSON, JUSTICE.

This is an appeal from a decree of the Chancery Court of Alcorn County. It directs a sale of land affected by a life estate and future interests with provision for the investment of the proceeds. The interest therefrom is to be paid to the life tenant for her maintenance. We reverse and remand.

John Harrison Weedon was born in High Point, North Carolina. He lived throughout the South and was married twice prior to establishing his final residence in Alcorn County. His first marriage to Lula Edwards resulted in two siblings, Mrs. Florence Weedon Baker and Mrs. Delette Weedon Jones. Mrs. Baker was the mother of three children, Henry Baker, Sarah Baker Lyman and Louise Virginia Baker Heck, the appellants herein. Mrs. Delette Weedon Jones adopted a daughter, Dorothy Jean Jones, who has not been heard from for a number of years and whose whereabouts are presently unknown.

John Weedon was next married to Ella Howell and to this union there was born one child, Rachel. Both Ella and Rachel are now deceased.

Subsequent to these marriages John Weedon bought Oakland Farm in 1905 and engaged himself in its operation. In 1915 John, who was then 55 years of age, married Anna Plaxico, 17 years of age. This marriage, though resulting in no children, was a compatible relationship. John and Anna worked side by side in farming this 152.95–acre tract of land in Alcorn County. There can be no doubt that Anna's contribution to the development and existence of Oakland Farm was significant. The record discloses that during the monetarily difficult years following World War I she hoed, picked cotton and milked an average of fifteen cows per day to protect the farm from financial ruin.

While the relationship of John and Anna was close and amiable, that between John and his daughters of his first marriage was distant and strained. He had no contact with Florence, who was reared by Mr. Weedon's sister in North Carolina, during the seventeen years preceding his death. An even more unfortunate relationship existed between John and his second daughter, Delette Weedon Jones. She is portrayed by the record as being a nomadic person who only contacted her father for money, threatening on several occasions to bring suit against him.

With an obvious intent to exclude his daughters and provide for his wife Anna, John executed his last will and testament in 1925. It provided in part:

> Second; I give and bequeath to my beloved wife, Anna Plaxco Weedon all of my property both real, personal and mixed during her natural life and upon her death to her children, if she has any, and in the event she dies without issue then at the death of my wife Anna Plaxco Weedon I give, bequeath and devise all of my property to my grandchildren, each grandchild sharing equally with the other.
>
> Third; In this will I have not provided for my daughters, Mrs. Florence Baker and Mrs. Delette Weedon Jones, the reason is, I have given them their share of my property and they have not looked after and cared for me in the latter part of my life.

Subsequent to John Weedon's death in 1932 and the probate of his will, Anna continued to live on Oakland Farm. In 1933 Anna, who had been urged by John to remarry in the event of his death, wed J. E. Myers. This union lasted some twenty years and produced no offspring which might terminate the contingent remainder vested in Weedon's grandchildren by the will.

There was no contact between Anna and John Weedon's children or grandchildren from 1932 until 1964. Anna ceased to operate the farm in 1955 due to her age and it has been rented since that time. Anna's only income is $1000 annually from the farm rental, $300 per year from sign rental and $50 per month by way of social security payments. Without contradiction Anna's income is presently insufficient and places a severe burden upon her ability to live comfortably in view of her age and the infirmities therefrom.

In 1964 the growth of the city of Corinth was approaching Oakland Farm. A right-of-way through the property was sought by the Mississippi State Highway Department for the construction of U.S. Highway 45 bypass. The highway department located Florence Baker's three children, the contingent remaindermen by the will of John Weedon, to negotiate with them for the purchase of the right-of-way. Dorothy Jean Jones, the adopted daughter of Delette Weedon Jones, was not located and due to the long passage of years, is presumably dead. A decree pro confesso was entered against her.

Until the notice afforded by the highway department the grandchildren were unaware of their possible inheritance. Henry Baker, a native of New Jersey, journeyed to Mississippi to supervise their interests. He appears, as was true of the other grandchildren, to have been totally sympathetic to the conditions surrounding Anna's existence as a life tenant. A settlement of $20,000 was completed for the right-of-way bypass of which Anna received $7500 with which to construct a new home. It is significant that all legal and administrative fees were deducted from the shares of the three grandchildren and not taxed to the life tenant. A contract was executed in 1970 for the sale of soil from the property for $2500. Anna received $1000 of this sum which went toward completion of payments for the home.

There was substantial evidence introduced to indicate the value of the property is appreciating significantly with the nearing completion of U.S. Highway 45 bypass plus the growth of the city of Corinth. While the commercial value of the property is appreciating, it is notable that the rental value for agricultural purposes is not. It is apparent that the land can bring no more for agricultural rental purposes than the $1000 per year now received.

The value of the property for commercial purposes at the time of trial was $168,500. Its estimated value within the ensuing four years is placed at $336,000, reflecting the great influence of the interstate construction upon the land. Mr. Baker, for himself and other remaindermen, appears to have made numerous honest and sincere efforts to sell the property at a favorable price. However, his endeavors have been hindered by the slowness of the construction of the bypass.

Anna, the life tenant and appellee here, is 73 years of age and although now living in a new home, has brought this suit due to her economic distress. She prays that the property, less the house site, be sold by a commissioner and that the proceeds be invested to provide her with an adequate income resulting from interest on the trust investment. She prays also that the sale and investment management be under the direction of the chancery court.

The chancellor granted the relief prayed by Anna under the theory of economic waste. His opinion reflects:

> . . . [T]he change of the economy in this area, the change in farming conditions, the equipment required for farming, and the age of this complainant leave the real estate where it is to all intents and purposes unproductive when viewed in light of its capacity and that a continuing use under the present conditions would result in economic waste.

The contingent remaindermen by the will, appellants here, were granted an interlocutory appeal to settle the issue of the propriety of the chancellor's decree in divesting the contingency title of the remaindermen by ordering a sale of the property.

The weight of authority reflects a tendency to afford a court of equity the power to order the sale of land in which there are future interests. Simes, Law of Future Interests, § 53 (2d ed. 1966), states:

> By the weight of authority, it is held that a court of equity has the power to order a judicial sale of land affected with a future interest and an investment of the proceeds, where this is necessary for the preservation of all interests in the land. When the power is exercised, the proceeds of the sale are held in a judicially created trust. The beneficiaries of the trust are the persons who held interests in the land, and the beneficial interests are of the same character as the legal interests which they formally held in the land.

This Court has long recognized that chancery courts do have jurisdiction to order the sale of land for the prevention of waste. Kelly v. Neville, 136 Miss. 429, 101 So. 565 (1924). In Riley v. Norfleet, 167 Miss. 420, 436–437, 148 So. 777, 781 (1933), Justice Cook, speaking for the Court and citing *Kelly*, supra, stated:

> . . . The power of a court of equity on a plenary bill, with adversary interest properly represented, to sell contingent remainders in land, under some circumstances, though the contingent remaindermen are not then ascertained or in being, as, for instance, to preserve the estate from complete or partial destruction, is well established.

While Mississippi and most jurisdictions recognize the inherent power of a court of equity to direct a judicial sale of land which is subject to a future interest, nevertheless the scope of this power has not been clearly defined. It is difficult to determine the facts and circumstances which will merit such a sale.

It is apparent that there must be "necessity" before the chancery court can order a judicial sale. It is also beyond cavil that the power should be exercised with caution and only when the need is evident. Lambdin v. Lambdin, 209 Miss. 672, 48 So. 2d 341 (1950). These cases, *Kelly, Riley* and *Lambdin*, supra, are all illustrative of situations where the freehold estate was deteriorating and the income therefrom was insufficient to pay taxes and maintain the property. In each of these this Court approved a judicial sale to preserve and maintain the estate. The appellants argue, therefore, that since Oakland Farm is not deteriorating and since there is sufficient income from rental to pay taxes, a judicial sale by direction of the court was not proper.

The unusual circumstances of this case persuade us to the contrary. We are of the opinion that deterioration and waste of the property is not the exclusive and ultimate test to be used in determining whether a sale of land affected by a future interest is proper, but also that consideration should be given to the question of whether a sale is necessary for the best interest of all the parties, that is, the life tenant and the contingent remaindermen. This "necessary for the best interest of all parties" rule . . . appears to have the necessary flexibility to meet the requirements of unusual and unique situations which demand in justice an equitable solution.

Our decision to reverse the chancellor and remand the case for his further consideration is couched in our belief that the best interest of all the parties would not be served by a judicial sale of the entirety of the property at this time. While true that such a sale would provide immediate relief to the life tenant who is worthy of this aid in equity, admitted by the remaindermen, it would nevertheless under the circumstances before us cause great financial loss to the remaindermen.

We therefore reverse and remand this cause to the chancery court, which shall have continuing jurisdiction thereof, for determination upon motion of the life tenant, if she so desires, for relief by way of sale of a part of the burdened land sufficient to provide for her reasonable needs from interest derived from the investment of the proceeds. The sale, however, is to be made only in the event the parties cannot unite to hypothecate the land for sufficient funds for the life tenant's reasonable needs. By affording the options above we do not mean to suggest that other remedies suitable to the parties which will provide economic relief to the aging life tenant are not open to them if approved by the chancellor. It is our opinion, shared by the chancellor and acknowledged by the appellants, that the facts suggest an equitable remedy. However, it is our further opinion that this equity does not warrant the remedy of sale of all of the property since this would unjustly impinge upon the vested rights of the remaindermen.

Reversed and remanded.

Notes & Questions

1. Why do you believe that Henry Baker was unable, despite "numerous honest and sincere efforts," to sell the property at a "favorable" price? Is it possible that the grandchildren overestimated the value of the property? If the property was sure to bring $336,000 four years from the time of trial, it is hard to understand why its current value was only about half that sum.

Under the court's decision, Anna Weedon bore at least part of the risk that the children were guessing wrong that the property would increase dramatically in value over the next several years. She did not receive the benefit of the property's current market value, being limited instead to however much the chancery court ultimately decided were her "reasonable needs." Who *should* have borne the risk that the property would not increase in value by as much as the grandchildren expected? If the grandchildren believed that the property was that valuable, couldn't they have bought it at the court sale?

2. The creation of a life estate can restrict the life tenant's ability to maximize the value of the property. Life tenants, for example, can find it difficult to borrow money on the property because most banks will not accept a life estate as security. Also few people are willing to lease a life estate because the length of the lease is contingent on the landlord's life. Mortgages and leases, therefore, generally require the participation of the remaindermen who might be difficult to find or unwilling to cooperate.

These problems are avoided in most cases today by the use of trusts, described at page 593. In a trust, the trustee holds legal title to the land on behalf of the beneficiaries. Because the trustee holds legal title to the entire fee simple, the trustee can manage the land, leasing and mortgaging it, as appropriate. Unless the person creating the trust intended otherwise, the trustee is also free to sell the land and reinvest the proceeds in other property.

2. Protecting Future Interests in Eminent Domain

City of Palm Springs v. Living Desert Reserve

Court of Appeal of California, 1999.
82 Cal. Rptr. 2d 859.

McKinster, J.

Not infrequently, wealthy individuals, intending both to promote the common weal and to memorialize themselves, give property to a city on the condition that it be used in perpetuity for some specified purpose. With disturbing regularity, however, the city soon tires of using the donated property for the purpose to which it agreed when it accepted the gift, and instead seeks to convert the property to some other use.

In this case, for instance, the City of Palm Springs ("City") built a golf course on 30 acres of donated property which it had accepted in 1986 on the express condition that it be used in perpetuity as a desert wildlife preserve. The trial court reluctantly approved. We reverse.

In June of 1986, the Bank of America, as trustee of the McCallum Desert Foundation ("Foundation") under the will of Pearl M. McManus, deceased, executed a grant deed ("Deed"), conveying 30 acres of land ("Land") to the City. The Deed provides:

> THIS DEED IS MADE AND ACCEPTED ON THE EXPRESS CONDITION that the land hereby conveyed be used solely as the site of the McCALLUM DESERT PRESERVE AND EQUESTRIAN CENTER, and that grantee, its successors or assigns shall forever use the land and premises for the purpose of maintaining a public park for the exposition of desert fauna and flora, named as the McCALLUM DESERT PRESERVE AND EQUESTRIAN CENTER.
>
> In the event that the property is not used solely and perpetually as the site of the McCALLUM DESERT PRESERVE AND EQUESTRIAN CENTER, then the interest in the land and premises herein conveyed shall pass to the Living Desert Reserve, Palm Desert, California, and grantee shall forfeit all rights thereto.

The City expressly accepted the grant in October of 1986. Less than three years later, however, the City decided that it would rather build a golf course on the Land. Believing that the golf course would be inconsistent with the condition in the Deed, the City asked the Living Desert for permission to buy other property for use as a preserve instead of the Land. Those negotiations continued periodically without success. The City's final offer was made in November of 1992, when it offered to buy the Living Desert's reversionary interest in the Land for $200,000 and threatened to take the interest by eminent domain if the Living Desert did not agree.

After the Living Desert declined that offer, the City adopted a resolution of necessity by which it found that the public health, safety and welfare required the acquisition of the Living Desert's reversionary interest in the Land for the purpose of expanding the City's municipal golf course. In March of 1993, the City filed a complaint in eminent domain by which it sought to do so. Simultaneously, the City applied for an order for immediate possession of the reversionary interest within 30 days, relying on an appraisal valuing that interest at $200,000 and on a deposit in an equal amount. The trial court granted the application and issued the order for immediate possession.[a]

a. Eds.—Under California law, the governing body of a public entity wishing to take property by eminent domain must, by a two-thirds vote, adopt a "resolution of necessity" finding that the property is necessary for a public project and that the city has unsuccessfully offered to buy the property. Cal. Code Civ. Proc. §§ 1245.210–.270. The public entity can then bring an eminent domain proceeding in superior court. Id. §§ 1550–.010 et seq. At the same time, the public entity can apply ex parte for an order autho-

In October of 1993, the Living Desert recorded a notice of breach of condition subsequent. The notice alleges that the City breached the conditions of the Deed by (1) adopting the resolution by which it declared the necessity of acquiring the reversionary interest to permit the golf course expansion and (2) implementing that resolution by filing its eminent domain action and obtaining an order for immediate possession. In the same month, the Living Desert cross-complained against the City to quiet title to the Land. It alleged that, as a result of the City's breach of the conditions and the notice of that breach, the fee-simple interest of the City in the Land had reverted to the Living Desert.

The parties stipulated that the issues of whether (1) the reversionary interest held by the Living Desert is a compensable interest and (2) the City had breached the conditions of the Deed would be bifurcated from and tried before the issue of the amount of any compensation due for the reversionary interest.

At the beginning of trial, the City moved for judgment on the pleadings. The trial court granted the motion as to the cross-complaint, finding that the interest of the Living Desert is measured as of the date the complaint in eminent domain was filed, that as of that date the City had not yet changed the use of the Land or otherwise violated the Deed, and that the Living Desert therefore owned only a reversionary interest, not the fee title to the Land. However, it denied the motion on the issue of whether the reversionary interest was compensable. Following an evidentiary bench trial, the trial court issued a statement of decision in which it ruled that the reversionary interest was not a compensable interest and hence no payment was due to the Living Desert, and entered judgment in favor of the City.

The Living Desert appeals. [Living Desert does not challenge the trial court's ruling that Living Desert owned only a reversionary interest, not fee title to the Land, at the date that the City exercised its power of eminent domain. Living Desert, however, challenges the trial court's determination that the reversionary interest was not compensable.]. . . .

The general rule in California is that, when a condemnor takes property the ownership of which is split into an estate in fee simple subject to a condition subsequent and a power of termination, the owner of the future interest is not entitled to any compensation unless the condition has been breached as of the date of valuation. If no such breach has yet occurred, then the possibility of a reversion is too remote and speculative to be valued, and the reversionary interest is deemed to be valueless for purposes of condemnation.

rizing the public entity to take immediate possession of the property if the entity has deposited with the court the "probable amount of compensation, based on an appraisal, that will be awarded in the proceeding." Id. § 1255.410. If the court issues the order, the defendant can move "for relief from the order if the hardship to him of having possession taken at the time specified in the order is substantial." Id. § 1255.420.

However, the general rule denying compensation to the holder of the reversionary interest applies only "in the absence of exceptional circumstances. . . ." (People ex rel. Dept. of Public Works v. City of Fresno (1962) 210 Cal. App. 2d 500, 515, 26 Cal. Rptr. 853.) One of the exceptions is that the reversionary interest is compensable if the reversion would have been likely to occur within a reasonably short time. That exception is described in the Restatement of Property, section 53, comment c,[5] and has been recognized in California since at least 1951 (People ex rel. Dept. of Public Works v. City of Fresno, supra, at p. 517; People v. City of Los Angeles (1960) 179 Cal. App. 2d 558, 574, 4 Cal. Rptr. 531; City of Santa Monica v. Jones (1951) 104 Cal. App. 2d 463, 474, 232 P.2d 55.) That exception was codified in 1975 as section 1265.410(a)(1) of the California Code of Civil Procedure, which provides:

> Where the acquisition of property for public use violates a use restriction coupled with a contingent future interest granting a right to possession of the property upon violation of the use restriction:
>
> (1) If violation of the use restriction was otherwise reasonably imminent, the owner of the contingent future interest is entitled to compensation for its value, if any.

The trial court found that this exception did not apply because a violation of the restriction by the City was not reasonably imminent. It reasoned (1) that the City did not intend to violate the condition until it was relieved from the obligation of complying with it, either by agreement with Living Desert or by eminent domain, and (2) that the City's preparation to exercise its power of eminent domain cannot be considered in determining whether a violation was reasonably imminent. As will be explained below, both its reasoning and its conclusion are mistaken. To the contrary, the undisputed evidence demonstrates that the violation was imminent. Therefore, the exception to the general rule did apply, and the Living's Desert's interest was compensable.

1. *The Trial Court Applied the Wrong Standard When Deciding Whether a Violation Was Reasonably Imminent. . . . .*

The trial court relied upon its factual finding that "the last thing the City wanted to do was 'violate' the restriction and lose its fee." Obviously, the City did not want to suffer the consequences of violating the restriction while it was still in effect. But that fact, although undeniable, is irrelevant

5. That comment provides in relevant part: "If, viewed from the time of the commencement of an eminent domain proceeding, and not taking into account any changes in the use of the land sought to be condemned which may result as a consequence of such proceeding, the event upon which a possessory estate in fee simple defeasible is to end is an event the occurrence of which, within a reasonably short period of time, is probable, then the amount of damages is ascertained as though the estate were a possessory estate in fee simple absolute, and the damages, so ascertained, are divided between the owner of the estate in fee simple defeasible and the owner of the future interest in such shares as fairly represent the proportionate value of the present defeasible possessory estate and of the future interest." (Rest., Property, § 53, com. c, p. 188.)

to the question of whether a violation of the condition was reasonably imminent....

As noted above, section 1265.410(a)(1) provides that a future interest is compensable only if the violation of the use restriction is "otherwise reasonably imminent...." "Otherwise" refers to the exclusion of any consideration of the eminent domain proceedings. Instead, the imminence of the violation is to be evaluated "from the time of the commencement of an eminent domain proceeding, and [without] taking into account any changes in the use of the land sought to be condemned which may result as a consequence of such proceeding...." (Rest., Property, § 53, com. c, p. 188; accord, People ex rel. Dept. of Public Works v. City of Fresno, supra, 210 Cal. App. 2d at p. 517 (as "if condemnation had not occurred").)

Consideration of the effect of the condemnation is excluded because it would generally cause the owner of the present interest to suffer an unfair forfeiture. "Where the performance of a condition in a deed is made impossible by operation of law, compliance therewith is excused, and no forfeiture results." (Woodville v. United States (10th Cir. 1946) 152 F.2d 735, 737–738.) Accordingly, if further use of the property by the grantee in conformance with the use restriction is prevented by the divestiture of the grantee's title through eminent domain, the failure to perform is excused as being involuntary on the part of the grantee, and the future interest is not compensated. (Romero v. Department of Public Works (1941) 17 Cal. 2d 189, 194, 109 P.2d 662; *Woodville*, p. 738; United States v. 2,086 Acres of Land (W.D.S.C. 1942) 46 F. Supp. 411, 413.)

In short, the statutory rule contemplates a situation in which the grantee of the conditional deed intends to continue to comply with the condition indefinitely, but is prevented from doing so because a paramount authority seizes title to the property through the power of eminent domain. And because it is designed to apply in situations in which the intentions and desires of the grantee of the present interest are contrary to and frustrated by the condemnor, it necessarily assumes that the grantee and the condemnor are separate entities dealing at arm's length.

The circumstances before us are radically different from those assumed by the statutory rule, for two reasons.

First, the grantee of the present interest and the condemnor are one and the same entity: the City. Given that identity, we cannot ignore the actions of the City as condemnor when considering whether a voluntary violation of the use restriction was reasonably imminent. Instead, we must evaluate the conduct of the grantee regardless of what other hats it may be wearing. When one of those hats is that of a condemnor, the actions of the condemnor are, and must be recognized to be, those of the grantee.

Second, the condemnation of the future interest did not divest the City of its present interest in the Land, and thus did not prevent the City from continuing to use the Land in conformance with the use restriction. That it did not plan to do so was not a decision forced upon it by the condemnation, but rather was its own voluntary choice, for which it should be held accountable.

For both of these reasons, that portion of section 1265.410(a)(1) which precludes the consideration of the condemnation proceedings to determine whether a violation of the use restriction is reasonably imminent, does not apply here.

2. The Violation of the Conditions of the Gift Was Imminent.

When the condemnation proceedings are considered, the undisputed evidence proves that a violation of the use restriction was reasonably imminent.

In its resolution of necessity, the City expressly found that the public welfare required the construction of a golf course on the Land, and that the acquisition of the future interest was necessary to do so. Similarly, in its application for an order for immediate possession, the City stated that it "must acquire the reversionary interest in order to devote the property to the public recreational uses" specified in the resolution of necessity.

Moreover, the City believed that the use of the Land as a golf course would violate the conditions of the gift. In one of its letters to the Living Desert, it offered to exchange adjacent property for the Land, explaining that "a golf course does not appear to be consistent with the intent of this grant. . . ."

Even in the absence of that express statement, the City's actions demonstrate its belief that the golf course would violate the use restriction: If a golf course was consistent with the conditions, then there would have been no need to buy the future interest. It is beyond belief that the City would have offered to pay $200,000 to purchase the future interest, and thereafter incurred the attorney's fees necessary to initiate the condemnation action, unless it believed that the planned golf course would violate the conditions. The only reason to do so was to attempt to eliminate the conditions by merging the present and future interest.[6]

Those circumstances establish that the violation of the conditions was reasonably imminent. Although we have found no California case involving similar facts, the Supreme Court of Texas has addressed that precise issue on a substantially identical factual record. (Leeco Gas & Oil Co. v. Nueces County (Tex. 1987) 736 S.W.2d 629.) In 1960, Leeco granted 50 acres of land to the county to be used as a park, retaining a reversionary interest. Pleading that its plans for the future development of the property included

6. Noting that the trial court expressly declined to decide whether use of the Land for a golf course would violate the conditions, the City argues that the issue must be remanded for trial. It is mistaken. Trials are reserved for disputed factual issues. No trial is necessary when a factual issue cannot be disputed. The Deed provides that the Land is to be used "solely" for the exhibition of desert flora and fauna. Even if we were to accept the City's questionable assertion that a golf course could be landscaped in such a fashion as to exhibit desert plants and animals, the fairways and greens would obviously not be devoted to such an exhibition, and thus such a course would not comply with the conditions of the Deed.

uses which may violate the grantor's conditions, in 1983 the county commenced condemnation proceedings to purchase Leeco's reversionary interest. The trial court awarded Leeco nominal damages of $10.

The Supreme Court reversed. Although noting that a future interest is generally not compensable unless the reversion is imminent (Rest., Property, § 53, coms. b & c), and that there was no evidence that the county intended to violate the condition so long as Leeco held the reversionary interest, the court explained that that evidence was not determinative of the issue. The evidence was undisputed that the county sought to purchase the reversionary interest in order to permit uses of the property which were inconsistent with the restrictive condition. "Thus, this is not a case of condemning a 'remote' possibility of reverter, but rather an attempt by the County to remove the 'burden' of the reversionary interest by condemning the interest and paying nominal damages."

In short, the Texas Supreme Court held that when the purpose of taking the future interest was to permit the holder of the present interest to use the property in a manner which violates the conditions under which the present interest was given to the condemnor, the violation of those conditions is imminent and the taking is compensable. The court explained that any other result would be contrary to public policy. "To allow a governmental entity, as grantee in a gift deed, to condemn the grantor's reversionary interest by paying only nominal damages would have a negative impact on gifts of real property to charities and governmental entities. It would discourage these types of gifts in the future. This is not in the best interests of the citizens of this State."

That analysis is persuasive, for several reasons. First, it is consistent with the concerns, voiced by this court and others, that if a public entity which had accepted a gift of property subject to a condition limiting the use of that property were permitted to avoid the force of the donor's restriction, donors would be discouraged from making such gifts in the future. (Save the Welwood Murray Memorial Library Com. v. City Council (1989) 215 Cal. App. 3d 1003, 1014, 263 Cal. Rptr. 896 (gift of land for library); Big Sur Properties v. Mott (1976) 62 Cal. App. 3d 99, 105, 132 Cal. Rptr. 835 (gift of land for park).)

Second, denying compensation under these facts would frustrate the public policy in favor of the enforcement of existing charitable gifts....

Finally, it does not reward the City's unfair and unseemly tactics. When offered 30 acres of valuable property on the condition that it be used exclusively and perpetually as a public park devoted to the display of desert plants and animals, the City eagerly accepted, apparently without voicing any objection to the condition imposed by the donor. In reliance upon the City's agreement to that condition, the Foundation conveyed the Land. But only a few years later, the City unilaterally renounced its agreement to devote the Land to the charitable use specified by the Foundation and hatched a plan not only to terminate that restrictive condition but to do so in a manner which would deprive the Living Desert of the means of carrying on the Foundation's charitable intent. Whether the City's refusal to comply with the condition is the result of promissory fraud or a subsequent change of heart, the unfairness to the donor is palpable.

One of the maxims of equity is that "he who takes the benefit must bear the burden." (Civ. Code, § 3521.) In this context, that means that the donee of a conditional gift may not keep the gift unless the donee complies with the conditions. That the donee in this case is a public entity, endowed with the power of eminent domain, does not exempt it from that rule. To the contrary, public entities should exemplify equitable conduct. "A public office is a public trust created in the interest and for the benefit of the people." (Terry v. Bender (1956) 143 Cal. App. 2d 198, 206, 300 P.2d 119.) As trustees for and representatives of the public, local public officials are required to discharge their responsibilities with the utmost fidelity and integrity. They should be "standard-bearers of public virtue." (People ex rel. Mosk v. Barenfeld (1962) 203 Cal. App. 2d 166, 173, 21 Cal. Rptr. 501, quoting People v. Harby (1942) 51 Cal. App. 2d 759, 773, 125 P.2d 874.)

The City, by contrast, has been unfaithful both to the Foundation's intent and to the spirit of the conditions under which it accepted the Foundation's gift. And whether the City's policymakers genuinely believed that the law might permit it to keep the Land without either complying with the Foundation's wishes or paying fair compensation—indeed, without paying any compensation whatsoever—the decision to assert that position did not display the high degree of fairness, justice, and virtue that should characterize public entities. We cannot condone such inequitable behavior.

In summary, we hold that if a public entity accepts a gift of property by the terms of which the public entity receives a fee simple subject to a condition subsequent restricting the use of the property to a particular charitable use, and if that same public entity thereafter seeks to eliminate the burden of complying with the condition by using the power of eminent domain to take the power of termination reserved by the donor or given by the donor to a third party in order to allow it to use the property in a manner which would violate the condition, then a violation of the condition is reasonably imminent. Accordingly, the public entity must pay compensation to the holder of the power of termination....

Had the condition been violated before the City commenced its condemnation action, the measure of compensation payable to the Living Desert would have been the fair market value of an estate in fee simple absolute. (Rest., Property, § 53, com. d, p. 190.) The violation here had not yet occurred when this action was filed but was reasonably imminent. Indeed, given that the City was requesting possession of the Land within 30 days, that violation was likely to occur within a matter of months. Under that circumstance, the trial court should apply the same measure of compensation to determine the value of Living Desert's power of termination, i.e., 100 percent of the value of the unrestricted fee in the Land. (Pa. Dept. of Transp. v. Montgomery Tp. (Pa. Cmwlth. 1995) 655 A.2d 1086, 1090 (6 months until violation).)....

Notes & Questions

1. No matter how strong the policy arguments were for awarding compensation to the Foundation, did the court ignore the language of section 1265.410(a)(1)? When, if at all, should courts be free to ignore the language of a statutory provision? Should it matter if the court believes that the language does not reflect the legislature's intent? If the court believes that the legislature did not contemplate the issue before the court? Was the court correct in awarding the Foundation 100 percent of the value of an *unrestricted* fee interest?

2. **Valuing Future Interests.** Future interests always have a present value. The value may be substantial and certain, as in the case of *A*'s reversion following a four-year leasehold estate in *B*. Or it may be equivalent to a lottery ticket. Wherever on the spectrum a particular future interest lies, lawyers may need to value the future interest for a wide variety of settings. One setting, illustrated by *Living Desert Reserve*, is where the government condemns the land. Another setting is where present and future interest holders agree to sell a parcel of land and then divide up the proceeds. Yet another setting is where the owner of the current possessory estate wishes to buy up outstanding future interests in order to make title marketable.

Valuing a Future Interest Following a Leasehold. In most cases, the basic approach to valuing the future interest will be the same. To start with a highly simplified example, suppose that *A* owns Greenacre in fee simple absolute, an interest worth $100,000 on today's market. She gives her son, *B*, an estate for four years in Greenacre, retaining the reversion to herself. *B*'s estate is clearly not worth $100,000 because all he has is the use of Greenacre for four years. Nor is *A*'s reversion worth $100,000 because she has only the right to receive the parcel four years from today and cannot enjoy the land in the interim. Taken together, however, *A*'s interest and *B*'s must add up to $100,000, the amount they would receive if they joined in a conveyance of the entire fee interest to a third party.

The first step in valuing *A*'s reversion at the time of the conveyance is to recognize that the present value of the right to receive $100,000 four years from now is the amount that, invested today at a specified interest rate based on today's investment market, would equal $100,000 in four years. (Can you see why?) Calculators and financial tables make computing this value quite easy. If we assume that the proper interest rate is 5% compounded annually, $82,270 is the present value of *A*'s reversion; invested today at 5% interest compounded annually, $82,500 will yield $100,000 four years from now. The closer *A* gets to the actual reversion date, the greater the value of her reversion. Thus, three years into *B*'s term, *A*'s reversion will be worth $95,238 (the amount that, if invested at 5%, would yield $100,000 at the end of one year).

The value of *B*'s estate is most easily calculated by subtracting the value of *A*'s reversion from $100,000, the value of the fee simple absolute.

At the beginning of *B*'s four year term, his leasehold estate is worth $17,730 ($100,000–$82,270). At the end of the third year of *B*s term, his leasehold estate will be worth only $4,762 ($100,000–$95,238). A conceptually more meaningful way to express this result is to say that the value of *B*'s estate at the beginning of its term is the present value of the right to receive $5,000 (5% interest on $100,000) per year for four years. (The amount is something less than $20,000 because the present value of $5,000 that *B* receives in the future is less than $5,000, reflecting the fact that *B* cannot earn interest or otherwise use the money today.) The value of *B*'s estate is thus the amount of money that, if invested at 5% interest, will pay $5,000 a year and be exhausted at the end of four years. The answer, readily ascertainable again by using a calculator or annuity table, is $17,730.

Valuing a Future Interest Following a Life Estate. The valuation principles would be the same if *A* gives *B* not a term of years, but a life estate. The value of *B*'s interest is the present value of the right to receive $5,000 per year over the course of his lifetime, and the value of *A*'s reversion is the present value of the right to receive $100,000 upon the death of *B*. The only complicating factor—that the length of *B*'s life is unknown—is resolved through the use of mortality tables that calculate average life expectancies. If at the time of valuation *B* is a 33–year–old male, for example, his life expectancy is approximately 40 years, and the value of his estate is $85,795 (the present value of the right to receive $5,000 a year over 40 years). The value of *A*'s reversion is $14,205 (the present value of the right to receive $100,000 40 years hence).

Valuing a Future Interest Following a Defeasible Fee. The calculation becomes more complicated if *A* gives *B* a defeasible fee (e.g., the right to possess Greenacre so long as he does not subdivide the property with a possibility of reverter in *A*). The value of the possibility of reverter is the full market value of Greenacre times the probability that *B* will subdivide the land and the property will revert to *A*. Because *B* is unlikely ever to try to do something that would strip him of all interest in the land, the probability of the property reverting to *A* is small and thus the possibility of reverter is effectively worthless.

3. **Splitting Condemnation Awards.** If the state had condemned the land in *Living Desert Reserve* for highway construction, how much compensation would the state owe to the City of Palm Springs for its defeasible fee? How much would the state owe the Living Desert Reserve for its remainder interest? Absent evidence that the city was likely to violate the condition in its defeasible fee, most courts would award the city the value of the land as a desert preserve (since that is all the city owns) and award the Living Desert Reserve nothing (since the probability that the land would ever revert to the Reserve was small). See Cal. Code Civ. Proc. § 1265.410(a)(1). Board of Transportation v. Charlotte Park & Recreation Comm'n, 248 S.E.2d 909 (N.C. App. 1978). Does this give the state a windfall—because the state receives an unrestricted fee interest for the value of a restricted fee? Are there other alternatives? See Ink v. City of

Canton, 212 N.E.2d 574 (Ohio 1965) (awarding the holders of a possibility of reverter in park land the difference between the value of an unrestricted fee and the value of the land as a park). Whatever amount is paid to the city, should the city be free to use the money for any purposes or only to create another desert preserve?

For an interesting discussion of how condemnation awards should be split between lessors and lessees, see Victor P. Goldberg, Thomas W. Merrill, & Daniel Unumb, Bargaining in the Shadow of Eminent Domain: Valuing and Apportioning Condemnation Awards Between Landlord and Tenant, 34 UCLA L. Rev. 1083 (1987).

CHAPTER 8

LANDLORD TENANT LAW

One of the most familiar estates, worthy of its own chapter, is the leasehold. Approximately a third of all Americans rent rather than own their residence. U.S. Census Bureau, 2004 American Community Survey. Although the law has long recognized the leasehold as an estate in land, the law does not consider it to be of the same high status as other estates. While fee simples, defeasible fees, and life estates are all considered *freehold estates*, leaseholds are considered *chattels real*—more akin to personal property than the other land estates.

Several recurring issues dominate the field of landlord-tenant law. First, should courts resolve landlord-tenant disputes by looking to traditional property doctrines, by turning instead to modern contract doctrines, or by employing a combination of these doctrinal fields? As you will see, landlord-tenant law today is an uneasy amalgam of property and contract doctrines (with a healthy dose of tort law thrown in). The problem of determining the appropriate body of law for resolving landlord-tenant conflicts is not a new phenomenon. The earliest tenants were *villeins* who, during England's feudal period, held neither by contract nor conveyance but rather at the will of their manorial lord. By the 16th century, courts had turned to property law to provide tenants with more secure rights, as well as the power to eject third-party trespassers. By the 18th and 19th centuries, American and English courts were using contract principles to interpret leases—only to return to treating leases mainly as estates in the early 20th century. Today, the contract theory of leaseholders is again in its ascendancy. The bottom line is that courts will borrow from whatever body of doctrine they believe leads to the best result.

Second, should commercial and residential leases be treated the same or differently? Courts have often concluded that legal rules developed in response to the special needs and concerns of residential tenancies may be entirely out of place in the context of commercial tenancies. Residential cases deal with the habitability and security of tenants' homes, and courts often perceive that residential landlords and tenants have disparate bargaining power. In residential cases, courts are therefore often willing to disregard the terms of a lease, in favor of implied provisions and public policy considerations. Courts, by contrast, are more willing to defer to the express agreement of the parties in commercial cases. As a result, cases decided in one context often have only limited authority in the other.

A. LEASEHOLD ESTATES

There are four common law landlord-tenant estates: the term of years tenancy, the periodic tenancy, the tenancy at will, and the tenancy at sufferance. Although these four share many attributes, they also possess important differences, principally in terms of duration and the steps needed to terminate or extend the tenancy.

1. Term of Years. The term of years tenancy (also called an estate for years) has a *fixed duration.* As a consequence, the tenant's possessory right automatically terminates, and the landlord's right to retake possession automatically accrues, at the end of the fixed term. Thus, "*A* to *B* for three years, to commence June 1, 2006," is a term of years tenancy and, without more, *B*'s right to possess the premises will terminate, and *A*'s right will begin, at midnight on May 31, 2009. The fixed term need not be measured in years. Had *A* conveyed to *B* for one year, three months, two weeks, or even one day, you would call it a term of years tenancy.

Term of years estates are often subject to two constraints that ordinarily do not apply to the other landlord-tenant estates. One is the Statute of Frauds which in most states requires leases for more than one year to be written and signed by the party to be charged; the Statute also typically requires the lease to specify the parties, the premises, the duration of the lease, and the rent to be paid. Second, statutes in many states impose a limit, commonly ninety-nine years, on the length of the lease term. See, e.g., Nev. Rev. Stat. § 111.200 (25 years for agricultural or grazing leases, 99 years for other leases). What purpose or purposes do you suppose these statutes serve?

2. Periodic Tenancy. Unlike the term of years, with its fixed duration, the periodic tenancy is *continuous,* renewing itself automatically at the end of each specified period, typically a month or a year, unless and until landlord or tenant terminates the tenancy by prior notice to the other. For example, *A*'s lease "to *B* from year to year, commencing June 1, 2006," will give *B* a periodic tenancy—specifically a tenancy from year to year. If *B,* having neither given nor received notice to terminate, continues in possession on June 1, 2007, he will be entitled—and bound—to the lease for another year, and for each succeeding year, every June 1, without prior notice.

When must a landlord or tenant give notice to the other in order to terminate a periodic tenancy? At common law, the notice required to terminate a year-to-year tenancy has to be given no later than six months before the end of the period. Thus, if *B* is a year to year tenant for a term beginning June 1, 2006, he must, to have his tenancy terminate on May 31, 2007, give *A* notice of his intent to terminate no later than November 30, 2006; otherwise, he will be bound for another one-year term, beginning June 1, 2007 and ending May 31, 2008. Periodic tenancies shorter than one year require notice that corresponds with the period: three months' notice to terminate a tenancy from quarter-to-quarter, and one month's notice to terminate a month-to-month tenancy. Statutes in a number of states have altered the common law notice requirements. See, e.g., Colo. Rev. Stat. § 13–40–107 (three months for year-to-year tenancy; one month for tenancies of six months or longer but less than one year; ten days for month-to-month tenancies; three days for week-to-week tenancies; one day for periods less than one week).

Although periodic tenancies can, as in the examples above, be created expressly, they are more commonly created by implication. If, for example, the parties fail to specify a fixed term, but apparently contemplate a continuing relationship, a periodic tenancy will be implied. Thus, the lease, "*A* to *B* at a monthly rental of $700.00," will create a month-to-month tenancy, and the lease, "*A* to *B* at an annual rental of $8,400," will create a year-to-year tenancy.

3. Tenancy at Will. A tenancy at will has neither fixed duration nor periodicity and *can be terminated at any time* by landlord or tenant without prior notice to the other. (Statutes in some states have introduced a requirement of prior notice ranging from three days to three months.) The arrangement may be express—"*A* to *B* subject to termination at the will of *A* or *B*"—or it may be implied. If the lease reads, "*A* to *B* at the will of *A*," most courts will imply a corresponding right to terminate in tenant *B*, and call it a tenancy at will.

Most often tenancies at will are entirely disconnected from the intent, express or implied, of the parties and represent instead a judicial or legislative patching over of the parties' failed effort at creating some other arrangement. Thus, if *B* enters Greenacre under a lease that violates the Statute of Frauds, he will be considered a tenant at will. See, e.g., Mass. Gen. Laws c. 183, § 3 ("An estate or interest in land created without an instrument in writing signed by the grantor or by his attorney shall have the force and effect of an estate at will only").

4. Tenancy at Sufferance. A tenancy at sufferance arises when *B*, who lawfully entered into possession of Greenacre, *wrongfully continues in possession* after his right to be there has ended. Thus, if *B* entered Greenacre under a valid lease, he will become a tenant at sufferance when he improperly holds over after the lease expires. The tenancy at sufferance provides landlords with a valuable election if their tenant remains on the property after the initial lease has expired: the landlord can treat the holdover tenant as a trespasser and sue to evict or as a tenant at sufferance who is responsible for paying rent.

B. TENANT RIGHTS AND REMEDIES

Unlike many other holders of current possessory and future interests, tenants and landlords are inherently bound together in a close relationship. Modern tenants generally depend on their landlords to provide safe and habitable premises. To the tenant, a good landlord who responds promptly to the tenant's concerns is a blessing. Landlords are equally interested in good tenants, who will pay their rent on a timely basis, not ruin the premises, and hopefully not complain too much. Landlords therefore will frequently want to meet prospective tenants and check out their creditworthiness before leasing to them.

Most states, as noted, require only leaseholds of more than one year to be in writing. Leases of less than one year—like the common month-to-month residential tenancy—typically do not need a written lease. Landlords, however, generally want each party's rights and obligations expressly spelled out, so most short-term leases today are also in writing. The typical lease spells out the rights and remedies of both the tenant and the landlord. The law, moreover, will imply a variety of rights, remedies, and restrictions even if they are not expressly spelled out in the lease.

Historically, the promises of landlords and tenants were independent. If a landlord failed to provide the tenant with access to the rented premises, for example, the tenant still had to pay rent. If the tenant failed to pay rent, the landlord could not evict the tenant. As you will see in this Chapter, courts today have rejected this approach for residential leases and, in most states, for commercial leases. If one party materially breaches the lease agreement, the other party is typically freed from performance.

So what are the tenant's rights? Start with the most fundamental right of importance to the tenant—possession of the leased premises.

1. THE RIGHT TO POSSESSION

A majority of states presume that, unless a lease says otherwise, the landlord implicitly covenants to give the tenant physical possession of the premises at the beginning of the lease term. See, e.g., Moore v. Cameron Parish School Bd., 563 So. 2d 347 (La. App. 1990); Uniform Residential Landlord & Tenant Act § 2.103. If a former tenant fails to move off the property at the end of her lease term, it is the landlord's responsibility to evict the former tenant and provide possession to the current tenant. In states following the majority rule (also known as the British Rule), a tenant who has been denied possession of any portion of the premises can generally rescind the lease unilaterally—so long as he has given prior notice to the landlord and immediately vacates any part of the premises to which he has gained possession In addition to any rental improperly paid, the rescinding tenant is entitled to recover "loss of bargain" damages (typically the difference between the contract rent and the cost of other comparable premises) and consequential damages (reasonable expenditures made by the tenant before the landlord's default, relocation expenses, and if the tenant is an established commercial enterprise, lost profits). If the tenant elects not to rescind, he can recover damages equal to the difference between the value of the lease without the default and with the default, as well as any lost profits, the cost of substitute premises during the period of default, and in some states the expense of bringing any legal action necessary to remove a holdover tenant.

The Restatement (Second) of Property, Landlord and Tenant, offers five rationales for the British Rule:

> (1) The landlord knows, or should know, the status of the possession of the leased property better than the tenant in the period before the date the tenant is entitled to possession.
>
> (2) The landlord knows, or should know, better than the tenant whether a person in possession of the leased property before the date the tenant is entitled to possession is properly or improperly on the leased property.
>
> (3) Before the date the tenant is entitled to possession of the leased property, the landlord is the only one of the two who can evict a person improperly in possession of the leased property.
>
> (4) In the situation where the person in possession of the leased property is entitled to be there until the date the tenant is entitled to possession, the case of the possible holdover prior tenant, the landlord is the only one of the two who has an opportunity to get some assurance that the prior tenant will not hold over.
>
> (5) The tenant will have received less than he bargained for if he must go forward with the lease and bear the cost of legal proceedings to clear the way for his entry on the leased property.

Id. § 6.2 cmt. a.

Do you agree? What counter-arguments, if any, can you muster in favor of requiring a new tenant to pay rent when a holdover tenant remains in possession of the premises? Although a majority of states excuse the tenant from paying rent, a minority follow the American Rule under which the landlord's only obligation is to provide the tenant with the legal right to the property, not physical possession.

What if the tenant rents an apartment or a lot with a house or other building on it and, before the tenant takes possession, the building burns down? In the 19th and early 20th centuries, most courts held that, absent an express provision in the lease insuring against loss of the building, the tenant was still obligated to pay full rent for the property. In the mind of the court, the tenant, not the landlord, bore the risk that the building might burn down or otherwise be unusable during the tenancy. See, e.g., Fowler v. Bott, 6 Mass. 63 (1809). Most states now hold that a tenant is not liable for the rent if a building burns down where (1) the tenant rents only a portion of the building (e.g., an apartment), or (2) the building is necessary to meet the purposes for which the property was expressly rented. See, e.g., Albert M. Greenfield & Co. v. Kolea, 380 A.2d 758 (Pa. 1977). As the Pennsylvania Supreme Court explained in *Kolea*, the original presumption that the tenant bore the risk of fire or other destruction

> developed in a society very different from ours today: one where the land was always more valuable than the buildings erected on it. Buildings are critical to the functioning of modern society.

> When the parties bargain for the use of a building, the soil beneath is generally of little consequence. Our laws should develop to reflect these changes.

Should courts treat the destruction of a building differently in residential and commercial leases?

What should happen if, before a tenant takes possession of a parcel of land, the landlord radically changes the environmental quality of the land? Assume that Henry David Thoreau rents a beautiful forested lot with a small home on it, and the landlord then harvests all of the trees before the leasehold begins. If the lease mentions the forest, should courts hold that Thoreau's promise to pay rent is dependent on the delivery of a forested property? What if the lease says nothing about the forest? Is there a reason to excuse a tenant from paying rent if a building burns down but not if major aesthetic elements of the leasehold estate change? There are no cases that we can find in which a tenant is relieved of paying rent because of an aesthetic change to the rented property. Is this because the law assumes that most tenants care more about buildings than about the environment. That people *should* care more? If so, do you agree? Are there other reasons to differentiate between the two situations?

2. THE RIGHT TO QUIET ENJOYMENT

Barash v. Pennsylvania Terminal Real Estate Corp.

Court of Appeals of New York, 1970.
256 N.E.2d 707.

BREITEL, JUDGE.

Defendant landlord appeals from an affirmed order denying its motion to dismiss tenant's complaint for legal insufficiency. The allegations for this purpose are accepted as true.

The first cause of action, alleging a partial actual eviction, is to relieve tenant from payment of rent, and, notably, is not a claim for damages. The second is for reformation of the lease to conform to alleged prior oral agreements.

With respect to the first cause of action, the question is whether landlord's allegedly wrongful failure to supply a continuous flow of fresh air on evenings and weekends to offices leased by tenant constitutes a partial actual eviction relieving tenant from the payment of rent or, at most, a constructive eviction requiring the tenant to abandon the premises before he may be relieved of the duty to pay rent. . . .

Plaintiff, a lawyer, alleges that on September 15, 1967, while the premises known as 2 Pennsylvania Plaza in New York City were being constructed, he entered into a written lease with defendant landlord for rental of office space to be used for the practice of law. Involved is a 29–story glass-enclosed, completely air-conditioned office building. Its windows are sealed and the supply and circulation of air inside the building is under the landlord's exclusive control.

Defendant landlord, through its authorized renting agents, had represented that the building would be open 24 hours a day, 7 days each week, to enable tenants and others to occupy the offices at all times. Prior to signing the lease, plaintiff inquired as to the manner in which air would be circulated "when the air-conditioning system was not in operation." He was informed, fraudulently he alleges, "that the offices in question would be constructed with a duct system, which would always provide a natural and continuous flow of air ... [making] the offices ... comfortable and usable at all evening hours and also on weekends, even when the air-conditioning and heating systems were not in operation." The tenant, on the basis of these representations, known by the landlord to be false, signed the lease.

The lease provides, in pertinent part: "As long as Tenant is not in default under any of the covenants of this lease Landlord shall furnish air cooling during the months of June, July, August and September on business days from 9 A.M. to 6 P.M. when in the judgment of the Landlord it may be required for the comfortable occupancy of the demised premises and at other times during business days and similar hours, ventilate the demised premises."

The lease also contains a general merger clause: "Landlord or Landlord's agents have made no representations or promises with respect to said building, the land upon which it is erected or the demised premises except as herein expressly set forth and no rights, easements or licenses are acquired by Tenant by implication or otherwise except as expressly set forth herein. The taking possession of the demised premises by Tenant shall be conclusive evidence, as against Tenant, that Tenant accepts the same, 'as is' and that said premises and the building of which the same form a part were in good and satisfactory condition at the time such possession was so taken."

Plaintiff tenant took possession on May 15, 1968 and that evening at 6:00 P.M. defendant "turned off all air" in the offices. By 7:00 P.M. the offices became "hot, stuffy, and unusable and uninhabitable". Upon protest the landlord refused to provide after hour ventilation unless paid for by the tenant at a rate of $25 per hour. The tenant refused to pay the reserved rent or the additional charge and brought the instant action. The landlord sought dispossession for the nonpayment. This was denied, but the tenant was directed to pay rent into court pending the outcome of the instant action.

The first cause of action, based on the unreformed lease, alleges a partial actual eviction. Even assuming that the leased premises became "hot, stuffy, and unusable and uninhabitable" so that no one was able to work or remain in the offices after 7:00 P.M., these allegations are insufficient, as a matter of law, to make out an actual eviction.

To be an eviction, constructive or actual, there must be a wrongful act by the landlord which deprives the tenant of the beneficial enjoyment or actual possession of the demised premises. Of course, the tenant must have been deprived of something to which he was entitled under or by virtue of the lease. A right to 24–hour ventilation cannot be established, in the absence of reformation of the lease, by alleging fraudulent representations concerning ventilation when the lease itself expressly limits ventilation rights.

But even if the lease were to be read to include the allegations concerning ventilation (the gravamen of the tenant's second cause of action in reformation), the facts alleged, and accepted as true, would still fall short of, and not constitute, an actual eviction.

An actual eviction occurs only when the landlord wrongfully ousts the tenant from physical possession of the leased premises. There must be a physical expulsion or exclusion. And where the tenant is ousted from a portion of the demised premises, the eviction is actual, even if only partial.

Thus, for example, where the landlord barred the tenant from entering the premises it has been held a partial actual eviction. Similarly, where the landlord changes the lock, or padlocks the door, there is an actual eviction.

On the other hand, constructive eviction exists where, although there has been no physical expulsion or exclusion of the tenant, the landlord's wrongful acts substantially and materially deprive the tenant of the beneficial use and enjoyment of the premises (City of New York v. Pike Realty Corp., 247 N.Y. 245, 160 N.E. 359). The tenant, however, must abandon possession in order to claim that there was a constructive eviction.

Thus, where the tenant remains in possession of the demised premises there can be no constructive eviction. It has been said to be inequitable for the tenant to claim substantial interference with the beneficial enjoyment of his property and remain in possession without payment of rent. In the case of actual eviction, even where the tenant is only partially evicted liability for all rent is suspended although the tenant remains in possession of the portion of the premises from which he was not evicted. In the leading case of Fifth Ave. Bldg. Co. v. Kernochan (221 N.Y. 370, 373, 117 N.E. 579, 580), the court stated: "We are dealing now with an eviction which is actual and not constructive. If such an eviction, though partial only, is the act of the landlord, it suspends the entire rent because the landlord is not permitted to apportion his own wrong."

This then presents the nub of the appeal. The tenant, who has not abandoned the premises, asserts that there has been an actual eviction, though partial only, thus permitting him to retain possession of the premises without liability for rent. To support this contention it is claimed that failure to supply fresh air constitutes actual eviction, if only, albeit, during the hours after 6:00 P.M. and on weekends.

There is no previous known reported case involving a like situation in a substantially sealed building. The resolution of this appeal turns therefore on the application of general principles to the novel complex of facts presented.

All that tenant suffered was a substantial diminution in the extent to which he could beneficially enjoy the premises. Although possibly more pronounced, tenant's situation is analogous to cases where there is a persistent offensive odor, harmful to health, arising from a noxious gas or defective plumbing. The possible odor-producing causes are innumerable. In all such cases there has been held to be only a constructive eviction.

In Tallman v. Murphy (120 N.Y. 345, 24 N.E. 716), which involved coal gas, the court stated: "In such a building as the one under consideration there is very much that remains under the charge and control of the landlord ... [I]f he persistently neglects them, and by reason of such neglect ... his apartments are filled with gas or foul odors ... and the apartments become unfit for occupancy, the tenant is deprived of the beneficial enjoyment thereof ... and there is a constructive eviction."

Given these well-established rules, proper characterization of the instant failure to ventilate follows easily, assuming there be such duty under the lease as written, or as reformed to conform to the representations. The tenant has neither been expelled nor excluded from the premises, nor has the landlord seized a portion of the premises for his own use or that of another. He has, by his alleged wrongful failure to provide proper ventilation, substantially reduced the beneficial use of the premises....

Tenant's reliance on Schulte Realty Co. v. Pulvino (179 N.Y.S. 371), which held that a tenant had suffered a partial actual eviction, is misplaced. The landlord, in that case, interfered with tenant's "easement" of light and air by allowing another to cover a large portion of an airshaft upon which tenant's windows opened. The court, relying on Adolphi v. Inglima (130 N.Y.S. 130), held that the lease included a right to light and air from the shaftway, and that there was, therefore, a partial eviction. It was observed that there could be no constructive eviction because the premises had not been rendered untenantable. In the *Adolphi* case a landlord had sealed up a window on the tenant's premises, and it was said to justify a finding of a partial eviction. On the other hand, in Solomon v. Fantozzi (43 Misc. 61, 86 N.Y.S. 754), the court held that blocking the ventilation of a water closet did not constitute a partial constructive eviction, let alone a partial actual eviction. The distinguishing feature of these cases, if indeed they be not anomalies, is that they deal with the destruction of an easement or appurtenance of light and air granted by the landlord. Here there is no claim to an appurtenant right to air external to the demised premises but rather the failure to provide an essential service within the demised premises, which failure traditionally constitutes a constructive eviction.

It would seem moreover, apart from or despite the cases last discussed, that interference with easements or appurtenances of light and air insofar as they diminish the tenant's beneficial enjoyment of the demised premises, constitutes a constructive and not an actual eviction. Thus in Two Rector St. Corp. v. Bein (226 App. Div. 73, 234 N.Y.S. 409), the substantial "diminution of light, air and view" constituted at most a constructive eviction requiring a surrender by the tenant.

Since the eviction, if any, is constructive and not actual, the tenant's failure to abandon the premises makes the first cause of action insufficient in law. The first cause of action, therefore, should have been dismissed.

[The court continued on in its opinion to reject the tenant's request for a reformation of the lease to provide for the "continuous flow of air" and the usability of the offices in the evenings and on weekends. The court held that reformation requires a unilateral mistake on the part of the tenant, which plaintiff had not alleged in his complaint. The court remanded, with instructions that the plaintiff should have leave to replead his complaint if he wished]

[FULD, CHIEF JUDGE, dissented in part. He would have held that the tenant's complaint sufficiently alleged a cause of action for reformation.]

East Haven Associates, Inc. v. Gurian

Civil Court of the City of New York, 1970.
313 N.Y.S.2d 927.

LEONARD H. SANDLER, JUDGE.

The most important of the several interesting issues presented by the proof in this case is whether or not the doctrine of constructive eviction is available to a residential tenant when a landlord is responsible for conditions that render part of the premises uninhabitable, and the tenant abandons that part but continues to reside in the rest of the premises. Put in another way, the question is whether New York Law should recognize the doctrine of partial constructive eviction as a counterpart to partial actual eviction precisely as it has recognized for over a century constructive eviction as a counterpart to actual eviction. See Dyett v. Pendleton, 8 Cow. 727 (Ct. of Errors, 1826).

After a careful review of the authorities, I have concluded that the concept of partial constructive eviction is sound in principle, is supported by compelling considerations of social policy and fairness, and is in no way precluded by controlling precedent.

On May 26, 1963, the defendant entered into a lease with the then owner of 301 East 69 Street, with respect to Apartment 18E under which the defendant agreed to pay rent for the apartment from Dec. 1, 1963 to November 30, 1966 in the amount of $425.00 per month. The apartment in question had a terrace.

In April, 1966, the plaintiff acquired the building. At the end of July, 1966, the defendant and his family vacated the apartment and refused to pay rent for the months of August, September, October and November, 1966, the remaining period of the lease. Accordingly, plaintiff sued for the total of the four months rent, for the reasonable value of legal services, and for specific items of damages allegedly caused by the defendants. As to the last, I find the proof wholly deficient and these claims are accordingly dismissed.

The defense to the suit for rent rests upon the claim that the defendant was constructively evicted from the apartment as a result of the misconduct and neglect of the landlord, which allegedly rendered the terrace uninhabitable . . . .

I find that from early 1965 the central air conditioner emitted quite steadily a green fluid and a stream of water overflow that fell in significant quantities on the terrace. I further find that the incinerator spewed forth particles of ash that were deposited in substantial part upon the terrace. The result was to render the terrace effectively unusable for its intended purposes, and the defendant and his family promptly abandoned the terrace, although it had been a prime factor in inducing them to enter the lease.

Nevertheless, I am unable to conclude that the departure of the defendant and his family from the apartment at the end of July, 1966 constituted their constructive eviction from the entire premises. The evidence clearly discloses that the terrace had become unusable no later than the early spring of 1965, and quite possibly earlier. The law is clear that the abandonment must occur with reasonable promptness after the conditions justifying it have developed.

Unquestionably, this rule should be given a flexible interpretation in light of the practical difficulties these days in finding satisfactory apartments. Moreover, tenants have a right to rely on assurances that the landlord will correct the objectionable conditions.

Although the question is troublesome, I have concluded that a delay of at least 17 months in moving, without any significant proof of an early sustained effort to find other apartments, cannot be reconciled with the current requirements of law.

Turning to the issue of partial eviction, the proof quite plainly established that the terrace had been promptly abandoned once the condition complained of had developed. I am satisfied that conforming the pleadings to the proof to permit consideration of the issue of partial eviction would serve the interests of justice.

Although the matter is not clear, I am inclined to believe that the proof before me spelled out an actual partial eviction. It seems to me that the tangible and concrete physical character of the substances falling on the terrace provides a substantial basis for such a finding.

However, I do not rest my decision on that ground in view of the decision of the New York Court of Appeals in Barash v. Pennsylvania Terminal Real Estate Corporation, 26 N.Y.2d 77, 308 N.Y.S.2d 649, 256 N.E.2d 707 (1970). Although the facts of the Barash case do not preclude such a finding, the wording of the opinion plainly suggests a disposition to define actual eviction rather narrowly. I therefore turn to consider the status of partial constructive eviction under New York law. . . .

The doctrine of constructive eviction was developed by analogy to actual eviction on the basis of a very simple and obvious proposition. If a tenant is effectively forced out of leased premises as a result of misconduct by a landlord that substantially impairs enjoyment of the leased premises, the same legal consequences should follow as though the evicted were physically evicted.

In the eloquent landmark decision that firmly established constructive eviction in New York law, Dyett v. Pendleton, 8 Cow. 727 (Ct. of Err. 1826) the following was said at p. 734:

> Suppose the landlord had established a hospital for the small pox, the plague, or the yellow fever, in the remaining part of the house; suppose he had made a deposit of gunpowder, under the tenant, or had introduced some offensive and pestilential materials of the most dangerous nature; can there be any hesitation in saying that if, by such means, he had driven the tenant from his habitation, he should not recover for the use of that house, of which, by his own wrong, he had deprived his tenant? It would need nothing but common sense and common justice to decide it.

Why should a different test be applied where the tenant, through comparable means, is effectively deprived of the use of part of his residence, and abandons that part? Ought not the same consequences to follow as would follow an "actual partial eviction"?

I am unable to see any basis in "common sense and common justice" for treating the two situations differently.

Support for this view appears in the careful phrasing of the first decision to establish the requirement of abandonment in constructive eviction cases: Edgerton v. Page, 20 N.Y. 281 (1859). The Court of Appeals squarely rested the requirement on the unfairness of suspending rent while the tenant continued to occupy the "entire premises."

> I cannot see upon what principle the landlord should be absolutely barred from a recovery of rent when his wrongful acts stop short of depriving the tenant of the possession of *any part* of the premises. The true Rule from all the authorities is that while the tenant remains in possession of the *entire premises* demised, his obligation to pay rent continues.

While some later opinions have been less carefully worded, I know of none that requires a different result.

While the view here expressed seems to me inherent in "common sense and common justice" that gave rise originally to the doctrine of constructive eviction, the result is independently compelled by considerations of fairness and justice in the light of present realities.

It cannot be seriously disputed that a major shortage in residential housing has prevailed in our metropolitan area for several decades. The clear effect has been to undermine so drastically the bargaining power of tenants in relation to landlords that grave questions as to the fairness and relevance of some traditional concepts of landlord-tenant law are presented.

The very idea of requiring families to abandon their homes before they can defend against actions for rent is a baffling one in an era in which decent housing is so hard to get, particularly for those who are poor and without resources. It makes no sense at all to say that if part of an apartment has been rendered uninhabitable, a family must move from the entire dwelling before it can seek justice and fair dealing.

Accordingly, I hold that when the defendant and his family ceased to use the terrace, a partial constructive eviction occurred with the same legal consequences as attends a partial "actual" eviction.

These consequences were comprehensively defined in Peerless Candy Co., Inc. v. Halbreich, 125 Misc. 889, 211 N.Y.S. 676, 213 N.Y.S. 49 (App. Term, 1925). It is clear that from the time of the partial eviction, the defendant had the right to stop paying rent. Accordingly, I find against the plaintiff on its action for rent and legal expenses, and for the defendant on his action to recover the security deposit of $425.00.

Judgment should be entered for the defendant for $425.00 with interest from Aug. 1, 1966.

Notes & Questions

1. **The Right to Quiet Enjoyment and the Right to Possession Compared.** Like the covenant to deliver possession, the covenant of quiet enjoyment is aimed at securing the tenant's right to exclusive possession of the leased premises and will, unless expressly waived, be implied into all leases. The principal distinction between the two covenants is that the covenant to deliver possession is breached, if at all, at the very outset of the lease, before the tenant goes into possession, while the covenant for quiet enjoyment can be breached only after the tenant has entered into possession.

2. What justification is there for the rule followed in *Barash* that, where the eviction is constructive rather than actual, the tenant must promptly abandon in order to maintain the quiet enjoyment defense? Is it that the claim of substantial interference is inconsistent with the fact that the tenant is staying on and managing to make the best of a bad situation?

Was *Gurian* overly cautious in reading *Barash* to prohibit a finding of partial, actual eviction under the facts? Was it overly ambitious in striking out on the new tack of partial constructive eviction? One clue to the court's motives is its observation that "the very idea of requiring families to abandon their homes before they can defend against actions for rent is a baffling one in an era in which decent housing is so hard to get, particularly for those who are poor and without resources." The neighborhood of 301 East 69th Street in Manhattan is comparatively plush and its inhabitants hardly qualify as "poor and without resources." But at the time *Gurian* arose there was considerable ferment elsewhere in New York City over the plight of poor tenants in deteriorating rental housing, plagued not by leaking air conditioners but by faulty wiring, malfunctioning plumbing, and peeling paint. It is entirely possible that Judge Sandler took *Gurian* as an opportunity to make new law aimed at resolving a social and economic problem that was far more compelling than the one raised by the immediate facts before him.

3. **What Constitutes Substantial Interference?** For the covenant of quiet enjoyment to be breached, the interference with the tenant's possession must be substantial. Although the substantiality requirement applies to all forms of claimed eviction—actual and constructive, partial and complete—and to all contexts—residential and commercial—the specific measure of substantiality differs depending on the setting in which the question is raised.

Constructive Eviction. In the setting of constructive eviction, the general test for substantiality is whether the tenant has been "deprived of the full use and enjoyment of the leased property for a material period of time." First Wisconsin Trust Co. v. L. Wiemann Co., 286 N.W.2d 360, 365 (Wis. 1980). In the residential context, this means landlord interferences such as noisy parties or noisome activities that seriously inhibit the premises' use as a dwelling. In the commercial context, it means landlord conduct, such as obstructing customer parking spaces, that injure the tenant's business. In both residential and commercial contexts the breach of a separate covenant imposing a specific duty on the landlord may also be held to result in constructive eviction.

Actual Eviction. The early actual eviction cases rarely confronted the substantiality question directly. So long as the physical intrusion was more than *de minimus,* the tenant would prevail. In the much-cited Smith v. McEnany, 48 N.E. 781 (Mass. 1897), the court ruled that an encroachment, estimated to be between nine inches and two feet wide, and thirty-four feet long, entitled tenant to a complete abatement; "this is partly due to the traditional doctrine that the rent issues out of the land, and that the whole rent is charged on every part of the land." The modern trend, at least in partial actual eviction cases, is to require the same proof of substantial interference as is required in constructive eviction cases. See, e.g., Cut–Outs, Inc. v. Man Yun Real Estate Corp., 729 N.Y.S.2d 107 (App. Div. 2001); Dussin Investment Co. v. Bloxham, 157 Cal. Rptr. 646, 651 (Cal. App. 1979).

4. **What Constitutes Landlord Conduct?** For an interference to breach the covenant of quiet enjoyment, it must not only be substantial, but must also be directly attributable to the landlord. If a third party, such as another tenant, caused a disturbance, courts historically did not hold the landlord liable, forcing the injured tenant to wage his cause directly against the third party, presumably on a nuisance ground. See, e.g., Stewart v. Lawson, 165 N.W. 716, 717 (Mich. 1917) (plaintiff landlord not liable for noise of other tenants, notwithstanding provision in all leases prohibiting each tenant from becoming a nuisance to other tenants).

There is, however, a growing inclination among courts to hold landlords liable for the acts of third parties where the landlord had the right to control the offensive use. In Blackett v. Olanoff, 358 N.E.2d 817 (Mass. 1977), for example, the court upheld the tenants' defense to an action for back rent that they had been constructively evicted by noise coming from nearby premises which their landlords had leased to others for use as a cocktail lounge. Against the landlords' claim that they were "not responsible for the conduct of the proprietors, employees, and patrons of the lounge," the court observed that the "landlords had a right to control the objectionable noise coming from the lounge," and concluded that, because "the disturbing condition was the natural and probable consequence of the landlords' permitting the lounge to operate where it did and because the landlords could control the actions at the lounge, they should not be entitled to collect rent for residential premises which were not reasonably habitable." Id. at 819–820. See also McNamara v. Wilmington Mall Realty Corp., 466 S.E.2d 324 (N.C. App. 1996) (constructive eviction where landlord did not control noise from aerobics studio to which it rented neighboring space).

Would, and should, the result in *Blackett* have differed if the lounge lease had not specifically prohibited the tenant from making excessive noise? Is a landlord under a duty to include such a clause in all her leases? Would the residential tenants have had a stronger or weaker case against the landlord if they could not demonstrate that the offending conduct constituted an actionable nuisance? As between landlord and tenant, who should bear the risk of loss arising from substantial interferences that fall outside the direct control of both—for example, when a city closes off one lane in the highway running past landlord's shopping center, substantially reducing the tenant's business?

3. THE WARRANTY OF HABITABILITY

The living conditions of the urban poor have long been a source of public concern. New York became the first city to address the problem through regulation with the New York Tenement House Act of 1867. Living conditions in New York City's tenement houses deteriorated dramatically following the acceleration of immigration to the city in the 1820s and 1830s. By the 1860s, the death rate in the slums of New York City was substantially higher than that in comparable American and European cities. The Tenement House Act sought to improve living conditions by requiring that tenement houses provide fire escapes, a "window or ventilator" in every sleeping room, watertight roofs, adequate chimneys, and "good and sufficient water-closets or privies." The act also required that new tenement houses be "graded and drained, and connected with the sewer." Other major eastern cities followed with their own tenement regulations and, by 1920, over ten states and forty municipalities had adopted some form of housing laws.

Following World War II, the federal government sped up the adoption of housing codes by requiring or encouraging municipalities to adopt housing codes as a condition of receiving urban redevelopment funds or federal housing subsidies. Today, thousands of cities and many states have adopted housing codes. These codes regulate, among other items,

> (1) structural elements such as walls, roofs, ceilings, floors, windows, and staircases; (2) facilities such as toilets, sinks, bathtubs, radiators or other heating fixtures, stoves, electrical outlets, window screens, and door and window locks; (3) services such as heat, hot and cold water, sanitary sewage disposal, electricity, elevator service, central air conditioning, and repair and maintenance services for each dwelling unit; and (4) occupancy standards setting limits on the number of occupants per dwelling or per bedroom.

William B. Stoebuck & Dale A. Whitman, The Law of Property § 6.37, at 295 (3d ed. 2000).

Many cities in the United States, however, particularly in more rural areas, remain without housing codes. Even in those cities with housing codes, enforcement is sometimes inadequate. Most codes authorize public housing officials to seek injunctive relief and to impose civil or criminal fines; in some jurisdictions, violations can even lead to incarceration. In practice, however, many violations go unprosecuted, and fines are often low. The reasons are multiple, including small numbers of inspectors, the problems of identifying and obtaining jurisdiction over landlords, delays in the criminal court system, and a continuing view among some judges even today that housing code violations are not serious offenses. See Samuel Bassett Abbott, Housing Policy, Housing Codes and Tenant Remedies: An Integration, 56 B.U.L. Rev. 1, 49–51 (1976). These deficiencies have led courts to ask what role the common law should play in providing more effective remedies for tenants in housing that violates the local housing code or is otherwise uninhabitable.

Javins v. First National Realty Corp.

United States Court of Appeals, District of Columbia Circuit, 1970.
428 F.2d 1071.

J. SKELLY WRIGHT, CIRCUIT JUDGE:

These cases present the question whether housing code violations which arise during the term of a lease have any effect upon the tenant's obligation to pay rent. The Landlord and Tenant Branch of the District of Columbia Court of General Sessions ruled proof of such violations inadmissible when proffered as a defense to an eviction action for nonpayment of rent. The District of Columbia Court of Appeals upheld this ruling.

Because of the importance of the question presented, we granted appellants' petitions for leave to appeal. We now reverse and hold that a warranty of habitability, measured by the standards set out in the Housing Regulations for the District of Columbia, is implied by operation of law into leases of urban dwelling units covered by those Regulations and that breach of this warranty gives rise to the usual remedies for breach of contract.

I

The facts revealed by the record are simple. By separate written leases, each of the appellants rented an apartment in a three-building apartment complex in Northwest Washington known as Clifton Terrace. The landlord, First National Realty Corporation, filed separate actions in the Landlord and Tenant Branch of the Court of General Sessions on April 8, 1966, seeking possession on the ground that each of the appellants had defaulted in the payment of rent due for the month of April. The tenants, appellants here, admitted that they had not paid the landlord any rent for April. However, they alleged numerous violations of the Housing Regulations as "an equitable defense or [a] claim by way of recoupment or set-off in an amount equal to the rent claim," as provided in the rules of the Court of General Sessions. They offered to prove

> [t]hat there are approximately 1500 violations of the Housing Regulations of the District of Columbia in the building at Clifton Terrace, where Defendant resides some affecting the premises of this Defendant directly, others indirectly, and all tending to establish a course of conduct of violation of the Housing Regulations to the damage of Defendants....

II

Since, in traditional analysis, a lease was the conveyance of an interest in land, courts have usually utilized the special rules governing real property transactions to resolve controversies involving leases. However, as the Supreme Court has noted in another context, "the body of private property law ..., more than almost any other branch of law, has been shaped by distinctions whose validity is largely historical."[6] Courts have a duty to reappraise old doctrines in the light of the facts and values of contemporary life—particularly old common law doctrines which the courts themselves created and developed. As we have said before, "[T]he continued vitality of the common law ... depends upon its ability to reflect contemporary community values and ethics."[8]

The assumption of landlord-tenant law, derived from feudal property law, that a lease primarily conveyed to the tenant an interest in land may have been reasonable in a rural, agrarian society; it may continue to be reasonable in some leases involving farming or commercial land. In these cases, the value of the lease to the tenant is the land itself. But in the case of the modern apartment dweller, the value of the lease is that it gives him a place to live. The city dweller who seeks to lease an apartment on the third floor of a tenement has little interest in the land 30 or 40 feet below, or even in the bare right to possession within the four walls of his

6. Jones v. United States, 362 U.S. 257, 266 (1960).

8. Whetzel v. Jess Fisher Management Co., 108 U.S. App. D.C. 385, 388, 282 F.2d 943, 946 (1960).

apartment. When American city dwellers, both rich and poor, seek "shelter" today, they seek a well known package of goods and services—a package which includes not merely walls and ceilings, but also adequate heat, light and ventilation, serviceable plumbing facilities, secure windows and doors, proper sanitation, and proper maintenance.

Professor Powell summarizes the present state of the law:

> ... The complexities of city life, and the proliferated problems of modern society in general, have created new problems for lessors and lessees and these have been commonly handled by specific clauses inserted in leases. This growth in the number and detail of specific lease covenants has reintroduced into the law of estates for years a predominantly contractual ingredient. In practice, the law today concerning estates for years consists chiefly of rules determining the construction and effect of lease covenants. ...[9]

Ironically, however, the rules governing the construction and interpretation of "predominantly contractual" obligations in leases have too often remained rooted in old property law.

Some courts have realized that certain of the old rules of property law governing leases are inappropriate for today's transactions. In order to reach results more in accord with the legitimate expectations of the parties and the standards of the community, courts have been gradually introducing more modern precepts of contract law in interpreting leases. Proceeding piecemeal has, however, led to confusion where "decisions are frequently conflicting, not because of a healthy disagreement on social policy, but because of the lingering impact of rules whose policies are long since dead."[12]

In our judgment the trend toward treating leases as contracts is wise and well considered. Our holding in this case reflects a belief that leases of urban dwelling units should be interpreted and construed like any other contract.

III

Modern contract law has recognized that the buyer of goods and services in an industrialized society must rely upon the skill and honesty of the supplier to assure that goods and services purchased are of adequate quality. In interpreting most contracts, courts have sought to protect the legitimate expectations of the buyer and have steadily widened the seller's responsibility for the quality of goods and services through implied warranties of fitness and merchantability. Thus without any special agreement a merchant will be held to warrant that his goods are fit for the ordinary purposes for which such goods are used and that they are at least of reasonably average quality. Moreover, if the supplier has been notified that

9. 2 R. Powell, Real Property ¶ 221[1] at 179 (1967).

12. Kessler, The Protection of the Consumer Under Modern Sales Law, 74 Yale L.J. 262, 263 (1964).

goods are required for a specific purpose, he will be held to warrant that any goods sold are fit for that purpose. These implied warranties have become widely accepted and well established features of the common law, supported by the overwhelming body of case law. Today most states as well as the District of Columbia have codified and enacted these warranties into statute, as to the sale of goods, in the Uniform Commercial Code.

Implied warranties of quality have not been limited to cases involving sales. The consumer renting a chattel, paying for services, or buying a combination of goods and services must rely upon the skill and honesty of the supplier to at least the same extent as a purchaser of goods. Courts have not hesitated to find implied warranties of fitness and merchantability in such situations. In most areas products liability law has moved far beyond "mere" implied warranties running between two parties in privity with each other.

The rigid doctrines of real property law have tended to inhibit the application of implied warranties to transactions involving real estate. Now, however, courts have begun to hold sellers and developers of real property responsible for the quality of their product. For example, builders of new homes have recently been held liable to purchasers for improper construction on the ground that the builders had breached an implied warranty of fitness. In other cases courts have held builders of new homes liable for breach of an implied warranty that all local building regulations had been complied with. And following the developments in other areas, very recent decisions and commentary suggest the possible extension of liability to parties other than the immediate seller for improper construction of residential real estate.

Despite this trend in the sale of real estate, many courts have been unwilling to imply warranties of quality, specifically a warranty of habitability, into leases of apartments. Recent decisions have offered no convincing explanation for their refusal; rather they have relied without discussion upon the old common law rule that the lessor is not obligated to repair unless he covenants to do so in the written lease contract. However, the Supreme Courts of at least two states, in recent and well reasoned opinions, have held landlords to implied warranties of quality in housing leases. In our judgment, the old no-repair rule cannot coexist with the obligations imposed on the landlord by a typical modern housing code, and must be abandoned in favor of an implied warranty of habitability. In the District of Columbia, the standards of this warranty are set out in the Housing Regulations.

IV

A.

In our judgment the common law itself must recognize the landlord's obligation to keep his premises in a habitable condition. This conclusion is compelled by three separate considerations. First, we believe that the old rule was based on certain factual assumptions which are no longer true; on its own terms, it can no longer be justified. Second, we believe that the consumer protection cases discussed above require that the old rule be abandoned in order to bring residential landlord-tenant law into harmony with the principles on which those cases rest. Third, we think that the nature of today's urban housing market also dictates abandonment of the old rule.

The common law rule absolving the lessor of all obligation to repair originated in the early Middle Ages. Such a rule was perhaps well suited to an agrarian economy; the land was more important than whatever small living structure was included in the leasehold, and the tenant farmer was fully capable of making repairs himself. These historical facts were the basis on which the common law constructed its rule; they also provided the necessary prerequisites for its application.

Court decisions in the late 1800's began to recognize that the factual assumptions of the common law were no longer accurate in some cases. For example, the common law, since it assumed that the land was the most important part of the leasehold, required a tenant to pay rent even if any building on the land was destroyed. Faced with such a rule and the ludicrous results it produced, in 1863 the New York Court of Appeals declined to hold that an upper story tenant was obliged to continue paying rent after his apartment building burned down.[35] The court simply pointed out that the urban tenant had no interest in the land, only in the attached building.

Another line of cases created an exception to the no-repair rule for short term leases of furnished dwellings. The Massachusetts Supreme Judicial Court, a court not known for its willingness to depart from the common law, supported this exception, pointing out:

> . . . [A] different rule should apply to one who hires a furnished room, or a furnished house, for a few days, or a few weeks or months. Its fitness for immediate use of a particular kind, as indicated by its appointments, is a far more important element entering into the contract than when there is a mere lease of real estate. One who lets for a short term a house provided with all furnishings and appointments for immediate residence may be supposed to contract in reference to a well-understood purpose of the hirer to use it as a habitation. . . . It would be unreasonable to hold, under such circumstances, that the landlord does not impliedly agree that what he is letting is a house suitable for occupation in its condition at the time. . . .[36]

These as well as other similar cases demonstrate that some courts began some time ago to question the common law's assumptions that the land was the most important feature of a leasehold and that the tenant could feasibly make any necessary repairs himself. Where those assumptions no longer reflect contemporary housing patterns, the courts have

35. Graves v. Berdan, 26 N.Y. 498 (1863).

36. Ingalls v. Hobbs, 156 Mass. 348, 31 N.E. 286 (1892).

created exceptions to the general rule that landlords have no duty to keep their premises in repair.

It is overdue for courts to admit that these assumptions are no longer true with regard to all urban housing. Today's urban tenants, the vast majority of whom live in multiple dwelling houses, are interested, not in the land, but solely in "a house suitable for occupation." Furthermore, today's city dweller usually has a single, specialized skill unrelated to maintenance work; he is unable to make repairs like the "jack-of-all-trades" farmer who was the common law's model of the lessee. Further, unlike his agrarian predecessor who often remained on one piece of land for his entire life, urban tenants today are more mobile than ever before. A tenant's tenure in a specific apartment will often not be sufficient to justify efforts at repairs. In addition, the increasing complexity of today's dwellings renders them much more difficult to repair than the structures of earlier times. In a multiple dwelling repair may require access to equipment and areas in the control of the landlord. Low and middle income tenants, even if they were interested in making repairs, would be unable to obtain any financing for major repairs since they have no long-term interest in the property.

Our approach to the common law of landlord and tenant ought to be aided by principles derived from the consumer protection cases referred to above. In a lease contract, a tenant seeks to purchase from his landlord shelter for a specified period of time. The landlord sells housing as a commercial businessman and has much greater opportunity, incentive and capacity to inspect and maintain the condition of his building. Moreover, the tenant must rely upon the skill and *bona fides* of his landlord at least as much as a car buyer must rely upon the car manufacturer. In dealing with major problems, such as heating, plumbing, electrical or structural defects, the tenant's position corresponds precisely with "the ordinary consumer who cannot be expected to have the knowledge or capacity or even the opportunity to make adequate inspection of mechanical instrumentalities, like automobiles, and to decide for himself whether they are reasonably fit for the designed purpose." Henningsen v. Bloomfield Motors, Inc., 32 N.J. 358, 375, 161 A.2d 69, 78 (1960).

Since a lease contract specifies a particular period of time during which the tenant has a right to use his apartment for shelter, he may legitimately expect that the apartment will be fit for habitation for the time period for which it is rented. We point out that in the present cases there is no allegation that appellants' apartments were in poor condition or in violation of the housing code at the commencement of the leases. Since the lessees continue to pay the same rent, they were entitled to expect that the landlord would continue to keep the premises in their beginning condition during the lease term. It is precisely such expectations that the law now recognizes as deserving of formal, legal protection.

Even beyond the rationale of traditional products liability law, the relationship of landlord and tenant suggests further compelling reasons for the law's protection of the tenants' legitimate expectations of quality. The inequality in bargaining power between landlord and tenant has been well documented. Tenants have very little leverage to enforce demands for better housing. Various impediments to competition in the rental housing market, such as racial and class discrimination and standardized form leases, mean that landlords place tenants in a take it or leave it situation. The increasingly severe shortage of adequate housing further increases the landlord's bargaining power and escalates the need for maintaining and improving the existing stock. Finally, the findings by various studies of the social impact of bad housing has led to the realization that poor housing is detrimental to the whole society, not merely to the unlucky ones who must suffer the daily indignity of living in a slum.

Thus we are led by our inspection of the relevant legal principles and precedents to the conclusion that the old common law rule imposing an obligation upon the lessee to repair during the lease term was really never intended to apply to residential urban leaseholds. Contract principles established in other areas of the law provide a more rational framework for the apportionment of landlord-tenant responsibilities; they strongly suggest that a warranty of habitability be implied into all contracts for urban dwellings.

B.

We believe, in any event, that the District's housing code requires that a warranty of habitability be implied in the leases of all housing that it covers. The housing code—formally designated the Housing Regulations of the District of Columbia—was established and authorized by the Commissioners of the District of Columbia on August 11, 1955. Since that time, the code has been updated by numerous orders of the Commissioners. The 75 pages of the Regulations provide a comprehensive regulatory scheme setting forth in some detail: (a) the standards which housing in the District of Columbia must meet; (b) which party, the lessor or the lessee, must meet each standard; and (c) a system of inspections, notifications and criminal penalties. The Regulations themselves are silent on the question of private remedies.

Two previous decisions of this court, however, have held that the Housing Regulations create legal rights and duties enforceable in tort by private parties. In Whetzel v. Jess Fisher Management Co., 108 U.S. App. D.C. 385, 282 F.2d 943 (1960), we followed the leading case of Altz v. Lieberson, 233 N.Y. 16, 134 N.E. 703 (1922), in holding (1) that the housing code altered the common law rule and imposed a duty to repair upon the landlord and (2) that a right of action accrued to a tenant injured by the landlord's breach of this duty.... Recently, in Kanelos v. Kettler, 132 U.S. App. D.C. 133, 135, 406 F.2d 951, 953 (1968), we reaffirmed our position in *Whetzel,* holding that "the Housing Regulations did impose maintenance obligations upon appellee [landlord] which he was not free to ignore."

The District of Columbia Court of Appeals gave further effect to the Housing Regulations in Brown v. Southall Realty Co., 237 A.2d 834 (1968).

There the landlord knew at the time the lease was signed that housing code violations existed which rendered the apartment "unsafe and unsanitary." Viewing the lease as a contract, the District of Columbia Court of Appeals held that the premises were let in violation of Sections 2304 and 2501 of the Regulations and that the lease, therefore, was void as an illegal contract. In the light of *Brown,* it is clear not only that the housing code creates privately enforceable duties as held in *Whetzel,* but that the basic validity of every housing contract depends upon substantial compliance with the housing code at the beginning of the lease term....

This principle of implied warranty is well established. Courts often imply relevant law into contracts to provide a remedy for any damage caused by one party's illegal conduct. In a case closely analogous to the present one, the Illinois Supreme Court held that a builder who constructed a house in violation of the Chicago building code had breached his contract with the buyer:

> ... [T]he law existing at the time and place of the making of the contract is deemed a part of the contract, as though expressly referred to or incorporated in it. ...
>
> The rationale for this rule is that the parties to the contract would have expressed that which the law implies "had they not supposed that it was unnecessary to speak of it because the law provided for it." ... Consequently, the courts, in construing the existing law as part of the express contract, are not reading into the contract provisions different from those expressed and intended by the parties, as defendants contend, but are merely construing the contract in accordance with the intent of the parties.[56]

We follow the Illinois court in holding that the housing code must be read into housing contracts—a holding also required by the purposes and the structure of the code itself. The duties imposed by the Housing Regulations may not be waived or shifted by agreement if the Regulations specifically place the duty upon the lessor. Criminal penalties are provided if these duties are ignored. This regulatory structure was established by the Commissioners because, in their judgment, the grave conditions in the housing market required serious action. Yet official enforcement of the housing code has been far from uniformly effective. Innumerable studies have documented the desperate condition of rental housing in the District of Columbia and in the nation....

56. Schiro v. W.E. Gould & Co., 18 Ill. 2d 538, 544, 165 N.E.2d 286, 290 (1960). As a general proposition, it is undoubtedly true that parties to a contract intend that applicable law will be complied with by both sides. We recognize, however, that reading statutory provisions into private contracts may have little factual support in the intentions of the particular parties now before us. But, for reasons of public policy, warranties are often implied into contracts by operation of law in order to meet generally prevailing standards of honesty and fair dealing. When the public policy has been enacted into law like the housing code, that policy will usually have deep roots in the expectations and intentions of most people.

V

In the present cases, the landlord sued for possession for nonpayment of rent. Under contract principles, however, the tenant's obligation to pay rent is dependent upon the landlord's performance of his obligations, including his warranty to maintain the premises in habitable condition. In order to determine whether any rent is owed to the landlord, the tenants must be given an opportunity to prove the housing code violations alleged as breach of the landlord's warranty.[59]

At trial, the finder of fact must make two findings: (1) whether the alleged violations[60] existed during the period for which past due rent is claimed, and (2) what portion, if any or all, of the tenant's obligation to pay rent was suspended by the landlord's breach. If no part of the tenant's rental obligation is found to have been suspended, then a judgment for possession may issue forthwith. On the other hand, if the jury determines that the entire rental obligation has been extinguished by the landlord's total breach, then the action for possession on the ground of nonpayment must fail.[61]

The jury may find that part of the tenant's rental obligation has been suspended but that part of the unpaid back rent is indeed owed to the landlord. In these circumstances, no judgment for possession should issue if the tenant agrees to pay the partial rent found to be due. If the tenant refuses to pay the partial amount, a judgment for possession may then be entered.

The judgment of the District of Columbia Court of Appeals is reversed and the cases are remanded for further proceedings consistent with this opinion.[67]

59. To be relevant, of course, the violations must affect the tenant's apartment or common areas which the tenant uses. Moreover, the contract principle that no one may benefit from his own wrong will allow the landlord to defend by proving the damage was caused by the tenant's wrongful action. However, violations resulting from inadequate repairs or materials which disintegrate under normal use would not be assignable to the tenant. Also we agree with the District of Columbia Court of Appeals that the tenant's private rights do not depend on official inspection or official finding of violation by the city government. Diamond Housing Corp. v. Robinson, 257 A.2d 492, 494 (1969).

60. The jury should be instructed that one or two minor violations standing alone which do not affect habitability are *de minimis* and would not entitle the tenant to a reduction in rent.

61. As soon as the landlord made the necessary repairs rent would again become due. Our holding, of course, affects only eviction for nonpayment of rent. The landlord is free to seek eviction at the termination of the lease or on any other legal ground.

67. Appellants in the present cases offered to pay rent into the registry of the court during the present action. We think this is an excellent protective procedure. If the tenant defends against an action for possession on the basis of breach of the landlord's warranty of habitability, the trial court may require the tenant to make future rent payments into the registry of the court as they become due; such a procedure would be appropriate only while the tenant remains in possession. The escrowed money will, however, represent rent for the period between the time the landlord files suit and the time the case comes to trial. In the normal course of litigation, the only factual question at trial would be the condition of the apartment during the time the landlord alleged rent was due and not paid.

As a general rule, the escrowed money should be apportioned between the landlord and the tenant after trial on the basis of the finding of rent actually due for the period at issue in the suit. To issue fair apportionment, however, we think either party should be permitted to amend its complaint or answer at any time before trial, to allege a change in the condition of the apartment. In this event, the finder of fact should make a separate finding as to the condition of the apartment at the time at which the amendment was filed. This new finding will have no effect upon the original action; it will only affect the distribution of the escrowed rent paid after the filing of the amendment.

Notes & Questions

1. Few common law rules have changed so quickly or definitively as the rule on landlord duties respecting habitability. The American Law of Property, published in 1952, stated flatly: "There is no implied covenant or warranty that at the time the term commences the premises are in a tenantable condition or that they are adapted to the purpose for which leased.... The reason assigned for this rule is that the tenant is a purchaser of an estate in land, subject to the doctrine of *caveat emptor*. He may inspect the premises and determine for himself their suitability or he may secure an express warranty." 1 American Law of Property § 3.45 (A. J. Casner, ed. 1952).

The implied warranty of habitability exists today in some form in virtually all states and the District of Columbia. Although many states and the District of Columbia initially crafted the warranty out of their common law, others have adopted a warranty of habitability by statute. The Uniform Residential Landlord and Tenant Act (URLTA), currently adopted in 15 jurisdictions, has been the single most powerful influence on state legislation, obligating landlords to "comply with the requirements of applicable building and housing codes materially affecting health and safety," to "do whatever is necessary to put and keep the premises in a fit and habitable condition," to keep all common areas and utilities clean, safe, and operative, to provide for garbage and other waste removal, and, under specified conditions, to "supply running water and reasonable amounts of hot water and heat." Uniform Residential Landlord and Tenant Act § 2.104 (1972). The URLTA also gives tenants a wide array of remedies for landlord breach, including rescission, self-help repair, and damages. Id. §§ 4.101 to 4.107.

2. **Habitability and Quiet Enjoyment Compared.** Which will better serve the interests of tenants living in substandard housing—the warranty of habitability endorsed in *Javins*, or the covenant of quiet enjoyment? Why do you suppose courts, determined to protect tenants from substandard premises, have chosen to adopt the warranty of habitability rather than to enlarge the well-worn covenant of quiet enjoyment?

Doubtless, one reason courts have ignored quiet enjoyment theory is that its traditional requirements might appear to block tenant relief in most cases. Unlike the warranty of habitability, the traditional quiet enjoyment rules require the tenant to show that he did not waive the covenant, that he promptly vacated the premises, and that the landlord actively participated in the interference. Yet, as East Haven Associates v.

Gurian, p. 666, illustrates, these quiet enjoyment requirements were being loosened at the time the first habitability decisions were being rendered.

3. **The Habitability Standard.** Some states follow *Javins* and hold residential landlords to the habitability standard imposed by the local housing code. See, e.g., Smith v. David, 176 Cal. Rptr. 112 (Cal. App. 1981). Other states apply *ad hoc* standards of health and safety, particularly in communities without housing codes. See, e.g., Glasoe v. Trinkle, 479 N.E.2d 915, 919 (Ill. 1985) (housing "should be habitable and fit for living," with no latent defects that are "vital to the life, health, and safety of the tenant"); Detling v. Edelbrock, 671 S.W.2d 265, 270 (Mo. 1984) (habitability "should be measured by community standards"). In practice, the two standards tend to merge. Courts following the *ad hoc* approach often look to the local housing code, if one exists, for evidence of a reasonable standard. See *Detling*, 671 S.W.2d at 270; Boston Housing Authority v. Hemingway, 293 N.E.2d 831 (Mass. 1973). And courts following the *Javins* approach generally hold that only those code violations that substantially threaten health and safety will be actionable and that substantial violations falling outside the code will also breach the warranty.

4. **Notice and Opportunity for Remedy.** All courts require, as a condition of finding a breach of the warranty of habitability, that a tenant provide the landlord with notice of the problem. How promptly must the landlord act to avoid breaching the warranty? Some courts allow the landlord a "reasonable" period of time within which to fix the problem. See, e.g., Chess v. Muhammad, 430 A.2d 928, 929 (N.J. Super. Ct. 1981). Other courts are less generous. In Berman & Sons, Inc. v. Jefferson, 396 N.E.2d 981 (Mass. 1979), for example, the Massachusetts Supreme Court held that the covenant is breached from the moment the landlord receives notice of the substandard condition, even though she then promptly moves to correct it. "The landlord may be correct in characterizing itself as an innocent party, and we are cognizant of the economic burdens that a landlord typically bears. Nevertheless, we note that the landlord's liability without fault is merely an economic burden; the tenant living in an uninhabitable building suffers a loss of shelter, a necessity." Id. at 984–985. See also Knight v. Hallsthammar, 623 P.2d 268, 273 (Cal. 1981).

5. **Remedies: Rescission & Damages.** If a landlord has breached the warranty of habitability, the tenant has the right to rescind the lease agreement, move out, and stop paying rent. See, e.g., Heutel v. Walker, 735 S.W.2d 196 (Mo. App. 1987). Courts also will award the tenant damages for the time during which a breach has taken place. Major appellate decisions, like *Javins*, however, have often sketched only the barest outlines for how damages should be calculated and offered few guidelines to trial courts faced with the difficult task of applying the damage remedy to the concrete facts of a particular case.

In Cazares v. Ortiz, 168 Cal. Rptr. 108 (Cal. App. 1980), the California Court of Appeal sought to provide greater guidance. The court began by identifying a number of methods suggested by courts or commentators to compute the tenant's damages in habitability cases:

(1) Use the difference between the premises' market rental value as impliedly warranted and its market rental value "as is."

(2) Take the percentage by which the tenant's use or enjoyment of the premises has been reduced as a result of the violation and multiply it by the originally agreed-upon rent.

(3) Use the difference between the agreed-upon rent and the rental value of the premises "as is."

(4) "Forget about market rent and agreed rent and just give the tenant a recovery for his 'discomfort and annoyance.' "

The court rejected the first, third and fourth approaches. The problem with the first approach was that "*market* rental value can properly be testified to only by experts who qualify by experience and the performance of market studies. In the usual small case like the present no one can afford to hire the experts." Id. at 110. The third approach, borrowed unwittingly from personal property warranty cases, ignored

> the public policy behind the adoption of the doctrine of implied warranty of habitability of residences. That purpose is to force the rehabilitation of substantially defective slum dwellings so that the poor may live decently. This third suggested method would only further this policy if the landlord was a "rent gouger" and charged high rents for defective housing. If he instead charged low rents because of the poor quality of his premises, the agreed rent and the market rent for the "as is" premises would differ little, if at all. A tenant living in a pigsty would recover nothing because he was paying pigsty rents. This is probably good contract law, but it is poor implied warranty of habitability law.

Id. at 111, 112. Finally, the court rejected the fourth approach: "A measure of damages which *bears no relation to the value of the lease contract to either party* . . . and which is so open-ended, will either drive landlords out of business (and thus dry up rental housing) or drive their insurance rates sky high (to be taken out of the hides of tenants)." Id. at 112 (emphasis in original).

Conceding that all the methods considered were "lamentable," the court concluded that the second—the method most widely employed across the country—"is the least of the evils, and the one selected by this court as (1) most likely to achieve the goals desired by the [California] Supreme Court in creating the implied warranty of habitability (residential), as (2) least likely to cause the shift of landlords' capital to the Zurich gold market, and (3) as manageable by trial courts." Id. at 113.

Do you agree? The *Cazares* court recognized that the second method

> does have a substantial possibility of injustice to the landlord in one situation, to wit: where he has by reason of premise defects set a low rent (by negotiation with a knowledgeable tenant or not) for the premises and later is faced with a bludgeon of even lower rents through a claim of a breach of the implied warranty of habitability.

> Thus, there is justice in forcing a landlord to disgorge $50 per month for premises that rented for $150 but were only worth $90 to $110. There is, however, a visceral queasiness in nailing a landlord who has rented the place for $90 because of the defects (perhaps after a discussion of the defects with the tenant), being forced to reimburse the tenant $30 a month because a court finds that the premises are 30 percent less habitable than a similar place in good condition. This, however, would be a result of the mandatory nature of the implied warranty of habitability and the policy of forcing the rehabilitation of markedly substandard dwellings.

Id. at 108.

6. **Remedies: Self–Help.** Standard contract remedies have little attraction for the typical tenant of substandard housing. Rescission, though speedy and cheap, leaves the tenant out on the street, usually with no better housing available at a price he can afford. A judicial award of damages or specific performance will rarely repay the time and expense of litigation. The tenant's real desire is for a quick and inexpensive remedy that will entitle him to stay on the premises at a reduced rent, or no rent, until needed repairs are made. Courts and legislatures have obliged tenants with three self-help remedies.

Rent Withholding. Many jurisdictions allow the tenant to remain on the premises and withhold her rent payment until the landlord remedies the breach. See, e.g., Napolski v. Champney, 667 P.2d 1013 (Ore. 1983). Escrow statutes, in force in several states, permit tenants in substandard dwellings to withhold rental payments owed to their landlord only on the condition that they deposit them into an escrow established by a court or some other designated agency. See, e.g., Mass. Gen. Laws. Ann. c. 111, § 127F. In some places, the rents deposited will be directly applied to repairing the premises. Elsewhere, the escrowed rents will be given to the landlord once she has repaired the defects. A few states have further systematized rent deposit procedures by providing for the appointment of a receiver to collect rents and oversee their expenditure toward upgrading the premises.

Abatement. If the landlord sues for damages or to evict the tenant, some courts will allow the tenant to continue occupying the premises while setting off the damages incurred against the monthly rent due. Thus, in a jurisdiction adopting the *Cazares* measure of damages (see Note 5 above), the tenant would be allowed to reduce his monthly rental payments by a fraction that corresponds to the premises' reduced habitability.

Repair and Deduct. If the dilapidations are reparable, and are located in or around the complaining tenant's apartment, many states allow the tenant, after notice to the landlord, to apply part or all of the rent due toward the expense of repair. In some places, the repair and deduct remedy was a judicial innovation. See, e.g., Marini v. Ireland, 265 A.2d 526 (N.J. 1970). Other states have authorized the remedy by statute. See, e.g., Cal. Civ. Code § 1942 (within a reasonable time—presumptively 30 or more days after giving landlord notice of the defective condition—tenant may repair and deduct up to one month's rent; tenant may not resort to this remedy more than twice in any twelve-month period).

7. **Can the Habitability Covenant Be Waived?** Most states hold that the warranty of habitability cannot be waived by the parties. Foisy v. Wyman, 515 P.2d 160 (Wash. 1973), for example, allowed a tenant who occupied a single family home under a six-month lease, with an option to buy, to assert breach of warranty even though he and the landlord had expressly negotiated a reduced rental to account for substantial defects in the premises. The Washington Supreme Court rested its decision on the ground that "this type of bargaining by the landlord with the tenant is contrary to public policy and the purpose of the doctrine of implied warranty of habitability. A disadvantaged tenant should not be placed in a position of agreeing to live in uninhabitable premises." Id. at 164. The Restatement would permit parties to modify or waive the warranty, so long as the agreement is not "unconscionable or significantly against public policy." Restatement (Second) of Property, Landlord and Tenant § 5.6 (1977). Which is the better approach?

8. **Retaliatory Evictions.** Tenants might well hesitate to assert the warranty of habitability if the landlord could respond by terminating the lease at the next opportunity, raising the rent, or otherwise retaliating against the tenant. Most states, as a result, prohibit retaliatory measures in some or all settings either by statute or judicial decision. In these settings, a landlord can evict the tenant or change the terms of the rental only if he can show that he is acting for a legitimate, nonretaliatory business reason. See, e.g., Hillview Assocs. v. Bloomquist, 440 N.W.2d 867 (Iowa 1989); Edwards v. Habib, 397 F.2d 687 (D.C. Cir. 1968); Cal. Civ. Code § 1942.5. But see Building Monitoring Systems, Inc. v. Paxton, 905 P.2d 1215 (Utah 1995) ("a tenant may be evicted anytime after repairs have been made, but ... courts 'should be generous in allowing the tenant sufficient time, without the pressure normally exerted in a holdover eviction proceeding, to find other suitable housing' ").

Who should have the burden of proving that the landlord's action is or is not in retaliation for the tenant's actions in asserting the warranty? The Uniform Residential Landlord and Tenant Act (URLTA) places the burden on the landlord for a year after the tenant has asserted the warranty, but then shifts the burden to the tenant. URLTA § 5.101. Some states similarly protect tenants from retaliatory actions only for limited periods of time. See, e.g., Cal. Civ. Code § 1942.5 (180 days).

9. **Commercial Leases.** Should the warranty of habitability apply to commercial leases. Most courts have said "no." See, e.g., Propst v. McNeill, 932 S.W.2d 766 (Ark. 1996); Chausse v. Coz, 540 N.E.2d 667 (Mass. 1989). The Texas Supreme Court, however, has held that commercial leases contain an implied warranty that the premises are suitable for their intended purposes. Davidow v. Inwood North Professional Group, 747 S.W.2d 373 (Tex. 1988). In response to the argument that implied warranties are unnecessary to protect commercial tenants, the Texas Supreme Court responded:

> It cannot be assumed that a commercial tenant is more knowledgeable about the quality of the structure than a residential tenant. A businessman cannot be expected to possess the expertise necessary to adequately inspect and repair the premises, and many commercial tenants lack the financial resources to hire inspectors and repairmen to assure the suitability of the premises. Additionally, because commercial tenants often enter into short-term leases, the tenants have limited economic incentive to make any extensive repairs to their premises. Consequently, commercial tenants generally rely on their landlords' greater abilities to inspect and repair the premises.

Id. at 376.

10. **Does the Warranty of Habitability Work?** In the wake of *Javins*, some legal experts warned that the warranty would probably harm many lower-income tenants. Employing a classical economic model of housing, for example, the late Dean Charles Meyers suggested that the warranty would have three different adverse effects. First, some landlords would improve their housing but then raise their rents to reflect the improvement. Tenants in these units "would either be forced out or be required to pay a higher proportion of their income for rent." Second, some landlords would not be able to raise rents sufficiently to pay for improvements and would be forced to abandon or tear down their buildings. Finally, some landlords would have sufficient income from their housing to improve it, but would not be able to raise their rents in the current housing market. "In these cases the tenants would enjoy a short-term wealth transfer, for they would enjoy better housing at no increase in rent. But low-income tenants as a class would not benefit in the long-run, for the covenant of habitability will retire this component of the housing stock sooner than would otherwise be the case and will discourage new investment in low-income housing." Charles J. Meyers, The Covenant of Habitability and the American Law Institute, 27 Stan. L. Rev. 879, 893 (1975).

Others have rejected this analysis, at least in part. Professor Duncan Kennedy, for example, has argued that there are situations where the warranty of habitability can improve housing conditions for poorer tenants. Kennedy agrees with Meyers that the warranty might be counter-productive (1) when buildings are "in such bad condition that their owners would abandon rather than comply with the warranty," or (2) when landlords can and will raise rent to reflect upgrades. In these cases, Kennedy would ignore the warranty and look for other possible approaches ("such as . . . expropriating [the housing] for the benefit of its occupants"). But Kennedy suggests that the warranty might benefit tenants where landlords are "milking" slum housing:

> I mean by milking the decision to reduce maintenance below the level necessary to keep a building in existence as a residential unit. . . . [The landlord] adopts a strategy of renting for what the market will bear as the building deteriorates, fully understanding that within some relatively short period of time he will be out of

> business. Either tenants will no longer pay him anything, or the authorities will close the building.... [The landlord at that point] will walk away from [the building], give it away, or lose it to tax foreclosure....

Courts could use the warranty

> to prevent landlords in declining neighborhoods from beginning to milk before falling rent offers make it necessary for them to do so to avoid a loss .... [T]here would be no reduction in supply due to abandonment and no rent increases due to upgrading. The warranty would extend the lives of low income buildings because it would force landlords to go on maintaining at the renewable level when they would otherwise have chosen to milk toward abandonment. Buildings in declining neighborhoods would still be milked and abandoned eventually, when rent offers fell below the renewable maintenance level. But no building would be milked or abandoned when there were still tenants willing to pay a sum in rent large enough to cover the landlord's cost.
>
> Under conventional assumptions, the increase in the supply of low income housing caused by life extension should depress rents. Since our ultraselective enforcement policy prevents warranty actions from ever increasing rents or inducing abandonment, the rent-depressing effect of life extension would be the only effect in the field. The overall impact of the warranty would be to make tenants as a group better off at the expense of landlords by increasing housing quantity while reducing its price.

Duncan Kennedy, The Effect of the Warranty of Habitability on Low Income Housing: "Milking" and Class Violence, 15 Fla. St. U. L. Rev. 485 (1987).

In the wake of the nationwide adoption of the warranty of habitability, several studies looked to see the impact of the warranty. The first study, conducted by two Stanford law students, examined the effect in San Francisco. Although the study found that the warranty was "not being extensively used" two years after the California Supreme Court's adoption of the warranty and had not yet had any impact on the housing market, the study also concluded that the warranty had shifted "some bargaining power from landlords to tenants in litigation." John Sabl & Ben Logan, the Great *Green* Hope: The Implied Warranty of Habitability in Practice, 28 Stan. L. Rev. 729, 776 (1976). A second study found that the warranty of habitability, at least in the short run, had adversely affected the welfare of African–American indigents but had no statistically significant impact on the welfare of elderly indigents. See Werner Z. Hirsch, Effect of Habitability and Anti-speedy Eviction Laws on Black and Aged Indigent Tenant Groups: An Economic Analysis, 3 Int'l Rev. L. & Econ. 121 (1983).

Given the uncertainties regarding the effects of the warranty of habitability, should courts have adopted the doctrine? Even if the warranty leads to less housing stock and higher rents, is the warranty bad policy? Is this an area where courts should have left new legal rights to the legislatures?

4. Tort Rights

Courts historically held that landlords were not liable for injuries suffered by tenants or third parties on leased premises. See Restatement (Second) of Torts §§ 355–356. This rule rested on the premise that a lease is predominantly a conveyance of an interest in land and that it is the tenant in possession of the land who is best placed to control the condition of the premises.

A number of exceptions, however, have riddled this general rule almost from the start. The landlord, for example, has long been liable for defects in common areas such as hallways and entrances over which she, rather than the tenant, is presumed to have control. Restatement (Second) Property, Landlord and Tenant § 17.3. The landlord is also liable for hidden defects of which she is aware but that she fails to disclose to the tenant (id. § 17.1) and for negligence in performing repairs voluntarily undertaken. The Restatement of Property also would waive a landlord's traditional immunity from liability where property is leased "for a purpose involving the admission of the public." Id. § 17.2. Courts in recent years have grappled with the question of whether to expand landlord liability even further. The following case deals with the liability of landlords for one of the most serious environmental dangers faced by children living in older apartments and homes—lead poisoning from peeling paint.

Gore v. People's Savings Bank

Supreme Court of Connecticut, 1995.
665 A.2d 1341.

KATZ, J.

The primary question on this certified appeal is whether the Appellate Court properly concluded that a landlord of a residential dwelling may be held strictly liable pursuant to General Statutes §§ 47a–7, 47a–8 & 47a–54f(b)[1] for personal injuries sustained by a minor tenant due to the minor's

1. General Statutes § 47a–7 provides in relevant part: "Landlord's responsibilities. (a) A landlord shall: (1) Comply with the requirements of chapter 368o and all applicable building and housing codes materially affecting health and safety of both the state or any political subdivision thereof; (2) make all repairs and do whatever is necessary to put and keep the premises in a fit and habitable condition, except where the premises are intentionally rendered unfit or uninhabitable by the tenant, a member of his family or other person on the premises with his consent, in which case such duty shall be the responsibility of the tenant...." This section has remained unchanged since 1985.

General Statutes § 47a–8 provides: "Paint not conforming to standards renders property unfit. The presence of paint which does not conform to federal standards as required in accordance with the Lead–Based Paint Poisoning Prevention Act, Chapter 63 of the Social Security Act, as amended, or of cracked, chipped, blistered, flaking, loose or peeling paint which constitutes a health hazard on accessible surfaces in any dwelling

exposure to lead-based paint in the landlord's dwelling. The plaintiffs, Thomas Gore and Wanda Copeland, brought an action on behalf of their minor son, Kendall Copeland, claiming, inter alia, that the defendants, People's Savings Bank and M.S.B. Real Estate Corporation, were strictly liable for the damages caused by their son's exposure to lead-based paint in the defendants' dwelling. The trial court granted the defendants' motion for a directed verdict on the strict liability count and, after the jury returned a verdict in favor of the defendants on the remaining counts, the court denied the plaintiffs' motion to set aside the verdict. The Appellate Court reversed the decision of the trial court, concluding that "§§ 47a–7 and 47a–8, when read together, and § 47a–54f provide for civil damages pursuant to a claim of strict liability" and, therefore, that the trial court should not have directed a verdict in favor of the defendants on the strict liability count. We granted the defendants' motion for certification to appeal and now reverse and remand the case to the Appellate Court for further proceedings.

The jury reasonably could have found the following facts. In 1984, the plaintiffs and Kendall Copeland moved into an apartment located at 400 Atlantic Street in Bridgeport. On May 22, 1985, Audrey Gaines, a program coordinator for the Bridgeport department of health, inspected the plaintiffs' apartment for the presence of lead. Gaines tested the surfaces of the apartment using a portable X-ray machine, which measured the amount of lead within the paint on the surfaces. This testing revealed that some surfaces contained more than five tenths of 1 percent lead by weight, the federal statutory standard then codified in 42 U.S.C. § 4841 and incorporated by § 47a–8. On the basis of the results of this inspection, Gaines sent notification to the landlord and requested that it abate the lead in the plaintiffs' apartment. On August 26, 1985, Gaines reinspected the apartment and determined that all lead hazards had been abated.

By amended complaint dated October 1, 1992, the plaintiffs brought an action against the defendants for injuries that Kendall had suffered due to his exposure to the lead-based paint. The plaintiffs claimed that the defendants negligently had failed to comply with certain state law pertaining to the health and safety of tenants. The plaintiffs also claimed that the defendants had failed to comply with the terms of their lease agreement requiring the defendants to comply with certain state laws pertaining to the health and safety of tenants. Finally, the plaintiffs alleged that the defendants were strictly liable for the damages caused by the lead-based paint violations. On October 20, 1992, after the close of evidence, the trial

unit, tenement or any real property intended for human habitation shall be construed to render such dwelling unit, tenement or real property unfit for human habitation and shall constitute a noncompliance with subdivision (2) of subsection (a) of section 47a–7." This section was repealed, effective July 1, 1994. Public Acts 1994. No. 94–220, § 11.

General Statutes § 47a–54f(b) provides: "Paint on the accessible surfaces of a tenement house shall not be cracked, chipped, blistered, flaking, loose, or peeling so as to constitute a health hazard." This provision has remained unchanged since 1985.

court granted the defendants' motion for a directed verdict on the strict liability count against each defendant.

With regard to the negligence counts, the trial court instructed the jury that the defendants were liable if, inter alia: (1) there was a violation of a warranty of habitability or state statute; (2) the landlord had constructive or actual notice of the violation; (3) the landlord had failed to repair the condition constituting the violation within a reasonable time after receiving notice of the violation; and (4) the landlord's failure to repair was a proximate cause of the plaintiffs' injuries....

The jury found the defendants not liable, finding that there was a violation of a warranty or statute and that the defendants had actual or constructive notice of the violation, but that the defendants had repaired the condition constituting the violation within a reasonable period of time....

In determining whether a violation of § 47a–8 constitutes negligence per se or provides a basis to subject the landlord to strict liability, we must first discuss traditional principles of landlord premises liability. We have recognized that, under the common law, landlords have a duty to use reasonable care to maintain in a reasonably safe condition those areas of their premises over which they exercise control. We stated in Cruz v. Drezek, 397 A.2d 1335 (Conn. 1978): "There could be no breach of the duty resting upon the [landlords] unless they knew of the defective condition or were chargeable with notice of it because, had they exercised a reasonable inspection of their premises, they would have discovered it." Thus, liability of a landlord for damages resulting from a defective condition in an area over which the landlord exercises control generally depends upon proof that the landlord received either actual or constructive notice of the condition prior to the time of the plaintiffs injuries. Liability also usually depends upon proof that the landlord failed to remedy the defective situation in a reasonable period of time after receipt of notice....

Although the common law imposes on landlords only a duty to maintain in a reasonably safe condition those areas of their premises over which they exercise control, statutes may impose on landlords additional duties or obligations. See Panaroni v. Johnson, 256 A.2d 246 (Conn. 1969) (New Haven housing code obligated landlord to maintain outside stairway in sound condition or good repair). Indeed, under general principles of tort law, a requirement imposed by statute may establish the applicable standard of care to be applied in a particular action. It is well established that "in order to establish liability as a result of a statutory violation, a plaintiff must satisfy two conditions. 'First, the plaintiff must be within the class of persons protected by the statute. Second, the injury must be of the type which the statute was intended to prevent.' Wright v. Brown, 356 A.2d 176 (Conn. 1975)." Berchtold v. Maggi, 464 A.2d 1 (Conn. 1983)....

In cases involving the doctrine of negligence per se, however, the defendant ordinarily may avoid liability upon proof of a valid excuse or justification. 2 Restatement (Second), Torts § 288A (1965). In particular, even if a defendant has contravened a statute the violation of which constitutes negligence per se, that defendant usually may avoid liability by showing that "he neither knows nor should know of the occasion for compliance." 2 Restatement (Second), Torts § 288A. The commentary to the Restatement explains that "where the actor neither knows nor should know of any occasion or necessity for action in compliance with the legislation or regulation, his violation of it will ordinarily be excused." Id., comment (f)....

Before applying these principles to the present situation, we first acknowledge that this court has not often construed a statutory provision in the landlord-tenant context as creating a standard the violation of which constitutes negligence per se. The majority of cases concluding that a statutory provision implicates the doctrine of negligence per se have arisen in the context of motor vehicle regulation. Such a history, however, should not be read to suggest that the negligence per se doctrine is relevant only in the context of statutes pertaining to motor vehicles. Indeed, in *Panaroni* v. *Johnson,* supra, we concluded that the trial court had not improperly charged the jury that certain provisions of the New Haven housing code imposed an affirmative duty on the landlord, beyond the requirements of the common law, the violation of which gave rise to civil liability....

In the specific circumstances of a case such as this, in which the plaintiffs claim that the landlord's violation of § 47a–8 caused damages resulting from their minor son's ingestion of lead-based paint in the apartment, we believe that the policies underlying the negligence per se doctrine apply and, therefore, we agree with the Appellate Court's conclusion that § 47a–8 imposes on landlords a standard of care the violation of which constitutes negligence per se....

The language of § 47a–8 provides: "The presence of paint which does not conform to federal [lead paint] standards ... or of cracked, chipped, blistered, flaking, loose or peeling paint which constitutes a health hazard on accessible surfaces in any dwelling unit, tenement or any real property intended for human habitation shall be construed to render such dwelling unit, tenement or real property unfit for human habitation and shall constitute a noncompliance with subdivision (2) of subsection (a) of section 47a–7." This language makes clear that the legislature intended to make a per se violation of § 47a–7 the presence of paint in violation of either the federal lead-based paint standards or the health hazard standards of § 47a–54f(b). The legislature's adoption of these specific hazards as per se violations of § 47a–7 suggests that the legislature considered the various risks and benefits associated with the continued use of lead-based paints and meant to hold landlords to a particular standard of conduct.

The purposes underlying the adoption of these per se violations are reflected in the provision's legislative history. Indeed, the Appellate Court aptly noted that "the legislative history reflects that a clear purpose of the act was to end the health problems arising specifically from the presence of lead-based paint." Children are those most likely to incur health problems as a result of exposure to lead-based paints. Consequently, we believe that the legislature intended to include children such as Kendall Copeland within the class of plaintiffs protected by the statute and that it intended to protect such plaintiffs from the hazards of lead poisoning. As a result, we agree with the Appellate Court that a violation of § 47a–8 constitutes negligence per se for the purposes of the plaintiffs' action.

We disagree, however, with the Appellate Court's further conclusion that the legislature intended not to permit excuses or justifications for such a per se violation. More specifically, we disagree that a landlord's lack of notice is not related to a cause of action based on § 47a–8. Moreover, we believe that the Appellate Court misconstrued the relationship between common law premises liability and the doctrine of negligence per se in resolving the question of the availability of excuses in this case.... The Appellate Court, after first concluding that the defendants' violation of § 47a–8 constituted negligence per se for the purposes of the plaintiffs' action, determined that it provided for strict liability because the statutory provision was "lacking any provision for an excuse for the violation...."....

[We] are unpersuaded that the legislature intended to create a standard the violation of which establishes a landlord's strict liability for injuries sustained by a minor plaintiff due to exposure to lead-based paint. Although the plaintiffs point to the language of §§ 47a–7 and 47a–8 and their legislative histories as indicating a legislative intent to provide strict liability, we can discern no such legislative intent. We agree that the language and histories of these sections indicate the legislature's intent to prohibit the use of lead-based paints and to prevent the existence of chipped or otherwise dilapidated paint for the protection of children, but the plaintiffs have shown us nothing to indicate that the legislature intended the extraordinary result of holding a landlord liable for injuries sustained by a minor due to exposure to lead-based paint regardless of a valid excuse or justification, such as lack of notice, for the violation. Absent such an indication, we do not "add" a notice requirement in declining to recognize strict liability; rather, we merely recognize that the legislature has not acted to eliminate the common law requirement of notice.

Our approach is supported by the position of the Restatement (Second) of Property. "A landlord is subject to liability for physical harm caused to the tenant and others upon the leased property with the consent of the tenant or his subtenant by a dangerous condition existing before or arising after the tenant has taken possession, if he has failed to exercise reasonable care to repair the condition and the existence of the condition is in violation of: (1) an implied warranty of habitability; or (2) a duty created by statute or administrative regulation." 2 Restatement (Second), Property, Landlord and Tenant § 17.6 (1977). The commentary clarifies the rationale underlying § 17.6:

> Insofar as a duty created by a statute or administrative regulation is concerned, the rule of this section is *based on the assumption that the statute or regulation represents a legislative determination of the standard of conduct required of the landlord, so that the violation constitutes negligence per se.* The tort liability

> of the landlord in this situation tends to increase the likelihood that the will of the legislature as expressed in the statute or regulation will be effectuated. . . .
>
> An overriding requirement of the rule of this section is that there be a dangerous condition on the leased property, the existence of which is in violation of either an implied warranty of habitability or a duty created by statute or administrative regulation.

Id., comment (a) (emphasis added).

The commentary to § 17.6 further explains the "reasonable care" aspect of the rule, stating that

> the landlord is subject to liability under the rules of this section only for conditions of which he is aware, or of which he could have known in the exercise of reasonable care. Ordinarily, the landlord will be chargeable with notice of conditions which existed prior to the time that the tenant takes possession. Where the condition arises after the tenant takes possession, the landlord may not be able, in the exercise of reasonable care, to discover the condition, in which case the landlord will not be liable under the rules of this section until he has had a reasonable opportunity to remedy the condition after the tenant notifies him of it. Where the landlord is able to discover the condition by the exercise of reasonable care, he is subject to liability after he has had a reasonable opportunity to discover the condition and to remedy it.

Id., comment (c). Thus, the Restatement (Second) of Property states that, even if the landlord violates a standard the violation of which constitutes negligence per se, no liability ordinarily attaches for injuries stemming from the violation unless the landlord had actual or constructive notice prior to the violation. . . .

[The] common law in Connecticut has always included a notice requirement as part of a tenant's cause of action. Furthermore, . . . the statutory scheme at issue in this case does not eliminate that requirement. Indeed, the statutory framework evinces a legislative intent to afford landlords the opportunity to remedy violations of housing standards after receipt of notice. General Statutes § 47a–58(a) provides, inter alia, that "any enforcing agency may issue a notice of violation to any person who violates any provision of this chapter or a provision of a local housing code. Such notice shall specify each violation and specify the last day by which such violation shall be corrected. . . . The enforcing agency may postpone the last day by which a violation shall be corrected upon a showing by the owner or other responsible person that he has begun to correct the violation but that full correction of the violation cannot be completed within the time provided because of technical difficulties, inability to obtain necessary materials or labor or inability to gain access to the dwelling unit wherein the violation exists." We agree with the defendants that this provision evinces a legislative intent to create a system based on notice rather than strict liability.... Moreover, we agree with the defendants that the legislature knows how to create strict liability when it chooses to do so; see, e.g., General Statutes § 22–357 (providing that dog owners "shall be liable" for damage to any person's body or property caused by dog); and that there is nothing to indicate that it chose to do so in this case.[22]

We acknowledge the weighty public policy arguments that may be advanced both in favor of and in opposition to holding landlords strictly liable for injuries sustained by children due to the presence of lead-based paint in their homes. Many of these arguments were raised by the parties and in the various briefs of the amici curiae. For example, some suggest that holding landlords strictly liable would best motivate them to eliminate the presence of lead-based paint in their rental properties and, therefore, would most effectively protect children from the often tragic consequences of lead ingestion.[24] Moreover, the Appellate Court reasoned that the notice requirement "would not fulfill the purpose of the statutes, namely, to curb the evils resulting from lead-based paint. In many cases, a landlord would not be notified of the danger until a child has already ingested the paint, become ill, and undergone medical tests, the results of which indicate an abnormal presence of lead in the body. There is no indication that the legislature intended that §§ 47a–8 and 47a–54f(b) be construed in a manner that would allow the potential harms caused by the presence of lead-

22. Because the provisions at issue here do not expressly provide for strict liability, this case is clearly distinguishable from the system of liability in Massachusetts. In Bencosme v. Kokoras, 43, 507 N.E.2d 748 (Mass. 1987), the Massachusetts Supreme Judicial Court concluded that landlords were strictly liable for compensatory damages resulting from violations of the lead-based paint laws. In doing so, however, the court noted that the language of Massachusetts General Laws c. 111, § 199, which created landlord liability, "virtually compelled the conclusion that neither negligence nor knowledge of the risk is an element of liability.... An owner 'shall be liable for all damages caused by his failure to perform the duties required of him pursuant to ... [§ 197].' G.L. c. 111, § 199...." The statutory scheme at issue in this case does not include such clear and unmistakable language. Thus, the existence of such liability in Massachusetts sheds little light on the question before us.

24. The Connecticut Trial Lawyers Association, in its brief, points us to the 1990 estimate of the Connecticut department of health services that more than 6000 children in the state have elevated lead levels. "The effects of high lead levels in children include decreased intelligence, slowed development, behavioral disturbances, impaired hearing, kidney ailments, changes in vitamin D Metabolism and disturbance of blood production including anemia. Most of these effects persist long after exposure has ended, perhaps for the lifetime of the affected child. Children who suffer lead related impairment will, throughout their lives, contribute less to themselves and to society." State of Connecticut, Department of Health Services, Lead Poisoning Fact Sheet (1990).

"High blood levels of lead cause various adverse effects. Severe lead exposure ... can cause coma, convulsions, and death. Moderate levels ... can adversely affect the central nervous system, kidneys, and hematopoietic system. Low levels ... can lower intelligence and impair neurobehavioral development.... The federal government estimates that at least three million children in the United States (approximately seventeen percent) are at risk from lead poisoning. A disproportionately high number of ethnic minority children live in poverty, in dilapidated housing, and are poisoned by lead paint. The government's neglect of this problem raises the issue of environmental racial inequity." J. Schukoske, "The Evolving Paradigm of Laws on Lead-Based Paint: From Code Violation to Environmental Hazard," 45 S.C. L. Rev. 511, 516–17 (1994).

based paint to proliferate." On the other hand, the defendants have suggested that a system of strict liability would motivate landlords, in fear of the substantial costs of lead abatement and limitless liability, to abandon their properties, which would stifle abatement and further cause children to be exposed to lead-based paint. See generally M. Gilligan & D. Ford, "Investor Response to Lead–Based Paint Abatement Laws: Legal and Economic Considerations," 12 Colum. J. Envtl. L. 243, 278–82 (1987) (discussing relationship between potential liability of landlords for injuries caused by lead-based paint and an investor's decision to invest or disinvest in urban rental housing).

These scenarios are plausible consequences of a system of strict liability. We are in no position, however, to weigh these economic and social arguments; it is the role of the legislature to consider these alternatives and enact legislation it deems appropriate. In the absence of a clear indication of legislative intent, it would be speculative for us to assume that the legislature intended to follow any of these particular policies....

Notes & Questions

1. **Strict Liability for Building Defects.** Most courts have rejected the view that landlords should be strictly liable for injuries to their tenants caused by a defect in a leased dwelling. In Becker v. IRM Corp., 698 P.2d 116 (Cal. 1985), the California Supreme Court disagreed and held a landlord strictly liable when a tenant fell against a shower door in his apartment, broke the glass, and severely lacerated his arm. Reasoning from the warranty of habitability and product liability cases, the court concluded that a landlord makes an "implied assurance of safety" in renting an apartment. As a result, "a landlord engaged in the business of leasing dwellings is strictly liable in tort for injuries resulting from a latent defect in the premises when the defect existed at the time the premises were let to the tenant."

Ten years later, however, the California Supreme Court overruled *Becker*. Noting that *Becker* had "received a chilly reception" from both other courts and commentators, the court concluded that neither product liability law nor the warranty of habitability justified holding landlords strictly liable for latent defects in rented premises.

> As noted in *Becker*, this court held in Greenman v. Yuba Power Products, Inc., 377 P.2d 897 (Cal. 1963), that "[a] manufacturer is strictly liable in tort when an article he places on the market, knowing that it is to be used without inspection for defects, proves to have a defect that causes injury to a human being." In Vandermark v. Ford Motor Co., 391 P.2d 168 (Cal. 1964), we held that a retailer of manufactured goods also is strictly liable in tort: "Retailers like manufacturers are engaged in the business of distributing goods to the public. They are an integral part of the overall producing and marketing enterprise that should bear the cost of injuries resulting from defective products. In some

cases the retailer may be the only member of that enterprise reasonably available to the injured plaintiff. In other cases the retailer himself may play a substantial part in insuring that the product is safe or may be in a position to exert pressure on the manufacturer to that end; the retailer's strict liability thus serves as an added incentive to safety. Strict liability on the manufacturer and retailer alike affords maximum protection to the injured plaintiff and works no injustice to the defendants, for they can adjust the costs of such protection between them in the course of their continuing business relationship."

Most of the preceding reasons for imposing strict liability upon a retailer of a defective product do not apply to landlords or hotel proprietors who rent residential premises. A landlord or hotel owner, unlike a retailer, often cannot exert pressure upon the manufacturer to make the product safe and cannot share with the manufacturer the costs of insuring the safety of the tenant, because a landlord or hotel owner generally has no "continuing business relationship" with the manufacturer of the defective product. As one commentator has observed: "If the objective of the application of the stream of commerce approach is to distribute the risk of providing a product to society by allowing an injured plaintiff to find a remedy for injury along the chain of distribution, it will probably fail in the landlord/tenant situation. The cost of insuring risk will not be distributed along the chain of commerce but will probably be absorbed by tenants who will pay increased rents. One could argue that this was not the effect sought by the court in earlier cases which anticipated that the cost of risk would be distributed vertically in the stream of commerce." (Note, Becker v. IRM Corporation: Strict Liability in Tort for Residential Landlords, 16 Golden Gate L. Rev. 349, 360 (1986).) . . . .

The implied warranty of habitability recognizes "the realities of the modern urban landlord-tenant relationship" and imposes upon the landlord the obligation to maintain leased dwellings in a habitable condition throughout the term of the lease. (Green v. Superior Court, 517 P.2d 1168 (Cal. 1974).) But deriving from this implied warranty an obligation on the part of the landlord to insure the safety of leased premises by imposing strict liability for injuries to tenants caused by defects in the premises goes far beyond this laudable goal. Rather than restore the parties to a reasonable balance, the doctrine of strict liability places an undue burden upon the landlord—regardless of fault or ability to avoid injury. Rather than obligate the landlord to promptly repair defects of which the landlord knows or should know, the doctrine often will impose an onerous burden to discover and correct defects that would not be disclosed by a reasonable inspection. Rather than obligate the landlord to comply with applicable housing codes and maintain the dwelling in a habitable condition, application of the products liability doctrine imposes strict liability

> upon the landlord, even when the landlord has taken all reasonable steps to render the dwelling safe.

Are the California Supreme Court's arguments for rejecting strict liability convincing?

2. **Liability for Criminal Actions.** Should landlords be liable for the criminal acts of third parties? In Kline v. 1500 Massachusetts Avenue Apt. Corp., 439 F.2d 477 (D.C. Cir. 1970), the landlord discontinued 24–hour security in its apartment building, following which there were an increasing number of assaults, larcenies, and robberies. When a tenant was assaulted and robbed, the Court of Appeals for the D.C. Circuit held that the landlord had breached its duty to provide reasonable protection for its tenants. "The landlord is no insurer of his tenants' safety, but he certainly is no bystander. And where, as here, the landlord has notice of repeated criminal assaults and robberies, has notice that these crimes occurred in the portion of the premises exclusively within his control, has every reason to expect like crimes to happen again, and has the exclusive power to take preventive action, it does not seem unfair to place upon the landlord a duty to take those steps which are within his power to minimize the predictable risk to his tenants."

Should it matter whether a landlord initially provides security and then discontinues it? Could a landlord avoid liability by simply leaving security up to his tenants from the very outset? The New Hampshire Supreme Court has held that landlords have a duty to avoid defective conditions that foreseeably enhance the risk of criminal assault. "Moreover, a landlord who undertakes, either gratuitously or by contract, to provide security will thereafter have a duty to act with reasonable care. Where, however, a landlord has made no affirmative attempt to provide security, and is not responsible for a physical defect that enhances the risk of crime, we will not find such a duty." Walls v. Oxford Mgmt. Co., 633 A.2d 103, 106–107 (N.H. 1993).

A Note on Indoor Environmental Contaminants

Most people feel safer from pollutants inside their homes than outside, particularly in large cities such as Houston and Los Angeles with well-known air pollution problems. But the exact opposite may often be true.

> Indoor air pollution may pose a greater danger to health than pollution of ambient air because people spend up to ninety percent of their time indoors. Groups that potentially are more likely to be adversely affected by air pollution, such as infants, the elderly, and the infirm, are indoors nearly all the time. Even low concentrations of air pollutants can be injurious to long-term health because exposure to indoor pollutants is more frequent and more prolonged than is ambient air exposure. Thus, a pound of pollution released indoors is usually more damaging to health than that amount released outdoors. It is even more dangerous to children, who

> breathe more air for their weight than adults and whose lungs and immune systems are still developing.

Arnold W. Reitze, Jr. & Sheryl–Lynn Carof, The Legal Control of Indoor Air Pollution, 25 B.C. Envtl. Aff. L. Rev. 247 (1998).

Indoor air pollution, however, is far less regulated than outdoor air pollution. The federal Clean Air Act, 42 U.S.C. §§ 7401 et seq., regulates the emission of a wide variety of pollutants by factories and automobiles, but does not regulate indoor air pollution. The Occupational Safety and Health Act, 29 U.S.C. §§ 650 et seq., protects workers from some forms of air pollution in the workplace, but does not address the significant health risks often found in residential housing. The major federal tool for dealing with indoor air pollution is the Toxic Substances Control Act (TSCA), 15 U.S.C. §§ 2600 et seq., which authorizes the Environmental Protection Agency to regulate and if necessary ban chemical substances that present an unreasonable risk of injury to health or the environment. TSCA, however, does not protect a tenant where a substance was in place in a rented dwelling prior to being banned, nor does it offer protection against naturally occurring contaminants, such as molds or radon (a clear, naturally occurring gas emitted from the ground in many areas around the United States).

A wide variety of indoor air pollutants, including lead, asbestos, radon, biological contaminants, and volatile organic compounds, present risks to both residential and commercial tenants. Most of these contaminants are artificially introduced to the indoor environment through paints, ceiling and floor treatments, rugs, and other fixtures. Other pollutants such as radon are naturally occurring, while others such as biological contaminants generally develop from insects, dirt, and moisture. Building deficiencies such as poor ventilation can increase indoor air pollution. The health impacts of indoor air pollution can range from relatively minor irritation of eyes, nose, and throat, to cancer, heart disease, chronic organ damage, and various respiratory diseases such as emphysema.

In recent years, lead has received the greatest attention of the indoor air pollutants because of the significant risk that it poses to young children.

> Humans have used lead for thousands of years because it has a number of desirable characteristics; however, they also have been aware for nearly as long of the fact that it poses human-health risks. Its toxicity was first reported by Eberhard Gochel in 1697. Nevertheless, it continued to be used as a food additive, as a glaze, and in pipes; thus human injury continues to the present day. Today, leadbased paint is the primary source of the indoor air health hazard created by the use of lead. From the turn of the century, lead was used as an ingredient in many oil-based paints because it improved the adherence, brightness, and durability of the paint. Two-thirds of the houses built before 1940, one-third of those built between 1940 and 1960, and some homes built after 1960 were painted with leadbased paints. The use of lead in paint produced for residential use was prohibited in 1978 because lead

> paint flakes off of walls and later is inhaled or ingested by children. . . .
>
> Lead affects virtually every system of the body. It can damage the brain, kidneys, peripheral nervous system, and red blood cells and may cause high blood pressure. While it is harmful to individuals of all ages, lead exposure can be especially damaging to children, fetuses, and women of childbearing age. This increased sensitivity to lead exposure is attributed to several factors. Children absorb lead more readily and their tissues are more sensitive. A child's lower body weight reduces the amount of lead necessary to generate higher concentrations at lower exposures. Children are more likely to encounter lead because they are inclined to place items in their mouths, including sources of lead such as paint chips. Lead contamination in children may lead to "delays in physical and mental development, lower IQ levels, shortened attention spans, and increased behavioral problems.". . . .
>
> In 1991, the Secretary of Health and Human Services said lead poisoning was the "number one environmental threat to the health of children in the United States." The percentage of children with elevated blood-lead levels has declined over the last twenty years, but millions of children have blood-lead levels high enough to threaten their health. . . .

Reitze & Carof, supra, at 301–305.

Courts have used a variety of doctrines, including tort liability and the warranty of habitability, to remedy tenant exposure to lead. See, e.g., Chapman v. Silber, 760 N.E.2d 329 (N.Y. 2001) (failure to remedy known lead problem can constitute actionable negligence). Legislation has provided additional protection. At the federal level, the Residential Lead–Based Paint Hazard Reduction Act, 42 U.S.C. §§ 4851 et seq., requires landlords who are renting property built before 1978 to disclose any lead-based paint known to be on the premises and to provide tenants with a pamphlet on lead hazards. As *Gore* illustrates, a number of states also have adopted laws designed to remedy or mitigate lead exposure in apartments and other residential housing. See, e.g., Mass. Gen. Laws ch. 111 §§ 190 et seq. (requiring landlords to abate lead exposure in any residential unit in which children under six years old live). Several state courts have held that their state lead-paint laws provide tenants with a cause of action against their landlords in strict liability. See Brooks v. Lewin Realty III, Inc., 835 A.2d 616 (Md. 2003); Ankiewicz v. Kinder, 563 N.E.2d 684 (Mass. 1990). For more on lead paint and the law, see Thomas J. Miceli, Katherine A. Pancak, & C.F. Sirmans, Protecting Children from Lead–Based Paint Poisoning: Should Landlords Bear the Burden?, 23 B.C. Envtl. Aff. L. Rev. 1 (1995); Martha Mahoney, Four Million Children at Risk: Lead Paint Poisoning Victims and the Law, 9 Stan. Envtl. L.J. 46 (1990).

Today, increasing attention is being paid to a diverse set of biological contaminants, including mold and spores, fungi, bacteria, dust mite fecal pellets, cockroach feces, animal danders, and pollens. Some experts believe that such biological contaminants are "the most significant source of indoor air pollution and . . . affect tens of millions of people in the United States." Reitze & Carof, supra, at 283. Biological contaminants can cause various diseases, respiratory allergies, and allergic or hypersensitive reactions.

A number of courts have held landlords liable for the negligent failure to abate problems of excessive moisture and mold infestation. See, e.g., Burnett v. Chimney Sweep, 20 Cal. Rptr. 3d 562 (Cal. App. 2004); Caldwell v. Curioni, 125 S.W.3d 784 (Tex. App. 2004); New Haverford P'ship v. Stroot, 772 A.2d 792 (Del. 2001). Other courts have held that mold and other biological contaminants can violate the warranty of habitability, allowing the tenant to rescind the lease or pursue other appropriate remedies. See, e.g., Geels v. Dunbar, 812 N.E.2d 857 (Ind. App. 2004). As in lead cases such as *Gore*, courts generally require that the landlord know of the biological contaminant before imposing liability for failing to abate the problem. See Krasnow v. JRBG Mgt. Corp., 808 N.Y.S.2d 75 (App. Div. 2006) (no liability for personal injuries where tenant failed to show that landlord had actual or constructive notice of toxic mold condition). For more on the growing number of lawsuits involving mold and other biological contaminants, see Gregory J. Johansen, Litigating Mold Claims: Crisis? What Crisis?, 19 J. Land Use & Envtl. L. 465 (2004); Stephen J. Henning & Daniel A. Berman, Mold Contamination, 8 Hastings W.-N.W. J. Envtl. L. & Pol'y 73 (2001).

5. THE RIGHT TO ASSIGN AND SUBLET

Leases, like other estates in land, are transferable. When a tenant wishes to transfer his right to use the leased premises to a third party, the tenant has two ways of doing so—assignment and subletting. An original tenant, *B*, is bound to his landlord, *A*, both by privity of contract (created by the lease covenants) and by privity of estate (created by transfer of the leasehold estate). When the tenant *assigns* the lease, he transfers his entire estate and thus is no longer in privity of estate with the landlord, but continues to be in privity of contract, and remains personally liable on his leasehold obligations throughout the lease term. The assignee, *C*, though not in privity of contract with the landlord, is in privity of estate, and is thus bound to perform all leasehold covenants, such as for rent and repairs, whose burdens run with the land. The assignee's privity of estate, and hence his obligations to the landlord, will end in the event that he transfers to yet another assignee.

When the original tenant, *B*, *subleases*, he transfers less than his entire estate—for example, six months out of a two year term—and thus continues to be both in privity of contract and privity of estate with his landlord, *A*. The sublessee, *C*, is neither in privity of contract nor privity of estate with the landlord, with the result that landlord *A* can enforce none of the covenants against sublessee *C* and the sublessee can enforce none of the landlord's covenants against her. But sublessee *C* is in privity of contract *and* of estate with *B* who, effectively, has become *C*'s landlord, retaining a reversionary interest entitling *B* to retake the premises at the end of *C*'s six-month term.

Assignments and subleases can affect the landlord's interests. The assignee or sublessee, for example, may not be as careful with the premises as the original tenant was. A landlord also might worry about his rent payments. Sublessees, as noted, are not responsible to the landlord for rent, and an assignee might not be as timely as the original tenant in paying the rent. Although the landlord can pursue the original tenant for his rent, the original tenant will no longer be living on the premises and may be more difficult to contact. The law therefore permits landlords to subject leaseholds to absolute restraints on alienation despite the law's general preference for free alienability. Courts will, however, interpret these restraints stringently. A lease provision that only prohibits assignments will generally be held to permit subletting, and a prohibition against subletting will be held to permit assignments.

Funk v. Funk

Supreme Court of Idaho, 1981.
633 P.2d 586.

SHEPARD, JUSTICE.

This is an appeal from a summary judgment which denied the relief sought by plaintiff-lessors, i.e., the termination of a farm lease. We affirm.

The principal question presented is the ability of a lessee to sublease without the consent of the lessor when the lease allows subletting conditioned on the lessor's consent and the lessor arbitrarily and capriciously withholds such consent.

In November of 1969, plaintiff-appellants Ewald and Pearl Funk [hereinafter lessors] leased certain farm land to Melvin and Diane Funk [hereinafter lessees] for a ten year period commencing January 1, 1970 and ending December 31, 1979. Semi-annual rental payments were required on or before March 1 and December 1 of each year. The written lease provided in pertinent part: "(e) That the Lessee shall have the right and privilege of sub-leasing or assigning this instrument provided that the consent of the Lessor is first obtained."

During early 1978 the lessees were desirous of subleasing the property for the 1978 crop year. In January, the then attorney for the lessees wrote a letter expressing the lessees' desire to sublet the property and indicated that the lessees would make both 1978 lease payments on March 1 to ensure that the entire 1978 rent was paid in advance. They also promised to supervise the subtenant's operations to assure that the land was farmed in a good and husbandry-like manner and that proper weed control was practiced. They also offered to provide any additional information concerning the sub-tenant that might be requested by the lessors.

In February, lessors responded "... that we cannot allow a sublease of any type" and declared "... that we do not intend to allow a sublease of this property." In response to further correspondence from lessees' attorney, the lessors in February expressed their belief that the rental fee was below the fair rental value and again emphasized their refusal to allow a sublease, stating: "... we do not now or in the future wish to honor any subleasing of this property. We already have more information concerning the proposed sublessees than you can possibly assemble." Thereafter, an additional letter was written on behalf of lessors indicating that a sublease would be allowed if the lessees would assign one-half of the sublease proceeds to the lessors, if the lessees would pay the 1978 property taxes and if the lessees would agree to terminate the underlying lease on December 31, 1978. Thereafter, the lessees indicated they would farm the property themselves and would not sublease it.

Lessees did, however, sublet at least a portion of the premises for the 1978 crop year. When lessors learned of that sublease in September of 1978 they served notice of termination of the lease agreement. When lessees refused to quit the premises, this action was commenced. In March, 1979, summary judgment was entered in favor of the lessees declaring the lease agreement to be in full force and effect. The lessees continued to farm the property through the final year of the lease, 1979, and lessors accepted semi-annual rental payments in March and December of both 1978 and 1979. ...

We now turn to the principal question presented here, *i.e.*, whether a lessor has an absolute right to withhold consent to a proposed sublease when the underlying lease grants to the lessee a right of assigning or subleasing upon the consent of a lessor.

A tenant holding under a lease for a definite period may sublet the premises in whole or in part in the absence of restrictions placed thereon by the parties or by statute. That common law right is limited to the extent that a lessee may not sublet premises to be used in a manner which is injurious to the property or inconsistent with the terms of the original lease.

In the case at bar the lessees' right to assign or sublet existed by virtue of the parties' written agreement, as well as by virtue of common law, but was also subject to a contractual restriction. The effect of such contractual restrictions on a right to assign or sublet has not been previously presented to this Court. In Enders v. Wesley W. Hubbard & Sons, Inc., 95 Idaho 590, 513 P.2d 992 (1973), a lease of grazing land was forfeited under a lease provision prohibiting assignment or subletting without the consent of the lessor. However, the sublease issue there was whether the actions of the lessee constituted a sublease or merely a granting of a license. In *Enders* the question of whether the consent of a lessor could be unreasonably withheld was not presented nor discussed.

The appellant-lessors correctly argue that the traditional majority position is that unless the lease provides that the lessors' consent shall not be unreasonably withheld, a provision against assignment or subletting without the lessors' consent authorizes the lessor to arbitrarily withhold consent for any reason or for no reason.

We find, however, an increasing number of jurisdictions departing from that traditional position and an increasing volume of authority that the consent of a lessor may not be *unreasonably* withheld. As stated in *Homa-Goff, supra*, "[the majority] rule, however, has been under steady attack in several states in the past twenty years; and this for the reason that, in recent times, the necessity of reasonable alienation of commercial building space has become paramount in our ever-increasing urban society."

We deem the principal enunciated in the minority position to be based on more solid policy rationale than is the traditional orthodox majority's position. A landlord may and should be concerned about the personal qualities of a proposed subtenant. A landlord should be able to reject a proposed subtenant when such rejection reflects a concern for the legitimate interest of the landlord, such as assurances of rent receipt, proper care of the property and in many cases the use of the property by the subtenant in a manner reasonably consistent with the usage of the original lessee. Such concerns by the landlord should result in the upholding of a withholding of consent by a landlord. However, no desirable public policy is served by upholding a landlord's arbitrary refusal of consent merely because of whim or caprice or where, as here, it is apparent that the refusal to consent was withheld for purely financial reasons and that the landlord wanted the lessees to enter into an entirely new lease agreement with substantial increased financial benefits to the landlord. If the lessor is allowed to arbitrarily refuse consent to a sublease for what is in effect no reason at all, such would virtually nullify the right of a lessee to sublet. The imposition of a reasonableness standard also gives greater credence to the doctrine that restraints on alienation of leased property are looked upon with disfavor and are strictly construed against the lessor.

The burden of proving that the landlord's conduct is unreasonable rests upon the party challenging that conduct. A standard of reasonableness has been applied in cases which have *implied* a reasonable standard as well as those cases in which the lease contained express language that consent could not be unreasonably withheld. "Arbitrary considerations of personal taste, sensibility, or convenience do not constitute the criteria of landlord's duty under an agreement such as this . . . the standard is the action of a reasonable man in the landlord's position." Chanslor–Western, 266 N.E.2d at 407, quoting Broad & Branford Place Corp. v. J.J. Hockenjos Co., 132 N.J. Law 229, 39 A.2d 80, 82 (1944).

In the instant case, the proper standard by which to review the lessors' refusal to consent to the proposed sublease is one of a reasonable person in the position of a landlord owning and leasing commercial farm land. Criteria to be utilized in application of that standard would include, but would not necessarily be limited to, assurances of proper farming practices and financial responsibility. In the instant case the record discloses no contentions by the landlord of the absence of these or any other criteria and hence we hold that the arbitrary refusal of the appellant-lessors in the instant case to grant their consent to the sublease was unreasonable.

We have considered appellants' remaining assignments of error and find them to be without merit.

BAKES, CHIEF JUSTICE, dissenting:

I must dissent from the majority's decision to rewrite the lease provision in question. The lessee's right to assign or sublease the premises was unambiguous and unconditional in its requirement that the lessor consent. For the members of this Court to inject a new requirement that "the consent of the lessor may not be unreasonably withheld" is in effect to say that this Court may at any time disregard the intentions of the parties as expressed in their unambiguous agreement and rewrite the contract because a majority of this Court is of the opinion that it should be altered. The action of the majority constitutes not only a severe encroachment upon the right of persons to freely contract and to maintain control over their own property, but is also a serious intrusion into the province of the legislature....

The rationale behind the [traditional] rule is supported by several basic concepts of property law.

> The reasons expressed in support of this rule are that, since the lessor has exercised a personal choice in the selection of a tenant for a definite term and has expressly provided that no substitute shall be acceptable without his written consent, no obligation rests upon him to look to anyone but the lessee for his rent ...; that a lease is a conveyance of an interest in real property and, when a lessor has delivered the premises to his lessee, the latter is bound to him by privity of estate as well as by privity of contract ...; that a lessor's right to reenter the premises upon lessee's default or abandonment thereof is at the lessor's option and not the lessee's ...; and that a lessee's unilateral action in abandoning leased premises, *unless accepted by his lessor*, does not terminate the lease or forfeit the estate conveyed thereby, nor the lessee's right to use and possess the leased premises and, by the same token, his obligation to pay the rent due therefor. [Gruman v. Investors Diversified Services, 247 Minn. 502, 78 N.W.2d 377, 380 (1956) (citations omitted, emphasis in original).]

The reasons given in the *Gruman* case are supported by the fundamental principle that the owner of property may transfer as much or as little control over his property as he sees fit. Freedom of ownership and control over one's own property forms the very basis of our social system. If that is to change, the proper forum for such changes is the legislature and not this Court.

The unsettling nature of the majority opinion is magnified when one realizes that the effect of the decision is to potentially subject every denial of consent to litigation and approval by a judge. Rather than the lessor being sure of his right to control his property by retaining an unrestricted right to deny consent to assign or sublease, by its decision today this Court has destroyed that right and vested in the courts the power to determine what the lessor *should have intended* and award control of the property based upon that determination. Certainly, as evidenced by this case, the parties will rarely agree on what is reasonable under particular circumstances. Is there any assurance that judges will be unified in their opinions on what is reasonable? The only assurance to be gained by the rule adopted by the majority today is that the parties' attempt to write their lease to avoid litigation will be frustrated. Had the parties wished or bargained to place a question mark on the lessor's right to withhold consent, they would have provided in the agreement that consent would not be arbitrarily or unreasonably withheld. This Court should not foist that uncertainty off on them....

When a court injects a new requirement that "the consent of the lessor may not be unreasonably withheld," as the majority has done in this case, it not only constitutes an interference with the right of persons to freely contract, but also interferes with the traditional rules for conveyancing real property. If, as the majority holds, it is against public policy for a lessor to provide in his lease that the lessee cannot assign his interest without the lessor's consent which may be denied for any reasons the lessor may give, including those which the majority concludes are arbitrary, the effect of such a rule is to modify the nature of the estate conveyed by the lessor. One wonders what the majority of this Court will do when faced with the conveyance of a fee conditional, the condition being an event which the majority might conclude is arbitrary or unreasonable. As an example, it is not uncommon for a benefactor to convey real property to a city in fee conditional, the condition being that the property be used perpetually for a park to be named after the benefactor, and in the event that any part of the park is not used for that purpose then the property reverts to the heirs of the benefactor. If this Court, as it has done today, can modify the conditions of a grant of a lease, then it is only a short step to stating that it can also modify the terms of a grant of a fee conditional estate. The decision of the Court today will have a tremendously unsettling effect not only upon the conveyancing of real property but also upon the execution of contracts in this state. ...

I would vote to carry out the contract as the parties negotiated it, and not as the majority of this Court thinks they should have negotiated it.

Notes & Questions

1. Did *Funk* hold that, at the time they signed the lease, landlord and tenant *intended* to require the landlord to behave reasonably in rejecting proposed sublessees? Or did it hold that because the parties *should* have had this intent, the court would ascribe it to them? Can Idaho landlords avoid the *Funk* rule by simply insisting on language to the effect that "landlord may withhold consent in its sole and absolute discretion, for any reason or for no reason at all"?

When is a landlord likely to behave unreasonably in withholding consent to an assignment or sublease? In *Funk*, the landlord was apparently trying to use the consent privilege as a lever to negotiate more favorable rent terms. Would the *Funk* majority enforce a lease provision that expressly gave the landlord the right to increase the rent periodically? Was the court simply saying that parties, though free to agree on any terms they wish, must be careful to draft them in specific rather than general terms?

2. Courts have split on whether a reasonableness requirement should be read into a lease provision requiring that the landlord consent to an assignment or sublease. Compare 21 Merchants Row Corp. v. Merchants Row, Inc., 587 N.E.2d 788 (Mass. 1992) (refusal to consent need not be reasonable) with Kendall v. Ernest Pestana, Inc., 709 P.2d 837 (Cal. 1985) (refusal must be reasonable) . Statutory provisions also diverge. Alaska, for example, allows a landlord to refuse consent only for a limited number of enumerated "reasonable grounds," including "insufficient credit standing or financial responsibility," the number of adults and children in the household, and "proposed maintenance of pets." Alaska Stat. § 34.03.060(d). New York allows landlords to withhold consent for assignments without cause, but if the landlord unreasonably withholds consent, the tenant can terminate the lease on thirty days' notice. New York does not allow landlords to unreasonably withhold consent for subleases. N.Y. Real Prop. Law § 226–b.

3. **The Reasonableness Standard.** What grounds will entitle a landlord who is under an implied or expressed obligation of reasonable behavior to reject a proposed assignee or sublessee? Courts will generally apply an objective standard, upholding refusals if the proposed transferee's questionable reputation, his intended use of the leased premises or, most commonly, his financial irresponsibility, are likely to depress the value of the premises. See, e.g., Julian v. Christopher, 575 A.2d 735, 739 (Md. 1990). Even in these circumstances, the original tenant can make the landlord's rejection appear unreasonable by offering to guarantee his proposed transferee's performance.

Courts applying an objective standard will question landlord motives founded on personal taste or an effort to obtain a collateral economic advantage. For example, lessor's affiliation with a religion opposed to birth control was held not to justify its refusal of a sublease to the Planned Parenthood Federation of America. American Book Co. v. Yeshiva University Development Foundation, Inc., 297 N.Y.S.2d 156 (N.Y. Sup. Ct. 1969) ("By 'objective' are meant those standards which are readily measurable criteria of a proposed subtenant's or assignee's acceptability, from the point of view of *any* landlord"). And in Krieger v. Helmsley–Spear, Inc., 302 A.2d 129 (N.J. 1973), the New Jersey Supreme Court held that the landlord could not reject an office sublease on the ground that the proposed sublessee was a tenant in another of the landlord's buildings whose lease there was about to expire and who was in the midst of negotiating a new term. "The clause [that lessor shall not unreasonably withhold consent] is for the protection of the landlord in its ownership and operation of the particular property—not for its general economic protection. Otherwise the landlord could refuse consent if it had vacancies in its other building." Id. at 424.

Should the reasonableness standard differ depending on whether the proposed transfer occurs in a residential or a commercial context? On whether the landlord's duty to act reasonably is imposed by the express terms of the lease or is imposed by judicial implication? Who should bear the burden of proof on the question of reasonableness? *Funk* appears to make the tenant bear the burden of proving that the landlord's refusal is unreasonable. Yet, the court concluded its decision against the landlord with the observation that "the record discloses no contention by the landlord of the absence of these or any other [reasonable] criteria...." Was the court in effect saying that it is the landlord who bears the burden of proving the reasonableness of her conduct? Who—tenant or landlord—is better placed to bear the burden in these cases? Note that, particularly on questions of intent and motive, placing the burden of proof on one party is often a gentle way of saying that party will lose the case.

C. LANDLORD RIGHTS AND REMEDIES

1. THE LANDLORD'S RIGHTS

Just as a well-drafted lease will spell out the landlord's agreed-upon obligations to the tenant, it will also detail the tenant's obligations to the landlord. Also, absent controlling language in the lease, the tenant, like the landlord, will be subject to a handful of implied obligations. The tenant's principal implied obligation is to return the premises to the landlord at the end of the term in substantially the condition the premises were in at the beginning of the term. Unless the lease provides otherwise, the tenant cannot commit acts, such as tearing out walls or doors, that will substantially impair the value of the premises (*affirmative waste*) or acts, such as adding a second story to a one-story house, that, though they will not impair the premises' value, will substantially alter their identity (*ameliorative waste*). These implied obligations are merely specific instances of the general law of waste discussed earlier at pages 634–646.

In addition to his obligations respecting affirmative and ameliorative waste, the tenant historically was under an implied obligation not to commit *permissive waste* by allowing the premises to fall into disrepair. Some modern courts and legislatures have shifted the obligation to keep residential premises in good repair from tenant to landlord.

> The rule that the tenant must make repairs was probably fair when applied in an agrarian economy where the materials for repair were simple and at hand, and the tenant capable of making them himself. At least as concerns the actual making of repairs, the rule seems archaic and completely out of harmony with the facts when applied in a complicated society to urban dwellings occupied by persons on salary or weekly wage.... It would seem that the lessor is in the better position, from the viewpoint of

> economic situation and interest, to make repairs, and that the tenant ought to have no duty in the absence of a specific covenant.

1 American Law of Property § 3.78 (A.J. Casner ed., 1952). Do you agree?

While the evolution from an agrarian to an urban economy may justify the reallocation of some responsibilities from tenant to landlord, it may also require the reallocation of other responsibilities in the opposite direction. For example, it was entirely consistent with an agrarian setting that the landlord should have no rights against the tenant's use of the premises in a noisy, noisome, or other offensive manner; these rights were more efficiently given to neighbors on a nuisance theory. Should the landlord be given these rights in an urban society? Does it matter whether the landlord could be held liable to other tenants for such behavior (see pp. 670–671)? See Howard Opera House Associates v. Urban Outfitters, Inc., 322 F.3d 125 (2d Cir. 2003) (violation of local noise ordinance breaches lease).

Should a landlord have a right to terminate a lease where the tenant is using the land in a manner that could violate environmental laws? Imagine, for example, that a tenant begins to store hazardous substances on the property, raising the specter of the waste getting out into the open environment. Landlords often can be held liable for environmental damage caused by their tenants and thus have a deep interest in how their land is being used. See, e.g., Comprehensive Emergency Response, Compensation and Liability Act, 42 U.S.C. § 9607(a) (holding the owners of land potentially responsible for hazardous waste cleanup); pp. 429–444 supra.

a. RENT

Tenants are not obligated to pay rent unless the lease expressly requires the tenant to do so. Some courts hold, however, that where there is no lease, the tenant must pay a fair rental value for the right to possess the property. See, e.g., Parkmerced Co. v. San Francisco Rent Stabilization & Arbitration Bd., 263 Cal. Rptr. 617, 621 (Ct. App. 1989).

Where the rent in a commercial lease is based at least in part on a percentage of the tenant's gross sales, does the tenant have an implicit obligation to continue operating? Where there is a significant minimum rental that must be paid no matter what, most courts conclude that the parties did not intend to obligate the tenant to continue operating. See, e.g., Nalle v. Taco Bell Corp., 914 S.W.2d 685 (Tex. App. 1996). By contrast, most courts will imply such an obligation in the case of a "pure" percentage lease, where the entire rental is based on a percentage of sales. See, e.g., Pequot Spring Water Co. v. Brunelle, 698 A.2d 920 (Conn. App. 1997). Courts similarly will often imply an obligation to continue operating where the lease provides for only a small base rental. See, e.g., Hornwood v. Smith's Food King No. 1, 807 P.2d 208 (Nev. 1991).

b. RENT CONTROL

Approximately 140 cities and other local governments in the United States currently limit the rent that landlords can charge to residential tenants. Rent control is not a modern idea. Dating back at least to medieval Europe, more than one hundred countries have employed rent control at one time or another. See John W. Willis, A Short History of Rent Control Laws, 36 Cornell L.Q. 54 (1950). In the United States, rent control ordinances first arose during the first World War to deal with wartime housing shortages and soaring rents. New York, which has perhaps the most famous (and controversial) rent control ordinance, adopted its War Emergency Tenant Protection Act during World War II in response to severe housing shortages and rising rents. Virtually every jurisdiction, except New York, phased out their war-time rent control ordinances during the 1950s. In the 1960s, growing pressure from tenants' organizations and scores of major rent strikes led to a "second generation" of rent control laws. See Anthony Downs, Residential Rent Controls: An Evaluation (1988). This second generation peaked in the 1980s when over 200 municipalities in the United States had rent control laws on their books.

Although rent control provisions vary considerably from jurisdiction to jurisdiction, they share some common features. First, while a number of older rent control laws set fixed rents that did not change over time, most modern rent control ordinances permit rents to increase over time in response to inflation. Some jurisdictions tie permitted rent increases to national or local inflation indices; others set fixed annual percentage increases; yet others allow landlord to increase rents in response to demonstrated increases in property taxes, operating expenses, and other costs. Second, rent control laws often permit landlords to increase rents when current tenants move out. Because such provisions obviously can give landlords an incentive to get rid of existing tenants, most rent control laws permit tenants to remain for as long as they want in their current rental units; landlords can evict a tenant only for a material breach of the lease. See generally Robert Schoshinski, American Law of Landlord and Tenant §§ 7.1–7.10 (1980); Richard E. Blumberg, Brian Quinn Robbins, & Kenneth K. Baar, The Emergence of Second Generation Rent Controls, 8 Clearinghouse Rev. 240 (1974).

Rent control has generated heated debate over its wisdom. Most of the debate has centered on the economics of rent control. Proponents of rent control make a number of arguments. One is that the structure of the rental housing market and the continued scarcity of rental housing puts landlords in a superior position, effectively disabling tenants from negotiating on price. Controlled rents, it is argued, will approximate the price upon which landlord and tenant would have agreed had they been able to bargain freely. A connected argument is that housing, like water and electricity, is a necessity of life and, like these other necessities, should be treated as a public utility, regulated in all respects including price.

Opponents of rent control argue that there is nothing in the normal structure of rental housing markets to give landlords the ability to set price substantially over cost. Rent control makes sense only during wartime and other unusual situations where the "demand for rental units rises sharply at the same time that new construction of such units has been legally restricted in order to conserve resources." Downs, supra, at 1. In the view of opponents, housing scarcity is often the result of—and not the justification for—rent control. If investors have the opportunity to receive unregulated returns they will quickly build additional housing. Rent controls make shortages worse by suppressing the construction of new rental housing. To try to address this concern, many rent control laws today exempt new units from their constraints. Opponents, however, still worry about the potential impact of rent control laws:

> Even if new construction is exempt from the statute, existing rent control laws give a loud and clear signal that old policies may be reversed so that future units may be subject to similar restrictions. That prospect is, moreover, far from negligible because once those units are occupied, their residents add a new class of voters to the rolls whose interests can no longer be ignored in the political calculus. All rent control statutes thus depress the future total return of any investment. Reduced returns mean reduced investments, so that rent control statutes only exacerbate the housing shortages they are said to alleviate.

Richard A. Epstein, Rent Control and the Theory of Efficient Regulation, 54 Brook. L. Rev. 741, 767 (1988).

Opponents also note that the prices of many other necessities, such as food and clothing, are not controlled, and that public utilities are regulated not because they provide necessities but because efficiency dictates that they be given a monopoly position in the areas they serve. Because there are no equivalent monopolies in the housing market, there is no need to prohibit monopoly pricing.

Opponents finally argue that price regulation will in fact harm tenants over the long run. As noted, rent control ordinances may reduce the stock of rental housing by depressing new construction. Guaranteed a minimum rental, landlords also will have little incentive to invest in cost-cutting innovations, and tenants will occupy more space than they really need, thus excluding others from needed housing.

> In addition, many of the short-term benefits of rent controls (reduced rents) aid affluent rather than poor households, and some of the costs (reduced access to vacant units) must be borne by very poor households. Where rent is eliminated as a basis for distinguishing among potential tenants, owners often use other factors such as credit-worthiness, race, sex, or ethnicity in allocating scarce rental units—even though most such discrimination is illegal.

Downs, supra, at 1.

Professor Peggy Radin has argued that rent control laws are more about competing claims to property than economics. According to Professor Radin, rent control laws are necessary to ensure that rent increases do not force out long term tenants, for whom their rental unit has become home and thus deeply personal property:

> Most of us, I think, feel that a tenant's interest in continuing to live in an apartment that she has made home for some time seems somehow a stronger or more exigent claim than a commercial landlord's interest in maintaining the same scope of freedom of choice regarding lease terms and in maintaining a high profit margin. Where rising rents are forcing out tenants and where landlords have significant economic rents, that is, one feels the tenant's claim is stronger than the landlord's. Even where significant economic rents are not present, so that some landlords are forced to leave the business, one may still feel that the tenant's expectation or desire to continue in her home is more important than the commercial landlord's expectation or desire to continue in the landlord business over some other business that will yield a better return. We do not recognize any general right to remain in a specific business such that regulation of the industry would be prohibited if regulation would operate to force some of the less efficient suppliers out of that market and into others.
>
> The intuitive general rule is that preservation of one's home is a stronger claim than preservation of one's business, or that noncommercial personal use of an apartment as a home is morally entitled to more weight than purely commercial landlording.

Margaret Jane Radin, Residential Rent Control, 15 Phil. & Pub. Aff. 350, 359–360 (1986). For other non-economic arguments for rent control, see William H. Simon, Social–Republican Property, 38 UCLA L. Rev. 1355 (1991) (emphasizing the importance of rent control to community); Mark Kelman, On Democracy–Bashing: A Skeptical Look at the Theoretical and "Empirical" Practice of the Public Choice Movement, 74 Va. L. Rev. 199, 271–273 (1988) (same).

There is a large, and largely inconclusive, theoretical and empirical literature on the economic effects of rent control. See, e.g., Richard J. Arnott, Tenancy Rent Control, 10 Swedish Econ. Pol'y Rev. 89 (2003); Richard J. Arnott, Time for Revisionism on Rent Control, 9 J. Econ. Perspectives 99 (1995); Choon–Geol Moon & Janet G. Stotsky, The Effect of Rent Control on Housing Quality Change: A Longitudinal Analysis, 101 J. Pol. Econ. 1114 (1993). In the late 1970s, however, a poll of 211 economists found that slightly more than 98 percent of United States respondents agreed that a "ceiling on rents reduces the quantity and quality of housing available." Bruno S. Frey et al., Consensus and Dissension Among Economists: An Empirical Inquiry, 74 Am. Econ. Rev. 986, 991 (1984). Although 95 percent of Canadian economists agreed, far fewer European economists agreed; indeed, only six percent of German economists and 11 percent of Austrian economists agreed. Id.

In some markets, landlords facing rent controls have an alternative: converting their buildings to condominiums and selling the individual units outright. Many proponents of rent control laws therefore have also lobbied for limits on condominium conversions. The legislative response has taken a variety of forms. The first response is generally a moratorium on conversions for a month, a year, or even longer, to allow the municipality to study the issue. Longer range programs require landlords (1) to give lengthy removal notices (e.g., three years) and aid displaced tenants in finding new housing; (2) to give tenants a right of first refusal to purchase their apartments; and/or (3) to obtain purchase commitments from a specified number of tenants. Other jurisdictions limit the total number of conversions that can occur in any year or prohibit any conversions at all if the rental vacancy rate falls below a specified figure.

Landlords have brought multiple challenges to rent control ordinances (and statutory limits on condominium conversions), primarily on the ground that rent control unconstitutionally takes the landlord's property without just compensation. To date, virtually all such takings challenges have failed. See, e.g., Yee v. City of Escondido, 503 U.S. 519 (1992); Pennell v. City of San Jose, 485 U.S. 1 (1988); Block v. Hirsch, 256 U.S. 135 (1921).

2. THE LANDLORD'S REMEDIES

Although modern leases are usually quite explicit in prescribing the tenant's obligations, they are often surprisingly bare when it comes to the equally important question of the remedies available to the landlord in the event the tenant breaches any of these obligations. Which obligations, if breached, will entitle the landlord to evict the tenant, and which will entitle him only to specific performance or damages? What are the landlord's remedies when a breaching tenant abandons the premises? Can the landlord recover the entire rental for the remainder of the lease term, or can she only obtain damages for her loss of bargain? Must she try to mitigate her damages by reletting the apartment? If the tenant breaches, but refuses to leave the premises, can the landlord employ self help to remove him? The following materials consider these and related questions.

a. REGAINING POSSESSION OF THE PREMISES

Forfeiture of the Lease. Unless a lease or applicable statute provided otherwise, the tenant's breach of his lease obligations traditionally did not entitle the landlord to terminate the lease and retake possession. The landlord's only recourse was an action for damages or, possibly, specific performance or injunctive relief. The rule rested on the traditional view that a lease is a conveyance of an interest in land rather than a bilateral contract containing mutually dependent covenants. See, e.g., State v. Brown, 282 N.W. 136, 137 (Minn. 1938). Despite the evolution of landlord-tenant law in other areas, this remains the common law rule in much of the United States today.

The only reason the common law rule has endured so long is that modern leases and statutes long ago emptied it of much consequence. Landlords and tenants, and the lease forms they employ, will usually be sufficiently farsighted to provide expressly that the tenant's default on any one or more specified covenants will terminate the lease either automatically or at the landlord's election. Further, statutes in more than forty states allow the landlord to summarily evict a tenant who fails to pay rent, even though the lease contains no express provision for forfeiture. Statutes in several states also allow the landlord to terminate for other specified breaches, such as waste, illegal use, or failure to obtain the landlord's required consent to an assignment or sublease. Some courts have abandoned the common law rule and now hold that a material breach by the tenant entitles the landlord to recover possession. See, e.g., Cain Partnership Ltd. v. Pioneer Investment Services Co., 914 S.W.2d 452, 456–458 (Tenn. 1996) (failure to pay assessed taxes, as required by lease, entitled landlord to terminate lease)

The traditional common law reluctance to terminate leases for failures to pay rent or for other material breaches remains relevant, however, in at least two contexts. First, courts in many states will narrowly interpret leases to limit the categories of breaches that can lead to forfeiture. For example, in Morris v. Austraw, 152 S.E.2d 155 (N.C. 1967), the landlord sought to terminate the lease for violation of an express covenant that the tenant would not use the premises for any "unlawful purpose or purposes." Although the lease did not contain any provision expressly terminating the lease for breach of this covenant, the landlord argued that termination was implicit in a provision entitling the landlord to attorney fees if he brought and won any "suit for the possession of the premises, for the recovery of any sum due hereunder, *or because of the breach of any covenant herein*" (emphasis added). The court disagreed: "Generally, unless there is an express stipulation for a forfeiture, the breach of a covenant in a lease does not work a forfeiture of the term. Moreover, the settled principle of both law and equity that contractual provisions for forfeitures are looked upon with disfavor applies with full force to stipulations for forfeitures found in leases; such stipulations are not looked upon with favor by the court, but on the contrary are strictly construed against the party seeking to invoke them."

Second, courts are often sympathetic to claims that the landlord has waived a breach by accepting rent without informing the tenant of an intent to terminate the lease. In Community Housing Alternatives, Inc. v. Latta, 362 S.E.2d 1 (N.C. App. 1987), for example, the landlord sought to terminate the lease because of the tenant's failure to maintain the apartment in a clean and sanitary condition. Because the landlord had continued to accept rent even after knowing of these conditions, the court held that the landlord had waived the right to terminate the lease. "It is the generally accepted rule that if the landlord receives rent from his tenant, after full notice or knowledge of a breach of a covenant or condition in his lease, for which a forfeiture might have been declared, such constitutes a waiver of the forfeiture which may not afterwards be asserted for that particular breach, or any other breach which occurred prior to the acceptance of the rent." See also Winslow v. Dillard Dept. Stores, Inc., 849 S.W.2d 862 (Tex. App. 1993) (finding waiver despite lease provision expressly stating that any delay in declaring a default does not waive the breach).

Summary Proceedings. Summary judicial proceedings, available in every state, give landlords a comparatively expeditious means for regaining possession of the leased premises when their tenants fail to pay rent, commit other specified breaches, or hold over after expiration of their term. States and cities first enacted these statutes, variously labeled "forcible entry and detainer," "unlawful detainer," "summary proceedings," or "summary ejectment," in the latter part of the nineteenth century in an effort to resolve the perennial conflict between landlords and tenants over eviction procedures. Landlords, frustrated by the lengthy and tortuous common law ejectment proceeding, typically used self-help to regain their premises. Tenants opposed self-help because of its potential for abuse. By giving landlords a simpler and safer procedural alternative, the new statutes reduced landlord incentives to pursue self-help evictions.

Although summary procedures vary from state to state, most follow the same general pattern. California's Forcible Entry and Detainer Statute, Cal. Civ. Proc. §§ 1159 et seq., is typical. The statute gives landlords a summary action against tenants holding over after their term, tenants who are in default of their rent payments, tenants who have breached other leasehold obligations, and tenants who are committing waste, engaging in a nuisance, or using the premises for an unlawful purpose. Id. § 1161. The landlord must give the tenant three days' notice before filing the action. Id. The landlord can then file a complaint, describing the premises and the nature of the unlawful detainer, along with a summons instructing the tenant that she has five days to respond to the complaint. Id. §§ 1166–1167. If the tenant fails to appear and defend the unlawful detainer action, the court will award the landlord a default judgment. Id. § 1169. If the tenant appears, the trial must take place "not later than the 20th day following the date that the request to set the time of trial is made." Id. § 1170.5(a). If the landlord prevails, the court is to immediately issue a writ of execution. Id. The landlord then turns to the local sheriff or marshal to execute the writ and evict the tenant.

Summary proceedings, however, are not always that summary. If a tenant does not fight eviction, landlords can sometimes recover possession of the premises in a few weeks time. In California, a landlord can theoretically recover the premises in 17 days—if the tenant does not answer the complaint and the marshal immediately evicts the tenant after the court issues the writ of execution. Randy G. Gerchick, No Easy Way Out: Making the Summary Eviction Process a Fairer and More Efficient Alternative to Landlord Self–Help, 41 UCLA L. Rev. 759, 807–808 (1994). But things are seldom this easy:

> In most cases in which the tenant is forcibly evicted by an officer of the court, the summary process will take substantially longer than the statutory minimum of seventeen days. Anecdotal evidence suggests that an eviction case may take from a few weeks to a few months, and in extreme cases of delay, may go on for a year or more. Statistical evidence suggests that eviction proceedings vary in length depending on a number of factors, but confirms that the summary eviction process usually takes over one month to complete.

> Studies of the duration of the eviction process in California have been conducted recently. It is difficult to reach a consensus as to the length of the eviction process based on these studies because of the differences in the manner in which the studies were conducted. For example, a study by [the California Apartment Law Information Foundation ("CALIF")] found that summary evictions in California during 1990 took an average of forty-eight days, with a median of thirty-three days, from filing of the unlawful detainer complaint to "final judicial disposition." The same study estimates that in the city of Los Angeles in 1990 the average length of an unlawful detainer case was 51.4 days with a median of 37 days. A different study of unlawful detainers in Los Angeles in 1991 conducted by the Los Angeles municipal courts ("LAMC") indicates a notably shorter period of thirty-four days from filing of [an unlawful detainer] complaint to "judicial disposition." This lower average, however, appears to reflect the duration of only the first main segment of the summary eviction process—the time from initial notice to judgment. The second segment of the eviction process—the period from obtaining the judgment to recovering actual possession of the rental unit—was found to take seventy-one days, more than twice as long as the first segment. All told, the LAMC study suggests that the summary eviction process takes an average of 108 days in Los Angeles, whereas the CALIF study reports a 51.4 day average. The difference in the results may be accounted for by the differences in how the results of the studies are reported or in the sample of cases that the two studies examined. Regardless of these differences in methodology and results, both studies demonstrate the eviction process often takes substantially longer than the seventeen-day statutory minimum. While these studies may prove useful in obtaining a general understanding of how long it takes to complete an eviction, it is important to recognize that the duration of any given case may vary drastically from the "averages" and will depend on a number of factors involving a complex combination of actions by tenants, landlords, attorneys, process servers, court clerks, judges, and marshals.

Id. at 808.

Self–Help. Can a landlord avoid this often lengthy process by exercising self-help and throwing the tenant off the premises immediately after a substantial breach occurs? Should a landlord be able to use self-help? If so, what type of self-help and under what circumstances? Consider the following case in this regard.

Berg v. Wiley

Supreme Court of Minnesota, 1978.
264 N.W.2d 145.

ROGOSHESKEM, Justice.

Defendant landlord, Wiley Enterprises, Inc., and defendant Rodney A. Wiley (hereafter collectively referred to as Wiley) appeal from a judgment upon a jury verdict awarding plaintiff tenant, A Family Affair Restaurant, Inc., damages for wrongful eviction from its leased premises. The issues for review are whether the evidence was sufficient to support the jury's finding that the tenant did not abandon or surrender the premises and whether the trial court erred in finding Wiley's reentry forcible and wrongful as a matter of law. We hold that the jury's verdict is supported by sufficient evidence and that the trial court's determination of unlawful entry was correct as matter of law, and affirm the judgment.

On November 11, 1970, Wiley, as lessor and tenant's predecessor in interest as lessee, executed a written lease agreement letting land and a building in Osseo, Minnesota, for use as a restaurant. The lease provided a 5-year term beginning December 1, 1970, and specified that the tenant agreed to bear all costs of repairs and remodeling, to "make no changes in the building structure" without prior written authorization from Wiley, and to "operate the restaurant in a lawful and prudent manner." Wiley also reserved the right "at [his] option [to] retake possession" of the premises "[s]hould the Lessee fail to meet the conditions of this Lease."[1] In early 1971, plaintiff Kathleen Berg took assignment of the lease from the prior lessee, and on May 1, 1971, she opened "A Family Affair Restaurant" on the premises. In January 1973, Berg incorporated the restaurant and assigned her interest in the lease to "A Family Affair Restaurant, Inc." As sole shareholder of the corporation, she alone continued to act for the tenant.

The present dispute has arisen out of Wiley's objection to Berg's continued remodeling of the restaurant without procuring written permission and her consequent operation of the restaurant in a state of disrepair with alleged health code violations. Strained relations between the parties came to a head in June and July 1973. In a letter dated June 29, 1973, Wiley's attorney charged Berg with having breached lease items 5 and 6 by making changes in the building structure without written authorization and by operating an unclean kitchen in violation of health regulations. The letter demanded that a list of eight remodeling items be completed within 2 weeks from the date of the letter, by Friday, July 13, 1973, or Wiley would retake possession of the premises under lease item 7. Also, a June 13 inspection of the restaurant by the Minnesota Department of Health had

1. The provisions of the lease pertinent to this case provide: "Item #5 The Lessee will make no changes to the building structure without first receiving written authorization from the Lessor. The Lessor will promptly reply in writing to each request and will cooperate with the Lessee on any reasonable request.

"Item #6 The Lessee agrees to operate the restaurant in a lawful and prudent manner during the lease period.

"Item #7 Should the Lessee fail to meet the conditions of this Lease the Lessor may at their option retake possession of said premises. In any such event such act will not relieve Lessee from liability for payment the rental herein provided or from the conditions or obligations of this lease."

produced an order that certain listed changes be completed within specified time limits in order to comply with the health code. The major items on the inspector's list, similar to those listed by Wiley's attorney, were to be completed by July 15, 1973.

During the 2–week deadline set by both Wiley and the health department, Berg continued to operate the restaurant without closing to complete the required items of remodeling. The evidence is in dispute as to whether she intended to permanently close the restaurant and vacate the premises at the end of the 2 weeks or simply close for about 1 month in order to remodel to comply with the health code. At the close of business on Friday, July 13, 1973, the last day of the 2–week period, Berg dismissed her employees, closed the restaurant, and placed a sign in the window saying "Closed for Remodeling." Earlier that day, Berg testified, Wiley came to the premises in her absence and attempted to change the locks. When she returned and asserted her right to continue in possession, he complied with her request to leave the locks unchanged. Berg also testified that at about 9:30 p.m. that evening, while she and four of her friends were in the restaurant, she observed Wiley hanging from the awning peering into the window. Shortly thereafter, she heard Wiley pounding on the back door demanding admittance. Berg called the county sheriff to come and preserve order. Wiley testified that he observed Berg and a group of her friends in the restaurant removing paneling from a wall. Allegedly fearing destruction of his property, Wiley called the city police, who, with the sheriff, mediated an agreement between the parties to preserve the status quo until each could consult with legal counsel on Monday, July 16, 1973.

Wiley testified that his then attorney advised him to take possession of the premises and lock the tenant out. Accompanied by a police officer and a locksmith, Wiley entered the premises in Berg's absence and without her knowledge on Monday, July 16, 1973, and changed the locks. Later in the day, Berg found herself locked out. The lease term was not due to expire until December 1, 1975. The premises were re-let to another tenant on or about August 1, 1973. Berg brought this damage action against Wiley and three other named defendants, including the new tenant, on July 27, 1973. A second amended complaint sought damages for lost profits, damage to chattels, intentional infliction of emotional distress, and other tort damages based upon claims in wrongful eviction, contract, and tort. Wiley answered with an affirmative defense of abandonment and surrender and counterclaimed for damage to the premises and indemnification on mechanics lien liability incurred because of Berg's remodeling. At the close of Berg's case, all defendants other than Rodney A. Wiley and Wiley Enterprises, Inc., were dismissed from the action. Only Berg's action for wrongful eviction and intentional infliction of emotional distress and Wiley's affirmative defense of abandonment and his counterclaim for damage to the premises were submitted by special verdict to the jury. With respect to the wrongful eviction claim, the trial court found as a matter of law that Wiley did in fact lock the tenant out, and that the lockout was wrongful.

The jury, by answers to the questions submitted, found no liability on Berg's claim for intentional infliction of emotional distress and no liability on Wiley's counterclaim for damages to the premises, but awarded Berg $31,000 for lost profits and $3,540 for loss of chattels resulting from the wrongful lockout. The jury also specifically found that Berg neither abandoned nor surrendered the premises. The trial court granted Wiley's post-trial motion for an order decreeing that Berg indemnify Wiley for any mechanics lien liability incurred due to Berg's remodeling by way of set-off from Berg's judgment and ordered the judgment accordingly amended.

On this appeal, Wiley seeks an outright reversal of the damages award for wrongful eviction, claiming insufficient evidence to support the jury's finding of no abandonment or surrender and claiming error in the trial court's finding of wrongful eviction as a matter of law.

The first issue before us concerns the sufficiency of evidence to support the jury's finding that Berg had not abandoned or surrendered the leasehold before being locked out by Wiley. Viewing the evidence to support the jury's special verdict in the light most favorable to Berg, as we must, we hold it amply supports the jury's finding of no abandonment or surrender of the premises. While the evidence bearing upon Berg's intent was strongly contradictory, the jury could reasonably have concluded, based on Berg's testimony and supporting circumstantial evidence, that she intended to retain possession, closing temporarily to remodel. Thus, the lockout cannot be excused on ground that Berg abandoned or surrendered the leasehold.

The second and more difficult issue is whether Wiley's self-help repossession of the premises by locking out Berg was correctly held wrongful as a matter of law.

Minnesota has historically followed the common-law rule that a landlord may rightfully use self-help to retake leased premises from a tenant in possession without incurring liability for wrongful eviction provided two conditions are met: (1) The landlord is legally entitled to possession, such as where a tenant holds over after the lease term or where a tenant breaches a lease containing a reentry clause; and (2) the landlord's means of reentry are peaceable. Under the common-law rule, a tenant who is evicted by his landlord may recover damages for wrongful eviction where the landlord either had no right to possession or where the means used to remove the tenant were forcible, or both. See, also, Minn. St. 566.01 (statutory cause of action where entry is not "allowed by law" or, if allowed, is not made "in a peaceable manner").

Wiley contends that Berg had breached the provisions of the lease, thereby entitling Wiley, under the terms of the lease, to retake possession, and that his repossession by changing the locks in Berg's absence was accomplished in a peaceful manner. In a memorandum accompanying the post-trial order, the trial court stated two grounds for finding the lockout wrongful as a matter of law: (1) It was not accomplished in a peaceable manner and therefore could not be justified under the common-law rule, and (2) any self-help reentry against a tenant in possession is wrongful under the growing modern doctrine that a landlord must always resort to the judicial process to enforce his statutory remedy against a tenant wrongfully in possession. Whether Berg had in fact breached the lease and whether Wiley was hence entitled to possession was not judicially determined. That issue became irrelevant upon the trial court's finding that Wiley's reentry was forcible as a matter of law because even if Berg had breached the lease, this could not excuse Wiley's nonpeaceable reentry. The finding that Wiley's reentry was forcible as a matter of law provided a sufficient ground for damages, and the issue of breach was not submitted to the jury.

In each of our previous cases upholding an award of damages for wrongful eviction, the landlord had in fact been found to have no legal right to possession. In applying the common-law rule, we have not before had occasion to decide what means of self-help used to dispossess a tenant in his absence will constitute a nonpeaceable entry, giving a right to damages without regard to who holds the legal right to possession. Wiley argues that only actual or threatened violence used against a tenant should give rise to damages where the landlord had the right to possession. We cannot agree.

It has long been the policy of our law to discourage landlords from taking the law into their own hands, and our decisions and statutory law have looked with disfavor upon any use of self-help to dispossess a tenant in circumstances which are likely to result in breaches of the peace. We gave early recognition to this policy in Lobdell v. Keene, 85 Minn. 90, 101, 88 N.W. 426, 430 (1901), where we said:

> The object and purpose of the legislature in the enactment of the forcible entry and unlawful detainer statute was to prevent those claiming a right of entry or possession of lands from redressing their own wrongs by entering into possession in a violent and forcible manner. All such acts tend to a breach of the peace, and encourage high-handed oppression. The law does not permit the owner of land, be his title ever so good, to be the judge of his own rights with respect to a possession adversely held, but puts him to his remedy under the statutes.

To facilitate a resort to judicial process, the legislature has provided a summary procedure in Minn. St. 566.02 to 566.17 whereby a landlord may recover possession of leased premises upon proper notice and showing in court in as little as 3 to 10 days. As we recognized in Mutual Trust Life Ins. Co. v. Berg, 187 Minn. 503, 505, 246 N.W. 9, 10 (1932), "[t]he forcible entry and unlawful detainer statutes were intended to prevent parties from taking the law into their own hands when going into possession of lands and tenements...." To further discourage self-help, our legislature has provided treble damages for forcible evictions, §§ 557.08 and 557.09, and has provided additional criminal penalties for intentional and unlawful exclusion of a tenant. § 504.25. In Sweeney v. Meyers, 199 Minn. 21, 270 N.W. 906 (1937), we allowed a business tenant not only damages for lost profits but also punitive damages against a landlord who, like Wiley, entered in the tenant's absence and locked the tenant out.

In the present case, as in *Sweeney*, the tenant was in possession, claiming a right to continue in possession adverse to the landlord's claim of breach of the lease, and had neither abandoned nor surrendered the premises. Wiley, well aware that Berg was asserting her right to possession, retook possession in her absence by picking the locks and locking her out. The record shows a history of vigorous dispute and keen animosity between the parties. Upon this record, we can only conclude that the singular reason why actual violence did not erupt at the moment of Wiley's changing of the locks was Berg's absence and her subsequent self-restraint and resort to judicial process. Upon these facts, we cannot find Wiley's means of reentry peaceable under the common-law rule. Our long-standing policy to discourage self-help which tends to cause a breach of the peace compels us to disapprove the means used to dispossess Berg. To approve this lockout, as urged by Wiley, merely because in Berg's absence no actual violence erupted while the locks were being changed, would be to encourage all future tenants, in order to protect their possession, to be vigilant and thereby set the stage for the very kind of public disturbance which it must be our policy to discourage.

Consistent with our conclusion that we cannot find Wiley's means of reentry peaceable under the common-law rule is Gulf Oil Corp. v. Smithey, 426 S.W.2d 262 (Tex. Civ. App.1968). In that case the Texas court, without departing from the common-law rule, held that a landlord's reentry in the tenant's absence by picking the locks and locking the tenant out, although accomplished without actual violence, was forcible as a matter of law. The Texas courts, by continuing to embrace the common-law rule, have apparently left open the possibility that self-help may be available in that state to dispossess a tenant in some undefined circumstances which may be found peaceable.

We recognize that the growing modern trend departs completely from the common-law rule to hold that self-help is never available to dispossess a tenant who is in possession and has not abandoned or voluntarily surrendered the premises. This growing rule is founded on the recognition that the potential for violent breach of peace inheres in any situation where a landlord attempts by his own means to remove a tenant who is claiming possession adversely to the landlord. Courts adopting the rule reason that there is no cause to sanction such potentially disruptive self-help where adequate and speedy means are provided for removing a tenant peacefully through judicial process. At least 16 states have adopted this modern rule, holding that judicial proceedings, including the summary procedures provided in those states' unlawful detainer statutes, are the exclusive remedy by which a landlord may remove a tenant claiming possession. While we would be compelled to disapprove the lockout of Berg in her absence under the common-law rule as stated, we approve the trial court's reasoning and adopt as preferable the modern view represented by the cited cases. To make clear our departure from the common-law rule for the benefit of future landlords and tenants, we hold that, subsequent to our decision in this case, the only lawful means to dispossess a tenant who has not abandoned nor voluntarily surrendered but who claims possession adversely to a landlord's claim of breach of a written lease is by resort to judicial process. We find that Minn. St. 566.02 to 566.17 provide the landlord with an adequate remedy for regaining possession in every such case. Where speedier action than provided in §§ 566.02 to 566.17 seems necessary because of threatened destruction of the property or other exigent circumstances, a temporary restraining order under Rule 65, Rules of Civil Procedure, and law enforcement protection are available to the landlord. Considered together, these statutory and judicial remedies provide a complete answer to the landlord. In our modern society, with the availability of prompt and sufficient legal remedies as described, there is no place and no need for self-help against a tenant in claimed lawful possession of leased premises.

Applying our holding to the facts of this case, we conclude, as did the trial court, that because Wiley failed to resort to judicial remedies against Berg's holding possession adversely to Wiley's claim of breach of the lease, his lockout of Berg was wrongful as a matter of law. The rule we adopt in this decision is fairly applied against Wiley, for it is clear that, applying the older common-law rule to the facts and circumstances peculiar to this case, we would be compelled to find the lockout nonpeaceable for the reasons previously stated. The jury found that the lockout caused Berg damage and, as between Berg and Wiley, equity dictates that Wiley, who himself performed the act causing the damage, must bear the loss.

Notes & Questions

1. Do you agree with the rule adopted in Berg v. Wiley? Who is better placed to bear the loss occasioned by the delays of judicial process—the tenant, removed by self-help, who may be wrongly deprived of his shelter or place of business before he can get possession back, or the landlord who, while awaiting trial of her summary proceeding, may see her investment further threatened by the acts of a breaching tenant? Should the answer depend upon whether the lease is for residential or commercial purposes? On whether one party is willing to indemnify the other for losses wrongfully suffered as a result of delay in the determination of rights?

2. Spurred by modern notions of due process, fairness, and civility, the vast majority of states today outlaw self-help measures. See, e.g., Unified Residential Landlord and Tenant Act § 4.207 (requiring landlords to use summary proceedings to regain possession). Some states bar self-help in residential leases, but still permit commercial landlords to exercise self-help. See, e.g., PRC Kentron, Inc. v. First City Center Associates, 762 S.W.2d 279 (Tex. App. 1988); Northfield Park Associates v. Northeast Ohio Harness, 521 N.E.2d 466 (Ohio App. 1987); Watson v. Brown, 686 P.2d 12 (Haw. 1984). A few states continue to permit self-help in both commercial and residential settings. See, e.g., Moriarty v. Dziak, 435 So. 2d 35 (Ala. 1983); Alaska Stat. § 09.45.690.

States that allow the landlord to employ self-help in some or all situations typically require that the self-help be "peaceable." See, e.g.,

Klosterman v. Hickel Investment Co., 821 P.2d 118 (Alaska 1991); Gargano v. Heyman, 525 A.2d 1343 (Conn. 1987). Judicial use of the concept, "peaceable," ranges from literal applications, permitting the landlord to take any steps that are neither injurious to the tenant nor a breach of the public peace, to applications so narrow and rigorous that they effectively bar any resort to self-help—for example, prohibiting such comparatively inoffensive measures as entry through an open window or by use of a passkey.

Faced with the difficulty of determining whether their acts will qualify as a "peaceable entry," how many landlords will risk the substantial damage award (and potential trespass charge) that may attend a retaking of possession by self-help? Does this pervasive uncertainty and ambiguity respecting the boundaries of legitimate self-help suggest that, as a practical matter, few landlords will employ self-help even where the law permits it?

3. Did *Berg* intend that its rule prohibiting landlord self-help be waivable by the parties? Should the prohibition be waivable? Although some courts have held that a lease provision expressly permitting the landlord to pursue reasonable self-help measures will supersede an applicable common law rule imposing a stricter standard, or outlawing self help entirely, a growing number of jurisdictions hold these provisions void as against public policy. Compare Rucker v. Wynn, 441 S.E.2d 417 (Ga. App. 1994) (upholding waiver in commercial lease) with McCrory v. Johnson, 755 S.W.2d 566 (Ark. 1988) (lease provisions authorizing self-help are illegal and invalid) and Jordan v. Talbot, 361 P.2d 20 (Cal. 1961) (same).

4. **Distress & Statutory Liens.** A landlord concerned that her defaulting, and possibly impecunious, tenant will be unable to satisfy a judgment for rental owed, may have one or two additional remedies in her arsenal: the common law remedy of *distress* (sometimes called the right of distraint), entitling her to seize personal property found on the premises as security for the rent, and a *statutory lien* on all personal property on the leased premises.

At early common law, the right of distress entitled the landlord to seize any chattels found on the leased premises belonging to the tenant, or even to a third party, and to hold them as security for rent. The statute, 2 Wm. & Mary, ch. 5 (1689), gave the landlord the additional right to sell the chattels. Distress with power of sale was widely imported into the American states and, although later abolished in many, is still available in others with a variety of statutory modifications. New Jersey and some other states, for example, allow distraint for commercial, but not residential, leases. See N.J. Stat. Ann. § 2A:33–1. The most pervasive statutory modification has been to eliminate or closely confine the landlord's ability to distrain through self-help rather than judicial process, and to surround the process with a number of procedural safeguards for the tenant.

Most states have, as an alternative or complement to distress, given landlords a statutory lien on their tenants' chattels as security for the tenants' obligation to pay rent. Unlike distress, which gives the landlord an interest in the chattels only upon the tenant's default, statutory liens typically attach at the beginning of the term. The landlord's right to enforce the lien does not, however, generally arise until the tenant defaults on the rental obligation.

5. **Constitutional Limitations.** Tenants have challenged self-help repossession, distraint, statutory liens, and summary proceedings as violating their right under the Fourteenth Amendment to the United States Constitution not to be deprived of property without due process of law. Ironically, the least proceduralized seizures are most immune from constitutional attack. If the landlord takes possession of the premises or the tenant's personal property without resorting to the state's judicial machinery, courts are likely to find that state action, required for the Fourteenth Amendment to apply, is missing. See, e.g., Luria Bros. & Co. v. Allen, 672 F.2d 347 (3d Cir. 1982) (posting of a notice of distraint does not constitute state action).

Unlawful detainer actions have proven more susceptible to constitutional challenge. In Lindsey v. Normet, 405 U.S. 56 (1972), tenants challenged three provisions of Oregon's summary proceeding statute: (1) the requirement that the trial be held between two and six days after service of the complaint, (2) the exclusion of habitability from the issues that are litigable in the proceeding, and (3) the requirement that tenants who wish to appeal must post a bond equal to twice the rent likely to be found due. The court upheld the first two provisions. A speedy trial was unlikely to prejudice the tenant, who "would appear to have as much access to relevant facts," such as whether the rent had been paid, as the landlord. As for any habitability claims that the tenant might have, the Oregon statute did not foreclose the tenant "from instituting his own action against the landlord and litigating his right to damages or other relief in that action." The bond, however, was unconstitutionally burdensome. The bond effectively "doubled the stakes" for a tenant wishing to appeal and discriminated against the poor. "For them, as a practical matter, appeal is foreclosed, no matter how meritorious their case may be." See also Greene v. Lindsey, 456 U.S. 444 (1982) (invalidating a Kentucky statute allowing service of process in a summary proceeding under the state's Forcible Entry and Detainer Act to be made by posting a summons on the tenant's apartment door).

b. DAMAGES

The last section addressed landlords' options where a tenant breaches the lease but refuses to move out. Landlords also face the risk that a tenant will announce that he is moving out and will no longer pay rent. In these cases, the landlord does not have to worry about getting rid of the tenant, but does not want to lose the economic advantage of the lease. In these cases, the landlord has at least three options.

Surrender of the Lease. If the landlord believes that he can lease the premises to someone else for the same or greater rent than he was charging the original tenant, the landlord can treat the tenant's actions as an offer to surrender the lease and accept the offer. In this case, the landlord regains possession of the premises, the original tenant is off the hook, and the landlord can relet the premises—potentially at a profit. The surrender of the lease, however, does not relieve the original tenant of liability for any back rent that is still owing, and the landlord can still sue the tenant to recover this amount.

Reletting on Tenant's Account. If the landlord does not believe that he can get a higher rental from a new tenant, the landlord also can refuse to accept the tenant's surrender and, after notice to the tenant, relet the premises *on the tenant's account*—in which case, the landlord "may recover from the original lessee the balance of the rent due under his lease less the rent received from the new lessee." Sagamore Corp. v. Willcutt, 180 A. 464 (Conn. 1935). If the lease, for example, provides for rent of $1000 per month and the landlord is able to relet the premises for only $600, she would be entitled to $400 per month in damages (discounted, where necessary, to reflect the fact that the landlord will be suffering the loss in the future). If the new tenant defaults and fails to pay the new rent, the original tenant is back on the hook for the full original rental. As its name suggests, the tenant's account approach rests on a conveyance view of leases: the premises belong to the tenant for the entire leasehold term and, in reletting them, the landlord is effectively acting as the tenant's agent.

Damages for Anticipatory Breach. Alternatively, the landlord can treat the tenant's actions as an anticipatory breach of the tenant's promise to pay rent in the future and can sue for damages. The landlord generally can recover the difference between the rent provided for in the lease and the reasonable rental value of the premises—the amount that a willing tenant would pay a willing landlord for the remainder of the term. If the lease, for example, again provides for rent of $1000 per month and the reasonable rental value is only $800 per month, the landlord would receive $200 in damages for the remainder of the lease term (discounted again as appropriate). Courts also will generally award the landlord reasonable expenses incurred in connection with finding a new tenant (e.g., brokerage or advertising expenses).

Can the landlord, rather than turning to one of these remedies, simply sit on the vacant apartment, not relet it, and sue the tenant for the rent payments as they become due and owing? Does the landlord, in short, need to try to mitigate the damages from the tenant's breach of the lease? Alternatively, can the landlord provide for other remedies in the lease agreement? The next two cases consider these questions.

Austin Hill Country Realty, Inc. v. Palisades Plaza, Inc.

Supreme Court of Texas, 1997.
948 S.W.2d 293.

JUSTICE SPECTOR delivered the opinion for a unanimous Court.

The issue in this case is whether a landlord has a duty to make reasonable efforts to mitigate damages when a tenant defaults on a lease.

The court of appeals held that no such duty exists at common law. We hold today that a landlord has a duty to make reasonable efforts to mitigate damages. Accordingly, we reverse the judgment of the court of appeals and remand for a new trial.

Palisades Plaza, Inc., owned and operated an office complex consisting of four office buildings in Austin. Barbara Hill, Annette Smith, and David Jones sold real estate in Austin as a Re/Max real estate brokerage franchise operating through Austin Hill Country Realty, Inc. On September 15, 1992, the Palisades and Hill Country executed a five-year commercial office lease for a suite in the Palisades' office complex. An addendum executed in connection with the lease set the monthly base rent at $3,128 for the first year, $3,519 for the second and third years, and $3,910 for the fourth and fifth years. The parties also signed an improvements agreement that called for the Palisades to convert the shell office space into working offices for Hill Country. The lease was to begin on the "commencement date," which was defined in the lease and the improvements agreement as either (1) the date that Hill Country occupied the suite, or (2) the date that the Palisades substantially completed the improvements or would have done so but for "tenant delay." All parties anticipated that the lease would begin on November 15, 1992.

By the middle of October 1992, the Palisades had nearly completed the improvements. Construction came to a halt on October 21, 1992, when the Palisades received conflicting instructions about the completion of the suite from Hill on one hand and Smith and Jones on the other. By two letters, the Palisades informed Hill Country, Hill, Smith, and Jones that it had received conflicting directives and would not continue with the construction until Hill, Smith, and Jones collectively designated a single representative empowered to make decisions for the trio. Hill, Smith, and Jones did not reply to these letters.

In a letter dated November 19, 1992, the Palisades informed Hill Country, Hill, Smith, and Jones that their failure to designate a representative was an anticipatory breach of contract. The parties tried unsuccessfully to resolve their differences in a meeting. The Palisades then sued Hill Country, Hill, Smith, and Jones (collectively, "Hill Country") for anticipatory breach of the lease.

At trial, Hill Country attempted to prove that the Palisades failed to mitigate the damages resulting from Hill Country's alleged breach. In particular, Hill Country introduced evidence that the Palisades rejected an offer from Smith and Jones to lease the premises without Hill, as well as an offer from Hill and another person to lease the premises without Smith and Jones. Hill Country also tried to prove that, while the Palisades advertised for tenants continuously in a local newspaper, it did not advertise in the commercial-property publication "The Flick Report" as it had in the past. Hill Country requested an instruction asking the jury to reduce the Palisades' damage award by "any amount that you find the [Palisades] could have avoided by the exercise of reasonable care." The trial judge rejected this instruction, stating, "Last time I checked the law, it was that a landlord doesn't have any obligation to try to fill the space." The jury returned a verdict for the Palisades for $29,716 in damages and $16,500 in attorney's fees. The court of appeals affirmed that judgment.

In its only point of error, Hill Country asks this Court to recognize a landlord's duty to make reasonable efforts to mitigate damages when a tenant breaches a lease. . . .

The traditional common law rule regarding mitigation dictates that landlords have no duty to mitigate damages. See Dawn R. Barker, Commercial Landlords' Duty upon Tenants' Abandonment—To Mitigate?, 20 J. Corp. L. 627, 629 (1995). This rule stems from the historical concept that the tenant is owner of the property during the lease term; as long as the tenant has a right to possess the land, the tenant is liable for rent. See Reid v. Mutual of Omaha Ins. Co., 776 P.2d 896, 902, 905 (Utah 1989). Under this rule, a landlord is not obligated to undertake any action following a tenant's abandonment of the premises but may recover rents periodically for the remainder of the term . . . .

In discerning the policy implications of a rule requiring landlords to mitigate damages, we are informed by the rules of other jurisdictions. Forty-two states and the District of Columbia have recognized that a landlord has a duty to mitigate damages in at least some situations: when there is a breach of a residential lease, a commercial lease, or both. Only six states have explicitly held that a landlord has no duty to mitigate in any situation.[2] In South Dakota, the law is unclear.

Those jurisdictions recognizing a duty to mitigate have emphasized the change in the nature of landlord-tenant law since its inception in medieval times. At English common law, the tenant had only contractual rights against the landlord and therefore could not assert common-law real property causes of action to protect the leasehold. Over time, the courts recognized a tenant's right to bring real property causes of action, and tenants were considered to possess an estate in land. The landlord had to give the tenant possession of the land, and the tenant was required to pay rent in return. As covenants in leases have become more complex and the structures on the land have become more important to the parties than the land itself, courts have begun to recognize that a lease possesses elements of both a contract and a conveyance. Under contract principles, the lease is

2. Ryals v. Laney, 338 So. 2d 413, 415 (Ala. Civ. App. 1976) (holding that there is no duty to mitigate in residential leases); Crestline Ctr. v. Hinton, 567 So. 2d 393, 396 (Ala. Civ. App. 1990) (commercial); Love v. McDevitt, 114 Ga. App. 734, 152 S.E.2d 705, 706 (Ga. Ct. App. 1966) (residential); Lamb v. Decatur Fed. Sav. & Loan Ass'n, 201 Ga. App. 583, 411 S.E.2d 527, 530 (Ga. Ct. App. 1991) (commercial); Markoe v. Naiditch & Sons, 303 Minn. 6, 226 N.W.2d 289, 291 (Minn. 1975) (residential and commercial); Alsup v. Banks, 68 Miss. 664, 9 So. 895, 895 (Miss. 1891) (residential); Duda v. Thompson, 169 Misc. 2d 649, 647 N.Y.S.2d 401, 403–04 (N.Y. Sup. Ct. 1996) (residential); Holy Properties, Ltd. v. Kenneth Cole Prods., Inc., 87 N.Y.2d 130, 661 N.E.2d 694, 696, 637 N.Y.S.2d 964 (N.Y. 1995) (commercial); Arbenz v. Exley, Watkins & Co., 52 W. Va. 476, 44 S.E. 149, 151 (W. Va. 1903) (commercial). Mississippi has reported no cases regarding a commercial landlord's duty to mitigate, and West Virginia has reported no cases regarding a residential landlord's duty to mitigate.

not a complete conveyance to the tenant for a specified term such that the landlord's duties are fulfilled upon deliverance of the property to the tenant. Rather, a promise to pay in a lease is essentially the same as a promise to pay in any other contract, and a breach of that promise does not necessarily end the landlord's ongoing duties. Because of the contractual elements of the modern lease agreement, these courts have imposed upon the landlord the contractual duty to mitigate damages upon the tenant's breach.

Public policy offers further justification for the duty to mitigate. First, requiring mitigation in the landlord-tenant context discourages economic waste and encourages productive use of the property. As the Colorado Supreme Court has written:

> Under traditional property law principles a landlord could allow the property to remain unoccupied while still holding the abandoning tenant liable for rent. This encourages both economic and physical waste. In no other context of which we are aware is an injured party permitted to sit idly by and suffer avoidable economic loss and thereafter to visit the full adverse economic consequences upon the party whose breach initiated the chain of events causing the loss.

Schneiker v. Gordon, 732 P.2d 603, 610 (Colo. 1987). A mitigation requirement thus returns the property to productive use rather than allowing it to remain idle. Public policy requires that the law "discourage even persons against whom wrongs have been committed from passively suffering economic loss which could be averted by reasonable efforts." Wright v. Baumann, 398 P.2d 119, 121 (Or. 1965) (quoting C. McCormick, Handbook on the Law of Damages § 33 (1935)).

Second, a mitigation rule helps prevent destruction of or damage to the leased property. If the landlord is encouraged to let the property remain unoccupied, "the possibility of physical damage to the property through accident or vandalism is increased." *Schneiker*, 732 P.2d at 610.

Third, the mitigation rule is consistent with the trend disfavoring contract penalties. Courts have held that a liquidated damages clause in a contract must represent a reasonable estimate of anticipated damages upon breach. See, e.g., Warner v. Rasmussen, 704 P.2d 559, 561, 563 (Utah 1985). "Similarly, allowing a landlord to leave property idle when it could be profitably leased and forcing an absent tenant to pay rent for that idled property permits the landlord to recover more damages than it may reasonably require to be compensated for the tenant's breach. This is analogous to imposing a disfavored penalty upon the tenant." Reid v. Mutual of Omaha Ins. Co., 776 P.2d 896, 902, 905–06 (Utah 1989).

Finally, the traditional justifications for the common law rule have proven unsound in practice. Proponents of the no-mitigation rule suggest that the landlord-tenant relationship is personal in nature, and that the landlord therefore should not be forced to lease to an unwanted tenant. Modern lease arrangements, however, are rarely personal in nature and are usually business arrangements between strangers. Further, the landlord's duty to make reasonable efforts to mitigate does not require that the landlord accept replacement tenants who are financial risks or whose business was precluded by the original lease.

The overwhelming trend among jurisdictions in the United States has thus been toward requiring a landlord to mitigate damages when a tenant abandons the property in breach of the lease agreement. Those courts adopting a mitigation requirement have emphasized the contractual elements of a lease agreement, the public policy favoring productive use of property, and the practicalities of the modern landlord-tenant arrangement as supporting such a duty.

We are persuaded by the reasoning of those courts that recognize that landlords must mitigate damages upon a tenant's abandonment and failure to pay rent. This Court has recognized the dual nature of a lease as both a conveyance and a contract. Under a contract view, a landlord should be treated no differently than any other aggrieved party to a contract. Further, the public policy of the state of Texas calls for productive use of property as opposed to avoidable economic waste. As Professor McCormick wrote over seventy years ago, the law

> which permits the landlord to stand idly by the vacant, abandoned premises and treat them as the property of the tenant and recover full rent, [should] yield to the more realistic notions of social advantage which in other fields of the law have forbidden a recovery for damages which the plaintiff by reasonable efforts could have avoided.

Charles McCormick, The Rights of the Landlord Upon Abandonment of the Premises by the Tenant, 23 Mich. L. Rev. 211, 221–22 (1925). Finally, we have recognized that contract penalties are disfavored in Texas. Stewart v. Basey, 245 S.W.2d 484, 486 (Tex. 1952) (landlord should not receive more or less than actual damages upon tenant's breach). A landlord should not be allowed to collect rent from an abandoning tenant when the landlord can, by reasonable efforts, relet the premises and avoid incurring some damages. We therefore recognize that a landlord has a duty to make reasonable efforts to mitigate damages when the tenant breaches the lease and abandons the property, unless the commercial landlord and tenant contract otherwise.

To ensure the uniform application of this duty by the courts of this state, and to guide future landlords and tenants in conforming their conduct to the law, we now consider several practical considerations that will undoubtedly arise. We first consider the level of conduct by a landlord that will satisfy the duty to mitigate. The landlord's mitigation duty has been variously stated in other jurisdictions. See, e.g., *Reid*, 776 P.2d at 906 ("objective commercial reasonableness"); *Schneiker*, 732 P.2d at 611 ("reasonable efforts"); Cal. Civ. Code § 1951.2(c)(2) ("reasonably and in a good-faith effort").... We hold that the landlord's duty to mitigate requires the landlord to use objectively reasonable efforts to fill the premises when the tenant vacates in breach of the lease.

We stress that this is not an absolute duty. The landlord is not required to simply fill the premises with any willing tenant; the replacement tenant must be suitable under the circumstances. Nor does the landlord's failure to mitigate give rise to a cause of action by the tenant. Rather, the landlord's failure to use reasonable efforts to mitigate damages bars the landlord's recovery against the breaching tenant only to the extent that damages reasonably could have been avoided. Similarly, the amount of damages that the landlord actually avoided by releasing the premises will reduce the landlord's recovery.

Further, we believe that the tenant properly bears the burden of proof to demonstrate that the landlord has mitigated or failed to mitigate damages and the amount by which the landlord reduced or could have reduced its damages. The traditional rule in other contexts is that the breaching party must show that the nonbreaching party could have reduced its damages. In the landlord-tenant context, although there is some split of authority, many other jurisdictions have placed the burden of proving mitigation or failure to mitigate upon the breaching tenant. . . .

The final issue to resolve regarding the duty to mitigate is to which types of actions by the landlord the duty will apply. Traditionally, Texas courts have regarded the landlord as having four causes of action against a tenant for breach of the lease and abandonment. First, the landlord can maintain the lease, suing for rent as it becomes due. Second, the landlord can treat the breach as an anticipatory repudiation, repossess, and sue for the present value of future rentals reduced by the reasonable cash market value of the property for the remainder of the lease term. Third, the landlord can treat the breach as anticipatory, repossess, release the property, and sue the tenant for the difference between the contractual rent and the amount received from the new tenant. Fourth, the landlord can declare the lease forfeited (if the lease so provides) and relieve the tenant of liability for future rent.

The landlord must have a duty to mitigate when suing for anticipatory repudiation. Because the cause of action is contractual in nature, the contractual duty to mitigate should apply. The landlord's option to maintain the lease and sue for rent as it becomes due, however, is more troubling. To require the landlord to mitigate in that instance would force the landlord to reenter the premises and thereby risk terminating the lease or accepting the tenant's surrender. We thus hold that, when exercising the option to maintain the lease in effect and sue for rent as it becomes due following the tenant's breach and abandonment, the landlord has a duty to mitigate only if (1) the landlord actually reenters, or (2) the lease allows the landlord to reenter the premises without accepting surrender, forfeiting the lease, or being construed as evicting the tenant. A suit for anticipatory repudiation, an actual reentry, or a contractual right of reentry subject to the above conditions will therefore give rise to the landlord's duty to mitigate damages upon the tenant's breach and abandonment.

In their first amended answer, Hill Country and Barbara Hill specifically contended that the Palisades failed to mitigate its damages. Because the court of appeals upheld the trial court's refusal to submit their mitigation instruction, we reverse the judgment of the court of appeals and remand for a new trial.

Aurora Business Park v. Michael Albert, Inc.

Supreme Court of Iowa, 1996.
548 N.W.2d 153.

ANDREASEN, Justice.

The district court entered judgment for the landlord on its action for the recovery of past unpaid rent and for future rent as damages under an acceleration clause in the parties' lease. The tenant contends that the acceleration clause constitutes an unenforceable penalty and that the court failed to award the proper damages. We affirm as modified and remand.

The defendants, Michael Albert, Inc. and Michael L. Albert (Albert), and the plaintiff, Aurora Business Park Associates, L.P. (Aurora), entered into a lease agreement in which Albert agreed to lease office and warehouse space in the Aurora Business Park. The lease term was from March 1, 1991 until February 28, 1996. Albert took possession of the property after signing the lease but vacated the premises some time in June or July of 1993. No June rent payment was made and notice of default was given to Albert. Shortly thereafter, Aurora served a notice to quit and retook possession of the premises. Aurora was unsuccessful in reletting the property.

The lease includes the following provision:

> In the event of termination of this Lease by reason of a violation of its terms by the Lessee, Lessor shall be entitled to prove claim for and obtain judgment against Lessee for the balance of the rent agreed to be paid for the term herein provided, plus all expenses of Lessor in regaining possession of the premises and the reletting thereof, including attorneys' fees and court costs, crediting against such claim, however, any amount obtained by reason of any such reletting.

In August 1993, Aurora brought an action to recover past unpaid rent and the balance of rent for the remaining term of the lease. The matter was tried before the district court on May 31, 1994. At the end of Aurora's case, Albert moved for a dismissal claiming Aurora failed to establish that it used reasonable diligence in attempting to relet the premises. The motion was denied. Albert also asserted that an award of future rent would be improper because the acceleration clause constituted an unenforceable penalty and, alternatively, that the court was required to offset any future rent by the reasonable value of the use of the premises to the landlord or a reasonable amount for rent the landlord would actually receive during the remaining term of the lease.

On August 31, the court entered judgment in favor of Aurora and against Albert in the amount of $221,692.28 with interest plus attorney fees and court costs. The court concluded that Albert had breached the lease by abandoning the property without giving notice and by defaulting on the rental payments. The court found the acceleration clause to be a valid liquidated damages provision rather than an unenforceable penalty. The court also found that Aurora had used reasonable diligence in attempting to relet the property. The court awarded damages for the remaining term of the lease without offset for a reasonable value of the use of the premises to Aurora or for rent which may be received from reletting the property during the remaining term of the lease. The court did not reduce the amount for future rent to its present value.

Albert contends that the judgment not only allows Aurora to recover the amount of rent due under the terms of the lease, but also allows Aurora to retain possession of the premises for its own use or relet the premises and retain any rents collected. Consequently, Aurora is placed in a better position than if the lease had been performed. Albert claims this not only violates the general principles of law against double recovery, but also violates the terms of the lease which specifically states that actual rents collected are to be offset against the amount of the claim. Additionally, Albert contends that the acceleration clause is an unenforceable penalty.

Some jurisdictions have held that provisions for the acceleration of payments of rent are invalid as unenforceable penalties. See, e.g., Kothe v. R.C. Taylor Trust, 280 U.S. 224, 226 (1930) (lease provision that lessee's bankruptcy terminates lease and lessor is entitled to damages equal to rent for remainder of term is an unenforceable penalty); Ricker v. Rombough, 261 P.2d 328, 331 (Cal. 1953) (rent acceleration provision in real property lease is unenforceable and void). Other jurisdictions, however, find specific acceleration clauses to be valid and enforceable. See, e.g., W & G Seafood Assocs. v. Eastern Shore Mkts., 714 F. Supp. 1336, 1346–49 (D. Del. 1989) (acceleration clause for rent under commercial lease is valid liquidated damages provision); Amacker v. Wedding, 363 So. 2d 223, 227–28 (La. Ct. App. 1978) (landlord entitled to liquidated damages equal to rent for one year pursuant to commercial lease clause); Frank Nero Auto Lease, Inc. v. Townsend, 411 N.E.2d 507, 512 (Ohio App. 1979) (weight of authority recognizes right of parties to contractually provide for repossession and acceleration of future rents where damages bear reasonable relationship to actual damages or lessor has obligation to mitigate damages); Woodhaven Apartments v. Washington, 907 P.2d 271, 273 (Utah App. 1995) (liquidated damages clause in residential lease is valid). The American Law Institute has recognized rent acceleration clauses as a valid expansion of a landlord's remedy:

> The parties may provide in the lease that if the tenant defaults in the payment of rent or fails in some other way to perform his obligations under the lease, the total amount of rent payable during the term of the lease shall immediately become due and payable.

Restatement (Second) of Property, Landlord & Tenant § 12.1 cmt. k (1977) . . . .

A landlord and tenant may agree to the landlord's remedies if the tenant abandons the property and fails to pay rent, as long as the provision does not constitute a penalty. See Restatement (Second) of Property, Landlord & Tenant § 12.1 cmt. j. We recognized the trend of favoring liquidated damages clauses in Rohlin Constr. Co. v. City of Hinton, 476 N.W.2d 78, 79 (Iowa 1991). In the past, we disfavored the use of liquidated damage clauses and favored interpretation of contracts that make stipulated sums penalties. Later, we relaxed this penalty rule and recognized that parties may fix damages by contract when the amount of damages is uncertain and the amount fixed is fair. We adopted the following test: "Damages for breach by either party may be liquidated in the agreement but only at an amount that is reasonable in the light of the anticipated or actual loss caused by the breach and the difficulties of proof of loss. A term fixing unreasonably large liquidated damages is unenforceable on grounds of public policy as a penalty." Id. at 80 (quoting Restatement (Second) of Contracts § 356(1) (1981)).

We first address whether the amount of actual damages resulting from a breach of the lease were uncertain. If a breach occurs, the ability to obtain another suitable tenant for the property is unknown. If Aurora was able to relet the property shortly after the breach, the resulting damages would be reduced. There is no guarantee, however, that Aurora would be able to relet the premises at any time during the remainder of the lease term. Under this scenario, Aurora would suffer substantial damages. Furthermore, the damages will vary depending upon when the breach occurs. We find there is considerable uncertainty as to the actual amount of damages resulting from a breach of the lease two and one-half years before the end of its agreed term.

We next address whether the amount of liquidated damages under the acceleration clause is reasonable. The amount fixed in a liquidated damages provision "is reasonable to the extent that it approximates the loss anticipated at the time of the making of the contract, even though it may not approximate the actual loss." Restatement (Second) of Contracts § 356 cmt. b (1981). Albert contends that the proper measure of damages is the remaining rent due under the lease less the reasonable fair market value of the premises for the remainder of the term. Although other courts have utilized this formula, we have not adopted this approach. In Becker v. Rute, 293 N.W. 18 (Iowa 1940), we rejected the tenants' argument that they "were entitled to credit on the rent due for the reasonable rental value of the use of the premises by [landlords] for the unexpired term." 293 N.W. at 20–21.

A landlord is entitled to recover from a tenant the damages sustained as a result of the tenant's abandonment and nonpayment of rent. Restatement (Second) of Property, Landlord & Tenant § 12.1 cmt. I; see also Iowa Code § 562A.32 (Under the Uniform Residential Landlord and Tenant Law "if the rental agreement is terminated, the landlord may have a claim for possession and for rent and a separate claim for actual damages for breach of the rental agreement."). In general, the purpose behind the allowance of damages for breach of a contract "is to place the injured party in the position he or she would have occupied if the contract had been performed." Macal v. Stinson, 468 N.W.2d 34, 36 (Iowa 1991). In Iowa "we are committed to the doctrine that when a tenant wrongfully abandons leased premises, the landlord is under a duty to show reasonable diligence has been used to relet the property at the best obtainable rent and thereby obviate or reduce the resulting damage." Vawter v. McKissick, 159 N.W.2d 538, 541 (Iowa 1968). Consequently, a landlord is entitled to damages equal to the amount of rent reserved in the lease, plus any other consequential damages, less amounts received in reletting the property. See Roberts v. Watson, 196 Iowa 816, 820, 195 N.W. 211, 212–13 (1923) (affirming judgment for landlord for full amount of unpaid rent plus subsequently accruing rent under five year lease less receipts from reletting).

The acceleration clause at issue here places Aurora in the position it would have occupied had Albert performed the entire lease. Furthermore, it takes into account the landlord's duty to mitigate damages by offsetting any claim by amounts received in reletting the property. We believe the acceleration clause reasonably approximates the anticipated or actual loss that resulted from Albert's abandonment and breach of the lease. Consequently, we hold that the acceleration clause is a valid and enforceable liquidated damages provision.

Albert urges the court should at least set off against the judgment any rents actually received by reletting the premises during the remainder of the lease. We agree. The acceleration clause explicitly provided a credit against the balance of the future rent for "any amount by reason of any such reletting." Furthermore, if a landlord regains possession of property abandoned by a tenant, courts "agree that a landlord may not keep both the accelerated rent and rent received from renting to a new tenant." Restatement (Second) of Property, Landlord & Tenant § 12.1 n.10.

We affirm the district court's judgment upholding the acceleration clause in the parties' lease as a valid liquidated damages provision. We modify the court's decision to provide for a credit against the judgment for rents received from reletting the property during the remainder of the lease term. We remand the case for the district court to determine if the property was relet during the remainder of the lease term. If so, Aurora must credit Albert for the rents obtained. Costs of appeal are taxed one-fourth against Aurora and three-fourths against Albert.

Notes & Questions

1. **Mitigation.** Should there be a landlord duty to mitigate? Do you find the reasons advanced in *Austin Hills* persuasive? Consider the opposing view, taken by the Restatement of Property, which imposes no duty to mitigate: "Abandonment of property is an invitation to vandalism, and the law should not encourage such conduct by putting a duty to mitigate of damages on the landlord." Restatement (Second) of Property, Landlord and Tenant § 12.1, cmt. (i) (1977). By allowing the landlord to let the premises

lie idle, at no cost to her, but at substantial cost to the tenant, what kinds of settlements between landlords and tenants is the Restatement position likely to encourage?

2. Why does the Texas Supreme Court conclude that the duty to mitigate should not apply where a landlord chooses to maintain the lease and sue for damages as rent payments come due over time? Is the court's reasoning convincing? Does this create a major loophole in the duty to mitigate? Most jurisdictions that require mitigation require it in all settings, not just where the landlord is suing for anticipatory breach. As a result, sitting on the lease and suing for rent as it comes due is not a viable option for landlords in a majority of jurisdictions.

3. Is there any reason to have different rules regarding mitigation for commercial and residential leases? The New York Court of Appeals has refused to abandon the traditional "no duty to mitigate" rule in the case of commercial leases, in part because businesses who engage in real estate transactions must be able to rely on the stability of legal precedents. "In business transactions, particularly, the certainty of settled rules is often more important than whether the established rule is better than another or even whether it is the 'correct' rule. This is perhaps true in real property more than any other area of the law, where established precedents are not lightly to be set aside." Holy Properties, Ltd. v. Kenneth Cole Productions, Inc., 661 N.E.2d 694, 696 (N.Y. 1995). What exactly would happen that is so bad if the court changed the mitigation rule for commercial leases?

4. Is there any connection between a landlord's duty to mitigate damages and her duty not to withhold consent to an assignment or sublease unreasonably? It is not unusual for a tenant who wishes to leave the premises before the expiration of his term to present the landlord with a proposed assignee for the remainder of the term. If the landlord withholds consent to the assignment, the tenant will often leave anyway and, in a later action by the landlord to recover rent, will defend that the landlord failed to mitigate damages, as evidenced by her refusal to accept the proposed assignee. Is it inconsistent for a jurisdiction to follow one rule but not the other?

5. Does a landlord who tries to mitigate damages by reletting the premises, or who chooses to "relet the premises on the tenant's account," risk accidentally accepting a surrender of the lease and ending the landlord-tenant relationship? Surrender requires a meeting of the minds between landlord and tenant. Courts, however, often find a surrender where the tenant performs some act, typically abandonment, indicating an offer to surrender, and the landlord performs some act, typically retaking the premises, indicating an acceptance of that offer. Other acts inconsistent with a continued tenancy, such as accepting back the keys, changing the locks, altering the premises, or reletting them for a longer term or higher rent, may also be treated as evidence of an accepted surrender. To avoid the risk that an act of mitigation might be viewed as an acceptance of a surrender, some states provide statutory protection to some landlord conduct. Wisconsin, for example, explicitly assures landlords that certain

actions will be deemed "privileged in mitigation" and will "not constitute an acceptance of surrender." Included in these privileged actions are "entry, with or without notice, for the purpose of inspecting, preserving, repairing, remodeling and showing the premises," reletting of the premises, and "any other act which is reasonably subject to interpretation as being in mitigation of rent or damages and which does not unequivocally demonstrate an intent to release the defaulting tenant." Wis. Stat. Ann. § 704.29(4).

6. **Acceleration Clauses.** Should landlords be able to contract around the mitigation requirement by including an acceleration clause in the lease? Is the Iowa Supreme Court in *Aurora Business Park* correct in concluding that the acceleration clause in that case took "into account the landlord's duty to mitigate damages by offsetting any claim by amounts received in reletting the property"? If the landlord in *Aurora Business Park* failed to relet the premises, what damages would it receive? If the landlord in *Austin Hills* did the same, what damages would it be entitled to receive?

7. **Security Deposits.** However effective the elaborate edifice of landlord remedies may be in the context of commercial leaseholds, it is only rarely employed in short-term residential tenancies. It is the unusual residential landlord who thinks she can be made whole by letting the premises lie idle or by reletting them at a lower rent and going after her departing tenant for the balance due. The costs of litigation are just too high, departing tenants too hard to find, and their pockets too often empty for the effort to be worthwhile. Rather, landlords will typically relet as quickly as possible, pocketing the one or two months' security deposit that most landlords are sufficiently farsighted to demand at the outset of the lease.

Security deposits help secure tenant performance of lease obligations. At the end of the term, the tenant is to receive the deposit back, less any amounts required to compensate the landlord for damages to the unit and unpaid rent. In the best of all possible worlds for landlords, the deposit could be as large as the landlord could convince the tenant to pay, the landlord could delay as long as she wished in returning the deposit at the end of the lease term, the landlord would be under no obligation to itemize or document her deductions for damage, and the fund would be hers to use throughout the lease term—an interest-free loan, with no strings on the landlord's power to invest it as she wishes or to commingle it with her other funds.

Although some elements of this landlord never-never land still exist in some places, common law developments and statutes enacted in a large majority of states have substantially curbed landlord prerogative. Arizona, to take one example, provides that the security deposit may not exceed one and one half months' rent and that the landlord must return the deposit, less accrued rent and itemized damages, if any, within fourteen days after the lease terminates; non-compliance entitles the tenant to recover the deposit together with damages equal to twice the amount wrongfully withheld. Ariz. Rev. Stat. § 33–1321. Most of these statutes apply only to residential leases.

Can a landlord escape these curbs by characterizing the tenant's front money as something other than a security deposit? As a general rule she can, although courts will resolve any doubt about the nature of the money by calling it a security deposit. A *bonus* paid by the tenant at the outset of the term as consideration for the landlord's entering into the lease belongs to the landlord free and clear, without any obligation to account or refund to the tenant. *Pre-paid rent*, typically for the last month of the term, also belongs exclusively to the landlord, although the tenant, of course, may occupy the premises for the prepaid period without further rental payments.

CHAPTER 9

SHARED OWNERSHIP

Land can be shared not only across time as seen in Chapters 7 and 8, but also simultaneously among individuals. The common law authorizes a number of *concurrent estates* or *cotenancies* in which several people hold common undivided interests in the same property. Rosalie Edge, for example, could give Greenacre to her children, Peter and Margaret, as *co-tenants*. Or a married couple could jointly own a home as co-tenants.

Cotenancy is widespread. In a spot sample of real estate records conducted by Professor Evelyn Lewis in the late 1980s, approximately two thirds of the residential properties were held in cotenancies. Professor Lewis identified at least three factors driving the high percentage of cotenancies. First, as discussed below, some forms of cotenancies provide a valuable form of estate planning that can reduce the costs of allocating someone's property when they die. Second, as land prices have skyrocketed in many parts of the United States, potential homebuyers have found cotenancy an effective way to pool resources with parents or others. Finally, "the rise in the incidence of unmarried cohabitants contributes to increased cotenancy prevalence. Real estate counsel are presented more frequently with 'unmarried couples who have married their financial affairs by purchasing property together.'" Evelyn Alicia Lewis, Struggling with Quicksand: The Ins and Outs of Cotenant Possession Value Liability and a Call for Default Rule Reform, 1994 Wis. L. Rev. 331, 399 n.204.

Section A examines two of the major forms of concurrent estates—the *tenancy in common* and the *joint tenancy*. Both types of cotenancies are open to anyone—whether husband or wife, siblings, relatives, friends, business partners, or complete strangers—although joint tenancies are used in almost all cases by married couples. Section B turns to special forms of marital property. Although the common law recognized a number of special property interests unique to marriage, only one—the *tenancy by the entirety*—remains of importance today and then in only a few states. In place of the common law interests, states have developed a variety of rules for dividing property between husband and wife in case of divorce or the death of one or the other spouse.

A. COMMON LAW CONCURRENT ESTATES

Cotenancies can be created in fee simples or in lesser estates, in future interests as well as present interests, and in any number of individuals. In the example

[8.1] "*A* to *B* for life, then to the children of *B* for their lives and, on the death of *B*'s last surviving child, to *C*, *D*, *E*, *F* and *G* in fee"

the children of *B* would be cotenants in a remainder life estate, while *C* through *G* would be cotenants in a remainder in fee simple absolute.

The most striking feature of concurrent estates is their *indivisibility*, or *unity of possession*. Each cotenant, no matter how small her interest, is entitled to possess the entire parcel. Thus, in the last example, *C*, *D*, *E*, *F* and *G* each would hold an undivided one-fifth interest in the remainder and, once the remainder becomes possessory, each would have the right to live on or otherwise use Greenacre.

As you might imagine, indivisibility creates great potential for conflict. For example, imagine that *X* in her will leaves the family house, on a quarter-acre lot, to her two children *Y* and *Z* as cotenants. If both *Y* and *Z* want to move into the house with their families, what rights does each child have? If *Y* unilaterally exercises his right to possession by moving his family into the house, what recourse does *Z* have? If only *Y* is interested in moving into the house, does *Z* nonetheless have a right to compensation for *Y*'s use of the property? After a brief introduction to the nature of the various common law concurrent interests, we explore these questions below.

1. TYPES OF CONCURRENT ESTATES

The common law today recognizes three concurrent estates: the *tenancy in common*, the *joint tenancy*, and the *tenancy by the entirety*. The early common law recognized a fourth concurrent estate: when heirs took equal undivided shares in land by descent from the same ancestor, they were said to take as *tenants in coparcenary*. Today, however, the heirs would be tenants in common.

The common law technically still recognizes another concurrent estate—the *tenancy in partnership*. Partnerships are one of two major legal structures used by individuals who wish to jointly own and manage a business—such as an apartment building or a manufacturing company. The other legal structure is the *corporation*. Although the common law once governed the formation of partnerships and the rights and liabilities of partners, today the Uniform Partnership Act and other state statutory provisions have largely displaced the common law tenancy in partnership. We therefore leave partnerships for business law courses that you might take.

Tenancy in Common. Of the three concurrent estates, the tenancy in common is the simplest. A tenant in common enjoys all of the rights of a holder of an estate, except that she shares those rights with her cotenants. Someone who owns a tenancy in common in fee simple absolute shares the right to use all of the property. She also can transfer her cotenancy interest inter vivos or, on her death, by will or intestacy. Thus, if *B*, *C*, and *D* hold Greenacre as tenants in common, each having a one-third undivided interest, and *B* dies, devising "all of my real property to *X*," *X*, *C*, and *D* will then each hold a one-third undivided interest in Greenacre.

Joint Tenancy. The main distinction between the tenancy in common and the joint tenancy lies in what happens to the cotenant's interest on death. Joint tenants hold a *right of survivorship*. On the death of one joint tenant, the decedent's interest passes instantly and automatically to the surviving cotenant(s), regardless of any attempted disposition by will. Thus, if *B*, *C*, and *D* own Greenacre as joint tenants, each holding a one-third undivided interest, and *B* dies, devising "all of my real property to *X*," *X* will take nothing, because *B*'s interest passes instantaneously to his surviving cotenants, *C* and *D*, who each now hold a one-half undivided interest. See, e.g., Huff v. Metz, 676 So. 2d 264 (Miss. 1996). If *C* then predeceases *D*, *D*, the final survivor, will take the entire fee interest.

Like a tenant in common, a joint tenant can transfer her interest inter vivos. As discussed in the next section, however, the transfer converts the joint tenancy into a tenancy in common. Thus, if *A* and *B* are joint tenants, and *B* transfers her interest to *C*, *A* and *C* will then share ownership as tenants in common. None of the parties will enjoy a right of survivorship. Like any other tenants in common, both *A* and *C* are free to transfer their interests to others inter vivos or by will or intestacy.

Tenancy by the Entirety. Tenants in the entirety, like joint tenants, hold a right of survivorship. But several features differentiate the tenancy by the entirety from both the tenancy in common and the joint tenancy. First, while any group of people can hold a tenancy in common, only a married couple can hold a tenancy by the entirety. Second, although tenants in common and joint tenants can sell or otherwise transfer their interests in their cotenancy, in most states neither a husband nor a wife can unilaterally sell, give away, or transfer his or her interest in a tenancy by the entirety. For this reason, creditors can reach the interest of a tenant in common or a joint tenant, but often cannot attach the interest of a tenant by the entirety. Finally, a tenant in common or joint tenant who wishes to end the cotenancy can petition a court to *partition* the estate—either by dividing the property physically into multiple units or by selling the property and dividing the proceeds among the former cotenants. Only a divorce can end a tenancy by the entirety.

This section of the Chapter looks at the law surrounding the tenancy in common and the joint tenancy. Because only husbands and wives can own a tenancy by the entirety, we save extended discussion of it for our discussion of marital property later in this Chapter.

2. JOINT TENANCIES

Historically, the common law favored joint tenancies over tenancies in common. Joint tenancies had a variety of advantages in the Middle Ages. By providing that 100 percent of the property ultimately went to the surviving co-tenant, the joint tenancy helped consolidate ownership in a few individuals, which made feudal services and incidents easier to enforce.

Until land wills were recognized, the joint tenancy was also the only means of estate planning. If Aldo Leopold were interested in passing his land at his death to Jessie Fremont, Aldo could simply establish a joint tenancy between himself and Jessie. Where grants of a cotenancy were ambiguous, the common law therefore presumed that the grantor intended to create a joint tenancy rather than a tenancy in common.

Beginning in the early 19th century, however, most states reversed the common law presumption in favor of a presumption for tenancies in common. The original virtues of the joint tenancy were no longer relevant. And modern courts and legislatures objected to the gambling aspect of the right of survivorship—"an 'odious thing' that too often deprived a man's heirs of their rightful inheritance." N. William Hines, Real Property Joint Tenancies: Law, Fact, and Fancy, 51 Iowa L. Rev. 582, 585 (1966).

A few states have abolished the joint tenancy completely or, while continuing technically to recognize the joint tenancy, abolished the right of survivorship. See, e.g., N.C. Gen. Stat. § 41–2; Pa. Cons. Stat. tit. 68, § 110. Most states simply provide that grants of cotenancies will be interpreted as creating a tenancy in common except where the grantor is clear that she intended to create a joint tenancy. See, e.g., 765 Ill. Comp. Stat. Ann. 1005/1; Iowa Code § 557.15. The exact language needed to create a joint tenancy varies from state to state, depending on statutory requirements and judicial decisions. In most states, it is adequate to state that the cotenants will hold "as joint tenants and not as tenants in common." In some, however, it is important to say that the cotenants hold "as joint tenants *with a right of survivorship*." See, e.g., Hoover v. Smith, 444 S.E.2d 546 (Va. 1994).

Despite the law's preference for tenancies in common, many private landowners prefer joint tenancies.[1] An exhaustive empirical study conducted in the 1960s by Dean William Hines found that joint tenancies in Iowa rose from less than 1 percent of land acquisitions in 1933 to over a third of farm acquisitions and over half of urban acquisitions in 1964. See Hines, supra, 51 Iowa L. Rev. at 586. Dean Hines also found that joint tenancies were created almost exclusively by married couples. At the time of his study, more than nine out of every ten joint tenancies were marital. "Joint tenancies between related persons other than husband and wives are rare, survivorship arrangements between unrelated persons virtually nonexistent." Id. at 623.

Other surveys have confirmed Hines' results. A study of real estate deeds in five California counties in 1959 and 1960 found that married couples held over two thirds of the property as cotenants. 85 percent of the couples held the property as joint tenants. See Yale B. Griffith, Community Property in Joint Tenancy Form, 14 Stan. L. Rev. 87, 88 & n.4 (1961). A more recent survey of a sample of deeds recorded in 1890, 1920, 1940, 1960,

1. The joint tenancy is sufficiently popular that some states that originally abolished the joint tenancy later decided to reinstitute the tenancy, including Georgia in 1976 (see Ga. Code Ann. § 44–6–190) and Washington in 1961 (see Wash. Rev. Code § 64.28.010).

and 1980 showed the percentage of land held in joint tenancies increasing from less than 1 percent in 1890 to almost 80 percent in 1960, before dropping slightly to 63.3 percent in 1980 (perhaps as a result of a drop in the percentage of married couples). See Carole Shammas et al., Inheritance in America from Colonial Times to the Present 171–72 (1987).

What explains the preference for joint tenancies, particularly by married couples? Perhaps the major reason is avoidance of *probate*. When property is transferred by will or intestate succession, most states require a probate court to oversee the process. The court will appoint an administrator or executor who locates and distributes all of the decedent's property. Probate can be a long and costly process, and most people are more than happy to avoid it. When a joint tenant dies, his interest in the land simply terminates; the co-tenant receives 100 percent of the land through her right of survivorship, not by receiving anything from the deceased.

Does the apparent predominance of joint tenancies suggest that the modern presumption favoring tenancies in common should be reversed?

a. CREATION OF JOINT TENANCIES

The common law originally required four "unities" to create a joint tenancy:

> *Unity of Interest.* All the tenants had to receive equal undivided shares in an identical type of estate. One tenant could not own a 1/3rd share, while the other held a 2/3rd share. And one tenant could not receive a fee simple, while another received a defeasible fee.
>
> *Unity of Title.* All the tenants had to acquire title by the same instrument or by the same joint act of adverse possession. Joint tenancy could not arise from intestate succession or other act of law.
>
> *Unity of Time.* The interests of the tenants had to be acquired or vest at the same time.
>
> *Unity of Possession.* All the tenants had to be entitled to possess the entire estate.

Only the last of these unities—unity of possession—was necessary to the creation of a tenancy in common. An attempt to create a joint tenancy that failed any of the first three unities therefore created a tenancy in common.

Although a few states have expressly abolished all unity requirements for joint tenancies except for unity of possession, the majority of states still insist that joint tenancies satisfy all four unities. This can sometimes trip up the ill advised layperson or the careless lawyer. The requirements of unity of title and unity of time also can make it difficult to create a joint tenancy in some settings. A wife who owns property individually, for example, may want to convert her sole ownership into a joint tenancy with her spouse. But the common law "delivery rule" holds that she cannot transfer title to herself. If she tries to create a cotenancy, her husband will receive a half interest in the property, but the law will view her interest in the property as predating her husband's interest. Unities of time and title thus would be absent, since wife and husband would have taken title at different times and by different acts. The attempted conveyance would create a tenancy in common, not a joint tenancy.

So how do property owners create a joint tenancy in this situation? Historically, the solution was for *A* to convey her entire fee interest to a strawman, *X*, who would immediately reconvey the property to *A* and *B* as joint tenants. Because it makes little sense to force a property owner to do in two steps what she can do in just one step, virtually all states have removed the need for the strawman. Some states have done so by abolishing the requirements of unity of title and time. See, e.g., Wis. Stat. § 700.19(5). Others have expressly authorized sole owners of a parcel of land to transfer the land directly to themselves and others in joint tenancy. See, e.g., Cal. Civ. Code § 683(a); Mass. Gen. Laws ch. 184, § 8.

b. SEVERANCE OF JOINT TENANCIES

Tenhet v. Boswell

Supreme Court of California, 1976.
554 P.2d 330.

MOSK, Justice.

A joint tenant leases his interest in the joint tenancy property to a third person for a term of years, and dies during that term. We conclude that the lease does not sever the joint tenancy, but expires upon the death of the lessor joint tenant.

Raymond Johnson and plaintiff Hazel Tenhet owned a parcel of property as joint tenants. Assertedly without plaintiff's knowledge or consent, Johnson leased the property to defendant Boswell for a period of 10 years at a rental of $150 per year with a provision granting the lessee an "option to purchase."[2] Johnson died some three months after execution of the lease, and plaintiff sought to establish her sole right to possession of the property as the surviving joint tenant. After an unsuccessful demand upon defendant to vacate the premises, plaintiff brought this action to have the lease declared invalid. The trial court sustained demurrers to the complaint, and plaintiff appealed from the ensuing judgment of dismissal....

II

An understanding of the nature of a joint interest in this state is fundamental to a determination of the question whether the present lease severed the joint tenancy. Civil Code section 683 provides in part: "A joint interest is one owned by two or more persons in equal shares, by a title

2. The lease did not disclose that the lessor possessed only a joint interest in the property. To the contrary, the "option to purchase" granted to the lessee, which might more accurately be described as a right of first refusal, implied that the lessor possessed a fee simple....

created by a single will or transfer, when expressly declared in the will or transfer to be a joint tenancy. . . ." This statute, requiring an express declaration for the creation of joint interests, does not abrogate the common law rule that four unities are essential to an estate in joint tenancy: unity of interest, unity of time, unity of title, and unity of possession.

The requirement of four unities reflects the basic concept that there is but one estate which is taken jointly; if an essential unity is destroyed the joint tenancy is severed and a tenancy in common results. Accordingly, one of two joint tenants may unilaterally terminate the joint tenancy by conveying his interest to a third person. Severance of the joint tenancy, of course, extinguishes the principal feature of that estate—the *jus accrescendi* or right of survivorship. Thus, a joint tenant's right of survivorship is an expectancy that is not irrevocably fixed upon the creation of the estate; it arises only upon success in the ultimate gamble—survival—and then only if the unity of the estate has not theretofore been destroyed by voluntary conveyance, by partition proceedings, by involuntary alienation under an execution, or by any other action which operates to sever the joint tenancy.

Our initial inquiry is whether the partial alienation of Johnson's interest in the property effected a severance of the joint tenancy under these principles. It could be argued that a lease destroys the unities of interest and possession because the leasing joint tenant transfers to the lessee his present possessory interest and retains a mere reversion. Moreover, the possibility that the term of the lease may continue beyond the lifetime of the lessor is inconsistent with a complete right of survivorship.

On the other hand, if the lease entered into here by Johnson and defendant is valid only during Johnson's life, then the conveyance is more a variety of life estate *pur autre vie* than a term of years. Such a result is inconsistent with Johnson's freedom to alienate his interest during his lifetime.

We are mindful that the issue here presented is "an ancient controversy, going back to Coke and Littleton." (2 Am. Law of Prop. (1952) § 6.2, p. 10.) Yet the problem is like a comet in our law: though its existence in theory has been frequently recognized, its observed passages are few. Some authorities support the view that a lease by a joint tenant to a third person effects a complete and final severance of the joint tenancy. Such a view is generally based upon what is thought to be the English common law rule.

Others adopt a position that there is a temporary severance during the term of the lease. If the lessor dies while the lease is in force, under this view the existence of the lease at the moment when the right of survivorship would otherwise take effect operates as a severance, extinguishing the joint tenancy. If, however, the term of the lease expires before the lessor, it is reasoned that the joint tenancy is undisturbed because the joint tenants resume their original relation. The single conclusion that can be drawn from centuries of academic speculation on the question is that its resolution is unclear.

As we shall explain, it is our opinion that a lease is not so inherently inconsistent with joint tenancy as to create a severance, either temporary or permanent.

Under Civil Code sections 683 and 686 a joint tenancy must be expressly declared in the creating instrument, or a tenancy in common results. This is a statutory departure from the common law preference in favor of joint tenancy. Inasmuch as the estate arises only upon express intent, and in many cases such intent will be the intent of the joint tenants themselves, we decline to find a severance in circumstances which do not clearly and unambiguously establish that either of the joint tenants desired to terminate the estate.

If plaintiff and Johnson did not choose to continue the joint tenancy, they might have converted it into a tenancy in common by written mutual agreement. They might also have jointly conveyed the property to a third person and divided the proceeds. Even if they could not agree to act in concert, either plaintiff or Johnson might have severed the joint tenancy, with or without the consent of the other, by an act which was clearly indicative of an intent to terminate, such as a conveyance of her or his entire interest. Either might also have brought an action to partition the property, which, upon judgment, would have effected a severance. Because a joint tenancy may be created only by express intent, and because there are alternative and unambiguous means of altering the nature of that estate, we hold that the lease here in issue did not operate to sever the joint tenancy.

III

Having concluded that the joint tenancy was not severed by the lease and that sole ownership of the property therefore vested in plaintiff upon her joint tenant's death by operation of her right of survivorship, we turn next to the issue whether she takes the property unencumbered by the lease.

In arguing that plaintiff takes subject to the lease, defendant relies on Swartzbaugh v. Sampson (1936) 11 Cal. App. 2d 451, 54 P.2d 73. In that case, one of two joint tenants entered into lease agreements over the objection of his joint tenant wife, who sought to cancel the leases. The court held in favor of the lessor joint tenant, concluding that the leases were valid.

But the suit to cancel the lease in *Swartzbaugh* was brought during the lifetime of both joint tenants, not as in the present case after the death of the lessor. Significantly, the court concluded that "a lease to all of the joint property by one joint tenant is not a nullity but is a valid and supportable contract *in so far as the interest of the lessor in the joint property is concerned*." (Italics added; id., at p. 458, 54 P.2d at p. 77.) During the lifetime of the lessor joint tenant, as the *Swartzbaugh* court perceived, her interest in the joint property was an undivided interest in fee simple that encompassed the right to lease the property.

By the very nature of joint tenancy, however, the interest of the nonsurviving joint tenant extinguishes upon his death. And as the lease is valid only "in so far as the interest of the lessor in the joint property is concerned," it follows that the lease of the joint tenancy property also expires when the lessor dies.

This conclusion is borne out by decisions in this state involving liens on and mortgages of joint tenancy property. In Zeigler v. Bonnell (1942) 52 Cal. App. 2d 217, 126 P.2d 118, the Court of Appeal ruled that a surviving joint tenant takes an estate free from a judgment lien on the interest of a deceased cotenant judgment debtor. The court reasoned that "The right of survivorship is the chief characteristic that distinguishes a joint tenancy from other interests in property.... The judgment lien of [the creditor] could attach only to the interest of his debtor.... That interest terminated upon [the debtor's] death." (Id. at pp. 219–220, 126 P.2d at p. 119.) After his death "the deceased joint tenant had no interest in the property, and his judgment creditor has no greater rights." (Id. at p. 220, 126 P.2d at p. 120.)

A similar analysis was followed in People v. Nogarr (1958) 164 Cal. App. 2d 591, 330 P.2d 858, which held that upon the death of a joint tenant who had executed a mortgage on the tenancy property, the surviving joint tenant took the property free of the mortgage. The court reasoned (at p. 594, 330 P.2d at p. 861) that "as the mortgage lien attached only to such interest as [the deceased joint tenant] had in the real property[,] when his interest ceased to exist the lien of the mortgage expired with it."

As these decisions demonstrate, a joint tenant may, during his lifetime, grant certain rights in the joint property without severing the tenancy. But when such a joint tenant dies his interest dies with him, and any encumbrances placed by him on the property become unenforceable against the surviving joint tenant. For the reasons stated a lease falls within this rule.

Any other result would defeat the justifiable expectations of the surviving joint tenant. Thus if A agrees to create a joint tenancy with B, A can reasonably anticipate that when B dies A will take an unencumbered interest in fee simple. During his lifetime, of course, B may sever the tenancy or lease his interest to a third party. But to allow B to lease for a term continuing *after* his death would indirectly defeat the very purposes of the joint tenancy. For example, for personal reasons B might execute a 99–year lease on valuable property for a consideration of one dollar a year. A would then take a fee simple on B's death, but would find his right to use the property—and its market value—substantially impaired. This circumstance would effectively nullify the benefits of the right of survivorship, the basic attribute of the joint tenancy.

On the other hand, we are not insensitive to the potential injury that may be sustained by a person in good faith who leases from one joint tenant. In some circumstances a lessee might be unaware that his lessor is not a fee simple owner but merely a joint tenant, and could find himself unexpectedly evicted when the lessor dies prior to expiration of the lease. This result would be avoided by a prudent lessee who conducts a title search prior to leasing, but we appreciate that such a course would often be economically burdensome to the lessee of a residential dwelling or a modest parcel of property. Nevertheless, it must also be recognized that every lessee may one day face the unhappy revelation that his lessor's estate in the leased property is less than a fee simple. For example, a lessee who innocently rents from the holder of a life estate is subject to risks comparable to those imposed upon a lessee of joint tenancy property.

More significantly, we cannot allow extraneous factors to erode the functioning of joint tenancy. The estate of joint tenancy is firmly embedded in centuries of real property law and in the California statute books. Its crucial element is the right of survivorship, a right that would be more illusory than real if a joint tenant were permitted to lease for a term continuing after his death. Accordingly, we hold that under the facts alleged in the complaint the lease herein is no longer valid....

Notes & Questions

1. As *Tenhet* highlights, courts historically have held that the four unities are required, not only to create a joint tenancy, but for a joint tenancy to continue. In all jurisdictions, a joint tenant's transfer of his entire interest to a third party will sever the joint tenancy and convert it into a tenancy in common, because it destroys the unities of title and time. Other acts that have been held to sever a joint tenancy include a joint tenant's unilateral execution of a contract of sale and the forced sale of a joint tenant's interest by his creditors. See 7 Richard R. Powell, Real Property § 51.04 (Michael Allan Wolf ed., 2005). In some jurisdictions, a unilateral lease by one joint tenant to a third person, as well as the issuance of a mortgage, severs the joint tenancy. See, e.g., Schaefer v. Peoples Heritage Savings Bank, 669 A.2d 185 (Me. 1996) (mortgage); Estate of Gulledge, 673 A.2d 1278 (D.C. 1996) (lease); General Credit Co. v. Cleck, 609 A.2d 553 (Pa. Sup. Ct. 1992) (mortgage)

2. On strictly technical grounds, was the court's decision in *Tenhet* correct? Was the court right to focus on the argument that a lease destroys the unities of *interest* and *possession*—rather than the unities of *title* and *time*? Did the court misconstrue the purport of sections 683 and 686 of the California Civil Code?

3. Which way do policy considerations cut? As a practical matter, would the expectations of all the parties have been better served by a finding of permanent severance? Of temporary severance that became permanent when Johnson died during the term of the lease? Does *Tenhet* increase the need for lessees to determine the title of the lessor (or should the wise lessee do that in any case)? Does *Tenhet* contradict the purpose behind the modern constructional presumption favoring tenancies in common?

4. Should the statutory relaxation of the four unities required for the *creation* of a joint tenancy also control decisions on the *continuation* of joint tenancies? If a joint tenant's conveyance of his interest has historically

been held to sever the joint tenancy because it destroys the unities of title and time, should severance be found in states that, like Wisconsin, have abolished the unities of title and time for purposes of creating a joint tenancy?

Riddle v. Harmon

Court of Appeal of California, 1980.
162 Cal. Rptr. 530.

We must decide whether Frances Riddle, now deceased, unilaterally terminated a joint tenancy by conveying her interest from herself as joint tenant to herself as tenant in common. The trial court determined, via summary judgment quieting title to her widower, that she did not. The facts follow.

Mr. and Mrs. Riddle purchased a parcel of real estate, taking title as joint tenants. Several months before her death, Mrs. Riddle retained an attorney to plan her estate. After reviewing pertinent documents, he advised her that the property was held in joint tenancy and that, upon her death, the property would pass to her husband. Distressed upon learning this, she requested that the joint tenancy be terminated so that she could dispose of her interest by will. As a result, the attorney prepared a grant deed whereby Mrs. Riddle granted to herself an undivided one-half interest in the subject property. The document also provided that "The purpose of this Grant Deed is to terminate those joint tenancies formerly existing between the Grantor, Frances P. Riddle, and Jack C. Riddle, her husband...." He also prepared a will disposing of Mrs. Riddle's interest in the property. Both the grant deed and will were executed on December 8, 1975. Mrs. Riddle died 20 days later.

The court below refused to sanction her plan to sever the joint tenancy and quieted title to the property in her husband. The executrix of the will of Frances Riddle appeals from that judgment.

The basic concept of a joint tenancy is that it is one estate which is taken jointly. Under the common law, four unities were essential to the creation and existence of an estate in joint tenancy: interest, time, title and possession ....

An indisputable right of each joint tenant is the power to convey his or her separate estate by way of gift or otherwise without the knowledge or consent of the other joint tenant and to thereby terminate the joint tenancy. If a joint tenant conveys to a stranger and that person reconveys to the same tenant, then no revival of the joint tenancy occurs because the unities are destroyed. The former joint tenants become tenants in common.

At common law, one could not create a joint tenancy in himself and another by a direct conveyance. It was necessary for joint tenants to acquire their interests at the same time (unity of time) and by the same conveyancing instrument (unity of title). So, in order to create a valid joint tenancy where one of the proposed joint tenants already owned an interest in the property, it was first necessary to convey the property to a disinterested third person, a "strawman," who then conveyed the title to the ultimate grantees as joint tenants.... By amendment to its Civil Code, California became a pioneer in allowing the creation of a joint tenancy by direct transfer. Under authority of Civil Code section 683, a joint tenancy conveyance may be made from a "sole owner to himself and others," or from joint owners to themselves and others as specified in the code.... This court is now asked to reexamine whether a strawman is required to *terminate* a joint tenancy.

Twelve years ago, in Clark v. Carter (1968) 265 Cal. App. 2d 291, 295, 70 Cal. Rptr. 923, the Court of Appeal considered the same question and found the strawman to be indispensable....

That "two-to-transfer" notion stems from the English common law feoffment ceremony with livery of seisin. If the ceremony took place upon the land being conveyed, the grantor (feoffor) would hand a symbol of the land, such as a lump of earth or a twig, to the grantee (feoffee). In order to complete the investiture of seisin it was necessary that the feoffor completely relinquish possession of the land to the feoffee. It is apparent from the requirement of livery of seisin that one could not enfeoff oneself—that is, one could not be both grantor and grantee in a single transaction. Handing oneself a dirt clod is ungainly. Just as livery of seisin has become obsolete, so should ancient vestiges of that ceremony give way to modern conveyancing realities.

.... [U]ndaunted by the *Clark* case, resourceful attorneys have worked out an inventory of methods to evade the rule that one cannot be both grantor and grantee simultaneously.

The most familiar technique for unilateral termination is use of an intermediary "strawman" blessed in the case of Burke v. Stevens (1968) 264 Cal. App. 2d 30, 70 Cal. Rptr. 87. There, Mrs. Burke carried out a secret plan to terminate a joint tenancy that existed between her husband and herself in certain real property. The steps to accomplish this objective involved: (1) a letter written from Mrs. Burke to her attorney directing him to prepare a power of attorney naming him as her attorney in fact for the purpose of terminating the joint tenancy; (2) her execution and delivery of the power of attorney; (3) her attorney's execution and delivery of a quitclaim deed conveying Mrs. Burke's interest in the property to a third party, who was an office associate of the attorney in fact; (4) the third party's execution and delivery of a quitclaim deed reconveying that interest to Mrs. Burke on the following day. The *Burke* court sanctioned this method of terminating the joint tenancy, noting at one point: "While the actions of the wife, from the standpoint of a theoretically perfect marriage, are subject to ethical criticism, and her stealthy approach to the solution of the problems facing her is not to be acclaimed, the question before the court is not what should have been done ideally in a perfect marriage, but whether the decedent and her attorneys acted in a legally permissible manner."....

In view of the rituals that are available to unilaterally terminate a joint tenancy, there is little virtue in steadfastly adhering to cumbersome feudal law requirements. "It is revolting to have no better reason for a rule of law than that so it was laid down in the time of Henry IV. It is still more revolting if the grounds upon which it was laid down have vanished long since, and the rule simply persists from blind imitation of the past." (Holmes, Collected Legal Papers (1920) p. 187.) Common sense as well as legal efficiency dictate that a joint tenant should be able to accomplish directly what he or she could otherwise achieve indirectly by use of elaborate legal fictions. . . .

Our decision does not create new powers for a joint tenant. A universal right of each joint tenant is the power to effect a severance and destroy the right of survivorship by conveyance of his or her joint tenancy interest to another "person." "If an indestructible right of survivorship is desired—that is, one which may not be destroyed by one tenant—that may be accomplished by creating a joint life estate with a contingent remainder in fee to the survivor; a tenancy in common in simple fee with an executory interest in the survivor; or a fee simple to take effect in possession in the future."

We discard the archaic rule that one cannot enfeoff oneself which, if applied, would defeat the clear intention of the grantor. . . .

Notes & Questions

1. A growing number of courts have chosen to follow *Riddle* and eliminate the need for a strawman transaction. See, e.g., Estate of Knickerbocker, 912 P.2d 969 (Utah 1996); Countrywide Funding Corp. v. Palmer, 589 So. 2d 994 (Fla. Dist. Ct. App. 1991); Minonk State Bank v. Grassman, 447 N.E.2d 822 (Ill. 1983).

In 1979, the Nebraska Supreme Court bucked this trend and held that a unilateral self-conveyance still would not sever a joint tenancy. See Krause v. Crossley, 277 N.W.2d 242 (Neb. 1979). A year later, however, the Nebraska legislature reversed the decision by statute. See Neb. Rev. Stat. § 76–118(4) (a conveyance by a joint tenant "to himself or herself as grantee, in which the intention to effect a severance of the joint tenancy expressly appears in the instrument, severs the joint tenancy").

2. Isn't the most troubling issue in *Riddle* the secrecy with which Mrs. Riddle destroyed the joint tenancy? Could a joint tenant convey property to herself without telling anyone, put the conveyance in a safe deposit box, and destroy the document if she outlives the other joint tenant? Of course, joint tenants have always been able to destroy the joint tenancy by conveying the property to a third party without telling the other tenant, but *Riddle* makes secret severances even easier than before. Should a joint tenant have to notify the other joint tenant if she engages in a self-conveyance as in *Riddle*? If she engages in any type of transfer that severs the joint tenancy?

Both California and Minnesota have adopted statutes providing that any transfer by a joint tenant, whether to himself or a third party, will not sever the joint tenancy and eliminate the right of survivorship of the other joint tenant unless the transfer is recorded. See Cal. Civ. Code § 683.2; Minn. Stat. § 500.19(5). Is this adequate protection in your view. The Minnesota Supreme Court has also suggested that a unilateral self-conveyance might not be sufficient to sever a joint tenancy if the other joint tenant has "taken some irrevocable action in reliance upon the creation or existence of the joint tenancy, or if some consideration was given or received when the joint tenancy was created." Hendrickson v. Minneapolis Fed. Sav. & Loan Ass'n, 161 N.W.2d 688, 692 (Minn. 1968). See generally Samuel M. Fetters, An Invitation to Commit Fraud: Secret Destruction of Joint Tenant Survivorship Rights, 55 Fordham L. Rev. 173 (1986).

3. A grantor can ensure that a cotenant cannot unilaterally destroy the right of survivorship by creating, not a joint tenancy, but a tenancy in common for the lives of the cotenants with a remainder interest in the surviving cotenant. See Durant v. Hamrick, 409 So. 2d 731 (Ala. 1981). In such a grant, the remainder interest following the concurrent life estates can be eliminated only through the agreement of all the remaindermen.

4. **Wills.** Could a joint tenant eliminate the other joint tenant's right of survivorship but keep his own by conveying his half of the property in his will? The answer, perhaps obviously, is no. See, e.g., Huff v. Metz, 676 So. 2d 264 (Miss. 1996); Powell v. American Charter Fed. Sav. & Loan Ass'n, 514 N.W.2d 326 (Neb. 1994).

5. **Divorce.** What should happen to a joint tenancy between a husband and wife if they divorce? Although traditionally a divorce did not sever a joint tenancy, most courts today find an intent to sever the joint tenancy in the divorce decree or other actions of the parties. See, e.g., Zulk v. Zulk, 502 N.W.2d 116 (S.D. 1993); Gaskie v. Hugins, 640 P.2d 248 (Colo. Ct. App. 1981). Is this consistent with the four unities? See R.H. Helmholz, Realism and Formalism in the Severance of Joint Tenancies, 77 Neb. L. Rev. 1, 23 (1998) (concluding that the four unities, while still cited in decisions, have ceased to control the outcome of most cases).

6. **Murder of a Cotenant.** Although the survivorship feature might appear to offer one joint tenant a unique incentive to murder her cotenant, we have found no cases outside of books and movies in which someone has murdered their joint tenant for the land. However, joint tenants, who are often spouses, occasionally kill each other for other reasons. If one joint tenant kills another, does the murderer still get the property? The principal approach today is to hold that the joint tenancy is severed, leaving a tenancy in common. See Uniform Probate Code § 2–803(c)(2). The decedent's share of the property thus becomes part of the decedent's estate and distributed per her will or testate laws.

7. **Simultaneous Deaths.** How should the survivorship feature be administered if it is impossible or impracticable to determine the order in which joint tenants have died? The question, which typically arises when

joint tenants die in a common accident, is resolved in most states under the terms of section 3 of the Uniform Simultaneous Death Act:

> Where there is no sufficient evidence that two joint tenants or tenants by the entirety have died otherwise than simultaneously the property so held shall be distributed one-half as if one had survived and one-half as if the other had survived. If there are more than two joint tenants and all of them have so died the property then distributed shall be in the proportion that one bears to the whole number of joint tenants.

3. DISAGREEMENTS AMONG COTENANTS

Despite the attractiveness of cotenancies, dividing ownership among multiple individuals can lead to disagreements over management of the land. One cotenant may want to rent the land for commercial use, while another cotenant might want to use the land for his personal residence. One cotenant might want to cash in on the land's value by selling it, while another cotenant might want to hold onto the land for appreciation. One cotenant might want to harvest trees on the property, while the other wants to preserve the land's natural condition and appearance. Although cotenants typically work out such disagreements, sometimes they cannot. This section looks at how the law deals with disagreements among cotenants. To what degree can a cotenant act unilaterally? Where cotenants disagree, what remedies does the law provide the warring cotenants? As discussed below, cotenants who want to end a cotenancy—because they are irreconcilably in disagreement or for any other reason—can ask a court to divide, or *partition*, the property either in kind or by selling the property and dividing the proceeds. In some situations, courts also can ensure an equitable sharing of the benefits and burdens of ownership by ordering payments, or an *accounting*, from one cotenant to another.

a. CAN A COTENANT ACT UNILATERALLY?

Carr v. Deking

Court of Appeals of Washington, 1988.
765 P.2d 40.

GREEN, J.

The primary issue presented by this appeal is whether a tenant in common who refuses to join in a lease executed by the other tenant in common is entitled to eject the lessee.

Joel Carr and his father, George Carr, now deceased, owned a parcel of land in Lincoln County as tenants in common. From 1974 through 1986 the Carrs leased the land to Richard Deking pursuant to a year-to-year oral agreement receiving one-third of the annual crop as rent. The Carrs paid for one-third of the fertilizer. In 1986, Joel Carr informed Mr. Deking he wanted cash rent beginning with the 1987 crop year. Mr. Deking was not receptive to this proposal.

In February 1987 Joel Carr wrote a letter to Mr. Deking to determine if he wanted to continue leasing the property. Mr. Deking did not respond. Instead he discussed the lease with George Carr. On February 18 Joel Carr went to his father's home and found Mr. Deking there discussing a possible 5–year lease. Joel Carr again indicated he wanted cash rent. Later that day, unbeknownst to Joel Carr, Mr. Deking and George Carr executed a written 10–year crop-share lease at the office of Mr. Deking's attorney. Under this lease, Mr. Deking agreed to pay all fertilizer costs. Joel Carr neither consented to nor ratified this lease and never authorized George Carr to act on his behalf.

In April Joel Carr gave notice to Mr. Deking that his tenancy would terminate at the end of the 1987 crop year. Mr. Deking responded that he would retain possession pursuant to the written lease with George Carr. In July Joel Carr commenced this action to declare that no valid lease existed, Mr. Deking had no right to farm the land and he should be required to vacate the land at the end of the 1987 crop year.

On August 21 Mr. Deking moved for summary judgment. He contended a lessee of one tenant in common cannot be ousted by the other tenant in common; and, therefore, Mr. Deking should be deemed a tenant in common with Joel Carr for the duration of the 10–year lease or until the premises are partitioned. Joel Carr also moved for summary judgment declaring the Deking–George Carr lease terminated. Additionally, he claimed his affidavit established an issue of fact as to whether George Carr had the mental capacity to enter into the lease. George Carr was never named as a party to this lawsuit. The court granted Mr. Deking's motion for summary judgment on October 7.

Before the judgment was formally entered, Joel Carr moved to amend his complaint to seek the right to lease his interest in the land to someone other than Mr. Deking if the lease was declared valid. He also sought a full one-third of the crop as rent should he acquiesce in the lease. On November 24, Joel Carr's motions were denied and he was granted as rental one-sixth of the crop grown on the land and one-sixth of a government conservation payment, but he was required to reimburse Mr. Deking for one-sixth of the fertilizer costs. Summary judgment was then entered declaring the lease valid as to all of the land for 10 years or until partition occurs. The court granted Mr. Deking's motion to strike portions of Joel Carr's affidavit as conclusionary statements about George Carr's mental capacity.

In reviewing a summary judgment, this court engages in the same inquiry as the trial court. Summary judgment under CR 56(c) can be granted only if the pleadings and depositions, together with affidavits, show there is no genuine issue as to any material fact and that the moving party is entitled to judgment as a matter of law. All facts submitted and all reasonable inferences must be considered in the light most favorable to the nonmoving party. Summary judgment should be granted only if, from all the evidence, reasonable persons could reach but one conclusion.

First, Joel Carr contends the court erred in refusing to eject Mr. Deking from the property on any of three bases: (1) He did not authorize or ratify the lease and, therefore, is not bound by it; (2) Mr. Deking is a stranger to the common title; and (3) the rights of Mr. Deking as lessee are subordinate to those of a nonjoining tenant in common. He argues public policy should prevent prospective lessees from going behind the back of one tenant in common to obtain a more favorable lease from the other.[1]....

It is well settled that each tenant in common of real property may use, benefit and possess the entire property subject only to the equal rights of cotenants. Rayonier, Inc. v. Polson, 400 F.2d 909, 919 (9th Cir. 1968); De La Pole v. Lindley, 131 Wash. 354, 258, 230 P. 144 (1924); 4A R. Powell, Real Property ¶ 603[1], at 50–14 (1986 & Supp. 1988); see Comment, The Inter Vivos Rights of Cotenants Inter Se, 37 Wash. L. Rev. 70 (1962). Thus, a cotenant may lawfully lease his own interest in the common property to another without the consent of the other tenant and without his joining in the lease. The nonjoining cotenant is not bound by this lease of the common property to third persons. The lessee "steps into the shoes" of the leasing cotenant and becomes a tenant in common with the other owners for the duration of the lease. *De La Pole*, at 358; 86 C.J.S. § 113(f), at 521; see Comment, 37 Wash. L. Rev. at 75. A nonjoining tenant may not demand exclusive possession as against the lessee, but may only demand to be let into copossession. Davis v. Shawler, 214 Kan. 501, 520 P.2d 1270, 1276 (1974); 3 G. Thompson, Real Property § 1071, at 259 (1980 repl.).

Applying these principles, we find Joel Carr is not entitled to eject Mr. Deking from the property. The proper remedy is partition and until that occurs, Mr. Deking is entitled to farm the land under the lease. There is no indication that this property is not amenable to physical partition. Joel Carr clearly has the right to that remedy....

Finally, Joel Carr moved to amend his complaint and for reconsideration or clarification of his relationship with Mr. Deking pending partition. The court denied the motions to amend and to reconsider, but clarified the parties' relationship by ruling that Joel Carr was entitled to one-sixth of the crop, one-sixth of the government conservation payment and was obligated to reimburse Mr. Deking for one-sixth of the fertilizer costs. Joel Carr claims this was error. His challenge is directed to the requirement he pay fertilizer costs when the lease with George Carr required that Mr. Deking pay all such costs....

In view of our holding that the trial court properly denied Joel Carr's effort to eject Mr. Deking, Joel Carr is entitled to the benefit of the Deking–George Carr lease, at his election, until a partition of the property occurs. However, Joel Carr cannot claim the benefits contained in the Deking–George Carr lease without also accepting the other terms of that lease. Consequently, we remand to the trial court to determine Joel Carr's election choice. If he elects to be governed until partition by the prior oral lease with Mr. Deking, then the trial court's ruling is affirmed. If Joel Carr

1. Joel Carr also argues Mr. Deking had no right to possession subsequent to the 1987 crop season because he was given timely notice to vacate under RCW 59.12.035 and this terminated the tenancy. This position is inconsistent with general cotenancy principles, as George Carr did not join in the notice to terminate....

elects to be governed until partition by the Deking–George Carr lease, then the judgment shall be so modified by the trial court.

Affirmed in part and remanded for further proceedings.

Threatt v. Rushing

Supreme Court of Mississippi, 1978.
361 So. 2d 329.

BROOM, Justice, for the Court.

Whether one whose interest in lands consists of (1) a life estate plus (2) an undivided one-fourth in the fee interest may, without consulting the cotenants, cut and sell timber is the chief issue of this cause appealed from the Chancery Court of Lauderdale County. Johnny Roy Rushing, Andrew Ray Rushing, and Mittie Edna Rushing Foster (appellees) sued appellant, Mittie Alice Cooper Rushing Threatt (Mrs. Threatt herein), Henry Cornish and Glen Cornish, seeking to enjoin Mrs. Threatt and the two Cornishes from cutting timber and seeking a judgment for timber already cut. The lower court granted the injunction and entered a money decree against Mrs. Threatt and the two Cornishes for $9,344.26. We affirm.

Mrs. Threatt owns a life estate in the timberlands in question, and an undivided one-fourth interest in the fee interest. She previously owned the lands in fee simple but later deeded the lands to her children (appellees), reserving a life estate. Afterward one of her daughters deeded back a one-fourth interest to her, leaving the three remaining children, Johnny Roy Rushing, Andrew Ray Rushing, and Mittie Rushing Foster owning an undivided one-fourth interest each.... According to Mrs. Threatt's testimony, in 1976 she decided to "improve" the timber by cutting out mature trees, leaving a good stand "that could reseed," and employed Henry Cornish (one of appellants) to selectively cut the mature trees....

Forester Goforth testified at trial that the lands had about 1,019,300 board feet of standing timber, of which 92,300 board feet of pine and 21,200 board feet of hardwood had been cut, the timber already cut being worth about $14,825.63. According to Goforth, the land was primarily used for growing timber and needed to be thinned or "you're taking a chance" on losing profit. Henry Cornish testified that his "thinning" made the smaller timber grow faster and improved the timber.... He admitted that the children had told him to quit cutting the trees....

Did Mrs. Threatt, the life tenant, waste the interests of the remaindermen (her children) by cutting the timber? The correct test may be stated thusly: Do the acts of the life tenant in cutting the timber damage or diminish the value of the chief inheritance? If so, such acts are actionable waste. This was the meaning of Learned v. Ogden, 80 Miss. 769, 32 So. 278 (1902), which stated that "the cutting down by the tenant of trees for sale is waste ... an injury to the inheritance...." Cannon v. Barry, 59 Miss. 289, 306 (1881), an earlier case, held that acts dictated by "good husbandry" are not in law waste. Under the common law, a life tenant (as is Mrs.

Threatt) may cut growing timber for estovers, making necessary repairs, for fuel, or to pay taxes, but cannot "lessen the value of the inheritance." 1 Thompson on Real Property, § 104 (1964).

Here, Mrs. Threatt holds a life estate, and by virtue of the fact that one of the daughters had deeded back her (the daughter's) one-fourth interest, Mrs. Threatt holds a one-fourth of the remainder interest along with her other three children (appellees). We cannot agree, given the facts of this case, that the lower court erred in holding that Mrs. Threatt's undertaking to cut the mature timber (leaving enough for reseeding) was simply not "good husbandry." Testimony shows there was over one million board feet of mature timber on the lands; to cut such a large part of the timber would obviously reduce the value of the chief estate. The cutting of timber here was of great magnitude and not for "estovers" or merely for the purpose of improving or maintaining the estate, but was in a large measure a commercial operation of Mrs. Threatt for profit and constitutes waste.

The second proposition argued on behalf of Mrs. Threatt is that as a cotenant, i.e., owner of an undivided one-fourth interest in the lands, she has a right, acting unilaterally, to harvest one-fourth of the mature timber and retain the proceeds. Mr. Goforth, appellees' witness, indicated that Mrs. Threatt and the Cornishes had not cut one-fourth of the mature timber on the property in dispute, but only about 92,300 board feet of pine and 21,200 board feet of hardwood out of a total mature timber of 1,019,300 board feet.

There is conflict among authorities as to whether or not a cotenant may cut timber from common property without the consent of the other cotenant(s) .... The rule of foreign jurisdictions varies widely, as indicated by the contrasting views cited in 86 C.J.S. Tenancy in Common § 54 (1954). In Rhode Island, timber is treated like crop income from the land and thus may be sold without liability for waste. Conversely, in the State of Washington timber is considered part of the realty and thus subject to an action for waste. Rayonier, Inc. v. Polson, 400 F.2d 909 (9th Cir. 1968); Buchanan v. Jencks, 38 R.I. 443, 96 A. 307 (1916)....

The 9th Circuit, in construing the rights of an assignee of a cotenant to remove timber, in Rayonier, Inc. v. Polson, supra, stated:

> [O]ne cotenant of real property may use and enjoy the entire property to the fullest extent consistent with the ordinary manner of deriving profits from property of like character ... and he may grant to other persons freely and without the necessity of the consent of his cotenants, his interest in the property and whatever rights he enjoys....

But:

> Courts generally hold that a cotenant has no right to remove substantial amounts of timber from land having a value primarily for its timber and that to do so constitutes waste for which he is liable.

In some jurisdictions a cotenant may cut his fractional share of the timber (not merely stumpage, but determined by commercial and other considerations) without consulting with or being accountable to the other cotenants. Such a rule seems to allow cotenants to vie or race with each other in the disposition of their estate, and could create a situation in which all the cotenants might descend on the property, taking what they individually seize upon so long as they limit themselves to their fractional share. How such a rule can be applied without pandemonium or chaos is not clear. We hold that the better rule which we now adopt is that a cotenant may not sever timber from the land without consent of the other cotenant(s). If a cotenant cannot obtain such consent, he may have to resort to partition proceedings or some other form of litigation, but he may not unilaterally partition the property himself by simply cutting timber, even though he cuts only his own fractional interest of timber ownership. . . .

Notes & Questions

1. Why should a cotenant be able to lease the property unilaterally but not remove timber without the permission of her cotenants? Considering the power to lease first, what is the effect of the lease between George Carr and Richard Deking? Can Joel Carr still use the property? Could he build a home in the middle of Deking's fields? If so, doesn't Joel Carr have the ability to make Deking's life quite miserable? Should the law encourage such self-help behavior, or instead require cotenants to agree on leases? What would be the disadvantage of requiring all cotenants to agree on leases?

2. What are the alternatives to permitting each co-tenant to act unilaterally? Where there are only two co-tenants, requiring both co-tenants to agree on leases and other major actions would seem a workable rule. How might the law deal with co-tenancies involving five, 15, 50, or even more co-tenants? Would it make sense to apply a majority rule in these cases: any action would require the assent of over 50 percent of the co-tenants?

3. Turning to timber cutting, a number of jurisdictions permit cotenants to cut a proportionate share of any timber found on the property. Is there any disadvantage to such a rule? *Threat* suggests that such a rule would "allow cotenants to vie or race with each other in the disposition of their estate"? If each cotenant is limited to her proportionate share, however, how would that create a destructive race?

4. **Conservation Issues.** What if some co-tenants want to exploit the timber or other resources found on their property, while the remaining co-tenants want to conserve the land without touching its resources? Who should prevail? In Chosar Corp. v. Owens, 370 S.E.2d 305 (Va. 1988), coal rights were held in cotenancy by approximately 90 heirs of Andrew and Crissie Willis. 85 percent of the owners wanted to develop the coal and so entered into a lease with Chosar Corporation; the other 15 percent of the

owners opposed any mining. Although Chosar carefully left in place a proportionate share of the coal for these 15 percent, the Virginia Supreme Court affirmed an injunction against the coal mining on the ground of waste. Justice Thomas dissented:

> The result of the majority opinion is that the rights of the 15% who do not want to mine have been made paramount to the rights of the 85% who want to mine. Indeed, the principle of the majority opinion is such that if the mineral rights here in dispute were jointly owned by 1,000,000 people and 999,999 of these co-owners wanted to mine, one solitary co-owner could enjoin all mining. The majority's position is neither required nor justified by existing Virginia law; moreover, it is not sound in principle or logic.

What are the arguments, if any, for letting the 15 percent minority decide not to permit mining?

5. Assume that Aldo Leopold and Jessie Fremont are co-tenants of a large undeveloped parcel of land, and Jessie wants to develop a shopping center on the property. If Aldo wants to protect the land in its natural state, can he block Jessie from building her shopping center and leasing space out to commercial stores? Is this hypothetical any different from *Chosar*?

Assume that, before Jessie begins any work on her shopping center, Aldo donates a "conservation easement" to The Nature Conservancy in which he promises that neither he nor anyone else who ever owns the land will develop it. Is this easement binding only on Aldo and anyone who acquires his undivided half-interest in the land, or is it also binding on Jessie?

b. ACCOUNTING TO COTENANTS

Martin v. Martin

Court of Appeals of Kentucky, 1994.
878 S.W.2d 30.

JOHNSTONE, Judge

Garis and Peggy Martin appeal from a judgment of the Pike Circuit Court which required them to pay rent to the cotenants of certain real estate. Reluctantly, we reverse.

Garis and Peggy own an undivided one-eighth interest in a tract of land in Pike County. This interest was conveyed to Garis by his father, Charles Martin, in 1971. Appellees, Charles and Mary Martin, own a life estate in the undivided seven-eighths of the property for their joint lives, with remainder to appellants.

In 1982, Charles Martin improved a portion of the property and developed a four lot mobile home park which he and Mary rented. In July of 1990, Garis and Peggy moved their mobile home onto one of the lots. It is undisputed that Garis and Peggy expended no funds for the improvement or maintenance of the mobile home park, nor did they pay rent for the lot that they occupied.

In 1990, Garis and Peggy filed an action which sought an accounting of their claimed one-eighth portion of the net rent received by Charles and Mary from the lots. The accounting was granted, however, the judgment of the trial court required appellants to pay "reasonable rent" for their occupied lot. It is that portion of the judgment from which this appeal arises.

The sole issue presented is whether one cotenant is required to pay rent to another cotenant. Appellants argue that absent an agreement between cotenants, one cotenant occupying premises is not liable to pay rent to a co-owner. Appellees respond that a cotenant is obligated to pay rent when that cotenant occupies the jointly owned property to the exclusion of his co-owner.

Appellants and appellees own the subject property as tenants in common. The primary characteristic of a tenancy in common is unity of possession by two or more owners. Each cotenant, regardless of the size of his fractional share of the property, has a right to possess the whole.

The prevailing view is that an occupying cotenant must account for outside rental income received for use of the land, offset by credits for maintenance and other appropriate expenses. See Barnes v. Kidwell, 245 Ky. 740, 54 S.W.2d 331 (1932). The trial judge correctly ordered an accounting and recovery of rent in the case *sub judice*.

However, the majority rule on the issue of whether one cotenant owes rent to another is that a cotenant is not liable to pay rent, or to account to other cotenants respecting the reasonable value of the occupancy, absent an ouster or agreement to pay. 51 A.L.R.2d 413 § 8; see also Taylor v. Farmers and Gardeners Market Association, 295 Ky. 126, 173 S.W.2d 803 (1943). . . .

The appellees reason that the award of rent was proper upon the premise that Garis and Mary ousted their cotenants. While the proposition that a cotenant who has been ousted or excluded from property held jointly is entitled to rent is a valid one, we are convinced that such ouster must amount to exclusive possession of the entire jointly held property. We find support for this holding in *Taylor*, supra, in which the Court stated at 807–08:

> But, however this may be, running throughout all the books will be found two essential elements which must exist before the tenant sought to be charged is liable. These are: (a) That the tenant sought to be charged and who is claimed to be guilty of an ouster must assert *exclusive* claim to the property in himself, thereby necessarily including a denial of *any* interest or any right or title in the supposed ousted tenant; (b) he must give notice to this effect to the ousted tenant, or his acts must be so open and notorious, positive and assertive, as to place it beyond doubt that

he is claiming the *entire* interest in the property. [Emphasis in original.]

We conclude that appellants' occupancy of one of the four lots did not amount to an ouster. To hold otherwise is to repudiate the basic characteristic of a tenancy in common that each cotenant shares a single right to possession of the entire property and each has a separate claim to a fractional share. 4a Richard R. Powell, Powell on Real Property § 601 (1986).

Accordingly, the judgment of the Pike Circuit Court is reversed as to the award of rent to the appellees.

Estate of Hughes

Court of Appeal of California, 1992.
7 Cal. Rptr. 2d 742.

WIENER, Acting P.J.

When Kathryn Marlow Hughes died on February 12, 1975, she and her husband, George Ervin Hughes, had been living in her separate property residence at 3438 Browning Street in San Diego. The house was worth about $45,000. Upon her death George, as a spouse omitted from Kathryn's November 15, 1965 will admitted to probate, acquired a one-third interest in the property pursuant to then Probate Code section 70.[a] The named beneficiaries under the will, Kathryn's two children, Victoria Wiseman and Charles Marlow, received the balance in equal shares. George, and later when he remarried, with his wife Sylvia, continued to live in the residence. Although they paid the monthly installments on the note secured on the property, they paid no additional rent. When George died on November 26, 1986, Sylvia remained in the house until July 31, 1988, living there rent-free until July 22, 1987, when the court ordered her to pay a monthly rental of $350.

[The principal issue on appeal was whether George had "ousted" his co-tenants, Victoria Wiseman and Charles Marlow, from the Browning Street Residence, and therefore was required to pay rent to his co-tenants. The trial court ruled that no rent was due either from George or later from his estate or widow. The Court of Appeal reversed.]

"An ouster, in the law of tenancy in common, is the wrongful dispossession or exclusion by one tenant of his cotenant or cotenants from the common property of which they are entitled to possession." (Zaslow v. Kroenert (1946) 29 Cal. 2d 541, 548 [176 P.2d 1].) Whether there has been an ouster is a legal question. Where the facts are disputed we must defer to the trial court's factual findings but we must nonetheless decide the legal issue de novo.

a. Under the law of some states, a husband or wife who is not included as a beneficiary in their spouse's will automatically receives a specified interest (in this case, a one-third undivided interest) in the family residence.—Eds.

Sometimes the facts will make it clear an ouster has occurred. For example, in Zaslow v. Kroenert, supra, the trial court and later the appellate court had no difficulty deciding that changing the locks on the doors, posting "no trespassing" signs on the property and denying the cotenant admittance on demand was an ouster. The facts, however, are not always so easy, and sometimes it is quite difficult for the cotenant in possession to decide whether there is an obligation to account to a cotenant or cotenants not in possession. "The practical borderline between privileged occupancy of the whole by a single cotenant and unprivileged greedy grabbing which subjects the greedy one to liability to his cotenants is not crystal clear." (4A Powell, The Law of Real Property (1982) § 603, p. 610.)

The problems associated with the difficulty of establishing an ouster prompted the California Law Revision Commission in 1983 to recommend a statutory procedure to simplify the process. Citing Brunscher v. Reagh (1958) 164 Cal. App. 2d 174 [330 P.2d 396] and De Harlan v. Harlan (1946) 74 Cal. App. 2d 555 [168 P.2d 985], the commission first explained that in California "in order for the cotenant in possession to be held to account for a proportionate share of the use value of the property, the cotenant must forcibly exclude or prevent use by the cotenant out of possession." (17 Cal. Law Revision Com. Rep. (1984) p. 1028.) It then recommended a statute "so that a tenant out of possession of property may establish an ouster and recover damages, without the need to show that the tenant in possession has forcibly excluded or prevented use of the property by the tenant out of possession." (Ibid.) Adopting the recommendation in 1984 the Legislature enacted Civil Code section 843 permitting a cotenant out of possession to make a written demand for concurrent possession of the property. An ouster is established if within 60 days after service of the demand, "the tenant in possession does not offer and provide unconditional concurrent possession of the property to the tenant out of possession." (Civ. Code, § 843(b).)

Our discussion of the legislative history of Civil Code section 843 is not to criticize [George's co-tenants] for failing to use this provision, but rather to emphasize the difficulties associated with determining when an ouster has occurred. The decision is particularly difficult in a case like the one before us where the conduct of the cotenant in possession for a substantial period consisted solely of his residing in the estate property, manifesting neither an intent to share possession nor to deprive other cotenants from sharing possession. In this analytical setting where the cotenants out of possession have the burden of establishing an ouster, the . . . court properly decided that absent any evidence George actually excluded Victoria or Charles, it could not find an ouster. . . . We therefore agree with the court that "George . . . did not physically oust Victoria and Charles nor [was there] any request to permit them to occupy the premises with him. . . ."

[The Court of Appeal next considered whether George had "ousted" his two co-tenants by filing a petition in the courts in late 1982 to have himself declared the owner of 100% of the Browning Street residence. George argued, incorrectly, that California marital property law gave him

100% of the property as the surviving spouse.] The referee dealt with this issue in the following manner:

> Although George apparently did not physically oust Victoria and Charles nor did he refuse any request to permit them to occupy the premises with him, does the fact that George filed a petition seeking to have the entire property set aside to him as community property amount to ouster or exclusion? Although no cases were found dealing with this question, it is difficult to see how it could do so, on policy grounds. Where a co-tenant has an unquestioned right to an undivided part interest in property and a colorable claim to the entire property it is difficult to see how he could proceed more reasonably than to seek a judicial resolution of the matter. He should be encouraged not to resort to self-help and should not be penalized (by being held liable to his co-tenants for rent) by seeking (even unsuccessfully) to establish his claim to the entire property in a peaceable manner.

Although there is a certain appeal to the referee's rationale we believe it is at odds with the underlying concept of ouster. As noted earlier, at common law ouster was established by a cotenant's unambiguous conduct manifesting an intent to exclude another cotenant from gaining or sharing possession of jointly owned property. Here George manifested a similar intent by categorically alleging in his petitions that he was the sole owner of the property and that Kathryn's two children had no interest in the property. On this basis we conclude the petitions were the functional equivalent of changing locks or posting "no trespassing" signs telling a cotenant out of possession that he or she may not enter the premises. It is one thing for the cotenant in possession to remain silent, but quite another for the cotenant to seek legal redress claiming entitlement to all the property to the exclusion of other claimants.

Support for this position is found in Zaslow v. Kroenert, supra, 29 Cal. 2d 541, where the court said an ouster is "proved by acts of an adverse character, such as *claiming the whole for himself, denying the title of his companion*, or refusing to permit him to enter. Actual or constructive possession of the ousted tenant in common at the time of the ouster is not necessary." (*Zaslow* at p. 548, italics added.) "An action by a tenant in common against his cotenant to be admitted into the possession, a denial in the answer of the plaintiff's title and right of entry is equivalent to an ouster." (Miller v. Myers (1873) 46 Cal. 535, 538.) George's petitions here, comparable to the pleadings in *Miller*, constituted an ouster.

In reaching this conclusion we disagree with the referee's observation that interpreting George's action in this manner penalizes the cotenant in possession because it will trigger an obligation to pay rent. Whenever an ouster occurs the rental obligation accrues. Consequently the manner of its accrual is irrelevant provided the cotenant in possession reasonably understands the effect of his or her behavior. In this case where George was represented by counsel when he filed his petition, we believe he should suffer the detriment in addition to receiving any potential benefit associated with his petition.

In addition, the fact that ouster may occur in a peaceful, nonaggressive manner through lawful means is consistent with the policy underlying the 1984 legislation resulting in the enactment of Civil Code section 843. More significantly, however, ouster furnishes the tenant in possession a reciprocal benefit since it starts the time in which the tenant in possession will hold the property adversely. "While there is a presumption that the possession of one cotenant is amicable and permissive, and not adverse to his cotenants, this presumption is not conclusive. Thus, under certain circumstances, the exclusive possession of one cotenant can 'ripen' into title against the other cotenants if the occupying cotenant otherwise satisfies all the requirements for title by adverse possession." (5 Miller & Starr, Cal. Real Estate 2d, supra, § 12:9, p. 113.) The ouster by one cotenant of others can result in the tenant in possession obtaining title to the property by adverse possession. . . .

Notes & Questions

1. In *Estate of Hughes*, is there any way that George Hughes could have sued to determine his interest in the property without ousting his cotenants? Could he have sued, but simultaneously sent a letter to his cotenants stating that he was just trying to assert his rights and did not intend to oust them if he was wrong? Why was the filing of the lawsuit an ouster? Couldn't George have filed the lawsuit without intending to oust his cotenants if the court ruled against him?

2. Several rules have evolved for allocating rights and liabilities between cotenants. Some of these rules make sense. Others rest on distinctions that are often arbitrary and almost always confusing. The various rules, explored at 7 Richard R. Powell, Powell on Real Property §§ 50.03–50.04 (Michael Allan Wolf ed., 2005) and 2 American Law of Property §§ 6.10–6.18 (A.J. Casner ed. 1952), are summarized in the notes that follow.

In allocating rights and liabilities, should courts distinguish between commercial and noncommercial cotenancies? Should the same accounting rules apply where a brother and sister have inherited a family home as tenants in common, where a husband and wife share their property as cotenants, and where two unrelated people acquire an office building in cotenancy? The law currently fails to distinguish among these various situations. In an excellent article, Professor Evelyn Lewis has argued that courts should factor into allocation rules the differences between family cotenancies and other forms of cotenancies. See Evelyn Alicia Lewis, Struggling with Quicksand: The Ins and Outs of Cotenant Possession Value Liability and a Call for Default Rule Reform, 1994 Wis. L. Rev. 331 (1994). In reading the following notes, consider whether the rules should vary based on the relationship between the cotenants and the type of property.

3. **Income**—*Rent*. Most American states today hold that while one cotenant is not liable to his cotenants for any part of the rental value he himself derives from possessing the whole, he must account to them for their proportional share of any rents he receives from a third-party occupant. A few states require the cotenant to apportion not only rents received but also the rental value of his own occupancy. See, e.g., McKnight v. Basilides, 143 P.2d 307 (Wash. 1943).

Is the result in *Martin*, which follows the majority distinction between outside rents and the rental value of a cotenant's occupancy, unfair? Why should Greg and Peggy Martin be entitled to their proportionate share of the mobile park rents, but not have to pay Charles and Mary Martin a proportionate share of the rental value of the mobile home lot that they occupy? Does the *Martin* rule encourage cotenants to live on the property even when the property could be more valuably used? Assume that Greg and Peggy Martin value the lot on which they live at $500 per month, but that the lot would rent for $800 per month. Because Greg and Peggy would receive only $100 per month if the lot were rented (1/8th of $800), Greg and Peggy would choose to stay on the lot even though other potential renters value the lot more highly.

Farming Income. The majority rules respecting income from crops generally follow the rules on income from occupancy. If one cotenant grows and harvests the crops herself, she will not be required to account to her cotenants for any part of their value, even though she may have realized cash profits from their sale. If, however, the cotenant leases the land to a third party for farming purposes, she must account to her cotenants for their fractional share of the rents received.

Natural Resources. When it is not crops, but depletable natural resources, such as minerals or timber, that are removed from the land, courts diverge in their results. As you have already seen, some courts will characterize any removal of depletable resources as waste and enjoin it. See Threatt v. Rushing, supra p. 754. Other courts will allow the cotenant to remove up to her fractional share of the resources, without any duty to account. Still others will allow the cotenant to remove resources from the entire parcel in a reasonable manner, with a duty to account to her cotenants for their fractional share of the profits. If the cotenant instead leases out the property, and authorizes the lessee to remove depletable resources, some courts will nullify the lease and enjoin the removal as waste, while others will honor the lease but require the cotenant to account to her cotenants for their fractional share of the rents received.

4. **Expenditures**—*Upkeep*. As a general principle, a cotenant who pays for upkeep expenses such as maintenance, taxes, insurance, and debt service, is entitled to have his cotenants contribute their fractional share. The general principle will be applied differently depending on whether the expenses are less or more than the rent or rental value the cotenant receives.

If the expenses are *less than* the rent received from a third party, the cotenant who pays the expenses can effectively obtain contribution by setting expenses off against rent and disbursing only the net profits to his cotenants. Similarly, if expenses are less than rental value, an occupying cotenant who is liable to his cotenants for rental value—either because he has ousted them or because the minority approach on rental value is followed—can deduct upkeep expenses from the rental value owed. However, an occupying cotenant who is not liable for rental value cannot charge his cotenants for upkeep expense that is less than the rental value. If upkeep expenses *exceed* rent or rental value received, the cotenant can bring an action for contribution against his cotenants, regardless of whether he is liable to them for any rent or rental value received. However, the amount of contribution will be reduced by the rent or rental value received and not shared with the cotenants.

Improvements: In principle, a cotenant who authorizes and pays for improvements on the common property has no right to contribution from cotenants who did not authorize the improvement. This principle will, however, be affected by the context in which it is applied. If the question of liability arises not in an action for contribution brought by the improving cotenant, but rather in an action for partition brought by another cotenant, the improver will often recoup the complete value of the improvement because courts will typically partition the land in a way that gives the improver the part that has the improvement on it; if physical partition is impracticable and a sale is ordered, courts will usually give the improver not only her fractional share of the sale proceeds attributable to the value of the land, but also the full amount of the proceeds attributable to the improvement.

5. **Ouster.** As explained in *Estate of Hughes*, ouster has two distinct consequences. First, upon proving that she has been ousted, the cotenant out of possession becomes entitled to recover her fractional share of the premises' rental value from the cotenant in possession. Second, ouster starts the statute of limitations running against the ousted cotenant, who must bring an action to establish her interest in the real property within the limitations period or else lose her interest by adverse possession. Should the rules that are employed to determine whether ouster has occurred differ depending on whether it is the first or the second issue that is to be resolved? Although courts do not expressly separate the two situations, the decisions suggest that a line is in fact being drawn.

Entitlement to Share of Rental Value. In Mastbaum v. Mastbaum, 9 A.2d 51, 53 (N.J. Eq. 1939), the question was whether an ouster had occurred entitling the cotenants out of possession to recover a fractional share of the rental value from the cotenants in possession. Under the facts, the premises, occupied by two of the cotenants, were too small to house the other cotenants. The court focused on whether, by his conduct, "the defendant in possession, while not claiming sole title ... deprives his cotenant of all benefit from the premises."

The court rested its holding that ouster had not occurred, and that the cotenants in possession were not liable to the cotenants out of possession for any part of the rental value, on the finding that the

> only way in which all the tenants could obtain an equal benefit from the apartment was by renting it to a third party. This, through the instrumentality of the executor, they tried unsuccessfully to do. If defendants had obstructed a leasing so as to obtain for themselves the sole benefit, they would be liable to account for the rental value under the cases cited above, but they did not do so. They moved into the property because it was advantageous for them to do so and because complainants did not desire to live there. Unless defendants had moved in, none of the parties would have received any benefit from the property. Tenants in common are not required to let their property stand vacant under penalty of paying rent to their cotenants.

Adverse Possession. Courts determining whether ouster has occurred for purposes of adverse possession generally focus on whether the cotenant out of possession has received adequate notice of the adverse claim. For example, in Nedry v. Morgan, 584 P.2d 1381 (Or. 1978), a cotenant with a one-half undivided interest in the property conveyed his interest to third-party transferees under a deed that purported to convey full title to the property. The transferor's cotenants brought suit after the transferees had been in exclusive possession of the property for twenty-five years, paying taxes, irrigating the land, and cultivating it. The court concluded that the transferees' exclusive possession of the property sufficed to put the cotenants out of possession on notice that "persons other than the original cotenants were in possession." The transferees were not required to give actual notice of ouster in order to qualify as adverse possessors.

Are *Mastbaum* and *Nedry* consistent? Should the court in *Nedry* have been more reluctant to find an ouster given the dire consequences to the other cotenant? Do the typical justifications for adverse possession, discussed in Chapter 2, also justify adverse possession in cases of ouster?

In *Estate of Hughes*, the court held that George Hughes had ousted his cotenants when he filed his judicial petitions in 1982? If so, did Sylvia (his second wife) gain adverse possession to the property in 1987 (California has a 5–year statute of limitations)?

6. **Constructive Ouster.** In cases of divorce, should courts require a spouse who inhabits jointly held property to pay rental for using the other spouse's half of the property? Is it realistic to expect that both spouses will jointly use the property after the divorce? A number of courts have held that occupancy by one or the other spouse in the case of a divorce can constitute a *constructive ouster* requiring an accounting for rent. See, e.g., Hertz v. Hertz, 657 P.2d 1169 (N.M. 1983). As the Florida Court of Appeals explained in Adkins v. Edwards, 317 So. 2d 770 (Fla. Ct. App. 1975),

> In cases like this there frequently exists an aura of hostility and awkwardness not necessarily common to co-tenancy of lands or other properties held for commercial purposes. While neither of the parties contended that he or she was ousted from possession, it is unrealistic to believe that parties who could not get along living together while they were married would be expected to enjoy common usage of the former marital home after their divorce.

A Massachusetts appellate court has also suggested that divorce raises a rebuttable presumption of ouster. See Stylianopoulos v. Stylianopoulos, 455

N.E.2d 477 (Mass. App. 1983). Most courts, however, reject the concept of constructive ouster and refuse to order an accounting absent evidence that one spouse has physically excluded the other spouse from the property. The Florida Supreme Court overruled *Adkins* in Barrow v. Barrow, 527 So. 2d 1373 (Fla. 1988). See also Reitmeier v. Kalinoski, 631 F. Supp. 565 (D.N.J. 1986) ("the mere fact that defendant does not wish to live with plaintiff on the premises is of no import. What counts is that she could physically live on the premises.").

7. **Statutory Ouster.** Two states have provided statutory procedures for establishing ousters. As discussed in *Estate of Hughes*, Section 843 of the California Civil Code provides that the failure of a cotenant to "offer and provide unconditional concurrent possession of the property, within 60 days of the service by another cotenant of a written demand for concurrent possession, conclusively demonstrates an ouster." Under section 700.23(3)(a) of the Wisconsin Statutes, a cotenant can recover rent from another cotenant in possession of the property if, following written demand for rent, "the occupying tenant manifests an intent to occupy the premises to the exclusion of the other cotenant." In both California and Wisconsin, a cotenant can still prove an ouster by showing other facts establishing an ouster under the common law. Do such statutory provisions represent a significant improvement over the case-by-case ouster approach of the common law? If so, is either the California or Wisconsin approach better? See Lewis, supra note 2, at 369–71.

8. Since cotenants are entirely free to contract around any of the legal rules allocating their rights and liabilities *inter se*, the question naturally arises whether these rules matter. The answer is that they probably do. Although cotenants can contract around the default rules, there is general consensus that cotenants seldom do. Why? A major factor almost certainly is ignorance. Few cotenants contemplate the potential for disagreements and are unaware of the rules that govern them. Another factor may be that the state, by supplying default rules, enhances the status of those rules and thus reduces the incentive to bargain and innovate. See Lewis, supra note 2, at 392 & n.190; Charles J. Goetz & Robert E. Scott, The Limits of Expanded Choice: An Analysis of the Interactions Between Express and Implied contract Terms, 73 Calif. L. Rev. 261 (1985). Finally, the large number of cotenants in some cases, or strategic behavior by one or more of them, may prevent the cotenants from reaching a unanimous agreement on rights and liabilities.

4. PARTITION

Schnell v. Schnell

Supreme Court of North Dakota, 1984.
346 N.W.2d 713.

SAND, J.

Joan G. Schnell appealed from a judgment granted in favor of her former husband, Robert D. Schnell, ordering the ranch property which the two hold as tenants in common be sold rather than partitioned in kind....

The Schnell ranch contains 4,420 acres. The Schnells also lease 1,600 acres, most of it contiguous. The ranch includes about 700 head of cattle, numerous pieces of machinery, and many buildings. The buildings include a sales barn, feed building, horse barn, machine shed, several pole barns, and three homes. The first home is an expansive ranch home in which the couple lived until their divorce. After the divorce, Joan remained in the home and Robert built a second, smaller home a short distance away. The third home is for the hired man.

The trial court found from the evidence presented that the value of each cotenant's share from a partition would be substantially less than the money each would receive from a sale of the whole. The court ordered that the property be sold and that the proceeds from the sale be equally divided between the parties.

The primary issue on appeal is whether or not the court erred in concluding that the ranch should be sold rather than partitioned in kind. . . .

Historically, an action for partition is in the nature of a chancery action, cognizable under equity powers. Current statutory law provides that a partition is a matter of right when several cotenants are in possession of real property as tenants in common. North Dakota Century Code § 32–16–01 . . . .

The test for determining whether real property should be sold or partitioned in kind is statutory. Section 32–16–12 of the North Dakota Century Code provides:

> If it is alleged in the complaint and established by evidence, or if it appears by the evidence without such allegation in the complaint, to the satisfaction of the court, that the property, or any part of it, *is so situated* that partition cannot be made *without great prejudice* to the *owners*, the court may order a sale thereof. Otherwise, upon the making of requisite proof, it must order a partition according to the respective rights of the parties as ascertained by the court and appoint three referees therefor, and must designate the portion to remain undivided for the owners whose interests remain unknown or unascertained. [Emphasis added.]

The legislative intent of §§ 32–16–01 and 32–16–12 is clear and is consistent with case law and statutory law in a majority of jurisdictions. The law favors partition in kind where it can be made without great prejudice to the parties. 68 C.J.S. Partition § 125 (1950); Pigeon River Lumber Co. v. McDougall, 169 Minn. 83, 210 N.W. 850, 851 (1926). The burden of proving that partition in kind cannot be made without great prejudice is on the party demanding a sale. Unless great prejudice is shown, a presumption prevails that partition in kind should be made. Forced sales are strongly disfavored. Richmond v. Dofflemyer, 105 Cal. App. 3d 745, 757, 164 Cal. Rptr. 727, 733 (1980).

In determining if great prejudice would result from a partition, the question is not which alternative would provide optimal economic value or maximum functional use. The resultant parcels need not be the economic, functional or aesthetic equivalent of the original parcel. Rather, great prejudice exists when "the value of the share of each in case of a partition would be materially less than his share of the money equivalent that could probably be obtained from the whole." Berg v. Kremers, 181 N.W.2d 730, 733 (N.D. 1970). Thus, sale of land in partition should not be ordered unless it is necessary to protect the parties from "serious pecuniary injury." Ibid. This applies to both Joan and Robert, not just Robert. Furthermore, owelty, NDCC § 32–16–41, may be employed in certain instances to bring about an equitable partition.[a]

The trial court's decision is based principally upon a concern that a partition would destroy the "usefulness" and "efficiency" of the ranch. In so holding, the court noted that the pastures were "grouped to efficiently accommodate year-round grazing," that the pastures were "planned and balanced," and that partition may result in decreased animal carrying capacity. The court also expressed concern that new machinery, wells, buildings, and fencing would be required if the ranch was partitioned. The court concluded that the Schnell Ranch was a "model" ranch and that "By partitioning the ranch the efficiency and balance planned and learned . . . would be lost."

While efficient agricultural management is a desirable objective, it is only one factor among several in an action for partition and sale. In determining if great prejudice would result by partition in kind, emphasis must also be placed upon the situation of the parties and their respective financial abilities, including the financial ability of one of the parties to purchase the property, the location and character of the property, and the size and utility of the respective shares. Sentimental reasons, particularly in the preservation of a home, may also be considered, although they are subordinate to the pecuniary interests of the parties.

The situation of the parties in the instant case is significant and their respective financial abilities are dissimilar. Robert, 53, has a degree in animal husbandry. In addition to his holdings on the Schnell Ranch he is a

a. Eds.—Where a parcel of property is partitioned in kind, one portion of the land is often worth more than another. Imagine, for example, a lot with a house on it. The only way to ensure that a division of the lot would yield two equally valuable pieces of property might well be to draw a line straight down the middle of the house, but that obviously would not make much sense. To ensure that each cotenant receives equal value when the property is partitioned, courts therefore will often require a cotenant who receives the more valuable portion of the land to pay compensation, or *owelty*, to the cotenant who receives the less valuable parcel. Section 32–16–41 of the North Dakota Century Code, for example, provides that "When it appears that the partition cannot be made equal between the parties according to their respective rights without prejudice to the rights and interests of some of them, and a partition is ordered, the court may adjudge compensation to be made by one party to another on account of the inequality."

member of a partnership that leases ranch land in Montana and South Dakota that contains about 1,500 cattle. Robert is also an accomplished auctioneer and was designated "World Champion Auctioneer" in 1967. Joan testified that Robert usually spent about two-thirds of each year away from the ranch with auctioneering duties.

Joan, 50, is employed by the United States Department of Agriculture and lives in Virginia. She stated that her position is a political appointment which she believes is temporary. Although Joan has a degree in fashion merchandising, the record does not reflect that she has ever been employed in that field. She has instead spent most of her adult life raising a family of four, developing and supervising the ranch, and learning the ranching business. She has no other particular job skills. Thus, in comparing the respective situation of the parties it appears that Robert's career opportunities are more diverse than Joan's.

The respective financial ability of the parties is also significant. Joan's financial worth is based almost exclusively on her interest in the ranch. Robert, in addition to his Schnell ranch interest and his South Dakota and Montana ranching operations, receives significant income from his work as an auctioneer. Further, there is currently a mortgage on the property in the amount of $267,000.00. While the mortgage reduces the net equity of both parties, it would probably affect Joan's financial status the most. There is also a $78,000.00 lien on the ranch property against Joan and in favor of Robert that was awarded during the divorce proceedings. Thus, Robert's superior financial status would likely enable him to more easily acquire the entire ranch if it is sold as one unit.

The record strongly suggests that Robert desires to continue operating the entire ranch and that a sale is one method of accomplishing that objective. No evidence or testimony was introduced indicating that someone other than Robert was interested in buying the ranch. The evidence and testimony support a finding that the ranch would be more beneficial to Robert if it is not partitioned in kind. However, the question in a partition action is whether or not partition can be accomplished without great prejudice to the owners; not to one of the owners, but to all of them.

.... [L]ogic tells us that the smaller and more compact the area or property and the greater the number of persons having an interest in the property the more difficult partitioning in kind will be. Conversely, the greater and more expansive the area or property and the smaller the number of persons having an interest in the property, the easier partitioning in kind will be....

Under Joan's proposed division of the ranch,[1] she would receive 1,977 acres, nearly 500 acres more than the average farm-ranch in Adams County. Robert would receive 2,421 acres, nearly 1,000 acres more than the average farm-ranch. The trial court overlooked or disregarded that fact.

1. We refer to Joan's proposal for division of the ranch only as a guide in analyzing whether or not the ranch could be partitioned without great prejudice to the parties. Our reference is not necessarily an endorsement.

While division based upon average acreage is not the dispositive factor in a partition action, it is worthy of consideration. In addition, Robert would retain the 1,600 acres of leased land. One thousand acres of the leased land consists of state school land that, by Robert's admission, is not subject to true competitive bidding. Robert explained that area school land bids are kept low because the ranchers have a "gentlemen's agreement" not to bid against each other. The likelihood that the school land will remain with Robert is supported by Robert's testimony that the land has been rented by the Schnells since at least 1955. In addition, there are 960 acres of adjacent private lands that are for sale. Robert has already bid upon the land and, under Joan's plan, the land would remain adjacent to Robert's parcel....

We also believe that a proposal by one of the owners to lease the land back to another owner is a factor in determining if partition in kind can be made without great prejudice to the owners. The memorandum decision indicates that the trial court gave little if any consideration to Joan's testimony indicating that she was willing to lease the land back to Robert and their son Carter. Joan testified that if Carter continued working with his father, she would be willing to lease the land back to Carter and Robert for $6.00 an acre. Consideration of Joan's proposal in this case negates many of the findings that the trial court made in determining that the land should be sold ....

Given the duration of Joan's involvement with the ranch and her sentimental attachment to the land, her resistance to a partition and sale is logical. In this respect we note that the sale of real property against the wishes of a joint owner can be likened to a forced sale. Forced sales seldom produce the highest return on the property. In Vesper v. Farnsworth, 40 Wis. 357, 362 (1876), the court said that the power to convert real estate into money against the will of an owner "is an extraordinary and dangerous power, and ought never to be exercised unless the necessity therefor is clearly established." Similarly, in Haggerty v. Nobles, 244 Ore. 428, 419 P.2d 9, 12 (1966), the court observed that although a court must occasionally order a sale in an appropriate case, "it is obnoxious to compel a person to sell his property."

If only two persons are owners of property and each treasures its heritage, partition in kind will generally preserve those personal interests better than a partition and sale. In this respect, Joan has an equal right to pursue her personal interests. She helped develop the ranch from its infancy and she frequently managed the ranch while Robert tended to auctioneering interests. Her rights in the property equal Robert's rights, and they include the right of ownership, the right to preserve the heritage of her labors, and the right to pass the property to her heirs. Indeed, the law favors partition in kind because it does not compel a person to sell property against a person's will and it does not disturb the existing form of inheritance. Phillips v. Phillips, 170 Neb. 733, 104 N.W.2d 52, 56 (1960).

In reviewing the situation of the parties, the location and character of the property, as well as the size and utility of the respective shares if a partition in kind were made, it appears that the ranch may be divisible in kind. The testimony, diagrams, and pictures introduced indicate that the ranch could be divided so that each parcel would have sufficient water, pasture, hay, barn, and corral facilities. The parties' two homes are about one-quarter mile apart and are separated by several shelter belts, buildings, and a small creek. Each home could have a separate access. About one and one-half mile of additional fencing and one or two easements may be required, but none of the alterations appear significant.

The foregoing factors compel the conclusion that the ranch can be partitioned in kind without doing great prejudice to the owners, Robert and Joan.

Accordingly, the case is remanded with directions that the district court vacate or set aside the judgment and appoint referees pursuant to NDCC § 32–16–12 to devise a plan to partition in kind the real and personal property. . . .

[The dissenting opinion of Justice Pederson is omitted.]

Notes & Questions

1. All, or virtually all, states today authorize courts to judicially partition lands held in cotenancy and, if necessary, to order sale of the lands and division of the proceeds. The form of cotenancy does not matter. See, e.g., Geib v. McKinney, 617 A.2d 1377 (Conn. 1992). Although these statutes generally make partition available on demand by any cotenant entitled to possession, they attempt to limit forced sales to those situations in which division in kind would be impracticable. The attempt has not been particularly successful. See 7 Richard R. Powell, Powell on Real Property § 50.07[5] (Michael Allan Wolf ed., 2005) (noting that most partitions today are in the form of sale and division of proceeds).

2. Why do you suspect that courts often ignore the presumption favoring partitions in kind and order forced sales? Do partitions by sale avoid economically inefficient "overfragmentation" of property? See Michael A. Heller, The Boundaries of Private Property, 108 Yale L.J. 1163, 1167 & n.13 (1999) (arguing that partition in kind can often lead to uneconomically small lots and resulting underuse of land). We will return to the problem of overfragmentation in the next section of the book.

3. Despite the economic arguments that might be made for a partition sale, are there social reasons to prefer divisions in kind? In Chuck v. Gomes, 532 P.2d 657 (Hawaii 1975), the Hawaii Supreme Court affirmed a trial court's decision that a partition in kind was impracticable and that a partition sale was therefore necessary. Testimony at trial showed that the Honolulu residential property would be difficult to subdivide into marketable lots and would be worth more if not divided. Citing the rule that "the law favors partitions in kind," Chief Justice Richardson dissented:

> It is especially important to restate this preference for partition in kind so that in Hawaii we preserve the right of the individual joint tenant or tenant in common to hold onto his parcel of land where he opposes any forced sale of such property. Indeed,

there are interests other than financial expediency which I recognize as essential to our Hawaiian way of life. Foremost is the individual's right to retain ancestral land in order to perpetuate the concept of the family homestead. Such right is derived from our proud cultural heritage wherein it was believed that:

> [T]he one guarantee of survival [was] land ... [which was] in short supply either because of the density of population or because of the large holdings of exploiting gentry landholders.
>
> Because peasants depend for their survival on specific plots of land, ownership is their goal and once land is owned it must be preserved and passed on intact to the children. All this makes for the great emphasis on the survival of the particular family line which owns the particular plot of land. Thus peasants stress the unity and continuity of the family—large number of children, particularly sons who will work the plots of land, inherit them, and perhaps add to them. [B. Horman, Hawaii's People in Transition, in Aspects of Hawaiian Life and Environment: Commentaries on Significant Hawaiian Topics by Fifteen Recognized Authorities 93, 98 (1971).]

Undoubtedly there will be circumstances which justify the invocation of partition by judicial sale. In the situation where the statutory grounds are met the preference for actual division of property must yield to partition by judicial sale. But let us recognize that such preference for partition in kind should not be so easily disregarded. "Mindful of our Hawaiian heritage," we must not lose sight of the cultural traditions which attach fundamental importance to keeping ancestral land in a particular family.

3. Between 1969 and 1978, farms run by African Americans disappeared at a rate two and a half times faster than the rate of decline of white-operated farms; indeed, during this period, the number of African American farms declined almost 94 percent, from 925,710 to 57,271. See U.S. Comm'n on Civil Rights, The Decline of Black Farming in America 2–3 (1982). One author has suggested that a reason may the prevalence of African American farms in cotenancies (with some cotenants holding very small shares of the farm) and the courts' preference for partition sales.

> These conditions provide a fertile environment for partitioning actions. Typically, an outsider to the cotenancy purchases one cotenant's interest, intending to force the sale of the entire cotenancy. Or, a cotentant, sometimes at the urging of a land speculator, will petition the court for a sale. In either situation, the court may order a sale of the entire estate on the basis that the property is indivisible among the cotenants. The property consequently is put up for sale, where it is purchased more often than not be local white lawyers or relatives of local officials. The economic inability of many black cotenants to purchase all the real estate provides speculators with an easy bidding market.

John C. Casagrande, Jr., Acquiring Property Through Forced Partitioning Sales: Abuses and Remedies, 27 B.C. L. Rev. 755 (1986).

4. **Owelty & Allotment.** What mechanisms could a court use to avoid a partition sale if partition in kind would be difficult either because the property is not easily divisible into equal portions or because fractional shares would be too small to be economically practical? One method of dealing with the first problem, mentioned in *Schnell*, is *owelty*—where the court orders one cotenant to pay the other cotenant for the higher value of his portion of the partitioned property. See, e.g., Steinbrecher v. Steinbrecher, 726 N.E.2d 1118 (Ill. App. 2000). Some state statutes also authorize *allotment*—where the court allocates part of the property to a cotenant (often with a required payment to other cotenants if the allocated portion represents more than the cotenant's share of the entire property) and then sells the remainder. See, e.g., 25 Del. Code § 730; S.C. Code Ann. § 15–61–50; Va. Code Ann. § 8.01–83. In some cases, a cotenant must demonstrate an equitable claim to the allotment before it can be awarded. See Haw. Rev. Stat. §§ 668–7(5)–(6).

5. How effective of an option is partition for cotenants who are warring? Does partition present a Hobbesian choice that is even worse than fighting? As discussed in the preceding notes, partitions in kind can lead to an overall loss in the value of the total property. But partition sales can lead to lost personal value where a cotenant who prizes the property is unable to bid at the sale for one reason or another. In a depressed real estate market, cotenants might even face the loss of some of their initial investment. See generally Evelyn Alicia Lewis, Struggling with Quicksand: The Ins and Outs of Cotenant Possession Value Liability and a Call for Default Rule Reform, 1994 Wis. L. Rev. 331, 395–98.

6. What was at stake in *Schnell*? One possibility, of course, is that Mrs. Schnell felt a special affection for her home and did not want to give it up. But note that, at the time of the case, Mrs. Schnell at least temporarily *was* living in Virginia and working for the Department of Agriculture. Are there other possible reasons why Mrs. Schnell might have opposed a partition sale? How does the decision in *Schnell* affect the relative bargaining power of the two ex-spouses? Should the motivation of the parties matter in determining how to partition the property?

7. **A Digression on Public Grazing Lands.** In *Schnell*, the husband leased 1600 acres of state school land. When admitting most western states to the Union, Congress awarded parcels of public land to the states as endowment for the states' public schools. Many western states lease some of these school lands to ranchers for cattle grazing. As the court notes, these leases are often not subject to competitive bidding. In recent years, environmental groups, worried by the potential environmental damage from grazing, have tried, with mixed success, to bid against ranchers for such leases. See Sally K. Fairfax, State Trust Lands: The Culture of Administrative Accountability, in Environmental Federalism 61 (Terry L. Anderson & Peter J. Hill eds., 1997). These efforts have set off a new series of "range wars" between environmental groups (who argue that they should be entitled to bid on the leases just like the ranchers) and ranchers

(who object to the new competition for the state lands). Ranchers have argued that grazing leases are for grazing not for conservation and that environmental groups therefore should not be able to bid on the state lands. State land agencies often have agreed. See Forest Guardians v. Wells, 34 P.3d 364 (Ariz. 2001) (rejecting the state land agency's decision not to allow environmental groups to bid).

5. The Problem of Fragmentation: American Indian Lands

Is there a danger of land ownership being shared among too many individuals? According to Thomas Jefferson, "Legislators cannot invent too many devices for subdividing property, only taking care to let their subdivisions go hand in hand with the natural affections of the human mind." 8 The Papers of Thomas Jefferson 682 (Julian P. Boyd ed., 1953). In a fascinating article, however, Professor Michael Heller has argued that fragmentation of ownership runs a variety of risks against which the law should and typically does protect:

> The danger with fragmentation is that it may operate as a one-way ratchet: Because of high transaction costs, strategic behaviors, and cognitive biases, people may find it easier to divide property than to recombine it. If too many people gain rights to use or exclude, then bargaining among owners may break down. With too many owners of property fragments, resources become prone to waste either through overuse in a commons or through underuse in an anticommons. In well-functioning property regimes, legislatures and courts prevent such waste by drawing boundaries that constrain owners' choices about fragmentation....

Michael A. Heller, The Boundaries of Private Property, 108 Yale L.J. 1163 (1999).

According to Heller, one example of overfragmentation occurred with the homesteading movement in the late 19th century. The government allocated homestead plots that were "too small to be economically viable, given local climate conditions and existing agricultural technology. Because homestead laws prevented sale prior to acquiring full ownership, people either stayed and starved or abandoned the land. A checkerboard of uneconomic and abandoned farms resulted, with no legal mechanisms to consolidate ownership to a viable scale." Id. at 1172. As explained in the following excerpt, the government has similarly encouraged overfragmentation of Native American lands through a series of policies and restrictions.

Katheleen R. Guzman, Give or Take an Acre: Property Norms and the Indian Land Consolidation Act

85 Iowa L. Rev. 595 (2000)

In 1887, Congress passed the General Allotment Act to privatize Indian reservations and advance the assimilationist sentiment of the day. The Act divested land from tribes to their members, each of whom received a tract of land on a wing and a prayer: become an autonomous Christian agrarian. With various goals (benign and otherwise) in mind, the Act's proponents envisioned its transformative ability to supplant communitarian tribal norms with the classical liberal virtues of self-sufficiency, individuality and private ownership. These hopes, however, did not materialize, and while allotment was soon abandoned in policy and practice, its legacy remains.

Fractionation is one critical consequence of allotment. Through confluent legal and sociological factors, multiple owners now share minuscule interests in the same original allotment tracts.[7] Consider an 1898 allotment of 80 acres, where the allottee and two successive generations die intestate leaving five heirs apiece. Roughly 125 tenants in common would each own a 1/125th equitable interest in one half of a quarter section. The scenario is plausible because many allotments exceed several hundred owners. As a result, "common denominators have reached 54 trillion, billions are not uncommon, and millions [approach the norm]."[9] Fractionation thus renders allotment development or other economically productive use monumentally elusive, and propels interested investors into a "Kafkaesque quagmire" of negotiation and statutory and regulatory compliance.

In response to this problem, Congress passed the Indian Land Consolidation Act ("ILCA") in 1983. To "improve the economy of the tribe and its members," the ILCA strictly foreclosed the testate or intestate transfer of extremely fractionated interests, and instead, mandated their noncompensated escheat to the tribe with jurisdiction.[11] Congress hoped that escheat would counteract the further atomization of allotments, encourage a consolidated tribal land base, and provide land for tribal programs. Despite laudable goals, the ILCA failed to pass constitutional muster. In *Hodel v. Irving*,[13] the Supreme Court rejected the ILCA's escheat provision as an unconstitutional taking; the amended version, which reached the Supreme Court in 1997 in *Babbitt v. Youpee*,[14] was similarly spurned. By holding that the ILCA violated the Fifth Amendment Takings Clause rather than the Fifth Amendment Due Process Clause, the Court grudgingly acceded federal power to mandate the escheat of the fractional property interests but

7. Burdensome administrative prerequisites to inter vivos transactions and initial prohibitions on testamentary ones meant that few allottees exercised transfer rights, forcing the allotment through intestacy to potentially numerous heirs as tenants in common. "First, testate succession was not permitted for many allottees until 1910. Even after wills were permitted, many Native Americans did not write them, again subjecting allotments to the intestacy scheme of the jurisdiction within which they were located." Alex Tallchief Skibine, In the U.S. Supreme Court: The Limits on the Government's Power to Regulate the Right to Distribute Property by Devise and Descent, Nov. 27, 1996, available in 1996 WL 680722.

9. Indian Land Consolidation Act Amendment, S. Rep. No. 98–632, at 82–83 (1984), reprinted in 1984 U.S.C.C.A.N. 5470. In fact, the lowest common denominator for some fractionalized ownership interests has reached a googol—a number containing 101 digits, or 10^{100} power.

11. Indian Land Consolidation Act of 1983, Pub. L. No. 97–459, 96 Stat. 2519 (codified as amended at 25 U.S.C. § 2206 (1994)).

13. 481 U.S. 704 (1987).

14. 519 U.S. 234 (1997).

implicitly conditioned its exercise upon just compensation to each affected decedent's estate.

. . . .

Undiluted economic analysis justifies the swift and expansive solution of escheat given the extent to which fractionation interferes with efficient land use. First, the transactional costs and demands of identifying, locating, negotiating with, and acquiring permission from all allotment cotenants are cumbersome and inefficient. It is difficult to identify and locate allottees, given the infamous multiple successive intestate estates, probate backlog, and outdated, incomplete, or irretrievable records with limited rights of access that often characterize allotted lands. Relatedly, there is little incentive for the cotenants to ensure that their interest is of record; that many cotenants neither know nor care about their proportionate ownership is both a cause and effect of the suboptimal return it generates. Unlike the routine cotenancy where any concurrent owner may lease, sell, or mortgage a fractional interest without procuring approval from the other owners, leasing an allotment ordinarily requires *unanimous* consent by *all* interest holders.[54] This arrangement creates enormous difficulties where lost or simply recalcitrant cotenants exist. The effect of these factors might be mitigated if significant blocks of willing owners were able to terminate the cotenancy through partition. However, unique contextual rules again limit that particular detour[55]. . . .

Second, allotments normally range from 80 to 160 acres. Their relatively small size impedes revenue-producing agricultural, industrial, or mining development—a difficulty exacerbated by the variegated ownership and jurisdictional patterns dominant in allotted reservations. The high information and transfer costs generated by such a complex scheme deter third parties from even entering negotiation, particularly where those costs might exceed the parcel's entire value. . . .

These already negligible returns diminish by degrees when weighed against the enormous administrative costs incurred by the Federal Bureau of Indian Affairs in managing the allotment lands and maintaining title records. Government, and by implication, taxpayer, dollars spent to maintain the allotments far exceed the income value of many individual owners' interests, with some allottees' checks cut for as little as a penny a month. The *Irving* Court aptly illustrates:

> Tract 1305 [of the Sisseton–Wahpeton Lake Traverse reservation] is forty acres and produces $1,080 in income annually. It is valued

54. Act of Aug. 9, 1955, ch. 615, 69 Stat. 539 (codified as amended at 25 U.S.C. § 415 (1999)) (non-mining allotment lease); Allotted Lands Leasing Act of 1909, ch. 263, 35 Stat. 783 (codified as amended at 25 U.S.C. § 396 (1999)) (mining allotment lease); McClanahan v. Hodel, 14 Indian L. Rptr. 3113 (D.N. Mo. 1987). . . .

55. Normally, any single cotenant may dissolve the concurrent estate through partition by sale (division of proceeds) or in kind (division of property). By contrast, allotments cannot be partitioned at all unless *all* cotenants agree. Act of May 14, 1948, ch. 293, 62 Stat. 236 (codified at 25 U.S.C. § 483 (1994)) (enabling secretary to partition allotments subject to the Indian Reorganization Act "upon approval of the Indian owners," construed to require the application of all co-owners in 25 C.F.R. § 121.33 (1980)).

> at $8000. It has 439 owners, one-third of whom receive less than $.05 in annual rent and two-thirds of whom receive less than $1. The largest interest holder receives $82.85 annually. The common denominator used to compute fractional interests in the property is 3,394,923,849,000. The smallest heir receives $.01 every 177 years. If the tract were sold (assuming the 439 owners could agree) for its estimated $8000 value, he would be entitled to $.000418. The administrative costs of handling this tract are estimated by the Bureau of Indian Affairs at $17,560 annually.[64]

. . . .

The original Indian Land Consolidation Act barred all allotment cotenants from testate or intestate transfers of any escheatable interest to any person, mandating its escheat to the tribe holding jurisdiction instead.... The forced escheat provision of the ILCA was intended to prevent the further fractionalization and reverse the pre-existing fractionation of allotments, in the hope that small, unproductive interests would gradually consolidate into economically and administratively manageable land units under the control of the tribes.

. . . .

[W]idespread fractionation did not spring forth overnight. It arose and proliferated only after Anglo–American property norms were imposed on the tribes through allotment. As one scholar observed in general terms, "once governments create anticommons property, it may be difficult for them to redefine rights without either paying compensation or suffering a blow to their credibility."[244] Such is the case with the ILCA. Although superficially remedial, the ILCA compounds the inequities of allotment by attempting to correct the difficulties spawned by its own past policies by again forcing a land ideology, but this time diametrical to that formerly proposed. The ILCA transmutes allotment's command to accept individual land parcels from the tribe into a command to return them, free of charge. This constitutes inverse allotment, barely disguised. While consolidation sounds good for strengthening collective rights, allotment rhetoric was as potent, yet view its effects....

After massive attempts to mold "the Indian land vision" into a Western and individualistic one, it is manifestly unfair to now divest individual property interests in favor of tribal ones, particularly when aside from a cultural inheritance, an interest in a fractionated allotment might be the only piece of property an allottee even has to devise....

Notes & Questions

1. Does the option of seeking a court-ordered partition sale help avoid overfragmentation outside the Native American setting? Is there any

64. Hodel v. Irving, 481 U.S. 704, 713 (1987).

244. Michael A. Heller, The Tragedy of the Anticommons: Property in the Transition from Marx to Markets, 111 Harv. L. Rev. 622, 687 (1998).

reason not to let allotment owners seek a partition? Would that cure the existing problem of overfragmentation?

2. How would you solve the existing fragmentation of allotments? Although Congress can avoid the constitutional takings problem by paying compensation to tribal members whose fractional interests are escheated to the tribe, would compensation be meaningful? Note that the value of the smallest interest in Tract 1305, as described in the excerpt, is only a small fraction of a cent.

Professor Guzman proposes giving the power to each tribe to decide issues of descent, distribution, and consolidation. According to her, tribes

> are best positioned to assess their own circumstances, including the necessity of land consolidation, the most appropriate means to achieve it, and the political consequences of that determination.... Allowing tribes to choose or avoid land consolidation and the means to reach it places the responsibility for ensuring tribal welfare on itself and its members. "Tribes should be empowered to take a candid look at what they are willing to compromise on—land, culture, environment—to gain employment or income. Sovereign nations should be allowed to choose inefficiency just as easily as they choose development. Perhaps that is true freedom for a people."

Guzman, supra, at 661 (quoting Seth H. Row, Tribal Sovereignty and Economic Development on the Reservation, 4 Geo. J. on Fighting Poverty 227, 236 (1996)).

4. **Indian Probate Reform Act.** Since Professor Guzman published her article, Congress has tried several more times to solve the problems posed by highly fragmented Indian land interests. Congress' most recent effort is the American Indian Probate Reform Act of 2004 (AIPRA). The United States Department of the Interior now operates an active Indian land consolidation program in which it buys back fractionated shares. By 2002, the program had purchased 184,000 individual interests, involving 200,000 acres of land; 87 percent of the interests involved less than a 2% ownership interest. Under the AIPRA, if Indian land would pass in a probate proceeding by intestate success, the Department of the Interior can purchase any interests in the land that would constitute less than a 5% holding. Interior is entitled to buy the interest even over the opposition of the heir (unless the heir is living on the land). Any of the decedent's heirs, as well as co-owners and the tribe where the land is located, can also purchase the land during probate, so long as they pay fair market value and have the consent of anyone holding more than a 5% interest.

B. PROPERTY RIGHTS OF HUSBAND AND WIFE

As a general rule, property belongs to the person who acquires it consensually from another. The wisdom of the general rule, self-evident in most cases, is sorely tested in others. Thus, in the case of wife and husband, one working at a salaried job and the other working without salary at managing a home, the salaried partner may use his or her cash income to acquire property throughout the marriage, while the homemaker, having no cash income, will be unable to do so. Husband and wife might seek to reset the balance by contract, agreeing to divide all property acquired during the marriage equally upon divorce or death, or assigning some dollar value to the homemaker's services and proportioning the property assignment to this value. But, at least historically, the marriage relationship has not proved to be a conducive setting for contract arrangements.

The American states have taken two approaches to property rights of husband and wife. The common law system, currently adopted in 41 states, takes as its starting point the proposition that each partner is entitled only to the property that he or she acquires individually. Thus, in the example just given, the wage earner would own all property acquired with his or her income and the homemaker would get none. By contrast, the community property system, adopted in eight states (Arizona, California, Idaho, Louisiana, Nevada, New Mexico, Texas, and Washington), starts from the proposition that all property acquired during the marriage belongs half to husband and half to wife without regard to which of the two received the income used to acquire the property. Wisconsin has adopted the Uniform Marital Property Act which closely resembles the community property system.

These are starting points only. In practice, and as the law has evolved through years of legislative and judicial modification, the two systems often approximate each other on all the points that matter: management and control of property during marriage, and disposition of the property on divorce or death. And just as it is important not to overstate the differences between the common law and community property systems, it is crucial not to understate the differences among states within each group. Specific rules differ, often dramatically, among both common law states and community property states.

Because marital property rules often differ in important ways among states, a critical issue in many judicial disputes is which state's law to apply where a couple has lived in two or more states over the course of their marriage, acquiring and disposing of assets in each. As a general matter, the law of the state in which a couple is domiciled when property is acquired determines the character of the property. The fact that the couple later moves to another state does not matter; unless both the husband and wife agree, the property retains its original status. Upon the death of a spouse, the law of the decedent's state governs distribution of personal property and the law of the state in which any real property is located governs its distribution.

For excellent overviews of the two systems, and their moves in the latter half of the 20th century toward resetting the property balance between husband and wife, see Herma Hill Kay, From the Second Sex to the Joint Venture: An Overview of Women's Rights and Family Law in the United States During the Twentieth Century, 88 Calif. L. Rev. 2017 (2000); Barbara Ann Kulzer, Law and the Housewife: Property, Divorce, and Death, 28 U. Fla. L. Rev. 1 (1975); Judith T. Younger, Community Property, Women and the Law School Curriculum, 48 N.Y.U. L. Rev. 211 (1973); Jack Johnston, Sex and Property: The Common Law Tradition, The Law School Curriculum, and Developments Toward Equality, 47 N.Y.U. L. Rev. 1033 (1972).

1. THE COMMON LAW SYSTEM

Throughout the feudal period, single women enjoyed essentially the same power to own, manage, and dispose of real property as did single men. Women lost these powers upon marriage. The feudal doctrine that sought to rationalize this result was *coverture:* "By marriage, the husband and wife are one person in law: that is, the very being or legal existence of the *woman* is suspended during the marriage, or at least is incorporated and consolidated into that of the husband. . . ." 1 William Blackstone, Commentaries on the Laws of England *442 (1766) (emphasis added). Upon marriage, a woman switched from being a *feme sole* to a *feme covert* under her husband's protection or "cover." Coverture meant that, during the marriage, the husband gained control of any freeholds that his wife owned at the time of marriage or later acquired. He had the exclusive right (his *jure uxoris*) to occupy these lands himself or to rent them; he had no duty to account to his wife for the profits; he could transfer this right to others; and the right could be reached by his creditors. If the wife brought any leasehold estates to the marriage, the husband was free not only to use these as he pleased, but also to sell them if he wished. Coverture also meant that the wife had no right unilaterally to transfer her property during the marriage.

To "justify" the disabilities imposed by coverture, the common law gave the wife the right to her husband's support. It also gave her *dower* (from the same root as the modern term "to endow")—the right, if she survived her husband, to a life estate in one-third of the lands that the husband had owned during the marriage. The right to dower attached at the moment of marriage and could not, without the wife's consent, be defeated by the husband's inter vivos or testamentary transfers. As a counterpart to dower, the common law gave the husband who survived his wife *curtesy*—a life estate in all her freehold lands, provided by "curtesy" of England. Unlike dower, curtesy was conditioned upon the birth of a child to the couple.

Eventually, equity offered prospective brides and their families devices to sequester the wife's estate from the husband's *jure uxoris.* One was the Chancellor's enforcement of antenuptial agreements, unenforceable at law, giving the wife the right to control, and to take the rents and profits from, the property that she brought to, or acquired during, the marriage. Another equitable device, the trust, enabled a concerned parent to place property in trust for the benefit of a married daughter and enabled the daughter, as beneficiary, to enjoy the income from the property and to enforce the terms of the trust against the trustee. The key advantage of these techniques was that, whether the wife obtained her equitable estate through contract or trust, she held it just as she would if she had been a single rather than a married woman.

The common law regime, subordinating the married woman's rights to her husband's *jure uxoris*, finally gave way in the latter part of the nineteenth century. Legislative reform centered on the Married Women's Property Acts, adopted in virtually all of the common law states by the end of the century, giving the married woman full control over all of the property that she brought to, or acquired during, the marriage. But the reform was by no means complete. Well into the twentieth century, several states continued to disable the married woman from conveying her own land, or engaging in business, without her husband's consent.

Dower and curtesy also began to crumble during this period, largely because they hindered the free marketability of land. In their place, the rules on descent were altered to entitle husband and wife to a portion of the other's estate should she or he die intestate. This change clearly prejudiced the homemaker, for the wage earner—typically at this time, the husband—could dispose of all of his property by will, thus depriving his widow of the portion that she would have taken under dower. The situation was partially corrected by legislation entitling the widow to choose between the amount, if any, that she was given under her husband's will, and a statutory "forced" share—typically the amount she would have taken had he died intestate. The husband, however, could still defeat these claims through inter vivos transfers.

a. THE TENANCY BY THE ENTIRETY

The common law fiction of spousal unity also underlies the tenancy by the entirety, a cotenancy between husband and wife resembling the joint tenancy, but with distinct attributes of its own. As in the joint tenancy, the surviving cotenant—husband or wife—takes the entire estate. Like the joint tenancy, the tenancy by the entirety requires the four unities of time, title, interest, and possession. It also requires that the cotenants be married at the time of the transfer. Not only death, but divorce, will terminate the tenancy, converting the relationship between the former spouses into a tenancy in common.

As originally designed, the tenancy by the entirety also differed from other cotenancies by vesting the exclusive rights of possession and management in one cotenant—the husband—without any duty to account to the other for rents and profits. Indeed, Blackstone failed to include the tenancy by the entirety in his original list of concurrent estates because he did not think of it as an estate involving a "plurality of tenants." The wife's only right was to take the land in the event that she survived her husband. Although the husband's powers in a tenancy by the entirety closely paralleled those that he enjoyed as a consequence of his *jure uxoris*, the Married Women's Property Acts did not eliminate the husband's authority over the tenancy by the entirety as completely as the Acts eliminated the *jure uxoris*. Three states held that since the Acts dealt only with separate property they had no effect on the unity of interest held by the entireties. Seventeen states held that the Acts had in varying degrees reduced the exclusivity of the husband's power over property held by the entireties. At least nine states held that the Acts, having obliterated the concept of spousal unity, effectively abolished the tenancy by the entirety. See Oval A. Phipps, Tenancy by Entireties, 25 Temp. L.Q. 24, 29–32 (1951).

The common law favored the tenancy by the entirety, erecting a strong presumption that any conveyance to husband and wife created a tenancy by the entirety rather than some other form of cotenancy. This common law presumption has since been reversed in favor of a presumption for a joint tenancy or tenancy in common. In one state, Minnesota, the statutory presumption favoring the tenancy in common has been held to abolish the tenancy by the entirety. Wilson v. Wilson, 45 N.W. 710 (Minn. 1890). Originally adopted in all but three of the American common law jurisdictions, the tenancy by the entirety today is still alive in approximately 30 states. See 7 Richard R. Powell, Powell on Real Property § 52.01[3] (Michael Allan Wolf ed., 2005).

For an excellent history of the tenancy by the entirety and the complexities of its modern application, see John V. Orth, Tenancy by the Entirety: The Strange Career of the Common–Law Marital Estate, 1997 BYU L. Rev. 35 (1997).

Sawada v. Endo

Supreme Court of Hawaii, 1977.
561 P.2d 1291.

MENOR, Justice.

This is a civil action brought by the plaintiffs-appellants, Masako Sawada and Helen Sawada, in aid of execution of money judgments in their favor, seeking to set aside a conveyance of real property from judgment debtor Kokichi Endo to Samuel H. Endo and Toru Endo, defendants-appellees herein, on the ground that the conveyance as to the Sawadas was fraudulent.

On November 30, 1968, the Sawadas were injured when struck by a motor vehicle operated by Kokichi Endo. On June 17, 1969, Helen Sawada filed her complaint for damages against Kokichi Endo. Masako Sawada filed her suit against him on August 13, 1969. The complaint and summons in each case was served on Kokichi Endo on October 29, 1969.

On the date of the accident, Kokichi Endo was the owner, as a tenant by the entirety with his wife, Ume Endo, of a parcel of real property situate at Wahiawa, Oahu, Hawaii. By deed, dated July 26, 1969, Kokichi Endo and his wife conveyed the property to their sons, Samuel H. Endo and Toru Endo. This document was recorded in the Bureau of Conveyances on December 17, 1969. No consideration was paid by the grantees for the conveyance. Both were aware at the time of the conveyance that their father had been involved in an accident, and that he carried no liability insurance. Kokichi Endo and Ume Endo, while reserving no life interests therein, continued to reside on the premises.

On January 19, 1971, after a consolidated trial on the merits, judgment was entered in favor of Helen Sawada and against Kokichi Endo in the sum of $8,846.46. At the same time, Masako Sawada was awarded judgment on her complaint in the amount of $16,199.28. Ume Endo, wife of Kokichi Endo, died on January 29, 1971. She was survived by her husband, Kokichi. Subsequently, after being frustrated in their attempts to obtain satisfaction of judgment from the personal property of Kokichi Endo, the Sawadas brought suit to set aside the conveyance which is the subject matter of this controversy. The trial court refused to set aside the conveyance, and the Sawadas appeal.

I

The determinative question in this case is, whether the interest of one spouse in real property, held in tenancy by the entireties, is subject to levy and execution by his or her individual creditors. This issue is one of first impression in this jurisdiction.

A brief review of the present state of the tenancy by the entirety might be helpful. Dean Phipps, writing in 1951,[1] pointed out that only nineteen states and the District of Columbia continued to recognize it as a valid and subsisting institution in the field of property law. Phipps divided these jurisdictions into four groups. He made no mention of Alaska and Hawaii, both of which were then territories of the United States.

In the Group I states (Massachusetts, Michigan, and North Carolina) the estate is essentially the common law tenancy by the entireties, unaffected by the Married Women's Property Acts. As at common law, the possession and profits of the estate are subject to the husband's exclusive dominion and control. In all three states, as at common law, the *husband* may convey the entire estate subject only to the possibility that the wife may become entitled to the whole estate upon surviving him. As at common law, the obverse as to the wife does not hold true. Only in Massachusetts, however, is the estate in its entirety subject to levy by the husband's creditors. In both Michigan and North Carolina, the use and income from the estate is not subject to levy during the marriage for the separate debts of either spouse.

In the Group II states (Alaska, Arkansas, New Jersey, New York, and Oregon) the interest of the debtor spouse in the estate may be sold or levied upon for his or her separate debts, subject to the other spouse's contingent right of survivorship. Alaska, which has been added to this group, has provided by statute that the interest of a debtor spouse in any type of estate, except a homestead as defined and held in tenancy by the entirety, shall be subject to his or her separate debts.

1. Phipps, "Tenancy by Entireties," 25 Temple L.Q. 24 (1951).

In the Group III jurisdictions (Delaware, District of Columbia, Florida, Indiana, Maryland, Missouri, Pennsylvania, Rhode Island, Vermont, Virginia, and Wyoming) an attempted conveyance by either spouse is wholly void, and the estate may not be subjected to the separate debts of one spouse only.

In Group IV, the two states of Kentucky and Tennessee hold that the contingent right of survivorship appertaining to either spouse is separately alienable by him and attachable by his creditors during the marriage. The use and profits, however, may neither be alienated nor attached during coverture.

It appears, therefore, that Hawaii is the only jurisdiction still to be heard from on the question. Today we join that group of states and the District of Columbia which hold that under the Married Women's Property Acts the interest of a husband or a wife in an estate by the entireties is not subject to the claims of his or her individual creditors during the joint lives of the spouses. In so doing, we are placing our stamp of approval upon what is apparently the prevailing view of the lower courts of this jurisdiction.

Hawaii has long recognized and continues to recognize the tenancy in common, the joint tenancy, and the tenancy by the entirety, as separate and distinct estates. That the Married Women's Property Act of 1888 was not intended to abolish the tenancy by the entirety was made clear by the language of Act 19 of the Session Laws of Hawaii, 1903 (now HRS § 509–1). The tenancy by the entirety is predicated upon the legal unity of husband and wife, and the estate is held by them in single ownership. They do not take by moieties, but both and each are seized of the whole estate.

A joint tenant has a specific, albeit undivided, interest in the property, and if he survives his cotenant he becomes the owner of a larger interest than he had prior to the death of the other joint tenant. But tenants by the entirety are each deemed to be seized of the entirety from the time of the creation of the estate. At common law, this taking of the "whole estate" did not have the real significance that it does today, insofar as the rights of the wife in the property were concerned. For all practical purposes, the wife had no right during coverture to the use and enjoyment and exercise of ownership in the marital estate. All she possessed was her contingent right of survivorship.

The effect of the Married Women's Property Acts was to abrogate the husband's common law dominance over the marital estate and to place the wife on a level of equality with him as regards the exercise of ownership over the whole estate. The tenancy was and still is predicated upon the legal unity of husband and wife, but the Acts converted it into a unity of equals and not of unequals as at common law. No longer could the husband convey, lease, mortgage or otherwise encumber the property without her consent. The Acts confirmed her right to the use and enjoyment of the whole estate, and all the privileges that ownership of property confers, including the right to convey the property in its entirety, jointly with her husband, during the marriage relation. They also had the effect of insulating the wife's interest in the estate from the separate debts of her husband.

Neither husband nor wife has a separate divisible interest in the property held by the entirety that can be conveyed or reached by execution. A joint tenancy may be destroyed by voluntary alienation, or by levy and execution, or by compulsory partition, but a tenancy by the entirety may not. The indivisibility of the estate, except by joint action of the spouses, is an indispensable feature of the tenancy by the entirety. . . .

We are not persuaded by the argument that it would be unfair to the creditors of either spouse to hold that the estate by the entirety may not, without the consent of both spouses, be levied upon for the separate debts of either spouse. No unfairness to the creditor is involved here. We agree with the court in Hurd v. Hughes, 109 A. 418 (Del. Ch. 1920):

> But creditors are not entitled to special consideration. If the debt arose prior to the creation of the estate, the property was not a basis of credit, and if the debt arose subsequently the creditor presumably had notice of the characteristics of the estate which limited his right to reach the property.

We might also add that there is obviously nothing to prevent the creditor from insisting upon the subjection of property held in tenancy by the entirety as a condition precedent to the extension of credit. Further, the creation of a tenancy by the entirety may not be used as a device to defraud existing creditors.

Were we to view the matter strictly from the standpoint of public policy, we would still be constrained to hold as we have done here today. In Fairclaw v. Forrest, 130 F.2d 829 (D.C. Cir. 1942), the court makes this observation:

> The interest in family solidarity retains some influence upon the institution [of tenancy by the entirety]. It is available only to husband and wife. It is a convenient mode of protecting a surviving spouse from inconvenient administration of the decedent's estate and from the other's improvident debts. It is in that protection the estate finds its peculiar and justifiable function.

It is a matter of common knowledge that the demand for single-family residential lots has increased rapidly in recent years, and the magnitude of the problem is emphasized by the concentration of the bulk of fee simple land in the hands of a few. The shortage of single-family residential fee simple property is critical and government has seen fit to attempt to alleviate the problem through legislation. When a family can afford to own real property, it becomes their single most important asset. Encumbered as it usually is by a first mortgage, the fact remains that so long as it remains whole during the joint lives of the spouses, it is always available in its entirety for the benefit and use of the entire family. Loans for education and other emergency expenses, for example, may be obtained on the security of the marital estate. This would not be possible where a third party has become a tenant in common or a joint tenant with one of the spouses, or where the ownership of the contingent right of survivorship of one of the spouses in a third party has cast a cloud upon the title of the marital estate, making it virtually impossible to utilize the estate for these purposes.

If we were to select between a public policy favoring the creditors of one of the spouses and one favoring the interests of the family unit, we would not hesitate to choose the latter. But we need not make this choice for, as we pointed out earlier, by the very nature of the estate by the entirety as we view it, and as other courts of our sister jurisdictions have viewed it, "[a] unilaterally indestructible right of survivorship, an inability of one spouse to alienate his interest, and, importantly for this case, a broad immunity from claims of separate creditors remain among its vital incidents." In re Estate of Wall, 440 F.2d at 218 (D.C. Cir. 1971).

Having determined that an estate by the entirety is not subject to the claims of the creditors of one of the spouses during their joint lives, we now hold that the conveyance of the marital property by Kokichi Endo and Ume Endo, husband and wife, to their sons, Samuel H. Endo and Toru Endo, was not in fraud of Kokichi Endo's judgment creditors.

Affirmed.

KIDWELL, Justice, dissenting.

This case has been well briefed, and the arguments against the conclusions reached by the majority have been well presented. It will not materially assist the court in resolving the issues for me to engage in an extensive review of the conflicting views. Appellants' position on the appeal was that tenancy by the entirety as it existed at common law, together with all of the rights which the husband had over the property of his wife by virtue of the common law doctrine of the unity of the person, was recognized by the early decisions; that the Married Women's Act of 1888 destroyed the fictional unity of husband and wife; that the legislature has recognized the continuing existence of the estate of tenancy by the entirety, but has not defined the nature or the incidents of that estate, HRS § 509–1, 509–2; that at common law the interest of the husband in an estate by the entireties could be taken by his separate creditors on execution against him, subject only to the wife's right of survivorship; and that the Married Women's Act merely eliminated any inequality in the positions of the spouses with respect to their interests in the property, thus depriving the husband of his former power over the wife's interest, without thereby altering the nature and incidents of the husband's interest. . . .

The majority reaches its conclusion by holding that the effect of the Married Women's Act was to equalize the positions of the spouses by taking from the husband his common law right to transfer his interest, rather than by elevating the wife's right of alienation of her interest to place it on a position of equality with the husband's. I disagree. I believe that a better interpretation of the Married Women's Acts is that offered by the Supreme Court of New Jersey in King v. Greene, 153 A.2d 49, 60 (N.J. 1959):

> It is clear that the Married Women's Act created an equality between the spouses in New Jersey, insofar as tenancies by the entirety are concerned. If, as we have previously concluded, the

> husband could alienate his right of survivorship at common law, the wife, by virtue of the act, can alienate her right of survivorship. And it follows, that if the wife takes equal rights with the husband in the estate, she must take equal disabilities. Such are the dictates of common equality. Thus, the judgment creditors of either spouse may levy and execute upon their separate rights of survivorship.
>
> . . . .

Notes & Questions

1. The Hawaii Supreme Court in *Sawada* lumps all creditors together, including tort creditors such as the Sawadas. Should contract and tort creditors be treated the same? Although the court is correct that contract creditors can protect themselves by checking title to the property ahead of extending credit and insisting on both the husband's and wife's signature if the property is a tenancy by the entirety, how can tort creditors protect themselves?

2. Subsequent to *Sawada*, the three states that had continued to give husbands exclusive dominion and control over estates in the entireties have adopted statutes giving both spouses equal control over such estates and any income therefrom. See Mass. Gen. Laws ch. 209, §§ 1 & 1A; Mich. Comp. Laws § 557.71; N.C. Gen. Stat. § 39–13.6. The North Carolina law expressly protects the property from seizure by a creditor of only one spouse; the Massachusetts statute protects a couple's principal residence from such seizure if the residence is held in a tenancy by the entirety. See In re Ulmer, 211 B.R. 523 (Bankr. E.D.N.C. 1997) (creditor of husband had no claim against tenancy by the entirety).

3. **Tax Liens.** In United States v. Craft, 535 U.S. 274 (2002), the United States Supreme Court addressed the question of whether a federal tax lien could attach to one spouse's interest in a tenancy by the entirety. After Don Craft ran up almost half a million dollars in unpaid income taxes, the federal government attached a lien to real estate held in a tenancy by the entirety by Craft and his wife, Sandra. The couple tried to escape the lien by quitclaiming the property to the wife for one dollar. By a five to four vote, the Court held that the husband's interest in the tenancy by the entirety was "property" or "rights to property" to which the government could attach a tax lien. According to the Court, any other holding would "allow spouses to shield their property from federal taxation by classifying it as entireties property, facilitating abuse of the federal tax system." In dissent, Justice Scalia objected that the Court was nullifying

> a form of property ownership that was of particular benefit to the stay-at-home spouse or mother. She is overwhelmingly likely to be the survivor that obtains title to the unencumbered property; and she (as opposed to her business-world husband) is overwhelmingly unlikely to be the source of the individual indebtedness against which a tenancy by the entirety protects. It is regrettable that the

Court has eliminated a large part of this traditional protection retained by many states.

Is there any reason to give the federal government greater rights than tort creditors over the tenancy by the entirety? Is the argument for shielding the tenancy by the entirety from creditors equally strong in *Craft* and *Sawada*?

4. **Civil Forfeitures.** A variety of statutes provide for forfeiture to the government of property used in connection with a crime. See, e.g., Drug Abuse Prevention and Control Act, 21 U.S.C. § 881 (providing for forfeiture of property used to commit or facilitate a drug offense). What if the property is held in a tenancy by the entirety and only one spouse is involved in the illegal activity? The answer depends on the provisions of the forfeiture statute. Where the statute exempts property used without the consent or knowledge of its owner (an "innocent owner" defense), several federal court of appeals have held that the innocent spouse should retain full use and possession of the property during his or her lifetime, as well as his or her right of survivorship. These courts split, however, in what right the federal government can claim against the property interest of the guilty spouse. Compare United States v. 1500 Lincoln Avenue, 949 F.2d 73 (3d Cir. 1991) (guilty spouse's interest is subject to forfeiture subject to innocent spouse's possession and survivorship rights) with United States v. 15621 S.W. 209th Avenue, 894 F.2d 1511 (11th Cir. 1990) (no current forfeiture, but government can file a *lis pendens* preserving its right to any interest that the guilty spouse receives upon the death of the innocent spouse or severance of the estate). Where a statute does not contain an innocent owner defense, however, the Supreme Court has held that there is no constitutional barrier to the government seizing and claiming the entire property. See Bennis v. Michigan, 516 U.S. 442 (1996) (rejecting takings and due process challenges to seizure and forfeiture of a car jointly held by husband and wife).

5. Is there any reason today to retain the tenancy by the entirety? If there are good policy reasons to retain the tenancy by the entirety, should it be limited to married couples or also extended to other longterm relationships?

b. DIVIDING UP PROPERTY ON DIVORCE OR DEATH

The common law system was relatively straight forward in its treatment of property at divorce or the death of one member of a married couple. At divorce, each spouse kept his or her separate property. Tenancies in common and joint tenancies remained in effect, although generally the couple would sell the property and split the proceeds or seek a judicial partition. Tenancies in the entirety converted to tenancies in common. But see Shepherd v. Shepherd, 336 So. 2d 497 (Miss. 1976) (holding that a tenancy by the entirety converts into a joint tenancy). Wives often received alimony if they had need for continuing support. At death, the surviving spouse would receive dower or curtesy, plus any property held in joint tenancy or tenancy by the entirety; the surviving spouse would also keep his or her share of any tenancy in common. Absent a will, the surviving spouse also would receive his or her intestate share of the decedent's separate property (including the decedent's share of any tenancy in common).

Today states have significantly restructured the traditional common law rules. Dower and curtesy have been abolished in all but about half a dozen states. And new systems have been adopted for dividing property at divorce or death.

Divorce. All common law states today follow a principle of "equitable distribution" when a marriage ends in divorce.[1] The exact details of equitable distribution vary tremendously among states. In some states, courts are authorized to divide all property belonging to either spouse, even if the property was acquired before marriage or was acquired by gift or inheritance during the marriage. In most states, courts divide only "marital property." Here again definitions vary. In some states, marital property includes all property acquired by either spouse during the marriage; in other states, marital property includes only that property acquired with money earned by one or the other spouse during the marriage.

The method by which courts determine an equitable division of property also differs among states. Some states provide for equal division of the property. Others employ a rebuttable presumption that an equal division is equitable, particularly in lengthy marriages. Finally, some states look to a variety of factors to determine the most equitable division of the property. Section 307 (alternative A) of the Uniform Marriage and Divorce Act, for example, provides:

> In making apportionment the court shall consider the duration of the marriage and prior marriage of either party, antenuptial agreement of the parties, the age, health, station, occupation, amount and sources of income, vocational skills, employability, estate, liabilities, and needs of each of the parties, custodial provisions, whether the apportionment is in lieu of or in addition to maintenance, and the opportunity of each for future acquisition of capital assets and income. The court shall also consider the contribution or dissipation of each party in the acquisition, preservation, depreciation, or appreciation in value of the respective estates, and the contribution of a spouse as a homemaker or to the family unit.

See also N.Y. Dom. Rel. Law § 236(B)(5)(d) (listing 13 factors to consider, including any "factor which the court shall expressly find to be just and proper").

Alimony awards also have changed. Only a fraction of women ever were awarded alimony in divorce proceedings. See Lenore J. Weitzman, The Divorce Revolution 144 (1985). But courts have tightened the stan-

1. Prior to 1970, courts granted divorces only on a showing of fault by one or both members of a couple. Beginning with California in 1970, however, virtually every state has adopted "no fault divorce" laws.

dards for alimony. Section 308(a) of the Uniform Marriage and Divorce Act provides for alimony only if the spouse who seeks the alimony:

> (1) lacks sufficient property to provide for his reasonable needs; and
>
> (2) is unable to support himself through appropriate employment or is the custodian of a child whose condition or circumstances make it appropriate that the custodian not be required to seek employment outside the home.

Today less than 20 percent of women in divorce cases receive alimony. See Mary E. O'Connell, Alimony after No–Fault: A Practice in Search of a Theory, 23 New Eng. L. Rev. 437, 437 n.1 (1988). Of more importance, courts now order alimony only for a short period during which the spouse is expected to enter the job market and become self-sufficient. Most alimony lasts for less than two years. See Weitzman, supra, at 165. Finding a well-paying job, however, often is difficult for women who have devoted years of marriage to homemaking, leaving them in a worse financial posture than the traditional common law system.

Death of a Spouse. Virtually every state also has replaced the common law rules for division of property upon death with *forced share legislation*. Under such legislation, the surviving spouse has a choice.[2] The surviving spouse can take whatever he or she is entitled to under the will, if any, of the decedent. Or the surviving spouse can renounce the will and take a *statutory share*, generally one-third to one-half, of all the property that the decedent owned at the time of death (other than joint tenancies or life insurance). A spouse's right to a statutory share in the case of death kicks in as soon as a couple is married. See Estate of Neiderhiser, 2 Pa. D. & C.3d 302 (1977) (widow entitled to force shared when husband dies during the wedding ceremony but after exchanging vows). In some states, however, the size of the statutory share varies with the length of the marriage. See, e.g., Haw. Rev. Stat. § 560:2–202(a). To protect against attempts to deprive a spouse of his or her statutory share, some courts will set aside any gifts made with the intent to evade the forced share legislation. Some courts will also invalidate attempts to alienate property without relinquishing control of the property (e.g., the creation of a revocable trust where the decedent appointed himself as trustee).

For interesting recent writings on forced share legislation, see Alan Newman, Incorporating the Partnership Theory of Marriage Into Elective–Share Law: The Approximation of the Uniform Probate Code and the Deferred–Community–Property Alternative, 49 Emory L.J. 487 (2000); Ronald R. Volkmen, The Complicated World of the Elective Spouse: *In re Estate of Myers* and Recent Statutory Developments, 33 Creighton L. Rev.

2. Hawaii extends its forced share legislation to same-sex partners who register as "reciprocal beneficiaries." See Haw. Rev. Stat. § 560:2–202(a); W. Brian Burnette, Hawaii's Reciprocal Beneficiaries Act: An Effective Step in Revoking the Controversy Surrounding Same Sex Marriage, 37 Brandeis L.J. 81 (1998/1999).

121 (1999); Ralph C. Brashier, Disinheritance and the Modern Family, 45 Case W. Res. L. Rev. 84 (1994).

Contractual Arrangements. To what degree can a couple vary the common law and statutory rules by contract? For many years, courts did not honor prenuptial agreements concerning property allocations at divorce for fear that they might encourage divorces either by being too stingy (in which case the spouse with the most property might feel comfortable abandoning the marriage) or too generous (in which case the spouse without the property might see a divorce as a lucrative opportunity). Courts were more open to prenuptial agreements dictating property distributions upon death, but only if they were fair to the surviving spouse and based on full and complete disclosure of property holdings.

In recent years, a growing number of courts have upheld prenuptial agreements dealing with divorce distributions where the provisions have seemed fair and there is again full disclosure. Approximately a third of the states have adopted the Uniform Premarital Agreement Act which permits prenuptial agreements except where the agreement is unconscionable and there has been inadequate disclosure. Uniform Premarital Agreement Act § 6. See also Uniform Marital Property Act § 10(g) (containing similar provisions); Jeffrey E. Stake, Mandatory Planning for Divorce, 45 Vand. L. Rev. 397 (1992); Judith T. Younger, Perspectives on Antenuptial Agreements, 40 Rutgers L. Rev. 1059 (1988).

In Borelli v. Brusseau, 16 Cal. Rptr. 2d 16 (Cal. App. 1993), a stroke victim orally promised his wife that he would leave her a significant portion of his separate property (as well as pay for the education of his wife's daughter by a prior marriage) if she continued to take care of him at home and did not place him in a rest home as his doctors recommended. After he died, his wife discovered that his will left her only a portion of the promised property, and so she sued. The court refused to enforce the oral agreement for lack of consideration. According to the court, the "marital duty of support" under California law "includes caring for a spouse who is ill.... Personal performance of a personal duty created by the contract of marriage does not constitute a new consideration supporting the indebtedness alleged in this case."

2. THE COMMUNITY PROPERTY SYSTEM

The eight community property states fashioned their laws from institutions tracing back to Spanish and French civil law traditions. The central premise of community property systems is that husband and wife contribute equally to the material successes and failures of their marriage and thus should share equally in the property—called *community property*—acquired through the labors of either or both spouses. One corollary is that property that is not acquired through community effort—*separate property*—belongs exclusively to the partner who acquired it.

Although rules differ from state to state, sometimes on the most fundamental points, a few rough generalizations are possible. As a general rule, community property is defined as all income, and all assets acquired with income, earned by either spouse during the course of the marriage, as well as all income derived from the investment or sale of property thus acquired.[3] Property acquired during marriage is presumed to be community, rather than separate, property. Separate property generally consists of the property that either spouse owned before the marriage or acquired during the marriage by gift, inheritance or devise, together with all income derived from such property.

Assume, for example, that John Burroughs and his wife, Ursula North, marry in 2000. At the time of their marriage, Ursula owns a house, mortgage free, into which the couple moves. In 2002, John inherits $200,000 which he uses several years later to purchase a vacation home in the mountains; he takes title in his name. To the degree that the couple saves money from their earnings during their marriage, they use the extra money to invest in a mutual fund. In 2005, John withdraws $20,000 from the mutual fund and uses the money to buy a new car; he again takes title in his name. When the couple divorces in 2006, their property includes their residence, the vacation property, the car, and $120,000 invested in the mutual fund. In most community property states, the residence would be the wife's separate property since she purchased it before the marriage. The vacation home would be the husband's separate property since the inheritance was his separate property and he used that property to purchase the vacation home. The money in the mutual fund would be community property since it is traceable to the earnings of the couple during the marriage. The car similarly would be community property, absent evidence that the wife agreed to donate the community property to the spouse. The fact that the husband took title in his name is irrelevant except to the degree that it reflects an agreement with his wife to convert the property.

Community property's sharing principle did not, historically, extend to questions of management and control. As in the common law states, the husband was traditionally vested with exclusive control not only of the community assets, but also of the wife's separate property. Although the husband could not transfer the wife's separate property without her consent, he could freely dispose of the community assets. The only legal limit on the husband's powers of management and control was that he not act in bad faith.

The Married Women's Acts partially curtailed the husband's management powers by giving wives full control over their separate property. But it was not until a century later, in the 1970s, that community property states first began to give wives a say in the management and control of community assets. California's legislation, passed in 1973, went as far as

3. States differ regarding the status of income earned from the investment or use of separate property. In most states, the income from separate property is itself separate property. Thus, if the husband's separate property is rented, the rent is separate property; if a book written by the wife before marriage brings in royalties, the royalties are separate property. In Idaho, Louisiana, and Texas, however, such income is community property if it is earned during the marriage.

any at the time, providing that, "either spouse has the management and control of the community personal property . . . with like absolute power of disposition, other than testamentary, as the spouse has of the separate estate of the spouse." Cal. Fam. Code § 1100(a). As to community real property, "either spouse has the management and control," but both spouses "must join in executing any instrument by which that community real property or any interest therein is leased for a longer period than one year, or is sold, conveyed, or encumbered." Id. § 5127(a).

Community property states still vary in their management rules. Most states, like California, give both the husband and wife the power to manage the community property, and both spouses must join together in transferring or mortgaging the property. Some states, however, give one or the other spouse sole management authority in some settings—e.g., if the community property is a business or is held in the name of only one spouse. The manager of community property must exercise his or her power in good faith for the benefit of the community.

Although community property starts with the premise that the spouses share equally in the community property, courts and statutes frequently depart from the equal sharing principle on divorce and death, with the result that community property dispositions often approximate those made in common law jurisdictions at these two critical points. Courts in most community property states have the power, frequently exercised, to divide community assets on divorce in such proportions as are "just and equitable." See, e.g., Rev. Code Wash. § 26.09.080.[4] In addition, they can award alimony. See, e.g., Cal. Fam. Code § 4320.

On death of a spouse, the surviving spouse is entitled to his or her half of the community property. If there is a will, the decedent's share of the community property (along with his or her separate property) is allocated according to the will's instructions. If there is not a will, the decedent's share of the community property goes to the surviving spouse in some states and is split 50–50 between the surviving spouse and children in the others.

In re Marriage of Lucas

Supreme Court of California, 1980.
614 P.2d 285.

Manuel, Justice.

Gerald E. Lucas appeals from an interlocutory judgment dissolving his marriage to Brenda G. Lucas, awarding child custody, fixing spousal and child support and dividing property. Gerald contests only the trial court's determination of the parties' ownership interests in their residence and in a vehicle, both of which were purchased with a combination of community

4. California, New Mexico, and Louisiana, however, require equal division of community property.

and separate funds. In this case we must resolve a conflict among the Courts of Appeal regarding the proper method of determining separate and community property interests in a single family dwelling acquired during the marriage with both separate property and community property funds.

Brenda and Gerald were married in March 1964 and lived together continuously until their separation in December 1976. At the time of their marriage Brenda was beneficiary of a trust. The trust corpus was distributed to her free of the trust in September 1964. She immediately established a revocable *inter vivos* trust of which she was trustor and beneficiary. The trust, conceded by Gerald to be Brenda's separate property, had a value of approximately $44,000 at the time of trial.

In November 1968, Brenda and Gerald bought a house for $23,300. Brenda used $6,351.57 from her trust for the down payment, and they assumed a loan of $16,948.43 for the balance of the purchase price. Title to the house was taken as "Gerald E. Lucas and Brenda G. Lucas, Husband and Wife as Joint Tenants." Brenda paid $2,962 from her trust funds for improvements to the property; the remainder of the expenses on the property was paid for with community funds. At the time of trial the residence had a fair market value of approximately $56,250 and a loan balance of approximately $14,600, leaving a net equity of approximately $41,650. The community had reduced the principal by $2,052.32 and paid $6,801.14 in interest and $5,146.20 for taxes.

The trial court findings describe the parties' intent regarding ownership of the residence as follows:

> The only discussions with regard to taking joint tenancy title to the property related to wife's understanding that title would pass to husband upon her death and that the children would benefit from this result; further, the parties contemplated that taking title in this manner would result in favorable tax consequences due to husband's veteran status. Wife did not intend to make a gift to the husband of any interest in the home purchased with her separate funds, nor did she know of any other legal significance of taking title to real property in the manner it was taken. Neither did husband intend to make a gift to wife of the payments made on the home from community funds during the period of ownership.

Brenda testified that she and Gerald did not discuss where the down payment would come from except to the extent that the payments would be higher if they did not use her trust fund and instead took a second trust deed on the house. Brenda said they had no agreement regarding the manner in which she would be disposing of the trust funds and that they did not discuss keeping the funds separate or using them to exhaust community debts. Brenda also testified that it was her intention at the time of the purchase to acquire the house for herself but that she did not discuss this with her husband.

In the interlocutory judgment entered in April 1978, the trial court deducted Brenda's $2,962 payment for improvements from the equity of

$41,650.50 and then awarded a community property interest in the residence of 24.42 percent with a value of $9,477.50. A separate property interest of 75.58 percent with a value of $29,241 was confirmed to Brenda.

The Courts of Appeal have taken conflicting approaches to the question of the proper method for determining the ownership interests in a residence purchased during the parties' marriage with both separate and community funds. In In re Marriage of Bjornestad (1974) 38 Cal. App. 3d 801, 113 Cal. Rptr. 576, the Court of Appeal allowed only reimbursement for separate property contributions to the down payment on the purchase of the parties' residence. In In re Marriage of Aufmuth (1979) 89 Cal. App. 3d 446, 152 Cal. Rptr. 668, the Court of Appeal developed a scheme of pro rata apportionment of the equity appreciation between the separate and community property contributions to the purchase price. The Court of Appeal in In re Marriage of Trantafello (1979) 94 Cal. App. 3d 533, 156 Cal. Rptr. 556, however, held that the residence was entirely community in nature in the absence of any evidence of an agreement or understanding between the parties to the contrary.

The beginning point of analysis in each case was the nature of title taken by the parties. In *Bjornestad* and *Trantafello,* title was taken by husband and wife as joint tenants; in *Aufmuth,* it was taken as community property. Until modified by statute in 1965, there was a rebuttable presumption that the ownership interest in property was as stated in the title to it. Thus a residence purchased with community funds, but held by a husband and wife as joint tenants, was presumed to be separate property in which each spouse had a half interest. The presumption arising from the form of title could be overcome by evidence of an agreement or understanding between the parties that the interests were to be otherwise. It could not be overcome, however, "solely by evidence as to the source of the funds used to purchase the property." (Gudelj v. Gudelj, 41 Cal. 2d at p. 212, 259 P.2d at p. 662.) Nor could it "be overcome by testimony of a hidden intention not disclosed to the other grantee at the time of the execution of the conveyance." (Ibid.)

The presumption arising from the form of title created problems upon divorce or separation when title to the parties' residence was held in joint tenancy. Unless the presumption of separate property created by the form of title could be overcome by evidence of a common understanding or agreement to the contrary, a house so held could not be awarded to the wife as a family residence for her and the children. In 1965 the Legislature considered various proposals to remedy this problem. The Legislature also noted that "husbands and wives take property in joint tenancy without legal counsel but primarily because deeds prepared by real estate brokers, escrow companies and by title companies are usually presented to the parties in joint tenancy form. The result is that they don't know what joint tenancy is, that they think it is community property, and then find out upon death or divorce that they didn't have what they thought they had all along and instead have something else which isn't what they had intended." (Final Rep. of Assem. Interim Com. on Judiciary Relating to Domestic Relations (1965), p. 124.)

In 1965, in an attempt to solve these problems, the Legislature added the following provision to Civil Code section 164: "[W]hen a single family residence of a husband and wife is acquired by them during marriage as joint tenants, for the purpose of the division of such property upon divorce or separate maintenance only, the presumption is that such single family residence is the community property of said husband and wife." (Stats. 1965, ch. 1710, p. 3843; see now Civ. Code § 5110.)[1] The effect of this provision was to change the presumptive form of ownership to that more closely matching the intent and assumptions of most spouses who acquire and hold their residence in joint tenancy. There is no indication that the Legislature intended in any way to change the rules regarding the strength and type of evidence necessary to overcome the presumption arising from the form of title.

The presumption arising from the form of title is to be distinguished from the general presumption set forth in Civil Code section 5110 that property acquired during marriage is community property. It is the affirmative act of specifying a form of ownership in the conveyance of title that removes such property from the more general presumption. It is because of this express designation of ownership that a greater showing is necessary to overcome the presumption arising therefrom than is necessary to overcome the more general presumption that property acquired during marriage is community property. In the latter situation, where there is no written indication of ownership interests as between the spouses, the general presumption of community property may be overcome simply by tracing the source of funds used to acquire the property to separate property. It is not necessary to show that the spouses understood or intended that property traceable to separate property should remain separate.

The rule requiring an understanding or agreement comes into play when the issue is whether the presumption arising from the form of title has been overcome. It is supported by sound policy considerations, and we decline to depart from it. To allow a lesser showing could result in unfairness to the spouse who has not made the separate property contribution. Unless the latter knows that the spouse contributing the separate property expects to be reimbursed or to acquire a separate property interest, he or she has no opportunity to attempt to preserve the joint ownership of the property by making other financing arrangements. The act of taking title in a joint and equal ownership form is inconsistent with

1. Section 164 was repealed in 1969 in connection with the enactment of the Family Law Act. (Stats.1969, ch. 1608, § 3, p. 3313.) It was replaced by section 5110 which contains an almost identical provision: "When a single-family residence of a husband and wife is acquired by them during marriage as joint tenants, for the purpose of the division of such property upon dissolution of marriage or legal separation only, the presumption is that such single-family residence is the community property of the husband and wife."

Although section 164 was the applicable statute when the parties in this case purchased their house, as a matter of convenience, future references in this opinion will be to the current statute, section 5110.

an intention to preserve a separate property interest. Accordingly, the expectations of parties who take title jointly are best protected by presuming that the specified ownership interest is intended in the absence of an agreement or understanding to the contrary. We therefore resolve the conflict in Court of Appeal opinions by following *Trantafello* and disapproving *Aufmuth* and *Bjornestad* to the extent they are inconsistent with this opinion.

In the present case there is no evidence of an agreement or understanding that Brenda was to retain a separate property interest in the house. Nor is there any finding by the trial court on the question. The only findings in this regard are that neither party intended a gift to the other. Such evidence and findings are insufficient to rebut the presumption arising from title set forth in Civil Code section 5110. The trial court's determination must therefore be reversed.

Neither the parties nor the court applied the correct rules to this case, and it is possible that had they done so the proof might have been different. In the interest of justice, therefore, the matter of the community or separate property character of the residence must be remanded for reconsideration in light of these rules.

If on reconsideration the house is found to be entirely community in nature, Brenda would also be barred from reimbursement for the separate property funds she contributed in the absence of an agreement therefor. It is a well-settled rule that a "party who uses his separate property for community purposes is entitled to reimbursement from the community or separate property of the other only if there is an agreement between the parties to that effect." (See v. See, 64 Cal. 2d at p. 785, 51 Cal. Rptr. at p. 893, 415 P.2d at p. 781; In re Marriage of Epstein (1979) 24 Cal. 3d 76, 82–86, 154 Cal. Rptr. 413, 592 P.2d 1165.) While the parties are married and living together it is presumed that, "unless an agreement between the parties specifies that the contributing party be reimbursed, a party who utilizes his separate property for community purposes intends a gift to the community." (In re Marriage of Epstein, supra, 24 Cal. 3d at p. 82, 154 Cal. Rptr. at p. 417, 592 P.2d at p. 1169.)

For guidance in the event that on reconsideration the court finds there was an understanding or agreement that Brenda was to retain a separate property interest in the residence, we discuss briefly the question of the proper method of calculating the community and separate interests. In these inflationary times when residential housing is undergoing enormous and rapid appreciation in value, we believe that the most equitable method of calculating the separate and community interests when the down payment was made with separate funds and the loan was based on a community or joint obligation is that set forth by Justice McGuire in In re Marriage of Aufmuth, supra, 89 Cal. App. 3d at pp. 456–457, 152 Cal. Rptr. 668. In brief, the *Aufmuth* formula gives the spouse who made the separate property down payment a separate property interest in the residence in the proportion that the down payment bears to the purchase price; the community acquires that percentage of the residence which the community loan bears to the purchase price.[3]

If the trial court finds no agreement or understanding that Brenda was to retain a separate property interest in the residence, Brenda's contribution of $2,962 of separate funds for improvements should have no effect on the determination of the parties' interests, and the presumption of section 5110 is controlling. If there was an understanding that Brenda's separate interest should be maintained, but no separate understanding with respect to improvements, Brenda should receive no additional credit for her expenditure for improvements, for it may be presumed that she intended that they redound to both the community and her separate interest in the property.

Gerald also challenges the trial court's determination that a 1976 Harvest Mini–Motorhome, purchased in January 1976 for a cash price of $10,388, was Brenda's separate property. A community property vehicle was traded in on the purchase for an allowance of $2,567. An additional cash payment of $100 was made on the purchase from community funds. The cost of insurance and license fees ($474) added to the cash price of the motorhome, less the trade-in allowance and cash down payment, left a total unpaid balance of $8,195. That sum was paid by check drawn on Brenda's separate checking account. The community contributed 24.6 percent of the cost and Brenda contributed 75.4 percent of the cost of the vehicle. The fair market value of it at the time of trial was $9,000.

The purchase contract was made out in the name of Gerald alone, but title and registration were taken in Brenda's name only. Brenda wished to have title in her name alone, and Gerald did not object. The motorhome was purchased for family use and was referred to and used by the parties as a "family vehicle."

3. The value of those interests is computed by first determining the amount of capital appreciation, which is computed by subtracting the purchase price from the fair market value of the residence. The separate property interest would be determined by adding the amount of capital appreciation attributable to separate funds to the amount of equity paid by separate funds. The community interest would be the amount of capital appreciation attributable to community funds plus the amount of equity paid by community funds; the amount of equity paid by community funds is represented by the amount by which the principal balance on the loan has been reduced.

These principles may be exemplified by considering a house purchased for $100,000, with the wife paying the entire down payment of $20,000 from separate property funds and the community contributing the rest of the purchase price in the amount of a loan for $80,000. There would be a 20 percent separate property interest and an 80 percent community property interest in the house. Assume that the fair market value of the house at the time of trial is $175,000, resulting in a capital appreciation of $75,000, and the mortgage balance at the time of separation was $78,000. The value of the separate property interest would be $35,000, which represents the amount of capital appreciation attributable to the separate funds (20 percent of $75,000) added to the amount of equity paid by separate funds ($20,000). The net value of the community property interest would be $62,000, which represents the amount of capital appreciation attributable to community funds (80 percent of $75,000) added to the amount of equity paid by community funds ($80,000 minus $78,000).

The trial court confirmed the motorhome to Brenda as her separate property. The interlocutory judgment stated that Gerald "had a de minimus community property interest therein which was made a gift to respondent [Brenda] at the time of the purchase."

Contrary to Gerald's contention, the trial court's determination that he made a gift of his interest is supported by substantial evidence. Title was taken in Brenda's name alone. Gerald was aware of this and did not object. This evidence constitutes substantial support for the trial court's conclusion that Gerald was making a gift to Brenda of his community property interest in the motorhome.

The judgment is reversed insofar as it determines the respective interests of the parties in the residence and divides the community property. It is affirmed in all other respects.

Notes & Questions

1. Do the California statutory presumptions comport with the likely intent of couples?

2. When property has been purchased with a combination of community and separate property, how should it be allocated upon death or divorce? There are several possibilities. First, the entire property can be treated as either community or separate property. Second, the property can be treated as community property with reimbursement of any contributions of separate property (or treated as separate property with reimbursement of any community contributions). Finally, the property can be allocated between community or separate property in proportion to the relative contributions from the two sources of funds. When is each approach appropriate? Why?

3. In the aftermath of *Lucas*, the California legislature passed a statute providing that, absent a written agreement to the contrary, a spouse who contributes separate property toward the acquisition of community property shall be reimbursed for the contribution. "The amount reimbursed shall be without interest or adjustment for change in monetary values and shall not exceed the net value of the property at the time of acquisition." Cal. Family Code § 2640(b).

4. What happens if someone acquires a piece of land before marriage, but uses community fund after marriage to help pay off an outstanding balance? Community property states differ in their approach. California follows the pro rata apportionment approach described in *Lucas*. Other states follow an "inception of right" rule and hold that the land is separate property because the purchase contract was signed before the marriage. Finally, some states follow a "time of vesting" rule and hold that the land is community property because title did not vest until the land has been paid for.

5. **Uniform Marital Property Act.** In 1983, the National Conference on Uniform State Laws adopted a Uniform Marital Property Act

largely tracking the community property system. The Act divides property into marital property (any property acquired during marriage from earnings of either spouse) and separate property (any property acquired before marriage or through gift, devise, or inheritance). Each spouse owns a one-half undivided interest in the marital property during marriage. On death, the decedent can dispose of his or her share of the marital property by will; the surviving spouse keeps his or her share. On divorce, marital property is allocated according to the state's distribution laws. To date, only Wisconsin has adopted the Uniform Marital Property Act. See Wis. Stat. §§ 766.001–.97.

3. What Is Marital Property?

In re Marriage of Graham

Supreme Court of Colorado, 1978.
574 P.2d 75.

Lee, Justice.

This case presents the novel question of whether in a marriage dissolution proceeding a master's degree in business administration (M.B.A.) constitutes marital property which is subject to division by the court. In its opinion, the Colorado Court of Appeals held that it was not. We affirm the judgment.

The Uniform Dissolution of Marriage Act requires that a court shall divide marital property, without regard to marital misconduct, in such proportions as the court deems just after considering all relevant factors. The Act defines marital property as follows:

> For purposes of this article only, "marital property" means all property acquired by either spouse subsequent to the marriage except:
>
> (a) Property acquired by gift, bequest, devise, or descent;
>
> (b) Property acquired in exchange for property acquired prior to the marriage or in exchange for property acquired by gift, bequest, devise, or descent;
>
> (c) Property acquired by a spouse after a decree of legal separation; and
>
> (d) Property excluded by valid agreement of the parties.

Section 14–10–113(2), C.R.S. 1973.

The parties to this proceeding were married on August 5, 1968, in Denver, Colorado. Throughout the six-year marriage, Anne P. Graham, wife and petitioner here, was employed full-time as an airline stewardess. She is still so employed. Her husband, Dennis J. Graham, respondent, worked part-time for most of the marriage, although his main pursuit was his education. He attended school for approximately three and one-half years of the marriage, acquiring both a bachelor of science degree in engineering physics and a master's degree in business administration at the University of Colorado. Following graduation, he obtained a job as an executive assistant with a large corporation at a starting salary of $14,000 per year.

The trial court determined that during the marriage petitioner contributed seventy percent of the financial support, which was used both for family expenses and for her husband's education. No marital assets were accumulated during the marriage. In addition, the Grahams together managed an apartment house and petitioner did the majority of housework and cooked most of the meals for the couple. No children were born during the marriage.

The parties jointly filed a petition for dissolution, on February 4, 1974, in the Boulder County District Court. Petitioner did not make a claim for maintenance or for attorney fees. After a hearing on October 24, 1974, the trial court found, as a matter of law, that an education obtained by one spouse during a marriage is jointly-owned property to which the other spouse has a property right. The future earnings value of the M.B.A. to respondent was evaluated at $82,836 and petitioner was awarded $33,134 of this amount, payable in monthly installments of $100.

The court of appeals reversed, holding that an education is not itself "property" subject to division under the Act, although it was one factor to be considered in determining maintenance or in arriving at an equitable property division.

I.

The purpose of the division of marital property is to allocate to each spouse what equitably belongs to him or her. The division is committed to the sound discretion of the trial court and there is no rigid mathematical formula that the court must adhere to. An appellate court will alter a division of property only if the trial court abuses its discretion. This court, however, is empowered at all times to interpret Colorado statutes.

The legislature intended the term "property" to be broadly inclusive, as indicated by its use of the qualifying adjective "all" in section 14–10–113(2). Previous Colorado cases have given "property" a comprehensive meaning, as typified by the following definition: "In short it embraces anything and everything which may belong to a man and in the ownership of which he has a right to be protected by law." Las Animas County High School District v. Raye, 144 Colo. 367, 356 P.2d 237.

Nonetheless, there are necessary limits upon what may be considered "property," and we do not find any indication in the Act that the concept as used by the legislature is other than that usually understood to be embodied within the term. One helpful definition is "everything that has an exchangeable value or which goes to make up wealth or estate." Black's Law Dictionary 1382 (rev. 4th ed. 1968). In Ellis v. Ellis, Colo., 552 P.2d 506, this court held that military retirement pay was not property for the reason that it did not have any of the elements of cash surrender value, loan value, redemption value, lump sum value, or value realizable after death. The court of appeals has considered other factors as well in deciding whether something falls within the concept, particularly whether it can be assigned, sold, transferred, conveyed, or pledged, or whether it terminates on the death of the owner.

An educational degree, such as an M.B.A., is simply not encompassed even by the broad views of the concept of "property." It does not have an exchange value or any objective transferable value on an open market. It is personal to the holder. It terminates on death of the holder and is not inheritable. It cannot be assigned, sold, transferred, conveyed, or pledged. An advanced degree is a cumulative product of many years of previous education, combined with diligence and hard work. It may not be acquired by the mere expenditure of money. It is simply an intellectual achievement that may potentially assist in the future acquisition of property. In our view, it has none of the attributes of property in the usual sense of that term.

II.

Our interpretation is in accord with cases in other jurisdictions. We have been unable to find any decision, even in community property states, which appears to have held that an education of one spouse is marital property to be divided on dissolution. This contention was dismissed in Todd v. Todd, 272 Cal. App. 2d 786, 78 Cal. Rptr. 131 (Ct. App.), where it was held that a law degree is not a community property asset capable of division, partly because it "cannot have monetary value placed upon it." Similarly, it has been recently held that a person's earning capacity, even where enhanced by a law degree financed by the other spouse, "should not be recognized as a separate, particular item of property." Stern v. Stern, 66 N.J. 340, 331 A.2d 257. . . .

III.

The trial court relied on Greer v. Greer, 32 Colo. App. 196, 510 P.2d 905, for its determination that an education is "property." In that case, a six-year marriage was dissolved in which the wife worked as a teacher while the husband obtained a medical degree. The parties had accumulated marital property. The trial court awarded the wife alimony of $150 per month for four years. The court of appeals found this to be proper, whether considered as an adjustment of property rights based upon the wife's financial contribution to the marriage, or as an award of alimony in gross. The court there stated that ". . . [i]t must be considered as a substitute for, or in lieu of, the wife's rights in the husband's property. . . ." We note that the court did not determine that the medical education itself was divisible property. The case is distinguishable from the instant case in that here there was no accumulation of marital property and the petitioner did not seek maintenance [alimony].

IV.

A spouse who provides financial support while the other spouse acquires an education is not without a remedy. Where there is marital property to be divided, such contribution to the education of the other spouse may be taken into consideration by the court. Here, we again note that no marital property had been accumulated by the parties. Further, if maintenance is sought and a need is demonstrated, the trial court may make an award based on all relevant factors. Section 14–10–114(2). Certainly, among the relevant factors to be considered is the contribution of the spouse seeking maintenance to the education of the other spouse from whom the maintenance is sought. Again, we note that in this case petitioner sought no maintenance from respondent.

The judgment is affirmed.

CARRIGAN, Justice, dissenting:

I respectfully dissent.

As a matter of economic reality the most valuable asset acquired by either party during this six-year marriage was the husband's increased earning capacity. There is no dispute that this asset resulted from his having obtained Bachelor of Science and Master of Business Administration degrees while married. These degrees, in turn, resulted in large part from the wife's employment which contributed about 70% of the couple's total income. Her earnings not only provided her husband's support but also were "invested" in his education in the sense that she assumed the role of breadwinner so that he would have the time and funds necessary to obtain his education.

The case presents the not-unfamiliar pattern of the wife who, willing to sacrifice for a more secure family financial future, works to educate her husband, only to be awarded a divorce decree shortly after he is awarded his degree. The issue here is whether traditional, narrow concepts of what constitutes "property" render the courts impotent to provide a remedy for an obvious injustice.

In cases such as this, equity demands that courts seek extraordinary remedies to prevent extraordinary injustice. If the parties had remained married long enough after the husband had completed his post-graduate education so that they could have accumulated substantial property, there would have been no problem. In that situation abundant precedent authorized the trial court, in determining how much of the marital property to allocate to the wife, to take into account her contributions to her husband's earning capacity. Greer v. Greer, 32 Colo. App. 196, 510 P.2d 905 (1973) (wife supported husband through medical school); In re Marriage of Vanet, 544 S.W.2d 236 (Mo. App. 1976) (wife was breadwinner while husband was in law school).

A husband's future income earning potential, sometimes as indicated by the goodwill value of a professional practice, may be considered in deciding property division or alimony matters, and the wife's award may be increased on the ground that the husband probably will have substantial future earnings. Todd v. Todd, 272 Cal. App. 2d 786, 78 Cal. Rptr. 131 (1969) (goodwill of husband's law practice); Golden v. Golden, 270 Cal. App. 2d 401, 75 Cal. Rptr. 735 (1969) (goodwill of husband's medical practice); Mueller v. Mueller, 144 Cal. App. 2d 245, 301 P.2d 90 (1956) (goodwill of husband's dental lab); In re Marriage of Goger, 27 Or. App. 729, 557 P.2d 46 (1976) (potential earnings of husband's dental practice); In re Marriage of Lukens, 16 Wash. App. 481, 558 P.2d 279 (1976) (goodwill of husband's medical practice indicated future earning capacity).

Similarly, the wife's contributions to enhancing the husband's financial status or earning capacity have been considered in awarding alimony and maintenance. The majority opinion emphasizes that in this case no maintenance was requested. However, the Colorado statute would seem to preclude an award of maintenance here, for it restricts the court's power to award maintenance to cases where the spouse seeking it is unable to support himself or herself.

While the majority opinion focuses on whether the husband's master's degree is marital "property" subject to division, it is not the degree itself which constitutes the asset in question. Rather it is the increase in the husband's earning power concomitant to that degree which is the asset conferred on him by his wife's efforts. That increased earning capacity was the asset appraised in the economist's expert opinion testimony as having a discounted present value of $82,000.

Unquestionably the law, in other contexts, recognizes future earning capacity as an asset whose wrongful deprivation is compensable. Thus one who tortuously destroys or impairs another's future earning capacity must pay as damages the amount the injured party has lost in anticipated future earnings.

Where a husband is killed, his widow is entitled to recover for loss of his future support damages based in part on the present value of his anticipated future earnings, which may be computed by taking into account probable future increases in his earning capacity.

The day before the divorce the wife had a legally recognized interest in her husband's earning capacity. Perhaps the wife might have a remedy in a separate action based on implied debt, quasi-contract, unjust enrichment, or some similar theory. Nevertheless, the law favors settling all aspects of a dispute in a single action where that is possible. Therefore I would affirm the trial court's award.

Dugan v. Dugan

Supreme Court of New Jersey, 1983.
457 A.2d 1.

SCHREIBER, J.

This case involves the equitable distribution of marital property upon divorce, more particularly the evaluation of an attorney's goodwill in his exclusively owned professional corporation.

Plaintiff, James P. Dugan, and defendant, Rosaleen M. Dugan, were married in 1958 and separated in 1978. They had no children. The plaintiff, a member of the New Jersey Bar, carries on his practice as a professional corporation. The defendant had served as a secretary in plaintiff's law office and attended college during the marriage, graduating in 1972. She is certified as a public school teacher, but as of the date of the divorce judgment was unemployed.

The judgment entered for dual no-fault divorce provided for distribution of property, alimony and other relief.... The trial court determined that the value of the material part of the marital estate was $606,966 as of December 29, 1978, the date the complaint was filed. It awarded the defendant $230,864 and the plaintiff $376,102 consisting of the following:

Real property	$ 285,400
Law practice	
Goodwill	$ 182,725
Accounts receivable	18,891
Pension plan	50,500
Common stock	1,000
Less	
Retained earnings deficit	1,780
Net value of law practice	*251,336*
Cash	55,313
Miscellaneous	14,917
	$606,966

A major asset in the joint estate was the plaintiff's law practice. It comprised more than 40% of the entire estate and over 70% of the value of that asset consisted of the value placed on goodwill....

We must determine whether goodwill is a part of the value of plaintiff's law practice; if so, whether it constitutes property subject to equitable distribution; and, if so, how it is to be evaluated.

I

In a divorce judgment a court may "effectuate an equitable distribution of the property, both real and personal," acquired during the marriage. N.J.S.A. 2A:34–23.[2] We have acknowledged that the Legislature intended that its reference to "property" be construed comprehensively. Painter v. Painter, 65 N.J. 196, 217 (1974). Determining the "property" subject to equitable distribution requires a marshalling of the parties' economic resources. Kruger v. Kruger, 73 N.J. 464, 468 (1977). These economic resources cover a broad spectrum. Initially a list of the parties' assets and liabilities upon a particular date should be prepared. Personal tangible property is clearly includable. Intangibles may also constitute property. See id. (stating "[t]he right to receive monies in the future is unquestionably such an economic resource") (emphasis in original). See also Kikkert v.

2. Gifts, devises or bequests, except interspousal gifts, are excluded. L.1980, c. 181, § 1.

Kikkert, 177 N.J. Super. 471 (App. Div.), aff'd, 88 N.J. 4 (1981) (holding a vested pension plan providing future monetary benefits to be equitably distributable).

As distinguished from tangible assets, intangibles have no intrinsic value, but do have a value related to the ownership and possession of tangible assets. Some intangibles, such as a trademark, trade name or patent, are related to an identifiable tangible asset. Goodwill, which is another intangible, is not. Often referred to as "the most 'intangible' of the intangibles," D. Kieso & J. Weygandt, Intermediate Accounting 570 (3d ed. 1980), goodwill is essentially reputation that will probably generate future business. Lord Eldon expressed that thought in Cruttwell v. Lye, 17 Ves. 335, 346, 34 Eng. Rep. 129, 134 (Ch. 1810): "The good-will, which has been the subject of sale, is nothing more than the probability, that the old customers will resort to the old place." . . . .

There can be no doubt that goodwill exists. It is a legally predictable interest. . . . Upon dissolution of a partnership, goodwill has been recognized as an element in determining value for purposes of liquidation. Blut v. Katz, 13 N.J. 374 (1953). . . .

The accounting profession has further expanded the concept of goodwill to encompass other advantages of an established business that contribute to its profitability. J. M. Smith & K. F. Skousen, Intermediate Accounting 283 (7th ed. standard vol. 1982), capture this thought in their definition:

> Goodwill is generally regarded as the summation of all the special advantages, not otherwise identifiable, related to a going concern. It includes such items as a good name, capable staff and personnel, high credit standing, reputation for superior products and services, and favorable location.

. . . .

Goodwill can be translated into prospective earnings. From an accounting standpoint goodwill has also been perceived of in terms of the extent to which future estimated earnings exceed the normal return on the investment. Walker, "Why Purchased Goodwill Should be Amortized on a Systematic Basis," 95 J. Acc'tancy 210, 213 (1953). When goodwill exists, it has value and may well be the most lucrative asset of some enterprises. . . .

II

Our limited concern involves the existence of goodwill as property and its evaluation for purposes of equitable distribution under N.J.S.A. 2A:34–23 with respect to attorneys and in particular individual practitioners. Though other elements may contribute to goodwill in the context of a professional service, such as locality and specialization, reputation is at the core. It does not exist at the time professional qualifications and a license to practice are obtained. A good reputation is earned after accomplishment and performance. Field testing is an essential ingredient before goodwill comes into being. Future earning capacity per se is not goodwill. However, when that future earning capacity has been enhanced because reputation leads to probable future patronage from existing and potential clients, goodwill may exist and have value. When that occurs the resulting goodwill is property subject to equitable distribution.

We held in Lynn v. Lynn, 91 N.J. 510 (1982), that a license to practice medicine and a medical degree were not property. They reflected only a possibility of future earnings. This holding was consonant with the proposition in Stern v. Stern, 66 N.J. 340, 345 (1975), that potential earning capacity is not property within the meaning of the statute, though relevant on the issues of alimony and of determining equitable proportions for the distribution of property.

When, however, the opportunity provided by the license is exercised, then goodwill may come into existence. Goodwill is to be differentiated from earning capacity. It reflects not simply a possibility of future earnings, but a probability based on existing circumstances. Enhanced earnings reflected in goodwill are to be distinguished from a license to practice a profession and an educational degree. In that situation the enhanced future earnings are so remote and speculative that the license and degree have not been deemed to be property. The possibility of additional earnings is to be distinguished from the existence of goodwill in a law practice and the probability of its continuation. Moreover, unlike the license and the degree, goodwill is transferable and marketable. Though there is an apparent limitation on the part of an individual practitioner to sell a law practice, the same is not true in a law firm.

After divorce, the law practice will continue to benefit from that goodwill as it had during the marriage. Much of the economic value produced during an attorney's marriage will inhere in the goodwill of the law practice. It would be inequitable to ignore the contribution of the non-attorney spouse to the development of that economic resource. An individual practitioner's inability to sell a law practice does not eliminate existence of goodwill and its value as an asset to be considered in equitable distribution. Obviously, equitable distribution does not require conveyance or transfer of any particular asset. The other spouse, in this case the wife, is entitled to have that asset considered as any other property acquired during the marriage partnership.

Other jurisdictions have accepted the principle that an attorney's goodwill is property subject to equitable distribution. In In re Marriage of Lopez, 38 Cal. App. 3d 93, 107, 113 Cal. Rptr. 58, 67 (1974), in discussing goodwill, the court quoted approvingly the following language from Golden v. Golden, 270 Cal. App. 2d 401, 405, 75 Cal. Rptr. 735, 738 (1969):

> [I]n a matrimonial matter, the practice of the sole practitioner husband will continue, with the same intangible value as it had during the marriage. Under principles of community property law, the wife, by virtue of her position of wife, made to that value the same contribution as does a wife to any of [the] husband's earnings and accumulations during marriage. She is as much entitled

to be recompensed for that contribution as if it were represented by the increased value of stock in a family business.

. . . .

In Stern v. Stern, we acknowledged that "[i]t may . . . be possible to prove that [goodwill] does exist and is a real element of economic worth. Concededly, determining its value presents difficulties." 66 N.J. at 346–47 n.5 (citation omitted). However, difficulty in fixing its value does not justify ignoring its existence. Goodwill should be valued with great care, for the individual practitioner will be forced to pay the ex-spouse "tangible" dollars for an intangible asset at a value concededly arrived at on the basis of some uncertain elements. . . .

One appropriate method to determine the value of goodwill of a law practice can be accomplished by fixing the amount by which the attorney's earnings exceed that which would have been earned as an employee by a person with similar qualifications of education, experience and capability. This is a fair manner in which to resolve the goodwill constituent. An attorney who earns $35,000 per year as an employee would, as any employee, not have goodwill properly ascribable to his employment. The same attorney earning a net income of the same amount from his individual practice should likewise not be considered to have property consisting of goodwill in ascertaining the value of his practice.

The court should first ascertain what an attorney of comparable experience, expertise, education and age would be earning as an employee in the same general locale. The effort that the practitioner expends on his law practice should not be overlooked when comparing his income to that of the hypothetical employee. A sole practitioner who, for example, works a regular sixty-hour week may have a significantly greater income than an employee who regularly works a forty-hour week, and the income may be due to greater productivity rather than the realization of income on the sole practitioner's goodwill. Next, the attorney's net income before federal and state income taxes for a period of years, preferably five, should be determined and averaged. The actual average should then be compared with the employee norm. If the attorney's actual average realistically exceeds the total of (1) the employee norm and (2) a return on the investment in the physical assets, the excess would be the basis for evaluating goodwill.

This excess is subject to a capitalization factor. The capitalization factor is generally perceived as the number of years of excess earnings a purchaser would be willing to pay for in advance in order to acquire the goodwill. 2 J. Bonbright, Valuation of Property 731 (1937). The minimum capitalization factor is zero. The precise capitalization factor would depend on other evidence. Such evidence could consist of a comparison of capitalization factors used to measure goodwill in other professions, such as medicine or dentistry, adjusted, however, for ingredients peculiar to law, such as the inability to sell the practice and nonavailability of a restrictive covenant. The age of a lawyer may be particularly important because a sole practitioner's goodwill would probably terminate upon death, contrary to that of a doctor. Subject to such adjustments, the method used in a comparable profession may be applied and a figure close to the true worth of the law practice's goodwill may be obtained.

Other approaches equally or more compelling may be used. If sufficient information about the average income of attorney employees with similar background and expertise is unavailable, partnership agreements covering comparable attorneys that set forth value in excess of capital accounts may disclose a useful figure for goodwill. See Cantor, "The Value of a Lawyer's Interest in His Practice," 43 N.Y. St. B.J. 47, 52–53 (1971) (referring to surveys of law firms to ascertain policies for valuing a terminating partner's interest). In *Stern* we agreed that the law partnership agreement may determine the worth of a lawyer's practice including goodwill upon proof that the books are well kept and the partner's interests are carefully reviewed periodically. 66 N.J. at 347.

There may well be other ways in which goodwill may be computed and we do not by the suggestions made herein intend to preclude their use....

The judgment is reversed and the cause remanded to the trial court for further proceedings to determine the value of plaintiff's law practice with respect to goodwill and accounts payable and for modification of equitable distribution, which may or may not affect the quantum of appropriate alimony.

Notes & Questions

1. **Professional Degrees.** Because a professional degree cannot be sold or transferred, it cannot be divided between spouses in the same way that land or most personal property might be. If a professional degree is marital property, therefore, a court can provide for its "distribution" only through the distribution of other property or, as the wife urged in *Graham*, by the awarding of a monetary sum.

Almost every court to consider whether a professional degree is marital property has agreed with *Graham*. See, e.g., Nelson v. Nelson, 736 P.2d 1145 (Alaska 1987); Drapek v. Drapek, 503 N.E.2d 946 (Mass. 1987); Petersen v. Petersen, 737 P.2d 237 (Utah App. 1987). The New York Court of Appeal, however, has held that, under New York's divorce statute, professional degrees are marital property and thus courts can "distribute ... other marital assets or ... make a distributive award in lieu of an actual distribution of the value of the professional spouse's license." O'Brien v. O'Brien, 489 N.E.2d 712 (N.Y. 1985). A Michigan court of appeal similarly has held that "where an advanced degree is the end product of a concerted family effort, involving the mutual sacrifice, effort, and contribution of both spouses, there arises a 'marital asset' subject to distribution, wherein the interest of the nonstudent spouse consists of an 'equitable claim' regarding the degree." Postema v. Postema, 471 N.W.2d 912 (Mich. App. 1991).

2. Courts have often found other ways of compensating spouses for the professional degrees that their mates earned during their marriage. In Mahoney v. Mahoney, 453 A.2d 527 (N.J. 1982), for example, the New Jersey Supreme Court concluded that a supporting spouse was entitled to "reimbursement alimony":

> In proper circumstances, ... courts should not hesitate to award reimbursement alimony. Marriage should not be a free ticket to professional education and training without subsequent obligations. This Court should not ignore the scenario of the young professional who after being supported through graduate school leaves his mate for supposedly greener pastures. One spouse ought not to receive a divorce complaint when the other receives a diploma. Those spouses supported through professional school should recognize that they may be called upon to reimburse the supporting spouses for the financial contributions they received in pursuit of their professional training. And they cannot deny the basic fairness of this result.

According to the New Jersey Supreme Court, reimbursement alimony should "cover *all* financial contributions used by the supported spouse in obtaining his or her degree or license." See also Hoak v. Hoak, 370 S.E.2d 473 (W. Va. 1988) (adopting New Jersey's "reimbursement alimony" approach).

Other courts have held that, even if a professional degree is not marital property, a supporting spouse is entitled to an equitable award reimbursing the spouse for his or her monetary contributions toward the degree (including living expenses paid for during the education). See, e.g., In re Marriage of DeLa Rosa, 309 N.W.2d 755 (Minn. 1981); Hubbard v. Hubbard, 603 P.2d 747 (Okla. 1979). See also Cal. Fam. Code § 2641 (providing for reimbursements of community contributions toward the education or training of one spouse).

Finally, a number of courts have held that the value of a professional degree should be taken into account in determining the equitable allocation of other marital property.

3. No matter the theory by which a supporting spouse is compensated for the professional degree of his or her mate, how much compensation should the supporting spouse receive? If the supporting spouse is reimbursed for his or her out-of-pocket contributions toward the professional degree, is that adequate?

In Haugan v. Haugan, 343 N.W.2d 796, 802 (Wis. 1984), Justice Abrahamson suggested that another possible approach would be to reimburse the supporting spouse for his or her opportunity costs. Because one member of the couple was attending school and not working, the couple earned less money during the marriage than it otherwise would have. Is there any reason why a spouse should be reimbursed for the direct costs of her mate's education, but not this "opportunity cost"? Should courts also take into account the fact that the supporting spouse was not able to earn a professional degree or perhaps advance his or her career in other ways while putting his or her mate through school?

In many cases, the supporting spouse is seeking a share of the "value" of the professional degree that his or her mate has earned. How could a court go about valuing a professional degree? Statistical studies show that individuals with professional degrees make more money on average than individuals without them. But does the higher earning capacity reflect the value of a professional degree or the intelligence and other innate attributes of the people who receive professional degrees?

4. **Goodwill.** In deciding whether goodwill is marital property, most courts distinguish between goodwill that is personal to the spouse (and thus will disappear if the spouse stops working) and goodwill that is intrinsic to the spouse's business separate and apart from the spouse's connection with it. Virtually all courts hold that the latter type of goodwill is marital property. See, e.g., Finch v. Finch, 825 S.W.2d 218 (Tex. App. 1992); Nicholson v. Nicholson, 669 S.W.2d 514 (Ark. Ct. App. 1984). But many courts have refused to hold that goodwill attributable to the spouse's continued involvement in the business is marital property:

> It should be emphasized that such goodwill, to be a marital property, must exist separate and apart from the reputation or continued presence of the marital litigant. If goodwill depends on the continued presence of a particular individual, such goodwill, by definition, is not a marketable asset distinct from the individual. Any value which attaches to the entity solely as a result of personal goodwill represents nothing more than probable future earning capacity, which, although relevant in determining alimony, is not a proper consideration in dividing the marital property. Therefore, "for professional goodwill to be marital property it must be a business asset having a value independent of the continued presence or reputation of any particular individual."

Thompson v. Thompson, 576 So. 2d 267, 270 (Fla. 1991) (citations omitted). See generally Scott Singley, Professional Goodwill: How Mississippi Produces an "Inequitable" Distribution of Property Pursuant to Divorce by Excluding Professional Goodwill, 68 Miss. L.J. 1053 (1999).

5. **Other Career Enhancements.** When John and Ursula first marry, Ursula is trying unsuccessfully to break into the movie business. Ten years later, Ursula has become a famous movie star, bringing in several million dollars per movie. During the ten year interim, John sacrificed his own career to take care of the family while Ursula worked hard to advance her movie career; John also gave Ursula advice on her acting and, in the early years, served as her informal, and uncompensated, business manager. If John and Ursula now divorce, is the enhanced value of Ursula's career "marital property" subject to equitable distribution? Should it be? See Elkus v. Elkus, 572 N.Y.S.2d 901 (N.Y. App. Div. 1991) (holding that appreciation in earning capacity as a singer is marital property to the extent that the appreciation is due at least in part to the spouse's efforts and contributions).

6. If a court concludes that a professional degree, goodwill, or enhanced career status is marital property, what happens if the spouse's earning capacity falls after the divorce? Can he or she seek reimbursement? Cf. Gastineau v. Gastineau, 573 N.Y.S.2d 819 (N.Y. Sup. Ct. 1991) (taking husband's professional football contract into account in distribution of property even though the husband had walked away from his contract, to be with his girlfriend while she underwent cancer treatment, and thereby forfeited his salary and probably any future he still had in football).

7. For more on the role of professional "capital" in divorce settings, see Carolyn J. Frantz & Hanoch Dagan, Properties of Marriage, 104 Colum. L. Rev. 75 (2004); Erik V. Wicks, Professional Degree Divorces: Of Equity Positions, Equitable Distributions, and Clean Breaks, 45 Wayne L. Rev. 1975 (2000).

4. Unmarried Couples

Connell v. Francisco

Supreme Court of Washington, 1995.
898 P.2d 831.

GUY, J.

This case requires us to decide how property acquired during a meretricious relationship is distributed.

Petitioner Richard Francisco and Respondent Shannon Connell met in Toronto, Canada, in June 1983. Connell was a dancer in a stage show produced by Francisco. She resided in New York, New York. She owned clothing and a leasehold interest in a New York apartment. Francisco resided in Las Vegas, Nevada. He owned personal property, real property, and several companies, including Prince Productions, Inc. and Las Vegas Talent, Ltd., which produced stage shows for hotels. Francisco's net worth was approximately $1,300,000 in February 1984.

Connell, at Francisco's invitation, moved to Las Vegas in, November 1983. They cohabited in Francisco's Las Vegas home from November 1983 to June 1986. While living in Las Vegas, Connell worked as a paid dancer in several stage shows. She also assisted Francisco as needed with his various business enterprises. Francisco managed his companies and produced several profitable stage shows.

In November 1985, Prince Productions, Inc. purchased a bed and breakfast, the Whidbey Inn, on Whidbey Island, Washington. Connell moved to Whidbey Island in June 1986 to manage the Inn. Shortly thereafter Francisco moved to Whidbey Island to join her. Connell and Francisco resided and cohabited on Whidbey Island until the relationship ended in March 1990.

While living on Whidbey Island, Connell and Francisco were viewed by many in the community as being married. Francisco acquiesced in Connell's use of his surname for business purposes. A last will and testament, dated December 11, 1987, left the corpus of Francisco's estate to Connell. Both Connell and Francisco had surgery to enhance their fertility. In the summer of 1986, Francisco gave Connell an engagement ring.

From June 1986 to September 1990 Connell continuously managed and worked at the Inn. She prepared breakfast, cleaned rooms, took reservations, laundered linens, paid bills, and maintained and repaired the Inn. Connell received no compensation for her services at the Inn from 1986 to 1988. From January 1989 to September 1990 she received $400 per week in salary.

Francisco produced another profitable stage show and acquired several pieces of real property during the period from June 1986 to September 1990. Property acquired by Francisco included: a condominium in Langley, Washington, for $65,000; a waterfront lot next to the Inn for $35,000; property identified as the Alan May property for $225,000; real property identified as the restaurant property for $320,000; a house in Langley, Washington, for $105,000; and a condominium in Las Vegas, Nevada, for $110,000. In addition to the real property acquired by Francisco, Prince Productions, Inc. acquired two pieces of real property next to the Inn. Connell did not contribute financially toward the purchase of any of the properties, and title to the properties was held in Francisco's name individually or in the name of Prince Productions, Inc.

Connell and Francisco separated in March 1990. When the relationship ended Connell had $10,000 in savings, $10,000 in jewelry, her clothes, an automobile, and her leasehold interest in the New York apartment. She continued to receive her $400 per week salary from the Inn until September 1990. In contrast, Francisco's net worth was over $2,700,000, a net increase since February 1984 of almost $1,400,000. In March 1990, he was receiving $5,000 per week in salary from Prince Productions, Inc.

Connell filed a lawsuit against Francisco in December 1990 seeking a just and equitable distribution of the property acquired during the relationship. The Island County Superior Court determined Connell and Francisco's relationship was sufficiently long term and stable to require a just and equitable distribution. The Superior Court limited the property subject to distribution to the property that would have been community in character had they been married. The trial court held property owned by each party prior to the relationship could not be distributed. In addition, the Superior Court required Connell to prove by a preponderance of the evidence that the property acquired during their relationship would have been community property had they been married.

The only property characterized by the Superior Court as being property that would have been community in character had Connell and Francisco been married was the increased value of Francisco's pension plan. The increased value of the pension plan, $169,000, was divided equally, with $84,500 distributed to Connell. The Superior Court, concluding Connell did not satisfy her burden of proof with respect to the remaining property, distributed to Francisco the remainder of the pension plan and all real property.

The Court of Appeals reversed, holding both property owned by each prior to the relationship and property that would have been community in character had the parties been married may be distributed following a meretricious relationship. The Court of Appeals also ruled the analogous application of RCW 26.09.080 by the Superior Court to meretricious relationships would be meaningless without a community-property-like presumption attaching to all property acquired during the relationship.[a] The Court of Appeals remanded the case to the Superior Court.

Francisco petitioned this court for discretionary review. He argues property owned by each party prior to the relationship may not be distributed following a meretricious relationship, and a community-property-like presumption is inapplicable when a trial court distributes property following a meretricious relationship. We granted discretionary review.

A meretricious relationship is a stable, marital-like relationship where both parties cohabit with knowledge that a lawful marriage between them does not exist. Relevant factors establishing a meretricious relationship include, but are not limited to: continuous cohabitation, duration of the relationship, purpose of the relationship, pooling of resources and services for joint projects, and the intent of the parties.... The Superior Court found Connell and Francisco were parties to a meretricious relationship. This finding is not contested.

Historically, property acquired during a meretricious relationship was presumed to belong to the person in whose name title to the property was placed. "In the absence of any evidence to the contrary, it should be presumed as a matter of law that the parties intended to dispose of the property exactly as they did dispose of it." Creasman v. Boyle, 31 Wash. 2d 345, 356, 196 P.2d 835 (1948). This presumption is commonly referred to as "the Creasman presumption."

To avoid inequitable results under "the Creasman presumption," Washington courts developed a number of exceptions.... In 1984, this court overruled Creasman. In re Marriage of Lindsey, 101 Wash. 2d 299, 304, 678 P.2d 328 (1984). In its place, the court adopted a general rule requiring a just and equitable distribution of property following a meretri-

a. Eds.—Section 26.09.080 of the Washington Revised Code provides:

"In a proceeding for dissolution of the marriage, legal separation, declaration of invalidity, or in a proceeding for disposition of property following dissolution of the marriage by a court which lacked personal jurisdiction over the absent spouse or lacked jurisdiction to dispose of the property, the court shall, without regard to marital misconduct, make such disposition of the property and the liabilities of the parties, either community or separate, as shall appear just and equitable after considering all relevant factors including, but not limited to:

"(1) The nature and extent of the community property;

"(2) The nature and extent of the separate property;

"(3) The duration of the marriage; and

"(4) The economic circumstances of each spouse at the time the division of property is to become effective, including the desirability of awarding the family home or the right to live therein for reasonable periods to a spouse with whom the children reside the majority of the time."

cious relationship. "We adopt the rule that courts must 'examine the [meretricious] relationship and the property accumulations and make a just and equitable disposition of the property.' " Id. at 304 (quoting Latham v. Hennessey, 87 Wash. 2d 550, 554, 554 P.2d 1057 (1976)).

In *Lindsey*, the parties cohabited for less than 2 years prior to marriage. When they subsequently divorced, the wife argued the increase in value of property acquired during the meretricious portion of their relationship was also subject to an equitable distribution as if the property were community in character. We agreed. . . .

Francisco contends the Court of Appeals misinterpreted *Lindsey* when it applied all the principles contained in RCW 26.09.080 to meretricious relationships. We agree. A meretricious relationship is not the same as a marriage. Davis v. Department of Employment Sec., 108 Wash. 2d. 272, 278–79, 737 P.2d 1262 (1987) (an unmarried cohabitant is ineligible for benefits triggered by a "marital status" provision under Washington's unemployment compensation statute). As such, the laws involving the distribution of marital property do not directly apply to the division of property following a meretricious relationship. Washington courts may look toward those laws for guidance.

Once a trial court determines the existence of a meretricious relationship, the trial court then: (1) evaluates the interest each party has in the property acquired during the relationship, and (2) makes a just and equitable distribution of the property. *Lindsey*, 101 Wash. 2d at 307. The critical focus is on property that would have been characterized as community property had the parties been married. This property is properly before a trial court and is subject to a just and equitable distribution.

While portions of RCW 26.09.080 may apply by analogy to meretricious relationships, not all provisions of the statute should be applied. The parties to such a relationship have chosen not to get married and therefore the property owned by each party prior to the relationship should not be before the court for distribution at the end of the relationship. However, the property acquired during the relationship should be before the trial court so that one party is not unjustly enriched at the end of such a relationship. We conclude a trial court may not distribute property acquired by each party prior to the relationship at the termination of a meretricious relationship. Until the Legislature, as a matter of public policy, concludes meretricious relationships are the legal equivalent to marriages, we limit the distribution of property following a meretricious relationship to property that would have been characterized as community property had the parties been married. This will allow the trial court to justly divide property the couple has earned during the relationship through their efforts without creating a common law marriage or making a decision for a couple which they have declined to make for themselves. Any other interpretation equates cohabitation with marriage; ignores the conscious decision by many couples not to marry; confers benefits when few, if any, economic risks or legal obligations are assumed; and disregards the explicit intent of the Legislature that RCW 26.09.080 apply to property distributions following a marriage.

Francisco argues the Court of Appeals erred in requiring the application of a community-property-like presumption to property acquired during a meretricious relationship. We disagree.

In a marital context, property acquired during marriage is presumptively community property. When no marriage exists there is, by definition, no community property. However, only by treating the property acquired in a meretricious relationship similarly can this court's reversal of "the Creasman presumption" be given effect. Failure to apply a community-property-like presumption to the property acquired during a meretricious relationship places the burden of proof on the non-acquiring partner. . . .

For the purpose of dividing property at the end of a meretricious relationship, the definitions of "separate" and "community" property found in RCW 26.16.010–.030 are useful and we apply them by analogy. Therefore, property owned by one of the parties prior to the meretricious relationship and property acquired during the meretricious relationship by gift, bequest, devise, or descent with the rents, issues and profits thereof, is not before the court for division. All other property acquired during the relationship would be presumed to be owned by both of the parties. Furthermore, when the funds or services owned by both parties are used to increase the equity or to maintain or increase the value of property that would have been separate property had the couple been married, there may arise a right of reimbursement in the "community." A court may offset the "community's" right of reimbursement against any reciprocal benefit received by the "community" for its use and enjoyment of the individually owned property.

In the case before us, the majority of real property was purchased during Connell and Francisco's meretricious relationship. This real property is presumed to be owned by both parties, notwithstanding the fact the real property is not held in both parties' names. Francisco may overcome this presumption with evidence showing the real property was acquired with funds that would have been characterized as his separate property had the parties been married.

With respect to any real property found by the trial court to be owned by Francisco, Connell may establish that any increase in value of Francisco's property occurred during their meretricious relationship and is attributable to "community" funds or efforts. If Connell can establish Francisco's property increased in value due to unreimbursed community funds or efforts, then there arises in the "community" a right of reimbursement for those contributions. Any such increase in value would be before the trial court for a just and equitable distribution. To the extent one, or both, of the parties received a fair wage for their efforts, the "community" may have already been reimbursed. Since these inquiries are factual, we leave their resolution to the trial court. . . .

[The dissenting opinion of UTTER, J. is omitted.]

Notes & Questions

1. **Common Law Marriage.** In the 19th century, most states recognized "common law marriages" where a couple intentionally and publicly lived as husband and wife, but had not met statutory marriage requirements. The doctrine made sense in the 19th century when traveling miles to get a marriage license could be difficult, but raised growing concerns over time about both immorality and potential perjury by people wishing to claim someone else's property. As a result, the vast majority of states have abolished the doctrine. Only 11 states, not including Washington, still recognize common law marriages. See Mary Louise Fellows, Committed Partners and Inheritance: An Empirical Study, 16 L. & Ineq. J. 1, 16 n.82 (1998); Cynthia Grant Bowman, A Feminist Proposal to Bring Back Common Law Marriage, 75 Or. L. Rev. 709 (1996).

2. What is the basis for the court's holding in *Connell*? Courts of other states have ordered property to be distributed at the termination of a meretricious relationship based on either a finding that a contract, express or implied, existed between the parties or on general equitable grounds. In Marvin v. Marvin, 557 P.2d 106 (Cal. 1976), for example, the California Supreme Court held that

> courts may inquire into the conduct of the parties to determine whether the conduct demonstrates an implied contract or implied agreement of partnership or joint venture, or some other tacit understanding between the parties. The courts may, when appropriate, employ principles of constructive trust or resulting trust. Finally, a nonmarital partner may recover in quantum meruit for the reasonable value of household services rendered less the reasonable value of support received if he can show that he rendered services with the expectation of monetary reward.

See also Goode v. Goode, 396 S.E.2d 430, 438 (W. Va. 1990) (courts may order a distribution based on "principles of contract, express or implied, or upon a constructive trust"); Morone v. Morone, 413 N.E.2d 1154 (N.Y. 1980) (courts may enforce an express, but not implied, contract).

Courts of a few states, however, have steadfastly refused to permit property distributions upon the termination of a meretricious relationship. Arguing that the question involves complex public policy considerations, for example, Illinois courts have left the issue to the state legislature. See Hewitt v. Hewitt, 394 N.E.2d 1204 (Ill. 1979); Ayala v. Fox, 564 N.E.2d 920 (Ill. App. 1990).

3. **Same–Sex Relationships.** Several courts have now held that courts can order property distributions at the conclusion of a same-sex relationship based on either contract or equity grounds. See, e.g., Crooke v. Gilden, 414 S.E.2d 645 (Ga. 1992); Whorton v. Dillingham, 248 Cal. Rptr. 405 (Cal. App. 1988).

A major legal question today is whether same-sex couples should have the right to marry or at least to form "civil unions" that entitle them to the same marital property rights as heterosexual couples. As of the publication of this book, Belgium, Canada, Netherlands, and Spain all authorize same-sex marriage. In the United States, only Massachusetts currently allows same-sex couples to enter into civil marriages. Like many states, Massachusetts had barred same-sex marriage, but the state supreme court held that this law violated the state constitution. In an advisory opinion, the state supreme court subsequently held that providing same-sex couples with a parallel institution, such as civil unions, is insufficient. See Goodridge v. Department of Pub. Health, 798 N.E.2d 941 (Mass. 2003) According to the court, "segregating same-sex unions from opposite-sex unions cannot possibly be held rationally to advance or 'preserve' ... the Commonwealth's legitimate interests in procreation, child rearing, and the conservation of resources. Because the proposed law by its express terms forbids same-sex couples entry into civil marriage, it continues to relegate same-sex couples to a different status." Opinions of the Justices to the Senate, 802 N.E.2d 565, 569 (Mass. 2004). Efforts are underway, however, to amend the Massachusetts constitution to prohibit same-sex marriages.

A majority of the states in the U.S. have laws expressly prohibiting same-sex marriages and refusing to recognize same-sex marriages from other jurisdictions. In 1996, Congress passed the Defense of Marriage Act defining "marriage" as "only a legal union between one man and one woman as husband and wife." 1 U.S.C. § 7; 28 U.S.C. § 1738C. The Defense of Marriage Act bars federal recognition of same-sex marriages and authorizes states to do the same.

While not recognizing same-sex marriages, Vermont and Connecticut provide for civil unions that entitle same-sex couples to many of the same rights and attributes as traditional marriages. For example, Vermont's Civil Union Law, passed in 2000, entitles gay and lesbian couples to enter into civil unions that provide the same state marital property rights as husbands and wives enjoy. 15 Vt. Stat. §§ 1201–1207. The state legislature acted in response to a ruling by the Vermont Supreme Court that the state constitution required the state to provide equivalent benefits to same-sex couples. See Baker v. Vermont, 744 A.2d 864 (Vt. 1999). In 2005, Connecticut also extended same-sex couples entering into civil unions the same rights and responsibilities as married couples.

A number of other states provide for "domestic partnerships" that often recognize at least some marital property rights. Domestic partners in Maine, for example, enjoy the right to inherit from one another without a will. 18A Me. Rev. Stat. §§ 2–102 et seq. Domestic partners in California enjoy effectively the same rights, protections, and benefits as a married spouse, including community property rights and the right to receive support from one's partner after separation. Cal. Fam. Code §§ 297 et seq.

For a valuable discussion of the issues raised by same-sex marriage, see William N. Eskridge, Jr., The Case for Same–Sex Marriage (1996). For a proposal to provide domestic partners with inheritance rights, see T.P. Gallanis, Inheritance Rights for Domestic Partners, 79 Tulane L. Rev. 55 (2004).

CHAPTER 10

NONPOSSESSORY INTERESTS IN LAND: EASEMENTS, COVENANTS, AND EQUITABLE SERVITUDES

Landowners sometimes acquire *nonpossessory interests* in their neighbors' lands. Imagine that Rachel Carson and John Wesley Powell are neighbors in a mountain subdivision built around a lake. Rachel owns Hillview, which has a nice view of the lake but does not border on it; John owns Lakefront, which is right on the lake. To swim in the lake, Rachel might purchase the right to cross John's parcel to get to the lake. Rachel might also obtain John's promise that he will clear and maintain a path to the lake. John might agree not to erect any structure on Lakefront that will interfere with Rachel's view. And to preserve the lake's rural residential character, John might promise Rachel that no commercial venture, such as a hotel or marina, will be ever be built or operated on Lakefront. These are all nonpossessory, rather than possessory, interests because they give their holder, Rachel, the right to use, but not to possess, part of Lakefront—to cross over the pathway to the lake, for example, or to enjoy an unobstructed view through the airspace over Lakefront.

It is necessary to distinguish among different types of nonpossessory interests. Much today can turn on whether the nonpossessory interest is classified as a *license*, an *easement*, a *profit à prendre*, a *covenant*, or an *equitable servitude* and, if an easement or a covenant, on whether it is *affirmative* or *negative*. As you will see, the differences often make little sense, and legal experts make a convincing case that the law should eliminate many of the distinctions. In most states, however, the differences are still critical.

Types of Nonpossessory Interests

Most states recognize a number of distinct nonpossessory interests.

Licenses. The most common form of nonpossessory interest is a license, which is a right to go onto someone else's property that is revokable at will by the property owner. If John invites Rachel over for dinner, John legally is giving Rachel a license to come onto his property for that purpose. When you buy a ticket to a movie, you are buying a license to go into the movie theater. Although most people do not think about it, they are being given licenses virtually every day. If sued for trespass, however, a license becomes an invaluable legal right.

Affirmative Easements. An affirmative easement entitles its holder to use another's land in a way that, absent the easement, would constitute a trespass or a nuisance and that either is irrevocable or is revocable only on the occurrence of a specific condition. In the example above, Rachel's right to cross Lakefront is an affirmative easement. Rachel would also have an affirmative easement in Lakefront if John grants her the right to run a water pipe across his land to transport water from the lake to Hillview for domestic use,[1] lay a drainage pipe or utility lines, or emit smoke or fumes that otherwise would interfere with John's property rights.

Profit à prendre. What if John gives Rachel the right not only to enter onto his property but also to take some resource—timber or minerals—off? Most courts would call the arrangement a profit à prendre or, just simply, a profit. The Restatement of Property describes a profit as an "easement '*plus*,' " i.e., an easement "plus the right to remove something from the land." Restatement (Third) of Property, Servitudes § 1.2, cmt. e (2000). Because the rules governing profits are largely the same as those governing easements, many other courts do not make a distinction and lump profits in with affirmative easements.

Negative Easements. A negative easement prohibits an otherwise lawful use of land. John's promise not to build a structure that would block the view from Rachel's property is a negative easement because it prohibits John from developing his land in an otherwise lawful manner. Courts historically limited the permissible forms of negative easements to a bare handful: easements for light and air, for subjacent and lateral support, and for the unimpeded flow of an artificial stream. Courts today generally recognize a variety of other forms of negative easements (including easements for a view, conservation easements, and historic preservation easements), and many courts have stated their general willingness to recognize a broad set of negative easements.

Affirmative Covenants. An affirmative covenant is a promise that a landowner will do something that he is otherwise not obligated to do. In the example above, John's promise to clear and maintain the pathway is an affirmative covenant. In other examples, John might agree to give Rachel a right of first refusal on the sale of Lakefront, or to pay an annual maintenance fee to the association that manages the subdivision in which Lakefront and Hillside are located.

1. If Hillview itself does not border the lake, will Rachel have a right to use water from the lake for domestic purposes? It will depend on the state in which Rachel lives. In the West, people can appropriate water from any waterway that has available water whether or not they own land bordering the waterway. In many eastern states, however, Rachel will not be able to withdraw water from the lake because her land is not "riparian" to the lake. In other eastern states, Rachel may be able to acquire the right to divert water from John or other riparians. If so, this right would also be considered an easement, in the form of a "profit."

Negative Covenants. Sometimes also called *restrictive covenants,* these are promises that a landowner will not do something that he is otherwise free to do—for example, a promise not to use Lakefront for other than residential purposes. Negative covenants are obviously similar to negative easements. Under English common law, a significant difference was that, while the law confined negative easements to a small handful of categories, courts imposed virtually no limits on the kinds of negative covenants that could be created. In many states today, however, the law governing negative covenants and negative easements is all but indistinguishable.

Equitable Servitudes. Equitable servitudes are negative covenants that are enforced by a court's equity side rather than by its law side. If Rachel seeks damages—a legal remedy—for John's violation of the residential restriction on Lakefront, she would call the restriction a negative covenant. If, however, she seeks an injunction, she would characterize the restriction as an equitable servitude in most jurisdictions. The difference historically was more than nominal, for courts imposed fewer requirements for enforcing equitable servitudes through injunctive relief than for enforcing negative covenants through damage awards. Today, however, the requirements are largely the same in most jurisdictions.

Is there an equitable counterpart to *affirmative* covenants? Some courts have seized on the *real obligation* as an equitable means for repairing the breach of affirmative obligations. But the device has not proved to be nearly as popular as the equitable servitude.

The Restatement (Third) of Property. Is there any reason to keep all these distinctions? Not only have they confused generations of law school students, but they often have confused the courts. Indeed, courts often have not even been consistent in the labels they use to distinguish between these different kinds of nonpossessory interests. The Restatement (Third) of Property proposes streamlining the list by eliminating the separate category of equitable servitudes (since the historical differences between real covenants and equitable servitudes have today all but disappeared) and by treating negative easements as negative covenants (since again the historical differences have disappeared in most states).

Unless and until courts and legislatures adopt the Restatement approach, however, lawyers must still learn and understand the existing differences between the various categories of nonpossessory interests. This will take some time. The current law has built up over decades and even centuries and consists of an interconnecting set of cases and statutes. Even if a state supreme court is interested in eliminating many or all of the distinctions among the various nonpossessory interests, they must work within the current statutory framework.

Should courts go even further than the Restatement and collapse all nonpossessory interests into one category of "servitudes" or "nonpossessory interests"? For some thoughtful views on unification, see Susan F. French, Toward a Modern Law of Servitudes: Reweaving the Ancient Strands, 55 S. Cal. L. Rev. 1261 (1982) and Uriel Reichman, Toward a Unified Concept of Servitudes, 55 S. Cal. L. Rev. 1179 (1982), along with the symposium issue of the Southern California Law Review of which the two articles are a part.

Elements of Nonpossessory Interests

Four pairs of characteristics help define a specific nonpossessory interest.

Benefit and *Burden.* Every nonpossessory interest creates both a benefit and a burden. The benefit is the right to use land possessed by another. The burden is the corresponding restriction on the possessor's use of his land. Rachel holds the benefit of a right of way easement over Lakefront in the example above; John, who owns Lakefront, bears the burden of having Rachel cross his land.

What are the benefit and the burden of John's agreement not to interfere with Rachel's view? Of the affirmative covenant to clear and maintain the pathway? Of the negative covenant not to use Lakefront for commercial purposes?

Appurtenant and *In Gross.* These two terms are used to describe how the benefit of an easement, covenant, or equitable servitude is held. A benefit is appurtenant—it appertains to a parcel of land—if it is intended to benefit that parcel of land. A benefit is in gross if, instead of attaching to some parcel of land, it is intended to benefit an individual.

Where the parties have not clearly expressed their intent as to how the benefit should be held, courts will determine intent by looking to the purpose behind the nonpossessory interest. Thus, absent a contrary expressed intent, a court would probably hold that the benefit of the right of way easement across Lakefront is appurtenant to Hillview since it increases the utility of Hillview by giving its occupant access to the nearby lake. The benefit of the affirmative covenant giving Rachel a right of first refusal to Lakefront might also be construed as appurtenant, but it would more likely be held to be in gross since it gives Rachel an economic benefit that is independent of the ownership of Hillview. Courts are generally guided by a strong presumption favoring appurtenant benefits.

Servient Estate and *Dominant Estate.* The servient estate is the parcel that bears the burden of an easement, covenant, or equitable servitude. In the examples above, Lakefront is the servient estate. The dominant estate is the parcel that enjoys the benefit of the easement, covenant, or equitable servitude. Obviously, there will be a dominant estate only if the benefit is appurtenant. In the examples above involving appurtenant benefits, Hillview is the dominant estate.

Does the Burden Run? Does the Benefit Run? Disputes between Rachel and John over enforcement of the agreements created in the examples above could properly be resolved under general contract principles, without resort to special real property doctrines. In each case, Rachel and John are in privity of contract, and contract law is all that is needed to interpret the agreements, to determine whether they have been breached, and to dispense the appropriate remedies.

But what if John sells Lakefront to George Washington Carver who refuses to honor John's undertakings: Does Rachel have an action against George? The answer under contract law is clearly no, for Rachel and George are not in privity of contract. Rachel will, however, have an action against George under real property doctrine if the burden of the particular interest "runs with the land"—i.e., if it's binding on successors in interest to the servient estate. The burden will be held to run with the land only if specific requirements, different for each form of nonpossessory interest, are met.

If Rachel sells Hillview to Black Kettle, can Black Kettle enforce the benefit against John or George, with whom he is not in privity of contract? Again the answer under real property law is yes, but only if the benefit is appurtenant, so that it passes with the dominant estate to Black Kettle, *and* only if specific requirements are met for the benefit to "run with the land." We return to these questions later in this Chapter.

A. EASEMENTS

1. EXPRESS EASEMENTS

The most common form of easements are express easements in which a property owner consciously and purposefully gives someone a nonpossessory interest in his or her land. Affirmative easements are limited only by the drafter's imagination. The most typical easements are utility easements (in which property owners give utilities the right to string or bury utility lines across their properties) and rights of way (in which property owners give others the right to cross their property to reach adjacent areas). Purchasers of interior lots, for example, need easements that connect their properties to public roads, sewers, and power, telephone, and cable lines. Subdivisions often use easements to assure home buyers access to common parking lots, laundry areas, swimming pools, tennis courts, and other common recreational facilities dispersed throughout the development. In shopping centers, Operation and Reciprocal Easement Agreements (or REA's) typically gives each tenant and its customers access to common facilities such as parking areas, entrances, exits, walkways, and commercial spaces.

In addition to these garden variety easements, a quick review of deeds or lawsuits reveals, to sample just a few: pasture easements, allowing ranchers to graze their livestock on the servient estate; drainage or flowage easements, allowing the owner of the dominant estate to divert flood waters over the surface of the servient estate; pollution easements, allowing the discharge of contaminants over and onto the servient estate; aviation easements, allowing aircraft to fly over the servient estate at low altitudes; and encroachment easements, allowing terraces, trees, and window air conditioners from adjacent buildings to overhang the servient estate.

As noted earlier, courts historically did not permit nearly as much variety or innovation in negative easements. The common law for many decades recognized only three—(1) easements for light and air, (2) easements for greater lateral and subjacent support than required by law, and (3) easements for the unimpeded flow of an artificial stream across the dominant estate. The common law, moreover, was slow to recognize new categories, apparently concerned that parties would too freely enter into restrictive land use arrangements that provided no countervailing social benefits.

States today are more receptive to new forms of negative easements, although legal questions linger. Courts in most states, for example, now recognize and enforce express *easements of view* in which the owner of property promises a neighbor not to obstruct her view. See, e.g., Dent v. Lovejoy, 857 A.2d 952 (Conn. App. 2004) (enforcing and liberally interpreting easement designed to protect view of water). State legislatures also have passed statutes authorizing a number of other negative easements (and thus avoiding any question whether the easements are valid under the common law). Prominent among these are conservation easements (see infra p. 927), historic preservation easements, and solar easements (designed to prohibit any improvement on the servient estate that prevents direct sunlight from reaching a solar collector located on the dominant estate).

Whether courts will recognize new forms of negative easements is generally inconsequential because most courts will enforce the same right as a covenant or equitable servitude. However, some differences between easements, on the one hand, and covenants and servitudes, on the other, may make the distinction important. Although American courts have long permitted easements to be held in gross, for example, many courts did not recognize covenants in gross until recently. This is one of the reason why statutes were passed authorizing conservation easements and historic preservation easements, where the benefit is held by non-profit organizations or governments rather than by neighbors. The Restatement proposes eliminating negative easements entirely and treating them as restrictive covenants; at the same time, it would loosen many of the historic restrictions on negative covenants. See Restatement (Third) of Property, Servitudes § 1.2(4) (2000).

A property owner can create an easement by grant or reservation. If Josephine Hensley signs a document giving her neighbor the right to cross her property to get to a public road, Josephine has created an easement by grant or conveyance. If Josephine sells her property to Red Cloud, on the other hand, but expressly retains the right to use the property for ingress or egress to other land she owns, Josephine has created an easement by reservation. For historical reasons, some courts refuse to recognize reservations of easements for the benefit of third parties. See, e.g., Potter v. Chadaz, 977 P.2d 533 (Utah App. 1999); Estate of Thomson, 509 N.E.2d 309 (N.Y. 1987). However, most states, as well as the Restatement of Property, recognize both easements by grant and by reservation. See Bolan

v. Avalon Farms Property Owners Ass'n, 735 A.2d 798 (Conn. 1999); Willard v. First Church of Christ, Scientist, 498 P.2d 987, 989 (Cal. 1972); Restatement (Third) of Property, Servitudes § 2.6(2) (2000).

Express grants or reservations of easements must comply with the same formalities as conveyances of fee simples and other possessory interests. The Statute of Frauds applies and usually requires a written instrument that accurately identifies the servient and the dominant estates and the location and extent of the easement. Parties who fail to reduce their agreement to writing or otherwise fail to comply with the other formalities of an express easement, however, are not necessarily out of luck. Many decisions that find no express easement go on to find an implied easement (see pp. 852–869 infra) or an easement by estoppel (pp. 847–852 infra). Courts, in short, look for other means of enforcing the apparent intent of the parties if the parties have failed to observe all the statutory niceties.

a. INTERPRETING AND APPLYING EXPRESS EASEMENTS

Express easements can raise a number of interpretation questions. Did the parties intend to create an easement, for example, or did they intend to create some form of possessory interest in land such as a fee simple? What is the scope of the easement? Can the easement be used for a new purpose that the parties might not have contemplated?

Railroad rights-of-way have provided a steady source of litigation on these questions in recent years. Railroads hold thousands of miles of rights-of-way across the nation. As rail service has declined, railroads have stopped using many of these rights-of-way to transport freight and passengers. If the railroad owns its right-of-way in fee simple absolute, ceasing to use the right-of-way does not pose a problem. The railroad continues to own the land and is free to use or transfer the land for other purposes. If the railroad owns only an easement, however, the railroad risks losing the right-of-way if it stops using it. As you will read later in this Chapter, if the holder of an easement ceases to use it, a court may in some situations find that the holder has "abandoned" and thus lost the easement. See pp. 948–950.

In 1983, Congress passed the Rails-to-Trails Act, 16 U.S.C. § 1247, to help save railroad rights-of-way and simultaneously meet growing public demand for recreational trails. Experts at the time predicted that approximately 3000 miles of railroad rights-of-way would be lost each year through 2000 as a result of abandonment. If these rights-of-way were ever needed in the future for transportation needs, railroads would find them extremely difficult to reassemble. Congress therefore encouraged railroads who planned to cease operating on particular lines to convey the rights-of-way to states, local governments, or qualified private organizations for recreational use, pending "future reactivation of rail service." Congress authorized the Interstate Commerce Commission (now the National Surface Transportation Board), which regulates railroads, to permit this "railbanking." The Rails-to-Trails Act and other more localized efforts to convert railway rights-of-way into recreational trails has generated a number of legal cases raising two related questions. First, are railroad rights-of-ways fee simple interests or easements? Second, if a particular railroad right-of-way is merely an easement, are biking, running, and other recreational uses within the legitimate scope of the easement?

Chevy Chase Land Company v. United States

Court of Appeals of Maryland, 1999.
733 A.2d 1055.

CHASANOW, J.

This case comes to us by a certified order pursuant to Maryland Code from the United States Court of Appeals for the Federal Circuit. That court seeks our resolution of the parties' state law property disputes.... The questions pertain to a right-of-way in Montgomery County called the "Georgetown Branch" that was granted to a railroad in 1911 and that has been converted for use as a hiker/biker trail under the federal "Rails-to-Trails" Act (the Act)....

I. BACKGROUND

The stipulated facts show the following. The property alleged to have been taken and for which the appellants seek compensation is a strip of land approximately one mile long and 100–feet wide, spanning some 12 acres in Montgomery County, Maryland, that lie on either side and across Connecticut Avenue in Chevy Chase. The mile-long stretch is a segment of an approximately 6.4 mile former railroad line in Montgomery County known as the Georgetown Branch, which runs from Silver Spring southwesterly into the District of Columbia.

The land company was founded in 1890 in part to develop the residential area now known as Chevy Chase and it then owned all the land relevant to this case. In 1891, the land company and the railroad entered into an agreement whereby the land company would convey the "right-of-way" over the mile-long stretch of land and a second parcel "for the purposes of a passenger and freight depot.".... In 1911, after the railroad line had been constructed and in operation for 19 years, the land company executed a deed conveying to the railroad, "its successors and assigns, a free and perpetual right of way" over the land referred to in the 1891 agreement. The deed also conveyed, in "fee simple," the parcel of land on which the depot was to have been built. The railroad paid $4,000 for the conveyance....

[In 1988, the railroad conveyed the entire Georgetown Branch to Montgomery County for a public hiker/biker tail in return for the County's payment of $10 million.] The plaintiffs/appellants assert that the 1911 deed conveyed an easement. They further argue that the proposed use of the easement as a hiker/biker trail is beyond its scope, which they contend is limited to railroad uses.... Defendants/appellees Montgomery County and the United States, on the other hand, argue that the 1911 deed conveyed to the railroad an interest in the right-of-way in fee simple absolute and therefore the appellants have had no interest in the property since 1911. Alternatively, should the deed be found to have conveyed an easement, they contend that the use of the right-of-way as a hiker/biker trail ... is within the scope of the easement....

II. THE RAILROAD'S PROPERTY INTEREST

The first question asks whether the 1911 deed conveyed an interest in fee simple absolute or an easement....

In railroad parlance, "the term 'right of way' has two meanings: in one sense it is 'the strip of land upon which the track is laid'; in the other sense it is 'the legal right to use such strip,' and in this sense it usually means the right of way *easement*." Ma. & Pa. RR. Co. v. Mer.–Safe, Etc., Co., 224 Md. 34, 36–37 n.1, 166 A.2d 247, 248 n.1 (1960) (quoting Quinn v. Pere Marquette Ry. Co., 256 Mich. 143, 239 N.W. 376, 379 (1931)). See also Joy v. City of St. Louis, 138 U.S. 1, 44 (1891) ("The term 'right of way' ... sometimes is used to describe a right belonging to a party, a right of passage over any tract; and it is also used to describe that strip of land which railroad companies take upon which to construct their road-bed.").

Nevertheless, it has generally been held by courts of this and other states that "deeds which in the granting clause convey a 'right of way' are held to convey an easement only." Deed to Railroad Company as Conveying Fee or Easement, Annotation, 6 A.L.R.3d 973, § 3, at 977 (1966). As explained in Professor Elliott's 1907 treatise on railroad law:

> " 'Right of way,' in its strict meaning, is 'the right of passage over another man's ground;' and in its legal and generally accepted meaning, in reference to a railway, it is a mere easement in the lands of others, obtained by lawful condemnation to public use or by purchase. It would be using the term in an unusual sense, by applying it to an absolute purchase of the fee-simple of lands to be used for a railway or any other kind of way."

2 Elliott on Railroads § 1158, at 628 n.77 (3d. ed. 1907)....

The general rule that the terms "right-of-way" and "easement" are synonymous came about because the rule is consistent with the likely intent of the parties to a deed when the term "right-of-way" is used. As we observed in Green Tr. v. Eldridge, 230 Md. 441, 448, 187 A.2d 674, 678 (1963): "The fact that the word 'easement' was not used to designate the property interest passing is not of particular significance, since use of the phrase 'right of way' is generally understood to mean that only an easement is being granted."

Furthermore, policy considerations support interpreting the conveyance of a "right-of-way" to a railroad as an easement where the intent to convey an estate in fee is not clearly expressed. A great number of railroad corridors have been abandoned in recent years. See Preseault v. ICC, 494 U.S. 1, 5 (1990)(observing that the nation's railway system has lost about 130,000 miles of track since 1920 and noting that "experts predict that 3,000 miles will be abandoned every year through the end of this century").

Whether a right-of-way is construed as an estate in fee simple or an easement has significant implications for the utility of the land upon abandonment. If the deed of a right-of-way is construed as an estate in fee simple, the railroad will retain the right-of-way even after it is no longer used for any transit purposes—effectively severing otherwise contiguous pieces of property, and for no useful purpose. As the Indiana Supreme Court has explained:

> "Public policy does not favor the conveyance of strips of land by simple titles to railroad companies for right-of-way purposes, either by deed or condemnation. This policy is based upon the fact that the alienation of such strips or belts of land from and across the primary or parent bodies of the land from which they are severed[] is obviously not necessary to the purpose for which such conveyances are made after abandonment of the intended uses as expressed in the conveyance, and that thereafter such severance generally operates adversely to the normal and best use of all the property involved."

Ross, Inc. v. Legler, 245 Ind. 655, 199 N.E.2d 346, 348 (Ind. 1964). We have previously recognized that the construction of a right-of-way as a fee simple would not further any significant interest that is not served by construction as an easement. See D. C. Transit Systems v. S.R.C., 259 Md. 675, 688, 270 A.2d 793, 800 (1970) (construing a deed to a railroad as an easement in part because it would not serve any useful purpose to convey "a strip of land 80 feet wide" as an estate in fee).

This is not to say that a deed conveying a "right of way" to a railroad cannot convey an estate in fee simple. It is well settled that a deed to a railroad, even though it characterizes the grant as conveying a right-of-way, may convey an estate in fee simple. However, when a deed conveying a right-of-way fails to express a clear intent to convey a different interest in land, a presumption arises that an easement was intended. . . .

In conclusion, the use of the term "right-of-way" in the deed provides a strong indication that the railroad and the land company intended the 1911 deed to convey an easement. Our cases and the cases from other states consistently have construed deeds to railroads of "rights-of-way" as conveying easements and not estates in fee simple absolute. The language of the deed at issue in this case provides no reason to deviate from our previous cases. This is especially the case in light of the dual granting clauses of Parcel A, conveying a "right of way" and Parcel B, conveying the parcel "in fee simple." Finally, the circumstances of the deed confirm the conclusion that the deed conveyed an easement only. In particular, . . . the nominal consideration given the land company by the railroad is a factor more consistent with the conveyance of an easement than an estate in fee simple absolute.

III. THE SCOPE OF THE EASEMENT

Since we have determined that the 1911 deed granted an easement, we must now consider the second certified question regarding the scope of the easement. We initially determine whether the express language of the deed limits the available uses of the right-of-way. After that determination, we consider the extent to which Maryland common law on railroad easements imposes any implied limits on use of the right-of-way that would prevent the right-of-way in the instant case from being used for a hiker/biker trail. This part then concludes with an examination of whether the use of the right-of-way for a hiker/biker trail unreasonably increases the burden of the easement on the servient estates.

Appellants contend that the proposed interim use of the right-of-way as a hiker/biker trail is beyond the scope of the easement. Instead of the language of the deed, appellants emphasize the circumstances at the time of the original agreement between the railroad and the land company in 1891, contending that the "evidence is clear" that the land company intended that the easement was for purposes of freight railroad only.... Appellees, on the other hand, emphasize the deed itself, which contains no express limitations on the right-of-way conveyed. They contend that the easement was for a right-of-way to be used for general transportation purposes and that its use as a recreational trail is consistent with those purposes and imposes no additional burden on the servient estates.

We agree with appellees that the primary consideration in construing the scope of an express easement is the language of the grant. "The extent of the rights [of an easement acquired by express grant] must necessarily depend upon a proper construction of the conveyance or that part of it by which the easement was created." Parker v. T & C Dev. Corp., 281 Md. 704, 709, 381 A.2d 679, 682 (1978). No language in the deed in the instant case suggests that the right-of-way was limited to railroad purposes only (and much less so to *freight* railroad purposes, as the land company contends). The deed conveyed a "free and perpetual right of way." The use of the terms "free" and "perpetual" provide a clear indication that few, if any, conditions were intended to be placed on the railroad's use of the right-of-way. "Free" is defined as "not [being] subject to [the] legal constraint of another." Black's Law Dictionary 663 (6th ed. 1990). The use of the term "perpetual" clearly indicates that the easement was intended to be of indefinite duration and, particularly when combined with the term "free," suggests that the use of the easement was to be dynamic, i.e., adaptable to the evolving circumstances and transit needs of those intended to benefit from the right-of-way—in particular the general public whom the land company was attempting to attract to the areas served by the railroad. The language making the easement transferable to "successors and assigns" further supports a broad construction of the deed language.

Unlike many of the grants of easements that we have addressed in the past, the deed in the instant case does not suggest any limit on the use of the right-of-way. It is clear that a right of passage was granted, and, as noted above in Part II, the circumstances clearly indicate that the original instrumentality was a railroad. But nowhere in the granting clause or elsewhere in the deed does the language suggest that a railroad was the only instrumentality for use of the perpetual right-of-way....

While the deed presents no express limitations on the use of the right-of-way, that does not end our analysis. Keeping in mind the broad language in the grant, we must determine whether the appellees have the right to substitute, at least for the interim, the use of the right-of-way as a recreational trail for the previous use of the right-of-way as a railroad corridor. We must consider whether the use of the right-of-way as a hiker/biker trail is of the same quality of use as anticipated in the original grant and whether it imposes any unreasonable new burdens on the dominant tenement. Before analyzing those questions, we note that because of the broad language of the grant any doubts about its use will be resolved in favor of the grantee, *i.e.*, the railroad:

> "If the grant contains no limitations, the court will attempt to discern what the parties would have reasonably expected, and will usually be generous in its interpretation. The language of the easement can grant to the easement holder a good deal of discretion in the use of the easement or limit the use very narrowly; if the grant is not clear, the court will interpret the scope of the easement in favor of 'free and untrammeled use of the land.'"

7 Thompson on Real Property § 60.04(a), at 451 (Thomas ed. 1994). . . .

Our highway cases have construed easements for public highways as including within their scope changing means of transportation. In Water Co. vs. Dubreuil, 105 Md. 424, 66 A. 439 (1907), we explained that

> "we have been governed by the fact that such [electric railway] uses, of both streets and rural highways, were only new modes of travel and transportation, and the right, originally acquired, to use them was not simply for the then existing modes, but for all such as might arise in the ordinary course of improvement. It could therefore be presumed that such improved modes of travel and transportation were within the contemplation of the parties. . . ."

. . . .

We believe it indisputable that use of the right-of-way as a trail is consistent with its essential nature relating to the "passing over land of another" and is a reasonable use of a general right of way. Accordingly, the scope of the right-of-way in the instant case encompasses use as a hiker/biker trail. It follows from our cases that the fact that a recreational trail may not have been actually contemplated by the parties when the deed was conveyed in 1911 is not outcome determinative. Rather, we assume that the parties anticipated that the use of the right-of-way would conform over time to the reasonable demands of the public. . . .

Use of the right-of-way as a hiker/biker trail constitutes a change in instrumentality consistent with the essential purpose anticipated at the time of the original grant in 1911—passage through Silver Spring, Chevy Chase, and Bethesda. The primary change is one of instrumentality from railcars to bikes and walking, and our highway cases make clear that changes in mode of use are presumed to be within the contemplation of the parties. Indeed, the state legislature has seen fit to define "highway" as including "bicycle and walking paths." Md. Code (1977, 1993 Repl. Vol., 1998 Supp.), Transportation Art., § 8–101(I)(1). As the South Dakota Supreme Court stated, "the Railroad has transferred the right-of-way to the State for use as a public highway. Hikers, bikers, skiers, and snowmobilers will use the right-of-way, and, as such, the right-of-way will continue to be used as a public highway compatible and consistent with its prior use as a public railway." Barney v. Burlington Northern R. Co., 490 N.W.2d 726, 732 (S.D. 1992).

We must next consider whether use of the right-of-way as a hiker/biker trail unreasonably increases the burden on the underlying fee simple estates. It is "the generally accepted rule that since an easement is a restriction upon the rights of the servient property owner, no alteration can be made by the owner of the dominant estate which would increase such restriction except by mutual consent of both parties." Reid v. Washington Gas Lt. Co., 232 Md. 545, 548–49, 194 A.2d 636, 638 (1963). As we explained in *Washington Gas Lt. Co.*, the test used to determine whether the restriction on the servient estate, *i.e.*, the burden imposed, is

> "whether the change is so substantial as to result in the creation and substitution of a different servitude from that which previously existed. In other words, if the alteration is merely one of quality and not substance there will be no resulting surcharge to the servient estate."

It is self-evident that the use of the right-of-way as a transportation corridor for walking, biking, and other transportation purposes, including its possible use in the future for light rail, imposes no new burdens on the servient tenements and does not result in the "substitution of a different servitude from that which previously existed." Id. . . .

In comparison to our public highway cases that have permitted a change in use from a highway to a horse or an electric railway, the change of use proposed in the instant case is considerably less burdensome. That use of the right-of-way by bikers and walkers poses less of a burden than the use required by a freight train is obvious. Bikers and walkers, even in large groups, simply cannot be said to be more burdensome than locomotive engines pulling truck-sized railroad cars through the corridor. . . . [Indeed,] the change in use in this case actually decreases the burden on the servient tenement because, *inter alia*, the shift is from an exclusive to a non-exclusive use. In this case, the owners of the underlying fee estates with property abutting the Georgetown Branch have access to a corridor to which they did not have access prior to conversion to a trail.

The fact that the right-of-way may be used for recreational as well as transportation purposes has no bearing on our analysis, since the "recreation" involved—biking and hiking—consists of the enjoyment one may have in transporting oneself. Indeed, that hiking and biking may be recreational in addition to fulfilling transportation needs is not all that different from the enjoyment that some derive from driving a car or even riding a train; the enjoyment that some derive from those activities does not detract from their essential character as transportation-related. Indeed, by the very nature of the right-of-way—a confined, narrow strip of land—the "recreational" use is limited to those uses involving *transportation* itself, including biking, running, and walking, each of which involves moving from one place to another. . . .

[In a final section of the option, the court considered and rejected the plaintiffs claim that the railroad had abandoned the easement prior to transferring it to the county for recreational use.]

Notes & Questions

1. **Easement Versus Fee Simple.** In City of Manhattan v. Superior Court, 914 P.2d 160 (Cal. 1996), the California Supreme Court found that a provision very similar to the language in *Chevy Chase Land Co.* created a fee simple rather than an easement. In 1888, the Redondo Land Company for a consideration of $1 "remise[d], release[d] and quit-claim[ed]" to the Atchison, Topeka, and Santa Fe Railway Company (Santa Fe) "the right of way for the construction, maintenance and operation of a Steam Railroad, upon, over and along" a strip of land running through what today is the Los Angeles suburb of Manhattan Beach. Santa Fe stopped using the strip for railroad purposes in 1982 and sold its interest to Manhattan Beach in 1986 for a jogging path and park. In 1987, heirs to the successors in interest of the Redondo Land Company sued to quiet title.[1] The key question was whether the quoted language created an easement or a fee simple.

The California Supreme Court found the language inconclusive. According to the court, the granting clause ("remise, release, and quit-claim") is more consistent with the grant of a fee simple than the conveyance of an easement, while the term "right of way," as well as the words "upon, over and along" usually refer to easements. Under California statutory law, however, "the law presumes '[a] fee simple title is . . . intended to pass by a grant of real property, unless it appears from the grant that a lesser estate was intended.' " Id. at 167, quoting Cal. Civ. Code § 1105. And documents subsequent to the grant suggested that the parties had intended a fee simple. Finally, the court concluded that a fee simple was more consistent with the Redondo Land Company's motivation to get the railroad to extend its tracks to Manhattan Beach. Three justices dissented.

What constructional preferences should courts use in interpreting ambiguous language? While the California Supreme Court adopted a fee-simple preference in *City of Manhattan*, the Maryland Court of Appeals argued that public policy favors easements. See also Brown v. Penn Central

1. The case was instigated by John P. Farquahar and Ricardo Bandini Johnson, two "hobbyist 'heir hunters' " who claimed to be heirs of the Redondo Land Company and set out to locate other heirs for purposes of filing the lawsuit. 914 P.2d 162 n.1. Claiming to be heirs to the original grantors of a 430-acre veterans' center in West Los Angeles, Farquahar and Johnson have also organized other heirs to object to the government's expanded use of that land. See Bob Pool, Seeking Tighter Control of VA Land, Los Angeles Times, January 23, 2000, p. B1.

Corp., 510 N.E.2d 641, 644 (Ind. 1987) (public policy favors easements when strips of land are involved).

2. **Scope of Railway Easements.** Courts also have split on the scope of railway rights-of-way, with some courts holding that the rights-of-way allow for recreational use and others holding that they permit only traditional railroad uses. In Preseault v. United States, 100 F.3d 1525 (Fed. Cir. 1996), for example, the Federal Circuit Court concluded that the grant of a right-of-way to a railroad for its "proper use, benefit and behoof forever" did not permit use as a recreational trail.

> When the easements here were granted to the Preseaults' predecessors in title at the turn of the century, specifically for transportation of goods and persons via railroad, could it be said that the parties contemplated that a century later the easements would be used for recreational hiking and biking trails, or that it was necessary to so construe them in order to give the grantee railroad that for which it bargained? We think not. Although a public recreational trail could be described as a roadway for the transportation of persons, the nature of the usage is clearly different. In the one case, the grantee is a commercial enterprise using the easement in its business, the transport of goods and people for compensation. In the other, the easement belongs to the public, and is open for use for recreational purposes, which happens to involve people engaged in exercise or recreation on foot or on bicycles. It is difficult to imagine that either party to the original transfers had anything remotely in mind that would resemble a public recreational trail.
>
> Furthermore, there are differences in the degree and nature of the burden imposed on the servient estate. It is one thing to have occasional railroad trains crossing one's land. Noisy though they may be, they are limited in location, in number, and in frequency of occurrence. Particularly is this so on a relatively remote spur. When used for public recreational purposes, however, in a region that is environmentally attractive, the burden imposed by the use of the easement is at the whim of many individuals, and, as the record attests, has been impossible to contain in numbers or to keep strictly within the parameters of the easement.

Should the scope of an easement ever include a use that the parties would not even have imagined at the time that the easement was negotiated? If so, how should a court go about determining whether the new use is within the scope of the easement?

3. What's the relevance in cases like *Chevy Chase Land Co.* of the public interest in recreational trails? The federal Rails-to-Trails Act has been enormously successful. As of 2001, the Act had created more than 100,000 miles of recreational trails throughout the United States. Richard A. Allen, Does the Rails-to-Trails Act Effect a Taking of Property?, 31 Transportation L.J. 35, 35 (2003).

4. For fascinating histories and discussions of the legal issues surrounding current ownership and use of railroad rights of way (including the question of what was originally conveyed), see Allen, supra note 3; Danaya C. Wright & Jeffrey M. Hester, Pipes, Wires, and Bicycles: Rails-to-Trails, Utility Licenses, and the Shifting Scope of Railroad Easements from the Nineteenth to the Twenty–First Centuries, 27 Ecology L.Q. 351 (2000).

Marcus Cable Associates v. Krohn

Supreme Court of Texas, 2002.
90 S.W.3d 697.

JUSTICE O'NEILL delivered the opinion of the Court.

In this case, we must decide whether an easement that permits its holder to use private property for the purpose of constructing and maintaining "an electric transmission or distribution line or system" allows the easement to be used for cable-television lines. We hold that it does not....

This case centers around the scope of a property interest granted over sixty years ago. In 1939, Alan and Myrna Krohn's predecessors in interest granted to the Hill County Electric Cooperative an easement that allows the cooperative to use their property for the purpose of constructing and maintaining "an electric transmission or distribution line or system." The easement further granted the right to remove trees and vegetation "to the extent necessary to keep them clear of said electric line or system."

In 1991, Hill County Electric entered into a "Joint Use Agreement" with a cable-television provider, which later assigned its rights under the agreement to Marcus Cable Associates, L.P. Under the agreement, Marcus Cable obtained permission from Hill County Electric to attach its cable lines to the cooperative's poles. The agreement permitted Marcus Cable to "furnish television antenna service" to area residents, and allowed the cable wires to be attached only "to the extent [the cooperative] may lawfully do so." The agreement further provided that the electric cooperative did not warrant or assure any "right-of-way privileges or easements," and that Marcus Cable "shall be responsible for obtaining its own easements and rights-of-way."

Seven years later, the Krohns sued Marcus Cable, alleging that the company did not have a valid easement and had placed its wires over their property without their knowledge or consent. The Krohns asserted a trespass claim, and alleged that Marcus Cable was negligent in failing to obtain their consent before installing the cable lines. The Krohns sought an injunction ordering the cable wires' removal, as well as actual and exemplary damages. In defense, Marcus Cable asserted a right to use Hill County Electric's poles under the cooperative's easement and under Texas statutory law....

We apply basic principles of contract construction and interpretation when considering an express easement's terms. The contracting parties' intentions, as expressed in the grant, determine the scope of the conveyed interest.

When the grant's terms are not specifically defined, they should be given their plain, ordinary, and generally accepted meaning. An easement's express terms, interpreted according to their generally accepted meaning, therefore delineate the purposes for which the easement holder may use the property. Thus, if a particular purpose is not provided for in the grant, a use pursuing that purpose is not allowed. If the rule were otherwise, "then the typical power line or pipeline easement, granted for the purpose of constructing and maintaining a power line or pipeline across specified property, could be used for any other purpose, unless the grantor by specific language negated all other purposes." Kearney & Son v. Fancher, 401 S.W.2d 897, 904–05 (Tex. Civ. App. 1966).

The common law does allow some flexibility in determining an easement holder's rights. In particular, the manner, frequency, and intensity of an easement's use may change over time to accommodate technological development. But such changes must fall within the purposes for which the easement was created, as determined by the grant's terms. Thus, contrary to Marcus Cable's argument, an express easement encompasses only those technological developments that further the particular purpose for which the easement was granted. Otherwise, easements would effectively become possessory, rather than nonpossessory, land interests.

The emphasis our law places upon an easement's express terms serves important public policies by promoting certainty in land transactions. In order to evaluate the burdens placed upon real property, a potential purchaser must be able to safely rely upon granting language. Similarly, those who grant easements should be assured that their conveyances will not be construed to undermine private-property rights—like the rights to "exclude others" or to "obtain a profit"—any more than what was intended in the grant.

Marcus Cable suggests that we should give greater weight to the public benefit that results from the wide distribution of cable-television services, arguing that technological advancement in Texas will be substantially impeded if the cooperative's easement is not read to encompass cable-television use. But even if that were so, we may not circumvent the contracting parties' intent by disregarding the easement's express terms and the specific purpose for which it was granted. Adhering to basic easement principles, we must decide not what is most convenient to the public or profitable to Marcus Cable, but what purpose the contracting parties intended the easement to serve....

Finally, Marcus Cable contends that its use should be allowed because attaching cable-television wires to Hill County Electric's utility poles does not materially increase the burden to the servient estate. But again, if a use does not serve the easement's express purpose, it becomes an unauthorized presence on the land whether or not it results in any noticeable burden to the servient estate. Thus, the threshold inquiry is not whether the proposed use results in a material burden, but whether the grant's terms authorize the proposed use. With these principles in mind, we turn to the easement at issue in this case. . . .

. . . . Marcus Cable cites a number of decisions in other jurisdictions that have allowed the use of easements predating cable technology to allow installation of cable transmission lines.

The cases Marcus Cable cites, however, involve different granting language and do not support the proposition that we may disregard the parties' expressed intentions or expand the purposes for which an easement may be used. To the contrary, those cases involve easements containing much broader granting language than the easement before us. Most of them involved easements granted for communications media, such as telegraph and telephone, in addition to electric utility easements. In concluding that the easements were broad enough to encompass cable, the reviewing courts examined the purpose for which the easement was granted and essentially concluded that the questioned use was a more technologically advanced means of accomplishing the same communicative purpose.

For example, in Salvaty v. Falcon Cable Television, 212 Cal. Rptr. 31 (Cal. App. 1985), the 1926 easement permitted its holder to maintain both electric wires *and* telephone wires. The court held that cable-television lines were within the easement's scope, observing that cable television is "part of the natural evolution of *communications* technology." Id. at 34–35 (emphasis added). Similarly, the Fourth Circuit held that an easement allowing its holder to use the land for the purpose of maintaining pole lines for "electrical and telephone service" was sufficiently broad to encompass cable-television lines. C/R TV, Inc. v. Shannondale, Inc., 27 F.3d 104, 106, 109–10 (4th Cir. 1994) (applying West Virginia law). In reaching its conclusion, the court relied on the similar communicative aspects of both "telephone services" and cable-television services. Id. at 109–10. Other cases Marcus Cable cites also involved easements granted for communications-transmission purposes.

We express no opinion about whether the cases Marcus Cable relies upon were correctly decided. But, unlike the cases Marcus Cable cites, Hill County Electric's easement does not convey the right to use the property for purposes of transmitting communications. While cable television may utilize electrical impulses to transmit communications, as Marcus Cable claims, television transmission is not a more technologically advanced method of delivering electricity. Thus, the above-referenced cases do not support Marcus Cable's argument that the easement here encompasses the additional purpose of transmitting television content to the public. . . .

In sum, the easement language here, properly construed, does not permit cable-television lines to be strung across the Krohns' land without their consent. However laudable the goal of extending cable service might be, we cannot disregard the easement's express terms to enlarge its purposes beyond those intended by the contracting parties. . . .

JUSTICE HECHT, dissenting.

The electric television (not its short-lived electro-mechanical predecessor) was conceived in 1921 by fourteen-year-old Philo Farnsworth, who made a working model in 1927, twelve years before RCA's National Broadcasting Company first began regular telecasts from the World's Fair in New York City, and H. W. and Ruth Curtis granted Hill County Electric Cooperative an easement on their land north of Sardis, Texas, "to place, construct, operate, repair, maintain, relocate and replace ... an electric transmission and distribution line or system." After 1939, television took off. Cable television is said to have originated in 1948 when John Walson of Mahanoy City, Pennsylvania, used a twin-lead wire to transmit an electric signal from a remote antenna to his store to demonstrate to his customers how reception could be improved and thereby increase his sales of the newfangled television sets. The Curtises no doubt intended that by granting the Co-op an easement, wires strung on poles erected on their property would be used to transmit electric current to power lights and appliances. They probably did not envision that one such appliance in the Sardis area would be a television set. And they could not possibly have imagined that televisions powered by the electric current carried by lines over their easement would have better reception if supplied with an electric signal transmitted over another look-alike line hung on the same poles, even if the Curtises had been as precocious as Philo Farnsworth himself.

So if the question is, what were the Curtises thinking in 1939 when they gave the Co-op an easement for "an electric transmission and distribution line or system," the answer is easy: they were thinking about electric power, not an electric cable television signal, even though both are electric. But that's not the question because, as the Court correctly holds, the scope of an easement is measured by the parties' intent as expressed in the words used, broadened by changes in the manner, frequency, and intensity of the intended use that are due to technological advances and do not unreasonably burden the servient estate. An easement need not accommodate unintended uses merely because they present no additional burden, nor can an easement be enlarged merely because additional uses would benefit the public. But a use that is within the language of an easement as it has come to be understood with changes in technology is not prohibited simply because it was not part of the parties' original thinking. So the question in this case is whether a cable carrying an electric television signal to various users is "an electric transmission and distribution line or system" as we have come to understand more of what those words entail.

Now if one were to stick just to the words, the answer would clearly be yes. A television cable is a "line." A television signal is "electric," assuming, as the Court does, that the cable is not fiber optic (although even if the cable were fiber optic, the signal would still start out electric at the transmitter and end up electric at the receiver). Sending the signal is "an electric transmission." Transmitting it among a number of users is "an electric distribution." Thus, a television cable is "an electric transmission and distribution line." Looking at a pole carrying lines transmitting electric power and a line transmitting television signals, a person unfamiliar with differences in the physics of the transmissions could not tell which was which....

In fact, Marcus Cable asserts that no case in the country has ever barred cable television from an easement for electric transmissions, and neither the Krohns nor the Court has found one. Today's decision stands alone in the nation athwart the path to providing cable television and related services to rural areas.... I would hold that the easement in the present case can be shared with a cable television provider if the servient estate is not additionally burdened....

Notes & Questions

1. *Marcus Cable Associates* poses the question of whether courts should help promote technological changes by interpreting easements flexibly or should ensure stability in property rights by interpreting easements more rigidly. So long as a new use of an easement will not expand the burden on the servient estate, is there any reason why courts should not interpret easements flexibly? As the dissent points out in *Marcus Cable Associates*, the vast majority of courts to have considered the issue have held that easements for power and/or telephone lines include cable television.

2. Does the Texas Supreme Court in *Marcus Cable Associates* take a narrower view of the scope of the electric cooperative's right-of-way than the Maryland Court of Appeals takes of the railroad right-of-way in *Chevy Chase Land Co.*? Recall that the Maryland Court of Appeals emphasized that railroad rights-of-way are like public highways and that courts have traditionally given broad scope to easements for public highways. Should easements with public purposes, such as easements for a roadway or railroad, be interpreted more flexibly than purely private easements? Was the purpose underlying the easement in *Marcus Cable Associates* public or private?

3. **Relocating Easements.** As a result of shifts in circumstance on the servient or dominant estate, the location of an easement that made sense a century ago may make little sense today. In Davis v. Bruk, 411 A.2d 660 (Me. 1980), the trial court decree relocated a right-of-way easement that had originally been located across defendant Bruk's land in 1896, on the ground that "the approved relocated route would not create an unreasonable burden upon the plaintiffs, and ... would alleviate Bruk's problems with dust and traffic hazards posed by the use of the existing right of way." The Maine Supreme Court reversed, noting that the "great majority" of state courts do not permit changes in the location of an easement unless the parties agree to a change or the easement expressly authorizes relocations. The court refused to carve out an exception, on the ground that it would "definitely introduce considerable uncertainty into land ownership, as well as upon the real estate market, and serve to proliferate litigation which the general rule as prevails in Maine has tended to prevent. Indeed, the owner of the dominant estate would be deprived of the

present security of his property rights in the servient estate and could be subjected to harassment by the servient owner's attempts at relocation to serve his own conveniences." Id. at 665. Accord Herren v. Pettengill, 538 S.E.2d 735 (Ga. 2000).

In Lewis v. Young, 705 N.E.2d 649 (N.Y. 1998), by contrast, the New York Court of Appeals decided that the owner of a servient estate should be entitled to, "consonant with the beneficial use and development of its property, ... move [a] right of way, so long as the landowner bears the expense of the relocation, and so long as the change does not frustrate the parties' intent or object in creating the right of way, does not increase the burden on the easement holder, and does not significantly lessen the utility of the right of way." See also Restatement (Third) of Property, Servitudes § 4.8 (authorizing the owner of the servient estate to "make reasonable changes in the location or dimensions of an easement" under similar circumstances); Note, The Right of Owners of Servient Estates to Relocate Easements Unilaterally, 109 Harv. L. Rev. 1693 (1996).

b. APPURTENANT EASEMENTS VERSUS EASEMENTS IN GROSS

O'Neill v. Williams

Supreme Judicial Court of Maine, 1987.
527 A.2d 322.

CLIFFORD, Justice.

Margaret Williams appeals the judgment of the Superior Court, Knox County, declaring that Thomas O'Neill had an easement over a narrow strip of land that Williams owns on Vinalhaven Island and which lies between O'Neill's land and a tidal cove locally known as the Basin. We affirm the judgment of the Superior Court.

The parties stipulated to the following facts. In 1882, Moses Webster, from whom O'Neill ultimately derives title, conveyed a narrow strip of land to Williams' predecessor in title. The strip of land lay along the margin of the Basin and deprived the land Webster retained of access to the sea. Nevertheless, the deed contained the following language: "Reserve being had for said Moses Webster the right of way by land or water."

O'Neill, who acquired his land in 1984, brought this action to establish his title to an easement over the narrow strip of land now owned by Williams, basing his claim on the clause in the 1882 deed. The Superior Court concluded that by the clause Webster reserved an easement appurtenant to the land he retained, which in turn passed to O'Neill as possessor of the dominant tenement.

The issue confronting us is whether the reservation clause in the 1882 deed created in Moses Webster an easement in gross or an easement appurtenant to the land that he retained. An easement in gross is a purely personal right, is not assignable, and terminates upon the death of the individual for whom it was created. By contrast, an easement appurtenant is created to benefit the dominant tenement and therefore runs with the land. The right and burden relative to an appurtenant easement respectively pass to grantees of the dominant and servient tenements, assuming the grantees of the servient tenement have actual or constructive notice of the easement.

The traditional rules of construction for grants or reservations of easements require that whenever possible an easement be fairly construed to be appurtenant to the land of the person for whose use the easement is created....

This approach should be followed here. As a littoral property owner Webster clearly intended that the easement across the land conveyed should benefit the land he retained. Otherwise access to water was cut off by the conveyance, appreciably diminishing the value of the retained land.... We conclude that the Superior Court correctly determined that the easement is appurtenant to O'Neill's land which is the dominant tenement.

Notes & Questions

1. **Is the Benefit Appurtenant or in Gross?** The question whether an easement is appurtenant or in gross involves a determination of the intent of those who created the easement. The Restatement suggests that the principal inquiry in determining the parties' intent is the relative value of the easement when appurtenant versus when held in gross. A servitude is appurtenant "if it serves a purpose that would be more useful to a successor to a property interest held by the original beneficiary of the servitude at the time that the servitude was created than it would be to the original beneficiary after transfer of that interest to a successor." Restatement (Third) of Property, Servitudes § 4.5(1)(a) (2000).

Most courts indulge a strong constructional preference for easements appurtenant. So long as there is a dominant estate to which the easement can be said to appertain, and so long as grantor and grantee have not clearly demonstrated an intent that the easement be in gross, the court will probably find an easement appurtenant. See id. § 4.5(2) ("In cases of doubt, a benefit should be construed to be appurtenant rather than in gross").

In cases of doubt, is there any reason why the law should prefer appurtenant easements over easement in gross? One argument is that the holder of an appurtenant easement, who is typically a neighbor and can always be tracked down through local property records, may often be easier to find than the holder of an easement in gross. Are there any counterarguments? If so, are there situations where they outweigh the arguments in favor of appurtenance?

2. **Does the Burden Run?** *O'Neill* deals with the question whether the benefit of an easement is held in gross or is appurtenant to a specific parcel of land. An equally important question is whether the burden of the

easement runs with the land. If John Wesley Powell grants a right-of-way across his property to his neighbor, Rachel Carson, does the easement last only so long as John owns the property? Or are all future owners of the property also bound by the easement?

As a general rule, the burden of an easement will run, and the future owners of the servient estate will be bound, if two requirements are met: (1) John and Rachel must have intended that the burden run, and (2) the current owner of the servient estate must have had notice of the easement at the time she acquired the property.

Intent. In the case of express easements, courts will divine the necessary intent from the language of the instrument and from the nature of the easement. Language of the following character clearly signifies an intent to bind successors:

[9.1] John, for himself, and for his successors, assigns, and licensees, grants a right-of-way across the property.

Even absent words of this nature, a court is likely to infer an intent that the burden run if Rachel's reasonable expectations, and the easement's utility, depend upon the easement's continued force, without regard to who owns the servient estate. Does the easement at issue in *O'Neill* run with the land? If you had been Margaret Williams, what arguments could you have made that it did not? How do you believe the Maine Supreme Court would have resolved the question?

Notice. To be bound, the current owner of the servient estate also must have had actual, constructive, or inquiry notice of the easement at the time she acquired the putative servient estate. See pages 445–469 supra.

c. TRANSFERRING EASEMENTS IN GROSS

Miller v. Lutheran Conference & Camp Association

Supreme Court of Pennsylvania, 1938.
200 A. 646.

Opinion By MR. JUSTICE STERN.

This litigation is concerned with interesting and somewhat novel legal questions regarding rights of boating, bathing and fishing in an artificial lake.

Frank C. Miller, his brother Rufus W. Miller, and others, who owned lands on Tunkhannock Creek in Tobyhanna Township, Monroe County, organized a corporation known as the Pocono Spring Water Ice Company, to which, in September, 1895, they made a lease for a term of ninety-nine years of so much of their lands as would be covered by the backing up of the water as a result of the construction of a 14–foot dam which they proposed to erect across the creek. The company was to have "the exclusive use of the water and its privileges." It was chartered for the purpose of "erecting a dam ..., for pleasure, boating, skating, fishing and the cutting, storing and selling of ice." The dam was built, forming "Lake Naomi," somewhat more than a mile long and about one-third of a mile wide.

By deed dated March 20, 1899, the Pocono Spring Water Ice Company granted to "Frank C. Miller, his heirs and assigns forever, the exclusive right to fish and boat in all the waters of the said corporation at Naomi Pines, Pa." On February 17, 1900, Frank C. Miller (his wife Katherine D. Miller not joining) granted to Rufus W. Miller, his heirs and assigns forever, "all the one-fourth interest in and to the fishing, boating, and bathing rights and privileges at, in, upon and about Lake Naomi . . . ; which said rights and privileges were granted and conveyed to me by the Pocono Spring Water Ice Company by their indenture of the 20th day of March, A.D. 1899." On the same day Frank C. Miller and Rufus W. Miller executed an agreement of business partnership, the purpose of which was the erection and operation of boat and bath houses on Naomi Lake and the purchase and maintenance of boats for use on the lake, the houses and boats to be rented for hire and the net proceeds to be divided between the parties in proportion to their respective interests in the bathing, boating and fishing privileges, namely, three-fourths to Frank C. Miller and one-fourth to Rufus W. Miller, the capital to be contributed and the losses to be borne in the same proportion. In pursuance of this agreement the brothers erected and maintained boat and bath houses at different points on the lake, purchased and rented out boats, and conducted the business generally, from the spring of 1900 until the death of Rufus W. Miller on October 11, 1925, exercising their control and use of the privileges in an exclusive, uninterrupted and open manner and without challenge on the part of anyone.

Discord began with the death of Rufus W. Miller, which terminated the partnership. Thereafter Frank C. Miller, and the executors and heirs of Rufus W. Miller, went their respective ways, each granting licenses without reference to the other. Under date of July 13, 1929, the executors of the Rufus W. Miller estate granted a license for the year 1929 to defendant, Lutheran Conference and Camp Association, which was the owner of a tract of ground abutting on the lake for a distance of about 100 feet, purporting to grant to defendant, its members, guests and campers, permission to boat, bathe and fish in the lake, a certain percentage of the receipts therefrom to be paid to the estate. Thereupon Frank C. Miller and his wife, Katherine D. Miller, filed the present bill in equity, complaining that defendant was placing diving floats on the lake and "encouraging and instigating visitors and boarders" to bathe in the lake, and was threatening to hire out boats and canoes and in general to license its guests and others to boat, bathe and fish in the lake. The bill prayed for an injunction to prevent defendant from trespassing on the lands covered by the waters of the lake, from erecting or maintaining any structures or other encroachments thereon, and from granting any bathing licenses. The court issued the injunction.

[The court began by finding that Frank C. Miller enjoyed an easement in gross for boating, fishing, and bathing. All parties agreed that Frank C.

Miller held an express easement for boating and fishing. The court also concluded that he also had gained an easement for bathing by prescription (see pages 869–881 infra).]

We are thus brought to a consideration of the next question, which is whether the boating, bathing and fishing privileges were assignable by Frank C. Miller to Rufus W. Miller. What is the nature of such rights?. . . . It has uniformly been held that a profit in gross—for example, a right of mining or fishing—may be made assignable: Funk v. Haldeman, 53 Pa. 229; Tinicum Fishing Co. v. Carter, 61 Pa. 21, 39. In regard to easements in gross generally, there has been much controversy in the courts and by textbook writers and law students as to whether they have the attribute of assignability. . . . There does not seem to be any reason why the law should prohibit the assignment of an easement in gross if the parties to its creation evidence their intention to make it assignable. Here, as in Tide Water Pipe Company v. Bell, 280 Pa. 104, the rights of fishing and boating were conveyed to the grantee—in this case Frank C. Miller—"his heirs and assigns," thus showing that the grantor, the Pocono Spring Water Ice Company, intended to attach the attribute of assignability to the privileges granted. Moreover, as a practical matter, there is an obvious difference in this respect between easements for personal enjoyment and those designed for commercial exploitation; while there may be little justification for permitting assignments in the former case, there is every reason for upholding them in the latter.

The question of assignability of the easements in gross in the present case is not as important as that of their divisibility. It is argued by plaintiffs that even if held to be assignable such easements are not divisible, because this might involve an excessive user or "surcharge of the easement" subjecting the servient tenement to a greater burden than originally contemplated. The law does not take that extreme position. It does require, however, that, if there be a division, the easements must be used or exercised as an entirety. This rule had its earliest expression in Mountjoy's Case, which is reported in Co. Litt. 164b, 165a. It was there said, in regard to the grant of a right to dig for ore, that the grantee, Lord Mountjoy, "might assign his whole interest to one, two, or more; but then, if there be two or more, they could make no division of it, but work together with one stock." In Caldwell v. Fulton, 31 Pa. 475, 477, 478, and in Funk v. Haldeman, 53 Pa. 229, that case was followed, and it was held that the right of a grantee to mine coal or to prospect for oil might be assigned, but if to more than one they must hold, enjoy and convey the right as an entirety, and not divide it in severalty. There are cases in other jurisdictions which also approve the doctrine of *Mountjoy's Case*, and hold that a mining right in gross is essentially integral and not susceptible of apportionment; an assignment of it is valid, but it cannot be aliened in such a way that it may be utilized by grantor and grantee, or by several grantees, separately; there must be a joint user, nor can one of the tenants alone convey a share in the common right: Grubb v. Baird, Federal Case No. 5849 (Circuit Court, Eastern District of Pennsylvania); Harlow v. Lake

Superior Iron Co., 36 Mich. 105, 121; Stanton v. T. L. Herbert & Sons, 141 Tenn. 440, 211 S.W. 353.

These authorities furnish an illuminating guide to the solution of the problem of divisibility of profits or easements in gross. They indicate that much depends upon the nature of the right and the terms of its creation, that "surcharge of the easement" is prevented if assignees exercise the right as "one stock," and that a proper method of enjoyment of the easement by two or more owners of it may usually be worked out in any given instance without insuperable difficulty.

In the present case it seems reasonably clear that in the conveyance of February 17, 1900, it was not the intention of Frank C. Miller to grant, and of Rufus W. Miller to receive, a separate right to subdivide and sublicense the boating, fishing and bathing privileges on and in Lake Naomi, but only that they should together use such rights for commercial purposes, Rufus W. Miller to be entitled to one-fourth and Frank C. Miller to three-fourths of the proceeds resulting from their combined exploitation of the privileges. They were to hold the rights, in the quaint phraseology of Mountjoy's Case, as "one stock.". . . . Defendant contends that, as a tenant in common of the privileges, Rufus W. Miller individually was entitled to their use, benefit and possession and to exercise rights of ownership in regard thereto, including the right to license third persons to use them, subject only to the limitation that he must not thereby interfere with the similar rights of his co-tenant. But the very nature of these easements prevents their being so exercised, inasmuch as it is necessary, because of the legal limitations upon their divisibility, that they should be utilized in common, and not by two owners severally, and, as stated, this was evidently the intention of the brothers.

Summarizing our conclusions, we are of opinion (1) that Frank C. Miller acquired title to the boating and fishing privileges by grant and he and Rufus W. Miller to the bathing rights by prescription; (2) that he made a valid assignment of a one-fourth interest in them to Rufus W. Miller; but (3) that they cannot be commercially used and licenses thereunder granted without the common consent and joinder of the present owners, who with regard to them must act as "one stock." It follows that the executors of the estate of Rufus W. Miller did not have the right, in and by themselves, to grant a license to defendant.

Notes & Questions

1. Under traditional English common law, easements could not be created in gross. American courts have not followed the English prohibition, but the prohibition may have influenced both the American presumption against easements in gross and American limitations on the assignment of easements in gross.

2. American courts initially took the position that easements in gross were entirely personal in character and could not be assigned or inherited. See, e.g., Stockdale v. Yerden, 190 N.W. 225 (Mich. 1922). Some courts

continue to assert in dictum that easements in gross cannot be transferred. For example, in O'Neill v. Williams, p. 839, the Maine Supreme Court stated without hesitation that "An easement in gross is a purely personal right, is not assignable, and terminates upon the death of the individual for whom it was created."

Despite such dicta, however, all jurisdictions now recognize the transferability of easements in gross in some situations. Economic reality initially drove courts away from an absolute prohibition on transfers. With the advent of electricity, telephones, sewage systems, and domestic water delivery, utilities needed rights of way across property to service their customers, and utilities often changed hands. This led a number of courts, as well as the first Restatement of Property, to draw a distinction between "commercial easements in gross" and "noncommercial easements in gross." Commercial easements were alienable in all situations, while the alienability of noncommercial easements was determined "by the manner or the terms of their creation." Restatement of Property §§ 489–91 (1944). The principal problem with this approach was the artificial distinction between commercial and noncommercial easements. In *Miller*, for example, was the original grant of the "exclusive right to fish and boat" a commercial or a noncommercial easement? Is the holder of the right relevant in determining whether an easement is commercial or noncommercial? If the grant in *Miller* had initially been to the Lutheran Conference & Camp Association, would the easement have been noncommercial? Does it matter whether the association charges its members and guests to use the lake? Even if one could readily distinguish between commercial and noncommercial easements, is there a good reason to distinguish? See generally Charles Clark, The American Law Institute's Law of Real Covenants, 52 Yale L.J. 699 (1943).

3. Today most courts look to the intent of the parties in determining whether an easement in gross is assignable. In O'Donovan v. McIntosh, 728 A.2d 681 (Me. 1999), the Maine Supreme Judicial Court rejected the dictum in *O'Neill* proscribing transfers of easements in gross and instead adopted an intent rule. Noting that a growing number of courts and authorities advocate looking to the intent of the parties, the court concluded that there are also good policy grounds for relaxing the historic bias against transfers of easements in gross:

> The conclusion that an easement in gross is assignable when the parties intend is consistent with our general policy favoring the free alienability of property. The alienability of an easement in gross promotes the free alienability of land, a general policy of property law. See Restatement of Property § 489 cmt. a (1944). The Restatement explains that "this policy arises from a belief that the social interest is promoted by the greater utilization of the subject matter of property resulting from the freedom of alienation of interests in it." Id. In furtherance of this policy, we have adhered to the traditional rule of construction that whenever possible an easement is construed to be appurtenant to the land of the person for whose use the easement is created, thereby ensur-

> ing that the easement is alienable. Similarly, we have held that a profit a prendre—the right to take from the land something that is a product of the soil—is freely assignable even when that right is in gross.... It is consistent with the policy of promoting a high degree of alienability that we hold an easement in gross may be assignable.

Id. at 684.

Many courts today presume that an easement in gross is assignable unless the parties intended or expected that the easement would be personal and thus not transferable. This is the position of the new Restatement. See Restatement (Third) of Property, Servitudes § 4.6 cmt. d, at 550 (2000).

4. Is there any justification for precluding the transferability of an easement in gross absent evidence that the parties intended or expected that the easement would be personal? The late Judge Charles Clark, probably the most vocal opponent of assignable easements in gross, argued that such easements, "usually of small value, and easily forgotten by the holder thereof, often are discovered many years later just at a time when they may hold up or prevent an advantageous sale of the servient estate.... Contrast this situation with that of an easement appurtenant to some dominant land. The latter is an interest hardly to be overlooked either upon death or removal elsewhere of the owner. Consequently it and the appurtenant easement will pass to some definitely ascertainable person." Charles Clark, Real Covenants and Other Interests Which "Run with the Land" 73 (2d ed. 1947). If this is the concern, are there better solutions to the problem?

5. Another concern with the assignability of easements in gross is that the new holder of an easement might increase the burden on the servient estate. Rachel Carson might willingly give her neighbor, George Washington Carver, the right to come onto her property to remove timber because she does not expect that George will want or be able to take very much timber, but she will feel quite differently if George transfers the right to a lumber company. Similarly, Rachel might be happy to grant George the right to use a lake found on her property, but is unlikely to sleep easily if George gives the right to his local lodge. What solutions are there to this problem?

Rachel, of course, can solve the problem by expressly prohibiting the alienability of the right or by expressly limiting the amount of timber that can be cut or the use that can be made of the lake. But what if Rachel does not, perhaps because she does not anticipate the problem? How does the Pennsylvania Supreme Court try to address the problem in *Miller*? Does the court's approach solve the problem? Should courts impose a "reasonableness" restriction on the use of easements in gross? How would courts determine what is "reasonable"?

6. **Divisibility of Appurtenant Easements.** Appurtenant easements also can lead to concerns over increased burdens. Imagine, for example, that the owner of a ten acre parcel of land holds an easement of right-of-way across a neighbor's property. If the owner subdivides his land

into 20 separate lots, do each of the subdivided lots enjoy a right-of-way across the neighbor's land? Most courts would say "yes" if the subdivision would not unreasonably increase the burden on the servient estate. See, e.g., Shooting Point, L.L.C. v. Wescoat, 576 S.E.2d 497 (Va. 2003). If allowing all owners of lots in the subdivision to use the right-of-way would unreasonably burden the servient estate, most courts require that the right-of-way be apportioned in order to reduce the burden. See Restatement (Third) of Property, Servitudes § 5.7 (2000).

7. **Riparian Rights.** Many lakes face a problem of growing recreational use, particularly as developers find ways of giving more and more property owners access to a lake. Most states follow the "civil law" rule that all the owners of property surrounding a lake, the "riparian" owners, have a right to make common use of the lake's surface.[1] Non-riparians have no right to utilize the lake. Developers, however, can readily squeeze in more "riparians" by building a club on the lake and giving memberships to everyone who purchases property in the development, by giving each purchaser a small sliver of lakefront just large enough to build a dock and set up a few deck chairs, by dredging a canal out from the lake and building homes along the canal, by constructing a condominium in which all owners share the waterfront in cotenancy, or by a multitude of other devices. The result often is more boats, more noise, more pollution, and less fish.

Courts hold that riparians are limited to a "reasonable" use of the lake; each riparian occupies a "correlative" status with all other riparians and cannot impose an "unreasonable" burden on overall usage of the lake. Does that mean that a developer cannot funnel more users onto a lake if a court finds that the total increased use is "unreasonable"? In Thompson v. Enz, 154 N.W.2d 473 (Mich. 1967), the court suggested that a developer could not add approximately 150 new "lakefront" homes by constructing a canal and placing the homes on the canal if the increased burden on the lake would be unreasonable. Other courts, however, have suggested that a riparian lot can be subdivided so long as each of the new owners makes only a reasonable use of the lake. See, e.g., Coleman v. Forister, 524 S.W.2d 899 (Tex. 1974). See also Three Lakes Ass'n v. Kessler, 285 N.W.2d 300 (Mich. App. 1979) (okay to give all residents of a subdivision access to a common boat dock so long as total use of the dock is limited to a reasonable amount).

2. Easements By Estoppel

Stoner v. Zucker

Supreme Court of California, 1906.
83 P. 808.

Henshaw, J.

[Plaintiff originally gave the defendants oral permission to enter onto his property and to construct and maintain a ditch to carry irrigation water

1. A few states, however, still follow the "common law" rule that, in the case of non-public waters, gives riparians only the right to use the portion of the lake overlying the land that they own. See, e.g., Lanier v. Ocean Pond Fishing Club, 322 S.E.2d 494 (Ga. 1984); People v. Emmert, 597 P.2d 1025 (Colo. 1979).

to their own and other lands. Defendants spent over $7,000—a princely sum at the time—to build the ditch. According to the plaintiff, all he ever gave to the defendants was a revocable license. The plaintiff claimed that he] never conveyed or agreed to convey to the defendants any right of way, easement, or interest in the land for the purpose, and their right to construct and maintain the ditch rested wholly upon this license; that in 1900 he served notice upon them that the license to construct and operate the ditch had been revoked and abrogated by him. Notwithstanding this notice of revocation and abrogation, the defendants, disregarding it, have continuously entered upon plaintiff's land, making repairs upon the ditch and restoring the same where it was broken and washed away, and defendants threaten to continue this trespass upon the lands of the plaintiff. Plaintiff therefore prayed that the defendants be adjudged trespassers and be enjoined from the use of the ditch or from in any manner entering upon the lands of the plaintiff to repair or otherwise maintain it.... So construing the findings, the question is squarely presented as to the revocability or nonrevocability of an executed parol license, whose execution has involved the expenditure of money, and where, from the very nature of the license given, it was to be continuous in use.

Appellant contends that a parol license to do an act upon the land of the licensor, while it justifies anything done by the licensee before revocation, is revocable at the option of the licensor, so that no further acts may be justified under it, and this, although the intention was to confer a continuing right, and money has been expended by the licensor upon the faith of the license, and that such a license cannot be changed into an equitable right on the ground of equitable estoppel. To the support of this proposition is offered authority of great weight and of the highest respectability. The argument in brief is that a license in its very nature is a revocable permission, that whoever accepts that permission does it with knowledge that the permission may be revoked at any time; that the rule cannot be changed, therefore, because the licensee has foolishly or improvidently expended money in the hope of a continuance of a license, upon the permanent continuance of which he has no right in law or in equity to rely; that to convert such a parol license into a grant or easement under the doctrine of estoppel is destructive of the statute of frauds, which was meant to lay down an inflexible rule; and, finally, that there is no room or play for the operation of the doctrine of estoppel, since the licensor has in no way deceived the licensee by revocation, has put no fraud upon him, and has merely asserted a right which had been absolutely reserved to him by the very terms of his permission. No one has stated this argument more clearly and cogently than Judge Cooley, who, holding to this construction of the law, has expressed it in his work on Torts. Cooley, Torts (2d Ed.) 364. But that the same eminent jurist recognized the injustice and the hardship which followed such a conclusion is plainly to be seen from his opinion in Maxwell v. Bay City Bridge Co., 41 Mich. 453, 2 N.W. 639, where, discussing this subject, he says: "But the injustice of a revocation after the licensee, in reliance upon the license, has made large and expensive improvements, is so serious that it seems a reproach to the law that it should fail to provide some adequate protection against it. Some of the courts have been disposed to enforce the license as a parol contract which has been performed on one side." Indeed, the learned jurist, with equal accuracy, might have stated that the majority of courts have so decided, in accordance with the leading case of Rerick v. Kern, 14 Serg. & R. 267, 16 Am. Dec. 497. That case was carefully considered, and it was held that it would be to countenance a fraud upon the part of the licensor if he were allowed, after expenditure of money by the licensees upon the faith of the license, to cut short by revocation the natural term of its continuance and existence, and that under the doctrine of estoppel, the licensor would not be allowed to do this. The decision was that the licensor would be held to have conveyed an easement commensurate in its extent and duration with the right to be enjoyed. In that case there was a parol license without consideration to use the waters of a stream for a sawmill, and it was held it could not be revoked at the grantor's pleasure, where the grantee, in consequence of the license, had erected a mill. The court in that case says, after discussion: "It is to be considered as if there had been a formal conveyance of the right, and nothing remains but to determine its duration and extent. A right under a license, when not specifically restricted, is commensurate with the thing of which the license is an accessory." And the court said further: "Having in view an unlimited enjoyment of the privilege, the grantee has purchased by the expenditure of money, a right indefinite in point of duration, which cannot be forfeited by a nonuser unless for a period sufficient to raise the presumption of a release. The right to rebuild in case of destruction or dilapidation and to continue the business on its original footing may have been in fact as necessary to his safety, and may have been an inducement of the particular investment in the first instance."

.... The recognized principle, therefore, is that where a licensee has entered under a parol license and has expended money, or its equivalent in labor, in the execution of the license, the license becomes irrevocable, the licensee will have a right of entry upon the lands of the licensor for the purpose of maintaining his structures or, in general, his rights under his license, and the license will continue for so long a time as the nature of it calls for. Thus, for example, where the license was to erect a lumber mill, the license came to an end when the timber available for use at that mill had been worked up into lumber. The same has been held as to a milldam, the right to maintain the dam continuing so long as there was use for the mill, and the right being lost by abandonment and disuse only when the nonuser had continued for a period sufficient to raise the presumption of release. In the case of irrigating ditches, drains, and the like, the license becomes, in all essentials, an easement, continuing for such length of time, under the indicated conditions, as the use itself may continue.

For these reasons the judgment and order appealed from are affirmed.

Notes & Questions

1. **Licenses.** At any given moment, more people occupy land under license than under any other form of legal arrangement. For every one person in possession of land, there are probably thousands more exercising licenses to enter movie theaters, ball parks, museums, rock concerts, shops, and restaurants. For every one who holds a right-of-way, there are probably tens of thousands licensed to enter the grounds of public schools, colleges, professional schools, hospitals, retirement homes, their places of work, and those of their doctors, lawyers, accountants, and auto mechanics.

Despite their widespread, indeed pervasive, use, licenses occupy only a small corner in real property law. The reason, of course, is that, because licenses can be revoked by either licensor or licensee at any time, they are too slender and fragile to support the kind of investment that is routinely made in easements, covenants, and servitudes. Although the theater owner who ejects a patron may be liable for breach of the contract implied in the ticket of admission, the patron's remedies are strictly contractual, for he has no enforceable interest in the land itself.

2. **Easements by Estoppel.** *Stoner* introduces the concept of an *irrevocable license*—or what many courts call an *easement by estoppel*. Courts recognize easements by estoppel in two situations. The first, illustrated by *Stoner*, is where the holder of a license substantially changes his position based on the reasonable belief that the owner of the servient estate will not revoke the license. In one of the most common scenarios, a property owner permits a neighbor to cross her property to get to his vacant lot, which does not have easy access to a public road. The neighbor builds a home on his lot, or takes other steps to utilize the easement such as paving a road, with full knowledge of the property owner, after which the property owner withdraws permission to cross her property. Virtually all courts hold that the neighbor has an easement by estoppel. See, e.g., Murphy v. Long, 170 S.W.3d 621 (Tex. App. 2005); Holbrook v. Taylor, 532 S.W.2d 763 (Ky. 1976); Cooke v. Ramponi, 239 P.2d 638 (Cal. 1952). A property owner can avoid estoppel by clearly informing the licensee that the license is revocable at will and that the licensee therefore makes any investment at his own risk. See Zimmerman v. Summers, 330 A.2d 722 (Md. App. 1975).

The second situation where courts recognize an easement by estoppel is where someone substantially changes their position in reasonable reliance on assurances by the owner of a piece of property that the property is subject to an easement or similar benefit. In Prospect Development Co. v. Bershader, 515 S.E.2d 291 (Va. 1999), a family of avid birdwatchers purchased a home in a new subdivision after the developer assured them that an adjacent lot, "Outlot B," could not be developed because it failed a water percolation test. Outlot B was designated "preserved land" on the subdivision tract. When the developer later received permission to build on Outlot B, the homebuyers successfully sued to enjoin construction. The court concluded that the homebuyers held a "negative easement by estoppel" to maintain Outlot B in its natural condition. According to the court,

> it would be manifestly unjust to permit Prospect Development to construct a house upon Outlot B. Relying upon the defendants' numerous representations and inducements that Outlot B would always remain as "preserved land," and that "there was no possibility" a house would be constructed on Outlot B, the Bershaders paid $500,000 to purchase Lot 23 with a house constructed thereon to enjoy the view and privacy afforded by Outlot B's status as "preserved land."

Id. at 299. See also Allee v. Kirk, 602 S.W.2d 922 (Mo. App. 1980) (homeowners enjoy easement by estoppel when developer informed them that they would have access to lake).

Even if courts believe that equity requires the creation of an easement by estoppel in these situations, should the courts require the plaintiff to compensate the defendant for the value of the resulting easement? Otherwise, doesn't the plaintiff receive a windfall?

3. Compare *Stoner* with Nelson v. American Telephone & Telegraph Co., 170 N.E. 416 (Mass. 1930), in which the Massachusetts Supreme Court ruled that defendant, AT & T, had obtained no rights under an unsealed and unacknowledged 1893 deed from plaintiff's predecessor purporting to grant AT & T, its successors and assigns, the right "to construct, operate and maintain its lines" over his property, even though AT & T had promptly installed thirty-two poles carrying thirty-four wires, and had maintained the installation for more than thirty years with the apparent acquiescence both of plaintiff's predecessor and of plaintiff. In the court's view,

> the defendant at all times must be held to have known that the instrument under which it was permitted to occupy and use the locus was a mere license which was revocable and gave it no estate or interest in the land. It was also bound to know when it entered upon and used the locus that the license was revocable not only at the will of the owner of the property on which it is to be exercised but by his death, by alienation, or demise of the land by him, and by whatever would deprive the original owner of the right to do the acts in question, or give permission to others to do them.

Id. at 420.

Which result is better, *Stoner* or *Nelson*? Can the cases be distinguished on the basis of AT & T's presumed superior expertise and bargaining power?

Should a distinction be drawn between cases in which the parties clearly intended a license and made no effort to execute an easement, and cases in which they did attempt an easement but failed to meet one or more of the formalities? If so, does the distinction suggest that both *Stoner* and *Nelson* were wrongly decided?

4. How long should an easement by estoppel last? *Stoner* states that it will last "for so long a time as the nature of it calls for." How long is that? Assume that Josephine Hensley asks John Wesley Powell whether she can

cross his land to get to her property, which otherwise has no ready access to public roads; that John agrees; and that Josephine then builds a house on her property with John's full knowledge. Most courts would award Josephine an easement by estoppel. If Josephine's house burns down, however, can she build a new house over John's objections and continue to use his land for access?

5. **Licenses Paired with an Interest.** Where a landowner conveys an interest in resources or personal property found on his land, courts also will imply a nonpossessory right to come onto the land to get the resources or property and will limit the landowner's authority to revoke the right. Assume, for example, that George Washington Carver sells Sitting Bull a cord of firewood that is sitting on George's land; Sitting Bull has an implied license to come onto George's land to remove the firewood. If George conveys to Sitting Bull ownership of coal found underneath George's land, Sitting Bull has an implied easement to come onto George's land to mine and remove the coal; the easement lasts until Sitting Bull has exhausted the coal supply.

3. EASEMENTS BY IMPLICATION AND NECESSITY

Williams Island Country Club, Inc. v. San Simeon at the California Club, Ltd.

Court of Appeals of Florida, 1984.
454 So. 2d 23.

SHARP, Associate Justice.

The issue in this case is whether appellant, Williams Island Country Club, Inc., made a prima facie showing at an evidentiary hearing sufficient to entitle it to a preliminary injunction. Williams sought to establish and preserve an easement for a golf cart path across appellees' entry strip: a block of land approximately 100 feet by 200 feet. The entry strip divides Williams' thirteenth hole green from its fourteenth hole tee. Without an easement leading from the thirteenth hole to the fourteenth, Williams could not operate his eighteen hole golf course, and its condominium and resort developments, which were built around the golf course, and for which the golf course was an important amenity, would be severely damaged. The lower court denied the injunctive relief primarily because there was no recorded easement for the golf cart path. We reverse because we think Williams made a prima facie showing it has an implied easement for a golf cart path across appellees' land.

The testimony at the hearing established that prior to 1979 the whole of the property, both appellant's golf course and appellees' development tract and entry strip, belonged to Sky Lake Development, Inc. Sky Lake built an eighteen hole golf course, and it used the entry strip for access from the thirteenth to the fourteenth hole for maintenance, and the flow of golfers playing the course. There is no practical or safe alternative route for golf carts to go from the thirteenth to the fourteenth hole other than by crossing the entry strip.[1]

In 1978 Sky Lake entered into a contract to sell the development tract and entry strip to an entity controlled by Harry Peisach. The contract stated that when sold, the grantee would give Sky Lake "certain reasonable easements for golf carts and maintenance." No specific easements were described in the contract or shown on the master plan attached to it. Burt Haft, president of Sky Lake, testified both parties to the contract intended that when the construction plans for the development tract and entry were set, an express easement would be granted for the golf cart path.

In 1980, the development tract and entry strip were sold to Nobata, N.V., another entity controlled by Harry Peisach. At that time the golf cart path was paved. It was nine feet wide, and was in constant use by golfers and maintenance workers. It was clearly visible from the development property, the four lane road bordering the entry strip, and the golf course.

When Williams purchased the golf course in 1983, its president was told that Williams had an easement across the entry strip for golf carts. Mr. Peisach agreed. But rather than developing the property himself, he entered into a contract to sell it to San Simeon At the Club, Ltd., one of the appellees.

A principal of San Simeon, Mr. Antin, called Haft four months before its purchase of the property from Nobata N.V., to obtain a copy of the plat of the golf course, which surrounded the development property. Haft reminded him about the golf cart easement across the entry strip. Mr. Antin replied, "No problem."

San Simeon purchased the development tract and entry strip in January of 1984. A dispute arose over the golf cart easement. When no agreement was reached, San Simeon bulldozed the cart path and blocked access at any point over the entry strip.

An easement, such as the golf cart path in this case, may be created by implication. When land is owned originally by the same owner, and part of the land is used for the benefit of another part, such use is termed a "quasi-easement," and it may become an implied easement when either part is severed from the other.

The easement may be created by implied reservation, as in this case, when the servient tenement is sold to a third party, or by implied grant, when the dominant tenement is sold.

> Where, during the unity of title, an apparently permanent and obvious servitude is imposed on one part of an estate in favor of another part, which servitude is in use at the time of severance and is necessary for the reasonable enjoyment of the other part, on

1. One suggested alternative route was to have the golfers cross a busy four lane highway, run along the sidewalk some 200 feet, and cross again to reach the fourteenth tee. Another was to run backwards against the flow of play a considerable distance, circumventing the balance of appellees' development tract.

> a severance of the ownership a grant of the right to continue such use arises by implication of law. Similarly, where the owner of property, one part of which has been subjected to such a use for the benefit of another part, sells both parts to different purchasers, the respective portions granted are subject to or benefitted by, as the case may be, an easement corresponding to such use.

25 Am. Jur. 2d Easements § 27 (1966). The majority view is that little distinction is made between implied grants and implied reservations. 25 Am. Jur. 2d Easements §§ 33, 21 (1966).

The rationale supporting implied easements is the court's conclusion that the parties must have intended to grant or reserve an easement as part of the conveyance of land based on the circumstances at the time of the conveyance. Restatement of Property § 476 (1944); 3 H. Tiffany, Real Property § 780 (3d ed. 1939). First, the use of the land for the easement must be apparent or visible, or reasonably discoverable at the time the unity of title was severed. Here the golf cart path was in existence and use, and was paved at the time of the conveyance to Nobata, N.V. Second, the use must be such that a permanent use was intended. 25 Am. Jur. 2d Easements § 31 (1966). Here, testimony of the original parties, and language in their contract supports the inference that a permanent golf cart easement was intended. Restatement of Property § 476 (1944).

Finally, the easement must be reasonably necessary for the use and benefit of the dominant tenement. 25 Am. Jur. 2d Easements §§ 24, 33 (1966); 28 C.J.S. Easements § 33 (1941). Strict necessity need not be shown. In this case a sufficient showing of need was made by establishing that without the golf cart easement, the dominant tenement could no longer be used as an eighteen hole golf course, its use at the time of severance of the servient tenement.

Whether or not a remote or subsequent grantor of the servient tenement is bound by an implied easement depends on whether he has notice of the dominant tenement's easement rights. In Kirma v. Norton, 102 So. 2d 653 (Fla. 2d DCA 1958), a subsequent grantor of the servient tenement was held bound by a sewer pipe easement which crossed his land and emptied into a river. Even though the pipes were underground, the court held the emergence of the pipes from the river bank should have put a prudent buyer on notice to inquire, and he was, therefore, bound by what he would have learned.

In this case, Williams established a sufficient physical presence and use of the golf cart easement at the time San Simeon purchased the servient tenement to impose on it a duty of inquiry. Further, Williams established actual knowledge of the easement by San Simeon's principal, before its purchase. Under either theory, appellant could prevail.

For the reasons stated in this opinion, we reverse the lower court's denial of a preliminary injunction and we direct that an appropriate injunction be entered to preserve the status quo of the easement pending a final determination on the merits.

Dupont v. Whiteside

Court of Appeal of Florida, 1998.
721 So. 2d 1259.

COBB, J.

C. E. Dupont and Joyce Dupont, his wife, plaintiffs below, appeal from an adverse final judgment granting an easement of necessity to Carl Whiteside and Leona Whiteside, his wife, over certain lands owned by the Duponts.

In 1980 the Duponts sold off a portion of their property to the Whitesides. The property purchased by the Whitesides, approximately 32 acres, included frontage on the St. Johns River. The Whitesides planned to build their home on the river front portion of the parcel; however, the public road accessing the property (School Street) was on the lower portion of the property away from the river and separated from it by wetlands. The Whitesides built their home in 1981 at a cost of approximately $240,000.00.

Mr. Whiteside testified that when considering the purchase of the property, his wife informed Mr. Dupont that they could not get to the portion of the property where they planned to situate their home. According to Mr. Whiteside, Mr. Dupont responded that he was putting "a road in right then." Dupont completed the road before the closing on September 24, 1980. This road traverses the Duponts' property, and provides direct access to the river front portion of the property acquired by the Whitesides. The Whitesides used this road to get to and from their home for some 14 years.

In July 1994, Mr. Dupont objected to the Whitesides' continued use of the roadway. Dupont gave the Whitesides 60 days within which to establish alternative access. The deed of conveyance to the Whitesides contains no grant of easement across any of the Duponts' land. The instant lawsuit was filed by the Duponts to enjoin the Whitesides from their continued use of the roadway over the Duponts' land. The Whitesides filed a counterclaim seeking an irrevocable license to use the roadway based on their expenditures in constructing their home, or, in the alternative, a common law or statutory way of necessity.

At trial the testimony centered primarily on two issues: (1) the parties' understanding at the time the Whitesides purchased the property; and (2) the availability of access to the Whiteside's home without traversing the Duponts' property. According to Mr. Dupont, the Whitesides never asked for an easement and he never offered them an easement. According to Dupont, the Whitesides said they were going to get to their home by building their own road. Dupont testified that he gave them temporary permission to use the roadway over the Dupont land until they could get their own roadway built, but they never attempted to build their own access way to the river front. Dupont sold off other river front parcels and included in those conveyances grants of easement over his lands.

As to the second point, the Duponts presented evidence from an engineer, Logan, that the Whitesides could construct a roadway over their land. Logan testified that although part of the Whitesides' land was possibly wetlands and a culvert would be required, a permit for the proposed construction was obtainable from the St. Johns Water Management District. Logan could not say how much such a road would cost to build.

The Whitesides presented testimony from Epsten, an environmental specialist with the St. Johns River Water Management District who handles permitting for the district. Epsten visited the property and concluded that approximately two-thirds of the distance from the Whitesides' river front home to their uplands was flood plain forest and inundated. He determined that a road through the Whitesides' property would have to be built through approximately 700 feet of wetlands and the Whitesides would likely have to execute a conservation easement to the district covering as many as 8 acres of other adjoining wetlands.

Turner, the Whitesides' other witness, testified that he is a surveyor with experience in wetlands determination and road-building through swamps. Turner testified that the cost of construction of a road on the Whitesides' land from their river front home to the uplands would be in the area of $40,000.00 to $50,000.00. Turner added that the most reasonable and practical route to the Whitesides' river front home is the one they have been using across the Duponts' land.

The trial court entered a final judgment finding that the Whitesides "have no 'practicable' way of egress or ingress to their property except by way of the constructed roadway across the property of the [Duponts]" and awarded the Whitesides an implied way of necessity easement over the existing roadway through the Duponts' property.

The evidence below was undisputed that the Duponts sold to the Whitesides a parcel of land which is located at the end of a public road. The Whitesides thus do not lack access to their property but they do lack convenient access to the river front portion of it where they built their home.

In Florida the common law rule of an implied grant of way of necessity has been codified at section 704.01, Florida Statutes:

> (1) **Implied grant of way of necessity.**—The common-law rule of an implied grant of a way of necessity is hereby recognized, specifically adopted, and clarified. Such an implied grant exists where a person has heretofore granted or hereafter grants lands to which there is no accessible right-of-way except over her or his land, or has heretofore retained or hereafter retains land which is inaccessible except over the land which the person conveys. In such instances a right-of-way is presumed to have been granted or reserved. Such an implied grant or easement in lands or estates exists where there is no other reasonable and practicable way of egress, or ingress and same is reasonably necessary for the beneficial use or enjoyment of the part granted or reserved. An implied grant arises only where a unity of title exists from a common

> source other than the original grant from the state or United Sates; provided, however, that where there is a common source of title subsequent to the original grant from the state or United States, the right of the dominant tenement shall not be terminated if title of either the dominant or servient tenement has been or should be transferred for nonpayment of taxes either by foreclosure, reversion, or otherwise.

Claimants such as the Whitesides seeking to establish a way of necessity have the burden of proof to establish that they have no practicable route of ingress or egress. The term "practicable" as used in 704.01(1) is defined to mean "without the use of bridge, ferry, turnpike road, embankment or substantial fill." § 704.03, Fla. Stat. Under section 704.01(1), no easement can be inferred from a conveyance that creates no necessity. . . .

In Tortoise Island Communities, Inc. v. Moorings Association, Inc., 489 So. 2d 22 (Fla. 1986), the supreme court held that absolute necessity, not merely reasonable necessity, is required for an implied grant of way of necessity. In Hunter v. Marquardt, Inc., 549 So. 2d 1095 (Fla. 1st DCA 1989), rev. denied, 560 So. 2d 234 (Fla. 1990), the First District applied the holding in *Tortoise Island* in reversing a final judgment and summarized the applicable law as follows:

> An implied easement of a way of necessity should not be granted where there is other reasonable access to the property that will enable the owner to achieve a beneficial use and enjoyment of the property. Roy v. Euro–Holland Vastgoed, B.V., 404 So. 2d 410 (Fla. 4th DCA 1981). The term "necessity," as used in the common law doctrine implying ways of necessity, means that no other reasonable mode of accessing the property exists without implying the easement, and the fact that one means of access is more convenient than another does not make the more convenient means a "necessity." Id. at 413. As stated by the supreme court in Tortoise Island Communities, Inc. v. Moorings Association, Inc., 489 So. 2d at 22, such an easement requires a showing of "an absolute necessity."

549 So. 2d at 1095. . . .

The Whitesides argue that section 704.01(1) should not be construed so as to deny them an easement to the portion of the land that was contemplated by the parties to be used for their home. The Whitesides point out that they were concerned about the lack of access to the river front portion of the property at the time they purchased the property and that Mr. Dupont put in a road to accommodate them, albeit over his own property. As the Whitesides point out, an easement by way of necessity is founded upon an implied grant which arises from the supposed intention of the parties. See Matthews v. Quarles, 504 So. 2d 1246 (Fla. 1st DCA 1986).

However, this presumed intention is not that the parties intended convenient access, only that it is presumed that a party conveying a landlocked parcel intends to convey what is necessary for the beneficial use of said property, i.e., access. In this case, the parcel conveyed to the Whitesides was not landlocked and the common law principle was thus never implicated. Furthermore, the evidence established below that the issue of access to the river front portion of the property was considered by the parties at the time of purchase. Unfortunately for the Whitesides, the access issue was resolved by the parties based upon what appears to have been an oral promise by Dupont to allow access across his land. Such an oral promise cannot form the basis for an enforceable easement because of the Statute of Frauds. See § 725.01, Fla. Stat. (1997).

Due to the trial court's disposition, it did not address the issue of whether the Whitesides enjoyed a license over the roadway crossing the Duponts' land which became irrevocable. In their counterclaim, the Whitesides alleged, inter alia, that they enjoy a continuing oral license to use the access road across the Duponts' property which they have been using since 1980. The Duponts concede that a license temporarily existed but argue it was revocable and was revoked.

An easement and license are fundamentally different in the law. An easement constitutes an interest in land, is subject to the statute of frauds, and runs with the land. A license, however, confers no interest in the land but merely gives one the authority to do a particular act on another's land; it may be created orally. A license in land is generally revocable at the pleasure of the grantor but an exception to this rule exists when permission is granted to use property for a particular purpose, or in a certain manner, and in the execution of that use the permittee has expended large sums or incurred heavy obligations for its permanent improvement. Dance v. Tatum, 629 So. 2d 127 (Fla. 1993). Here, evidence was presented that the Whitesides were concerned about access to the river front portion of the property and in reliance on Dupont's assurance that he was putting "a road in right then" closed on the property and proceeded to construct a $240,000 home. This evidence, if believed by the trial court, could support the granting of an irrevocable license. The cause is remanded for retrial on the license issue.

HARRIS, J., dissenting.

I respectfully dissent. While I agree with the general statement of law expressed in the majority, I do not agree that access to the bottom portion of the 32 acres purchased by the Whitesides from the DuPonts is either a "reasonable [or] practicable" way of access to the upper portion of the subject property. The majority acknowledges that the term "practicable" would contemplate an implied easement if the upper portion of the 32 acres was separated from the bottom portion by a river requiring a bridge. I submit that with the advent of environmental laws and the creation of regulatory agencies such as the St. Johns River Water Management District, it might be easier to traverse a river by walking across the surface of the water than to obtain a dredge and fill permit to construct a road through some 700 feet of wetlands. Even if the permit is obtainable, the added cost of construction of the roadway because of the environmental problems and the value of the property lost by having to give a conservation easement to the District in mitigation for the wetlands destroyed would render the purported access unreasonable and impracticable. The access sought (and obtained) below is not a mere convenience. It is, in the words of Tortoise Island Communities, Inc. v. Moorings Association, Inc., 489 So. 2d 22 (Fla. 1986), truly a "necessity." I would simply affirm the trial court.

Notes & Questions

1. Both *Williams Island* and *Dupont* involve easements created when a parcel of land was split into two pieces and the use of one piece was needed, to one degree or another, for enjoyment of the other piece. In *Williams Island*, the use preexisted the separation. In cases where one part of a parcel of land has been used for the benefit of another part, and the two parts are then separated, courts have long been willing to find an *easement implied from prior use* where the use was apparent and reasonably necessary. In these cases, the use of one part of the land to benefit the other prior to separation is often called a *quasi-easement*. (It is not a regular easement because a property owner cannot enjoy an easement in his own land). Easements implied from prior use are therefore sometimes called *easements implied from quasi-easements*.

In *DuPont*, the use did not preexist the separation, so the Whitesides could not argue that they held an easement implied from prior use. To demonstrate an *easement by necessity*, courts insist on a greater showing of necessity than in cases of easements implied from prior use.

2. The courts in both *Williams Island* and *Dupont* claim to be divining the intent of the parties. Are easements by necessity based only on the implied intent of the parties, or is their also an important public policy consideration—that land should be economically usable? Consider the following discussion of the issue in Hurlocker v. Medina, 878 P.2d 348, 351–52 (N.M. App. 1994):

> English courts began to develop general principles to deal with the conveyance of landlocked realty as early as the fourteenth century. From an early date it was a recognized legal maxim that "anyone who grants a thing to someone is understood to grant that without which the thing cannot be or exist." Id. In the seventeenth century Chief Justice Glyn added, "it is not only a private inconvenience, but it is also to the prejudice of the public weal, that land should lie fresh and unoccupied[.]" Id. at 574 (quoting from Packer v. Welsted, 2 Sid. 39, 111 (1658)). Public policy remained the stated basis for the servitude of necessity until the nineteenth century when the focus shifted back to the intent of the parties.
>
> Several factors dictate that the easement by necessity rests more heavily upon the intent of the parties than a public policy in favor of productive land use. First, it may well be questioned

whether it is still universally in the public interest to prohibit land from lying "fresh and unoccupied."

Second, it is clear that if the imposition of easements by necessity were truly required by public policy, those conveyances which clearly negated any access would be void. However, "the public policy favoring the productive use of land does not override the landowner's freedom to give up the right to ingress and egress." Jon W. Bruce & James W. Ely, Jr., The Law of Easements and Licenses in Land § 4.02[3], at 4–26 (1988); see also Gerald Korngold, Private Land Use Arrangements § 3.10, at 44 (1990).

Third, the law allows landlocked parcels to remain in that condition where they do not meet the requirements for imposition of an easement by necessity. See, e.g., Amoco Prod. Co. v. Sims, 97 N.M. 324, 639 P.2d 1178 (1981).

Fourth, operational rules by which easements by necessity are construed also indicate that the implied intent of the parties, rather than public policy, is the basic rationale underlying easements by necessity. For example, the required necessity must exist at the time of severance. This requirement is based on the concept that if the estate is readily accessible by other means at the time of severance, there can be little basis to infer intent to preserve access. See State v. Innkeepers of New Castle, Inc., 271 Ind. 286, 392 N.E.2d 459, 463–64 (Ind. 1979); see also Stewart E. Sterk, Neighbors in American Land Law, 87 Colum. L. Rev. 55, 64 (1987).

Finally, the imposition of an easement for public policy reasons can raise questions of compensation. Compensation problems are avoided by viewing the common grantor of the two estates, rather than governmental policy, as the source of the burden upon the servient tenement.

Therefore, the implied intention of the parties is a more reliable foundation than public policy upon which to build the analytical framework necessary to sustain easements by necessity; it is only when the record provides absolutely no insight from which an inference as to the intent of the parties can be drawn that public policy is employed as a significant factor.

Should easements by necessity rest on public policy rather than intent? Assume William Clark divides his property into two parcels, one of which is land-locked. Under what, if any, circumstances should the law permit Clark to sell the land-locked parcel with an explicit proviso that the parcel will enjoy no right of access across his remaining parcel?

3. **Degree of Necessity.** Necessity, although not the only factor involved in finding an easement implied from prior use or an easement by necessity, is often the central one. How much, and what kind of, necessity is needed? As *Dupont* illustrates, courts generally say that "strict" or "absolute" necessity must be shown in the case of an easement by necessity; only "reasonable" or "some" necessity typically need be shown

to find an easement implied from a prior use. But how strict is "strict," and how much less so is "reasonable"?

Easements by Necessity. Virtually all cases hold that access to a landlocked parcel meets a strict necessity test. But is it necessary that the land be accessible by car? See Thompson v. Whinnery, 895 P.2d 537 (Colo. 1995) (access by foot and horseback sufficient where parties originally contemplated that land would be used only for fishing and hunting).

What other needs might fit the test? Although the first Restatement of Property translated strict necessity as easements without which "the land cannot be effectively used," the current Restatement rejects this approach in favor of inquiring whether the right is "reasonably required to make effective use of the property. If the property cannot otherwise be used without disproportionate effort or expense, the rights are necessary within the meaning of this section." Compare Restatement of Property § 676, cmt. g (1944) with Restatement (Third) of Property, Servitudes § 2.15, cmt. d (2000). Should there be an easement by necessity for electricity and other utilities? Compare Morrell v. Rice, 622 A.2d 1156 (Me. 1993) (yes) with Helms v. Tullis, 398 So. 2d 253 (Ala. 1981) (no).

Easements Implied from Prior Use. Courts have found easements implied from a diversity of prior uses, including roadways, sewer and utility connections, overhanging tree limbs, and cattle grazing. According to the current Restatement, "Reasonable necessity usually means that alternative access or utilities cannot be obtained without a substantial expenditure of money or labor. It may also be measured by the amount of waste involved in duplicating facilities or the cost of reestablishing an entitlement to make the prior use." Restatement (Third) of Property, Servitudes § 2.12, cmt. e (2000).

Was there "reasonable necessity" in *Williams Island*? As noted in footnote 1 of the decision, golfers could always cross the street and walk along the sidewalk.

Is an easement for access to a recreational lake "reasonably necessary" under this standard? In Russakoff v. Scruggs, 400 S.E.2d 529 (Va. 1991), plaintiffs purchased homes in a subdivision surrounding an artificial lake; their deeds contained no express easements of access to the lake. When the developer stopped paying local property taxes, the state sold the developer's property, including the lake, to the Scruggs who immediately built a fence around the lake. The court found an implied easement. Compare Drye v. Eagle Rock Ranch, Inc., 364 S.W.2d 196 (Tex. 1962) (no implied easement for recreational privileges in open areas of a subdivision).

4. **Changes in Necessity.** What if, as a result of a new state law protecting wetlands, the Whitesides are forbidden from building a road across their wetlands several years after purchasing the land from the Duponts? Can the Whitesides claim an easement by necessity at that point? Courts uniformly hold that necessity is measured at the time of severance. See, e.g., State v. Innkeepers of New Castle, 392 N.E.2d 459 (Ind. 1979). The Whitesides thus would be out of luck. For similar reason, if land has

been subdivided several times and becomes "landlocked" only when severed the last time, the parcel has an easement by necessity only across the last parcel of land from which it was severed; it cannot claim an easement by necessity across other parcels of land to which it was once connected. See Godfrey v. Pilon, 529 P.2d 1372 (Mont. 1974).

What should happen in the reverse situation? If an easement was originally necessary for a landlocked parcel of land, but the necessity later disappeared because the owner obtained an express easement from someone else, should the owner still be able to claim an easement by necessity? The general rule is that easements by necessity cease to exist when the necessity for the easement disappears. See Hancock v. Henderson, 202 A.2d 599, 603 (Md. 1964).

5. **Grants Versus Reservations.** Courts deciding whether to imply an easement based on prior use will sometimes consider whether the claimed easement was created by grant or by reservation. An easement is implied by *grant* when Josephine Hensley, who is using one part of her land to benefit another part, sells the part benefitted (sometimes called the "quasi-dominant" estate) and retains the part burdened (the "quasi-servient" estate); the benefit is said to be granted along with the conveyance of the benefitted parcel. An easement is implied by *reservation* when Josephine conveys the quasi-servient estate and retains the quasi-dominant estate; the grantor is said to have reserved the benefit to himself.

Many states are more willing to imply an easement by grant than by reservation. See, e.g., Hillary Corp. v. U.S. Cold Storage, Inc., 550 N.W.2d 889 (Neb. 1996); Daniel v. Fox, 917 S.W.2d 106 (Tex. App. 1996). Suffield v. Brown, 4 DeGex, J. & S. 185 (Ch. 1864), the landmark case for this position, explains the principle behind the preference: "It seems to me more reasonable and just to hold that if the grantor intends to reserve any right over the property granted, it is his duty to reserve it expressly in the grant, rather than to limit and cut down the operation of a plain grant (which is not pretended to be otherwise than in conformity with the contract between the parties), by the fiction of an implied reservation." Id. at 190. Does this constructional principle accurately reflect modern conveyancing and title insurance practices under which the subject of easements is more likely to be the object of bargaining between grantor and grantee than of unilateral imposition by the grantor alone? A growing number of courts, along with the current Restatement, hold that the same level of necessity is required in cases of grants and reservations except "in circumstances where the knowledge of the grantor or unfairness to the grantee would make implication of an easement unreasonable." Restatement (Third) of Property, Servitudes § 2.12, cmt. e (2000).

6. **Negative Easements.** *Williams Island* and *Dupont* involve affirmative easements. Can a *negative* easement be implied by necessity or from prior use? Say that Rachel Carson and Black Kettle own adjoining lots acquired from a common grantor and that Rachel erects a ten-foot high wall, three inches away from the property line, that obstructs the passage of light and air through Black Kettle's kitchen windows. Can Black Kettle

succeed in establishing an implied easement, based on either the prior allowance of light and air or necessity, that will require Rachel to remove the obstructing portion of the wall?

In Maioriello v. Arlotta, 73 A.2d 374 (Pa. 1950), the lower court ordered that the defendant reduce the height of the wall from ten feet to six feet on the ground that, "because title to *both* premises had become vested in the same individual in 1916, and subsequently such owner conveyed the two properties separately, the grantor thereby created an easement of light and air, *by implication because of necessity.*" Id. at 375 (emphasis added). The Pennsylvania Supreme Court reversed. Although concluding that an easement of light and air can be implied from necessity, the court held that the plaintiff's claim fell short in several respects, including the showing of necessity:

> [E]ven if an easement of light and air would be *implied* in circumstances which reveal an absolute necessity, the finding of the learned Chancellor was that while a small amount of light and air was admitted into the kitchen, it was insufficient for the reasonable comfort, enjoyment and health of the plaintiff. This would constitute but a *partial* obstruction of light and air. But it was testified that a skylight can be placed in the ceiling of the kitchen, which would supply an ample amount of light and air. As it clearly appears that there exists no absolute necessity, no implied easement of light and air can be decreed.

Id. at 375–376.

7. **Notice.** Even if a property owner can establish an implied easement, will the burden of the easement run to future owners of the servient estate? The issue here is notice: courts will find that the burden runs if the purchaser received notice of the easement. In most cases involving an easement implied from prior existing use, the use of the easement will provide sufficient *inquiry notice*—facts that would lead a reasonable buyer to inquire into the existence of an easement. But what if the easement involves underground utilities that cannot be seen from the surface? Some courts will struggle to find something visible, like a manhole, that might support a finding of inquiry notice; others hold that the existence of underground utilities in a neighborhood puts all purchasers on inquiry notice; yet others simply ignore the requirement. See Joel Eichengrun, The Problem of Hidden Easements and the Subsequent Purchaser Without Notice, 40 Okla. L. Rev. 3 (1987).

The notice requirement can also be problematic in cases of easements by necessity. Where the owner of the landlocked property is actually using the servient estate for access, that use again should provide inquiry notice. In some cases, however, the lack of any current use has led to a finding that a purchaser of the servient estate is not subject to the easement. See, e.g., Tiller v. Hinton, 482 N.E.2d 946 (Ohio 1985). Should a property owner have an obligation to investigate whether there are any landlocked parcels of land bordering his land? To examine local land records to see what parcels of land were once held jointly with his own and whether they now have access to roads? See Backhausen v. Mayer, 234 N.W. 904 (Wis. 1931) ("Such a doctrine would be unreasonable").

8. **Statutory Solutions.** Several states have sought to remedy situations where property becomes landlocked through private condemnation statutes. For example, section 24–9–101 of the Wyoming Statutes provides that "Any person whose land has no outlet to, nor connection with a public road, may file an application in writing with the board of county commissioners in the county where his land is located for a private road leading from his land to some convenient public road." Upon a finding of necessity, the board appoints three appraisers to "locate and mark out a private road" that does "not exceed thirty (30) feet in width from a certain point on the premises of the applicant to some certain point on the public road" and that does "the least possible damage to the lands through which such private road is located." The appraisers also set damages to be paid by the applicant equal to the loss in value of the land across which the road will run. See generally Warren R. Darrow, Acquiring Access to Private Landlocked Tracts: Wyoming's Statutory Right-of-Way, 16 Land & Water L. Rev. 281 (1981).

Does the Wyoming statute violate the constitutional injunction against takings of property for other than a public purpose (see pp. 179–198 supra)? In Estate of Waggoner v. Gleghorn, 378 S.W.2d 47 (Tex. 1964), the Texas Supreme Court invalidated Vernon's Ann. Civil St., art. 1377b § 2, which gave the owner of land, wholly or partially surrounded by the land of another, the right to an ingress and egress easement over the surrounding land. Although the statute did not require that the surrounding landowner be fairly compensated for the easement, the Texas court made clear that this was not the statute's only constitutional defect: "the permanent appropriation of an easement for a right of way for travel across a tract of land constitutes a 'taking' within the purview of Article 1, Section 17 of the Constitution. In our opinion Article 1377b is unconstitutional and void to the extent that it purports to authorize the taking of private property for a private purpose." 378 S.W.2d at 50. How would you respond?

What should be the consequence of private condemnation statutes on the easement by necessity?

Leo Sheep Co. v. United States

Supreme Court of the United States, 1979.
440 U.S. 668.

MR. JUSTICE REHNQUIST delivered the opinion of the Court.

This is one of those rare cases evoking episodes in this country's history that, if not forgotten, are remembered as dry facts and not as adventure. Admittedly the issue is mundane: Whether the Government has an implied easement to build a road across land that was originally granted to the Union Pacific Railroad under the Union Pacific Act of 1862—a grant that was part of a governmental scheme to subsidize the construction of the transcontinental railroad. But that issue is posed against the backdrop of a fascinating chapter in our history....

The early 19th century—from the Louisiana Purchase in 1803 to the Gadsden Purchase in 1853—saw the acquisition of the territory we now regard as the American West. During those years, however, the area remained a largely untapped resource for the settlers on the eastern seaboard of the United States did not keep pace with the rapidly expanding western frontier. A vaguely delineated area forbiddingly referred to as the "Great American Desert" can be found on more than one map published before 1850, embracing much of the United States' territory west of the Missouri River. As late as 1860, for example, the entire population of the State of Nebraska was less than 30,000 persons, which represented one person for every five square miles of land area within the State.

With the discovery of gold at Sutter's Mill in California in 1848, the California gold rush began and with it a sharp increase in settlement of the West. Those in the East with visions of instant wealth, however, confronted the unenviable choice among an arduous 4–month overland trek, risking yellow fever on a 35–day voyage via the Isthmus of Panama, and a better than 4–month voyage around Cape Horn. They obviously yearned for another alternative, and interest focused on the transcontinental railroad.

The idea of a transcontinental railroad predated the California gold rush. From the time that Asa Whitney had proposed a relatively practical plan for its construction in 1844, it had, in the words of one of this century's leading historians of the era, "engaged the eager attention of promoters and politicians until dozens of schemes were in the air."[2] The building of the railroad was not to be the unalloyed product of the free-enterprise system. There was indeed the inspiration of men like Thomas Durant and Leland Stanford and the perspiration of a generation of immigrants, but animating it all was the desire of the Federal Government that the West be settled. This desire was intensified by the need to provide a logistical link with California in the heat of the Civil War. That the venture was much too risky and much too expensive for private capital alone was evident in the years of fruitless exhortation; private investors would not move without tangible governmental inducement.

In the mid–19th century there was serious disagreement as to the forms that inducement could take. Mr. Justice Story, in his Commentaries on the Constitution, described one extant school of thought which argued that "internal improvements," such as railroads, were not within the enumerated constitutional powers of Congress. Under such a theory, the direct subsidy of a transcontinental railroad was constitutionally suspect—an uneasiness aggravated by President Andrew Jackson's 1830 veto of a bill appropriating funds to construct a road from Maysville to Lexington within the State of Kentucky.

The response to this constitutional "gray" area, and source of political controversy, was the "checkerboard" land-grant scheme. The Union Pacific

2. 2 A. Nevins, Ordeal of the Union 82 (1947).

Act of 1862 granted public land to the Union Pacific Railroad for each mile of track that it laid. Land surrounding the railway right-of-way was divided into "checkerboard" blocks. [See Figure 10–1.] Odd-numbered lots were granted to the Union Pacific; even-numbered lots were reserved by the Government. As a result, Union Pacific land in the area of the right-of-way was usually surrounded by public land, and vice versa. The historical explanation for this peculiar disposition is that it was apparently an attempt to disarm the "internal improvement" opponents by establishing a grant scheme with "demonstrable" benefits. As one historian notes in describing an 1827 federal land grant intended to facilitate private construction of a road between Columbus and Sandusky, Ohio:

> Though awkwardly stated, and not fully developed in the Act of 1827, this was the beginning of a practice to be followed in most future instances of granting land for the construction of specific internal improvements: donating alternate sections or one half of the land within a strip along the line of the project and reserving the other half for sale.... In later donations the price of the reserved sections was doubled so that it could be argued, as the *Congressional Globe* shows *ad infinitum*, that by giving half the land away and thereby making possible construction of the road, canal, or railroad, the government would recover from the reserved sections as much as it would have received from the whole.

P. Gates, History of Public Land Law Development 345–346 (1968)....

This case is the modern legacy of these early grants. Petitioners, the Leo Sheep Co. and the Palm Livestock Co., are the Union Pacific Railroad's successors in fee to specific odd-numbered sections of land in Carbon County, Wyo. These sections lie to the east and south of the Seminoe Reservoir, an area that is used by the public for fishing and hunting. Because of the checkerboard configuration, it is physically impossible to enter the Seminoe Reservoir sector from this direction without some

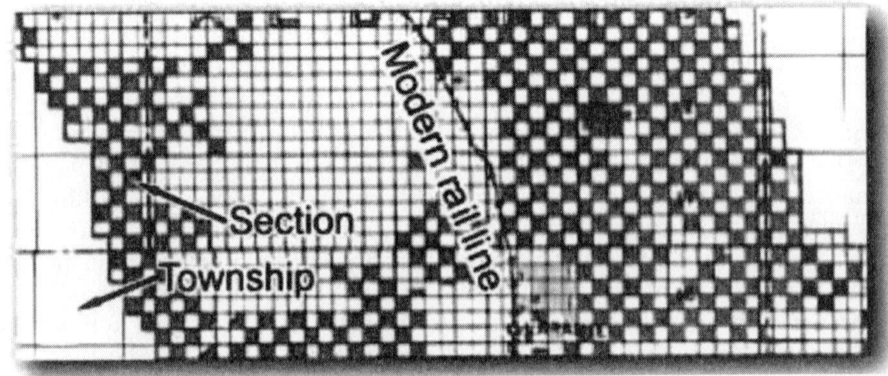

Figure 10–1
Map of Union Pacific Land Grant North of Laramie, Wyoming
(Shows typical checkerboard pattern of land grants—
railroad lands are dark squares)

minimum physical intrusion upon private land. In the years immediately preceding this litigation, the Government had received complaints that private owners were denying access over their lands to the reservoir area or requiring the payment of access fees. After negotiation with these owners failed, the Government cleared a dirt road extending from a local county road to the reservoir across both public domain lands and fee lands of the Leo Sheep Co. It also erected signs inviting the public to use the road as a route to the reservoir.

Petitioners initiated this action pursuant to 28 U. S. C. § 2409a to quiet title against the United States....

The Government does not claim that there is any express reservation of an easement in the Union Pacific Act that would authorize the construction of a public road on the Leo Sheep Co.'s property.... Where a private landowner conveys to another individual a portion of his lands in a certain area and retains the rest, it is presumed at common law that the grantor has reserved an easement to pass over the granted property if such passage is necessary to reach the retained property. These rights-of-way are referred to as "easements by necessity." There are two problems with the Government's reliance on that notion in this case. First of all, whatever right of passage a private landowner might have, it is not at all clear that it would include the right to construct a road for public access to a recreational area. More importantly, the easement is not actually a matter of necessity in this case because the Government has the power of eminent domain. Jurisdictions have generally seen eminent domain and easements by necessity as alternative ways to effect the same result. For example, the State of Wyoming no longer recognizes the common-law easement by necessity in cases involving landlocked estates. It provides instead for a procedure whereby the landlocked owner can have an access route condemned on his behalf upon payment of the necessary compensation to the owner of the servient estate. For similar reasons other state courts have held that the "easement by necessity" doctrine is not available to the sovereign.

The applicability of the doctrine of easement by necessity in this case is, therefore, somewhat strained, and ultimately of little significance. The pertinent inquiry in this case is the intent of Congress when it granted land to the Union Pacific in 1862. The 1862 Act specifically listed reservations to the grant, and we do not find the tenuous relevance of the common-law doctrine of ways of necessity sufficient to overcome the inference prompted by the omission of any reference to the reserved right asserted by the Government in this case. It is possible that Congress gave the problem of access little thought; but it is at least as likely that the thought which was given focused on negotiation, reciprocity considerations, and the power of eminent domain as obvious devices for ameliorating disputes. So both as a matter of common-law doctrine and as a matter of construing congressional intent, we are unwilling to imply rights-of-way, with the substantial impact that such implication would have on property rights granted over 100 years ago, in the absence of a stronger case for their implication than the Government makes here. . . .

. . . . Generations of land patents have issued without any express reservation of the right now claimed by the Government. Nor has a similar right been asserted before. When the Secretary of the Interior has discussed access rights, his discussion has been colored by the assumption that those rights had to be purchased. This Court has traditionally recognized the special need for certainty and predictability where land titles are concerned, and we are unwilling to upset settled expectations to accommodate some ill-defined power to construct public thoroughfares without compensation. The judgment of the Court of Appeals for the Tenth Circuit is accordingly

Reversed.

MR. JUSTICE WHITE took no part in the consideration or decision of this case.

Notes & Questions

1. If the question in *Leo Sheep* is the intent of the parties, do you believe that Congress intended to create landlocked parcels of public land when it awarded railroads every other section in a checkerboard pattern? The Tenth Circuit had concluded in *Leo Sheep* that Congress had intended to reserve a right of access. "To hold to the contrary would be to ascribe to Congress a degree of carelessness or lack of foresight which in our view would be unwarranted." Leo Sheep Co. v. United States, 570 F.2d 881, 885 (10th Cir. 1977).

If the question is instead one of public policy, is the United States' claim to an easement of necessity to access public lands a stronger or weaker case than a private property owner's claim to an easement of necessity? Although the government's power of eminent domain cuts in one direction, does the public's interest in being able to utilize federal lands cut the other? The United States Supreme Court historically has held that land grants should be "construed favorably to the Government," with any doubts regarding the grants "resolved for the Government, not against it." United States v. Union Pacific R. Co., 353 U.S. 112, 116 (1957). How would you have resolved *Leo Sheep*?

2. Assume that the Leo Sheep Company lacked access to its lands because of the checkerboard pattern of land ownership. Would the Leo Sheep Company be entitled to an easement of necessity across the federal government's lands? Should the federal government be treated any differently when it seeks an easement of necessity?

If the government transferred the public lands at issue in *Leo Sheep* to a third party, would the new owner be entitled to an easement of necessity? The new owner, after all, would not enjoy the federal government's power of eminent domain. If the United States did not originally enjoy an easement by necessity, however, can someone who purchases the land hold such an easement? In Granite Beach Holdings v. State ex rel. Dept. of Natural Resources, 11 P.3d 847 (Wash. App. 2000), several private plaintiffs bought federal lands that were completely surrounded by trust land belonging to the State of Washington and could only be accessed by logging roads running across the state land. Relying on *Leo Sheep*, the Washington State Court of Appeals held that the property owners did not enjoy an easement of necessity across the state land.

4. EASEMENTS BY PRESCRIPTION

MacDonald Properties, Inc. v. Bel–Air Country Club

Court of Appeal of California, 1977.
140 Cal. Rptr. 367.

FLEMING, Acting Presiding Judge

Plaintiffs appeal an adverse summary judgment in this action for declaratory relief and to quiet title to real property bordering defendant Bel–Air Country Club's golf course. The judgment (1) declared valid and binding on plaintiffs certain building restrictions in the deed by which Bel–Air conveyed the subject property in 1936 to Hilda Weber, plaintiffs' predecessor in interest, and (2) granted Bel–Air a prescriptive easement in the subject property.

The undisputed facts reveal the following: In 1936 Bel–Air owned a golf course, portions of which abutted lot 35, block 3, tract 7656, in the County of Los Angeles. Hilda Weber owned the bulk of lot 35, a wooded plateau of over 7 acres jutting south from Bellagio Road almost 800 feet into Bel–Air's golf course. Weber had constructed a large mansion on lot 35 but was dissatisfied with the entrance to her property from Bellagio Road. Her entryway was steep, curving, and hazardous, and she wished to acquire a portion of the golf course to provide safer, more convenient access from Bellagio Road. In 1936 Bel–Air likewise had cause for dissatisfaction in that Weber's frontage on Bellagio Road separated the fifth green of its golf course from its sixth tee, thereby making surface movement between these two points difficult. Accordingly, Weber and Bel–Air entered into an arrangement for their mutual satisfaction. Bel–Air undertook to convey to Weber the subject property of this action, approximately four-fifths of an acre of portions of lots 33, 34, and 35 of tract 7656, comprising a long strip of land bounded by Bellagio Road on the northeast and by Bel–Air's sixth fairway on the southwest. Acquisition of the property would give Weber the entranceway she desired. However, the property served as rough for Bel–Air's sixth fairway, and misdirected golf balls fell on it every day. To prevent interference with this use of the property for golfing purposes Bel–Air inserted certain building restrictions in its deed of conveyance to Weber, restrictions hereinafter discussed in detail. In her turn, Weber agreed to convey to Bel–Air a permanent easement and right of way for the construction, operation, and maintenance of a pedestrian tunnel under her portion of lot 35 adjoining Bellagio Road, a tunnel which would link the fifth green of Bel–Air's golf course with its sixth tee.

.... In November 1950 plaintiff Hilton purchased the entire Weber property and mansion, including the subject property, and in March 1963 Hilton transferred a remainder interest in the property to plaintiff MacDonald Properties.

[The court began by upholding the validity of the set-back restrictions.]

The question of a prescriptive easement to use the subject property as rough for Bel–Air's golf course and to allow players to enter upon the property to retrieve golf balls is more difficult. A prescriptive easement in property may be acquired by open, notorious, continuous, adverse use, under claim of right, for a period of five years. (Code Civ. Proc., § 321; Civ. Code, § 1007; Lynch v. *Glass* (1975) 44 Cal. App. 3d 943, 950.) The owner of the servient property must have actual knowledge of its use. Once knowledge of use is established, as was done here without contradiction, the key issue becomes one of permissive use under license as against adverse use under claim of right. The decisions on the burden of proving adverse use are widely divergent. Clarke v. Clarke (1901) 133 Cal. 667, puts the burden on the person asserting the easement to establish that his use was adverse under claim of right; whereas Fleming v. Howard (1906) 150 Cal. 28, holds that undisputed use of an easement for the prescriptive period raises a presumption of claim of right and puts the burden on the party resisting the easement to prove permissive use. Each decision has acquired a following....

We think the better and more widely held rule is that continuous use of an easement over a long period of time without the landowner's interference is presumptive evidence of its existence. This rule ... was quoted as controlling in Miller v. Johnston (1969) 270 Cal. App. 2d 289, 294, as follows:

> "It is true that title to an easement for the use of a private roadway must be established by clear and satisfactory evidence that it was used for more than the statutory period of five years openly, notoriously, visibly, continuously and without protest, opposition or denial of right to do so. But clear and satisfactory evidence of the use of the road in that manner creates a *prima facie* title to the easement by prescription. Such evidence raises a presumption that the road is used with an adverse claim of right to do so, and in the absence of evidence of mere permissive use of the road, it will be sufficient upon which to sustain a judgment quieting title to the easement therein." (Wallace v. Whitmore (1941) 47 Cal. App. 2d 369, 372–373.)

At bench, the affidavits of both parties establish without contradiction that Bel–Air's use of the area as rough for its sixth hole continued for over forty years—from sometime prior to 1936 to the filing of suit in 1974—and was well known to plaintiffs. Furthermore, in addition to the evidence of open and continuous use referred to in Miller v. Johnston, supra, we have at bench the crucial fact of the Weber deed with its building restrictions on the subject property designed to preserve Bel–Air's then existing use of its sixth hole. Extrinsic evidence established that such was the motivation for the restrictions, and no other plausible justification for them exists. The conduct of Bel–Air subsequent to the execution of the deed manifests the open and continuous use inferentially contemplated by the parties to the deed and effectuated through the creation of building restrictions. It is true that the deed does not in so many words grant an easement to Bel–Air to continue to use the property as rough for the sixth hole of its golf course. But the deed's existence, coupled with Weber's acquiescence in Bel–Air's use of the subject property as rough for many years (1936 to 1950), provides conclusive evidence that Bel–Air's use was adverse, under claim of right, and accepted as such by the owner of the subject property.

Plaintiffs did not acquire their interest in the subject property until later—1950 for Hilton, 1963 for MacDonald. Accordingly, if open and continuous use of property for five years is presumed to be adverse and in the absence of other evidence establishes an easement, Bel–Air had already perfected its easement against plaintiffs' predecessor in title (Weber). Even if we disregard the historic record and assume that prescription did not begin until title to the servient property was acquired by its present owners, the evidence establishes that plaintiffs knew of the fall of golf balls on the subject property and their retrieval by defendant's players and agents (knowledge which plaintiffs concede) and failed to protest Bel–Air's continuous use of the subject property as rough, a failure that lasted 24 years in respect to Hilton and 11 years in respect to MacDonald. Nor did plaintiffs erect permissive use signs or take other steps to preserve their rights as they might have done (see Civ. Code, § 1008), a significant evidentiary fact in most jurisdictions. (See 28 C.J.S., Easements, § 70, p. 745, fn. 19; e.g., Burnham v. Burnham (1931) 130 Me. 409.) Clearly, it did not occur to plaintiffs to challenge Bel–Air's right to use the subject property until challenge acquired the appearance of profitability in the context of plaintiffs' desire to build.

Plaintiffs raise the spectre that if Bel–Air prevails on the easement issue, all homeowners living near golf courses on whose property golf balls sometimes fall will find themselves subject to easements in favor of the golf course property if they permit players to retrieve golf balls. However, it is unlikely that many homes are so situated as to show the continuous usage without protest that occurred here (a minimum of "several balls per day frequently and regularly" driven onto the property and retrieved therefrom, amounting to "between three and five percent of the balls teed off from" a given location) or that the written record of the relationship between adjoining landowners will show as clearly as here what the intended use of the property had been. As discussed earlier, the Weber deed furnishes powerful evidence of the parties' actual intent that Bel–Air should continue to use the subject property as rough in the same fashion that it had when it owned the property in fee. Continuity of usage is really all the trial court granted Bel–Air by way of this unusual, but under the circumstances not incredible, prescriptive easement....

Lyons v. Baptist School of Christian Training

Supreme Judicial Court of Maine, 2002.
804 A.2d 364.

ALEXANDER, J.

The Baptist School of Christian Training appeals from a judgment entered in the Superior Court after a nonjury trial finding that a public, prescriptive easement exists across the Baptist School's property located in the Town of Chapman. The Baptist School argues that the Superior Court erred in finding a public, prescriptive easement because there is insufficient evidence of adversity and because the court did not apply Maine's presumption of permissive use regarding recreational uses of open lands. We vacate the Superior Court's judgment because the record fails to support the finding of adversity necessary to establish a public, prescriptive easement.

For the past fifty years, the Baptist School has owned a lot consisting of approximately 150 acres of mostly wooded land in the Town of Chapman (Chapman lot). The Chapman lot adjoins another large lot owned by the Baptist School in the Town of Mapleton (Mapleton lot). Until the 1940s, there was a residence on the Chapman lot, and four to six acres of the Chapman lot immediately abutting the Mapleton lot were cultivated for potatoes and other uses. Only a foundation remains today, and the formerly cultivated areas are now significantly overgrown. Beginning in the 1950s, the Baptist School developed and expanded a summer camp for children on the Mapleton lot, constructing a number of buildings and open areas for camp activities and recreation.

The Baptist School's properties are accessed from the Carvel Road, a public way, onto the Baptist Park Road. The Baptist Park Road runs through the Mapleton and Chapman lots and has provided access to other properties south of the Chapman lot and to the Presque Isle Stream. The portion of the Baptist Park Road within the Town of Mapleton is a public way maintained by the Town of Mapleton. The Town of Chapman has not been involved in maintaining the portion of Baptist Park Road within the Town of Chapman. There is no evidence that, within the Town of Chapman, the Baptist Park Road exists as anything other than a private way across the land of the Baptist School and other owners within the Town of Chapman.

The programs on the Baptist School's property have expanded considerably in recent years from approximately 200 campers in the mid–1950s to nearly 1000 campers in the year 2000. In addition, the nature of the programs has expanded from weekly summer camp offerings for children to larger weekly camp sessions in the summers. There are also weekend sessions for children and adults at other times of the year. Most of the camp-related activities have been conducted on the Mapleton lot. In the past several years, however, the Baptist School has added an archery course, a climbing wall, and trails for cross-country skiing and mountain biking that use the Chapman lot. . . .

In 2000, after increasing concern about abusive uses of their property by all-terrain vehicles and large-tire, four-wheel drive vehicles, the Baptist School placed a barrier across the Baptist Park Road. Initially, this barrier was placed across the road on the Mapleton lot. Later, because the road on the Mapleton lot is a public way, the barrier was moved back to the Chapman line. The plaintiffs, all of whom own property in the vicinity of the Baptist School, then brought suit alleging that a public easement by prescription had been established on the portion of the Baptist Park Road located on the Chapman lot....

All of the witnesses testified that through the years, they and other members of the public frequently used the Baptist Park Road for hunting, fishing, snowmobiling, and other recreational activities as well as to access the Presque Isle Stream and other properties south of the Chapman lot.... All of the plaintiffs' witnesses testified that they currently or had previously used the road within the Town of Chapman with some frequency and, when they used it, they neither requested permission nor believed they needed to receive permission to use the road....

Plaintiffs contend that an owner of open fields or woodlands who, over a twenty-year period, knows of and does not object to recreational crossings and/or uses of that land, forfeits a public easement and forfeits the owner's rights to object to a continuation and even an expansion of those uses by the public. Maine's public, prescriptive easement law is not so quick to deprive landowners of rights to control access to their land. The tradition of acquiescence in public access to nonposted fields and woodlands, acknowledged by six of the plaintiffs' witnesses, can, as a matter of law, remain alive and well in comity with Maine law governing public, prescriptive easements.

The party asserting a public, prescriptive easement must prove: (1) continuous use; (2) by people who are not separable from the public generally; (3) for at least twenty years; (4) under a claim of right adverse to the owner; (5) with the owner's knowledge and acquiescence; or (6) a use so open, notorious, visible, and uninterrupted that knowledge and acquiescence will be presumed.

In this case, there is no serious dispute that the road crossing the Chapman lot was subject to continuous public recreational use for at least twenty years and that this use was known and allowed by the Baptist School until 2000. The question before us is whether that public use was under a claim of right adverse to the Baptist School....

In cases involving claims of private, prescriptive easements, we have stated that where there has been unmolested, open and continuous use of a way for twenty years or more, with the knowledge and acquiescence of the owner of the servient estate, the use will be presumed to have been adverse and under a claim of right. However, application of such a presumption to a public, prescriptive easement claim for recreational uses is inappropriate when that claim applies to open fields or woodlands and the ways traversing them.

Under our precedents, public recreational uses of unposted open fields or woodlands and the ways through them are presumed permissive. Thus, in S.D. Warren v. Vernon, 697 A.2d 1280, 1283–84 (Me. 1997), we affirmed a finding of a private prescriptive easement, but we vacated a finding of a public prescriptive easement based on evidence of use of a way for hunting or recreation, woods work and access by abutting landowners. We held that "use of the road by the public for hunting or recreation is presumed permissive." In Town of Manchester v. Augusta Country Club, 477 A.2d 1124 (Me. 1984), we addressed a way maintained by the town through a golf course and used by the public for nearly fifty years to access a beach maintained by the country club. We affirmed a trial court finding that a public prescriptive easement was not proven because the evidence was insufficient to "rebut the presumption that such use was permissive." We also noted that our rule that public recreational uses are presumed to be permissive "is predicated on the notion that such use by the general public is consistent with, and in no way diminishes, the rights of the owner in his land." This observation is consistent with the testimony about traditions underlying recreational uses of land that was offered by several of the plaintiffs' witnesses in this case.

Some of our past decisions may not have been entirely clear as to whether the presumption of permissive use is generated by the public, recreational use itself, or by the nature of the land on which the use occurs, which we have sometimes characterized as "wild and uncultivated.".... [I]t is the public recreational uses of land, not the nature of the land alone, that triggers application of the rebuttable presumption of permissive use in public prescriptive easement cases. The presumption that public recreational uses of open, unposted land are permissive applies equally to children playing on a vacant lot in town, hunters and snowmobilers crossing a cultivated field after the harvest, or families camping on privately owned wood lots, and it applies to the uses testified to by the plaintiffs in this case.[6]

In this case, the long history of public, recreational uses of the Chapman lot and the way through it, creates a presumption of permissive use, not a presumption of adversity.... In this record, there is no evidence of an open and demonstrated hostile intent to limit the Baptist School's rights in the land. A majority of the plaintiffs' witnesses acknowledged the tradition of landowner acquiescence in public recreational uses of open, unposted fields and woodlands. Seven of plaintiffs' witnesses acknowledged that they would have respected no trespassing signs, had they been posted. Even those witnesses who stated that they believed they had a right to use the property, either acknowledged the tradition of acquiescence or acknowl-

6. To promote and continue Maine's tradition of presumptive landowner permission for public access for recreational uses of open fields and woodlands, the legislature has adopted limitations on landowner liability for injuries to the public that may occur in the course of such recreational uses. See 14 M.R.S.A. § 159–A (Supp. 2001); Robbins v. Great N. Paper Co., 557 A.2d 614, 616–17 (Me. 1989) (stating that the purpose of § 159–A "is to encourage landowners to allow recreational use of the Maine woodlands that are rich with opportunities for hunting, fishing, and other recreational activities").

edged that they would have respected no trespassing signs had they been posted. None of the witnesses testified to any overt act of hostility that could have placed the Baptist School on notice that the plaintiffs' use was extending beyond the accepted land use traditions and was seeking to establish a public easement or otherwise limit the Baptist School's capacity to control access to and through its property....

CALKINS, J., with whom CLIFFORD and RUDMAN, JJ., join, dissenting.

I respectfully dissent. I do so because the Court has failed to give the proper deference to the trial court's factual findings and because the Court has created a new and unwarranted presumption in the law of prescriptive easements.

I agree with the Court that the elements required to prove a public prescriptive easement are continuous public use for twenty years under a claim of right adverse to the owner, with the owner's knowledge or acquiescence, or a use so open, notorious, visible, and uninterrupted that knowledge and acquiescence are presumed. These are the same elements required to prove a private prescriptive easement with the addition of proving public use. Public use is shown by the use of the road by people who are inseparable from the public generally....

The Court today creates a new presumption to negate the presumption of adversity in prescriptive easement cases, holding that public recreational use of private land is presumed to be permissive. Because this new presumption is based on the use of the land instead of the character of the land, it departs significantly from our established case law.

The Court justifies its new presumption by claiming that it is not new, but rooted in our precedents. This is incorrect. From Maine's first year as a state, we have recognized that the law of prescriptive easements developed in the improved, agricultural terrain of England could not be applied without change to the wild lands of Maine. We first held over one hundred and thirty years ago that use of "open and unenclosed" land is presumed permissive .... In none of our early cases did we indicate that the presumption had anything to do with the use rather than the character of the land. We subsequently applied the presumption to land with a variety of uses, both recreational and nonrecreational. E.g., Littlefield v. Hubbard, 128 A. 285, 288 (Me. 1925) (applying presumption of permission to use of uncultivated, unenclosed seashore property by hunters, commercial fishermen, people harvesting seaweed, and others)....

Further indication that a presumption of permission based on the use of the land is an unprecedented innovation comes from looking at authorities from outside Maine, which strongly support a presumption based on the character of the land. Restatement (Third) of Property, Servitudes § 2.16 cmt. g (2000) ("Evidence that the claimed servient estate was wild, unenclosed, vacant land overcomes the presumption of adverse use in many states, creating a presumption that the use was permissive."); 4 Powell on Real Property § 34.10[2][c] (2001) (citing cases from sixteen states holding that presumption of adversity does not apply where land is "open, unenclosed, and unimproved"); 25 Am. Jur. 2d Easements & Licenses § 53 (1996) (citing cases from eleven states holding that there is presumption of permission and/or no presumption of adversity for use of "wild or unenclosed land"); J.J. Marticelli, Annotation, Acquisition by user or prescription of right of way over uninclosed land, 46 A.L.R.2d 1140, 1142–43 & n.9 (1956) (citing cases from twenty-five states for "prevailing rule" that no presumption of adversity arises for use of unenclosed land). The Court's holding thus not only departs from our own precedents, but also puts us out of step with the law in other states.

The justification offered for this change is that the Court desires to give property owners more protection than our existing law provides against the acquisition of easements by prescription. In one important respect, however, today's holding apparently makes it *easier* to acquire a prescriptive easement. Under our case law, any use of wild and uncultivated land has been presumed permissive. By replacing the traditional presumption of permission with one that only applies to public recreational use, the Court gives those who use wild and uncultivated land for private or nonrecreational uses the benefit of the presumption of adversity. The effect of this change in the law is to shift the burden to landowners to prove that, for example, private use for commercial timber harvesting or public use for transportation purposes was permissive....

Notes & Questions

1. Is the practical lesson of prescriptive easement cases that you shouldn't be a good neighbor? That property owners should not let strangers cross or otherwise come onto their land? Is that good public policy?

2. **Adversity.** In most prescriptive easement cases, the determinative yet most issue is whether the use was adverse or permissive. Courts split on whether uses of someone else's property should be presumed to be adverse (in which case the land owner has the burden of showing that she gave the claimant permission to use the land) or permissive (in which case the claimant has the burden of proof). Compare United States v. Platt, 730 F. Supp. 318, 321 (D. Ariz. 1990) ("the law presumes the use to be under a claim of right and not permissive") with McGill v. Wahl, 839 P.2d 393, 397 (Alaska 1992) ("There is a presumption that the use of land by an alleged easement holder was permissive"). Some courts assume that uses are nonpermissive, but reverse the presumption where land is undeveloped, wild, or remote. See, e.g., Carson v. County of Drew, 128 S.W.3d 423, 426–427 (Ark. 2003). As *Lyons* illustrates, the Maine Supreme Court now presumes that public recreational use of land is permissive. What are the likely consequences of the various alternative presumptions?

3. **The Other Elements of Prescription.** The other elements required to prove an easement by prescription bear many obvious similarities to the requirements for adverse possession (see pages 102–128 supra). As *MacDonald Properties* and *Lyons* discuss, most of the required elements for prescription and adverse possession are the same. Yet, there are a number

of differences stemming from fundamental differences between possession and use.

Most importantly, prescription requires *use* of someone else's land for the statutory period, while adverse possession requires the *occupation* of someone else's land with the intent to control it. In most cases, the distinction is clear. If Rachel Carson crosses John Wesley Powell's property periodically to get to her favorite fishing spot, she may ultimately gain a prescriptive easement, but she will not gain adverse possession to his property. If Rachel builds a house on John's property and lives in it, she ultimately may gain possessory title to the property by adverse possession.

Some cases, however, are more difficult. Imagine, for example, that Rachel paves a road from the street to her property across John's land and uses it for a driveway. Rachel even plants trees on either side of the driveway. After the statutory period has passed, does Rachel have a prescriptive easement to use the driveway as a right of way, or has she gained title to the land on which the driveway is found? Compare McDonald v. Harris, 978 P.2d 81 (Alaska 1999) (prescriptive easement) with Palazzolo v. Malba Estates, Inc., 500 N.Y.S.2d 327 (App. Div. 1986) (title by adverse possession).

Continuous. Both prescription and adverse possession require that the use or possession be "continuous." Continuity of possession, however, is physically different from continuity of use. A claimant's house which encroaches on a neighbor's parcel will physically deprive the neighbor of possession *throughout* the limitations period. By contrast, claimant's use of a neighbor's pathway will characteristically be discontinuous, for there will be many times during the limitations period when the claimant is not actually present on the land. As a result, courts have been far less rigorous in applying the continuity requirement in prescriptive easement cases than in adverse possession cases.

What limits should be placed on this comparatively relaxed attitude? What if claimant uses two paths with identical terminal points, changing from one path to the other midway through the prescription period? See Algermissen v. Sutin, 61 P.3d 176, 184 (N.M. 2002) ("Plaintiffs must show that the location of the alleged easement did not change during the prescriptive period").

Known or Open and Notorious. Because land uses are characteristically discontinuous, and often covert, courts generally require more open and obvious conduct in prescriptive easement cases than in adverse possession cases. Actual knowledge, if shown, obviates proof that the use was open and notorious. Absent actual knowledge, the requisite notice will be implied only if the claimant's use was sufficiently open and notorious to make a reasonable neighbor aware of it. See, e.g., Mavromoustakos v. Padussis, 684 A.2d 51 (Md. Ct. Spec. App. 1996); Hopkins v. Hill, 68 N.W.2d 678 (Neb. 1955).

Exclusive. Like the California Court of Appeal in *MacDonald Properties*, most courts do not require that a use be "exclusive" in order to establish a prescriptive easement. See, e.g., Neyland v. Hunter, 668 S.W.2d 530, 531 (Ark. 1984). Easements, after all, are nonpossessory interests in land that do not preclude the landowner from also using her property. A few courts do list "exclusivity" as a requirement for prescription, but they define exclusivity to mean that the claimant's right must not depend on a similar right in others. Thus, a claimant's use, along with use by the owner of the servient estate or by adjoining landowners, will be exclusive so long as the use is based on an individual claim. But see Vrazel v. Skrabanek, 725 S.W.2d 709 (Tex. 1987) (no prescriptive easement where both claimant and landowner used the roadway).

4. **Scope of Prescriptive Easements.** What is the extent of use permitted by a prescriptive easement? Aztec Ltd., Inc. v. Creekside Investment Co., 602 P.2d 64, 66 (Idaho 1979), states the general rule: "an easement acquired by prescription is confined to the right as exercised during the prescriptive period. It is limited by the purpose for which it is acquired and the use to which it is put." At the same time, the court reaffirmed "a single and narrow exception" stated in an earlier decision, Gibbens v. Weisshaupt, 570 P.2d 870, 876 (Idaho 1977): "some changes in the character of the dominant estate are foreseeable and will necessitate changes in the use of a prescriptive easement. We emphasize, however, that any changes in the use of a prescriptive easement cannot result in an unreasonable increased burden on the servient estate and that the increase in use must be reasonably foreseeable at the time the easement is established."

Applying the rule and its exception to the case before it, the *Aztec* court held that a prescriptive easement to use a twenty-foot roadway for access to and from three or four private homes could not be expanded to include access to 200 apartment units. The court also ruled that it was impermissible to widen the roadway: "any increase in width of a prescriptive easement would constitute an impermissible expansion even if a contemporaneous increase in traffic over the easement would not. An increase in width does more than merely increase the burden upon the servient estate; it has the effect of enveloping additional land." 602 P.2d at 67.

5. **Rejection of Negative Prescriptive Easements.** Does the requirement of open, actual, and notorious use leave any room for prescriptive *negative* easements, such as an easement for light and air? Because negative easements involve no physical use of the servient estate, how could courts determine the extent of the prescriptive easement? What steps could a landowner take to prevent her parcel from becoming the servient estate burdened by a negative easement?

In England, the doctrine of ancient lights gives a landowner who has continuously received light and air from across his neighbor's land a prescriptive right, entitling him to an injunction against his neighbor's subsequent obstruction of the light and air reaching his windows. Although the doctrine of ancient lights enjoyed an early, tentative foothold in the United States, it was soon rejected throughout the country. The "doctrine was out of place—or so the courts thought. America was bent on economic growth—on trying to promote, not curb, the intensive use of land." Lawrence Friedman, History of American Law 310 (3d ed. 2005).

6. **Easements to Pollute.** Should a company that has polluted for many years gain a prescriptive easement entitling it to continue to pollute? In Hoffman v. United Iron & Metal Co., 671 A.2d 55 (Md. Spec. App. 1996), 35 property owners sued a scrap metal yard and automobile shredding facility, arguing that noise and pollution from the facility was an illegal nuisance. The court held that the owners of the facility, by running it for over twenty years, had gained a prescriptive right to maintain a nuisance—even though the pollution violated state laws.

> [A]ppellants contend that a party may not obtain a prescriptive easement to perform an illegal act.... The Supreme Court of Mississippi held that the enactment of a state pollution law "tolled any prescriptive right gained by [defendant] or its predecessor in ownership." Vicksburg Chemical Co. v. Thornell, 355 So. 2d 299, 301 (Miss. 1978). Appellants argue that, when Maryland enacted [air pollution regulations], it became impossible for the appellees to obtain a prescriptive right to maintain a nuisance. We reject appellants' argument. Just as the legality of a business is not conclusive as to whether its operation constitutes a nuisance, illegality of certain conduct is not conclusive as to the same question. We see no reason to hold that the passage of regulations controlling air pollution in 1980 tolled the prescriptive period.

Id. at 66. Should courts recognize a prescriptive right to engage in an activity that is illegal? Should it matter if the alleged prescriptive right poses health risks to the neighbors? In a footnote, the court noted that no one can acquire a prescriptive right to maintain a *public* nuisance, but concluded that the question whether the facility constituted a public nuisance was not properly before it. Id. at 64 n.9. Should the resolution of cases like *Hoffman* depend on whether the plaintiff is a public official, suing to enjoin a public nuisance, or a private landowner, suing to stop a private nuisance?

7. **Public Prescriptive Easements.** Many courts historically did not recognize public prescriptive easements. See, e.g., Mihalczo v. Borough of Woodmont, 400 A.2d 270, 272 (Conn. 1978). However, a growing number of courts today, as well as the Restatement of Property, recognize public prescriptive easements. See, e.g., Carson v. County of Drew, 128 S.W.3d 423 (Ark. 2003); Breiner v. Holt Cty., 581 N.W.2d 89, 94 (Neb. App. 1998); Swandel Ranch Co. v. Hunt, 915 P.2d 840, 844 (Mont. 1996); Fears v. YJ Land Corp., 539 N.W.2d 306, 308 (N.D. 1995); Opinion of the Justices, 649 A.2d 604, 610 (N.H. 1994); Weidner v. State Dept. of Transp. & Pub. Facilities, 860 P.2d 1205, 1209 (Alaska 1993); Restatement (Third) of Property, Servitudes § 2.18 (2000).

Should the standards for establishing public prescriptive easements differ from those for private prescriptive easements (other than any differences in the exclusiveness of use)? Should courts that generally presume that uses are nonpermissive switch the presumption when the public at large is asserting a prescriptive right, as the Maine Supreme Court did for recreational uses in *Lyons*?

8. **Beach Access: Public Prescriptive Easements, Dedication, and Custom.** Public demand for access to coastal beaches is increasing. Some courts have used the doctrine of public prescriptive easements to open up beaches to recreational use by the public. See, e.g., Villa Nova Resort, Inc. v. State, 711 S.W.2d 120 (Tex. Ct. Civ. App. 1986). Courts also have used two related doctrines—*implied dedication* and *custom*—to achieve the same goal.

The general doctrine of *dedication* permits property owners to offer and governments to accept real property, including rights of way and other easements, on behalf of the public. In a typical situation, a developer offers to dedicate roadways in its subdivision to the public; once the government accepts the offer, the government controls and maintains the roadways. Where the public has made lengthy use of a private beach, some courts have held that the lengthy use is evidence of an implicit dedication of the beach to public use. See, e.g., Gion v. City of Santa Cruz, 465 P.2d 50 (Cal. 1970); *Villa Nova Resort*, supra, 711 S.W.2d at 128. Should it matter whether the property owner has acquiesced in the public's use or, alternatively, objected to the use and tried to stop it?

Other courts have used the common law doctrine of custom to open up private beaches to public use. Under custom, English courts protect usages of property that have lasted so long "that the memory of man runneth not to the contrary." 1 William Blackstone, Commentaries on the Laws of England *75–*78 (1766). Because of the United States' relatively young history, few American courts have found the doctrine of custom relevant to property disputes in the nation. Americans' memory simply does not "runneth" long enough. In State ex rel. Thornton v. Hay, 462 P.2d 671 (Ore. 1969), however, the Oregon Supreme Court held that the public's long-standing use of that state's beaches gave the public a customary right to continue to use the beaches.

> So long as there has been an institutionalized system of land tenure in Oregon, the public has freely exercised the right to use the dry-sand area up and down the Oregon coast.... On the score of the brevity of our political history, it is true that the Anglo–American legal system on this continent is relatively new. Its newness has made it possible for government to provide for many of our institutions by written law rather than by customary law. This truism does not, however, militate against the validity of a custom when the custom does in fact exist. If antiquity were the sole test of validity of a custom, Oregonians could satisfy that requirement by recalling that the European settlers were not the first people to use the dry-sand area as public land.

Recall from Chapter 2 that the New Jersey Supreme Court has used the public trust doctrine to provide the public with reasonable access to dry-sand beaches. Pp. 94–102. In determining whether to open dry-sand beaches to the public and which beaches to open, what are the relative advantages and disadvantages of the four doctrines used by courts to date—public prescriptive easements, dedication, custom, and public trust?

9. **Statutory Protections of Property Owners.** Some state legislatures have taken steps to protect landowners from claims for private or public prescriptive easements, or implied dedication, across their lands. California, for example, provides that no use of someone else's property can ever ripen into a prescriptive easement "if the owner of such property posts at each entrance to the property or at intervals of not more than 200 feet along the boundary a sign reading substantially as follows: 'Right to pass by permission, and subject to control, of owner.' " Cal. Civ. Code § 1008. California also prohibits public claims to the use of land, except in the case of coastal properties. Owners of coastal properties can protect themselves by (1) posting the signs described in section 1008, (2) recording a notice that the right of the public to use the land is "by permission, and subject to control, of owner," or (3) entering into a "written agreement with any federal, state, or local agency providing for the public use of such land." Id. § 1009. What's the rationale for such laws?

B. COVENANTS AND SERVITUDES

As explained earlier, real covenants are promises that a property owner will or will not do something that the law otherwise does not compel or prohibit. Covenants can take a variety of forms. For example, Rachel, who owns Greenacre, may promise John that she will erect and maintain a boundary wall running between the two parcels, or that she will not place any improvement on Greenacre that obstructs her neighbor's scenic view. The Zion's Cooperative Mercantile Institution (ZCMI), a major department store tenant in a suburban shopping center, may promise the center's small retail tenants that it will actively conduct its business during regular shopping center hours, seven days a week; each tenant may in turn promise ZCMI and the other tenants not to sell competing lines of merchandise.

Subdivisions make extensive use of real covenants. For example, property in the White Oakdale Subdivision in Woodford County, Illinois, is subject to over a dozen separate covenants, including promises that the property owner will:[1]

- Use his land only for single family residential purposes,
- Erect a residence that contains at least 1400 square feet of enclosed living space (if a single level residence) and 1800 square feet (if a multiple level residence),
- Use only new material in construction projects,
- Keep his lot free of all "new or used construction materials or supplies, junk, wrecked or unused machinery, inoperable vehicles, commercial

1. You can read the full "Declaration of Covenants, Conditions, and Restrictions" at http://www.germantownhills.com/wola/covenents.htm.

property or equipment or the like," except as part of a construction project, and

- Complete his residence and any other buildings within one year of the commencement of construction.

A property owner in the White Oakdale Subdivision also promises not to:

- Maintain any "pre-built residential structure or house trailers" on his property,
- Use basements or garages as living quarters,
- Raise, breed, or keep any animals, livestock, or poultry on his property, except for "dogs, cats, or other household pets ..., provided they are not kept, bred, or maintained for any commercial purpose,"
- Allow weeds or grass to grow more than 12 inches high, or permit any other "unsightly growth,"
- Erect or maintain any commercial sign ("except for a single 'for sale' or 'for rent' sign not exceeding sixteen (16) square feet in size"),
- Permit the "development of any unclean, unsightly or unkempt conditions of the residence or grounds on his lot which shall tend to substantially decrease the beauty of the neighborhood as a whole or the specific area," and
- Engage in any "noxious or offensive activity" or do anything "tending to cause embarrassment, discomfort, annoyance or nuisance to the neighborhood."

The English courts of law that developed the law of real covenants wanted to promote the marketability of land and therefore limited the ability of property owners to subject future owners of the property to restrictive covenants. As discussed in the next section, courts of law accomplished this goal by imposing a number of conditions on the running of the burden of real covenants. Those property owners who wanted to get around these limitations turned to courts of equity, which agreed to enforce a broader set of covenants as "equitable servitudes" and allow those servitudes to run with the land.

A landowner's promise to do something or not to do something in connection with land ownership can thus be a real covenant, an equitable servitude, or both. The choice of what to call the promise depends, in part, on the type of relief that the plaintiff is seeking. The remedy for breach of a real covenant is damages. The remedy for breach of an equitable servitude is a prohibitory injunction in the case of negative undertakings and a mandatory injunction in the case of affirmative undertakings. Equity, however, also will exercise its "cleanup" jurisdiction and award damages when needed to make the beneficiary whole. Equally important in determining what to call the promise are the requirements for real covenants and equitable servitudes running with the land. As discussed below, it is still harder in many jurisdictions to get a real covenant to run with the land than to have an equitable servitude do the same.

In many jurisdictions today, the differences between real covenants and equitable servitudes have begun to disappear. See Susan F. French, Toward a Modern Law of Servitudes: Reweaving the Ancient Strands, 55 S. Cal. L. Rev. 1261 (1982). The Restatement of Property would abolish the distinctions entirely and treat both of them as covenants running with the land. Restatement (Third) of Property, Servitudes § 1.4 (2000). "Because continued use of the terms 'real covenant' and 'equitable servitude' perpetuates the idea that there is a difference between covenants at law and in equity, which at best tends to generate confusion, and at worst may lead lawyers and judges to focus on irrelevant questions or reach erroneous results, those terms have been dropped in this Restatement in favor of the term 'covenant running with land.' " Id. § 1.4, cmt. a, at 30. Under the Restatement, any servitude

> may be enforced by any appropriate remedy or combination of remedies, which may include declaratory judgment, compensatory damages, punitive damages, nominal damages, injunctions, restitution, and imposition of liens. Factors that may be considered in determining the availability and appropriate choice of remedy include the nature and purpose of the servitude, the conduct of the parties, the fairness of the servitude and the transaction that created it, and the costs and benefits of enforcement to the parties, to third parties, and to the public.

Id. § 8.3(1).

1. RUNNING OF THE BENEFIT AND BURDEN

English courts, from an early stage in the law of covenants, allowed the *benefit* of a covenant to run to nonpromisees who subsequently acquired an interest in the dominant estate. They were reluctant, however, to allow the *burden* of a covenant to run to nonpromisors who subsequently acquired the servient estate. One reason for this reluctance was the courts' reasonable belief that it was a much larger step to impose the burden of promises on nonpromisors than to shower their benefits on nonpromisees.

Although American courts were more generous than their English counterparts in allowing the burden of a real covenant to run with the land, they succeeded only by replacing parsimony with prolixity. Piling requirement upon requirement for the burden to run, American courts produced what one observer characterized "an unnecessarily complicated, cumbersome and unpredictable complex of rules." Lawrence Berger, A Policy Analysis of Promises Respecting the Use of Land, 55 Minn. L. Rev. 167, 169 (1970). American courts, however, like their English counterparts, were more willing to enforce equitable servitudes against subsequent landowners.

Figure 10–2 on the next page shows the traditional requirements for the benefits and burdens of covenants and equitable servitudes to run with the land. As you will see in the notes following the next case, courts are increasingly abandoning several of these requirements, including horizontal privity and "touch or concern." States, moreover, always varied to some degrees in the exact requirements that they imposed. You may want to refer to this chart as you read the remaining materials in this section.

Requirements	Burdens of Real Covenants	Benefits of Real Covenants	Burdens of Equitable Servitudes	Benefits of Equitable Servitudes
Intent	√	√	√	√
Notice to Subsequent Purchaser	√		√	
Horizontal Privity	√	Generally not required		
Vertical Privity	Succession to estate of same duration	Succession to any part of the estate		
Touch or Concern Land	√	√	Laxer than for real covenants	Laxer than for real covenants

Figure 10–2
Traditional Requirements for Benefits and Burdens to Run

Runyon v. Paley

Supreme Court of North Carolina, 1992.
416 S.E.2d 177.

MEYER, J.

This case involves a suit to enjoin defendants from constructing condominium units on their property adjacent to the Pamlico Sound on Ocracoke Island. Plaintiffs maintain that defendants' property is subject to restrictive covenants that prohibit the construction of condominiums. The sole question presented for our review is whether plaintiffs are entitled to enforce the restrictive covenants.

On 17 May 1937, Ruth Bragg Gaskins acquired a four-acre tract of land located in the Village of Ocracoke bounded on the west by the Pamlico Sound and on the east by Silver Lake. [In 1954, Mrs. Gaskins conveyed a 1½-acre parcel of the land to the plaintiffs Runyons. In 1960, the Runyons reconveyed the property to Mrs. Gaskins. Two days later, she conveyed a small lake-front parcel of the property to the Runyons, and the following day, conveyed the remainder of the 1½-acre parcel to the Brughs. The deed of conveyance from Mrs. Gaskins to the Brughs included the following:]

> But this land is being conveyed subject to certain restrictions as to the use thereof, running with said land by whomsoever owned, until removed as herein set out; said restrictions, which

are expressly assented to by [the Brughs], in accepting this deed, are as follows:

(1) Said lot shall be used for residential purposes and not for business, manufacturing, commercial or apartment house purposes; provided, however, this restriction shall not apply to churches or to the office of a professional man which is located in his residence, and

(2) Not more than two residences and such outbuildings as are appurtenant thereto, shall be erected or allowed to remain on said lot. This restriction shall be in full force and effect until such time as adjacent or nearby properties are turned to commercial use, in which case the restrictions herein set out will no longer apply. The word "nearby" shall, for all intents and purposes, be construed to mean within 450 feet thereof. . . .

Prior to the conveyance of this land to the Brughs, Mrs. Gaskins had constructed a residential dwelling in which she lived on lake-front property across the road from the property conveyed to the Brughs. Mrs. Gaskins retained this land and continued to live on this property until her death in August 1961. Plaintiff Williams, Mrs. Gaskins' daughter, has since acquired the property retained by Mrs. Gaskins.

By mesne conveyances, defendant Warren D. Paley acquired the property conveyed by Mrs. Gaskins to the Brughs. Thereafter, defendant Warren Paley and his wife, defendant Claire Paley, entered into a partnership with defendant Midgett Realty and began constructing condominium units on the property.

Plaintiffs [Williams and the Runyons] brought this suit, seeking to enjoin defendants from using the property in a manner that is inconsistent with the restrictive covenants included in the deed from Mrs. Gaskins to the Brughs. In their complaint, plaintiffs alleged that the restrictive covenants were placed on the property "for the benefit of [Mrs. Gaskins'] property and neighboring property owners, specifically including and intending to benefit the Runyons." Plaintiffs further alleged that the "restrictive covenants have not been removed and are enforceable by plaintiffs." . . .

I. Real Covenants at Law

A restrictive covenant . . . runs with the land of the dominant and servient estates only if (1) the subject of the covenant touches and concerns the land, (2) there is privity of estate between the party enforcing the covenant and the party against whom the covenant is being enforced, and (3) the original covenanting parties intended the benefits and the burdens of the covenant to run with the land. Elements

A. Touch and Concern

As noted by several courts and commentators, the touch and concern requirement is not capable of being reduced to an absolute test or precise definition. Focusing on the nature of the burdens and benefits created by a 

covenant, the court must exercise its best judgment to determine whether the covenant is related to the covenanting parties' ownership interests in their land.

For a covenant to touch and concern the land, it is not necessary that the covenant have a physical effect on the land. It is sufficient that the covenant have some economic impact on the parties' ownership rights by, for example, enhancing the value of the dominant estate and decreasing the value of the servient estate. It is essential, however, that the covenant in some way affect the legal rights of the covenanting parties as landowners. Where the burdens and benefits created by the covenant are of such a nature that they may exist independently from the parties' ownership interests in land, the covenant does not touch and concern the land and will not run with the land.

Although not alone determinative of the issue, the nature of the restrictive covenants at issue in this case (building or use restrictions) is strong evidence that the covenants touch and concern the dominant and servient estates. As recognized by some courts, a restriction limiting the use of land clearly touches and concerns the estate burdened with the covenant because it restricts the owner's use and enjoyment of the property and thus affects the value of the property. A use restriction does not, however, always touch and concern the dominant estate. See Stegall v. Housing Authority, 278 N.C. 95, 178 S.E.2d 824 (1971) (holding that covenant did not meet the touch and concern requirement where the record failed to disclose the location of the grantor's property "in the area" or the distance from the grantor's property to the restricted property). To meet the requirement that the covenant touch and concern the dominant estate, it must be shown that the covenant somehow affects the dominant estate by, for example, increasing the value of the dominant estate.

In the case at bar, plaintiffs have shown that the covenants sought to be enforced touch and concern not only the servient estate owned by defendants, but also the properties owned by plaintiffs. The properties owned by defendants, plaintiff Williams, and plaintiffs Runyon comprise only a portion of what was at one time a four-acre tract bounded on one side by the Pamlico Sound and on the other by Silver Lake. If able to enforce the covenants against defendants, plaintiffs would be able to restrict the use of defendants' property to uses that accord with the restrictive covenants. Considering the close proximity of the lands involved here and the relatively secluded nature of the area where the properties are located, we conclude that the right to restrict the use of defendants' property would affect plaintiffs' ownership interests in the property owned by them, and therefore the covenants touch and concern their lands.

B. Privity of Estate

In order to enforce a restrictive covenant as one running with the land at law, the party seeking to enforce the covenant must also show that he is in privity of estate with the party against whom he seeks to enforce the covenant. Although the origin of privity of estate is not certain, the privity requirement has been described as a substitute for privity of contract, which exists between the original covenanting parties and which is ordinarily required to enforce a contractual promise. Thus, where the covenant is sought to be enforced by someone not a party to the covenant or against someone not a party to the covenant, the party seeking to enforce the covenant must show that he has a sufficient legal relationship with the party against whom enforcement is sought to be entitled to enforce the covenant.

For the enforcement at law of a covenant running with the land, most states require two types of privity: (1) privity of estate between the covenantor and covenantee at the time the covenant was created ("horizontal privity"), and (2) privity of estate between the covenanting parties and their successors in interest ("vertical privity"). The majority of jurisdictions have held that horizontal privity exists when the original covenanting parties make their covenant in connection with the conveyance of an estate in land from one of the parties to the other. A few courts, on the other hand, have dispensed with the showing of horizontal privity altogether, requiring only a showing of vertical privity.

Vertical privity, which is ordinarily required to enforce a real covenant at law, requires a showing of succession in interest between the original covenanting parties and the current owners of the dominant and servient estates....

We adhere to the rule that a party seeking to enforce a covenant as one running with the land at law must show the presence of both horizontal and vertical privity. In order to show horizontal privity, it is only necessary that a party seeking to enforce the covenant show that there was some "connection of interest" between the original covenanting parties, such as, here, the conveyance of an estate in land.

In the case *sub judice*, plaintiffs have shown the existence of horizontal privity. The record shows that the covenants at issue in this case were created in connection with the transfer of an estate in fee of property then owned by Mrs. Gaskins....

To review the sufficiency of vertical privity in this case, it is necessary to examine three distinct relationships: (1) the relationship between defendants and the Brughs as the covenantors; (2) the relationship between plaintiff Williams and the covenantee, Mrs. Gaskins; and (3) the relationship between plaintiffs Runyon and Mrs. Gaskins. The evidence before us shows that the Brughs conveyed all of their interest in the restricted property and that by mesne conveyances defendant Warren Paley succeeded to a fee simple estate in the property. Thus, he is in privity of estate with the covenantors. Any legal interests held by the other defendants were acquired by them from defendant Warren Paley. As successors to the interest held by defendant Warren Paley, they too are in privity of estate with the covenantors. Plaintiff Williams has also established a privity of estate between herself and the covenantee. Following the death of Mrs. Gaskins, the property retained by Mrs. Gaskins was conveyed by her heirs to her daughter, Eleanor Gaskins. Thereafter, Eleanor Gaskins conveyed to plaintiff Williams a fee simple absolute in that property .... Such would be true even if the parties had succeeded to only a part of the land burdened and benefitted by the covenants. Plaintiffs Runyon have not, however, made a sufficient showing of vertical privity. The Runyons have not succeeded in any interest in land held by Mrs. Gaskins at the time the covenant was created. The only interest in land held by the Runyons was acquired by them prior to the creation of the covenant. Therefore, they have not shown vertical privity of estate between themselves and the covenantee with respect to the property at issue in this case. Because the Runyons were not parties to the covenant and are not in privity with the original parties, they may not enforce the covenant as a real covenant running with the land at law.

C. Intent of the Parties

Defendants argue that plaintiff Williams is precluded from enforcing the restrictive covenants because the covenanting parties who created the restrictions intended that the restrictions be enforceable only by Mrs. Gaskins, the original covenantee. According to defendants, such a conclusion is necessitated where, as here, the instrument creating the covenants does not expressly state that persons other than the covenantee may enforce the covenants. We disagree.

Defendants correctly note that our law does not favor restrictions on the use of real property. It is generally stated that "[r]estrictions in a deed will be regarded as for the personal benefit of the grantor unless a contrary intention appears, and the burden of showing that they constitute covenants running with the land is upon the party claiming the benefit of the restriction." Stegall v. Housing authority, 178 S.E.2d 824, 828 (1971). This, however, does not mean that we will always regard a restriction as personal to the covenantee unless the restriction expressly states that persons other than the covenantee may enforce the covenant.

"Whether restrictions imposed upon land ... create a personal obligation or impose a servitude upon the land enforceable by subsequent purchasers [of the covenantee's property] is determined by the intention of the parties at the time the deed containing the restriction was delivered." *Stegall*, 178 S.E.2d at 828. The question of the parties' intention is one that the court must decide by applying our well-established principles of contract construction....

Ordinarily, the parties' intent must be ascertained from the deed or other instrument creating the restriction. However, when the language used in the instrument is ambiguous, the court, in determining the parties' intention, must look to the language of the instrument, the nature of the restriction, the situation of the parties, and the circumstances surrounding their transaction.

We conclude that the language of the deed creating the restrictions at issue here is ambiguous with regard to the intended enforcement of the restrictions. The deed from Mrs. Gaskins to the Brughs provided that the property conveyed was being made "subject to certain restrictions as to the use thereof, running with said land by whomsoever owned, until removed [due to a change of conditions in the surrounding properties] as herein set out." As noted by the dissent in the Court of Appeals, this provision unequivocally expresses the parties' intention that the burden of the restrictions runs with the land conveyed by the deed. In the habendum clause of the deed, the parties also included language providing that the estate granted shall be "*subject always* to the restrictions as to use as hereinabove set out." (Emphasis added.) We conclude that the language of the deed creating the restrictions is such that it can reasonably be interpreted to establish an intent on the part of the covenanting parties not only to bind successors to the covenantor's interest, but also to benefit the property retained by the covenantee.

Having determined that the instrument creating the restrictions at issue here is ambiguous as to the parties' intention that the benefit of the covenants runs with the land, we must determine whether plaintiff Williams has produced sufficient evidence to show that the covenanting parties intended that the covenants be enforceable by the covenantee's successors in interest. . . . As noted by some courts, restrictions limiting the use of property to residential purposes have a significant impact on the value of neighboring land, and thus the very nature of such a restriction suggests that the parties intended that the restriction benefit land rather than the covenantee personally. . . . We need not decide whether the nature of a building or use restriction, in and of itself, is sufficient evidence of the parties' intent that the benefit run with the land, however.

In this case, the evidence also shows that the property now owned by defendants was once part of a larger, relatively secluded tract bounded by Silver Lake and the Pamlico Sound. . . . [It] is reasonable to assume that Mrs. Gaskins, by later restricting the use of defendants' property, intended to preserve the residential character and value of the relatively secluded area. This evidence is further supported by the fact that Mrs. Gaskins retained land across the road from the property now owned by defendants and continued to reside in her dwelling located on the retained land. We believe that this evidence of the parties' situation and of the circumstances surrounding their transaction strongly supports a finding that the covenanting parties intended that the restrictive covenants inure to the benefit of Mrs. Gaskins' land and not merely to Mrs. Gaskins personally.

Moreover, we conclude that the language of the deed creating the restrictive covenants supports a finding that the parties intended the benefit of the covenants to attach to the real property retained by Mrs. Gaskins. The pertinent language of the deed provides that the property was conveyed subject to certain use restrictions "running with said land by whomsoever owned, until removed," and that the property is "subject always to the restrictions." That the deed expressly stated that the covenants were to run with the land and continue indefinitely, unless and until the surrounding property is "turned to commercial use," indicates that the parties intended the covenants to be enforceable by Mrs. Gaskins as the owner of the land retained by her or by her successors in interest to the retained land. . . .

II. Equitable Servitudes

With regard to plaintiffs Runyon, we must go further because, in certain circumstances, a party unable to enforce a restrictive covenant as a real covenant running with the land may nevertheless be able to enforce the covenant as an equitable servitude. . . .

In this case, plaintiffs seek injunctive relief, which is available for the breach of an equitable servitude. Therefore, we now examine the question of whether plaintiffs Runyon, although unable to enforce the covenants as covenants running with the land, may nevertheless enforce the covenants against defendants on the theory of equitable servitudes.

"Even though a promise is unenforceable as a covenant at law because of failure to meet one of the requirements, the promise may be enforced as an equitable servitude against the promisor or a subsequent taker who acquired the land with notice of the restrictions on it." Traficante v. Pope, 341 A.2d 782, 784 (N.H. 1975). In order to enforce a restrictive covenant on the theory of equitable servitude, it must be shown (1) that the covenant touches and concerns the land, and (2) that the original covenanting parties intended the covenant to bind the person against whom enforcement is sought and to benefit the person seeking to enforce the covenant.

A. Touch and Concern

. . . .

Plaintiffs Runyon have shown that the covenants at issue here meet the legal requirement that the covenants touch and concern defendants' property as well as the property owned by the Runyons. Because a covenant that touches and concerns the land at law will also touch and concern the land in equity, we need not further examine this requirement.

B. Intent of the Parties

A party who seeks to enforce a covenant as an equitable servitude against one who was not an original party to the covenant must show that the original covenanting parties intended that the covenant bind the party against whom enforcement is sought. To meet this requirement, the party seeking to enforce the covenant must show that the covenanting parties intended that the burden run to successors in interest of the covenantor's land. . . .

Applying these principles as well as the rules of construction used to determine the parties' intent that a covenant run with the land, which likewise apply here, we conclude that plaintiffs Runyon have failed to show that the original covenanting parties intended that they be permitted to enforce the covenants either in a personal capacity or as owners of any land they now own. The Runyons were not parties to the covenants, and neither they nor their property are mentioned, either explicitly or implicitly, as intended beneficiaries in the deed creating the covenants or in any other instrument in the public records pertaining to defendants' property. Although they own property closely situated to defendants', in an area which was primarily residential at the time the restrictive covenants were created, they did not acquire their property as part of a plan or scheme to develop the area as residential property. In fact, they acquired their property free of any restrictions as to the use of their property. Finally, the Runyons purchased their property prior to the creation of the restrictive covenants at issue here, and thus they cannot be said to be successors in interest to any property retained by the covenantee that was intended to be benefitted by the covenants.

An affidavit filed by Mr. Runyon is the only evidence tending to support the Runyons' claim that they were intended beneficiaries of the covenants. This affidavit, filed with plaintiffs' motion for summary judgment, states that the covenants were created as a result of a "three-party land swap" whereby the Runyons conveyed their sound-front property to effectuate two transfers of the property: the transfer of a fifteen-foot-wide strip of land to the Runyons for access to the Pamlico Sound and the transfer of the remainder of the property to the Brughs, defendants' predecessors in interest. Mr. Runyon alleges in his affidavit that the covenants were included in the deed of conveyance to the Brughs "for the benefit of the land retained by [Mrs.] Gaskins and neighboring property owners, specifically including and intending to benefit [the Runyons]."

This affidavit by Mr. Runyon, no matter how informative of the parties' intent, is not competent evidence to support the Runyons' claim. Unlike the evidence relied upon to support plaintiff Williams' claim, the allegations contained in this affidavit reference no matters of public record that tend to explain ambiguous deed language by showing the parties' situation or the circumstances surrounding their transaction. The Runyons' reliance on this affidavit is an attempt to use inadmissible parol evidence to add to or vary the terms of the instrument to include the Runyons, who owned no interest in the property conveyed, as named beneficiaries to the covenants. Moreover, even if the allegations of the affidavit were admissible to explain some ambiguous language of the instrument, the affidavit would still be incompetent under our well-established rule that declarations and testimony of the parties are not admissible to prove the covenanting parties' intent.

III. Notice

It is well settled in our state that a restrictive covenant is not enforceable, either at law or in equity, against a subsequent purchaser of property burdened by the covenant unless notice of the covenant is contained in an instrument in his chain of title. N.C.G.S. § 47–18(a) provides:

> No . . . conveyance of land . . . shall be valid to pass any property interest as against . . . purchasers for a valuable consideration . . . but from the time of registration thereof in the county where the land lies. . . .

Notwithstanding the fact that the covenants at issue here were created in a properly recorded deed of conveyance from Mrs. Gaskins to defendants' predecessors, defendants contend that they are purchasers for value and that N.C.G.S. § 47–18 precludes enforcement of the restrictions against them. Relying on Reed v. Elmore, 98 S.E.2d 360, defendants argue that a restrictive covenant is not enforceable against a subsequent purchaser of the property unless the instruments in the chain of title *expressly* state "*both* an intention to bind succeeding grantees and an intention to permit enforcement by successors of the grantor or named beneficiaries."

While it would be advisable to include an express provision with respect to the rights of enforcement in the conveyance that creates them, we do not agree that such notice, as defendants demand, is required. An examination of our case law reveals that we have required the certainty of an express statement in the chain of title only with respect to the *existence* of a restrictive covenant. . . . Where, however, the restriction is contained in the chain of title, we have not hesitated to enforce the restriction against a subsequent purchaser when the court may reasonably infer that the covenant was created for the benefit of the party seeking enforcement. . . .

In this case, a proper search of the public records pertaining to defendants' property would have revealed not only the existence of the restrictive covenants, but also that prior to the conveyance the property was part of a larger tract owned by Mrs. Gaskins. Upon conveying the property to defendants' predecessors, Mrs. Gaskins did not part with all of her property but retained adjacent or nearby property that would be benefitted by the restrictive covenants. From this evidence, it reasonably may be inferred that the restrictive covenants were intended to benefit the property retained by Mrs. Gaskins. Therefore, plaintiff Williams, Mrs. Gaskins' successor in title, has shown that the public records provided sufficient notice to defendants to enable her to enforce the restrictive covenants against them. . . .

For the reasons stated herein, we conclude that the restrictive covenants contained in the deed from Mrs. Gaskins to defendants' predecessors are not personal covenants that became unenforceable at Mrs. Gaskins' death but are real covenants appurtenant to the property retained by Mrs. Gaskins at the time of the conveyance to defendants' predecessors in interest. As a successor in interest to the property retained by Mrs. Gaskins, plaintiff Williams is therefore entitled to seek enforcement of the restrictive covenants against defendants. . . . We further conclude that the Runyons have not proffered sufficient evidence to show that they have standing to enforce the restrictive covenants, either personally or as owners of any land intended to be benefitted by the restrictions. . . .

Notes & Questions

1. Apart from tradition, what reason is there to require anything more than intent and notice for the burden of a covenant to run? These are, you will recall, the only requirements traditionally imposed to determine whether the burden of an easement runs.

2. **Intent and Notice.** For the burden and benefit of either a covenant or equitable servitude to run, the promisee and promisor must have intended that the burden and benefit would run, and the promisor's

successor, who is sought to be charged with the burden, must have had notice of the covenant at the time she acquired the servient estate. The standard way to indicate that the burden will run is for the promisor to covenant, "for herself, her heirs, successors and assigns." But any clear expression of intent will do. And if the parties do not express their intent, courts may infer it from the circumstances surrounding the covenant's creation.

In most states, the notice required for the burden of a covenant or equitable servitude to run may be actual, inquiry or constructive, as in the law of easements and conveyancing generally. But notice of what? Although most covenants and equitable servitudes will explicitly prescribe the conduct they require, some subdivision covenants today will vest general rulemaking authority in a homeowner's association or architectural review board. Is the homeowner bound by rules that the association adopts after she acquires her parcel? In Davis v. Huey, 620 S.W.2d 561 (Tex. 1981), plaintiff neighbors sought to enjoin defendants from building a house in a manner that violated standards adopted under the subdivision's architectural review covenant. Even though the defendant knew of the covenant, the court found that the defendants did not have adequate notice of the specific standards to which they were being held and thus were not required to comply with the subdivision's architectural review. Earlier purchases in the subdivision had not been held to the same standards. Does *Davis* prevent architectural and other standards from evolving over time to meet new conditions? Is this bad?

3. **Horizontal Privity.** As *Runyon* illustrates, courts historically examined both horizontal and vertical privity in deciding whether the benefit and burden of a real covenant run with the dominant and servient estates respectively. As shown in Figure 10–3 on the next page, horizontal privity refers to the relationship between the original promisor and promisee. Vertical privity refers to the relationship between the original covenanting parties and the current parties holding interests in the dominant and servient estates.

Covenants. When the first Restatement of Property was published in 1944, the vast majority of courts held that the burden of a covenant would not run absent horizontal privity between the original covenanting parties; most courts, however, did not require horizontal privity for the benefit to run. See Restatement of Property § 534 (1944). Some courts still require horizontal privity for the running of the burden of a real covenant. See, e.g., Waynesboro Village v. BMC Properties, 496 S.E.2d 64, 68 (Va. 1998). Courts have historically differed in the precise degree and form of horizontal privity required. English courts originally required *tenurial privity*: the original covenanting parties had to be present and future interest holders in the servient property—a landlord and tenant, for example, or a life tenant and a reversioner. Only a few American courts ever followed this rule, and the cases adopting it are now quite old. See, e.g., McIntosh v. Vail, 28 S.E.2d 607 (W. Va. 1943). A second test, *substituted privity,* allows an

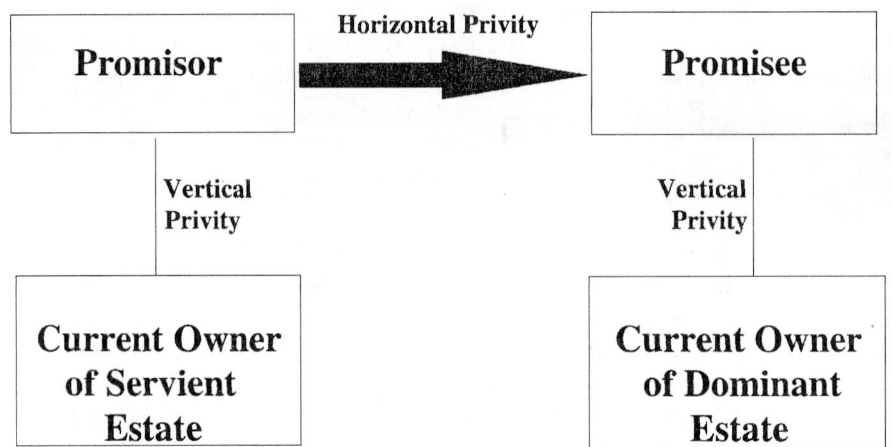

Figure 10–3
Horizontal & Vertical Privity

easement to substitute for the tenurial relationship. If John Wesley Powell holds a right-of-way easement across Rachel Carson's property, for example, John and Rachel have substituted privity, and Rachel could promise to keep the trees trimmed along the easement. This test is sometimes called "Massachusetts privity" after the state that first adopted it. See, e.g., Whitinsville Plaza, Inc. v. Kotseas, 390 N.E.2d 243 (Mass. 1979). The least demanding and almost universally used test today, *instantaneous privity*, expands horizontal privity to include promises made in connection with land transactions between the covenanting parties—e.g., a sale or lease of the property, or the conveyance of an easement or, arguably, even another covenant. Thus, if John buys land from Rachel, they have instantaneous privity, and John or Rachel can make a series of promises that run with the land.

Is there any reason to require horizontal privity? Is horizontal privity another way of determining whether the parties intended the burden of the covenant to run with the land—using the tenurial, easement, or grantor-grantee relationship as evidence of the original parties' seriousness about their intent to bind successors? Neighbors are the group that the horizontal privity requirement principally excludes. If neighbors want to mutually agree to use their properties only for single-family residential purposes, the horizontal privity requirement would exclude the burden of the covenants from running with the land. Is there any reason to prevent neighbors from entering into real covenants that run with the land?

A growing number of courts no longer require horizontal privity for the running of the burden of real covenants, and the new Restatement of Property would abolish the requirement. Restatement (Third) of Property, Servitudes § 2.4 (2000).

> Application of the horizontal-privity requirement prevents enforcement at law of covenants entered into between neighbors and between other parties who do not transfer or share some other interest in the land. The rule can easily be circumvented by conveyance to a strawperson, who imposes the covenant in the reconveyance. Since the rule serves no necessary purpose and simply acts as a trap for the poorly represented, it has been abandoned. As a matter of common law, horizontal privity between the covenanting parties is no longer required to create a servitude obligation.

Id. § 2.4, cmt. b.

Equitable Servitudes. Courts have never insisted on horizontal privity to enforce equitable servitudes. See Tulk v. Moxhay, 41 Eng. Rep. 1143 (1848).

4. **Vertical privity:** *Covenants.* Most courts still require vertical privity to enforce a real covenant against a subsequent buyer of the servient estate: the buyer must have acquired the same interest in the servient estate as the original promisor held. What policies underlie this requirement? Can vertical privity again be viewed as just another device for measuring the force of the covenanting parties' intent to bind the promisor's successor in interest? For example, if John Wesley Powell and Rachel Carson enter into a twenty-year lease for an office building, obligating John to pay an annual rent, perform necessary repairs on the premises, and reconstruct the building's facade, is it likely that they intended Black Kettle, a one-year subtenant of John, to perform all these obligations? If Black Kettle is instead an assignee, who succeeds to John's entire interest, is it more or less likely that they intended her to perform these obligations?

Merging vertical privity into the intent requirement might have two immediate advantages. First, in the example just given, it would allow some differentiation among the duties with which Rachel seeks to charge the one-year subtenant. Presumably John and Rachel did not intend the tenant to undertake capital repairs whose value would extend over the full twenty-year term, while they probably did intend that he pay the annual rent. Second, John and Rachel can control the issue of intent by express language in the instrument creating the covenant. Thus, if they want to make the one-year subtenant liable for the cost of repairs, they can accomplish this by saying so in the lease. Black Kettle will doubtless take this heavy burden into account in determining how much he is willing to pay—or accept from—John in consideration for taking the sublease with all of its burdens.

Most courts also require vertical privity for the benefit of a real covenant to run with the dominant estate. In the case of the benefit, however, courts generally require that the person seeking to enforce the promise have succeeded merely to *some* estate, even if of lesser duration, in the property of the original grantor. If John makes a promise to Rachel and Rachel then rents her property to William Clark, for example, Clark generally would be entitled to enforce the promise. Courts also have long recognized an exception to the vertical privity requirement for homeowner associations that have the express authority to enforce covenants within a subdivision. See, e.g., Neponsit Property Owners' Ass'n v. Emigrant Industrial Savings Bank, 15 N.E.2d 793 (N.Y. 1938).

The Restatement, along with a growing number of courts, again have rejected the vertical privity requirement entirely. See Restatement (Third) of Property, Servitudes §§ 5.2–5.4 (2000) (rejecting vertical privity in favor of a number of more nuanced standards for determining what types of promises should bind lessees and life tenants).

Equitable Servitudes. The running of equitable servitudes never has required vertical privity.

5. **Touch or Concern.** One of the most problematic (and confusing) requirements for the burden or benefit of a real covenant to run with the land is the requirement that the burden or benefit "touch or concern" the servient or dominant estate, respectively. Compounding the problem and confusion, courts have traditionally also required that equitable servitudes "touch or concern" the land, although the standard used in making this determination has often been looser in the case of equitable servitudes. As the next case illustrates, a growing number of courts have rejected the "touch or concern" requirement in favor of a more general requirement that covenants and equitable servitudes be "reasonable."

Davidson Brothers, Inc. v. D. Katz & Sons, Inc.

Supreme Court of New Jersey, 1990.
579 A.2d 288.

Opinion by GARIBALDI, J.

This case [presents the issue of] whether a restrictive covenant in a deed, providing that the property shall not be used as a supermarket or grocery store, is enforceable against the original covenantor's successor, a subsequent purchaser with actual notice of the covenant....

I

The facts are not in dispute. Prior to September 1980 plaintiff, Davidson Bros., Inc., along with Irisondra, Inc., a related corporation, owned certain premises located at 263–271 George Street and 30 Morris Street in

New Brunswick (the "George Street" property). Plaintiff operated a supermarket on that property for approximately seven to eight months. The store operated at a loss allegedly because of competing business from plaintiff's other store, located two miles away (the "Elizabeth Street" property). Consequently, plaintiff and Irisondra conveyed, by separate deeds, the George Street property to defendant D. Katz & Sons, Inc., with a restrictive covenant not to operate a supermarket on the premises. Specifically, each deed contained the following covenant:

> The lands and premises described herein and conveyed hereby are conveyed subject to the restriction that said lands and premises shall not be used as and for a supermarket or grocery store of a supermarket type, however designated, for a period of forty (40) years from the date of this deed. This restriction shall be a covenant attached to and running with the lands.

The deeds were duly recorded in Middlesex County Clerk's office on September 10, 1980. According to plaintiff's complaint, its operation of both stores resulted in losses in both stores. Plaintiff alleges that after the closure of the George Street store, its Elizabeth Street store increased in sales by twenty percent and became profitable....

According to defendants New Brunswick Housing Authority (the "Authority") and City of New Brunswick (the "City"), the closure of the George Street store did not benefit the residents of downtown New Brunswick. Defendants allege that many of the residents who lived two blocks away from the George Street store in multi-family and senior-citizen housing units were forced to take public transportation and taxis to the Elizabeth Street store because there were no other markets in downtown New Brunswick, save for two high-priced convenience stores.

The residents requested the aid of the City and the Authority in attracting a new food retailer to this urban-renewal area.... Despite its actual notice of the covenant the Authority, on October 23, 1986, purchased the George Street property from Katz for $450,000, and agreed to lease from Katz at an annual net rent of $19,800.00, the adjacent land at 263–265 George Street for use as a parking lot. The Authority invited proposals for the lease of the property to use as a supermarket. C–Town was the only party to submit a proposal at a public auction.... The Authority accepted the proposal in 1987. All the defendants in this case had actual notice of the restrictions contained in the deed and of plaintiff's intent to enforce the same. Not only were the deeds recorded but the contract of sale between Katz and the Housing Authority specifically referred to the restrictive covenant and the pending action.

Plaintiff filed this action in the Chancery Division against defendants D. Katz & Sons, Inc., the City of New Brunswick, and C–Town. The first count of the complaint requested a declaratory judgment that the noncompetition covenant was binding on all subsequent owners of the George Street property ....

II

. . . .

New Jersey courts ... continue to focus on the "touch and concern" requirement as the pivotal inquiry in ascertaining whether a covenant runs with the land. Under New Jersey law, a covenant that "exercise[s] [a] direct influence on the occupation, use or enjoyment of the premises" satisfies the "touch and concern" rule. Caullett v. Stanley Stilwell & Sons, Inc., 67 N.J. Super. 111, 116, 170 A.2d 52 (App. Div.1961). The covenant must touch and concern both the burdened and the benefitted property in order to run with the land....

Unlike New Jersey, which has continued to rely on the "touch and concern" requirement, most other jurisdictions have omitted "touch and concern" from their analysis and have focused instead on whether the covenant is reasonable ....

The "touch and concern" test has, thus, ceased to be, in most jurisdictions, intricate and confounding.... The time has come to cut the gordian knot that binds this state's jurisprudence regarding covenants running with the land. Rigid adherence to the "touch and concern" test as a means of determining the enforceability of a restrictive covenant is not warranted. Reasonableness, not esoteric concepts of property law, should be the guiding inquiry into the validity of covenants at law. We do not abandon the "touch and concern" test, but rather hold that the test is but one of the factors a court should consider in determining the reasonableness of the covenant.

A "reasonableness" test allows a court to consider the enforceability of a covenant in view of the realities of today's commercial world and not in the light of out-moded theories developed in a vastly different commercial environment. Originally strict adherence to "touch and concern" rule ... was to effectuate the then pervasive public policy of restricting many, if not all, encumbrances of the land. Courts today recognize that it is not unreasonable for parties in commercial-property transactions to protect themselves from competition by executing noncompetition covenants. Businesspersons, either as lessees or purchasers may be hesitant to invest substantial sums if they have no minimal protection from a competitor starting a business in the near vicinity. Hence, rather than limiting trade, in some instances, restrictive covenants may increase business activity.

We recognize that "reasonableness" is necessarily a fact sensitive issue involving an inquiry into present business conditions and other factors specific to the covenant at issue. Nonetheless, as do most of the jurisdictions, we find that it is a better test for governing commercial transactions than are obscure anachronisms that have little meaning in today's commercial world. The pivotal inquiry, therefore, becomes what factors should a court consider in determining whether such a covenant is "reasonable" and hence enforceable. We conclude that the following factors should be considered:

1. The intention of the parties when the covenant was executed, and whether the parties had a viable purpose which did not at the time interfere with existing commercial laws, such as antitrust laws, or public policy.

2. Whether the covenant had an impact on the considerations exchanged when the covenant was originally executed. This may provide a measure of the value to the parties of the covenant at the time.

3. Whether the covenant clearly and expressly sets forth the restrictions.

4. Whether the covenant was in writing, recorded, and if so, whether the subsequent grantee had actual notice of the covenant.

5. Whether the covenant is reasonable concerning area, time or duration. Covenants that extend for perpetuity or beyond the terms of a lease may often be unreasonable.

6. Whether the covenant imposes an unreasonable restraint on trade or secures a monopoly for the covenantor. This may be the case in areas where there is limited space available to conduct certain business activities and a covenant not to compete burdens all or most available locales to prevent them from competing in such an activity.

7. Whether the covenant interferes with the public interest.

8. Whether, even if the covenant was reasonable at the time it was executed, "changed circumstances" now make the covenant unreasonable....

The concurrence maintains that the initial validity of the covenant is a question of contract law while its subsequent enforceability is one of property law. The result is that the concurrence uses reasonableness factors in construing the validity of the covenant between the original covenantors, but as to successors-in-interest, claims to adhere strictly to a "touch and concern" test. Such strict adherence to a "touch and concern" analysis turns a blind eye to whether a covenant has become unreasonable over time. Indeed many past illogical and contorted applications of the "touch and concern" rules have resulted because courts have been pressed to twist the rules of "touch and concern" in order to achieve a result that comports with public policy and a free market. Most jurisdictions acknowledge the reasonableness factors that affect enforcement of a covenant concerning successors-in-interest, instead of engaging in the subterfuge of twisting the touch and concern test to meet the required result. New Jersey should not remain part of the small minority of States that cling to an anachronistic rule of law.

There is insufficient evidence in this record to determine whether the covenant is reasonable.... The fact-sensitive nature of a "reasonableness" analysis make resolution of this dispute through summary judgment inappropriate. We therefore remand the case to the trial court for a thorough analysis of the "reasonableness" factors delineated herein.

The trial court must first determine whether the covenant was reasonable at the time it was enacted. If it was reasonable then, but now adversely affects commercial development and the public welfare of the people of New Brunswick, the trial court may consider whether allowing damages for breach of the covenant is an appropriate remedy. C–Town could then continue to operate but Davidson would get damages for the value of his covenant. On the limited record before us, however, it is impossible to make a determination concerning either reasonableness of the covenant or whether damages, injunctive relief, or any relief is appropriate.

. . . .

POLLOCK, J., concurring.

The Court reverses the Appellate Division's affirmance of the Chancery Division's grant of summary judgment invalidating the restrictive covenant and remands the matter to the Chancery Division for a plenary hearing. Although I concur in the judgment of remand, I believe it should be on different terms. . . .

I

I begin by questioning the majority's formulation and application of a reasonableness test for determining whether the covenant runs with the land. The law has long distinguished between the validity of a covenant between original-contracting parties from the enforceability of a covenant against the covenantor's successor-in-interest. Initial validity is a question of contract law; enforceability against subsequent parties is one of property law. That distinction need not foreclose a subsequent owner of the burdened property from challenging the validity of the contract between the original parties. The distinction, however, sharpens the analysis of the effect of the covenant.

In this case, the basic issue is enforceability of the covenant against the Authority and C–Town, successors in interest to Katz. Thus, the only relevant consideration is whether the covenant "touches and concerns" the benefitted and burdened properties. . . . Scholars have written that a covenant's benefit touches and concerns land if it renders the owner's interest in the land more valuable, Bigelow, The Content of Covenants in Leases, 12 Mich. L. Rev. 639, 645 (1914), or if "the parties as laymen and not as lawyers" would naturally view the covenant as one that aids "the promisee as landowner," C. Clark, Real Covenants and Other Interests Which Run with the Land 99 (2d ed. 1947); see also 5 R. Powell & P. Rohan, Powell on Real Property ¶ 673[2][a] (1990) (inclining towards Clark's view). Like most courts, leading scholars believe that under the "touch and concern" test, the benefit of non-competition covenants should run with the land.

The conclusion that this covenant "touches and concerns" the land should end the inquiry about enforceability against the Authority and C–Town. The majority, however, holds that the "touch and concern" test is "but one of the factors a court should consider in determining the reasonableness of the covenant." The majority's inquiry about reasonableness, however, confuses the issue of validity of the original contract between Davidson and Katz with enforceability against the subsequent owner, the Authority. This confusion of validity with enforceability threatens to add uncertainty to an already troubled area of the law....

As between the vendor and purchaser, a noncompetition covenant generally should be treated as valid if it is reasonable in scope and duration, and neither an unreasonable restraint on trade nor otherwise contrary to public policy. A covenant would contravene public policy if, for example, its purpose were to secure a monopoly, or to carry out an illegal object, such as invidious discrimination....

II

For me the critical issue is whether the appropriate remedy for enforcing the covenant is damages or an injunction. Ordinarily, as between competing land users, the more efficient remedy for breach of a covenant is an injunction. If Katz still owned the George Street property, the efficient remedy, therefore, would be an injunction. The Authority, which took title with knowledge of the covenant, is in no better position than Katz insofar as the binding effect of the covenant is concerned. Although an injunction might be the most efficient form of relief, it would however deprive the residents of access to the George Street store....

Money damages would compensate Davidson for the wrong done by the opening of the George Street supermarket. Davidson would be "given what plaintiffs are given in many types of cases—relief measured, so far as the court reasonably may do so, in damages." The award of money damages, rather than an injunction, might be the more appropriate form of relief for several reasons. First, a damages award is "particularly applicable to a case, such as this, wherein we are dealing with two commercial properties...." Gilpin v. Jacob Ellis Realties, 135 A.2d 204 (N.J. App. Div. 1957). Second, the award of damages in a single proceeding would provide more efficient justice than an injunction in the present case, with a condemnation suit to follow. Davidson would be compensated for the loss of the covenant and the needy residents would enjoy more convenient shopping. That solution is both efficient and just.

I can appreciate why New Brunswick residents want a supermarket and why the Authority would come to their aid. Supermarkets may be essential for the salvation of inner cities and their residents. The Authority's motives, however noble, should not vitiate Davidson's right to compensation. The fair result, it seems to me, is for the Authority to compensate Davidson in damages for the breach of its otherwise valid and enforceable covenant.

Notes & Questions

1. On remand, a New Jersey court held that the restrictive covenant at issue in *Davidson Brothers* was unreasonable and contrary to public

policy. See Davidson Bros., Inc. v. D. Katz & Sons, Inc., 643 A.2d 642 (N.J. Super. Ct. App. Div. 1994). The court concluded that the promise not to use the property for a grocery store or supermarket would cause personal hardship to local residents and damage "the ongoing efforts of government and private enterprise to revitalize the city. We are persuaded, therefore, that, in the absence of any equivalent reciprocal benefit to the city, Davidson's scorched earth policy is so contrary to the public interest in these circumstances that the covenant is unreasonable and unenforceable." Id. At 648. Do you agree? Was the dissent in *Davidson Brothers* correct that courts should have addressed these concerns by awarding damages rather than an injunction?

2. The Restatement of Property would abolish the touch and concern requirement. See Restatement (Third) of Property, Servitudes § 3.1 (2000). Is there any justification for the touch or concern requirement? Does the requirement give courts the opportunity to evaluate covenants and equitable servitudes to determine whether they are fair, efficient, or otherwise appropriate? If so, should courts be more explicit in their goals, rather than talking in vague and oddly anthropomorphic terms about promises "touching or concerning" the land?

One perceived value of the touch or concern requirement is that it prevents all but the most physically evident and geographically confined covenants from encumbering title over a period that may well outlast the covenant's utility. For articles defending the touch or concern requirement, see A. Dan Tarlock, Touch and Concern Is Dead, Long Live the Doctrine, 77 Neb. L. Rev. 804 (1998); Jeffrey E. Stake, Toward an Economic Understanding of Touch and Concern, 1988 Duke L.J. 925.

3. **Tests.** What does it mean for a promise to "touch or concern" land? All courts agree that the promise need not involve physical actions on the land. A variety of different tests have been suggested for determining what it does mean. One of the most common tests, stated in *Runyon*, supra p. 884, is whether the promise in some fashion "affects the legal rights of the covenanting parties as landowners. Where the burdens and benefits created by the covenant are of such a nature that they may exist independently from the parties' ownership interests in land, the covenant does not touch and concern the land and will not run with the land." The late Judge Charles Clark suggested a somewhat similar test: "Where the parties, as laymen and not as lawyers, would naturally regard the covenant as intimately bound up with the land, aiding the promisee as landowner or hampering the promisor in similar capacity, the requirement should be held fulfilled." Charles E. Clark, Real Covenants and Other Interests Which "Run With the Land" 99 (2d ed. 1947).

Courts have found it easy to apply the rule in some settings. For example, promises concerning how land is to be used or not used clearly meet the requirement. As the next few notes examine, however, other types of promises have proven harder.

4. **Covenants to Make Payments.** When does a promise to pay money "touch or concern" land? In Neponsit Property Owners' Ass'n v.

Emigrant Industrial Sav. Bank, 15 N.E.2d 793 (N.Y. 1938), the New York Court of Appeals held that a promise by a landowner to pay money to a local property owners' association, to maintain roads, paths, parks, beaches, sewers, and other common amenities in the area, touched or concerned the land.

> [I]t seems clear that the covenant may properly be said to touch and concern the land of the defendant and its burden should run with the land. True, it calls for payment of a sum of money to be expended for "public purposes" upon land other than the land conveyed . . . to plaintiff's predecessor in title. By that conveyance the grantee, however, obtained not only title to particular lots, but an easement or right of common enjoyment with other property owners in roads, beaches, public parks, or spaces and improvements in the same tract. For full enjoyment in common by the defendant and other property owners of these easements or rights, the roads and public places must be maintained. In order that the burden of maintaining public improvements should rest upon the land benefitted by the improvements, the grantor exacted from the grantee of the land with its appurtenant easement or right of enjoyment a covenant that the burden of paying the cost should be inseparably attached to the land which enjoys the benefit. It is plain that any distinction or definition which would exclude such a covenant from the classification of covenants which "touch" or "concern" the land would be based on form and not on substance.

In Eagle Enterprises, Inc. v. Gross, 349 N.E.2d 816 (N.Y. 1976), by contrast, the same court held that a covenant to pay for well water provided by a neighbor between May 1 and October 1 of each year did not "touch or concern" the defendant's land and thus did not run. The court in *Eagle Enterprises* rested its decision on the conclusion that the covenant "does not substantially affect the ownership interest of landowners in the Orchard Hill subdivision. The covenant provides for the supplying of water for only six months of the year; no claim has been advanced by appellant that the lands in the subdivision would be waterless without the water it supplies." According to the court, the record did "not demonstrate that other property owners in the subdivision would be deprived of water from appellant or that the price of water would become prohibitive for other property owners if respondent terminated appellant's service. Thus, the agreement for the seasonal supply of water does not seem to us to relate in any significant degree to the ownership rights of respondent and the other property owners in the subdivision of Orchard Hill."

Is there a legitimate distinction between *Neponsit* and *Eagle Enterprises*? Does a promise to pay for a golf course maintained by a local homeowners' association "touch or concern" a homeowner's land if the homeowner is not interested in playing golf? Compare Raintree Corp. v. Rowe, 248 S.E.2d 904 (N.C. App. 1978) (promise does not touch and concern the land: landowner might not use the golf course) with Anthony v. Brea Glenbrook Club, 130 Cal. Rptr. 32 (Cal. App. 1976) (promise does touch and concern land: even if landowner does not use club, its facilities increased the value of everyone's lots). How would all of these cases be decided under the *Davidson Brothers* reasonableness test?

5. **Covenants Against Competition.** Do covenants against competition meet the touch or concern requirement? In a landmark case, Norcross v. James, 2 N.E. 946 (Mass. 1885), the Massachusetts Supreme Court held that a grantor's covenant not to operate a competing quarry on his neighboring land did not touch or concern the land, and thus did not bind the grantor's successors. Writing for the court, Justice Holmes observed that the covenant did not "make the use or occupation" of plaintiff's alleged dominant estate "more convenient."

> It does not in any way affect the use or occupation; it simply tends indirectly to increase its value, by excluding a competitor from the market for its products. If it be asked what is the difference in principle between an easement to have land unbuilt upon, such as was recognized in Brooks v. Reynolds, 106 Mass. 31, and an easement to have a quarry left unopened, the answer is, that, whether a difference of degree or of kind, the distinction is plain between a grant or covenant that looks to direct physical advantage in the occupation of the dominant estate, such as light and air, and one which only concerns it in the indirect way which we have mentioned.

After almost a century of following *Norcross*, but expressing growing discomfort with its limitations, the Massachusetts Supreme Court finally overruled it and joined the mainstream of American decisions in Whitinsville Plaza, Inc. v. Kotseas, 390 N.E.2d 243 (Mass. 1979). Enforcing a covenant not to compete with plaintiff's neighboring discount store, the court ruled that "reasonable covenants against competition *may* be considered to run with the land when they serve a purpose of facilitating orderly and harmonious development for commercial use." Id. at 250. In part the court rested its decision on the fact that "[w]ith respect to covenants in commercial leases, we have long held that reasonable anticompetitive covenants are enforceable by and against successors to the original parties." Id. at 249. What relevant differences, if any, are there between the leasehold and fee context?

Does *Davidson Brothers* complicate the issue of when the burden of a covenant against competition runs with the land? Is Justice Pollock correct in his concurring opinion that the majority confuses the question of the validity of the original covenant with the question of whether the burden of the covenant should run with the land?

6. **Covenants Not to Sue.** If a buyer of contaminated land promises not to sue the seller for any future cleanup costs or any damages resulting from exposure to the contaminants, does this promise touch and concern and thus run with the land? In El Paso Refinery L.P. v. TRMI Holdings, Inc., 302 F.3d 343 (5th Cir. 2002), the purchaser (El Paso) of an oil refinery promised the seller (TRMI) never to pursue TRMI to clean up the property if it turned out to be contaminated; the covenant expressly stated that it

was to bind all future owners of the property. When a future owner of the property (RHC) sought contribution toward cleanup costs from TRMI, TRMI argued that the covenant precluded liability. The Fifth Circuit, however, concluded that the covenant did not touch and concern the land and therefore was not binding on RHC.

> Any burden or benefit created by the TRMI Deed affects only TRMI personally and has no direct impact upon the land itself. The Refinery's owner may, in accordance with the deed's provisions, take remedial action or not take remedial action, pollute or not pollute, as long as contribution is not sought from TRMI. The covenant does not compel nor preclude the promisor or any subsequent owner from doing anything on the land itself. The covenant is not predicated upon an agreement to refrain from taking any action on the land, as in the case of a negative covenant. Nor does it permit TRMI, the promisee, to enter or utilize the land for any purpose. Rather, it is a continuing and non-contingent contractual agreement under which [RHC] agrees to refrain from seeking environmental remediation or damages from TRMI. A personal contractual arrangement does not qualify as a covenant.

Id. at 356–357.

Covenants in Gross

Many courts historically would not enforce the benefit of a covenant in gross. Assume, for example, that George Washington Carver owns a seafood restaurant and is planning to move to a larger location several blocks away. When he sells his current location to Josephine Hensley, he may want to include a covenant not to compete, and anticipating that he might plan to move again, he would probably prefer to hold the benefit of the covenant in gross rather than have it attach permanently to his new location. Most courts would not have permitted George to do this. See, e.g., Matter of Turners Crossroad Development Co., 277 N.W.2d 364 (Minn. 1979) (refusing to permit a covenant not to sell alcohol to be held in gross). Is there any good reason for the rule?

According to the first Restatement of Property, the requirement reflected the law's belief that covenants should not restrict and burden a parcel of land if the covenants do not benefit other land. Courts, in short, were willing to tolerate a covenant where the net impact on land might be positive, but not where the covenant only burdened and did not benefit land. "The requirement of 'reciprocal benefit' . . . is based upon a social policy adverse to the placing of undue restrictions upon the freedom of alienation of land. If the burden of a promise runs with land, the freedom of alienation of that land is to some extent restricted. The resulting restriction is permitted only when there is a countervailing benefit in the use of either the burdened land or of some other land." Restatement of Property § 543, cmt. c (1944).

Virtually all states today recognize, either by judicial decision or statute, an exception to the traditional ban on covenants in gross where the benefit is held by the government, a charity, or a homeowner's association with power to enforce covenants on behalf of its members. See, e.g., Bennett v. Commissioner of Food & Ag., 576 N.E.2d 1365, 1367 (Mass. 1991). The new Restatement would permit easements in gross, so long as the person who seeks to enforce the easement has a "legitimate interest in enforcing the servitude." Restatement (Third) of Property, Servitudes § 2.6 & cmt. d, § 8.1 (2000).

2. SUBDIVISIONS, CONDOMINIUMS, AND OTHER COMMON INTEREST COMMUNITIES

The last century has seen tremendous change in the types of neighborhoods in which people live, with covenants and other servitudes becoming of increasing importance over time. In the 19th century, most Americans still lived in rural environments. In cities, people typically developed their properties home by home, with little attention to common plans or schemes. Most properties were subject to few, if any, covenants.

Beginning in the 1910s, however, developers began to construct large suburban subdivisions in which homes shared common characteristics and amenities. In the middle of the 20th century, the Federal Housing Administration encouraged subdivisions to adopt common covenants and restrictions that were binding on all homeowners in the subdivision. In the same period, developers of large subdivisions began increasingly to create homeowner associations that could enforce these restrictions, hold title to and manage parks and other common areas within the subdivision, impose financial assessments on property owners to pay for the upkeep and management of the subdivision, and provide general governance for the subdivision. This was the birth of "common interest communities" in which homeowners share common rights and obligations and engage in limited self-governance.

Central to the modern subdivision are the *Covenants, Conditions, and Restrictions* (CC&Rs) that provide the common rules and limitations for land use in the subdivision. These CC&Rs deal with a wide variety of subjects including how property can be used, the permissible size and other characteristics of homes and other structures on lots within the subdivision, and the upkeep of property. The CC&Rs also provide necessary easements for utilities, common pathways, and other amenities. Finally, the CC&Rs typically set out the powers of any local homeowner association, as well as homeowners' rights in any common areas of the subdivision.

In the late 1950s and 1960s, states enacted laws authorizing the construction of *condominiums*, in which homeowners own personal living space in a multi-unit development and share ownership of common spaces (e.g., pools, lawns, clubhouses, and hallways) as tenants in common with the other residents. Just as homeowner associations govern a growing number of subdivisions, condominiums are governed by *management asso-*

ciations. The governing document for a condominium is typically the *Declaration*. The Declaration provides a legal description of the project and of the individual units and common areas, as well as setting out CC&Rs for the development. The Declaration also establishes guidelines for the condominium *bylaws*, which outline the procedures that the management association must use in selecting a board of managers to supervise the condominium's ongoing activities, in authorizing expenditures for maintenance and reconstruction of common areas and facilities, and in adopting house rules governing day-to-day life in the condominium.

Some states also have a third type of common interest community—the *cooperative*. Cooperatives, like condominiums, are multi-unit residential developments. In a cooperative, however, a single, non-profit cooperative corporation owns and governs not only the common areas, but also the individual residential units. Unlike the condominium owner who receives a deed conveying fee title to his unit and an undivided interest in the common areas, each *cooperator* receives two instruments—a perpetually renewable proprietary lease to her unit (with the cooperative as landlord), and shares of stock in the cooperative corporation. Each cooperator's rights and duties are set out in the corporate charters, bylaws, and proprietary leases.

a. SERVITUDES IMPLIED FROM COMMON PLANS

These various forms of modern housing developments have generated a variety of legal issues. In the case of subdivisions, for example, what happens if a developer intends to subject all residential lots to common covenants, but stops doing so halfway through the development? In most situations, a developer will prepare a general plan for the development, containing all of the CC&Rs, prior to beginning development of the subdivision. The developer will typically record the general plan for the development, including the CC&Rs, at the outset of the development and will then include the CC&Rs in the deed for each individual property that is sold. These CC&Rs are then enforceable as covenants and equitable servitudes that run with the land.

What happens, however, if the developer fails to include the CC&Rs in the deeds for some of the lots that are sold? In Citizens for Covenant Compliance v. Anderson, 906 P.2d 1314 (Cal. 1995), the developer of a California subdivision in the late 1950's recorded a general plan and a set of CC&Rs for the entire subdivision before selling any home sites. In selling individual properties, however, the developer sometimes failed to include the CC&Rs in the deed of sale, and some of these property owners later claimed that they were free to ignore the CC&Rs. The California Supreme Court disagreed and held that property owners are bound by common CC&Rs recorded for a subdivision, whether or not the CC&Rs appear in the deed for individual properties. According to the court, this rule has many advantages:

> The first advantage is simplicity itself. One document, recorded for all purchasers to review, would establish the rules for all

> parcels, not many documents that may or may not be mutually consistent. There would be no bewildering mosaic of enforceability and nonenforceability. . . .
>
> Having a single set of recorded restrictions that apply to the entire subdivision would also no doubt fulfill the intent, expectations, and wishes of the parties and community as a whole. . . . The rule would also better enable the community to protect its interests. Here, for example, [the town of] Woodside's approval of the Friar's subdivision was conditioned on the town attorney's review of the CC&Rs. Thus the community was able to exercise oversight as to the original recorded declaration. But it is unrealistic to expect such oversight of all subsequent individual deeds. The community should be able to expect that restrictions it requires as a condition of approving the subdivision will take effect, and not run the risk that they will fall victim to careless deed drafting.
>
> By requiring recordation before execution of the contract of sale, the rule would also be fair. All buyers could easily know exactly what they were purchasing. Title searches would be easier, requiring only a search of restrictions of record, not of all deeds to all properties in the subdivision. . . .
>
> Some of the prior cases, however, simply assumed that the deeds must *expressly* refer to the restrictions to evidence the purchaser's intent and agreement. On the contrary, it is reasonable to conclude that property conveyed after the restrictions are recorded is subject to those restrictions even without further mention in the deed. "The issue in these cases is the intent of the grantors and grantees at the time of the conveyance." (Fig Garden Park etc. Assn. v. Assemi Corp., 233 Cal. App. 3d 1704, 1709.) This intent can be inferred from the recorded uniform plan. It is express on the part of the seller, implied on the part of the purchaser. The law may readily conclude that a purchaser who has constructive notice, and therefore knowledge, of the restrictions, takes the property with the understanding that it, as well as all other lots in the tract, is subject to the restrictions, and intends and agrees to accept their burdens and benefits, even if there is no additional documentation evidencing the intent at the time of the conveyance.

Id. at 1325–1327.

What if a developer does not record a general plan and, after including common CC&Rs in some of the early property sales, fails to include the CC&Rs in later sales? Where there is evidence that the developer meant for the entire subdivision to be subject to a general plan and that early purchasers relied on this plan, courts have sometimes held that all properties in the subdivision are subject to implied servitudes. Courts sometimes refer to such servitudes as "implied negative servitudes" or, quite confusingly, as "implied negative reciprocal easements." The following case considers how far the doctrine of implied negative servitudes can be stretched.

Schovee v. Mikolasko

Court of Appeals of Maryland, 1999.
737 A.2d 578.

Opinion by WILNER, J.

The basic issue before us is whether the Circuit Court for Howard County erred in its application of the doctrine of implied negative reciprocal easement. The court subjected a 50–acre lot that was included in the subdivision plat of a 25–lot development community to restrictive covenants contained in a separately recorded Declaration of Covenants, Easements, Conditions and Restrictions, notwithstanding that the lot was not included in that Declaration, upon a finding from other evidence that the lot was intended by the developer to be part of the community. The Court of Special Appeals held that the circuit court erred in that regard, and we shall affirm that holding.

BACKGROUND

We are concerned here with a 168–acre development in Howard County known as Chapel Woods II, developed by J.J.M. Partnership (JJMP). The original subdivision plat for the development was recorded in November, 1989; it was amended, in a non-substantive way, by a Revision Plat recorded in April, 1990. The plat showed a development of 25 lots.... In conformance with then-existing zoning requirements, each of the lots comprised at least three acres. Lots 1 through 5 and 8 through 25 were generally between three and four acres, although two of them—Lots 17 and 25—contained over six acres. Lot 6 comprised nearly 20 acres and Lot 7—the one at issue here—contained about 50 acres....

Contemporaneously with the recording of the initial subdivision plat, JJMP recorded the Declaration. In a preamble to the Declaration, JJMP stated that it was the owner of a parcel of land known as Chapel Woods II, "(hereinafter referred to as 'the Community'), which is more particularly described in Exhibit A attached hereto and hereby made a part hereof." The declarant stated further its intent to create "on such real property" a residential community of single family homes for the benefit of the owners of such homes, and, to that end, declared that *the land described in Exhibit A* would be sold and conveyed subject to the easements, restrictions, covenants, and conditions thereafter set forth in the Declaration. Exhibit A described the property subject to the Declaration as "Lot Nos. 1 through 5 (inclusive) and 8 through 25 (inclusive) as shown on [the recorded plat]." In so defining the property, and thus "the Community," the Declaration clearly did not include Lots 6 and 7.

Among the restrictions stated in § 4.1.1 of the Declaration were that no lot could be devoted to a use other than a residential use and that no lot may contain more than one detached residential structure at any time.

Section 7.5.1 provided that the covenants and restrictions were to run with and bind upon the property for 40 years, subject to amendments approved by certain percentages of the owners, and were thereafter to be automatically renewed for successive terms of 10 years. . . .

Following the recording of the plat and the Declaration, JJMP began to sell the lots, eventually selling all 23 that were included under the Declaration . . . . The contract of sale specifically referred to the Declaration, which by then had been recorded and was attached to the contract as an exhibit. The contract also contained an integration clause, stating that the written agreement represented "the complete understanding between the parties" and superseded all prior negotiations, representations, promises, and statements as to the property, "or any other matter whatsoever," made or furnished by any real estate broker or other person representing or purporting to represent either party. As indicated, the Declaration, when coupled with Exhibit A, informed the buyer that Lots 6 and 7, which were shown on the plat of the development, were not subject to the Declaration and thus were not part of "the Community," as defined in the Declaration.

The deed also made specific reference to the Declaration. The parties acknowledged that title to the lot being conveyed was subject to the Declaration, which was specifically identified, that the provisions of the Declaration constitute a general plan or scheme of development and use "for all of that real property, situate and lying in said County, which is *therein* and hereinafter *referred to as the community* . . . including the lot (*but not for any real property not within the Community*, as from time to time constituted)," and that the provisions of the Declaration were covenants running with, binding, burdening, and benefitting "the title to both the lot and the remainder of the Community." (Emphasis added.) Although not normally the case, the buyers of these lots signed the deeds to their respective lots.

The plaintiffs/petitioners consist of seven couples who purchased lots in the development between 1989 and 1991. Notwithstanding that each received a copy of the Declaration prior to signing the contract of sale and the deed, they claimed in their complaint that they had been led to believe that Lot 7 was part of "the community" and thus subject to the Declaration.

At some point, Mikolasko decided to embark on a Chapel Woods III development by combining Lots 7 and 8 and subdividing the whole into nine new lots of between one and one-and-a-third acres each. Apparently, the county zoning law had been changed to permit lots of less than three acres, for no complaint of zoning violation has been made. Although the plat for that resubdivision was not recorded until February, 1996, it appears that construction, or pre-construction, work was commenced in 1995. That work, on Lot 7, caused concern among some of the homeowners, who met with Mikolasko in protest. At the time, Mikolasko took the position that . . . Lot 7 was not included in the Declaration and thus was not subject to the restrictions contained in the Declaration. . . . That led the plaintiffs to file a six-count complaint seeking a variety of declaratory and injunctive relief. Although a number of issues were presented to the trial court, the essential [question is] whether Lot 7 was encumbered by the restrictions in the Declaration. . . .

The evidence from the plaintiffs concerned representations allegedly made to them either by John Mikolasko or the real estate broker, Ms. Ramelmeier, and the plat that was shown to them when they were in the process of deciding whether to buy a lot in Chapel Woods II. Ms. Schovee, a banker, testified that she looked at the Chapel Woods II property several times, beginning in 1988, and that it was her "understanding" that the community was going to be "an exclusive community of twenty-five lots that were at least three acres in size, heavily wooded, private community." She was shown the as-yet-unrecorded plat that depicted 25 lots. Ms. Ramelmeier, she said, told her that the Mikolaskos were going to build their own homes on Lots 7 and 8, and that Lot 7 would be "part of the Chapel Woods Two community." Ms. Schovee said that she had read the Declaration and Exhibit A to it, but, notwithstanding its reference to Lots 1–5 and 8–25, she "focused on Lots 1 through 25 as the community." Her belief that all 25 lots, including even Lot 6, were part of the community and subject to the Declaration, was based on what was "represented on the map" when she walked the area prior to signing the lot reservation agreement and on a representation by Ms. Ramelmeier that "Lots 1 through 25 were going to be developed in the common scheme of the community according to the covenants.". . . . Mr. Schovee, a non-practicing member of the Bar, gave similar testimony. . . .

Like the Schovees . . . , Mr. Kramer, a certified public accountant, said that he was interested in Chapel Woods II because of the three-acre wooded lots that afforded privacy. He had expressed an interest in Lot 7 but was told by Ms. Ramelmeier that John Mikolasko was going to put his "estate lot" there. She added further, however, that Lot 7 was to be "part of the community plan" for Chapel Woods II. Kramer said that he read the Declaration—although he "could have missed a few words"—but that he nonetheless thought that "the community" consisted of the 25 lots shown on the plat.

[Both John Mikolasko and Ms. Ramelmeir denied telling anyone that Lot 7 would be part of the overall subdivision scheme.]

[Based on the evidence, the trial court concluded that, despite the express terms of the Declaration, Lot 7 was meant to be part of a "common scheme" of development. In holding that Lot 7 was subject to the restrictive covenants of the Declaration, the trial court relied on the doctrine of "implied negative reciprocal easements." Under this doctrine,] restrictions may be enforced against land not expressly subject to them if the party seeking that enforcement shows that (1) a common owner subdivided property into a number of lots for sale, (2) the common owner had an intention to create a general scheme of development for the property as a whole, in which the use of the land was restricted, (3) the vast majority of subdivided lots contain restrictive covenants that reflect the general scheme, (4) the property against which application of an implied covenant is sought was intended to be part of the general scheme of development, and (5) the purchaser of the lot in question had notice, actual or constructive, of the condition....

There have been a plethora of cases in Maryland, dating back to *Thruston v. Minke*, 32 Md. 487 (1870), in which someone has attempted to subject land retained by a common grantor to restrictions not expressly applicable to that land, often, but not always, on a theory that the retained land was part of a general plan of development. Nearly all of the cases in which that theory has been asserted have rested on a determination of whether (1) there was, in fact, a general plan of development, and (2) if so, the retained land was intended to be a part of the development....

The device of *implying* restrictive covenants on land retained by a grantor, as a matter of property law, in those situations avoided some thorny problems that arose when enforcement was sought under contract theories. As the Restatement and some commentators point out, the implied negative reciprocal easement or servitude doctrine arose before the advent of comprehensive zoning in order to provide a measure of protection for those who bought lots in what they reasonably expected was a general development in which all of the lots would be equally burdened and benefitted. In those early days, it was uncommon for the developer to evidence the development or impose uniform restrictions through a recorded Declaration that would later be incorporated in individual deeds. They often filed subdivision plats of one kind or another but did not take the extra step of using one instrument to impose the restrictions. The common, almost universal, practice, instead, was for the developer to place the restrictions in the deeds to individual lots and, sometimes, to represent to the purchasers of those lots that the same restrictions would be placed in subsequent deeds to the other lots. Litigation arose most frequently when the developer then neglected to include the restrictions in one or more of the subsequent deeds and those buyers proceeded or proposed to use their property in a manner that would not be allowed by the restrictions....

We need to keep in mind both the function of the implied negative reciprocal easement doctrine, which is to serve as a basis for subjecting land not otherwise burdened by them to restrictions applicable generally throughout a planned development, and its historical context. To the extent that land is expressly subjected to restrictions by an instrument forming part of its chain of title, the doctrine would ordinarily have no application, for there is no reason to *imply* a burden that is already *expressly* imposed.... Absent some compelling circumstance, purchasers cannot be allowed to claim ignorance of that which is clearly set forth in a recorded instrument in the chain of title to their respective lots, especially when that instrument (1) is actually given to them, and (2) is specifically referred to in their contracts of sale and deeds. Indeed, the Restatement now takes the position that "the implied reciprocal servitudes doctrine comes into play *only* when the developer does not follow the practice of recording a declaration of servitudes applicable to the entire subdivision *or other general plan area.*" Restatement (Third) of Property Servitudes § 2.14, cmt. i (Tentative Draft No. 1, 1989) (emphasis added).

We need not, and do not, go so far as the Restatement in holding the doctrine inherently inapplicable in the case of a recorded Declaration, for there may be instances in which the developer, through its conduct, creates a basis for implying restrictions to retained land that was not included in the Declaration. When the developer uses such an instrument to create the restrictions and define the land subject to them, however, that instrument is not merely a piece of evidence, to be viewed with other evidence in determining whether there was a general plan of development and what property is subject to the restrictions imposed on that development. The instrument ordinarily suffices to establish both facts.

The Declaration at issue here, especially when coupled with the language in the various deeds, establishes with virtually unimpeachable clarity both that JJMP did not intend to subject Lot 7 to the restrictions imposed on Lots 1 through 5 and 8 through 25, and that the purchasers of those lots knew, at least constructively, that Lot 7 was excluded from the Declaration. Not only did the Declaration specify the lots to be included, it also expressly defined "the Community" as encompassing only those lots. The deeds made specific reference to the Declaration and characterized it as constituting a general plan of development for the property defined in it as "the Community," and as excluding "any real property not within the Community."

The only issue, then, is whether JJMP, directly or through its agents, acted inconsistently with its exclusion of Lot 7 from "the Community," and, through its conduct, afforded a basis to apply the doctrine. We see no such basis in this record.... Whatever expectations the four buyers may have had prior to signing their contracts of sale, there was no reasonable basis upon which they could believe, when they signed those contracts and when they later signed their deeds, that Lot 7 was part of "the Community" and was therefore subject to the restrictions set forth in the Declaration. The Court of Special Appeals was entirely correct in holding that the presumption of non-inclusion of Lot 7 had not been rebutted.

Cathell, Judge, dissenting:

I respectfully dissent.... Every witness for the plaintiffs testified as to the representations made by the developer's agents, which were entirely consistent with a developmental scheme including all of the twenty-five lots. That evidence, if believed by the trier of fact, as apparently it was, was sufficient to support the trial court's decision.

What occurred in the case *sub judice* is a real estate developer's version of tactics similar to "bait and switch," which we ought to condemn. The developer's agent showed prospective buyers an initial plat that displayed twenty-five lots under circumstances that can lead to no other conclusion but that it is a twenty-five lot subdivision. Then by a subsequent document, in this case a declaration, the developer uses the omission of textual language to delete, by nondescription, one or more of the lots from the limitations of the development, knowing the tendency of purchasers to focus on maps and plats, rather than the omissions in the text of a subsequent document.

It is interesting that rather than including prominent language on the initial plats indicating to purchasers that Lot 7 was omitted or making an express statement in the declaration that Lot 7 was to be omitted or putting a prominent notation on "Exhibit A" that Lot 7 was omitted, the developer elected to use a tactic that had a high probability of not being noticed. He just left Lot 7 out: "Lots Nos.1 through 5 (inclusive) and 8 through 25 (inclusive) as shown on [the recorded] plat. . . ." New purchasers and their title attorneys would be examining the documents looking for the inclusion of their lots in the subdivision, not for what was excluded by mere omission.

The trial court considered that the evidence before it met the . . . standard for representing to purchasers that there was a common scheme of development that included Lot 7. In my view, although there was evidence to the contrary, the evidence supporting the trial court's decision was sufficient. The trial court, not this Court, is the weigher of fact and credibility. The lower court should be affirmed and the Court of Special Appeals reversed.

Moreover, the holding of the majority may encourage unscrupulous developers to use deceptive tactics in the sale of lots in their subdivisions. All a developer has to do now is use the services of an agent to offer something in the sales process, and then take it away by purposely omitting it in the extensive postsales period documentation. . . .

Notes & Questions

1. In the typical case of implied servitudes, a homebuyer, say Rachel Carson, purchases her lot subject to an express negative covenant and upon the developer's representation that all other parcels in the subdivision will be subjected to the same restriction. When someone later tries to use another parcel in violation of the covenant, Rachel sues to enjoin the violation. In deciding whether to imply a servitude in such situations, should it matter whether the developer still owns the other parcel and is trying to develop it in violation of the covenant (as in *Schovee*) or has sold it to a third party who now wishes to use the property in violation of the covenant?

2. Courts differ on the level of proof required to establish a common neighborhood plan. Some courts hold that uniform restrictions appearing in deeds to a substantial number of lots in the subdivision will suffice. Others require additional direct evidence of intent—typically the subdivider's representation to home buyers that the restrictions appearing in their deeds will also appear in the deeds to all other parcels in the subdivision. A few courts will not allow these representations to be proved by parol evidence, such as oral statements or declarations in documents or maps, and require that the representation appear in the homebuyer's deed.

3. How can decisions that infer common neighborhood plans from such fugitive evidence as sales brochures and advertisements, and that imply restrictive servitudes based on these plans into deeds absolute on their face, be reconciled with the policies behind the Statute of Frauds and the parol evidence rule? In Riley v. Bear Creek Planning Committee, 551 P.2d 1213 (Cal. 1976), the California Supreme Court held that the plaintiff, who acquired a subdivision parcel through a deed containing no restrictions, was not bound by CC&Rs recorded for the subdivision nine months *after* the conveyance to him. The court reached this result even though extrinsic evidence "tended to prove that the grantor intended to convey and plaintiffs intended to purchase a parcel which both parties assume to be governed by building restrictions." The court acknowledged that the parol evidence rule had been liberalized to a point at which it might allow such evidence to be used in construing the deed. Nonetheless, the court held that the continuing force of the Statute of Frauds required that the evidence be given no weight. "Any other rule would make important questions of the title to real estate largely dependent upon the uncertain recollection and testimony of interested witnesses. The [exclusion of extrinsic evidence] is supported by every consideration of sound public policy which has led to the enactment and enforcement of statutes of frauds in every English-speaking commonwealth." Id. at 1220.

4. For a successor in interest to the putative servient estate to be bound by an implied servitude, she must have had notice of the servitude at the time she acquired the parcel. Courts in their occasional zeal to imply and enforce residential negative servitudes sometimes overlook or distort the standard notice requirements.

Sanborn v. McLean, 206 N.W. 496 (Mich. 1925), is an example. The court there enforced an implied servitude that land would be used only for residential purposes, even though the plaintiff had failed to demonstrate that the defendant had actual notice of the servitude, and even though the defendant had no constructive notice since, the servitude being implied, no instrument in the defendant's chain of title referred to it. The court held that the defendant had inquiry notice of the implied restriction. "Considering the [residential] character of use made of all the lots open to a view of Mr. McLean when he purchased, we think he was put thereby to inquiry, beyond asking his grantor whether there were restrictions. . . . he could not avoid noticing the strictly uniform residence character given the lots by the expensive dwellings thereon, and the least inquiry would have quickly developed the fact that lot 86 was subjected to a reciprocal negative easement. . . ." Id. at 498.

Representing a subdivision lot buyer in Michigan after *Sanborn*, what steps would you take to protect your client against implied negative servitudes? Will the absence of dogs in the subdivision put your client under a duty to inquire whether there is an implied servitude prohibiting dogs? Will the absence of large dogs create a duty to inquire about a servitude excluding large dogs only?

b. PROTECTING LANDOWNERS FROM UNREASONABLE RESTRICTIONS

According to the Community Association Institute, more than 54 million Americans today live in common interest communities (up from approximately 10 million in 1980 and about 30 million in 1990). Slightly less than two-thirds live in subdivisions governed by homeowner associations; about 35–40 percent live in condominiums; and about five percent live in cooperatives.[1] As more and more Americans have moved into such common interest communities, CC&Rs and governing associations have assumed a greater role in regulating people's use and enjoyment of their homes. In many cases, the importance of CC&Rs and governing associations in determining the use of property is equal to or greater than that of governmental zoning. Should there be limits on what types of covenants and restrictions can be imposed, either initially when the housing development is built or later by the governing association?

Nahrstedt v. Lakeside Village Condominium Association

Supreme Court of California, 1994.
878 P.2d 1275.

KENNARD, J.

A homeowner in a 530-unit condominium complex sued to prevent the homeowners association from enforcing a restriction against keeping cats, dogs, and other animals in the condominium development. The owner asserted that the restriction, which was contained in the project's declaration recorded by the condominium project's developer, was "unreasonable" as applied to her because she kept her three cats indoors and because her cats were "noiseless" and "created no nuisance."....

I

Lakeside Village is a large condominium development in Culver City, Los Angeles County. It consists of 530 units spread throughout 12 separate 3-story buildings. The residents share common lobbies and hallways, in addition to laundry and trash facilities.

The Lakeside Village project is subject to certain covenants, conditions and restrictions (hereafter CC&R's) that were included in the developer's declaration recorded with the Los Angeles County Recorder on April 17, 1978, at the inception of the development project. Ownership of a unit includes membership in the project's homeowners association, the Lakeside Village Condominium Association (hereafter Association), the body that enforces the project's CC&R's, including the pet restriction, which provides in relevant part: "No animals (which shall mean dogs and cats), livestock, reptiles or poultry shall be kept in any unit."

1. See Community Associations Institute, Data on U.S. Community Associations, at www.caionline.org/about/facts.cfm <visited March 29, 2006>.

In January 1988, plaintiff Natore Nahrstedt purchased a Lakeside Village condominium and moved in with her three cats. When the Association learned of the cats' presence, it demanded their removal and assessed fines against Nahrstedt for each successive month that she remained in violation of the condominium project's pet restriction. . . .

II

Today, condominiums, cooperatives, and planned-unit developments with homeowners associations have become a widely accepted form of real property ownership. These ownership arrangements are known as "common interest" developments. The owner not only enjoys many of the traditional advantages associated with individual ownership of real property, but also acquires an interest in common with others in the amenities and facilities included in the project. It is this hybrid nature of property rights that largely accounts for the popularity of these new and innovative forms of ownership in the 20th century. . . .

Use restrictions are an inherent part of any common interest development and are crucial to the stable, planned environment of any shared ownership arrangement. The viability of shared ownership of improved real property rests on the existence of extensive reciprocal servitudes, together with the ability of each co-owner to prevent the property's partition.

The restrictions on the use of property in any common interest development may limit activities conducted in the common areas as well as in the confines of the home itself. Commonly, use restrictions preclude alteration of building exteriors, limit the number of persons that can occupy each unit, and place limitations on—or prohibit altogether—the keeping of pets.

Restrictions on property use are not the only characteristic of common interest ownership. Ordinarily, such ownership also entails mandatory membership in an owners association, which, through an elected board of directors, is empowered to enforce any use restrictions contained in the project's declaration or master deed and to enact new rules governing the use and occupancy of property within the project. Because of its considerable power in managing and regulating a common interest development, the governing board of an owners association must guard against the potential for the abuse of that power.[2] As Professor Natelson observes, owners associations "can be a powerful force for good or for ill" in their members' lives. (Natelson, Comments on the Historiography of Condominium: The Myth of Roman Origin (1987) 12 Okla. City U. L. Rev. 17, 43.) Therefore, anyone who buys a unit in a common interest development with knowledge of its owners association's discretionary power accepts "the risk that the power may be used in a way that benefits the commonality but harms the individual." (Id. at p. 67.) Generally, courts will uphold decisions made by the governing board of an owners association so long as they represent

2. The power to regulate pertains to a "wide spectrum of activities," such as the volume of playing music, hours of social gatherings, use of patio furniture and barbecues, and rental of units.

good faith efforts to further the purposes of the common interest development, are consistent with the development's governing documents, and comply with public policy. (Id. at p. 43.)

Thus, subordination of individual property rights to the collective judgment of the owners association together with restrictions on the use of real property comprise the chief attributes of owning property in a common interest development. As the Florida District Court of Appeal observed in Hidden Harbour Estates, Inc. v. Norman (Fla. Dist. Ct. App. 1975) 309 So. 2d 180, a decision frequently cited in condominium cases: "[I]nherent in the condominium concept is the principle that to promote the health, happiness, and peace of mind of the majority of the unit owners since they are living in such close proximity and using facilities in common, each unit owner must give up a certain degree of freedom of choice which he [or she] might otherwise enjoy in separate, privately owned property. Condominium unit owners comprise a little democratic subsociety of necessity more restrictive as it pertains to use of condominium property than may be existent outside the condominium organization." (Id. at pp. 181–182.)

Notwithstanding the limitations on personal autonomy that are inherent in the concept of shared ownership of residential property, common interest developments have increased in popularity in recent years, in part because they generally provide a more affordable alternative to ownership of a single-family home. One significant factor in the continued popularity of the common interest form of property ownership is the ability of homeowners to enforce restrictive CC&R's against other owners (including future purchasers) of project units. Generally, however, such enforcement is possible only if the restriction that is sought to be enforced meets the requirements of equitable servitudes or of covenants running with the land. . . .

When restrictions limiting the use of property within a common interest development satisfy the requirements of covenants running with the land or of equitable servitudes, what standard or test governs their enforceability? In California, . . . our Legislature has made common interest development use restrictions contained in a project's recorded declaration "enforceable . . . *unless unreasonable*." (§ 1354, subd. (a), italics added.)

In states lacking such legislative guidance, some courts have adopted a standard under which a common interest development's recorded use restrictions will be enforced so long as they are "reasonable." Although no one definition of the term "reasonable" has gained universal acceptance, most courts have applied what one commentator calls "equitable reasonableness," upholding only those restrictions that provide a reasonable means to further the collective "health, happiness and enjoyment of life" of owners of a common interest development. (Note, *Community Association Use Restrictions: Applying the Business Judgment Doctrine* (1988) 64 Chi.-Kent L. Rev. 653, 655.) Others would limit the "reasonableness" standard only to those restrictions adopted by majority vote of the homeowners or enacted under the rulemaking power of an association's governing board, and would not apply this test to restrictions included in a planned development project's recorded declaration or master deed. Because such restrictions are presumptively valid, these authorities would enforce them regardless of reasonableness. . . .

In Hidden Harbour Estates v. Basso (Fla. Dist. Ct. App. 1981) 393 So. 2d 637, the Florida court distinguished two categories of use restrictions: use restrictions set forth in the declaration or master deed of the condominium project itself, and rules promulgated by the governing board of the condominium owners association or the board's interpretation of a rule. The latter category of use restrictions, the court said, should be subject to a "reasonableness" test, so as to "somewhat fetter the discretion of the board of directors." (Id. at p. 640.) Such a standard, the court explained, best assures that governing boards will "enact rules and make decisions that are reasonably related to the promotion of the health, happiness and peace of mind" of the project owners, considered collectively. (Ibid.)

By contrast, restrictions contained in the declaration or master deed of the condominium complex, the Florida court concluded, should not be evaluated under a "reasonableness" standard. (Id. at pp. 639–640.) Rather, such use restrictions are "clothed with a very strong presumption of validity" and should be upheld even if they exhibit some degree of unreasonableness. (Id. at pp. 639, 640.) Nonenforcement would be proper only if such restrictions were arbitrary or in violation of public policy or some fundamental constitutional right. . . .

Indeed, giving deference to use restrictions contained in a condominium project's originating documents protects the general expectations of condominium owners "that restrictions in place at the time they purchase their units will be enforceable." (Note, Judicial Review of Condominium Rulemaking (1981) 94 Harv. L. Rev. 647, 653; Ellickson, Cities and Homeowners' Associations (1982) 130 U. Pa. L. Rev. 1519, 1526–1527 [stating that association members "unanimously consent to the provisions in the association's original documents" and courts therefore should not scrutinize such documents for "reasonableness."].) This in turn encourages the development of shared ownership housing—generally a less costly alternative to single-dwelling ownership—by attracting buyers who prefer a stable, planned environment. It also protects buyers who have paid a premium for condominium units in reliance on a particular restrictive scheme.

To what extent are these general principles reflected in California's statutory scheme governing condominiums and other common interest developments? We shall explore that in the next section.

III

In California, common interest developments are subject to the provisions of the Davis–Stirling Common Interest Development Act (hereafter Davis–Stirling Act or Act). . . . Pertinent here is the Act's provision for the enforcement of use restrictions contained in the project's recorded declaration. That provision, subdivision (a) of section 1354, states in relevant part: "The covenants and restrictions in the declaration shall be enforceable equitable servitudes, *unless unreasonable*, and shall inure to the benefit of and bind all owners of separate interests in the development." (Italics added.) . . . .

As we have mentioned in the preceding paragraph, section 1354 states that covenants and restrictions appearing in the recorded declaration of a common interest development are "enforceable equitable servitudes, unless unreasonable." . . . . In choosing equitable servitude law as the standard for enforcing CC&R's in common interest developments, the Legislature has manifested a preference in favor of their enforcement. This preference is underscored by the use of the word "shall" in the first phrase of section 1354: "The covenants and restrictions shall be enforceable equitable servitudes. . . ."

The Legislature did, however, set a condition for the mandatory enforcement of a declaration's CC&R's: a covenant, condition or restriction is "enforceable . . . *unless unreasonable*." (§ 1354, subd. (a), italics added.) The Legislature's use of the phrase "unless unreasonable" in section 1354 was a marked change from the prior version of that statutory provision, which stated that "restrictions shall be enforceable equitable servitudes *where reasonable*." (Former § 1355, italics added.) Under settled principles of statutory construction, such a material alteration of a statute's phrasing signals the Legislature's intent to give an enactment a new meaning. Here, the change in statutory language, from "where reasonable" to "unless unreasonable," cloaked use restrictions contained in a condominium development's recorded declaration with a presumption of reasonableness by shifting the burden of proving otherwise to the party challenging the use restriction.

How is that burden satisfied? To answer this question, we must examine the principles governing enforcement of equitable servitudes. . . . [W]hen enforcing equitable servitudes, courts are generally disinclined to question the wisdom of agreed-to restrictions. This rule does not apply, however, when the restriction does not comport with public policy. Equity will not enforce any restrictive covenant that violates public policy. Nor will courts enforce as equitable servitudes those restrictions that are arbitrary, that is, bearing no rational relationship to the protection, preservation, operation or purpose of the affected land.

These limitations on the equitable enforcement of restrictive servitudes that are either arbitrary or violate fundamental public policy are specific applications of the general rule that courts will not enforce a restrictive covenant when "the harm caused by the restriction is so disproportionate to the benefit produced" by its enforcement that the restriction "ought not to be enforced." When a use restriction bears no relationship to the land it burdens, or violates a fundamental policy inuring to the public at large, the resulting harm will always be disproportionate to any benefit. . . .

This interpretation of section 1354 is consistent with the views of legal commentators as well as judicial decisions in other jurisdictions that have applied a presumption of validity to the recorded land use restrictions of a common interest development. As these authorities point out, and as we discussed previously, recorded CC&R's are the primary means of achieving the stability and predictability so essential to the success of a shared ownership housing development. In general, then, enforcement of a common interest development's recorded CC&R's will both encourage the development of land and ensure that promises are kept, thereby fulfilling both of the policies identified by the Restatement.

When courts accord a presumption of validity to all such recorded use restrictions and measure them against deferential standards of equitable servitude law, it discourages lawsuits by owners of individual units seeking personal exemptions from the restrictions. This also promotes stability and predictability in two ways. It provides substantial assurance to prospective condominium purchasers that they may rely with confidence on the promises embodied in the project's recorded CC&R's. And it protects all owners in the planned development from unanticipated increases in association fees to fund the defense of legal challenges to recorded restrictions.

How courts enforce recorded use restrictions affects not only those who have made their homes in planned developments, but also the owners associations charged with the fiduciary obligation to enforce those restrictions. When courts treat recorded use restrictions as presumptively valid, and place on the challenger the burden of proving the restriction "unreasonable" under the deferential standards applicable to equitable servitudes, associations can proceed to enforce reasonable restrictive covenants without fear that their actions will embroil them in costly and prolonged legal proceedings. Of course, when an association determines that a unit owner has violated a use restriction, the association must do so in good faith, not in an arbitrary or capricious manner, and its enforcement procedures must be fair and applied uniformly.

There is an additional beneficiary of legal rules that are protective of recorded use restrictions: the judicial system. Fewer lawsuits challenging such restrictions will be brought, and those that are filed may be disposed of more expeditiously, if the rules courts use in evaluating such restrictions are clear, simple, and not subject to exceptions based on the peculiar circumstances or hardships of individual residents in condominiums and other shared-ownership developments. . . .

V

Under the holding we adopt today, the reasonableness or unreasonableness of a condominium use restriction that the Legislature has made subject to section 1354 is to be determined *not* by reference to facts that are specific to the objecting homeowner, but by reference to the common interest development as a whole. . . .

We conclude, as a matter of law, that the recorded pet restriction of the Lakeside Village condominium development prohibiting cats or dogs but allowing some other pets is not arbitrary, but is rationally related to health, sanitation and noise concerns legitimately held by residents of a high-density condominium project such as Lakeside Village, which includes 530 units in 12 separate 3–story buildings.

Nahrstedt's complaint alleges no facts that could possibly support a finding that the burden of the restriction on the affected property is so disproportionate to its benefit that the restriction is unreasonable and should not be enforced. Also, the complaint's allegations center on Nahrstedt and her cats (that she keeps them inside her condominium unit and that they do not bother her neighbors), without any reference to the effect on the condominium development as a whole, thus rendering the allegations legally insufficient to overcome section 1354's presumption of the restriction's validity.

.... [We] discern no fundamental public policy that would favor the keeping of pets in a condominium project. There is no federal or state constitutional provision or any California statute that confers a general right to keep household pets in condominiums or other common interest developments.[12]....

ARABIAN, J., dissenting.

.... In relevant part, plaintiff has alleged that she is the owner of a condominium unit located in Lakeside Village; that she has three cats which she brought with her when she moved there; that she maintains her cats entirely within the confines of her unit and has "never released [them] in any common area"; that they are "noiseless, create no nuisance, [and] have not destroyed any portion of [her] unit, or the common area"; and that they provide her companionship. She further alleges the homeowners association is seeking to enforce a recorded restriction that prohibits keeping any pets except domestic fish and birds....

Our true task in this turmoil is to strike a balance between the governing rights accorded a condominium association and the individual freedom of its members. To fulfill that function, a reviewing court must view with a skeptic's eye restrictions driven by fear, anxiety, or intolerance. In any community, we do not exist *in vacuo*. There are many annoyances which we tolerate because not to do so would be repressive and place the freedom of others at risk.

In contravention, the majority's failure to consider the real burden imposed by the pet restriction unfortunately belittles and trivializes the interest at stake here. Pet ownership substantially enhances the quality of life for those who desire it. When others are not only undisturbed by, but *completely unaware of*, the presence of pets being enjoyed by their neighbors, the balance of benefit and burden is rendered disproportionate and unreasonable, rebutting any presumption of validity. Their view, shorn of grace and guiding philosophy, is devoid of the humanity that must temper the interpretation and application of all laws, for in a civilized society that

12. With respect to either disabled individuals living in rented housing or elderly persons living in publicly funded housing, the situation is otherwise. The Legislature has declared its intent that, in specified circumstances, these two classes of Californians be allowed to keep pets.... Because this case does not involve a disabled person needing guide dog assistance or an elderly person living in public housing, we do not address the public policy implications of recorded CC&R's that are in conflict with these statutes.

is the source of their authority. As judicial architects of the rules of life, we better serve when we construct halls of harmony rather than walls of wrath....

Notes & Questions

1. Should courts be in the business of evaluating the reasonableness of covenants to which homeowners expressly agree? Nahrstedt presumably could have found condominium complexes that did not prohibit pets, and other condominium owners in the Lakeside Village development may have purchased units there in the expectation of living in a pet-free community. Having agreed to the covenant in purchasing her property, why should Nahrstedt be able to complain later? Should courts review such covenants even to determine whether they are "reasonable"? See Hidden Harbour Estates v. Basso, 393 So. 2d 637 (Fla. Dist. Ct. App. 1981) (even "unreasonable" restrictions should be upheld if they are not "wholly arbitrary" or in violation of public policy or constitutional rights).

2. Looking at the case from Ms. Nahrstedt's perspective, should condominium developers and subdividers ever be able to limit what a homeowner does in the privacy of her own unit, so long as the behavior does not affect activities outside the unit? A covenant might be permissible, for example, if it limits loud noises (including meowing cats and barking dogs) or prevents cats in the common areas. But should a covenant be able to prohibit Ms. Nahrstedt from keeping purportedly meowless cats in her condominium? Should a condominium complex be able to impose a covenant prohibiting people from drinking coffee in their units? Even if rational, do such covenants intrude too deeply into personal freedom?

3. As noted in *Nahrstedt*, many common-interest communities authorize homeowner associations or similar organizations to review construction plans and adopt specific rules and restrictions governing the community. Many common-interest communities also permit property owners by majority or super-majority vote to amend or adopt new covenants. Should new restrictions be judged by the same standard as covenants that are in place at the time that a homeowner buys into a common-interest community?

As the California Supreme Court notes in *Nahrstedt*, many courts apply a heightened standard to later-adopted restrictions. As *Nahrstedt* observes, the Florida Court of Appeal set out a two-tier standard in Hidden Harbour Estates v. Basso, 393 So. 2d 637 (Fla. Dist. Ct. App. 1981). According to *Hidden Harbour*, restrictions to which homeowners expressly agree should be clothed

> with a very strong presumption of validity which arises from the fact that each individual unit owner purchases his unit knowing of and accepting the restrictions to be imposed.... [By contrast], where a use restriction is not mandated by the declaration of condominium per se, but is instead created by the board of directors of the condominium association, the rule of reasonable-

> ness comes into vogue. The requirement of "reasonableness" in these instances is designed to somewhat fetter the discretion of the board of directors. By imposing such a standard, the board is required to enact rules and make decisions that are reasonably related to the promotion of the health, happiness and peace of mind of the unit owners. In cases like the present one where the decision to allow a particular use is within the discretion of the board, the board must allow the use unless the use is demonstrably antagonistic to the legitimate objectives of the condominium association, i.e., the health, happiness and peace of mind of the individual unit owners.

Id. at 640.

California uses the same statutory "reasonableness" standard applied in *Nahrstedt* to evaluate covenants adopted after a homeowner purchases a unit in a common-interest community. See Villa de Las Palmas Homeowners Ass'n v. Terifaj, 90 P.3d 1223 (Cal. 2004) (upholding rule banning pets of all kinds).

4. Some courts have suggested that new rules and restrictions agreed upon by a homeowners' or management association after someone has purchased property in a common-interest community should be subjected to a less restrictive test than the reasonableness standard. In Levandusky v. One Fifth Avenue Apt. Corp., 553 N.E.2d 1317 (N.Y. 1990), for example, the New York Court of Appeals rejected a reasonableness standard in favor of a "business judgment standard" that defers to the judgment of the homeowners' or management association and places the burden of proof on the complaining property owner.

> The more limited judicial review embodied in the business judgment rule is preferable. In the context of the decisions of a for-profit corporation, "courts are ill equipped and infrequently called on to evaluate what are and must be essentially business judgments.... [B]y definition the responsibility for business judgments must rest with the corporate directors; their individual capabilities and experience peculiarly qualify them for the discharge of that responsibility." (Auerbach v. Bennett, 47 N.Y.2d 619, 630–631.) Even if decisions of a cooperative board do not generally involve expertise beyond the usual ken of the judiciary, at the least board members will possess experience of the peculiar needs of their building and its residents not shared by the court.
>
> Several related concerns persuade us that such a rule should apply here. As this case exemplifies, board decisions concerning what residents may or may not do with their living space may be highly charged and emotional. A cooperative or condominium is by nature a myriad of often competing views regarding personal living space, and decisions taken to benefit the collective interest may be unpalatable to one resident or another, creating the prospect that board decisions will be subjected to undue court involvement and judicial second-guessing. Allowing an owner who is simply dissatis-

> fied with particular board action a second opportunity to reopen the matter completely before a court, which—generally without knowing the property—may or may not agree with the reasonableness of the board's determination, threatens the stability of the common living arrangement.
>
> Moreover, the prospect that each board decision may be subjected to full judicial review hampers the effectiveness of the board's managing authority. The business judgment rule protects the board's business decisions and managerial authority from indiscriminate attack.

Id. at 1322–1323.

5. Although courts have been generally deferential to covenants imposed in common interest communities, legislatures have occasionally stepped in and protected homeowners from particular types of restrictions. See, e.g., Cal. Civ. Code § 1353.5 (prohibiting covenants that restrict the display of the American flag); Cal. Civ. Code § 1360.5 (authorizing residents of common interest communities to keep at least one pet—enacted after *Nahrstedt*).

6. For insightful discussions of common interest communities and the role of judicial review in overseeing private covenants imposed by common interest communities on their property owners, see Robert Jay Dilger, Neighborhood Politics: Residential Community Associations in American Governance (1992); Gregory S. Alexander, Dilemmas of Group Autonomy: Residential Associations and Community, 75 Cornell L. Rev. 1 (1989); Note, the Rule of Law in Residential Associations, 99 Harv. L. Rev. 472 (1985); Robert C. Ellickson, Cities and Homeowners Associations, 130 U. Pa. L. Rev. 1519 (1982).

3. Discriminatory Covenants

Racial Covenants. The law today is clear that, under the equal protection clause of the Fourteenth Amendment, courts cannot enforce racially restrictive covenants that prohibit a property owner from selling or leasing the property to minorities. A century ago, however, courts were split on whether the Fourteenth Amendment reached private restrictive covenants. The California Supreme Court took the position that private restrictive covenants that discriminated against minorities involved no state action and therefore were not unconstitutional. Los Angeles Investment Co. v. Gary, 186 P. 596 (Cal. 1919). A federal district court in California, by contrast, held that the Fourteenth Amendment did reach private covenants and barred any covenant that discriminated on the basis of race. According to the court,

> It would be a very narrow construction of the constitutional amendment in question . . . and a very restricted application of the broad principles under which . . . the amendment . . . proceeds, to hold that, while state and municipal legislatures are forbidden to discriminate against the Chinese in their legislation, a citizen of

> the state may lawfully do so by contract, which the courts may enforce. Such a view is ... entirely inadmissible. Any result inhibited by the constitution can no more be accomplished by contract of individual citizens than by legislation, and the courts should no more enforce the one than the other. This would seem to be very clear.

Gandolfo v. Hartman, 49 F. 181, 182 (S.D. Cal 1892) (invalidating a covenant prohibiting the landowner from renting to "Chinamen").

In Shelley v. Kraemer, 334 U.S. 1 (1948), the Supreme Court held that courts could not enforce racially restrictive covenants through injunctive relief without violating the Fourteenth Amendment. "We have no doubt that there has been state action in these cases in the full and complete sense of the phrase .... It is clear that but for the active intervention of the state courts, supported by the full panoply of state power, petitioners would have been free to occupy the properties in question without restraint." Id. at 19. Because the Supreme Court did not hold that the covenants themselves were unconstitutional, some state courts continued to award damages for violations of racially restrictive covenants. Five years later, the Supreme Court held that courts could not award damages either. Barrows v. Jackson, 346 U.S. 249 (1953).

Today the federal Fair Housing Act of 1968 (42 U.S.C. §§ 3601 et seq.), the federal Civil Rights Act of 1866 (42 U.S.C. §§ 1981 et seq.), and various state civil rights laws almost certainly prohibit even the creation of a racially restrictive covenant. Reaching beyond *Shelley* and *Barrows*, moreover, these laws have helped eliminate the remaining vestiges of those covenants already on the books. In 1969, for example, the U.S. Department of Justice concluded in a letter to 18 major title insurance companies that the 1968 Fair Housing Act "broadened the *Shelley* prohibition to cover not only judicial enforcement of such covenants, but also their inclusion in public documents such as deeds or insurance policies." The Department

> informed the companies that they were violating the law by their practice of reporting the existence of racial restrictions appearing in the records of title on property for which they were issuing title insurance policies. All eighteen title companies replied that in future policies they would eliminate any reference to such restrictions.

Mayers v. Ridley, 465 F.2d 630, 649 (D.C. Cir. 1972) (Wilkey, J., concurring). In the early 1970s, the federal Court of Appeals held that the Civil Rights Act prohibits recorders of deeds from accepting and recording any racially restrictive covenant. Id.

Age Discrimination. Restrictive covenants in various "retirement communities," which often prohibit children from living in the community, have spawned considerable litigation in recent years. In O'Connor v. Village Green Owners Ass'n, 662 P.2d 427 (Cal. 1983), the California Supreme Court held that a covenant in a condominium complex that limited residency to persons over the age of 18 violated the state's civil rights law prohibiting arbitrary discrimination. Two justices dissented. In their view, the result was "disastrous for the many well-conceived, constructively operated developments" that sought to provide "comfort and peace of mind" to the elderly. Id. at 804 (Mosk, J., dissenting). A year later, the California legislature enacted a narrow exception to the civil rights law for certain retirement communities. Cal. Civ. Code § 51.3.

The federal Fair Housing Act also exempts from its purview discrimination against families in connection with "housing for older persons." Such housing is defined as including communities "intended for, and solely occupied by, persons 62 years of age or older" and communities intended for persons 55 and over if at least one person who is 55 or over occupies at least 80 percent of the occupied units. 42 U.S.C. § 3607(b). Do such exemptions deny equal protection to the young? See Taylor v. Rancho Santa Barbara, 206 F.3d 932 (9th Cir. 2000) (no).

C. Conservation Easements

Nonprofit *land trusts* are playing an increasingly important role in preserving and enhancing land for open space, recreation, biodiversity, and other uses in the United States. Over 1500 land trusts now operate throughout the nation. As of 2000, these land trusts protected almost four million acres of land. The Nature Conservancy (TNC) dwarfs every other land trust in the amount of land that it has protected—over 1.5 million acres, or two-third of the total land protected by land trusts. However, other land trusts, including such major organizations as Ducks Unlimited, the Rocky Mountain Elk Foundation, and the Wildlands Conservancy, play an essential role in protecting land. The role of private land trusts in preserving habitat and other open space, moreover, is increasing geometrically. During the 1990s, the number of land trusts increased by 63% and the amount of land and conservation easements owned by the trusts increased by 135%.

Conservation easements, under which a land trust or other entity obtains a servitude requiring a property owner to protect various natural or historical characteristics of his or her land, are the principal tool that land trusts use to preserve habitat and open space. Although land trusts often own extensive amounts of land in fee simply absolute, approximately 60 percent of all the property protected by land trusts in 2000 was held in the form of conservation easements. Such easements generally prohibit the property owner from engaging in a wide variety of activities that might harm the particular environmental, aesthetic, historical, or recreational amenities of the land meant to be protected:

> For example, subdivision, development, significant commercial use (other than agriculture), clear-cutting of timber, strip mining, and billboard advertisements are commonly prohibited. Landowners are routinely able, however, to negotiate terms that will allow them to own, occupy, and perform a variety of activities on the property. These permitted activities may include, without limita-

> tion, residential occupancy, construction of new residential structures, construction of new agricultural structures, farming, hunting, camping, private airstrips, and equestrian activities.

Tennessee Envt'l Council v. Bright Par 3 Associates, 2004 WL 419720 at 2.

William Whyte was one of the first persons to coin the term "conservation easement." In 1959, he published a major study entitled *Conservation Easements* in which he argued that states should pass legislation authorizing and encouraging private land conservation. Even before Whyte's study, the national government, as well as a variety of private organizations, acquired easements to protect lands that were valuable to the public for aesthetic, recreational, historical, environmental, or other reasons. "By the time Whyte coined the term 'conservation easement,' the property interest he described was already relatively well established. In the 1930s and 1940s, the National Park Service purchased easements encumbering almost 1,500 acres in North Carolina and Virginia to protect scenic vistas along the Blue Ridge Parkway, and easements encumbering another 4,500 acres in Alabama, Mississippi, and Tennessee to protect scenic vistas along the Natchez Trace Parkway." Frederico Cheever & Nancy A. McLaughlin, Why Environmental Lawyers Should Know (and Care) About Land Trusts and Their Private Land Conservation Transactions, 34 Envtl. L. Rep. 10223, 10224 (2004).

The legitimacy of conservation easements, however, was in doubt under the traditional common law rules of servitudes. The common law historically recognized negative easements for only a limited number of purposes (see page 820)—and conservation was not one of them. The assignability of noncommercial easements in gross was also in doubt (see page 841). This left the possibility of structuring conservation easements as negative covenants or equitable servitudes. If the burden was to run with the land, however, negative covenants typically required that there be horizontal privity between the original parties to the covenant (see page 893), making it difficult for land trusts or governments to acquire a conservation servitude except as part of a real estate transaction. And the common law historically prohibited the enforcement of a restrictive covenant held in gross (see page 905).

Starting in the late 1950s, therefore, states began enacting legislation authorizing the creation and enforcement of conservation easements that could run with the land. California passed the first statute in 1959, followed a year later by New York. See Cal. Govt. Code § 6953; N.Y. Gen. Mun. Law § 247. Although every state has now passed such a statute, some of the statutes are quite limited, and the validity of conservation servitudes created before such statutes were passed remains an open question in most states.

United States v. Blackman

Supreme Court of Virginia, 2005.
613 S.E.2d 442.

Opinion by JUSTICE LAWRENCE L. KOONTZ, JR.

Pursuant to Article VI, Section 1 of the Constitution of Virginia and our Rule 5:42, the United States District Court for the Western District of

Virginia ("district court") . . . certified to this Court the following question of law:

> A. In Virginia in 1973, would a conveyance of a negative easement in gross by a private property owner to a private party for the purpose of land conservation and historic preservation be valid?. . . .

The relevant facts are recited in the order of certification as follows:

> The Green Springs Historic District (the "District") is an area of roughly 14,000 acres in Louisa County that was settled in the 1700s. Much of the land in this area has historically been used for agricultural purposes, and this agricultural setting remains today. Because the land has been continuously farmed for almost three centuries, many of the homes and farms have been preserved in their original context with little alteration. . . . The Green Springs Historic District was listed on the National Register of Historic Places in March of 1973, and was ultimately designated as a National Historic Landmark in 1974.
>
> By a "Deed of Easement" dated March 19, 1973 (the "Easement"), D.L. Atkins and Frances Atkins granted to [a non-profit group dubbed Historic Green Springs, Inc. ("HGSI")] an assignable easement over several parcels of their property, including Eastern View Farm. The Easement states in part that "in consideration of the grant to the Grantee of similar easements in gross by other owners of land in the said Green Springs Historic District for similar purposes, the Grantors [D.L. Atkins and Frances Atkins] do hereby grant and convey to the Grantee [HGSI] an easement in gross restricting in perpetuity, in the manner hereinafter set forth, the use of the following described tracts of land, together with the improvements erected thereon." In 1978, HGSI decided to convey its entire portfolio of easements to the United States. In the resulting deed of easement to the United States, all of the original grantors of similar easements within the District acknowledged their agreement to the conveyance by affixing their signatures to the deed. The National Park Service ("NPS") now administers these easements, including the Easement at issue, on behalf of the United States as part of the Green Springs National Historic Landmark District. The Easement at issue provides that the manor house on Eastern View Farm:
>
>> will be maintained and preserved in its present state as nearly as practicable, though structural changes, alterations, additions, or improvements as would not in the opinion of the Grantee fundamentally alter its historic character or its setting may be made thereto by the owner, provided that the prior written approval of the Grantee to such change, alteration, addition, or improve-

> ments shall have been obtained. This provision applies as well to those 18th and 19th Century outbuildings located on the described property.
>
> Peter F. Blackman ("Blackman") purchased Eastern View Farm on July 1, 2002. Blackman wishes to renovate and rehabilitate the manor house. Specifically, Blackman, inter alia, seeks to remove the existing front porch on the manor house, replace the siding, and create an addition. In support of these intended alternations, Blackman submitted several sets of renovation plans to the NPS for review, but the NPS repeatedly denied certain aspects of his plans. Rather than working with the NPS for final approval of his plan, Blackman's attorney stated in a latter dated January 13, 2004 that Blackman would "commence the Rehabilitation at a time of his choosing, without further notice to [NPS], in accordance with the attached elevations." Subsequently, Blackman removed the porch from his house. The United States filed the complaint in this case June 14, 2004, and on June 16, 2004 Judge James C. Turk issued a temporary restraining order restraining Blackman from "commencing and/or continuing renovation work to the manor house located on the Eastern View Parcel, in the Green Springs National Historic Landmark District, unless he has first obtained written approval from the National Park Service."

In defense of his actions, Blackman argues that, inter alia, the original deed of easement granted to HGSI was invalid because at the time it was purportedly created, Virginia law did not recognize any kind of negative easement in gross, including such easements for the purpose of land conservation and historic preservation. . . .

Although previously we have not addressed the issue of the validity of a negative easement in gross under the law existing in 1973, the issue is of considerable significance beyond the specific historic district involved in this case. By the brief of amici curiae filed in this case, we are advised that at least seven other charitable entities hold conservation or historic preservation easements, many of them easements in gross, conveyed prior to 1973. Underlying the issue is a degree of apparent conflict between the common law preference for unrestricted rights of ownership of real property and the public policy of this Commonwealth as expressed in Article XI of the Constitution of Virginia, ratified by the people of this Commonwealth in 1970, that "it shall be the policy of this Commonwealth to conserve . . . its historical sites and buildings." Accordingly, we take this opportunity to discuss in some detail the relevant law. . . .

At common law, an owner of land was not permitted at his pleasure to create easements of every novel character and annex them to the land so that the land would be burdened with the easement when the land was conveyed to subsequent grantees. Rather, the landowner was limited to the creation of easements permitted by the common law or by statute. The traditional negative easements recognized at common law were those created to protect the flow of air, light, and artificial streams of water, and to ensure the subjacent and lateral support of buildings or land. See Andrew Dana & Michael Ramsey, Conservation Easements and the Common Law, 8 Stan. Envtl. L.J. 2, 13 (1989).

Easements, whether affirmative or negative, are classified as either "appurtenant" or "in gross."…. The four negative easements traditionally recognized at common law are, by their nature, easements appurtenant, as their intent is to benefit an adjoining or nearby parcel of land. See Federico Cheever, Environmental Law: Public Good and Private Magic in the Law of Land Trusts and Conservation Easements: A Happy Present and a Troubled Future, 73 Denv. U. L. Rev. 1077, 1081 (1996).

In contrast, an easement in gross, sometimes called a personal easement, is an easement "which is not appurtenant to any estate in land, but in which the servitude is imposed upon land with the benefit thereof running to an individual." Lester Coal Corp. v. Lester, 122 S.E.2d 901, 904 (Va. 1961). At common law, easements in gross were strongly disfavored because they were viewed as interfering with the free use of land. Thus, the common law rule of long standing is that an easement is "never presumed to be in gross when it [can] fairly be construed to be appurtenant to land." French v. Williams, 4 S.E. 591, 594 (Va. 1886)….

Because easements in gross were disfavored by the common law, they could neither be transferred by the original grantee nor pass by inheritance. By statute, however, Virginia long ago abrogated common law restrictions on the transfer of interests in land "by declaring that any interest in or claim to real estate may be disposed of by deed or will." Carrington v. Goddin, 54 Va. (13 Gratt.) 587, 599–600 (1857). Pursuant to this statutory change in the common law rule, currently embodied in Code § 55–6, we have recognized that an affirmative easement in gross is an interest in land that may be disposed of by deed or will. Following this Court's decision in *Lester Coal Corp.*, which in dictum made reference to the common law rule that easements in gross remained non-transferable by deed or will, Code § 55–6 was amended "to make clear the transferability of easements in gross." 1962 Va. Acts ch. 169. Since 1962, Code § 55–6, in pertinent part, has expressly provided that "any interest in or claim to real estate, including easements in gross, may be disposed of by deed or will."

The 1962 amendment and clarification of Code § 55–6 with regard to the transferability of easements in gross has facilitated, in part, Virginia's long recognition of the value of conserving and preserving the natural beauty and historic sites and buildings in which it richly abounds. In 1966, the General Assembly enacted the Open–Space Land Act, 1966 Va. Acts ch. 461. This Act, currently found in Code § § 10.1–1700 through–1705, is intended to encourage the acquisition by certain public bodies of fee simple title or "easements in gross or such other interests in real estate" that are designed to maintain the preservation or provision of open-space land. Code § 10.1–1703. By definition, open-space land includes land that is preserved for "historic or scenic purposes." Code § 10.1–1700. Additionally, in 1966, the General Assembly enacted statutes creating the Virginia Outdoors Foundation, 1966 Va. Acts. ch. 525, and the Virginia Historic Landmarks

Commission, 1966 Va. Acts ch. 632. As currently expressed in Code § 10.1–1800, the purpose of the Virginia Outdoors Foundation is "to promote the preservation of open-space lands." The Virginia Historic Landmarks Commission, now known as the Virginia Board of Historic Resources, was charged with the designation of historic landmarks and districts. 1966 Va. Acts ch. 632, § 4(A). These statutes evince a strong public policy in favor of land conservation and preservation of historic sites and buildings.

As noted above, this public policy was expressly embodied in Article XI of the Constitution of Virginia which, since 1970, has provided:

> § 1. To the end that the people have clean air, pure water, and the use and enjoyment for recreation of adequate public lands, waters, and other natural resources, it shall be the policy of the Commonwealth to conserve, develop, and utilize its natural resources, its public lands, and its historical sites and buildings. Further, it shall be the Commonwealth's policy to protect its atmosphere, lands, and waters from pollution, impairment, or destruction, for the benefit, enjoyment, and general welfare of the people of the Commonwealth.
>
> § 2. In the furtherance of such policy, the General Assembly may undertake the conservation, development, or utilization of lands or natural resources of the Commonwealth, the acquisition and protection of historical sites and buildings, and the protection of its atmosphere, lands, and waters from pollution, impairment, or destruction, by agencies of the Commonwealth or by the creation of public authorities, or by leases or other contracts with agencies of the United States, with other states, with units of government in the Commonwealth, or with private persons or corporations.

In further support of this public policy, the General Assembly in 1988 enacted the Virginia Conservation Easement Act ("VCEA"), Code §§ 10.1–1009 through –1016. In pertinent part, as defined in the VCEA a conservation easement is "a nonpossessory interest of a holder in real property, whether easement appurtenant or in gross ... the purposes of which include retaining or protecting natural or open-space values of real property ... or preserving the historical, architectural or archaeological aspects of real property." Code § 10.1–1009.

Mindful of this background, we now consider the validity of the negative easement in gross granted to HGSI by the Atkinses in the 1973 deed and subsequently conveyed, with the Atkinses' concurrence, to the United States in 1978. . . . Blackman contends that a negative easement in gross for the purpose of land conservation and historic preservation was not valid in this Commonwealth until 1988 with the enactment of the VCEA. The thrust of this contention is that the VCEA would have been unnecessary if such easements were already valid. We are not persuaded by this contention.

Blackman's contention suggests an analysis devoid of due consideration of the pertinent statutory and constitutional provisions in effect in the Commonwealth long before the 1988 enactment of the VCEA. As discussed supra, Code § 55–6 since at least 1962 has recognized easements in gross, whether affirmative or negative, as interests in real property capable of being transferred by deed or will.... Moreover, in the subsequent 1966 enactment of the Open–Space Land Act, the General Assembly specifically recognized easements in gross when it authorized acquisition by certain public bodies of easements in gross in real property which is preserved for historic purposes. Such easements under that Act, under certain circumstances, would be negative easements in gross. Accordingly, while we continue to be of opinion that "the law will not permit a landowner to create easements of every novel character and attach them to the soil," Tardy v. Creasy, 81 Va. (6 Hans.) 553, 557 (1886), the easement at issue in the present case is not of a novel character and is consistent with the statutory recognition of negative easements in gross for conservation and historic purposes....

In enacting the VCEA, the General Assembly undertook to comprehensively address various land interests that can be used for conserving and preserving the natural and historical nature of property.... The readily apparent purpose of the VCEA was to codify and consolidate the law of conservation easements to promote the granting of such easements to charitable organizations. When so viewed, it is clear that the VCEA did not create a new right to burden land by a negative easement in gross for the purpose of land conservation and historic preservation. Rather, it facilitated the continued creation of such easements by providing a clear statutory framework under which tax exemptions are made available to charitable organizations devoted to those purposes and tax benefits and incentives are provided to the grantors of such easements....

For these reasons, we hold that the law of Virginia in 1973 did recognize as valid a negative easement in gross created for the purpose of land conservation and historic preservation. Accordingly, we answer the first certified question in the affirmative....

Notes & Questions

1. While upholding conservation easements created before the Virginia Conservation Easement Act, the Virginia Supreme Court expresses continued skepticism regarding new forms of negative easements. Is there any reason why the law should not recognize any form of negative easement to which property owners now wish to agree? Other significant negative easements still in doubt in some jurisdictions include view easements and solar energy easements.

2. All states have now adopted statutes authorizing conservation easements. About half of the states have adopted versions of the Uniform Conservation Easement Act of 1981, 12 U.L.A. (1981) (UCEA). The UCEA provides that a conservation easement is valid even though it "is not of a

character that has been recognized traditionally at common law," is held in gross, provides a benefit that "does not touch or concern real property," and imposes a negative burden. Id. § 4. The UCEA applies not only to interests created after the effective date of the act in a state, but to pre-existing interests "unless retroactive application contravenes the constitution or laws of this State or the United States." Id. § 4(a)–(b). Does it violate the takings protection of the federal constitution to validate pre-existing conservation easements that would not have been permissible under the common law?

3. **Purposes of Conservation Easements.** Should there be any limitations on the purposes for which conservation easements can be created? The UCEA authorizes conservation easements for multiple purposes, including "retaining or protecting natural, scenic, or open-space values of real property, assuring its availability for agricultural, forest, recreational, or open-space use, protecting natural resources, maintaining or enhancing air or water quality, or preserving the historical, architectural, archaeological, or cultural aspects of real property." UCEA § 1(1). Most states are equally inclusive, although different statutes add or exclude specific purposes. See Todd D. Mayo, A Holistic Examination of the Law of Conservation Easements, in Protecting the Land: Conservation Easements Past, Present, and Future 26 (Julie Ann Gustanski & Roderick H. Squires eds., 2000).

4. **Beneficiaries.** Who should be entitled to hold a conservation easement? The UCEA authorizes any governmental body, charitable corporation, charitable association, or charitable trust to hold a conservation easement. UCEA § 1(2). New Mexico precludes governments from holding conservation easements (N.M. Stat. Ann. § 47–12–2(A)), while Mississippi expressly authorizes private and educational corporations to hold conservation easements so long as the corporation's purposes include conservation (Miss. Code Ann. § 89–19–3(2)(b)). Is there any reason not to permit anyone to hold a conservation easement?

5. **Length.** The UCEA provides that "a conservation easement is unlimited in duration unless the instrument creating it otherwise provides." UCEA § 2(c). The perpetual nature of most conservation easements has come under recent challenge, as discussed in the following two law review articles.

Julia D. Mahoney, The Illusion of Perpetuity and the Preservation of Privately Owned Lands

44 Nat. Resources J. 573, 573–574 (2004).

For centuries, the law of property has grappled with a "basic paradox" at the core of the idea that owners exert dominion over their holdings. The power to control one's property includes the ability to limit the choices available to one's successors in interest (or even to oneself at a later date).

Imposing such constraints has the effect of denying later owners the full range of options enjoyed by earlier owners.

With respect to real property, a consensus has emerged that this conundrum should be resolved by disfavoring the "dead hand" of the past. Taking to heart the maxim that the earth belongs to the living, a number of courts and commentators have embraced the notion that each generation should be free, with limited exceptions, to make its own decisions regarding the disposition and use of land. Thus, restrictions purportedly designed to limit the ability of landholders to transfer their property rights to others, commonly known as restraints on alienation, are regarded with disfavor. Similarly, American property law discourages attempts to control future land uses through the creation of estates in land that are subject to forfeiture in the event that an owner fails to abide by conditions imposed by an earlier owner. While it is true that the law of servitudes allows owners to exercise substantial influence over future uses of their properties through the imposition of easements, real covenants, and equitable servitudes, the fact that servitudes can "impose significant dead hand controls over land use"[7] is regarded as a shortcoming of these instruments.

The suspicion generally evinced toward efforts of private owners of real property to influence the future use and disposition of their holdings rarely extends to measures aimed at "preserving" the land, however. Property holders who take steps to ensure that their lands remain undeveloped in perpetuity or for a substantial time period are widely regarded as having bestowed benefits not only upon their immediate communities and society as a whole, but also on future generations. This response is a curious one, for it means that the very aspect of private land preservation that might be expected to trigger the greatest concern—to wit, its explicit goal of reducing or even extinguishing the possibility that certain choices made today will be revisited—instead forms the basis of its appeal. . . .

The fact that land preservation by private holders entails more than simple inaction deserves our attention and analysis. In effect, land preservation is regarded as a mechanism by which present owners serve as a bridge between the past and the future. According to this view, those in possession of lands deemed worthy of "preservation" shoulder the awesome responsibility of ensuring that what remains of the natural world does not vanish but is instead enjoyed and passed on in an unspoiled state to those who follow. Because what is thought to be at stake is nothing less than making sure that the world's last, best places do not disappear altogether, the prospect of "dead hand" influence fails to arouse serious concern. We are confident that our successors will share our preferences or, at the very least, that they ought to share them. Either way, the institutional roadblocks put in place today to frustrate future development are a cause for celebration. Land preservation, in short, is implicitly assumed to present a

7. Susan F. French, Toward a Modern Law of Servitudes: Reweaving the Ancient Strands, 55 S. Cal. L. Rev. 1261, 1265 (1982).

special case, one in which the usual worries about the lingering influence of earlier actors can be put aside.

The trouble with this line of thought is that there are compelling reasons to think that those who follow us will have different ideas regarding which lands warrant preservation. What's more, our successors are likely to be justified in wishing to reconsider many of today's policy choices. Future decision makers, after all, will reap the benefits of advances in ecological understanding and technological capabilities, leading them to question the advisability of preservation decisions that today appear obviously well founded. In addition, changes in aesthetic tastes may severely reduce or even obliterate the amenity value of some conserved lands, thereby making development of these lands an attractive option. Finally, the fact that nature is not equilibrial means that over time many preserved lands will change, no matter how vigorously human impact is curtailed. As a result, keeping lands undeveloped may no longer promote the goals that motivated their preservation in the first place.

These insights have important ramifications for public policy. Instead of assuming that the specific land preservation choices made now will (and should) prove eternal, or at least very long-lasting, decision makers should understand that many conservation actions will in all likelihood be revisited. The costs of undoing or modifying preservation choices . . . will vary significantly and will depend on the institutional structures set up to restrain development as well as the anticipated changes in land use. Whether and to what extent a choice regarding land is reversible will hinge on the particular circumstances of each case, not on whether that choice, when made, caused the land in question to be labeled "preserved" or "developed." In short, it is wrong to assume that reversing choices to conserve land will necessarily prove cheaper and easier than revisiting decisions to develop. The implication of this analysis is far reaching and, to some, no doubt disquieting: a number of today's choices to preserve privately held lands will not inure to the benefit of those who follow.

Barton H. Thompson, Jr., The Trouble with Time: Influencing the Conservation Choices of Future Generations

44 Nat. Resources J. 601 (2004).

There may be affirmative and legitimate reasons . . . why someone might want to make future development difficult for both themselves and others. Even if one concludes that the creation of conservation easements or other forms of intergenerational conservancies strips future generations of the ability to make their own conservation decisions, this "dead hand" problem must be weighed against a number of potential justifications for "perpetual" conservation. . . . Although individual property owners might try to create intergenerational conservancies for reasons that arguably are illegitimate (e.g., a desire simply to dictate the moral norms of future generations), there are strong rationales in many, if not most, cases for moving beyond "at will" or short-term conservation and adopting some form of intergenerational conservancy.

A. Reducing Transaction Costs

[One] possible justification for using an intergenerational conservancy [is] minimization of transaction costs. [Land] conservation inevitably involves large transaction costs because of its public-good character. Large numbers of people generally benefit from land that is conserved for its aesthetic, recreational, historic, or cultural values or for the ecosystem services that it generates. As is the case of any public good, however, each beneficiary is tempted to free ride off of others' efforts to preserve the land, undermining effective collective action. The most realistic options for conserving the land—lobbying the government to acquire and preserve the land or raising money through a private land trust—are administratively costly.

If one expects that conservation will be the most valuable use of a parcel of land for a lengthy and indefinite period of time, an intergenerational conservancy is likely to minimize transaction costs. If a new agreement has to be worked out every X years (in the case of fixed-term conservation instruments) or each time the land changes hands through market transfers, wills, or intestate succession (in the case of conservation agreements personal to the current owner), the transaction costs would mount quickly. Although an intergenerational conservancy makes it more costly to move the land back out of conservation, the low probability that development will become in the public interest in the future makes it less troubling than having to negotiate new conservation agreements every time the land is transferred.

B. Avoiding Temptation

Like Odysseus and the Sirens, a property owner also may wish to avoid the future temptation to make a quick and sizable profit by developing her land. Imagine a farmer who owns several acres of wetlands in the middle of a rural area. The farmer may believe that preserving the wetlands in "perpetuity" will maximize the long-term value of the wetlands to society as a whole, including the value of the ecosystem services and aesthetic delight that the wetlands provide. The farmer, however, does not trust herself to make the "right" decision if, 30 years from now when suburbs are encroaching, a developer approaches the farmer to purchase the land for hundreds of millions of dollars in hard cash. Nor does the farmer trust her heirs to make the "right" decision if confronted by that same "big bucks" option or if forced to raise money to pay estate taxes upon the farmer's death. In these situations, the farmer fears that when "temptation knocks," she (or her successors) will be "weak willed" and act largely if not entirely out of self-interest. Because no developer is knocking on her door at the moment, however, the farmer is willing to transfer a conservation easement today to a local land trust....

C. Private Ordering

[P]roperty owners frequently use "perpetual" servitudes as part of private land-use regimes—and for good reason. To see their relevance to conservation, assume that you are developing a new subdivision of summer homes along the northern coast of California. You know that you can maximize the value of the subdivision by setting aside much of the land as a "perpetual" wildlife preserve, so that the buyers of your homes can sit in their hot tubs and observe the deer and birds in their natural habitat. After all, beauty and nature are values for which buyers will pay extra. Each of the purchasers, however, will want to know that they are not buying a pig in a poke, that the land indeed will be preserved for a long, long time, and that the land will not be subject to the whims of their neighbors (who they do not entirely trust). Like many developers before and after, the coastal developer may find it profit-maximizing to deed a "perpetual" conservation easement to a newly formed land trust or even to the local government. The motivation here is no different from the motivation underlying scenic easements, park dedications, and subdivision CC&Rs (covenants, conditions, and restrictions). If the conservation easement were of only limited duration, home buyers (or their successors) would have to renegotiate the easement in 50 or 100 years, at which time the successor to the developer would have significant monopoly power (given that the homes already would exist).

At a more general level, intergenerational conservancies can promote land use planning by private developers, governmental regulators, and environmentalists by providing both stability and security. In deciding where to build, developers will find it valuable to know that certain lands are part of an intergenerational conservancy because neighboring lands will sell for a premium. In deciding whether to permit Riverside County, California, to build a new hospital directly on top of the sand dune habitat of an endangered species, both environmentalists and governmental regulators will find it valuable to know that other land in the area that provides valuable habitat for the species is protected by an intergenerational conservancy. If this other habitat is protected only for a limited time, environmentalists and governmental regulators may hesitate to let the hospital build because, after the hospital destroys the sand dunes on its property, the owners of the other habitat might develop their lands some day as well. For this reason, developers also might favor "perpetual" conservation of habitat, increasing the chances that the government and environmental groups will permit them to build on some areas of habitat in return for the preservation of other areas of habitat through conservation easements. Stability, in short, can be a virtue and not just a vice.

D. A Temporal Tragedy of the Commons

There also may be some situations in which a landowner will not preserve his land unless permitted to preserve it "perpetually." Assume that a rancher owns a particularly beautiful valley that is rich in biodiversity and Indian artifacts. Assume further that the rancher believes that the valley should be preserved for centuries to come for the enjoyment of everyone and that, based on everything we currently know, the valley will be more valuable to society as open space than as the site of a new subdivision. The rancher may be willing to tell interested developers to take a hike (despite the obvious financial advantage of selling the land and moving to the good life in Newport Beach) if he can be assured that the land will remain preserved in "perpetuity," but not if his "good for nothing" son or grandson can sell the land as soon as he dies. "Why," the rancher will say, "should I sacrifice if my sacrifice will not do any permanent good?"

The problem that the rancher faces is akin to the tragedy of the commons or prisoners' dilemma, but looked at temporally rather than spatially. To remove time from the analysis, assume that the rancher, his son, his grandson, and several more generations are all currently alive and that each owns a fraction of the valley. Assume also that a developer wants to build in the valley and will offer more money to the first person who sells his land than to later sellers. Finally, assume that, if anyone develops the valley, the valley is effectively destroyed. All the generations of ranchers might want to preserve the valley, but each, nevertheless, will be tempted to sell his land to the developer before one of his relatives sells and gets the most money. In deciding whether to sell, the rancher thinks, "If I don't, my son probably will, so I might as well sell and get the premium myself." Each generation evaluates the decision in the same way and thus will sell out to the developer, even though every generation might prefer to preserve the valley in its current state. This is the traditional tragedy of the commons.

Now assume that the various generations own the valley seriatim across time. Even if every generation would prefer to save the valley, each generation will be tempted to sell out to a developer because, if that generation does not sell, the next generation is likely to do so. Each generation, in short, is likely to decide that, if the valley is going to be destroyed anyway, he might as well be the one to benefit financially. The coordination problem is worse, in fact, than in our single-time-frame example because the different generations in this second hypothetical cannot communicate effectively with each other. This is a temporal tragedy of the commons.

Perpetual conservation easements are a solution to the temporal tragedy of the commons. By entering into a perpetual conservation easement, the current property owner is able to bind both himself and future generations. As a result, the current property owner does not need to worry that he will give up economic profit by refusing to develop his land today only to find the land developed by the next generation or the generation after that.

Notes & Questions

1. Does Professor Mahoney's argument underestimate the difficulty of restoring land to its natural condition once land has been developed?

Once land is developed for a shopping center, for example, it's unlikely that society will tear it down and restore the natural environment. In many cases, moreover, restoration of the natural environmental will be difficult if not impossible. Does this provide another justification for perpetual conservation easements?

2. Even if there are good arguments for perpetual conservation easements, should the law presume that conservation easements are perpetual absent evidence to the contrary? Although the UCEA and most states presume that conservation easements are perpetual, some states reverse the presumption and provide that conservation easements are limited in duration unless otherwise stated. See, e.g., Ala. Code § 35–18–2(c) (30 years or the life of the grantor); Kan. Stat. Ann. § 58–3811(d) (lifetime of the grantor). Four states (California, Colorado, Florida, and Hawaii), however, actually mandate that conservation easements be perpetual, no matter what the parties may prefer. See Jeffrey Tapick, Threats to the Continued Existence of Conservation Easements, 27 Colum. J. Envtl. L. 257, 274 n.66 (2002).

3. The federal government strongly encourages perpetual conservation easements. The federal tax code, for example, provides charitable tax deductions and estate tax benefits for property owners who create conservation easements in their land, but only if the easements are perpetual. I.R.C. §§ 170, 203(c). The Department of Agriculture also pays farmers to establish perpetual conservation easements in agricultural lands through the Conservation Reserve Enhancement Program (CREP). Why should the federal government insist that conservation easements be perpetual in order to qualify for tax deductions and other tax advantages?

4. No easement is truly "perpetual" in the sense that there is no way to eliminate the easement if conditions significantly change. For example, if a parcel of land loses its conservation value (e.g., because of development in the region or a change in land conditions), a land trust can release the owner of the underlying land from the conservation easement in return, perhaps, for money that the land trust can use to promote conservation elsewhere (although such releases can have adverse tax consequences). Or the owner of the underlying land can argue that courts should not enforce the easement because "changed circumstances" make the purposes of the easement impossible or impracticable to accomplish. See Nancy A. McLaughlin, Rethinking the Perpetual Nature of Conservation Easements, 29 Harv. Envtl. L. Rev. 421 (2005); Barton H. Thompson, Jr., The Trouble with Time: Influencing the Conservation Choices of Future Generations, 44 Nat. Resources J. 601, 609–610 (2004); Melissa Waller Baldwin, Conservation Easements: A Viable Tool for Land Preservation, 32 Land & Water L. Rev. 89, 119–120 (1997). Does this change your view of whether or not the law should encourage perpetual conservation easements?

5. If a land trust wishes to amend or release an existing conservation easement, should it need to get the permission of a court? Of the state attorney general or some other public official? In 1975, for example, Margaret Donoho, whose family had owned an historic 160–acre former

tobacco plantation known as Myrtle Grove on Maryland's eastern shore for eight generations, donated a perpetual conservation easement on the land to the National Trust for Historic Preservation in the United States (the "National Trust"). The National Trust assured Donoho that a "landowner who gives an easement can enjoy the feeling of knowing that his land will be forever protected from the pressure of destructive change." Almost twenty years later, a subsequent owner of Myrtle Grove, sought to subdivide it into eight large residential lots. The National Trust agreed to modify the conservation easement to permit the subdivision, in return for an easement on a neighboring piece of property and $68,700 in funding to enforce the restrictions that would be imposed on the new lots. Should the National Trust be able to unilaterally do this?

In a fascinating article, Professor Nancy McLaughlin has argued that conservation easements should be treated as "restricted charitable gifts or charitable trusts" and thus subject to the "well-settled rule that, except to the extent granted the power in the gift or trust instrument, the donee of a restricted charitable gift or charitable trust may not deviate from the administrative terms or charitable purpose thereof without receiving court approval therefor under the doctrine of administrative deviation or *cy pres*." McLaughlin, supra note 4, at 428. As Professor McLaughlin notes, most conservation easements grant the holder discretion to "amend the easement in manners that are consistent with the charitable purpose of the easement" (e.g., by deleting restrictions that advances in ecology show are not needed for effective conservation and perhaps are even counterproductive). Id. at 429. If a land trust wishes to go beyond such changes, however, Professor McLaughlin argues that the land trust must convince a court that, as a result of changed circumstances, achievement of the easement's conservation purposes has become "impossible or impracticable." Id. at 433. If the land trust can make this showing, the court can formulate a "substitute plan" for the use of the easement that comes "as near as possible" to achieving the original charitable purpose of the donor or settlor. Id. The state attorney general, as representative of the public's interest, would be a necessary party to any such proceeding.

Professor McLaughlin in her article also relates the Myrtle Grove story. Faced by a storm of controversy, the National Trust backed away from its agreement to amend the conservation easement, acknowledging that "it had made a 'serious mistake' in allowing development of the lush, waterfront Myrtle Grove." Id. at 454.

> Almost three years later, in February of 1997, the [landowner] sued the National Trust for breach of contract. In July of 1998, the attorney general for the state of Maryland filed a separate, collateral suit asserting that Donoho's donation of the easement created a charitable trust for the benefit of the people of Maryland and asking the court to enforce the terms of the trust.
>
> Both cases were settled in December of 1998, with the National Trust agreeing to pay the [landowner] $225,000, and the parties agreeing that no action would be taken to amend, release (in whole

> or in part), or extinguish the Myrtle Grove easement without the express written consent of the attorney general, except consent of the attorney general is not required for approvals carried out pursuant to the ordinary administration of the easement in accordance with its terms. The Washington Post reported that the settlement ended an "embarrassing episode" for the National Trust.

Id. at 454–455.

Tennessee Environmental Council v. Bright Par 3 Associates, L.P.

Court of Appeals of Tennessee, 2004.
2004 WL 419720.

WILLIAM H. INMAN, SR. J.

On May 1, 1996, the East Ridge Development Co., conveyed to the City of Chattanooga a conservation easement affecting 40 acres of land adjacent to Chickamauga Creek. . . .

The creation of a conservation easement is authorized by Tennessee Code Annotated § 66–9–307 which provides, inter alia, and as pertinent here, that

> conservation easements may be enforced by injunction or proceedings in equity by the holders and/or beneficiaries of the easement, or their bona fide representatives, heirs, or assigns.

The complaint, as amended, alleges that the "Property" is owned and is being developed by the Defendants. The "Property" is alleged to be commercially zoned, and that it contains or has adjoining it wetland and conservation easement areas, protected under state and federal law, which drain directly into South Chickamauga Creek, a waterway subject to contaminant and discharge limitations under state and federal law. Further allegations are that a Wal–Mart Supercenter and adjoining strip mall are being constructed on the "Property" which would result in an illegal discharge of pollutants into South Chickamauga Creek and/or illegal alteration of the protected areas, and that site preparation has already resulted in damage to the protected areas. Irreparable harm is forecast unless the Defendants are restrained from further construction.

A temporary restraining order was issued on July 7, 2003, in accordance with the demand for relief, and scheduled for hearing on July 15, 2003. The Defendants filed motions to dissolve the temporary restraining order, alleging that the Plaintiffs cannot succeed on the merits, that there is no imminent threat of irreparable injury to the Plaintiffs or to the protected areas, and that the proposed injunction is contrary to the public interest.

At the July 15, 2003 hearing, the sole issue for resolution was whether the individual plaintiff, Ms. Kurtz, had the requisite standing to maintain this action. The Chancellor stated "... we need to find out whether Ms. Kurtz has any injury separate and apart from that of the member of the public." Ms. Kurtz thereupon testified at length about her environmental concerns, her dedication and devotion to the preservation of the flora and fauna of the property described in the easement, that she was an independent, environment education consultant, that she serves on the Board of the Tennessee Environmental Council and related organizations. She conducts nature walks through the easement property, and generally enjoys its solace and solitude.

The Chancellor made a finding of fact that Ms. Kurtz suffered no injury "separate or different" from an injury that the public at large has sustained, and that under settled law in Tennessee she had no standing to file the action. The Chancellor further found that only the grantee, the City of Chattanooga, has standing to enforce the easement and accordingly dismissed the complaint.

The Plaintiffs appeal and present for review the issue of whether Ms. Kurtz or the [Tennessee Environmental Council, a non-profit environmental group] have standing to enforce the conservation easement....

We stress the language of the Act which provides that the conservation easement may be enforced by injunction or proceedings in equity by the holder and/or beneficiaries of the easement. The City of Chattanooga is the grantee, and thus the holder of the easement and obviously entitled to enforce the easement. Who are the beneficiaries?

We are bound to ascertain and give effect to the Legislative intent with no undue restriction or expansion of the statutory language. We think it evident that the phrase "by the holder and/or beneficiaries" means someone in addition to the grantee; otherwise, the words "and/or beneficiaries" would be utterly meaningless, and we are not at liberty to ignore this language. The word "beneficiaries" has a commonly accepted dictionary meaning: "those who benefit from the act of another." Who benefits from the act of the grantor in creating this easement? A conservation easement is "held for the benefit of the people of Tennessee." Tenn. Code Ann. § 66–9–303. We hold that any resident of Tennessee has standing to enforce it. This interpretation is consistent with the terms of the deed and the Act, both of which require a liberal construction of the word "beneficiaries." Superimposed is that the Act is a remedial one, and must be liberally construed to further and give effect to its purpose. Further superimposed is the fact that the Legislature chose not to adopt the verbiage of the Uniform Act which precludes the enforcement of a conservation easement by any entity other than a governmental body, charitable corporation or association with the specific right granted in the document.[5]

5. A number of states have enacted a form of the Uniform Conservation Easement Act. Research indicates that in each instance third parties cannot enforce the easement unless the right is expressly granted. Tennessee appears, thus far, to be the only state to grant enforcement power to "beneficiaries" of the easement. See, e.g., Ala. Code § 35–18–1: Ky. Rev. Stat. 382.800; La. Rev. Stat. 9:1272; Miss. Code Ann. § 89–19–3; Va. Code Ann. § 10.1–1009.

Notes & Questions

1. If conservation easements are intended to benefit the public, shouldn't state law provide that any member of the public has the right to enforce an easement? See generally Jessica E. Jay, Third–Party Enforcement of Conservation Easements, 29 Vt. L. Rev. 757 (2005).

That said, is the Tennessee law clear on this point? If the legislature had wanted to give enforcement power to any member of the public, why didn't the legislature expressly say that? Assume a Tennessee resident living 100 miles from Chickamauga Creek wants to enforce the easement. Should he be entitled to sue? Or should the power to sue be reserved to those living near the easement? Does the answer depend on the purpose of the easement? The related question of what individuals and private groups should have standing to enforce federal environmental laws has generated a tremendous body of commentary. See, e.g., Cass Sunstein, What's Standing After *Lujan*? Of Citizen Suits, "Injuries," and Article III, 91 Mich. L. Rev. 163 (1992).

2. As noted in *Tennessee Environmental Council*, the UCEA does not authorize general public enforcement. Under the UCEA, a third party has a right of enforcement only if the conservation easement expressly provides for such enforcement and if the third party is "a governmental body, charitable corporation, charitable association, or charitable trust, which, although eligible to be a holder, is not a holder." UCEA §§ 1(3) & 3(3). Why limit enforcement to these entities?

D. TERMINATING EASEMENTS, COVENANTS, AND SERVITUDES

Pergament v. Loring Properties, Ltd.

Supreme Court of Minnesota, 1999.
599 N.W.2d 146.

. . . .

In this case, respondent, Brian A. Pergament, brought an action in district court seeking declaratory judgment that he was entitled to an easement to eight parking spaces in the parking lot of appellant, Loring Properties, Ltd . . . .

On September 19, 1986, BSR Properties entered into a contract for deed with Willow Street Properties to purchase property that included an apartment building, an office building and a parking lot. On November 20, 1987, the City of Minneapolis approved a plan to subdivide the property into two separate parcels, one parcel containing the apartment building, the other parcel containing the office building and parking lot. On December 22, 1987, BSR acquired fee title to the apartment building. To obtain the purchase money for this transaction, BSR obtained a loan from Midwest Federal Savings and Loan and agreed to secure the loan with a mortgage to the apartment building. Before lending BSR the money, Midwest Federal required that BSR obtain from Willow ... a parking easement for the benefit of the apartment building, allowing use of eight parking spaces in the parking lot adjacent to the office building. This easement was created by a declaration dated December 22, 1987.

On July 28, 1988, BSR paid to Willow the balance due on the contract for deed and acquired fee title to the remaining property, the office building and parking lot. BSR financed the transaction with a loan from Canada Life Assurance Company and, to secure the loan, BSR gave Canada Life a mortgage to the office building and parking lot. By becoming fee owner of the office building/parking lot, as well as the apartment building, BSR united title to the easement's dominant and servient estates.

On December 20, 1990, BSR conveyed the office building/parking lot to Canada Life by deed in lieu of foreclosure. The parking easement was mentioned in the deed. On September 30, 1993, Canada Life sold the office building/parking lot to Loring Properties. The easement was not mentioned in the deed but was referred to in the title insurance policy.

On February 28, 1997, BSR sold the apartment property to Pergament and, incidental to the transaction, Midwest Federal's mortgage was satisfied. Although the deed from BSR to Pergament mentioned the easement, Pergament admitted that he was unaware of it when he purchased the apartment building. From the date the easement was created, all parking spaces in the parking lot were used exclusively in conjunction with the office building and were never assigned to nor used by apartment residents.

When Pergament discovered that the easement was mentioned in his deed, he requested that Loring Properties designate eight of the parking spaces in its parking lot for use by apartment residents. Pergament's request was denied and he brought an action in district court for a judgment declaring that he was entitled to an easement for the parking spaces. The district court granted Pergament's motion for summary judgment and the court of appeals affirmed....

Under the merger doctrine, an easement that benefits the dominant estate and burdens the servient estate is extinguished when fee title to each estate is united in one owner. In his treatise, *The Law Of Real Property*, Professor Powell explains that the reason for the doctrine is that one cannot have, indeed has no need for, an easement in property one owns in fee. See 4 Richard R. Powell, The Law of Real Property § 34.22 (Patrick J. Rohan ed., 1997). Thus, in July 1988 when BSR obtained fee title to the servient estate (the office building/parking lot), BSR held fee title to both the dominant estate (the apartment building) and the servient estate and, under the merger doctrine, the parking easement was extinguished as to BSR and its successors in interest.

Once extinguished, an easement is not revived or reinstated when referred to in a subsequent conveyance. See Caroga Realty Co. v. Tapper, 274 Minn. 164, 180 n.3, 143 N.W.2d 215, 226 n.3 (1966); see also Werner v. Sample, 259 Minn. 273, 275, 107 N.W.2d 43, 44 (1961) (concluding that reference to an extinguished easement does not create or revive an easement, "it presupposes an existing easement"). Therefore, the extinguished parking easement was not revived as to BSR or its successors simply because the deeds conveying the property mentioned the easement.

Under the mortgage exception to the merger doctrine, the mortgagee of the dominant estate is protected from losing its interest in an easement otherwise extinguished when fee title to the dominant estate and fee title to the servient estate have been united in one fee owner. This exception is grounded in equity and is intended to protect the mortgagee of the dominant estate from losing the value of its interest in an easement that is otherwise extinguished. See Duval v. Becker, 81 Md. 537, 32 A. 308, 309–10 (1895) (stating that allowing an extinguishment of the mortgagee's interest "would jeopardize, if not wholly destroy the stability of every mortgage as security"). Thus, even though fee ownership of the dominant and servient estates was eventually merged in BSR, Midwest Federal's interest in the parking easement was not extinguished. If Midwest Federal's mortgagee interest in the apartment building would have become possessory, Midwest Federal would have had the benefit of the parking easement and the servient estate, the office building/parking lot, would have had the burden of the easement. Therefore, under the mortgage exception, Midwest Federal retained its inchoate interest in the parking easement until the mortgage was satisfied.

Pergament argues, however, that the mortgage exception to the merger doctrine prevented BSR's interest in the easement from being extinguished and therefore prevents his interest, as BSR's successor, from being extinguished. Pergament would extend the mortgage exception to the merger doctrine so that as long as Midwest Federal had a protected mortgage interest in the parking easement, the easement could not be extinguished as to anyone who later acquired the apartment property. Under Pergament's theory, a mortgage acts as a shield to defeat the merger doctrine. Relying on Schwoyer v. Smith, 388 Pa. 637, 131 A.2d 385 (1957), both the district court and the court of appeals agreed with Pergament that the mortgagee's interest in the easement prevented the merger doctrine from extinguishing the easement even as to the fee owner and its successors.

Upon close reading, however, *Schwoyer* does not support the lower courts' expansion of the mortgage exception to the merger doctrine. In *Schwoyer*, as in our case, the dominant and servient estates were united in one ownership, then sold to separate owners. One of the owners sought to enforce an easement running to the benefit of the dominant estate and burdening the servient estate. The owner of the servient estate argued that the merger doctrine extinguished the easement because the previous owner of the servient estate had acquired the dominant estate. The Pennsylvania Supreme Court rejected the merger argument and held that the easement was not extinguished.

The critical distinction between *Schwoyer* and our case is that in *Schwoyer*, the dominant estate was acquired by mortgage foreclosure. Therefore, the party that acquired the dominant estate by mortgage foreclosure obtained all the rights and interests the mortgagee held, including the rights and interests in the easement. By contrast, Pergament acquired the apartment property from the mortgagor, BSR, and therefore acquired only those interests BSR held at the time of the conveyance. Under the doctrine of merger, BSR's interest in the easement was extinguished and therefore BSR's successor in interest, Pergament, could not have acquired any interest in the easement from BSR. . . .

We conclude that the easement was extinguished as to BSR and its assigns and successors, including Pergament, when BSR united fee title to the dominant and servient estates and we reverse and remand to the district court and direct that judgment be entered accordingly.

Reversed.

GILBERT, Justice (dissenting).

I concur with the majority's discussion of the mortgage exception to the merger doctrine, but believe that the analysis stops short of considering all of the facts and law presented in this case. Therefore, I dissent as to the result and would remand this case to the trial court.

Our case law has firmly established that application of the merger doctrine depends on the equities of the case. For over one hundred years we have recognized that "the doctrine of merger is a flexible, equitable doctrine" the application of which depends on the facts or circumstances of the particular case at issue, including the intent of the parties. Connecticut Mut. Life Ins. Co. v. King, 72 Minn. 287, 291, 75 N.W. 376, 378 (1898).

Contrary to this modern view of merger, no consideration is given to the intent of the parties and the impact of the majority's decision on all of the entities involved with the properties. The majority fails to consider or acknowledge the restrictions imposed on the properties by the City of Minneapolis. By law, the lot division of the original Willow Street property into separate apartment and office parcels could not have occurred without the prior approval of the Minneapolis City Planning Commission. . . . [The] record shows that the subdivision, as proposed to and accepted by the Commission, required the parking easement at issue in this case. . . .

Prior to this subdivision, the parking rights at issue in the present case were shared by the entire Willow Street property. An easement requiring the continued sharing of parking between the office and apartment parcels was an express condition of the subdivision. The easement was to continue so long as the apartment building continued in existence and was to run with the land and bind not only present owners but also future owners.

While the record does not show that the tenants of the apartment parcel ever used the parking rights, the existence of those parking rights was nevertheless preserved for future "need or intent" and was a valuable commodity to whomever held the parcel. The record contains evidence that on-site parking was a desired and valuable commodity to both the apartment and office tenants. In the Loring Park area, parking space is at a premium. The elimination of parking rights may significantly affect the already intense competition for scarce parking space.

Despite the extensive role the city played in creating the restricted property interests at stake here and the potentially adverse effect elimination of the parking easement could have on the Loring Park neighborhood, appellant admitted that the city has not even been notified of this action. The majority now continues this inequity by summarily eliminating the easement, contrary to the city's prohibition. . . .

Hatcher v. Chesner

Supreme Court of Pennsylvania, 1966.
221 A.2d 305.

EAGEN, Justice.

This is an appeal from a final decree in equity enjoining the defendant from obstructing a right of way over his land. . . .

The plaintiff and the defendant are owners of bordering pieces of improved land. In 1894, the then common owner of both properties created by deed a perpetual ten foot right of way over the land, now owned by the defendant, for the benefit of the owners and occupiers of the land, now owned by the plaintiff.

The plaintiff acquired title to his land on March 22, 1961; the defendant title to his land on July 31, 1957. Both the deeds of the plaintiff and the defendant and, in fact, all deeds in the chain of title since 1894 have unequivocally stated that title was subject to the reservation and the right of way.

Both pieces of land front on the same street and extend back therefrom a distance of 140 feet. On defendant's land, along the line common to that of plaintiff's, there exists a continuous row of out buildings. At one point where the right of way should exist, there is a small frame shed or garage 18 feet long with double doors, approximately 9 feet in width, on both ends. On one end, these doors, when opened, extend out on plaintiff's land. For the right of way to be usable, the double doors on both ends of the garage would necessarily have to be opened and the right of way would then extend through the garage for a distance of 18 feet.

The right of way has not been used since at least 1932. Also, a tree has been permitted to grow on plaintiff's property for at least 35 years in such close proximity to the double doors of the garage, which open on his property, as to preclude their use. A board has also been nailed across both doors on plaintiff's side which completely bars their use.

The defendant contends here, as he did below, that under the facts the plaintiff has lost the right to use of the easement by non-use, abandonment and adverse possession.

Mere non-use, no matter how long extended, will not result in extinguishment of an easement created by deed.

The problems raised by the defenses of abandonment and adverse possession are so interrelated that they must be considered together.

The Restatement of Property, § 504 (1944), recognizes that an easement may be lost by abandonment. It states "an easement may be extinguished by an intentional relinquishment thereof indicated by conduct respecting the use authorized thereby." The comments to this section make it clear that failure to use the easement is a fact from which an inference of abandonment can be drawn and found to exist. A number of states adhere to this view....

Pennsylvania, however, has always been reluctant to accept this theory. Instead, where an easement is created by deed, Pennsylvania has required not only intent to abandon by the dominant tenement, but adverse possession by the servient tenement as well. Thus the Pennsylvania courts look not only to the actions and intentions of the dominant tenement with which the Restatement limits its consideration, but also to the *intentions and actions* of the servient tenement as well. The rationale behind the Pennsylvania rule was stated in Lindeman v. Lindsey, 69 Pa. 93, 100 (1871), wherein this Court said: "A man ought not to be obliged unless he requires it, actually to use a right or privilege secured to him by deed, nor resort to legal proceedings unless his title is denied, and he is actually ousted, disseised, obstructed or prevented by some wrongdoer from an enjoyment of it when he requires and demands such enjoyment." It is clear from this and later cases that our courts equate ownership of an easement with ownership of a fee for these purposes. See, Weaver v. Getz, 16 Pa.Super. 418 (1901). Another factor in the view held by this state is the general dislike of forfeiture by our courts....

The lower court decreed that the plaintiff had not lost the legal right to use the easement. While it found the evidence convincing, if not conclusive, as to an intent to abandon by the plaintiff and his predecessors in title, it based its final judgment on the conclusion that the necessary adverse possession on the part of the owner or owners of the servient tenement had not been established. This conclusion was dictated by language in the deeds in the defendant's chain of title, wherein the existence of the right to use the easement was continuously recognized and kept alive. In this the lower court was ... correct.

However, we disagree with one crucial conclusion of the lower court wherein it stated, that the existence of the tree on plaintiff's land, as described before, and the board nailed across the garage doors had no effect on the outcome of the case. In this connection the lower court failed to recognize and apply one exception that exists in Pennsylvania to the rule of abandonment. It is this: If the owner of the easement by his own affirmative act renders use thereof impossible, or if he obstructs it in a manner that is inconsistent with its further enjoyment, the easement will be deemed to have been abandoned, even in the absence of adverse use on the part of the owner of the servient tenement.

In the instant case, the plaintiff, or his predecessors in title by whose actions in relation to the property he is bound, planted or permitted a tree to grow on the land now owned by the plaintiff which obstructed use of the easement to a material extent. Further, the same parties placed, or permitted to be placed, a bar across the doors of the garage serving as the only entrance to the easement right of way. These acts, in our opinion, were not mere inaction, but rather affirmative acts on the part of the plaintiff and his predecessors in title, which were sufficiently inconsistent with further use of the easement to constitute an abandonment thereof. . . .

Decree reversed. Each side to pay own costs.

Morris v. Nease

Supreme Court of West Virginia, 1977.
238 S.E.2d 844.

NEELY, Justice:

In this appeal from the Circuit Court of Cabell County Dr. William F. Nease, a chiropractor, challenges the enforcement against him of restrictive covenants affecting property he owns in Huntington. In 1972 Dr. Nease opened a chiropractic clinic at 2703 Third Avenue, and a number of his neighbors brought suit against him to have the clinic closed. They contended that Dr. Nease's clinic violated applicable restrictive covenants, and the Circuit Court agreed, issuing a permanent injunction that prohibits Dr. Nease from operating a chiropractic clinic at 2703 Third Avenue. We reverse.

The land owned by Dr. Nease, as well as that owned by the neighbors seeking to enforce the restrictive covenants, was originally developed by the Huntington Land Company in the early 1900s. At that time the following restrictions were imposed:

> [T]here shall be left an open space or courtyard bounding on Third Avenue of not less than forty feet in depth exclusive of porch in front of any building erected on said premises, which space shall extend the entire width of said premises; that there shall not be erected on said premises hereby conveyed more than one single dwelling, and any dwelling erected thereon shall not cost less than three thousand dollars; that there shall not be erected on said premises any building other than for dwelling or residence purposes, or purposes of like nature, and the necessary outbuildings pertaining thereto, nor shall any building erected thereon be used for other than dwelling or residence purposes, or purposes of like nature, and as such outbuildings pertaining thereto; that these covenants and agreements shall run with the land.

It was conceded that all parties to this action, including Dr. Nease, had record notice of these restrictions and took their property subject to the restrictions. Dr. Nease, accordingly, accepts the fact that he is bound by the restrictions to the extent they remain in force, but he argues that the restrictions have been effectively nullified through changes in the character of the neighborhood where his clinic is located. Alternatively, Dr. Nease has raised personal equitable defenses which would prevent the complainants from enforcing the restrictive covenants against him, in the event the Court finds that the covenants remain in force.

I

West Virginia recognizes the commonly accepted legal proposition that changes in a neighborhood's character can nullify restrictive covenants affecting neighborhood property. Technically, there is a distinction between changes which occur within the restricted neighborhood itself and changes in the surrounding, unrestricted area. The "problem of *change of conditions* arises where the complainant's and defendant's lots lie within a restricted subdivision, but the area surrounding the restricted subdivision has been so changed by the acts of third persons that the building scheme for the subdivision has been frustrated through no fault of the lot owners themselves." 2 American Law of Property 445–446 (A.J. Casner ed. 1952, emphasis added) [hereinafter cited as 2 American Law of Property]. When, however, the change in the neighborhood's character is a result of "violations within the subdivision itself, a problem of *abandonment* rather than change of conditions is involved." 2 American Law of Property 446 (emphasis added).

Some of the evidence in this case concerns the complainants' own violations of the restrictive covenants. This evidence properly goes to the question of abandonment, since the complainants' property clearly lies within the restricted area. Other evidence concerns non-residential uses of nearby property, some of which may lie within, and some outside, the restricted area. This evidence could show either abandonment or change of conditions, depending on the exact location of the property having the non-residential use. We will consider all the evidence relating to the changing character of the neighborhood here, and we will refrain from drawing technical distinctions between abandonment and change of conditions. Regardless of how it is characterized or labeled, the fundamental issue of this case is the viability of restrictive covenants in a changing neighborhood.

The evidence shows that a substantial amount of commercial property is located a short distance from Dr. Nease's clinic. Twenty-seventh Street, the nearest cross street to his Third Avenue clinic, has a maintenance company, a brokerage company, a repair shop, and a beauty shop, all within two blocks of Third Avenue. Another beauty shop is located on Twenty-eighth Street within half a block of Third Avenue. The 2800 block of Third Avenue itself has a service station, a laundry, and a church, while the 2600 block has an antique shop, a church, and a ball field.

These properties significantly change the original residential character of the neighborhood. It does not follow, however, that the entire neighborhood is perforce released from the burden of the restrictive covenants. On the contrary, every effort must be exerted to protect the unchanged portions of residential neighborhoods when businesses begin to encroach on the fringes. The obvious danger is that restrictions throughout an entire area can eventually be destroyed through succeeding block-by-block changes in the neighborhood's character:

> [A]s soon as the border lots are freed, the next tier of lots is put in the same position as that in which the border lots were originally. Thus by a step-by-step process the restrictions must be relaxed until the plan is totally defeated. [2 American Law of Property 446]

To guard against such an eventuality courts in a majority of jurisdictions have evolved the rule that "if the benefits of the original plan for a restricted subdivision can still be realized for the protection of interior lots, the restrictions should be enforced against the border lots, notwithstanding the fact that such lot owners are deprived of the most valuable use of their lots." 2 American Law of Property 447. West Virginia has adopted the essence of this salutary rule by holding that "changed conditions of the neighborhood will not be sufficient to defeat the right [to enforce restrictive covenants] unless the changes are 'so radical as practically to destroy the essential objects and purposes of the agreement.' " Wallace v. St. Clair, 147 W. Va. 377 at 399, 127 S.E.2d 742 at 757 (1962). Based on the evidence thus far discussed, we can say that the non-residential uses of property in the complainants' neighborhood have not destroyed the essential objects and purposes of the restrictive covenants and that the benefits of the original plan can still be realized for that portion of the neighborhood which retains its residential character. In this respect we note that protection against covenant violations can be afforded to an area as small as one block.

There are additional changes affecting the character of the neighborhood which remain to be considered. These changes have occurred in the block where the complainants reside and the chiropractic clinic is located. On a corner property at one end of the block is the Highlawn United Methodist Church. The evidence shows that the church building was constructed in compliance with neighborhood setback requirements, and with the permission of the property owners in the 2700 block of Third Avenue. The church blends well with the character of the neighborhood; nonetheless, it is a non-residential use. Another change in the neighborhood is the shift in the use of many properties from single-family occupancy to multi-family occupancy, apparently in violation of the applicable restrictive covenants. This change for the most part stems from the conversion into apartment units of garage-stable facilities formerly used by servants or guests. The evidence shows that a number of such apartment units existed in the 2700 block of Third Avenue, and that these units were in various stages of occupancy including unoccupied but available for rent, occupied by extended family members related to the main dwelling's owners, and occupied by unrelated tenants. In addition, at least one main house on the block was divided into two rental units. Despite these significant departures from the neighborhood plan of limiting the occupancy of each lot to single families, the 2700 block of Third Avenue has retained the residential character which was also an important and essential part of the original plan. Even the church, which represents the most drastic change in the block, complements the residential character of the area in a manner that business enterprises do not. Accordingly, we find that the changes in the neighborhood's character, both in the 2700 block of Third Avenue and in the nearby area, have not been so radical that the restrictive covenants involved here are nullified.

II

Having found Dr. Nease's arguments concerning the neighborhood's changing character to be unconvincing, we turn now to the personal equitable defenses he raised in this proceeding. The foremost among these defenses is acquiescence, which may be described as follows:

> The equitable defense of acquiescence arises where the complainant has acquiesced in the violation of the same type of restriction by third parties. Where the complainant has failed to enforce a similar equitable servitude against third parties, he has debarred himself from obtaining equitable relief against the defendant for subsequent violations of the same character. The reason for allowing this defense of acquiescence is the belief that the complainant, by his conduct in failing to seek enforcement against similar violations by third parties, has induced the defendant to assume that the restrictions are no longer in effect. Thus, acquiescence by the complainant to the violations of dissimilar restrictions cannot be a bar to enforcement where the restrictions are essentially different so that abandonment of one would not induce a reasonable person to assume that the other was also abandoned. Likewise, failure to sue for prior breaches by others where the breaches were noninjurious to the complainant cannot be treated as an acquiescence sufficient to bar equitable relief against a more serious and damaging violation. [2 American Law of Property 441–442, footnotes omitted]

This defense is recognized in West Virginia. In analyzing this defense, we must compare Dr. Nease's covenant violations with other violations in the same neighborhood in which the complainants have acquiesced. The violations outside the 2700 block of Third Avenue are too remote to be considered injurious to the complainants' interests. Accordingly, these violations do not provide the basis for the defense of acquiescence. Likewise, the apparent violations in the 2700 block itself, such as the rental of garage apartments and the construction of a church, are not so similar in character to Dr. Nease's clinic, or so injurious to the complainants, that they entitle Dr. Nease to raise the defense of acquiescence. There is one significant violation, however, which we find to be critical to Dr. Nease's defense of acquiescence, namely the use of Dr. Nease's property by his predecessor in title before Dr. Nease established his clinic.

The evidence shows that the property Dr. Nease purchased was divided into five rental units, four in the main structure and one in an outbuilding. There is a very fine line between residential and commercial use in this instance, and Dr. Nease could fairly have assumed that the neighborhood acquiesced in a commercial use of 2703 Third Avenue. This assumption was warranted, we believe, by the fact that in this particular neighborhood the operation of five rental units on one lot is essentially a commercial undertaking. Although the character of Dr. Nease's business differs from that of the preceding business at the same location, the similarities between the businesses are sufficient in our view to entitle Dr. Nease to raise the defense of acquiescence. Both businesses brought added traffic into the neighborhood and resulted in other minor disruptions which are out of the ordinary. Furthermore, it would appear that both businesses resulted in about the same injury to the complainants. In any case it does not seem that the clinic is a significantly more serious and damaging covenant violation than the five-unit rental property.

We can only judge the similarities between Dr. Nease's clinic and the preceding use of the same property on the basis of the record before us. The record indicates that Dr. Nease rehabilitated his property in such a manner that it harmonizes well with other dwellings on the block. In addition there was testimony that Dr. Nease did not conduct a high-volume practice. Furthermore, the discreet sign which identifies the clinic is placed on the building itself, rather than at the curb, where it would call more attention to the commercial character of the property. In short, Dr. Nease's commercial use of the property appears to be restrained and dignified, and we note that the complainants have acquiesced in only such a use. Should Dr. Nease significantly alter the character of his clinic, or should some other less restrained business move into the property, the complainants would have cause to reexamine the situation and take whatever action they deem appropriate to protect their interests.

We need not consider the other errors assigned by Dr. Nease because our decision with respect to the defense of acquiescence is dispositive of the case. Accordingly, for the foregoing reasons, the judgment of the Circuit Court of Cabell County is reversed.

Notes & Questions

1. **Consensual Termination.** A nonpossessory interest may be terminated or modified at any time through a release executed by the owner of the benefit to the owner of the servient estate. Restatement (Third) of Property, Servitudes § 7.3 (2000). The release must comply with the Statute of Frauds and with all other formalities required for the creation of the interest being terminated. Id. cmt. a. If, as is commonly the case in subdivisions, there is more than one benefit holder, a release, to be effective, must be executed by all. Negotiations, relatively simple when only a single servient and dominant estate are involved, can become extraordinarily complex when the interests of all the homeowners in a subdivision—each owning a parcel that is both dominant and servient—must be accommodated. Although most, or even all, may desire a complete release,

negotiation costs and strategic behavior may very well block the transaction.

Parties drafting an easement, covenant, or servitude sometimes anticipate the transaction costs that will surround efforts at termination and expressly provide shortcuts to termination in the instrument itself. The most obvious method is to provide that the interest will expire after a specified period. Another method, sometimes employed in subdivisions, is to limit the initial duration of the covenants but provide that they will automatically be extended for successive periods unless a specified majority of homeowners in the subdivision votes to amend or rescind the covenants. Some subdivisions also permit a majority or super-majority of the homeowners to amend or extinguish covenants. Do you see any problems with such provisions?

2. If the parties who created the nonpossessory interest failed to express their full intent respecting the conditions under which the interest should end, courts will attempt to determine this intent from the instrument's language and surrounding circumstances. Do the rules of merger, abandonment, acquiescence, and changed neighborhood conditions, applied in the principal cases, attempt to approximate the results the original parties would have dictated had they contemplated the events that later occurred on the servient and dominant estates? Or are these rules of law, followed on principle, without regard for the original parties' intent?

3. **Merger.** The doctrine of merger applies to easements in gross as well as to easements appurtenant, and to covenants and servitudes as well as to easements. See Restatement (Third) of Property, Servitudes § 7.5 (2000). Once a servitude terminates as a result of merger, it does not revive if the two properties are reseparated; if the owner of the former dominant estate wants the benefit of the previous servitude, he must negotiate the creation of a new servitude. If the owner of the dominant estate merely leases the servient estate, however, most courts will only suspend the nonpossessory interest for the period of the lease, and the interest will revive once the lease term expires. Id. § 7.5, ill. 6. Similarly, if the owner of the dominant estate acquires only a portion of the servient estate, the nonpossessory interest will be terminated or suspended only with respect to that portion.

To what extent do merger rules approximate the original parties' probable intent as to what should happen when Greenacre and Whiteacre are owned by a single person? Is it likely they intended that the interest be terminated, and not just suspended during the period of unitary ownership?

4. **Abandonment.** What rationale underlies (a) the general rule on abandonment; (b) the Pennsylvania rule on abandonment applied in Hatcher v. Chesner; (c) the exception to the Pennsylvania rule, also applied in *Hatcher*? What difference, if any, is there between the general rule and the Pennsylvania rule when it is taken together with its exception? Is the general rule or the Pennsylvania rule better calculated to encourage the productive use of the servient estate and of the easement's benefit? Does

the exception to the Pennsylvania rule add to, or detract from, its ability to encourage productive land use?

5. **Equitable Defenses Based on the Passage of Time.** Abandonment is not the only doctrine under which elapsed time will prevent the holder of a nonpossessory interest from enforcing it. A benefit owner who stops using his nonpossessory interest may be barred by *estoppel* from later enforcing the interest against a servient owner who relied to her detriment on the benefit holder's representation that he did not intend to resume use. See Restatement (Third) of Property, Servitudes § 7.6. A benefit holder who delays filing suit against a servient owner who is violating the nonpossessory interest may be barred on the equitable ground of *laches* if the delay prejudices the defendant. And, as noted in Morris v. Nease, a benefit owner who fails to proceed against some violators may, by his *acquiescence* in their conduct, later be barred from relief against another servient owner who has committed the same violation.

6. **Prescription.** Easements and other servitudes also can be lost by prescription. According to the Restatement, "To the extent that a use of property violates a servitude burdening the property and the use is maintained adversely to a person entitled to enforce the servitude for the prescriptive period, that person's beneficial interest in the servitude is modified or extinguished." Restatement (Third) of Property, Servitudes § 7.7.

7. **Changed Conditions.** Courts divide on whether changed neighborhood conditions constitutes only an equitable defense—immunizing the servient owner from injunctive but not monetary relief—or constitutes a ground for terminating the interest entirely. Although the first view once predominated, the second is gaining increased support. One practical effect of the distinction is that, since an equitable defense will not terminate the restriction, the defense offers no basis for removing the restriction as a continuing cloud on title. However, by limiting the benefit holder to damages, the equitable defense should make it less costly for the servient owner to buy him off. Did *Nease* offer another, preferable alternative by allowing defendant to continue his practice, so long as it was "restrained and dignified"?

Does termination on the ground of changed conditions unfairly deprive the benefit holder of a property interest while conferring a windfall on the owner of the servient estate? Is the older equitable approach, which gives damages to the benefit holder, fairer? Can courts justify termination on this ground as simply effectuating the intent of the original parties who, had they contemplated the change in neighborhood conditions, would have provided for termination of the interest? Is it preferable to disregard presumed intent and to rest these decisions on the assumption that when individuals acquire land they take into account not only the nature and limits of the applicable land use restrictions, but also the legal rules that will be applied in terminating these restrictions? Under this view, termination produces neither a wipe-out nor a windfall for benefit owner and servient owner since each can be expected to have taken the possibility of termination into account at the time he purchased his interest. Is this a plausible view of investment behavior?

8. **Statutory Approaches.** Several states have by statute augmented the common law methods for terminating nonpossessory interests. Statutes in New York and Massachusetts, for example, authorize courts to extinguish obsolete restrictions. N.Y. Real Prop. Acts & Proc. Law § 1951 provides that no restriction on the use of land created by "covenant, promise or negative easement" shall be enforced "if, at the time the enforceability of the restriction is brought in question, it appears that the restriction is of no actual and substantial benefit to the persons seeking its enforcement or seeking a declaration or determination of its enforceability, either because the purpose of the restriction has already been accomplished or, by reason of changed conditions or other cause, its purpose is not capable of accomplishment, or for any other reason." Upon a finding of unenforceability, the court may extinguish the interest, "upon payment, to the person or persons who would otherwise be entitled to enforce it in the event of a breach at the time of the action, of such damages, if any, as such person or persons will sustain from the extinguishment of the restriction."

Mass. Gen. Laws c. 184, § 30 starts from the same position as its New York counterpart, terminating restrictions that have no "actual and substantial benefit," but adds a presumption, with specified exceptions, against the existence of an "actual and substantial benefit," if "any part of the subject land lies within a city or town having a population greater than 100,000 persons." Further, no restriction determined to be of benefit shall be enforced, other than by an award of damages, if, among other alternatives, "changes in the character of the properties affected or their neighborhood, in available construction materials or techniques, in access, services or facilities, in applicable public controls of land use or construction, or in any other conditions or circumstances, reduce materially the need for the restriction or the likelihood of the restriction accomplishing its original purposes or render it obsolete or inequitable to enforce except by award of money damages," or "continuation of the restriction on the parcel against which enforcement is claimed or on parcels remaining in a common scheme with it or subject to like restrictions would impede reasonable use of land for purposes for which it is most suitable, and would tend to impair the growth of the neighborhood or municipality in a manner inconsistent with the public interest or to contribute to deterioration of properties or to result in decadent or substandard areas or blighted open areas." See also Mass. Gen. Laws c. 184, §§ 23–29.

*

PART IV

PUBLIC CONTROL OF USE

For the first century and a half of this nation's history, land use management was largely the province of nuisance law and private servitudes. When landowners sought to control how land was being used in their neighborhood, they sued to enforce nuisance rules or acquired easements and covenants in their neighbors' land. To the degree that cities became involved, they generally confined their land use control efforts to excluding noxious industries from residential districts, setting maximum building heights, and specifying safe building materials. It was not until 1916 that New York City enacted the country's first comprehensive zoning ordinance, regulating the location of office buildings, apartment houses, and commercial facilities.

The development of land use planning principles in the United States closely paralleled the development of governmental land use controls. Throughout the nineteenth century, cities engaged in only a rough-hewn sort of planning by laying out the grids for prospective streets and avenues, effectively "drawing up a giant chessboard on which the forces of the market would build the future city." U.S. National Commission on Urban Problems, Building the American City 200 (1968). Then, the 1893 Chicago World's Fair sparked the so-called "City Beautiful" movement and gave planners a grander object: the incorporation of parks, plazas, boulevards, and other such amenities into city life. Although the City Beautiful movement succeeded in crystallizing an ideal vision of the city, it ultimately had far less impact on urban design than the "City Practical" movement that followed it, which focused planners' efforts on good engineering principles and the efficient allocation of land uses within a city.

The evolution toward comprehensive public land use controls and planning, though steady, has not been uniform. Voters in Houston, Texas, for example, have rejected zoning on three separate occasions, in 1948, 1962, and 1993. Although the City has subdivision controls, a building code, and a planning department, it relies primarily on private restrictive covenants to manage land uses. Occasionally, voters have tried to cast off land use controls altogether. In November 1982, the voters of Tehama County, California, narrowly approved an initiative measure, the "Landowner's Bill of Rights," designed to repeal virtually all land use controls in the county, as well as to prohibit the county from enacting new ones. Proponents of the measure promised that it would expose the "fallacy of governmentally dictated land use," Sample Ballot, General Election, Nov. 2, 1982, County of Tehama 52–14. The California Court of Appeal later invalidated the initiative on the ground that it violated the state's mandatory land use planning statute. Patterson v. County of Tehama, 235 Cal. Rptr. 867 (Cal. App. 1987).

A new wave of land use scholars has also asked whether market forces and private arrangements may, at least in some contexts, produce better results than centralized planning and control. Using Houston, Texas as a case study, for example, Professor Bernard Siegan has argued that private covenants can provide a more effective means than zoning of coordinating land uses. Bernard Siegan, Land Use Without Zoning (1972). See also Orlando E. Delogu, Local Land Use Controls: An Idea Whose Time Has Passed, 36 Me. L. Rev. 261 (1984); Douglas W. Kmiec, Deregulating Land Use, 130 U. Pa. L. Rev. 28 (1981); Jan Z. Krasnowiecki, Abolish Zoning, 31 Syracuse L. Rev. 719 (1980); Robert C. Ellickson, Alternatives to Zoning: Covenants, Nuisance Rules, and Fines as Land Use Controls, 40 U. Chi. L. Rev. 681 (1973). For a spirited defense of zoning, see Bradley C. Karkkainen, Zoning: A Reply to Critics, 10 J. Land Use & Envtl. L. 45 (1994).

Several of the themes and issues already considered in this book's discussion of nuisance law and private land use arrangements recur in the context of public land use controls. Like nuisance law, for example, public land use regulation must balance the competing interests of land owners; protecting one property owner's use of her land often requires limiting others' use of their land. The goals of zoning laws also sometimes raise legitimacy questions that parallel judicial concerns over the lawful reach of private servitudes. Communities, for example, have used both zoning and servitudes at different points in time to try to exclude unwanted residents. Public land use control, however, also raises new issues. Because public controls necessarily involve governmental action, land use measures often raise constitutional questions regarding the extent of governmental authority to restrict land uses. Public land use controls also raise concerns that naked political power, rather than legitimate public concerns, may sometimes motivate regulatory decisions.

Chapter 11 examines *local* land use regulation, the mainstay of land use management for the last century. Chapter 11 looks not only at the mechanics of local zoning, but also at some of the newer uses of local regulation, including aesthetic and architectural oversight, historic preservation, environmental protection, and growth control. Chapter 11 also scrutinizes the exclusionary effects that zoning can have on minorities and the poor.

As Chapter 12 explores, federal environmental regulations are playing an increasingly important role in land use decisions throughout the United States. Although the federal government briefly considered and rejected national land use regulation in the early 1970s, a number of federal statutes today have as great of an impact as local zoning ordinances on many land use decisions. Chapter 12 looks at two of the major federal statutes with land use implications—the Clean Water Act's protection of wetlands, and the Endangered Species Act.

Chapter 13 examines the question of when governmental land use regulations unconstitutionally "take" property. As discussed in Chapter 2 at pp. 178–213, the United States Constitution, as well as the constitutions of all fifty states, prohibit governments from taking property without paying "just compensation." From the beginning of modern land use management, the United States Supreme Court has recognized that land use regulations, if they go too far in limiting a property owner's rights, can constitute unconstitutional "takings." Determining when a land use regulation constitutes a taking and requires compensation, however, has proven one of the most vexing constitutional issues that courts have faced.

CHAPTER 11

LOCAL LAND USE CONTROL

A. THE CONSTITUTIONAL FRAMEWORK

New York City adopted the first comprehensive zoning law in 1916. Skyscrapers were multiplying and cutting off the light to many property owners. Garment factories, moreover, were impinging on Fifth Avenue, forcing well-to-do shoppers to mingle with immigrant workers. New York's answer was to segregate land uses and impose bulk and height limits on buildings. Zoning "made an almost instant appeal to the American people." U.S. Dept. of Commerce, A Standard State Zoning Enabling Act iii (rev. ed. 1926). Within a decade, over 500 other cities followed suit and adopted their own zoning programs.

The constitutionality of local zoning, however, was initially in doubt. Courts split on whether land use regulation fell within the traditional police power of state and local governments. The issue finally made its way to the United States Supreme Court in the following landmark decision.

Village of Euclid v. Ambler Realty Co.

Supreme Court of the United States, 1926.
272 U.S. 365.

MR. JUSTICE SUTHERLAND delivered the opinion of the Court.

[In this case, a real estate company sued to enjoin the zoning ordinance of the Village of Euclid as unconstitutional. The Village zoning ordinance divided the entire village] into six classes of use districts, denominated U–1 to U–6, inclusive; three classes of height districts, denominated H–1 to H–3, inclusive; and four classes of area districts, denominated A–1 to A–4, inclusive. The use districts are classified in respect of the buildings which may be erected within their respective limits, as follows: U–1 is restricted to single family dwellings, public parks, water towers and reservoirs, suburban and interurban electric railway passenger stations and rights of way, and farming, noncommercial greenhouse nurseries, and truck gardening; U–2 is extended to include two-family dwellings; U–3 is further extended to include apartment houses, hotels, churches, schools, public libraries, museums, private clubs, community center buildings, hospitals, sanitariums, public playgrounds, and recreation buildings, and a city hall and courthouse; U–4 is further extended to include banks, offices, studios, telephone exchanges, fire and police stations, restaurants, theaters and moving picture shows, retail stores and shops, sales offices, sample rooms, wholesale stores for hardware, drugs, and groceries, stations for gasoline and oil (not exceeding 1,000 gallons storage) and for ice delivery, skating rinks and dance halls, electric substations, job and newspaper printing, public garages for motor vehicles, stables and wagon sheds (not exceeding five horses, wagons or motor trucks), and distributing stations for central store and commercial enterprises; U–5 is further extended to include billboards and advertising signs (if permitted), warehouses, ice and ice cream manufacturing and cold storage plants, bottling works, milk bottling and central distribution stations, laundries, carpet cleaning, dry cleaning, and dyeing establishments, blacksmith, horseshoeing, wagon and motor vehicle repair shops, freight stations, street car barns, stables and wagon sheds (for more than five horses, wagons or motor trucks), and wholesale produce markets and salesrooms; U–6 is further extended to include plants for sewage disposal and for producing gas, garbage and refuse incineration, scrap iron, junk, scrap paper, and rag storage, aviation fields, cemeteries, crematories, penal and correctional institutions, insane and feeble-minded institutions, storage of oil and gasoline (not to exceed 25,000 gallons), and manufacturing and industrial operations of any kind other than, and any public utility not included in, a class U–1, U–2, U–3, U–4, or U–5 use. There is a seventh class of uses which is prohibited altogether. . . .

[The real estate company, which was the appellee before the Supreme Court, owned a 68–acre vacant tract of land, abutting on Euclid Avenue to the south and the Nickel Plate Railroad to the north. There were residential subdivisions both to the east and west of the company's land, and the Village zoned a large portion of the company's land U–2 or U–3. The company alleged that it had held the land] for years for the purpose of selling and developing it for industrial uses, for which it is especially adapted, being immediately in the path of progressive industrial development; that for such uses it has a market value of about $10,000 per acre, but if the use be limited to residential purposes the market value is not in excess of $2,500 per acre; that the first 200 feet of the parcel back from Euclid avenue, if unrestricted in respect of use, has a value of $150 per front foot, but if limited to residential uses, and ordinary mercantile business be excluded therefrom, its value is not in excess of $50 per front foot. . . .

The record . . . show[s], as the lower court found, that the normal and reasonably to be expected use and development of that part of appellee's land adjoining Euclid avenue is for general trade and commercial purposes, particularly retail stores and like establishments, and that the normal and reasonably to be expected use and development of the residue of the land is for industrial and trade purposes. . . .

Building zone laws are of modern origin. They began in this country about 25 years ago. Until recent years, urban life was comparatively simple; but, with the great increase and concentration of population, problems have developed, and constantly are developing, which require, and will continue to require, additional restrictions in respect of the use and occupation of private lands in urban communities. Regulations, the wisdom, necessity, and validity of which, as applied to existing conditions, are so apparent that they are now uniformly sustained, a century ago, or even half a century ago, probably would have been rejected as arbitrary and oppressive. Such regulations are sustained, under the complex conditions of our day, for reasons analogous to those which justify traffic regulations, which, before the advent of automobiles and rapid transit street railways, would have been condemned as fatally arbitrary and unreasonable. And in this there is no inconsistency, for, while the meaning of constitutional guaranties never varies, the scope of their application must expand or contract to meet the new and different conditions which are constantly coming within the field of their operation. In a changing world it is impossible that it should be otherwise. But although a degree of elasticity is thus imparted, not to the *meaning,* but to the *application* of constitutional principles, statutes and ordinances, which, after giving due weight to the new conditions, are found clearly not to conform to the Constitution, of course, must fall.

The ordinance now under review, and all similar laws and regulations, must find their justification in some aspect of the police power, asserted for the public welfare. The line which in this field separates the legitimate from the illegitimate assumption of power is not capable of precise delimitation. It varies with circumstances and conditions. A regulatory zoning ordinance, which would be clearly valid as applied to the great cities, might be clearly invalid as applied to rural communities. In solving doubts, the maxim "sic utere tuo ut alienum non laedas," which lies at the foundation of so much of the common law of nuisances, ordinarily will furnish a fairly helpful clew. And the law of nuisances, likewise, may be consulted, not for the purpose of controlling, but for the helpful aid of its analogies in the process of ascertaining the scope of, the power. Thus the question whether the power exists to forbid the erection of a building of a particular kind or for a particular use, like the question whether a particular thing is a nuisance, is to be determined, not by an abstract consideration of the building or of the thing considered apart, but by considering it in connection with the circumstances and the locality. A nuisance may be merely a right thing in the wrong place, like a pig in the parlor instead of the barnyard. If the validity of the legislative classification for zoning purposes be fairly debatable, the legislative judgment must be allowed to control....

It is said that the village of Euclid is a mere suburb of the city of Cleveland; that the industrial development of that city has now reached and in some degree extended into the village, and in the obvious course of things will soon absorb the entire area for industrial enterprises; that the effect of the ordinance is to divert this natural development elsewhere, with the consequent loss of increased values to the owners of the lands within the village borders. But the village, though physically a suburb of Cleveland, is politically a separate municipality, with powers of its own and authority to govern itself as it sees fit, within the limits of the organic law of its creation and the state and federal Constitutions. Its governing authorities, presumably representing a majority of its inhabitants and voicing their will, have determined, not that industrial development shall cease at its boundaries, but that the course of such development shall proceed within definitely fixed lines. If it be a proper exercise of the police power to relegate industrial establishments to localities separated from residential sections, it is not easy to find a sufficient reason for denying the power because the effect of its exercise is to divert an industrial flow from the course which it would follow, to the injury of the residential public, if left alone, to another course where such injury will be obviated. It is not meant by this, however, to exclude the possibility of cases where the general public interest would so far outweigh the interest of the municipality that the municipality would not be allowed to stand in the way.

We find no difficulty in sustaining restrictions of the kind thus far reviewed. The serious question in the case arises over the provisions of the ordinance excluding from residential districts apartment houses, business houses, retail stores and shops, and other like establishments. This question involves the validity of what is really the crux of the more recent zoning legislation, namely, the creation and maintenance of residential districts, from which business and trade of every sort, including hotels and apartment houses, are excluded. Upon that question this court has not thus far spoken. The decisions of the state courts are numerous and conflicting; but those which broadly sustain the power greatly outnumber those which deny it altogether or narrowly limit it, and it is very apparent that there is a constantly increasing tendency in the direction of the broader view....

The matter of zoning has received much attention at the hands of commissions and experts, and the results of their investigations have been set forth in comprehensive reports. These reports, which bear every evidence of painstaking consideration, concur in the view that the segregation of residential, business and industrial buildings will make it easier to provide fire apparatus suitable for the character and intensity of the development in each section; that it will increase the safety and security of home life, greatly tend to prevent street accidents, especially to children, by reducing the traffic and resulting confusion in residential sections, decrease noise and other conditions which produce or intensify nervous disorders, preserve a more favorable environment in which to rear children, etc. With particular reference to apartment houses, it is pointed out that the development of detached house sections is greatly retarded by the coming of apartment houses, which has sometimes resulted in destroying the entire section for private house purposes; that in such sections very often the apartment house is a mere parasite, constructed in order to take advantage of the open spaces and attractive surroundings created by the residential character of the district. Moreover, the coming of one apartment house is followed by others, interfering by their height and bulk with the free circulation of air and monopolizing the rays of the sun which otherwise would fall upon the smaller homes, and bringing, as their necessary accompaniments, the disturbing noises incident to increased traffic and business, and the occupation, by means of moving and parked automobiles, of larger portions of the streets, thus detracting from their safety and depriving children of the privilege of quiet and open spaces for play, enjoyed by those in more favored localities—until, finally, the residential character of the neighborhood and its desirability as a place of detached residences are utterly destroyed. Under these circumstances, apartment houses, which in a different environment would be not only entirely unobjectionable but highly desirable, come very near to being nuisances.

If these reasons, thus summarized, do not demonstrate the wisdom or sound policy in all respects of those restrictions which we have indicated as pertinent to the inquiry, at least, the reasons are sufficiently cogent to preclude us from saying, as it must be said before the ordinance can be declared unconstitutional, that such provisions are clearly arbitrary and unreasonable, having no substantial relation to the public health, safety, morals, or general welfare. . . .

. . . . What would be the effect of a restraint imposed by one or more or the innumerable provisions of the ordinance, considered apart, upon the value or marketability of the lands, is neither disclosed by the bill nor by the evidence, and we are afforded no basis, apart from mere speculation, upon which to rest a conclusion that it or they would have any appreciable effect upon those matters. Under these circumstances, therefore, it is enough for us to determine, as we do, that the ordinance in its general scope and dominant features, so far as its provisions are here involved, is a valid exercise of authority, leaving other provisions to be dealt with as cases arise directly involving them.

And this is in accordance with the traditional policy of this court. In the realm of constitutional law, especially, this court has perceived the embarrassment which is likely to result from an attempt to formulate rules or decide questions beyond the necessities of the immediate issue. It has preferred to follow the method of a gradual approach to the general by a systematically guarded application and extension of constitutional principles to particular cases as they arise, rather than by out of hand attempts to establish general rules to which future cases must be fitted. This process applies with peculiar force to the solution of questions arising under the due process clause of the Constitution as applied to the exercise of the flexible powers of police, with which we are here concerned.

Notes & Questions

1. What vision of the public's "health, safety, welfare, and morals" lay behind the Village of Euclid's zoning ordinance? *Whose* health, safety, welfare, and morals was the village trying to protect? Consider the view of the trial court in *Euclid*:

> The plain truth is that the true object of the ordinance in question is to place all the property in an undeveloped area of 16 square miles in a strait-jacket. The purpose to be accomplished is really to regulate the mode of living of persons who may hereafter inhabit it. In the last analysis, the result to be accomplished is to classify the population and segregate them according to their income or situation in life. The true reason why some persons live in a mansion and others in a shack, why some live in a single-family dwelling and others in a double-family dwelling, why some live in a two-family dwelling and others in an apartment, or why

> some live in a well-kept apartment and others in a tenement, is primarily economic. It is a matter of income and wealth, plus the labor and difficulty of procuring adequate domestic service.

Ambler Realty Co. v. Village of Euclid, 297 F. 307, 316 (N.D. Ohio 1924). One of the early proponents of zoning was Robert Whitten, who favored using zoning to segregate cities by race. Whitten helped draft a number of zoning ordinances for Cleveland suburbs, and these in turn influenced the Village of Euclid's zoning scheme.

2. *Euclid* is, by any measure, a landmark—probably *the* landmark—in American land use control law. One paradox of *Euclid* is that this sweeping paean to the supremacy of state regulation over private property was written by an ardent conservative, Justice George Sutherland, who would later vote as one of the "Four Horsemen" to invalidate much of the New Deal's social legislation. The mystery is deepened by the fact that, after the initial oral argument, the Court had apparently voted 5–4 *against* the ordinance, with Justice Sutherland writing the majority opinion. What explains Sutherland's change of heart? According to Justice Stone's law clerk, "talks with his dissenting brethren (principally Stone, I believe) shook his convictions and led him to request a reargument, after which he changed his mind and the ordinance was upheld." Alfred McCormack, A Law Clerk's Recollections, 46 Colum. L. Rev. 710, 712 (1946).

Others have speculated that it was a request for reargument and an *amicus* brief filed by Alfred Bettman, one of the leading municipal reformers of the day, on behalf of the National Conference on City Planning that made the difference. Bettman warned that zoning was essential to protect the health and happiness of the upper-class and their children. Explaining the need to exclude apartments from U–1 districts, Bettman argued that "children are likely to grow mentally, physically, and morally more healthful" in a neighborhood with only single-family residences than "in a disorderly, noisy, slovenly, blighted and slum-like district." Richard H. Chused, *Euclid*'s Historical Imagery, 51 Case W. Res. L. Rev. 597, 612–613 (2001) (quoting from Bettman's brief). See also Robert A. Walker, The Planning Function in Urban Government 77–78 (2d ed. 1950).

Sutherland's biographer suggests that it was scholarly reflection that led the Justice to conclude that the ordinance was

> not the deprivation of property, but its enhancement. A distinction observed by [Judge Thomas] Cooley long before was . . . pertinent. It pointed out "the line between what would be a clear invasion of right on the one hand, and regulation not lessening the value of the right" on the other. On this basis the common law had allowed the abatement of nuisances, and the forbidden industrial plants would approximate nuisances in a residential area such as Euclid. The result of the statute, then, was beneficial to property, and grounded as it was on the ultimate fact of overcrowding, it could not be set aside.

Joel F. Paschal, Mr. Justice Sutherland 127 (1951).

3. The plaintiff in *Euclid* challenged the village's zoning ordinance on its face. Two years later, a landowner challenged the specific application of Cambridge, Massachusetts's zoning ordinance to his land—and won. In Nectow v. City of Cambridge, 277 U.S. 183, the city zoned plaintiff's land R–3, which permitted only residential dwellings and related low-intensity uses such as churches, schools, and clubs. Because the land was close to a Ford Motor Company auto assembling factory, a soap factory, and a railroad line, the land was of little value for these residential and related uses. The United States Supreme Court unanimously held that the decision to zone plaintiff's land R–3 was an "arbitrary and irrational exercise of power" and thus unconstitutional:

> The governmental power to interfere by zoning regulations with the general rights of the land owner by restricting the character of the use, is not unlimited, and, other questions aside, such restriction cannot be imposed if it does not bear a substantial relation to the public health, safety, morals, or general welfare. Here, the express finding of the master ... is that the health, safety, convenience, and general welfare of the inhabitants of the part of the city affected will not be promoted by the disposition made by the ordinance of [plaintiff's land].... That the invasion of the property of plaintiff ... was serious and highly injurious is clearly established; and, since a necessary basis for the support of the invasion is wanting, the action of the zoning authorities comes within the ban of the Fourteenth Amendment and cannot be sustained.

After *Euclid* and *Nectow*, the Supreme Court did not address the constitutionality of a local zoning measure for half a century. Instead, the Supreme Court left the development of zoning law to state and lower federal courts. *Euclid* and *Nectow*, however, established a pattern in the resolution of zoning cases that remains true today: landowners seldom win facial challenges to zoning laws, but are far likelier to win as-applied challenges.

4. Taking its name from the case that approved it, the style of zoning approved in *Euclid*, which segregates uses by dividing a city into separate districts in which only specific land uses are permitted, is now known as Euclidian zoning. Most Euclidian zoning sets out a hierarchy of uses (with single-family residential at the top, followed by multi-family dwellings, commercial, and industrial); districts zoned for a lower use generally allow any higher use also. A city's zoning system, for example, might permit only single-family residential homes in R1 districts, both single-family dwellings and apartments in R2 districts, residential and commercial uses in C, and all types of uses, including manufacturing plants, in M. The name "Euclidian zoning," of course, seems particularly appropriate when describing a zoning scheme based on plane geometry.

5. For interesting histories and discussion of *Euclid*, see David Callies, *Villae of Euclid v. Ambler Realty Co.*, in Property Stories 323 (Gerald Korngold & Andrew P. Morris eds., 2004); Charles M. Haar & Michael

Allan Wolf, *Euclid* Lives: The Survival of Progressive Jurisprudence, 115 Harv. L. Rev. 2158 (2002); Symposium on the Seventy–Fifth Anniversary of *Euclid v. Ambler*, 51 Case W. Res. L. Rev. 593 (2001); Joseph Gordon Hylton, Prelude to *Euclid*: The United States Supreme Court and the Constitutionality of Land Use Regulation, 1900–1920, 3 Wash. U. J.L. & Pol'y 1 (2000); Michael Allan Wolf, "Compelled by Conscientious Duty": *Village of Euclid v. Ambler Realty Co.* As Romance, 2 J. Sup. Ct. Hist. 88 (1997).

B. THE ZONING SYSTEM

1. THE STATE ZONING ENABLING ACT

Constitutionally, the power to plan and to zone resides in state, not local, government. States therefore must delegate zoning authority to cities and other local governments before they can engage in zoning efforts. In the early 1920's, Secretary of Commerce (later President) Herbert Hoover organized a committee of experts to develop a Standard Zoning Enabling Act (SZEA). Released initially in 1922 and published in a revised form in 1926, the SZEA has served as a model for zoning authorization statutes at one time or another in all 50 states. U.S. Dept. of Commerce, A Standard State Zoning Enabling Act (rev. ed. 1926). Many states still use variants of the SZEA to authorize zoning at the municipal level.

The SZEA provides that cities can engage in zoning "to regulate and restrict the height, number of stories, and size of buildings and other structures, the percentage of lot that may be occupied, the size of yards, courts, and other open spaces, the density of population, and the location and use of buildings, structures, and land for trade, industry, residence, or other purposes." SZEA § 1. To accomplish these goals, the SZEA authorizes municipalities to create an appropriate number of geographical zones or "districts" in which buildings and land uses are regulated. Id. § 2.

A city's council or legislative body has the ultimate power under the SZEA to establish the city's districts and the regulations governing each district. Id. § 4. To implement the zoning, however, the SZEA provides for a number of other local governmental bodies. A *zoning (or planning) commission*, appointed by the legislative body, recommends the boundaries of the districts and "appropriate regulations to be enforced therein." Id. § 6. A *board of adjustment* (or *board of zoning appeals*), again appointed by the legislative body, (1) hears appeals of zoning decisions and orders, (2) makes *special exceptions* to the zoning regulations as appropriate, and (3) issues *variances* from the zoning ordinance "where, owing to special conditions, a literal enforcement of the provisions of the ordinance will result in unnecessary hardship." Id. § 7. Anyone who is aggrieved by a zoning decision, as well as any governmental official or taxpayer, is entitled to appeal a zoning decision. Id. Anyone who loses before the board of adjustment can petition the state court for review. Id.

The SZEA places a premium on planning, process, and uniformity. All zoning, for example, must be "made in accordance with a comprehensive plan." Id. § 3. According to notes to the SZEA, this requirement "will prevent haphazard or piecemeal zoning. No zoning should be done without such a comprehensive study." Id. at 6 n.22. Before creating districts and adopting regulations, the city's legislative body also must hold a public hearing, "in which parties in interest and citizens shall have an opportunity to be heard." Id. § 4. "This permits any person to be heard, and not merely property owners.... It is right that every citizen should be able to make his voice heard and protest against any ordinance that might be detrimental to the best interests of the city." Id. at 7 n.28. The zoning commission similarly must conduct public hearings before submitting recommendations to the legislative body. Id. § 6. Within any district, regulations must be "uniform for each class or kind of buildings." Id. § 2.

Although the SZEA and similar authorizing statutes provided cities with the power to zone, they also served as legal straitjackets well into the middle of the 20th century. The SZEA, as noted, lists specific purposes, such as height control and the regulation of land uses, for which cities can engage in zoning. On the premise that municipalities possess only those powers specifically delegated to them by the state, or those necessarily implied, most courts initially refused to enlarge the local zoning power to include objects or methods not specified in the SZEA, such as aesthetic regulation or historic preservation. The SZEA therefore often constrained local governments from embarking on innovative land use control programs.

An increasing number of states have abandoned the SZEA's rigid format in favor of more flexible enabling acts. At the same time, courts have become more generous in interpreting the powers delegated by state enabling acts. Many municipalities have also gained increased freedom to plan and zone as a result of state constitutional and statutory provisions giving them broad home rule powers. As a result, the basic authority of cities to engage in a wide range of zoning activities is seldom today in any doubt.

2. THE COMPREHENSIVE PLAN

The Standard Zoning Enabling Act, as noted in the last section, requires zoning to be "made in accordance with a comprehensive plan," in order to prevent "haphazard or piecemeal zoning." SZEA § 3, at 6 & n.22. What does this requirement mean?

Udell v. Haas

Court of Appeals of New York, 1968.
235 N.E.2d 897.

KEATING, Judge.

The issue on this appeal is whether a 1960 amendment to the Building Zone Ordinance (altering the Zoning Map) of the Village of Lake Success, which reclassified appellant's property from Business "A" and "B" to Residence "C", is valid. Appellant claims that the rezoning was discriminatory, confiscatory and *ultra vires*.

The background of the dispute is this: The Village of Lake Success is a small, suburban community in the extreme westerly portion of Nassau County. It has a rather irregular shape, but generally is bounded on the south by the Northern State Parkway and on the north and east by the Town of North Hempstead. To the west lies its giant neighbor, the City of New York.

The village is approximately two square miles in size. Running through it in a generally north-south direction is the main artery of the village, Lakeville Road. That street intersects with Northern Boulevard, a major east-west thoroughfare in this section of Long Island.

The village's northern boundary appears to be completely arbitrary. For the most part, it is to the south of Northern Boulevard. However, along Lakeville Road, the village reaches out in a northerly direction to touch Northern Boulevard. The area is not large and is neck-like in shape, consisting of several hundred feet on either side of Lakeville Road extending from Northern Boulevard some 750 feet to University Road on the west side of Lakeville Road and some 600 feet to Cumberland Avenue on the east. Cumberland Avenue and University Road form what may be described as the base of the neck.

Prior to the 1960 rezoning in question, almost the entire neck was zoned for business. For a distance of some 400 feet south of Northern Boulevard, the area was zoned Business "A" which permitted retailing and similar uses as well as laboratories and office and public buildings. The rest of the neck was zoned Business "B" where essentially the only nonresidential use allowed was neighborhood retailing.

[This litigation involves two parcels of property in this neck—the "east parcel" and the "west parcel." Each parcel is about 2½ acres in size and was originally zoned for business use. One parcel is used as a restaurant; both abut gas stations.

[In 1960, the Village of Lake Success adopted a zoning amendment that] placed the entire neck, except for a 100–foot-wide strip adjacent to Northern Boulevard, in a Residence "C" category.... Permitted uses in the new classification include public and religious buildings and residences with minimum plot size set at 13,000 square feet and minimum frontage of 100 feet on Lakeville Road....

We hold that ordinance No. 60 is invalid.... We have concluded that the rezoning was discriminatory and that it was not done "in accordance with [the] comprehensive plan" of the Village of Lake Success (Village Law, § 177). In our view, sound zoning principles were not followed in this case, and the root cause of this failure was a misunderstanding of the nature of zoning, and, even more importantly, of its relationship to the statutory requirement that it be "in accordance with a comprehensive plan."

Zoning is not just an expansion of the common law of nuisance. It seeks to achieve much more than the removal of obnoxious gases and unsightly uses. Underlying the entire concept of zoning is the assumption that zoning can be a vital tool for maintaining a civilized form of existence only if we employ the insights and the learning of the philosopher, the city planner, the economist, the sociologist, the public health expert and all the other professions concerned with urban problems.

This fundamental conception of zoning has been present from its inception. The almost universal statutory requirement that zoning conform to a "well-considered plan" or "comprehensive plan" is a reflection of that view. (See Standard State Zoning Enabling Act, U. S. Dept. of Commerce [1926].) The thought behind the requirement is that consideration must be given to the needs of the community as a whole. In exercising their zoning powers, the local authorities must act for the benefit of the community as a whole following a calm and deliberate consideration of the alternatives, and not because of the whims of either an articulate minority or even majority of the community. (De Sena v. Gulde, 24 A.D.2d 165 [2d Dept., 1965].) Thus, the mandate of the Village Law (§ 177) is not a mere technicality which serves only as an obstacle course for public officials to overcome in carrying out their duties. Rather, the comprehensive plan is the essence of zoning. Without it, there can be no rational allocation of land use. It is the insurance that the public welfare is being served and that zoning does not become nothing more than just a Gallup poll.

Moreover, the "comprehensive plan" protects the landowner from arbitrary restrictions on the use of his property which can result from the pressures which outraged voters can bring to bear on public officials. "With the heavy presumption of constitutional validity that attaches to legislation purportedly under the police power, and the difficulty in judicially applying a 'reasonableness' standard, there is danger that zoning, considered as a self-contained activity rather than as a means to a broader end, may tyrannize individual property owners. Exercise of the legislative power to zone should be governed by rules and standards as clearly defined as possible, so that it cannot operate in an arbitrary and discriminatory fashion, and will actually be directed to the health, safety, welfare and morals of the community. The more clarity and specificity required in the articulation of the premises upon which a particular zoning regulation is based, the more effectively will courts be able to review the regulation, declaring it ultra vires if it is not in reality 'in accordance with a comprehensive plan.' " (Haar, "In Accordance With a Comprehensive Plan," 68 Harv. L. Rev. 1154, 1157–1158.)

As Professor Haar points out, zoning may easily degenerate into a talismanic word, like the "police power," to excuse all sorts of arbitrary infringements on the property rights of the landowner. To assure that this does not happen, our courts must require local zoning authorities to pay more than mock obeisance to the statutory mandate that zoning be "in accordance with a comprehensive plan." There must be some showing that the change does not conflict with the community's basic scheme for land use.

One of the key factors used by our courts in determining whether the statutory requirement has been met is whether forethought has been given to the community's land use problems. Where a community, after a careful and deliberate review of "the present and reasonably forseeable needs of the community," adopts a general developmental policy for the community as a whole and amends its zoning law in accordance with that plan, courts can have some confidence that the public interest is being served (Rodgers v. Village of Tarrytown, 302 N.Y. 115, 121–122; Thomas v. Town of Bedford, 11 N.Y.2d 428, 434). Where, however, local officials adopt a zoning amendment to deal with various problems that have arisen, but give no consideration to alternatives which might minimize the adverse effects of a change on particular landowners, and then call in the experts to justify the steps already taken in contemplation of anticipated litigation, closer judicial scrutiny is required to determine whether the amendment conforms to the comprehensive plan.

The role of these experts must be more than that of giving rationalizations for actions previously decided upon or already carried out. In recent years, many experts on land use problems have expressed the pessimistic view that the task of bringing about a rational allocation of land use in an ever more urbanized America will prove impossible. But of one thing, we may all be certain. The difficulties involved in developing rational schemes of land use controls become insuperable when zoning or changes in zoning are followed rather than preceded by study and consideration.

By this statement, we do not mean to imply that the courts should examine the motives of local officials. What we do mean is that the courts must satisfy themselves that the rezoning meets the statutory requirement that zoning be "in accordance with [the] comprehensive plan" of the community.

Exactly what constitutes a "comprehensive plan" has never been made clear. Professor Haar in his article discusses most of the meanings which courts have given the term. In the conclusion of his article he notes (68 Harv. L. Rev. 1173): "As we have seen, the courts have taken a number of rather different approaches in testing zoning measures for consonance with the enabling act mandate of 'accordance with a comprehensive plan.' None of the meanings suggested—broad geographical coverage, 'policy' of the planning or zoning commission, the zoning ordinance itself, the rational basis underlying the ordinance—do extreme violence to the statutory wording. But all of them share a common defect: they emphasize the question whether the zoning ordinance is a comprehensive plan, not whether it is in accordance with a comprehensive plan. Thus construed, the enabling act demands little more than that zoning be 'reasonable,' and impartial in treatment, to satisfy the constitutional conditions for exercise of the state's police power."

No New York case has defined the term "comprehensive plan." Nor have our courts equated the term with any particular document. We have found the "comprehensive plan" by examining all relevant evidence. As the trial court noted, generally New York cases "have analyzed the ordinance ... in terms of consistency and rationality." While these elements are important, the "comprehensive plan" requires that the rezoning should not conflict with the fundamental land use policies and development plans of the community. These policies may be garnered from any available source, most especially the master plan of the community, if any has been adopted, the zoning law itself and the zoning map.

In the case at bar, the search for the village's "comprehensive plan" is relatively easy. It may be found both in the village's zoning ordinance and in its zoning map. In 1925 the Village of Lake Success adopted its first zoning ordinance. At least since 1938, appellant's parcel has been placed in a business use district. Over the years, various amendments were passed, none of them, however, affecting appellant's property. If anything, the changes tended to reinforce the conclusion that the community had decided that the neck of land was most appropriately fitted for business use because of its proximity to Northern Boulevard. Thus, in the early 1950s the west side of University Place near Northern Boulevard was rezoned for business use. When appellants acquired the parcel, it had been zoned for business use for some 12 or 13 years and so it remained for the next 8 or 9 years.

In 1958 the village undertook to set forth expressly the essential development goals of the community. It did so in the form of an amendment to the zoning ordinance and entitled the statement a "developmental policy." According to the statement, Lake Success was and was to remain a suburban community of low density, one-family residential development. Other uses were to be permitted only to the extent that they were related to residential use, e.g., schools, churches and community institutions, or as they might contribute to the strengthening of the tax base of the community.

If one examines the zoning map of the village as it stood prior to June, 1960, this policy is carried out almost perfectly. Only a small portion of the community's land was zoned for business use. It is important to note that almost, if not, every piece of property in the nonresidential category was located on the periphery of the community, usually adjacent to lands in neighboring communities with similar nonresidential use. Consistent with this "developmental policy," a portion of the northeast section of the community had previously been rezoned for commercial use.

Thus, as matters stood on the morning of June 21, 1960, the village had a zoning plan with stated community goals and a zoning map which consistently carried out these policies.

On June 21, 1960 Fred Rudinger, an associate of the appellant, appeared at the village's offices with a preliminary sketch for the development of the vacant west parcel with a bowling alley and a supermarket or discount house. That same evening, the village planning board recommended a change in zoning from business to residential use.

The minutes of that meeting indicate that, following a discussion of the severe traffic problem which had developed on Lakeville Road, a proposed amendment to the zoning map was recommended to the village trustees. A month or so later, this proposal became, in slightly modified form, ordinance No. 60.

Next, the following comment appears in the minutes: "Mr. Klein informed the Board that *by coincidence*, this morning, an informal preliminary sketch was submitted to him by Mr. Fred Rudinger for the development of the area with a bowling alley and a supermarket or discount house. The Board gave no opinion on this informal sketch and no further action was considered necessary." (Emphasis supplied.) The reference to Mr. Rudinger's visit as being "by coincidence" appears somewhat odd since no zoning amendments had been considered previously. It is significant that no consideration was given to other possible alternatives for alleviating the traffic problem.

Only after adopting this recommendation did the planning board vote to ask the board of trustees to retain a planning expert to review the village's master plan. On July 5, 1960 the trustees retained Mr. Hugh Pomeroy to make just such an investigation. Later that same day, the planning board and the trustees met in joint session, and it was agreed that a required public hearing should be held promptly. On July 27, 1960 ordinance No. 60 became law following the holding of a public hearing two days earlier.

This history of ordinance No. 60 must immediately raise doubts whether this race to the statute books was in accord with sound zoning principles or was a subversion of them for the process by which a zoning revision is carried out is important in determining the validity of the particular action taken. The village argues that there was no longer any need for shopping facilities in the area. Assuming that to be so, this does not explain why consideration was only given to zoning the area as "Residence C." A fair respect for the community's need for taxables, as set forth in its "developmental policy," required that some thought be given to other possible land use controls.

A more substantial justification for the rezoning was the serious traffic conditions on Lakeville Road. However, at the trial, the village's own expert, Mr. Frederick P. Clark, who was retained by the village after Mr. Pomeroy's death, admitted that business use of the east parcel would create less of a traffic problem than business use of the west parcel would. The reason for this was that access to the east parcel could be restricted to Northern Boulevard, while access to the west parcel would probably have to be from Lakeville Road.

The point here is not only that the expert's argument does not support the village's position, but that his testimony also conflicted sharply with the community's "developmental policy" and his own earlier recommendations for modifications of that policy, which he had made in 1962 when he drafted a proposed "Comprehensive Zoning Plan" for the community. In that report, Mr. Clark had recommended the rezoning of various perimeter areas in the community for commercial and light manufacturing use to take account of property developments outside the community and to strengthen the tax base. For example, he suggested that the entire area of the community south of the Northern State Parkway be rezoned for commercial or light manufacturing. On cross-examination, Mr. Clark admitted that the east parcel was in a perimeter area. The fair implication, therefore, is that commercial use of this property would conform with his recommendations for land use control.

More pertinent is Mr. Clark's testimony at the trial: "In my opinion the property on the east side, the Andre property, could be used either for residential purposes as presently zoned or for business. I do not find in my study of it a marked superiority of one over the other. I believe it could be used for either as an appropriate use."

He later modified this statement to include the proviso that there should be no access from Lakeville Road. This concession by Mr. Clark was no mistake. In light of the recommendations of his "Comprehensive Zoning Plan of 1962," he had to agree that commercial use was at least equally desirable. Otherwise, he would have discredited his own planning work for the community. Mr. Clark's testimony establishes that the zoning amendment was neither in 1960 nor afterwards in harmony with the community's over-all land use plan.

Aside from this testimony, examining the zoning map, one would find it difficult to locate a more fitting area to use for commercial purposes than this isolated neck near Northern Boulevard of which the subject parcel is part.

Viewing the village's plans on a temporal basis, there is a consistency predating ordinance No. 60 and post-dating the change. In 1958 a large area in the northeast section of the village had been zoned for nonresidential use. After 1960 other changes of a similar nature were recommended in conformity with a policy of expanding areas of commercial use on the periphery of the community. The only significant deviation was the ordinance No. 60.

It is not disputed that the village officials faced a traffic problem in the Northern Boulevard–Lakeville Road area. Nevertheless, we can come to no other conclusion that the rezoning was not "accomplished in a proper, careful and reasonable manner" (Rodgers v. Village of Tarrytown, 302 N.Y. 115, 122, supra). Ordinance No. 60 not only did not conform to the village's general "developmental policy," but it was also inconsistent with what had been the fundamental rationale of the village's zoning law and map. The amendment was not the result of a deliberate change in community policy and was enacted without sufficient forethought or planning. The particular conditions existing in the area did not support the radical change, which ordinance No. 60 embodied.

More than 60% of the value, of appellant's property, or $260,000, was wiped out because, to use the words of the village's first expert, "in his discussions he had found *it is the feeling of the Village* that it does not want extensive business in that area." (Emphasis supplied.)

These vague desires of a segment of the public were not a proper reason to interfere with the appellant's right to use his property in a manner which for some 20 odd years was considered perfectly proper. If there is to be any justification for this interference with appellant's use of his property, it must be found in the needs and goals of the community as articulated in a rational statement of land use control policies known as the "comprehensive plan". We find that appellant has demonstrated that ordinance No. 60 did not conform to the established "comprehensive plan" of the village. Hence, ordinance No. 60 must be held to be *ultra vires* as not meeting the requirement of section 177 of the Village Law that zoning be "in accordance with a comprehensive plan."....

Notes & Questions

1. State courts have traditionally been quite cavalier about enforcing the Standard State Zoning Enabling Act's requirement that zoning be "in accordance with a comprehensive plan." For example, in the influential case of Kozesnik v. Township of Montgomery, 131 A.2d 1 (N.J. 1957), the New Jersey Supreme Court held that a municipality which had not adopted a separate comprehensive plan could treat its zoning ordinance as itself a comprehensive plan; amendments to the zoning ordinance were thus viewed as amendments to—and necessarily in conformity with—the comprehensive plan. As courts have often noted, the SZEA does not specifically require the preparation of a separate comprehensive plan and indeed no where even defines what a comprehensive plan is.

2. *Udell* may reflect a contemporary judicial trend to take comprehensive plans more seriously. "The definite trend appears to be toward finding the plan as a sort of impermanent constitution, flexible in its interpretation, but more than a guide to growth that may be rejected in some circumstances." Edward J. Sullivan, The Role of the Comprehensive Plan, 31 Urb. Law. 915, 924 (1999). According to the Iowa Supreme Court, however, a majority of courts in states requiring zoning to be "in accordance with a comprehensive plan" still "hold a plan external to the zoning ordinance is not required." Wolf v. City of Ely, 493 N.W.2d 846 (Iowa 1992)

3. State legislatures are increasingly trying to breath life into comprehensive planning, ordering local governments to prepare separate comprehensive plans, setting out detailed standards for such plans, and requiring that land use regulations be not only "in accordance with," but "consistent with" such plans. See Stuart Meck, The Legislative Requirement that Zoning and Land Use Controls Be Consistent with an Independently Adopted Local Comprehensive Plan: A Model Statute, 3 Wash. U. J.L. & Pol'y 295 (2000). Florida, for example, requires all municipalities to adopt comprehensive plans that address future land uses, housing (including low-income housing and the "elimination of substandard dwelling conditions"), traffic circulation (including bicycle and pedestrian paths), sewage and solid

waste, water supplies, conservation (including the "conservation, use, and protection of natural resources"), recreation, open space, and coastal management. Fla. Stat. Ann. § 163.3177(6).

States that require comprehensive planning take different approaches to enforcing the requirement. In Florida, for example, regional planning agencies can prepare a comprehensive plan for a local government that fails to meet its statutory requirements. Fla. Stat. Ann. § 163.3167(3). California, by contrast, authorizes courts to order local governments to prepare an adequate comprehensive plan (or *general plan*, using California's terminology) and to suspend the government's authority to issue building permits and zoning approvals until the deficiency is cured. Cal. Gov't Code §§ 65754–65755. What are the relative advantages and disadvantages of these approaches? How else might a state encourage local governments to prepare adequate comprehensive plans?

4. Why require comprehensive planning? One function of comprehensive planning is to force municipalities to think about local land use patterns and demographics over the longer term. Another function is to clarify goals and to systematize the land use control devices employed to reach those goals. And, as *Udell* indicates, the plan also serves an important political function, protecting the landowner from "arbitrary restrictions on the use of his property which can result from the pressure which outraged voters can bring to bear on public officials." Do local governments, however, have sufficient foresight and information to engage in effective comprehensive planning? Are the potential values of comprehensive planning worth the substantial time and expense needed to prepare a comprehensive plan?

5. Can a developer use a comprehensive plan affirmatively to argue that her parcel should be rezoned from its present use to one that is less restrictive? In City of Louisville v. Kavanaugh, 495 S.W.2d 502 (Ky. 1973), a landowner had unsuccessfully argued that the city should rezone his property from single family to multifamily residential, noting that the city's comprehensive plan projected multifamily use for his parcel. The Kentucky Supreme Court ordered the City Board of Aldermen to rezone the property.

3. The Zoning Ordinance

United States National Commission on Urban Problems, Building the American City

201–202, 205 (1968).

Despite increasingly important changes, the form of today's land use regulations, and often their substance as well, still commonly fall within the conventional patterns established in the 1920's. Of course, no one local regulation is typical of these patterns: Objectives, techniques, and administrative practices reflect the varying desires of thousands of local governments. A rudimentary zoning regulation in a rural village may do little more than exclude a few noxious uses from residential areas, while a regulation for a large city or a prosperous suburb may establish an array of districts and a complex administrative process. There are, however, some elements that are common to most of the current regulations that fall within the conventional pattern.

The Zoning Ordinance

a. *Regulated subjects.*

A zoning ordinance typically prescribes how each parcel of land in a community may be used. Most regulations cover at least these subjects—

Use: First, zoning ordinances designate permitted "uses" (activities). Many divide uses into three basic categories: Dwellings, businesses, and industry. These basic categories are usually divided into subcategories. It is common practice, for example, to distinguish between one-family detached houses and apartment buildings, between "light" and "heavy" industry. Over the years ordinances have tended to establish more and more use categories. Ordinances with more than 20 different use categories are now common, and many ordinances now make specific provision for hundreds of listed uses.

Population density: A limitation on population density is also part of today's accepted zoning pattern. Most ordinances establish this limitation by setting a minimum required size for each lot. Alternatively, they may limit the number of families per acre or set a minimum required lot area for each dwelling unit on a lot. Some, particularly in large cities, establish more refined density controls that try to take account of the likelihood that more people will live in larger apartment units than in smaller ones.

Building bulk: Zoning regulations also limit building bulk. Usually, they do this by requiring yards along lot boundaries, by limiting building height, and by limiting the proportion of lot area that may be covered by buildings. Refinements of these devices have become common, in recent years, as communities have recognized that rigid yard and height requirements often deter imaginative design. "Floor area ratio" and "usable open space" requirements are among the increasingly common refinements.

Offstreet parking: As an addition to the original pattern, most zoning ordinances now contain offstreet parking requirements. These are intended to assure that new development provides for at least some of its own parking needs rather than adding to the number of parked cars on already crowded streets.

Other subjects: Many other requirements also appear in zoning regulations. Minimum house size, landscaping, signs, appearance of buildings, offstreet loading, view protection, and grading are just a few of the other subjects sometimes regulated.

b. *The zoning map.*

In recognition of differing conditions and planning policies in different parts of each community, zoning regulations establish "zones" or "districts." Within each of these districts a uniform set of regulations dealing with uses, bulk and the like apply. Thus, for example, stores may be permitted in one district but not in another. To show the location and boundaries of these districts, the ordinance includes a zoning map.

The number of districts and the nature of the differences between them vary greatly from town to town. Most ordinances contain at least one district in which single-family detached dwellings are the only permitted residential use. Often there are several such "single family" districts, distinguished from each other primarily by differences in the required minimum lot size; one district may require each lot to contain at least 2 acres, another at least 1 acre, and so on. Many ordinances also contain general residence districts, in which other types of dwellings are also permitted; these, too, are often differentiated by density requirements. Ordinances also commonly contain a variety of commercial districts bearing such names as neighborhood retail, central business, heavy commercial, and commercial recreation. They are commonly distinguished from one another by variations in permitted activity, bulk, and parking requirements. And industrial districts may differ from each other with respect to permitted activities, bulk regulations, and "performance" regulations limiting the amount of smoke, noise, or odor that industries may produce.

In addition to the basic districts—those based on the traditional triad of dwellings, business and industry—scores of other kinds of districts have been devised since the early days of zoning and are now commonly used to fit local conditions and policies. Agricultural districts, industrial-park districts, and special districts for public land are examples. Some of the newer districts allow a mixture of traditionally separated uses, such as residential-office and residential-commercial districts. Others are intended to meet unique conditions of a particular area, such as flood plain districts....

Evolution of the Regulatory Pattern

Although today's regulations still normally resemble those of the 1920's in some respects, many also show marked differences from the early pattern. Regulatory techniques have been substantially refined, and standards have been generally raised. Objectives have become more ambitious, particularly where the old negativism has given way to the view that regulations should be part of a process to guide development affirmatively toward desired public objectives. And both techniques and objectives have been adapted to changes in the process of city building itself....

One direction of change has been toward refinement of regulatory techniques. Among the many common examples of such refinement are these:

Specification of permitted uses: Instead of listing prohibited uses in each district, as the oldest ordinances did, regulations now normally list uses permitted in each district and prohibit all others. This plugs loopholes and establishes more clearly the intent of the regulations to guide development affirmatively in desired directions.

Noncumulative regulations: Old zoning ordinances set up a kind of use pyramid. Residences were "highest," businesses next, and industry was at the bottom. Each district permitted all the "higher" uses but excluded the "lower" ones. Thus, while industry was prohibited in residence zones, residences were permitted in industrial zones. Recent ordinances, however, attempting to assure that land is put to its planned use are much more likely to prohibit residences in industrialized zones as well as *vice versa.*

More districts: Another sign of increasing refinement of control is the ever-increasing number of districts. A small suburban community that may have had half a dozen districts 30 years ago may have several times that many today.

More subjects regulated: There is a tendency to regulate more characteristics of development. Landscaping and screening provisions, for example, are now common. Many community regulations reflect public concern about such diverse matters as the appearance of buildings, the economic compatibility of the uses permitted in business areas, or the unwelcome glare from lights in parking lots.

Performance standards: Finally, a number of regulations contain performance standards. Performance standards fashion regulations more precisely to public objectives than do traditional or conventional regulations. Industrial performance standards, for example, may establish odor limits instead of prohibiting all paint plants. Performance standards hold great promise wherever the regulatory purpose is clear, where a standard can be precisely determined, and where compliance with it can be objectively and easily measured. Nevertheless, standards of this type are not even potentially available to govern many of the most important land-use relationships; there are simply too many purposes to be weighed in each situation and too many that defy objective measurement.

C. PROTECTION OF EXPECTATIONS

Should the law protect property owners who have been using their land, perhaps for many years, in a fashion that zoning authorities now wish to proscribe? What about property owners who were told that they could build, only to find that zoning authorities have changed their mind? State courts have often held that zoning authorities must protect landowner's expectations in these settings. In some cases, courts have rested their rulings on the constitutional protections against uncompensated takings of private property. As you will see in Chapter 13, the United States Supreme Court has held that regulations that interfere too greatly with landowners' reasonable, investment-backed expectations can constitute a taking for which the government must pay compensation. In other cases, courts have relied on explicit or implied statutory protections. In yet other cases, courts assert their general equity authority. The cases in this section investigate the circumstances in which courts require zoning authorities to protect landowners' expectations and what forms that protection takes.

1. NONCONFORMING STRUCTURES AND USES

Village of Valatie v. Smith

Court of Appeals of New York, 1994.
632 N.E.2d 1264.

SIMONS, J.

This appeal challenges the facial validity of chapter 85 of the Village Code of the Village of Valatie, a local law that terminates the nonconforming use of a mobile home upon the transfer of ownership of either the mobile home or the land upon which it sits. Defendant argues that it is unconstitutional for the Village to use a change in ownership as the termination date for a nonconforming use. We conclude, however, that defendant has failed to carry her burden of showing that the local law is unreasonable on its face. Accordingly, we modify the order of the Appellate Division by denying defendant's cross motion for summary judgment.

In 1968, the Village enacted chapter 85 to prohibit the placement of mobile homes outside mobile home parks. Under the law, any existing mobile home located outside a park which met certain health standards was allowed to remain as a nonconforming use until either ownership of the land or ownership of the mobile home changed. According to the Village, six mobile homes, including one owned by defendant's father, fell within this exception at the time the law was passed.

In 1989, defendant inherited the mobile home from her father and the Village instituted this action to enforce the law and have the unit removed. Both the Village and defendant moved before Supreme Court for summary judgment. The court granted defendant's motion and denied the Village's. The court characterized defendant's mobile home as a lawful nonconforming use—a use that was legally in place at the time the municipality enacted legislation prohibiting the use. Reasoning that the right to continue a nonconforming use runs with the land, the court held that the portion of the ordinance setting termination at the transfer of ownership was unconstitutional. The Appellate Division affirmed. The Court acknowledged that a municipality had the authority to phase out a nonconforming use with an "amortization period," but it concluded that this particular law was unreasonable, and therefore unconstitutional, because the period of time allowed "bears no relationship to the use of the land or the investment in that use."

Preliminarily, it is important to note that the question presented is the facial validity of the local law. The Court is not called upon to decide whether the local law *as applied* so deprived defendant of the value of her property as to constitute a governmental taking under the Fifth Amendment. Nor does defendant challenge the power of a municipality to regulate land use, including the placement of mobile homes, as a valid exercise of the police power. Finally, there is no question that municipalities may enact laws reasonably limiting the duration of nonconforming uses.

Thus, the narrow issue is whether the Village acted unreasonably by establishing an amortization period that uses the transfer of ownership as an end point.

The policy of allowing nonconforming uses to continue originated in concerns that the application of land use regulations to uses existing prior to the regulations' enactment might be construed as confiscatory and unconstitutional. While it was initially assumed that nonconforming uses would disappear with time, just the opposite proved to be true in many instances, with the nonconforming use thriving in the absence of any new lawful competition. In light of the problems presented by continuing nonconforming uses, this Court has characterized the law's allowance of such uses as a "grudging tolerance," and we have recognized the right of municipalities to take reasonable measures to eliminate them.

Most often, elimination has been effected by establishing amortization periods, at the conclusion of which the nonconforming use must end. As commentators have noted, the term "amortization period" is somewhat misleading (see, e.g., 4 Rathkopf, Zoning and Planning § 51B.05[1], at 51B–44, n 3 [Ziegler 4th ed]). "Amortization" properly refers to a liquidation, but in this context the owner is not required to take any particular financial step. "Amortization period" simply designates a period of time granted to owners of nonconforming uses during which they may phase out their operations as they see fit and make other arrangements (id.). It is, in effect, a grace period, putting owners on fair notice of the law and giving them a fair opportunity to recoup their investment. Though the amortization period is typically discussed in terms of protecting the owners' financial interests, it serves more generally to protect "an individual's interest in maintaining the present use" of the property (Modjeska Sign Studios v. Berle, 43 NY2d 468, 479).

The validity of an amortization period depends on its reasonableness (Matter of Harbison v. City of Buffalo, 4 NY2d 553, 562–563). We have avoided any fixed formula for determining what constitutes a reasonable period. Instead, we have held that an amortization period is presumed valid, and the owner must carry the heavy burden of overcoming that presumption by demonstrating that the loss suffered is so substantial that it outweighs the public benefit to be gained by the exercise of the police power (Matter of Town of Islip v. Caviglia, 73 NY2d 544, 561; Modjeska Sign Studios v. Berle, supra, at 480). Using this approach, courts have declared valid a variety of amortization periods (see 6 Rohan, Zoning and Land Use Controls § 41.04[2], at 41–158)....

Defendant here does not challenge the local law's constitutionality under our established balancing test for amortization periods—i.e., whether the individual loss outweighs the public benefit. Instead, the challenge is a more basic due process claim: that the means of eliminating nonconforming uses is not reasonably related to the Village's legitimate interest in land use planning. More particularly, defendant makes two arguments: first, that the length of an amortization period must be related either to land use objectives or to the financial recoupment needs of the owner and, second, that the local law violates the principle that zoning is to regulate land use rather than ownership. Neither argument withstands analysis.

We have never required that the length of the amortization period be based on a municipality's land use objectives. To the contrary, the periods are routinely calculated to protect the rights of individual owners *at the temporary expense of* public land use objectives. Typically, the period of time allowed has been measured for reasonableness by considering whether the owners had adequate time to recoup their investment in the use (see, e.g., Modjeska Sign Studios v. Berle, 43 NY2d 468, 474; accord, Matter of Town of Islip v. Caviglia, 73 NY2d 544, 561). Patently, such protection of an individual's interest is unrelated to land use objectives. Indeed, were land use objectives the only permissible criteria for scheduling amortization, the law would require immediate elimination of nonconforming uses in all instances. Instead, the setting of the amortization period involves balancing the interests of the individual and those of the public. Thus, the real issue here is whether it was irrational for the Village, in striking that balance, to consider a nonfinancial interest of the individual owners—the individual's interest in not being displaced involuntarily.

It is significant that the six properties involved here are residential. In our previous cases dealing with amortization, we have focused almost exclusively on commercial properties, where the owner's interest is easily reduced to financial considerations. The same may not be true for the owners of residential properties, especially in instances where the property is the primary residence of the owner. Simply being able to recoup one's financial investment may be a secondary concern to staying in a neighborhood or remaining on a particular piece of land. Indeed, when mobile homes are involved, there may actually be little or no financial loss, given that the owner often will be able to relocate the structure and sell the land for legal development. Here, rather than focusing solely on financial recoupment, the Village apparently took a broader view of "an individual's interest in maintaining the present use" of the property (see, Modjeska Sign Studios v. Berle, 43 NY2d 468, 479). It enacted a law that allowed owners to keep their mobile homes in place until they decided to sell, even though they may have recouped their investment long ago. By doing so, it saved the owners from a forced relocation at the end of a predetermined amortization period set by the Village. Defendant has not demonstrated why such an approach is irrational or explained why a municipality should be barred constitutionally from considering the nonfinancial interests of the owners in setting an amortization schedule. Thus, on this motion for summary judgment and the present record, defendant has failed to overcome the presumption of the law's validity and prove, as she must, unconstitutionality beyond a reasonable doubt. . . .

Defendant's second argument is premised on the "fundamental rule that zoning deals basically with land use and not with the person who owns or occupies it" (Matter of Dexter v. Town Bd., 36 NY2d 102, 105). In essence, the rule is a prohibition against *ad hominem* zoning decisions. In *Dexter,* for instance, a zoning change needed to allow a supermarket was to be effective only if a certain corporation developed the site. We voided the action on the ground that the identity of the site's owner was irrelevant to its suitability for a certain type of development. Likewise, variances to accommodate the personal physical needs of the occupants have been denied on the basis that such needs are unrelated to land use (see Matter of Fuhst v. Foley, 45 NY2d 441). In the present case, defendant claims that the Village's amortization scheme is similarly personal in that the right to the nonconforming use is enjoyed only by those who owned the property in 1968 and cannot be transferred.

Defendant misconstrues the nature of the prohibition against *ad hominem* zoning. The hallmark of cases like *Dexter* and *Fuhst* is that an identifiable individual is singled out for special treatment in land use regulation. No such individualized treatment is involved in the present case. All similarly situated owners are treated identically. . . .

In fact, what defendant is actually arguing is that the Village should not be allowed to infringe on an owner's ability to transfer the right to continue a nonconforming use. It is true that, in the absence of amortization legislation, the right to continue a nonconforming use runs with the land. However, once a valid amortization scheme is enacted, the right ends at the termination of the amortization period. As a practical matter, that means the owner of record during the amortization period will enjoy a right that cannot be transferred to a subsequent owner once the period passes. In such circumstances, the law is not rendered invalid because the original owner no longer has a right to transfer or because the original owner and subsequent owners have received disparate treatment under the land use regulations. . . .

Thus, we conclude that defendant has failed to prevail on her facial challenge to the Village law. As to the remaining issues raised, further factual development is necessary. . . .

Notes & Questions

1. What is the legal justification in *Village of Valatie* for requiring the village to allow the nonconforming use to continue? The court notes at the outset of its decision that the policy of allowing an amortization period "originated in concerns that the application of land use regulations to uses existing prior to the regulations' enactment might be construed as confiscatory and unconstitutional." But the court subsequently suggests that prohibiting the use of a mobile home may involve "little or no financial loss" because a landowner can sell or relocate the mobile home and then develop her property for other uses. If the constitutional takings protections and concerns about confiscation do not require allowing the mobile home to remain in use for a period of time, what does? Does the decision in *Village of Valatie* rest on general notions of due process?

2. **Amortization.** What is a reasonable amortization period where the nonconforming structure is not a mobile home that can be readily moved? Statutory amortization periods can be as short as one or two

years—typically for nonconforming uses—and as long as fifty or sixty years—typically for nonconforming structures. Courts will generally approve an amortization period if it is sufficiently long to enable the landowner to recover all or most of her original investment.

> The distinction between an ordinance restricting future uses and one requiring the termination of present uses within a reasonable period of time is merely one of degree, and constitutionality depends on the relative importance to be given to the public gain and to the private loss. Zoning as it affects every piece of property is to some extent retroactive in that it applies to property already owned at the time of the effective date of the ordinance. The elimination of existing uses within a reasonable time does not amount to a taking of property.... Use of a reasonable amortization scheme provides an equitable means of reconciliation of the conflicting interests in satisfaction of due process requirements. As a method of eliminating existing nonconforming uses it allows the owner of the nonconforming use, by affording an opportunity to make new plans, at least partially to offset any loss he might suffer.... If the amortization period is reasonable the loss to the owner may be small when compared with the benefit to the public.

City of Los Angeles v. Gage, 274 P.2d 34, 44 (Cal. App. 1954). What factors should a court consider in determining whether an amortization period is reasonable?

3. Not all courts approve of amortization periods. Some courts have rejected amortization and required local governments to protect nonconforming uses and structures indefinitely. In their view forcing a landowner to end his or her nonconforming use after a specified number of years still cuts too deeply into property rights:

> To our knowledge, no one has, as yet, been so brash as to contend that such a pre-existing lawful nonconforming use properly might be terminated *immediately*. In fact, the contrary is implicit in the amortization technique itself which would validate a taking *presently* unconstitutional by the simple expedient of *postponing* such taking for a "reasonable" time.... [I]t would be a strange and novel doctrine indeed which would approve a municipality taking private property for public use without compensation if the property was not too valuable and the taking was not too soon ...

Hoffmann v. Kinealy, 389 S.W.2d 745, 753 (Mo. 1965). See also PA Northwestern Distributors, Inc. v. Zoning Hearing Bd., 584 A.2d 1372 (Pa. 1991). In some cases, state statutes appear to preclude amortization. See, e.g., Ariz. Rev. Stat. Ann. § 9–462.02 (zoning authority shall not affect preexisting uses or structures). If the state enabling statute is silent regarding nonconforming uses, is amortization permissible? See State v. Bates, 305 N.W.2d 426 (Iowa 1981) (no).

4. As property owners get toward the end of an amortization period, they are likely to put little money into maintaining and repairing nonconforming structures. Few landowners want to pour money into a structure when they will soon need to tear it down. The result can be a public eyesore or worse. Are there any ways to avoid this problem?

5. **Changes or Increases in Use.** Most courts also prohibit the owner of a nonconforming use from changing or increasing the use. Changes or increases in use can increase any harm to the local neighborhood from the nonconforming use. Changes in use also sometimes extend the economic life of the use, lengthening the period of time during which the local government must tolerate the nonconforming use. What, however, is a change in use for purposes of the prohibition? In Belleville v. Parrillo's, Inc., 416 A.2d 388 (N.J. 1980), a nonconforming restaurant with a dance floor and live bands hired a DJ, added "psychedelic" and mirrored lighting, and started advertising itself as a discothetique. The transformation was extremely effective, and the disco became very popular. Lines outside the establishment grew with the volume of the music, and neighbors started to complain. The New Jersey Supreme Court held that the transformation constituted a substantial change and therefore was impermissible. "The entire character of the business has been altered. What was once a restaurant is now a dancehall. Measured by the zoning ordinance the general welfare of the neighborhood has been demonstrably affected adversely by the conversion of defendant's business. Our strong public policy restricting nonconforming uses requires" that the new use be prohibited.

Are there any circumstances under which courts should allow changes in a nonconforming use? See Adolphson v. Zoning Board of Appeals, 535 A.2d 799 (Conn. 1988) (allowing the owner of an aluminum casting foundary to change to an automobile repair shop—a "less offensive" use).

6. **Remodeling and Repairs.** Should courts permit the owners of nonconforming structures to repair or remodel the structures, even though that may increase the life of the structure? What types of restrictions, if any, should be placed on remodeling or repairs? See Ariz. Rev. Stat. Ann. § 9–462.02 (authorizing "reasonable repairs or alterations"). Should courts permit a manufacturing facility to make significant modifications to its plant in order to come into compliance with pollution laws—or refuse to permit the modifications in which case the plant must either close down or operate illegally?

7. **Destruction.** Most states provide that, if a nonconforming structure burns down or is otherwise destroyed, it cannot be rebuilt. What, however, if the structure is seriously damaged but not totally destroyed? For example, what if an earthquake causes serious structural damage that would require substantial repair work, but the walls of the building are still standing? See Ruby v. Carlisle Zoning Hearing Bd., 488 A.2d 655 (Pa. Commw. Ct. 1985) (local ordinance that terminated nonconforming structures upon damage to 50 percent of the structure was unconstitutional).

8. **Abandonment.** If a property owner stops using his land for a nonconforming use, should he be able to restart the use in the future? Most

courts hold that "abandonment" ends nonconforming uses, but this leaves open the question of what constitutes abandonment. Should intent to abandon the nonconforming use, for example, be required? If so, what evidence of intent should a court require? See Stokes v. Board of Permit Appeals, 61 Cal. Rptr. 2d 181 (Ct. App. 1997) (closure of gay bathhouse for seven years, combined with application to convert to a homeless shelter, constituted intentional abandonment).

2. Vested Rights

Western Land Equities, Inc. v. City of Logan

Supreme Court of Utah, 1980.
617 P.2d 388.

Stewart, Justice.

Defendants appeal from a ruling of the district court that the City of Logan unlawfully withheld approval of plaintiffs' proposed residential plan and was estopped from enforcing a zoning change that prohibits plaintiffs' proposed use. We affirm the trial court's order.

In February 1969 plaintiffs purchased 18.53 acres of property within the City of Logan. In April 1976, pursuant to a new land use ordinance, the property was zoned M–1, a manufacturing zone which permitted single-family dwellings. Plaintiffs' intent was to use the property for moderately priced single-family housing.

The procedure for securing approval of single-family residential subdivisions is established by city ordinance. The ordinance requires consultation with the city planning commission, preparation and submittal of a preliminary plan showing compliance with minimum requirements of the subdivision ordinance, and approval of both preliminary and final plans by the city planning commission. The planning commission's practice is to introduce the preliminary plan at one meeting ("first reading") and discuss its merits and take action in a second meeting. Plaintiffs' project was introduced on July 13, 1977; the second reading was scheduled for August 10, at which time the advisability of the residential development was questioned and the matter was tabled and referred to the municipal council. On August 18, the municipal council reviewed the matter and referred it back to the planning commission with a recommendation that protective covenants be drawn up and that more roadways in and out of the proposed subdivision be provided. The second reading of the preliminary plan occurred before the planning commission on September 14, and the matter was tabled for 60 days. On October 12 the planning commission went on record as opposing subdivisions in M–1 zones, and on November 9 the commission rejected the proposed subdivision on the following grounds:

(1) Development of the proposed residential subdivision was contrary to the land use ordinance and to the city's master plan;

(2) The access roads provided by the plan were inadequate;

(3) The location of the railroad on three sides of the proposed subdivision made it an inappropriate site for housing.

In November plaintiffs unsuccessfully appealed the decision of the planning commission to the municipal council, and in December plaintiffs filed a complaint in district court. A restraining order was issued on January 3, 1978, enjoining the city from amending its zoning ordinance. The injunction was lifted on April 18, 1978, at which time a change in the zoning ordinance that had been enacted on January 19, 1978, became effective as it applied to plaintiffs' property. . . .

The trial court in its findings of fact and conclusions of law held that plaintiffs' proposed development was permissible under the zoning regulations in existence prior to January 31, 1978, that plaintiffs had substantially complied with procedural requirements and had a vested right to develop the proposed subdivision, and that defendants were estopped from withholding approval of plaintiffs' subdivision on the basis of the amended ordinance enacted after the application for subdivision approval had been submitted.

On appeal defendants argue that . . . the application for approval of a subdivision does not create vested rights in the owner which immunize him from subsequent zoning changes. Since the decision of the court below was based on a finding that plaintiffs did have such a vested right, . . . we deal only with the issue of whether the amendment to the zoning ordinance enacted by the city could be retroactively applied to plaintiffs' application for subdivision approval.

It is established that an owner of property holds it subject to zoning ordinances enacted pursuant to a state's police power. Euclid v. Ambler Realty Co., 272 U.S. 365 (1926). With various exceptions legislative enactments, other than those defining criminal offenses, are not generally subject to the constitutional prohibitions against retroactive application. The legality of retroactive civil legislation is tested by general principles of fairness and by due process considerations.

This Court has previously dealt with the issue of retroactive application of zoning laws in Contracts Funding & Mortgage Exchange v. Maynes, Utah, 527 P.2d 1073 (1974). In *Contracts Funding* the plaintiff arranged to purchase property which was unzoned, and the application to construct mobile homes on the property was conditionally approved. Following a period of further review, during which time the objections of neighbors were considered, the building permit was denied, and soon thereafter a zoning ordinance was passed which excluded plaintiff's proposed use. This Court held that the date of application for a building permit fixed the applicable zoning laws and that the application could not be denied on the basis of a subsequently-enacted ordinance. There was no contention in that case that there were countervailing public interests that outweighed the right of the property owner to use his land pursuant to the law in effect at the time of application for a permit.

The holding of *Contracts Funding* is not in accord with the rule generally accepted in other jurisdictions that an applicant for a building permit or subdivision approval does not acquire any vested right under existing zoning regulations prior to the issuance of the permit or official approval of a proposed subdivision. Generally, denial of an application may be based on subsequently-enacted zoning regulations. See 8 McQuillin, Municipal Corporations § 25.155 (1976); 1 Anderson, American Law of Zoning § 6.23 2d ed. (1976).

However, for the reasons discussed below, we are of the view that the majority rule fails to strike a proper balance between public and private interests and opens the area to so many variables as to result in unnecessary litigation. We hold instead that an applicant for subdivision approval or a building permit is entitled to favorable action if the application conforms to the zoning ordinance in effect at the time of the application, unless changes in the zoning ordinances are pending which would prohibit the use applied for, or unless the municipality can show a compelling reason for exercising its police power retroactively to the date of application.

In the present case, the trial court found that plaintiffs had acquired a vested development right by their substantial compliance with procedural requirements and that the city was estopped from withholding approval of the proposed subdivision. The court used the language of zoning estoppel, a principle that is widely followed. That principle estops a government entity from exercising its zoning powers to prohibit a proposed land use when a property owner, relying reasonably and in good faith on some governmental act or omission, has made a substantial change in position or incurred such extensive obligations or expenses that it would be highly inequitable to deprive the owner of his right to complete his proposed development.

The focus of zoning estoppel is primarily upon the conduct and interests of the property owner. The main inquiry is whether there has been substantial reliance by the owner on governmental actions related to the superseded zoning that permitted the proposed use. The concern underlying this approach is the economic hardship that would be imposed on a property owner whose development plans are thwarted. Some courts hold that before a permit is issued no action of the owner is sufficient reliance to bar application of changes in zoning ordinances because there has been no governmental act sufficient to support an estoppel. Accordingly, a landowner is held to have no vested right in existing or anticipated zoning. Avco Community Developers, Inc. v. South Coast Regional Comm'n, 17 Cal. 3d 785, 132 Cal. Rptr. 386, 553 P.2d 546 (1976). Other courts consider any substantial change of position in determining the estoppel issue. This Court in Wood v. North Salt Lake, 15 Utah 2d 245, 390 P.2d 858 (1964), held a zoning ordinance change requiring larger lots unenforceable because water mains and sewer connections had already been provided for lots that conformed in size to a previous ordinance. The Court stated that enforcement of the new ordinance in those circumstances would be unfair and inequitable.

Generally, "substantial reliance" is determined by various tests employed by the courts—for example, the set quantum test, the proportionate test, and a balancing test. The set quantum test, used by the majority of courts, determines that an owner is entitled to relief from new, prohibitory zoning if he has changed his position beyond a certain point, measured quantitatively. A related test is the proportionate test, which determines the percentage of money spent or obligations incurred before the zoning change as compared with the total cost. The problem with both of these tests is that there is no predictable point short of adjudication which separates reliance that is less than "substantial" from the reliance sufficient to result in a vested right or to support an estoppel.

The balancing test, although likely to produce a more fair outcome in a particular case, also results in little predictability. The test weighs the owner's interest in developing his property and the reasonableness of his proposed use against the interests of public health, safety, morals, or general welfare. If the gain to the public is small when compared to the hardship that would accrue to the property owner, the actions of the owner in preparation for development according to a formerly permitted use may be seen as sufficiently substantial to justify the issuance of a permit or continuation of development despite an amendment to the zoning ordinances.

An additional requirement generally considered in zoning estoppel cases is that of the existence of some physical construction as an element of substantial reliance. Preconstruction activities such as the execution of architectural drawings or the clearing of land and widening of roads are not sufficient to create a vested right, nor generally are activities that are not exclusively related to the proposed project. Fairlawns Cemetery Ass'n v. Zoning Comm'n, 138 Conn. 434, 86 A.2d 74 (1952); F.L.D. Construction Corp. v. Walsh, 357 N.Y.S.2d 112, 45 A.D.2d 832 (1974); Edelbeck v. Town of Theresa, 57 Wis. 2d 172, 203 N.W.2d 694 (1973).

If the substantial reliance requirement of zoning estoppel were applied to the facts of the present case, we could not agree with the trial court that plaintiffs' "substantial compliance" with procedural requirements justified the estoppel of the city's enforcement of a new zoning ordinance. Although plaintiffs allege they proceeded with subdivision plans and incurred significant costs with the encouragement of certain city officials, they had not yet received official approval of their plan, and their expenditures were merely for surveying and preliminary plans. The record indicates that plaintiffs spent $1,335 for a boundary survey and $890 for the preparation of a preliminary subdivision plat. The boundary survey has value regardless of the city's approval or disapproval of the plaintiffs' proposal. The expenditure of $890 for the plat is not significant in relation to the size of the parcel and is not substantial enough to justify an estoppel with regard to the enforcement of valid zoning ordinances that became effective before official approval of plaintiffs' proposed subdivision....

Courts in several states have adopted the view, not unlike that stated in Contracts Funding & Mortgage Exchange v. Maynes, Utah, 527 P.2d

1073 (1974), that an application for a building permit creates a vested right as of the time of application.... In Ready-to-Pour, Inc. v. McCoy, 95 Idaho 510, 511 P.2d 792 (1973), the [Idaho Supreme] court ruled that the elimination of an industrial zone after an applicant had sought a building permit for erection of a concrete batch plant did not alter the applicant's right to a building permit. The zoning change was found to be confiscatory, arbitrary, and capricious. The court upheld the applicant's right to a permit to build in a formerly authorized industrial district and stated, "People are entitled to rely upon the law." [511 P.2d at 797.] The applicant in the case had purchased its property in reliance on the city council's previous action in creating the industrial district and was held to be entitled to a permit to proceed.

In Pure Oil Division v. City of Columbia, 254 S.C. 28, 173 S.E.2d 140 (1970), the South Carolina court stated that in the absence of "intervening considerations of public necessity,"

> we see no sound reason to protect vested rights acquired after a permit is issued, and to deny such protection to similar rights acquired under an ordinance as it existed at the time a proper application for a permit is made. In both instances, the right protected is the same, that is, the good faith reliance by the owner on the right to use his property as permitted under the Zoning Ordinance in force at the time of the application for a permit. [173 S.E.2d at 143.]

The State of Washington has also refused to follow the general rule that building permits are not protected against revocation by subsequent zoning change unless a permittee has gained a vested right through a substantial change in position in reliance on the permit. As stated in Hull v. Hunt, 53 Wash. 2d 125, 331 P.2d 856, 859 (1958):

> Notwithstanding the weight of authority, we prefer to have a date certain upon which the right vests to construct in accordance with the building permit. We prefer not to adopt a rule which forces the court to search through "the moves and countermoves of ... parties ... by way of passing ordinance and bringing actions for injunctions"—to which may be added the stalling or acceleration of administrative action in the issuance of permits—to find that date upon which the substantial change of position is made which finally vests the right. The more practical rule to administer, we feel, is that the right vests when the party, property owner or not, applies for his building permit, if that permit is thereafter issued. This rule, of course, assumes that the permit applied for and granted be consistent with the zoning ordinances and building codes in force at the time of application for the permit.

The court met the argument that its rule would result in speculation in building permits by noting that the cost of preparing plans and meeting permit requirements was such that an applicant would generally have a good faith expectation of proceeding according to his application, and, furthermore, that the city building code renders a permit null and void if work authorized by the permit does not commence within 180 days. . . .

In our view the tests employed by most other jurisdictions tend to subject landowners to undue and even calamitous expense because of changing city councils or zoning boards or their dilatory action and to the unpredictable results of burdensome litigation. The majority rule permits an unlimited right to deny permits when ordinances are amended after application and preliminary work. It allows government in many cases broader power with regard to land regulation than may be justified by the public interests involved. A balancing test, though geared toward promoting fairness, must be applied on a case-by-case basis and offers no predictable guidelines on which landowners can intelligently base their decisions regarding extensive development projects. Tests currently followed by the majority of states are particularly unsatisfactory in dealing with the large multistage projects. The threat of denial of a permit at a late stage of development makes a developer vulnerable to shifting governmental policies and tempts him to manipulate the process by prematurely engaging in activities that would establish the substantial reliance required to vest his right to develop when inappropriate.

The economic waste that occurs when a project is halted after substantial costs have been incurred in its commencement is of no benefit either to the public or to landowners. In a day when housing costs have severely escalated beyond the means of many prospective buyers, governmental actions should not be based on policies that exacerbate a severe economic problem without compelling justification. Governmental powers should be exercised in a manner that is reasonable and, to the extent possible, predictable.

On the other hand, a rule which vests a right unconditionally at the time application for a permit is made affords no protection for important public interests that may legitimately require interference with planned private development. If a proposal met zoning requirements at the time of application but seriously threatens public health, safety, or welfare, the interests of the public should not be thwarted.

The above competing interests are best accommodated in our view by adopting the rule that an applicant is entitled to a building permit or subdivision approval if his proposed development meets the zoning requirements in existence at the time of his application and if he proceeds with reasonable diligence, absent a compelling, countervailing public interest. Furthermore, if a city or county has initiated proceedings to amend its zoning ordinances, a landowner who subsequently makes application for a permit is not entitled to rely on the original zoning classification. . . .

In the present case, the zoning of the property in question was found by the trial court to have permitted the proposed use at the time of the application. The owners had received encouragement from city officials, although no official approval was rendered. After the application, the city council members decided to reexamine the pertinent zoning regulation and thereafter voted to amend or "clarify" the zoning ordinance to disallow subdivisions in an M–1 zone and permit residences only by special permit. Their actions may have had a reasonable basis. It was argued that fire protection would be undermined because of limited access roads, but it does not appear the problem would be any less serious if the unarguably-permitted manufacturing facilities were erected instead of single-family houses. Objections as to inadequate sidewalks and other problems can be handled by requiring modification of specifications that do not meet city subdivision requirements. Indeed, the order of the trial court stated that the developers must comply with all the reasonable requirements of the city's subdivision ordinance.

We do not find the reasons given by the city for withholding approval of plaintiffs' proposed subdivision to be so compelling as to overcome the presumption that an applicant for a building permit or subdivision approval is entitled to affirmative official action if he meets the zoning requirements in force at the time of his application.

Notes & Questions

1. Once construction of an improvement is completed in compliance with an applicable zoning ordinance, the rules respecting prior nonconforming structures and uses protect the improvement and its permitted uses against zoning changes. Courts in most states have adopted the doctrine of *vested rights* to protect developers from changes in zoning and other land use controls that arise before construction is finished. In deciding whether a developer enjoys a vested right, most courts focus on two factors: the extent to which the developer has obtained the required governmental approvals, up to and including the final building permit, and the extent to which the developer has irretrievably committed time and money in good faith reliance on the existing zoning.

Judicial treatment of these two factors varies widely. Some courts, like the Utah Supreme Court in *Western Land Equities*, do not require a developer to have obtained any permits, while others ignore even the issuance of a final building permit. Some courts require good faith expenditures on the actual construction of improvements, while others credit expenditures made on planning alone or do not require any expenditures at all. Most courts require that a developer have made substantial planning expenditures in reliance on a building permit or its equivalent in order to have a vested right to continue. *Western Land Equities*, by contrast, provides for very early vesting by requiring only that the property owner have applied for a building permit before the zoning change. How should courts balance the competing interests of the property owner, who has acted in good faith reliance on existing zoning law, and the interests of the public in the zoning changes? See generally Daniel R. Mandelker, Land Use Law §§ 6.12–6.22 (5th ed. 2003).

2. What are the legal grounds for protecting a developer from zoning changes that occur before construction is complete? See Valley View Industrial Park v. City of Redmond, 733 P.2d 182 (Wash. 1987) (due process

"requires governments to treat citizens in a fundamentally fair manner"). In some states, statutes protect developers from zoning changes that occur during the planning and construction of improvements. Texas, for example, provides that the laws in effect at the time of the first application for development "shall be the sole basis for consideration of all subsequent permits required for the completion of the project." Tex. Local Gov't Code Ann. § 245.002.

3. Is there a principled distinction between the rule that categorically permits prior nonconforming structures to continue, and the rule that a developer can continue building a nonconforming structure only if she has relied on a building permit or equivalent permit issued before the change in zoning? Is it fair or efficient to allow the developer who completes her building before rezoning to continue occupying it, while requiring her counterpart, whom the rezoning fortuitously catches in the middle of development, to scrap his investment?

4. **Zoning Estoppel.** As the Utah Supreme Court notes, the doctrine of vested rights is closely related to the principle of *zoning estoppel*. Some courts hold that local governments are estopped from applying a zoning change to a property owner who has substantially changed her position or incurred significant expenses in good faith reliance on an act or omission of the government, on the ground that it would be "highly inequitable and unjust." Town of Largo v. Imperial Homes Corp., 309 So. 2d 571, 573 (Fla. Dist. Ct. App. 1975). See generally Richard B. Cunningham & David H. Kremer, Vested Rights, Estoppel, and the Land Development Process, 29 Hastings L.J. 625 (1978).

5. **Mistakes.** If a local official mistakenly grants a building permit in violation of an applicable zoning ordinance, may the municipality, once it discovers the mistake, revoke the permit and require the developer to remove any improvements built in reliance on it? As a general rule, the answer is that the municipality can revoke the permit. See, e.g., Pettitt v. City of Fresno, 110 Cal. Rptr. 262, 268 (Cal. App. 1973) (to prevent a city from revoking the permit "would not punish the City but it would assuredly injure the area residents, who in no way can be held responsible for the City's mistake"). Some courts, however, hold that the developer has acquired a vested right in the improvement erected under the illegal permit. See Petrosky v. Zoning Hearing Board of Upper Chichester Township, 402 A.2d 1385 (Pa. 1979).

The decisions in these cases have a "damned if you do, damned if you don't" character. To hold that the municipality is not estopped penalizes the developer who has relied to her detriment on an authoritative governmental act. But to hold that the municipality is estopped penalizes the neighbors who must live with any nonconforming structure and use. Would it be better in these cases to allow the municipality to revoke the permit and require the developer to remove any illegal improvement, but also to require that the municipality indemnify the developer for any losses suffered? Such an approach would make the developer whole and would give the municipality an incentive to be more careful in its issuance of permits. Would nuisance law's gravity-utility calculus (see page 134) offer a useful approach to this problem—balancing the costs to the developer of compliance against the cost to neighbors of noncompliance?

D. FLEXIBILITY IN ZONING

1. ADMINISTRATIVE CHANGES—VARIANCES AND SPECIAL EXCEPTIONS

North Shore Steak House, Inc. v. Board of Appeals

Court of Appeals of New York, 1972.
282 N.E.2d 606.

BURKE, Judge.

In this article 78 proceeding, appellant North Shore Steak House, Inc. (hereafter North Shore) seeks to review a decision of the Board of Appeals of the Village of Thomaston (hereafter the Board) denying North Shore's application for: (1) a special exception permit to extend its parking area, on its split zoned lot, 25 feet into a single-family residence district, and (2) a hardship variance permitting accessory parking on the residentially zoned property beyond the 25–foot strip.

North Shore is the lessee of a plot of land used for a restaurant on the northwest corner of Northern Boulevard and Summer Street, in the Village of Thomaston in Great Neck, Long Island. The lease term is from May 1, 1961 to February 28, 2003. The premises front 181 feet on Northern Boulevard, a heavily traveled State highway, and have a depth of 286 feet along Summer Street. The zoning map provides that the Business "B" District has a depth of 200 feet and, therefore, the lot is split zoned, the rear 86 feet being in Residence "B" District zoned for single-family homes. The plot has been in single and separate ownership since 1903 and is improved with a main building, used as a restaurant since 1940, and an old stable, in the back of the premises, approximately 5 feet from the rear line.

All available space within the 200 feet business district has been blacktopped for parking during the past nine years. North Shore has made two small extensions to the main building which did not increase the seating capacity but did result in the loss of several parking spaces. The restaurant has seats for 170 people at the tables and an additional 18 at the bar. At present, there are parking spaces for 75 to 85 cars.

In December, 1969, North Shore, joined by the owner-lessor, Herman Weinman, made an application for a special exception permit, pursuant to article X (§ 3) of the Zoning Ordinance, which states:

> Section 3. They *may* in appropriate cases, after public notice and hearing, and subject to appropriate conditions and safeguards, and in harmony with the general purpose and intent of this ordinance, in addition to the powers and duties set forth in the

Village Law of the State of New York and such powers as are heretofore in this ordinance given to them:

(e) Where a zone boundary line divides a lot in single ownership at the effective date of this ordinance affecting a use district, as the case may be, permit a use authorized on either portion of such lot to extend to the entire lot, but not more than twenty-five (25) feet beyond the boundary line of the greater restricted zone. [Emphasis supplied.]

In addition, the application sought a variance for the balance of the rear 86 feet beyond the 25–foot strip, except for a 50–foot by 100–foot plot on the northeast corner, to be improved with a new one-family house fronting on Summer Street.

In rejecting the application for a variance, the Board found, among others, that (1) the premises were not unique or different from other split zoned property in the village (2) that the hardship, if any, was self-created (3) that the evidence that the variance would have an adverse effect on the adjoining property was not rebutted and (4) that a ratio of one car to every three or four seats is all that should be reasonably required. Based on these findings, the Board also concluded, without any additional findings or conditions, that the special exception permit "would not be in harmony with the general purpose and intent of the zoning plan and scheme."....

On this record, it cannot be said that the hardship variance was improperly denied. It was sought for accessory parking on the northwest corner of the property (measuring approximately 61 feet by 81 feet) beyond the 25–foot special exception area and next to the 50–foot by 100–foot plot on the northeast corner on which the owner-lessor planned to erect a new, conforming one-family house fronting on Summer Street. North Shore's contention, no doubt true, that this plot is more valuable as accessory parking is insufficient to warrant a hardship variance since the property, located in a residential zone, may be reasonably employed for that use as evidenced by the proposed new house on the adjoining parcel.

The denial of the special exception permit, based on factual findings used to support denial of the variance, ignores the fundamental difference between a variance and a special exception permit. A variance is an authority to a property owner to use property in a manner forbidden by the ordinance while a special exception allows the property owner to put his property to a use expressly permitted by the ordinance. The inclusion of the permitted use in the ordinance is tantamount to a legislative finding that the permitted use is in harmony with the general zoning plan and will not adversely affect the neighborhood. Denial of the permit on the ground that the extension of the parking lot 25 feet into the residential zone is "not ... in harmony with the general purpose and intent of the zoning plan" is, thus, patently inconsistent.

The burden of proof on an applicant for a special exception permit is much lighter than that required for a hardship variance. It does not require the applicant to show that it has been denied any reasonable use of the property but only that the use is contemplated by the ordinance subject only to "conditions" attached to its use to minimize its impact on the surrounding area. North Shore has met that burden. The president of North Shore testified that 22 parking spaces are needed for employees' cars. Despite the employment of parking attendants at all times, a severe shortage of parking space exists at peak dining periods on weekends. A 25–foot by 81–foot extension would accommodate approximately 25 to 30 more cars. Because of congestion in the parking lot, cars tend to back up on Summer Street waiting to get into the parking area. This problem is further aggravated by the fact that a median was installed on Northern Boulevard three years ago preventing traffic traveling eastward from turning left into the driveway on Northern Boulevard. Instead, the traffic must proceed to Summer Street and make a left turn, adding to the congestion there.

The Board's expert, Mr. Reuter, conceded that North Shore had a parking problem and the restaurant needs 100 parking spaces. He admitted that there was an adjacent water tower, 80 feet to 100 feet tall, but declined to estimate the impact of the tower on residential values. In addition, he admitted that Briggs Auto Leasing had been issued a permit to extend a large parking area beyond the 200–foot business district on a plot less than two blocks from the restaurant and that the Methodist Church fronting on Northern Boulevard in the vicinity had parking well beyond the 200–foot line without harm to anyone. He, nonetheless, concluded that granting the permit would adversely affect property values and generate more traffic on Northern Boulevard.

In view of the changes which have already taken place in the immediate area, there is no basis for the conclusion that the addition of parking spaces for 25 or 30 cars, to be used primarily on weekends, will adversely affect property values or greatly increase traffic in the area. On the contrary, the uncontroverted evidence is that granting of the permit will have a beneficial impact by relieving traffic on Summer Street during peak dining hours while preventing any spillback onto heavily traveled Northern Boulevard by cars traveling eastward and unable to enter the front entrance of the parking lot. Nor does there appear to be any reasonable basis for the conclusion that the additional cars will increase noise or gas fumes in the immediate area, since North Shore has agreed to provide a 10–foot screen of shrubs or trees at the rear of the extension to protect the neighboring residences. Absent any support in the record for the conclusions advanced by the Board justifying the denial, and in view of the "erroneous standard" used, namely that applicable to a hardship variance, the decision of the Board with respect to the special permit, must be deemed arbitrary and capricious....

In sum, North Shore has advanced sufficient proof of compliance with the ordinance justifying issuance of the special permit by the Board. The testimony of North Shore is virtually uncontroverted. As a result it would appear there is no room for the exercise of discretion on the part of the Board and no purpose would be served by remanding the matter for further hearings.

Accordingly the order of the Appellate Division should be modified to the extent of reversing the denial of the special exception permit and directing the Board to issue the permit subject to any reasonable conditions it deems appropriate and the remainder of the order insofar as it denied the application for a use variance should be affirmed.

Notes & Questions

1. What difference in standards does *North Shore* suggest local boards of adjustment and zoning appeals should observe in acting on applications for variances and applications for special exceptions? Should courts apply a different standard in reviewing these two types of administrative decisions? Should there be any difference between the standard that administrative agencies apply in determining whether to grant a variance and the standard that courts apply in determining whether a zoning ordinance is unconstitutional as applied to a particular parcel?

2. In rejecting North Shore's application, the Village Board of Appeals relied in part on the ground that the applicant's hardship, if any, "was self-created" because North Shore had acquired its parcel knowing of the applicable zoning restriction. This disqualification finds some scattered support in judicial decisions. See, e.g., Abel v. Zoning Board of Appeals, 374 A.2d 227 (Conn. 1977). Does the "self-created hardship" disqualification make sense? Say that your client, John Muir, wishes to buy Greenacre from Caroline Nichols Churchill to develop a mobile home park. At the time Churchill acquired the parcel, it was zoned to allow mobile home parks, but the parcel has since been rezoned to prohibit them. Under the self-created hardship rule, Muir would be barred from obtaining a variance, but Churchill would not, and you would probably advise Muir to condition his purchase of Greenacre on Churchill's obtaining the necessary variance. (The value of the variance to Muir would doubtless be reflected in the purchase price.) Does this suggest that the only effect of the self-created hardship rule is to shift the risk of not obtaining a variance from the buyer, who acquires after the rezoning, to the seller who acquired before the rezoning? Who—seller or buyer—has better access to the information needed to pursue the administrative action?

3. **Variances.** Variances, authorized by the 1926 Standard State Zoning Enabling Act, represent the earliest administrative device for flexing the rigid framework of Euclidean zoning. As noted earlier, the SZEA gives boards of adjustment the power to "authorize, upon appeal in specific cases, such variance from the terms of the ordinance as will not be contrary to the public interest, where, owing to special conditions, a literal enforcement of the provisions of the ordinance will result in unnecessary hardship, and so that the spirit of the ordinance shall be observed and substantial justice done." U.S. Dept. of Commerce, Standard State Zoning Enabling Act § 7(3) (rev. ed. 1926).

How and by what standard should "unnecessary hardship" be measured? Courts have historically demanded a showing of exceptional hardship. According to the New Jersey Supreme Court in Commons v. Westwood Zoning Bd. of Adjustment, 410 A.2d 1138, 1142 (N.J. 1980), for example, undue hardship "involves the underlying notion that no effective use can be made of the property in the event the variance is denied." Some courts have more recently begun to move to less restrictive standards for variances. According to the New Hampshire Supreme Court, for example,

> Inevitably and necessarily there is a tension between zoning ordinances and property rights, as courts balance the right of citizens to the enjoyment of private property with the right of municipalities to restrict property use. In this balancing process, constitutional property rights must be respected and protected from unreasonable zoning restrictions. . . .
>
> We believe our definition of unnecessary hardship has become too restrictive in light of the constitutional protections by which it must be tempered. In consideration of these protections, therefore, we depart today from the restrictive approach that has defined unnecessary hardship and adopt an approach more considerate of the constitutional right to enjoy property. Henceforth, applicants for a variance may establish unnecessary hardship by proof that: (1) a zoning restriction as applied to their property interferes with their reasonable use of the property, considering the unique setting of the property in its environment; (2) no fair and substantial relationship exists between the general purposes of the zoning ordinance and the specific restriction on the property; and (3) the variance would not injure the public or private rights of others.

Simplex Technologies v. Town of Newington, 766 A.2d 713, 716–717 (N.H. 2001).

Should it matter whether the property owner is seeking a *use variance* (i.e., the right to use the property in a way not permitted by local zoning laws) or an *area variance* (i.e., the right to deviate from non-use restrictions such as limits on height, size, density, or lot coverage)? Some states explicitly prohibit or limit the granting of use variances. See, e.g., Cal. Gov't Code § 65906 (prohibiting use variances); N.J. Stat. Ann. § 40:55D–70 (requiring a super-majority vote of the board of adjustment for use variances). Many courts, moreover, require a higher showing of hardship in the case of use variances than for area variances. See, e.g., State v. Waushara County Bd. of Adjustment, 679 N.W.2d 514 (Wis. 2004); Consolidated Edison Co. v. Hoffman, 374 N.E.2d 105 (N.Y. 1978) (requiring "unnecessary hardship" in the case of use variances, but only "practical difficulties" in the case of area variances). Is there any real difference between use variances and area variances? Should courts instead consider the relative impact of each individual variance, no matter how characterized, on the public interest?

3. **Special Exceptions (sometimes called Conditional Uses).** Like variances, special exceptions seek to make zoning more flexible. Yet, as indicated in *North Shore,* the two devices rest on different premises.

Variances aim to protect landowners from economic hardship. Special exceptions, by contrast,

> are designed to meet the problem which arises where certain uses, although generally compatible with the basic use classification of a particular zone, should not be permitted to be located as a matter of right in every area included within the zone because of hazards inherent in the use itself or special problems which its proposed location may present. By this device, certain uses (e.g., gasoline service stations, electric substations, hospitals, schools, churches, country clubs, and the like) which may be considered essentially desirable to the community, but which should not be authorized generally in a particular zone because of considerations such as current and anticipated traffic congestion, population density, noise, effect on adjoining land values, or other considerations involving public health, safety, or general welfare, may be permitted upon a proposed site depending upon the facts and circumstances of the particular case.

Zylka v. City of Crystal, 167 N.W.2d 45, 48–49 (Minn. 1969).

4. Professor Jan Krasnowiecki begins his provocative article, Abolish Zoning, 31 Syracuse L. Rev. 719 (1980), with the truism that the "fundamental idea of zoning is that development is best controlled by a set of 'self-administering' rules laid down by the legislative body of a municipality long in advance of actual development." He then asserts that zoning in practice bears no resemblance to this idea. All "intensive development, certainly all residential development involving densities of more than four units to the acre, is occurring, if at all, only through a zoning change, variance, or some other form of administrative relaxation that is *applied for and granted on the threshold of development.*" From this, Krasnowiecki concludes that "zoning cannot work, especially in a developing community. Failure to perceive this fact has led the courts on a wild goose chase in pursuit of an ideal that is not capable of attainment and that is, in any event, unsound. This failure has led commentators and statutory drafters on the same chase and has significantly delayed finding any realistic solution to the problem."

If Krasnowiecki's perception is correct, should zoning be abolished? If so, what kind of system should replace it? Unconstrained, *ad hoc* decision-making by local legislatures and administrative agencies? *Ad hoc* decisions constrained only by the goals set forth in the community's comprehensive plan? Since the battles in most of these cases involve developers pitted against their neighbors, would it be preferable to leave decisions to neighborhood referenda?

5. The main problem with the statutory standards governing variances and special exceptions, and with the judicial decisions that construe them, is not that they are too vague or too precise, nor that they are too heavily biased toward developers or toward neighbors, but is simply that they are probably irrelevant to the vast, unreviewed bulk of administrative decisions rendered by local boards. Political and economic pressures doubtless play a far larger role in these decisions than does the rule of law.

2. LEGISLATIVE DECISIONS

a. REZONING

City of Pharr v. Tippitt

Supreme Court of Texas, 1981.
616 S.W.2d 173.

POPE, Justice.

E.A. Tippitt and fourteen other landowners filed suit against the City of Pharr, Mayfair Minerals, Inc., and Urban Housing Associates seeking a judgment declaring a zoning ordinance invalid. The district court upheld the ordinance, but the court of civil appeals nullified it. We reverse the court of civil appeals judgment and affirm that of the trial court.

Mayfair Minerals, Inc. is the owner of 10.1 acres of land which the City of Pharr rezoned from R–1, single-family residence use to R–3, multi-family residence use. Urban Housing Associates, the developer, made the application for change of the single-family classification so that it could build fifty family units consisting of duplexes and quadruplexes. The Planning and Zoning Commission rejected its staff's recommendation that the zoning request be approved; but the City Council, by a four to one vote, enacted an ordinance which rezoned the property. After the district court upheld the validity of the zoning ordinance, Tippitt was the only person who appealed from that judgment. Tippitt's single point of error, which point was sustained by the court of civil appeals, was that the City acted arbitrarily because the amendatory ordinance was spot zoning that was not warranted by any change in conditions in the area.

The land in question is a rectangular 10.1–acre tract. It is on the west side of a larger 60–acre tract. The 60–acre tract and additional large expanses of land to the south and southeast are vacant farmlands. The lands were zoned in 1974 for single-family residences. The tract in question is about two blocks east of Highway 281, a major highway that runs from north to south toward Mexico. The land along the highway is rapidly developing as a commercial strip by reason of a proposed new bridge that will cross the Rio Grande River into Mexico. Sam Houston Street is a major traffic artery that runs from west to east. The tract in question is south of and separated from Sam Houston Street by a 2.6–acre tract of land known as the Aycock tract. Moving clockwise from the north around the 10.1–acre tract, the Aycock tract is zoned for single-family residences. Farther north of there, on the north side of Sam Houston, there are many city blocks of land that were zoned for multiple-family residences. That area, however, was built as single-family residences. The land on the east, southeast, south, and southwest are undeveloped farmlands, all zoned for single-family residences. Bordering the 10.1–acre tract on the west is Richmond Heights Subdivision, which has been developed as single-family residences on the north end, but is not yet developed toward the south. Three hundred feet to the northeast of the tract, but south of Sam Houston, there is an area that is zoned for multiple housing. Two hundred feet to the west of the 10.1–acre tract is a small area that is zoned for industrial use.

Zoning is an exercise of a municipality's legislative powers. The validity of an amendment to the City of Pharr's comprehensive zoning ordinance presents a question of law, not fact. In making its determination, courts are governed by the rule stated in Hunt v. City of San Antonio, 462 S.W.2d 536, 539 (Tex.1971): "If reasonable minds may differ as to whether or not a particular zoning ordinance has a substantial relationship to the public health, safety, morals or general welfare, no clear abuse of discretion is shown and the ordinance must stand as a valid exercise of the city's police power."....

The burden on the party attacking the municipal legislative action is a heavy one. As expressed in Weaver v. Ham, 149 Tex. 309, 232 S.W.2d 704 (1950):

> The City had the power to enact the basic zoning ordinance, and to amend it, if a public necessity demanded it. While the presumption would be that the enactment of the amendatory ordinance was valid, that presumption disappears when the facts show and it was determined by the court that the City acted arbitrarily, unreasonably, and abused its discretion; that the ordinance is discriminatory and violates the rights of petitioners under the basic ordinance, and does not bear any substantial relation to the public health, safety, morals or general welfare; that it "constitutes unjustifiable spot zoning"; and that the ordinance is void.

These general rules for review of zoning ordinances have often been stated, but there has been little discussion of the actual legal criteria or standards against which legislative action should be tested. It has been suggested that such a statement would help to restrain arbitrary, capricious and unreasonable actions by city legislative bodies; improve the quality of the legislation; assist in eliminating *ad hoc* decisions, and focus the evidence from interested parties upon the real issues. We call attention to some of the important criteria:

First: A comprehensive zoning ordinance is law that binds the municipal legislative body itself. The legislative body does not, on each rezoning hearing, redetermine as an original matter, the city's policy of comprehensive zoning. The law demands that the approved zoning plan should be respected and not altered for the special benefit of the landowner when the change will cause substantial detriment to the surrounding lands or serve no substantial public purpose. The duty to obey the existing law forbids municipal actions that disregard not only the pre-established zoning ordinance, but also long-range master plans and maps that have been adopted by ordinance.

The adoption of a comprehensive zoning ordinance does not, however, exhaust the city's powers to amend the ordinance as long as the action is not arbitrary, capricious and unreasonable.

Second: The nature and degree of an adverse impact upon neighboring lands is important. Lots that are rezoned in a way that is substantially inconsistent with the zoning of the surrounding area, whether more or less restrictive, are likely to be invalid. For example, a rezoning from a residential use to an industrial use may have a highly deleterious effect upon the surrounding residential lands.

Third: The suitability or unsuitability of the tract for use as presently zoned is a factor. The size, shape and location of a lot may render a tract unusable or even confiscatory as zoned. An example of this is found in City of Waxahachie v. Watkins, 154 Tex. 206, 275 S.W.2d 477 (1955), in which we approved the rezoning of a residential lot for local retail use, because the lot was surrounded by a de facto business area. This factor, like the others, must often be weighed in relation to the other standards, and instances can exist in which the use for which land is zoned may be rezoned upon proof of a real public need or substantially changed conditions in the neighborhood.

Fourth: The amendatory ordinance must bear a substantial relationship to the public health, safety, morals or general welfare or protect and preserve historical and cultural places and areas. The rezoning ordinance may be justified, however, if a substantial public need exists, and this is so even if the private owner of the tract will also benefit.

Mr. Tippitt's attack upon the amendatory ordinance in this case is that it is spot zoning. The term, "spot zoning," is used in Texas and most states to connote an unacceptable amendatory ordinance that singles out a small tract for treatment that differs from that accorded similar surrounding land without proof of changes in conditions. Mr. Tippitt's present complaint of spot zoning invokes mainly inquiries about the second and third criteria stated above. Spot zoning is regarded as a preferential treatment which defeats a pre-established comprehensive plan. It is piecemeal zoning, the antithesis of planned zoning.

Spot zoning has uniformly been denied when there is a substantial adverse impact upon the surrounding land. The size of a rezoned tract in relation to the affected neighboring lands has been said by some authorities to be the most significant consideration in rezoning.

Amendatory ordinances which have rezoned a single city lot when there have been no intervening changes or other saving characteristic, have almost always been voided in Texas.

Proof that a small tract is unsuitable for use as zoned or that there have been substantial changes in the neighborhood have justified some amendatory ordinances. Here, too, the size, shape and characteristics of the tract have been determinative factors in upholding the amendments....

We do not regard the ordinance as spot zoning. The ten-acre tract is located in an undeveloped farming area. Large expanses of rural lands are located to the east, south and southeast, the direction in which the town must grow. To hold that the undeveloped land cannot be used for anything other than single-family residences (R–1) would mean, for all practical purposes, that there can be no more multiple housing in Pharr within its present city limits, since there is almost no presently undeveloped area which is available for R–3 housing. The size of this tract is large enough for planning as a self-contained orderly development which can in advance provide for the direction and the flow of traffic and assure a careful development of necessary public utilities. The development will not cause that measure of disharmony that occurs when there is a rezoning ordinance that permits a use that affects lands or tracts that are already developed. This is not an instance of an unplanned or piecemeal zoning of an isolated lot or small tract.

There is also evidence that rezoning would benefit and promote the general welfare of the community. The City of Pharr has a great need for multiple housing, the population has markedly increased since 1974, and there are only three small areas in Pharr that are presently zoned for multiple housing (R–3) which are not fully developed. The mayor testified that the need for multi-family housing will continue to grow. The City of Pharr, from the data included in the minutes of the zoning hearing, has 703 acres zoned for residential purposes of all kinds. Only 49 acres are actually used for multiple housing (R–3), and nine acres are actually used for duplexes (R–2). To relieve the City of Pharr's housing and utility needs, the City had agreed with the Housing and Urban Development Department to provide more space for multiple housing (R–3) construction. A block grant to the City of $3,000,000 had been made which included sums to provide needed extensions of sewer and water lines and the construction of a water reservoir. From the record it does not appear that the one complaining of the rezoning ordinance discharged his burden to prove that the City of Pharr acted arbitrarily, capriciously or unreasonably.

The judgment of the court of civil appeals is reversed and the judgment of the district court upholding the ordinance rezoning the tract in question is affirmed.

McGee, J., notes his dissent.

Notes & Questions

1. How much freedom should municipalities have in rezoning individual parcels? Would the *Tippitt* court have reached the same result if it had been reviewing the grant of a variance instead of a rezoning?

Tippitt reflects what is probably the majority view on piecemeal rezonings. Maryland and a few other states apply a more rigorous standard, allowing municipalities to rezone individual parcels only if they can demonstrate that the rezoning is necessary to correct a mistake in the original zoning ordinance or to accommodate substantially changed neighborhood conditions. Md. Code art. 66B, § 4.05(a)(2).

Should the rezoning standard differ depending on whether it is a developer or a neighbor who seeks the piecemeal rezoning? In *Tippitt,* the developer sought the rezoning over the opposition of his neighbors. In other cases, neighbors may seek the rezoning over the opposition of a developer.

Apartment house owners in an R–3 (multi-family residential) district, for example, might seek to rezone the developer's parcel from R–3 to R–1 (single family residential) on the ground that more multiple family dwellings in the area would produce intolerable increases in traffic, noise, and the demand for public services and facilities.

2. **Is Rezoning Legislative or Adjudicatory Decisionmaking?** A few states take the position that piecemeal rezonings should not be treated as legislative acts at all, but rather as judicial decisions, and should therefore be encumbered by all the trappings of the judicial process. The position has dramatic procedural implications—shifting the burden of proof from landowner to legislature, widening and intensifying the standard of review on appeal, and requiring such due process guarantees as adequate notice to all concerned parties, a fair and public hearing, the right to cross-examination, and written fact findings.

Fasano v. Board of County Commissioners, 507 P.2d 23 (Or. 1973), is the leading case for this position. The court there struck down a zoning amendment that would have changed a parcel's permitted use from single-family residential to mobile home park, observing that it "would be ignoring reality to rigidly view all zoning decisions by local governing bodies as legislative acts to be accorded a full presumption of validity and shielded from less than constitutional scrutiny by the theory of separation of powers. Local and small decision groups are simply not the equivalent in all respects of state and national legislatures." Specifically, the court ruled that:

> Ordinances laying down general policies without regard to a specific piece of property are usually an exercise of legislative authority, are subject to limited review, and may only be attacked upon constitutional grounds for an arbitrary abuse of authority. On the other hand, a determination whether the permissible use of a specific piece of property should be changed is usually an exercise of judicial authority and its propriety is subject to an altogether different test....
>
> Because the action of the commission in this instance is an exercise of judicial authority, the burden of proof should be placed, as is usual in judicial proceedings, upon the one seeking change. The more drastic the change, the greater will be the burden of showing that it is in conformance with the comprehensive plan as implemented by the ordinance, that there is a public need for the kind of change in question, and that the need is best met by the proposal under consideration. As the degree of change increases, the burden of showing that the potential impact upon the area in question was carefully considered and weighed will also increase. If other areas have previously been designated for the particular type of development, it must be shown why it is necessary to introduce it into an area not previously contemplated and why the property owners there should bear the burden of the departure.

Id. at 26, 29. The Oregon Supreme Court subsequently limited the reach of *Fasano* in Neuberger v. City of Portland, 603 P.2d 771 (Or. 1979).

A handful of states and the American Law Institute have adopted the *Fasano* approach. See, e.g., Board of County Comm'rs v. Snyder, 627 So. 2d 469 (Fla. 1993); American Law Institute, A Model Land Development Code § 2–312 (1976). Most states, however, have expressly rejected the approach, and even some states that initially adopted it subsequently changed their minds. See, e.g., Cabana v. Kenai Peninsula Borough, 21 P.3d 833 (Alaska 2001); State by Rochester Ass'n v. City of Rochester, 268 N.W.2d 885 (Minn. 1978); William B. Stoebuck & Dale A. Whitman, The Law of Property 620 (3d ed. 2000). ("[O]ur narrow scope of review reflects a policy decision that a legislative body can best determine which zoning classifications best serve the public welfare").

For an insightful and provocative analysis of piecemeal land use decisions, see Carol Rose, Planning and Dealing: Piecemeal Land Controls as a Problem of Local Legitimacy, 71 Calif. L. Rev. 837 (1983). According to Professor Rose, "piecemeal local land decisions should not be classed as either 'legislative' or 'judicial'; these rubrics are drawn from a separation-of-powers doctrine more appropriate to larger governmental units. Piecemeal changes are quintessentially local matters, and any jurisprudential test of the reasonableness of piecemeal changes must identify and build upon the factors that lend legitimacy and institutional competence to local decisionmaking." Id. at 846.

3. **"Contract" and "Conditional" Zoning.** Municipalities will sometimes condition a parcel's rezoning on its owner's agreement to mitigate a development's adverse effects on neighboring parcels by such steps as building and maintaining an attractive buffer or providing a specified amount of off-street parking. These undertakings usually take the form of covenants executed and recorded by the developer either before or after the rezoning, depending on local practice.

In zoning's early years, courts generally condemned these arrangements on the ground that the state cannot bargain away its police power. Although some courts still take this view, most today hold that, within prescribed limits, conditional zoning is not only tolerable but desirable. The New York Court of Appeals decision in Church v. Town of Islip, 168 N.E.2d 680 (N.Y. 1960), marked the beginning of this modern trend, upholding a rezoning from residential to business use that had been conditioned on the parcel owner's execution of covenants respecting maximum density and the installation of a fence and shrubbery buffer. Noting that the Town Board could have rezoned the parcel for business use without any restrictions, the court failed "to see how reasonable conditions invalidate the legislation." Further, the court observed

> [a]ll legislation "by contract" is invalid in the sense that a Legislature cannot bargain away or sell its powers. But we deal here with actualities, not phrases. To meet increasing needs of Suffolk County's own population explosion, and at the same time to make as gradual and as little of an annoyance as possible the change from residence to business on the main highways, the Town Board imposes conditions.

Id. at 683.

Even in states that allow the type of *conditional zoning* just described, a failure to structure the arrangement properly may lead to its invalidation as illegal *contract zoning*. Many courts distinguish between unilateral promises of a developer to restrict his property in return for rezoning (conditional zoning) and agreements between municipal governments and developers in which the government promises that it will rezone land in return for the developer's promises to restrict the land (contract zoning).

> We hold that when a city itself makes an agreement with a landowner to rezone, the contract is invalid. However, when the agreement is made by others than the city to conform the property in a way or manner which makes it acceptable for the requested rezoning and the city is not committed to rezone, it is not contract zoning in the true sense and does not vitiate the zoning if it is otherwise valid.

State ex rel. Zupancic v. Schimenz, 174 N.W.2d 533, 538 (Wis. 1970). See also Old Canton Hills Homeowners Ass'n v. City of Jackson, 749 So. 2d 54 (Miss. 1999); Dacy v. Village of Ruidoso, 845 P.2d 793 (N.M. 1992); Baylis v. City of Baltimore, 148 A.2d 429 (Md. 1959).

The distinction between valid conditional zoning and invalid contract zoning creates a dilemma both for developers and municipalities. Neither will be willing to act—by recording a covenant or rezoning the parcel—unless and until it is certain that the other will be equally forthcoming. Yet, the most effective vehicle for creating that certainty—conditions in a mutually binding executory contract—is unavailable because of the contract zoning bar. Can a city rezone the developer's parcel and then rescind the rezoning if the developer does not record its covenant? Can the developer record its covenant and later rescind it if the municipality fails to rezone? How would you try to structure the arrangement to satisfy the interests of both sides?

Is there anything truly wrong with contract zoning? See Lee Anne Fennell, Hard Bargains and Real Steals: Land Use Exactions Revisited, 86 Iowa L. Rev. 1 (2000); Jennifer G. Brown, Concomitant Agreement Zoning: An Economic Analysis, 1 U. Ill. L. Rev. 89 (1985).

Who should hold the benefit of these covenants? If only neighboring landowners hold the benefit, they and the parcel's developer can later agree to terminate the covenant, possibly against the city's wishes. Yet, if the municipality holds the benefit, does it have an enforceable interest? Can a city seeking to enforce one of these covenants successfully rebut the argument that the benefit is unenforceable because it is held in gross (see pp. 905–906 supra)? That the burden of the covenant does not run because it does not touch or concern the land (see pp. 896–905 supra)?

b. CLUSTER ZONING AND PUDs

Traditional Euclidean zoning achieves density goals by spreading homes out over the zoning map's grid with specified set-back, frontage, and yard requirements. Large-scale developers will often prefer the freedom to meet density goals by clustering homes in one or more areas and providing significant open space in between the clusters. By clustering homes, developers can economize on street, sidewalk, and public utility installations, as well as reduce grading and other site preparation costs by leaving many of the parcel's natural features, such as hills and trees, untouched. Many homebuyers, too, prefer cluster developments, and are happy to trade the privacy of a small backyard for the pleasures of far larger, shared open space and recreation areas such as parks, playgrounds, pools, and tennis courts.

Many zoning ordinances therefore now permit cluster zoning and planned unit developments (or PUDs). In cluster zoning, municipal governments allow developers to deviate from the specific area requirements of the zoning ordinance so long as they meet overall density goals. In PUDs, zoning authorities also permit the developer to deviate from use requirements and mix single-family residential, apartments, and even retail and office uses as part of a carefully planned development.

Courts today generally accept the concept of cluster zoning and PUDs. See, e.g., Cheney v. Village 2 at New Hope, Inc., 241 A.2d 81 (Pa. 1968). Questions, however, continue to surround the concept's implementation. Conflict often arises when the developer submits its final development plans for government approval. The developer will want the plans to consist only of rough guidelines, enabling it to alter the development to meet problems that arise in the course of construction. The city will want the final plans to indicate not only the height, bulk, and location of improvements and common areas, but also their design.

What recourse do neighbors have when a development, as built, violates the terms of the final approved plan? In Frankland v. City of Lake Oswego, 517 P.2d 1042, 1055 (Or. 1973), the court found that defendant developer's project did not conform to its final plan, and ruled that plaintiff neighbors would be entitled to recover damages for the diminution in value of their parcels resulting from "the difference between the apartment constructed and the apartment represented in the sketches which have been approved by the City."

Does the evolution from Euclidean zoning to cluster zoning suggest that the next evolutional step will be for government to keep its hands entirely off large-scale cluster developments or to set only broad standards, trusting developers to follow plans that will keep homebuyers happiest?

3. COMMUNITY DECISIONS

Eastlake v. Forest City Enterprises, Inc.

Supreme Court of the United States, 1976.
426 U.S. 668.

MR. CHIEF JUSTICE BURGER delivered the opinion of the Court.

The question in this case is whether a city charter provision requiring proposed land use changes to be ratified by 55% of the votes cast violates the due process rights of a landowner who applies for a zoning change.

The city of Eastlake, Ohio, a suburb of Cleveland, has a comprehensive zoning plan codified in a municipal ordinance. Respondent, a real estate developer, acquired an eight-acre parcel of real estate in Eastlake zoned for "light industrial" uses at the time of purchase.

In May 1971, respondent applied to the City Planning Commission for a zoning change to permit construction of a multi-family high-rise apartment building. The Planning Commission recommended the proposed change to the City Council, which under Eastlake's procedures could either accept or reject the Planning Commission's recommendation. Meanwhile, by popular vote, the voters of Eastlake amended the city charter to require that any changes in land use agreed to by the Council be approved by a 55% vote in a referendum. The City Council approved the Planning Commission's recommendation for reclassification of respondent's property to permit the proposed project. Respondent then applied to the Planning Commission for "parking and yard" approval for the proposed building. The Commission rejected the application, on the ground that the City Council's rezoning action had not yet been submitted to the voters for ratification.

Respondent then filed an action in state court, seeking a judgment declaring the charter provision invalid as an unconstitutional delegation of legislative power to the people. While the case was pending, the City Council's action was submitted to a referendum, but the proposed zoning change was not approved by the requisite 55% margin. Following the election, the Court of Common Pleas and the Ohio Court of Appeals sustained the charter provision.

The Ohio Supreme Court reversed. Concluding that enactment of zoning and rezoning provisions is a legislative function, the court held that a popular referendum requirement, lacking standards to guide the decision of the voters, permitted the police power to be exercised in a standardless, hence arbitrary and capricious manner. . . .

We reverse.

I

The conclusion that Eastlake's procedure violates federal constitutional guarantees rests upon the proposition that a zoning referendum involves a delegation of legislative power. A referendum cannot, however, be characterized as a delegation of power. Under our constitutional assumptions, all power derives from the people, who can delegate it to representative instruments which they create. In establishing legislative bodies, the people can reserve to themselves power to deal directly with matters which might otherwise be assigned to the legislature.

The reservation of such power is the basis for the town meeting, a tradition which continues to this day in some States as both a practical and symbolic part of our democratic processes. The referendum, similarly, is a means for direct political participation, allowing the people the final decision, amounting to a veto power, over enactments of representative bodies. The practice is designed to "give citizens a voice on questions of public policy." James v. Valtierra, supra, 402 U.S., at 141.

In framing a state constitution, the people of Ohio specifically reserved the power of referendum to the people of each municipality within the State.

> The initiative and referendum powers are hereby reserved to the people of each municipality on all questions which such municipalities may now or hereafter be authorized by law to control by legislative action.... [Ohio Const., Art. II, § 1f.]

To be subject to Ohio's referendum procedure, the question must be one within the scope of legislative power. The Ohio Supreme Court expressly found that the City Council's action in rezoning respondent's eight acres from light industrial to high-density residential use was legislative in nature. Distinguishing between administrative and legislative acts, the court separated the power to zone or rezone, by passage or amendment of a zoning ordinance, from the power to grant relief from unnecessary hardship. The former function was found to be legislative in nature.

II

The Ohio Supreme Court further concluded that the amendment to the city charter constituted a "delegation" of power violative of federal constitutional guarantees because the voters were given no standards to guide their decision. Under Eastlake's procedure, the Ohio Supreme Court reasoned, no mechanism existed, nor indeed could exist, to assure that the voters would act rationally in passing upon a proposed zoning change. This meant that "appropriate legislative action [would] be made dependent upon the potentially arbitrary and unreasonable whims of the voting public." 41 Ohio St. 2d, at 195, 324 N.E.2d, at 746. The potential for arbitrariness in the process, the court concluded, violated due process.

Courts have frequently held in other contexts that a congressional delegation of power to a regulatory entity must be accompanied by discernible standards, so that the delegatee's action can be measured for its fidelity to the legislative will. Assuming, *arguendo,* their relevance to state governmental functions, these cases involved a delegation of power by the legislature to regulatory bodies, which are not directly responsible to the people; this doctrine is inapplicable where, as here, rather than dealing with a delegation of power, we deal with a power reserved by the people to themselves.

In basing its claim on federal due process requirements, respondent also invokes Euclid v. Ambler Realty Co., 272 U.S. 365 (1926), but it does not rely on the direct teaching of that case. Under *Euclid,* a property owner can challenge a zoning restriction if the measure is "clearly arbitrary and unreasonable, having no substantial relation to the public health, safety, morals, or general welfare." Id., at 395. If the substantive result of the referendum is arbitrary and capricious, bearing no relation to the police power, then the fact that the voters of Eastlake wish it so would not save the restriction. As this Court held in invalidating a charter amendment enacted by referendum:

> The sovereignty of the people is itself subject to those constitutional limitations which have been duly adopted and remain unrepealed. [Hunter v. Erickson, 393 U.S., at 392.]

But no challenge of the sort contemplated in Euclid v. Ambler Realty is before us. The Ohio Supreme Court did not hold, and respondent does not argue, that the present zoning classification under Eastlake's comprehensive ordinance violates the principles established in Euclid v. Ambler Realty. If respondent considers the referendum result itself to be unreasonable, the zoning restriction is open to challenge in state court, where the scope of the state remedy available to respondent would be determined as a matter of state law, as well as under Fourteenth Amendment standards. That being so, nothing more is required by the Constitution.

Nothing in our cases is inconsistent with this conclusion. Two decisions of this Court were relied on by the Ohio Supreme Court in invalidating Eastlake's procedure. The thread common to both decisions is the delegation of legislative power, originally given by the people to a legislative body, and in turn delegated by the legislature to a *narrow segment* of the community, not to the people at large. In Eubank v. Richmond, 226 U.S. 137 (1912), the Court invalidated a city ordinance which conferred the power to establish building setback lines upon the owners of two-thirds of the property abutting any street. Similarly, in Washington ex rel. Seattle Title Trust Co. v. Roberge, 278 U.S. 116 (1928), the Court struck down an ordinance which permitted the establishment of philanthropic homes for the aged in residential areas, but only upon the written consent of the owners of two-thirds of the property within 400 feet of the proposed facility.

Neither *Eubank* nor *Roberge* involved a referendum procedure such as we have in this case; the standardless delegation of power to a limited group of property owners condemned by the Court in *Eubank* and *Roberge* is not to be equated with decision-making by the people through the referendum process. The Court of Appeals for the Ninth Circuit put it this way:

> A referendum, however, is far more than an expression of ambiguously founded neighborhood preference. It is the city itself legislating through its voters—an exercise by the voters of their traditional right through direct legislation to override the views of their elected representatives as to what serves the public interest. [Southern Alameda Spanish Speaking Organization v. Union City, California, 424 F.2d 291, 294 (1970).]

Our decision in James v. Valtierra, upholding California's mandatory referendum requirement, confirms this view. Mr. Justice Black, speaking for the Court in that case, said:

> This procedure ensures that *all the people* of a community will have a voice in a decision which may lead to large expenditures of local governmental funds for increased public services.... [402 U.S., at 143 (emphasis added).]

Mr. Justice Black went on to say that a referendum procedure, such as the one at issue here, is a classic demonstration of "devotion to democracy...." Id., at 141. As a basic instrument of democratic government, the referendum process does not, in itself, violate the Due Process Clause of the Fourteenth Amendment when applied to a rezoning ordinance. Since the rezoning decision in this case was properly reserved to the People of Eastlake under the Ohio Constitution, the Ohio Supreme Court erred in holding invalid, on federal constitutional grounds, the charter amendment permitting the voters to decide whether the zoned use of respondent's property could be altered.

The judgment of the Ohio Supreme Court is reversed, and the case is remanded for further proceedings not inconsistent with this opinion.

Reversed and remanded.

MR. JUSTICE POWELL, dissenting.

There can be no doubt as to the propriety and legality of submitting generally applicable legislative questions, including zoning provisions, to a popular referendum. But here the only issue concerned the status of a single small parcel owned by a single "person." This procedure, affording no realistic opportunity for the affected person to be heard, even by the electorate, is fundamentally unfair. The "spot" referendum technique appears to open disquieting opportunities for local government bodies to bypass normal protective procedures for resolving issues affecting individual rights.

MR. JUSTICE STEVENS, with whom MR. JUSTICE BRENNAN joins, dissenting.

....

Although this Court has decided only a handful of zoning cases, literally thousands of zoning disputes have been resolved by state courts. Those courts have repeatedly identified the obvious difference between the adoption of a comprehensive citywide plan by legislative action and the decision of particular issues involving specific uses of specific parcels. In the former situation there is generally great deference to the judgment of the legislature; in the latter situation state courts have not hesitated to correct manifest injustice....

The essence of fair procedure is that the interested parties be given a reasonable opportunity to have their dispute resolved on the merits by reference to articulable rules. If a dispute involves only the conflicting rights of private litigants, it is elementary that the decision-maker must be impartial and qualified to understand and to apply the controlling rules.

I have no doubt about the validity of the initiative or the referendum as an appropriate method of deciding questions of community policy. I think it is equally clear that the popular vote is not an acceptable method of adjudicating the rights of individual litigants. The problem presented by this case is unique, because it may involve a three-sided controversy, in which there is at least potential conflict between the rights of the property owner and the rights of his neighbors, and also potential conflict with the public interest in preserving the city's basic zoning plan. If the latter aspect of the controversy were predominant, the referendum would be an acceptable procedure. On the other hand, when the record indicates without contradiction that there is no threat to the general public interest in preserving the city's plan—as it does in this case, since respondent's proposal was approved by both the Planning Commission and the City Council and there has been no allegation that the use of this eight-acre parcel for apartments rather than light industry would adversely affect the community or raise any policy issue of citywide concern—I think the case should be treated as one in which it is essential that the private property owner be given a fair opportunity to have his claim determined on its merits.

As Justice Stern [pointed] out in his concurring opinion [in the decision of the Ohio Supreme Court], it would be absurd to use a referendum to decide whether a gasoline station could be operated on a particular corner in the city of Cleveland. The case before us is not that clear because we are told that there are only 20,000 people in the city of Eastlake. Conceivably, an eight-acre development could be sufficiently dramatic to arouse the legitimate interest of the entire community; it is also conceivable that most of the voters would be indifferent and uninformed about the wisdom of building apartments rather than a warehouse or factory on these eight acres. The record is silent on which of these alternatives is the more probable. Since the ordinance places a manifestly unreasonable obstacle in the path of every property owner seeking any zoning change, since it provides no standards or procedures for exempting particular parcels or claims from the referendum requirement, and since the record contains no justification for the use of the procedure in this case, I am persuaded that we should respect the state judiciary's appraisal of the fundamental fairness of this decisionmaking process in this case.

I therefore conclude that the Ohio Supreme Court correctly held that Art. VIII, § 3, of the Eastlake charter violates the Due Process Clause of the Fourteenth Amendment, and that its judgment should be affirmed.

Notes & Questions

1. Is *Eastlake* a good decision? Are the procedural safeguards that surround legislative acts necessary when the electorate votes directly? Can a court overturn a land use referendum or initiative on the ground that it is not "in accordance with a comprehensive plan"? Compare Kaiser Hawaii Kai Development Co. v. City of Honolulu, 777 P.2d 244 (Haw. 1989)

("zoning by initiative is inconsistent with the goal of long range comprehensive planning") with R.G. Moore Building Corp. v. Committee for Repeal, 391 S.E.2d 587 (Va. 1990) (initiatives are not inconsistent with comprehensive planning requirement). Are referenda and initiatives inconsistent with the requirement of the Standard State Zoning Enabling Act that notice and public hearings precede any zoning decision? Compare Transamerica Title Ins. Co. v. City of Tucson, 757 P.2d 1055 (Ariz. 1988) (initiative to establish a buffer zone around open space violated procedural zoning requirements) with Associated Home Builders v. City of Livermore, 557 P.2d 473 (Cal. 1976) (process requirements do not apply to initiatives).

2. Should it matter whether an initiative or referendum deals with general zoning standards or with a specific parcel of property? The Supreme Court, in both *Eastlake* and City of Cuyahoga Falls v. Buckeye Community Hope Found., 538 U.S. 188, 199 (2003), has held that it does not make a difference as to federal due process rights. State constitutions, however, sometimes limit initiatives and referenda to legislative issues. In Buckeye Community Hope Found. v. City of Cuyahoga Falls, 697 N.E.2d 181 (Ohio 1998), the city council ratified a decision of the planning commission to permit the construction of a 72–unit apartment complex on land zoned for multifamily use. Voters organized a referendum to reject the city council's decision, and the landowner sued. The Ohio Supreme Court held that the referendum was invalid because it involved an administrative rather than legislative decision, and the Ohio Constitution allowed referenda only in regard to legislative actions. The city council "merely approve[d] the planning commission's application of existing zoning regulations to the plan submitted by the appellants. The ordinance has no general, prospective application such that the action would fit within the usual and customary meaning of the phrase 'legislative action.' " See also Garvin v. Ninth Judicial District Ct., 59 P.3d 1180 (Nev. 2002) (zoning changes are not legislative decisions subject to referendum); Leonard v. City of Bothell, 557 P.2d 1306 (Wash. 1976) (rezoning of 141–acre lot was "quasi-judicial" action and thus not subject to a referendum).

3. Ignoring constitutional questions, should states permit residents of cities to vote directly on zoning issues? Should zoning decisions be the subject of the "unreflective, nondeliberative aggregate will of the electorate"? See Lawrence Gene Sager, Insular Majorities Unabated, 91 Harv. L. Rev. 1373, 1411 (1978).

4. For interesting insights into zoning by ballot box, see Daniel P. Selmi, Reconsidering the Use of Direct Democracy in Making Land Use Decisions, 19 UCLA J. Envtl. L. & Pol'y 293 (2001–2002); David L. Callies et al., Ballot Box Zoning: Initiative, Referendum, and the Law, 39 Wash. U.J. Urb. & Contemp. L. 53 (1991); Peter G. Glenn, State Law Limitations on the Use of Initiatives and Referenda in Connection with Zoning Amendments, 51 S. Cal. L. Rev. 265 (1978).

5. **Neighbor Consent Requirements.** As discussed in *Eastlake*, the Supreme Court in 1912 invalidated a statute that allowed two thirds of the property owners on any street to request the establishment of a set-back

line. See Eubank v. Richmond, 226 U.S. 137 (1912). In Cusack Co. v. City of Chicago, 242 U.S. 526 (1917), however, the Supreme Court upheld an ordinance that allowed a majority of the property owners on a block to consent to the erection of billboards, which otherwise were impermissible. According to the Court, the Chicago ordinance was clearly distinguishable from the ordinance that had been invalidated in *Eubank*. "The one ordinance permits two-thirds of the lot owners to impose restrictions upon the other property in the block, while the other permits one-half of the lot owners to remove a restriction from the other property owners." Id. at 531. To further muddle the picture, the Supreme Court ten years later invalidated a statute that permitted a landowner to run a "philanthropic home for children or for old people" in a residential neighborhood if two-thirds of property owners near the home consented. The difference from *Cusack Co.*? Philanthropic homes are not nuisances, while billboard are "by reason of their nature ... liable to be offensive"? Are these various distinctions meaningful? Courts continue to invalidate laws permitting neighbors to control zoning decisions, but only where courts conclude that the laws give neighbors the ability to impose rather than waive restrictions or involve uses that are not noxious.

E. Review of Environmental Impacts

In recent years, a growing number of states have required planning authorities to engage in extensive reviews of the potential environmental impacts of a zoning or development decision before making the decision. The genesis of this requirement was the passage in 1969 of the National Environmental Policy Act (NEPA), 42 U.S.C. §§ 4321 et seq., which is designed to improve the environmental decisions of federal agencies. NEPA was the first major environmental statute that Congress passed in the modern era of environmental law. Unlike most of the environmental statutes that followed, NEPA does not try to improve the environment by directly regulating the actions of federal agencies. Instead, "NEPA relies on information, forcing [federal] agencies to consider the environmental impacts of their proposed actions and alternatives. This approach reflects a New Deal faith in agency management—the belief that a bureaucracy will do the right thing if it considers the proper issues." James Salzman & Barton H. Thompson, Jr., Environmental Law and Policy 275 (2003).

Although NEPA applies only to the actions of federal agencies, almost half the states have adopted their own versions of NEPA—known as *little NEPAs* or *SEPAs* (for *state environmental policy acts*)—that govern the decisionmaking of state and, in some cases, local governmental agencies. See 5 Zoning and Land Use Controls §§ 28.01, 28.02[1] (Patrick J. Rohan ed., 2004); Daniel Mandelker, NEPA Law and Litigation, ch. 12 (2d ed. 1994). Although SEPA requirements vary from state to state, the basic requirements are generally the same. Before a governmental agency takes any major action such as issuing a building permit for a large subdivision, the agency must consider whether the action could significantly impact the environment. If the agency decides that the action might have such an impact, the agency must prepare an *environmental impact statement* (EIS)—known in some jurisdictions as an *environmental impact report* (EIR). In the EIS, the agency must typically discuss:

(1) the environmental impact of the proposed action,

(2) any adverse environmental effects that cannot be avoided should the agency go forward with the action, and, most importantly,

(3) alternatives to the proposed action, as well as the comparative environmental effects of the various alternatives.

Most SEPA litigation focuses on the adequacy of EISs and their discussion of environmental impacts and potential alternatives. The following case deals with the California Environmental Quality Act, Cal. Pub. Resources Code §§ 21000 et seq., and its requirement that state and local agencies prepare an EIR. More specifically, the case deals with the adequacy of an EIR's discussion of the water resources needed for a large subdivision in the northern part of Los Angeles County. The region receives most of its water from the California State Water Project (SWP), which transports water from the Sacramento River and its tributaries in Northern California hundreds of miles down to the burgeoning communities of Southern California. Because of environmental constraints, California has never built the SWP out to its planned capacity, and many water suppliers hold contracts to water from the SWP that the project can only partially deliver. The case therefore also raises the question of the role that water scarcity should play in local land use planning.

Santa Clarita Organization for Planning the Environment v. County of Los Angeles

Court of Appeal of California, 2003.
131 Cal. Rptr. 2d 186.

GILBERT, P.J.

An environmental impact report for a housing development must contain a thorough analysis that reasonably informs the reader of the amount of water available. The dream of water entitlements from the incomplete State Water Project (SWP) is no substitute for the reality of actual water the SWP can deliver.

This appeal arises under the California Environmental Quality Act. (hereafter CEQA.) The Santa Clarita Organization for Planning the Environment and the Friends of the Santa Clara River (hereafter collectively SCOPE) petitioned the trial court for a writ of mandate. The petition requested that the court order the County of Los Angeles (hereafter County) to vacate its resolution certifying the final environmental impact report (EIR) and related resolutions approving the West Creek development project.

The trial court denied SCOPE's petition. We conclude the County erred in approving the EIR because the water service portion of the EIR is inadequate. We reverse.

Facts

West Creek is a proposed mixed residential and commercial development in the Santa Clarita Valley area of northern Los Angeles County. The project includes 2,545 housing units, 180,000 square feet of commercial retail space and 46 acres of community facilities. The County served as the lead agency in preparing the EIR for the project. The project developers are The Newhall Land and Farming Company and Valencia Corporation (hereafter collectively Newhall).

The water service portion of the EIR states that the Castaic Lake Water Agency (Castaic) is the water wholesaler for the Santa Clarita area. It provides water to four local suppliers including the Valencia Water Company (Valencia). Valencia will provide water to West Creek. The EIR estimates West Creek will demand 2,194 acre feet of water per year (afy).

The draft EIR states that Castaic has an "existing water supply" of 107,000 afy. More specifically, a chart indicates Castaic's existing water supply is between 97,700 and 106,700 afy. This supply is composed of 32,500 afy from the Alluvial Aquifer; between 11,000 and 20,000 afy from the Saugus Aquifer; and 54,200 afy as "current entitlements" from the SWP. In addition, Castaic predicts that it will be able to add 18,000 afy of recycled water to its supply. Because current water demand within the Castaic service area is only 48,858 afy, the draft EIR concludes that Castaic presently has sufficient water to meet current demand including West Creek. The draft EIR states that Valencia has an existing water supply of 45,000 afy and a current demand of 22,000 afy. Thus West Creek would have sufficient water under current supply and demand.

The draft EIR then discusses long-term cumulative impact of development on water supply. The report considers two "scenarios." The first scenario considers existing and projected development, including West Creek, within the Valencia service area. Considering a buildout of the Valencia service area only, the report projects a total water demand of 32,811 afy and a supply of 45,000 afy. The report therefore concludes Valencia has sufficient water to meet present and future needs.

The second scenario considers not only the Valencia service area, but present and projected development of the entire Santa Clarita Valley. This would generate a demand for 157,500 afy. But the total supply including 54,200 afy of state water entitlements will only be between 115,700 to 124,700 afy. The draft EIR concludes a buildout of the entire valley will create a water shortage of between 32,800 to 41,800 afy. Even without West Creek, the water supply will be inadequate to meet projected demand.

The draft EIR states, however: "[Castaic] has the opportunity . . . to purchase additional entitlement [from the SWP] at the present time. [Castaic] has undertaken negotiations to acquire additional . . . entitlement of 41,000 acre feet per year.... In the long term, the receipt of this additional entitlement along with the addition of water banking and other storage opportunities will provide the water needed for planned growth within the Santa Clarita Valley."

Under the heading "Unavoidable Significant Impacts," the report states in part, "[E]ach development project in the Santa Clarita Valley, including the proposed project, would be required to demonstrate water availability as part of the subdivision approval process. So long as each proposed development demonstrates water availability prior to the project approval, cumulative development would not result in an unavoidable significant cumulative impact on Santa Clarita Valley water resources."

In the comment and response portion of the EIR, SCOPE claimed there is no guarantee water purveyors would receive 100 percent of their SWP entitlements, and that Castaic uses 50 percent for planning purposes.

The EIR responded that after the draft EIR was released, Castaic purchased an additional SWP entitlement of 41,000 afy from the Kern County Water Agency. That increased Castaic's "wet year supply" to 156,900 afy, consisting of 40,000 afy from the Alluvial Aquifer, 20,000 afy from the Saugus Aquifer, 95,200 afy from the SWP and 1,700 afy from recycled water. The figures were taken from Castaic's most recent water report.

The response stated the "dry year" supply is 142,800 afy, taking into account a 50 percent reduction in the state water supply and a lower draft from the aquifers. Even assuming a 50 percent delivery factor for periods of "extreme drought," Castaic will still have adequate supplies for a buildout of the Santa Clarita Valley.

The response also stated that the 50 percent figure suggested by SCOPE was flawed. Castaic is currently collecting funding for a capital improvement program that includes the acquisition of new water supplies and water banking. In light of this program and other state programs, the response concluded it is entirely appropriate to consider 100 percent of SWP entitlement for long-term planning purposes.

The final EIR incorporated the draft EIR and the comments and response to the draft. A summary table of project impacts and mitigation measures contained in the final EIR states in part: "On a cumulative basis, buildout of the Santa Clarita Valley would result in a mid-point demand that could exceed 157,000 AFY. In comparison, [Castaic] and Valencia Water Company can only account for supplies ranging from 156,700 to 165,700 AFY.... While [Castaic] has undertaken programs to increase future water supplies, based on current conditions there could be a deficit of supply.... However, ... each development project in the Santa Clarita Valley, including the proposed project, would be required to demonstrate water availability as part of the subdivision approval process. So long as each proposed development demonstrates water availability prior to the project approval, cumulative development would not result in an unavoidable significant cumulative impact on Santa Clarita Valley water resources."

Discussion

SCOPE contends the EIR is inadequate in that it fails to state accurately the amount of water available. The contention is based on the EIR's use of state water "entitlements" to calculate the water supply. SCOPE points out that in Planning & Conservation League v. Department of Water Resources (2000) 83 Cal. App. 4th 892, 908, footnote 5 [100 Cal. Rptr. 2d 173], the appellate court noted the difference between water entitlements and the amount of water the SWP can actually deliver:

> The original long-term contracts between DWR [Department of Water Resources] and the water contractors were predicated on the state's contractual obligation to build out the SWP so as to deliver 4.23 maf [million acre feet] of water to the contractors annually. Each of the contractors is allocated a percentage of the 4.23 maf in table A of the long-term contracts. The allocation is referred to as an entitlement. Therefore, cumulatively, the contractors are "entitled" to 4.23 maf of water annually.
>
> The SWP, however, has never been completed and the state cannot deliver 4.23 maf of water annually. The entitlements represent nothing more than hopes, expectations, water futures or, as the parties refer to them, "paper water." Actual, reliable water supply from the SWP is more in the vicinity of 2 to 2.5 maf of water annually. Consequently, there is a huge gap between what is promised and what can be delivered. . . .

The purpose of an EIR is to inform the public and its responsible officials of the environmental consequences of decisions before they are made. Among the matters that the EIR must consider is the cumulative impact of past, present and probable future projects. (§ 21083.)

In reviewing an agency's determination under CEQA, we must determine whether an agency prejudicially abused its discretion. (§ 21168.5.) An abuse of discretion occurs where the agency has not proceeded in a manner required by law, or its decision that the EIR is adequate is not supported by substantial evidence. To be adequate, the EIR must include sufficient detail to enable those who did not participate in its preparation to understand and "meaningfully" consider the issues raised by the proposed project.

Here the EIR attempts to analyze the cumulative impact of past, present and future development on the amount of water available. The EIR relies heavily on SWP entitlements in calculating the total available water supply. As the court in *Planning & Conservation League* points out, the entitlements are based on a state water system that has not been completed. There is a vast difference between entitlements and the amount of water that SWP can actually deliver.

The draft EIR makes no attempt to calculate or even discuss the differences between entitlement and actual supply. The final EIR contains a response to SCOPE's concern about the reliability of SWP water, but the response is inadequate. In calculating the wet year supply, the response included 100 percent of Castaic's SWP entitlement. But because the entitlement is based on a water system that is not completed, there is no justification for believing the SWP will be able to deliver 100 percent of all entitlements, even in wet years. As for periods of "extreme drought," the response used 50 percent of the entitlement in calculating the amount of water available. But there is nothing to suggest the SWP will be able to deliver 50 percent of all entitlements during periods of extreme drought.

Significantly, the response contains no estimates from the DWR, the agency that manages the SWP, as to how much water it can deliver, whether in wet years, average years and in periods of drought. It may be that no such reliable estimates are available. If that is the case, the EIR should say so. Instead, the comment and response portion of the EIR attempts to dismiss SCOPE's concerns. It states a program undertaken by Castaic and other state programs justify considering 100 percent of SWP entitlements in long-term planning. But the response gives no details of such programs or an estimate of how much water they might make available if they ever get past the funding stage. A reasonable correlation between water to be produced by these projects and SWP entitlements is left to the imagination. Even taking these programs into account, a reliable estimate of SWP deliveries is crucial to an understanding of the cumulative impact of development.

In an effort to show the EIR provides sufficient information on the reliability of SWP supplies, Newhall points to portions of the record in addition to SCOPE's comment and the response. Much of the information Newhall points to is in the administrative record, but is not in the EIR. Most of the remaining information was submitted by project opponents in response to the draft EIR and is scattered here and there in EIR appendices. For example, Newhall cites a page from a brief submitted by Friends of the Santa Clara River in a different case; a page from a trial court's statement of decision in an unrelated case; and a page from a Valencia document stating generally that the SWP is not complete "and supplies are subject to reduction when state-wide droughts occur." Only one report, prepared by consultants, purports to analyze the reliability of water supplies using a DWR computer model. It purports to analyze SWP's ability to deliver only 25,000 afy. It is buried in an appendix. The EIR contains no response to that report or any of the other submissions beyond that given to SCOPE's comment.

It is not enough for the EIR simply to contain information submitted by the public and experts. Problems raised by the public and responsible experts require a good faith reasoned analysis in response. (Cleary v. County of Stanislaus (1981) 118 Cal. App. 3d 348, 357 [173 Cal. Rptr. 390].) The requirement of a detailed analysis in response ensures that stubborn problems or serious criticism are not "swept under the rug." (Ibid.)

Here the draft EIR gives no hint that SWP entitlements cannot be taken at face value. It is only in response to comments and submissions by project opponents such as SCOPE that the EIR obliquely acknowledges that the entitlements may not be all they seem. Instead of undertaking a serious and detailed analysis of SWP supplies, the EIR does little more than dismiss project opponents' concerns about water supply. Water is too important to receive such cursory treatment.

The final EIR's acknowledgement that there "could be a deficit of supply" does not cure the defect. Without some reasonably accurate estimate of SWP's ability to deliver water, it is impossible to judge how likely or how deep the deficit might be.

Nor is the inadequacy cured by the requirement that Newhall demonstrate an adequate supply of water before the tract map is recorded. An EIR's purpose is to inform. This purpose is not satisfied by simply stating information will be provided in the future. . . .

Newhall expends much effort in an attempt to convince us that there will be sufficient water. The attempt misses the point. The EIR acknowledges that water service for a buildout of the Santa Clarita Valley will depend to a large extent on SWP deliveries. But the EIR fails to undertake an adequate analysis of how much water the SWP can actually deliver in wet, average and dry years. Without such information, the general public and its responsible officials cannot make an informed decision on whether to approve the project. The County's approval of the West Creek EIR is not supported by substantial evidence.

Because the water services portion of the EIR is inadequate, the judgment is reversed. The trial court shall issue a writ of mandate vacating the certification of the EIR, shall retain jurisdiction until the county certifies an EIR complying with CEQA consistent with the views expressed in this opinion, and shall consider such orders it deems appropriate. . . .

Notes & Questions

1. What must Los Angeles County do now to meet the requirements of CEQA? Do you believe that the county is likely to make a better decision regarding the West Creek development in light of the court's decision?

2. **Are SEPAs Substantive?** The United States Supreme Court has concluded that NEPA imposes no substantive requirements on federal agencies. Once an agency completes an adequate EIS, the agency is free to make any decision that it believes is appropriate—even if the EIS suggests that another decision would be better. "NEPA merely prohibits uninformed—rather than unwise—agency action." Robertson v. Methow Valley Citizens Council, 490 U.S. 332, 351 (1989). . Some SEPAs, however, go further and impose various substantive requirements on state or local agencies. See, e.g., Minn. Stat. § 116D.04(6) (prohibiting the issuance of permits that are "likely to cause pollution, impairment, or destruction of . . . natural resources . . ., so long as there is a feasible and prudent alternative"). Some states courts also have shown more willingness than the United States Supreme Court not only to require that agencies prepare

adequate EISs, but also to require the agencies "to consider fully the environmental consequences revealed in an EIS and to take these consequences into account when reaching a decision whether or not to approve an action." Town of Henrietta v. Department of Envtl. Conservation, 430 N.Y.S.2d 440, 449 (App. Div. 1980).

3. What's the value of requiring agencies to prepare an EIS or EIR? Was Professor Joseph Sax correct when he once commented in connection with NEPA that the "emphasis on the redemptive quality of procedural reform is about nine parts myth and one part coconut oil"? See Joseph L. Sax, The (Unhappy Truth) About NEPA, 26 Okla. L. Rev. 239, 239 (1973).[1] According to one environmental policy text, the fundamental goal of an EIS

> is to *educate* decisionmakers, ideally by sensitizing them to environmental issues and helping the agencies find easy, inexpensive means of mitigating environmental impacts. From an *advocacy* perspective, an EIS can provide a source of leverage for internal agency opposition. A study by the National Science Foundation in the 1980s, for example, concluded that EISs give agency personnel a tool "to resist political importunities to pursue environmentally harmful measures." Moreover, it provides information that can be used to fight an agency's decision in court, and the information is not easily dismissed. It's hard, after all, for an agency to explain why its own EIS is incorrect. In relying on the EIS, in some instances litigants may be able to show that an agency action is "arbitrary and capricious".... From a *political* perspective, the EIS can be used to educate the public and provide information that can be used to fight the decision through [legislative bodies or the] voting booth. Finally, [EIS] litigation can *delay* a project (particularly if the EIS must be done again), allowing time to organize opposition and, in some cases, making the project so costly that it expires on its own.

James Salzman & Barton H. Thompson, Jr., Environmental Law and Policy 276 (2003). There are many insightful articles on the potential value of EIS requirements, including Bradley C. Karkkainen, Toward a Smarter NEPA: Monitoring and Managing Government's Environmental Performance, 102 Colum. L. Rev. 903 (2002); Stewart E. Sterk, Environmental Review in the Land Use Process: New York's Experience with SEQRA, 13 Cardoza L. Rev. 2041 (1992); William H. Rodgers, Jr., NEPA at Twenty: Mimicry and Recruitment in Environmental Law, 20 Envtl. L. 485 (1990).

4. **Wet Growth.** Land use planning historically ignored water issues. Land use planners decided where development should take place and left finding the water up to water suppliers. Water suppliers, moreover, were happy with the arrangement. In the 1950s, the giant Metropolitan Water District of Southern California, which supplies water to Los Angeles, San

1. Professor Sax later reconsidered his somewhat harsh assessment of NEPA and concluded that he had "underestimated the influence of NEPA's 'soft law' elements." Joseph L. Sax, More Than Just a Passing Fad, 29 U. Mich. J.L. Reform 797, 804 (1986).

Diego, and other coastal communities in Southern California, issued a formal statement known as the Laguna Declaration promising to provide water for any needs that arose within its service area. Today, however, there is growing recognition that land use planning and water planning must go hand in hand.

> One of the problems with land development is its *location*. In general, the greatest growth in the United States is, and has been, occurring in arid and semi-arid regions, especially in the American West, but also in other areas of water stress in the eastern United States. In areas where the demand for water is high and the supply of water is scarce, the pressures to over-exploit sources of water and to make trans-basin (out-of-watershed) transfers are great. For example, the Los Angeles metroplex grew and sprawled at the cost of water, biodiversity, and ecosystem health in locations far from the urban area: Owens Lake (now dry), Mono Lake (now protected and rising after 25 years of environmental activism) [see p. 255 supra], and the Colorado River (overdrawn but now the subject of an agreement by California appropriators to reduce diversions). Likewise, the fast-growing Phoenix metropolitan area depends on water from the Colorado, Salt, and Verde rivers and from overdrafting (or mining) groundwater with significant environmental and economic costs. . . .
>
> But the West is not the only place of growth and water scarcity. Water stress has come to the eastern United States, where water was always thought to be plentiful. Many eastern Massachusetts communities, for example, lack sufficient water supplies. . . . The Florida Everglades' water flow has been altered to supply and protect a thriving, thirsty Miami's drinking water, adversely changing the Everglades' water flows and composition, natural vegetation, and wildlife habitat, among other biological factors. Connecticut has experienced episodes of insufficient stream flows to supply its urban area populations, and Georgia cities are eyeing the Alabama–Coosa–Tallapoosa River Basin in Georgia and Alabama, even though damming the river for urban water supply would harm mussels, snails, and fish dependent on instream flow. . . .

Craig Anthony (Tony) Arnold, Introduction: Integrating Water Controls and Land Use Controls: New Ideas and Old Obstacles, in Wet Growth: Should Water Law Control Land Use? 1, 24–25 (Craig Anthony (Tony) Arnold ed., 2005).

5. Should local governments authorize developers to build new subdivisions without knowing where residents will obtain their water in future years? California now prohibits local cities and counties from issuing a construction permit for a subdivision of 500 or more homes unless and until the local water supplier demonstrates that it can provide the subdivision with water for at least 20 years. Cal. Gov't Code § 66473.7.

Some states also require cities and other local governments to consider water supplies in developing and revising comprehensive plans. Florida, for example, requires each local government in its comprehensive plan to address "the water supply sources necessary to meet and achieve the existing and projected water use demand for the established planning period." Fla. Stat. § 163.3167(13); see also id. § 163.3177(6)(c) (requiring comprehensive plans to include elements addressing potable water and natural ground water aquifer recharge).

6. For interesting and informative discussions of the relationship between water and land use, see the various essays collected in Wet Growth: Should Water Law Control Land Use? (Craig Anthony (Tony) Arnold ed., 2005), particularly the articles by Professors Arnold, A. Dan Tarlock, Barton Thompson, Janet Neuman, Eileen Gauna, Robert Adler, Holly Doremus, Eric Freyfogle, and David Callies.

F. EXPANDING THE GOALS OF ZONING

The 1926 Standard State Zoning Enabling Act, as discussed earlier, recognized only a limited number of zoning goals, including land use, density, and the size and location of buildings. Over the past fifty years, growing interest in environmental and aesthetic issues has led to new uses of land use regulation. This section examines how courts have responded to some of these uses.

1. AESTHETIC AND ARCHITECTURAL REGULATION

Anderson v. City of Issaquah

Court of Appeals of Washington, 1993.
851 P.2d 744.

KENNEDY, J.

Appellants M. Bruce Anderson, Gary D. LaChance, and M. Bruce Anderson, Inc. (hereinafter referred to as Anderson), challenge the denial of their application for a land use certification, arguing, inter alia, that the building design requirements contained in Issaquah Municipal Code (IMC) 16.16.060 are unconstitutionally vague. The Superior Court rejected this constitutional challenge. We reverse and direct that Anderson's land use certification be issued....

Facts

Anderson owns property located at 145 N.W. Gilman Boulevard in the city of Issaquah (City). In 1988, Anderson applied to the City for a land use certification to develop the property. The property is zoned for general commercial use. Anderson desired to build a 6,800–square-foot commercial building for several retail tenants.

After obtaining architectural plans, Anderson submitted the project to various City departments for the necessary approvals. The process went smoothly until the approval of the Issaquah Development Commission (Development Commission) was sought. This commission was created to administer and enforce the City's land use regulations. It has the authority to approve or deny applications for land use certification.

Section 16.16.060 of the IMC enumerates various building design objectives which the Development Commission is required to administer and enforce. Insofar as is relevant to this appeal, the Development Commission is to be guided by the following criteria:

IMC 16.16.060(B). Relationship of Building and Site to Adjoining Area.

> 1. Buildings and structures shall be made compatible with adjacent buildings of conflicting architectural styles by such means as screens and site breaks, or other suitable methods and materials.
>
> 2. Harmony in texture, lines, and masses shall be encouraged. . . .

IMC 16.16.060(D). Building Design.

> 1. Evaluation of a project shall be based on quality of its design and relationship to the natural setting of the valley and surrounding mountains.
>
> 2. Building components, such as windows, doors, eaves and parapets, shall have appropriate proportions and relationship to each other, expressing themselves as a part of the overall design.
>
> 3. Colors shall be harmonious, with bright or brilliant colors used only for minimal accent.
>
> 4. Design attention shall be given to screening from public view all mechanical equipment, including refuse enclosures, electrical transformer pads and vaults, communication equipment, and other utility hardware on roofs, grounds or buildings.
>
> 5. Exterior lighting shall be part of the architectural concept. Fixtures, standards and all exposed accessories shall be harmonious with the building design.
>
> 6. Monotony of design in single or multiple building projects shall be avoided. Efforts should be made to create an interesting project by use of complimentary details, functional orientation of buildings, parking and access provisions and relating the development to the site. In multiple building projects, variable siting of individual buildings, heights of buildings, or other methods shall be used to prevent a monotonous design.

As initially designed, Anderson's proposed structure was to be faced with off-white stucco and was to have a blue metal roof. It was designed in a "modern" style with an unbroken "warehouse" appearance in the rear, and large retail-style windows in the front. The City moved a Victorian era residence, the "Alexander House," onto the neighboring property to serve as a visitors' center. Across the street from the Anderson site is a gasoline station that looks like a gasoline station. Located nearby and within view from the proposed building site are two more gasoline stations, the First Mutual Bank Building built in the "Issaquah territorial style," an Elks hall which is described in the record by the Mayor of Issaquah as a "box building," an auto repair shop, and a veterinary clinic with a cyclone-fenced dog run. The area is described in the record as "a natural transition area between old downtown Issaquah and the new village style construction of Gilman [Boulevard]."

The Development Commission reviewed Anderson's application for the first time at a public hearing on December 21, 1988. Commissioner Nash commented that "the facade did not fit with the concept of the surrounding area." Commissioner McGinnis agreed. Commissioner Nash expressed concern about the building color and stated that he did not think the building was compatible with the image of Issaquah. Commissioner Larson said that he would like to see more depth to the building facade. Commissioner Nash said there should be some interest created along the blank back wall. Commissioner Garrison suggested that the rear facade needed to be redesigned.

At the conclusion of the meeting, the Development Commission voted to continue the hearing to give Anderson an opportunity to modify the building design.

On January 18, 1989, Anderson came back before the Development Commission with modified plans which included changing the roofing from metal to tile, changing the color of the structure from off-white to "Cape Cod" gray with "Tahoe" blue trim, and adding brick to the front facade. During the ensuing discussion among the commissioners, Commissioner Larson stated that the revisions to the front facade had not satisfied his concerns from the last meeting. In response to Anderson's request for more specific design guidelines, Commissioner McGinnis stated that the Development Commission had "been giving direction; it is the applicant's responsibility to take the direction/suggestions and incorporate them into a revised plan that reflects the changes." Commissioner Larson then suggested that "the facade can be broken up with sculptures, benches, fountains, etc." Commissioner Nash suggested that Anderson "drive up and down Gilman and look at both good and bad examples of what has been done with flat facades."

As the discussion continued, Commissioner Larson stated that Anderson "should present a [plan] that achieves what the Commission is trying to achieve through its comments/suggestions at these meetings" and stated that "architectural screens, fountains, paving of brick, wood or other similar methods of screening in lieu of vegetative landscaping are examples of design suggestions that can be used to break up the front facade." Commissioner Davis objected to the front facade, stating that he could not see putting an expanse of glass facing Gilman Boulevard. "The building is not compatible with Gilman." Commissioner O'Shea agreed. Commissioner

Nash stated that "the application needs major changes to be acceptable." Commissioner O'Shea agreed. Commissioner Nash stated that "this facade does not create the same feeling as the building/environment around this site."

Commissioner Nash continued, stating that he "personally liked the introduction of brick and the use of tiles rather than metal on the roof." Commissioner Larson stated that he would like to see a review of the blue to be used: "Tahoe blue may be too dark." Commissioner Steinwachs agreed. Commissioner Larson noted that "the front of the building could be modulated [to] have other design techniques employed to make the front facade more interesting."

With this, the Development Commission voted to continue the discussion to a future hearing.

On February 15, 1989, Anderson came back before the Development Commission. In the meantime, Anderson's architects had added a 5-foot overhang and a 7-foot accent overhang to the plans for the front of the building. More brick had been added to the front of the building. Wood trim and accent colors had been added to the back of the building and trees were added to the landscaping to further break up the rear facade.

Anderson explained the plans still called for large, floor to ceiling windows as this was to be a retail premises: "[A] glass front is necessary to rent the space. . . ." Commissioner Steinwachs stated that he had driven Gilman Boulevard and taken notes. The following verbatim statement by Steinwachs was placed into the minutes:

> *"My General Observation From Driving Up and Down Gilman Boulevard."*
>
> I see certain design elements and techniques used in various combinations in various locations to achieve a visual effect that is sensitive to the unique character of our Signature Street. I see heavy use of brick, wood, and tile. I see minimal use of stucco. I see colors that are mostly earthtones, avoiding extreme contrasts. I see various methods used to provide modulation in both horizontal and vertical lines, such as gables, bay windows, recesses in front faces, porches, rails, many vertical columns, and breaks in roof lines. I see long, sloping, conspicuous roofs with large overhangs. I see windows with panels above and below windows. I see no windows that extend down to floor level. This is the impression I have of Gilman Boulevard as it relates to building design.

Commissioner Nash agreed stating, "There is a certain feeling you get when you drive along Gilman Boulevard, and this building does not give this same feeling." Commissioner Steinwachs wondered if the applicant had any option but to start "from scratch." Anderson responded that he would be willing to change from stucco to wood facing but that, after working on the project for 9 months and experiencing total frustration, he was not willing to make additional design changes.

At that point, the Development Commission denied Anderson's application, giving four reasons:

> 1. After four [sic] lengthy review meetings of the Development Commission, the applicant has not been sufficiently responsive to concerns expressed by the Commission to warrant approval or an additional continuance of the review.
>
> 2. The primary concerns expressed relate to the building architecture as it relates to Gilman Boulevard in general, and the immediate neighborhood in particular.
>
> 3. The Development Commission is charged with protecting, preserving and enhancing the aesthetic values that have established the desirable quality and unique character of Issaquah, reference IMC 16.16.010C.
>
> 4. We see certain design elements and techniques used in various combinations in various locations to achieve a visual effect that is sensitive to the unique character of our Signature Street. On Gilman Boulevard we see heavy use of brick, wood and tile. We see minimal use of stucco. We see various methods used to provide both horizontal and vertical modulation, including gables, breaks in rooflines, bay windows, recesses and protrusions in front face. We see long, sloping, conspicuous roofs with large overhangs. We see no windows that extend to ground level. We see brick and wood panels at intervals between windows. We see earthtone colors avoiding extreme contrast.

Anderson, who by this time had an estimated $250,000 into the project, timely appealed the adverse ruling to the Issaquah City Council (City Council). After a lengthy hearing and much debate, the City Council decided to affirm the Development Commission's decision by a vote of 4 to 3. . . .

Constitutionality of IMC 16.16.060
(Building Design Provisions)

> [A] statute which either forbids or requires the doing of an act in terms so vague that men [and women] of common intelligence must necessarily guess at its meaning and differ as to its application, violates the first essential of due process of law.

Connally v. General Constr. Co., 269 U.S. 385, 391 (1926). In the field of regulatory statutes governing business activities, statutes which employ technical words which are commonly understood within an industry, or which employ words with a well-settled common law meaning, generally will be sustained against a charge of vagueness. The vagueness test does not require a statute to meet impossible standards of specificity. . . .

Looking first at the face of the building design sections of IMC 16.16.060, we note that an ordinary citizen reading these sections would learn only that a given building project should bear a good relationship with the Issaquah Valley and surrounding mountains; its windows, doors, eaves and parapets should be of "appropriate proportions," its colors should be "harmonious" and seldom "bright" or "brilliant"; its mechanical equipment should be screened from public view; its exterior lighting should be "harmonious" with the building design and "monotony should be avoided." The project should also be "interesting." IMC 16.16.060(D)(1)–(6). If the building is not "compatible" with adjacent buildings, it should be "made compatible" by the use of screens and site breaks "or other suitable methods and materials." "Harmony in texture, lines, and masses [is] encouraged." The landscaping should provide an "attractive ... transition" to adjoining properties. IMC 16.16.060(B)(1)–(3).

As is stated in the brief of amicus curiae, we conclude that these code sections "do not give effective or meaningful guidance" to applicants, to design professionals, or to the public officials of Issaquah who are responsible for enforcing the code. Although it is clear from the code sections here at issue that mechanical equipment must be screened from public view and that, probably, earthtones or pastels located within the cool and muted ranges of the color wheel are going to be preferred, there is nothing in the code from which an applicant can determine whether his or her project is going to be seen by the Development Commission as "interesting" versus "monotonous" and as "harmonious" with the valley and the mountains. Neither is it clear from the code just what else, besides the valley and the mountains, a particular project is supposed to be harmonious with, although "harmony in texture, lines, and masses" is certainly encouraged. IMC 16.16.060(B)(2).

In attempting to interpret and apply this code, the commissioners charged with that task were left with only their own individual, subjective "feelings" about the "image of Issaquah" and as to whether this project was "compatible" or "interesting." The commissioners stated that the City was "making a statement" on its "signature street" and invited Anderson to take a drive up and down Gilman Boulevard and "look at good and bad examples of what has been done wit h flat facades." One commissioner drove up and down Gilman, taking notes, in a no doubt sincere effort to define that which is left undefined in the code.

The point we make here is that neither Anderson nor the commissioners may constitutionally be required or allowed to guess at the meaning of the code's building design requirements by driving up and down Gilman Boulevard looking at "good and bad" examples of what has been done with other buildings, recently or in the past. We hold that the code sections here at issue are unconstitutionally vague on their face. The words employed are not technical words which are commonly understood within the professional building design industry. Neither do these words have a settled common law meaning....

Anderson has argued strenuously in this appeal that a municipality has no power to deny a proposed development for aesthetic reasons alone. Anderson argues this issue is "settled" by Washington case law....

We believe the issue of whether a community can exert control over design issues based solely on accepted community aesthetic values is far from "settled" in Washington case law. The possibility certainly has not been foreclosed by our Supreme Court. See Polygon Corp. v. Seattle, 90 Wash. 2d 59, 70, 578 P.2d 1309 (1978) ("While this court has not held that aesthetic factors alone will support an exercise of the police power, such considerations taken together with other factors can support such action."). See also Duckworth v. Bonney Lk., 91 Wash. 2d 19, 30, 586 P.2d 860 (1978) ("While we have indicated that aesthetic considerations alone *may* not support invocation of the police powers ...". (Italics ours.))

Clearly, however, aesthetic standards are an appropriate *component* of land use governance. Whenever a community adopts such standards they can and must be drafted to give clear guidance to all parties concerned. Applicants must have an understandable statement of what is expected from new construction. Design professionals need to know in advance what standards will be acceptable in a given community. It is unreasonable to expect applicants to pay for repetitive revisions of plans in an effort to comply with the unarticulated, unpublished "statements" a given community may wish to make on or off its "signature street." It is equally unreasonable, and a deprivation of due process, to expect or allow a design review board such as the Issaquah Development Commission to create standards on an *ad hoc* basis, during the design review process.

Conclusion

It is not disputed that Anderson's project meets all of the City's land use requirements except for those unwritten and therefore unenforceable requirements relating to building design which the Development Commission unsuccessfully tried to articulate during the course of several hearings. We order that Anderson's land use certification be issued, provided however, that those changes which Anderson agreed to through the hearing before the City Council may validly be imposed.

Notes & Questions

1. What vision of public health, safety, welfare, and morals underlay the enactment of the city ordinance in *Anderson*?

2. The preservation or creation of such amenities as scenic highways and architecturally homogeneous neighborhoods has only gradually and partially obtained a secure foothold in the police power. Courts originally took a jaundiced view of aesthetic regulations, holding that the presence of an aesthetic objective would defeat an otherwise valid land use control measure. Virtually all courts in the country have since decided that the presence of an aesthetic objective will not defeat an ordinance so long as some other, more acceptable element of the police power—safety or the protection of property values—also justifies the measure. Most states now hold that aesthetic objects are a legitimate goal of the state police power and thus sufficient by themselves to sustain land use legislation. See generally Beverly A. Rowlett, Aesthetic Regulation Under the Police Power: The New General Welfare and the Presumption of Constitutionality, 34

Vand. L. Rev. 603 (1981); Samuel Bufford, Beyond the Eye of the Beholder: A New Majority of Jurisdictions Authorize Aesthetic Regulation, 48 U.M.K.C. L. Rev. 125 (1980).

3. **Architectural Controls.** The principal criticism leveled today against architectural review provisions like that in *Anderson* is that they are vague and delegate excessive discretionary authority to administrative agencies, exposing landowners to arbitrary and standardless decisions. What type of guidance would have saved the Issaquah ordinance from invalidation? Are aesthetic regulations inherently vague and subjective?

Courts will sometimes look outside the express terms of the applicable legislation to find the necessary constraining standards. Standard architectural principles provide one external source of guidelines. Where an expert architectural review board implements the standards, courts also sometimes emphasize the expertise of the board members in holding that the review provisions are sufficiently clear. See, e.g., Reid v. Architectural Bd. of Review, 192 N.E.2d 74, 77 (Ohio App. 1963) ("When borne in mind that the members of the Board are highly trained experts in the field of architecture, the instruction that they resolve these questions on 'proper architectural principles' is profoundly reasonable since such expression has reference to the basic knowledge on which their profession is founded").

4. **Aesthetics and the First Amendment.** Aesthetic regulations sometimes run head-on into free speech interests protected under the First Amendment to the United States Constitution, as applied to the states under the Fourteenth Amendment. Indeed, the early reluctance to validate these regulations stemmed in part from the concern that to allow city councils to legislate what is beautiful, as well as what is safe and healthful, might improperly chill artistic and political expression.

Ironically, one of the first decisions to accept aesthetics as a legitimate, independent object of local regulation, and to reject the First Amendment claim, upheld an ordinance that was directly aimed at curbing political speech. In People v. Stover, 191 N.E.2d 272 (N.Y. 1963), the defendants had placed a clothesline, "filled with old clothes and rags," in their front yard as a form of protest against local taxes. The city prosecuted the defendants for violating a city ordinance that prohibited front yard clotheslines. While acknowledging that the clothesline was a form of nonverbal expression protected under the First Amendment, the New York Court of Appeals held that it was subject to reasonable regulation, allegedly intended to reduce traffic hazards by providing clear visibility at street corners.

The United States Supreme Court has addressed the constitutionality of aesthetic controls in a series of cases dealing with bans on billboards and other signs. In Metromedia, Inc. v. City of San Diego, 453 U.S. 490 (1981), a 6–3 decision that generated five separate opinions, the Court held that San Diego, in the interests of "traffic safety and beauty," could constitutionally ban off-site commercial billboards, while permitting on-site advertising. (Advertising is "on-site" when it touts goods or services available on the property where the advertising is located.) The Court, however, invalidated San Diego's ban on signs carrying noncommercial speech, both because the Constitution provides greater protection to noncommercial speech and because San Diego permitted some noncommercial signs but not others.

A decade later, the Court unanimously overturned a local ordinance that banned the displaying of any signs other than "residence identification" signs, "for sale" signs, and signs warning of safety hazards. City of Ladue v. Gilleo, 512 U.S. 43 (1994). The city had refused to grant a variance for a sign protesting the first Persian Gulf war. While the court conceded that the city's "interest in minimizing the visual clutter associated with signs" was valid, the ordinance "almost completely foreclosed a venerable means of communication" and thus was unconstitutional.

> A special respect for individual liberty in the home has long been part of our culture and our law; that principle has special resonance when the government seeks to constrain a person's ability to speak there. Most Americans would be understandably dismayed, given that tradition, to learn that it was illegal to display from their window an 8–by 11–inch sign expressing political views.... It bears mentioning that individual residents themselves have strong incentives to keep their own property values up and to prevent "visual clutter" in their own yards and neighborhoods.... Residents' self-interest diminishes the danger of the "unlimited" proliferation of residential signs that concerns the City of Ladue.

5. **Zoning Adult Entertainment.** To what degree can a city use zoning to limit the amount and location of adult entertainment? In Young v. American Mini Theatres, Inc., 427 U.S. 50 (1976), the Court by a 5–4 vote upheld a Detroit zoning ordinance that prohibited "adult" movie theatres, bookstores, and peep shows from locating within 1000 feet of each other. Justice Stevens' plurality opinion started from the premise that society's interest in protecting erotic expression is less compelling than its interest in protecting political expression, and concluded that "[w]e are not persuaded that the Detroit zoning ordinances will have a significant deterrent effect on the exhibition of films protected by the First Amendment." Id. at 60. Justice Powell, writing separately on the point, viewed the case as "presenting an example of innovative land-use regulation, implicating First Amendment concerns only incidentally and to a limited extent." Id. at 73.

The Supreme Court did not intend the municipal power validated in *Young* to be "infinite or unchallengeable," and in Schad v. Borough of Mt. Ephraim, 452 U.S. 61 (1981), the Court overturned appellant's conviction under a zoning ordinance that prohibited all live entertainment, including live nude dancing, in the borough. Writing for the majority, Justice White asserted that "when a zoning law infringes upon a protected liberty, it must be narrowly drawn and must further a sufficiently substantial governmental interest." Id. at 69. Justice Blackmun, concurring, thought that "the presumption of validity that traditionally attends a local government's exercise of its zoning powers carries little, if any weight where the zoning regulation trenches on rights of expression protected under the First

Amendment." Id. at 77. Chief Justice Burger, joined by Justice Rehnquist, dissented. "At issue here is the right of a small community to ban an activity incompatible with a quiet, residential atmosphere. The Borough of Mount Ephraim did nothing more than employ traditional police power to provide a setting of tranquility." Id. at 85.

Finally, in City of Renton v. Playtime Theatres, Inc., 475 U.S. 41 (1986), the Supreme Court upheld a local ordinance that prohibited adult motion picture theaters from locating within 1,000 feet of any residential zone, church, park, or school—even though this limited such theatres to only about 5 percent of the city. The Court concluded that the ordinance was "the essence of zoning." The city "sought to make some areas available for adult theaters and their patrons, while at the same time preserving the quality of life in the community at large by preventing those theaters from locating in other areas." Id. at 54.

6. For interesting observations on the relationship of zoning and the First Amendment, see Shelley Ross Saxer, Zoning Away First Amendment Rights, 53 Wash. U. J. Urb. & Contemp. L. 1 (1998).

2. HISTORIC PRESERVATION

A–S–P Associates v. City of Raleigh

Supreme Court of North Carolina, 1979.
258 S.E.2d 444.

Plaintiff brought this action seeking a declaratory judgment the two ordinances adopted on 3 June 1975 by the City of Raleigh are invalid both on constitutional and statutory grounds. The two ordinances (hereinafter referred to collectively as the Oakwood Ordinance) amended the City's zoning ordinance to create a 98 acre, overlay historic district in the City's Oakwood neighborhood (hereinafter referred to as the Historic District), established the Raleigh Historic District Commission (hereinafter referred to as the Historic District Commission), adopted architectural guidelines and design standards to be applied by the Historic District Commission in its administration of the Oakwood Ordinance, and provided civil and criminal penalties for failure to comply with the Oakwood Ordinance.

The Ordinance was adopted pursuant to G.S. § § 160A–395 through 399, which authorize municipalities to designate historic districts and to require that after the designation of a historic district any property owner within it who desires to erect, alter, restore, or move the exterior portion of any building or other structure first obtain a certificate of appropriateness from a historic district commission. A historic district commission's action is limited by G.S. § 160A–397 to "preventing the construction, reconstruction, alteration, restoration, or moving of buildings, structures, appurtenant fixtures, or outdoor advertising signs in the historic district which would be incongruous with the historic aspects of the district."

In May of 1974, the Division of Archives and History of the North Carolina Department of Cultural Resources nominated Raleigh's Oakwood neighborhood for inclusion on the United States Department of Interior's National Register of Historic Places. In the required statement of significance, the Division's Survey and Planning Unit observed:

> Oakwood, a twenty-block area representing the only intact nineteenth century neighborhood remaining in Raleigh, is composed predominantly of Victorian houses built between the Civil War and 1914. Its depressed economic state during most of the twentieth century preserved the neighborhood until 1971, when individuals began its revitalization. The great variety of Victorian architectural styles represented by the houses reflects the primarily middle-class tastes of the business and political leaders of Raleigh for whom they were built, as well as the skill of local architects and builders. Oakwood is a valuable physical document of Southern suburban life during the last quarter of the nineteenth century.

On 25 June 1974, the Oakwood neighborhood was placed on the National Register. . . .

The Historic District thus created is an overlay zoning district. All zoning regulations in the area in effect prior to passage of the Oakwood Ordinance remain in effect. Compliance with the Oakwood Ordinance is required in addition to compliance with the pre-existing, underlying zoning regulations. Most of the area covered by the Historic District is zoned residential. A relatively small portion of the area covered by it is zoned as office and institutional. Associates own a vacant lot, located within the Historic District at 210 North Person Street. The lot is within the office and institutional zoning district.

On 22 July 1975 Associates brought this action challenging the validity of the Ordinance on constitutional and statutory grounds. . . .

BROCK, J.

. . . .

Associates' first contentions are that the Oakwood Ordinance deprives them of their property without due process of law in contravention of the Fourteenth Amendment to the United States Constitution, and that it deprives them of their property otherwise than by the law of the land in contravention of Article I, Section 19, of the North Carolina Constitution. The terms "law of the land" and "due process of law" are synonymous. Horton v. Gulledge, 277 N.C. 353, 177 S.E. 2d 885 (1970).

Associates' claim is premised on a line of cases in which this Court has indicated that a statute or ordinance based purely on aesthetic considerations, without any real or substantial relation to the public health, safety or morals, or the general welfare, deprives individuals of due process of law. State v. Vestal, 281 N.C. 517, 189 S.E. 2d 152 (1972); Little Pep Delmonico Restaurant, Inc. v. Charlotte, 252 N.C. 324, 113 S.E. 2d 422 (1960); State v. Brown, 250 N.C. 54, 108 S.E. 2d 74 (1959); In Re O'Neal, 243 N.C. 714, 92

S.E. 2d 189 (1956). Associates contend that the Oakwood Ordinance falls within the scope of such impermissible exercise of the police power because it focuses entirely on the exterior appearance of structures within the Historic District. Associates further contend that even if the Ordinance is a valid exercise of the police power insofar as it is applied to historic structures, it is invalid when applied to new construction on property such as Associates' vacant lot.

The police power is inherent in the sovereignty of the State. Winston–Salem v. Southern R.R. Co., 248 N.C. 637, 105 S.E. 2d 37 (1958). It is as extensive as may be required for the protection of the public health, safety, morals and general welfare. State v. Hales, 256 N.C. 27, 122 S.E. 2d 768 (1961)....

Legislative exercise of the police power to regulate private property in the interest of historic preservation has met with increasing acceptance by the courts of other jurisdictions. E.g., Maher v. City of New Orleans, 516 F. 2d 1051 (5th Cir. 1975); Bohannan v. City of San Diego, 30 Cal. App. 3d 416, 106 Cal. Rptr. 333 (1973); Figarsky v. Historic District Comm., 171 Conn. 198, 368 A. 2d 163 (1976); Rebman v. City of Springfield, 111 Ill. App. 2d 430, 250 N.E. 2d 282 (1969); City of New Orleans v. Levy, 223 La. 14, 64 So. 2d 798 (1953); Opinion of the Justices, 333 Mass. 773, 128 N.E. 2d 557 (1955); Opinion of the Justices, 333 Mass. 783, 128 N.E. 2d 563 (1955); and City of Santa Fe v. Gamble–Skogmo, Inc., 73 N.M. 410, 389 P.2d 13 (1964). Historic district legislation similar to the provisions of G.S. §§ 160A–395 through 399 has now been enacted by at least thirty-nine states. More than 500 cities and towns have passed local landmark or historic district ordinances. National Trust for Historic Preservation, Historic Preservation and the Law, Part IV, ch. 5, p. 3 (1978)....

In State v. Vestal, 281 N.C. 517, 189 S.E. 2d 152 (1972), we took note of the growing body of authority in other jurisdictions recognizing that the police power may be broad enough to include reasonable regulation of property for aesthetic reasons alone. Although we are not now prepared to endorse such a broad concept of the scope of the police power, we find no difficulty in holding that the police power encompasses the right to control the exterior appearance of private property when the object of such control is the preservation of the State's legacy of historically significant structures. "While most aesthetic ordinances are concerned with good taste and beauty ... a historic district zoning ordinance ... is not primarily concerned with whether the subject of regulation is beautiful or tasteful, but rather with preserving it as it is, representative of what it was, for such educational, cultural, or economic values as it may have. Cases dealing with purely aesthetic regulations are distinguishable from those dealing with preservation of a historical area or a historical style of architecture." A. Rathkopf, The Law of Zoning and Planning, § 15.01, p. 15–4, (4th ed. 1975).

The preservation of historically significant residential and commercial districts protects and promotes the general welfare in distinct yet intricately related ways. It provides a visual, educational medium by which an understanding of our country's historic and cultural heritage may be imparted to present and future generations. That understanding provides in turn a unique and valuable perspective on the social, cultural, and economic mores of past generations of Americans, which remain operative to varying degrees today. Historic preservation moreover serves as a stimulus to protection and of the general welfare in related, more tangible respects. It can stimulate revitalization of deteriorating residential and commercial districts in urban areas, thus contributing to their economic and social stability. It tends to foster architectural creativity by preserving physical examples of outstanding architectural techniques of the past. It also has the potential, documented in numerous instances, e.g., in the Vieux Carre section of New Orleans, of generating substantial tourism revenues. Although it is also recognized that historic preservation legislation, particularly historic district ordinances, may adversely affect the welfare of certain segments of society and infringe on individual liberty, the wisdom of such legislation is "fairly debatable," precluding substitution of our judgment for that of the General Assembly....

Associates next contend that the superior court erred as a matter of law in ruling that the Oakwood Ordinance does not delegate legislative power to the Historic District Commission. Legislative power is vested exclusively in the General Assembly by Article II, Section 1, of the North Carolina Constitution. From this provision and from Article I, Section 6, derives the principle that the General Assembly may not delegate its power to any other department or body. This principle, however, is not absolute.

> Since legislation must often be adapted to complex conditions involving numerous details with which the Legislature cannot deal directly, the constitutional inhibition against delegating legislative authority does not deny to the Legislature the necessary flexibility of enabling it to lay down policies and establish standards, while leaving to designated governmental agencies and administrative boards the determination of facts to which the policy as declared by the Legislature shall apply. (Citation omitted.) Without this power, the Legislature would often be placed in the awkward situation of possessing a power over a given subject without being able to exercise it.

Coastal Highway v. Turnpike Authority, 237 N.C. 52, 60, 74 S.E.2d 310, 316 (1953). Associates contend that adequate standards have not been established in this instance....

The delegation of legislative power to municipal governing bodies is not in this instance, however, an unlimited delegation. G.S. § 160A-396 provides that before a city or county may designate one or more historic districts it must establish a historic district commission. n2 G.S. § 160A-396 further limits the delegation of power by specifying that, "a majority of the members of such a commission shall have demonstrated special interest, experience, or education in history or architecture...." G.S. § 160A-397 imposes another limitation by specifying the method by which a historic district ordinance adopted by a city or county is to be enforced:

> From and after the designation of a historic district, no exterior portion of any building or other structure (including stone walls, fences, light fixtures, steps and pavement, or other appurtenant features) nor above-ground utility structure nor any type of outdoor advertising sign shall be erected, altered, restored, or moved within such district until after an application for a certificate of appropriateness as to exterior architectural features has been submitted to and approved by the historic district commission.

G.S. § 160A–397 then establishes the standard by which a historic district commission is to be bound in its administration of a historic district by approving or disapproving applications for Certificates of Appropriateness:

> The commission shall not consider interior arrangement and shall take no action under this section except for the purpose of preventing the construction, reconstruction, alteration, restoration, or moving of buildings, structures, appurtenant fixtures, or outdoor advertising signs in the historic district *which would be incongruous with the historic aspects of the district.* (Emphasis added.)

The statutory authorization of historic district ordinances is, therefore, a mixture of delegated legislative and administrative power. A municipal governing body has unlimited discretion to determine whether or not to establish a historic district or districts. Once it chooses to do so, however, its discretion insofar as the method and the standard by which a historic district ordinance is to be administered is, by contrast, extremely limited. A historic district ordinance is to be administered by a historic district commission, the composition of which is specified by the General Assembly, in accordance with the standard of "incongruity" set directly by the General Assembly in G.S. § 160A–397. . . .

In the recent case of Adams v. Dept. of N.E.R., 295 N.C. 683, 698, 249 S.E. 2d 402, 411 (1978) we observed with respect to the delegation of power to an administrative agency:

> When there is an obvious need for expertise in the achievement of legislative goals the General Assembly is not required to lay down a detailed agenda covering every conceivable problem which might arise in the implementation of the legislation. It is enough if general policies and standards have been articulated which are sufficient to provide direction to an administrative body possessing the expertise to adapt the legislative goals to varying circumstances.

We also joined in *Adams* a growing trend of authority by recognizing that "the presence or absence of procedural safeguards is relevant to the broader question of whether a delegation of authority is accompanied by adequate guiding standards." Id.

The general policy and standard of "incongruity," adopted by both the General Assembly and the Raleigh City Council, in this instance is best denominated as "a contextual standard." A contextual standard is one which derives its meaning from the objectively determinable, interrelated conditions and characteristics of the subject to which the standard is to be applied. In this instance the standard of "incongruity" must derive its meaning, if any, from the total physical environment of the Historic District. That is to say, the conditions and characteristics of the Historic District's physical environment must be sufficiently distinctive and identifiable to provide reasonable guidance to the Historic District Commission in applying the "incongruity" standard.

Although the neighborhood encompassed by the Historic District is to a considerable extent an architectural melange, that heterogeneity of architectural style is not such as to render the standard of "incongruity" meaningless. The predominant architectural style found in the area is Victorian, the characteristics of which are readily identifiable....

It will be remembered that G.S. § 160A–396 requires that a majority of the members of a historic district commission shall have demonstrated special interest, experience, or education in history or architecture. There is no evidence that Raleigh's Historic District Commission is not so constituted. To achieve the ultimate purposes of historic district preservation, it is a practical necessity that a substantial degree of discretionary authority guided by policies and goals set by the legislature, be delegated to such an administrative body possessing the expertise to adapt the legislative policies and goals to varying, particular circumstances. It is a matter of practical impossibility for a legislative body to deal with the host of details inherent in the complex nature of historic district preservation.

It is therefore sufficient that a general, yet meaningful, contextual standard has been set forth to limit the discretion of the Historic District Commission. Strikingly similar standards for administration of historic district ordinances have long been approved by courts of other jurisdictions....

For the reasons stated, the superior court's ruling that the Oakwood Ordinance does not impermissibly delegate legislative power to the Historic District Commission is affirmed....

Notes & Questions

1. As *A–S–P Associates* illustrates, historic preservation efforts have raised the same two basic issues as architectural controls have generated: is the ordinance a legitimate exercise of the state police, and do the statutory standards provide adequate guidance to the implementing agency? Courts, however, have generally been more receptive to historic preservation laws than to architectural review statutes. Why? Is there any basis for distinguishing historic preservation from architectural review?

On the question of constitutional authority, are historic preservation efforts grounded on broader and more established principles of public welfare than are architectural controls? Consider in this regard Professor Carol Rose's summary of the major themes that have dominated the evolution of historic preservation efforts over the last century or so:

> The first [major theme], especially characteristic of the nineteenth century, is the idea that historic preservation should seek to inspire the observer with a sense of patriotism. Thus, nineteenth-century preservation activities revolved around structures associated with famous individuals or events; the movement to save Mount Vernon is perhaps the epitome of this approach. The second theme has a cultural, artistic, and architectural focus emerging at about the turn of the century with the entry of professional artists and architects into historic preservation. The protagonists of this view thought preservation activities should focus on the artistic merit of buildings or groups of buildings and on the integrity of their architectural style. In recent years a third strand has appeared that incorporates some elements of the earlier two. Its most notable characteristic is a concern for the environmental and psychological effects of historic preservation. Indeed, this approach to preservation coincided with the environmental movement, and like that movement centers on the relationship of human beings to their physical surroundings. It stresses the "sense of place" that older structures lend to a community, giving individuals interest, orientation, and a sense of familiarity in their surroundings.

Carol Rose, Preservation and Community: New Directions in the Law of Historic Preservation, 33 Stan. L. Rev. 473, 479–480 (1981).

On the question of administrative discretion, does the architectural style of particular historic locations and periods help confine an agency's discretion? See, e.g., City of New Orleans v. Impastato, 3 So. 2d 559 (La. 1941) (upholding architectural controls for New Orleans' historic French Quarter).

2. Although the federal government indicated a programmatic interest in historic preservation as early as the Antiquities Act of 1906, 16 U.S.C. §§ 431 et seq., all levels of government did not become actively involved until the 1960s. By the mid–1970s, however, all fifty states and more than 500 municipalities, including many of the nation's largest cities, had enacted laws aimed at preserving landmark buildings and historic districts.

Federal efforts at historic preservation combine a variety of techniques. The 1966 Historic Preservation Act, 16 U.S.C. §§ 470 et seq., authorizes grants in aid for preservation and, probably more importantly, establishes a National Register of Historic Places to list landmarks nominated by the states. As of the middle of 2006, the register listed almost 79,000 sites. Any federally-assisted project affecting a registered landmark must take the project's effects into account, and the responsible agency must give the Advisory Council on Historic Preservation the opportunity to comment on these effects. 16 U.S.C. §§ 470(a) & (f). The federal tax code also provides tax incentives for the designation of a building as an historic landmark. See Roberta F. Mann, Tax Incentives for Historic Preservation: An Antidote for Sprawl?, 8 Widener L. Symp. J. 207 (2002)

Cities and other local governments provide the most active protection of historic structures. Many local governments provide for the designation and protection of both individual buildings and entire communities or districts. Historic district regulations typically prohibit any new construction or demolition that is inconsistent with buildings already in the district. See, e.g., Mass. Gen. Laws Ann. ch. 40C. Because preservation ordinances typically have a substantial impact on landowners within designated historic districts, these ordinances sometimes give local residents a say in the designation decision—for example, by requiring a specified percentage of residents to agree to the designation.

3. **Gentrification.** Some observers have raised concerns that historic designations can lead to *gentrification*. See David B. Fein, Historic Districts: Preserving City Neighborhoods for the Privileged, 60 N.Y.U. L. Rev. 64 (1985). The historical designation of a run-down area is sometimes the prelude to a dramatic social upheaval: the eviction of lower income tenants, restoration of buildings, and the sale or rental of the restored buildings to middle or upper income residents. How might historic preservation ordinances address this problem?

4. **Freedom of Religion.** Can the government restrict the ability of a religious order to tear down or modify a church, synagogue, or other religious facility? In the 1980s, St. Bartholomew's Episcopal Church in New York City sought to replace its community house, a designated historic landmark, with a 47-story office tower and use the revenue to help support its religious activities and its programs for the needy. When New York City's Landmarks Preservation Commission denied permission, the church sued, arguing that the city's landmark law violated the church's First Amendment rights to "carry on and expand the ministerial and charitable activities that are central to its religious mission." The Second Circuit disagreed. Although fifteen percent of New York City's landmarked sites at the time were religious properties, there was no evidence that the city's landmarks law intended to or did discrimination against religion or particular religious beliefs. "Because of the importance of religion, and of particular churches, in our social and cultural history, and because many churches are designed to be architecturally attractive, many religious structures are likely to fall within the neutral criteria—having 'special character or special historical or aesthetic interest or value'—set forth by the Landmarks Law." Rector of St. Bartholomew's Church v. City of New York, 914 F.2d 348 (2d Cir. 1990).

In 2000, Congress passed the Religious Land Use and Institutionalized Persons Act, 42 U.S.C. §§ 2000c et seq., which provides that no government "shall impose or implement a land use regulation in a manner that imposes a substantial burden" on a religious institution, "unless the government demonstrates that imposition of the burden ... (A) is in furtherance of a compelling government interest; and (B) is the least restrictive means of furthering that compelling governmental interest." Id. § 2000cc(a)(1). Does the designation of a church as a historic landmark, preventing its congregation from tearing it down to build a larger church, "substantially burden" the free exercise rights protected by the Act? See Episcopal Student Found. v. City of Ann Arbor, 341 F. Supp. 2d 691 (E.D. Mich. 2004) (no).

3. Growth Control

Many cities in recent years have sought to address the impacts of rapid growth. Growth raises several issues. The first is how to deal with the increased demand on public funding and resources that growth brings. As a city's population grows, the city must provide more classrooms, hospitals, libraries, and other public facilities. Growth, moreover, can increase pollution levels and traffic. Growth also can place pressure on existing water supplies (forcing the city either to restrict water use or obtain new supplies from distant watersheds), as well as sewage systems and other infrastructure. A second issue is growth patterns. As families began to flee cities in the second half of the 20th century, they settled in large new suburban subdivisions—destroying valuable open space and creating *urban sprawl*. See Patrick Gallagher, The Environmental, Social, and Cultural Impacts of Sprawl, 15 Nat. Resources & Env't 219 (2001).

What steps can a city take to manage growth? Can a city declare a moratorium on new development, at least for a long enough period of time to study the problems of growth and determine how best to address them or to ensure that the city can handle the growth?

Associated Home Builders, Inc. v. City of Livermore

Supreme Court of California, 1976.
557 P.2d 473.

Tobriner, Justice.

We face today the question of the validity of an initiative ordinance enacted by the voters of the City of Livermore which prohibits issuance of further residential building permits until local educational, sewage disposal, and water supply facilities comply with specified standards. Plaintiff, an association of contractors, subdividers, and other persons interested in residential construction in Livermore, brought this suit to enjoin enforcement of the ordinance. The superior court issued a permanent injunction, and the city appealed....

The initiative ordinance in question was enacted by a majority of the voters at the Livermore municipal election of April 11, 1972, and became effective on April 28, 1972. The ordinance states that it was enacted to further the health, safety, and welfare of the citizens of Livermore and to contribute to the solution of air pollution. Finding that excessive issuance of residential building permits has caused school overcrowding, sewage pollution, and water rationing, the ordinance prohibits issuance of further permits until three standards are met: "1. Educational Facilities—No double sessions in the schools nor overcrowded classrooms as determined by the California Education Code. 2. Sewage—The sewage treatment facilities and capacities meet the standards set by the Regional Water Quality Control Board. 3. Water Supply—No rationing of water with respect to human consumption or irrigation and adequate water reserves for fire protection exist."

Plaintiff association filed suit to enjoin enforcement of the ordinance and for declaratory relief.... Plaintiff contends that the ordinance proposes, and will cause, the prevention of nonresidents from migrating to Livermore, and that the ordinance therefore attempts an unconstitutional exercise of the police power, both because no compelling state interest justifies its infringement upon the migrant's constitutionally protected right to travel, and because it exceeds the police power of the municipality.

The ordinance on its face imposes no absolute prohibition or limitation upon population growth or residential construction. It does provide that no building permits will issue unless standards for educational facilities, water supply and sewage disposal have been met, but plaintiff presented no evidence to show that the ordinance's standards were unreasonable or unrelated to their apparent objectives of protecting the public health and welfare. Thus, we do not here confront the question of the constitutionality of an ordinance which limits or bars population growth either directly in express language or indirectly by the imposition of prohibitory standards; we adjudicate only the validity of an ordinance limiting building permits in accord with standards that reasonably measure the adequacy of public services....

Many writers have contended that exclusionary land use ordinances tend primarily to exclude racial minorities and the poor, and on that account should be subject to strict judicial scrutiny. These writers, however, are concerned primarily with ordinances which ban or limit less expensive forms of housing while permitting expensive single family residences on large lots. The Livermore ordinance is not made from this mold; it impartially bans all residential construction, expensive or inexpensive. Consequently plaintiff at bar has eschewed reliance upon any claim that the ordinance discriminates on a basis of race or wealth.

Plaintiff's contention that the Livermore ordinance must be tested by a standard of strict scrutiny, and can be sustained only upon a showing of a compelling state interest, thus rests solely on plaintiff's assertion that the ordinance abridges a constitutionally protected right to travel. As we shall explain, however, the indirect burden imposed on the right to travel by the ordinance does not warrant application of the plaintiff's asserted standard of "compelling interest."

In asserting that legislation which burdens a right to travel requires strict scrutiny, and can be sustained only upon proof of compelling need, plaintiff relies on recent decisions of this court (In re King (1970) 3 Cal. 3d 226 [90 Cal. Rptr. 15, 474 P.2d 983]) and the United States Supreme Court (Memorial Hospital v. *Maricopa County* (1974) 415 U.S. 250; Dunn v. Blumstein (1972) 405 U.S. 330; Shapiro v. Thompson (1969) 394 U.S. 618). The legislation held invalid by those decisions, however, directly burdened the right to travel by distinguishing between nonresidents or newly arrived residents on the one hand and established residents on the other, and imposing penalties or disabilities on the former group.

Both the United States Supreme Court and this court have refused to apply the strict constitutional test to legislation, such as the present ordinance, which does not penalize travel and resettlement but merely makes it more difficult for the outsider to establish his residence in the place of his choosing. (See Village of Belle Terre v. Boraas (1973) 416 U.S. 1, 7; Ector v. City of Torrance (1973) 10 Cal. 3d 129, 135 [109 Cal. Rptr. 849, 514 P.2d 433].). . . .

Most zoning and land use ordinances affect population growth and density. As commentators have observed, to insist that such zoning laws are invalid unless the interests supporting the exclusion are compelling in character, and cannot be achieved by an alternative method, would result in wholesale invalidation of land use controls and endanger the validity of city and regional planning. "Were a court to . . . hold that an inferred right of any group to live wherever it chooses might not be abridged without some compelling state interest, the law of zoning would be literally turned upside down; presumptions of validity would become presumptions of invalidity and traditional police powers of a state would be severely circumscribed." (Comment, Zoning, Communes and Equal Protection, 1973 Urban L. Ann. 319, 324.)

We conclude that the indirect burden upon the right to travel imposed by the Livermore ordinance does not call for strict judicial scrutiny. The validity of the challenged ordinance must be measured by the more liberal standards that have traditionally tested the validity of land use restrictions enacted under the municipal police power.

This conclusion brings us to plaintiff's final contention: that the Livermore ordinance exceeds the authority conferred upon the city under the police power. The constitutional measure by which we judge the validity of a land use ordinance that is assailed as exceeding municipal authority under the police power dates in California from the landmark decision in Miller v. Board of Public Works (1925) 195 Cal. 477 [234 P. 381, 38 A.L.R. 1479]. Upholding a Los Angeles ordinance which excluded commercial and apartment uses from certain residential zones, we declared that an ordinance restricting land use was valid if it had a "real or substantial relation to the public health, safety, morals or general welfare." (195 Cal. at p. 490.). . . . Later California decisions confirmed that a land use restriction lies within the public power if it has a "reasonable relation to the public welfare." (Lockard v. City of Los Angeles (1949) 33 Cal. 2d 453, 461 [202 P.2d 38, 7 A.L.R.2d 990].). . . . Most previous decisions applying this test, however, have involved ordinances without substantial effect beyond the municipal boundaries. The present ordinance, in contrast, significantly affects the interests of nonresidents who are not represented in the city legislative body and cannot vote on a city initiative. We therefore believe it desirable for the guidance of the trial court to clarify the application of the traditional police power test to an ordinance which significantly affects nonresidents of the municipality.

When we inquire whether an ordinance reasonably relates to the public welfare, inquiry should begin by asking *whose* welfare must the ordinance serve. In past cases, when discussing ordinances without significant effect beyond the municipal boundaries, we have been content to assume that the ordinance need only reasonably relate to the welfare of the enacting municipality and its residents. But municipalities are not isolated islands remote from the needs and problems of the area in which they are located; thus an ordinance, superficially reasonable from the limited viewpoint of the municipality, may be disclosed as unreasonable when viewed from a larger perspective.

These considerations impel us to the conclusion that the proper constitutional test is one which inquires whether the ordinance reasonably relates to the welfare of those whom it significantly affects. If its impact is limited to the city boundaries, the inquiry may be limited accordingly; if, as alleged here, the ordinance may strongly influence the supply and distribution of housing for an entire metropolitan region, judicial inquiry must consider the welfare of that region....

We explain the process by which a trial court may determine whether a challenged restriction reasonably relates to the regional welfare. The first step in that analysis is to forecast the probable effect and duration of the restriction. In the instant case the Livermore ordinance posits a total ban on residential construction, but one which terminates as soon as public facilities reach specified standards. Thus to evaluate the impact of the restriction, the court must ascertain the extent to which public facilities currently fall short of the specified standards, must inquire whether the city or appropriate regional agencies have undertaken to construct needed improvements, and must determine when the improvements are likely to be completed.

The second step is to identify the competing interests affected by the restriction. We touch in this area deep social antagonisms. We allude to the conflict between the environmental protectionists and the egalitarian humanists; a collision between the forces that would save the benefits of nature and those that would preserve the opportunity of people in general to settle. Suburban residents who seek to overcome problems of inadequate schools and public facilities to secure "the blessing of quiet seclusion and clean air" and to "make the area a sanctuary for people" (Village of Belle Terre v. Boraas, supra, 416 U.S. 1, 9) may assert a vital interest in limiting immigration to their community. Outsiders searching for a place to live in the face of a growing shortage of adequate housing, and hoping to share in the perceived benefits of suburban life, may present a countervailing interest opposing barriers to immigration.

Having identified and weighed the competing interests, the final step is to determine whether the ordinance, in light of its probable impact, represents a reasonable accommodation of the competing interests. We do not hold that a court in inquiring whether an ordinance reasonably relates to the regional welfare, cannot defer to the judgment of the municipality's legislative body. But judicial deference is not judicial abdication. The ordinance must have a *real and substantial* relation to the public welfare. . . .

The burden rests with the party challenging the constitutionality of an ordinance to present the evidence and documentation which the court will require in undertaking this constitutional analysis. Plaintiff in the present case has not yet attempted to shoulder that burden. . . . Without an evidentiary record to demonstrate the validity and significance of the asserted interests, we cannot determine whether the instant ordinance attempts a reasonable accommodation of those interests. . . . That issue can only be resolved by a trial at which evidence is presented to document the probable impact of the ordinance upon the municipality and the surrounding region.

The judgment of the superior court is reversed, and the cause remanded for further proceedings consistent with the views expressed herein.

MOSK, Justice (dissenting).

Limitations on growth may be justified in resort communities, beach and lake and mountain sites, and other rural and recreational areas; such restrictions are generally designed to preserve nature's environment for the benefit of all mankind. They fulfill our fiduciary obligation to posterity. As Thomas Jefferson wrote, the earth belongs to the living, but in usufruct.

But there is a vast qualitative difference when a suburban community invokes an elitist concept to construct a mythical moat around its perimeter, not for the benefit of mankind but to exclude all but its fortunate current residents. . . .

Exclusion of unwanted outsiders, while a more frequent phenomenon recently, is not entirely innovative. The State of California made an abortive effort toward exclusivity back in the 1930s as part of a scheme to stem the influx of poor migrants from the dust bowl states of the southwest. The additional burden these indigent new residents placed on California services and facilities was severely aggravated by the great depression of that period. In Edwards v. California (1941) 314 U.S. 160, the Supreme Court held, however, that the nature of the union established by the Constitution did not permit any one state to "isolate itself from the difficulties common to all of them by restraining the transportation of persons and property across its borders." The sanction against immigration of indigents was invalidated.

If California could not protect itself from the growth problems of that era, may Livermore build a Chinese Wall to insulate itself from growth problems today? And if Livermore may do so, why not every municipality in Alameda County and in all other counties in Northern California? With a patchwork of enclaves the inevitable result will be creation of an aristocracy housed in exclusive suburbs while modest wage earners will be confined to declining neighborhoods, crowded into sterile, monotonous, multifamily projects, or assigned to pockets of marginal housing on the urban fringe. The overriding objective should be to minimize rather than exacerbate social and economic disparities, to lower barriers rather than raise them, to emphasize heterogeneity rather than homogeneity, to increase choice rather than limit it. . . .

Whatever the motivation, total exclusion of people from a community is both immoral and illegal. Courts have a duty to prevent such practices, while at the same time recognizing the validity of genuine conservationist efforts.

The problem is not insoluble, nor does it necessarily provoke extreme results. Indeed, the solution can be relatively simple if municipal agencies would consider the aspirations of society as a whole, rather than merely the effect upon their narrow constituency. Accommodation between environmental preservation and satisfaction of housing needs can be reached through rational guidelines for land-use decision-making. Ours, of course, is not the legislative function. But two legal inhibitions must be the benchmark of any such guidelines. First, any absolute prohibition on housing development is presumptively invalid. And second, local regulations, based on parochialism, that limit population densities in growing suburban areas may be found invalid unless the community is absorbing a reasonable share of the region's population pressures.

Under the foregoing test, the Livermore ordinance is fatally flawed. I would affirm the judgment of the trial court.

Notes & Questions

1. What is the likely effect of a growth moratorium such as the Livermore initiative? Do local moratoria simply push the problems of growth to neighboring areas? By prohibiting new construction within the community, do moratoria exacerbate the problem of urban sprawl by forcing growth out into undeveloped areas without effective land use controls?

2. Some states prohibit or closely restrict the use of local growth moratoria. See, e.g., Ariz. Rev. Stat. § 9–463.06 (requiring cities to find "irrevocable public harm" before imposing moratoria); N.J. Stat. Ann. § 40:55D–90(a) (precluding cities from using moratoria to provide time to prepare master plans and development regulations); Naylor v. Township of Hellam, 773 A.2d 770 (Pa. 2001) (municipalities have no authority to impose a growth moratorium). Most states, moreover, permit moratoria only for limited periods of time and require cities to make good faith efforts to eliminate the need for the moratoria as quickly as possible. See, e.g., Q.C. Construction Co. v. Gallo, 649 F. Supp. 1331 (D.R.I. 1986) (finding a three-year moratorium unconstitutional where no effort had been made during this period to increase sewage capacity).

3. **Growth Rate Caps.** Another form of local growth control measure limits the amount of new housing built each year. In the early 1970s, for example, the City of Petaluma in Northern California adopted a plan that capped new housing at 500 units per year. To allocate the limited development rights, the city developed a Residential Development Control

System that gave preference to builders whose developments conformed closely to the city's general and environmental design plans, employed good architectural design, and provided low-and moderate-income housing and recreational facilities. A federal court of appeals upheld the plan against due process challenges:

> Although we assume that some persons desirous of living in Petaluma will be excluded under the housing permit limitation and that, thus, the Plan may frustrate some legitimate regional housing needs, the Plan is not arbitrary or unreasonable. We agree with appellees that unlike the situation in the past most municipalities today are neither isolated nor wholly independent from neighboring municipalities and that, consequently, unilateral land use decisions by one local entity affect the needs and resources of an entire region. It does not necessarily follow, however, that the due process rights of builders and landowners are violated merely because a local entity exercises in its own self-interest the police power lawfully delegated to it by the state. If the present system of delegated zoning power does not effectively serve the state interest in furthering the general welfare of the region or entire state, it is the state legislature's and not the federal courts' role to intervene and adjust the system.... [T]he federal court is not a super zoning board and should not be called on to mark the point at which legitimate local interests in promoting the welfare of the community are outweighed by legitimate regional interests.

Construction Industry Ass'n v. City of Petaluma, 522 F.2d 897, 908 (9th Cir. 1975).

4. **Concurrency.** Yet another approach adopted by some local governments is to link growth to the availability of necessary infrastructure. As the city develops new infrastructure, it permits additional development. Developers often can increase the allowed rate of growth by installing needed infrastructure at their own expense. Such an approach is sometimes known as *concurrency*, because development is concurrent with available infrastructure. The New York Court of Appeals rejected a constitutional challenge to a statute limiting growth to the available infrastructure in Golden v. Planning Bd., 285 N.E.2d 291 (N.Y. 1972). Florida has adopted a statewide concurrency requirement that forbids local governments from permitting any new development that reduces public services below levels specified in their comprehensive plans. Fla. Stat. §§ 163.3161 et seq. Is concurrency a better or worse approach than growth rate caps?

5. **Growth Boundaries.** A number of jurisdictions have tried to address the problem of urban sprawl by drawing *urban growth boundaries* around metropolitan areas. New development generally must occur within these boundaries, reducing the need to extend infrastructure beyond existing service areas and preserving rural lands and open space. In 1973, Oregon embarked on one of the first statewide efforts to draw and enforce urban growth boundaries. Over a hundred such urban constraint programs are now in place around the United States. Studies of the effectiveness of

urban growth boundaries have found mixed results. Urban growth boundaries appear to reduce sprawl and create often vibrant urban communities. Buoyed by market pressure and citizen preferences for low-density development, however, new development still often leaks out of the growth boundaries into the countryside. See Robert Stacey, Urban Growth Boundaries: Saying "Yes" to Strengthening Communities, 34 Conn. L. Rev. 597 (2002); Douglas R. Porter, State Growth Management: The Intergovernmental Experiment, 13 Pace L. Rev. 481 (1993); Keith W. Dearborn & Ann M. Bygi, Planner's Panacea or Pandora's Box: A Realistic Assessment of the Role of Urban Growth Areas in Achieving Growth Management Goals, 16 U. Puget Sound L. Rev. 975 (1993).

6. By restricting the overall supply of housing, does growth control harm the poor? We will return to this issue later in the Chapter.

G. PROTECTING AGAINST DISCRIMINATION IN ZONING

1. DIRECT DISCRIMINATION

As noted earlier, a number of local governments used zoning in the early 20th century to segregate communities by race. Indeed, efforts to restrict minorities to specific areas predated comprehensive zoning. See, e.g., In re Lee Sing, 43 F. 359 (N.D. Cal. 1890) (invalidating a San Francisco law requiring Chinese to live in a specified city neighborhood). Cities in over ten states ultimately adopted zoning ordinances establishing separate districts for blacks and whites. In Buchanan v. Warley, 245 U.S. 60 (1917), however, the Supreme Court held that racial zoning violates the Fourteenth Amendment to the United States Constitution. To what degree does the United States Constitution protect other groups from discriminatory treatment under local zoning ordinances?

Village of Belle Terre v. Boraas

Supreme Court of the United States, 1974.
416 U.S. 1.

MR. JUSTICE DOUGLAS delivered the opinion of the Court.

Belle Terre is a village on Long Island's north shore of about 220 homes inhabited by 700 people. Its total land area is less than one square mile. It has restricted land use to one-family dwellings excluding lodging houses, boarding houses, fraternity houses, or multiple-dwelling houses. The word "family" as used in the ordinance means, "one or more persons related by blood, adoption, or marriage, living and cooking together as a single housekeeping unit, exclusive of household servants. A number of persons but not exceeding two (2) living and cooking together as a single housekeeping unit though not related by blood, adoption, or marriage shall be deemed to constitute a family."

Appellees the Dickmans are owners of a house in the village and leased it in December 1971 for a term of 18 months to Michael Truman. Later Bruce Boraas became a colessee. Then Anne Parish moved into the house along with three others. These six are students at nearby State University at Stony Brook and none is related to the other by blood, adoption, or marriage. When the village served the Dickmans with an "Order to Remedy Violations" of the ordinance, the owners plus three tenants thereupon brought this action under 42 U. S. C. § 1983 for an injunction and a judgment declaring the ordinance unconstitutional. The District Court held the ordinance constitutional, and the Court of Appeals reversed, one judge dissenting. The case is here by appeal, and we noted probable jurisdiction....

The present ordinance is challenged on several grounds: that it interferes with a person's right to travel; that it interferes with the right to migrate to and settle within a State; that it bars people who are uncongenial to the present residents; that it expresses the social preferences of the residents for groups that will be congenial to them; that social homogeneity is not a legitimate interest of government; that the restriction of those whom the neighbors do not like trenches on the newcomers' rights of privacy; that it is of no rightful concern to villagers whether the residents are married or unmarried; that the ordinance is antithetical to the Nation's experience, ideology, and self-perception as an open, egalitarian, and integrated society.

We find none of these reasons in the record before us. It is not aimed at transients.... It involves no "fundamental" right guaranteed by the Constitution, such as voting, Harper v. Virginia Board, 383 U.S. 663; the right of association, NAACP v. Alabama, 357 U.S. 449; the right of access to the courts, NAACP v. Button, 371 U.S. 415; or any rights of privacy, cf. Griswold v. Connecticut, 381 U.S. 479; Eisenstadt v. Baird, 405 U.S. 438, 453–454. We deal with economic and social legislation where legislatures have historically drawn lines which we respect against the charge of violation of the Equal Protection Clause if the law be " 'reasonable, not arbitrary' " (quoting Royster Guano Co. v. Virginia, 253 U.S. 412, 415) and bears "a rational relationship to a [permissible] state objective." Reed v. Reed, 404 U.S. 71, 76.

It is said, however, that if two unmarried people can constitute a "family," there is no reason why three or four may not. But every line drawn by a legislature leaves some out that might well have been included. That exercise of discretion, however, is a legislative, not a judicial, function.

It is said that the Belle Terre ordinance reeks with an animosity to unmarried couples who live together. There is no evidence to support it; and the provision of the ordinance bringing within the definition of a "family" two unmarried people belies the charge.

The ordinance places no ban on other forms of association, for a "family" may, so far as the ordinance is concerned, entertain whomever it likes.

The regimes of boarding houses, fraternity houses, and the like present urban problems. More people occupy a given space; more cars rather continuously pass by; more cars are parked; noise travels with crowds.

A quiet place where yards are wide, people few, and motor vehicles restricted are legitimate guidelines in a land-use project addressed to family needs. This goal is a permissible one within Berman v. Parker, 348 U.S. 26 (1954). The police power is not confined to elimination of filth, stench, and unhealthy places. It is ample to lay out zones where family values, youth values, and the blessings of quiet seclusion and clean air make the area a sanctuary for people....

Reversed.

[The opinion of Mr. Justice Brennan, dissenting, is omitted.]

Mr. Justice Marshall, dissenting....

I am in full agreement with the majority that zoning is a complex and important function of the State. It may indeed be the most essential function performed by local government, for it is one of the primary means by which we protect that sometimes difficult to define concept of quality of life. I therefore continue to adhere to the principle of Euclid v. Ambler Realty Co., 272 U.S. 365 (1926), that deference should be given to governmental judgments concerning proper land-use allocation....

I would also agree with the majority that local zoning authorities may properly act in furtherance of the objectives asserted to be served by the ordinance at issue here: restricting uncontrolled growth, solving traffic problems, keeping rental costs at a reasonable level, and making the community attractive to families. The police power which provides the justification for zoning is not narrowly confined. And, it is appropriate that we afford zoning authorities considerable latitude in choosing the means by which to implement such purposes. But deference does not mean abdication. This Court has an obligation to ensure that zoning ordinances, even when adopted in furtherance of such legitimate aims, do not infringe upon fundamental constitutional rights.

When separate but equal was still accepted constitutional dogma, this Court struck down a racially restrictive zoning ordinance. Buchanan v. Warley, 245 U.S. 60 (1917). I am sure the Court would not be hesitant to invalidate that ordinance today. The lower federal courts have considered procedural aspects of zoning, and acted to insure that land-use controls are not used as means of confining minorities and the poor to the ghettos of our central cities. These are limited but necessary intrusions on the discretion of zoning authorities. By the same token, I think it clear that the First Amendment provides some limitation on zoning laws. It is inconceivable to me that we would allow the exercise of the zoning power to burden First Amendment freedoms, as by ordinances that restrict occupancy to individuals adhering to particular religious, political, or scientific beliefs. Zoning officials properly concern themselves with the uses of land—with, for example, the number and kind of dwellings to be constructed in a certain neighborhood or the number of persons who can reside in those dwellings. But zoning authorities cannot validly consider who those persons are, what they believe, or how they choose to live, whether they are Negro or white, Catholic or Jew, Republican or Democrat, married or unmarried.

My disagreement with the Court today is based upon my view that the ordinance in this case unnecessarily burdens appellees' First Amendment freedom of association and their constitutionally guaranteed right to privacy. Our decisions establish that the First and Fourteenth Amendments protect the freedom to choose one's associates. NAACP v. Button, 371 U.S. 415, 430 (1963).... The selection of one's living companions involves similar choices as to the emotional, social, or economic benefits to be derived from alternative living arrangements.

The freedom of association is often inextricably entwined with the constitutionally guaranteed right of privacy. The right to "establish a home" is an essential part of the liberty guaranteed by the Fourteenth Amendment. And the Constitution secures to an individual a freedom "to satisfy his intellectual and emotional needs in the privacy of his own home." Stanley v. Georgia, 394 U.S. 557, 565 (1969). Constitutionally protected privacy is, in Mr. Justice Brandeis' words, "as against the Government, the right to be let alone ... the right most valued by civilized man." Olmstead v. United States, 277 U.S. 438, 478 (1928) (dissenting opinion). The choice of household companions—of whether a person's "intellectual and emotional needs" are best met by living with family, friends, professional associates, or others—involves deeply personal considerations as to the kind and quality of intimate relationships within the home. That decision surely falls within the ambit of the right to privacy protected by the Constitution.

The instant ordinance discriminates on the basis of just such a personal lifestyle choice as to household companions. It permits any number of persons related by blood or marriage, be it two or twenty, to live in a single household, but it limits to two the number of unrelated persons bound by profession, love, friendship, religious or political affiliation, or mere economics who can occupy a single home. Belle Terre imposes upon those who deviate from the community norm in their choice of living companions significantly greater restrictions than are applied to residential groups who are related by blood or marriage, and compose the established order within the community. The village has, in effect, acted to fence out those individuals whose choice of lifestyle differs from that of its current residents.

This is not a case where the Court is being asked to nullify a township's sincere efforts to maintain its residential character by preventing the operation of rooming houses, fraternity houses, or other commercial or high-density residential uses. Unquestionably, a town is free to restrict such uses. Moreover, as a general proposition, I see no constitutional infirmity in a town's limiting the density of use in residential areas by zoning regulations which do not discriminate on the basis of constitutionally suspect criteria. This ordinance, however, limits the density of occupancy of only those homes occupied by unrelated persons. It thus reaches beyond control of the use of land or the density of population, and undertakes to regulate the way people choose to associate with each other within the privacy of their own homes. . . .

By limiting unrelated households to two persons while placing no limitation on households of related individuals, the village has embarked upon its commendable course in a constitutionally faulty vessel. I would find the challenged ordinance unconstitutional. But I would not ask the village to abandon its goal of providing quiet streets, little traffic, and a pleasant and reasonably priced environment in which families might raise their children. Rather, I would commend the village to continue to pursue those purposes but by means of more carefully drawn and even-handed legislation.

I respectfully dissent.

Notes & Questions

1. How far will the Supreme Court let a municipality go in regulating the relationship, as well as the number, of individuals living in a single unit? In Moore v. City of East Cleveland, 431 U.S. 494 (1977), the Court, in a 5–4 decision, drew the line at prohibiting true families from living together and overturned appellant's state court conviction, under which she had been sentenced to five days in jail and a $25 fine for living together with her son and two grandsons. East Cleveland, unlike Belle Terre, defined "family" in a way that excluded cousins from living together, and appellant's two grandsons were cousins rather than brothers. "When a city undertakes such intrusive regulation of the family, neither *Belle Terre* nor *Euclid* governs; the usual judicial deference to the legislature is inappropriate. This Court has long recognized that freedom of personal choice in matters of marriage and family life is one of the liberties protected by the Due Process Clause of the Fourteenth Amendment." Id. at 499.

2. Both before and after *Belle Terre,* state courts have invoked state constitutions to invalidate zoning ordinances that restrict the number of unrelated individuals that can constitute a "family" for purposes of single-family residential districts. These state courts have generally accepted the legitimacy of promoting "family values" and a "family style of living" through the maintenance of low density residential areas, but disagreed with the proposition that consanguinity is necessary to attain these goals. In the view of the California Supreme Court, for example

> "residential character" can be and is preserved by restrictions on transient and institutional uses (hotels, motels, boarding houses, clubs, etc.). Population density can be regulated by reference to floor space and facilities. Noise and morality can be dealt with by enforcement of police power ordinances and criminal statutes. Traffic and parking can be handled by limitations on the number of cars (applied evenly to all households) and by off-street parking requirements. *In general, zoning ordinances are much less suspect when they focus on the use than when they command inquiry into who are the users.*

City of Santa Barbara v. Adamson, 610 P.2d 436, 441–442 (Cal. 1980) (emphasis in original). See also McMinn v. Town of Oyster Bay, 488 N.E.2d 1240 (N.Y. 1985); State v. Baker, 405 A.2d 368, 375 (N.J. 1979) ("Given the availability of less restrictive alternatives, such regulations are insufficiently related to the perceived social ills which they were intended to ameliorate").

3. **Discrimination Against the Mentally Retarded.** Can a local government insist that group homes for the mentally retarded obtain a special use permit? In City of Cleburne v. Cleburne Living Center, 473 U.S. 432 (1985), the Supreme Court held that the retarded are not a "quasi-suspect class" entitled to a heightened standard of scrutiny under the federal Equal Protection Clause. The Court concluded, however, that the requirement of a special use permit was an "irrational prejudice against the mentally retarded" and thus unconstitutional. Could the city get around the Supreme Court's decision by zoning the Cleburne Living Center's property for single-family residential use and defining "family" to exclude groups of people who are unrelated?

4. **Statutory Protections.** Various federal and state civil rights statutes may also preclude zoning ordinances from excluding certain individuals or groups from a neighborhood. For example, the federal Fair Housing Act (FHA), 42 U.S.C. §§ 3601 et seq., makes it unlawful "to discriminate in the sale or rental, or to otherwise make unavailable or deny, a dwelling to any buyer or renter because of a handicap of . . . that buyer or renter." Id. § 3604(f)(1). Discrimination includes a "refusal to make reasonable accommodations in rules, policies, practices, or services, when such accommodations may be necessary to afford such person equal opportunity to use and enjoy a dwelling." Id. § 3604(f)(3)(B). In Smith & Lee Associates v. City of Taylor, 102 F.3d 781 (6th Cir. 1996), the federal Court of Appeals held that the City of Taylor had violated the reasonable accommodation provision by refusing to rezone land in an R–1A district so that elderly disabled adults could live in a group home.

2. EXCLUSIONARY ZONING

Southern Burlington County N.A.A.C.P. v. Township of Mount Laurel

Supreme Court of New Jersey, 1975.
336 A.2d 713.

HALL, J.

This case attacks the system of land use regulation by defendant Township of Mount Laurel on the ground that low and moderate income families are thereby unlawfully excluded from the municipality. The trial court so found and declared the township zoning ordinance totally invalid. . . .

Plaintiffs represent the minority group poor (black and Hispanic)[3] seeking such quarters. But they are not the only category of persons barred from so many municipalities by reason of restrictive land use regulations. We have reference to young and elderly couples, single persons and large, growing families not in the poverty class, but who still cannot afford the only kinds of housing realistically permitted in most places—relatively high-priced, single-family detached dwellings on sizeable lots and, in some municipalities, expensive apartments. We will, therefore, consider the case from the wider viewpoint that the effect of Mount Laurel's land use regulation has been to prevent various categories of persons from living in the township because of the limited extent of their income and resources. In this connection, we accept the representation of the municipality's counsel at oral argument that the regulatory scheme was not adopted with any desire or intent to exclude prospective residents on the obviously illegal basis of race, origin or believed social incompatibility. . . .

Extensive oral and documentary evidence was introduced at the trial, largely informational, dealing with the development of Mount Laurel, including the nature and effect of municipal regulation, the details of the region of which it is a part and the recent history thereof, and some of the basics of housing, special reference being directed to that for low and moderate income families. . . . This evidence was not contradicted by the township, except in a few unimportant details. Its candid position is that, conceding its land use regulation was intended to result and has resulted in economic discrimination and exclusion of substantial segments of the area population, its policies and practices are in the best present and future fiscal interest of the municipality and its inhabitants and are legally permissible and justified. . . .

I
The Facts

Mount Laurel is a flat, sprawling township, 22 square miles, or about 14,000 acres, in area, on the west central edge of Burlington County. . . .

In 1950, the township had a population of 2817, only about 600 more people than it had in 1940. It was then, as it had been for decades, primarily a rural agricultural area with no sizeable settlements or commercial or industrial enterprises. The populace generally lived in individual houses scattered along country roads. There were several pockets of pover-

3. Plaintiffs fall into four categories: (1) present residents of the township residing in dilapidated or substandard housing; (2) former residents who were forced to move elsewhere because of the absence of suitable housing; (3) nonresidents living in central city substandard housing in the region who desire to secure decent housing and accompanying advantages within their means elsewhere; (4) three organizations representing the housing and other interests of racial minorities. The township originally challenged plaintiffs' standing to bring this action. The trial court properly held that the resident plaintiffs had adequate standing to ground the entire action and found it unnecessary to pass on that of the other plaintiffs. The issue has not been raised on appeal. We merely add that both categories of nonresident individuals likewise have standing. No opinion is expressed as to the standing of the organizations.

ty, with deteriorating or dilapidated housing (apparently 300 or so units of which remain today in equally poor condition). After 1950, as in so many other municipalities similarly situated, residential development and some commerce and industry began to come in. By 1960 the population had almost doubled to 5249 and by 1970 had more than doubled again to 11,221. These new residents were, of course, "outsiders" from the nearby central cities and older suburbs or from more distant places drawn here by reason of employment in the region. The township is now definitely a part of the outer ring of the South Jersey metropolitan area, which area we define as those portions of Camden, Burlington and Gloucester Counties within a semicircle having a radius of 20 miles or so from the heart of Camden city. And 65% of the township is still vacant land or in agricultural use.

The growth of the township has been spurred by the construction or improvement of main highways through or near it. . . .

The location and nature of development has been, as usual, controlled by the local zoning enactments. The general ordinance presently in force, which was declared invalid by the trial court, was adopted in 1964. We understand that earlier enactments provided, however, basically the same scheme but were less restrictive as to residential development. The growth pattern dictated by the ordinance is typical.

Under the present ordinance, 29.2% of all the land in the township, or 4,121 acres, is zoned for industry. This amounts to 2,800 more acres than were so zoned by the 1954 ordinance. . . . Only industry meeting specified performance standards is permitted. The effect is to limit the use substantially to light manufacturing, research, distribution of goods, offices and the like. Some non-industrial uses, such as agriculture, farm dwellings, motels, a harness racetrack, and certain retail sales and service establishments, are permitted in this zone. At the time of trial no more than 100 acres . . . were actually occupied by industrial uses. They had been constructed in recent years, mostly in several industrial parks, and involved tax ratables of about 16 million dollars. The rest of the land so zoned has remained undeveloped. If it were fully utilized, the testimony was that about 43,500 industrial jobs would be created, but it appeared clear that, as happens in the case of so many municipalities, much more land has been so zoned than the reasonable potential for industrial movement or expansion warrants. At the same time, however, the land cannot be used for residential development under the general ordinance.

The amount of land zoned for retail business use under the general ordinance is relatively small—169 acres, or 1.2% of the total. . . . While the greater part of the land so zoned appears to be in use, there is no major shopping center or concentrated retail commercial area—"downtown"—in the township.

The balance of the land area, almost 10,000 acres, has been developed until recently in the conventional form of major subdivisions. The general ordinance provides for four residential zones, designated R–1, R–1D, R–2 and R–3. All permit only single-family, detached dwellings, one house per lot—the usual form of grid development. Attached townhouses, apartments (except on farms for agricultural workers) and mobile homes are not allowed anywhere in the township under the general ordinance. This dwelling development, resulting in the previously mentioned quadrupling of the population, has been largely confined to the R–1 and R–2 districts in two sections—the northeasterly and southwesterly corners adjacent to the turnpike and other major highways. The result has been quite intensive development of these sections, but at a low density. The dwellings are substantial; the average value in 1971 was $32,500 and is undoubtedly much higher today.

The general ordinance requirements, while not as restrictive as those in many similar municipalities, nonetheless realistically allow only homes within the financial reach of persons of at least middle income. The R–1 zone requires a minimum lot area of 9,375 square feet, minimum lot width of 75 feet at the building line, and a minimum dwelling floor area of 1,100 square feet if a one-story building and 1,300 square feet if one and one-half stories or higher. Originally this zone comprised about 2,500 acres. Most of the subdivisions have been constructed within it so that only a few hundred acres remain (the testimony was at variance as to the exact amount). The R–2 zone, comprising a single district of 141 acres in the northeasterly corner, has been completely developed. While it only required a minimum floor area of 900 square feet for a one-story dwelling, the minimum lot size was 11,000 square feet; otherwise the requisites were the same as in the R–1 zone.

The general ordinance places the remainder of the township, outside of the industrial and commercial zones and the R–1D district (to be mentioned shortly), in the R–3 zone. This zone comprises over 7,000 acres—slightly more than half of the total municipal area—practically all of which is located in the central part of the township extending southeasterly to the apex of the triangle. The testimony was that about 4,600 acres of it then remained available for housing development. Ordinance requirements are substantially higher, however, in that the minimum lot size is increased to about one-half acre (20,000 square feet). (We understand that sewer and water utilities have not generally been installed, but, of course, they can be.) Lot width at the building line must be 100 feet. Minimum dwelling floor area is as in the R–1 zone. Presently this section is primarily in agricultural use; it contains as well most of the municipality's substandard housing. . . .

[Mount Laurel also has approved four planned unit developments (PUDs.)] If completed as planned, they will in themselves ultimately quadruple the 1970 township population, but still leave a good part of the township undeveloped. (The record does not indicate how far development in each of the projects has progressed.) While multi-family housing in the form of rental garden, medium rise and high rise apartments and attached townhouses is for the first time provided for, as well as single-family detached dwellings for sale, it is not designed to accommodate and is beyond the financial reach of low and moderate income families, especially those with young children. The aim is quite the contrary; as with the single-family homes in the older conventional subdivisions, only persons of medium and upper income are sought as residents.

A few details will furnish sufficient documentation. Each of the resolutions of tentative approval of the projects contains a similar fact finding to the effect that the development will attract a highly educated and trained population base to support the nearby industrial parks in the township as well as the business and commercial facilities. The approvals also sharply limit the number of apartments having more than one bedroom. Further, they require that the developer must provide in its leases that no school-age children shall be permitted to occupy any one-bedroom apartment and that no more than two such children shall reside in any two-bedroom unit. The developer is also required, prior to the issuance of the first building permit, to record a covenant, running with all land on which multi-family housing is to be constructed, providing that in the event more than .3 school children per multi-family unit shall attend the township school system in any one year, the developer will pay the cost of tuition and other school expenses of all such excess numbers of children. In addition, low density, required amenities, such as central air conditioning, and specified developer contributions help to push rents and sales prices to high levels. These contributions include fire apparatus, ambulances, fire houses, and very large sums of money for educational facilities, a cultural center and the township library....

All this affirmative action for the benefit of certain segments of the population is in sharp contrast to the lack of action, and indeed hostility, with respect to affording any opportunity for decent housing for the township's own poor living in substandard accommodations, found largely in the section known as Springville (R–3 zone). The 1969 Master Plan Report recognized it and recommended positive action. The continuous official reaction has been rather a negative policy of waiting for dilapidated premises to be vacated and then forbidding further occupancy. An earlier non-governmental effort to improve conditions had been effectively thwarted. In 1968 a private non-profit association sought to build subsidized, multi-family housing in the Springville section with funds to be granted by a higher level governmental agency. Advance municipal approval of the project was required. The Township Committee responded with a purportedly approving resolution, which found a need for "moderate" income housing in the area, but went on to specify that such housing must be constructed subject to all zoning, planning, building and other applicable ordinances and codes. This meant single-family detached dwellings on 20,000 square foot lots. (Fear was also expressed that such housing would attract low income families from outside the township.) Needless to say, such requirements killed realistic housing for this group of low and moderate income families.

The record thoroughly substantiates the findings of the trial court that over the years Mount Laurel "has acted affirmatively to control development and to attract a selective type of growth" and that "through its zoning ordinances has exhibited economic discrimination in that the poor have been deprived of adequate housing and the opportunity to secure the construction of subsidized housing, and has used federal, state, county and local finances and resources solely for the betterment of middle and upper-income persons."

There cannot be the slightest doubt that the reason for this course of conduct has been to keep down local taxes on *property* (Mount Laurel is not a high tax municipality) and that the policy was carried out without regard for nonfiscal considerations with respect to *people*, either within or without its boundaries.... This policy of land use regulation for a fiscal end derives from New Jersey's tax structure, which has imposed on local real estate most of the cost of municipal and county government and of the primary and secondary education of the municipality's children. The latter expense is much the largest, so, basically, the fewer the school children, the lower the tax rate. Sizeable industrial and commercial ratables are eagerly sought and homes and the lots on which they are situate are required to be large enough, through minimum lot sizes and minimum floor areas, to have substantial value in order to produce greater tax revenues to meet school costs. Large families who cannot afford to buy large houses and must live in cheaper rental accommodations are definitely not wanted, so we find drastic bedroom restrictions for, or complete prohibition of, multi-family or other feasible housing for those of lesser income.

This pattern of land use regulation has been adopted for the same purpose in developing municipality after developing municipality. Almost every one acts solely in its own selfish and parochial interest and in effect builds a wall around itself to keep out those people or entities not adding favorably to the tax base, despite the location of the municipality or the demand for varied kinds of housing. There has been no effective intermunicipal or area planning or land use regulation.... One incongruous result is the picture of developing municipalities rendering it impossible for lower paid employees of industries they have eagerly sought and welcomed with open arms (and, in Mount Laurel's case, even some of its own lower paid municipal employees) to live in the community where they work.

The other end of the spectrum should also be mentioned because it shows the source of some of the demand for cheaper housing than the developing municipalities have permitted. Core cities were originally the location of most commerce and industry. Many of those facilities furnished employment for the unskilled and semi-skilled. These employees lived relatively near their work, so sections of cities always have housed the majority of people of low and moderate income, generally in old and deteriorating housing. Despite the municipally confined tax structure, commercial and industrial ratables generally used to supply enough revenue to provide and maintain municipal services equal or superior to those furnished in most suburban and rural areas.

The situation has become exactly the opposite since the end of World War II. Much industry and retail business, and even the professions, have left the cities. Camden is a typical example. The testimonial and documentary evidence in this case as to what has happened to that city is depressing indeed. For various reasons, it lost thousands of jobs between 1950 and 1970, including more than half of its manufacturing jobs (a reduction from 43,267 to 20,671, while all jobs in the entire area labor market increased from 94,507 to 197,037). A large segment of retail business faded away with the erection of large suburban shopping centers. The economically better situated city residents helped fill up the miles of sprawling new housing developments, not fully served by public transit. In a society which came to depend more and more on expensive individual motor vehicle transportation for all purposes, low income employees very frequently could not afford to reach outlying places of suitable employment and they certainly could not afford the permissible housing near such locations. These people have great difficulty in obtaining work and have been forced to remain in housing which is overcrowded, and has become more and more substandard and less and less tax productive. There has been a consequent critical erosion of the city tax base and inability to provide the amount and quality of those governmental services—education, health, police, fire, housing and the like—so necessary to the very existence of safe and decent city life. This category of city dwellers desperately needs much better housing and living conditions than is available to them now, both in a rehabilitated city and in outlying municipalities. They make up, along with the other classes of persons earlier mentioned who also cannot afford the only generally permitted housing in the developing municipalities, the acknowledged great demand for low and moderate income housing.

II
The Legal Issue

The legal question before us, as earlier indicated, is whether a developing municipality like Mount Laurel may validly, by a system of land use regulation, make it physically and economically impossible to provide low and moderate income housing in the municipality for the various categories of persons who need and want it and thereby, as Mount Laurel has, exclude such people from living within its confines because of the limited extent of their income and resources. Necessarily implicated are the broader questions of the right of such municipalities to limit the kinds of available housing and of any obligation to make possible a variety and choice of types of living accommodations.

We conclude that every such municipality must, by its land use regulations, presumptively make realistically possible an appropriate variety and choice of housing. More specifically, presumptively it cannot foreclose the opportunity of the classes of people mentioned for low and moderate income housing and in its regulations must affirmatively afford that opportunity, at least to the extent of the municipality's fair share of the present and prospective regional need therefor. These obligations must be met unless the particular municipality can sustain the heavy burden of demonstrating peculiar circumstances which dictate that it should not be required so to do.

We reach this conclusion under state law and so do not find it necessary to consider federal constitutional grounds urged by plaintiffs. We begin with some fundamental principles as applied to the scene before us.

.... Frequently the decisions in this state ... have spoken only in terms of the interest of the enacting municipality, so that it has been thought, at least in some quarters, that such was the only welfare requiring consideration. It is, of course, true that many cases have dealt only with regulations having little, if any, outside impact where the local decision is ordinarily entitled to prevail. However, it is fundamental and not to be forgotten that the zoning power is a police power of the state and the local authority is acting only as a delegate of that power and is restricted in the same manner as is the state. So, when regulation does have a substantial external impact, the welfare of the state's citizens beyond the borders of the particular municipality cannot be disregarded and must be recognized and served....

It is plain beyond dispute that proper provision for adequate housing of all categories of people is certainly an absolute essential in promotion of the general welfare required in all local land use regulation. Further the universal and constant need for such housing is so important and of such broad public interest that the general welfare which developing municipalities like Mount Laurel must consider extends beyond their boundaries and cannot be parochially confined to the claimed good of the particular municipality. It has to follow that, broadly speaking, the presumptive obligation arises for each such municipality affirmatively to plan and provide, by its land use regulations, the reasonable opportunity for an appropriate variety and choice of housing, including, of course, low and moderate cost housing, to meet the needs, desires and resources of all categories of people who may desire to live within its boundaries. Negatively, it may not adopt regulations or policies which thwart or preclude that opportunity.

It is also entirely clear, as we pointed out earlier, that most developing municipalities, including Mount Laurel, have not met their affirmative or negative obligations, primarily for local fiscal reasons....

Without further elaboration at this point, our opinion is that Mount Laurel's zoning ordinance is presumptively contrary to the general welfare and outside the intended scope of the zoning power in the particulars mentioned. A facial showing of invalidity is thus established, shifting to the municipality the burden of establishing valid superseding reasons for its action and non-action. We now examine the reasons it advances.

The township's principal reason in support of its zoning plan and ordinance housing provisions, advanced especially strongly at oral argument, is the fiscal one previously adverted to, i.e., that by reason of New Jersey's tax structure which substantially finances municipal governmental and educational costs from taxes on local real property, every municipality may, by the exercise of the zoning power, allow only such uses and to such extent as will be beneficial to the local tax rate. In other words, the position is that any municipality may zone extensively to seek and encourage the "good" tax ratables of industry and commerce, and limit the permissible types of housing to those having the fewest school children or to those providing sufficient value to attain or approach paying their own way taxwise.

We have previously held that a developing municipality may properly zone for and seek industrial ratables to create a better economic balance for the community *vis-a-vis* educational and governmental costs engendered by residential development, provided that such was "... done reasonably as part of and in furtherance of a legitimate comprehensive plan for the zoning of the entire municipality." Gruber v. Mayor and Township Committee of Raritan Township, 39 N.J. 1, 9–11 (1962). We adhere to that view today. But we were not there concerned with, and did not pass upon, the validity of municipal exclusion by zoning of types of housing and kinds of people for the same local financial end. We have no hesitancy in now saying, and do so emphatically, that, considering the basic importance of the opportunity for appropriate housing for all classes of our citizenry, no municipality may exclude or limit categories of housing for that reason or purpose. While we fully recognize the increasingly heavy burden of local taxes for municipal governmental and school costs on homeowners, relief from the consequences of this tax system will have to be furnished by other branches of government. It cannot legitimately be accomplished by restricting types of housing through the zoning process in developing municipalities.

The propriety of zoning ordinance limitations on housing for ecological or environmental reasons seems also to be suggested by Mount Laurel in support of the one-half acre minimum lot size in that very considerable portion of the township still available for residential development. It is said that the area is without sewer or water utilities and that the soil is such that this plot size is required for safe individual lot sewage disposal and water supply. The short answer is that, this being flat land and readily amenable to such utility installations, the township could require them as improvements by developers or install them under the special assessment or other appropriate statutory procedure. The present environmental situation of the area is, therefore, no sufficient excuse in itself for limiting housing therein to single-family dwellings on large lots. This is not to say that land use regulations should not take due account of ecological or environmental factors or problems. Quite the contrary. Their importance, at last being recognized, should always be considered. Generally only a relatively small portion of a developing municipality will be involved, for, to have a valid effect, the danger and impact must be substantial and very real (the construction of every building or the improvement of every plot has some environmental impact)—not simply a makeweight to support exclusionary housing measures or preclude growth—and the regulation adopted must be only that reasonably necessary for public protection of a vital interest. Otherwise difficult additional problems relating to a "taking" of a property owner's land may arise.

By way of summary, what we have said comes down to this. As a developing municipality, Mount Laurel must, by its land use regulations, make realistically possible the opportunity for an appropriate variety and choice of housing for all categories of people who may desire to live there, of course including those of low and moderate income. It must permit multi-family housing, without bedroom or similar restrictions, as well as small dwellings on very small lots, low cost housing of other types and, in general, high density zoning, without artificial and unjustifiable minimum requirements as to lot size, building size and the like, to meet the full panoply of these needs. Certainly when a municipality zones for industry and commerce for local tax benefit purposes, it without question must zone to permit adequate housing within the means of the employees involved in such uses. (If planned unit developments are authorized, one would assume that each must include a reasonable amount of low and moderate income housing in its residential "mix," unless opportunity for such housing has already been realistically provided for elsewhere in the municipality.) The amount of land removed from residential use by allocation to industrial and commercial purposes must be reasonably related to the present and future potential for such purposes. In other words, such municipalities must zone primarily for the living welfare of people and not for the benefit of the local tax rate.[20]

We have earlier stated that a developing municipality's obligation to afford the opportunity for decent and adequate low and moderate income housing extends at least to ". . . the municipality's fair share of the present and prospective regional need therefor." Some comment on that conclusion is in order at this point. Frequently it might be sounder to have more of such housing, like some specialized land uses, in one municipality in a region than in another, because of greater availability of suitable land, location of employment, accessibility of public transportation or some other significant reason. But, under present New Jersey legislation, zoning must be on an individual municipal basis, rather than regionally. So long as that situation persists under the present tax structure, or in the absence of some kind of binding agreement among all the municipalities of a region, we feel that every municipality therein must bear its fair share of the regional burden. . . .

The composition of the applicable "region" will necessarily vary from situation to situation and probably no hard and fast rule will serve to furnish the answer in every case. Confinement to or within a certain county appears not to be realistic, but restriction within the boundaries of the state seems practical and advisable. (This is not to say that a developing municipality can ignore a demand for housing within its boundaries on the part of people who commute to work in another state.) Here we have

20. This case does not properly present the question of whether a developing municipality may time its growth and, if so, how. . . . We now say only that, assuming some type of timed growth is permissible, it cannot be utilized as an exclusionary device or to stop all further development and must include early provision for low and moderate income housing.

already defined the region at present as "those portions of Camden, Burlington and Gloucester Counties within a semicircle having a radius of 20 miles or so from the heart of Camden City." The concept of "fair share" is coming into more general use and, through the expertise of the municipal planning adviser, the county planning boards and the state planning agency, a reasonable figure for Mount Laurel can be determined, which can then be translated to the allocation of sufficient land therefor on the zoning map....

III
The Remedy

As outlined at the outset of this opinion, the trial court invalidated the zoning ordinance *in toto* and ordered the township to make certain studies and investigations and to present to the court a plan of affirmative public action designed "to enable and encourage the satisfaction of the indicated needs" for township related low and moderate income housing. Jurisdiction was retained for judicial consideration and approval of such a plan and for the entry of a final order requiring its implementation.

We are of the view that the trial court's judgment should be modified in certain respects. We see no reason why the entire zoning ordinance should be nullified. Therefore we declare it to be invalid only to the extent and in the particulars set forth in this opinion. The township is granted 90 days from the date hereof, or such additional time as the trial court may find it reasonable and necessary to allow, to adopt amendments to correct the deficiencies herein specified. It is the local function and responsibility, in the first instance at least, rather than the court's, to decide on the details of the same within the guidelines we have laid down. If plaintiffs desire to attack such amendments, they may do so by supplemental complaint filed in this cause within 30 days of the final adoption of the amendments.

We are not at all sure what the trial judge had in mind as ultimate action with reference to the approval of a plan for affirmative public action concerning the satisfaction of indicated housing needs and the entry of a final order requiring implementation thereof. Courts do not build housing nor do municipalities. That function is performed by private builders, various kinds of associations, or, for public housing, by special agencies created for that purpose at various levels of government. The municipal function is initially to provide the opportunity through appropriate land use regulations and we have spelled out what Mount Laurel must do in that regard. It is not appropriate at this time, particularly in view of the advanced view of zoning law as applied to housing laid down by this opinion, to deal with the matter of the further extent of judicial power in the field or to exercise any such power. The municipality should first have full opportunity to itself act without judicial supervision. We trust it will do so in the spirit we have suggested, both by appropriate zoning ordinance amendments and whatever additional action encouraging the fulfillment of its fair share of the regional need for low and moderate income housing may be indicated as necessary and advisable. (We have in mind that there is at least a moral obligation in a municipality to establish a local housing agency pursuant to state law to provide housing for its resident poor now living in dilapidated, unhealthy quarters.) The portion of the trial court's judgment ordering the preparation and submission of the aforesaid study, report and plan to it for further action is therefore vacated as at least premature. Should Mount Laurel not perform as we expect, further judicial action may be sought by supplemental pleading in this cause.

The judgment of the Law Division is modified as set forth herein.

[The opinions of Mountain and Pashman, JJ., concurring, are omitted.]

Notes & Questions

1. The Township of Mt. Laurel is situated in southern New Jersey, about fifteen minutes by car from Philadelphia, Pennsylvania. Doubtless, the two municipalities lie within the same "region." Are Philadelphia suburbs likely to take on a "fair share" of the regional need, absent a mandate from *their* supreme court or legislature? Does the problem of adequate housing for the poor call for interstate compacts as are sometimes employed in the management of air quality problems that cross state boundaries? Are states likely to enter into compacts addressing the problem of low- and moderate-income housing? Is this a federal problem that Congress should address?

2. Mt. Laurel's response to the supreme court's 1975 decision was weak: it rezoned 20 acres—less than one-quarter of one per cent of the town's entire area—to allow construction of low-income units. Developers failed to respond at all: not a single unit of low income housing was built in the community. Reviewing this quiescence almost twenty years after its initial decision, the New Jersey Supreme Court concluded that, after "all this time, ten years after the trial court's initial order invalidating its zoning ordinance, Mt. Laurel remains afflicted with a blatantly exclusionary ordinance. Papered over with studies, rationalized by hired experts, the ordinance at its core is true to nothing but Mount Laurel's determination to exclude the poor." Southern Burlington County NAACP v. Township of Mount Laurel, 456 A.2d 390 (N.J. 1983) (*Mt. Laurel II*).

In a 248–page opinion, Chief Justice Wilentz sought to "put some steel" into *Mt. Laurel I.* The new decision declared that "every municipality's land use regulations should provide a realistic opportunity for decent housing for at least some part of its resident poor who now occupy dilapidated housing," and that already-developed communities are no longer immune from the *Mt. Laurel* mandate. To facilitate the efficient and informed determination of regional need and fair share, the court also held that a group of three judges to be selected by the Chief Justice should handle any future *Mt. Laurel* litigation. Each judge would be responsible for a different region of the state.

The court ordered cities to permit mobile homes, unless there is "solid proof that sound planning in a particular municipality requires [their] prohibition." The court also recognized that the "municipal obligation to provide a realistic opportunity for the construction of its fair share of low and moderate income housing may require more than the elimination of unnecessary cost-producing requirements and restrictions." The court suggested that cities consider mandatory set-asides and lower-income density bonuses, where developers who build low- and moderate-income housing are entitled to build more units.

3. Is there any effective way that courts can force communities to accept low-and moderate-income residents? After *Mt. Laurel II,* what stratagems might wealthy suburban residents be expected to employ in order to keep the poor from entering their communities? Could they vote to double or triple property taxes—to levels well beyond what lower income families can afford—and spend the increased tax revenues on golf, tennis and polo clubs for community use? Could they do just the opposite, reducing taxes to a point at which no public services—police, fire, or sanitation—are provided at all, so that each household must contract for these services with private firms? What if wealthy residents seek to preserve the amenities offered by large-lot zoning by buying up private restrictive covenants on all vacant parcels in the township, limiting the development of these parcels to a one-acre minimum lot size?

4. *Mt. Laurel II* was not popular. In 1985, the New Jersey legislature passed the New Jersey Fair Housing Act to try to address the continuing controversy over the *Mt. Laurel* decisions. N.J. Stat. Ann. §§ 52:27D–301 et seq. Taking the issue out of the hands of the courts, the Fair Housing Act created a Council on Affordable Housing to define and enforce local obligations under *Mt. Laurel.* The Act also created a trading system in which a suburb can pay a city to take over up to half of the suburb's fair-share obligation. See Harold A. McDougall, Regional Contribution Agreements: Compensation for Exclusionary Zoning, 60 Temp. L.Q. 665 (1987). The New Jersey Supreme Court upheld the Fair Housing Act in Hills Dev. Co. v. Bernards Township, 510 A.2d 621 (N.J. 1986).

5. A few other state courts have taken roughly the approach adopted in *Mt. Laurel I.* See, e.g., Surrick v. Zoning Hearing Board of the Township of Upper Providence, 382 A.2d 105 (Pa. 1977); Berenson v. Town of New Castle, 341 N.E.2d 236 (N.Y. 1975). Most state courts, however, have avoided active involvement.

6. All zoning is potentially exclusionary. Height, bulk, setback, and minimum lot size requirements exclude denser land uses that will often be more profitable to the developer and more economical to prospective occupants. Although *Mt. Laurel I* was the first state high court decision to overturn an ordinance on strictly exclusionary grounds, earlier state court decisions had invalidated specific ordinance provisions for cutting too deeply into landowners' potential profits, or for excluding more economical uses, or both.

a. **Minimum Lot Size.** Courts widely accept minimum lot size requirements as a legitimate means for enhancing visual amenities, reducing congestion, and lowering the costs of water supply and sewage treatment. Yet, if the minimum is too large, some courts may invalidate it as confiscatory or exclusionary. In National Land & Investment Co. v. Kohn, 215 A.2d 597 (Pa. 1965), the Pennsylvania Supreme Court invalidated an Easttown ordinance that required a minimum area of four acres per building lot in residential districts in approximately 30% of the Township. One factor influencing the court's decision was that the regulation reduced the value of plaintiff's land from $260,000 to $175,000. The court was even more troubled by the question

> whether the township can stand in the way of the natural forces which send our growing population into hitherto undeveloped areas in search of a comfortable place to live. We have concluded not. A zoning ordinance whose primary purpose is to prevent the entrance of newcomers in order to avoid future burdens, economic and otherwise, upon the administration of public services and facilities can not be held valid.

Id. at 612. But see Johnson v. Town of Edgartown, 680 N.E.2d 37 (Mass. 1997) (upholding 3–acre minimum).

b. **Minimum Floor Area.** Courts early upheld ordinances imposing minimum floor space requirements in residential developments as reasonably aimed at controlling density, preserving neighborhood amenities, and promoting public health by assuring that families would not live in cramped housing. See, e.g., Lionshead Lake, Inc. v. Wayne Township, 89 A.2d 693 (N.J. 1952). Concerned, no doubt, by the requirements' exclusion of more modest and economical housing, however, a few courts have invalidated floor space minima on the ground that they bear no rational relationship to legitimate police power objects. See, e.g., Home Builders League, Inc. v. Township of Berlin, 405 A.2d 381 (N.J. 1979).

c. **Restrictions on Multiple Family Dwellings.** In Appeal of Girsh, 263 A.2d 395 (Pa. 1970), the Pennsylvania Supreme Court invalidated a zoning ordinance that effectively prohibited apartment houses anywhere in the township. The court relied on its earlier decision in National Land & Investment Co. v. Kohn, above, to reject the township's argument that "apartment uses would cause a significant population increase with a resulting strain on available municipal services and roads, and would clash with the existing residential neighborhood." The court conceded that the town

> can protect its attractive character by requiring apartments to be built in accordance with (reasonable) setback, open space, height, and other light-and-air requirements, but it cannot refuse to make any provision for apartment living. The simple fact that someone is anxious to build apartments is strong indication that the location of this township is such that people are desirous of moving in, and we do not believe Nether Providence can close its doors to those people.

Id. at 399.

d. **Restrictions on Mobile Homes and Mobile Home Parks.** Although conditions have improved substantially since the 1930s and 1940s, when mobile homes were dinky trailers and trailer courts were cramped and ill-kept, even the most gracious suburban governments still seek to exclude individual mobile homes or to confine them to carefully segregated mobile home parks. Courts have often invalidated efforts at complete exclusion and, in some states, have also stricken ordinances limiting mobile homes to designated mobile home parks. See, e.g., Cannon v. Coweta County, 389 S.E.2d 329 (Ga. 1990); Robinson Township v. Knoll, 302 N.W.2d 146, 150 (Mich. 1981).

e. **Growth Controls.** What of the growth control measures studied earlier in this Chapter? In Golden v. Planning Board of Town of Ramapo, 285 N.E.2d 291 (N.Y. 1972), discussed at p. 1048, the New York Court of Appeals upheld a local ordinance that conditioned subdivision approval on the availability to the subdivision of sewers, drainage facilities, public parks, schools, roads, and firehouses. Noting that it would "not countenance" any "community efforts at immunization or exclusion," the court emphasized that,

> far from being exclusionary, the present amendments merely seek, by the implementation of sequential development and timed growth, to provide a balanced cohesive community dedicated to the efficient utilization of land. The restrictions conform to the community's considered land use policies as expressed in its comprehensive plan and represent a bona fide effort to maximize population density consistent with orderly growth.

Id. at 301.

7. Federal courts have been far less hospitable to exclusionary claims than state courts. In the early 1970's, housing activists had hoped that the United States Supreme Court would overturn exclusionary ordinances on the ground that, by discriminating against the poor in search of housing, they violated the Constitution's Equal Protection Clause and interfered with consumers' freedom of travel. The Supreme Court soon dashed these hopes. In Lindsey v. Normet, 405 U.S. 56 (1972), the Court held that housing is not a fundamental right. In San Antonio Independent School District v. Rodriguez, 411 U.S. 1 (1973), it held that wealth is not necessarily a suspect classification. In Belle Terre v. Boraas, 416 U.S. 1 (1974), the Court dismissed the argument that zoning regulations inhibit the right to travel. And in Warth v. Seldin, 422 U.S. 490 (1975), it ruled that plaintiffs—nonprofit organizations, local taxpayers, low-income minority residents living in the general area, and a local homebuilders' association—lacked standing to attack the local zoning ordinance.

Federal courts will, however, overturn exclusionary zoning ordinances shown to discriminate on the basis of race. In Village of Arlington Heights v. Metropolitan Housing Corp., 429 U.S. 252 (1977), the Supreme Court rejected a claim that, because the village's refusal to rezone plaintiff's property to permit the construction of federally-financed low income housing had a racially discriminatory impact, it violated the equal protection clause. In the Court's view, plaintiff had to show discriminatory *intent,* not just *impact,* to prevail on the constitutional claim. On remand, however, the Seventh Circuit Court of Appeals held that the village's refusal to rezone violated the Fair Housing Act: "under the circumstances of this case defendant has a statutory obligation to refrain from zoning policies that effectively foreclose the construction of any low-cost housing within its corporate boundaries." At least in some situations, "a violation of section 3604(a) can be established by a showing of discriminatory effect without a showing of discriminatory intent." Metropolitan Housing Development Corp. v. Village of Arlington Heights, 558 F.2d 1283, 1285, 1290 (1977).

CHAPTER 12

FEDERAL ENVIRONMENTAL LAND USE REGULATION

Land use controls have historically been the province of local governments. In recent years, however, the federal government also has become increasingly involved in private land use regulation. While local land use controls focus primarily on the effect of land uses on other property owners and community members, federal regulations focus more on protecting the natural environment from harmful development. This Chapter provides a short introduction to the two federal statutes with perhaps the greatest land use implications—the Clean Water Act, which restricts development of wetlands, and the Endangered Species Act. We touch here only on some of the principal land use aspects of these statutes, leaving broader and more detailed discussions of these statutes to courses in environmental and natural resources law.

A. WETLANDS PRESERVATION & THE CLEAN WATER ACT

Protection of wetlands under section 404 of the Clean Water Act, 33 U.S.C. § 1344, regularly involves the federal government in land use decisions throughout the nation. Section 404(a) authorizes the Army Corps of Engineers to "issue permits, after notice and opportunity for public hearings, for the discharge of dredged or fill material into the navigable waters" of the United States. 33 U.S.C. § 1344(a). As discussed below, navigable waters include most wetlands. Before a private landowner can fill and develop wetlands on his property, the landowner therefore must obtain a permit from the Army Corps of Engineers. The Corps in turn must determine that the development will not unnecessarily harm the environment.

Wetlands are land areas that are saturated or inundated with water long enough each year to support hydrophilic (water loving) plants. Although generations of Americans eagerly filled "swamps" and "bogs" in the nation's efforts to grow and develop, wetlands provide a variety of valuable services to society.

> To start, wetlands help protect waterways, and thus drinking water, from a variety of contaminants. Wetlands, for example, filter out nutrients and other contaminants from water running off of neighboring lands into a waterway. Studies indicate that wetlands retain 80 percent of the phosphorous and 89 percent of

> the nitrogen found in runoff. Forested wetlands also lower water temperature in hot summer months, reducing harmful algal blooms. In addition, wetlands reduce the risk of floods (which in an average year cause over $4 billion in damages and dozens of deaths). Wetlands act as natural sponges, soaking up water during peak runoffs and then releasing the water slowly over time. A 1993 study by the Illinois State Water Survey estimated that every one percent increase in wetlands along a stream corridor decreased peak streams by an average of almost four percent. A Wisconsin study found that watersheds consisting of 30 percent or more wetlands enjoy 60 to 80 percent lower flood-water levels compared to watersheds with no wetlands. By storing water during periods of high precipitation and then releasing the water during the dry season, wetlands also serve as natural reservoirs.
>
> Wetlands also provide crucial habitat for migrating birds and other species. Approximately a third of the domestic species listed as endangered or threatened under the federal Endangered Species Act use wetlands as habitat. Half of the nation's migratory bird species use wetlands as nesting, migratory, or wintering areas. Wetlands also provide nursery or spawning habitat for 60 to 90 percent of the nation's commercial fish species. Because wetlands attract so much wildlife, they serve as an important source of recreation. Each year millions of people use wetlands for nature watching, hunting, hiking, and canoeing. In 1980, 55 million people spent $10 billion observing and photographing waterfowl and other wetlands species.

James Salzman & Barton H. Thompson, Jr., Environmental Law and Policy 243–244 (2003).

Despite wetlands' value, the nation enjoys only a fraction of the wetlands that existed on the North American Continent when European settlers first arrived. For years, the nation has lost wetlands to urban development, agriculture, peat mining, and other activities. Of the 220 million acres of wetlands in the lower 48 states in the 1600s, fewer than 110 million acres remain. California and Iowa have lost approximately 90 percent of their wetlands. Those wetlands that remain are often degraded, reducing their ability to provide the valuable services described above.

Since 1988, the United States has pursued a policy of "no net loss" of wetlands. Section 404 of the Clean Water Act is the federal government's principal tool for achieving this policy. Because it is difficult if not impossible to develop wetlands without filling or otherwise discharging materials into the wetlands, any landowner wishing to develop a wetland on his property must typically obtain a permit from the Corps under section 404 (as well as obtain whatever other land use and construction permits she needs from local, regional, or state permitting authorities).

1. THE REACH OF FEDERAL WETLANDS AUTHORITY

Section 404 prohibits nonpermitted discharges of dredged or fill materials into "navigable waters"—which the Clean Water Act defines as all "waters of the United States." 33 U.S.C. §§ 1344(a), 1362(7). What wetlands does this language cover? Initially, the Corps of Engineers concluded that it had jurisdiction over only historically navigable waters—which would exclude most wetlands, including virtually all freshwater wetlands. An environmental group, however, challenged this narrow interpretation and won in Natural Resources Defense Council v. Callaway, 392 F. Supp. 685 (D.D.C. 1975). The Corps responded by issuing new regulations that asserted jurisdiction not only over actually navigable waters, but also adjacent wetlands, interstate wetlands, and intrastate "wetlands, sloughs, prairie potholes, wet meadows, playa lakes, or natural ponds, the use of which could affect interstate or foreign commerce." 33 C.F.R. § 328.3(a), 40 C.F.R. § 230.3(s).

In United States v. Riverside Bayview Homes, Inc., 474 U.S. 121 (1985), the United States Supreme Court unanimously agreed that the Corps could assert jurisdiction over wetlands that are not themselves navigable, but that are adjacent to and integrally connected to actually navigable waters.

> Congress chose to define the waters covered by the Act broadly. Although the Act prohibits discharges into "navigable waters," the Act's definition of "navigable waters" as "the waters of the United States" makes it clear that the term "navigable" as used in the Act is of limited import.... In view of the breadth of federal regulatory authority contemplated by the Act itself and the inherent difficulties of defining precise bounds to regulable waters, the Corps' ecological judgment about the relationship between waters and their adjacent wetlands provides an adequate basis for a legal judgment that adjacent wetlands may be defined as waters under the Act.

Id. at 133–134.

In Solid Waste Agency of Northern Cook County v. United States Army Corps of Engineers (SWANCC), 531 U.S. 159 (2001), the Court addressed the Corps' jurisdiction over isolated wetlands that sit apart from any navigable waters. Under its "Migratory Bird Rule," the Corps asserted jurisdiction over isolated wetlands that are the actual or potential habitat for migratory birds. These wetlands are especially important because over half of all migratory bird species use wetlands as habitat. In *SWANCC*, however, the Supreme Court by a 5–4 vote held the Migratory Bird Rule exceeded the Corps' authority under the Clean Water Act. The Court concluded that neither the language nor the legislative history of the Clean Water Act support the Migratory Bird Rule. The Court also worried that the Migratory Bird Rule pushed the outer limits of Congress' constitutional authority. (We look at the issue of Congress' authority over local land use in more detail later in this Chapter at page 1102.) "This concern is heightened where the administrative interpretation alters the federal-state framework by permitting federal encroachment upon a traditional state power"—land use regulation. Id. at 173.

The Supreme Court addressed the Corps' jurisdiction once again in a fractured set of opinions in Rapanos v. United States, 126 S. Ct. 2208 (2006). In *Rapanos*, the question was the Corps' jurisdiction over wetlands that were hydrologically connected, through various ditches, drains, and creeks, to major waterways that were sometimes miles away. Lower courts had upheld the Corps' assertion of jurisdiction. By a 5–4 vote, however, the Supreme Court reversed. Justice Scalia, writing for himself and three other justices, adopted a narrow interpretation of the Corps' jurisdiction. According to Scalia, " 'the waters of the United States' include only relatively permanent, standing or flowing bodies of water," not "transitory puddles or ephemeral flows of water." Any broader interpretation would raise federalism concerns:

> As we noted in *SWANCC*, the Government's expansive interpretation would "result in a significant impingement of the States' traditional and primary power over land and water use." Regulation of land use ... is a quintessential state and local power.... The extensive federal jurisdiction urged by the Government would authorize the Corps to function as a *de facto* regulator of immense stretches of intrastate land—an authority the agency has shown its willingness to exercise with the scope of discretion that would befit a local zoning board. We ordinary expect a "clear and manifest" statement from Congress to authorize an unprecedented intrusion into traditional state authority. See BFP v. Resolution Trust Corporation, 511 U.S. 531, 544 (1994). The phrase "the waters of the United States" hardly qualifies.

Justice Kennedy provided the fifth vote to reverse. According to Justice Kennedy, the Corps can establish jurisdiction over isolated wetlands on a case by case basis by demonstrating the "existence of a significant nexus between the wetland in question and navigable waters in the traditional sense." The Corps can demonstrate this nexus by showing that the "wetland, either alone or in combination with similarly situated lands in the region, significantly affects the chemical, physical, and biological integrity of the covered waters more readily understood as 'navigable.' "

Are there good policy reasons for the federal government to regulate isolated wetlands with no close geographic connection to traditional navigable waters?

Does the Corps enjoy regulatory authority over purely artificial wetlands? Courts have permitted the Corps to assert jurisdiction over artificial wetlands, at least where the Corps did not itself help to create the wetlands. See Leslie Salt Co. v. United States, 896 F.2d 354 (9th Cir. 1990) (approving jurisdiction); United States v. Fort Pierre, 747 F.2d 464 (8th Cir. 1984) (rejecting jurisdiction where the Corps created the wetland). Why exclude wetlands that the Corps helped create?

2. WHAT ACTIVITIES ARE REGULATED?

Although a wide range of activities can harm wetlands, section 404 regulates only "discharges" of fill and other materials into wetlands.

Section 404 therefore requires a landowner who wants to fill in a wetland and build on it to obtain a permit from the Corps. But what if a landowner can figure out a way to develop or use a wetland without filling it in? Does section 404 apply and, if so, when?

In Avoyelles Sportsmen's League v. Marsh, 715 F.2d 897 (5th Cir. 1983), the owners of a 20,000–acre tract of land in Louisiana wanted to use wetlands on their property to grow soybeans. To do this, however, they needed to remove trees and other vegetation from the area. "Using bulldozers with shearing blades that *floated* along the ground, the defendants cut the timber and vegetation at or just above ground level. The trees were then raked into windrows, burned, and the stumps and ashes were disced into the ground by other machinery." Id. at 901. The defendants argued that they did not need a 404 permit because they were removing objects from the wetlands not discharging anything into them. The Fifth Circuit Court of Appeals disagreed. As the defendants cut timber and other vegetation, they inevitably redeposited and disced some of the vegetation back into the wetland. They also filled in some small sloughs to help level the land. Section 404 therefore applied.

In Borden Ranch Partnership v. United States Army Corps of Engineers, 261 F.3d 810 (9th Cir. 2001), a California real estate developer purchased a large ranch with the intent to convert the ranch into vineyards and orchards and then subdivide it into upscale residential parcels. During rainy seasons, a shallow layer of impermeable clay formed vernal pools, swales, and other intermittent wetlands on parts of the property. Because vineyards have deep roots, the developer needed to "deep rip" the land by dragging tractors with lengthy metal prongs through the soil, tearing open the clay layer and, as an unfortunate byproduct, destroying the wetlands. The Ninth Circuit held that the developer needed a 404 permit because the deep ripping moved and redeposited soil as the prongs passed through the soil. The United States Supreme Court affirmed by an equally divided vote. Borden Ranch Partnership v. United States Army Corps of Engineers, 537 U.S. 99 (2002). But see National Mining Ass'n v. United States Army Corps of Engineers, 145 F.3d 1399 (D.C. Cir. 1998) (holding that the mining of dredged material from a wetland does not require a 404 permit even if some of the material incidentally falls back into the wetland).

Could a landowner drain a wetland without getting permission from the Corps? Is there any way of draining a wetland without incidentally depositing or redepositing some materials into the wetland? Are such incidental deposits a sufficient basis to require a permit? If Congress had meant to regulate the draining of wetlands through section 404, couldn't Congress have simply said so? Is *Borden Ranch* an example of a court stretching the terms of a statute to reach what it perceives to be a socially beneficial result?

3. THE PERMITTING PROCESS

Section 404 of the Clean Water Act provides little direct guidance on the standards that the Corps should use in issuing permits to landowners who wish to discharge fill or other material into wetlands on their property. Instead, Congress instructed the federal Environmental Protection Agency (EPA), in conjunction with the Corps, to develop appropriate guidelines. Under those guidelines, the Corps can issue a permit only after finding that

> (1) there is no practicable alternative to the proposed discharge that would have less adverse impact on the aquatic ecosystem;
>
> (2) the proposed activity will not have significant adverse impacts on aquatic resources;
>
> (3) all "appropriate and practicable" mitigation will be employed; and
>
> (4) the proposed activity will not violate any other state or federal laws (such as the Endangered Species Act).

40 C.F.R. § 230.10. Even if a landowner shows that she would meet these standards, the Corps also will scrutinize the activity to see if it would be "contrary to the public interest." In making this determination, the Corps will consider a broad range of factors, including the effect of the activity on fish, wildlife, water quality, flood control, recreation, and aesthetics. Id. § 320.4.

The Administrator of EPA also can veto a permit whenever he or she "determines, after notice and opportunity for public hearings, that the discharge of such materials into such area will have an unacceptable adverse effect on municipal water supplies, shellfish beds and fishery areas (including spawning and breeding areas), wildlife, or recreational areas." Before making this determination, the Administrator must consult with the Corps. The Administrator of EPA has seldom used this power.

Of the various standards for a 404 permit, the requirement that there be no "practicable alternative to the proposed discharge that would have less adverse impact on the aquatic ecosystem" has generated the most litigation and confusion. Although the presence or absence of practicable alternatives might seem a straightforward inquiry, whether something is a practicable alternative can depend on *how* you define the purpose of the proposed activity and *when* you ask the question.

Sylvester v. Army Corps of Engineers

United States Court of Appeals for the Ninth Circuit, 1989.
882 F.2d 407.

JOSEPH T. SNEED, Circuit Judge.

[In this case, the Perini Land & Development Co. (Perini) sought to develop a proposed resort, including a golf course, in Squaw Valley, California. Construction of the golf course would have involved filling eleven acres of wetlands along Squaw Creek. Perini applied for a permit from the Army Corps of Engineers under section 404 of the Clean Water Act, which was granted. Sylvester filed suit seeking to invalidate the permit and sought a preliminary injunction to halt construction of the golf course. The district court denied the injunction, and Sylvester appealed.] We affirm....

We review the district court's refusal to grant injunctive relief for abuse of discretion. See Friends of the Earth, Inc. v. Coleman, 518 F.2d 323, 327 (9th Cir. 1975). This court will set aside the Corps' decision only if it is "arbitrary, capricious, an abuse of discretion, or otherwise not in accordance with [the] law."

[Sylvester argues that the Corps violated section 404 of the Clean Water Act and its own regulations] in issuing a permit to Perini to fill eleven acres of wetlands in the process of building a golf course.

A. Practicable Alternative under the CWA

First, we turn to Sylvester's claim that the Corps impermissibly accepted Perini's definition of the project as necessitating an on-site, eighteen hole golf course. By accepting this definition, Sylvester contends that the Corps' evaluation of practicable alternatives was skewed in favor of Perini.

The regulations implementing § 404 of the CWA provide that "no discharge of dredged or fill material shall be permitted if there is a *practicable alternative* to the proposed discharge which would have less adverse impact on the aquatic ecosystem, so long as the alternative does not have other significant adverse environmental consequences." The Corps defines a practicable alternative as an alternative that "is available and capable of being done after taking into consideration cost, existing technology, and logistics in light of overall project purposes." Further, because the golf course is not a water dependent activity, the Corps' regulations presume that practicable alternatives are available "unless clearly demonstrated otherwise."

In its Environmental Assessment (EA), the Corps defined the project's purpose as follows:

> To construct an 18–hole, links style, championship golf course and other recreational amenities in conjunction with the development of the proposed Resort at Squaw Creek. Research conducted for the applicant has indicated that a quality 18–hole golf course is an essential element for a successful alpine destination resort.

Sylvester protests that the use of this definition impermissibly skewed the "practicable alternatives" analysis in favor of Perini. Specifically, Sylvester objects to the Corps' failure to consider off-site locations for the golf course, i.e., a site that was not contiguous to the rest of the resort complex. The Corps rejected consideration of such an alternative because it "did not meet [Perini's] basic purpose and need." The Corps did note, however, that two off-site locations were considered but rejected because of insufficient size and the potential for more severe environmental impacts.

In evaluating whether a given alternative site is practicable, the Corps may legitimately consider such facts as cost to the applicant and logistics. In addition, the Corps has a duty to consider the applicant's purpose. As the Fifth Circuit observed: "The Corps has a duty to take into account the objectives of the applicant's project. Indeed, it would be bizarre if the Corps were to ignore the purpose for which the applicant seeks a permit and to substitute a purpose it deems more suitable." Louisiana Wildlife Fed'n, Inc. v. York, 761 F.2d 1044, 1048 (5th Cir. 1985) (per curiam) (footnote omitted).

Obviously, an applicant cannot define a project in order to preclude the existence of any alternative sites and thus make what is practicable appear impracticable. This court [in prior cases has] quite properly suggested that the applicant's purpose must be "legitimate." Yet, in determining whether an alternate site is practicable, the Corps is not entitled to reject Perini's genuine and legitimate conclusion that the type of golf course it wishes to construct is economically advantageous to its resort development.

By contrast, an alternative site does not have to accommodate components of a project that are merely incidental to the applicant's basic purpose. For example, in Shoreline Assocs. v. Marsh, 555 F. Supp. 169, 179 (D. Md. 1983), aff'd, 725 F.2d 677 (4th Cir. 1984), the Corps refused to issue a permit to a developer for building a number of waterfront town houses together with a boat storage and launching facility. The developer argued that the Corps' proposed alternative site for the town houses could not accommodate the boat storage and launch area. The court upheld the Corps' denial of the permit, observing that the boat facilities were merely "incidental" to the town house development.

In this case, it is not the resort buildings that are at issue as were the town houses in Shoreline. The location of the resort buildings was fixed by decisions not involving the Corps of Engineers.... Rather the issue in this case is whether this proposed location ignores other reasonable and practicable alternatives, including no golf course at all. Resolution of this issue requires that the relationship of the course to the entire project be considered. The Corps of Engineers did consider this relationship. Doing so was neither arbitrary nor capricious....

B. Evaluation of the Benefits of the Golf Course

.... Sylvester contends that the Corps limited its consideration of the impact of the proposed development to only those of the golf course while simultaneously including the benefits from the entire resort complex.... Sylvester argues that the Corps' CWA "public interest analysis" was likewise skewed in favor of the project.

.... The Corps did not, as Sylvester argues, weigh the benefits of the entire project against the environmental impacts of the golf course. The EA makes plain that the Corps followed its regulations and weighed only the benefits of the golf course to the resort.

We conclude, therefore, that the Corps quite properly did measure the benefit of the golf course in terms of its contribution to making the resort an economically viable year-round facility with all of its attendant advantages. This analysis was proper under ... the CWA....

Notes & Questions

1. Was the result in *Sylvester* preordained once the Army Corps of Engineers accepted the Perini Land & Development Company's characterization of the project's purpose as building an "alpine destination resort"? Why did Perini have to build a destination resort? If there were other potential uses of the land (e.g., condominiums), wasn't this an "alternative"?

2. In National Wildlife Federation v. Whistler, 27 F.3d 1341 (8th Cir. 1994), a developer wanted to dredge an old river channel in order to provide a planned housing development with boat access to the Missouri River. Because the old river channel was now wetland, the developer applied for and received a 404 permit. The National Wildlife Federation challenged the Corps' finding that there was no practicable alternative. "The Corps concluded that the project's purpose was to provide boat access to the Missouri River from [the] planned development. Given this purpose, ... [no] other alternative ... would serve [the developer's] purpose." The Eighth Circuit Court of Appeals agreed. Given where the housing development was located, the court reasoned, there was no other site that would provide direct boat access to the Missouri River. Was there really no alternative? Why couldn't the residents of the new development have used a public boat ramp? Why did the residents need boat access at all? And why did the housing development need to be where the developer placed it?

3. A developer is not entitled to a permit just because he can show that there is no practicable alternative. As noted above, the developer also must show that the discharge will not have a "significant adverse impact on aquatic resources" and that "all reasonable mitigation measures will be employed." In *Whistler*, supra Note 2, for example, the developer agreed to 42 conditions, including the enhancement of a 20–acre mitigation area. Given that the Corps will issue a permit only if the proposed activity will not significantly harm aquatic resources, why should the Corps even worry whether there is a practicable alternative?

4. **Citizen Suits.** The plaintiff in *Sylvester* was a local activist who opposed the proposed development. The Clean Water Act, like most federal environmental statutes, authorizes "any citizen" to sue "any person ... who is alleged to be in violation of" section 404 or any order issued thereunder. 33 U.S.C. § 1365(a). Courts, moreover, can award attorney fees to prevailing plaintiffs. 33 U.S.C. § 1365(d). Should anyone be able to sue to enforce section 404? Recall that historically only public officials, and private plaintiffs suffering special damages, were able to sue for a public nuisance. See p. 146 supra.

Bersani v. Robichaud

United States Court of Appeals for the Second Circuit, 1988.
850 F.2d 36.

TIMBERS, Circuit Judge.

Appellants John A. Bersani, the Pyramid Companies, Newport Galleria Group and Robert J. Congel ("Pyramid", collectively) appeal from a judgment entered October 23, 1987 in the Northern District of New York, granting summary judgment in favor of appellees, the United States Environmental Protection Agency ("EPA"), the United States Army Corps of Engineers (the "Corps"), Lee Thomas, the Administrator of the EPA, Richard K. Dawson, Assistant Secretary for Civil Works, United States Army, and Jennifer Joy Wilson, Assistant Administrator for External Affairs of the EPA (the "Federal Appellees" collectively), and denying Pyramid's motion for summary judgment.

This case arises out of Pyramid's attempt to build a shopping mall on certain wetlands in Massachusetts known as Sweedens Swamp. Acting under the Clean Water Act, EPA vetoed the approval by the Corps of a permit to build the mall because EPA found that an alternative site had been available to Pyramid at the time it entered the market to search for a site for the mall. The alternative site was purchased later by another developer and arguably became unavailable by the time Pyramid applied for a permit to build the mall.

On appeal, the thrust of Pyramid's argument is a challenge to what it calls EPA's "market entry" theory, i.e., the interpretation by EPA of the relevant regulation, which led EPA to consider the availability of alternative sites at the time Pyramid entered the market for a site, instead of at the time it applied for a permit.... 40 C.F.R. § 230.10(a) covers "non-water dependent activities" (i.e., activities that could be performed on non-wetland sites, such as building a mall) and provides essentially that the Corps must determine whether an alternative site is available that would cause less harm to the wetlands. Specifically, it provides that "no discharge of dredged or fill material shall be permitted if there is a practicable alternative" to the proposal that would have a "less adverse impact" on the "aquatic ecosystem." It also provides that a practicable alternative may include "an area not presently owned by the applicant which could reasonably be obtained, utilized, expanded or managed in order to fulfill the basic purpose of the proposed activity." It further provides that, "unless clearly demonstrated otherwise," practicable alternatives are (1) "presumed to be available" and (2) "presumed to have less adverse impact on the aquatic ecosystem." Thus an applicant such as Pyramid must rebut both of these presumptions in order to obtain a permit....

Sweedens Swamp is a 49.5 acre wetland which is part of an 80 acre site near Interstate 95 in South Attleboro, Massachusetts. Although some illegal dumping and motorbike intrusions have occurred, these activities have been found to have had little impact on the site which remains a "high-quality red maple swamp" providing wildlife habitat and protecting the area from flooding and pollution.

The effort to build a mall on Sweedens Swamp was initiated by Pyramid's predecessor, the Edward J. DeBartolo Corporation ("DeBartolo"). DeBartolo purchased the Swamp some time before April 1982. At the time of this purchase an alternative site was available in North Attleboro (the "North Attleboro site").... Pyramid took over the project in 1983....

One of the key issues in dispute in the instant case is just when did Pyramid begin searching for a suitable site for its mall. EPA asserts that Pyramid began to search in the Spring of 1983. Pyramid asserts that it began to search several months later, in September 1983. The difference is crucial because on July 1, 1983—a date between the starting dates claimed by EPA and Pyramid—a competitor of Pyramid, the New England Development Co. ("NED"), purchased options to buy the North Attleboro site. This site was located upland and could have served as a "practicable alternative" to Sweedens Swamp, if it had been "available" at the relevant time....

In December 1983, Pyramid purchased Sweedens Swamp from DeBartolo. In August 1984, Pyramid applied under § 404(a) to the New England regional division of the Corps (the "NE Corps") for a permit. It sought to fill or alter 32 of the 49.6 acres of the Swamp; to excavate nine acres of uplands to create artificial wetlands; and to alter 13.3 acres of existing wetlands to improve its environmental quality. Later Pyramid proposed to mitigate the adverse impact on the wetlands by creating 36 acres of replacement wetlands in an off-site gravel pit....

In November 1984, EPA and FWS submitted official comments to the NE Corps recommending denial of the application because Pyramid's proposal was inconsistent with the 404(b)(1) guidelines. Pyramid had failed (1) to overcome the presumption of the availability of alternatives and (2) to mitigate adequately the adverse impact on wildlife. EPA threatened a § 404(c) review. Pyramid then proposed to create additional artificial wetlands at a nearby upland site, a proposal it eventually abandoned.

In January 1985, the NE Corps hired a consultant to investigate the feasibility of Sweedens Swamp and the North Attleboro site. The consultant reported that either site was feasible but that from a commercial standpoint only one mall could survive in the area. On February 19, 1985, the NE Corps advised Pyramid that denial of its permit was imminent. On May 2, 1985, the NE Corps sent its recommendation to deny the permit to the national headquarters of the Corps. Although the NE Corps ordinarily makes the final decision on whether to grant a permit, in the instant case, because of widespread publicity, General John F. Wall, the Director of Civil Works at the national headquarters of the Corps, decided to review the NE Corps' decision. Wall reached a different conclusion. He decided to grant the permit after finding that Pyramid's offsite mitigation proposal would reduce the adverse impacts sufficiently to allow the "practicable alternative" test to be deemed satisfied. He stated:

> In a proper case, mitigation measures can be said to reduce adverse impacts of a proposed activity to the point where there is no "easily identifiable difference in impact" between the proposed activity (including mitigation) versus the alternatives to that activity.

Although he did not explicitly address the issue, Wall apparently assumed that the relevant time to determine whether there was a practicable alternative was the time of the application, not the time the applicant entered the market. In other words, Wall appears to have assumed that the market entry theory was not the correct approach. For example, while addressing the traditional "practicable alternatives" analysis as an alternative ground for his decision, Wall found that the North Attleboro site was unavailable "because it has been optioned by another developer."....

On March 4, 1986, the RA recommended that EPA veto the permit because of adverse impacts on wildlife and available "practicable alternatives.".... On May 13, 1986, EPA issued its final determination, which prohibited Pyramid from using Sweedens Swamp. It found (1) that the filling of the Swamp would adversely affect wildlife; (2) that the North Attleboro site could have been available to Pyramid at the time Pyramid investigated the area to search for a site; (3) that considering Pyramid's failure or unwillingness to provide further materials about its investigation of alternative sites, it was uncontested that, at best, Pyramid never checked the availability of the North Attleboro site as an alternative; (4) that the North Attleboro site was feasible and would have a less adverse impact on the wetland environment; and (5) that the mitigation proposal did not make the project preferable to other alternatives because of scientific uncertainty of success. In the second of these findings, EPA used what Pyramid calls the "market entry" approach....

One of Pyramid's principal contentions is that the market entry approach is inconsistent with both the language of the 404(b)(1) guidelines and the past practice of the Corps and EPA.

With regard to the language of the regulations, Pyramid reasons that the 404(b)(1) guidelines are framed in the present tense, while the market entry approach focuses on the past by considering whether a practicable alternative was available at the time the applicant entered the market to search for a site. To support its argument that the 404(b)(1) guidelines are framed in the present tense, Pyramid quotes the following language:

> An alternative is practicable if it is available.... If it is otherwise a practicable alternative, an area not presently owned by the applicant which could reasonably be obtained, utilized, expanded or managed in order to fulfill the basic purpose of the proposed activity may be considered.

It then argues that EPA says "is" means "was."....

While this argument has a certain surface appeal, we are persuaded that it is contrary to a common sense reading of the regulations; that it entails an overly literal and narrow interpretation of the language; and that it creates requirements not intended by Congress.

First, while it is true that the language is in the present tense, it does not follow that the "most natural" reading of the regulations would create a time-of-application rule. As EPA points out, "the regulations do not indicate when it is to be determined whether an alternative 'is' available," i.e., the "present" of the regulations might be the time the application is submitted; the time it is reviewed; or any number of other times. Based upon a reading of the language in the context of the controlling statute and the regulations as a whole, moreover, we conclude that when the agencies drafted the language in question they simply were not thinking of the specific issues raised by the instant case, in which an applicant had available alternatives at the time it was selecting its site but these alternatives had evaporated by the time it applied for a permit. We therefore agree with the district court that the regulations are essentially silent on the issue of timing and that it would be appropriate to consider the objectives of the Act and the intent underlying the promulgation of the regulations.

Second, as EPA has pointed out, the preamble to the 404(b)(1) guidelines states that the purpose of the "practicable alternatives" analysis is "to recognize the special value of wetlands and to avoid their unnecessary destruction, particularly where practicable alternatives *were* available in non-aquatic areas to achieve the basic purpose of the proposal." In other words, the purpose is to create an incentive for developers to avoid choosing wetlands when they could choose an alternative upland site. Pyramid's reading of the regulations would thwart this purpose because it would remove the incentive for a developer to search for an alternative site at the time such an incentive is needed, i.e., at the time it is making the decision to select a particular site. If the practicable alternatives analysis were applied to the time of the application for a permit, the developer would have little incentive to search for alternatives, especially if it were confident that alternatives soon would disappear. Conversely, in a case in which alternatives were not available at the time the developer made its selection, but became available by the time of application, the developer's application would be denied even though it could not have explored the alternative site at the time of its decision....

In short, we conclude that a common-sense reading of the statute can lead only to the use of the market entry approach used by EPA....

PRATT, Circuit Judge, dissenting....

In this case I have no problem with EPA's basic approach. It conscientiously attempted to weigh the economic advantages against the ecological disadvantages of developing Sweedens Swamp and, in approaching this determination, it properly looked to alternate available sites. However, EPA went wrong—seriously wrong—when it adopted the market entry theory to decide whether an alternate site was available. By focusing on the decision-making techniques and tactics of a particular developer, instead of the actual alternatives to disturbing the wetland, EPA ignored the statute's central purpose.

The market entry theory in effect taints a particular developer with respect to a particular site, while ignoring the crucial question of whether the site itself should be preserved. Under the market entry theory, developer A would be denied a permit on a specific site because when he entered the market alternatives were available, but latecomer developer B, who entered the market after those alternatives had become unavailable, would be entitled to a permit for developing the same site. In such a case, the theory no longer protects the land, but instead becomes a distorted punitive device: it punishes developer A by denying him a permit, but grants developer B a permit for the same property—and the only difference between them is when they "entered the market".

The market entry theory has further problems. In this case, for example, if a Donald Trump had "entered the market" after NED took the option on the North Attleboro site and made it unavailable, under EPA's approach he apparently would have been entitled to a permit to develop Sweedens Swamp. But after obtaining the permit and the land, could Trump then sell the package to Pyramid to develop? Or could he build the mall and then sell the developed site to Pyramid? If, on the one hand, the answer to these questions is "yes," then the market entry theory is no more than a troublesome mirage that could easily be circumvented by Pyramid's using a second party to buy the land and obtain the permit. If, on the other hand, the answer is "no," then Pyramid is forever tainted, forever prohibited—somewhat like a bill of attainder—from owning this particular site, and only because at some time in the past it had "entered the market" while an alternative was still available.

Furthermore, in a business that needs as much predictability as possible, the market entry theory will regrettably inject equisite vagueness. When does a developer enter the market? When he first contemplates a development in the area? If so, in what area—the the neighborhood, the village, the town, the state or the region? Does he enter the market when he first takes some affirmative action? If so, is that when he instructs his staff to research possible sites, when he commits money for more intensive study of those sites, when he contacts a real estate broker, when he first visits a site, or when he makes his first offer to purchase? Without answers to these questions a developer can never know whether to proceed through the expense of contracts, zoning proceedings, and EPA applications. Such a vague standard as "market entry" falls far short of the requirement that an agency articulate its standards with sufficient clarity so that the affected community may know what those standards are.

Even more important, the result reached by EPA and the majority is contrary to what Congress sought to achieve when it passed § 1344. Pyramid has been "punished" for beginning its quest when the North Attleboro site was still available; but Sweedens Swamp nevertheless could be destroyed through an identical application by some other developer who happened to enter the market after that alternate site became unavailable. And this would be so even if another, better-suited site should become available after the second developer enters the market, because the "common sense" market entry theory looks only, and blindly, to the alternatives available at the time the applicant "entered the market."....

Notes & Questions

1. Assume that John Muir has owned a large piece of property, consisting largely of wetlands, since 1965. Muir originally purchased the

property as an investment, with no particular development ideas in mind. In 2005, Muir decides to develop the property as a shopping center. In deciding whether to grant Muir a 404 permit, must the Corps look to see what properties were available to buy in 1965? Would such an inquiry make any sense? Is someone who has owned a wetland for a lengthy period of time at a disadvantage in seeking a 404 permit to develop it? If Muir sells the property to Mary Austin, does she stand a better chance of getting a 404 permit?

2. Note in *Bersani* that the New England Development Co. had purchased the North Attleboro site and was planning to develop it as a shopping center. Given this, and given that there apparently was not enough business in the area to support two malls, why permit Pyramid to destroy wetlands on the Sweedens Swamp site no matter when Pyramid entered the market? Looked at from the perspective of the section 404 standards, wasn't there a practicable alternative to putting a shopping center on Sweedens Swamp, even if that alternative wasn't available to Pyramid?

3. Is the inquiry into the availability of practicable alternatives hopelessly flawed? Rather than asking whether the applicant has a practicable alternative to filling a wetland, should the law instead ask whether filling the wetland is essential to meet an important public need? For thoughts on how to reform the inquiry, see William K. McGreevey, A Public Availability Analysis to Section 404(b)(1) Alternatives Analysis: A Practical Definition for Practicable Alternatives, 59 Geo. Wash. L. Rev. 379 (1991).

4. **Mitigation.** If the Corps concludes that there is no practicable alternative, it then will turn to ensuring that the proposed project will not have significant adverse impacts on aquatic resources and employ all reasonable mitigation. The Corps "first makes a determination that potential impacts have been avoided to the maximum extent practicable." It then looks to determine if "remaining unavoidable impacts will . . . be mitigated to the extent appropriate and practicable by requiring steps to minimize impacts." To the extent that significant adverse impacts remain, the Corps will seek compensatory mitigation "for aquatic resource values." Memorandum of Agreement Between the EPA and the Department of the Army Concerning the Determination of Mitigation Under the Clean Water Act Section 404(b)(1) Guidelines, at 3, Feb. 6, 1990. The Corps, in short, follows a pecking order or sequencing of approaches to protecting wetlands: (1) avoidance of impact, (2) minimization of impact, and (3) compensatory mitigation. Note that, in *Bersani*, Pyramid agreed to protect about 17 acres of onsite wetlands (minimization of impact) and to both create artificial wetlands and enhance existing wetlands (compensatory mitigation). In evaluating proposed mitigation, the Corps prefers restoration of prior wetlands, followed by the creation of new wetlands, with the protection of existing off-site wetlands being the least favored method.

5. **Mitigation Banking.** To help provide compensatory mitigation for lost wetlands, both public and private entities have created large wetland restoration and enhancement projects to which developers and

others can turn to meet 404 mitigation requirements. The following excerpt from an article by Professor J.B. Ruhl explains the logic behind these *mitigation banks*:

> Notwithstanding its official status as the least-favored alternative in the agencies' sequencing pecking order, compensatory mitigation has been used frequently in the 404 program. Compensatory mitigation frees up highly valued wetlands for more comprehensive and flexible development. While attractive for these purposes, ... project-by-project compensatory mitigation ... has been widely regarded as having failed miserably in terms of environmental protection. Whether mitigation was accomplished onsite or near-site, [this] piecemeal approach complicated the Corps' ability to articulate mitigation performance standards, monitor success, and enforce conditions; not surprisingly, the success rate for this approach suffered as a result.
>
> In light of these problems, during the late 1980s the Corps and EPA started shifting compensatory activities increasingly from on-site to off-site mitigation, thus opening the door to the wetlands mitigation banking technique. This approach, its proponents argued, would prove advantageous both in terms of economic efficiency and ecological integrity, aggregating small wetlands threatened by development into larger restored wetlands in a different location. It is defined generally as "a system in which the creation, enhancement, restoration, or preservation of wetlands is recognized by a regulatory agency as generating compensatory credits allowing the future development of other wetland sites." In its most basic form, wetlands mitigation banking allows a developer to protect wetlands at one site in advance of development and then draw down the resulting bank of mitigation "credits" as development is implemented and wetlands at another site are filled. Indeed, the concept has progressed beyond this personal bank model. Today, large commercial and public wetlands banks, not tied to a particular development, sell mitigation piecemeal to third-party developers in need of compensatory mitigation.

J.B. Ruhl & R. Juge Gregg, Integrating Ecosystem Services Into Environmental Law: A Case Study of Wetlands Mitigation Banking, 20 Stan. Envtl. L.J. 365, 370–372 (2001). For more on wetlands banking, see Environmental Law Institute, Wetland Mitigation Banking (1993); Royal C. Gardner, Banking on Entrepreneurs: Wetlands, Mitigation Banking, and Takings, 81 Iowa L. Rev. 527 (1996).

6. **General Permits.** To help relieve the administrative burden of applying for individual 404 permits, the Corps has created a number of *general permits* that provide blanket coverage across the nation to specified activities, so long as a landowner complies with the conditions set out in the general permit. The most controversial permit for many years was Nationwide Permit 29, which authorized the filling of up to three acres of isolated wetlands for commercial or residential purposes. Faced by mount-

ing criticism that Nationwide Permit 29 was leading to significant cumulative reductions in wetland acreage, the Corps allowed the permit to expire in 2000. The Corps replaced it with Nationwide Permit 39, which authorizes the filling of half an acre or less of land subject to significant restrictions and mitigation measures, including the maintenance of a vegetation buffer.

7. **State Regulation.** Almost half of the states also have enacted statutes to regulate the conversion and use of wetlands. See Linda Malone, Environmental Regulation of Land Use § 4.29[1] (2002). Could state officials also sue to enjoin the development of a wetland on the ground that development would constitute a public nuisance?

B. THE ENDANGERED SPECIES ACT

The Endangered Species Act (ESA), 16 U.S.C. §§ 1531 et seq., is perhaps the most controversial environmental statute in the United States and, like section 404 of the Clean Water Act, it strongly influences many private land use decisions. The members of Congress who passed the ESA in 1973 had no idea of how controversial the law would become. No Senator and only four members of the House of Representatives voted against the ESA. Most legislators thought that the ESA simply protected charismatic birds and megafauna, such as grizzly bears, bald eagles, and alligators, against hunters and poachers. But they were wrong. The ESA today affects not only the actions of all federal agencies, but development decisions throughout the United States.

Protection of endangered species is of immense importance:

> Most scientists agree that the world is experiencing the highest rate of species extinction since dinosaurs died out sixty-five million years ago, although the exact size of the current extinction "crisis" is uncertain. Some scientists estimate that, at the current rate of extinction, only half of the world's existing species will survive to the end of this century. Even conservative estimates peg current species loss to be three or four orders of magnitude greater than the historical average. In the United States alone over the last century some sixty species of mammals and forty species of freshwater fish have died out.

James Salzman & Barton H. Thompson, Jr., Environmental Law and Policy 254 (2003). Some people believe that the nation must protect endangered species because species have an intrinsic right to exist and thrive. To others, the nation must protect species because of their potential genetic and other value to humans. When Congress passed the ESA in 1973, a House report on the legislation concluded that the "value of this genetic heritage is, quite literally, incalculable.... Who knows, or can say, what potential cures for cancer or other scourges, present or future, may lie locked up in the structures of plants which may yet be undiscovered, much less analyzed." H.R. Rep. No. 93–412, 93d Cong., 1st Sess. 4–5 (1973).

1. OVERVIEW

The ESA protects *endangered* and *threatened species*. A species is endangered if it is "in danger of extinction throughout all or a significant portion of its range" (16 U.S.C. § 1532(6)) and threatened if it is "likely to become an endangered species in the foreseeable future" (id. § 1532(20)). Species gain protected status in several ways. First, the federal Fish and Wildlife Service (FWS) (or the National Marine Fisheries Service in the case of marine species) can decide on its own initiative to list a species as endangered or threatened. Second, anyone can petition the FWS to list a species as endangered or threatened. In either case, the FWS must use the "best scientific and commercial data available" in deciding whether the species is endangered or threatened and cannot consider the potential economic consequences of listing the species.

As of May 2006, the federal government had listed over 1800 endangered or threatened species; 1300 of these species live in the United States. Every state contains at least a handful or two of endangered or threatened species, and most contain far more. States with more than 50 endangered or threatened species include Alabama (117), Arizona (57), California (308), Florida (112), Georgia (71), Hawaii (the grand prize winner with 317), North Carolina (63), Oregon (56), Tennessee (91), Texas (94), and Virginia (66).

The ESA tries to protect endangered and threatened species in several ways. First, the FWS must prepare *recovery plans* for listed species. 16 U.S.C. § 1533(f). These plans serve as blueprints for the conservation and recovery of listed species and for funding requests to Congress to support recovery work. The federal government often works with state and local governments in the development and implementation of these plans. Second, the FWS under section 5 of the ESA can acquire needed land and water for a species "by purchase, donation, or otherwise." Id. § 1534.

One of the most important tools of the ESA is section 7(a)(2), which requires all federal agencies to consult with the FWS before taking any action that might affect an endangered or threatened species. 16 U.S.C. § 1536(a)(2). Under section 7(a)(2), federal agencies must ensure that their actions are not "likely" either (1) to "jeopardize the continued existence" of a listed species or (2) to "result in the destruction or adverse modification of [the critical] habitat of such species." The *critical habitat* of a species is the geographic area "essential to the conservation of the species." Id. § 1533(b)(3)(A). The FWS determines the critical habitat of endangered or threatened species, often at the time that it lists the species.

Section 7(a)(2) requires federal agencies to take whatever steps are needed to avoid jeopardizing listed species or adversely modifying their critical habitat—no matter what the cost. In the famous case of TVA v. Hill, 437 U.S. 153 (1978), the Supreme Court ordered construction stopped on a dam in the Tennessee Valley that was almost finished because the dam threatened a little known species of perch, called the snail darter, that is about three inches long. "The plain intent of Congress in enacting [the

ESA] was to halt and reverse the trend towards species extinction, whatever the cost." Id. at 184. "Congress intended endangered species to be afforded the highest priorities," adopting a policy which the House Report on the ESA described as the "institutionalization of ... caution." Id. at 174, quoting H.R. Rep. No. 93–412, at 4–5 (1973).

2. LAND USE REGULATION

For landowners, the most important provision of the ESA is probably section 9, 16 U.S.C. § 1538. Section 9 proscribes a variety of activities, including selling, importing, or exporting endangered species. Of most importance to landowners, section 9(a)(1) makes it unlawful to *take* an endangered species of fish or wildlife, while section 3 in turn defines "take" as "to harass, harm, pursue, hunt, shoot, wound, kill, trap, capture, or collect, or to attempt to engage in any such conduct." Id. §§ 1538(a)(1), 1532(13). In 1975, the Department of the Interior issued regulations that defined "harm" to include any

> act or omission which actually injures or kills wildlife, including acts which annoy it to such an extent as to significantly disrupt essential behavioral patters, which include, but are not limited to, breeding, feeding or sheltering; *significant environmental modification or degradation which has such effects is included within the meaning of "harm."*

40 Fed. Reg. 44412, 44416 (1975) (emphasis added).

Palila v. Hawaii Dept. of Land & Natural Resources, 639 F.2d 495 (9th Cir. 1981), was the first case to illustrate the potential importance of section 9 for landowners. In that case, the Sierra Club and other environmental interests argued that the State of Hawaii was "taking" the palila bird by maintaining a population of feral sheep and goats on state land that also happened to be habitat for the palila; the sheep and goats harmed the mamane trees in which the palila nested. Relying on the Department of the Interior's regulation, the trial court agreed with the Sierra Club, and the Ninth Circuit affirmed. While *Palila* dealt with state lands, any types of land uses, whether on private or public lands, that threatened endangered species were now fair game.

When the Department of the Interior recognized that its definition of "harm" could potentially restrict private use of land throughout the United States, the Department proposed eliminating the reference to "significant environmental modification or degradation." When this proposal generated a heated political backlash, the Department instead adopted the following definition:

> "Harm" in the definition of "take" in the Act means an act which actually kills or injures wildlife. Such act may include significant habitat modification or degradation where it actually kills or injures wildlife by significantly impairing essential behavior patterns, including breeding, feeding or sheltering.

50 C.F.R. § 17.3 (1995).

Under what circumstances would a property owner's modification of the habitat of an endangered species violate this definition? Is the definition consistent with the Endangered Species Act? The latter question reached the Supreme Court in the following case.

Babbitt v. Sweet Home Chapter of Communities for a Great Oregon

United States Supreme Court, 1995.
515 U.S. 687.

JUSTICE STEVENS delivered the opinion of the Court.

The Endangered Species Act of 1973 contains a variety of protections designed to save from extinction species that the Secretary of the Interior designates as endangered or threatened. Section 9 of the Act makes it unlawful for any person to "take" any endangered or threatened species. The Secretary has promulgated a regulation that defines the statute's prohibition on takings to include "significant habitat modification or degradation where it actually kills or injures wildlife." This case presents the question whether the Secretary exceeded his authority under the Act by promulgating that regulation....

Respondents in this action are small landowners, logging companies, and families dependent on the forest products industries in the Pacific Northwest and in the Southeast, and organizations that represent their interests. They brought this declaratory judgment action against petitioners, the Secretary of the Interior and the Director of the Fish and Wildlife Service, in the United States District Court for the District of Columbia to challenge the statutory validity of the Secretary's regulation defining "harm," particularly the inclusion of habitat modification and degradation in the definition. Respondents challenged the regulation on its face. Their complaint alleged that application of the "harm" regulation to the red-cockaded woodpecker, an endangered species, and the northern spotted owl, a threatened species, had injured them economically....

The text of the Act provides three reasons for concluding that the Secretary's interpretation is reasonable. First, an ordinary understanding of the word "harm" supports it. The dictionary definition of the verb form of "harm" is "to cause hurt or damage to: injure." Webster's Third New International Dictionary 1034 (1966). In the context of the ESA, that definition naturally encompasses habitat modification that results in actual injury or death to members of an endangered or threatened species. Respondents argue that the Secretary should have limited the purview of "harm" to direct applications of force against protected species, but the dictionary definition does not include the word "directly" or suggest in any way that only direct or willful action that leads to injury constitutes "harm." Moreover, unless the statutory term "harm" encompasses indirect as well as direct injuries, the word has no meaning that does not duplicate the meaning of other words that § 3 uses to define "take." A reluctance to treat statutory terms as surplusage supports the reasonableness of the Secretary's interpretation.

Second, the broad purpose of the ESA supports the Secretary's decision to extend protection against activities that cause the precise harms Congress enacted the statute to avoid. In TVA v. Hill, 437 U.S. 153 (1978), we described the Act as "the most comprehensive legislation for the preservation of endangered species ever enacted by any nation." Whereas predecessor statutes enacted in 1966 and 1969 had not contained any sweeping prohibition against the taking of endangered species except on federal lands, the 1973 Act applied to all land in the United States and to the Nation's territorial seas. As stated in § 2 of the Act, among its central purposes is "to provide a means whereby the ecosystems upon which endangered species and threatened species depend may be conserved."....

Third, the fact that Congress in 1982 authorized the Secretary to issue permits for takings that § 9(a)(1)(B) would otherwise prohibit, "if such taking is incidental to, and not the purpose of, the carrying out of an otherwise lawful activity," 16 U.S.C. § 1539(a)(1)(B), strongly suggests that Congress understood § 9(a)(1)(B) to prohibit indirect as well as deliberate takings. The permit process requires the applicant to prepare a "conservation plan" that specifies how he intends to "minimize and mitigate" the "impact" of his activity on endangered and threatened species, making clear that Congress had in mind foreseeable rather than merely accidental effects on listed species. No one could seriously request an "incidental" take permit to avert § 9 liability for direct, deliberate action against a member of an endangered or threatened species, but respondents would read "harm" so narrowly that the permit procedure would have little more than that absurd purpose. "When Congress acts to amend a statute, we presume it intends its amendment to have real and substantial effect." Stone v. INS, 514 U.S. 386, 397 (1995). Congress' addition of the § 10 permit provision supports the Secretary's conclusion that activities not intended to harm an endangered species, such as habitat modification, may constitute unlawful takings under the ESA unless the Secretary permits them.

[Respondents argue that Congress intended the government to buy habitat under section 5 of the ESA when necessary to prevent habitat degradation. According to respondents, section 5 would have been unnecessary if the government can regulate habitat modification under section 9.] Respondents' argument that the Government lacks any incentive to purchase land under § 5 when it can simply prohibit takings under § 9 ignores the practical considerations that attend enforcement of the ESA. Purchasing habitat lands may well cost the Government less in many circumstances than pursuing civil or criminal penalties. In addition, the § 5 procedure allows for protection of habitat before the seller's activity has harmed any endangered animal, whereas the Government cannot enforce the § 9 prohibition until an animal has actually been killed or injured. The Secretary may also find the § 5 authority useful for preventing modification of land that is not yet but may in the future become habitat for an endangered or threatened species....

When it enacted the ESA, Congress delegated broad administrative and interpretive power to the Secretary.... The proper interpretation of a term such as "harm" involves a complex policy choice. When Congress has entrusted the Secretary with broad discretion, we are especially reluctant to substitute our views of wise policy for his. In this case, that reluctance accords with our conclusion, based on the text, structure, and legislative history of the ESA, that the Secretary reasonably construed the intent of Congress when he defined "harm" to include "significant habitat modification or degradation that actually kills or injures wildlife." In the elaboration and enforcement of the ESA, the Secretary and all persons who must comply with the law will confront difficult questions of proximity and degree; for, as all recognize, the Act encompasses a vast range of economic and social enterprises and endeavors. These questions must be addressed in the usual course of the law, through case-by-case resolution and adjudication.

JUSTICE O'CONNOR, concurring.

My agreement with the Court is founded on two understandings. First, the challenged regulation is limited to significant habitat modification that causes actual, as opposed to hypothetical or speculative, death or injury to identifiable protected animals. Second, even setting aside difficult questions of scienter, the regulation's application is limited by ordinary principles of proximate causation, which introduce notions of foreseeability.... Because there is no need to strike a regulation on a facial challenge out of concern that it is susceptible of erroneous application, however, and because there are many habitat-related circumstances in which the regulation might validly apply, I join the opinion of the Court.

In my view, the regulation is limited by its terms to actions that actually kill or injure individual animals. Justice Scalia disagrees, arguing that the harm regulation "encompasses injury inflicted, not only upon individual animals, but upon populations of the protected species." At one level, I could not reasonably quarrel with this observation; death to an individual animal always reduces the size of the population in which it lives, and in that sense, "injures" that population. But by its insight, the dissent means something else. Building upon the regulation's use of the word "breeding," Justice Scalia suggests that the regulation facially bars significant habitat modification that actually kills or injures hypothetical animals (or, perhaps more aptly, causes potential additions to the population not to come into being). Because "impairment of breeding does not 'injure' living creatures," Justice Scalia reasons, the regulation must contemplate application to "a population of animals which would otherwise have maintained or increased its numbers."

I disagree. As an initial matter, I do not find it as easy as Justice Scalia does to dismiss the notion that significant impairment of breeding injures living creatures. To raze the last remaining ground on which the piping plover currently breeds, thereby making it impossible for any piping plovers to reproduce, would obviously injure the population (causing the species' extinction in a generation). But by completely preventing breeding, it would also injure the individual living bird, in the same way that sterilizing the creature injures the individual living bird. To "injure" is, among other things, "to impair." Webster's Ninth New Collegiate Dictionary 623 (1983). One need not subscribe to theories of "psychic harm" to recognize that to make it impossible for an animal to reproduce is to impair its most essential physical functions and to render that animal, and its genetic material, biologically obsolete. This, in my view, is actual injury.

In any event, even if impairing an animal's ability to breed were not, in and of itself, an injury to that animal, interference with breeding can cause an animal to suffer other, perhaps more obvious, kinds of injury. The regulation has clear application, for example, to significant habitat modification that kills or physically injures animals which, because they are in a vulnerable breeding state, do not or cannot flee or defend themselves, or to environmental pollutants that cause an animal to suffer physical complications during gestation. Breeding, feeding, and sheltering are what animals do. If significant habitat modification, by interfering with these essential behaviors, actually kills or injures an animal protected by the Act, it causes "harm" within the meaning of the regulation. In contrast to Justice Scalia, I do not read the regulation's "breeding" reference to vitiate or somehow to qualify the clear actual death or injury requirement, or to suggest that the regulation contemplates extension to nonexistent animals. . . .

By the dissent's reckoning, the regulation at issue here imposes liability for any habitat-modifying conduct that ultimately results in the death of a protected animal, "regardless of whether that result is intended or even foreseeable, and no matter how long the chain of causality between modification and injury." Even if § 1540(a)(1) does create a strict liability regime (a question we need not decide at this juncture), I see no indication that Congress, in enacting that section, intended to dispense with ordinary principles of proximate causation. Strict liability means liability without regard to fault; it does not normally mean liability for every consequence, however remote, of one's conduct. I would not lightly assume that Congress, in enacting a strict liability statute that is silent on the causation question, has dispensed with this well-entrenched principle. In the absence of congressional abrogation of traditional principles of causation, then, private parties should be held liable under § 1540(a)(1) only if their habitat-modifying actions proximately cause death or injury to protected animals. The regulation, of course, does not contradict the presumption or notion that ordinary principles of causation apply here. Indeed, by use of the word "actually," the regulation clearly rejects speculative or conjectural effects, and thus itself invokes principles of proximate causation.

Proximate causation is not a concept susceptible of precise definition. It is easy enough, of course, to identify the extremes. The farmer whose fertilizer is lifted by a tornado from tilled fields and deposited miles away in a wildlife refuge cannot, by any stretch of the term, be considered the proximate cause of death or injury to protected species occasioned thereby.

At the same time, the landowner who drains a pond on his property, killing endangered fish in the process, would likely satisfy any formulation of the principle. We have recently said that proximate causation "normally eliminates the bizarre," and have noted its "functionally equivalent" alternative characterizations in terms of foreseeability and duty. Proximate causation depends to a great extent on considerations of the fairness of imposing liability for remote consequences. The task of determining whether proximate causation exists in the limitless fact patterns sure to arise is best left to lower courts. But I note, at the least, that proximate cause principles inject a foreseeability element into the statute, and hence, the regulation, that would appear to alleviate some of the problems noted by the dissent.

In my view, then, the "harm" regulation applies where significant habitat modification, by impairing essential behaviors, proximately (foreseeably) causes actual death or injury to identifiable animals that are protected under the Endangered Species Act. Pursuant to my interpretation, *Palila II*—under which the Court of Appeals held that a state agency committed a "taking" by permitting mouflon sheep to eat mamane-naio seedlings that, when full grown, might have fed and sheltered endangered palila—was wrongly decided according to the regulation's own terms.[a] Destruction of the seedlings did not proximately cause actual death or injury to identifiable birds; it merely prevented the regeneration of forest land not currently sustaining actual birds.

This case, of course, comes to us as a facial challenge. We are charged with deciding whether the regulation on its face exceeds the agency's statutory mandate. I have identified at least one application of the regulation (*Palila II*) that is, in my view, inconsistent with the regulation's own limitations. That misapplication does not, however, call into question the validity of the regulation itself. One can doubtless imagine questionable applications of the regulation that test the limits of the agency's authority. However, it seems to me clear that the regulation does not on its terms exceed the agency's mandate, and that the regulation has innumerable valid habitat-related applications. Congress may, of course, see fit to revisit this issue. And nothing the Court says today prevents the agency itself from narrowing the scope of its regulation at a later date.

With this understanding, I join the Court's opinion.

JUSTICE SCALIA, with whom THE CHIEF JUSTICE and JUSTICE THOMAS join, dissenting.

I think it unmistakably clear that the legislation at issue here (1) forbade the hunting and killing of endangered animals, and (2) provided federal lands and federal funds for the acquisition of private lands, to

a. Eds.—In a followup to the original *Palila* decision, a federal district court held that a finding of "harm" under the ESA did not require that the plaintiffs show that sheep grazing had actually killed any Palila birds or led to a decline in population numbers. "If the habitat modification prevents the population from recovering, then this causes injury to the species and should be actionable under section 9." Palila v. Hawaii Dept. of Land & Natural Resources, 649 F. Supp. 1070, 1077 (D. Haw. 1986). The Ninth Circuit Court of Appeals affirmed. 639 F.2d 495 (9th Cir. 1981) (*Palila II*).

preserve the habitat of endangered animals. The Court's holding that the hunting and killing prohibition incidentally preserves habitat on private lands imposes unfairness to the point of financial ruin—not just upon the rich, but upon the simplest farmer who finds his land conscripted to national zoological use. I respectfully dissent....

The regulation has three features which ... do not comport with the statute. First, it interprets the statute to prohibit habitat modification that is no more than the cause-in-fact of death or injury to wildlife. Any "significant habitat modification" that in fact produces that result by "impairing essential behavioral patterns" is made unlawful, regardless of whether that result is intended or even foreseeable, and no matter how long the chain of causality between modification and injury....

Second, the regulation does not require an "act": The Secretary's officially stated position is that an omission will do. The previous version of the regulation made this explicit. When the regulation was modified in 1981 the phrase "or omission" was taken out, but only because (as the final publication of the rule advised) "the [Fish and Wildlife] Service feels that 'act' is inclusive of either commissions or omissions which would be prohibited by section."....

The third and most important unlawful feature of the regulation is that it encompasses injury inflicted, not only upon individual animals, but upon populations of the protected species. "Injury" in the regulation includes "significantly impairing essential behavioral patterns, including breeding." Impairment of breeding does not "injure" living creatures; it prevents them from propagating, thus "injuring" a population of animals which would otherwise have maintained or increased its numbers. What the face of the regulation shows, the Secretary's official pronouncements confirm. The Final Redefinition of "Harm" accompanying publication of the regulation said that "harm" is not limited to "direct physical injury to an individual member of the wildlife species," and refers to "injury to a population."....

None of these three features of the regulation can be found in the statutory provisions supposed to authorize it. The term "harm" in § 1532(19) has no legal force of its own. An indictment or civil complaint that charged the defendant with "harming" an animal protected under the Act would be dismissed as defective, for the only operative term in the statute is to "take." If "take" were not elsewhere defined in the Act, none could dispute what it means, for the term is as old as the law itself. To "take," when applied to wild animals, means to reduce those animals by killing or capturing, to human control.... And that meaning fits neatly with the rest of § 1538(a)(1), which makes it unlawful not only to take protected species, but also to import or export them; to possess, sell, deliver, carry, transport, or ship any taken species; and to transport, sell, or offer to sell them in interstate or foreign commerce....

In response to the points made in this dissent, the Court's opinion stresses two points, neither of which is supported by the regulation, and so cannot validly be used to uphold it. First, the Court and the concurrence suggest that the regulation should be read to contain a requirement of proximate causation or foreseeability, principally because the statute does—and "nothing in the regulation purports to weaken those requirements [of the statute]." I quite agree that the statute contains such a limitation, because the verbs of purpose in § 1538(a)(1)(B) denote action directed at animals. But the Court has rejected that reading. The critical premise on which it has upheld the regulation is that, despite the weight of the other words in § 1538(a)(1)(B), "the statutory term 'harm' encompasses indirect as well as direct injuries." Consequently, unless there is some strange category of causation that is indirect and yet also proximate, the Court has already rejected its own basis for finding a proximate-cause limitation in the regulation. In fact "proximate" causation simply means "direct" causation....

The second point the Court stresses in its response seems to me a belated mending of its holding. It apparently concedes that the statute requires injury to particular animals rather than merely to populations of animals. The Court then rejects my contention that the regulation ignores this requirement, since, it says, "every term in the regulation's definition of 'harm' is subservient to the phrase 'an act which actually kills or injures wildlife.' ".... [T]his reading is incompatible with the regulation's specification of impairment of "breeding" as one of the modes of "killing or injuring wildlife."....

But since the Court is reading the regulation and the statute incorrectly in other respects, it may as well introduce this novelty as well—law *a la carte*. As I understand the regulation that the Court has created and held consistent with the statute that it has also created, habitat modification can constitute a "taking," but only if it results in the killing or harming of individual animals, and only if that consequence is the direct result of the modification. This means that the destruction of privately owned habitat that is essential, not for the feeding or nesting, but for the breeding, of butterflies, would not violate the Act, since it would not harm or kill any living butterfly. I, too, think it would not violate the Act—not for the utterly unsupported reason that habitat modifications fall outside the regulation if they happen not to kill or injure a living animal, but for the textual reason that only action directed at living animals constitutes a "take."

The Endangered Species Act is a carefully considered piece of legislation that forbids all persons to hunt or harm endangered animals, but places upon the public at large, rather than upon fortuitously accountable individual landowners, the cost of preserving the habitat of endangered species. There is neither textual support for, nor even evidence of congressional consideration of, the radically different disposition contained in the regulation that the Court sustains. For these reasons, I respectfully dissent.

Notes & Questions

1. After *Sweet Home*, what constitutes a "take" of an endangered animal? Does a "take" require actual harm to a species? Would habitat

modification that leads to the death of one member of a species constitute a "take" if that one death does not constitute significant harm to the species? Does the prohibition on the taking of a species apply to actions that result in indirect injury? Do the "Justices' opinions in *Sweet Home* raise as many questions as they answer with regard to the meaning of the harm regulation"? Michael J. Bean & Melanie J. Rowland, The Evolution of National Wildlife Law 219 (3d ed. 1997).

2. Based on *Sweet Home*, how would you rule in the following cases:

a. The owner of a 240–acre parcel of old-growth forest has begun to harvest the trees. Because of the age of the forest and its proximity to the ocean, the forest is suitable nesting habitat for the marbled murrelet, an endangered bird species; scores of recent surveys of the property have detected the presence of the marbled murrelet. Can a court issue an injunction against the harvesting if there is no evidence that the harvesting has yet killed or harmed a marbled murrelet? See Marbled Murrelet v. Environmental Protection Improvement Center, 83 F.3d 1060 (9th Cir. 1996) (a "reasonably certain threat of imminent harm to a protected species is sufficient for issuance of an injunction under section 9 of the ESA"). But see United States v. West Coast Forest Resources Ltd. Partnership, 2000 WL 298707 (D. Or. 2000) (" 'Mere speculation' is not sufficient; there must be 'a definite threat of future harm to [a] protected species' ").

b. John Muir plans to construct a lounge, restaurant, and hotel complex in the vicinity of the endangered Perdido Key Beach mouse. A biologist sues to enjoin the construction, arguing that the complex is likely to lead to an "influx of house mice, feral and house cats and human foot traffic on critical beach mouse habitat." Another biologist testifies that these intrusions will "eventually lead to the extinction of the Perdido Key beach mouse." See Morrill v. Lujan, 802 F. Supp. 424 (S.D. Ala. 1992) (no taking).

3. By potentially limiting the use and development of property on which an endangered species of fish or wildlife is found, does section 9 encourage property owners to extirpate the endangered species from their property before the species is listed or while no one is looking? Does section 9 also encourage property owners to destroy any potentially attractive habitat on their land?

> Section 9 regulates only *existing* habitat of *listed* species. Property owners facing significant economic costs therefore may try to develop habitat before a species is listed or ensure that listed species do not reside on their lands. Because the government has limited monitoring capabilities, many property owners also will try to eliminate endangered species or destroy potential habitat while the government is not looking. Because property owners obviously do not report such behavior, estimating its exact incidence is impossible. But reports of its occurrence are frequent enough, and arise from enough different sectors, that the phenomenon has picked up its own appellation: "shoot, shovel, and shut up," or the "Three–S Syndrome."

Barton H. Thompson, Jr., People or Prairie Chickens: The Uncertain Search for Optimal Biodiversity, 51 Stan. L. Rev. 1127, 1153–1154 (1999). See also Dean Lueck, Preemptive Habitat Destruction under the Endangered Species Act, 46 J.L. & Econ. 27 (2003) (empirical study finding that the ESA encourages property owners to destroy habitat before it attracts endangered species); Michael J. Bean, The Endangered Species Act and Private Land: Four Lessons Learned from the Past Quarter Century, 28 Env. L. Rep. 1071 (1998); Barton H. Thompson, Jr., The Endangered Species Act: A Case Study in Takings and Incentives, 49 Stan. L. Rev. 305 (1997).

How might the federal government eliminate the perverse incentive created by the ESA? Under a *safe harbor program* created in the mid–1990s, the federal government will promise property owners who wish to create or enhance habitat on their land that their actions will not lead to greater restrictions under the ESA. The program, which is meant to encourage property owners to manage their land in a way that is beneficial to endangered species, has been very successful to date. See Bean, supra, at 10707.

4. Section 9 applies only to actions that would take an *endangered* species of fish or wildlife, not to actions that would take a *threatened* species. Section 4(d), however, authorizes the Secretary of the Interior to "issue such regulations as he deems necessary and advisable to provide for the conservation" of threatened species. 16 U.S.C. § 1533(d). The Secretary has used this authority to extend the basic protections of section 9 to most threatened species of fish and wildlife.

5. Section 9 originally did not apply to endangered plants. In the 1980s, however, Congress amended the Act to make it a violation to (1) maliciously damage, destroy, or remove endangered plants from federal land, or (2) "remove, cut, dig up, or damage or destroy" any endangered plant on nonfederal land "in knowing violation of any law or regulation of any state or in the course of any violation of a state criminal trespass law." 16 U.S.C. § 1538(a)(2). Why, do you believe, does section 9 provide narrower protection for endangered plants?

To mitigate section 9's potential restrictions on the use of private property, Congress in 1982 authorized the issuance to property owners of *incidental take permits*. Under section 10(a) of the ESA, the FWS can issue a permit for an otherwise unlawful taking of a species if (1) the taking is merely incidental to an otherwise lawful activity (such as building a subdivision or an apartment house), and (2) the permit applicant has developed an acceptable *habitat conservation plan* (HCP). 16 U.S.C. § 1539(a)(1). An HCP must (1) minimize the impact of the taking "to the maximum extent practicable," (2) ensure that the taking will not "appreciably reduce the likelihood of the survival and recovery of the species in the wild," and (3) be adequately funded. Id. § 1539(a)(2).

Challenges to incidental take permits and habitat conservation plans have been few but growing. Soon after Congress passed the 1982 amendment that added incidental take permits, environmental groups challenged an incidental take permit issued for the development of land on San Bruno Mountain, an area south of San Francisco that is home to the endangered mission blue butterfly. The plaintiffs' principal challenge was to the adequacy of the field studies underlying the government's decision to issue the permit. Although there were conflicting views on the sufficiency of the proposed conservation measures, the Ninth Circuit refused to disturb the government's judgment. Friends of Endangered Species, Inc. v. Jantzen, 760 F.2d 976 (9th Cir. 1985). Courts today continue to defer in most cases to the government's expert judgment in deciding the adequacy of an HCP. There are limits, however, to this deference.

Sierra Club v. Babbitt

United States District Court for the District of Alabama, 1998.
15 F. Supp. 2d 1274.

This action commenced in April of 1997 in the United States District Court of the District of Columbia when the original plaintiff's filed this action seeking declaratory injunctive relief regarding two incidental take permits ("ITP's") issued by the Fish & Wildlife Service ("FWS") for the construction of two separate high density housing complexes in habitat of the endangered Alabama Beach Mouse ("ABM"), alleging that the FWS violated numerous provisions of the Endangered Species Act ("ESA")....

Because this case involves a challenge to the final administrative action of the FWS in issuing the two ITPs in question, the appropriate standard of review is whether actions of the FWS were "arbitrary, capricious, an abuse of discretion, or otherwise not in accordance with the law."....

.... [It] is unlawful to "take" an endangered species without first obtaining, from the FWS, an ITP pursuant to ESA § 10(a)(1)(B). The ITP must include, among other things, "a conservation plan," and the steps the applicant will take to minimize and mitigate the impact to the species or its habitat. The director of the FWS considers certain criteria and "shall issue" the permit if he finds that: "(i) the taking will be incidental; (ii) the applicant will, to the maximum extent practicable, minimize and mitigate the impact of such taking; (iii) the applicant will insure that adequate funding for the conservation plan ... will be provided; (iv) the taking will not appreciably reduce the likelihood of the survival ... of the species...." It is criteria (ii) around which this dispute largely focuses: whether "to the maximum extent practicable" the developers' HCPs adequately minimize and mitigate the impacts likely to result from the proposed takings. Once an application for an ITP is submitted, the FWS must conduct a biological assessment (BA) in accordance with ESA which must include a discussion of the effects of the action on the ABM and the FWS's opinion of whether the action is likely to jeopardize the continued existence of the ABM or result in the destruction or adverse modification of critical habitat. FWS has developed a handbook which guides them through the statutory and regulatory maze involved in the permit process and requires early coordination between the regional office and the applicable field office.

The ABM was listed as endangered in 1985, and at that time the FWS concluded that the species' habitat was being drastically destroyed "by residential and commercial development, recreational activity, and tropical storms." The FWS determined that on the portion of the Alabama coast known as the Fort Morgan Peninsula, there was in 1985 a total baseline habitat of approximately 671 acres of which approximately 402 are known as fore dunes, 269 scrub dunes. Between 1985, when the ABM was listed, and January 1996, when the FWS issued an ITP for construction of the first of the two developments at issue in this case—the 52 acre Aronov project—another 8.5% of dwindling ABM habitat was lost due to additional commercial development and damage from Hurricane Opal. Indeed, during that time, the FWS issued four other ITPs allowing further habitat loss in the area, including two permits for the construction of single family residences and two permits for the construction of an additional 110 multi-family residential development—the 64-lot "Laguna Key" development, and the 60-unit "Kiva Dunes" residential community and golf course. According to the FWS, the four ITPS issued prior to Aronov resulted in the destruction of a total of 41.3 acres of ABM habitat. The remaining ABM habitat has also been reduced by a series of hurricanes, and in January 1996 the FWS concluded that the "designated critical habitat may be an inadequate area for ABM recovery and delisting." In the final biological opinion, the FWS noted that the net direct effect of the Fort Morgan project will be the permanent destruction of 37 acres of currently occupied ABM habitat, of which 25 are scrub dunes habitat and an undetermined number of ABM will be incidentally taken during destruction. The FWS also determined that as to the Aronov Project the net direct effect will be the permanent destruction of 7.5 acres currently occupied by ABM, 6.5 of which is scrub dune habitat, and an undetermined number of ABM incidentally taken during construction. During the internal coordinating process among the FWS and its regional field office in Jackson, Mississippi, the field office received a draft of the BO for the Fort Morgan project and concurred that the ITP "will not jeopardize the ABM or adversely modify its critical habitat . . . ," but goes further and states its "primary concern" is over the "level of mitigation provided," or "whether the mitigation has been to the maximum extent practicable." The field office also received a draft of the BO for the Aronov project and concurred that the ITP should be issued.

The primary bone of contention in this lawsuit evolves around the proposals in the HCPs incorporated into the Aronov Realty Management, Inc. ITP at paragraph H(5) that there be $60,000 collected from the developer for offsite mitigation "to acquire property of quantity and quality sufficient to compensate for and minimize unavoidable impacts of the project area," and incorporated in the Fort Morgan ITP at paragraph G(5) that there be $150,000 collected from the developer for offsite mitigation. The plaintiffs first contend that the level of off site mitigation funding is inadequate, and cannot be supported by any rational basis in the Administrative Record. In addition, the plaintiffs challenge the inconsistent application of the FWS's off site mitigation policies. Finally, the Plaintiffs contend that the FWS's reliance on speculative unnamed sources to contribute additional funds in order to make up for the inadequacy of the amounts of off site mitigation funding the FWS required the developers to pay is arbitrary and capricious, and otherwise not in accordance with the law.

First, the plaintiffs maintain that the level of mitigation funding for both projects is inadequate, and that the agency's determination of these amounts is arbitrary and capricious. The lack of any analysis in the Administrative Record concerning whether the amount or level of offsite mitigation funding is to the maximum extent practicable supports the plaintiff's contention. Moreover, the Jackson field office supervisor voiced much concern over the inadequacy of the level of funding for offsite mitigation required by the HCP for the Fort Morgan project: "Overall, our primary concern is the amount or level of mitigation provided." The field office based these concerns on consideration of the biological effects of the project and a comparison of such effects to the level of mitigation provided by other ITPs with high density real estate development. Based on these considerations the field office stated that, "we believe the amount of mitigation provided is low.".... As the Court finds that there is no sufficient basis in the Administrative Record to support the amount of offsite mitigation funding, the issuance of the ITPs was arbitrary and capricious.

In addition, the plaintiffs contend that the inconsistency in the amounts of offsite mitigation funding that the FWS has required for various high density developments on the Alabama coast indicates that the FWS has failed to develop an appropriate standard for determining what levels of mitigation will mitigate the effects of these two projects to the maximum extent practicable. The FWS's Habitat Conservation Planning Handbook is intended to guide the agency through complex determinations such as the establishment of mitigation measures for HCPs. The Handbook states that "mitigation measures required by individual FWS or NMFS offices should be as consistent as possible for the same species," and that consistency is "essential." The Handbook goes on further and states that consistency is to be accomplished by (1) establishing good communication between offices, and (2) establishing "specific standards." Moreover, "the Service should not apply inconsistent mitigation policies for the same species, unless differences are based on biological or other good reasons and are clearly explained." The Court can find no evidence that the FWS paid any attention to its own guidelines. The Court searched the Administrative Record thoroughly in search of any evidence that the FWS applied its own internal guidelines, but finds that first of all the FWS never explained or provided any analysis of whether the amount of offsite mitigation required is "to the maximum extent practicable." In addition, despite the explicit directive in the FWS Handbook not to apply inconsistent mitigation policies and to provide good reasons for or to explain clearly any inconsistent applications, the agency never provided "good reasons" for or "clearly explained" why the FWS applied inconsistent mitigation policies for the ABM in the same geographic area. Moreover, the FWS's complete disregard of the experts, who cautioned the agency that the level of mitigation was not to the maximum extent practicable, only serves to amplify the arbitrariness of the FWS's decision that such levels of offsite mitigation were in compliance with the law. Although neither Congress nor the FWS Handbook requires the FWS to develop one specific formula for determining the level of mitigation required for all projects, the Administrative Record must contain some analysis of why the level or amount selected is appropriate for the particular project at issue, and the FWS should not apply inconsistent mitigation policies for the same species in the same geographic area, unless differences are based on biological or other good reasons and are clearly explained. The Court finds on the basis of the record for these two projects that the agency's inconsistent application of offsite mitigation measures for the same species in the same geographic area is arbitrary and capricious, as the record is devoid of any "biological or other good reasons to justify such findings."

Finally, the FWS's speculative reliance on other unnamed sources to contribute funds to make up for the inadequacy of the amounts of offsite mitigation funding required is simply contrary to the law and unsupported by any factually reliable basis in the Administrative Record. In the Biological Opinions the FWS states that the Applicant's offsite mitigation funding would have to be combined with additional funds from a non-profit organization in order to purchase a large tract or several tracts for mitigation purposes. The BO does not establish how much those funds would be, who they would come from, or whether it is likely they could be acquired. Nevertheless, the FWS issued the two ITPs at issue by relying on funding from an unknown source for an unknown amount, and accepts that this will "minimize and mitigate" the effects of the projects to the maximum extent practicable. Because the Administrative Record does not establish what level of funding has been offered by "other sources," the FWS cannot demonstrate any basis in the Administrative Record upon which the level or amount of offsite mitigation measures are "to the maximum extent practicable." Moreover, the law establishes that the FWS cannot comply with the strict ESA mandate that the HCP "minimize and mitigate" the effects of the projects to the "maximum extent practicable" simply by relying on speculative future actions by others.

Based upon all of the above considerations, the Court finds that the Administrative Record is devoid of any rational basis upon which the FWS could have reasonably relied in deciding to issue the ITPs for these two projects. Therefore, because the Court finds that the permits at issue fall short of both the ESA and APA standards, they must be remanded to the agency for review and re-issuance....

Notes & Questions

1. Do the relatively weak provisions of the HCPs in *Sierra Club v. Babbitt* surprise you? The FWS often faces significant political pressure to

approve HCPs for new developments in growing regions. Many environmentalists believe that, as a result, HCPs often provide inadequate protection for listed species. See, e.g., Patrick Parenteau, Rearranging the Deck Chairs: Endangered Species Act Reforms in an Era of Mass Extinction, 22 Wm. & Mary Envtl. L. & Pol'y Rev. 227 (1998).

2. As of May 2006, the FWS had approved almost 450 HCPs and issued over 700 incidental take permits, covering an area of over thirty million acres and over 200 listed species. The FWS has issued most of the permits to individual property owners wishing to develop or otherwise use their land in a manner that might be construed to be a violation of section 9. For more on HCPs, see Timothy Beatley, Habitat Conservation Planning: Endangered Species and Urban Growth (1994); Barton H. Thompson, Jr., Managing the Working Landscape, in The Endangered Species Act at Thirty (Dale D. Goble et al eds., 2006); Albert C. Lin, Participants' Experiences with Habitat Conservation Plans and Suggestions for Streamlining the Process, 23 Ecology L.Q. 369 (1996).

3. **Regional HCPs.** A number of communities have developed *regional HCPs* that permit property owners in a region to develop their land subject to regional protections of imperiled species found in the area. Regional HCPs relieve individual landowners of the burden of developing individual HCPs, and they enable more comprehensive and coherent planning for species protection. Federal, state, and local governmental officials, property owners, and environmental representatives generally meet over a lengthy period of time to hammer out the terms of regional HCPs.

4. **No Surprises Policy.** Property owners and developers generally want security. Although they are willing to dedicate land and pay fees to develop their lands, they want to be sure that the government will not come back midway through a development and insist on greater protections for listed species. To help provide property owners with that security, the FWS has adopted a *no surprises policy* in which the government promises landowners who receive incidental take permits that the government will pay for any new habitat or actions that might be needed to meet unforeseen circumstances that later arise. 63 Fed. Reg. 8859 (Feb. 23, 1998).

C. THE REACH OF FEDERAL REGULATION

Does the federal government have any business intruding into local land use decisions? Why should the federal government care if a developer in Kansas destroys an isolated wetland? Why should it care whether an endangered species found only in Texas goes extinct? Aren't these local questions? More importantly, does the federal government have the constitutional authority to regulate private land uses when only isolated wetlands or local species are involved?

The following case deals with Congress' authority to regulate local land use decisions in Riverside County, California under the ESA to protect the endangered Delhi Sands flower-loving fly, which is found in no other state.

The federal government threatened to hold up a new hospital that the county was building in the middle of the fly's habitat, leading the county and other groups to challenge the constitutionality of the ESA in court. At the time the litigation was brought, the fly also threatened a number of other proposed land developments, including

- A $2.8 million square foot Wal–Mart distribution facility.
- A 27 hole golf course and accompanying 202 home development, which a city official defended because the sighting of a couple of Flies there over a two-year period is "just not enough science to put people's land at risk."
- A truck stop and industrial center to be built by Kaiser Ventures, which estimates that the project could create 5,300 jobs and $75 million per year for the local economy.
- A cement plant and a facility that produces sidewalk pavers that was blocked by a federal court when the FWS claimed that the plant would wipe out a major portion of the Fly's habitat, but which the FWS approved in 1999 when the company agreed to set aside 30.5 acres of land for Fly habitat.
- A large project that would include new homes, theaters, and restaurants.

John Copeland Nagle & J.B. Ruhl, The Law of Biodiversity and Ecosystem Management 8 (2002).

National Association of Home Builders v. Babbitt

United States Court of Appeals for the District of Columbia Circuit, 1997.
130 F.3d 1041.

WALD, Circuit Judge.

[The plaintiffs seek] a declaration that the application of section 9 of the ESA to the Delhi Sands Flower–Loving Fly ("the Fly"), which is located only in California, exceeds Congress' Commerce Clause power.... This dispute arose when the Fish and Wildlife Service ("FWS") placed the Fly, an insect that is native to the San Bernardino area of California, on the endangered species list. The listing of the Fly, the habitat of which is located entirely within an eight mile radius in southwestern San Bernardino County and northwestern Riverside County, California, forced San Bernardino County to alter plans to construct a new hospital on a recently purchased site that the FWS had determined contained Fly habitat....

The Delhi Sands Flower–Loving Fly ... is the only remaining subspecies of its species. The other subspecies, the El Segundo Flower–Loving Fly, is believed to be extinct due to destruction of its habitat through urban development. The Fly is also one of only a few North American species in the "mydas flies" family and one of only a few species in that family that visit flowers in search of nectar, thereby pollinating native plant species.

Over 97 percent of the historic habitat of the Fly has been eliminated, and, prior to its listing as endangered, its remaining habitat was threatened by urban development, unauthorized trash dumping, and off-road vehicle use. There are currently 11 known populations of the Fly, all of which occur within an eight mile radius of one another. The size of the entire population of Flies was recently estimated in the low hundreds.

Appellants' Commerce Clause challenge to the application of section 9(a)(1) of the ESA to the Fly rests on the Supreme Court's decision in United States v. Lopez, 514 U.S. 549 (1995). In *Lopez,* the Court held that the Gun–Free School Zones Act of 1990, 18 U.S.C. § 922(q), which made possession of a gun within a school zone a federal offense, exceeded Congress' Commerce Clause authority. Drawing on its earlier Commerce Clause jurisprudence, the *Lopez* Court explained that Congress could regulate three broad categories of activity: (1) "the use of the channels of interstate commerce," (2) "the instrumentalities of interstate commerce, or persons or things in interstate commerce, even though the threat may come only from intrastate activities," and (3) "those activities having a substantial relation to interstate commerce ... i.e., those activities that substantially affect interstate commerce." *Lopez,* 514 U.S. at 558–59 (citations omitted)....

It is clear that, in this instance, section 9(a)(1) of the ESA is not a regulation of the instrumentalities of interstate commerce or of persons or things in interstate commerce. As a result, only the first and the third categories of activity discussed in *Lopez* will be examined....

A. *Channels of Interstate Commerce*

Application of section 9(a)(1) of the ESA to the Fly can be viewed as a proper exercise of Congress' Commerce Clause power over the first category of activity that the *Lopez* Court identified: the use of the "channels of interstate commerce." *Lopez,* 514 U.S. at 558. Although this category is commonly used to uphold regulations of interstate transport of persons or goods, it need not be so limited. Indeed, the power of Congress to regulate the channels of interstate commerce provides a justification for section 9(a)(1) of the ESA for two reasons. First, the prohibition against takings of an endangered species is necessary to enable the government to control the transport of the endangered species in interstate commerce. Second, the prohibition on takings of endangered animals falls under Congress' authority " 'to keep the channels of interstate commerce free from immoral and injurious uses.' " Id. (quoting Heart of Atlanta Motel Inc. v. United States, 379 U.S. 241, 256 (1964)).

.... [In this case, Congress used this latter authority] to prevent the eradication of an endangered species by a hospital that is presumably being constructed using materials and people from outside the state and which will attract employees, patients, and students from both inside and outside the state. Thus, like regulations preventing racial discrimination or labor exploitation, regulations preventing the taking of endangered species prohibit interstate actors from using the channels of interstate commerce to "promote or spread evil, whether of a physical, moral or economic nature." North American Co. v. S.E.C., 327 U.S. 686, 705 (1946)....

B. *Substantially Affects Interstate Commerce*

The takings clause in the ESA can also be viewed as a regulation of the third category of activity that Congress may regulate under its commerce power. According to *Lopez,* the test of whether section 9(a)(1) of the ESA is within this category of activity "requires an analysis of whether the regulated activity 'substantially affects' interstate commerce." 514 U.S. at 559. A class of activities can substantially affect interstate commerce regardless of whether the activity at issue—in this case the taking of endangered species—is commercial or noncommercial....

The Committee Reports on the ESA reveal that one of the primary reasons that Congress sought to protect endangered species from "takings" was the importance of the continuing availability of a wide variety of species to interstate commerce. As the House Report explained:

> .... As we homogenize the habitats in which these plants and animals evolved, and as we increase the pressure for products that they are in a position to supply (usually unwillingly) we threaten their—and our own—genetic heritage. The value of this genetic heritage is, quite literally, incalculable....
>
> From the most narrow possible point of view, it is in the best interests of mankind to minimize the losses of genetic variations. The reason is simple: they are potential resources. They are keys to puzzles which we cannot solve, and may provide answers to questions which we have not yet learned to ask....
>
> Who knows, or can say, what potential cures for cancer or other scourges, present or future, may lie locked up in the structures of plants which may yet be undiscovered, much less analyzed? More to the point, who is prepared to risk being [sic] those potential cures by eliminating those plants for all time? Sheer self interest impels us to be cautious.

H.R. Rep. No. 93–412, at 4–5 (1973)....

Approximately 521 of the 1082 species in the United States currently designated as threatened or endangered are found in only one state. The elimination of all or even some of these endangered species would have a staggering effect on biodiversity—defined as the presence of a large number of species of animals and plants—in the United States and, thereby, on the current and future interstate commerce that relies on the availability of a diverse array of species.

The variety of plants and animals in this country are, in a sense, a natural resource that commercial actors can use to produce marketable products. In the most narrow view of economic value, endangered plants and animals are valuable as sources of medicine and genes. Fifty percent of the most frequently prescribed medicines are derived from wild plant and animal species. Such medicines were estimated in 1983 to be worth over

$15 billion a year. In addition, the genetic material of wild species of plants and animals is inbred into domestic crops and animals to improve their commercial value and productivity....

Each time a species becomes extinct, the pool of wild species diminishes. This, in turn, has a substantial effect on interstate commerce by diminishing a natural resource that could otherwise be used for present and future commercial purposes.... Because our current knowledge of each species and its possible uses is limited, it is impossible to calculate the exact impact that the loss of the option value of a single species might have on interstate commerce. In the aggregate, however, we can be certain that the extinction of species and the attendant decline in biodiversity will have a real and predictable effect on interstate commerce....

The taking of the Fly and other endangered animals can also be regulated by Congress as an activity that substantially affects interstate commerce because it is the product of destructive interstate competition. It is a principle deeply rooted in Commerce Clause jurisprudence that Congress is empowered to act to prevent destructive interstate competition. As the Supreme Court explained in Hodel v. Virginia Surface Mining & Reclamation Ass'n, 452 U.S. 264 (1981) ("*Hodel v. Virginia*"), a case that the *Lopez* Court cited repeatedly, "prevention of ... destructive interstate competition is a traditional role for congressional action under the Commerce Clause." 452 U.S. at 282.

.... In *Hodel v. Virginia,* the Supreme Court considered a challenge to the constitutionality of the Surface Mining Control and Reclamation Act of 1977. The Surface Mining Act required mine operators to restore the land after mining to its prior condition, including its approximate original contour, topsoil, hydrologic balance, and vegetation in order to "protect society and the environment from the adverse effects of surface coal mining operations." 452 U.S. 264 at 268.... The Court held that the Act was a valid exercise of Congress' power under the Commerce Clause....

The parallels between *Hodel v. Virginia* and the case at hand are obvious. The ESA and the Surface Mining Act both regulate activities—destruction of endangered species and destruction of the natural landscape—that are carried out entirely within a State and which are not themselves commercial in character. The activities, however, may be regulated because they have destructive effects, on environmental quality in one case and on the availability of a variety of species in the other, that are likely to affect more than one State. In each case, moreover, interstate competition provides incentives to states to adopt lower standards to gain an advantage vis-a-vis other states: In *Hodel v. Virginia,* the states were motivated to adopt lower environmental standards to improve the competitiveness of their coal production facilities, and in this case, the states are motivated to adopt lower standards of endangered species protection in order to attract development....

KAREN LECRAFT HENDERSON, Circuit Judge, concurring.

I agree with Judge Wald's conclusion that the "taking" prohibition in section 9(a)(1) of the Endangered Species Act (ESA) constitutes a valid exercise of the Congress's authority to regulate interstate commerce under the Commerce Clause. I cannot, however, agree entirely with either of her grounds for reaching the result and instead arrive by a different route.

Judge Wald first asserts that section 9(a)(1) is a proper regulation of the "channels of commerce." . . . The Delhi Sands Flower-loving Flies the Department of the Interior seeks to protect are (along with many other species no doubt) entirely *intra*state creatures. They do not move among states either on their own or through human agency. As a result, like the Gun–Free School Zones Act in *Lopez,* the statutory protection of the flies "is not a regulation of the use of the channels of interstate commerce." 514 U.S. 549 at 559.

Judge Wald also justifies the protection of endangered species on the ground that the loss of biodiversity "substantially affects" interstate commerce because of the resulting loss of potential medical or economic benefit. Yet her opinion acknowledges that it is "impossible to calculate the exact impact" of the economic loss of an endangered species. As far as I can tell, it is equally impossible to ascertain that there will be any such impact at all. It may well be that no species endangered now or in the future will have any of the economic value proposed. Given that possibility, I do not see how we can say that the protection of an endangered species has any effect on interstate commerce (much less a substantial one) by virtue of an uncertain potential medical or economic value. Nevertheless, I believe that the loss of biodiversity itself has a substantial effect on our ecosystem and likewise on interstate commerce. In addition, I would uphold section 9(a)(1) as applied here because the Department's protection of the flies regulates and substantially affects commercial development activity which is plainly interstate.

First, I agree with Judge Wald that biodiversity is important to our understanding of ESA and its relation to interstate commerce. As Judge Wald's opinion notes:

> Every species is part of an ecosystem, an expert specialist of its kind, tested relentlessly as it spreads its influence through the food web. To remove it is to entrain changes in other species, raising the populations of some, reducing or even extinguishing others, risking a downward spiral of a larger assemblage.

The effect of a species' continued existence on the health of other species within the ecosystem seems to be generally recognized among scientists. Some studies show, for example, that the mere presence of diverse species within an ecosystem (biodiversity) by itself contributes to the ecosystem's fecundity. The Congress recognized the interconnection of the various species and the ecosystems when it declared that the "essential purpose" of ESA, which protects endangered species, is in fact "to protect the ecosystem upon which we and other species depend." H.R. Rep. No. 93–412, at 10 (1973). Given the interconnectedness of species and ecosystems, it is reasonable to conclude that the extinction of one species affects others and their ecosystems and that the protection of a purely intrastate species (like the Delhi Sands Flower-loving Fly) will therefore substantially affect land and objects that are involved in interstate commerce. There is, therefore, "a rational basis" for concluding that the "taking" of endangered species "substantially affects" interstate commerce so that section 9(a)(1) is within the Congress's Commerce Clause authority. *See Lopez,* 514 U.S. 549.

.... In enacting ESA, the Congress expressed an intent to protect not only endangered species but also the habitats that they, and we, occupy. At the same time, the Congress expressly found that "economic growth and development untempered by adequate concern and conservation" was the cause for "various species of fish, wildlife, and plants in the United States having been rendered extinct." 16 U.S.C. § 1531(a)(1). It is plain, then, that at the time it passed ESA the Congress contemplated protecting endangered species through regulation of land and its development, which is precisely what the Department has attempted to do here. Such regulation, apart from the characteristics or range of the specific endangered species involved, has a plain and substantial effect on interstate commerce....

SENTELLE, Circuit Judge, dissenting.

This case concerns the efforts of San Bernardino County, California ("the County"), to construct a hospital and supporting infrastructure for its citizens and other humans. Unfortunately, those efforts discomfit an insect—the Delhi Sands Flower–Loving Fly. According to the parties in this case, there are fewer than 300 breeding individuals of this species, all located within forty square miles in southern California. These flies live as larvae for nearly two years under Delhi Sands, a particular type of grit, apparently found only in those forty square miles of southern California, after which they emerge to feed and breed for two weeks before dying.

.... Can Congress under the Interstate Commerce Clause regulate the killing of flies, which is not commerce, in southern California, which is not interstate? Because I think the answer is "no," I can not join my colleagues' decision to affirm the district court's conclusion that it can.

The proposition that the federal government can, under the Interstate Commerce Clause, regulate an activity which is neither interstate nor commerce, reminds me of the old chestnut: If we had some ham, we could fix some ham and eggs, if we had some eggs. With neither ham nor eggs, the chances of fixing a recognizable meal requiring both amount to nil. Similarly, the chances of validly regulating something which is neither commerce nor interstate under the heading of the interstate commerce power must likewise be an empty recitation. I recognize that for some decades of jurisprudential development, the Commerce Clause has been used as the justification for the regulation of a plethora of activities not apparently within its text. So wide-ranging has been the application of the Clause as to prompt one writer to "wonder why anyone would make the mistake of calling it the Commerce Clause instead of the 'hey-you-can-do-whatever-you-feel-like clause.' " Judge Alex Kozinski, Introduction to Volume 19, 19 Harv. J.L. Pub. Pol. 1, 5 (1995). However, in 1995, the Supreme Court brought an end to the galactic growth of the Clause's application and reminded Congress that the words of that Clause, like the rest of the Constitution, have content, in *Lopez.* While I would have found the present application of the ESA to be outside the enumerated powers of Congress under the Commerce Clause even in the world before *Lopez,* after that controlling decision, I think there can be no doubt. . . .

Though Judge Henderson rejects Judge Wald's "biodiversity" rationale, she relies on a related justification of her own, which is to me indistinguishable in any meaningful way from that of Judge Wald. As I understand her rationale, it depends on "the interconnectedness of species and ecosystems," which she deems sufficient for us "to conclude that the extinction of one species affects others and their ecosystems and that the protection of a purely intrastate species [concededly including the Delhi Sands Flower–Loving Fly] will therefore substantially affect land and objects that are involved in interstate commerce." I see this as no less of a stretch than Judge Wald's rationale. First, the Commerce Clause empowers Congress "to regulate commerce" not "ecosystems." The Framers of the Constitution extended that power to Congress, concededly without knowing the word "ecosystems," but certainly knowing as much about the dependence of humans on other species and each of them on the land as any ecologist today. An ecosystem is an ecosystem, and commerce is commerce.

Granted, years of jurisprudence have extended that regulatory authority to encompass "activities having a substantial effect on interstate commerce," the third category of *Lopez* legitimacy, but Judge Henderson's rationale fails the analysis of this third category as completely as does Judge Wald's. . . . There is no showing, but only the rankest of speculation, that a reduction or even complete destruction of the viability of the Delhi Sands Flower–Loving Fly will in fact "affect land and objects that are involved in interstate commerce," let alone do so substantially. Nothing in the statute certainly necessitates such a nexus, nor has my colleague supplied a reason why this basis of regulation would apply to the preservation of a species any more than any other act potentially affecting the continued and stable existence of any other item of a purely intrastate nature upon which one might rest a speculation that its loss or change could somehow affect some other object, land, or otherwise, that might be involved in interstate commerce. . . .

In the end, attempts to regulate the killing of a fly under the Commerce Clause fail because there is certainly no interstate commerce in the Delhi Sands Flower–Loving Fly. . . .

Notes & Questions

1. Under the reasoning of Judges Wald and Henderson, is there anything stopping the federal government from adopting a system of national land use regulation? Should the federal government nationalize land use planning? In the 1970s, the federal government briefly considered

enacting a system of national land use controls, but the idea lost steam when President Richard Nixon withdrew his support. See Richard J. Lazarus, The Making of Environmental Law 78 (2004). Short of nationalizing all land use planning, should the federal government take over specific aspects of land use—e.g., coastal protection—where there is arguably a strong national interest? What types of land use programs might fall into this category?

2. *National Home Builders* deals with Congress' Commerce Clause authority. Could the ESA be justified under one of Congress' other constitutional powers? The United States has signed a number of treaties dealing with biodiversity protection, including the Convention on Biological Diversity and the Migratory Bird Treaty. Does Congress' treaty power provide adequate support for the ESA? See Gavin R. Villareal, One Leg to Stand On: The Treaty Power and Congressional Authority for the Endangered Species Act After *United States v. Lopez*, 75 Texas L. Rev. 1125 (1998).

3. The question of the ESA's constitutionality generated Chief Justice John Roberts' famous "hapless toad" quotation. While still on the D.C. Circuit Court of Appeals, Chief Justice Roberts dissented from the denial of a petition for the rehearing en banc of a case challenging the constitutionality of the ESA. According to Chief Justice Roberts,

> The panel's approach in this case leads to the result that regulating the taking of a hapless toad that, for reasons of its own, lives its entire life in California constitutes regulating "Commerce ... among the several States." To be fair, the panel faithfully applied National Association of Home Builders v. Babbitt.... [En banc] review would ... afford the opportunity to consider alternative grounds for sustaining application of the Act that may be more consistent with Supreme Court precedent.

Rancho Viejo, LLC v. Norton, 334 F.3d 1158, 1160 (D.C. Cir. 2003).

4. The Supreme Court has yet to rule on the constitutionality of local land use restrictions imposed under either section 404 of the Clean Water Act or the ESA.

CHAPTER 13

REGULATORY TAKINGS

Chapter 2 introduced you to the takings protections of the United States Constitution, which requires the government to pay compensation when it takes private property for a public use. See pp. 178–213. The government must pay compensation when it takes title to someone's property or occupies it for a public use like an army barracks. But what if the government regulates property in a way that reduces the economic value of the land? Is that ever a "taking" for which the government must pay compensation. If regulations can constitute "takings," does any regulation that reduces the value of a piece of property mandate compensation? If not, what differentiates regulations that require compensation from those that do not?

Complicating these questions is the fact that regulatory taking claims arise most frequently in connection with legal transitions. As you have seen throughout this book, property law has changed dramatically over the last two centuries and continues to change. While the law used to encourage people to fill in "swamps," for example, the law today recognizes the ecological value of these same "wetlands" and restricts their destruction. While the law once permitted landowners to develop their property with few restrictions, landowners today may not be able to develop their property as they wish because of endangered species, historic buildings, local growth concerns, and dozens of other environmental and aesthetic factors. Changes of this nature can undermine the expectations of property owners who acquired their land thinking that they could develop it. If the changes are sufficiently dramatic, the property owners may claim that the change has "taken" their property in violation of the Constitution. Most of the cases in this Chapter address the question of the circumstances in which new legislation or government regulation that diminishes the rights of some land owners constitutes a "taking" for which just compensation must be paid. See generally Holly Doremus, Takings and Transitions, 19 J. Land Use & Envtl. L. 1 (2003).

A. ANTECEDENTS AND FOUNDATIONS

Prior to the Civil War, the takings provision of the United States Constitution applied only to actions of the federal government.[1] Because the federal government seldom regulated land use, the Supreme Court had

1. As noted in Chapter 2, the key provision was the Fifth Amendment: "nor shall private property be taken for public use without just compensation."

little occasion to consider the question of whether and when regulations could constitute takings. In the late 19th century, however, the United States Supreme Court concluded that the due process clause of the Fourteenth Amendment incorporates the takings provision and thus requires the states also to pay just compensation when they take private property. This extension of the takings provision to the states set the stage for federal takings challenges to state land use regulations.

Mugler v. Kansas

Supreme Court of the United States, 1887.
123 U.S. 623.

MR. JUSTICE HARLAN delivered the opinion of the Court.

[Mugler and his fellow defendants owned and operated a brewery in Saline County, Kansas. In 1881, the Kansas legislature passed a statute that provided that] all places where intoxicating liquors are manufactured, sold, bartered, or given away . . . [are] common nuisances [and] that upon the judgment of any court having jurisdiction finding such place to be a nuisance, the proper officer shall be directed to shut up and abate the same. [When Mugler and the other defendants continued to operate their brewery in defiance of the statute, the state sued to have the brewery declared a nuisance and shut down.]

The buildings and machinery constituting these breweries are of little value if not used for the purpose of manufacturing beer; that is to say, if the statutes are enforced against the defendants the value of their property will be very materially diminished. . . .

[The defendants contend that] as their respective breweries were erected when it was lawful to engage in the manufacture of beer for every purpose; as such establishments will become of no value as property, or, at least, will be materially diminished in value, if not employed in the manufacture of beer for every purpose; the prohibition upon their being so employed is, in effect, a taking of property for public use without compensation, and depriving the citizen of his property without due process of law. In other words, although the State, in the exercise of her police powers, may lawfully prohibit the manufacture and sale, within her limits, of intoxicating liquors to be used as a beverage, legislation having that object in view cannot be enforced against those who, at the time, happen to own property, the chief value of which consists in its fitness for such manufacturing purposes, unless compensation is first made for the diminution in the value of their property, resulting from such prohibitory enactments.

This interpretation of the Fourteenth Amendment is inadmissible. It cannot be supposed that the States intended, by adopting that Amendment, to impose restraints upon the exercise of their powers for the protection of the safety, health, or morals of the community. . . .

The principle, that no person shall be deprived of life, liberty, or property, without due process of law, was embodied, in substance, in the constitutions of nearly all, if not all, of the States at the time of the adoption of the Fourteenth Amendment; and it has never been regarded as incompatible with the principle, equally vital, because essential to the peace and safety of society, that all property in this country is held under the implied obligation that the owner's use of it shall not be injurious to the community. . . .

It is supposed by the defendants that the doctrine for which they contend is sustained by Pumpelly v. Green Bay Co., 13 Wall. 166. . . . That was an action for the recovery of damages for the overflowing of the plaintiff's land by water, resulting from the construction of a dam across a river. The defence was that the dam constituted a part of the system adopted by the State for improving the navigation of Fox and Wisconsin rivers; and it was contended that as the damages of which the plaintiff complained were only the result of the improvement, under legislative sanction, of a navigable stream, he was not entitled to compensation from the State or its agents. . . . This court said it would be a very curious and unsatisfactory result, were it held that, "if the government refrains from the absolute conversion of real property to the uses of the public, it can destroy its value entirely, can inflict irreparable and permanent injury to any extent, can, in effect, subject it to total destruction, without making any compensation, because, in the narrowest sense of that word, it is not taken for the public use. . . ." Pp. 177–178.

These principles have no application to the case under consideration. The question in Pumpelly v. Green Bay Company arose under the State's power of eminent domain; while the question now before us arises under what are, strictly, the police powers of the State, exerted for the protection of the health, morals, and safety of the people. . . . [*Pumpelly*] was a case in which there was a "permanent flooding of private property," a "physical invasion of the real estate of the private owner, and a practical ouster of his possession." His property was, in effect, required to be devoted to the use of the public, and, consequently, he was entitled to compensation.

As already stated, the present case must be governed by principles that do not involve the power of eminent domain, in the exercise of which property may not be taken for public use without compensation. A prohibition simply upon the use of property for purposes that are declared, by valid legislation, to be injurious to the health, morals, or safety of the community, cannot, in any just sense, be deemed a taking or an appropriation of property for the public benefit. Such legislation does not disturb the owner in the control or use of his property for lawful purposes, nor restrict his right to dispose of it, but is only a declaration by the State that its use by any one, for certain forbidden purposes, is prejudicial to the public interests. . . . The power which the States have of prohibiting such use by individuals of their property as will be prejudicial to the health, the morals, or the safety of the public, is not—and, consistently with the existence and safety of organized society, cannot be—burdened with the condition that the State must compensate such individual owners for pecuniary losses they may sustain, by reason of their not being permitted, by a noxious use of their property, to inflict injury upon the community. The exercise of the police power by the destruction of property which is itself a public nuisance, or the prohibition of its use in a particular way, whereby its value becomes depreciated, is very different from taking property for public use, or from depriving a person of his property without due process of law. In the one case, a nuisance only is abated; in the other, unoffending property is taken away from an innocent owner.

It is true, that, when the defendants in these cases purchased or erected their breweries, the laws of the State did not forbid the manufacture of intoxicating liquors. But the State did not thereby give any assurance, or come under an obligation, that its legislation upon that subject would remain unchanged....

[The dissenting opinion of MR. JUSTICE FIELD is omitted. In his view, the Kansas legislation "crossed the line which separates regulation from confiscation."]

Notes & Questions

1. **Physical Invasions.** What is the basis for Justice Harlan's conclusion that the Kansas law did not take Mugler's property? Does *Mugler* stand for the proposition that only a physical invasion of someone's property that results in the actual ouster of the landowner from possession of at least some of his land can constitute a taking? Is this a reasonable line to draw?

Parts of Justice Harlan's opinion, particularly his effort to distinguish *Pumpelly*, certainly suggest that mere governmental regulation of land use can never amount to a taking. A number of other late 19th century Supreme Court cases involving physical actions by the government that reduced the value of private land also suggested that the takings protections embody a physical invasion principle. If the government physically appropriated or occupied someone's land, it had to pay compensation, but governmental actions—no matter how burdensome on landowners—did not require compensation if they did not physically deprive the owner of some or all of his land. Thus, the flooding of the plaintiff's land was a taking in *Pumpelly* because it "invaded" his land "by superinduced additions of water, earth, sand or other materials." 80 U.S. (13 Wall.) at 181. On the other hand, the Supreme Court held that there was no taking where a municipal construction project interfered with plaintiff's access to his land because there was "no entry ... upon the plaintiff's lot. All that was done was to render for a time its use more inconvenient." Northern Transportation Co. v. City of Chicago, 99 U.S. 635, 642 (1879).[2] See also William Michael Treanor, The Original Understanding of the Takings Clause and the Political Process, 95 Colum. L. Rev. 782 (1995) (arguing that the early understanding of the takings protection was that it applied only to interfer-

2. As discussed in Chapter 2 (pp. 203–213), it is still the rule today that the government does not need to compensate property owners for the indirect effects of their actions.

ences with physical ownership); James W. Ely, Jr., "That Due Satisfaction May Be Made": The Fifth Amendment and the Origins of the Compensation Principle, 36 Am. J. Legal Hist. 1 (1992).

Commentators have criticized the physical invasion test for its "anachronistic reliance on precommercial conceptions of property, ones which stressed title and dominion while tending to ignore the less tangible prerogatives of ownership such as use and enjoyment." The physical invasion test "treats two parties, both of whom may have lost the same amount of value, differently merely because the government 'touched' the land of the one but not the other. By compensating only the former property holder, the test ignores the fact that both intrusions leave their victim in the same aggrieved position." Developments in the Law—Zoning, 91 Harv. L. Rev. 1427, 1468–69 (1978).

2. For purposes of the takings protections, under what circumstances does a governmental action physically appropriate someone's property and oust them from possession? Consider the following two hypotheticals.

a. **Protection of Instream Water Flows.** Assume that Mary Austin owns a farm in California and holds an appropriative water right (see p. 249) that she uses to irrigate her crops. In order to protect endangered fish in the river from which Mary appropriates her water, the federal government tells Mary that she must reduce her diversions from the river by 50 percent. Has the government physically taken that water from Mary, or has the government merely regulated her use of the water? Should she receive compensation for the water? In Tulare Lake Basin Water Storage Dist. v. United States, 49 Fed. Cl. 313 (2001), the Court of Federal Claims held that such a regulation is a "physical taking" of the water. "In the context of water rights, a mere restriction on use—the hallmark of a regulatory action—completely eviscerates the right itself since the plaintiffs' sole entitlement is to the use of the water.... Thus, by limiting plaintiffs' ability to use an amount of water to which they would otherwise be entitled, the government has essentially substituted itself as the beneficiary of the [water rights] ... and totally displaced the [water user]." Do you agree? For criticisms of the *Tulare* decision, see Brian E. Gray, The Property Right in Water, 9 Hastings W.-N.W. J. Envtl. L. & Pol'y 1 (2002).

b. **Predatory and Marauding Species.** Assume that Jim Bridger owns a sheep ranch in Montana. In recent years, he has lost almost 100 sheep to grizzly bears. He would like to shoot any grizzly bear that comes near his sheep, but grizzly bears are endangered, and the federal Endangered Species Act prohibits him from harming, harassing, or killing them. Has the federal government physically taken his sheep by preventing him from protecting them? Would this be a taking under *Mugler*? In Christy v. Hodel, 857 F.2d 1324, the federal Court of Appeals rejected exactly such a takings claim; according to the court, the bears, not the government, took the rancher's property. When the Supreme Court declined to hear the case, Justice White dissented: "[I]f the government decided ... to enact a law barring grocery store owners from 'harassing, harming, or pursuing' people who wish to take food off the grocery shelves without paying for it, such a law might well be suspect under the Fifth Amendment." Christy v. Lujan, 490 U.S. 1114, 1116 (White, J., dissenting). Who has the better part of this argument?

3. **Airplanes.** The physical invasion test also has played a role in government liability for airplane noise. In United States v. Causby, 328 U.S. 256 (1946), the Supreme Court held that Causby, a chicken farmer whose land lay directly beneath the flight path used by military aircraft from a neighboring airport, was entitled to recover against the government for the diminution in value of his residence and poultry business. The Court stressed that, for compensation to be paid, flights must be "so low and so frequent as to be a direct and immediate interference with the enjoyment and use of the land." Courts have split, however, on whether compensation must be paid where a plane does not fly directly over the property owner's land. Federal courts hold that no compensation is owed where there is no physical invasion of the property owner's air space. See, e.g., Batten v. United States, 306 F.2d 580 (10th Cir. 1962). Some states, however, have disagreed. As the Washington State Supreme Court has asked, why should compensation depend on "anything as irrelevant as whether the wing tip of the aircraft passes through some fraction of an inch of the airspace directly above the plaintiff's land"? Martin v. Port of Seattle, 391 P.2d 540, 545 (Wash. 1964). For interesting insights into these constitutional issues, see Abraham Bell & Gideon Parchomovsky, Takings Reassessed, 87 Va. L. Rev. 277 (2001). For a superb study of the aircraft noise problem, see William F. Baxter & Lillian R. Altree, Legal Aspects of Airport Noise, 15 J.L. & Econ. 1 (1972).

4. **A Nuisance Exception?** Alternatively, did Justice Harlan conclude that the Kansas statute was not a taking because it merely outlawed a nuisance? See Hadacheck v. Sebastian, 239 U.S. 394 (1915) (suggesting that laws designed to abate nuisances are not takings unless arbitrary). As you'll recall from Chapter 2, the law has long outlawed private and public nuisances, and judicial exercise of the nuisance doctrine to limit land uses has never been regarded as a taking. Is the brewing of beer, however, a traditional common law nuisance? Should it matter in *Mugler* that it was the legislature rather than the judiciary that determined that breweries are a nuisance? In his dissenting opinion in *Mugler*, Justice Fields suggested that the distinction between judicial decision and legislative fiat is important. By the challenged statute, the Kansas legislature

> without notice to the owner or hearing of any kind, declares every ... brewery ... to be a common nuisance; and then prescribes what shall follow, upon a court having jurisdiction finding one of such places to be what the legislature has already pronounced it. The court is not to determine whether the place is a common nuisance in fact, but is to find it to be so if it comes within the definition of the statute, and, having thus found it, the executive officers of the court are to be directed to shut up and abate the place.... No discretion is left in the judge or in the officer.

123 U.S. at 677. Why, however, should it matter whether the legislature, versus a court, decides that something is a nuisance and should be prohibited? Unless the legislature's determination is arbitrary, shouldn't courts uphold the legislation without requiring compensation?

For recent thoughts on whether the courts should employ a nuisance approach to determining whether or not governmental regulations are takings, see Eric R. Claeys, Takings and Private Property on the Rehnquist Court, 99 Nw. U.L. Rev. 187 (2004) (advocating a nuisance approach); Stewart E. Sterk, The Inevitable Failure of Nuisance–Based Theories of the Takings Clause: A Reply to Professor Claeys, 99 Nw. U.L. Rev. 231 (2004).

5. **Harms versus Benefits.** Another potential interpretation of *Mugler*, similar to the nuisance test, is that governmental regulations are not takings if they merely prohibit land uses that are harmful. Under this test for a taking, a governmental regulation that proscribes a harmful activity does not require compensation, but a regulation designed to achieve a benefit to society does require compensation.

The major problem with the harm-benefit distinction, as the Supreme Court has recognized in a number of its modern decisions, is that it is arbitrary. Whether a regulation prohibits a harm or provides a benefit depends on what you believe is an acceptable land use. Assume, for example, that the government passes a new law barring any construction on wetlands. If a court believes that a landowner should not have the right to destroy a wetland, the new law prohibits a harm and is not a taking. See, e.g., Just v. Marinette Cty., 201 N.W.2d 761 (Wis. 1972) (concluding that a state law protecting wetlands was not a taking because it merely prevented a harm). If the court believes that property owners should ordinarily have the right to develop any lands they own, however, the new law provides a benefit to society by protecting wetlands that otherwise could have been converted. See generally Glynn S. Lunney, Jr., Responsibility, Causation, and the Harm–Benefit Line in Takings Jurisprudence, 6 Fordham Envtl. L.J. 433 (1995).

Pennsylvania Coal Co. v. Mahon

Supreme Court of the United States, 1922.
260 U.S. 393.

MR. JUSTICE HOLMES delivered the opinion of the Court.

This is a bill in equity brought by the defendants in error to prevent the Pennsylvania Coal Company from mining under their property in such way as to remove the supports and cause a subsidence of the surface and of their house. The bill sets out a deed executed by the Coal Company in 1878, under which the plaintiffs claim. The deed conveys the surface but in express terms reserves the right to remove all the coal under the same and the grantee takes the premises with the risk and waives all claim for damages that may arise from mining out the coal. But the plaintiffs say that whatever may have been the Coal Company's rights, they were taken away by an Act of Pennsylvania, approved May 27, 1921, commonly known there as the Kohler Act....

The statute forbids the mining of anthracite coal in such way as to cause the subsidence of, among other things, any structure used as a human habitation, with certain exceptions, including among them land where the surface is owned by the owner of the underlying coal and is distant more than one hundred and fifty feet from any improved property belonging to any other person. As applied to this case the statute is admitted to destroy previously existing rights of property and contract. The question is whether the police power can be stretched so far.

Government hardly could go on if to some extent values incident to property could not be diminished without paying for every such change in the general law. As long recognized some values are enjoyed under an implied limitation and must yield to the police power. But obviously the implied limitation must have its limits or the contract and due process clauses are gone. One fact for consideration in determining such limits is the extent of the diminution. When it reaches a certain magnitude, in most if not in all cases there must be an exercise of eminent domain and compensation to sustain the act. So the question depends upon the particular facts. The greatest weight is given to the judgment of the legislature but it always is open to interested parties to contend that the legislature has gone beyond its constitutional power.

This is the case of a single private house. No doubt there is a public interest even in this, as there is in every purchase and sale and in all that happens within the commonwealth. Some existing rights may be modified even in such a case. But usually in ordinary private affairs the public interest does not warrant much of this kind of interference. A source of damage to such a house is not a public nuisance even if similar damage is inflicted on others in different places. The damage is not common or public. The extent of the public interest is shown by the statute to be limited, since the statute ordinarily does not apply to land when the surface is owned by the owner of the coal. Furthermore, it is not justified as a protection of personal safety. That could be provided for by notice. Indeed the very foundation of this bill is that the defendant gave timely notice of its intent to mine under the house. On the other hand the extent of the taking is great. It purports to abolish what is recognized in Pennsylvania as an estate in land—a very valuable estate—and what is declared by the Court below to be a contract hitherto binding the plaintiffs. If we were called upon to deal with the plaintiffs' position alone we should think it clear that the statute does not disclose a public interest sufficient to warrant so extensive a destruction of the defendant's constitutionally protected rights.

But the case has been treated as one in which the general validity of the act should be discussed. The Attorney General of the State, the City of Scranton and the representatives of other extensive interests were allowed to take part in the argument below and have submitted their contentions here. It seems, therefore, to be our duty to go farther in the statement of our opinion, in order that it may be known at once, and that further suits should not be brought in vain.

It is our opinion that the act cannot be sustained as an exercise of the police power, so far as it affects the mining of coal under streets or cities in places where the right to mine such coal has been reserved. As said in a Pennsylvania case, "For practical purposes, the right to coal consists in the right to mine it." Commonwealth v. Clearview Coal Co., 256 Pa. 328, 331, 100 Atl. 820. What makes the right to mine coal valuable is that it can be exercised with profit. To make it commercially impracticable to mine certain coal has very nearly the same effect for constitutional purposes as appropriating or destroying it. This we think that we are warranted in assuming that the statute does.

It is true that in Plymouth Coal Co. v. Pennsylvania, 232 U.S. 531, it was held competent for the legislature to require a pillar of coal to be left along the line of adjoining property, that with the pillar on the other side of the line would be a barrier sufficient for the safety of the employees of either mine in case the other should be abandoned and allowed to fill with water. But that was a requirement for the safety of employees invited into the mine, and secured an average reciprocity of advantage that has been recognized as a justification of various laws.

The rights of the public in a street purchased or laid out by eminent domain are those that it has paid for. If in any case its representatives have been so short sighted as to acquire only surface rights without the right of support we see no more authority for supplying the latter without compensation than there was for taking the right of way in the first place and refusing to pay for it because the public wanted it very much. The protection of private property in the Fifth Amendment presupposes that it is wanted for public use, but provides that it shall not be taken for such use without compensation. A similar assumption is made in the decisions upon the Fourteenth Amendment. When this seemingly absolute protection is found to be qualified by the police power, the natural tendency of human nature is to extend the qualification more and more until at last private property disappears. But that cannot be accomplished in this way under the Constitution of the United States.

The general rule at least is that while property may be regulated to a certain extent, if regulation goes too far it will be recognized as a taking. It may be doubted how far exceptional cases, like the blowing up of a house to stop a conflagration, go—and if they go beyond the general rule, whether they do not stand as much upon tradition as upon principle. In general it is not plain that a man's misfortunes or necessities will justify his shifting the damages to his neighbor's shoulders. We are in danger of forgetting that a strong public desire to improve the public condition is not enough to warrant achieving the desire by a shorter cut than the constitutional way of paying for the change. As we already have said this is a question of degree—and therefore cannot be disposed of by general propositions....

We assume, of course, that the statute was passed upon the conviction that an exigency existed that would warrant it, and we assume that an exigency exists that would warrant the exercise of eminent domain. But the question at bottom is upon whom the loss of the changes desired should fall. So far as private persons or communities have seen fit to take the risk of acquiring only surface rights, we cannot see that the fact that their risk has become a danger warrants the giving to them greater rights than they bought.

Decree reversed.

MR. JUSTICE BRANDEIS, dissenting.

The Kohler Act prohibits, under certain conditions, the mining of anthracite coal within the limits of a city in such a manner or to such an extent "as to cause the ... subsidence of ... any dwelling or other structure used as a human habitation, or any factory, store, or other industrial or mercantile establishment in which human labor is employed." Coal in place is land, and the right of the owner to use his land is not absolute. He may not so use it as to create a public nuisance, and uses, once harmless, may, owing to changed conditions, seriously threaten the public welfare. Whenever they do, the Legislature has power to prohibit such uses without paying compensation; and the power to prohibit extends alike to the manner, the character and the purpose of the use. Are we justified in declaring that the Legislature of Pennsylvania has, in restricting the right to mine anthracite, exercised this power so arbitrarily as to violate the Fourteenth Amendment?

Every restriction upon the use of property imposed in the exercise of the police power deprives the owner of some right theretofore enjoyed, and is, in that sense, an abridgment by the state of rights in property without making compensation. But restriction imposed to protect the public health, safety or morals from dangers threatened is not a taking. The restriction here in question is merely the prohibition of a noxious use. The property so restricted remains in the possession of its owner. The state does not appropriate it or make any use of it. The state merely prevents the owner from making a use which interferes with paramount rights of the public. Whenever the use prohibited ceases to be noxious—as it may because of further change in local or social conditions—the restriction will have to be removed and the owner will again be free to enjoy his property as heretofore.

.... If by mining anthracite coal the owner would necessarily unloose poisonous gases, I suppose no one would doubt the power of the state to prevent the mining, without buying his coal fields. And why may not the state, likewise, without paying compensation, prohibit one from digging so deep or excavating so near the surface, as to expose the community to like dangers? In the latter case, as in the former, carrying on the business would be a public nuisance.

It is said that one fact for consideration in determining whether the limits of the police power have been exceeded is the extent of the resulting diminution in value, and that here the restriction destroys existing rights of property and contract. But values are relative. If we are to consider the value of the coal kept in place by the restriction, we should compare it with the value of all other parts of the land. That is, with the value not of the coal alone, but with the value of the whole property. The rights of an owner as against the public are not increased by dividing the interests in his property into surface and subsoil. The sum of the rights in the parts can not be greater than the rights in the whole. The estate of an owner in land is grandiloquently described as extending *ab orco usque ad coelum*. But I suppose no one would contend that by selling his interest above 100 feet from the surface he could prevent the state from limiting, by the police power, the height of structures in a city. And why should a sale of underground rights bar the state's power? For aught that appears the value of the coal kept in place by the restriction may be negligible as compared with the value of the whole property, or even as compared with that part of it which is represented by the coal remaining in place and which may be extracted despite the statute....

This case involves only mining which causes subsidence of a dwelling house. But the Kohler Act contains provisions in addition to that quoted above; and as to these, also, an opinion is expressed. These provisions deal with mining under cities to such an extent as to cause subsidence of—

(a) Any public building or any structure customarily used by the public as a place of resort, assemblage, or amusement, including, but not limited to, churches, schools, hospitals, theaters, hotels, and railroad stations.

(b) Any street, road, bridge, or other public passageway, dedicated to public use or habitually used by the public.

(c) Any track, roadbed, right of way, pipe, conduit, wire, or other facility, used in the service of the public by any municipal corporation or public service company as defined by the Public Service Law.

A prohibition of mining which causes subsidence of such structures and facilities is obviously enacted for a public purpose; and it seems, likewise, clear that mere notice of intention to mine would not in this connection secure the public safety. Yet it is said that these provisions of the act cannot be sustained as an exercise of the police power where the right to mine such coal has been reserved. The conclusion seems to rest upon the assumption that in order to justify such exercise of the police power there must be "an average reciprocity of advantage" as between the owner of the property restricted and the rest of the community; and that here such reciprocity is absent. Reciprocity of advantage is an important consideration, and may even be an essential, where the state's power is exercised for the purpose of conferring benefits upon the property of a neighborhood, as in drainage projects, or upon adjoining owners, as by party wall provisions. But where the police power is exercised, not to confer benefits upon property owners but to protect the public from detriment and danger, there is in my opinion, no room for considering reciprocity of advantage. There was no reciprocal advantage to the owner prohibited from using his oil tanks in 248 U.S. 498; his brickyard, in 239 U.S. 394; his livery stable, in 237 U.S. 171; his billiard hall, in 225 U.S. 623; his oleomargarine factory, in 127 U.S. 678; his brewery, in 123 U.S. 623; unless it be the advantage of living and doing business in a civilized community. That reciprocal advantage is given by the act to the coal operators.

Notes & Questions

1. Was the Kohler Act in *Pennsylvania Coal* needed to protect the owners of surface land? Why shouldn't the government leave the relative rights of surface and subsurface rights up to the property owners? When Mahon purchased his property, the Pennsylvania Coal Company expressly reserved the right to remove all the coal from underneath it. If Mahon did not acquire the right to maintain a certain amount of the subsurface in place for subjacent support, why should the state later intervene? If Mahon has changed his mind, couldn't he simply re-purchase sufficient subsurface rights from Pennsylvania Coal to protect his property?

In response to calls for regulation, Pennsylvania Coal and other coal companies had volunteered to repair any subsidence damage to homes valued at less than $5000 and to public roads. In the case of homes worth more than $5000, the coal companies had offered to sell to the homeowners "such pillar of coal as they may reasonably desire to purchase for the support" of their homes "for a fair consideration" (which, in practice, was less than the value of the lost coal). William A. Fischel, Regulatory Takings 30 (1995). The coal companies continued to offer to repair subsidence damages even after they won in the Supreme Court. Id. at 40.

2. Does *Pennsylvania Coal* implicitly overrule *Mugler*? Although Justice Holmes never mentions *Mugler*, it seems hard to reconcile the two opinions.

3. Assume that Mary Austin owns the right to remove an asbestos-like mineral from land in Ohio. Scientists discover that the mineral is highly carcinogenic when freed from the rock in which it is found. If the United States bans the mining and sale of the mineral, is the law a taking under *Pennsylvania Coal*? Should it be a taking?

4. **Diminution in Value.** How does Justice Holmes suggest that a court should determine whether a governmental regulation is an unconstitutional taking of private property? Justice Holmes' opinion in *Pennsylvania Coal* is often read as suggesting that regulations are takings when they lead to too large of a diminution in the value of property. As Justice Holmes noted, the Kohler Act, by making it "commercially impracticable to mine certain coal," had "very nearly the same effect for constitutional purposes as appropriating or destroying it." This diminution-in-value test has obvious roots in the physical invasion test, but substitutes the more sophisticated notion of economic detriment for the rudimentary concept of physical deprivation. As a result, it replaces a bright line (has there been a physical appropriation?) with a far more sensitive and flexible inquiry (has value been diminished too far?).

Although the diminution-in-value test has obvious advantages over the various tests suggested by the *Mugler* opinion (physical invasion, nuisance, and harm-benefit), it has substantial problems of its own. To say that the test is sensitive and flexible is also to say that it is uncertain. In 1978, for example, the editors of the Harvard Law Review observed that laws "which variously diminished property values from $1,500,000 to $275,000, $450,000 to $50,000, and $65,000 to $5000 have all been upheld. Ordinances which reduced property values from about $48,750 to about $11,250 and from $350,000 to $100,000 have been struck down." Developments in the Law—Zoning, 91 Harv. L. Rev. 1427, 1480 (1978). Justice Holmes' opinion in *Pennsylvania Coal* also leaves open whether the takings question should be determined by the amount of value lost, as in the examples just given, or by the amount of value remaining—whether, that is, the claimant can still earn a reasonable return on her investment after the regulation.

As Justice Brandeis suggests in his dissenting opinion in *Pennsylvania Coal*, the diminution-in-value test also raises questions about how to apply it when a regulation dramatically reduces the value of some rights in a parcel of land but not all of the rights. The Kohler Act would probably not have significantly reduced the value of a lot where the surface and subsurface rights were owned by the same person. The Pennsylvania Coal Company, by contrast, had purchased only subsurface rights and thus suffered a substantial percentage loss. Should the two cases be treated differently? As you will see, all of these various issues have come back to haunt the Supreme Court in later takings cases.

5. **Public Use Redux.** Could the Pennsylvania Coal Company have argued that the Kohler Act was unconstitutional even if the government had paid compensation to the coal companies? Did the Kohler Act take the subsurface rights of one group of private citizens (the coal companies) and give them to another (the surface owners)? Is that a taking for a private rather than public use? Review in this regard the discussion in Chapter 2 of the "public use" requirement. See pp. 179–198.

6. **Average Reciprocity of Advantage.** Justices Holmes and Brandeis both mention "average reciprocity of advantage." What do they mean by this term? How, if at all, is it relevant to the question of whether a regulation is a taking?

7. ***Keystone Bituminous Coal.*** Sixty five years after *Pennsylvania Coal*, the United States Supreme Court narrowly upheld a similar Pennsylvania statute designed to avoid subsidence from coal mining. Keystone Bituminous Coal Ass'n v. DeBenedictis, 480 U.S. 470 (1987). The 1966 Bituminous Mine Subsidence and Land Conservation Act required mining companies to keep up to half of their coal in place and to repair subsidence damage. In the view of Chief Justice Rehnquist and three other justices, this act was "strikingly similar" to the Kohler Act and equally unconstitutional. Justice Stevens, however, writing for the majority of the Court, distinguished *Pennsylvania Coal* on two grounds. First, while the purpose of the Kohler Act was primarily to protect the private economic interest of surface owners, the purpose of the 1966 act, according to Justice Stevens, was to protect the public interest in health, environmental quality, and fiscal integrity. Second, the mining companies in *Keystone* had failed to

show that the 1966 act had the required economic impact on their property. In *Pennsylvania Coal*, Justice Holmes had found that the Kohler Act made it "commercially impracticable" to mine coal. In *Keystone*, by contrast, the mining companies had failed to show that the legislation denied them all economically viable use of their property. Justice Stevens rejected the mining companies' argument that the Court should look only at the economic impact on the companies' subsurface estate, since this is only "part of the entire bundle of rights possessed by the owner of either the coal or the surface." For challenges to Justice Stevens' reading of *Pennsylvania Coal*, see Douglas W. Kmiec, The Original Understanding of the Takings Clause Is Neither Weak Nor Obtuse, 88 Colum. L. Rev. 1630 (1988); Richard Epstein, Takings: Descent and Resurrection, 1987 Sup. Ct. Rev. 1.

8. As the first Supreme Court case holding that a regulation was a taking, *Pennsylvania Coal* has not surprisingly generated a great deal of scholarly comment. Among just some of the interesting commentaries, see William Michael Treanor, Jam for Justice Holmes: Reassessing the Significance of *Mahon*, 86 Geo. L.J. 813 (1998); Lawrence M. Friedman, A Search for Seizure: *Pennsylvania Coal Co. v. Mahon* in Context, 4 Law & Hist. Rev. 1 (1986); Carol M. Rose, *Mahon* Reconstructed: Why the Takings Issue Is Still a Muddle, 57 S. Cal. L. Rev. 561 (1984).

B. THE *PENN CENTRAL* BALANCING TEST

Penn Central Transportation Co. v. New York City

Supreme Court of the United States, 1978.
438 U.S. 104.

MR. JUSTICE BRENNAN delivered the opinion of the Court.

The question presented is whether a city may, as part of a comprehensive program to preserve historic landmarks and historic districts, place restrictions on the development of individual historic landmarks—in addition to those imposed by applicable zoning ordinances—without effecting a "taking" requiring the payment of "just compensation." Specifically, we must decide whether the application of New York City's Landmarks Preservation Law to the parcel of land occupied by Grand Central Terminal has "taken" its owners' property in violation of the Fifth and Fourteenth Amendments.

I

[New York City passed its Landmarks Preservation Law in 1965. The purposes of the law include protecting New York's "standing . . . as a world-wide tourist center and world capital of business, culture and government," fostering "civic pride in the beauty and noble accomplishments of the past," and strengthening the city's economy.

[An 11–member Landmarks Preservation Commission determines which buildings and areas to designate as "historic landmarks" and "historic districts." If a building is designated an historic landmark, the owner must keep the building's exterior in "good repair." The owner also has to obtain the Commission's approval to make any alteration in the building's exterior architectural features or to make any exterior improvement. Owners who wish to make alterations or improvements have three options. First, the owner can apply for a "certificate of no effect on protected architectural features" if the alteration or improvement would not change any architectural feature of the landmark. Second, the owner can apply for a "certificate of appropriateness" if the alteration or improvement "would not unduly hinder the protection, enhancement, perpetuation, and use of the landmark." Finally, the owner can seek a certificate of appropriateness on the ground of insufficient financial return.

[If the restrictions of the Landmarks Preservation Law prevent the owner of an historic landmark from developing his property to the full extent permitted by applicable zoning laws, the city provides the owner with"Transferable Development Rights" (TDRs). The owner can use the TDRs to develop other properties that he owns beyond what applicable zoning restrictions would allow, or he can sell them to other landowners who wish to do so. Initially, the Landmarks Preservation Law permitted owners to use TDRs only on contiguous parcels in the same city block. Later amendments of the law, however, expanded the parcels on which the TDRs can be used to noncontiguous properties.

[In 1967, the Commission designated Grand Central Terminal an historic landmark. The Terminal, which is owned by the Penn Central Transportation Co. and its affiliates (Penn Central), is "one of New York City's most famous buildings. Opened in 1913, it is regarded not only as providing an ingenious engineering solution to the problems presented by urban railroad stations, but also as a magnificent example of the French beaux-arts style." In 1968, Penn Central applied to the Commission for approval to construct an office building on top of the Terminal. Penn Central presented two separate plans. "Breuer I" provided for the construction of a 55–story office building, to be cantilevered above the existing facade and to rest on the roof of the Terminal. "Breuer II" called for tearing down part of the Terminal, stripping off some of Terminal's facade, and constructing a 53–story office building. Although both plans complied with applicable zoning restrictions, the Commission denied approval. The Commission found neither proposal close to acceptable. In its decision, for example, the Commission wrote, "to balance a 55–story office tower above a flamboyant Beaux–Arts facade seems nothing more than an aesthetic joke. Quite simply, the tower would overwhelm the Terminal by its sheer mass."

[Penn Central sued in state court for injunctive and declaratory relief, arguing that the Landmark Preservation Law took its property without just compensation.]

Figure 13–1
1968 Design by Marcel Breuer
(Breuer I)

II

The issues presented by appellants are (1) whether the restrictions imposed by New York City's law upon appellants' exploitation of the Terminal site effect a "taking" of appellants' property for a public use within the meaning of the Fifth Amendment, which of course is made applicable to the States through the Fourteenth Amendment, and, (2), if so, whether the transferable development rights afforded appellants constitute "just compensation" within the meaning of the Fifth Amendment. We need only address the question whether a "taking" has occurred.

A

Before considering appellants' specific contentions, it will be useful to review the factors that have shaped the jurisprudence of the Fifth Amendment injunction "nor shall private property be taken for public use, without just compensation." The question of what constitutes a "taking" for purposes of the Fifth Amendment has proved to be a problem of considerable difficulty. While this Court has recognized that the "Fifth Amendment's guarantee . . . [is] designed to bar Government from forcing some people alone to bear public burdens which, in all fairness and justice, should be borne by the public as a whole," Armstrong v. United States, 364 U.S. 40, 49 (1960), this Court, quite simply, has been unable to develop any "set formula" for determining when "justice and fairness" require that economic injuries caused by public action be compensated by the government, rather than remain disproportionately concentrated on a few persons. Indeed, we have frequently observed that whether a particular restriction will be rendered invalid by the government's failure to pay for any losses proximately caused by it depends largely "upon the particular circumstances [in that] case." United States v. Central Eureka Mining Co., 357 U.S. 155, 168 (1958).

In engaging in these essentially ad hoc, factual inquiries, the Court's decisions have identified several factors that have particular significance. The economic impact of the regulation on the claimant and, particularly, the extent to which the regulation has interfered with distinct investment-backed expectations are, of course, relevant considerations. So, too, is the character of the governmental action. A "taking" may more readily be found when the interference with property can be characterized as a physical invasion by government, than when interference arises from some public program adjusting the benefits and burdens of economic life to promote the common good.

"Government hardly could go on if to some extent values incident to property could not be diminished without paying for every such change in the general law," Pennsylvania Coal Co. v. Mahon, 260 U.S. 393, 413 (1922), and this Court has accordingly recognized, in a wide variety of contexts, that government may execute laws or programs that adversely affect recognized economic values. Exercises of the taxing power are one obvious example. A second are the decisions in which this Court has dismissed "taking" challenges on the ground that, while the challenged government action caused economic harm, it did not interfere with interests that were sufficiently bound up with the reasonable expectations of the claimant to constitute "property" for Fifth Amendment purposes. See, e.g., United States v. Willow River Power Co., 324 U.S. 499 (1945) (interest in high-water level of river for runoff for tailwaters to maintain power head is not property); United States v. Chandler–Dunbar Water Power Co., 229 U.S. 53 (1913) (no property interest can exist in navigable waters).

More importantly for the present case, in instances in which a state tribunal reasonably concluded that "the health, safety, morals, or general welfare" would be promoted by prohibiting particular contemplated uses of land, this Court has upheld land-use regulations that destroyed or adversely affected recognized real property interests. Zoning laws are, of course, the classic example which have been viewed as permissible governmental action even when prohibiting the most beneficial use of the property....

B

In contending that the New York City law has "taken" their property in violation of the Fifth and Fourteenth Amendments, appellants make a series of arguments, which, while tailored to the facts of this case, essentially urge that any substantial restriction imposed pursuant to a landmark law must be accompanied by just compensation if it is to be constitutional....

They first observe that the airspace above the Terminal is a valuable property interest, citing United States v. Causby, 328 U.S. 256 (1946). They urge that the Landmarks Law has deprived them of any gainful use of their "air rights" above the Terminal and that, irrespective of the value of the remainder of their parcel, the city has "taken" their right to this superadjacent airspace, thus entitling them to "just compensation" measured by the fair market value of these air rights.

Apart from our own disagreement with appellants' characterization of the effect of the New York City law, the submission that appellants may establish a "taking" simply by showing that they have been denied the ability to exploit a property interest that they heretofore had believed was available for development is quite simply untenable.... "Taking" jurisprudence does not divide a single parcel into discrete segments and attempt to determine whether rights in a particular segment have been entirely abrogated. In deciding whether a particular governmental action has effected a taking, this Court focuses rather both on the character of the action and on the nature and extent of the interference with rights in the parcel as a whole—here, the city tax block designated as the "landmark site."

Secondly, appellants, focusing on the character and impact of the New York City law, argue that it effects a "taking" because its operation has significantly diminished the value of the Terminal site. Appellants concede that the decisions sustaining other land-use regulations, which, like the New York City law, are reasonably related to the promotion of the general welfare, uniformly reject the proposition that diminution in property value, standing alone, can establish a "taking," see Euclid v. Ambler Realty Co., 272 U.S. 365 (1926) (75% diminution in value caused by zoning law); Hadacheck v. Sebastian, 239 U.S. 394 (1915) (87½% diminution in value); and that the "taking" issue in these contexts is resolved by focusing on the uses the regulations permit. Appellants, moreover, also do not dispute that a showing of diminution in property value would not establish a taking if the restriction had been imposed as a result of historic-district legislation, but appellants argue that New York City's regulation of individual landmarks is fundamentally different from zoning or from historic-district legislation because the controls imposed by New York City's law apply only to individuals who own selected properties.

Stated baldly, appellants' position appears to be that the only means of ensuring that selected owners are not singled out to endure financial hardship for no reason is to hold that any restriction imposed on individual landmarks pursuant to the New York City scheme is a "taking" requiring the payment of "just compensation." Agreement with this argument would, of course, invalidate not just New York City's law, but all comparable landmark legislation in the Nation. We find no merit in it. . . .

C

Rejection of appellants' broad arguments is not, however, the end of our inquiry, for all we thus far have established is that the New York City law is not rendered invalid by its failure to provide "just compensation" whenever a landmark owner is restricted in the exploitation of property interests, such as air rights, to a greater extent than provided for under applicable zoning laws. We now must consider whether the interference with appellants' property is of such a magnitude that "there must be an exercise of eminent domain and compensation to sustain [it]." Pennsylvania Coal Co. v. Mahon, 260 U.S. at 413. That inquiry may be narrowed to the question of the severity of the impact of the law on appellants' parcel, and its resolution in turn requires a careful assessment of the impact of the regulation on the Terminal site.

. . . . [The] New York City law does not interfere in any way with the present uses of the Terminal. Its designation as a landmark not only permits but contemplates that appellants may continue to use the property precisely as it has been used for the past 65 years: as a railroad terminal containing office space and concessions. So the law does not interfere with what must be regarded as Penn Central's primary expectation concerning the use of the parcel. More importantly, on this record, we must regard the New York City law as permitting Penn Central not only to profit from the Terminal but also to obtain a "reasonable return" on its investment.

Appellants, moreover, exaggerate the effect of the law on their ability to make use of the air rights above the Terminal in two respects. First, it simply cannot be maintained, on this record, that appellants have been prohibited from occupying *any* portion of the airspace above the Terminal. While the Commission's actions in denying applications to construct an office building in excess of 50 stories above the Terminal may indicate that it will refuse to issue a certificate of appropriateness for any comparably sized structure, nothing the Commission has said or done suggests an intention to prohibit *any* construction above the Terminal. The Commission's report emphasized that whether any construction would be allowed depended upon whether the proposed addition "would harmonize in scale, material and character with [the Terminal]." Since appellants have not sought approval for the construction of a smaller structure, we do not know that appellants will be denied any use of any portion of the airspace above the Terminal.

Second, to the extent appellants have been denied the right to build above the Terminal, it is not literally accurate to say that they have been denied *all* use of even those pre-existing air rights. Their ability to use these rights has not been abrogated; they are made transferable to at least eight parcels in the vicinity of the Terminal, one or two of which have been found suitable for the construction of new office buildings. Although appellants and others have argued that New York City's transferable development-rights program is far from ideal, the New York courts here supportably found that, at least in the case of the Terminal, the rights afforded are valuable. While these rights may well not have constituted "just compensation" if a "taking" had occurred, the rights nevertheless undoubtedly mitigate whatever financial burdens the law has imposed on appellants and, for that reason, are to be taken into account in considering the impact of regulation.

On this record, we conclude that the application of New York City's Landmarks Law has not effected a "taking" of appellants' property. The restrictions imposed are substantially related to the promotion of the general welfare and not only permit reasonable beneficial use of the landmark site but also afford appellants opportunities further to enhance not only the Terminal site proper but also other properties.

Affirmed.

MR. JUSTICE REHNQUIST, with whom THE CHIEF JUSTICE and MR. JUSTICE STEVENS join, dissenting.

Of the over one million buildings and structures in the city of New York, appellees have singled out 400 for designation as official landmarks.[1] The owner of a building might initially be pleased that his property has been chosen by a distinguished committee of architects, historians, and city planners for such a singular distinction. But he may well discover, as appellant Penn Central Transportation Co. did here, that the landmark designation imposes upon him a substantial cost, with little or no offsetting benefit except for the honor of the designation. The question in this case is whether the cost associated with the city of New York's desire to preserve a limited number of "landmarks" within its borders must be borne by all of its taxpayers or whether it can instead be imposed entirely on the owners of the individual properties....

Appellees have ... destroyed—in a literal sense, "taken"—substantial property rights of Penn Central. While the term "taken" might have been narrowly interpreted to include only physical seizures of property rights, "the construction of the phrase has not been so narrow. The courts have held that the deprivation of the former owner rather than the accretion of a right or interest to the sovereign constitutes the taking." United States v.

1. A large percentage of the designated landmarks are public structures (such as the Brooklyn Bridge, City Hall, the Statue of Liberty and the Municipal Asphalt Plant) and thus do not raise Fifth Amendment taking questions....

General Motors Corp., 323 U.S. 373, 378 (1945). Because "not every destruction or injury to property by governmental action has been held to be a 'taking' in the constitutional sense," Armstrong v. United States, 364 U.S. 40, 48 (1960), however, this does not end our inquiry. But an examination of the two exceptions where the destruction of property does not constitute a taking demonstrates that a compensable taking has occurred here.

As early as 1887, the Court recognized that the government can prevent a property owner from using his property to injure others without having to compensate the owner for the value of the forbidden use.... Thus, there is no "taking" where a city prohibits the operation of a brickyard within a residential area, see Hadacheck v. Sebastian, 239 U.S. 394 (1915), or forbids excavation for sand and gravel below the water line, see Goldblatt v. Hempstead, 369 U.S. 590 (1962). Nor is it relevant, where the government is merely prohibiting a noxious use of property, that the government would seem to be singling out a particular property owner....

Appellees are not prohibiting a nuisance. The record is clear that the proposed addition to the Grand Central Terminal would be in full compliance with zoning, height limitations, and other health and safety requirements. Instead, appellees are seeking to preserve what they believe to be an outstanding example of beaux arts architecture. Penn Central is prevented from further developing its property basically because too good a job was done in designing and building it. The city of New York, because of its unadorned admiration for the design, has decided that the owners of the building must preserve it unchanged for the benefit of sightseeing New Yorkers and tourists.

Even where the government prohibits a noninjurious use, the Court has ruled that a taking does not take place if the prohibition applies over a broad cross section of land and thereby "[secures] an average reciprocity of advantage." Pennsylvania Coal Co. v. Mahon, 260 U.S., at 415. It is for this reason that zoning does not constitute a "taking." While zoning at times reduces individual property values, the burden is shared relatively evenly and it is reasonable to conclude that on the whole an individual who is harmed by one aspect of the zoning will be benefited by another.

Here, however, a multimillion dollar loss has been imposed on appellants; it is uniquely felt and is not offset by any benefits flowing from the preservation of some 400 other "landmarks" in New York City. Appellees have imposed a substantial cost on less than one one-tenth of one percent of the buildings in New York City for the general benefit of all its people. It is exactly this imposition of general costs on a few individuals at which the "taking" protection is directed. The Fifth Amendment

> prevents the public from loading upon one individual more than his just share of the burdens of government, and says that when he surrenders to the public something more and different from that which is exacted from other members of the public, a full and just equivalent shall be returned to him. [Monongahela Navigation Co. v. United States, 148 U.S. 312, 325 (1893).]

Less than 20 years ago, this Court reiterated that the

> Fifth Amendment's guarantee that private property shall not be taken for a public use without just compensation was designed to bar Government from forcing some people alone to bear public burdens which, in all fairness and justice, should be borne by the public as a whole. [Armstrong v. United States, 364 U.S., at 49.]

As Mr. Justice Holmes pointed out in Pennsylvania Coal Co. v. Mahon, "the question at bottom" in an eminent domain case "is upon whom the loss of the changes desired should fall." The benefits that appellees believe will flow from preservation of the Grand Central Terminal will accrue to all the citizens of New York City. There is no reason to believe that appellants will enjoy a substantially greater share of these benefits. If the cost of preserving Grand Central Terminal were spread evenly across the entire population of the city of New York, the burden per person would be in cents per year—a minor cost appellees would surely concede for the benefit accrued. Instead, however, appellees would impose the entire cost of several million dollars per year on Penn Central. But it is precisely this sort of discrimination that the Fifth Amendment prohibits. . . .

Notes & Questions

1. *Penn Central* represents the high point for ad hoc, balancing approaches in the Supreme Court's takings cases. The Supreme Court confesses its inability to come up with a "set formula" for resolving regulatory taking cases and endorses instead "essentially ad hoc, factual inquiries" under which a variety of factors get balanced. What guidance does the Court give lower courts in engaging in these ad hoc inquiries? If you were a lower court, how easy would you find it to apply the *Penn Central* standards to a challenged regulation? If you were a land use planner wondering whether a new regulation would get you into trouble, or a property owner wondering whether you should sue to invalidate a new regulation, how much counsel does *Penn Central* provide you?

2. **Investment-Backed Expectations.** One factor that *Penn Central* suggests courts consider in deciding whether a regulation is a taking in any particular case is the property owner's "distinct investment-backed expectations." What does that mean? By emphasizing "investment," is the Court suggesting that gifts and inheritance are entitled to less protection than purchased property?

The Supreme Court borrowed the term "investment-backed expectations" from Professor Frank Michelman. See Frank Michelman, Property, Utility, and Fairness: Comments on the Ethical Foundations of "Just Compensation" Law, 80 Harv. L. Rev. 1165, 1229–1234 (1967). Michelman used the term to describe one method for determining when interference with a mere subset of property rights, like the subsurface estate in *Pennsylvania Coal* or the air rights in *Penn Coal*, might be a taking. In Michelman's view, unless a property owner has invested explicitly in these rights, a court should look at the entire property, not just the subset of rights, in deciding whether there is a taking. Holmes therefore was right in looking at the subsurface estate in *Pennsylvania Coal* because the coal companies had specifically purchased that estate. But *Penn Central* was right in emphasizing the "parcel as a whole" rather than just the air rights because the Penn Central Corporation had not acquired the land specifically for its air rights.

The term "investment-backed expectations," however, has acquired broader significance in the Supreme Court's takings jurisprudence. In Hodel v. Irving, 481 U.S. 704 (1987), for example, the Court examined whether a federal law that prohibited the devise or intestate transfer of highly fractionated interests in Indian lands was an unconstitutional taking. See pp. 774–778 (discussing the problem of fractionated Indian interest), pp. 1144–1145 (discussing *Hodel*). Although the Court concluded the law was a taking, the Court suggested that the plaintiffs' investment-backed expectations were exceptionally weak because the plaintiffs had not purchased their property rights:

> The extent to which any of appellees' decedents had "investment-backed expectations" in passing on the property is dubious. Though it is conceivable that some of these interests were purchased with the expectation that the owners might pass on the remainder to their heirs at death, the property has been held in trust for the Indians for 100 years and is overwhelmingly acquired by gift, descent, or devise. ... None of the appellees here can point to any specific investment-backed expectations beyond the fact that their ancestors agreed to accept allotments only after ceding to the United States large parts of the original Great Sioux Reservation.

Id. at 715. The concept of "investment-backed expectations" has also played a role in the Court's evaluation of whether landowners who purchase property after a regulatory system is in place can complain that the regulation has taken their property. See Pallazzolo v. Rhode Island, p. 1169.

For interesting discussions of the use of "investment-backed expectations" in takings law, see Robert M. Washburn, "Reasonable Investment Backed Expectations" as a Factor in Defining Property Interest, 49 Wash. U.J. Urb. & Contemp. L. 63 (1996); Daniel R. Mandelker, Investment–Backed Expectations in Taking Law, 27 Urb. Law. 215 (1995).

3. **Alternative Takings Tests.** Why has it been so difficult for the Supreme Court to identify "set formula" for determining when a regulation is a taking? At the time the Court decided the *Penn Central* case, courts and commentators had suggested a number of takings tests—all of which suffer from analytical or other problems:

a. *Physical Invasion.* See *Mugler* and the discussion at pp. 1114–1115 supra.

b. *Nuisance.* See *Mugler* and the discussion at pp. 1116–1117 supra.

c. *Harm–Benefit.* See *Mugler* and the discussion at p. 1117 supra.

d. *Diminution in Value.* See *Pennsylvania Coal* and the discussion at pp. 1122–1123 supra.

e. *Cost–Benefit Balancing.* Justice Holmes' reference in *Pennsylvania Coal* to "average reciprocity of advantage" planted the seed for a test that balances a regulation's public benefits against its private costs. Employing the same sort of cost-benefit calculus as is used in nuisance cases, the test upholds a regulation if it is "efficient"—i.e., if the public benefits derived from the regulation outweigh its costs to the regulated landowner. See, e.g., State, Department of Ecology v. Pacesetter Construction Co., Inc., 571 P.2d 196 (Wash. 1977).

The balancing test suffers from several problems. First, determining the economic benefits of particular regulations can be extremely difficult. Second, does the economic efficiency of regulations have anything to do with whether the government should compensate property owners negatively affected by the regulations? As the Supreme Court said in the most cited passage in takings law, the purpose of the constitutional takings provisions is to prevent the "government from forcing some people alone to bear public burdens which, in all fairness and justice, should be borne by the public as a whole." Armstrong v. United States, 364 U.S. 40, 49 (1960). If efficiency were the criterion, government would be excused from compensating for physical appropriations of land for public uses such as parks, roads, schools, and police stations, any time the public benefit derived from these uses outweighed their private costs.

f. *Utility and Fairness.* In an important 1967 article, Professor Frank Michelman formulated a test that incorporated and refined the efficiency calculus of the balancing test. Michelman, supra Note 2. The test employs three factors:

(i) "efficiency gains"—the excess of a regulatory measure's benefits over the losses it inflicts;

(ii) "demoralization costs"—the total dollar value of (1) the discomfort to the regulated property owner and her "sympathizers" for not being paid and (2) the diminished productivity, "reflecting either impaired incentives or social unrest," resulting from the discomfort; and

(iii) "settlement costs"—the dollar cost of the "time, effort and resources" required to compensate affected parties in order to avoid the demoralization costs.

Under Michelman's formulation, the government should not undertake a regulation if the measure would yield no efficiency gains, or if both demoralization costs and settlement costs would exceed efficiency gains. If the measure passes this first hurdle, then compensation should be paid if demoralization costs exceed settlement costs.

To this efficiency calculus, Michelman also posed a fairness alternative, arguing that the denial of compensation "is not unfair as long as the disappointed claimant ought to be able to appreciate how such decisions might fit into a consistent practice which holds forth a lesser long-run risk to people like him than would any consistent practice which is naturally suggested by the opposite decision." 80 Harv. L. Rev. at 1223.

One obvious problem with Michelman's efficiency approach is that it relies so heavily on the quantification of factors that courts and regulators are ill-equipped to measure. How, for example, are demoralization costs to be computed? And *whose* demoralization is to be taken into account? Is Michelman's fairness alternative any easier to apply?

g. *Externalities.* In 1971, Professor Sax suggested that the government need not compensate property owners when a regulation merely prohibits or moderates an externality. See Joseph Sax, Takings, Private Property, and Public Rights, 81 Yale L.J. 149 (1971). If the government orders a factory not to pollute, for example, no compensation is owed to the factory. Under Sax's test, what types of regulations would not require compensation? Is Sax's test any different than the discredited harm-benefit test?

4. **TDRs.** Transferable development rights (TDRs) have been widely used to ameliorate the effects of landmark preservation programs like the one in *Penn Central.* They have also been frequently used in programs aimed at preserving ecologically or aesthetically important open spaces. Indeed, TDRs can be employed any time a landowner is prohibited from developing land to the bulk and height limits that generally apply in its zoning district. The concept of TDRs is simple and straight-forward. To compensate for regulations on historical landmarks, for example, a city can give Mary Austin, who owns a regulated 18–story landmark in a district that is generally zoned to allow buildings thirty stories high, a transferable development right for twelve stories. Mary can then sell this right to Jim Bridger, another landowner in the district, enabling Jim to build to forty-two stories—twelve stories over the generally applicable limit. Alternatively, the city can buy the development rights from Mary for cash and then resell the rights to some other landowner in the district, also for cash. The TDR concept is considered in two essays by its leading academic exponent, John Costonis, The Chicago Plan: Incentive Zoning and the Preservation of Urban Landmarks, 85 Harv. L. Rev. 574 (1972); John Costonis, Development Rights Transfer: An Exploratory Essay, 83 Yale L.J. 75 (1973). For more recent discussions of TDRs, see Dorothy J. Glancy, Preserving Rockefeller Center, 24 Urb. Law. 423 (1992); James T.B. Tripp & Daniel J. Dudek, Institutional Guidelines for Designing Successful Transferable Rights Programs, 6 Yale J. Reg. 369 (1989).

5. According to *Penn Central*, what is the role of TDRs in takings cases? If a regulation is a taking, can the government compensate property owners in TDRs rather than cash? Can the government avoid a finding that the regulation is a taking by providing property owners with TDRs? Assume that Parley Pratt owns a parcel of land on which there is a prehistoric tar pit in which many dinosaur fossils have been found. Parley's land is now in the middle of a major city, and he would like to develop his land. The city, however, wants to protect the tar pit. If the government forbids Parley from using his land in any way, a court would probably find

that the regulation has gone "too far" and is a taking. See Lucas v. South Carolina Coastal Council, p. 1145 infra. Parley would then be entitled to the full fair market value of his property as "just compensation." Should it make a difference to the takings finding if the government provides Parley with TDRs? What if the TDRs are worth less than the fair market value of Parley's property?

In Suitum v. Tahoe Regional Planning Agency, 520 U.S. 725 (1997), a landowner near Lake Tahoe argued that regulations preventing her from using her land were a taking even though the government had provided her with TDRs that she had never used. Although the Court concluded that the takings claim was not ripe for adjudication, Justice Scalia in a concurring opinion addressed the role of TDRs in evaluating a takings claim. In Justice Scalia's view, the provision of TDRs to a regulated property owner is irrelevant to the question of whether the regulation has gone "too far" and is a taking. In deciding whether there is a taking, the focus should be

> on ascertaining the extent of the governmental restriction on land use, not what the government has given the landowner in exchange for that restriction.... Just as a cash payment from the government would not relate to whether the regulation "goes too far" (i.e., restricts use of the land so severely as to constitute a taking), but rather to whether there has been adequate compensation for the taking; and just as a chit or coupon from the government, redeemable by and hence marketable to third parties, would relate not to the question of taking but to the question of compensation; so also the marketable TDR, a peculiar type of chit which enables a third party not to get cash from the government but to use his land in ways the government would otherwise not permit, relates not to taking but to compensation....
>
> Putting TDRs on the taking rather than the just-compensation side of the equation (as the Ninth Circuit did below) is a clever, albeit transparent, device that seeks to take advantage of a peculiarity of our takings-clause jurisprudence: Whereas once there *is* a taking, the Constitution requires just (*i.e.*, full) compensation, a regulatory taking generally does not *occur* so long as the land retains substantial (albeit not its full) value. If money that the government-regulator gives to the landowner can be counted on the question of whether there *is* a taking (causing the courts to say that the land retains substantial value, and has thus not been taken), rather than on the question of whether the compensation for the taking is adequate, the government can get away with paying much less....

Id. at 747–748.

C. BRIGHT LINE RULES & *PER SE* TAKINGS

Frustrated at the lack of certainty provided by the *Penn Central* balancing test, some justices on the Supreme Court have continued to look for the "set formula" that *Penn Central* found elusive. This section explores several cases in which the Supreme Court has established *per se* tests for regulatory takings.

Loretto v. Teleprompter Manhattan CATV Corp.

Supreme Court of the United States, 1982.
458 U.S. 419.

JUSTICE MARSHALL delivered the opinion of the Court.

This case presents the question whether a minor but permanent physical occupation of an owner's property authorized by government constitutes a "taking" of property for which just compensation is due under the Fifth and Fourteenth Amendments of the Constitution. New York law provides that a landlord must permit a cable television company to install its cable facilities upon his property. In this case, the cable installation occupied portions of appellant's roof and the side of her building. The New York Court of Appeals ruled that this appropriation does not amount to a taking. Because we conclude that such a physical occupation of property is a taking, we reverse.

I

Appellant Jean Loretto purchased a five-story apartment building located at 303 West 105th Street, New York City, in 1971. The previous owner had granted appellees Teleprompter Corp. and Teleprompter Manhattan CATV (collectively Teleprompter) permission to install a cable on the building and the exclusive privilege of furnishing cable television (CATV) services to the tenants. The New York Court of Appeals described the installation as follows:

> On June 1, 1970 TelePrompter installed a cable slightly less than one-half inch in diameter and of approximately 30 feet in length along the length of the building about 18 inches above the roof top, and directional taps, approximately 4 inches by 4 inches by 4 inches, on the front and rear of the roof. By June 8, 1970 the cable had been extended another 4 to 6 feet and cable had been run from the directional taps to the adjoining building at 305 West 105th Street.

Teleprompter also installed two large silver boxes along the roof cables. The cables are attached by screws or nails penetrating the masonry at approximately two-foot intervals, and other equipment is installed by bolts. . . .

Prior to 1973, Teleprompter routinely obtained authorization for its installations from property owners along the cable's route, compensating the owners at the standard rate of 5% of the gross revenues that Teleprompter realized from the particular property. To facilitate tenant access to CATV, the State of New York enacted § 828 of the Executive Law, effective January 1, 1973. Section 828 provides that a landlord may not "interfere with the installation of cable television facilities upon his property or premises," and may not demand payment from any tenant for permitting CATV, or demand payment from any CATV company "in excess of any amount which the [State Commission on Cable Television] shall, by regulation, determine to be reasonable." The landlord may, however, require the CATV company or the tenant to bear the cost of installation and to indemnify for any damage caused by the installation. Pursuant to § 828(1)(b), the State Commission has ruled that a one-time $1 payment is the normal fee to which a landlord is entitled. . . .

On appeal, the Court of Appeals, over dissent, upheld the statute. . . . The court . . . ruled that the law serves a legitimate police power purpose—eliminating landlord fees and conditions that inhibit the development of CATV, which has important educational and community benefits. Rejecting the argument that a physical occupation authorized by government is necessarily a taking, the court stated that the regulation does not have an excessive economic impact upon appellant when measured against her aggregate property rights, and that it does not interfere with any reasonable investment-backed expectations.

II

. . . . We have no reason to question [the New York Court of Appeals'] determination [that § 828 serves a legitimate state purpose]. It is a separate question, however, whether an otherwise valid regulation so frustrates property rights that compensation must be paid. We conclude that a permanent physical occupation authorized by government is a taking without regard to the public interests that it may serve. Our constitutional history confirms the rule, recent cases do not question it, and the purposes of the Takings Clause compel its retention.

A

In Penn Central Transportation Co. v. New York City, the Court surveyed some of the general principles governing the Takings Clause. The Court noted that no "set formula" existed to determine, in all cases, whether compensation is constitutionally due for a government restriction of property. Ordinarily, the Court must engage in "essentially ad hoc, factual inquiries." But the inquiry is not standardless. . . . [W]e have long considered a physical intrusion by government to be a property restriction of an unusually serious character for purposes of the Takings Clause. Our cases further establish that when the physical intrusion reaches the extreme form of a permanent physical occupation, a taking has occurred. In such a case, "the character of the government action" not only is an important factor in resolving whether the action works a taking but also is determinative.

When faced with a constitutional challenge to a permanent physical occupation of real property, this Court has invariably found a taking. As early as 1872, in Pumpelly v. Green Bay Co., 13 Wall. 166, this Court held that the defendant's construction, pursuant to state authority, of a dam which permanently flooded plaintiff's property constituted a taking....

More recent cases confirm the distinction between a permanent physical occupation, a physical invasion short of an occupation, and a regulation that merely restricts the use of property. In United States v. Causby, 328 U.S. 256 (1946), the Court ruled that frequent flights immediately above a landowner's property constituted a taking, comparing such overflights to the quintessential form of a taking....

Although this Court's most recent cases have not addressed the precise issue before us, they have emphasized that physical invasion cases are special and have not repudiated the rule that any permanent physical occupation is a taking. The cases state or imply that a physical invasion is subject to a balancing process, but they do not suggest that a permanent physical occupation would ever be exempt from the Takings Clause....

In Kaiser Aetna v. United States, 444 U.S. 164 (1979), the Court held that the Government's imposition of a navigational servitude requiring public access to a pond was a taking where the landowner had reasonably relied on Government consent in connecting the pond to navigable water. The Court emphasized that the servitude took the land-owner's right to exclude, "one of the most essential sticks in the bundle of rights that are commonly characterized as property." The Court explained:

> This is not a case in which the Government is exercising its regulatory power in a manner that will cause an insubstantial devaluation of petitioner's private property; rather, the imposition of the navigational servitude in this context will result in an actual physical invasion of the privately owned marina.... And even if the Government physically invades only an easement in property, it must nonetheless pay compensation.

Although the easement of passage, not being a permanent occupation of land, was not considered a taking per se, *Kaiser Aetna* reemphasizes that a physical invasion is a government intrusion of an unusually serious character.

Another recent case underscores the constitutional distinction between a permanent occupation and a temporary physical invasion. In PruneYard Shopping Center v. Robins, 447 U.S. 74 (1980), the Court upheld a state constitutional requirement that shopping center owners permit individuals to exercise free speech and petition rights on their property, to which they had already invited the general public. The Court emphasized that the State Constitution does not prevent the owner from restricting expressive activities by imposing reasonable time, place, and manner restrictions to minimize interference with the owner's commercial functions. Since the invasion was temporary and limited in nature, and since the owner had not exhibited an interest in excluding all persons from his property, "the fact that [the solicitors] may have 'physically invaded' [the owners'] property cannot be viewed as determinative."

In short, when the "character of the governmental action," *Penn Central*, 438 U.S., at 124, is a permanent physical occupation of property, our cases uniformly have found a taking to the extent of the occupation, without regard to whether the action achieves an important public benefit or has only minimal economic impact on the owner.

B

The historical rule that a permanent physical occupation of another's property is a taking has more than tradition to commend it. Such an appropriation is perhaps the most serious form of invasion of an owner's property interests. To borrow a metaphor, the government does not simply take a single "strand" from the "bundle" of property rights: it chops through the bundle, taking a slice of every strand.

Property rights in a physical thing have been described as the rights "to possess, use and dispose of it." To the extent that the government permanently occupies physical property, it effectively destroys each of these rights. First, the owner has no right to possess the occupied space himself, and also has no power to exclude the occupier from possession and use of the space. The power to exclude has traditionally been considered one of the most treasured strands in an owner's bundle of property rights. Second, the permanent physical occupation of property forever denies the owner any power to control the use of the property; he not only cannot exclude others, but can make no nonpossessory use of the property. Although deprivation of the right to use and obtain a profit from property is not, in every case, independently sufficient to establish a taking, it is clearly relevant. Finally, even though the owner may retain the bare legal right to dispose of the occupied space by transfer or sale, the permanent occupation of that space by a stranger will ordinarily empty the right of any value, since the purchaser will also be unable to make any use of the property.

Moreover, an owner suffers a special kind of injury when a stranger directly invades and occupies the owner's property. Property law has long protected an owner's expectation that he will be relatively undisturbed at least in the possession of his property. To require, as well, that the owner permit another to exercise complete dominion literally adds insult to injury. Furthermore, such an occupation is qualitatively more severe than a regulation of the use of property, even a regulation that imposes affirmative duties on the owner, since the owner may have no control over the timing, extent, or nature of the invasion.

The traditional rule also avoids otherwise difficult line-drawing problems. Few would disagree that if the State required landlords to permit third parties to install swimming pools on the landlords' rooftops for the convenience of the tenants, the requirement would be a taking. If the cable installation here occupied as much space, again, few would disagree that the occupation would be a taking. But constitutional protection for the rights of private property cannot be made to depend on the size of the area permanently occupied. Indeed, it is possible that in the future, additional cable installations that more significantly restrict a landlord's use of the roof of his building will be made. . . .

Finally, whether a permanent physical occupation has occurred presents relatively few problems of proof. The placement of a fixed structure on land or real property is an obvious fact that will rarely be subject to dispute. Once the fact of occupation is shown, of course, a court should consider the extent of the occupation as one relevant factor in determining the compensation due. For that reason, moreover, there is less need to consider the extent of the occupation in determining whether there is a taking in the first instance.

C

Teleprompter's cable installation on appellant's building constitutes a taking under the traditional test. The installation involved a direct physical attachment of plates, boxes, wires, bolts, and screws to the building, completely occupying space immediately above and upon the roof and along the building's exterior wall. . . .

[W]e do not agree with appellees that application of the physical occupation rule will have dire consequences for the government's power to adjust landlord-tenant relationships. This Court has consistently affirmed that States have broad power to regulate housing conditions in general and the landlord-tenant relationship in particular without paying compensation for all economic injuries that such regulation entails. . . . [O]ur holding today in no way alters the analysis governing the State's power to require landlords to comply with building codes and provide utility connections, mailboxes, smoke detectors, fire extinguishers, and the like in the common area of a building. So long as these regulations do not require the landlord to suffer the physical occupation of a portion of his building by a third party, they will be analyzed under the multifactor inquiry generally applicable to nonpossessory governmental activity.[19]

III

. . . . [O]ur conclusion that § 828 works a taking of a portion of appellant's property does not presuppose that the fee which many landlords had obtained from Teleprompter prior to the law's enactment is a proper measure of the value of the property taken. The issue of the amount of

19. If § 828 required landlords to provide cable installation if a tenant so desires, the statute might present a different question from the question before us, since the landlord would own the installation. Ownership would give the landlord rights to the placement, manner, use, and possibly the disposition of the installation. The fact of ownership is, contrary to the dissent, not simply "incidental"; it would give a landlord (rather than a CATV company) full authority over the installation except only as government specifically limited that authority. The landlord would decide how to comply with applicable government regulations concerning CATV and therefore could minimize the physical, esthetic, and other effects of the installation. Moreover, if the landlord wished to repair, demolish, or construct in the area of the building where the installation is located, he need not incur the burden of obtaining the CATV company's cooperation in moving the cable.

compensation that is due, on which we express no opinion, is a matter for the state courts to consider on remand.

JUSTICE BLACKMUN, with whom JUSTICE BRENNAN and JUSTICE WHITE join, dissenting.

If the Court's decisions construing the Takings Clause state anything clearly, it is that "[there] is no set formula to determine where regulation ends and taking begins." Goldblatt v. Town of Hempstead, 369 U.S. 590, 594 (1962).

In a curiously anachronistic decision, the Court today acknowledges its historical disavowal of set formulae in almost the same breath as it constructs a rigid per se takings rule: "a permanent physical occupation authorized by government is a taking without regard to the public interests that it may serve." To sustain its rule against our recent precedents, the Court erects a strained and untenable distinction between "temporary physical invasions," whose constitutionality concededly "is subject to a balancing process," and "permanent physical occupations," which are "[takings] without regard to other factors that a court might ordinarily examine."

In my view, the Court's approach "reduces the constitutional issue to a formalistic quibble" over whether property has been "permanently occupied" or "temporarily invaded." Sax, Takings and the Police Power, 74 Yale L.J. 36, 37 (1964)....

The Court's recent Takings Clause decisions teach that nonphysical government intrusions on private property, such as zoning ordinances and other land-use restrictions, have become the rule rather than the exception. Modern government regulation exudes intangible "externalities" that may diminish the value of private property far more than minor physical touchings....

Precisely because the extent to which the government may injure private interests now depends so little on whether or not it has authorized a "physical contact," the Court has avoided per se takings rules resting on outmoded distinctions between physical and nonphysical intrusions. As one commentator has observed, a takings rule based on such a distinction is inherently suspect because "its capacity to distinguish, even crudely, between significant and insignificant losses is too puny to be taken seriously." Michelman, Property, Utility, and Fairness: Comments on the Ethical Foundations of "Just Compensation" Law, 80 Harv. L. Rev. 1165, 1227 (1967)....

The Court reaffirms that "States have broad power to regulate housing conditions in general and the landlord-tenant relationship in particular without paying compensation for all economic injuries that such regulation entails."....§ 828 merely defines one of the many statutory responsibilities that a New Yorker accepts when she enters the rental business. If appellant occupies her own building, or converts it into a commercial property, she becomes perfectly free to exclude Teleprompter from her one-eighth cubic foot of roof space. But once appellant chooses to use her property for rental purposes, she must comply with all reasonable government statutes regulating the landlord-tenant relationship. If § 828 authorizes a "permanent" occupation, and thus works a taking "without regard to the public interests that it may serve," then all other New York statutes that require a landlord to make physical attachments to his rental property also must constitute takings, even if they serve indisputably valid public interests in tenant protection and safety.[7]

.... [H]istory teaches that takings claims are properly evaluated under a multifactor balancing test. By directing that all "permanent physical occupations" automatically are compensable, "without regard to whether the action achieves an important public benefit or has only minimal economic impact on the owner," the Court does not further equity so much as it encourages litigants to manipulate their factual allegations to gain the benefit of its per se rule. I do not relish the prospect of distinguishing the inevitable flow of certiorari petitions attempting to shoehorn insubstantial takings claims into today's "set formula."....

Notes & Questions

1. On remand, the New York courts concluded that the New York Commission on Cable Television was entitled to determine the compensation due Mrs. Loretto and other landlords for the taking of their property. Loretto v. Teleprompter Manhattan CATV Corp., 446 N.E.2d 428 (N.Y. 1983). The commission, after concluding that the cable box actually increased the value of Mrs. Loretto's apartment house, awarded her $1 in nominal damages. Why all the fuss to start with about a small cable box on a roof?

2. The Court in *Loretto* distinguishes between "permanent physical occupations" (*per se* taking) and "temporary physical invasion" (perhaps, but not necessarily, a taking). What is the difference between the two types of physical interference, and should the difference matter in takings cases? If the United States Environmental Protection Agency issues an order requiring a landowner to provide access to his property to governmental scientists wishing to sample and monitor groundwater contamination by hazardous wastes, is that a "temporary physical invasion" or a "permanent physical occupation"? Should it be a taking? See Hendler v. United States, 952 F.2d 1364 (Fed. Cir. 1991). What result if the government forbids the owner of a private beach from excluding members of the public from crossing the land in order to reach a public beach? See Nolan v. California Coastal Comm'n, infra p. 1178.

3. ***Per Se* Rules Versus Balancing Standards.** *Loretto* and *Penn Central* present two approaches to resolving takings claims—"bright line"

7. See, e.g., N.Y. Mult. Dwell. Law § 35 (McKinney 1974) (requiring entrance doors and lights); § 36 (windows and skylights for public halls and stairs); § 50–a (Supp. 1982) (locks and intercommunication systems); § 50–c (lobby attendants); § 51–a (peepholes); § 51–b (elevator mirrors); § 53 (fire escapes); § 57 (bells and mail receptacles); § 67(3) (fire sprinklers)....

rules and balancing standards. What are the advantages and disadvantages of each? For interesting insights into this question, see F. Patrick Hubbard et al., Do Owners Have a Fair Chance of Prevailing Under the Ad Hoc Regulatory Takings Test of *Penn Central Transportation Company*?, 14 Duke Envtl. L. & Pol'y F. 121 (2003); Marc Poirier, The Virtue of Vagueness in Takings Doctrine, 24 Cardozo L. Rev. 93 (2002); Frank Michelman, Takings, 1987, 88 Colum. L. Rev. 1600 (1988); Susan Rose–Ackerman, Against Ad Hocery: A Comment on Michelman, 88 Colum. L. Rev. 1697 (1988).

4. **Endangered Species.** Assume that one of the last remaining colonies of Delhi sands flower-loving flies, a species listed as endangered under the federal Endangered Species Act, lives on your property. When you try to develop your property, the federal government orders you to stop and also tells you that you cannot do anything on your property that would remove the fly colony from your land. Is this a taking under *Loretto?*

In Southview Associates v. Bongartz, 980 F.2d 84 (2d Cir. 1992), a developer challenged Vermont's refusal to let him construct a vacation home project on the last remaining deeryard in a 10.7 square mile watershed. The developer argued that the case was identical to *Loretto* except that the government was authorizing a permanent physical occupation by deer rather than cable television equipment. The court disagreed. According to its opinion, "no absolute, exclusive physical occupation exists.... To the extent that [the State] has allowed the deer to 'invade' Southview's land, this 'invasion' is relatively minor, consisting of an occasional, seasonal, and limited habitation by no more than 20 deer." In a footnote, the court also expressed uneasiness with treating animals in their natural habitat as an invasive force giving rise to governmental liability. While *Loretto* involved physical occupation by a "stranger," the deer in *Bongartz* were not "strangers to their winter habitat—the deeryard." See also Florida Game & Fresh Water Fish Comm'n v. Flotilla, Inc., 636 So. 2d 761 (Fla. Dist. Ct. App. 1994) (same result, noting that the government "neither owns nor controls the migration of the wildlife species it protects"). Is the latter distinction relevant to the takings question? Why?

5. **Rent Control.** Many rent control ordinances that protect current, but not new, tenants from rent increases also restrict landlords' ability to toss current tenants out; otherwise, landlords could easily evade the rent control by evicting tenants and leasing out the apartments at a higher rent. Under *Loretto*, are such ordinances unconstitutional takings? See Yee v. City of Escondido, 503 U.S. 519 (1992) (no taking.)

6. **Are There Other Essential Sticks?** According to the Supreme Court in *Loretto*, physical occupations and invasions constitute particularly serious intrusions into property because the right to exclude is "one of the most essential sticks in the bundle of rights that are commonly characterized as property." Are there other "essential sticks" in a property owner's bundle of rights that, like the right to exclude, should be absolutely protected against takings without compensation? In Hodel v. Irving, 481 U.S. 704, the Court strongly suggested that the "right to pass on property"

is a core property interest that is strongly protected against governmental abrogation, although it emphasized that the government has long enjoyed the ability to "adjust the rules governing the descent and devise of property."

Lucas v. South Carolina Coastal Council

Supreme Court of the United States, 1992.
505 U.S. 1003.

JUSTICE SCALIA delivered the opinion of the Court.

In 1986, petitioner David H. Lucas paid $975,000 for two residential lots on the Isle of Palms in Charleston County, South Carolina, on which he intended to build single-family homes. In 1988, however, the South Carolina Legislature enacted the Beachfront Management Act which had the direct effect of barring petitioner from erecting any permanent habitable structures on his two parcels.[a] A state trial court found that this prohibition rendered Lucas's parcels "valueless." This case requires us to decide whether the Act's dramatic effect on the economic value of Lucas's lots accomplished a taking of private property under the Fifth and Fourteenth Amendments requiring the payment of "just compensation."....

Figure 13–2
Lucas' Lots (Nov. 1994)

(Lucas' lots are on either side of the rectangular house in the middle)

Source: William A. Fischel

a. Eds.—As the Court noted in a later footnote, the "Act did allow the construction of certain nonhabitable improvements, e.g., 'wooden walkways no larger in width than six feet,' and 'small wooden decks no larger than one hundred forty-four square feet.' "

In the late 1970's, Lucas and others began extensive residential development of the Isle of Palms, a barrier island situated eastward of the city of Charleston. Toward the close of the development cycle for one residential subdivision known as "Beachwood East," Lucas in 1986 purchased the two lots at issue in this litigation for his own account.... His intention with respect to the lots was to do what the owners of the immediately adjacent parcels had already done: erect single-family residences....

The Beachfront Management Act brought Lucas's plans to an abrupt end. Under that 1988 legislation, the Council was directed to establish a "baseline" connecting the landwardmost "points of erosion ... during the past forty years" in the region of the Isle of Palms that includes Lucas's lots. In action not challenged here, the Council fixed this baseline landward of Lucas's parcels. That was significant, for under the Act construction of occupyable improvements was flatly prohibited seaward of a line drawn 20 feet landward of, and parallel to, the baseline. The Act provided no exceptions.

state supreme court

The Supreme Court of South Carolina [held that the Act did not constitute an unconstitutional "taking" of Lucas' property.] It found dispositive what it described as Lucas's concession "that the Beachfront Management Act [was] properly and validly designed to preserve ... South Carolina's beaches." Failing an attack on the validity of the statute as such, the court believed itself bound to accept the "uncontested ... findings" of the South Carolina legislature that new construction in the coastal zone—such as petitioner intended—threatened this public resource. The Court ruled that when a regulation respecting the use of property is designed "to prevent serious public harm," no compensation is owing under the Takings Clause regardless of the regulation's effect on the property's value....

In [the Court's] 70–odd years of ... "regulatory takings" jurisprudence, we have generally eschewed any "set formula" for determining how far is too far, preferring to "engage in ... essentially ad hoc, factual inquiries." Penn Central Transportation Co. v. City of New York, 438 U.S. 104, 124 (1978). We have, however, described at least two discrete categories of regulatory action as compensable without case-specific inquiry into the public interest advanced in support of the restraint. The first encompasses regulations that compel the property owner to suffer a physical "invasion" of his property. In general (at least with regard to permanent invasions), no matter how minute the intrusion, and no matter how weighty the public purpose behind it, we have required compensation.

The second situation in which we have found categorical treatment appropriate is where regulation denies all economically beneficial or productive use of land. As we have said on numerous occasions, the Fifth Amendment is violated when land-use regulation "does not substantially advance legitimate state interests or denies an owner economically viable use of his land."[7] Agins v. City of Tiburon, 447 U.S. 255, 260 (1980).

7. Regrettably, the rhetorical force of our "deprivation of all economically feasible use" rule is greater than its precision, since the rule does not make clear the "property

We have never set forth the justification for this rule. Perhaps it is simply, as Justice Brennan suggested, that total deprivation of beneficial use is, from the landowner's point of view, the equivalent of a physical appropriation.... Surely, at least, in the extraordinary circumstance when no productive or economically beneficial use of land is permitted, it is less realistic to indulge our usual assumption that the legislature is simply "adjusting the benefits and burdens of economic life," in a manner that secures an "average reciprocity of advantage" to everyone concerned. And the functional basis for permitting the government, by regulation, to affect property values without compensation—that "Government hardly could go on if to some extent values incident to property could not be diminished without paying for every such change in the general law"—does not apply to the relatively rare situations where the government has deprived a landowner of all economically beneficial uses.

On the other side of the balance, affirmatively supporting a compensation requirement, is the fact that regulations that leave the owner of land without economically beneficial or productive options for its use—typically, as here, by requiring land to be left substantially in its natural state—carry with them a heightened risk that private property is being pressed into some form of public service under the guise of mitigating serious public harm. As Justice Brennan explained: "From the government's point of view, the benefits flowing to the public from preservation of open space through regulation may be equally great as from creating a wildlife refuge through formal condemnation or increasing electricity production through a dam project that floods private property." San Diego Gas & Electric Co. v. City of San Diego, 450 U.S. 621, 652 (1981) (dissenting opinion). The many statutes on the books, both state and federal, that provide for the use of eminent domain to impose servitudes on private scenic lands preventing developmental uses, or to acquire such lands altogether, suggest the practical equivalence in this setting of negative regulation and appropriation.... [8]

interest" against which the loss of value is to be measured. When, for example, a regulation requires a developer to leave 90% of a rural tract in its natural state, it is unclear whether we would analyze the situation as one in which the owner has been deprived of all economically beneficial use of the burdened portion of the tract, or as one in which the owner has suffered a mere diminution in value of the tract as a whole.... The answer to this difficult question may lie in how the owner's reasonable expectations have been shaped by the State's law of property—i.e., whether and to what degree the State's law has accorded legal recognition and protection to the particular interest in land with respect to which the takings claimant alleges a diminution in (or elimination of) value. In any event, we avoid this difficulty in the present case, since the "interest in land" that Lucas has pleaded (a fee simple interest) is an estate with a rich tradition of protection at common law, and since the South Carolina Court of Common Pleas found that the Beachfront Management Act left each of Lucas's beachfront lots without economic value.

8. Justice Stevens criticizes the "deprivation of all economically beneficial use" rule as "wholly arbitrary", in that "[the] landowner whose property is diminished in value 95% recovers nothing," while the landowner who suffers a complete elimination of value "recovers the land's full value." This analysis errs in its assumption that the landowner whose deprivation is one step short of com-

[The Court next rejects the argument of the South Carolina Supreme Court that there was no taking because the Act was designed to "prevent serious public harm." The] distinction between "harm-preventing" and "benefit-conferring" regulation is often in the eye of the beholder. It is quite possible, for example, to describe in either fashion the ecological, economic, and aesthetic concerns that inspired the South Carolina legislature in the present case. One could say that imposing a servitude on Lucas's land is necessary in order to prevent his use of it from "harming" South Carolina's ecological resources; or, instead, in order to achieve the "benefits" of an ecological preserve. Whether one or the other of the competing characterizations will come to one's lips in a particular case depends primarily upon one's evaluation of the worth of competing uses of real estate....

Where the State seeks to sustain regulation that deprives land of all economically beneficial use, we think it may resist compensation only if the logically antecedent inquiry into the nature of the owner's estate shows that the proscribed use interests were not part of his title to begin with.... This accords, we think, with our "takings" jurisprudence, which has traditionally been guided by the understandings of our citizens regarding the content of, and the State's power over, the "bundle of rights" that they acquire when they obtain title to property. It seems to us that the property owner necessarily expects the uses of his property to be restricted, from time to time, by various measures newly enacted by the State in legitimate exercise of its police powers; "as long recognized, some values are enjoyed under an implied limitation and must yield to the police power." Pennsylvania Coal Co. v. Mahon, 260 U.S. at 413.... In the case of land, however, we think the notion pressed by the Council that title is somehow held subject to the "implied limitation" that the State may subsequently eliminate all economically valuable use is inconsistent with the historical compact recorded in the Takings Clause that has become part of our constitutional culture.

.... [Where regulations prohibit all economically beneficial use of land, the government can sustain its regulation only by showing that the restriction] inheres in the title itself, in the restrictions that background principles of the State's law of property and nuisance already place upon land ownership. A law or decree with such an effect must, in other words, do no more than duplicate the result that could have been achieved in the courts—by adjacent landowners (or other uniquely affected persons) under the State's law of private nuisance, or by the State under its complementary power to abate nuisances that affect the public generally, or otherwise.

On this analysis, the owner of a lake bed, for example, would not be entitled to compensation when he is denied the requisite permit to engage

plete is not entitled to compensation. Such an owner might not be able to claim the benefit of our categorical formulation, but, as we have acknowledged time and again, "the economic impact of the regulation on the claimant and ... the extent to which the regulation has interfered with distinct investment-backed expectations" are keenly relevant to takings analysis generally....

in a landfilling operation that would have the effect of flooding others' land. Nor the corporate owner of a nuclear generating plant, when it is directed to remove all improvements from its land upon discovery that the plant sits astride an earthquake fault. Such regulatory action may well have the effect of eliminating the land's only economically productive use, but it does not proscribe a productive use that was previously permissible under relevant property and nuisance principles. The use of these properties for what are now expressly prohibited purposes was *always* unlawful, and (subject to other constitutional limitations) it was open to the State at any point to make the implication of those background principles of nuisance and property law explicit. In light of our traditional resort to "existing rules or understandings that stem from an independent source such as state law" to define the range of interests that qualify for protection as "property" under the Fifth and Fourteenth Amendments, this recognition that the Takings Clause does not require compensation when an owner is barred from putting land to a use that is proscribed by those "existing rules or understandings" is surely unexceptional. When, however, a regulation that declares "off-limits" all economically productive or beneficial uses of land goes beyond what the relevant background principles would dictate, compensation must be paid to sustain it.

The "total taking" inquiry we require today will ordinarily entail (as the application of state nuisance law ordinarily entails) analysis of, among other things, the degree of harm to public lands and resources, or adjacent private property, posed by the claimant's proposed activities, see, e.g., Restatement (Second) of Torts §§ 826, 827, the social value of the claimant's activities and their suitability to the locality in question, see, e.g., id., §§ 828(a) and (b), 831, and the relative ease with which the alleged harm can be avoided through measures taken by the claimant and the government (or adjacent private landowners) alike, see, e.g., id., §§ 827(e), 828(c), 830. The fact that a particular use has long been engaged in by similarly situated owners ordinarily imports a lack of any common-law prohibition (though changed circumstances or new knowledge may make what was previously permissible no longer so, see Restatement (Second) of Torts, supra, § 827, comment g). So also does the fact that other landowners, similarly situated, are permitted to continue the use denied to the claimant.

It seems unlikely that common-law principles would have prevented the erection of any habitable or productive improvements on petitioner's land; they rarely support prohibition of the "essential use" of land. The question, however, is one of state law to be dealt with on remand. We emphasize that to win its case South Carolina must do more than proffer the legislature's declaration that the uses Lucas desires are inconsistent with the public interest, or the conclusory assertion that they violate a common-law maxim such as *sic utere tuo ut alienum non laedas*. As we have said, a "State, by *ipse dixit*, may not transform private property into public property without compensation...." Webb's Fabulous Pharmacies, Inc. v. Beckwith, 449 U.S. 155, 164 (1980). Instead, as it would be required to do if it sought to restrain Lucas in a common-law action for public nuisance, South Carolina must identify background principles of nuisance and property law that prohibit the uses he now intends in the circumstances in which the property is presently found. Only on this showing can the State fairly claim that, in proscribing all such beneficial uses, the Beachfront Management Act is taking nothing.

The judgment is reversed and the cause remanded for proceedings not inconsistent with this opinion.

JUSTICE KENNEDY, concurring in the judgment.

.... Where a taking is alleged from regulations which deprive the property of all value, the test must be whether the deprivation is contrary to reasonable, investment-backed expectations.

In my view, reasonable expectations must be understood in light of the whole of our legal tradition. The common law of nuisance is too narrow a confine for the exercise of regulatory power in a complex and interdependent society. The State should not be prevented from enacting new regulatory initiatives in response to changing conditions, and courts must consider all reasonable expectations whatever their source. The Takings Clause does not require a static body of state property law; it protects private expectations to ensure private investment. I agree with the Court that nuisance prevention accords with the most common expectations of property owners who face regulation, but I do not believe this can be the sole source of state authority to impose severe restrictions. Coastal property may present such unique concerns for a fragile land system that the State can go further in regulating its development and use than the common law of nuisance might otherwise permit.

The Supreme Court of South Carolina erred, in my view, by reciting the general purposes for which the state regulations were enacted without a determination that they were in accord with the owner's reasonable expectations and therefore sufficient to support a severe restriction on specific parcels of property....

JUSTICE BLACKMUN, dissenting.

.... The Beachfront Management Act includes a finding by the South Carolina General Assembly that the beach/dune system serves the purpose of "protecting life and property by serving as a storm barrier which dissipates wave energy and contributes to shoreline stability in an economical and effective manner." The General Assembly also found that "development unwisely has been sited too close to the [beach/dune] system. This type of development has jeopardized the stability of the beach/dune system, accelerated erosion, and endangered adjacent property."

If the state legislature is correct that the prohibition on building in front of the setback line prevents serious harm, then, under this Court's prior cases, the Act is constitutional. "Long ago it was recognized that all property in this country is held under the implied obligation that the owner's use of it shall not be injurious to the community, and the Takings Clause did not transform that principle to one that requires compensation whenever the State asserts its power to enforce it." Keystone Bituminous Coal Assn. v. DeBenedictis, 480 U.S. 470, 491–492 (1987)....

The Court rejects the notion that the State always can prohibit uses it deems a harm to the public without granting compensation because "the distinction between harm-preventing' and benefit-conferring' regulation is often in the eye of the beholder." . . . . [However, in] determining what is a nuisance at common law, state courts make exactly the decision that the Court finds so troubling when made by the South Carolina General Assembly today: they determine whether the use is harmful. There is nothing magical in the reasoning of judges long dead. They determined a harm in the same way as state judges and legislatures do today. If judges in the 18th and 19th centuries can distinguish a harm from a benefit, why not judges in the 20th century, and if judges can, why not legislators? There simply is no reason to believe that new interpretations of the hoary common-law nuisance doctrine will be particularly "objective" or "value free." Once one abandons the level of generality of *sic utere tuo ut alienum non laedas, ante*, one searches in vain, I think, for anything resembling a principle in the common law of nuisance. . . .

JUSTICE STEVENS, dissenting.

. . . . The Court's holding today effectively freezes the State's common law, denying the legislature much of its traditional power to revise the law governing the rights and uses of property. Until today, I had thought that we had long abandoned this approach to constitutional law. More than a century ago we recognized that "the great office of statutes is to remedy defects in the common law as they are developed, and to adapt it to the changes of time and circumstances." Munn v. Illinois, 94 U.S. 113, 134 (1877). . . .

Arresting the development of the common law is not only a departure from our prior decisions; it is also profoundly unwise. The human condition is one of constant learning and evolution—both moral and practical. Legislatures implement that new learning; in doing so they must often revise the definition of property and the rights of property owners. Thus, when the Nation came to understand that slavery was morally wrong and mandated the emancipation of all slaves, it, in effect, redefined "property." On a lesser scale, our ongoing self-education produces similar changes in the rights of property owners: New appreciation of the significance of endangered species, the importance of wetlands, and the vulnerability of coastal lands shapes our evolving understandings of property rights.

Of course, some legislative redefinitions of property will effect a taking and must be compensated—but it certainly cannot be the case that every movement away from common law does so. There is no reason, and less sense, in such an absolute rule. We live in a world in which changes in the economy and the environment occur with increasing frequency and importance. If it was wise a century ago to allow Government "the largest legislative discretion" to deal with "the special exigencies of the moment," *Mugler*, 123 U.S. at 669, it is imperative to do so today. . . .

Notes & Questions

1. On remand, the South Carolina Supreme Court concluded that building on the two lots would not violate nuisance law or any other

common law doctrine and that the Beachfront Management Act's ban on construction was thus a taking of Lucas' property. Lucas v. South Carolina Coastal Council, 424 S.E.2d 484 (S.C. 1992). After paying Lucas $850,000 in compensation for the two lots, South Carolina proceeded to sell the lots to private parties for development. Large homes now sit on both lots. See Vicki Been, Lucas v. The Green Machine: Using the Takings Clause to Promote More Efficient Regulation?, in Property Stories 221 (Gerald Korngold & Andrew P. Morriss, eds. 2004).

2. **Fiscal Illusion.** Does South Carolina's decision to sell the two lots suggest that the Beachfront Management Act's original ban on construction was ill advised? One argument for requiring the government to provide compensation when its actions reduce the value of property is that the compensation will force the government to recognize and take into account the full costs of its actions. If the government does not have to pay compensation when it bans development of coastal property, for example, the government might ignore or underestimate the cost of that ban on private property owners—or, in the words of some articles, the government might suffer from "fiscal illusion." As a result, the government might decide to regulate property even though the monetary costs exceed the monetary benefits. Looked at in slightly different terms, forcing the government to pay compensation in these settings ensures that regulators "internalize" the cost of their actions. See, e.g., William A. Fischel, Takings and Public Choice: The Persuasion of Price, in The Encyclopedia of Public Choice 549 (Charles Kershaw Rowley, ed. 2003); Richard A. Posner, Economic Analysis of Law 54–57 (6th ed. 2003); Blume & Rubinfeld, Compensation for Takings: An Economic Analysis, 72 Calif. L. Rev. 569, 620–622 (1984). Will forcing the government to pay compensation really lead to better governmental decisionmaking? See Daryl J. Levinson, Making Government Pay: Markets, Politics, and the Allocation of Constitutional Costs, 67 U. Chi. L. Rev. 345 (2000).

3. **Protecting Barrier Islands.** The Supreme Court spends virtually no time in *Lucas* discussing the public policy lying behind the Beachfront Management Act. As Figure 13–3 shows, Lucas' lots were on one of a number of highly unstable barrier islands that line the coast of South Carolina and many other coastal states. As the beach on the Isle of Palms has built up, eroded, and built up again, the waterline has moved back and forth; the waterline at times has been significantly inland of Lucas' lots. What are the consequences of building on the beaches of barrier islands?

> Much of the East and Gulf coast is protected from the brunt of storms and their resultant destruction by narrow strips of sand and wetlands known as barrier islands. The 2,700 miles of barrier islands stretching along the coastline also buffer the mainland from the normal scour of waves and currents. However, coastal barrier islands are especially vulnerable to erosion since they follow a process that geologists refer to as island migration. These islands basically roll over themselves as sand, carried by storm waves during frequent flooding, is taken from the beach and offshore areas and is redistributed across the island.

Despite the fragile nature of barrier islands, these coastal areas have experienced widespread development as well.... On undeveloped beaches, although shorelines erode or accurate over time, a beach is generally healthy as long as it is permitted to move.... With increased population, income, and mobility, growing numbers of people have moved to the seashore in recent decades. Coastal areas have also been developed to meet the needs of the millions of seasonal visitors that flock to beaches.

Much of the beach erosion problem is linked to the growth in coastal development. The recent growth in coastal development, and some of the accompanying problems, are clearly illustrated at Myrtle Beach, the vacation Mecca for many summer sojourners along South Carolina's Grand Strand. Until the late 1950s most of the three mile stretch of beach that is now the center of Myrtle Beach was populated with cottages, set well back from the ocean. Through the 1960s and 1970s the cottages, along with the sand dunes separating them from the ocean, were replaced with the many motels that now crowd the beach. Locating too near to the

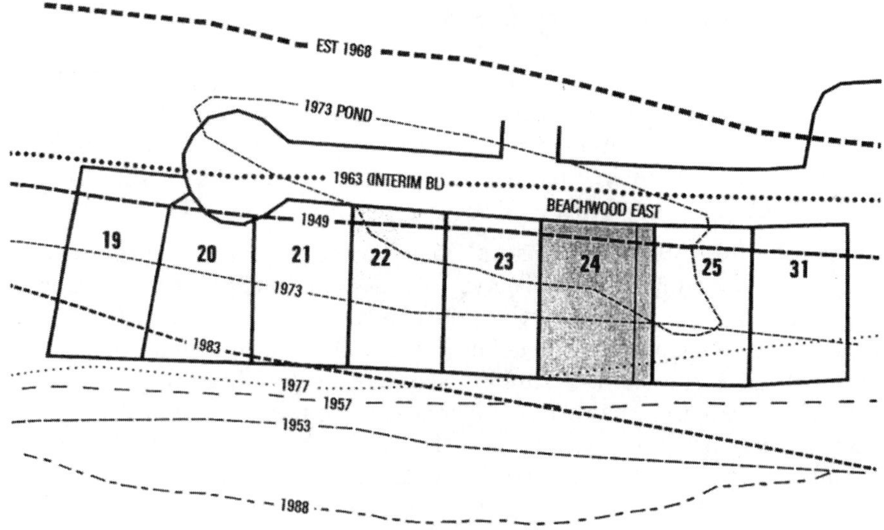

Figure 13–3
Map of Lucas Lots & Waterlines

(The various dotted lines show the local waterline in select years since 1949. Lucas owned lots 22 & 24.)

Source: Douglas R. Porter, The *Lucas* Case, Urb. Land, Sept. 1992, at 27, 29.

ocean and removing natural beach protection such as sand dunes and vegetation leads to erosion. Sand dunes, along with offshore sandbars, provide valuable reservoirs for beaches, replenishing sand that has been washed away. In addition to building closer to the ocean, many of the motels built seawalls to protect against the increased erosion, further exacerbating the problem of erosion. Construction near the beach also compacts the sand, which increases erosion.

Jeffrey Pompe, The Nature of Sand: South Carolina's Shifting Shoreline, S.C. Pol'y F. Mag., Summer 199, at 4.

4. **The Denominator Issue.** The *Lucas* opinion raises and leaves open a number of difficult questions for future litigation. First, what is the relevant parcel of property in determining whether the owner has been deprived of "all economically beneficial use"? For example, if a property owner buys a piece of property composed of two adjacent lots and the state prohibits her from building on one of the lots because it is a wetlands, has she been deprived of all use of one lot or only partial use of the entire parcel? Would it make any difference if the property were one lot, subdividable into two? One lot that is not subdividable?

Lower courts have not always found these questions easy. In 1988, for example, the Washington Supreme Court concluded that a court could split a piece of property into two or more parts for purposes of deciding whether a regulation had deprived one portion of so much economic value that it should have to pay compensation. See Allingham v. Seattle, 749 P.2d 160, 163 (Wash. 1988) Two years later, however, the court overruled *Allingham* and concluded that a parcel of regulated property must be examined "in its entirety" rather than in "pieces." Presbytery of Seattle v. King County, 787 P.2d 907, 914–915 (Wash. 1990).

5. **Economically Beneficial Use.** What does the Court mean by "*economically* beneficial use of land"? Must a property owner be deprived of all use of his land? Or does the Court mean something special by its use of the term "economically beneficial use"? And if so, what? The Court repeatedly uses the term or similar modifiers in its *Lucas* opinion, but the Court never explains the terms' relevance to the takings issue. Perhaps the Court meant merely to exclude uses that would be open to any member of the public (e.g., looking at the land or enjoying its undeveloped nature). But *Lucas* also suggests that a regulation can constitute a *per se* taking even though the property owner can make some minimal *private* use of his land. Lucas, after all, could still use his land for recreation, exclude the public from his land, and even build walkways, platforms, and perhaps even a tent on his land. Compare Loveladies Harbor, Inc. v. United States, 15 Cl. Ct. 381, 394–95 (1988) (test is whether regulation deprives owner of all "viable commercial *or recreational* uses").

6. **Partial Deprivations of Use.** Is there a taking if a property owner is deprived of *virtually* all of the "economically beneficial use" of his land, even if some economic value remains? If so, how much deprivation is needed? See Rith Energy v. United States, 270 F.3d 1347 (Fed. Cir. 2001)

(no categorical taking where 91% of property value lost due to regulation); Loveladies Harbor, Inc. v. United States, 15 Cl. Ct. 381 (1988) & 21 Cl. Ct. 153 (1990), aff'd, 28 F.3d 1171 (Fed. Cir. 1994) (denial of permit to develop wetlands under section 404 of the Clean Water Act was a taking where value declined 99 percent, even though remaining value of the wetlands was still $1000 per acre); Formanek v. United States, 26 Cl. Ct. 332 (1992) (permit denial that "rendered the property all but worthless" was a taking).

7. **Determining the Background Property Rights.** Does the Court mean to freeze the state common law of property and nuisance (except to the limited extent that applying preexisting legal rules to new knowledge can lead courts to different results)? If this is correct, must the Supreme Court police the decisions of state courts to make sure that they don't evade the takings rules by misstating or stretching the background principles of property law?

Stevens v. City of Cannon Beach, 510 U.S. 1207 (1994), raised this latter question. In *Stevens*, owners of beachfront Oregon property sued in inverse condemnation when the city and state denied a building permit for construction of a seawall on the dry-sand portion of their property. The Oregon courts dismissed the claim on the ground that, under State ex rel. Thornton v. Hay, 462 P.2d 671 (Ore. 1969), the owners never held the right to build a seawall; *Hay* had held that, under the common law doctrine of "custom," private landowners could not obstruct the public's right to use the dry-sand areas of Oregon beaches. (See p. 880 supra.) Although the Supreme Court denied certiorari, Justice Scalia (joined by Justice O'Connor) dissented. In Scalia's view, the Oregon court's application of "custom" looked surprisingly like a legal "fiction" that could not justify the regulation:

> As a general matter, the Constitution leaves the law of real property to the States. But just as a State may not deny rights protected under the Federal Constitution through pretextual procedural rulings, neither may it do so by invoking nonexistent rules of state substantive law. Our opinion in *Lucas*, for example, would be a nullity if anything that a State court chooses to denominate "background law"—regardless of whether it is really such—could eliminate property rights.... No more by judicial decree than by legislative fiat may a State transform private property into public property without compensation.... To say that this case raises a serious Fifth Amendment takings issue is an understatement. The issue is serious in the sense that it involves a holding of questionable constitutionality; and it is serious in the sense that the land-grab (if there is one) may run the entire length of the Oregon coast.

8. **Judicial Takings.** If a court all by itself changes the law of property in a way that deprives a property owner of all the economically viable use of her land, is this a taking? Assume, for example, that the common law in a state has never precluded the development of wetlands. If

the state supreme court now decides that building on a wetland is a private nuisance because of the flood risks to other property owners, is this a taking if it leaves a property owner without an economically viable use of her land? Is the Constitution's ban on the taking of private property without compensation only applicable to the legislature, or does it also apply to courts. In one of the few opinions to address this question, Justice Stewart suggested that a state "cannot be permitted to defeat the constitutional prohibition against taking property without due process of law by the simple device of asserting retroactively that the property it has taken never existed at all." Hughes v. Washington, 389 U.S. 290, 296–297 (1967) (Stewart, J., concurring). Do you agree? For thoughts on whether courts can "take" property, see W. David Sarratt, Judicial Takings and the Course Pursued, 90 Va. L. Rev. 1487 (2004); Barton H. Thompson, Jr., Judicial Takings, 76 Va. L. Rev. 1449 (1990).

9. **Lucas' Impact.** Given its narrow focus on regulations that have deprived landowners of *all* economic value, is *Lucas* likely to have much impact? In one study of state takings cases in the two and a half years after *Lucas*, Professor Ronald Rosenberg found that *Lucas* "has not had a major impact on the state courts and has not resulted in more than a trivial number of constitutional invalidations of state and local regulations." Ronald H. Rosenberg, The Non–Impact of the United States Supreme Court Regulatory Takings Cases on the State Courts: Does the Supreme Court Really Matter, 6 Fordham Envtl. L.J. 523, 548 (1995).

D. TAKINGS AND TIME

Time adds yet another level of complexity to regulatory takings law. If a governmental regulation permanently deprives a property owner of all the economic use of her property, that's a taking according to the *Lucas* decision. Is it still a taking if the regulation is only in place for a short period of time? Does it matter *why* the regulation is only temporary? Can a property owner ever claim a taking, moreover, when he purchases his land after the government has imposed the challenged regulation? What if the property owner purchases land before the government imposes the regulation, but the owner knew that the government was considering the regulation? Is there a "coming to the takings" defense similar to the "coming to the nuisance" defense studied in Chapter 2 at pages 164–165? The cases in this section explore these issues.

1. TAKINGS REMEDIES

First English Evangelical Lutheran Church v. County of Los Angeles. If a court concludes that a governmental regulation constitutes a taking, the government generally has two basic options. First, the government can keep the regulation in place and pay just compensation to affected property owners. Second, the government can repeal the regulation or, if it's possible, amend the regulation so that it's no longer a taking. If the government chooses to repeal or amend the regulation, is the property owner entitled to compensation for the period of time during which the regulation was in place?

The Supreme Court addressed this question in First English Evangelical Lutheran Church v. County of Los Angeles, 482 U.S. 304 (1987). In *First English*, the County of Los Angeles prohibited the First English Evangelical Lutheran Church from building on a parcel of land that presented a serious flood risk. The Church alleged that the Los Angeles County ordinance deprived it of all the use of its property and thus had taken the property. In an opinion written by Chief Justice Rehnquist, the Court concluded that, if a court ultimately held that the ordinance was indeed a taking, the Church would be entitled to just compensation for the period of time during which the ordinance was in effect, even if the county chose to repeal it. The Court began by noting that a number of World War II era Supreme Court cases had held that property owners are entitled to compensation when the government temporarily appropriates the owner's land for government use. See Kimball Laundry Co. v. United States, 338 U.S. 1 (1949); United States v. Petty Motor Co., 327 U.S. 372 (1946); United States v. General Motors Corp., 323 U.S. 373 (1945).

> These cases reflect the fact that "temporary" takings which, as here, deny a landowner all use of his property, are not different in kind from permanent takings, for which the Constitution clearly requires compensation. It is axiomatic that the Fifth Amendment's just compensation provision is "designed to bar Government from forcing some people alone to bear public burdens which, in all fairness and justice, should be borne by the public as a whole." Armstrong v. United States, 364 U.S. 40, 49 (1960). In the present case the . . . ordinance was adopted by the County of Los Angeles in January 1979, and became effective immediately. Appellant filed suit within a month after the effective date of the ordinance and yet when the California Supreme Court denied a hearing in the case on October 17, 1985, the merits of appellant's claim had yet to be determined. The United States has been required to pay compensation for leasehold interests of shorter duration than this. The value of a leasehold interest in property for a period of years may be substantial, and the burden on the property owner in extinguishing such an interest for a period of years may be great indeed. Where this burden results from governmental action that amounted to a taking, the Just Compensation Clause of the Fifth Amendment requires that the government pay the landowner for the value of the use of the land during this period. Invalidation of the ordinance or its successor ordinance after this period of time, though converting the taking into a "temporary" one, is not a sufficient remedy to meet the demands of the Just Compensation Clause. . . .
>
> Nothing we say today is intended to abrogate the principle that the decision to exercise the power of eminent domain is a

> legislative function "for Congress and Congress alone to determine." Hawaii Housing Authority v. Midkiff, 467 U.S. 229, 240 (1984), quoting Berman v. Parker, 348 U.S. 26, 33 (1954). Once a court determines that a taking has occurred, the government retains the whole range of options already available—amendment of the regulation, withdrawal of the invalidated regulation, or exercise of eminent domain. Thus we do not, as the Solicitor General suggests, "permit a court, at the behest of a private person, to require the ... Government to exercise the power of eminent domain...." We merely hold that where the government's activities have already worked a taking of all use of property, no subsequent action by the government can relieve it of the duty to provide compensation for the period during which the taking was effective.
>
> We also point out that the allegation of the complaint which we treat as true for purposes of our decision was that the ordinance in question denied appellant all use of its property. We limit our holding to the facts presented, and of course do not deal with the quite different questions that would arise in the case of normal delays in obtaining building permits, changes in zoning ordinances, variances, and the like which are not before us. We realize that even our present holding will undoubtedly lessen to some extent the freedom and flexibility of land-use planners and governing bodies of municipal corporations when enacting land-use regulations. But such consequences necessarily flow from any decision upholding a claim of constitutional right; many of the provisions of the Constitution are designed to limit the flexibility and freedom of governmental authorities, and the Just Compensation Clause of the Fifth Amendment is one of them. As Justice Holmes aptly noted more than 50 years ago, "a strong public desire to improve the public condition is not enough to warrant achieving the desire by a shorter cut than the constitutional way of paying for the change." Pennsylvania Coal Co. v. Mahon, 260 U.S., at 416.

482 U.S. at 318–322.

Justice Stevens, writing for himself and Justices Blackmun and O'Connor, dissented. Stevens began by conceding that physical takings require compensation even if only temporary.

> But our cases also make it clear that regulatory takings and physical takings are very different in this, as well as other, respects. While virtually all physical invasions are deemed takings, a regulatory program that adversely affects property values does not constitute a taking unless it destroys a major portion of the property's value. This diminution of value inquiry is unique to regulatory takings. Unlike physical invasions, which are relatively rare and easily identifiable without making any economic analysis, regulatory programs constantly affect property values in countless ways, and only the most extreme regulations can constitute tak-

> ings. Some dividing line must be established between everyday regulatory inconveniences and those so severe that they constitute takings. The diminution of value inquiry has long been used in identifying that line. As Justice Holmes put it: "Government hardly could go on if to some extent values incident to property could not be diminished without paying for every such change in the general law." *Pennsylvania Coal*, 260 U.S. at 413. It is this basic distinction between regulatory and physical takings that the Court ignores today.
>
> Regulations are three dimensional; they have depth, width, and length. As for depth, regulations define the extent to which the owner may not use the property in question. With respect to width, regulations define the amount of property encompassed by the restrictions. Finally, and for purposes of this case, essentially, regulations set forth the duration of the restrictions. It is obvious that no one of these elements can be analyzed alone to evaluate the impact of a regulation, and hence to determine whether a taking has occurred. For example, in *Keystone Bituminous* we declined to focus in on any discrete segment of the coal in the petitioners' mines, but rather looked to the effect that the restriction had on their entire mining project. Similarly, in *Penn Central*, the Court concluded that it was error to focus on the nature of the uses which were prohibited without also examining the many profitable uses to which the property could still be put. Both of these factors are essential to a meaningful analysis of the economic effect that regulations have on the value of property and on an owner's reasonable investment-based expectations with respect to the property.
>
> Just as it would be senseless to ignore these first two factors in assessing the economic effect of a regulation, one cannot conduct the inquiry without considering the duration of the restriction. For example, while I agreed with the Chief Justice's view that the permanent restriction on building involved in *Penn Central* constituted a taking, I assume that no one would have suggested that a temporary freeze on building would have also constituted a taking. Similarly, I am confident that even the dissenters in *Keystone Bituminous* would not have concluded that the restriction on bituminous coal mining would have constituted a taking had it simply required the mining companies to delay their operations until an appropriate safety inspection could be made....

482 U.S. at 329–331.

Justice Stevens also worried about the potential impact that the Court's ruling would have on land use planners:

> The policy implications of today's decision are obvious and, I fear, far reaching. Cautious local officials and land-use planners may avoid taking any action that might later be challenged and

> thus give rise to a damages action. Much important regulation will never be enacted,[17] even perhaps in the health and safety area. Were this result mandated by the Constitution, these serious implications would have to be ignored. But the loose cannon the Court fires today is not only unattached to the Constitution, but it also takes aim at a long line of precedents in the regulatory takings area. It would be the better part of valor simply to decide the case at hand instead of igniting the kind of litigation explosion that this decision will undoubtedly touch off.

482 U.S. at 339.

Erroneous Takings. Assume that the government denies Jim Bridger the right to build on his property because they mistakenly believe that Jim's land is in the critical habitat for endangered red legged frogs. After consulting their maps, the government realizes that Jim's lot falls outside the critical habitat and allows him to proceed with his development plans. If it took the government two months to realize its mistake, should Jim be entitled to compensation under *First English*? Most state courts have concluded that mistaken assertions of governmental jurisdiction do not justify compensation. See, e.g., Landgate, Inc. v. California Coastal Comm'n, 953 P.2d 1188 (Cal. 1998). Is there any reason to distinguish mistaken jurisdiction cases from *First English*?

2. "TEMPORARY TAKINGS" AND MORATORIA

Tahoe–Sierra Preservation Council v. Tahoe Regional Planning Agency

Supreme Court of the United States, 2002.
535 U.S. 302.

JUSTICE STEVENS delivered the opinion of the Court.

The question presented is whether a moratorium on development imposed during the process of devising a comprehensive land-use plan constitutes a *per se* taking of property requiring compensation under the Takings Clause of the United States Constitution. This case actually involves two moratoria ordered by respondent Tahoe Regional Planning Agency (TRPA) to maintain the status quo while studying the impact of development on Lake Tahoe and designing a strategy for environmentally sound growth. The first, Ordinance 81–5, was effective from August 24, 1981, until August 26, 1983, whereas the second more restrictive Resolution 83–21 was in effect from August 27, 1983, until April 25, 1984. As a

17. It is no answer to say that "after all, if a policeman must know the Constitution, then why not a planner?" San Diego Gas & Electric Co. v. San Diego, 450 U.S. 621, 661, n.26 (1981) (Brennan, J., dissenting). To begin with, the Court has repeatedly recognized that it itself cannot establish any objective rules to assess when a regulation becomes a taking. How then can it demand that land planners do any better? However confusing some of our criminal procedure cases may be, I do not believe they have been as open-ended and standardless as our regulatory takings cases are. . . .

result of these two directives, virtually all development on a substantial portion of the property subject to TRPA's jurisdiction was prohibited for a period of 32 months. Although the question we decide relates only to that 32–month period, a brief description of the events leading up to the moratoria and a comment on the two permanent plans that TRPA adopted thereafter will clarify the narrow scope of our holding.

I

The relevant facts are undisputed. The Court of Appeals, while reversing the District Court on a question of law, accepted all of its findings of fact, and no party challenges those findings. All agree that Lake Tahoe is "uniquely beautiful," that President Clinton was right to call it a " 'national treasure that must be protected and preserved,' " and that Mark Twain aptly described the clarity of its waters as "not *merely* transparent, but dazzlingly, brilliantly so" (quoting M. Twain, Roughing It 174–175 (1872)).

Lake Tahoe's exceptional clarity is attributed to the absence of algae that obscures the waters of most other lakes. Historically, the lack of nitrogen and phosphorous, which nourish the growth of algae, has ensured the transparency of its waters. Unfortunately, the lake's pristine state has deteriorated rapidly over the past 40 years; increased land development in the Lake Tahoe Basin (Basin) has threatened the "noble sheet of blue water" beloved by Twain and countless others. As the District Court found, "dramatic decreases in clarity first began to be noted in the 1950's/early 1960's, shortly after development at the lake began in earnest." The lake's unsurpassed beauty, it seems, is the wellspring of its undoing.

The upsurge of development in the area has caused "increased nutrient loading of the lake largely because of the increase in impervious coverage of land in the Basin resulting from that development."

"Impervious coverage—such as asphalt, concrete, buildings, and even packed dirt—prevents precipitation from being absorbed by the soil. Instead, the water is gathered and concentrated by such coverage. Larger amounts of water flowing off a driveway or a roof have more erosive force than scattered raindrops falling over a dispersed area—especially one covered with indigenous vegetation, which softens the impact of the raindrops themselves."

Given this trend, the District Court predicted that "unless the process is stopped, the lake will lose its clarity and its trademark blue color, becoming green and opaque for eternity."[3]

Those areas in the Basin that have steeper slopes produce more runoff; therefore, they are usually considered "high hazard" lands. Moreover, certain areas near streams or wetlands known as "Stream Environment Zones" (SEZs) are especially vulnerable to the impact of development because, in their natural state, they act as filters for much of the debris

3. The District Court added: "Or at least, for a very, very long time. Estimates are that, should the lake turn green, it could take over 700 years for it to return to its natural state, if that were ever possible at all."

that runoff carries. Because "the most obvious response to this problem . . . is to restrict development around the lake—especially in SEZ lands, as well as in areas already naturally prone to runoff," conservation efforts have focused on controlling growth in these high hazard areas.

In the 1960's, when the problems associated with the burgeoning development began to receive significant attention, jurisdiction over the Basin, which occupies 501 square miles, was shared by the States of California and Nevada, five counties, several municipalities, and the Forest Service of the Federal Government. In 1968, the legislatures of the two States adopted the Tahoe Regional Planning Compact, which Congress approved in 1969. The compact set goals for the protection and preservation of the lake and created TRPA as the agency assigned "to coordinate and regulate development in the Basin and to conserve its natural resources."

Pursuant to the compact, in 1972 TRPA adopted a Land Use Ordinance that divided the land in the Basin into seven "land capability districts," based largely on steepness but also taking into consideration other factors affecting runoff. Each district was assigned a "land coverage coefficient—a recommended limit on the percentage of such land that could be covered by impervious surface." Those limits ranged from 1% for districts 1 and 2 to 30% for districts 6 and 7. Land in districts 1, 2, and 3 is characterized as "high hazard" or "sensitive," while land in districts 4, 5, 6, and 7 is "low hazard" or "non-sensitive." The SEZ lands, though often treated as a separate category, were actually a subcategory of district 1.

Unfortunately, the 1972 ordinance allowed numerous exceptions and did not significantly limit the construction of new residential housing. California became so dissatisfied with TRPA that it withdrew its financial support and unilaterally imposed stricter regulations on the part of the Basin located in California. Eventually the two States, with the approval of Congress and the President, adopted an extensive amendment to the compact that became effective on December 19, 1980. Pub. L. 96–551, 94 Stat. 3233.

The 1980 Tahoe Regional Planning Compact (Compact) redefined the structure, functions, and voting procedures of TRPA and directed it to develop regional "environmental threshold carrying capacities"—a term that embraced "standards for air quality, water quality, soil conservation, vegetation preservation and noise." 94 Stat. 3235, 3239. The Compact provided that TRPA "shall adopt" those standards within 18 months, and that "within 1 year after" their adoption (i.e., by June 19, 1983), it "shall" adopt an amended regional plan that achieves and maintains those carrying capacities. Id. at 3240. The Compact also contained a finding by the Legislatures of California and Nevada "that in order to make effective the regional plan as revised by [TRPA], it is necessary to halt temporarily works of development in the region which might otherwise absorb the entire capability of the region for further development or direct it out of harmony with the ultimate plan." Id. at 3243. Accordingly, for the period prior to the adoption of the final plan ("or until May 1, 1983, whichever is earlier"), the Compact itself prohibited the development of new subdivisions, condominiums, and apartment buildings, and also prohibited each city and county in the Basin from granting any more permits in 1981, 1982, or 1983 than had been granted in 1978.

During this period TRPA was also working on the development of a regional water quality plan to comply with the Clean Water Act, 33 U.S.C. § 1288 (1994 ed.). Despite the fact that TRPA performed these obligations in "good faith and to the best of its ability," after a few months it concluded that it could not meet the deadlines in the Compact. On June 25, 1981, it therefore enacted Ordinance 81–5 imposing the first of the two moratoria on development that petitioners challenge in this proceeding. The ordinance provided that it would become effective on August 24, 1981, and remain in effect pending the adoption of the permanent plan required by the Compact....

Given the complexity of the task of defining "environmental threshold carrying capacities" and the division of opinion within TRPA's governing board, the District Court found that it was "unsurprising" that TRPA failed to adopt those thresholds until August 26, 1982, roughly two months after the Compact deadline. Under a liberal reading of the Compact, TRPA then had until August 26, 1983, to adopt a new regional plan. 94 Stat. 3240. "Unfortunately, but again not surprisingly, no regional plan was in place as of that date." TRPA therefore adopted Resolution 83–21, "which completely suspended all project reviews and approvals, including the acceptance of new proposals," and which remained in effect until a new regional plan was adopted on April 26, 1984. Thus, Resolution 83–21 imposed an 8–month moratorium prohibiting all construction on high hazard lands in either State. In combination, Ordinance 81–5 and Resolution 83–21 effectively prohibited all construction on sensitive lands in California and on all SEZ lands in the entire Basin for 32 months, and on sensitive lands in Nevada (other than SEZ lands) for eight months. It is these two moratoria that are at issue in this case.

On the same day that the 1984 plan was adopted, the State of California filed an action seeking to enjoin its implementation on the ground that it failed to establish land-use controls sufficiently stringent to protect the Basin. The District Court entered an injunction that was upheld by the Court of Appeals and remained in effect until a completely revised plan was adopted in 1987. Both the 1984 injunction and the 1987 plan contained provisions that prohibited new construction on sensitive lands in the Basin. As the case comes to us, however, we have no occasion to consider the validity of those provisions.

II

Approximately two months after the adoption of the 1984 Plan, petitioners filed parallel actions against TRPA and other defendants in federal courts in Nevada and California that were ultimately consolidated for trial in the District of Nevada. The petitioners include the Tahoe Sierra Preservation Council, a nonprofit membership corporation representing about

2,000 owners of both improved and unimproved parcels of real estate in the Lake Tahoe Basin, and a class of some 400 individual owners of vacant lots located either on SEZ lands or in other parts of districts 1, 2, or 3. Those individuals purchased their properties prior to the effective date of the 1980 Compact, primarily for the purpose of constructing "at a time of their choosing" a single-family home "to serve as a permanent, retirement or vacation residence." When they made those purchases, they did so with the understanding that such construction was authorized provided that "they complied with all reasonable requirements for building."....

III

Petitioners make only a facial attack on Ordinance 81–5 and Resolution 83–21. They contend that the mere enactment of a temporary regulation that, while in effect, denies a property owner all viable economic use of her property gives rise to an unqualified constitutional obligation to compensate her for the value of its use during that period. Hence, they "face an uphill battle," Keystone Bituminous Coal Ass'n v. DeBenedictis, 480 U.S. 470, 495 (1987), that is made especially steep by their desire for a categorical rule requiring compensation whenever the government imposes such a moratorium on development. Under their proposed rule, there is no need to evaluate the landowners' investment-backed expectations, the actual impact of the regulation on any individual, the importance of the public interest served by the regulation, or the reasons for imposing the temporary restriction. For petitioners, it is enough that a regulation imposes a temporary deprivation—no matter how brief—of all economically viable use to trigger a *per se* rule that a taking has occurred. Petitioners assert that our opinions in *First English* and *Lucas* have already endorsed their view, and that it is a logical application of the principle that the Takings Clause was "designed to bar Government from forcing some people alone to bear burdens which, in all fairness and justice, should be borne by the public as a whole." Armstrong v. United States, 364 U.S. 40, 49 (1960)....

IV

.... As we noted in *Lucas,* it was Justice Holmes' opinion in Pennsylvania Coal Co. v. Mahon, 260 U.S. 393 (1922), that gave birth to our regulatory takings jurisprudence.... In the decades following that decision, we have "generally eschewed" any set formula for determining how far is too far, choosing instead to engage in " 'essentially ad hoc, factual inquiries.' " *Lucas*, 505 U.S. at 1015 (quoting *Penn Central,* 438 U.S. at 124). Indeed, we still resist the temptation to adopt *per se* rules in our cases involving partial regulatory takings, preferring to examine "a number of factors" rather than a simple "mathematically precise" formula. Justice Brennan's opinion for the Court in *Penn Central* did, however, make it clear that even though multiple factors are relevant in the analysis of regulatory takings claims, in such cases we must focus on "the parcel as a whole":

" 'Taking' jurisprudence does not divide a single parcel into discrete segments and attempt to determine whether rights in a particular segment have been entirely abrogated. In deciding whether a particular governmental action has effected a taking, this Court focuses rather both on the character of the action and on the nature and extent of the interference with rights in the parcel as a whole—here, the city tax block designated as the 'landmark site.' " 438 U.S. at 130–131.

This requirement that "the aggregate must be viewed in its entirety" explains why, for example, a regulation that prohibited commercial transactions in eagle feathers, but did not bar other uses or impose any physical invasion or restraint upon them, was not a taking. Andrus v. Allard, 444 U.S. 51, 66 (1979). It also clarifies why restrictions on the use of only limited portions of the parcel, such as set-back ordinances, Gorieb v. Fox, 274 U.S. 603 (1927), or a requirement that coal pillars be left in place to prevent mine subsidence, Keystone Bituminous Coal Ass'n v. DeBenedictis, 480 U.S. at 498, were not considered regulatory takings. In each of these cases, we affirmed that "where an owner possesses a full 'bundle' of property rights, the destruction of one 'strand' of the bundle is not a taking." Andrus, 444 U.S. at 65–66.

While the foregoing cases considered whether particular regulations had "gone too far" and were therefore invalid, none of them addressed the separate remedial question of how compensation is measured once a regulatory taking is established. [*First English* held that governments must pay compensation for a temporary regulation that it decides to rescind after a court holds that the regulation is a taking.] *First English* was certainly a significant decision, and nothing that we say today qualifies its holding. Nonetheless, it is important to recognize that we did not address in that case the quite different and logically prior question whether the temporary regulation at issue had in fact constituted a taking.

In *First English*, the Court unambiguously and repeatedly characterized the issue to be decided as a "compensation question" or a "remedial question." 482 U.S. at 311. . . . And the Court's statement of its holding was equally unambiguous: "We merely hold that where the government's activities *have already worked a taking* of all use of property, no subsequent action by the government can relieve it of the duty to provide compensation for the period during which the taking was effective." Id. at 321 (emphasis added). . . .

The categorical rule that we applied in *Lucas* states that compensation is required when a regulation deprives an owner of "*all* economically beneficial uses" of his land. 505 U.S. at 1019. Under that rule, a statute that "wholly eliminated the value" of Lucas' fee simple title clearly qualified as a taking. But our holding was limited to "the extraordinary circumstance when *no* productive or economically beneficial use of land is permitted." Id. at 1017. . . .

Certainly, our holding that the permanent "obliteration of the value" of a fee simple estate constitutes a categorical taking does not answer the question whether a regulation prohibiting any economic use of land for a 32-month period has the same legal effect. Petitioners seek to bring this case under the rule announced in *Lucas* by arguing that we can effectively sever a 32-month segment from the remainder of each landowner's fee simple estate, and then ask whether that segment has been taken in its entirety by the moratoria. Of course, defining the property interest taken in terms of the very regulation being challenged is circular. With property so divided, every delay would become a total ban; the moratorium and the normal permit process alike would constitute categorical takings. Petitioners' "conceptual severance" argument is unavailing because it ignores *Penn Central*'s admonition that in regulatory takings cases we must focus on "the parcel as a whole." 438 U.S. at 130–131. . . .

An interest in real property is defined by the metes and bounds that describe its geographic dimensions and the term of years that describes the temporal aspect of the owner's interest. Both dimensions must be considered if the interest is to be viewed in its entirety. Hence, a permanent deprivation of the owner's use of the entire area is a taking of "the parcel as a whole," whereas a temporary restriction that merely causes a diminution in value is not. Logically, a fee simple estate cannot be rendered valueless by a temporary prohibition on economic use, because the property will recover value as soon as the prohibition is lifted. . . .

V

. . . . In rejecting petitioners' *per se* rule, we do not hold that the temporary nature of a land-use restriction precludes finding that it effects a taking; we simply recognize that it should not be given exclusive significance one way or the other.

A narrower rule that excluded the normal delays associated with processing permits, or that covered only delays of more than a year, would certainly have a less severe impact on prevailing practices, but it would still impose serious financial constraints on the planning process. Unlike the "extraordinary circumstance" in which the government deprives a property owner of all economic use, *Lucas*, 505 U.S. at 1017, moratoria like Ordinance 81–5 and Resolution 83–21 are used widely among land-use planners to preserve the status quo while formulating a more permanent development strategy. In fact, the consensus in the planning community appears to be that moratoria, or "interim development controls" as they are often called, are an essential tool of successful development. . . .

The interest in facilitating informed decisionmaking by regulatory agencies counsels against adopting a *per se* rule that would impose such severe costs on their deliberations. Otherwise, the financial constraints of compensating property owners during a moratorium may force officials to rush through the planning process or to abandon the practice altogether. To the extent that communities are forced to abandon using moratoria, landowners will have incentives to develop their property quickly before a comprehensive plan can be enacted, thereby fostering inefficient and ill-conceived growth. . . .

CHIEF JUSTICE REHNQUIST, with whom JUSTICE SCALIA and JUSTICE THOMAS join, dissenting.

For over half a decade petitioners were prohibited from building homes, or any other structures, on their land. Because the Takings Clause requires the government to pay compensation when it deprives owners of all economically viable use of their land, see Lucas v. South Carolina Coastal Council, 505 U.S. 1003 (1992), and because a ban on all development lasting almost six years does not resemble any traditional land-use planning device, I dissent.

.... *Lucas* reaffirmed our "frequently expressed" view that "when the owner of real property has been called upon to sacrifice *all* economically beneficial uses in the name of the common good, that is, to leave his property economically idle, he has suffered a taking." 505 U.S. at 1019.... The Court does not dispute that petitioners were forced to leave their land economically idle during this period. But the Court refuses to apply *Lucas* on the ground that the deprivation was "temporary."

Neither the Takings Clause nor our case law supports such a distinction. For one thing, a distinction between "temporary" and "permanent" prohibitions is tenuous. The "temporary" prohibition in this case that the Court finds is not a taking lasted almost six years. The "permanent" prohibition that the Court held to be a taking in *Lucas* lasted less than two years. The "permanent" prohibition in *Lucas* lasted less than two years because the law, as it often does, changed. The South Carolina Legislature in 1990 decided to amend the 1988 Beachfront Management Act to allow the issuance of " 'special permits' for the construction or reconstruction of habitable structures seaward of the baseline." Id. at 1011–1012. Land-use regulations are not irrevocable.... Under the Court's decision today, the takings question turns entirely on the initial label given a regulation, a label that is often without much meaning. There is every incentive for government to simply label any prohibition on development "temporary," or to fix a set number of years. As in this case, this initial designation does not preclude the government from repeatedly extending the "temporary" prohibition into a long-term ban on all development. The Court now holds that such a designation by the government is conclusive even though in fact the moratorium greatly exceeds the time initially specified. Apparently, the Court would not view even a 10–year moratorium as a taking under *Lucas* because the moratorium is not "permanent."

More fundamentally, even if a practical distinction between temporary and permanent deprivations were plausible, to treat the two differently in terms of takings law would be at odds with the justification for the *Lucas* rule. The *Lucas* rule is derived from the fact that a "total deprivation of use is, from the landowner's point of view, the equivalent of a physical appropriation." 505 U.S. at 1017. The regulation in *Lucas* was the "practical equivalence" of a long-term physical appropriation, i.e., a condemnation, so the Fifth Amendment required compensation. The "practical equivalence," from the landowner's point of view, of a "temporary" ban on all economic use is a forced leasehold. For example, assume the following situation: Respondent is contemplating the creation of a National Park around Lake Tahoe to preserve its scenic beauty. Respondent decides to take a 6–year leasehold over petitioners' property, during which any human activity on the land would be prohibited, in order to prevent any further destruction to the area while it was deciding whether to request that the area be designated a National Park.

Surely that leasehold would require compensation. In a series of World War II-era cases in which the Government had condemned leasehold interests in order to support the war effort, the Government conceded that it was required to pay compensation for the leasehold interest. See United States v. Petty Motor Co., 327 U.S. 372 (1946); United States v. General Motors Corp., 323 U.S. 373, 376 (1945). From petitioners' standpoint, what happened in this case is no different than if the government had taken a 6–year lease of their property. The Court ignores this "practical equivalence" between respondent's deprivation and the deprivation resulting from a leasehold. In so doing, the Court allows the government to "do by regulation what it cannot do through eminent domain—i.e., take private property without paying for it." 228 F.3d 998, 999 (CA9 2000) (Kozinski, J., dissenting from denial of rehearing en banc)....

The Court worries that applying *Lucas* here compels finding that an array of traditional, short-term, land-use planning devices are takings. But since the beginning of our regulatory takings jurisprudence, we have recognized that property rights "are enjoyed under an implied limitation." Pennsylvania Coal v. Mahon, 260 U.S. 393, 413 (1922). Thus, in *Lucas*, after holding that the regulation prohibiting all economically beneficial use of the coastal land came within our categorical takings rule, we nonetheless inquired into whether such a result "inhered in the title itself, in the restrictions that background principles of the State's law of property and nuisance already place upon land ownership." 505 U.S. at 1029....

When a regulation merely delays a final land use decision, we have recognized that there are other background principles of state property law that prevent the delay from being deemed a taking. We thus noted in *First English* that our discussion of temporary takings did not apply "in the case of normal delays in obtaining building permits, changes in zoning ordinances, variances, and the like." 482 U.S. at 321.... But a moratorium prohibiting all economic use for a period of six years is not one of the longstanding, implied limitations of state property law....

Lake Tahoe is a national treasure and I do not doubt that respondent's efforts at preventing further degradation of the lake were made in good faith in furtherance of the public interest. But, as is the case with most governmental action that furthers the public interest, the Constitution requires that the costs and burdens be borne by the public at large, not by a few targeted citizens. Justice Holmes' admonition of 80 years ago again rings true: "We are in danger of forgetting that a strong public desire to improve the public condition is not enough to warrant achieving the desire by a shorter cut than the constitutional way of paying for the change." *Mahon*, 260 U.S. at 416.

[The separate dissenting opinion of JUSTICE THOMAS is omitted.]

Notes & Questions

1. Is *Tahoe–Sierra* consistent with *First English*? Note that Justice Stevens, who wrote the dissent in *First English*, wrote the majority opinion in *Tahoe–Sierra*, and that Chief Justice Rehnquist, who wrote the majority opinion in *First English*, wrote the dissent in *Tahoe–Sierra*.

2. If a moratorium lasts long enough, will it ultimately become a taking? If so, how should a court determine when a moratorium reaches that point? Note that some landowners were still unable to develop their Tahoe properties at the time *Tahoe–Sierra* reached the Supreme Court.

3. *Tahoe–Sierra* returns once again to the question that has confronted courts since *Pennsylvania Coal*—should courts ever separate out portions of a property right and look at just one portion in deciding whether there has been a taking? Professor Peggy Radin has called this "conceptual severance." See Margaret Jane Radin, The Liberal Conception of Property: Cross Currents in the Jurisprudence of Takings, 88 Colum. L. Rev. 1667 (1988). In the case of physical takings, the answer has always been that the physical appropriation of just a portion of a property owner's land—or the appropriation of the land for a limited period of time—is a taking for which compensation should be paid. Does *Tahoe–Sierra* settle the question once and for all that in the case of regulatory takings, courts should always look at the whole parcel?

4. For interesting insights into *Tahoe–Sierra* and the issues that it raises, see Steven J. Eagle, Planning Moratoria and Regulatory Takings: The Supreme Court's Fairness Mandate Benefits Landowners, 31 Fla. St. U.L. Rev. 429 (2004); Danaya C. Wright, A New Time for Denominators: Toward a Dynamic Theory of Property in the Regulatory Takings Relevant Parcel Analysis, 34 Envtl. L. 175 (2004).

3. Coming to the Regulation

Palazzolo v. Rhode Island

Supreme Court of the United States, 2001.
533 U.S. 606.

Justice Kennedy delivered the opinion of the Court.

Petitioner Anthony Palazzolo owns a waterfront parcel of land in the town of Westerly, Rhode Island. Almost all of the property is designated as coastal wetlands under Rhode Island law. After petitioner's development proposals were rejected by respondent Rhode Island Coastal Resources Management Council (Council), he sued in state court, asserting the Council's application of its wetlands regulations took the property without compensation in violation of the Takings Clause of the Fifth Amendment, binding upon the State through the Due Process Clause of the Fourteenth

Amendment. Petitioner sought review in this Court, contending the Supreme Court of Rhode Island erred in rejecting his takings claim. We granted certiorari....

In 1959 petitioner, a lifelong Westerly resident, decided to invest in three undeveloped, adjoining parcels along [the] eastern stretch of Atlantic Avenue. To the north, the property faces, and borders upon, Winnapaug Pond; the south of the property faces Atlantic Avenue and the beachfront homes abutting it on the other side, and beyond that the dunes and the beach. To purchase and hold the property, petitioner and associates formed Shore Gardens, Inc. (SGI). After SGI purchased the property petitioner bought out his associates and became the sole shareholder. In the first decade of SGI's ownership of the property the corporation submitted a plat to the town subdividing the property into 80 lots; and it engaged in various transactions that left it with 74 lots, which together encompassed about 20 acres. During the same period SGI also made initial attempts to develop the property and submitted intermittent applications to state agencies to fill substantial portions of the parcel. Most of the property was then, as it is now, salt marsh subject to tidal flooding. The wet ground and permeable soil would require considerable fill—as much as six feet in some places—before significant structures could be built. SGI's proposal, submitted in 1962 to the Rhode Island Division of Harbors and Rivers (DHR), sought to dredge from Winnapaug Pond and fill the entire property. The application was denied for lack of essential information. A second, similar proposal followed a year later. A third application, submitted in 1966 while the second application was pending, proposed more limited filling of the land for use as a private beach club. These latter two applications were referred to the Rhode Island Department of Natural Resources, which indicated initial assent. The agency later withdrew approval, however, citing adverse environmental impacts. SGI did not contest the ruling.

No further attempts to develop the property were made for over a decade. Two intervening events, however, become important to the issues presented. First, in 1971, Rhode Island enacted legislation creating the Council, an agency charged with the duty of protecting the State's coastal properties. Regulations promulgated by the Council designated salt marshes like those on SGI's property as protected "coastal wetlands," on which development is limited to a great extent. Second, in 1978 SGI's corporate charter was revoked for failure to pay corporate income taxes; and title to the property passed, by operation of state law, to petitioner as the corporation's sole shareholder.

In 1983 petitioner, now the owner, renewed the efforts to develop the property. An application to the Council, resembling the 1962 submission, requested permission to construct a wooden bulkhead along the shore of Winnapaug Pond and to fill the entire marsh land area. The Council rejected the application, noting it was "vague and inadequate for a project of this size and nature." The agency also found that "the proposed activities will have significant impacts upon the waters and wetlands of Winnapaug Pond," and concluded that "the proposed alteration ... will conflict with the Coastal Resources Management Plan presently in effect." Petitioner did not appeal the agency's determination.

Petitioner went back to the drawing board, this time hiring counsel and preparing a more specific and limited proposal for use of the property. The new application, submitted to the Council in 1985, echoed the 1966 request to build a private beach club. The details do not tend to inspire the reader with an idyllic coastal image, for the proposal was to fill 11 acres of the property with gravel to accommodate "50 cars with boat trailers, a dumpster, port-a-johns, picnic tables, barbecue pits of concrete, and other trash receptacles."

The application fared no better with the Council than previous ones. Under the agency's regulations, a landowner wishing to fill salt marsh on Winnapaug Pond needed a "special exception" from the Council. In a short opinion the Council said the beach club proposal conflicted with the regulatory standard for a special exception. To secure a special exception the proposed activity must serve "a compelling public purpose which provides benefits to the public as a whole as opposed to individual or private interests." This time petitioner appealed the decision to the Rhode Island courts, challenging the Council's conclusion as contrary to principles of state administrative law. The Council's decision was affirmed.

Petitioner filed an inverse condemnation action in Rhode Island Superior Court, asserting that the State's wetlands regulations, as applied by the Council to his parcel, had taken the property without compensation in violation of the Fifth and Fourteenth Amendments. The suit alleged the Council's action deprived him of "all economically beneficial use" of his property, resulting in a total taking requiring compensation under Lucas v. South Carolina Coastal Council, 505 U.S. 1003 (1992). He sought damages in the amount of $3,150,000, a figure derived from an appraiser's estimate as to the value of a 74–lot residential subdivision. The State countered with a host of defenses. After a bench trial, a justice of the Superior Court ruled against petitioner, accepting some of the State's theories.

The Rhode Island Supreme Court affirmed. Like the Superior Court, the State Supreme Court recited multiple grounds for rejecting petitioner's suit. The court held, first, that petitioner's takings claim was not ripe; second, that petitioner had no right to challenge regulations predating 1978, when he succeeded to legal ownership of the property from SGI; and third, that the claim of deprivation of all economically beneficial use was contradicted by undisputed evidence that he had $200,000 in development value remaining on an upland parcel of the property. In addition to holding petitioner could not assert a takings claim based on the denial of all economic use the court concluded he could not recover under the more general test of Penn Central Transp. Co. v. New York City, 438 U.S. 104 (1978). On this claim, too, the date of acquisition of the parcel was found determinative, and the court held he could have had "no reasonable investment-backed expectations that were affected by this regulation" because it predated his ownership.

We disagree with the Supreme Court of Rhode Island as to the first two of these conclusions; and, we hold, the court was correct to conclude that the owner is not deprived of all economic use of his property because the value of upland portions is substantial. We remand for further consideration of the claim under the principles set forth in *Penn Central*....

[The Court started by deciding that Palazzolo's claim was ripe for consideration.]

We turn to the second asserted basis for declining to address petitioner's takings claim on the merits. When the Council promulgated its wetlands regulations, the disputed parcel was owned not by petitioner but by the corporation of which he was sole shareholder. When title was transferred to petitioner by operation of law, the wetlands regulations were in force. The state court held the postregulation acquisition of title was fatal to the claim for deprivation of all economic use and to the *Penn Central* claim. While the first holding was couched in terms of background principles of state property law, see *Lucas,* 505 U.S. at 1015, and the second in terms of petitioner's reasonable investment-backed expectations, see *Penn Central,* 438 U.S. at 124, the two holdings together amount to a single, sweeping, rule: A purchaser or a successive title holder like petitioner is deemed to have notice of an earlier-enacted restriction and is barred from claiming that it effects a taking.

The theory underlying the argument that post-enactment purchasers cannot challenge a regulation under the Takings Clause seems to run on these lines: Property rights are created by the State. So, the argument goes, by prospective legislation the State can shape and define property rights and reasonable investment-backed expectations, and subsequent owners cannot claim any injury from lost value. After all, they purchased or took title with notice of the limitation.

The State may not put so potent a Hobbesian stick into the Lockean bundle. The right to improve property, of course, is subject to the reasonable exercise of state authority, including the enforcement of valid zoning and land-use restrictions. The Takings Clause, however, in certain circumstances allows a landowner to assert that a particular exercise of the State's regulatory power is so unreasonable or onerous as to compel compensation. Just as a prospective enactment, such as a new zoning ordinance, can limit the value of land without effecting a taking because it can be understood as reasonable by all concerned, other enactments are unreasonable and do not become less so through passage of time or title. Were we to accept the State's rule, the postenactment transfer of title would absolve the State of its obligation to defend any action restricting land use, no matter how extreme or unreasonable. A State would be allowed, in effect, to put an expiration date on the Takings Clause. This ought not to be the rule. Future generations, too, have a right to challenge unreasonable limitations on the use and value of land.

Nor does the justification of notice take into account the effect on owners at the time of enactment, who are prejudiced as well. Should an owner attempt to challenge a new regulation, but not survive the process of ripening his or her claim (which, as this case demonstrates, will often take years), under the proposed rule the right to compensation may not by asserted by an heir or successor, and so may not be asserted at all. The State's rule would work a critical alteration to the nature of property, as the newly regulated landowner is stripped of the ability to transfer the interest which was possessed prior to the regulation. The State may not by this means secure a windfall for itself. See Webb's Fabulous Pharmacies, Inc. v. Beckwith, 449 U.S. 155, 164 (1980) ("[A] State, by *ipse dixit*, may not transform private property into public property without compensation"); cf. Ellickson, Property in Land, 102 Yale L. J. 1315, 1368–1369 (1993) (right to transfer interest in land is a defining characteristic of the fee simple estate). The proposed rule is, furthermore, capricious in effect. The young owner contrasted with the older owner, the owner with the resources to hold contrasted with the owner with the need to sell, would be in different positions. The Takings Clause is not so quixotic. A blanket rule that purchasers with notice have no compensation right when a claim becomes ripe is too blunt an instrument to accord with the duty to compensate for what is taken.

Direct condemnation, by invocation of the State's power of eminent domain, presents different considerations than cases alleging a taking based on a burdensome regulation. In a direct condemnation action, or when a State has physically invaded the property without filing suit, the fact and extent of the taking are known. In such an instance, it is a general rule of the law of eminent domain that any award goes to the owner at the time of the taking, and that the right to compensation is not passed to a subsequent purchaser. A challenge to the application of a land-use regulation, by contrast, does not mature until ripeness requirements have been satisfied, under principles we have discussed; until this point an inverse condemnation claim alleging a regulatory taking cannot be maintained. It would be illogical, and unfair, to bar a regulatory takings claim because of the post-enactment transfer of ownership where the steps necessary to make the claim ripe were not taken, or could not have been taken, by a previous owner....

We have no occasion to consider the precise circumstances when a legislative enactment can be deemed a background principle of state law or whether those circumstances are present here. It suffices to say that a regulation that otherwise would be unconstitutional absent compensation is not transformed into a background principle of the State's law by mere virtue of the passage of title. This relative standard would be incompatible with our description of the concept in *Lucas,* which is explained in terms of those common, shared understandings of permissible limitations derived from a State's legal tradition, see *Lucas*, supra, at 1029–1030. A regulation or common-law rule cannot be a background principle for some owners but not for others. The determination whether an existing, general law can limit all economic use of property must turn on objective factors, such as the nature of the land use proscribed. See *Lucas*, supra, at 1030 ("The 'total taking' inquiry we require today will ordinarily entail ... analysis of, among other things, the degree of harm to public lands and resources, or adjacent private property, posed by the claimant's proposed activities"). A law does not become a background principle for subsequent owners by enactment itself. . . .

For reasons we discuss next, the state court will not find it necessary to explore these matters on remand in connection with the claim that all economic use was deprived; it must address, however, the merits of petitioner's claim under *Penn Central.* That claim is not barred by the mere fact that title was acquired after the effective date of the state-imposed restriction.

As the case is ripe, and as the date of transfer of title does not bar petitioner's takings claim, we have before us the alternative ground relied upon by the Rhode Island Supreme Court in ruling upon the merits of the takings claims. It held that all economically beneficial use was not deprived because the uplands portion of the property can still be improved. On this point, we agree with the court's decision. Petitioner accepts the Council's contention and the state trial court's finding that his parcel retains $200,000 in development value under the State's wetlands regulations. He asserts, nonetheless, that he has suffered a total taking and contends the Council cannot sidestep the holding in *Lucas* "by the simple expedient of leaving a landowner a few crumbs of value."

Assuming a taking is otherwise established, a State may not evade the duty to compensate on the premise that the landowner is left with a token interest. This is not the situation of the landowner in this case, however. A regulation permitting a landowner to build a substantial residence on an 18–acre parcel does not leave the property "economically idle." *Lucas*, supra, at 1019.

In his brief submitted to us petitioner attempts to revive this part of his claim by reframing it. He argues, for the first time, that the upland parcel is distinct from the wetlands portions, so he should be permitted to assert a deprivation limited to the latter. This contention asks us to examine the difficult, persisting question of what is the proper denominator in the takings fraction. Some of our cases indicate that the extent of deprivation effected by a regulatory action is measured against the value of the parcel as a whole, see, e.g., Keystone Bituminous Coal Assn. v. DeBenedictis, 480 U.S. 470, 497 (1987); but we have at times expressed discomfort with the logic of this rule, see *Lucas*, supra, at 1016–1017, n.7, a sentiment echoed by some commentators, see, e.g., Epstein, Takings: Descent and Resurrection, 1987 Sup. Ct. Rev. 1, 16–17 (1987); Fee, Unearthing the Denominator in Regulatory Takings Claims, 61 U. Chi. L. Rev. 1535 (1994). Whatever the merits of these criticisms, we will not explore the point here. Petitioner did not press the argument in the state courts, and the issue was not presented in the petition for certiorari. The case comes to us on the premise that petitioner's entire parcel serves as the basis for his takings claim, and, so framed, the total deprivation argument fails.

For the reasons we have discussed, the State Supreme Court erred in finding petitioner's claims were unripe and in ruling that acquisition of title after the effective date of the regulations barred the takings claims.

The court did not err in finding that petitioner failed to establish a deprivation of all economic value, for it is undisputed that the parcel retains significant worth for construction of a residence. The claims under the *Penn Central* analysis were not examined, and for this purpose the case should be remanded.

The judgment of the Rhode Island Supreme Court is affirmed in part and reversed in part, and the case is remanded for further proceedings not inconsistent with this opinion.

Justice O'Connor, concurring.

. . . . Today's holding does not mean that the timing of the regulation's enactment relative to the acquisition of title is immaterial to the *Penn Central* analysis. Indeed, it would be just as much error to expunge this consideration from the takings inquiry as it would be to accord it exclusive significance. Our polestar instead remains the principles set forth in *Penn Central* itself and our other cases that govern partial regulatory takings. Under these cases, interference with investment-backed expectations is one of a number of factors that a court must examine. Further, the regulatory regime in place at the time the claimant acquires the property at issue helps to shape the reasonableness of those expectations. . . .

If investment-backed expectations are given exclusive significance in the *Penn Central* analysis and existing regulations dictate the reasonableness of those expectations in every instance, then the State wields far too much power to redefine property rights upon passage of title. On the other hand, if existing regulations do nothing to inform the analysis, then some property owners may reap windfalls and an important indicium of fairness is lost. As I understand it, our decision today does not remove the regulatory backdrop against which an owner takes title to property from the purview of the *Penn Central* inquiry. It simply restores balance to that inquiry. Courts properly consider the effect of existing regulations under the rubric of investment-backed expectations in determining whether a compensable taking has occurred. As before, the salience of these facts cannot be reduced to any "set formula." The temptation to adopt what amount to *per se* rules in either direction must be resisted. The Takings Clause requires careful examination and weighing of all the relevant circumstances in this context. The court below therefore must consider on remand the array of relevant factors under *Penn Central* before deciding whether any compensation is due.

Justice Scalia, concurring.

I write separately to make clear that my understanding of how the issues discussed in . . . the Court's opinion must be considered on remand is not Justice O'Connor's.

The principle that underlies her separate concurrence is that it may in some (unspecified) circumstances be "unfai[r]," and produce unacceptable "windfalls," to allow a subsequent purchaser to nullify an unconstitutional partial taking (though, inexplicably, not an unconstitutional total taking) by the government. The polar horrible, presumably, is the situation in which a sharp real estate developer, realizing (or indeed, simply gambling on) the unconstitutional excessiveness of a development restriction that a naive landowner assumes to be valid, purchases property at what it would be worth subject to the restriction, and then develops it to its full value (or resells it at its full value) after getting the unconstitutional restriction invalidated.

This can, I suppose, be called a windfall—though it is not much different from the windfalls that occur every day at stock exchanges or antique auctions, where the knowledgeable (or the venturesome) profit at the expense of the ignorant (or the risk averse). There is something to be said (though in my view not much) for pursuing abstract "fairness" by requiring part or all of that windfall to be returned to the naive original owner, who presumably is the "rightful" owner of it. But there is nothing to be said for giving it instead to the *government*—which not only did not lose something it owned, but is both the *cause* of the miscarriage of "fairness" and the only one of the three parties involved in the miscarriage (government, naive original owner, and sharp real estate developer) which *acted unlawfully*—indeed *unconstitutionally*. Justice O'Connor would eliminate the windfall by giving the malefactor the benefit of its malefaction. It is rather like eliminating the windfall that accrued to a purchaser who bought property at a bargain rate from a thief clothed with the indicia of title, by making him turn over the "unjust" profit *to the thief*.

In my view, the fact that a restriction existed at the time the purchaser took title (other than a restriction forming part of the "background principles of the State's law of property and nuisance," Lucas v. South Carolina Coastal Council, 505 U.S. 1003, 1029 (1992)) should have no bearing upon the determination of whether the restriction is so substantial as to constitute a taking. The "investment-backed expectations" that the law will take into account do not include the assumed validity of a restriction that in fact deprives property of so much of its value as to be unconstitutional. Which is to say that a *Penn Central* taking, see Penn Central Transp. Co. v. New York City, 438 U.S. 104 (1978), no less than a total taking, is not absolved by the transfer of title.

JUSTICE STEVENS, concurring in part and dissenting in part.

....

To the extent that the adoption of the regulations constitute the challenged taking, petitioner is simply the wrong party to be bringing this action. If the regulations imposed a compensable injury on anyone, it was on the owner of the property at the moment the regulations were adopted. Given the trial court's finding that petitioner did not own the property at that time, in my judgment it is pellucidly clear that he has no standing to claim that the promulgation of the regulations constituted a taking of any part of the property that he subsequently acquired.

His lack of standing does not depend, as the Court seems to assume, on whether or not petitioner "is deemed to have notice of an earlier-enacted restriction." If those early regulations changed the character of the owner's title to the property, thereby diminishing its value, petitioner acquired only the net value that remained after that diminishment occurred. Of course, if, as respondent contends, even the prior owner never had any right to fill wetlands, there never was a basis for the alleged takings claim in the first place. But accepting petitioner's theory of the case, he has no standing to complain that preacquisition events may have reduced the value of the property that he acquired.... A new owner may maintain an ejectment action against a trespasser who has lodged himself in the owner's orchard but surely could not recover damages for fruit a trespasser spirited from the orchard before he acquired the property....

[The dissenting opinions of JUSTICE GINSBURG, with whom JUSTICES SOUTER and BREYER joined, and of JUSTICE BREYER, are omitted.]

Notes & Questions

1. On remand, the Rhode Island Superior Court found that there was no taking of Palazzolo's property under *Penn Central* for three reasons. First, Palazzolo's proposed development would be an "ecological disaster" and thus a public nuisance; Palazzolo therefore had no right to develop his property as he proposed. Second, Palazzolo's property was subject to the public trust doctrine, limiting his reasonable investment-backed expectations. Finally, the court concluded that Palazzolo's property had not lost any value because developing the property for multiple homes would have encountered serious engineering difficulties. Selling the land for a single house, which was permitted, would still bring Palazzolo about $200,000. See Palazzolo v. Rhode Island, 2005 WL 1645974 (R.I. Super. Ct. July 5, 2005).[1]

2. Note that the United States Supreme Court in *Palazzolo* chooses not to address the property owner's argument that the wetlands upon which he was prohibited from building was "distinct" from the rest of his property and thus could be the focus alone of a *Lucas* inquiry. Does this mean that the "whole parcel" issue, seemingly closed after Tahoe–Sierra (see p. 1169, Note 3), is open for debate again?

3. How would you address the issue of notice and investment-backed expectations in *Palazzolo*? How should courts treat property owners who purchase their land after a regulatory scheme is in effect? What if the regulatory system was not yet in place when they purchased their property but they should have reasonably anticipated the change? On remand in *Palazzolo*, the Rhode Island Superior Court found that the existence of a "well publicized and growing nationwide movement toward the preservation of ecologically valuable sites during the last half of the twentieth century," among other factors, limited Palazzolo's reasonable investment-backed expectations.

1. The Rhode Island Superior Court's decision is available on the web at http://www.courts.state.ri.us/superior/pdf/880297.pdf

4. For insights into *Palazzolo* and the question of notice, see Holly Doremus, Takings and Transitions, 19 J. Land Use & Envtl. L. 1 (2003); Daniel R. Mandelker, The Notice Rule in Investment-Backed Expectations, in Taking Sides on the Takings Issue: Public and Private Perspectives 21 (Thomas E. Roberts, ed. 2002). Steven J. Eagle, The 1997 Regulatory Takings Quartet: Retreating from the "Rule of Law," 42 N.Y.L. Sch. L. Rev. 345 (1998).

E. EXACTIONS

Local governments often condition proposed real estate development on either the developer's provision of various public goods (e.g., the dedication of land for a public school, or the construction and dedication of utility lines) or the payment of a fee to be used to fund such goods. Such exactions sometimes raise constitutional concerns, as the following Supreme Court case demonstrates.

Nollan v. California Coastal Commission

United States Supreme Court, 1987.
483 U.S. 825.

JUSTICE SCALIA delivered the opinion of the Court.

James and Marilyn Nollan appeal from a decision of the California Court of Appeal ruling that the California Coastal Commission could condition its grant of permission to rebuild their house on their transfer to the public of an easement across their beachfront property. . . .

The Nollans own a beachfront lot in Ventura County, California. A quarter-mile north of their property is Faria County Park, an oceanside public park with a public beach and recreation area. Another public beach area, known locally as "the Cove," lies 1,800 feet south of their lot. A concrete seawall approximately eight feet high separates the beach portion of the Nollans' property from the rest of the lot. The historic mean high tide line determines the lot's oceanside boundary.

The Nollans originally leased their property with an option to buy. The building on the lot was a small bungalow, totaling 504 square feet, which for a time they rented to summer vacationers. After years of rental use, however, the building had fallen into disrepair, and could no longer be rented out.

The Nollans' option to purchase was conditioned on their promise to demolish the bungalow and replace it. In order to do so, under Cal. Pub. Res. Code Ann. §§ 30106, 30212, and 30600, they were required to obtain a coastal development permit from the California Coastal Commission. On February 25, 1982, they submitted a permit application to the Commission in which they proposed to demolish the existing structure and replace it with a three-bedroom house in keeping with the rest of the neighborhood.

The Nollans were informed that their application had been placed on the administrative calendar, and that the Commission staff had recommended that the permit be granted subject to the condition that they allow the public an easement to pass across a portion of their property bounded by the mean high tide line on one side, and their seawall on the other side. This would make it easier for the public to get to Faria County Park and the Cove. The Nollans protested imposition of the condition, but the Commission overruled their objections and granted the permit subject to their recordation of a deed restriction granting the easement. . . .

Had California simply required the Nollans to make an easement across their beachfront available to the public on a permanent basis in order to increase public access to the beach, rather than conditioning their permit to rebuild their house on their agreeing to do so, we have no doubt there would have been a taking. . . . In *Loretto* we observed that where governmental action results in "[a] permanent physical occupation" of the property, by the government itself or by others, "our cases uniformly have found a taking to the extent of the occupation, without regard to whether the action achieves an important public benefit or has only minimal economic impact on the owner," 458 U.S. at 434–435. We think a "permanent physical occupation" has occurred, for purposes of that rule, where individuals are given a permanent and continuous right to pass to and fro, so that the real property may continuously be traversed, even though no particular individual is permitted to station himself permanently upon the premises. . . .[2]

Given, then, that requiring uncompensated conveyance of the easement outright would violate the Fourteenth Amendment, the question becomes whether requiring it to be conveyed as a condition for issuing a land-use permit alters the outcome. We have long recognized that land-use regulation does not effect a taking if it "substantially advance[s] legitimate state interests" and does not "den[y] an owner economically viable use of his land," Agins v. Tiburon, 447 U.S. 255, 260 (1980). Our cases have not elaborated on the standards for determining what constitutes a "legitimate state interest" or what type of connection between the regulation and the state interest satisfies the requirement that the former "substantially advance" the latter. They have made clear, however, that a broad range of governmental purposes and regulations satisfies these requirements. See Agins v. Tiburon, supra, at 260–262 (scenic zoning); Penn Central Transportation Co. v. New York City, 438 U.S. 104 (1978) (landmark preservation); Euclid v. Ambler Realty Co., 272 U.S. 365 (1926) (residential zoning); Laitos & Westfall, Government Interference with Private Interests in Public Resources, 11 Harv. Envtl. L. Rev. 1, 66 (1987). The Commission argues that among these permissible purposes are protecting the public's

2. . . . . Nor are the Nollans' rights altered because they acquired the land well after the Commission had begun to implement its policy. So long as the Commission could not have deprived the prior owners of the easement without compensating them, the prior owners must be understood to have transferred their full property rights in conveying the lot.

ability to see the beach, assisting the public in overcoming the "psychological barrier" to using the beach created by a developed shorefront, and preventing congestion on the public beaches. We assume, without deciding, that this is so—in which case the Commission unquestionably would be able to deny the Nollans their permit outright if their new house (alone, or by reason of the cumulative impact produced in conjunction with other construction)[4] would substantially impede these purposes, unless the denial would interfere so drastically with the Nollans' use of their property as to constitute a taking.

The Commission argues that a permit condition that serves the same legitimate police-power purpose as a refusal to issue the permit should not be found to be a taking if the refusal to issue the permit would not constitute a taking. We agree. Thus, if the Commission attached to the permit some condition that would have protected the public's ability to see the beach notwithstanding construction of the new house—for example, a height limitation, a width restriction, or a ban on fences—so long as the Commission could have exercised its police power (as we have assumed it could) to forbid construction of the house altogether, imposition of the condition would also be constitutional. Moreover (and here we come closer to the facts of the present case), the condition would be constitutional even if it consisted of the requirement that the Nollans provide a viewing spot on their property for passersby with whose sighting of the ocean their new house would interfere. Although such a requirement, constituting a permanent grant of continuous access to the property, would have to be considered a taking if it were not attached to a development permit, the Commission's assumed power to forbid construction of the house in order to protect the public's view of the beach must surely include the power to condition construction upon some concession by the owner, even a concession of property rights, that serves the same end. If a prohibition designed to accomplish that purpose would be a legitimate exercise of the police power rather than a taking, it would be strange to conclude that providing the owner an alternative to that prohibition which accomplishes the same purpose is not.

The evident constitutional propriety disappears, however, if the condition substituted for the prohibition utterly fails to further the end advanced as the justification for the prohibition. When that essential nexus is eliminated, the situation becomes the same as if California law forbade shouting fire in a crowded theater, but granted dispensations to those willing to contribute $100 to the state treasury. While a ban on shouting fire can be a core exercise of the State's police power to protect the public

4. If the Nollans were being singled out to bear the burden of California's attempt to remedy these problems, although they had not contributed to it more than other coastal landowners, the State's action, even if otherwise valid, might violate either the incorporated Takings Clause or the Equal Protection Clause. One of the principal purposes of the Takings Clause is "to bar Government from forcing some people alone to bear public burdens which, in all fairness and justice, should be borne by the public as a whole." Armstrong v. United States, 364 U.S. 40, 49 (1960). But that is not the basis of the Nollans' challenge here.

safety, and can thus meet even our stringent standards for regulation of speech, adding the unrelated condition alters the purpose to one which, while it may be legitimate, is inadequate to sustain the ban. Therefore, even though, in a sense, requiring a $100 tax contribution in order to shout fire is a lesser restriction on speech than an outright ban, it would not pass constitutional muster. Similarly here, the lack of nexus between the condition and the original purpose of the building restriction converts that purpose to something other than what it was. The purpose then becomes, quite simply, the obtaining of an easement to serve some valid governmental purpose, but without payment of compensation. Whatever may be the outer limits of "legitimate state interests" in the takings and land-use context, this is not one of them. In short, unless the permit condition serves the same governmental purpose as the development ban, the building restriction is not a valid regulation of land use but "an out-and-out plan of extortion." J. E. D. Associates, Inc. v. Atkinson, 121 N. H. 581, 584, 432 A.2d 12, 14–15 (1981).

The Commission claims that it concedes as much, and that we may sustain the condition at issue here by finding that it is reasonably related to the public need or burden that the Nollans' new house creates or to which it contributes. We can accept, for purposes of discussion, the Commission's proposed test as to how close a "fit" between the condition and the burden is required, because we find that this case does not meet even the most untailored standards. The Commission's principal contention to the contrary essentially turns on a play on the word "access." The Nollans' new house, the Commission found, will interfere with "visual access" to the beach. That in turn (along with other shorefront development) will interfere with the desire of people who drive past the Nollans' house to use the beach, thus creating a "psychological barrier" to "access." The Nollans' new house will also, by a process not altogether clear from the Commission's opinion but presumably potent enough to more than offset the effects of the psychological barrier, increase the use of the public beaches, thus creating the need for more "access." These burdens on "access" would be alleviated by a requirement that the Nollans provide "lateral access" to the beach.

Rewriting the argument to eliminate the play on words makes clear that there is nothing to it. It is quite impossible to understand how a requirement that people already on the public beaches be able to walk across the Nollans' property reduces any obstacles to viewing the beach created by the new house. It is also impossible to understand how it lowers any "psychological barrier" to using the public beaches, or how it helps to remedy any additional congestion on them caused by construction of the Nollans' new house. We therefore find that the Commission's imposition of the permit condition cannot be treated as an exercise of its land-use power for any of these purposes. . . .

Reversed.

JUSTICE BRENNAN, with whom JUSTICE MARSHALL joins, dissenting.

Appellants in this case sought to construct a new dwelling on their beach lot that would both diminish visual access to the beach and move private development closer to the public tidelands. The Commission reasonably concluded that such "buildout," both individually and cumulatively, threatens public access to the shore. It sought to offset this encroachment by obtaining assurance that the public may walk along the shoreline in order to gain access to the ocean. The Court finds this an illegitimate exercise of the police power, because it maintains that there is no reasonable relationship between the effect of the development and the condition imposed....

Even if we accept the Court's unusual demand for a precise match between the condition imposed and the specific type of burden on access created by the appellants, the State's action easily satisfies this requirement. First, the lateral access condition serves to dissipate the impression that the beach that lies behind the wall of homes along the shore is for private use only. It requires no exceptional imaginative powers to find plausible the Commission's point that the average person passing along the road in front of a phalanx of imposing permanent residences, including the appellants' new home, is likely to conclude that this particular portion of the shore is not open to the public. If, however, that person can see that numerous people are passing and repassing along the dry sand, this conveys the message that the beach is in fact open for use by the public. Furthermore, those persons who go down to the public beach a quarter-mile away will be able to look down the coastline and see that persons have continuous access to the tidelands, and will observe signs that proclaim the public's right of access over the dry sand. The burden produced by the diminution in visual access—the impression that the beach is not open to the public—is thus directly alleviated by the provision for public access over the dry sand. The Court therefore has an unrealistically limited conception of what measures could reasonably be chosen to mitigate the burden produced by a diminution of visual access.

The second flaw in the Court's analysis of the fit between burden and exaction is more fundamental. The Court assumes that the only burden with which the Coastal Commission was concerned was blockage of visual access to the beach. This is incorrect. The Commission specifically stated in its report in support of the permit condition that "the Commission finds that the applicants' proposed development would present an increase in view blockage, *an increase in private use of the shorefront*, and that this impact would burden the public's ability to traverse to and along the shorefront." It declared that the possibility that "the public may get the impression that the beachfront is no longer available for public use" would be "due to *the encroaching nature of private use immediately adjacent to the public use, as well as* the visual 'block' of increased residential build-out impacting the visual quality of the beachfront" (emphasis added)....

The deed restriction on which permit approval was conditioned would directly address this threat to the public's access to the tidelands. It would provide a formal declaration of the public's right of access, thereby ensuring that the shifting character of the tidelands, and the presence of private development immediately adjacent to it, would not jeopardize enjoyment of that right....

[The dissenting opinions of Justice Blackman and Justice Stevens is omitted.]

Notes & Questions

1. The Court in *Nollan* seems to hold that, if a regulation does not "substantially advance" a "legitimate state interest," it is an unconstitutional taking. What does the relationship between a regulation and legitimate governmental goals have to do with whether a regulation is a taking? Isn't the relationship really a question of substantive due process? In Lingle v. Chevron U.S.A. Inc., 544 U.S. 528 (2005), Hawaii, concerned about high gasoline prices, passed a law that limited the rent oil companies could charge gasoline dealers that leased stations from the companies. In a challenge to the law brought by Chevron, a federal district court held that the law was an unconstitutional taking because it did not substantially advance Hawaii's asserted interest in controlling retail gas prices. The Supreme Court disagreed. While acknowledging that prior opinions had suggested that regulations are takings if they don't substantially advance a legitimate state interest, the Court concluded that these opinions had been wrong:

> The "substantially advances" formula suggests a means-ends test: It asks, in essence, whether a regulation of private property is *effective* in achieving some legitimate public purpose. An inquiry of this nature has some logic in the context of a due process challenge, for a regulation that fails to serve any legitimate governmental objective may be so arbitrary or irrational that it runs afoul of the Due Process Clause. But such a test is not a valid method of discerning whether private property has been "taken" for purposes of the Fifth Amendment.
>
> In stark contrast to [the Court's other] regulatory takings tests ..., the "substantially advances" inquiry reveals nothing about the *magnitude or character of the burden* a particular regulation imposes upon private property rights. Nor does it provide any information about how any regulatory burden is *distributed* among property owners. In consequence, this test does not help to identify those regulations whose effects are functionally comparable to government appropriation or invasion of private property; it is tethered neither to the text of the Takings Clause nor to the basic justification for allowing regulatory actions to be challenged under the Clause.
>
> Finally, the "substantially advances" formula is not only *doctrinally* untenable as a takings test—its application as such would also present serious practical difficulties. [Some of our prior opinions] can be read to demand heightened means-ends review of

> virtually any regulation of private property. If so interpreted, it would require courts to scrutinize the efficacy of a vast array of state and federal regulations—a task for which courts are not well suited. Moreover, it would empower—and might often require—courts to substitute their predictive judgments for those of elected legislatures and expert agencies.
>
> Twenty-five years ago, the Court posited that a regulation of private property "effects a taking if [it] does not substantially advance [a] legitimate state interest." Agins v. City of Tiburon, 447 U.S. 255, 260 (1980). The lower courts in this case took that statement to its logical conclusion, and in so doing, revealed its imprecision. Today we correct course. We hold that the "substantially advances" formula is not a valid takings test, and indeed conclude that it has no proper place in our takings jurisprudence. In so doing, we reaffirm that a plaintiff seeking to challenge a government regulation as an uncompensated taking of private property may proceed under one of the other theories discussed [in our prior cases]—by alleging a "physical" taking, a *Lucas*-type "total regulatory taking," a *Penn Central* taking, or a land-use exaction violating the standards set forth in *Nollan* and *Dolan*.

Id. at 542–548. See D. Benjamin Barros, At Last, Some Clarity: The Potential Long–Term Impact of *Lingle v. Chevron* and the Separation of Takings and Substantive Due Process, 69 Alb. L. Rev. 343 (2005). For earlier thoughts on the role of substantive due process in takings inquiries, see Ronald J. Krotoszynski, Jr., Expropriatory Intent: Defining the Proper Boundaries of Substantive Due Process and the Takings Clause, 80 N.C. L. Rev. 713 (2002); Steven J. Eagle, Substantive Due Process and Regulatory Takings: A Reappraisal, 51 Ala. L. Rev. 977 (2000); Edward J. Sullivan, Emperors and Clothes: The Genealogy and Operation of the *Agins*' Tests, 33 Urb. Law. 343 (2001);

2. At the heart of *Nollan*, is there a disagreement among the justices about the typical motivations of local legislators and officials? If so, how can courts resolve this disagreement? Does the Constitution itself embody one view or the other?

3. Is *Nollan* likely to help or hurt property owners interested in developing their property? Could California constitutionally have decided that the Nollans could not build a new structure on their property? If so, isn't it better for the Nollans to permit the State to condition the construction of a new house? See generally Lee Anne Fennell, Hard Bargains and Real Steals: Land Use Exactions Revisited, 86 Iowa L. Rev. 1 (2000).

Dolan v. City of Tigard

United States Supreme Court, 1994.
512 U.S. 374.

CHIEF JUSTICE REHNQUIST delivered the opinion of the Court.

Petitioner challenges the decision of the Oregon Supreme Court which held that the city of Tigard could condition the approval of her building permit on the dedication of a portion of her property for flood control and traffic improvements. We granted certiorari to resolve a question left open by our decision in Nollan v. California Coastal Comm'n, 483 U.S. 825 (1987), of what is the required degree of connection between the exactions imposed by the city and the projected impacts of the proposed development.

The State of Oregon enacted a comprehensive land use management program in 1973. The program required all Oregon cities and counties to adopt new comprehensive land use plans that were consistent with the statewide planning goals. . . . Pursuant to the State's requirements, the city of Tigard, a community of some 30,000 residents on the southwest edge of Portland, developed a comprehensive plan and codified it in its Community Development Code (CDC). The CDC requires property owners in the area zoned Central Business District to comply with a 15% open space and landscaping requirement, which limits total site coverage, including all structures and paved parking, to 85% of the parcel. After the completion of a transportation study that identified congestion in the Central Business District as a particular problem, the city adopted a plan for a pedestrian/bicycle pathway intended to encourage alternatives to automobile transportation for short trips. The CDC requires that new development facilitate this plan by dedicating land for pedestrian pathways where provided for in the pedestrian/bicycle pathway plan.

The city also adopted a Master Drainage Plan (Drainage Plan). The Drainage Plan noted that flooding occurred in several areas along Fanno Creek, including areas near petitioner's property. The Drainage Plan also established that the increase in impervious surfaces associated with continued urbanization would exacerbate these flooding problems. To combat these risks, the Drainage Plan suggested a series of improvements to the Fanno Creek Basin, including channel excavation in the area next to petitioner's property. Other recommendations included ensuring that the floodplain remains free of structures and that it be preserved as greenways to minimize flood damage to structures. The Drainage Plan concluded that the cost of these improvements should be shared based on both direct and indirect benefits, with property owners along the water-ways paying more due to the direct benefit that they would receive.

Petitioner Florence Dolan owns a plumbing and electric supply store located on Main Street in the Central Business District of the city. The store covers approximately 9,700 square feet on the eastern side of a 1.67–acre parcel, which includes a gravel parking lot. Fanno Creek flows through the southwestern corner of the lot and along its western boundary. The year-round flow of the creek renders the area within the creek's 100–year floodplain virtually unusable for commercial development. The city's comprehensive plan includes the Fanno Creek floodplain as part of the city's greenway system.

Petitioner applied to the city for a permit to redevelop the site. Her proposed plans called for nearly doubling the size of the store to 17,600 square feet and paving a 39–space parking lot. The existing store, located on the opposite side of the parcel, would be razed in sections as construction progressed on the new building. In the second phase of the project, petitioner proposed to build an additional structure on the northeast side of the site for complementary businesses and to provide more parking. The proposed expansion and intensified use are consistent with the city's zoning scheme in the Central Business District.

The City Planning Commission (Commission) granted petitioner's permit application subject to conditions imposed by the city's CDC.... Thus, the Commission required that petitioner dedicate the portion of her property lying within the 100–year floodplain for improvement of a storm drainage system along Fanno Creek and that she dedicate an additional 15–foot strip of land adjacent to the floodplain as a pedestrian/bicycle pathway. The dedication required by that condition encompasses approximately 7,000 square feet, or roughly 10% of the property. In accordance with city practice, petitioner could rely on the dedicated property to meet the 15% open space and landscaping requirement mandated by the city's zoning scheme. The city would bear the cost of maintaining a landscaped buffer between the dedicated area and the new store....

The Commission made a series of findings concerning the relationship between the dedicated conditions and the projected impacts of petitioner's project. First, the Commission noted that "it is reasonable to assume that customers and employees of the future uses of this site could utilize a pedestrian/bicycle pathway adjacent to this development for their transportation and recreational needs." The Commission noted that the site plan has provided for bicycle parking in a rack in front of the proposed building and "it is reasonable to expect that some of the users of the bicycle parking provided for by the site plan will use the pathway adjacent to Fanno Creek if it is constructed." In addition, the Commission found that creation of a convenient, safe pedestrian/bicycle pathway system as an alternative means of transportation "could offset some of the traffic demand on [nearby] streets and lessen the increase in traffic congestion."

The Commission went on to note that the required floodplain dedication would be reasonably related to petitioner's request to intensify the use of the site given the increase in the impervious surface. The Commission stated that the "anticipated increased storm water flow from the subject property to an already strained creek and drainage basin can only add to the public need to manage the stream channel and floodplain for drainage purposes." Based on this anticipated increased storm water flow, the Commission concluded that "the requirement of dedication of the floodplain area on the site is related to the applicant's plan to intensify development on the site." The Tigard City Council approved the Commission's final order....

Petitioner contends that the city has forced her to choose between the building permit and her right under the Fifth Amendment to just compensation for the public easements. Petitioner does not quarrel with the city's authority to exact some forms of dedication as a condition for the grant of a building permit, but challenges the showing made by the city to justify these exactions. She argues that the city has identified "no special benefits" conferred on her, and has not identified any "special quantifiable burdens" created by her new store that would justify the particular dedications required from her which are not required from the public at large.

In evaluating petitioner's claim, we must first determine whether the "essential nexus" exists between the "legitimate state interest" and the permit condition exacted by the city. *Nollan*, 483 U.S. at 837. If we find that a nexus exists, we must then decide the required degree of connection between the exactions and the projected impact of the proposed development. We were not required to reach this question in *Nollan*, because we concluded that the connection did not meet even the loosest standard. Here, however, we must decide this question.

[An "essential nexus" exists in this case.] Undoubtedly, the prevention of flooding along Fanno Creek and the reduction of traffic congestion in the Central Business District qualify as the type of legitimate public purposes we have upheld. It seems equally obvious that a nexus exists between preventing flooding along Fanno Creek and limiting development within the creek's 100–year floodplain. Petitioner proposes to double the size of her retail store and to pave her now-gravel parking lot, thereby expanding the impervious surface on the property and increasing the amount of storm water runoff into Fanno Creek.

The same may be said for the city's attempt to reduce traffic congestion by providing for alternative means of transportation. In theory, a pedestrian/bicycle pathway provides a useful alternative means of transportation for workers and shoppers....

The second part of our analysis requires us to determine whether the degree of the exactions demanded by the city's permit conditions bears the required relationship to the projected impact of petitioner's proposed development.... In some States, very generalized statements as to the necessary connection between the required dedication and the proposed development seem to suffice. See, e.g., Billings Properties, Inc. v. Yellowstone County, 144 Mont. 25, 394 P.2d 182 (1964); Jenad, Inc. v. Scarsdale, 18 N.Y.2d 78, 218 N.E.2d 673, 271 N.Y.S.2d 955 (1966). We think this standard is too lax to adequately protect petitioner's right to just compensation if her property is taken for a public purpose.

Other state courts require a very exacting correspondence, described as the "specific and uniquely attributable" test. The Supreme Court of Illinois first developed this test in Pioneer Trust & Savings Bank v. Mount Prospect, 22 Ill. 2d 375, 380, 176 N.E.2d 799, 802 (1961). Under this standard, if the local government cannot demonstrate that its exaction is directly proportional to the specifically created need, the exaction becomes "a veiled exercise of the power of eminent domain and a confiscation of private property behind the defense of police regulations." Id., at 381, 176 N.E.2d at 802. We do not think the Federal Constitution requires such exacting scrutiny, given the nature of the interests involved.

A number of state courts have taken an intermediate position, requiring the municipality to show a "reasonable relationship" between the required dedication and the impact of the proposed development. Typical is the Supreme Court of Nebraska's opinion in Simpson v. North Platte, 206 Neb. 240, 245, 292 N.W.2d 297, 301 (1980), where that court stated:

> The distinction, therefore, which must be made between an appropriate exercise of the police power and an improper exercise of eminent domain is whether the requirement has some reasonable relationship or nexus to the use to which the property is being made or is merely being used as an excuse for taking property simply because at that particular moment the landowner is asking the city for some license or permit.

Thus, the court held that a city may not require a property owner to dedicate private property for some future public use as a condition of obtaining a building permit when such future use is not "occasioned by the construction sought to be permitted." Id., at 248, 292 N.W.2d at 302.... Some form of the reasonable relationship test has been adopted in many other jurisdictions....

We think the "reasonable relationship" test adopted by a majority of the state courts is closer to the federal constitutional norm than either of those previously discussed. But we do not adopt it as such, partly because the term "reasonable relationship" seems confusingly similar to the term "rational basis" which describes the minimal level of scrutiny under the Equal Protection Clause of the Fourteenth Amendment. We think a term such as "rough proportionality" best encapsulates what we hold to be the requirement of the Fifth Amendment. No precise mathematical calculation is required, but the city must make some sort of individualized determination that the required dedication is related both in nature and extent to the impact of the proposed development.[8]....

It is axiomatic that increasing the amount of impervious surface will increase the quantity and rate of storm water flow from petitioner's property. Therefore, keeping the floodplain open and free from development would likely confine the pressures on Fanno Creek created by petitioner's development. In fact, because petitioner's property lies within the Central Business District, the CDC already required that petitioner leave 15% of it as open space and the undeveloped floodplain would have nearly satisfied that requirement. But the city demanded more—it not only wanted petitioner not to build in the floodplain, but it also wanted petitioner's property along Fanno Creek for its greenway system. The city

8. Justice Stevens' dissent takes us to task for placing the burden on the city to justify the required dedication. He is correct in arguing that in evaluating most generally applicable zoning regulations, the burden properly rests on the party challenging the regulation to prove that it constitutes an arbitrary regulation of property rights. Here, by contrast, the city made an adjudicative decision to condition petitioner's application for a building permit on an individual parcel. In this situation, the burden properly rests on the city....

has never said why a public greenway, as opposed to a private one, was required in the interest of flood control.

The difference to petitioner, of course, is the loss of her ability to exclude others. As we have noted, this right to exclude others is "one of the most essential sticks in the bundle of rights that are commonly characterized as property." Kaiser Aetna v. United States, 444 U.S. 164, 176 (1979). It is difficult to see why recreational visitors trampling along petitioner's floodplain easement are sufficiently related to the city's legitimate interest in reducing flooding problems along Fanno Creek, and the city has not attempted to make any individualized determination to support this part of its request....

With respect to the pedestrian/bicycle pathway, we have no doubt that the city was correct in finding that the larger retail sales facility proposed by petitioner will increase traffic on the streets of the Central Business District. The city estimates that the proposed development would generate roughly 435 additional trips per day. Dedications for streets, sidewalks, and other public ways are generally reasonable exactions to avoid excessive congestion from a proposed property use. But on the record before us, the city has not met its burden of demonstrating that the additional number of vehicle and bicycle trips generated by petitioner's development reasonably relate to the city's requirement for a dedication of the pedestrian/bicycle pathway easement. The city simply found that the creation of the pathway "could offset some of the traffic demand ... and lessen the increase in traffic congestion."

As Justice Peterson of the Supreme Court of Oregon explained in his dissenting opinion, however, "the findings of fact that the bicycle pathway system '*could* offset some of the traffic demand' is a far cry from a finding that the bicycle pathway system *will*, or is *likely to*, offset some of the traffic demand." 317 Ore. at 127, 854 P.2d at 447 (emphasis in original). No precise mathematical calculation is required, but the city must make some effort to quantify its findings in support of the dedication for the pedestrian/bicycle pathway beyond the conclusory statement that it could offset some of the traffic demand generated.

Cities have long engaged in the commendable task of land use planning, made necessary by increasing urbanization, particularly in metropolitan areas such as Portland. The city's goals of reducing flooding hazards and traffic congestion, and providing for public greenways, are laudable, but there are outer limits to how this may be done. "A strong public desire to improve the public condition [will not] warrant achieving the desire by a shorter cut than the constitutional way of paying for the change." Pennsylvania Coal Co. v. Mahon, 260 U.S. 393, 416 (1922).

The judgment of the Supreme Court of Oregon is reversed, and the case is remanded for further proceedings not inconsistent with this opinion.

JUSTICE STEVENS, with whom JUSTICE BLACKMUN and JUSTICE GINSBURG, join, dissenting....

The Court's assurances that its "rough proportionality" test leaves ample room for cities to pursue the "commendable task of land use planning"—even twice avowing that "no precise mathematical calculation is required"—are wanting given the result that test compels here. Under the Court's approach, a city must not only "quantify its findings" and make "individualized determinations" with respect to the nature *and* the extent of the relationship between the conditions and the impact, but also demonstrate "proportionality." The correct inquiry should instead concentrate on whether the required nexus is present and venture beyond considerations of a condition's nature or germaneness only if the developer establishes that a concededly germane condition is so grossly disproportionate to the proposed development's adverse effects that it manifests motives other than land use regulation on the part of the city....

In our changing world one thing is certain: uncertainty will characterize predictions about the impact of new urban developments on the risks of floods, earthquakes, traffic congestion, or environmental harms. When there is doubt concerning the magnitude of those impacts, the public interest in averting them must outweigh the private interest of the commercial entrepreneur. If the government can demonstrate that the conditions it has imposed in a land use permit are rational, impartial and conducive to fulfilling the aims of a valid land use plan, a strong presumption of validity should attach to those conditions. The burden of demonstrating that those conditions have unreasonably impaired the economic value of the proposed improvement belongs squarely on the shoulders of the party challenging the state action's constitutionality. That allocation of burdens has served us well in the past. The Court has stumbled badly today by reversing it.

[The dissenting opinions of JUSTICE SOUTER is omitted.]

Notes & Questions

1. **Legislative Exactions.** Both *Nollan* and *Dolan* involved individualized exactions imposed by an administrative agency. Should the courts apply the same constitutional requirements to across-the-board development fees set by a legislative body? Assume that a city, for example, imposes a per-acre fee on all developments, to be used to pay for new roads, schools, etc. Can a developer escape the fee by showing that, in its case, the fee is not "roughly proportional" to its impacts on the community? State courts have split on the issue. Compare Northern Ill. Home Buildings Ass'n v. County of DuPage, 649 N.E.2d 384 (Ill. 1995) (*Dolan* applicable) with Home Builders Ass'n v. City of Scottsdale, 930 P.2d 993 (Ariz. 1997) (*Dolan* inapplicable).

2. **Regulations Generally.** Does the "rough proportionality" test apply only to exactions or to all regulations? According to the Supreme Court in City of Monterey v. Del Monte Dunes, 526 U.S. 687, 703 (1999), *Dolan* "was not designed to address, and is not readily applicable to, the much different questions arising where, as here, the landowner's challenge

is based not on excessive exactions but on denial of development." For criticisms of the Supreme Court's differential treatment of exactions and regulatory takings, see Mark Fenster, Takings Formalism and Regulatory Formulas: Exactions and the Consequences of Clarity, 96 Calif. L. Rev. 609 (2004); Lee Anne Fennell, Hard Bargains and Real Steals: Land Use Exactions Revisited, 86 Iowa L. Rev. 1 (2000)

3. **Endangered Species.** The Endangered Species Act permits property owners to build in the habitat of a listed species if they prepare a habitat conservation plan (HCP) that minimizes the risk of the development to the species. See pp. 1097–1102. Assume that Mary Austin wants to develop her 40–acre property and is told by the United States Fish and Wildlife Service (F&WS) that she can do so only by agreeing to an HCP in which she sets aside 38 acres of her land as a wildlife refuge. Can Mary challenge the F&WS's position on the ground that this requirement is disproportionate to the risk that her project poses to the species? Are HCPs a form of exaction? In many cases, the species will be at risk of extinction only because prior development destroyed most of the species' habitat. Can Mary argue that the F&WS's demand violates *Dolan* because the prior developers, not Mary, caused most of the problem? See Barton H. Thompson, Jr., The Endangered Species Act: A Case Study in Takings & Incentives, 49 Stan. L. Rev. 305, 339–343 (1997) (suggesting that *Nollan* and *Dolan* may restrict the types of HCPs that can be imposed on property owners).

4. **Likely Impact.** What is the likely impact of *Nollan* and *Dolan* on land use planning? Professor Ann Carlson, in a fascinating study, finds that *Nollan* and *Dolan* may have actually increased the level of exactions being imposed on some developers in California. Forced to more closely examine the impacts of developments in order to meet the *Nollan* and *Dolan* tests, land use planners in high-growth regions have found that their prior exactions were actually too low. By forcing land use planners to look more closely at their exactions, in short, *Nollan* and *Dolan* appear to have encouraged land use planners in these areas to set higher fees. Carlson finds, however, that *Nollan* and *Dolan* have constrained exactions in highly built-out urban communities. See Ann E. Carlson & Daniel Pollack, Takings on the Ground: How the Supreme Court's Takings Jurisprudence Affects Local Land Use Decisions, 35 U.C. Davis L. Rev. 103 (2001). See also David A. Dana, Land Use Regulation in an Age of Heightened Scrutiny, 75 N.C. L. Rev. 1243 (1997) (arguing that the theoretical effect of *Nollan* and *Dolan* on land use decisions is ambiguous).

*

INDEX

References are to Pages.

†